SIPRI Yearbook 2020
Armaments, Disarmament and International Security

www.sipriyearbook.org

STOCKHOLM INTERNATIONAL PEACE RESEARCH INSTITUTE
Signalistgatan 9
SE-169 72 Solna, Sweden
Telephone: + 46 8 655 9700
Email: sipri@sipri.org
Internet: www.sipri.org

SIPRI Yearbook 2020

Armaments, Disarmament and International Security

**STOCKHOLM INTERNATIONAL
PEACE RESEARCH INSTITUTE**

OXFORD UNIVERSITY PRESS
2020

OXFORD

UNIVERSITY PRESS

Great Clarendon Street, Oxford OX2 6DP,
United Kingdom

Oxford University Press is a department of the University of Oxford.
It furthers the University's objective of excellence in research, scholarship,
and education by publishing worldwide. Oxford is a registered trade mark of
Oxford University Press in the UK and in certain other countries

British Library Cataloguing in Publication Data

Data available

Library of Congress Cataloging in Publication Data

Data available

ISBN 978–0–19–886920–7

Typeset and originated by SIPRI
Maps in chapter 6 by Hugo Ahlenius, Nordpil, <https://nordpil.se/>

Printed in Great Britain by Bell & Bain Ltd., Glasgow

Published in the United States of America by Oxford University Press
198 Madison Avenue, New York, NY 10016, United States of America

SIPRI Yearbook 2020 is also published online at
<http://www.sipriyearbook.org>

Contents

Part II. Military spending and armaments, 2019

Part III. Non-proliferation, arms control and disarmament, 2019

Annexes

Preface

This, the 51st edition of the SIPRI Yearbook, was finalized against the background of the unfolding and multidimensional impact of the coronavirus disease 2019 (COVID-19) pandemic. At the time of writing, the world is in the midst of a global public health emergency on a scale not seen for a century—over 4 million cases of infection and over 300 000 deaths, according to statistics that are almost uniformly agreed to be incomplete. The consequences are far-reaching in economic, social and political terms, and, in the longer term, probably also their cultural and social psychological ramifications. The pandemic has exacerbated existing geopolitical struggles, prompting a disinformation war that has drawn in China, Russia, the United States and other powers.

However, in a Yearbook that is concerned with events in 2019, COVID-19 is only a minor, albeit highly lethal, postscript to the year. The COVID-19 virus was first detected in Wuhan, China, and reported to the World Health Organization on the last day of 2019. Accordingly, while it will undoubtedly feature strongly in the next edition of the Yearbook, it is not part of the narrative when reflecting on events in 2019. As always, this edition of the Yearbook presents the evidence that is needed to identify the approaches that are needed to address challenges to human security and international stability. The Yearbook's focus on the facts is vital in an era of misinformation and 'fake news'. It will also be crucial for mapping cooperative approaches to the building of a more peaceful and resilient world when dealing with the consequences of the COVID-19 pandemic.

The introduction (chapter 1) reflects on a year in which the negative trends continued to outweigh the positive. Despite the need for cooperation on a range of major challenges—climate, cyber, peace and trade—international tensions increased during 2019 and exacerbated an already insecure global order. Similarly, despite the complexity and transboundary nature of the COVID-19 pandemic, governments appear to have at least initially retreated into isolationism, nationalism and protectionism. However, as with the more traditional security challenges discussed in this Yearbook, the pandemic requires multilateral solutions and instruments, and leaders will need to champion initiatives that forge new international health security mechanisms and institutions.

Part I of the Yearbook covers armed conflicts and conflict management in 2019. It aims to catch key moments and trends in conflict escalation and peacebuilding. Chapter 2 focuses on armed conflicts and peace processes, looking at the multifaceted root causes of both and summarizing their latest developments. Multilateral peace operations feature prominently. Active armed conflicts occurred in at least 32 states in 2019: 2 in the Americas, 7 in Asia and Oceania, 1 in Europe, 7 in the Middle East and North Africa, and 15 in sub-Saharan Africa (chapters 3–7). Nevertheless, the reduction in the severity of several armed conflicts in 2019 led to a further reduction in conflict fatalities, continuing a recent downward trend since 2014.

Parts II and III focus on issues related to armament and disarmament. Much of the Institute's work in these areas is based on original, rigorous data collection, which forms the foundation of SIPRI's databases. Part II is devoted to military spending and armaments, including comprehensive assessments of recent trends in military expenditure (chapter 8), international arms transfers and arms production (chapter 9), and world nuclear forces and the current nuclear modernization programmes (chapter 10).

Part III covers non-proliferation, arms control and disarmament. In it, chapter 11 looks at North Korean–US nuclear diplomacy, developments in US–Russian nuclear arms control, including the INF Treaty, and Iran's continued implementation of the Joint Comprehensive Plan of Action to limit its nuclear programme. Chapter 12 discusses the use of chemical weapons in Syria and other developments in chemical and biological security threats. Chapter 13 includes a round-up of the global instruments for controlling conventional weapons in 2019, including the latest discussions on how to regulate lethal autonomous weapon systems and the dialogue on preventing an arms race in outer space. Chapter 14 reports on efforts to strengthen controls on the trade in conventional arms and dual-use items.

Taken together, this compendium addresses some of the most urgent matters that confronted humanity in 2019. SIPRI continues to look for ways to make best use of the Yearbook and its contents as a tool of transparency and accountability. To that end, the Yearbook has been translated for many years into Arabic, Chinese, Russian and Ukrainian.

The SIPRI Yearbook depends on many people's work. This year's edition features contributions from 29 authors. Its content is refereed extensively, and a dedicated editorial team ensures that it conforms to the highest publishing standards. The communications, library, operations and IT staff at SIPRI all contribute in different ways to the Yearbook's production and distribution. I would like to take this opportunity to express my gratitude to everybody involved, within SIPRI and beyond.

The SIPRI Yearbook remains the starting place for in-depth and authoritative open-source information on critical issues of international security, armaments and disarmament. Even in this digital age, when 'facts' are only a click away, SIPRI's commitment to authenticating the facts means that the volume remains an indispensable global public good. This will continue to be the case as the institute assesses the consequences of the COVID-19 pandemic and helps to chart a course for emerging from the crisis with more equitable, resilient and sustainable societies.

Dan Smith
Director, SIPRI
Stockholm, May 2020

Abbreviations and conventions

ABM	Anti-ballistic missile	CTBTO	Comprehensive Nuclear-Test-Ban Treaty Organization
ACLED	Armed Conflict Location & Event Data Project		
AG	Australia Group	CW	Chemical weapon/warfare
ALCM	Air-launched cruise missile	CWC	Chemical Weapons Convention
APC	Armoured personnel carrier		
APM	Anti-personnel mine	DDR	Disarmament, demobilization and reintegration
ASAT	anti-satellite		
ASEAN	Association of Southeast Asian Nations	DPKO	UN Department of Peacekeeping Operations
ATT	Arms Trade Treaty	DPRK	Democratic People's Republic of Korea (North Korea)
AU	African Union		
BCC	Bilateral Consultative Commission (of the Russian–US New START treaty)		
		DRC	Democratic Republic of the Congo
		EAEC	European Atomic Energy Community (Euratom)
BMD	Ballistic missile defence		
BWC	Biological and Toxin Weapons Convention	EAPC	Euro-Atlantic Partnership Council
CAR	Central African Republic	ECOWAS	Economic Community of West African States
CBM	Confidence-building measure		
		EDA	European Defence Agency
CBW	Chemical and biological weapon/warfare	ERW	Explosive remnants of war
		EU	European Union
CCM	Convention on Cluster Munitions	EWIPA	Explosive weapons in populated areas
CCW	Certain Conventional Weapons (Convention)	FATF	Financial Action Task Force
		FFM	Fact-finding mission
CD	Conference on Disarmament	FMCT	Fissile material cut-off treaty
CFE	Conventional Armed Forces in Europe (Treaty)		
		FSC	Forum for Security Cooperation (of the OSCE)
CFSP	Common Foreign and Security Policy (of the EU)		
		FY	Financial year
CIS	Commonwealth of Independent States	G7	Group of Seven (industrialized states)
CSBM	Confidence- and security-building measure		
		GBV	Gender-based violence
CSDP	Common Security and Defence Policy (of the EU)	GCC	Gulf Cooperation Council
		GDP	Gross domestic product
CSP	Conference of States Parties	GGE	Group of governmental experts
CSTO	Collective Security Treaty Organization		
		GHG	Greenhouse gas
CTBT	Comprehensive Nuclear-Test-Ban Treaty	GLCM	Ground-launched cruise missile

HCOC	Hague Code of Conduct	OAS	Organization of American States
HEU	Highly enriched uranium		
IAEA	International Atomic Energy Agency	OCCAR	Organisation Conjointe de Coopération en matière d'Armement (Organisation for Joint Armament Cooperation)
ICBM	Intercontinental ballistic missile		
ICC	International Criminal Court	OECD	Organisation for Economic Co-operation and Development
ICJ	International Court of Justice		
		OEWG	Open-ended working group
IED	Improvised explosive device	OHCHR	Office of the UN High Commissioner for Human Rights
IGAD	Intergovernmental Authority on Development		
IHL	International humanitarian law	OIC	Organisation of Islamic Cooperation
INF	Intermediate-range Nuclear Forces (Treaty)	OPCW	Organisation for the Prohibition of Chemical Weapons
ISAF	International Security Assistance Force		
		OPEC	Organization of the Petroleum Exporting Countries
ISU	Implementation Support Unit		
JCG	Joint Consultative Group (of the CFE Treaty)	OSCC	Open Skies Consultative Commission
JCPOA	Joint Comprehensive Plan of Action	OSCE	Organization for Security and Co-operation in Europe
LAWS	Lethal autonomous weapon systems	P5	Five permanent members of the UN Security Council
LEU	Low-enriched uranium	PAROS	Prevention of an arms race in outer space
MENA	Middle East and North Africa		
		PFP	Partnership for Peace
MIRV	Multiple independently targetable re-entry vehicle	POA	Programme of Action to Prevent, Combat and Eradicate the Illicit Trade in Small Arms and Light Weapons in All its Aspects (UN)
MRBM	Medium-range ballistic missile		
MSP	Meeting of States Parties		
MTCR	Missile Technology Control Regime	PSC	Peace and Security Council (of the African Union)
MX	Meeting of Experts		
NAM	Non-Aligned Movement	PSI	Proliferation Security Initiative
NATO	North Atlantic Treaty Organization		
		R&D	Research and development
NGO	Non-governmental organization	SADC	Southern African Development Community
NNWS	Non-nuclear weapon state	SALW	Small arms and light weapons
NPT	Non-Proliferation Treaty		
NSG	Nuclear Suppliers Group	SAM	Surface-to-air missile
NWS	Nuclear weapon state	SCO	Shanghai Cooperation Organisation

SLBM	Submarine-launched ballistic missile	UNDP	UN Development Programme
SLCM	Sea-launched cruise missile	UNHCR	UN High Commissioner for Refugees
SORT	Strategic Offensive Reductions Treaty	UNODA	UN Office for Disarmament Affairs
SRBM	Short-range ballistic missile		
START	Strategic Arms Reduction Treaty	UNROCA	UN Register of Conventional Arms
TPNW	Treaty on the Prohibition of Nuclear Weapons	UNSC	UN Security Council
		WA	Wassenaar Arrangement
UAE	United Arab Emirates	WHO	World Health Organization
UAV	Unmanned aerial vehicle	WMD	Weapon(s) of mass destruction
UN	United Nations		
UNASUR	Unión de Naciones Suramericanas (Union of South American Nations)		

Conventions

..	Data not available or not applicable
–	Nil or a negligible figure
( )	Uncertain data
b.	Billion (thousand million)
kg	Kilogram
km	Kilometre (1000 metres)
m.	Million
th.	Thousand
tr.	Trillion (million million)
$	US dollars
€	Euros

Geographical regions and subregions

Africa	Consisting of North Africa (Algeria, Libya, Morocco and Tunisia, but excluding Egypt) and sub-Saharan Africa
Americas	Consisting of North America (Canada and the USA), Central America and the Caribbean (including Mexico), and South America
Asia and Oceania	Consisting of Central Asia, East Asia, Oceania, South Asia (including Afghanistan) and South East Asia
Europe	Consisting of Eastern Europe (Armenia, Azerbaijan, Belarus, Georgia, Moldova, Russia and Ukraine) and Western and Central Europe (with South Eastern Europe)
Middle East	Consisting of Egypt, Iran, Iraq, Israel, Jordan, Kuwait, Lebanon, Syria, Turkey and the states of the Arabian peninsula

SIPRI Yearbook online

www.sipriyearbook.org

The full content of the SIPRI Yearbook is also available online. With the SIPRI Yearbook online you can

- access the complete SIPRI Yearbook on your desktop or handheld device for research on the go
- navigate easily through content using advanced search and browse functionality
- find content easily: search through the whole SIPRI Yearbook and within your results
- save valuable time: use your personal profile to return to saved searches and content again and again
- share content with colleagues and students easily via email and social networking tools
- enhance your research by following clearly linked references and web resources

How to access the SIPRI Yearbook online

Institutional access

The SIPRI Yearbook online is available to institutions worldwide for a one-time fee or by annual subscription. Librarians and central resource coordinators can contact Oxford University Press to receive a price quotation using the details below or register for a free trial at <http://www.oxford online.com/freetrials/>.

Individuals can recommend this resource to their librarians at <http://www.oup.com/library-recommend/>.

Individual subscriptions

The SIPRI Yearbook online is available to individuals worldwide on a 12-month subscription basis. Purchase details can be found at <http://www.oup.com/>.

Contact information

Customers within the Americas

Email: oxfordonline@oup.com
Telephone: +1 (800) 624 0153
Fax: +1 (919) 677 8877

Customers outside the Americas

Email: institutionalsales@oup.com
Telephone: +44 (0) 1865 353705
Fax: +44 (0) 1865 353308

Introduction

Chapter 1. Introduction: International stability and human security in 2019

1. Introduction: International stability and human security in 2019

DAN SMITH

As the second decade of the 21st century ended, there was little sign of relief from the generally disturbed and concerning state of international security that has characterized it. Recent editions of the annual review by SIPRI of developments in armaments, disarmament, arms control and security—of which this is the 51st edition—have set out the evidence of that deterioration in the conditions for international stability. Not all developments across the years have been negative. Some elements of international cooperation—a major precondition for stability—remain in place, functional and vibrant. However, while an overall judgement of how the evidence weighs up necessarily contains aspects of subjectivity, it is a widely shared view that the deterioration continued in 2019.[1]

As in previous years in the decade, this trend is reflected in the continued rise in military spending and estimated value of global arms transfers, as well as in an unfolding crisis of arms control that has now become chronic. Forming a malign part of the context is the increasingly toxic nature of global geopolitics, which is especially visible in relations between China and the United States, and in regional rivalries. These produced flashpoints during 2019, especially in the Middle East and South Asia, that an increasingly divided international community appeared to lack capacity or will to manage safely. The deficiencies of international crisis management that these moments revealed were striking. This was perhaps especially concerning because there remains a stubbornly high number of armed conflicts worldwide. The indications were that lethality levels were lower than in earlier years—according to one report, there were 17 per cent fewer conflict-related fatalities in 2019 than in 2018, driven largely by a decrease in battle-related events.[2] However, there were few signs of negotiated settlements in view.

In the background, the climate crisis has continued to unfold. Scientific evidence has advanced and the impact of climate change is becoming more

---

[1] See e.g. the assessment by the Science and Security Board of the Bulletin of the Atomic Scientists, reviewing the international scene at the start of 2020, to set the time on the 'doomsday clock' closer to midnight than ever before: Bulletin of the Atomic Scientists, 'Closer than ever: It is 100 seconds to midnight', 23 Jan. 2020.

[2] Kishi, R. et al., *Year in Review* (Armed Conflict Location & Event Data Project: Mar. 2020). For analysis of all armed conflicts and peace processes in 2019, see chapters 2–7 in this volume.

visible in the form of extreme weather events. An apparently growing public awareness of climate change and other environmental issues during the course of 2019, combined with high-level declarations of intent such as those articulated during the United Nations Climate Action Summit in September, were welcome signs that opinion was moving decisively towards support for serious action to address the problem. However, action remains hard to organize and stimulate, and there will be a considerable time lag between action and impact. Further increase in average global temperatures is inevitable, no matter how much and how quickly greenhouse gas (GHG) emissions are reduced. As important and urgent as such measures are, adapting to the impact of climate change and building resilience in the short to medium term are just as necessary. Without them, the security agenda of the 2030s risks being so full of shocks and stresses as to be essentially unmanageable for many countries in all regions of the world.

Arguably, there has never been more need of international cooperation for jointly responding to shared challenges. Yet there appears to be a declining appetite for it among the great powers and a worrying amount of drift in international politics. No single one of the challenges alluded to here is incapable of solution. True enough, the complexity of many of today's armed conflicts poses great difficulties for efforts to reduce violence and resolve conflicts. Similarly, the onward march of technology is hard to restrain, in part because there are many benefits, some of them of world-changing importance. And responding successfully to climate change is an enormous task because the problem is a product of core economic features of how contemporary societies are organized. But in conflicts, similar problems have been faced and managed in the past. There is a solid history of successful regulation of technological development. And the instruments for reducing GHG emissions and adapting to the pressures on human society produced by unavoidable climate change are well established and available. What is missing so far is the will to work practically, cooperatively and on an international scale to address these diverse issues.

The following chapters of this Yearbook set out the data and analysis on which these broad conclusions are built. This introductory chapter offers an overview of trends and issues that require action by the major powers, and in particular cooperation among them, in order to avoid major insecurities and conflicts. The chapter shows how the international response to key flash-points during 2019 and the approach to arms control lacked the cooperative dimension. International cooperation is likewise a key ingredient for success in minimizing and managing the negative security consequences of climate change. As 2020 began and the threat of coronavirus disease 2019 (COVID-19) emerged—the most serious immediate global challenge faced in a long time—international cooperation was again deficient.

Respect for the international laws and norms that underpin cooperation has declined in recent years. Their importance cannot be neglected if the international system is to function on the basis of cooperation rather than confrontation.

I. Flashpoints

More than in recent years, events in 2019 raised the prospect of war between major powers in the Middle East and in South Asia. Such a war did not occur and was at no time the probable outcome in either setting. Yet, as missile strikes, proxy attacks and challenges to freedom of navigation in the Persian Gulf unfolded in mid-2019, it was not unreasonable to contemplate the possibility that Iran might be at war with Saudi Arabia and other regional powers, and potentially with the USA. Armed clashes also increased between two nuclear-armed states, India and Pakistan, over Kashmir. Again, escalation did not appear completely out of the question. Although in both cases the crisis calmed, the kind of crisis management that has in the past been achieved through high-level diplomacy conducted by the UN or an uninvolved major power was not visible. In the case of events in the Gulf region, this may be largely traceable to Russia and the USA positioning themselves to back opposing sides in regional politics; in the case of Kashmir, it might rather be understood as a case of the global powers being unwilling to attempt to impose a compromise on two major regional powers. It is perhaps too soon to conclude that this indicates an international systemic deficiency of worrying proportions. Nonetheless, the world seemed to get too close for comfort to a situation of considerable danger more than once in 2019.

Crisis in the Strait of Hormuz

The Strait of Hormuz is the narrow seaway between the northern tip of the peninsula of the United Arab Emirates (UAE) and, to its north, the coast of Iran. It is the world's most important choke point in the sea transport of oil: approximately 19 per cent of the world's total petroleum oil supply, or about one third of what is traded internationally, passes through the strait each year.[3] From May to July, attacks against oil tankers in the strait highlighted the risk of a regional conflagration and put the principle of freedom of navigation in jeopardy. This principle is of paramount importance in an interconnected, trade-dependent world economy characterized by just-in-time supply chains.

---

[3] US Energy Information Administration, 'World oil transit chokepoints', 25 July 2017, updated 15 Oct. 2019. The Energy Information Administration defines world oil chokepoints as 'narrow channels along widely used global sea routes'.

The background to the incidents lay in part in the regional rivalry between Iran and Saudi Arabia, and in part in the termination of the Joint Comprehensive Plan of Action (JCPOA), often known as the Iran nuclear deal. In early May 2019 the USA tightened sanctions on Iran by revoking waivers on all remaining oil exports from Iran. Previously, Iran had threatened to close the Strait of Hormuz in response to such sanctions.[4] At the same time, the USA strengthened its regional naval presence with an additional aircraft carrier strike group.[5] It also reportedly updated its military plans for the region, including a provision to send up to 120 000 troops to the Middle East should Iran attack US forces.[6] Tensions rose sharply thereafter and a series of armed actions began that continued throughout the year. Iran responded to the increased economic sanctions by suspending some of its own nuclear restrictions and threatened to exit the 2015 nuclear deal altogether.[7]

Four commercial vessels, including two Saudi Arabian oil tankers, were attacked off the coast of the UAE on 12 May and two more on 13 June. Rejecting US allegations that Iran was responsible for the attacks, Iranian Foreign Minister Mohammad Javad Zarif nonetheless warned that the USA 'cannot expect to stay safe' in what he described as a US 'economic war' against Iran.[8] Escalation continued on 4 July when the British navy seized a tanker off the coast of Gibraltar. The United Kingdom justified the action by arguing that the tanker was carrying Iranian oil to a refinery in Syria in violation of European Union (EU) sanctions.[9] Six days later Iran attempted to seize a British oil tanker in the Strait of Hormuz before successfully seizing two foreign oil tankers and their crews on 18 and 31 July.[10] The USA responded by seeking to expand its international coalition to protect merchant vessels in and around the Strait of Hormuz. However, only Australia, Bahrain and the UK initially joined the coalition force, with Saudi Arabia and the UAE joining later.[11] In the months following, despite a reported attack on an Iranian vessel

---

[4] *The Guardian*, 'Iran threatens to block Strait of Hormuz over US oil sanctions', 5 July 2018.

[5] Lubold, G. and Gordon, M. R., 'US deploys forces to Mideast to deter Iran', *Wall Street Journal*, 5 May 2019.

[6] Schmitt, E. and Barnes, J. E., 'White House reviews military plans against Iran, in echoes of Iraq war', *New York Times*, 13 May 2019.

[7] Sanger, D. E. et al., 'US issues new sanctions as Iran warns it will step back from nuclear deal', *New York Times*, 8 May 2019. On developments in the Iran nuclear deal, see chapter 11, section III, in this volume.

[8] Wintour, P., 'Iran's foreign minister warns US "cannot expect to stay safe"', *The Guardian*, 10 June 2019.

[9] BBC, 'Oil tanker bound for Syria detained in Gibraltar', 4 July 2019.

[10] Starr, B. and Browne, R., 'Iranian boats attempted to seize a British tanker in the Strait of Hormuz', CNN, 11 July 2019; France 24, 'Iran seizes foreign tanker with 12 crew "smuggling fuel" in Gulf', 18 July 2019; and Yee, V. et al., 'Iran says it has seized another oil tanker in Persian Gulf', *New York Times*, 4 Aug. 2019.

[11] Morgan, W. and Toosi, N., 'US-led Gulf maritime coalition "rebranded" to attract more countries', Politico, 5 Aug. 2019; UK Cabinet Office et al., 'UK joins international maritime security mission in the Gulf', 5 Aug. 2019; and Neuman, S., 'Australia joins US-led maritime force protecting Persian Gulf shipping', National Public Radio, 22 Aug. 2019.

in the Red Sea in October, some of the heat seemed to go out of the maritime side of the aggravated confrontation in the Gulf region.[12] However, the action had merely moved to other arenas.

There was a dramatic increase in Iranian–US tensions in June when Iran shot down a US surveillance drone, stating it was in Iranian airspace.[13] The USA denied the intrusion. US President Donald J. Trump reportedly authorized military strikes against Iranian radar and missile batteries, only to reverse his decision some minutes before the attack was due to be launched.[14] Instead, the USA carried out cyberattacks against Iran's missile control systems and an Iranian intelligence organization that it believed responsible for the June attacks on the two oil tankers.[15]

Saudi Arabia had already accused Iran of a drone and missile attack on a Saudi Arabian oil pipeline in May, despite the strikes being claimed by Houthi forces in Yemen (see chapter 6, section V).[16] Tensions spiked again in the wake of a series of drone and cruise missile attacks on Saudi Arabian oil facilities on 14 September. The strikes temporarily shut down about half of Saudi Arabian oil production. Again, the Houthi rebels in Yemen claimed responsibility for the attacks, but some EU member states, Saudi Arabia and the USA accused Iran.[17] President Trump weighed up the option of retaliatory air strikes—tweeting the day after the attack that the USA was 'locked and loaded'—before choosing instead to pursue a more cautious approach: imposing new sanctions on Iran and increasing military aid to Saudi Arabia.[18]

Efforts by French President Emmanuel Macron to broker a meeting between the Iranian and US presidents in September came to nothing, yet tensions appeared to ease somewhat in October and November. Iran and Saudi Arabia were reported to be working through intermediaries to establish a dialogue, and in early December Iran and the USA exchanged prisoners.[19] However, the final month of the year was more notable for an escalating

---

[12] BBC, 'Iranian oil tanker attacked off Saudi coast, foreign ministry says', 11 Oct. 2019; and *Times of Israel*, 'Iran says 3 tankers attacked in Red Sea in six-month period, warns route unsafe', 7 Nov. 2019.

[13] Deeks, A. and Anderson, S. R., 'Iran shoots down a US drone: Domestic and international legal implications', Lawfare, 20 June 2019.

[14] Shear, M. D. et al., 'Strikes on Iran approved by Trump, then abruptly pulled back', *New York Times,* 20 June 2019.

[15] Barnes, J. E. and Gibbons-Neff, T., 'US carried out cyberattacks on Iran', *New York Times,* 22 June 2019.

[16] Deutsche Welle, 'Houthi rebels attack Saudi oil pipeline', 14 May 2019.

[17] Kirkpatrick, D. D. et al., 'Who was behind the Saudi oil attack? What the evidence shows', *New York Times*, 16 Sep. 2019; and International Crisis Group, 'After the Aramco attack: A Middle East one step closer to its "1914 moment"', Commentary, 20 Sep. 2019.

[18] Quilantan, B., 'Trump says US "locked and loaded" after attack on Saudi oil', Politico, 15 Sep. 2019; and Gibbons-Neff, T., 'New US aid to Saudi Arabia will include 200 troops', *New York Times*, 26 Sep. 2019. On US military bases in the Middle East, see Musto, P., 'US–Iran dispute brings attention to military bases in Middle East', Voice of America, 6 Sep. 2019.

[19] Fassihi, F. and Hubbard, B., 'Saudi Arabia and Iran make quiet openings to head off war', *New York Times*, 4 Oct. 2019; and Crowley, M., 'In prisoner swap, Iran frees American held since 2016', *New York Times*, 7 Dec. 2019.

series of military clashes in Iraq between Iran's allies and US forces. These culminated just after 2020 began in the targeted killing of General Qasem Soleimani, a senior commander in the Islamic Revolutionary Guards Corps, who was regarded as one of Iran's most effective generals and influential individuals.[20]

Escalation raised the prospect of asymmetric warfare unfolding. Those regional powers that looked most likely to be involved—Iran on one side and Israel, Saudi Arabia and the UAE opposing it—would each be vulnerable to attacks on their homelands. Were Russia or the USA to be engaged, their greatest vulnerabilities would presumably lie in their regional military, diplomatic and economic presence. Strikes and counterstrikes in cyberspace would, judging from the track record, play a considerable part, likely including attacks on critical infrastructure. If nothing else, while underlining the need for a stable settlement—or at least a reliable management—of the differences among the disputants, this also indicated the need for rules of the road for cyberspace to be introduced.[21]

Crisis in Kashmir

During 2019 the conflict between India and Pakistan over the contested territory of Kashmir escalated. Its particular significance lay not only in the immediate violence but also in the protracted and intractable nature of the dispute between India and Pakistan, and in the fact that both powers are nuclear armed.

Since their independence India and Pakistan have fought three wars over Kashmir in 1947–48, 1965 and 1999, as well as one in 1971 over the independence of Bangladesh. In addition, there have been numerous armed clashes. Both countries claim the entirety of the territory of Jammu and Kashmir, but India currently controls approximately 55 per cent of the land area, in which about 70 per cent of the population lives, Pakistan controls about 30 per cent of the area and China the remaining 15 per cent. Since the First Kashmir War in 1947–48 a military 'line of control' (LOC) has divided India- and Pakistan-administered Jammu and Kashmir. A UN observer mission, the UN Military Observer Group in India and Pakistan (UNMOGIP), has monitored ceasefires in the region since 1949.[22]

---

[20] O'Driscoll, D., 'Tensions on Iraqi soil likely to overshadow anti-government protest demands', SIPRI Commentary, 9 Jan. 2020.

[21] See chapter 13, section I, in this volume.

[22] See the UNMOGIP website. On the conflict in Kashmir and armed conflicts in India and Pakistan, also see chapter 4, section II, in this volume.

The 1950 Constitution of India granted Jammu and Kashmir special status and a degree of autonomy.[23] Since the late 1980s Kashmiri separatists—some seeking independence and others fighting to join neighbouring Pakistan—have periodically fought an armed campaign against around 500 000 Indian security forces in Jammu and Kashmir, resulting in tens of thousands of deaths.[24] Combined with clashes between the regular forces of India and Pakistan, this has made the region one of the most dangerous in the world.

Following the Kargil War in 1999, a 2003 ceasefire was agreed but was persistently unstable. It was reinstated in 2018 after two particularly difficult years and then swept aside in a new surge of tensions in 2019. Over 40 Indian paramilitary police were killed in a bomb attack in February. It was the deadliest such attack in Indian-administered Kashmir for over three decades.[25] In response, later that same month, India carried out its first air strikes across the LOC since 1971 (when they occurred in the context of major war between India and Pakistan over the independence of Bangladesh), targeting a suspected training camp of the group that claimed responsibility for the attack on the Indian police. Pakistan responded in kind with airstrikes in Indian-administered Kashmir.

Along with escalating violence there was also a further political entrenchment of the dispute. In August, in keeping with a long-standing goal of the ruling Bharatiya Janata Party, the Indian Government revoked Kashmir's special status.[26] About 38 000 additional troops were deployed to the region, there was a temporary communications and media blackout, and local leaders were arrested.[27] Protests broke out and more than 500 people were arrested.[28]

There was no progress during the year in bilateral or international diplomacy on the issue. Pakistan's request in August for a formal, open meeting of the UN Security Council failed to gain sufficient support, and there was

---

[23] Noorani, A. G., *Article 370: A Constitutional History of Jammu and Kashmir* (Oxford University Press: Oxford, 2011).

[24] According to the Indian Government, the conflict has killed about 42 000 civilians, militants and security personnel since 1989, while independent estimates suggest 70 000 or more deaths. Kronstadt, K. A., 'Kashmir: Background, recent developments, and US policy', Congressional Research Service Report R45877, 16 Aug. 2019. On the number of Indian security personnel in Kashmir, see Shukla, A., 'India has 700,000 troops in Kashmir? False!!!', rediff.com, 17 July 2018.

[25] BBC, 'Kashmir attack: Bomb kills 40 Indian paramilitary police in convoy', 14 Feb. 2019; and Miller, L., 'Deadly Kashmir suicide bombing ratchets up India–Pakistan tensions', International Crisis Group Q&A, 22 Feb. 2019.

[26] Gettleman, J., 'Narenda Modi, India's "watchman", captures historic election victory', *New York Times*, 23 May 2019; Kalra, A. et al., 'India scraps special status for Kashmir in step Pakistan calls illegal', Reuters, 5 Aug. 2019; Fair, C. C., 'India's move in Kashmir: Unpacking the domestic and international motivations and implications', Lawfare, 12 Aug. 2019; and Maheshwari, L., 'How the Indian Government changed the legal status of Jammu and Kashmir', Lawfare, 12 Aug. 2019.

[27] Dutta, P. K., 'Kashmir: Why centre is sending additional 38000 troops to J&K', *India Today*, 2 Aug. 2019; and Human Rights Watch, 'India: Basic freedoms at risk in Kashmir', 6 Aug. 2019.

[28] Gettleman, J. et al., 'Modi defends revoking Kashmir's statehood as protests flare', *New York Times*, 8 Aug. 2019.

no official UN statement.[29] At the annual UN General Assembly high-level session in September, Pakistani Prime Minister Imran Khan condemned India's decision to remove Kashmir's special status and expressed his worry that even nuclear weapons might be used if violence continued and escalated further.[30] However, in keeping with India's view of the conflict as an internal issue, Indian Prime Minister Narendra Modi did not mention it in his General Assembly speech.[31] By the end of 2019 there appeared to be no reason to expect an agreed settlement of this long-contentious issue.

II. Arms control

In 2019 there were no gains and some setbacks in nuclear arms control. The USA withdrew from the 1987 Intermediate Nuclear Forces Treaty (INF Treaty), and Russia formally suspended its obligations under it.[32] At the same time, uncertainty continued about whether the Russian–US bilateral treaty on strategic nuclear force, normally known as New START, would be extended beyond its current expiry date of February 2021. In addition, the challenge of new technologies—including cyber, machine learning and additive manufacturing technologies—has yet to be fully factored into discussion of arms control, even though they are already part of weapons development. A bright spot of 2018—the détente on the Korean peninsula and initial discussions on denuclearization between the Democratic People's Republic of Korea (DPRK, North Korea) and the USA—dimmed during 2019. After having abandoned the 2015 JCPOA, in 2018 the USA continued to impose additional sanctions against Iran. In response to these measures, during 2019 Iran progressively disowned the constraints it had accepted under the agreement, announcing it no longer regarded itself as bound by those commitments.[33]

From arms control to arms race?

Shortly after finalizing its withdrawal from the INF Treaty in August 2019, which was followed by Russia suspending its own obligations under the treaty, the USA tested a ground-launched cruise missile of a range that was

---

[29] Parashar, S., 'No formal UNSC meeting on J&K but closed-door consultations after China intervenes', *Times of India*, 16 Aug. 2019; and UN News, 'UN Security Council discusses Kashmir, China urges India and Pakistan to ease tensions', 16 Aug. 2019.

[30] *Business Recorder*, 'Full transcript of Prime Minister Imran Khan's speech at the UNGA', 27 Sep. 2019.

[31] *India Today*, 'Full text of PM Narendra Modi's UNGA speech', 28 Sep. 2019.

[32] For a summary and other details of the INF Treaty and other arms control treaties in this section, see annex A, sections I–III, in this volume.

[33] On developments in the JCPOA in 2019, see chapter 11, section III, in this volume.

prohibited by the treaty.[34] Together with a continued lack of action on the possible extension of the New START agreement, this raised concerns about a new arms race. At the same time, there was increasing discussion of whether and how arms control between Russia and the USA could be revived. The USA suggested that this would require China joining talks so the bilateral framework became a trilateral one.[35]

There are signs that the US–Russian strategic competition could intensify.[36] They were evident already in 2018 in the USA's Nuclear Posture Review and in Russian President Vladimir Putin's dramatic unveiling of new weapon systems in March.[37] There is a range of technologies in which an arms competition could occur, including not only nuclear weapons and dual-capable nuclear-conventional weapons platforms, but also hypersonic glide technology, ballistic missile defence (BMD), systems in outer space and the contest for cyber supremacy.[38] However, it may be a mistake to anticipate a repetition of the 1960s and 1970s arms race between the USA and the Union of Soviet Socialist Republics (USSR). Each side was then trying to match or beat the other's numbers in specific categories of weapon systems—bombers, missiles, multi-warhead technology and BMD. While nuclear parity still matters to Russia and the USA, there is also an asymmetric competition between measure, countermeasure and counter-countermeasure. At the same time, non-nuclear systems are increasingly important in shaping the strategic balance. These two factors suggest future arms control agreements may not be based on symmetrical reductions and may not be solely focused on nuclear weapons. It cannot be forecast with any confidence whether the outcome will be more or less stable than the cold war version.

Given China's growing role in the global strategic dynamics and in US threat perceptions, the political cogency of the US argument for trilateral arms control is easy to understand. However, there is also logic in China's rejection of the idea because the size of its nuclear arsenal is hardly comparable to that of Russia and the USA: Russian and US nuclear holdings account for over 90 per cent of the global stockpile of nuclear warheads; China's stockpile, while

---

[34] US Department of Defense, 'DOD conducts ground launch cruise missile test', News release, 19 Aug. 2019; and Deutsche Welle, 'US test-fires cruise missile after INF treaty pullout', 19 Aug. 2019.

[35] Panda, A., 'Thanks, but no thanks: China pushes back on trilateral strategic nuclear arms control', *The Diplomat*, 7 May 2019.

[36] See e.g. Arbatov, A., 'A new era for arms control: Myths, realities and options', Carnegie Moscow Center, 24 Oct. 2019.

[37] Office of the Secretary of Defense, *Nuclear Posture Review 2018* (US Department of Defense: Washington, DC, 2018); Osborn, A., 'Russia names Putin's new "super weapons" after a quirky public vote', Reuters, 23 Mar. 2018; and President of Russia, 'Presidential address to the Federal Assembly', 1 Mar. 2018.

[38] See e.g. Oelrich, I., 'Hypersonic missiles: Three questions every reader should ask', Bulletin of the Atomic Scientists, 17 Dec. 2019; Wilkening, D., 'Hypersonic weapons and strategic stability', *Survival*, vol. 61, no. 5 (2019), pp. 129–48; and Hambling, D., 'China, Russia and the US are all racing to produce hypersonic weapons', *New Scientist*, 6 July 2019. On the developing arms race in space, see chapter 13, section III, in this volume.

growing, is approximately 2 per cent. Indeed, the French nuclear arsenal is bigger than China's. That raises questions about whether there should be an arms control framework that includes not only China but also France, India, Israel, North Korea, Pakistan and the UK.

The current period sees a potential fork in the road for arms control. Agreeing during the course of 2020 to extend New START and coming up with an agreed way forward would suggest shared recognition in the US and Russian governments on the need for limits on the military and nuclear dimension of their relationship, even while some degree of antagonism and rivalry continues.

It may be worth reminding a contemporary policy audience that, as arms control faltered at the end of the 1970s and a new cold war developed with the Soviet invasion of Afghanistan and new nuclear deployments in Europe, the USA and the USSR nonetheless agreed informally to abide by the limits of the 1979 Strategic Arms Limitation Treaty (SALT II), although it was never ratified.[39] In addition to reducing risks, this recognition of a mutual interest in constraints around their rivalry helped to pave the way for improvement in their relationship from 1985 and subsequent agreements on arms reduction. Without a similar display of mutual self-restraint today, the road ahead looks increasingly treacherous for all sides.

The Joint Comprehensive Plan of Action

The JCPOA came under pressure from the moment the Trump presidency was inaugurated in January 2017. The 2015 agreement was made between China, France, Iran, Russia, the UK, the USA and the EU, and endorsed by a binding resolution of the UN Security Council.[40] It was technically sound and implemented fully by Iran.[41] The criticism made by the Trump administration among others that the JCPOA did not cover Iran's missiles or restrain Iranian regional policies is a political objection to the agreement, not a valid comment on its technical merit or the implementation record. In May 2018 the USA gave notice it would no longer adhere to the agreement. In August and November 2018 the USA reimposed the sanctions on Iran that it had lifted as part of the JCPOA.[42]

---

[39] 'SALT II: An analysis of the agreements', *SIPRI Yearbook 1980*, pp. 209–44; and Arms Control Association, 'US–Russian nuclear arms control agreements at a glance', Fact sheet, Aug. 2019.

[40] UN Security Council Resolution 2231, 20 July 2015, 'Annex A: Joint Comprehensive Plan of Action (JCPOA), Vienna, 14 July 2015'.

[41] On the technical soundness of the JCPOA, see Rauf, T., 'Resolving concerns about Iran's nuclear programme', *SIPRI Yearbook 2016*, chapter 17, section I, pp 675–80; on implementation up to US withdrawal, see International Atomic Energy Agency, 'Iran is implementing nuclear-related JCPOA commitments, Director General Amano tells IAEA Board', 5 Mar. 2018·

[42] See Erästö, T., *SIPRI Yearbook 2018*, pp. 337–46; *SIPRI Yearbook 2019*, pp. 378–86; and chapter 11, section III, in this volume.

US sanctions on Iran are applied extraterritorially via the international banking system so any entity trading with or investing in Iran faces the risk of penalties. The EU initially sought to establish a way round the sanctions so European trade with and investment in Iran could continue. However, legal measures the EU had adopted in the 1990s to prevent European companies from observing extraterritorial US sanctions now lack efficacy because of the size of the US commercial market and the global role of the US dollar.[43] The EU established a financial Instrument in Support of Trade Exchanges (INSTEX), which was initially intended to allow continuation of oil imports from Iran but did not achieve that aim.[44] It offered no room for manoeuvre for European companies inclined to do business with or in Iran. It therefore offered Iran no respite from the pressure of sanctions. On the grounds that the other side had not lived up to its commitments regarding sanctions relief, in May 2019 Iran decided to reduce its commitments under the JCPOA.[45]

By the end of 2019, although Iran and all the parties to the JCPOA except the USA remained parties to it, the deal was largely non-functional. The paradox was that the US administration, while apparently worried about the possibility of Iran developing nuclear weapons capability, had successfully undermined an agreed instrument that would prevent that from happening.[46]

North Korea–United States nuclear diplomacy

One of the bright points of 2018 was the breakthrough in relations between North Korea and the USA. In the Singapore Joint Declaration on 12 June 2018, President Trump committed to provide security guarantees to North Korea while Chairman Kim Jong Un reaffirmed his 'firm and unwavering commitment to the complete denuclearization of the Korean Peninsula'. The two leaders pledged to hold follow-on negotiations to 'join their efforts to build a lasting and stable peace regime' on the peninsula.[47]

By the end of 2019 these bright prospects had dimmed.[48] A second North Korea–US summit meeting in Hanoi ended with a cancelled press conference and no joint statement. The primary problem was a disagreement over US sanctions relief for North Korea. A third meeting between President Trump and Chairman Kim, arranged at short notice, took place at the end of June in Panmunjon in the de-militarized zone between North Korea and the

---

[43] Geranmayeh, E. and Rapnouil, M. L., 'Meeting the challenge of secondary sanctions', European Council on Foreign Relations, 25 June 2019.

[44] Deutsche Welle, 'EU mechanism for trade with Iran "now operational"', 28 June 2019; and chapter 11, section III, in this volume.

[45] See chapter 11, section III, in this volume.

[46] Arnold, A. et al., *The Iran Nuclear Archive: Impressions and Implications* (Belfer Center for Science and International Affairs, Harvard Kennedy School: Apr. 2019).

[47] Kile, S. N., 'North Korean–US nuclear diplomacy', *SIPRI Yearbook 2019*, pp. 361–68.

[48] See chapter 11, section II, in this volume.

Republic of Korea (South Korea). However, the goodwill generated by the meeting did not last long. An October meeting between North Korean and US negotiators in Stockholm ended after eight hours with a sharp verbal attack by North Korea on the USA.[49] North Korea gave the USA until the end of the year to change its attitude and warned that it would have an unwelcome 'Christmas surprise' if it did not change its approach.[50] The USA, perhaps not surprisingly, did not announce any change of attitude and showed little sign of taking the deadline seriously.

With limited information coming out from either side, it is not possible to have any degree of clarity about what went wrong. A preparatory meeting in Stockholm in January 2019 before the Hanoi summit meeting appeared to generate a good atmosphere and agreement that progress would be through a series of incremental steps. However, at that point the two sides had different interpretations of the term 'denuclearization' and how to get there.[51] With the negotiating agenda also including the conclusion of a genuine settlement of the Korean War some 70 years on—hardly a straightforward task—there was clearly a need for hard work and lots of it. It may therefore appear that one of the critical deficiencies of the North Korean–US diplomatic process in 2018–19 was a lack of will to put in that detailed work, and perhaps a lack of belief on the part of either leader—or both—that it was necessary or desirable to take that rather traditional, diplomatic approach to working out issues that have been profoundly contentious for decades.

By the end of 2019 while the USA expressed willingness to return to talks whenever an opportunity would arise, North Korea offered no grounds for expecting such an opportunity to arise. One glimmer of hope was perhaps to be found in the fact that North Korea did not come up with the threatened 'Christmas surprise'. At the end of the year the diplomatic process may have stalled, but the resumption of testing of more nuclear devices or long-range missiles by North Korea had not occurred.

The 2020 Review Conference of the Nuclear Non-Proliferation Treaty

The 1968 Treaty on the Non-Proliferation of Nuclear Weapons (Non-Proliferation Treaty, NPT) entered force in 1970. The year 2020 is thus its fiftieth anniversary as well as being the year for the quinquennial review

---

[49] Pak, J. H., 'Why North Korea walked away from negotiations in Sweden', Brookings Institution, 18 Oct. 2019.

[50] Korea Central News Agency, 'DPRK Vice Foreign Minister for US Affairs issues statement', 3 Dec. 2019.

[51] Kim, J. and Smith, J., 'North Korea media says denuclearization includes ending "US nuclear threat"', Reuters, 20 Dec. 2018; and Mason, J. and Holland, S., 'US, North Korea to seek understanding on denuclearization at summit', Reuters, 21 Feb. 2019.

conference (RevCon) as specified under the NPT. Preparations for the 2020 RevCon have unfolded in a difficult context.

The 2020 RevCon is regarded as being especially important because the 2015 iteration was unproductive.[52] This was not unusual; it was the ninth RevCon and the fifth that failed to produce a consensus final document on implementation of the NPT.[53] However, the differences this time seemed to run particularly deep. A key bottleneck issue in 2015 concerned efforts to establish a Middle East zone free of weapons of mass destruction. Several NPT members also expressed deep concern about the pace of nuclear arms reductions.[54] Reductions from an estimated global total of between 65 000 and 70 000 nuclear warheads in the 1980s before the end of the cold war down to 13 865 by 2019 were significant.[55] However, Article VI of the NPT commits the parties to 'negotiations in good faith on effective measures relating to cessation of the nuclear arms race at an early date and to nuclear disarmament'. This has been widely interpreted as giving the nuclear-weapon states (NWSs) the specific responsibility to undertake negotiations with the aim of eliminating all nuclear weapons.

The charge that arms control efforts by the NWSs have been inadequate has encouraged a significant number of states to support and join the 2017 Treaty on the Prohibition of Nuclear Weapons (TPNW). By the end of 2019 the TPNW had been signed by 81 states and ratified by 35; it will enter force for states that are party to it after 50 states have ratified it.[56] Turkish President Recep Tayyip Erdoğan gave a different angle on the argument but expressed the same frustration when, at the start of his speech to the UN General Assembly in September 2019, he asserted that nuclear weapons 'should be forbidden for all or should be permissible for all'. To wide applause, he said: 'The world is bigger than five.'[57]

Against that background, it is worth placing today's non-proliferation concerns in historical perspective. In the early 1970s SIPRI's assessment was that some 15 states had 'near nuclear' status.[58] At the time six states possessed nuclear weapons: China, France, the UK, the USA and the USSR, together with Israel whose possession of nuclear weapons was secret (and officially remains unconfirmed). Three additional states now possess nuclear weapons—India, North Korea and Pakistan—while three states—Belarus,

---

[52] Kulesa, L., 'Five years that will decide the fate of the NPT', European Leadership Network commentary, 1 June 2015·

[53] Duarte, S., 'Unmet promise: The challenges awaiting the 2020 NPT Review Conference', *Arms Control Today*, vol. 48 (Nov. 2018).

[54] For further details, see chapter 11, section IV, in this volume.

[55] See chapter 10, table 10.1, in this volume.

[56] On developments in the TPNW in 2019, see chapter 11, section IV, in this volume.

[57] Gilinsky, V. and Sokolski, H., 'Taking Erdogan's critique of the Nuclear Non-Proliferation Treaty seriously', Bulletin of the Atomic Scientists, 14 Nov. 2019.

[58] 'The near-nuclear countries and the Non-Proliferation Treaty', *SIPRI Yearbook 1972*, pp. 290–98.

Kazakhstan and Ukraine—gave up nuclear weapons that they had a legal right to retain at the time the USSR broke up in 1991. South Africa abandoned its nuclear weapon development during the final years of the apartheid regime, while Iraq's nuclear weapon programme was dismantled under international supervision during the 1990s and Libya's in 2003–2004.[59] Thus, taken overall, non-proliferation has had some success; the NPT has been at the heart of that relatively positive record, and a significant erosion of support for it would be a serious blow against global stability.

Preparations for the 2020 RevCon therefore unfold in a three-part context: the crisis of arms control, the importance and success of the NPT, and the disillusion about the NPT process among many states parties. Unfortunately, the April 2019 preparatory committee for the 2020 RevCon did nothing to dispel the sense that there were weak prospects of progress towards further nuclear arms reductions, in implementing previous commitments related to a zone free of weapons of mass destruction in the Middle East, or building consensus on a wide range of other contentious issues.[60] In an effort to break the logjam of disappointment, disillusion and pessimism, in June 2019 the Swedish Government convened a ministerial conference to discuss a phased, 'stepping stone' approach to nuclear disarmament.[61]

III. Climate change

The pressure of climate change continues to build. The year 2019 was the second hottest on record and concluded a decade 'of exceptional global heat and high-impact weather' according to the World Meteorological Organization.[62] Each decade since the 1980s has been warmer than the previous one. Like the 2010s as a whole, parts of the world experienced retreating ice, record sea levels, increasing ocean heat and acidification, and extreme weather in 2019. Authoritative international reports continued to explore the impact of global temperature increase and associated interlinkages. A

[59] Friedman, U., 'Why one president gave up his country's nukes', *The Atlantic*, 9 Sep. 2017; Atomic Heritage Foundation, 'South African nuclear program', 15 Aug. 2018; and Hart, J. and Kile, S. N., 'Libya's renunciation of nuclear, biological and chemical weapons and ballistic missiles', *SIPRI Yearbook 2005*, pp. 629–48.

[60] Sanders-Zakre, A., 'Deep divisions challenge NPT meeting', *Arms Control Today*, vol. 49 (Apr. 2019); and Einhorn, R., 'The 2020 NPT Review Conference: Prepare for plan B', United Nations Institute for Disarmament Research, [n.d.].

[61] Government Offices of Sweden, 'The Stockholm Ministerial Meeting on Nuclear Disarmament and the Non-Proliferation Treaty', Ministerial declaration, Stockholm, 11 June 2019. See also Ingram, P. and Downman, M., *Stepping Stones to Disarmament: Making Progress in a Polarised International Climate* (The British American Security Information Council: Apr. 2019).

[62] World Meteorological Organization, '2019 concludes a decade of exceptional global heat and high-impact weather', Press release, 3 Dec. 2019; and World Meteorological Organization, 'WMO confirms 2019 as second hottest year on record', Press release, 15 Jan. 2020. See also National Aeronautics and Space Administration, 'NASA, NOAA analyses reveal 2019 second warmest year on record', Press release, 15 Jan. 2020.

definitive intergovernmental report on the state of nature and ecosystems, the first such since 2005, identified a rate of change in nature during the last half century that is without precedent. Changes in the way that sea and land are used have been identified as the driver of change with the greatest impact; climate change was regarded as the third most important driver.[63]

The average global temperature in 2019 was approximately 1°C above the average for 1850–1900, a period often referred to as 'pre-industrial times'. According to the Intergovernmental Panel on Climate Change (IPCC), the current rate of increase is about 0.2°C each decade.[64] At this rate, an average temperature 1.5°C above pre-industrial times will be reached soon after 2040 and the 2°C mark just over two decades later. These are the targets established by the 2015 Paris Agreement on climate change, in which parties agreed to limit global warming to a maximum of 2°C and to try to keep it below 1.5°C.[65] The latter and lower level is often regarded as the maximum amount of global heating before sea-level rise threatens low-lying habitats by the sea, such as islands and coastal plains. It is perhaps salutary to note that the 1.5°C mark has already been reached in the global average temperature on land; it is the sea and ocean averages that keep the global average overall a fraction under 1°C.[66]

Population estimates for low-lying coastal and island areas range from 800 million to 1 billion.[67] Some small island developing states (SIDS) face an existential challenge.[68] There are 570 coastal cities in low-lying coastal areas, including 20 with populations over 10 million.[69] Some analyses raise the prospect of sea-level rise 'all but' erasing some major cities including major financial centres by 2050.[70] However, the more likely risk in those areas stems from the impact of sudden surges in sea level; the IPCC concludes

[63] Díaz, S. et al. (eds), *The Global Assessment Report on Biodiversity and Ecosystem Services: Summary for Policymakers* (Intergovernmental Science-Policy Platform on Biodiversity and Ecosystem Services: Bonn, 2019), p. 12.

[64] IPCC, *Global Warming of 1.5°C* (IPCC: Geneva, 2018), para. A.1.1.

[65] The Paris Agreement opened for signature on 22 Apr. 2016 and entered into force on 4 Nov. 2016, see UN, *Paris Agreement* (UN: 2015).

[66] Shukla, P. R. et al. (eds), 'Summary for policymakers', *Climate Change and Land: An IPCC Special Report on Climate Change, Desertification, Land Degradation, Sustainable Land Management, Food Security, and Greenhouse Gas Fluxes in Terrestrial Ecosystems* (IPCC: Geneva, 2019), paras A.2 and A.2.1.

[67] UN Office of the High Representative for the Least Developed Countries, Landlocked Developing Countries and Small Island Developing States, 'Small island developing states (SIDS) statistics', [n.d.]; C40 Cities, 'Staying afloat: The urban response to sea level rise', [n.d.]; and 'The uncertain future of the coasts', *World Ocean Review*, vol. 1, chapter 3 (2010).

[68] Climate & Development Knowledge Network, The IPCC's Fifth Assessment Report: What's in it for Small Island Developing States? (Climate & Development Knowledge Network: London, 2014); and UN Development Programme, 'Small island nations at the frontline of climate action', 18 Sep. 2017.

[69] C40 Cities (note 68).

[70] Lu, D. and Flavelle, C., 'Rising seas will erase more cities by 2050, new research shows', *New York Times*, 29 Oct. 2019.

that extreme sea-level events that are historically rare (once per century) are likely to occur at least once a year in many places by 2050.[71]

There are clear risks for human security and political stability in the affected regions. If GHG emissions continue to increase at their current rate and if there is no preparation to help communities adapt to the unavoidable consequences of climate change, the humanitarian and security challenges of the 2030s and beyond risk being essentially unmanageable. Yet this is not simply a challenge for the medium-term future. As recent examples in the Middle East have shown, challenges for human security in the form of insecurity of food and water availability can all too quickly and tragically become part of what triggers major upheaval and violence.[72] It has also become clear that the impact of climate change often needs to be addressed amid the tricky business of building peace in war-torn settings. In Somalia for example, SIPRI research has shown how extreme weather events such as floods and droughts undermine efforts to build the institutions of law and governance and strengthen the hand of militia groups and insurgents.[73] And in a different way, 2019 saw many examples of how the impact of climate change was undermining ordinary people's everyday security—in the Australian bush fires from September 2019 to February 2020, and in similar if somewhat less-widespread conflagrations in the Amazon forests, Indonesia and Siberia.[74] During 2019 the UN secretary-general's special representative on disaster risk reduction assessed the rate of climate-related disasters as one per week.[75]

The impact and risks of climate change were confirmed in 2019 as a global issue of the highest priority. Decision makers and experts were in increasing agreement on this, with social movements expressing themselves in school strikes, rallies and marches.[76] In September the UN Climate Action Summit was an effort to raise the level of ambition to reduce GHG emissions and to provide financing for climate action. With some exceptions, few actionable

---

[71] Pörtner, H.-O. et al. (eds), 'Summary for policymakers', *Special Report on the Ocean and Cryosphere in a Changing Climate* (IPCC: Geneva, 25 Sep. 2019).

[72] See e.g. Krampe, F. and Smith, D., 'Climate-related security risks in the Middle East', eds Jägerskog, A. et al., *Routledge Handbook on Middle East Security* (Routledge: Abingdon, 2019); and Schaar, J., 'A confluence of crises: On water, climate and security in the Middle East and North Africa', SIPRI Insights on Peace and Security no. 2019/4, July 2019.

[73] Eklöw, K. and Krampe, F., 'Climate-related security risks and peacebuilding in Somalia', SIPRI Policy Paper no. 53, Oct. 2019. On the armed conflict in Somalia, see chapter 7, section IV, in this volume.

[74] Hughes, L., *Summer of Crisis* (Climate Council of Australia Ltd: Potts Point, 2020); and Pierre-Louis, K., 'The Amazon, Siberia, Indonesia: A world of fire', *New York Times*, 28 Aug. 2019. Some 11 hectares of bush, farmland and towns were affected by the Australian bushfires; in the Amazon fires, it was estimated that almost 1 million hectares were lost to fire.

[75] Harvey, F., 'One climate crisis disaster happening every week, UN warns', *The Guardian*, 7 July 2019.

[76] Collins, A., *The Global Risks Report 2019* (World Economic Forum: Geneva, Feb. 2019); Granados, F., *The Global Risks Report 2020* (World Economic Forum: Geneva, Feb. 2020); and Marris, E., 'Why young climate activists have captured the world's attention', *Nature*, 18 Sep. 2019.

commitments were made at the summit meeting.[77] And the security dimension of climate risk was wholly absent even though the secretary-general himself later described climate change as 'a dramatic threat' to security.[78]

The practical challenge of slowing global warming and avoiding the worst consequences is immense because the average global temperature has risen as a direct result of economic growth and progress. The surface temperatures of land and sea will continue to increase for as long as GHG emissions continue. Most scenarios for limiting global warming to 1.5°C involve exceeding that level before dropping back below it.[79] To achieve that, the global economy needs to be carbon neutral by 2050, with deep cuts—often thought to be about 45 per cent—by 2030. This is the approximate range of targets in the EU long-term strategy, for example.[80] If global warming is never to rise above the 1.5°C target, the cuts in GHG emissions must come earlier and bite deeper. Even the less ambitious path to the 1.5°C target means reversing the last century's increase in GHG emissions and doing so at greater speed. At the same time, economic output has to meet the needs and expectations of a growing global population.[81] By the end of 2019, although plenty of ambitions had been stated, only two governments were on course to meet those targets: Gambia and Morocco.[82] It therefore appears certain that the world will face climate-related security challenges in the 2030s and thereafter, for which it is currently unready, and yet for which there is plenty of time to prepare. In the effort to reduce GHG emissions so the scale of the problems posed by climate change is minimized, and in the effort to adapt to the impact of climate change so its unavoidable consequences are managed, including with the realm of security, the key ingredient for success is international cooperation. There is today an unprecedented level of need for greater cooperation.

IV. The international system and law

The need for cooperation on climate is matched by a similar need on other major challenges of our age—for example in the cyber realm or the risk of

---

[77] Sengupta, S. and Friedman, L., 'At UN climate summit, few commitments and US silence', *New York Times*, 23 Sep. 2019.

[78] UN Climate Change, 'António Guterres calls for increased ambition and commitment at COP25', 1 Dec. 2019.

[79] Levin, K., '8 things you need to know about the IPCC 1.5°C report', World Resources Institute, 7 Oct. 2018.

[80] European Commission, 'A clean planet for all: A European strategic long-term vision for a prosperous, modern, competitive and climate neutral economy', Communication from the Commission to the European Parliament, the European Council, the Council, the European Economic and Social Committee, the Committee of the Regions and the European Investment Bank, COM(2018) 773 final, 28 Nov. 2018.

[81] *The Economist*, 'The past, present and future of climate change', 21 Sep. 2019.

[82] Climate Action Tracker, [n.d.]; Climate Action Tracker, 'Gambia', [n.d.]; and Climate Action Tracker, 'Morocco', [n.d.].

pandemics—as well as on the traditional and major issues of peace and trade. The degree to which international politics are characterized by tensions and disagreements among the major players is a serious cause for concern. There are various issues in dispute among China, Russia and the USA, which also has difficult relations on some issues with France and the UK, its allies. Disharmony at the heart of the international system has been increasingly marked during the last decade.[83] Its contours are made sharper by what is, as remarked upon in the 2019 edition of this Yearbook, an oddity of today's international scene, namely that none of the three great powers—China, Russia and the USA—is a committed status quo power. Each challenges aspects of the world political order. This makes international politics less predictable. In particular, there is more uncertainty than only a few years ago about whether the laws, rules and norms of the international order, such as it is, will be respected. This makes cooperation a more complex and less attractive approach to some key international problems than a more unilateral approach.

There are striking instances in recent years of international law, agreements and norms being ignored and abused. An egregious example is the premeditated murder of the Saudi Arabian journalist Jamal Khashoggi, in October 2018, in the Saudi Arabian Consulate in Istanbul.[84] The US Department of State included the murder among its catalogue of human rights abuses in Saudi Arabia, stating that government agents carried out the killing.[85] The UN went further and described the killing as 'a deliberate, premeditated execution, an extrajudicial killing for which the state of Saudi Arabia is responsible under international human rights law'.[86]

Few incidents of illegal behaviour by states and their representatives carry as much power to shock as that, although there are, of course, other examples of arbitrary behaviour by states, including imprisonment without trial, torture and extrajudicial executions. And there are many other violations of international legal norms—so many that they begin to lack much impact. Russia's 2014 annexation of Crimea from Ukraine is regarded as illegal by the EU, which continues to apply sanctions, but that does not seem to disturb the pattern of Russia's international relations.[87] A UN report finding that Russia—a permanent member of the UN Security Council—has

---

[83] International Crisis Group, 'Council of despair? The fragmentation of UN diplomacy', Special Briefing no. 1, 30 Apr. 2019.

[84] BBC, 'Jamal Khashoggi: All you need to know about Saudi journalist's death', 19 June 2018.

[85] US Department of State, '2018 country reports on human rights practices: Saudi Arabia', 11 Mar. 2019.

[86] UN Office of the High Commissioner for Human Rights, Annex to the report of the special rapporteur on extrajudicial, summary or arbitrary executions: Investigation into the unlawful death of Mr Jamal Khashoggi, A/HRC/41/CRP.1, 19 June 2019, para. 235.

[87] Council of the European Union, 'Illegal annexation of Crimea and Sevastopol: EU extends sanctions by one year', Press release, 20 June 2019.

committed war crimes in Syria during the period from July 2019 to January 2020 elicited little comment or audible outrage.[88] In part this might be due to the deficiencies of the international response to an earlier war crime issue in Syria: the government's alleged use of chemical weapons (CWs) in March and April 2018 in the Douma suburb of Damascus.[89] Less than a week later, France, the UK and the USA launched punitive missile attacks on suspected CW sites in Syria, pre-empting the investigation by the Organisation for the Prohibition of Chemical Weapons.[90] Deciding not to wait for the legally mandated process to unfold was no way for the three governments to support international law; it politicized the issue and made it much less likely that there would eventually be international unity over the incident, regardless of what evidence might emerge. Among other examples of selective approaches to the international legal process is China's rejection in 2016 of the findings of the Permanent Court of Arbitration in a case brought by the Philippines over disputed islets and islands in the South China Sea.[91]

Some of the incidents and issues referred to earlier in this chapter also reflect an over casual attitude to issues of law. On the US withdrawal from the JCPOA, the question of whether the USA could merely ignore a binding resolution of the UN Security Council never figured in official US discussion. India's decision to change the status of Jammu and Kashmir put aside the fragile balance that the constitutional provision on the province was designed to support and may also have diverged from the letter of the law. The move has been challenged in the Supreme Court of India, and the case was still going through the system some six months later.[92] British and Iranian seizures of ships in the Strait of Gibraltar and Strait of Hormuz, respectively, also suggested an attitude that the rule of law could be set aside if the moment was regarded as opportune.

In its own way, one of the stranger incidents of international politics in 2019 revealed the same tendency. A US musician, Rakim Myers, known as A$AP Rocky, and two others were arrested in Stockholm, charged with assault. President Trump's response was to phone the Swedish prime minis-

---

[88] UN General Assembly, Report of the Independent International Commission of Inquiry on the Syrian Arab Republic, A/HRC/43/57, 28 Jan. 2020, paras 21–25, and annex II, paras 6, 15–17.

[89] Hubbard, B., 'Dozens suffocate in Syria as government is accused of chemical attack', *New York Times*, 8 Apr. 2018; and Sanders-Zakre, A, 'More chemical attacks reported in Syria', *Arms Control Today*, vol. 48 (Apr. 2018).

[90] Collins, K. et al., 'What we know about the three sites targeted in Syria', *New York Times*, 14 Apr. 2018.

[91] Permanent Court of Arbitration, 'PCA case no. 2013-19 in the matter of the South China Sea arbitration before an arbitral tribunal constituted under annex VII to the 1982 United Nations Convention on the Law of the Sea between the Republic of the Philippines and the People's Republic of China: Award', 12 July 2016.

[92] Mohanty, S, 'India's top court to hear legal challenges on Kashmir in October', Reuters, 28 Aug. 2019; and Firstpost, 'SC on Article 370 abrogation: Apex court says "five-judge bench competent to hear case", turns down pleas to move matter to larger bench', 2 Mar. 2020.

ter to ask for the musician's release, to tweet that Sweden was ungrateful for all the USA does for it, and to send the special presidential envoy for hostage affairs, Robert O'Brien, to Stockholm at the time of the trial.[93] An official US Government letter on 31 July 2019 warned the Swedish Prosecution Authority of 'negative consequences to the US–Swedish bilateral relationship' if the case was not satisfactorily resolved.[94] The idea that the legal system operates independently of the government is, of course, a basic principle in the USA as well as in Sweden and other countries. In August Myers was found guilty and given a suspended sentence; he returned to Sweden to perform later in the year.[95]

If at the A$AP end of the spectrum, the problem seems to be a frivolous attitude to the law, which may not be taken seriously, it is hard to deny that at the other end of the spectrum there is something truly dangerous. Arguably, states have always behaved like this, when the incentives were strong enough and the disincentives weak. Similarly, and equally arguably, one of the hallmarks of the modern era of international relations has been a steady shift towards there being an increasing number of international laws and regulations to constrain the behaviour of states. Just as with the development of legal systems within countries, so between them, accepting constraints reduces the frequency of arbitrary behaviour. It is easy to exaggerate this historical process. Comments about the importance of the rules-based international system generally overstate the coherence of international relations, just as the once modish term 'international community' overstated the degree of togetherness among the main actors. There is more than one rules-based system governing relations of different kinds among states.[96] Nonetheless, the foundation of the UN at the end of the 1939–45 World War II marked an important moment in a changing global landscape.

It may seem that the disincentives against arbitrary behaviour by states are weakening. If so, that is a serious problem because the current critical challenges raise a requirement for cooperation that is only possible on the basis of a functioning international system. Facing the problems of today, a go-it-alone approach is fantasy; in international relations cooperation is the new realism. Indeed, the evidence that cooperation works for individuals,

---

[93] Donald J. Trump (@realDonaldTrump), 'Give A$AP Rocky his freedom. We do so much for Sweden but it doesn't seem to work the other way round. Sweden should focus on its real crime problem! #FreeRocky', Twitter, 25 July 2019; see also BBC, 'ASAP Rocky: President Trump demands Sweden free US rapper', 26 July 2019; and Heil, E., 'Trump sends envoy for hostage affairs to Sweden "on a mission" to bring back A$AP Rocky', Washington Post, 31 July 2019.

[94] O'Brien, R., Letter from the Embassy of the USA to the Prosecution Authority of the Kingdom of Sweden, 31 July 2019.

[95] Williams, J., 'ASAP Rocky trial verdict: Rapper found guilty of assault in Sweden', Newsweek, 14 Aug. 2019; and Legaspi, A., 'Watch A$AP Rocky return to Sweden to perform in a cage', Rolling Stone, 11 Dec. 2019.

[96] Chalmers, M., 'Which rules? Why there is no single "rules-based international system"', Royal United Services Institute for Defence and Security Studies, Occasional paper, Apr. 2019.

communities, organizations, governments and international institutions is simply too powerful to ignore. Despite everything the practise and institutions of diplomacy are still strong. Even governments whose leaders express loathing of diplomatic means find it next to impossible to do without them. Out of that continued need, however reluctantly recognized, it is more probable than not that new cooperative approaches to shared problems will develop. The spread of COVID-19 will underline the message that other global challenges today also carry, the message that cooperation is essential for human security and international stability.

Part I. Armed conflict and conflict management, 2019

Chapter 2. Global developments in armed conflict, peace processes and peace operations

Chapter 3. Armed conflict and peace processes in the Americas

Chapter 4. Armed conflict and peace processes in Asia and Oceania

Chapter 5. Armed conflict and peace processes in Europe

Chapter 6. Armed conflict and peace processes in the Middle East and North Africa

Chapter 7. Armed conflict and peace processes in sub-Saharan Africa

2. Global developments in armed conflict, peace processes and peace operations

Overview

This chapter describes general developments in 2019 in armed conflicts and peace processes (for detailed regional coverage see chapters 3–7), and global and regional trends and developments in multilateral peace operations.

Section I explores definitions and some of the main features and consequences of the active armed conflicts that occurred in at least 32 states in 2019: 2 in the Americas, 7 in Asia and Oceania, 1 in Europe, 7 in the Middle East and North Africa and 15 in sub-Saharan Africa. As in preceding years, most took place within a single country (intrastate), between government forces and one or more armed non-state groups. Three were major armed conflicts (with more than 10 000 conflict-related deaths in the year)—Afghanistan, Yemen and Syria—and 15 were high-intensity armed conflicts (with 1000–9999 conflict-related deaths)—Mexico, Nigeria, Somalia, the Democratic Republic of the Congo (DRC), Iraq, Burkina Faso, Libya, Mali, South Sudan, the Philippines, India, Myanmar, Cameroon, Pakistan and Egypt. Only one armed conflict was fought between states (border clashes between India and Pakistan), and two were fought between state forces and armed groups that aspired to statehood. All three major armed conflicts and most of the high-intensity armed conflicts were internationalized.

The reduction in the severity of several armed conflicts in 2019 led to a further reduction in conflict fatalities, continuing a recent downward trend since 2014. The number of forcibly displaced people worldwide at the beginning of 2019 was 70.8 million (including more than 25.9 million refugees). Protracted displacement crises continued in Afghanistan, the Central African Republic (CAR), the DRC, Myanmar, Somalia, South Sudan, Syria, Venezuela and Yemen, as well as in the Sahel region. In 2019 almost 30 million people in five countries (Afghanistan, the CAR, Haiti, Somalia and South Sudan) and two regions (the Lake Chad Basin and central Sahel) needed urgent food, nutrition and livelihood assistance.

Of the 21 new peace agreements in 2019, 10 relate to local agreements and 11 to national agreements, although most of the latter were renewal or implementation accords. Two new substantive national peace agreements were signed in sub-Saharan Africa: in the CAR and in Mozambique. Relatively peaceful transitions of power in Ethiopia (in 2018) and Sudan (in 2019) and the implementation of a 2018 peace agreement in South Sudan led to significant decreases in armed violence in those three states. Peace processes

SIPRI Yearbook 2020: Armaments, Disarmament and International Security
www.sipriyearbook.org

in two of the most protracted and complex armed conflicts had mixed results in 2019: in Afghanistan the Taliban–United States peace talks collapsed, before resuming in November 2019; and in Yemen the 2018 Stockholm Agreement was supplemented by a new peace accord, the November 2019 Riyadh Agreement.

Section II describes the trends in multilateral peace operations. With 61 active operations in 2019, there was an increase of one compared to the previous year. Two ended in 2019. These were the Temporary International Presence in Hebron and the United Nations Mission for Justice Support in Haiti (MINUJUSTH). Three started in 2019. These were the UN Integrated Office in Haiti, which succeeded MINUJUSTH, the UN Mission to Support the Hodeidah Agreement in Yemen and the European Union Integrated Border Assistance Mission in Libya, which qualified as a multilateral peace operation under SIPRI's definition following the entry into force of its new mandate.

In spite of this slight increase in the number of multilateral peace operations, the number of personnel deployed in them decreased. This reduction was mainly driven by peace operations conducted by the UN and drawdowns in sub-Saharan Africa. Nonetheless, being responsible for over one-third of all multilateral peace operations and nearly two-thirds of all personnel deployed in them, the UN remains the leading organization in the field.

In spite of a force reduction, the African Union Mission in Somalia remains the largest multilateral peace operation in 2019. In addition, the top three troop contributors were unchanged from the previous year, with Ethiopia leading, followed by the USA and Uganda. The latter two owe their high ranking primarily to their contributions to non-UN operations. In 2019 the annual hostile death rates in UN peacekeeping operations remained relatively stable, but at higher levels than in the preceding decade. However, all but one of the hostile deaths among uniformed UN personnel were recorded in the UN Multidimensional Integrated Stabilization Mission in Mali. The table in section III provides further details on the different multilateral peace operations and the organizations deploying them.

IAN DAVIS AND JAÏR VAN DER LIJN

I. Tracking armed conflicts and peace processes

IAN DAVIS

In 2019, active armed conflicts occurred in at least 32 states: 2 in the Americas, 7 in Asia and Oceania, 1 in Europe, 7 in the Middle East and North Africa, and 15 in sub-Saharan Africa (see chapters 3–7, respectively).[1] As in preceding years most took place within a single country (intrastate), between government forces and one or more armed non-state groups. Only one was fought between states (the border clashes between India and Pakistan), and two were fought between state forces and armed groups that aspired to statehood, with the fighting sometimes spilling outside the recognized state's borders.

Of the intrastate conflicts, three were major armed conflicts (with more than 10 000 conflict-related deaths in the year)—Afghanistan (approximately 41 900 reported fatalities), Yemen (25 900) and Syria (15 300)—and 15 were high-intensity armed conflicts (with 1000–9999 conflict-related deaths in the year)—Mexico (9400), Nigeria (5400), Somalia (4000), the Democratic Republic of the Congo (DRC, 3700), Iraq (3600), Burkina Faso (2200), Libya (2100), Mali (1900), South Sudan (1800), the Philippines (1700), India (1500), Myanmar (1500), Cameroon (1200), Pakistan (1100) and Egypt (1000)—see figure 2.1. The others were low-intensity armed conflicts (with fewer than 1000 conflict-related deaths). However, these categorizations should be considered tentative as fatality information is unreliable.[2] All three major armed conflicts and most of the high-intensity armed conflicts were internationalized; that is, they involved foreign elements that may have led to the conflict being prolonged or exacerbated.[3]

This section discusses the definitions of 'armed conflict' and related terms used in chapters 2–7, and then highlights salient (and largely continuing) features of the armed conflicts and some of their main consequences in 2019, as well as key developments in peace processes during the year.

---

[1] For the definitions of 'armed conflict' and related terms used in chapters 2–7, see the subsection 'Defining armed conflict' and box 2.1 below.

[2] Armed Conflict Location & Event Data Project (ACLED), 'Data export tool', [n.d.]; and ACLED, 'FAQs: ACLED fatality methodology', 27 Jan. 2020. On casualty counting, see also Giger, A., 'Casualty recording in armed conflict: Methods and normative issues', *SIPRI Yearbook 2016*, pp. 247–61.

[3] See e.g. the conclusions in American Bar Association's Center for Human Rights & Rule of Law Initiative, *The Legal Framework Regulating Proxy Warfare* (American Bar Association's Center for Human Rights & Rule of Law Initiative: Dec. 2019), p. 1.

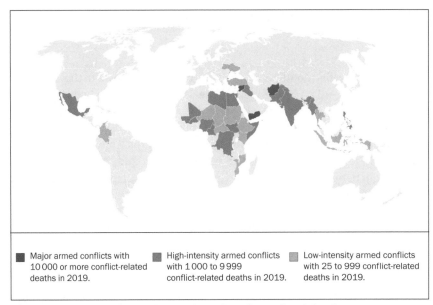

Major armed conflicts with
10 000 or more conflict-related
deaths in 2019.

High-intensity armed conflicts
with 1 000 to 9 999
conflict-related deaths in 2019.

Low-intensity armed conflicts
with 25 to 999 conflict-related
deaths in 2019.

Figure 2.1. Armed conflicts by number of conflict-related deaths, 2019

Defining armed conflict

Armed conflicts are often complex and multifaceted, with multiple actors that have diverse and changeable objectives.[4] This complexity can be a major challenge for the conceptual and legal categorization of armed conflict, as well as thinking on peacebuilding and conflict prevention.[5] Determining the existence of an 'armed conflict' within the framework of international law, for example, differs according to whether the conflict occurs between states (interstate or international armed conflict) or between a state and one or more non-state groups or among two or more non-state groups (intrastate armed conflict, or 'non-international armed conflict' under international humanitarian law).[6] Qualifying the situation as an 'armed conflict' and further defining the nature of the armed conflict—international or non-international—is also crucial for determining the level of protection that

[4] See Davis, I., 'Tracking armed conflicts and peace processes in 2017', *SIPRI Yearbook 2018*, pp. 30–31.

[5] The complexity is captured in United Nations and World Bank, *Pathways for Peace: Inclusive Approaches to Preventing Violent Conflict* (International Bank for Reconstruction and Development/ The World Bank: Washington, DC, 2018).

[6] For a primary source on the definition of armed conflicts, see the 1949 Geneva Conventions common Article 2 and 1977 Additional Protocol I, Article 1 (international), and 1949 Geneva Conventions common Article 3 and Additional Protocol II, Article 1 (non-international). Also see e.g. International Committee of the Red Cross, 'How is the term "armed conflict" defined in international humanitarian law?', Opinion Paper, Mar. 2008; and International Committee of the Red Cross, *International Humanitarian Law and the Challenges of Contemporary Armed Conflicts* (International Committee of the Red Cross: Oct. 2019), pp. 50–52, 58–59, 75–76.

should be granted to non-combatants, for defining the status of a combatant and for determining the level of obligations towards captured adversaries.

Not every situation of armed violence amounts to an armed conflict. For example, although criminal violence can threaten the authority and capability of a state as much as an armed conflict, law enforcement activities unconnected to an armed conflict fall outside the scope of international humanitarian law (even if a state's military is involved). If, however, the criminal violence meets the threshold of a non-international armed conflict—as was the case in 2019 for the armed conflict between the Jalisco New Generation Cartel, an organized crime group, and the Mexican Government (see chapter 3, section III)—then international humanitarian law applies.

In 2019 most armed conflicts occurred within states. While there can be complications in grading an international armed conflict—for example, intervention of foreign or multinational forces in armed conflicts not otherwise of an international character or extraterritorial uses of force by a state—classifying non-international armed conflicts is usually more complex. There is often no clear dividing line between intrastate armed conflicts and usually smaller-scale incidents of internal violence, such as riots and organized crime gangs. The threshold for an intrastate armed conflict must be evaluated on a case-by-case basis by weighing a range of indicative data. The two key thresholds relevant to the classification of a non-international armed conflict are: (*a*) protracted armed violence and (*b*) one or more organized armed groups. This evaluation might include whether explicit political goals are stated by the actors, the duration of the conflict, the frequency and intensity of the acts of violence and military operations and the degree of continuity between them, the nature of the weapons used, displacement of civilians, territorial control by opposition forces and the number of victims (including the dead, wounded and displaced people).[7] In the Americas in 2019 it was particularly difficult to distinguish between high levels of political violence and armed conflict (see chapter 3).

This complexity in defining an armed conflict also contributes in part to the differences among the main data sets on violence and conflict—including the one that is predominantly used in chapters 2–7 of this Yearbook, the Armed Conflict Location & Event Data Project (ACLED)—each of which has its own definitions and methodology.[8] This part of the Yearbook offers a primarily descriptive (rather than quantitative) synopsis of trends and events in 2019

---

[7] Vité, S., 'Typology of armed conflicts in international humanitarian law: Legal concepts and actual situations', *International Review of the Red Cross*, vol. 91, no. 873 (Mar. 2009), pp. 69–94.

[8] For an overview of the major advances in the collection and availability of armed conflict data, see Brzoska, M., 'Progress in the collection of quantitative data on collective violence', *SIPRI Yearbook 2016*, pp. 191–200.

Box 2.1. Definitions and types of armed conflict

Armed conflict involves the use of armed force between two or more states or non-state organized armed groups. For the purpose of Part I of this Yearbook, there is a threshold of violence causing 25 or more deaths in a given year. With the caveat that data on conflict deaths is often imprecise and tentative, the chapters categorize such conflicts, based on the number of conflict-related deaths in the current year, as *major* (10 000 or more deaths), *high-intensity* (1000–9999 deaths) or *low-intensity* (25–999 deaths).

Armed conflict can be further categorized as follows:

Interstate armed conflict, the use of armed force by one or more states against another state or states, is now rare and mostly occurs at lower intensities or shorter durations. While territorial, border and other disputes persist among states, they are unlikely to escalate to armed conflict.

Intrastate armed conflict, the most common form of armed conflict today, usually involves sustained violence between a state and one or more non-state groups fighting with explicitly political goals (e.g. taking control of the state or part of the territory of the state)—although the question of goals is not relevant to the legal classification. It can also be classified as follows:

- *Subnational armed conflict* is typically confined to particular areas within a sovereign state, with economic and social activities in the rest of the country proceeding relatively normally. This kind of conflict often takes place in stable, middle-income countries with relatively strong state institutions and capable security forces. Sometimes it takes place in a troubled border region in a large country that expanded geographically in the past or has arbitrarily drawn borders.

- *Civil war* involves most of the country and results in at least 1000 conflict-related deaths in a given year.

- Either type of conflict is considered *internationalized* if there is significant involvement of a foreign entity (excluding United Nations peace operations) that is clearly prolonging or exacerbating the conflict—such as armed intervention in support of, or provision of significant levels of weapons or military training to, one or more of the conflict parties by a foreign government or foreign non-state actor.

Extrastate armed conflict occurs between a state and a political entity that is not widely recognized as a state but has long-standing aspirations of statehood (e.g. the Israeli–Palestinian conflict). Such conflicts, which are rare, may take place inside and outside of the state boundaries recognized by the international community.

Note: These definitions apply to chapters 2 to 7 of this volume. They are not legal definitions, so conclusions based on them can be political only; it is not possible to draw legal conclusions from such definitions, including on the applicability or otherwise of international humanitarian law to the armed violence in question.

---

affecting key armed conflicts.[9] It uses a loose framework to characterize and distinguish armed conflicts within the three major categories: interstate, intrastate and extrastate (see box 2.1). It also differentiates them from other kinds of organized group violence (such as criminal violence). To define a series of violent events as an armed conflict, a threshold of 25 conflict-related deaths in a year is used.

---

[9] For more on events in 2019 related to armaments, disarmament and international security, see annex C in this volume.

Significant features of armed conflicts in 2019

Most armed conflicts since the cold war are fought by regular armies and also militias and armed civilians. Fighting is often intermittent with a wide range of intensities and brief ceasefires, and rarely occurs on well-defined battlefields. The nature of most armed conflicts is context specific; this subsection highlights some of the most significant features of several armed conflicts in 2019.

While evidence suggests that violence is becoming increasingly concentrated in urban areas, this largely relates to political and criminal violence (issues that are largely outside the scope of the Yearbook).[10] The picture regarding armed conflicts is mixed. While many post-cold war armed conflicts tend to be fought primarily in urban areas, others retain a strong rural dimension. Civilians are at great risk from urban and rural armed conflicts, but the risks multiply in urban settings: when explosive weapons were used in populated areas, for the ninth consecutive year over 90 per cent of the casualties in 2019 were civilians.[11] The use of explosive weapons in urban areas—especially explosive weapons with a large destructive radius, inaccurate delivery system or capacity to deliver multiple munitions over a wide area—is a growing concern and the focus of some humanitarian arms control efforts.[12]

The number of armed groups involved in conflict has increased over the past 70 years, from an average of 8 per intrastate conflict in 1950 to 14 in 2010, according to a joint United Nations–World Bank study.[13] Despite the growing numbers of non-state armed groups, state forces remained the most powerful and violent actors in 2019, and were responsible for the largest number of civilian fatalities according to ACLED.[14]

As was the case in 2018, organized violence, as measured by ACLED, decreased overall in 2019 but spread to more places. Five armed conflicts—in Afghanistan, Yemen, Syria, Mexico and Nigeria—had the highest fatality estimates, with a combined total of nearly 98 000 fatalities in 2019 (about 78 per cent of the total conflict-related fatalities).[15] Although battle-related events decreased by 15 per cent in 2019 compared with 2018, all other ACLED categories of political violence events increased: explosions/remote violence

---

[10] Organisation for Economic Co-operation and Development, *States of Fragility 2016: Understanding Violence* (Organisation for Economic Co-operation and Development: Paris, 2016); Anthony, I., 'International humanitarian law: ICRC guidance and its application in urban warfare', *SIPRI Yearbook 2017*, pp. 545–53; and International Committee of the Red Cross, 'War in cities', [n.d.].

[11] Action on Armed Violence, 'Explosive violence in 2019', 7 Jan. 2020.

[12] See chapter 13, section I, in this volume. See also Overton, I. et al., *Wide-Area Impact: Investigating the Wide-Area Effect of Explosive Weapons* (Action on Armed Violence: Feb. 2016).

[13] UN and World Bank (note 5), p. 15.

[14] Kishi, R. et al., *Year in Review* (ACLED: Mar. 2020), pp. 31–34.

[15] Kishi et al. (note 14), pp. 18–23.

by 5 per cent, violence against civilians by 7 per cent and mob violence by 47 per cent.[16]

Conflict-affected populations often play a role in attempting to secure their own protection via 'avoidance' (escaping or moving away from the threat), 'containment' (managing the threat locally, such as by paying taxes or engaging in direct negotiations with local power holders) or 'confrontation' (aligning with one of the conflict parties or by forming local armed self-defence groups).[17] For example, in the Sahel region in 2019, ethnic and village 'self-defence' militias were increasingly widespread.[18]

The forced recruitment and use of child soldiers and sexual violence are widely perpetrated in armed conflict. In 2018 (the last year for which data is available) Somalia remained the country with the highest number of cases of the recruitment and use of children (2300) followed by Nigeria (1947).[19] In an annual report on conflict-related sexual violence, the UN secretary-general described 19 countries of concern and an updated list of 50 parties to conflict that were credibly suspected of having committed or instigated sexual violence in 2018 (the year covered by the report), as well as a 'disturbing trend' of sexual violence perpetrated against very young girls and boys in Afghanistan, Burundi, the Central African Republic (CAR), the DRC, Myanmar, Somalia, South Sudan, Sri Lanka, Sudan and Yemen.[20] ACLED found there were twice as many targeted political violence events—a broader category than just armed conflicts—against women in the first quarter of 2019 compared with the first quarter of 2018.[21]

In February 2019 the UN and the International Committee of the Red Cross pledged to strengthen efforts to combat sexual violence in conflict settings, while UN Security Council Resolution 2467 (2019), adopted on 23 April 2019, called for a survivor-centred approach in the prevention and response to the problem.[22]

During many of the armed conflicts, especially the major and high-intensity conflicts, other international humanitarian law violations were also committed, including the use of starvation to achieve military ends, the denial of humanitarian aid, forced displacement, and attacks on aid and

---

[16] Kishi et al. (note 14), p. 2.

[17] Bonwick, A., 'Who really protects civilians?' *Development in Practice*, vol. 16, no. 3–4 (2006), pp. 270–77; and Metcalfe-Hough, V., *Localising Protection Responses in Conflicts: Challenges and Opportunities*, Humanitarian Policy Group Report (Overseas Development Institute: Nov. 2019).

[18] See chapter 7, section II, in this volume.

[19] UN General Assembly and UN Security Council, 'Children and armed conflict', Report of the Secretary-General, A/73/907–S/2019/509, 20 June 2019.

[20] UN Security Council, 'Conflict related sexual violence', Report of the UN Secretary-General, S/2019/280, 29 Mar. 2019, p. 6.

[21] Kishi, R. et al., *'Terribly and Terrifyingly Normal': Political Violence Targeting Women* (ACLED: May 2019).

[22] Schlein, L., 'UN, ICRC address sexual, gender-based violence in conflict situations', Voice of America, 25 Feb. 2019; and UN Security Council Resolution 2467, 23 Apr. 2019.

health workers, hospitals and schools. Such violations appear to be on the increase—the rules that are meant to protect civilians in war are being broken regularly and systematically, while in remarks to the UN Security Council on the protection of civilians in armed conflict, the UN secretary-general said compliance with international humanitarian law had 'deteriorated'.[23]

Consequences of armed conflicts in 2019

Armed conflicts result in loss of life and life-changing injuries, displacement of civilian populations and destruction of infrastructure and institutions. They also have long-term economic, developmental, political, environmental, health and social consequences.

The reduction in the severity of several armed conflicts in 2019 led to a further reduction in conflict fatalities in 2019, continuing a recent downward trend since 2014. Total deaths from organized violence, as measured by the Uppsala Conflict Data Program (UCDP), reached a 15-year high in 2014 with about 103 000 deaths. UCDP's most recent data, for 2018, showed almost 76 000 deaths, a decrease for the fourth successive year to a level 43 per cent lower than the latest peak in 2014.[24] More limited in its geographic coverage (for 2019 it covered all regions except Latin America and parts of Europe) but broader in scope in the forms of violence and conflict events covered, ACLED reported a 17 per cent reduction in fatalities from political violence from about 152 000 fatalities in 2018 to 126 000 in 2019, confirming a continuation in the downward trend. According to ACLED, reported fatalities decreased most substantially in the Middle East in 2019 (by 34 per cent), particularly in Iraq and Syria. However, significant increases in conflict-related fatalities were recorded in Burkina Faso (an increase of 625 per cent), Myanmar (582 per cent), Mozambique (197 per cent), Libya (74 per cent) and the DRC (18 per cent).[25]

Armed conflict is also a major driver of displacement.[26] The number of forcibly displaced people worldwide at the end of 2018 was 70.8 million (including 25.9 million refugees), up from 68.5 million in 2017 and twice as many people as 20 years ago.[27] It seems likely that these record numbers

---

[23] See e.g. UN Security Council, 'Women and peace and security', Report of the Secretary-General, S/2019/800, 9 Oct. 2019; UN Secretary-General, 'Secretary-general's remarks to the Security Council on the protection of civilians in armed conflict', 23 May 2019; and Safeguarding Health in Conflict, *Impunity Remains: 2018 Attacks on Health Care in 23 Countries in Conflict* (Safeguarding Health in Conflict: May 2019).

[24] Pettersson, T. et al., 'Organized violence, 1989–2018 and peace agreements', *Journal of Peace Research*, vol. 56, no. 4 (2019), pp. 589–603.

[25] Kishi et al. (note 14), pp. 13–14, 26–29.

[26] See Grip, L., 'Coping with crises: Forced displacement in fragile contexts', *SIPRI Yearbook 2017*, pp. 253–83.

[27] UN High Commissioner for Refugees, *Global Trends: Forced Displacement in 2018* (UN High Commissioner for Refugees: Geneva, 2019).

continued into 2019 (for which global figures were not yet available at the time of publication). In 2019, for example, the armed conflict in Syria continued to drive the world's largest refugee crisis, with 6.7 million refugees (up from 5.6 million in 2018) and more than 6 million Syrians internally displaced at the beginning of 2019—out of a total estimated population of 22 million people at the start of the civil war in 2011.[28] Displacement also dramatically increased in the Sahel region, and protracted displacement crises continued in many other places, including Afghanistan, the CAR, the DRC, Myanmar, Somalia, South Sudan, Venezuela and Yemen. Many displaced people crossed international borders in search of protection and assistance as refugees, although most were displaced within their own countries.[29]

In 2019 almost 30 million people in five countries (Afghanistan, the CAR, Haiti, Somalia and South Sudan) and two regions (the Lake Chad Basin and central Sahel) were experiencing protracted conflict (or other forms of instability) and insecurity, and needed urgent food, nutrition and livelihood assistance. The DRC, Sudan, Syria and Yemen were almost certainly food insecure as well, but there was no updated acute food insecurity data for late 2019 available for them.[30] At the beginning of 2019, for example, more than half the population of Yemen (15.9 million people) were in urgent need of food and livelihood assistance.[31]

Large numbers of children suffer the consequences of armed conflicts: in 2018 (the latest year for which figures are available), 415 million children, almost one fifth of children worldwide, were living in areas affected by armed conflict (3 per cent fewer children than in 2017)—149 million in high-intensity or major armed conflict zones (i.e. those with 1000 or more conflict-related deaths in a year).[32] Hundreds of thousands of children die every year as a result of the indirect effects of conflict, including malnutrition, disease and the breakdown of healthcare, water supply and sanitation. The UN secretary-general's annual report on children and armed conflict documented more than 25 000 incidents of 'grave violations' against children in conflicts around the world in 2018—1000 less than in 2017 (which had been the highest ever recorded). The six categories of grave violations covered in the report are: killing and maiming of children, recruitment and use of children as soldiers,

---

[28] On the armed conflict in Syria, see chapter 6, section II, in this volume.

[29] UN Office for the Coordination of Humanitarian Affairs (UNOCHA), *Global Humanitarian Overview 2020* (UNOCHA: Geneva, Dec. 2019), p. 13.

[30] Food and Agriculture Organization of the UN and World Food Programme, 'Monitoring food security in countries with conflict situations: A joint FAO/WFP update for the members of the United Nations Security Council', issue no. 7, Jan. 2020. See the relevant conflict chapters in this volume for the situations in the DRC, Sudan, Syria and Yemen.

[31] UNOCHA (note 29), p. 12.

[32] Østby, G. et al., 'Children affected by armed conflict, 1990–2018', Conflict Trends no. 1, Peace Research Institute Oslo, 2020. For an overview of the literature on the use of children in armed conflict, see Haer, R., 'Children and armed conflict: Looking at the future and learning from the past', *Third World Quarterly*, vol. 40, no. 1 (2019), pp. 74–91.

sexual violence against children, abduction of children, attacks on schools and hospitals, and denial of humanitarian access.[33]

New data in 2019 from the World Health Organization suggested that one in five people living in conflict zones have mental health conditions. This is a figure substantially higher than previously thought—data it published in 2016 suggested that 1 in 16 people suffered from such problems in conflict zones.[34]

Armed conflict also imposes substantial economic costs on society. While calculating the economic costs of violence is extremely difficult, one study estimated the global cost to be $14.1 trillion in 2018, or 11.2 per cent of the global gross domestic product (GDP). This was a slight improvement on the 2017 calculation, mainly due to significant reductions in the economic impact of armed conflict and terrorism in 2018. The economic impact of violence in the 10 most affected countries was equivalent to 35 per cent of their GDP; the economic costs of violence in Syria, Afghanistan and the CAR in 2018 were equivalent to 67, 47 and 42 per cent of GDP, respectively.[35]

Finally, armed conflict also contributes to the deteriorating condition of the global environment, with consequences for sustainable development, human security and ecosystems—vulnerabilities that are being amplified by increasingly unpredictable climate patterns.[36] In South Sudan, for example, efforts to rebuild globally important protected areas in 2019 were hampered by insecurity and small arms proliferation.[37] States and armed groups also used the environment as a weapon to target vulnerable populations. In Syria, for example, crop fields were deliberately set on fire, resulting in wildfires that affected food security.[38] In July 2019 the International Law Commission (ILC)—a body of experts established in 1947 by the UN General Assembly to help develop and codify international law—adopted 28 legal principles intended to enhance the protection of the environment in relation to armed conflicts.[39] The ILC has been working on this initiative since 2013, and many other independent experts have called for a Fifth Geneva Convention relative

[33] UN General Assembly and UN Security Council, A/73/907–S/2019/509 (note 19), p. 2.

[34] Charlson, F. et al., 'New WHO prevalence estimates of mental disorders in conflict settings: A systematic review and meta-analysis', *The Lancet*, vol. 394, no. 10194 (2019), pp. 240–48.

[35] Institute for Economics and Peace, *Global Peace Index 2019: Measuring Peace in a Complex World* (Institute for Economics and Peace: Sydney, June 2019), p. 3. Also see Iqbal, M. et al., 'Estimating the global economic cost of violence: Methodology improvement and estimate updates', *Defence and Peace Economics* (2019).

[36] Schaar, J., 'A confluence of crises: On water, climate and security in the Middle East and North Africa', SIPRI Insights on Peace and Security, no. 2019/4, July 2019; and *The Economist*, 'How climate change can fuel wars', 23 May 2019.

[37] Mednick, S., 'South Sudan tries to protect wildlife after long conflict', Associated Press, 27 July 2019.

[38] Parker, B., 'As crops burn in Syria conflict zone, hunger warnings for civilians', New Humanitarian, 7 June 2019.

[39] Pantazopoulos, S., 'UN lawyers approve 28 legal principles to reduce the environmental impact of war', Conflict and Environment Observatory, 16 July 2019; and UN General Assembly, 'Protection of the environment in relation to armed conflicts', International Law Commission, 6 June 2019.

Table 2.1. Number of peace agreements, 2010–19

2010	2011	2012	2013	2014	2015	2016	2017	2018	2019
33	51	62	42	79	69	75	74	69	21[a]

[a] At the time of writing, the PA-X database contained 19 peace agreements and excluded the two peace accords in Mozambique because the texts were not publicly available (see table 2.2).

Source: PA-X, 'Peace agreements database and access tool, version 3', Political Settlements Research Programme, University of Edinburgh, [n.d.], <https://www.peaceagreements.org>.

to the Protection of Civilian Persons in Time of War on the environment.[40] States debated the draft principles during the UN General Assembly Sixth Committee meeting in November 2019, and a final version of the principles is expected to be adopted in 2021.[41]

Peace processes in 2019

Like the conflicts they attempt to address, peace processes are also increasingly complex, multidimensional and highly internationalized, with a wide range of actors, activities and outcomes.[42] There is also a growing number of peace agreement databases and collections, although the evidence suggests that there have been fewer peace agreements, despite increasing numbers of armed conflicts in recent years.[43] According to the UCDP, for example, in the period 1991–94 the peak in the number of armed conflicts corresponded with a similar peak in peace agreements (82 peace agreements

[40] See e.g. an open letter from a group of conservation biologists who witnessed the impact on wildlife in the Sahel from arms proliferation: Durant, S. M. and Brito, J. C., 'Stop military conflicts from trashing environment', *Nature*, vol. 571 (25 July 2019); and Gleick, P., 'Protecting the environment in times of war', Bulletin of the Atomic Scientists, 20 Sep. 2019.

[41] UN General Assembly, Sixth Committee, 'Sixth Committee speakers debate scope for draft texts on Protection of Environment in Armed Conflict, as International Law Commission review continues', GA/L/3610, 5 Nov. 2019; and Conflict and Environment Observatory, 'Report: 2019's UN General Assembly debate on the protection of the environment in relation to armed conflicts', Dec. 2019.

[42] Wolff, S., 'The making of peace: Processes and agreements', *Armed Conflict Survey*, vol. 4, no. 1 (2018), pp. 65–80. On the role of donor support, see Ross, N. and Schomerus, M., 'Donor support to peace processes: A lessons for peace literature review', Overseas Development Institute Working Paper 571, Feb. 2020. On implementation measures for peace agreements, see Molloy, S. and Bell, C., *How Peace Agreements Provide for Implementation* (Political Settlements Research Programme: 2019). On the role of human rights in peace agreements, see Lacatus, C. and Nash, K., 'Peace agreements and the institutionalisation of human rights: A multi-level analysis', *International Journal of Human Rights* (2019).

[43] Examples include: UN Peacemaker, 'Peace agreements database', [n.d.], <https://peacemaker.un.org/document-search>; UN Peacemaker and University of Cambridge, 'Language of peace database', [n.d.], <https://www.languageofpeace.org/#/>; University of Edinburgh, Political Settlements Research Programme, 'PA-X peace agreements database', [n.d.], <https://www.peaceagreements.org/search>; University of Notre Dame, Kroc Institute for International Peace Studies, 'Peace accords matrix', [n.d.], <https://peaceaccords.nd.edu>; and UCDP, 'UCDP peace agreement dataset', [n.d.], <https://ucdp.uu.se/downloads/>.

in 192 active 'conflict years'). However, in the 207 conflict years recorded in the period 2015–18, only 23 peace agreements were concluded.[44]

The PA-X database, which contains 1832 peace agreements found in more than 150 peace processes in the period 1990–2019 (including agreements from a wider variety of negotiation practices than covered by the UCDP), shows a particularly strong decrease in 2019 compared to the previous nine years (see table 2.1). A less effective and less influential UN Security Council may be partly to blame for the lower number of peace agreements in 2019. For example, the International Crisis Group cited three geopolitical trends affecting the UN Security Council in 2019: worsening Western tensions with China, diverging United States and European strategies, and tensions over how to deal with crises in Africa, including between the UN and the African Union.[45]

The 21 new peace agreements in 2019 are listed in table 2.2. Ten relate to local agreements and 11 to intrastate (national agreements), although most of the latter were renewal or implementation accords. Two new substantive national peace agreements were signed in sub-Saharan Africa: in the CAR and in Mozambique. In the latter, former armed opposition group, the Mozambican National Resistance (RENAMO), signed a ceasefire and a separate peace deal with the government, formally ending an armed conflict that first began in the late 1970s. In addition, relatively peaceful transitions of power in Ethiopia (in 2018) and Sudan (in 2019) and the implementation of a 2018 peace agreement in South Sudan led to significant decreases in armed violence in those three states.[46] Political change in Ukraine in 2019 also brought new vitality to efforts to end the six-year conflict with Russian-backed separatists in the country's eastern Donbas region.[47] Peace processes in two of the most protracted and complex armed conflicts had mixed results in 2019: in Afghanistan the Taliban–US peace talks collapsed in September 2019, before resuming in November 2019; and in Yemen the 2018 Stockholm Agreement was supplemented by a new peace accord, the November 2019 Riyadh Agreement, although much work was still needed to implement the two agreements.[48] On the Korean peninsula, discussions between the

---

[44] Pettersson et al. (note 24), pp. 594–95.

[45] Gowan, R., 'Three troubling trends at the UN Security Council', International Crisis Group commentary, 6 Nov. 2019; and International Crisis Group, 'Council of despair? The fragmentation of UN diplomacy', Special Briefing no. 1, 30 Apr. 2019. On the lack of cooperation in the international system, and specifically Western tensions with China, also see chapter 1 and chapter 4, section I, in this volume.

[46] On the peace processes in sub-Saharan Africa, see chapter 7 in this volume.

[47] On the peace process in Ukraine, see chapter 5, section II, in this volume.

[48] On the peace process in Afghanistan, see chapter 4, section II, in this volume; on the peace process in Yemen, see chapter 6, section V, in this volume.

Table 2.2. Peace agreements in 2019

Country	Date of agreement	Agreement	Conflict level	Stage
Afghanistan	8 July 2019	Resolution of Intra Afghan Peace Conference in Doha, Qatar (Doha Roadmap for Peace)	Intrastate	Pre-negotiation/ process
Central African Republic	6 March 2019	Compte Rendu des Activities du Comite de Suivi de L'Accord de Paix a Bangassou	Local	Implementation/ renegotiation (addresses new or outstanding issues)
	5 February 2019	Political Agreement for Peace and Reconciliation in the Central African Republic (Khartoum Accord)	Intrastate	Framework/ substantive— comprehensive (agreement)
	21 January 2019	Proces verbal de gestion de conflit	Local	Framework/ substantive—partial (core issue)
	9 January 2019	Accord Entre Les Groupes Armes de Batangafo	Local	Framework/ substantive—partial (multiple issues)
Libya	22 January 2019	Statement from the Sheikhs and Dignitaries of the Tribes of Tarhunah Regarding the Events Taking Place in Southern Tripoli	Local	Framework/ substantive—partial (multiple issues)
Mali	1 August 2019	Humanitarian agreement between Bambara and Bozo farmers, Fulani herders as well as hunters from the area ('circle') of Djenné	Local	Framework/ substantive—partial (core issue)
	25 July 2019	Agreement between the Dafing, Samogo, Fulani, Dogon and Bozo communities of the Baye municipality, located in the area ('circle') of Bankass and the region of Mopti (Baye agreement)	Local	Framework/ substantive—partial (core issue)
Mozambique[a]	6 August 2019	Peace and National Reconciliation Agreement, between the Government of Mozambique and Renamo, signed at Praça da Paz in Maputo	Intrastate	Unknown

Country	Date of agreement	Agreement	Conflict level	Stage
Mozambique *continued*	1 August 2019	Agreement between the Government of Mozambique and RENAMO to definitively cease military hostilities, signed in Chitengo, Gorongosa National Park	Intrastate	Ceasefire
Philippines	22 December 2019	Context and premises of the CPP declaration of ceasefire (December 23, 2019 to January 7, 2020)	Intrastate	Ceasefire/related (ceasefire)
South Sudan	7 November 2019	Communique on the occasion of the tripartite summit on the Revitalised Agreement on Resolution of the Conflict in Republic of South Sudan	Intrastate	Renewal (renewal implementation)
Sudan	17 July 2019	Political agreement on establishing the structures and institutions of the transitional period between the Transitional Military Council and the Declaration of Freedom and Change Forces	Intrastate	Framework/substantive—partial (multiple issues)
Syria	8 February 2019	Agreement of reconciliation between Hurras al-Din and Hayat Tahrir al-Sham in the countryside of Aleppo	Local	Other
	10 January 2019	Agreement for a ceasefire and exchange of prisoners between Tahrir al-Sham and the National Liberation Front (NLF) in Idlib	Local	Ceasefire/related (ceasefire)
Ukraine	9 December 2019	Paris 'Normandie' Summit Common agreed conclusions	Intrastate	Implementation/renegotiation (addresses new or outstanding issues)
	17 July 2019	Statement of the Trilateral Contact Group as of 17 July 2019	Intrastate	Renewal (renewal implementation)
Yemen	5 November 2019	Riyadh agreement between the legitimate Government of Yemen and the Southern Transitional Council (STC)	Intrastate	Framework/substantive—partial (multiple issues)

Country	Date of agreement	Agreement	Conflict level	Stage
Yemen *continued*	26 April 2019	Document of Reconciliation between areas of al-Mahariq and al-Saliyah, Sheikh Othman, Aden	Local	Ceasefire/related (ceasefire)
	7 April 2019	Document of Reconciliation and Forgiveness Between the Families of the Al Ali bin Ahmad Al Awlaqi Clan	Local	Framework/ substantive— comprehensive (agreement)
	16 January 2019	United Nations Security Council Resolution 2452	Intrastate	Ceasefire/related (related)

[a] The two peace agreements in Mozambique were not publicly available at the time of writing.

Notes: Pre-negotiation/process: Agreements that aim to get parties to the point of negotiating over the incompatibilities at the heart of the conflict.

Framework/substantive—partial: Agreements that concern parties that are engaged in discussion and agreeing to substantive issues to resolve the conflict, but only deal with some of the issues in ways that appear to contemplate future agreements to complete.

Framework/substantive—comprehensive: Agreements that concern parties that are engaged in discussion and agreeing to substantive issues to resolve the conflict, and appear to be set out as a comprehensive attempt to resolve the conflict.

Implementation/renegotiation: Aiming to implement an earlier agreement.

Renewal: These are short agreements (typically of just one page), which do nothing other than 'renew' previous commitments.

Ceasefire/related: This category contains agreements which provide in their entirety for a ceasefire, or association demobilization, or an agreement that is purely providing a monitoring arrangement for, or extension, of a ceasefire.

Other: This is a residual category, capturing all agreements that do not fit the definitions above.

Sources: PA-X, 'Peace agreements database and access tool, version 3', Political Settlements Research Programme, University of Edinburgh, [n.d.], <https://www.peaceagreements.org>; Bell, C. et al., 'Peace agreement database and dataset v3, codebook', 31 Jan. 2020, <https://www.peaceagreements.org/files/PA-X%20codebook%20Version3.pdf>; Government of Mozambique, 'Presidente da República e Presidente da Renamo assinam acordo' [President of the Republic and President of Renamo sign agreement], [n.d.]; and Government of Mozambique, '"Hoje é dia da celebração da paz e da concórdia entre os moçambicanos"—PR' ["Today is the day for the celebration of peace and harmony between Mozambicans"—PR], [n.d.].

Democratic People's Republic of Korea (DPRK, North Korea) and the USA that had seemed promising in 2018 stalled in 2019.[49]

Peacebuilding efforts typically include: disarmament, demobilization and reintegration (DDR) of former combatants; ceasefire negotiations; signing of peace agreements; multilateral peace operations; power-sharing arrangements; and state-building measures. These are all designed to

---

[49] On the North Korean–US talks, see chapter 1, chapter 4, section I, and chapter 11, section II, in this volume.

bring about sustainable peace among parties to a conflict.[50] Many of the DDR programmes are supported as part of UN peace operations.[51] There has also been more effort in recent years to make peace processes more inclusive, especially by promoting increased representation of women. However, women continue to be under-represented in the political–military hierarchies at the centre of peace negotiations.[52] Efforts at increasing women's participation in peace operations and in improving gender training for peacekeepers have had similarly limited results.[53]

Not all peace processes lead to sustainable peace. Inconclusive political settlements, failure to address the root causes of a conflict, and ongoing insecurity and tensions have often led to non-compliance, violations and a recurrence of armed conflict.[54] Many contemporary peace processes are long, drawn-out affairs that 'institutionalise forms of disagreement' to contain rather than resolve the conflict.[55] Indeed, this may be the best option where resolution of the conflict is not possible. Some peace agreements break down and hostilities resume, whereas others achieve a relatively stable ceasefire but not a sustainable conflict settlement (such as the unresolved armed conflicts in the post-Soviet space, see chapter 5). Even relatively successful peace agreements, such as the 2016 agreement in Colombia, face continuing challenges (see chapter 3).

Since the mid-1990s most armed conflicts have been new outbreaks of old conflicts rather than conflicts over new issues. One study of 216 peace agreements signed during 1975–2011 revealed that 91 were followed by a resumption of violence within five years. This indicates that peace processes

---

[50] On multilateral peace operations, see section II in this chapter. On various interpretations of the term 'peace' as well as other tools for realizing peace, see Caparini, M. and Milante, G., 'Sustaining peace and sustainable development in dangerous places', *SIPRI Yearbook 2017*, pp. 211–52; and Caplan, R., *Measuring Peace: Principles, Practices and Politics* (Oxford: Oxford University Press, 2019).

[51] UN Peacekeeping, 'Disarmament, demobilization and reintegration', [n.d.]. Also see Bussmann, M., 'Military integration, demobilization, and the recurrence of civil war', *Journal of Intervention and Statebuilding*, vol. 13, no. 1 (2019), pp. 95–111.

[52] Bell, C. and McNicholl, K., 'Principled pragmatism and the "Inclusion Project": Implementing a gender perspective in peace agreements', *feminists@law*, vol. 9, no. 1 (2019). Also see Wise, L. et al., 'Local peace processes: Opportunities and challenges for women's engagement', PA-X Spotlight, University of Edinburgh, 2019; Bell, C. and Forster, R., 'Women and the renegotiation of transitional governance arrangements', PA-X Spotlight, University of Edinburgh, 2019; and Forster, R. and Bell, C., 'Gender mainstreaming in ceasefires: Comparative data and examples', PA-X Spotlight, University of Edinburgh, 2019.

[53] Smit, T. and Tidblad-Lundholm, K., *Trends in Women's Participation in UN, EU and OSCE Peace Operations*, SIPRI Policy Paper no. 47 (SIPRI: Stockholm, Oct. 2018); Ferrari, S. S., 'Is the United Nations Uniformed Gender Parity Strategy on track to reach its goals', SIPRI Commentary, 12 Dec. 2019; and Caparini, M., 'Gender training for police peacekeepers: Approaching two decades of United Nations Security Council Resolution 1325', SIPRI Commentary, 31 Oct. 2019.

[54] Bell, C. and Pospisil, J., 'Navigating inclusion in transitions from conflict: The formalised political unsettlement', *Journal of International Development*, vol. 29, no. 5 (2017), pp. 576–93.

[55] See e.g. Pospisil, J., *Peace in Political Unsettlement: Beyond Solving Conflict* (Palgrave Macmillan: 2019); and Wittke, C., 'The Minsk Agreements—more than "scraps of paper"?', *East European Politics*, vol. 35, no. 3 (2019), pp. 264–90.

are difficult, complex and multifaceted, but that more peace agreements succeed than fail.[56] It may also indicate that root causes of conflicts are not being sufficiently addressed. Finally, this blurred boundary between war and peace also makes it difficult to identify and conceptualize the end of an armed conflict.[57]

[56] Högbladh, S., 'Peace agreements 1975–2011—Updating the UCDP peace agreement dataset', eds T. Pettersson and L. Themnér, *States in Armed Conflict 2011*, Department of Peace and Conflict Research Report no. 99 (Uppsala University: Uppsala, 2012), pp. 39–56.
[57] De Franco, C. et al., 'How do wars end? A multidisciplinary enquiry', *Journal of Strategic Studies*, vol. 42, no. 7 (2019), pp. 889–900. Also see Krause, J., 'How do wars end? A strategic perspective', *Journal of Strategic Studies*, vol. 42, no. 7 (2019), pp. 920–45.

II. Global and regional trends and developments in multilateral peace operations

TIMO SMIT, SOFÍA SACKS FERRARI AND JAÏR VAN DER LIJN

In 2019, United Nations peace operations continued to suffer from budget cuts. Despite research showing positive contributions by UN peacekeeping operations, there was increasing cynicism in the political arena regarding their effectiveness. In addition, concerns remained about the physical security of UN personnel. These developments affect the global and regional trends in multilateral peace operations—their numbers, the organizations leading them, the personnel deployed in them, their locations, the personnel contributors to them and the fatalities they suffer, as well as developments in other multilateral operations.

Multilateral peace operations in 2019

Sixty-one multilateral peace operations were active globally in 2019 (see figure 2.2).[1] This was one more than in the previous year.[2] The UN led 22 operations, regional organizations and alliances led 33 operations, and ad hoc coalitions of states led 6 operations.[3] Most of the operations have been deployed for a long time: 50 of them have been active for more than five years and 32 for longer than 10 years.

Two multilateral peace operations ended in 2019. These were the Temporary International Presence in Hebron (TIPH), which withdrew involuntarily after its mandate expired on 31 January 2019, and the UN Mission for Justice Support in Haiti (MINUJUSTH), which terminated as planned on 15 October 2019. TIPH was established pursuant to the 1995 Oslo II Accord between Israel and the Palestinian Liberation Organization and had been active in its then-current form since 1997.[4] The exit of TIPH in 2019 was the consequence of a unilateral decision by the Government of Israel to

---

[1] The quantitative analysis draws on data collected by SIPRI to examine trends in peace operations. According to SIPRI's definition, a multilateral peace operation must have the stated intention of: (*a*) serving as an instrument to facilitate the implementation of peace agreements already in place, (*b*) supporting a peace process or (*c*) assisting conflict prevention or peacebuilding efforts. Good offices, fact-finding or electoral assistance missions and missions comprising non-resident individuals or teams of negotiators are not included. Since all SIPRI data is reviewed on a continual basis and adjusted when more accurate information becomes available, the statistics in this chapter may not always fully correspond with data found in previous editions of the SIPRI Yearbook or other SIPRI publications.

[2] See Smit, T., 'Global trends and developments in peace operations', *SIPRI Yearbook 2019*, pp. 147–58.

[3] The UN–African Union (AU) Hybrid Operation in Darfur (UNAMID) is included in the totals for the UN and excluded from the totals for the AU.

[4] A previous version of TIPH was active in Hebron between May and Aug. 1994.

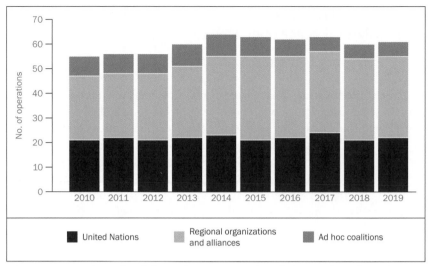

Figure 2.2. Number of multilateral peace operations by type of conducting organization, 2010–19

not extend its mandate.[5] MINUJUSTH was established in 2017 to succeed the UN Stabilization Mission in Haiti (MINUSTAH) for the intended duration of two years.[6] Its closure was the last step in the gradual withdrawal of UN peacekeepers from Haiti that began eight years earlier in 2011.

Three multilateral peace operations started in 2019. These were: the European Union (EU) Integrated Border Assistance Mission (EUBAM) in Libya, which henceforth qualified as a multilateral peace operation following the entry into force of its new mandate on 1 January 2019; the UN Mission to Support the Hodeidah Agreement (UNMHA) in Yemen, which was established on 16 January 2019; and the UN Integrated Office in Haiti (BINUH), which succeeded MINUJUSTH on 16 October 2019.

None of these operations came about unexpectedly. The expansion of EUBAM Libya's mandate and the planning for a UN mission in Yemen had been authorized in December 2018, while the timeline for the transition into a UN non-peacekeeping presence in Haiti had been known since 2017. EUBAM Libya had been active since 2013 but did not previously qualify as a multilateral peace operation due to its narrow focus on border management. As of 1 January 2019 it was also mandated to support capacity building and institutional reform in law enforcement and criminal justice in Libya (see chapter 6). UNMHA was mandated to support the implementation of the Agreement on the City of Hodeidah and the Ports of Hodeidah, Salif, and Ras Issa, which was part of the December 2018 Stockholm Agreement.

---

[5] BBC, 'Hebron: Palestinians denounce Israeli decision to end observer mission', 30 Jan. 2019.
[6] UN Security Council Resolution 2350, 13 Apr. 2017, para. 22.

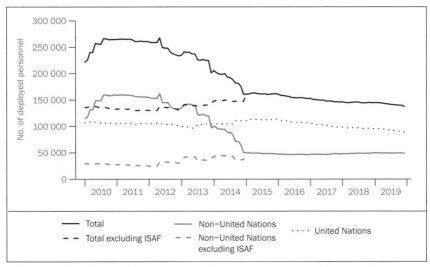

Figure 2.3. Number of personnel in multilateral peace operations, 2010–19

ISAF = International Security Assistance Force

Personnel deployments

The number of personnel deployed in multilateral peace operations decreased by 4.8 per cent during 2019, from 144 791 on 31 December 2018 to 137 781 on 31 December 2019 (see figure 2.3).[7] Aggregate personnel levels at the global level declined for the fourth consecutive year and for the eighth time in the past decade. As a consequence, the number of personnel that were serving in peace operations was lower in December 2019 than in any other month in 2010–19. The high number of personnel deployed and the relatively large year-on-year changes thereof during 2010–14 were primarily attributable to the International Security Assistance Force (ISAF) in Afghanistan, which was led by the North Atlantic Treaty Organization (NATO). From 2015 onwards, when ISAF was no longer active, the developments in terms of personnel deployments were primarily driven by peace operations conducted by the UN and deployed in sub-Saharan Africa. This was also the case in 2019 (see below).

---

[7] The analyses of personnel levels in this chapter are based on estimates of the number of international personnel (military, police and international civilian staff) deployed at the end of each month in each of the multilateral peace operations that were active in the period Jan. 2010 to Dec. 2019. In previous editions of the SIPRI Yearbook, similar analyses used annual snapshot data on the number of international personnel in multilateral peace operations at the end of each year or, in the case of an operation terminated during a calendar year, on the number at their closure. Consequently, the data in this chapter does not exactly match the data used in previous editions of the SIPRI Yearbook.

Organizations conducting multilateral peace operations

United Nations

The UN conducted 22 multilateral peace operations in 2019, which was 1 more than in the previous year.[8] The closure of MINUJUSTH brought to an end the continuous presence of UN peacekeepers in Haiti that began with the deployment of MINUSTAH in 2004. This followed the ending of similar, long-running and once-major UN peacekeeping efforts in Liberia in 2018 and Côte d'Ivoire in 2017. The two peace operations that the UN established in 2019—BINUH and UNMHA—are relatively small-sized special political missions (SPMs), similar to the SPMs that were established in Colombia in 2016 and 2017. The UN has not established a major new peacekeeping operation since 2014.

The number of personnel serving in UN operations decreased by 7.0 per cent during 2019, from 95 488 on 31 December 2018 to 88 849 on 31 December 2019 (see figure 2.3).[9] The last time that the UN had fewer people in its peace operations was in 2007, before the deployment of the UN–African Union (AU) Hybrid Operation in Darfur (UNAMID). The number of personnel deployed in UN peace operations peaked at 115 000 in 2015 and decreased in the four consecutive years thereafter.

Most of the change in 2019 can be attributed to the closure of MINUJUSTH and to the downscaling of UNAMID, the UN Interim Security Force for Abyei (UNISFA), the UN Multidimensional Integrated Stabilization Mission in Mali (MINUSMA) and the UN Organization Stabilization Mission in the Democratic Republic of the Congo (MONUSCO). MONUSCO and UNAMID faced decreased personnel ceilings implemented in 2019 due to scheduled gradual drawdowns. The UN Security Council decided to reduce the number of authorized military personnel in lieu of police personnel for MINUSMA and UNISFA. These five operations together cut deployments by approximately 6500 personnel. Nonetheless, the UN continued to deploy far more personnel in peace operations than any other organization in 2019.

While the total number of personnel serving in all UN peace operations decreased during 2019, the number and proportion of women among the personnel of UN peace operations (military, police and international civilian staff) increased for the third year in a row, from 6304 (6.6 per cent of total) on 31 December 2018 to 6914 (7.7 per cent of total) on 31 December 2019. With regard to personnel deployments in UN operations in sub-Saharan Africa, which decreased by 7.0 per cent during 2019, the number of deployed women increased by 12 per cent from 4953 (6.2 per cent of total) on 31 December

---

[8] This includes UNAMID.
[9] This includes only international personnel in UN peace operations that meet the SIPRI definition of a multilateral peace operation.

2018 to 5552 (7.5 per cent of total) on 31 December 2019. In particular, the number of women deployed to the UN Multidimensional Integrated Stabilization Mission in the Central African Republic (MINUSCA) increased by 26 per cent (from 748 to 943).

Regional organizations and alliances

Regional organizations and alliances conducted 33 multilateral peace operations in 2019, which is the same number as in the previous year. The number of personnel serving in these operations decreased by 0.6 per cent during the year, from 46 842 on 31 December 2018 to 46 569 on 31 December 2019. The main development behind this was the withdrawal of 575 troops from the AU Mission in Somalia (AMISOM). Since the termination of ISAF in 2014, the number of personnel in regional peace operations has been stable at about 45 000 on average.

The EU and the Organization for Security and Co-operation in Europe (OSCE) conducted many multilateral peace operations while deploying relatively few personnel in 2019. The EU conducted 13 Common Security and Defence Policy missions and operations that qualified as multilateral peace operations, in which it deployed approximately 2700 personnel on average during the year. The OSCE conducted nine field operations that qualified as multilateral peace operations, in which it deployed approximately 1100 personnel. Most of them were part of the Special Monitoring Mission to Ukraine. In other words, the EU and the OSCE were responsible for two-thirds of all regional operations in 2019 but accounted for less than a tenth of their personnel.

By contrast, the AU and NATO conducted fewer multilateral peace operations than the EU and the OSCE while deploying relatively large numbers of personnel in 2019. The AU deployed 20 370 personnel in four peace operations, although nearly all of them were part of AMISOM.[10] NATO deployed 20 624 personnel in three peace operations. It was the first time since the end of ISAF that NATO was the regional organization which deployed the most personnel in peace operations. The AU previously held this position, but was overtaken by NATO during 2019 as a consequence of AMISOM's troop reduction.

The other regional organizations that conducted multilateral peace operations were the Economic Community of West African States (ECOWAS), the Intergovernmental Authority on Development (IGAD) and the Organization of American States (OAS). ECOWAS deployed 1658 personnel in two peace operations, while IGAD and OAS led one peace operation each, in which they deployed 86 and 29 personnel, respectively.

---

[10] This does not include UNAMID.

Table 2.3. Number of multilateral peace operations and personnel deployed, by region and type of organization, 2019

Conducting organization	Americas	Asia and Oceania	Europe	Middle East and North Africa	Sub-Saharan Africa	World
Operations	**4**	**5**	**18**	**14**	**20**	**61**
United Nations[a]	3	2	2	7	8	22
Regional organization or alliance	1	1	14	5	12	33
Ad hoc coalition	–	2	2	2	–	6
Personnel	**275**	**17 086**	**7 819**	**15 082**	**97 519**	**137 781**
United Nations[a]	246	346	1 007	13 161	74 089	88 849
Regional organization or alliance	29	16 705	5 751	654	23 430	46 569
Ad hoc coalition	–	35	1 061	1 267	–	2 363

– = not applicable.

[a] UN figures include the UN–African Union Hybrid Operation in Darfur.

Notes: Numbers of operations cover the year 2019; personnel figures are as of 31 Dec. 2019.

Source: SIPRI Multilateral Peace Operations Database, <http://www.sipri.org/databases/pko/>.

Ad hoc coalitions

Ad hoc coalitions of states conducted six multilateral peace operations in 2019, all of which had been active for many years: the International Monitoring Team (IMT) in Mindanao, the Philippines, since 2004; TIPH since 1997; the Office of the High Representative (OHR) in Bosnia and Herzegovina since 1995; the Joint Control Commission (JCC) Joint Peacekeeping Forces in Trans-Dniester, Moldova, since 1992; the Multinational Force and Observers (MFO) in the Sinai peninsula since 1982; and the Neutral Nations Supervisory Commission (NNSC) on the Korean peninsula since 1953.

The number of personnel serving in these operations remained relatively constant during 2019, at around 2250. The JCC and MFO consisted of approximately 1100 personnel each; the IMT, NNSC and OHR were much smaller and had fewer than 25 personnel. Until its closure in January 2019, TIPH had around 60 personnel.

Multilateral peace operations by region

Most of the 61 multilateral peace operations in 2019 were active in sub-Saharan Africa, Europe, and the Middle East and North Africa (MENA) region (see table 2.3). Sub-Saharan Africa continued to host the most peace operations and the most peace operations personnel of all regions

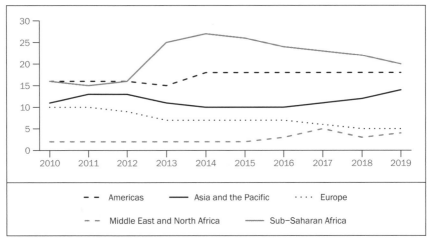

Figure 2.4. Number of multilateral peace operations by region, 2010–19

(see figures 2.4 and 2.5). The personnel levels decreased in all regions during the year except for in MENA.[11]

The largest multilateral peace operations

Although there were 61 multilateral peace operations active in 2019, the 10 largest ones accounted for 90 per cent of all deployed personnel (124 274 personnel on 31 December). Of the 10 largest operations, 7 were UN peace-keeping operations and 7 were deployed in sub-Saharan Africa. While most of the operations reduced their size throughout 2019, their ranking remained mostly constant except for MONUSCO, which moved from second to fourth place in November.

For the fifth year in a row, AMISOM was the largest multilateral peace operation in 2019 (see figure 2.6). This was despite a force reduction authorized in October 2018 and enacted by March 2019, which set the total size of AMISOM to 20 370 personnel. Six additional multilateral peace operations had more than 10 000 personnel as of 31 December 2019 (see figure 2.6). With fewer than 10 000 personnel, UNAMID, UNISFA and the NATO-led Kosovo Force were also among the 10 largest multilateral peace operations, with the latter two being considerably smaller than the other operations in the top 10.

---

[11] For regional discussions of multilateral peace operations, see the following chapters in this volume: the Americas, chapter 3, section I; Asia and Oceania, chapter 4, section I; Europe, chapter 5, section I; MENA, chapter 6, section I; and sub-Saharan Africa, chapter 7, section I.

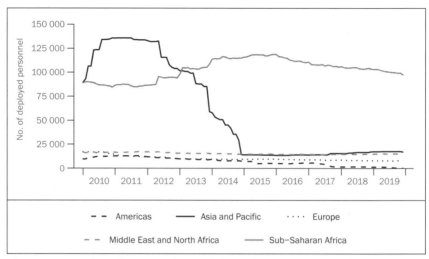

Figure 2.5. Number of personnel in multilateral peace operations by region, 2010–19

The main troop-contributing countries

There was little change in terms of which were the main troop-contributing countries (TCCs) in 2019 compared with 2018. Ethiopia remained the highest TCC to multilateral peace operations in 2019 (see figure 2.7). In December 2019 it was contributing 10 727 military personnel across all operations, mostly to operations in its neighbouring countries, such as AMISOM in Somalia, UNISFA in Abyei and the UN Mission in South Sudan. Although Ethiopia's contribution has been declining since 2018, it has been the highest TCC since 2014, the year in which it joined AMISOM.

The United States was the second-highest TCC to multilateral peace operations in 2019, and the only one from the Global North in the top 10. As of 31 December 2019, it was contributing 9091 personnel, most of which were serving in the NATO-led Resolute Support Mission. It contributed few personnel to UN operations. In comparison to 2018, the USA's contribution decreased slightly, mostly due to 475 personnel withdrawn from Afghanistan.

The remaining countries among the top 10 TCCs to multilateral peace operations as of 31 December 2019 were all from sub-Saharan Africa (Burundi, Kenya, Rwanda and Uganda) or South Asia (Bangladesh, India, Nepal and Pakistan). Burundi, Kenya and Uganda rank highly because of large troop contributions to AMISOM. Overall, the top 10 TCCs accounted for half of all military personnel deployed in multilateral peace operations as of 31 December 2019.

There was a decrease in the number of deployed police in multilateral peace operations in 2019, mainly due to the closure of MINUJUSTH. As of 31 December 2019 Senegal was the top police-contributing country (PCC)

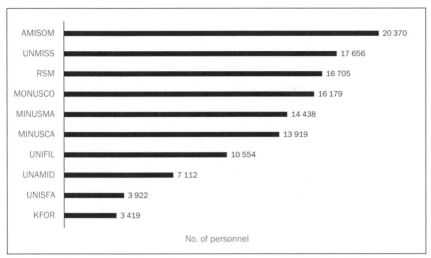

Figure 2.6. Largest multilateral peace operations as of 31 Dec. 2019

AMISOM = African Union (AU) Mission in Somalia; UNMISS = United Nations Mission in South Sudan; RSM = Resolute Support Mission; MONUSCO = UN Organization Stabilization Mission in the Democratic Republic of the Congo; MINUSMA = UN Multidimensional Integrated Stabilization Mission in Mali; MINUSCA = UN Multidimensional Integrated Stabilization Mission in the Central African Republic; UNIFIL = UN Interim Force in Lebanon; UNAMID = UN–AU Hybrid Operation in Darfur; UNISFA = UN Interim Security Force for Abyei; KFOR = Kosovo Force.

to police operations, with a contribution of 1204 police personnel—a 12 per cent decrease compared to a year earlier (see figure 2.8). Senegal has been the largest PCC since April 2016, with most of its personnel deployed to the ECOWAS Mission in Guinea-Bissau, MINUSCA, MINUSMA and MONUSCO. Out of the 10 largest TCCs, 3 were also among the 10 largest PCCs as of 31 December 2019: Bangladesh, Nepal and Rwanda. The 10 largest PCCs accounted for more than 65 per cent of the police serving in multi-lateral peace operations as of 31 December 2019.

Fatalities in United Nations peace operations

There were 102 fatalities of UN peace operations personnel in 2019 (see figure 2.9). This was three more than in the previous year, but fewer than in other years in the period 2010–17. The fatalities in 2019 included 28 that resulted from malicious acts (hereafter termed 'hostile deaths'), which was 1 more than in 2018. Other known causes of death included accidents, illness and suicides.

Uniformed personnel accounted for 65 of the 102 fatalities and 23 of the 28 hostile deaths. This corresponded to a rate of 0.8 fatalities per 1000 uniformed personnel and of 0.3 hostile deaths per 1000 uniformed

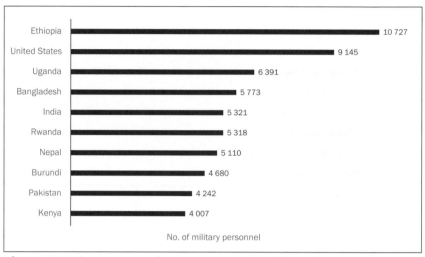

Figure 2.7. Main troop-contributing countries to multilateral peace operations as of 31 Dec. 2019

personnel. These annual rates were very similar to those recorded in 2018 (see figure 2.10).

MINUSMA has been the deadliest concurrent UN peace operation since it was established in 2013. Of the 23 military and police peacekeeper hostile deaths in 2019, 22 were part of MINUSMA. Sixteen of the deaths were due to four different attacks, of which the deadliest was a complex attack against the Aguelhoc camp in northern Mali on 20 January 2019 that killed 9 peacekeepers from Chad and wounded 25 more. Al-Qaeda in the Islamic Maghreb claimed responsibility for the attack, which it stated was 'in reaction' to the visit to Chad of the prime minister of Israel, Benjamin Netanyahu, on the same day.[12]

Whereas MINUSMA continued to experience a high number of hostile deaths, there were relatively few hostile deaths among the personnel in other UN peace operations. One notable event was the death of three civilian personnel from the UN Support Mission in Libya—two international and one local—in a car bomb explosion in Benghazi on 10 August 2019.[13] The remaining two non-uniformed hostile deaths in UN peace operations in 2019 were one staff member from MINUSCA and one from BINUH. There was only one hostile death among uniformed personnel outside MINUSMA, in UNISFA. As a consequence, the annual hostile death rate of uniformed personnel in all UN peace operations except MINUSMA was 0.01 per 1000—far lower than in any other year since 1990.

[12] Al Jazeera, '10 UN peacekeepers killed in attack on Mali's Aguelhoc camp', 21 Jan. 2019.
[13] Al-Warfalli, A., 'Car bomb explodes in Libya's Benghazi, killing three UN staff', Reuters, 10 Aug. 2019.

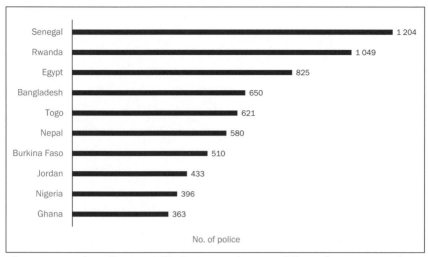

Figure 2.8. Main police-contributing countries to multilateral peace operations as of 31 Dec. 2019

Other multilateral operations

A number of other multilateral organizations were conducting security-related missions and operations in addition to or instead of ordinary multilateral peace operations (as defined by SIPRI). Some of these other multilateral operations play only minor coordinating roles in peacebuilding at the low end of the spectrum of conflict. The high-end other multilateral operations, which are more involved in counter-insurgency and war fighting, have become increasingly visible in the contemporary multilateral operations landscape. These operations are generally either co-located and operating in parallel with multilateral peace operations to execute tasks that peace operations cannot perform, or they are deployed in contexts where or when the deployment of a multilateral peace operation is not appropriate or feasible.

The French-led military Operation Barkhane is one of the most significant examples of an other multilateral operation. Operation Barkhane consisted of 4700 soldiers as well as military ground and air assets in 2019, deployed across the Group of Five for the Sahel (G5S) countries of Burkina Faso, Chad, Mali, Mauritania and Niger. It conducted counterterrorism operations in the G5S countries and provided training to their armed forces. In Mali, the operation was co-located with MINUSMA and authorized by the UN Security Council to intervene in support of the UN operation when it is under 'imminent and serious threat'.[14] The United Kingdom and Denmark joined

---

[14] UN Security Council Resolution 2480, 28 June 2019, para. 42. On developments within the armed conflicts in the Sahel and Lake Chad regions, see chapter 7, section II.

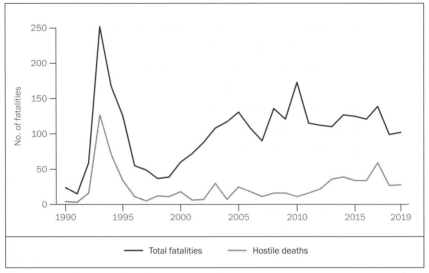

Figure 2.9. Number of fatalities in United Nations peace operations, 1990–2019

Operation Barkhane in 2018 and 2019, respectively, both contributing transport helicopters and supporting military units. Estonia started contributing a force protection platoon to Barkhane in August 2018, and in November 2019 announced its intention to increase its contribution from 50 to 95 troops.[15] Germany, Spain and the USA have been supporting the operation with fixed-wing transport aircraft.[16] France further decided in 2019 to establish a Special Operations Task Force called Takuba as part of Operation Barkhane, to train, advise and accompany into battle military units from G5S countries. The task force is expected to be launched in 2020, and it is envisioned that several of France's European partners will contribute to it.[17]

Further other multilateral operations that warrant mention are the 5000-strong Joint Force of the Group of Five of the Sahel (JF-G5S) and the 10 500-strong Multinational Joint Task Force (MNJTF) against Boko Haram led by the Lake Chad Basin Commission (LCBC). These operations are both authorized by the AU Peace and Security Council but not by the UN Security Council. They do not qualify as multilateral peace operations under the SIPRI definition, because they comprise national units operating primarily within their own national territories. The nature of their operations is primarily military counterterrorism or counter-insurgency. The JF-G5S comprises all the G5S countries, whereas the MNJTF comprises Benin and LCBC member

[15] Kelly, F., 'Estonia parliament approves Mali troop increase for Operation Barkhane', Defense Post, 8 Nov. 2019.

[16] Ministry of the Armed Forces, 'Dossier de presse Barkhane.ENG', [n.d.].

[17] Kelly, F., 'France expects new international task force Takuba to deploy in Mali "by 2020"', Defense Post, 6 Nov. 2019.

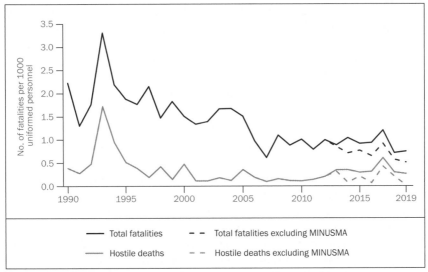

Figure 2.10. Fatality rates for uniformed personnel in United Nations peace operations, 1990–2019

MINUSMA = United Nations Multidimensional Integrated Stabilization Mission in Mali.

states Chad, Cameroon, Niger and Nigeria, and operates in the border areas of these countries adjacent to Lake Chad. Unlike the JF-G5S, the MNJTF is not co-located with any peace operations. Operation Barkhane, the JF-G5S and the MNJTF together added approximately 20 000 personnel to 97 000 personnel that were deployed in 20 multilateral peace operations in sub-Saharan Africa in 2019.

Events in 2019 also drew renewed attention to the deployment of multilateral or multinational naval operations, which do not qualify as multilateral peace operations. The EU maintained its anti-piracy naval operation along the coast of Somalia—Operation Atalanta. Although the Council of the EU extended EUNAVFOR MED Operation Sophia until March 2020, it suspended the deployment of naval assets until an appropriate solution is found for the disembarkation of rescued migrants. It reinforced surveillance by air assets and support to the Libyan navy and coastguard.[18]

Conclusions

Many trends and developments in multilateral peace operations of the past few years continued during 2019. Three are worth highlighting below.

---

[18] Council of the EU, 'EUNAVFOR MED Operation Sophia: Mandate extended until 31 March 2020', Press Release 609/19, 26 Sep. 2019. On armed conflicts in the Horn of Africa, see chapter 7, section IV, in this volume.

A first trend is that although the total number of multilateral peace operations has remained stable, in the low 60s, since 2015 many of the larger UN peacekeeping operations have continued to draw down or have closed. The total number of UN peace operations during the period 2010–19 has remained relatively stable, at around 22, while the number of multilateral peace operations conducted by ad hoc coalitions has declined and the number of operations deployed by regional organizations has risen. Successor operations and newly established multilateral peace operations tend to be relatively small in size. As a consequence, personnel numbers deployed in UN peacekeeping operation have continued to drop, while those deployed by regional organizations have remained stable except for a personnel reduction in AMISOM. Some of the global capacity to contribute to multilateral peace operations has been deployed to other multilateral operations.

A second trend, which started in 2015 and continued in 2019, is that the attention of multilateral peace operations is moving away from focusing on sub-Saharan Africa. While this region continues to host by far the most multilateral peace operations personnel, the numbers of personnel and operations it hosts have been declining steadily in recent years. Again, this development is mainly explained by the closure of some of the larger UN peacekeeping operations. Some of the attention has shifted to the MENA region. While personnel numbers there have remained stable, the number of often smaller peace operations in this region has increased significantly: there were two more operations active in 2019 than in 2018.

A third trend is that since 2013 the annual hostile death rates in UN peace operations have remained relatively stable but at higher levels than in most years in the preceding decade of the 2000s. These higher levels are mainly explained by the establishment of MINUSMA in 2013, which has been the main UN peace operation suffering from hostile deaths. In fact, excluding MINUSMA, a number of years since 2012 have had the lowest annual rates of hostile deaths since 1990. Remarkably, in 2019 all but one of the hostile deaths among uniformed UN personnel were recorded in MINUSMA. This strongly qualifies one of the main criticisms of UN peacekeeping operations—that they suffer from high numbers of hostile deaths.

III. Table of multilateral peace operations, 2019

SOFÍA SACKS FERRARI AND TIMO SMIT

Table 2.4 provides data on the 61 multilateral peace operations conducted in 2019, including operations that were either launched or terminated during the year.

The table lists operations conducted under the authority of the United Nations, operations conducted by regional organizations and alliances, and operations conducted by ad hoc coalitions of states. UN operations are divided into three subgroups: (*a*) observer and multidimensional peace-keeping operations run by the Department of Peace Operations, (*b*) special political and peacebuilding missions, and (*c*) the joint UN–African Union Hybrid Operation in Darfur.

The table draws on the SIPRI Multilateral Peace Operations Database, <http://www.sipri.org/databases/pko>, which provides information on all UN and non-UN peace operations conducted since 2000, such as location, dates of deployment and operation, mandate, participating countries, number of personnel, budget and fatalities.

Table 2.4. Multilateral peace operations, 2019

Unless otherwise stated, all figures are as of 31 Dec. 2019. Operations that closed in 2019 are shown in italic type and are not included in the aggregate figures.

Operation	Start	Location	Mil.	Pol.	Civ.
UN peacekeeping operations[a]			**68 677**	**6 877**	**3 807**
UNTSO	1948	Middle East	148	0	77
UNMOGIP	1951	India/Pakistan	42	0	23
UNFICYP	1964	Cyprus	796	65	37
UNDOF	1974	Syria (Golan Heights)	1 070	0	49
UNIFIL	1978	Lebanon	10 315	0	239
MINURSO	1991	Western Sahara	202	0	75
MONUSCO	1999	DRC	14 155	1 191	833
UNMIK	1999	Kosovo	8	8	93
UNISFA	2011	Abyei	3 759	27	136
UNMISS	2011	South Sudan	14 962	1 799	895
MINUSMA	2013	Mali	11 951	1 744	743
MINUSCA	2014	CAR	11 269	2 043	607
MINUJUSTH	*2017*	*Haiti*	–	–	–
UN special political missions[a]			**1 180**	**97**	**1 099**
UNAMA	2002	Afghanistan	1	0	280
UNAMI	2003	Iraq	237	0	306
UNIOGBIS	2010	Guinea-Bissau	1	0	62
UNSMIL	2011	Libya	232	0	174
UNSOM	2013	Somalia	633	15	152
UNVMC	2017	Colombia	51	66	125
UNMHA	2019	Yemen	25	12	..
BINUH	2019	Haiti	0	4	..
UN–AU[a]			**4 332**	**2 150**	**630**
UNAMID	2007	Sudan (Darfur)	4 332	2 150	630
AU			**19 586**	**718**	**66**
AMISOM	2007	Somalia	19 586	718	66
MISAHEL	2013	Mali	–	–	..
MISAC	2014	CAR	–	–	..
AU Observer Mission in Burundi	2015	Burundi	..	–	..
ECOWAS			**1 248**	**410**	**0**
ECOMIB	2012	Guinea-Bissau	398	285	0
ECOMIG	2017	Gambia	850	125	0
EU[b]			**1 612**	**..**	**1 073**
EUFOR ALTHEA	2004	Bosnia and Herzegovina	553	–	16
EUBAM Rafah	2005	Palestinian territories (Rafah Crossing Point)	–	..	6
EUPOL COPPS	2005	Palestinian territories	–	..	57
EULEX Kosovo	2008	Kosovo	–	..	280
EUMM Georgia	2008	Georgia	–	–	213
EUTM Somalia	2010	Somalia	137	–	12

Operation	Start	Location	Mil.	Pol.	Civ.
EUCAP Sahel Niger	2012	Niger	–	..	115
EUTM Mali	2013	Mali	697	–	3
EUAM Ukraine	2014	Ukraine	–	..	153
EUBAM Libya	2013^c	Libya	–	..	36
EUCAP Sahel Mali	2015	Mali	–	..	127
EUTM RCA	2016	CAR	225	–	0
EUAM Iraq	2017	Iraq	–	..	55
NATO			20 624	–	–
KFOR	1999	Kosovo	3 419	–	–
RSM	2015	Afghanistan	16 705	–	–
NMI	2018	Iraq	500	–	–
IGAD			–	–	86
CTSAMVM	2015	South Sudan	–	–	86
OAS			–	–	29
MAPP/OEA	2004	Colombia	–	–	29
OSCE			–	–	1 117
OSCE Mission to Skopje	1992	North Macedonia	–	–	37
OSCE Mission to Moldova	1993	Moldova	–	–	13
OSCE PRCIO	1995	Azerbaijan (Nagorno-Karabakh)	–	–	6
OSCE Mission to Bosnia and Herzegovina	1995	Bosnia and Herzegovina	–	–	29
OSCE Presence in Albania	1997	Albania	–	–	16
OMIK	1999	Kosovo	–	–	90
OSCE Mission to Serbia	2001	Serbia	–	–	19
OSCE SMM	2014	Ukraine	–	–	885
OSCE Observer Mission at the Russian checkpoints Gukovo and Donetsk	2014	Russia (Gukovo and Donetsk checkpoints)	–	–	22
Ad hoc coalition of states			2 235	3	125
NNSC	1953	South Korea	10	–	–
MFO	1982	Egypt (Sinai)	1 156	–	111
JCC	1992	Moldova (Transnistria)	1 050	–	–
OHR	1995	Bosnia and Herzegovina	–	–	11
TIPH	*1997*	*Palestinian territories (Hebron)*	–	–	–
IMT	2004	Philippines (Mindanao)	19	3	3

– = not applicable; .. = information not available; AMISOM = African Union Mission in Somalia; AU = African Union; BINUH = United Nations Integrated Office in Haiti; CAR = Central African Republic; Civ.= international civilian personnel; CTSAMVM = Ceasefire and Transitional Security Arrangements Monitoring and Verification Mechanism; DRC = Democratic Republic of the Congo; ECOMIB = ECOWAS Mission in Guinea-Bissau; ECOMIG = ECOWAS Mission in the Gambia; ECOWAS = Economic Community of West African States; EU = European Union; EUAM Iraq = EU Advisory Mission in Support of Security Sector Reform in Iraq; EUAM Ukraine = EU Advisory Mission for Civilian Security Sector Reform Ukraine; EUBAM Rafah = EU Border Assistance Mission for the Rafah Crossing Point; EUCAP Sahel Mali = EU Common Security and Defence Policy (CSDP) Mission in Mali; EUCAP Sahel Niger = EU CSDP Mission in

Niger; EUFOR ALTHEA = EU Military Operation in Bosnia and Herzegovina; EULEX Kosovo = EU Rule of Law Mission in Kosovo; EUMM Georgia = EU Monitoring Mission in Georgia; EUPOL COPPS = EU Police Mission for the Palestinian Territories; EUTM Mali = EU Training Mission Mali; EUTM RCA = EU Training Mission in the CAR; EUTM Somalia = EU Training Mission Somalia; IGAD = Intergovernmental Authority on Development; IMT = International Monitoring Team; JCC = Joint Control Commission Peacekeeping Force; KFOR = Kosovo Force; MAPP/OEA = Organization of American States Mission to Support the Peace Process in Colombia; MFO = Multinational Force and Observers; Mil. = military personnel (troops and military observers); MINUJUSTH = UN Mission for Justice Support in Haiti; MINURSO = UN Mission for the Referendum in Western Sahara; MINUSCA = UN Multidimensional Integrated Stabilization Mission in the CAR; MINUSMA = UN Multidimensional Integrated Stabilization Mission in Mali; MISAC = AU Mission for the CAR and Central Africa; MISAHEL = AU Mission for Mali and the Sahel; MONUSCO = UN Organization Stabilization Mission in the DRC; NATO = North Atlantic Treaty Organization; NMI = NATO Mission Iraq; NNSC = Neutral Nations Supervisory Commission; OAS = Organization of American States; OHR = Office of the High Representative; OMIK = OSCE Mission in Kosovo; OSCE = Organization for Security and Co-operation in Europe; OSCE SMM = OSCE Special Monitoring Mission in Ukraine; Pol. = police; PRCIO = Personal Representative of the Chairman-in-Office on the Conflict Dealt with by the OSCE Minsk Conference; RSM = Resolute Support Mission; TIPH = Temporary International Presence in Hebron; UN = United Nations; UNAMA = UN Assistance Mission in Afghanistan; UNAMI = UN Assistance Mission in Iraq; UNAMID = UN–AU Hybrid Operation in Darfur; UNDOF = UN Disengagement Observer Force; UNFICYP = UN Peacekeeping Force in Cyprus; UNMHA = UN Mission to Support the Hodeidah Agreement; UNIFIL = UN Interim Force in Lebanon; UNIOGBIS = UN Integrated Peacebuilding Office in Guinea-Bissau; UNISFA = UN Interim Security Force for Abyei; UNMIK = UN Interim Administration Mission in Kosovo; UNMISS = UN Mission in South Sudan; UNMOGIP = UN Military Observer Group in India and Pakistan; UNSMIL = UN Support Mission in Libya; UNSOM = UN Assistance Mission in Somalia; UNTSO = UN Truce Supervision Organization; UNVMC = UN Verification Mission in Colombia.

[a] Figures on international civilian staff are as of 31 Dec. 2018.

[b] Figures on international civilian staff may include uniformed police.

[c] EUBAM Libya was established in 2013 but did not qualify as a multilateral peace operation prior to 1 Jan. 2019.

Source: SIPRI Multilateral Peace Operations Database, <http://www.sipri.org/databases/pko/>. Data on multilateral peace operations is obtained from the following categories of open source: (*a*) official information provided by the secretariat of the organization concerned; (*b*) information provided by the operations themselves, either in official publications or in written responses to annual SIPRI questionnaires; and (*c*) information from national governments contributing to the operation under consideration. In some instances, SIPRI researchers may gather additional information on an operation from the conducting organizations or governments of participating states by means of telephone interviews and email correspondence. These primary sources are supplemented by a wide selection of publicly available secondary sources consisting of specialist journals, research reports, news agencies, and international, regional and local newspapers.

3. Armed conflict and peace processes in the Americas

Overview

In 2019 non-international armed conflicts, as defined under international humanitarian law, were present in two countries in the Americas: Colombia and Mexico. Implementation of the 2016 Colombian peace agreement with the Revolutionary Armed Forces of Colombia–People's Army continued throughout 2019. At the same time the Government of Colombia was involved in several non-international armed conflicts with non-signatory non-state armed groups, while there were additional conflicts among such groups. The fragmentation and growing presence of these groups threaten to destabilize the fragile peace that has sustained since ratification of the peace agreement. In Mexico amid record levels of homicides, a non-international armed conflict has also emerged between the state and the criminal syndicate Jalisco New Generation Cartel. Beyond the strict definitions of international humanitarian law, various forms of armed violence affected these and other countries across the region.

There were four multilateral peace operations active in the Americas in 2019: the new United Nations Integrated Office in Haiti; the UN Mission for Justice Support in Haiti; the UN Verification Mission in Colombia; and the Organization of American States (OAS) Mission to Support the Peace Process in Colombia. Additionally, the OAS established a special commission on Nicaragua. However, the OAS Mission to Support the Fight against Corruption and Impunity in Honduras failed to reach agreement on renewal of its mandate with the Government of Honduras.

According to the UN Office on Drugs and Crime, global deaths caused by criminal activity far exceeded those caused by conflicts and terrorism combined. By the metric of homicides, in which organized crime has a significant role, the Americas remained the world's most violent region in 2019. Armed criminal violence continued to affect key parts of the region from Mexico to Brazil. In 2019 Mexico experienced the highest number of homicides in a century.

Dubbed the 'year of rage', 2019 saw marked political unrest in which waves of mass demonstrations swept across many of the region's countries. While triggered by differing issues or events, many of the protests had similar underlying causes, including economic pressures from slow rates of economic growth since 2015, persistently high levels of inequality, discontent with the functioning of democratic institutions and processes, and enduring problems of corruption and abuse of power by political and economic elites.

MARINA CAPARINI

SIPRI Yearbook 2020: Armaments, Disarmament and International Security
www.sipriyearbook.org

I. Key general developments in the region

MARINA CAPARINI

Two states in the Americas—Colombia and Mexico—experienced non-international armed conflict in 2019 according to the threshold set out under international humanitarian law.[1] However, several other states (including Brazil, El Salvador, Guatemala, Honduras and Venezuela) experienced levels of violence among armed groups of a similar magnitude. By some measures, those conflicts might also be considered armed conflicts.[2]

In the wake of the 2016 Colombian peace agreement and demobilization of the Revolutionary Armed Forces of Colombia–People's Army (Fuerzas Armadas Revolucionarias de Colombia–Ejército del Pueblo, FARC–EP), several organized armed groups have clashed in seeking to fill the resulting power vacuum. The International Committee of the Red Cross identified five 'non-international armed conflicts' in Colombia that involve fighting between government forces and non-state armed groups, or among the groups themselves.[3] The Government of Colombia is involved in non-international armed conflicts with the National Liberation Army (Ejército de Liberación Nacional, ELN), the FARC–EP dissident groups (Eastern Bloc), the Popular Liberation Army (Ejército Popular de Liberación, EPL) and the Gaitanista Self-Defense Forces of Colombia (Autodefensas Gaitanistas de Colombia, AGC, also known as the Gulf Clan). Additional conflicts continue among armed non-state actors, namely the AGC, ELN and EPL.[4] Section II discusses the armed conflicts in Colombia in more detail.

Experts have debated whether the high levels of violence and record levels of homicides mean that an armed conflict exists in Mexico.[5] Recent developments suggest this classification now applies at least in regard to one armed group. Based on the level of armed violence between government forces and the extremely violent criminal syndicate Jalisco New Generation Cartel (Cártel Jalisco Nueva Generación, CJNG), and the latter's well-organized structure, international legal experts deemed in early 2019 that the threshold for a non-international armed conflict between the Government

---

[1] International Committee of the Red Cross, 'How is the term "armed conflict" defined in international humanitarian law?', International Committee of the Red Cross Opinion Paper, Mar. 2008.

[2] On the difficulties of defining an armed conflict, see chapter 2, section I, and box 2.1, in this volume.

[3] International Committee of the Red Cross, 'Colombia: Five armed conflicts—What's happening?', 30 Jan. 2019.

[4] Rule of Law in Armed Conflicts (RULAC), 'Non-international armed conflicts in Colombia', 22 Jan. 2020.

[5] Enciso, F., 'Mexico's worsening war without a name', International Crisis Group commentary, 15 June 2017.

of Mexico and the CJNG has been passed.[6] Section III discusses the armed conflict in Mexico in more detail.

There were four multilateral peace operations active in the Americas in 2019. The United Nations Mission for Justice Support in Haiti terminated on 15 October 2019, bringing to an end 15 consecutive years of UN uniformed peacekeeper presence in Haiti. A special political mission, the UN Integrated Office in Haiti, was established in June 2019 with a presence only in Port-au-Prince, mandated to support the Government of Haiti in promoting stability and good governance, including the rule of law. The UN Verification Mission in Colombia, a special political mission established in July 2017, continues to verify implementation of the peace agreement by the Government of Colombia and FARC–EP. The long-running Organization of American States (OAS) Mission to Support the Peace Process in Colombia, which is in its 15th year, continues to monitor security conditions, peacebuilding and transitional justice in the areas most affected by armed conflict. As a consequence of the closure of the UN Mission for Justice Support in Haiti the number of personnel serving in multilateral peace operations in the Americas fell by 81 per cent during 2019, from 1433 to 275. Personnel deployments fell for the third year in a row.[7]

The OAS was unable to reach agreement with the Government of Honduras on an extension of the four-year old Mission to Support the Fight against Corruption and Impunity in Honduras (MACCIH), and the mission was terminated in January 2020. MACCIH sought to replicate the success of the UN-backed International Commission against Impunity in Guatemala (Comisión Internacional contra la Impunidad en Guatemala, CICIG), which since 2007 had combated corruption and helped strengthen the integrity of the judicial and political system. CICIG assisted local prosecutors to investigate and successfully prosecute over 100 cases involving over 700 political, business and organized crime figures including former president Otto Pérez Molina.[8] In January 2019 Guatemalan President Jimmy Morales unilaterally terminated the agreement with the UN, but this was overturned by the constitutional court.[9] The CICIG was subsequently shut down by Morales in September on the grounds it had overreached its authority in its investigations of Morales and his family and associates.[10]

---

[6] RULAC, 'International humanitarian law applies to confrontations between Mexico and the Jalisco Cartel New Generation', Geneva Academy of International Law and Human Rights, 12 Feb. 2019; and RULAC, 'Non-international armed conflict in Mexico', 3 June 2019.

[7] On peace operations, see also chapter 2, sections II and III, in this volume.

[8] Malkin, E., 'Guatemala's anti-corruption fight inspired Latin America: It may be shut down', *New York Times*, 18 May 2019.

[9] *The Guardian*, 'Guatemala: Court blocks president's expulsion of UN anti-corruption group', 9 Jan. 2019.

[10] Abbott, J., 'Guatemala's CICIG: UN-backed anti-corruption body shuts its doors', Al Jazeera, 3 Sep. 2019.

Additionally, in August 2019 the OAS established a special commission on Nicaragua to seek, through diplomatic efforts, a peaceful solution to the political and social crisis building since protests began in April 2018. The protests were triggered by tax increases and pension reductions, but developed into widespread unrest against anti-democratic and corrupt governance under the Ortega administration. The protests were suppressed after several months by a crackdown by the National Police and pro-government militias, resulting in over 300 deaths, including 22 police officers, 2000 injured, and hundreds arbitrarily arrested and detained.[11] President Daniel Ortega, a former Marxist guerrilla leader, and his wife, Vice President Rosario Murillo, have dismantled institutional checks on presidential power, circumvented electoral term limits, and suppressed political opposition and dissenting voices through imprisonment.[12] Anti-government protests erupted through 2019 despite a ban on public demonstrations.[13] In September an OAS commission established to help resolve the crisis was denied entry into the country.[14] Following allegations of torture and murder of detained activists,[15] international pressure including United States sanctions against members of the Ortega regime and family members who hold key posts were applied.[16] Consequently, 91 of 148 political prisoners held since the 2018 demonstrations on a variety of alleged serious criminal charges were released in late December 2019.[17] As a result of the continuing social unrest and international sanctions, the economy was estimated by the International Monetary Fund to have abruptly contracted by 5.7 per cent in 2019.[18] By the end of November 2019 over 92 000 people had fled the country since the beginning of the crisis in April 2018.[19]

The two most significant cross-cutting issues affecting the Americas in 2019 were the high levels of armed criminal violence and mass political protests. These two issues are discussed briefly below. As noted by Peter Maurer, the president of the International Committee of the Red Cross, 'The impact of war on disappearances, the displacement of people and the rupture of communities is the same whether the violence is derived from war, [or]

---

[11] Human Rights Watch, 'Nicaragua: Events of 2019', World Report 2020.

[12] Human Rights Watch (note 11).

[13] Reuters, 'Anti-government protests erupt in Nicaragua after extended pause', 17 Mar. 2019; Voice of America, 'Good Friday processions become protests in Nicaragua', 19 Apr. 2019; and Deutsche Welle, 'Nicaragua police quash opposition protest', 22 Sep. 2019.

[14] Reuters, 'OAS peace mission to Nicaragua says denied entry by Ortega government', 16 Sep. 2019.

[15] UN News, 'Nicaragua "crisis" still cause for concern amid murder, torture allegations: Bachelet', 10 Sep. 2019.

[16] US Department of State, 'Nicaragua sanctions', [n.d.].

[17] France 24, 'Nicaragua releases dozens of political prisoners', 31 Dec. 2019; and Robles, F., 'Nicaragua frees political prisoners after international pressure', New York Times, 30 Dec. 2019.

[18] International Monetary Fund, 'Nicaragua: Staff concluding statement of the 2019 Article IV Mission', 20 Nov. 2019.

[19] UN High Commissioner for Refugees, 'UNHCR Nicaragua situation fact sheet (1–30 November 2019)', 12 Dec. 2019.

is instigated or is generated by a conflict between the state and organized crime groups'.[20] Widespread protests indicate deep public anger at the failure of political systems and governing elites to resolve their economic and social problems. As seen in past waves of 'colour revolutions', protesters have the potential to overturn governing elites and precipitate reform of political systems. However, failure of political authorities to accommodate protester demands or their suppression by state forces, and grievances fed by inequalities, corrupt governance and impunity may also result in protracted social unrest or violence.

Armed criminal violence

The Americas region continued to be deeply affected by violent crime in 2019, and is ranked as the most violent region in the world based on homicide rates.[21] According to figures collected by the UN, the Americas accounted for 13.3 per cent of the world's population, but 37.4 per cent of its homicides in 2017.[22] Young men are especially at risk: the homicide rate for men aged 18–19 years in the Americas is estimated at 46 per 100 000 people, which is far higher than the risk faced by their peers in other regions of the world.[23] Moreover, the male homicide rate in the Americas is 10 times that of females in the region.[24]

In the 'Northern Triangle' states of Central America (El Salvador, Guatemala and Honduras) gang violence, poverty and extreme inequality combine with fragile institutions and corrupt governance to foster instability and drive refugee and migration flows, mostly towards the USA. While the number of people fleeing from this region averaged 265 000 people per year between 2014 and 2018, it had doubled between October 2018 and June 2019.[25] There was an increase in homicides in Honduras in 2019; at 41.2 per 100 000 people, it has the third-highest rate of homicides in the Americas, exceeded only by Venezuela (60.3 per 100 000) and Jamaica (47.4 per 100 000).[26]

Brazil is prioritizing counter-crime efforts under right-wing populist President Jair Bolsonaro. In 2017 violent crime spiked, with over 63 000 people losing their lives—a result of inter-factional drug gang rivalry

---

[20] Asmann, P., 'Is the impact of violence in Mexico similar to war zones?', InSight Crime, 23 Oct. 2017.

[21] UN Office on Drugs and Crime (UNODC), *Global Study on Homicide: Executive Summary* (Vienna: UNODC, July 2019), p. 11.

[22] UNODC, *Global Study on Homicide: Homicide Extent, Patterns, Trends and Criminal Justice Response* (Vienna: UNODC, July 2019), p. 16.

[23] UNODC (note 21), p. 19.

[24] UNODC (note 21), p. 18.

[25] Congressional Research Service, 'Central American migration: Root causes and US policy', 13 June 2019.

[26] Asmann, P. and O'Reilly, P., 'InSight Crime's 2019 homicide round-up', InSight Crime, 28 Jan. 2020.

over control of the drug trade and an upsurge in cocaine production in neighbouring Colombia and Peru.[27] President Bolsonaro initiated a severe crackdown on crime upon taking office on 1 January 2019, accompanied by a series of decrees loosening Brazil's strict gun control laws, ostensibly to enable citizens to better defend themselves.[28] Homicide rates declined by over 20 per cent in 2019. However, this trend began in early 2018 before the Bolsonaro administration took office. Experts attribute it to the cumulative impact of several factors such as state programmes, initiated well before President Bolsonaro's election, to improve police coordination and training and increase community involvement in planning and implementing of public safety, as well as general improvement of economic conditions.[29]

However, President Bolsonaro's harsh war-on-crime rhetoric and support for shielding police from prosecution for shooting alleged offenders have contributed to the rise in use of excessive and lethal force by police. Brazil witnessed an 18 per cent increase in people killed by police in 2019, reaching the highest level in Rio de Janeiro state in over 20 years.[30] In addition to having the world's highest rate of people killed by police, Brazil is also where the highest number of indigenous leaders and environmental activists have been killed, in the context of the Bolsonaro administration's efforts to weaken environmental protection and enforcement efforts.[31]

Mass protests

Over the course of the 2019 'year of rage', citizens of Bolivia, Peru and Venezuela took to the streets in political unrest, while in Argentina, Chile, Colombia, Ecuador and Puerto Rico protests and in some cases mass movements were triggered by inequality, economic policies and conditions, and corruption. In Venezuela between January and May, opposition protests against Nicolás Maduro's presidential inauguration and efforts to replace him with opposition leader, National Assembly leader and self-declared interim president Juan Guaidó often met with counterdemonstrations in support of Maduro and against foreign intervention.[32] The UN Office of the High Commissioner for Human Rights cites figures ranging from 1569 to 2124 individuals killed by state forces for 'resistance to authority' in the first

[27] Muggah, R., 'What explains Brazil's homicide decline?', openDemocracy, 17 Sep. 2019.

[28] Deutsche Welle, 'Brazil's Bolsonaro signs decree further easing gun rules', 8 May 2019.

[29] Muggah (note 27); and Associated Press, 'Rio de Janeiro 2019 homicides fall as police killings surge', 22 Jan. 2020.

[30] Associated Press (note 29); and The Economist, 'Police killings in the state of Rio de Janeiro are at a 20-year high', 3 Sep. 2019.

[31] Hanbury, S., 'Murders of indigenous leaders in Brazilian Amazon hits highest level in two decades', Mongabay, 14 Dec. 2019.

[32] Mcdonnell, P. J. and Mogollon, M., 'In Venezuela, clashes continue as protestors for and against Maduro fill the streets', Los Angeles Times, 1 May 2019.

five months of 2019, many of which may have been extrajudicial killings.[33] By the end of the year Venezuela remained in a political impasse, with Maduro retaining control of the presidency. Ever-worsening economic conditions resulted in a severe humanitarian crisis and refugee flows that saw 4.6 million or 16 per cent of the population living abroad as refugees and migrants by November 2019. Projections, based on current trends, predict that as many as 6.5 million people will be living abroad by the end of 2020.[34]

Protesters in Bolivia demonstrated against President Evo Morales follow-ing accusations of fraud in the October presidential election, which would have given him a fourth term in office, resulting in over 30 deaths.[35] The loss of support by the army resulted in his resignation and him fleeing the country.[36] An independent audit by the OAS subsequently confirmed 'inten-tional manipulation' and 'serious irregularities' in the election.[37] In Peru, facing an opposition-held congress that refused to pass his anti-corruption reforms, President Martín Vizcarra dissolved congress in late September to call early parliamentary elections. The political crisis pitted the executive against the legislative branch, as legislators suspended Vizcarra and installed Vice President Mercedes Aráoz as acting president.[38] Vizcarra had replaced former president Pedro Pablo Kuczynski, who is under investigation in connection to the corruption scandal involving Odebrecht, the Brazilian con-struction company. Another former president, Alan García, killed himself in April before being arrested also in relation to Odebrecht.[39]

Elsewhere in the Americas region, masses protested the effects of auster-ity, precarity and corruption. In Argentina beginning in February mass crowds demonstrated against high unemployment and austerity policies that cut government subsidies under centre-right President Mauricio Macri in a context of high inflation and recession.[40] Weeks of protests resulted in passage of an emergency law in September to provide financial support for

---

[33] United Nations Human Rights Council, 'Human rights in the Bolivarian Republic of Venezuela', Report of the United Nations High Commissioner for Human Rights on the situation of human rights in the Bolivarian Republic of Venezuela, A/HRC/41/18, 5 July 2019, para. 50.

[34] UN High Commissioner for Refugees and International Organization for Migration, 'US$1.35 billion needed to help Venezuelan refugees and migrants and host countries', Joint press release, 13 Nov. 2019.

[35] Angee, G. and Berlinger, J., 'Bolivia's death toll rises as protests continue', CNN, 20 Nov. 2019.

[36] Bristow, M. and Martin, E., 'Bolivian President Evo Morales resigns after army tells him to go', Bloomberg, 10 Nov. 2019.

[37] OAS, 'Final report of the audit of the elections in Bolivia: Intentional manipulation and serious irregularities made it impossible to validate the results', Press release, 4 Dec. 2019.

[38] BBC, 'Peru in turmoil after President Vizcarra dissolves Congress', 1 Oct. 2019.

[39] Nurena, C. and Helfgott, F., 'Rings of corruption in Peru', North American Congress on Latin America, 27 June 2019.

[40] Jourdan, A., 'Tens of thousands march in Buenos Aires against austerity, tariffs', Reuters, 13 Feb. 2019.

food programmes in view of a doubling of people living in grave food insecurity from 2.5 to 5 million over the preceding four years.[41]

In July in the US territory of Puerto Rico people took to the streets after the leak of demeaning personal chat messages between Governor Ricardo Rosselló and his inner circle. Building on outrage from a corruption scandal, and frustrations over the weak economy and inadequate disaster response, the protests resulted in the fall of the government.[42] In Ecuador transport workers, students and indigenous groups protested in early October against austerity measures of cutting state fuel subsidies and public workers' wages, which were part of an economic reform package agreed in a financing deal with the International Monetary Fund.[43] In Haiti demonstrators marched daily against the government to protest about crippling economic conditions and corruption.[44] An increase in subway fares in Santiago triggered months of demonstrations in which over 1 million Chileans protested against the high cost of living, low wages, an inadequate pension system and pronounced inequality.[45] In Colombia a national strike by labour unions against rumoured pension cuts and student protests against corruption and cuts in education grew into a series of wider protests against inadequate social services, inequality and corruption.[46]

In Honduras protests against President Juan Orlando Hernández's plans to further privatize health and education, which could result in mass lay-offs, began in April and developed over months into a broader anti-government movement demanding the resignation of Hernández. The military was deployed nationwide in June, and security forces shot and killed several protesters, although support of the security forces may be weakening as indicated by the refusal of several hundred police special forces to leave the barracks for two days in order to avoid repressing the people.[47] US Government support for Hernández also appeared to be weakening when the president's brother was found guilty of trafficking large quantities of cocaine into the USA in a New York court in 2019, with the president himself identified by the US Government as a co-conspirator in the case. Drug traffickers testified that Hernández accepted millions of dollars, including from Mexican cartel

[41] Alcoba, N., 'Argentine Senate approves emergency food law after mass protests', Al Jazeera, 18 Sep. 2019.

[42] Romero, S. et al., '15 days of fury: How Puerto Rico's government collapsed', New York Times, 27 July 2019.

[43] Guy, J. and de Moura, H., 'Ecuador government leaves capital city amid violent protests', CNN, 8 Oct. 2019.

[44] Krygier, R., 'Daily protests are paralyzing Haiti. Here's why', Washington Post, 14 Oct. 2019.

[45] Taub, A., '"Chile woke up": Dictatorship's legacy of inequality triggers mass protests', New York Times, 3 Nov. 2019, updated 18 Nov. 2019.

[46] Grattan, S., 'Colombia protests: What prompted them and where are they headed?', Al Jazeera, 26 Nov. 2019.

[47] Breda, T., 'Crackdown raises stakes as Honduran protestors march on', International Crisis Group Q&A, 2 July 2019.

leader Joaquín Guzmán Loera ('El Chapo'), to fund political campaigns, including his 2013 electoral campaign, in exchange for protection from police and military forces.[48]

Economic and political roots

Economic and political frustrations were the cause of many of the region's public protests. These were rooted in increasing vulnerabilities, persistently high levels of inequalities and constraints on social mobility, and rising discontent with political elites and dysfunctional democratic institutions. Regional economic growth slowed from 1.0 per cent in 2018 to only 0.2 per cent in 2019.[49] The slowdown came after a decade of commodities-driven expansion that had lifted 100 million people out of poverty; between 2002 and 2012 economic growth and redistributive policies in the region had lifted over 10 million people into the middle class every year.[50] From 2013 a slowdown in economic growth translated into society's 'vulnerable' (not living in poverty, but not yet in the middle class) becoming the largest segment of the population in the region.

With the region's persistently high rate of social inequalities, the prolonged economic slump has tipped many of the new middle class back into poverty.[51] This has provoked widespread anger over the hardships of daily life and lack of opportunities. Furthermore, scandals linked to corruption, electoral fraud and abuse of power have fed dissatisfaction with the state of democracy and eroded trust in political institutions. According to *The Economist*, Latinobarómetro data indicates that Latin Americans have felt increasing dissatisfaction with democracy in their countries, rising from 52 per cent in 2010 to 71 per cent in 2018.[52] When citizens were asked whether they would like to move to another country permanently if they could, 31 per cent of a representative sample of respondents throughout Latin America and the Caribbean responded with 'yes' in 2019, a steady increase from 19 per cent in 2010.[53]

---

[48] Palmer, E. and Malkin, E., 'Honduran president's brother is found guilty of drug trafficking', *New York Times*, 18 Oct. 2019; and Guthrie, A., 'US prosecutors accuse Honduran president of drug conspiracy', Associated Press, 4 Aug. 2019.

[49] International Monetary Fund, *Regional Economic Outlook: Stunted by Uncertainty* (International Monetary Fund: Washington, DC, Oct. 2019).

[50] Calvo-González, O., 'Economic slow-down puts the brakes on middle class growth in Latin America', World Bank Datablog, 7 Apr. 2016.

[51] UN, *World Economic Situation and Prospects 2020* (New York: UN, 2020), p. 153.

[52] *The Economist*, 'Nearly a third of Latin Americans want to emigrate', 7 Sep. 2019.

[53] *The Economist* (note 52).

II. Armed conflict and the peace process in Colombia

JOSÉ ALVARADO CÓBAR

Colombia experienced over five decades of armed conflict before the biggest guerrilla group in the country—the Revolutionary Armed Forces of Colombia–People's Army (Fuerzas Armadas Revolucionarias de Colombia–Ejército del Pueblo, FARC–EP)—signed a peace agreement in November 2016. Since then, the Government of Colombia and FARC–EP have taken a series of steps to implement the peace agreement. In 2019 more than two thirds of the commitments set out in the agreement had been initiated, and more than one third had been completed or made substantial progress.[1] Overall, the agreement has been effective at ending the conflict, sustaining peace between both parties and transforming the FARC–EP into a democratic political party.[2] Nevertheless the process has become more complex due to the aggravating security situation in the country, particularly in relation to the protection of demobilized FARC–EP soldiers and human rights activists, and the power vacuum being filled by diverse non-state armed groups.

Fragile peace and implementation of the Colombian peace agreement

Modest progress has been made in terms of implementing the peace agreement. The United Nations Verification Mission in Colombia, responsible for verifying the implementation of the agreement between the FARC–EP and the Colombian Government, highlighted that the establishment of development programmes with a territorial focus advanced as part of comprehensive rural reform measures; 780 projects of the 1207 planned have been implemented in 76 municipalities across the country.[3] The Special Jurisdiction for Peace, an institution created to investigate, prosecute and punish those responsible for human rights violations during the armed conflict, accredited more than 60 000 victims as of December 2019—this includes the first collective accreditations of ethnic communities as victims during the conflict.[4] FARC–EP (renamed the Common Alternative Revolutionary Force) political party members also participated in their first local and departmental elections in October 2019; 12 candidates were elected for different offices, including 3 for mayor.[5]

---

[1] Kroc Institute for International Peace Studies, 'State of implementation of the Colombian Final Accord December 2016–April 2019', University of Notre Dame, Apr. 2019, p. 1.

[2] Kroc Institute for International Peace Studies (note 1), p. 2.

[3] UN Security Council, 'United Nations Verification Mission in Colombia', Report of the Secretary-General, S/2019/988, 26 Dec. 2019, p. 3.

[4] UN Security Council, S/2019/988 (note 3), p. 4.

[5] UN Security Council, S/2019/988 (note 3), p. 6.

Nevertheless, other aspects of the agreement saw setbacks throughout the year. Adequate funding for the full implementation of gender actions and the targeting of women participating in political, social and peacebuilding processes by illegal armed groups remain major concerns.[6] Additionally, as of August 2019 only 42 per cent of commitments aimed at improving gender equality have been either initiated or implemented, compared to 73 per cent of the general commitments in the peace agreement.[7] The right-wing government of President Iván Duque Márquez has also led a forceful coca eradication strategy. In February the government revealed plans to increase the annual goal of eradicated land, via the army and anti-narcotics police, to 100 000 hectares, an increase of 43 per cent from the previous year. This undermined alternatives such as the crop substitution programme, known as the National Comprehensive Program for the Substitution of Illicit Crops (Programa Nacional Integral de Sustitución de Cultivos de Uso Ilícito, PNIS), to which over 100 000 families signed up as part of the government and former FARC–EP negotiations.[8] Further aggravating the PNIS, the Organization of American States (OAS) Mission to Support the Peace Process in Colombia (MAPP/OAS) has documented cases of extortion by the National Liberation Army (Ejército de Liberación Nacional, ELN) guerrilla group and other criminal groups, such as the Gaitanista Self-Defense Forces of Colombia (Autodefensas Gaitanistas de Colombia, also known as the Gulf Clan), to families receiving funds under the PNIS.[9]

Additionally, in the 2019 national budget the Duque administration announced a cut of around $140 million to the development funding established in the peace accords, which includes institutions such as the Rural Development Agency and the Territorial Renovation Agency, and an increase in military spending.[10] Another mechanism contemplated in the peace accords, the Territorial Training and Reintegration Spaces legally ended its transitionary period on 15 August 2019 and officially transformed into 24 permanent settlements spread across the country. Nevertheless, 69 per cent of the 13 202 former FARC–EP combatants have left these spaces and settled elsewhere. Of those who have left, 154 ex-combatants have been killed in 2018 and 2019, 113 have also been threatened and 11 forcibly disappeared as of December 2019.[11]

---

[6] UN Security Council, S/2019/988 (note 3), p. 11.

[7] Kroc Institute for International Peace Studies, *Gender Equality for Sustainable Peace, Second Report on the Monitoring of the Gender Perspective in the Implementation of the Colombian Peace Accord* (University of Notre Dame: Dec. 2019), p. 11.

[8] Puerta, F. and Chaparro, M. P., 'Aggressive coca eradication threatens voluntary substation efforts in Colombia', InSight Crime, 19 Feb. 2019.

[9] OAS, Twenty-sixth report of the Secretary General to the Permanent Council on the Organization of American States Mission to Support the Peace Process in Colombia, 10 May 2019, p. 4.

[10] Puerto and Chaparro (note 8).

[11] Semana, 'Farc: En qué va la reincorporación' [FARC: Dealing with reincorporation], 16 Nov. 2019.

In terms of human rights protections, the Office of the UN High Commissioner for Human Rights verified that there were 86 killings of human rights defenders and social leaders (including 12 women) in 2019.[12] The UN has identified human rights defenders advocating on behalf of community-based and specific ethnic groups such as indigenous peoples and Afro-Colombians as the single most-targeted group; there was also an increase by almost 50 per cent of female human rights defenders killed in 2019 compared with 2018.[13] The UN places half of all killings concentrated in four departments: Antioquia, Arauca, Cauca and Caquetá. Three of these are located in border areas, while Cauca also borders the Pacific Ocean. The urgency to address killings in border provinces is highlighted by the MAPP/OAS, which links the presence and activities of illegal armed groups in these areas to increases in violent crime and homicide.

Dissident Revolutionary Armed Forces of Colombia groups in Colombia

Disillusionment with the post-conflict reintegration process has resulted in the emergence of a broad spectrum of different criminal groups with ties to former FARC–EP commanders. Most dissident FARC–EP groups that did not join the political wing of the group have pledged allegiance to two former FARC–EP commanders leading different criminal enterprises in Colombia: Miguel Botache Santillan (alias Gentil Duarte) and Luciano Marín (alias Iván Márquez). Botache Santillan, along with Géner García Molina (alias John 40) and Nestor Gregorio Vera Fernández (alias Iván Mordisco), are the most powerful dissident FARC–EP commanders and are said to control large parts of drug-trafficking and illegal mining networks in the southern part of Colombia. The group led by Botache Santillan is known as the Eastern Bloc of the FARC–EP, which had originally rejected the peace accords with the government.[14] In 2019 the group coordinated efforts to bring together diverse dissident FARC–EP units into a single fighting force; operating more as a federation rather than a single, insurgent force. It currently runs a criminal syndicate across 8 of the 32 departments in Colombia.[15]

On 29 August 2019 FARC–EP's former second in command, Márquez, alongside other high-profile former FARC–EP combatants involved in the peace process in Havana, denounced the slow pace of implementation, including the lack of promised vocational training and reintegration

---

[12] UN Security Council, S/2019/988 (note 3), p. 9.

[13] UN Office of the High Commissioner for Human Rights, 'Colombia: Human rights activists killings', 14 Jan. 2020.

[14] Rule of Law in Armed Conflicts, 'Non-international armed conflicts in Colombia', 22 Jan. 2020.

[15] InSight Crime, 'The tipping point: Iván Márquez deserts the peace process', 11 Nov. 2019.

programmes, and announced that they would rearm.[16] It is also believed that the current number of former FARC–EP combatants that have rearmed as of September 2019 is between 1000 and 3000.[17] The splintering of the organization, in addition to numerous diverse actors vying for power and influence, has created a loose network of dissident groups that divides criminal incomes and territory, and agrees to work together to push for shared criminal interests, rather than ideology or a shared vision.[18]

The Colombian state and the National Liberation Army rebel group

President Duque formally took office on 7 August 2018. Since the beginning of his mandate he showed reluctance to engage with the ELN and its factions unless they suspended all criminal activity and abandoned the coca trade.[19] The ELN, now the country's largest Marxist rebel group, continued to target state and private infrastructure in Colombia in 2019.[20] It is also believed that the ELN controls most cocaine routes on the border between Venezuela and Colombia's Arauca department.[21] The contentious relationship with the government ultimately led to the ELN suspending a unilateral ceasefire imposed from 23 December 2018 to 3 January 2019 and resuming hostilities against the state.[22]

On 17 January 2019 José Aldemar Rojas Rodríguez, a member of the ELN, escalated hostilities against the Colombian state, and a car bomb was detonated outside a police academy in Bogotá, killing 21 people.[23] Soon thereafter, the Colombian Government reactivated arrest warrants for members of the ELN leadership and asked Cuba to collaborate with extraditions.[24] It is believed that FARC–EP dissidents and the ELN cooperate on drug trafficking and other illicit activities in overlapping territories; however, the extent of that cooperation is unknown.[25] There is a fear that with the splintering of FARC–EP into many dissident groups, levels of violent conflict among FARC–EP dissident groups and ELN will increase.

[16] Charles, M., 'Why Colombia's dissident FARC rebels are taking up arms again', World Politics Review, 4 Sep. 2019.

[17] Charles (note 16).

[18] InSight Crime (note 15).

[19] Olaya, Á. et al., 'Colombia President Duque's 5 "hot potatoes"', InSight Crime, 8 Aug. 2018.

[20] Latin News, 'Colombia: Government dialogue remains far off as ELN ceasefire ends', Jan. 2019.

[21] Venezuela Investigative Unit, 'FARC dissidents and the ELN turn Venezuela into criminal enclave', InSight Crime, 10 Dec. 2018.

[22] Latin News (note 20).

[23] González, J. C. and Casey, N., 'Colombia car bombing suspect belonged to rebel group, government says', New York Times, 18 Jan. 2019.

[24] González and Casey (note 23).

[25] InSight Crime, 'Ex-FARC Mafia, Venezuela and the current international climate', 11 Nov. 2019.

The worsening security situation was evident in the latest statistics for 2018; for the first time in eight years, the Colombian homicide rate saw an increase, to 12 311 from 11 381 in 2017.[26] The increase in levels of violence is associated with new and old armed groups, such as the ELN, and FARC–EP dissidents, and it is likely that those figures continued with an upward trajectory in 2019.

---

[26] Dalby, C. and Carranza, C., 'InSight Crime's 2018 homicide round-up', InSight Crime, 22 Jan. 2019.

III. Armed conflict in Mexico

MARINA CAPARINI

Mexico experienced a record number of people murdered in 2019—nearly 35 000 people, or an average of 95 people per day.[1] Approximately 9400 people were killed as a result of political violence in 2019, predominantly as violence against civilians (7400) and secondarily in battles involving armed groups (1900).[2] New figures estimate that over 61 000 people have disappeared in Mexico since 1964, the majority since 2006 when Mexico began a crackdown on narcotrafficking and pursued it with a militarized approach.[3] The administrations of Felipe Calderón (2007–12) and Enrique Peña Nieto (2013–18) implemented the 'kingpin strategy' of arresting or killing the leaders of major organized crime cartels. Driven by record homicides rates in Mexico and drug-related deaths in the United States, this strategy was reaffirmed by the Nieto administration in 2018 in a joint Mexican–US initiative to investigate the financial infrastructure of the drug cartels and target their leaders through the offer of large monetary rewards for information leading to their capture.[4] However, mounting evidence indicates that the kingpin strategy has directly increased rather than decreased violence by triggering often violent reprisals and creating leadership vacuums that result in the splintering and fragmentation of cartels and the emergence of small, extremely violent armed groups.[5] The elevated level of cartel-related violence in 2019 led the Armed Conflict Location & Event Data Project to warn that Mexico is at 'high risk' of the cartel 'criminal market developing into insurgency'.[6]

Whether cartel violence amounts to armed conflict has been a matter of continuing debate among experts.[7] In 2019 an expert group on international humanitarian law concluded that due to the level of armed violence perpetrated by the Jalisco New Generation Cartel (Cártel Jalisco Nueva Generación, CJNG) and its level of internal organization, a non-international

---

[1] Al Jazeera, 'Mexico murder rate hits record high in 2019', 21 Jan. 2020.
[2] Armed Conflict Location & Event Data Project (ACLED), 'Data export tool', [n.d.].
[3] Villegas, P., 'A new toll in Mexico's drug war: More than 61,000 vanished', *New York Times*, 6 Jan. 2020.
[4] Green, E., 'Joint US–Mexico effort to focus on drug kingpins' financial infrastructure', Public Radio International, 20 Aug. 2018.
[5] Phillips, B. J., 'How does leadership decapitation affect violence? The case of drug trafficking organizations in Mexico', *Journal of Politics*, vol. 77, no. 2 (2015), pp. 324–36; and Calderón, G. et al., 'The beheading of criminal organizations and the dynamics of violence in Mexico', *Journal of Conflict Resolution*, vol. 59, no. 8 (2015), pp. 1455–85.
[6] ACLED, 'Ten conflicts to worry about in 2020', 23 Jan 2020.
[7] Phillips, B. J., 'Is Mexico the second-deadliest "conflict zone" in the world? Probably not', Monkey Cage, Washington Post, 18 May 2017; and Redman, N. et al., 'Armed conflict survey 2018: Revisions and review', International Institute for Strategic Studies, 4 July 2018.

armed conflict existed between the Mexican armed forces and the CJNG.[8] The group reasoned that armed violence involving the CJNG had reached a level that went beyond internal disturbances and tensions, and its capacity to purchase and manufacture weapons and to organize and carry out military operations, as well as its control of some parts of the Mexican territory, satisfied the organizational requirement for a non-international armed conflict under international humanitarian law.[9]

CJNG's well-disciplined and heavily armed members have employed extreme violence in killing rivals from other cartels and have launched attacks on state police and armed forces, including the shooting down of a military helicopter in 2015.[10] In October 2019 CJNG was responsible for an ambush that killed 14 state police officers.[11]

Advocating in his electoral campaign an approach of 'hugs not bullets', President Andrés Manuel López Obrador, who took office in December 2018, sought to break with the kingpin strategy and shift the focus from confronting criminal organizations to a more holistic approach that includes addressing the root causes of insecurity such as poverty through social security programmes and the social reintegration of criminal actors.[12] On 17 October Ovidio Guzmán López, who is a son of Joaquín Guzmán Loero ('El Chapo') and a high-ranking member of the Sinaloa cartel, was captured in Culiacán, capital city of Sinaloa, resulting in an estimated 375 armed individuals attacking state security forces.[13] The violence lasted several days and resulted in at least 13 deaths before Ovidio Guzmán was released by authorities in order to minimize further loss of life.[14] That incident, followed by the deaths of nine members, including six children, of a Mexican–US Mormon family in early November in an ambush by alleged members of an organized crime gang, increased criticism that the López Obrador administration lacked an effective public security policy to deal with the cartels and the record level of lethal violence.[15]

---

[8] Rule of Law in Armed Conflict (RULAC), 'IHL applies to the armed confrontations between Mexico and the Jalisco Cartel New Generation', Geneva Academy of International Humanitarian Law and Human Rights, 12 Feb. 2019.

[9] RULAC (note 8).

[10] RULAC, 'Non-international armed conflicts in Mexico', 9 Mar. 2020; CBS News, 'Ruthless Mexican cartel led by DEA's most-wanted fugitive is "taking over everywhere"', 18 Mar. 2020; and InSight Crime, 'Jalisco Cartel New Generation', 21 May 2019.

[11] Malkin, E., '14 police officers killed in an ambush in Mexico', New York Times, 14 Oct. 2019.

[12] Cruz, O., 'AMLO's peace and security plan', Infographic, Wilson Center Mexico Institute, 4 Jan. 2019.

[13] Sandin, L. and McCormick, G., '"Abrazos no belazos"—Evaluating Amlo's security initiatives', Center for Strategic International Studies commentary, 13 Dec. 2019.

[14] McGinnis, T., 'The capture and release of Ovidio Guzmán in Culicán, Sinaloa', Justice in Mexico, 5 Nov. 2019.

[15] Ahmad, A. et al., '9 members of Mormon family in Mexico are killed in ambush', New York Times, 5 Nov. 2019; and Tuckman, J., 'Mexico's president under pressure over "hugs not bullets" cartel policy', The Guardian, 5 Nov. 2019.

Over 1 million people were internally displaced between 2017 and 2018, moving to protect themselves from crime in Mexico.[16] Additionally, unprecedented numbers of US-bound migrants transited Mexico. The migrant flows featured many women and children, largely fleeing high levels of violence in Guatemala and Honduras, moving individually and later in caravans. Initially vowing to assist the migrants and grant them humanitarian visas, President López Obrador bowed to pressure by US President Donald J. Trump to impose damaging tariffs on Mexican imports if Mexico did not crack down on migrants arriving at the US border.

After reaching agreement with the USA in June to control migration from Central America in order to avert escalating import tariffs on Mexican goods, President López Obrador ordered the deployment of 6000 members of the newly established National Guard to the southern border with Guatemala, with some 20 000 becoming tasked in 2019 with migration enforcement.[17] By December Mexico's migration control efforts had contributed to reducing migrant arrests at the US border by 75 per cent.[18]

The role and structure of the National Guard is controversial: established under the Secretariat of Security and Civilian Protection to prevent and combat crime, it is ostensibly under civilian control. Over 100 000 personnel were to be recruited by the end of 2019, drawn from the army, navy and federal police. However, it is a militarized body in that it is composed predominantly of military and naval personnel, who retain their military status, and is led by military officers.[19] The end target is 150 000 personnel, to be achieved by 2023, in an organization that, according to the National Plan for Peace and Security, 'will follow with the discipline, hierarchy and rank of the armed forces'.[20] By October 80 per cent of its personnel was military, growing primarily through the transfer of military personnel rather than civilian recruitment.[21]

---

[16] Telesur, 'México reporta 1.13 millones de desplazados por la violencia' [Mexico reports 1.13 million displaced by violence], 23 Apr. 2019; and Díaz Pérez, M. C. and Viramontes, R. M., *La violencia como causa de desplazamiento interno forzado. Aproximaciones a su análisis en México* [*Violence as a Cause of Forced Internal Displacement. Approaches to its Analysis in Mexico*] (Consejo Nacional de Población: Mar. 2019).

[17] Cabezas, J., 'Mexico says National Guard deployment to southern border starts on Wednesday', Reuters, 12 June 2019; and Beittel, J. S., 'Mexico: Organized crime and drug trafficking organizations', Congressional Research Service R41576, 20 Dec. 2019, p. 7.

[18] Webber, J., 'Amlo bows to Trump in a relationship of unequals', *Financial Times*, 18 Dec. 2019.

[19] Moyano, I. G., *Mexico's National Guard: When Police are Not Enough* (Wilson Center: Jan. 2020).

[20] Melimopolous, E., 'Mexico's National Guard: What, who and when', Al Jazeera, 30 June 2019.

[21] Wilson Center Mexico Institute, 'Comments of Alejandro Hope, Eighth Annual US–Mexico Security Conference: Taking stock of Mexico's security landscape one year on', 15 Jan. 2020.

4. Armed conflict and peace processes in Asia and Oceania

Overview

Seven countries in Asia and Oceania experienced active armed conflicts in 2019—three in South Asia: Afghanistan (major internationalized civil war), India (high-intensity interstate border and subnational armed conflicts) and Pakistan (high-intensity interstate border and subnational armed conflicts); and four in South East Asia: Indonesia (low-intensity subnational armed conflict), Myanmar (high-intensity subnational armed conflict), the Philippines (high-intensity subnational armed conflict) and Thailand (low-intensity subnational armed conflict). Two emerging trends remained cause for concern in 2019: (a) the growing violence related to identity politics, based on ethnic and/ or religious polarization, and (b) the increase in transnational violent jihadist groups.

Two peace processes deteriorated in 2019: discussions between the Democratic People's Republic of Korea and the United States stalled; and the Taliban–USA peace talks collapsed in September 2019—leading to renewed pessimism about the prospects of ending the long-running war in Afghanistan (despite the resumption of talks in November 2019). The war in Afghanistan was the deadliest armed conflict in the world, with nearly 42 000 fatalities in 2019. The increased use of suicide and improvised explosive device attacks by anti-government groups, in particular the Taliban, and an expansion in US air strikes, contributed to increased civilian casualties.

There were five multilateral peace operations active in Asia and Oceania in 2019, the same number as in 2018. The number of personnel serving in peace operations in the region decreased only slightly during 2019, from 17 296 in 2018 to 17 086 in 2019. Most of these were part of the Resolute Support Mission in Afghanistan, led by the North Atlantic Treaty Organization.

Tensions between China and the USA continued during 2019, with serious disagreements across economic, political, security and human rights dimensions. In addition to their roller-coaster trade war, strategic competition between the two countries continued in the South China Sea and across the Taiwan Strait. Tensions in Hong Kong resurfaced in June 2019, when hundreds of thousands of people protested against a proposed new extradition law, and clashes between police and protesters continued to the end of the year.

A February suicide attack by a Pakistan-based militant group in Indian-administered Kashmir—the worst in Kashmir for over three decades—sparked a sharp but short escalation in the conflict between the nuclear-armed neigh-

bours of India and Pakistan. Although the immediate crisis thawed, tensions continued throughout the year as India indicated that the episode had brought to an end its unstated policy of strategic restraint, and that retaliation for any attack perceived to be linked to Pakistan was now the 'new normal'.

Some of the most organized Islamist extremist groups are active in South East Asia, most notably in Indonesia, Malaysia and the Philippines. In Myanmar, an ongoing peace process made little headway during the year against a backdrop of rising violence, especially in Rakhine state. The voluntary return of almost a million Rohingya people forcibly displaced in 2017 seemed even less likely, despite worsening humanitarian conditions in refugee camps in Bangladesh. Accountability and justice for alleged atrocities committed against the Rohingya people and other ethnic minorities in Myanmar remained elusive, despite legal efforts pending at the International Criminal Court and the International Court of Justice. Developments to end the long-running Moro insurgency in the southern Philippines were more promising.

IAN DAVIS

I. Key general developments in the region

IAN DAVIS

Seven countries in Asia and Oceania experienced active armed conflicts in 2019—three in South Asia: Afghanistan (major internationalized civil war), India (high-intensity as a result of combined interstate border and subnational armed conflicts) and Pakistan (high-intensity as result of combined interstate border and subnational armed conflicts), as discussed in section II; and four in South East Asia: Indonesia (low-intensity subnational armed conflict), Myanmar (high-intensity subnational armed conflict), the Philippines (high-intensity as a result of combined subnational armed conflict and high levels of violence against civilians in a 'war on drugs') and Thailand (low-intensity subnational armed conflict), as discussed in section III.[1] Alongside these armed conflicts parts of Asia and Oceania continued to be affected by instability arising from a variety of causes, with no single unifying trend (other than China–United States rivalry), and important subregional differences.

While Asia, especially East Asia, has experienced a dramatic reduction in armed conflict and mass-atrocity crimes in the last 40 years, a reversal of this positive trend appears to be under way.[2] Two emerging trends remained cause for concern in 2019: (*a*) the growing violence related to identity politics, based on ethnic and/or religious polarization (some of which has long-term roots) and (*b*) the increase in transnational violent jihadist groups—including the presence of actors linked to the Islamic State in Afghanistan, Bangladesh, China, India, Indonesia, Malaysia, Pakistan, the Philippines and Sri Lanka.[3] In some countries (such as India) Islamic State presence is minimal, while in others (such as Afghanistan) the presence is more entrenched and groups are more capable of carrying out armed attacks.

Only a few of the armed conflicts discussed in this chapter were being addressed in 2019 by ongoing or new peace processes. One significant peace development in 2018—the peace process on the Korean peninsula—deteriorated in 2019 (see below), while the Taliban–USA peace talks collapsed in September 2019. This was followed by an increase in violence in the long-running war in Afghanistan, despite a resumption of the peace talks in November 2019 (see section II). There is no noticeable peace process

---

[1] For conflict definitions and typologies, see chapter 2, section I, in this volume.

[2] World Bank Group and United Nations, *Pathways for Peace: Inclusive Approaches for Preventing Violent Conflict* (International Bank for Reconstruction and Development/The World Bank: Washington, DC, 2018), pp. 11–12, 19; and Bellamy, A. J., *East Asia's Other Miracle: Explaining the Decline of Mass Atrocities* (Oxford University Press: 2017).

[3] Marshall, W., 'Islamic State's South Asia pivot: Rhetoric or reality?', Geopolitical Monitor, 18 June 2019.

between India and Pakistan with regard to their ongoing interstate armed conflict over Kashmir. This conflict also witnessed a significant uptick in violence in 2019 and growing tensions between the two nuclear-armed states (see section II).

Developments to end the long-running Moro insurgency in the southern Philippines (see section III) and in Papua New Guinea, where the Autonomous Region of Bougainville voted in December 2019 for independence from Papua New Guinea, were more promising. The vote, which had been delayed twice in 2019, was part of the 2001 Bougainville Peace Agreement, which ended 10 years of armed conflict over revenues from mining and its environmental impact. However, as the referendum result was non-binding further negotiations will be required before the group of islands becomes the world's newest nation.[4]

There were five multilateral peace operations active in Asia and Oceania in 2019. This was the same number as in 2018. The number of personnel serving in peace operations in the region decreased only slightly during 2019, from 17 296 in 2018 to 17 086 in 2019. Most of these were part of the Resolute Support Mission in Afghanistan, led by the North Atlantic Treaty Organization. The other multilateral peace operations in the region were the International Monitoring Team on the Philippine island of Mindanao, the Neutral Nations Supervisory Commission on the Korean peninsula, the United Nations Assistance Mission in Afghanistan and the UN Military Observer Group in India and Pakistan.

Geopolitical developments involving China and the Democratic People's Republic of Korea (DPRK, North Korea) continued to take a prominent place in regional and global affairs in 2019, as discussed briefly below.

China

China marked the 70th anniversary of its official formation on 1 October 2019.[5] The country's rapid development—including its most high-profile political and development project, the Belt and Road Initiative—and especially its development of a modern military force, has been accompanied by internal and external challenges and controversies.[6] These include growing domestic political repression, increased economic, military and political competition with the USA (and some neighbouring states, especially Taiwan), and tensions in Hong Kong and the South China Sea.

---

[4] Lyons, K., 'Bougainville referendum: Region votes overwhelmingly for independence from Papua New Guinea', *The Guardian*, 11 Dec. 2019; and Powles, A., 'Bougainville has voted to become a new country, but the journey to independence is not yet over', The Conversation, 12 Dec. 2019.

[5] BBC, 'China anniversary: Beijing celebrations mark 70 years of Communist rule', 1 Oct. 2019.

[6] BBC, 'Belt and Road: China showcases initiative to world leaders', 25 Apr. 2019; and Perlez, J., 'China retools vast global building push criticized as bloated and predatory', *New York Times*, 25 Apr. 2019. On China's growth in military expenditure, see chapter 8, section I, in this volume.

Repression of ethnic minorities in Xinjiang

International censure of a large-scale programme for the mass surveillance, incarceration and forced re-education of many hundreds of thousands of Uighurs (Turkic Muslims), Kazakhs and other ethnic minorities in the autonomous region of Xinjiang continued in 2019.[7] In June the vice-governor of Xinjiang defended the state-run detention camps, arguing that they were vocational training centres which helped protect people from extremist influences.[8] In July an international diplomatic divide emerged over the issue at the UN Human Rights Council. Twenty-two Western states signed a letter criticizing China's actions, while 50 states, including many Muslim-majority states, such as Pakistan and Saudi Arabia, endorsed an alternative letter backing China.[9] Neither Turkey, which shares a related language with the Uighurs and earlier in the year had stepped up criticism of China's policy towards them, or the USA signed either letter.[10] Nonetheless, the USA announced new visa restrictions on certain Chinese officials allegedly involved in human rights abuses against the Uighurs and other minority groups in October.[11] However, the overall international response has been largely muted.[12]

[7] Smith Finley, J., 'Securitization, insecurity and conflict in contemporary Xinjiang: Has PRC counter-terrorism evolved into state terror?', *Central Asian Survey*, vol. 38, no. 1 (2019), pp. 1–26; Hasmath, R., 'What explains the rise of majority–minority tensions and conflict in Xinjiang?', *Central Asian Survey*, vol. 38, no. 1 (2019), pp. 46–60; *The Economist*, 'To suppress news of Xinjiang's gulag, China threatens Uighurs abroad', 24 Oct. 2019; and Ramzy, A. and Buckley, C., 'The Xinjiang papers, "Absolutely no mercy": Leaked files expose how China organized mass detentions of Muslims', *New York Times*, 16 Nov. 2019.

[8] Nebehay, S., 'Xinjiang vice-governor defends centers for Uighurs at UN rights forum', Reuters, 25 June 2019.

[9] UN General Assembly, Human Rights Council Forty-first session, Letter dated 8 July 2019 from the Permanent Representatives of Australia, Austria, Belgium, Canada, Denmark, Estonia, Finland, France, Germany, Iceland, Ireland, Japan, Latvia, Lithuania, Luxembourg, the Netherlands, New Zealand, Norway, Spain, Sweden, Switzerland and the United Kingdom of Great Britain and Northern Ireland to the United Nations Office at Geneva addressed to the President of the Human Rights Council, A/HRC/41/G/11, 23 July 2019; and UN General Assembly, Human Rights Council Forty-first session, Letter dated 12 July 2019 from the representatives of Algeria, Angola, Bahrain, Bangladesh, Belarus, the Plurinational State of Bolivia, Burkina Faso, Burundi, Cambodia, Cameroon, Comoros, the Congo, Cuba, the Democratic People's Republic of Korea, the Democratic Republic of the Congo, Djibouti, Egypt, Equatorial Guinea, Eritrea, Gabon, the Islamic Republic of Iran, Iraq, Kuwait, the Lao People's Democratic Republic, Mozambique, Myanmar, Nepal, Nigeria, Oman, Pakistan, the Philippines, the Russian Federation, Saudi Arabia, Serbia, Somalia, South Sudan, Sri Lanka, the Sudan, the Syrian Arab Republic, Tajikistan, Togo, Turkmenistan, Uganda, the United Arab Emirates, Uzbekistan, the Bolivarian Republic of Venezuela, Yemen, Zambia, Zimbabwe and the State of Palestine to the United Nations Office at Geneva addressed to the President of the Human Rights Council, A/HRC/41/G/17, 9 Aug. 2019. Also see Putz, C., 'Which countries are for or against China's Xinjiang policies?', The Diplomat, 15 July 2019.

[10] Pitel, L., 'Turkey steps up criticism of China over crackdown on Uighurs', *Financial Times*, 25 Feb. 2019.

[11] Hansler, J., 'US announces visa restrictions on China for Xinjiang abuses', CNN, 9 Oct. 2019.

[12] Storey, H., 'Why nobody is taking action on Xinjiang and why it matters', Australian Institute of International Affairs, 30 Dec. 2019; and Blanchard B. and Emmott, R., 'EU's proposed ambassadorial visit to Xinjiang seen unlikely to happen', Reuters, 14 Nov. 2019.

China–United States tensions

Tensions between China and the USA continued during 2019, with serious disagreements across economic, political, security and human rights dimensions.[13] A truce in the 2018 China–USA trade war was agreed in December 2018, and the two governments undertook not to impose further tariffs for 90 days while working out a broad trade agreement.[14] Although trade talks stalled in May 2019, a temporary halt in the trade war was agreed after talks at the Group of Twenty (G20) summit at the end of June.[15] In October Chinese–US trade negotiators reached a preliminary agreement to ease tensions, and in December they reportedly reached a 'deal in principle'. However, it remained unclear whether this represented a comprehensive settlement of the dispute.[16]

A significant area of disagreement remains over the development of next-generation 5G communication networks, with the USA urging allies not to use China's Huawei Technologies Co. Ltd because of the risk that the company's equipment could be used by China for spying, which the company has repeatedly denied.[17]

In addition to their roller-coaster trade war, strategic competition between the two countries continued in the South China Sea and across the Taiwan Strait.[18] Tensions in the South China Sea between China and its Association of Southeast Asian Nations neighbours generally eased during 2019 as the parties sought to resolve issues peacefully. An exception was a fishing dispute between China and Indonesia.[19] However, various challenges and uncertainties remained, largely due to Chinese–US military competition. The USA increased the frequency of its freedom of navigation operations (FONOPs)—transits of US naval vessels to challenge what the USA considers excessive territorial claims on the world's oceans—in the South China Sea and the Taiwan Strait during 2019, while an expanding navy and improving

---

[13] See e.g. World Politics Review, 'US–China rivalry in the Trump era', 19 Aug. 2019.

[14] See Smith, D., 'Introduction: International stability and human security in 2018', *SIPRI Yearbook 2019*, pp. 19–20; and BBC, 'A quick guide to the US–China trade war', 16 Jan. 2020.

[15] Bradsher, K. and Swanson, A., 'Trump's trade war threat poses problems for China and investors', *New York Times*, 6 May 2019; and Davis, B. et al., 'Trump allows US sales to Huawei as trade talks resume', *Wall Street Journal*, 29 June 2019.

[16] Kuo, L., 'Beijing silent on US reports of China trade deal', *The Guardian*, 13 Dec. 2019.

[17] Halpern, S., 'The terrifying potential of the 5G network', *New Yorker*, 26 Apr. 2019.

[18] On China's strategy towards the South China Sea, see Rosyidin, M., 'The *Dao* of foreign policy: Understanding China's dual strategy in the South China Sea', *Contemporary Security Policy*, vol. 40, no. 2 (2019), pp. 214–38.

[19] Ng, J., 'The Natuna Sea incident: How Indonesia is managing its bilateral relationship with China', The Diplomat, 15 Jan. 2020; and Shicun, W., 'What's next for the South China Sea?', The Diplomat, 1 Aug. 2019.

Chinese missile technology provided a perceived threat to US naval supremacy in the region.[20]

China–Taiwan relations continued to deteriorate in 2019, and proposed US arms sales, including 66 F-16V combat aircraft, Abrams tanks and Stinger missiles, to Taiwan worth over $10 billion further exacerbated tensions.[21]

Protests in Hong Kong

The former British colony of Hong Kong is a special administrative region of China that, unlike the Chinese mainland's provinces, has certain political and economic freedoms. However, in recent years there have been growing fears that Hong Kong's significant autonomy could erode. China increased its efforts to restrict political dissent following the Umbrella Movement protests in 2014 and the electoral victories of pro-democracy factions in 2016.[22] Tensions resurfaced in June 2019, when hundreds of thousands of people protested against a proposed new extradition law.[23]

In July the protesters temporarily occupied the Legislative Council building, while the Chinese Government called the protests an 'undisguised challenge' to Hong Kong's system of governance, and damaging to the rule of law and social order.[24] In August, the Chinese Government deployed the People's Armed Police, a paramilitary force, to Shenzhen, across the border from Hong Kong, in an apparent warning that China could use force in response to the protests.[25] By the end of September it was reported that China had more than doubled the number of troops stationed in Hong Kong

---

[20] Kelly, T., 'US, UK conduct first joint drills in contested South China Sea', Reuters, 16 Jan. 2019; Browne, R., 'US Navy sails warships through Taiwan Strait', 24 Jan. 2019; Ali, I., 'Two US Navy warships sail through strategic Taiwan Strait', Reuters, 29 Apr. 2019; Lague, D. and Kang Lim, B., 'New missile gap leaves US scrambling to counter China', Reuters, 25 Apr. 2019; and Lague, D. and Kang Lim, B., 'China's vast fleet is tipping the balance in the Pacific', Reuters, 30 Apr. 2019. The US Department of Defense publishes annual reports on FONOPs, see Under Secretary of Defense for Policy, DOD Annual Freedom of Navigation (FON) Reports, [n.d.].

[21] Reuters, 'China to impose sanctions on US firms that sell arms to Taiwan', 12 July 2019; and Chan, M., 'Taiwan's plan to buy 66 F-16 Viper fighter jets from US still on track, defence ministry says', *South China Morning Post*, 6 Apr. 2019. On the risk of a conflict over Taiwan, see Taylor, B., *Dangerous Decade: Taiwan's Security And Crisis Management* (Routledge: 2019); *The Economist*, 'China's might is forcing Taiwan to rethink its military strategy', 26 Jan. 2019; and 'Tensions in the Taiwan Strait', *Strategic Comments*, vol. 25, no. 3 (2019), pp. vi–viii. On US arms sales to Taiwan, see chapter 9, section III, in this volume.

[22] Buckley, C. et al., 'Violence erupts in Hong Kong as protesters are assaulted', *New York Times*, 3 Oct. 2014.

[23] Bodeen, C. and Wang, Y., 'Extradition bill pushes Hong Kong to a political crisis', Associated Press, 10 June 2019; Victor, D., 'Hong Kong protests resume as police headquarters is surrounded', *New York Times*, 20 June 2019; and *The Economist*, 'Hong Kong remains crucially important to mainland China', 8 Aug. 2019.

[24] Westcott, B. and Fang, N., 'Beijing says "radical" Hong Kong protests are an "undisguised challenge"', CNN, 2 July 2019; and Associated Press, 'Hong Kong leader condemns protest in legislature', 2 July 2019.

[25] Myers, S. L. and Hernández, J. C., 'With troop buildup, China sends a stark warning to Hong Kong', *New York Times*, 19 Aug. 2019.

since the protests began (up from 3000–5000 to 10 000–12 000 military personnel).[26]

In mid-November the protesters occupied several university campuses amid growing violence.[27] In local elections, pro-democracy candidates won 347 of the 452 district council seats, with a high turnout of over 71 per cent.[28] Clashes between police and protesters continued to the end of the year, and the future outlook remained uncertain.[29]

Democratic People's Republic of Korea

There were further developments in two parallel and closely related diplomatic processes initiated in 2018: one between North Korea and the Republic of Korea (South Korea) that aimed to promote peace and reconciliation between the two states, and the other between North Korea and the USA that sought to achieve denuclearization of the Korean peninsula and a peace agreement to formally end the Korean War (1950–53) as part of normalizing their relations.[30] These developments affect the future of all Korean citizens, regional and global peace and security, the international nuclear non-proliferation regime, China–USA relations and the balance of power in East Asia.

Despite a second North Korea–USA nuclear summit in Hanoi, Viet Nam, in February 2019, and meetings between President Donald J. Trump and North Korean leader Kim Jong Un at the demilitarized zone at the end of June, and between officials from both sides in Stockholm in October, it proved impossible to break the deadlocked negotiations over the North Korean nuclear programme.[31] At the end of the year, the prospects that North Korea and the USA could make progress towards resolving the impasse on a denuclearization agreement remained uncertain.

Humanitarian needs and the human rights situation in North Korea remained acute in 2019. In February the country issued an international appeal for food aid to help combat the worsening impact of international

---

[26] Torode, G. et al., 'China quietly doubles troop levels in Hong Kong, envoy says', Reuters, 30 Sep. 2019; and Walden, M. and Li, M., 'Why does Beijing have a military garrison in Hong Kong and what could that mean for protesters?', ABC News, 30 Aug. 2019.

[27] Ives, M. and Li, K., 'Hong Kong students ready bows and arrows for battles with police', New York Times, 14 Nov. 2019; and The Economist, 'Hong Kong stares into the abyss amid growing violence', 21 Nov. 2019.

[28] BBC, 'Hong Kong elections: Carrie Lam promises "open mind" after election rout', 25 Nov. 2019.

[29] Jim, C. and Jiang, X., 'Hong Kong to end year with multiple protests, kick off 2020 with big march', Reuters, 30 Dec. 2019.

[30] For developments in 2018, see Smith (note 14), pp. 9–10; and Davis, I., 'Armed conflict and peace processes in Asia and Oceania', SIPRI Yearbook 2019, pp. 53.

[31] On negotiations on North Korea's nuclear programme, see chapter 1, section II, and chapter 11, section II, in this volume.

sanctions and a poor harvest.[32] According to a UN report released in May 2019, 4 in 10 North Koreans were chronically short of food, and further cuts to already minimal rations were expected after the worst harvest in a decade.[33]

Japan–Russia territorial dispute

Relations between Japan and Russia improved in 2018 following several meetings between the two leaders to discuss a possible peace accord for the 70-year dispute over the South Kuril Islands (also known in Japan as the Northern Territories). However, three further summit meetings in 2019 between Japanese Prime Minister Shinzo Abe and Russian President Vladimir Putin (in January, June and September) failed to produce any significant progress.[34]

---

[32] *The Guardian*, 'North Korea appeals for food aid as regime cuts rations due to drought and sanctions', 22 Feb. 2019.

[33] World Food Programme, 'After worst harvest in ten years, 10 million people in DPRK face imminent food shortages', 3 May 2019.

[34] 'Why Japan's prime minister pines for four desolate islands', *The Economist*, 7 Feb. 2019; Tsuruoka, M., 'Making sense of Japan's approach to Russia', The Diplomat, 5 Sep. 2019; and 'Vladimir Putin rebuffs Shinzo Abe's call to sign peace treaty over Tokyo's ties with US military, unresolved territorial issues', *South China Morning Post*, 5 Sep. 2019.

II. Armed conflict and peace processes in South Asia

IAN DAVIS AND TIMO SMIT

The security threats facing the states in South Asia—Afghanistan, Bangladesh, Bhutan, India, Maldives, Nepal, Pakistan and Sri Lanka—are complex and diverse. Security challenges include interstate rivalry, border disputes, nuclear risks, terrorism and internal threats arising from a combination of ethnic, religious and political tensions.[1] Environmental challenges, such as climate change, water scarcity and energy security, are also an increasingly common reality for the region.[2] In 2019 for example, drought and over-extraction of groundwater caused the Indian city of Chennai (with 10 million inhabitants) to nearly run out of water, while the controversy over water resources also formed part of India–Pakistan tensions.[3]

This section focuses on two important issues that are crucial barometers for peace and stability in South Asia: the long-running and devastating war in Afghanistan, and the territorial dispute between India and Pakistan over the Kashmir region. In the former, initial optimism that a peace process led by the United States would pave the way to a settlement of the conflict was replaced by renewed pessimism following the collapse of the peace talks in September 2019 (despite their resumption in November). In the latter, a February suicide attack by the Pakistan-based militant group Jaish-e-Mohammad (JEM) in Indian-administered Kashmir—the worst in Kashmir for over three decades—sparked a sharp but short escalation in the conflict between the nuclear-armed neighbours of India and Pakistan.

South Asia remains one of the regions most affected by attacks by non-state groups. For example, the *Global Terrorism Index 2019* notes that Afghanistan, Pakistan, India and the Philippines were among the top 10 countries most affected by terrorism worldwide (with Afghanistan, India and Pakistan appearing in the top 10 for over a decade).[4] Major non-state armed groups operating in the region included: al-Qaeda, the Islamic State in the Khorasan Province (IS-KP), Lashkar-e-Jhangvi (LEJ) and the Taliban in Afghanistan; Lashkar-e-Taiba (LET), LEJ and the Taliban Movement in Pakistan (Tehreek-e-Taliban, TEP); LET and the Maoists in India; and various home-grown Islamist extremist groups affiliated with al-Qaeda and the Islamic

---

[1] Staniland, P., 'The future of democracy in South Asia: Why citizens must stay vigilant', *Foreign Affairs*, 4 Jan. 2019.

[2] Nordqvist, P. and Krampe, F., 'Climate change and violent conflict: Sparse evidence from South Asia and South East Asia', SIPRI Insights on Peace and Security no. 2018/4, Sep. 2018.

[3] Pathak, S., 'No drips, no drops: A city of 10 million is running out of water', National Public Radio, 25 June 2019; and Reuters, 'India again threatens to restrict flow of river water to Pakistan as tension builds', *The Guardian*, 22 Feb. 2019.

[4] Institute for Economics & Peace, *Global Terrorism Index 2019: Measuring the Impact of Terrorism* (Institute for Economics & Peace: Nov. 2019), p. 18.

State. In Sri Lanka for example, over 250 people were killed and 500 injured in suicide bombings at churches and hotels on 21 April 2019, Easter Sunday, in Colombo. The Islamic State claimed responsibility for the attack, but the Sri Lankan Government said it was carried out by a local radical Islamist group, National Thowheeth Jama'ath, with foreign support. The attack led to heightened intercommunal tensions and anti-Muslim violence in the country.[5]

Armed conflict in Afghanistan

The war in Afghanistan continued unabatedly in 2019. By some accounts it was the deadliest armed conflict in the world, ahead of the wars in Syria and Yemen. According to the Armed Conflict Location & Event Data Project (ACLED) there were nearly 42 000 fatalities due to the conflict over the course of the year (see table 4.1).[6] Most of these were combat related and involved Afghan Government forces and the Taliban. Meanwhile, the United Nations Assistance Mission in Afghanistan (UNAMA) continued to document high levels of violence against civilians. It recorded 8239 civilian casualties (2563 fatalities and 5676 injuries) in the first nine months of 2019, of which 4313 (1174 fatalities and 3139 injuries) were between 1 July and 30 September. This was the largest number of civilian casualties that UNAMA had recorded in a three-month period since it started tracking them in 2009.[7]

The spike in civilian casualties in the third quarter of 2019 was attributed primarily to an increase in suicide and improvised explosive device (IED) attacks by anti-government groups, in particular the Taliban.[8] The Taliban was in advanced stages of peace negotiations with the USA at this point, and was stepping up its attacks against military and civilian targets as a means of creating additional leverage as the talks were progressing.[9] The Taliban was also responsible for most of the civilian casualties resulting from electoral violence in the run-up to and on the day of the Afghan presidential elections, which took place on 28 September.[10]

Another factor that explained the high level of civilian casualties was that the USA further expanded its use of air strikes. US aircraft and unmanned

---

[5] Keenan, A., 'Sri Lanka's Easter bombings: Peaceful coexistence under attack', International Crisis Group commentary, 23 Apr. 2019; The Economist, 'Sri Lanka responds to Islamist terrorism by terrorising Muslims', 6 June 2019; and Safi, M., 'Death toll in Sri Lanka bombings revised down to 253', The Guardian, 25 Apr. 2019.

[6] ACLED, 'Data export tool', [n.d.].

[7] UNAMA, 'Quarterly report on the protection of civilians in armed conflict: 1 January to 30 September 2019', 17 Oct. 2019.

[8] UNAMA (note 7).

[9] George, S., 'The past three months in Afghanistan have been the deadliest for civilians in a decade', The Washington Post, 17 Oct. 2019.

[10] UNAMA (note 7).

Table 4.1. Estimated conflict-related fatalities in Afghanistan, 2017–19

Event type	2017	2018	2019
Battles	26 200	31 769	26 686
Explosions/remote violence	9 517	10 891	14 647
Protests, riots and strategic developments	268	297	197
Violence against civilians	433	369	388
Total	**36 418**	**43 326**	**41 918**

Notes: The first available year for data on Afghanistan in the Armed Conflict Location & Event Data Project (ACLED) database is 2017. For definitions of event types, see ACLED, 'ACLED definitions of political violence and protest', 11 Apr. 2019.

Source: ACLED, 'Data export tool', [n.d.].

aerial vehicles released more munitions on targets in Afghanistan than in any other year since the US Department of Defense began publishing this type of statistics.[11] According to UNAMA air strikes killed 579 civilians in the first nine months of 2019—more than any other type of incident—of which 74 per cent was attributed to the USA.[12]

The IS-KP was less active than in previous years due to successive military campaigns against it by the Afghan Government, the Taliban and the USA. It suffered a major defeat in its stronghold province Nangarhar in November when 243 IS-KP fighters and several hundred of their relatives surrendered to the Afghan Government.[13] Although the IS-KP conducted fewer suicide attacks in 2019 than in 2018, it was responsible for the largest mass-casualty single incident, namely the terrorist attack at a wedding in a Shia district of Kabul in August 2019, which killed 92 and injured 142 civilians.[14]

The conflict displaced 345 000 people in the first nine months of 2019, and an estimated 4 million people displaced since 2012 have not returned to their communities. In 2020 an estimated 14.3 million people are expected to be in either crisis or emergency levels of food insecurity.[15]

The peace process

The Taliban and the USA conducted several rounds of peace talks in Doha, Qatar, in 2019. The Trump administration had taken the initiative to reopen these bilateral direct talks with the Taliban in July 2018, hoping this would break the deadlock and pave the way for meaningful negotiations to end the war in Afghanistan. The USA had previously been unwilling to participate

---

[11] Borger, J., 'US dropped record number of bombs on Afghanistan last year', *The Guardian*, 28 Jan. 2020; and US Central Command, 'Combined Forces Air Component Commander 2013–2019 Airpower statistics as of 31 December 2019', [n.d.].

[12] George (note 9).

[13] Gibbons-Neff, T. and Mashal, M., 'ISIS is losing Afghan territory. That means little for its victims', *New York Times*, 2 Dec. 2019.

[14] BBC, 'Afghanistan war: Tracking the killings in August 2019', 16 Sep. 2019.

[15] UN Office for the Coordination of Humanitarian Affairs, *Global Humanitarian Overview 2020* (UN Office for the Coordination of Humanitarian Affairs: Geneva, Dec. 2019), p. 32.

in peace talks that did not include the Afghan Government. However, the Taliban does not recognize the government in Kabul and has hitherto refused to negotiate with it.[16]

These talks between the Taliban and the USA were the most prominent of the various Afghan peace talks that were ongoing, and they also appeared to be the most promising.[17] The Taliban and the USA settled on a draft framework of an agreement in January 2019, in which the USA would agree to withdraw from Afghanistan militarily in exchange for credible assurances from the Taliban that it would prohibit terrorist groups from operating from Afghanistan.[18] Ever since the USA intervened in Afghanistan in 2001, it has stated that the strategic objective of its military presence there is to prevent the country from becoming a safe haven for terrorist groups again. The USA also made clear that the withdrawal of US troops would be conditional on that the Taliban would agree to a ceasefire and to hold direct talks with the Afghan Government.[19]

The Taliban and the USA were seemingly close to an agreement in September 2019. The US special representative for Afghanistan reconciliation and chief negotiator, Zalmay Khalilzad, confirmed that the Taliban and the USA had reached an agreement 'in principle' and subject to the approval of US President Donald J. Trump.[20] The agreement stipulated that upon its entry into force, the USA would gradually withdraw its 14 000 troops from Afghanistan within 16 months, 5400 of which within 135 days. This would be conditional on the Taliban adhering to the terms of the agreement, including counterterrorism assurances and a partial ceasefire to facilitate the withdrawal of US troops from military bases.[21] Following the conclusion of this agreement, direct negotiations between the Afghan Government and the Taliban on a permanent ceasefire and comprehensive peace agreement would commence.[22]

However, the peace talks between the Taliban and the USA collapsed shortly thereafter. On 8 September President Trump suddenly announced that he had called off peace negotiations with the Taliban, which he later declared 'dead'.[23] The reason he gave was that the Taliban had claimed

---

[16] Thomas, C., 'Afghanistan: Background and US policy in brief', Congressional Research Service, 31 Jan. 2020.

[17] For more information on the various international peace processes in Afghanistan, see Davis, I., 'Armed conflict and peace processes in Asia and Oceania', *SIPRI Yearbook 2019*, pp. 62–65.

[18] Mashal, M., 'US and Taliban agree in principle to peace framework, envoy says', *New York Times*, 28 Jan. 2019.

[19] Mashal (note 18).

[20] Mashal, M., 'To start Afghan withdrawal, US would pull 5,400 troops in 135 days', *New York Times*, 2 Sep. 2019.

[21] Hamid, S. and Qadir Sediqi, A., 'US to withdraw 5,000 troops from Afghanistan, close bases: US negotiator', Reuters, 2 Sep. 2019; and Mashal (note 20).

[22] Al Jazeera, 'Intra-Afghan negotiations to follow US-Taliban deal: Khalidzad', 28 July 2019.

[23] Jakes, L., 'Trump declares Afghan peace talks with Taliban "dead"', *New York Times*, 9 Sep. 2019.

responsibility for a major bomb attack in Kabul a few days earlier, which had killed 11 including a US soldier.[24]

The collapse of the Taliban–USA talks in September led to renewed pessimism about peace in Afghanistan. The Taliban maintained that it would not engage in intra-Afghan peace talks before it had reached an agreement with the USA.[25] Towards the end of the year there were indications that the talks between the Taliban and the USA might be revived.[26] During a surprise visit to Afghanistan in November, President Trump said that the Taliban and the USA were talking about an agreement again while implying that the USA was also demanding a ceasefire now.[27] Official talks resumed in Doha in December 2019.[28]

The United States and North Atlantic Treaty Organization military presence

The withdrawal of the US military forces from Afghanistan—and the conditions and timing thereof—was one of the key issues in the negotiations between the Taliban and the USA in 2019. In December 2018 President Trump reportedly ordered the withdrawal of 7000 of the approximately 14 000 US troops in Afghanistan.[29] However, neither the USA nor the Resolute Support Mission (RSM), which was led by the North Atlantic Treaty Organization, significantly reduced their presence in Afghanistan during 2019. The USA withdrew approximately 2000 troops towards the end of the year, of which around 500 were part of the RSM.[30] The RSM consisted of 16 705 troops at the end of 2019, of which 8000 were from the USA. The remaining US troops were deployed in Afghanistan as part of the parallel US counterterrorism operation Freedom's Sentinel.[31]

Presidential elections

Afghanistan held presidential elections on 28 September 2019. Initially scheduled to take place in April, the elections were carried out after two delays due to problems with registration requirements and biometric

---

[24] Baker, P. et al., 'How Trump's plan to secretly meet with the Taliban came together, and fell apart', *New York Times*, 8 Sep. 2019.

[25] UN General Assembly and UN Security Council, 'The situation in Afghanistan and its implications for international peace and security', Report of the Secretary-General, A/74/582–S/2019/935, 10 Dec. 2019, para. 15.

[26] Thomas (note 16); and Crowley, M., 'Trump visits Afghanistan and says he reopened talks with Taliban', *New York Times*, 28 Nov. 2019.

[27] Crowley (note 26).

[28] Al Jazeera, 'First round of resurrected US-Taliban peace talks open in Qatar', 7 Dec. 2019.

[29] Gibbons-Neff, T. and Mashal, M., 'US to withdraw about 7,000 troops from Afghanistan, officials say', *New York Times*, 20 Dec. 2018.

[30] Thomas (note 16).

[31] SIPRI Multilateral Peace Operations Database, <https://www.sipri.org/databases/pko>; North Atlantic Treaty Organization, 'Resolute Support Mission: Key facts and figures', Feb. 2020; and US Department of Defense, *Enhancing Security and Stability in Afghanistan*, Report to Congress (US Department of Defense: Dec. 2019).

software (as had been the case during the country's parliamentary election in October 2018, which was also disrupted by the Islamic State and the Taliban).[32] Nearly 1 million of the initial 2.7 million votes were excluded due to irregularities, meaning the election saw by far the lowest turnout of any Afghan poll.[33] Moreover, the elections were also marred by violence, which fostered the low turnout.[34]

The announcement of the results was also repeatedly delayed, with Independent Election Commission (IEC) officials citing technical issues, allegations of fraud and protests from candidates. In December 2019 the IEC finally announced the preliminary election results in which the incumbent president, Ashraf Ghani, won 50.64 per cent of the votes. Ghani's main contender in the elections and the chief executive officer of the previous unity government, Abdullah Abdullah, disputed the preliminary outcome and stated that he would not accept this result.[35] This raised concerns of the prospect of another post-electoral political crisis in Afghanistan similar to that in 2014. The final results are scheduled to be announced in February 2020.[36]

India, Pakistan and the territorial dispute in Kashmir

The Kashmir conflict and several military conflicts fought between India and Pakistan have largely defined relations between them. Since their independence, the two countries have fought three of their four wars over Kashmir (1947–48, 1965 and 1999)—and the other one over Bangladeshi independence (1971)—and have been involved in numerous armed clashes and military stand-offs. There have also been many talks and confidence-building measures over the years that sought to improve the relationship, but no current peace process.[37] Tensions between India and Pakistan surged again in 2019, especially as a result of the military confrontation across the de facto border in Kashmir in February 2019 (see chapter 1, section I).

In addition to the February 2019 air strikes conducted by India and Pakistan against targets in each other's territory, exchanges of artillery fire across the line of control are a regular part of the conflict, and ACLED

---

[32] Al Jazeera, 'Afghan presidential elections postponed until July 20: Official', 30 Dec. 2018.

[33] Al Jazeera, 'Afghanistan presidential election: All the latest updates', 28 Sep. 2019.

[34] New York Times, 'Afghanistan election draws low turnout amid Taliban threats', 28 Sep. 2019.

[35] Mashal, M. and Faizi, F., 'Afghan president leads in disputed vote as opposition protests', New York Times, 22 Dec. 2019.

[36] BBC, 'Afghan presidential election: Tense wait after day of attacks', 30 Sep. 2019.

[37] See e.g. International Crisis Group, India/Pakistan Relations and Kashmir: Steps Towards Peace, Asia Report no. 79 (International Crisis Group: Islamabad/New Delhi/Brussels, 24 June 2004); and Rashid, A., 'A peace plan for India and Pakistan already exists', New York Times, 7 Mar. 2019.

Table 4.2. Estimated conflict-related fatalities in India, 2016–19

Event type	2016	2017	2018	2019
Battles	1 007	844	1 203	563
Explosions/remote violence	69	64	148	116
Protests, riots and strategic developments	282	209	224	299
Violence against civilians	301	317	525	545
Total	**1 659**	**1 434**	**2 100**	**1 523**

Notes: The first available year for data on India in the Armed Conflict Location & Event Data Project (ACLED) database is 2016. For definitions of event types, see ACLED, 'ACLED definitions of political violence and protest', 11 Apr. 2019.

Source: ACLED, 'Data export tool', [n.d.].

recorded 582 such events in 2019, up from 349 in 2018.[38] There were 280 battle-related fatalities in Jammu and Kashmir in 2019.[39] According to the Indian Government, the conflict in Kashmir has killed about 42 000 civilians, militants and security personnel since 1989, while independent estimates suggest 70 000 or more deaths.[40] The UN High Commissioner for Human Rights has reported serious human rights violations and patterns of impunity in India-administered Kashmir and significant human rights concerns in Pakistan-administered Kashmir.[41]

India's internal security threats

In 2019 India also continued to face internal security threats, notably from the Naxalite insurgency (Maoist rebels in rural areas of central and eastern India), which started in 1967 and entered its current phase in 2004, and also intercommunal (mainly Hindu–Muslim) tensions. For example, Maoist rebels killed five police officers in Jharkhand state in June and 15 police officers and a civilian during an attack in Maharashtra state in May 2019.[42] The Indian security forces claim to have inflicted heavy losses on the Maoist rebels in recent years and the insurgency appears to be using more remote technologies, including unmanned aerial vehicles and IEDs.[43] The

[38] ACLED, *Ten Conflicts to Worry About in 2020* (ACLED: Jan. 2020), p. 12; and BBC, 'India and Pakistan blame each other over Kashmir shelling', 21 Oct. 2019.

[39] ACLED, 'Data export tool', [n.d.].

[40] Kronstadt, K. A., 'Kashmir: Background, recent developments, and US policy', Congressional Research Service Report R45877, 16 Aug. 2019. On the number of Indian security personnel in Kashmir, see Shukla, A., 'India has 700,000 troops in Kashmir? False!!!', rediff.com, 17 July 2018.

[41] See e.g. Office of the United Nations High Commissioner for Human Rights, *Update of the Situation of Human Rights in Indian-administered Kashmir and Pakistan-administered Kashmir from May 2018 to April 2019* (Office of the United Nations High Commissioner for Human Rights: 8 July 2019).

[42] Reuters, 'Maoist rebels kill five policemen in eastern India', 14 June 2019. On the history of the conflict, see Sahoo, N., 'Half a century of India's Maoist insurgency: An appraisal of state response', Observer Research Foundation, June 2019.

[43] Mukherjee, U., 'IEDs and the Maoist insurgency', Institute for Defence Studies and Analyses Comment, 7 May 2019; and Kujur, R. K., 'The CPI-Maoist tech onslaught: Early warnings—analysis', Eurasia Review, 27 Nov. 2019. On attempts to regulate IEDs, see chapter 13, section I, in this volume.

Maoist conflict accounted for 20 per cent of the 1523 conflict-related fatalities in India in 2019 (see table 4.2), while the fatalities in Jammu and Kashmir accounted for 26 per cent.[44] According to ACLED, India had the fifth-highest number of political violence events in the world in 2019, mainly mob violence (riots) with links to political parties.[45]

However, there were hopes that the Nagaland insurgency (in north-east India) might be nearing resolution. In particular, peace talks between the Indian Government and the National Socialist Council of Nagaland-Isak-Muivah (NSCN-IM), the main separatist group in Nagaland, may help to finalize a framework peace accord signed with the NSCN-IM in 2015.[46]

The Hindu–Muslim divide in India remains a potential source of communal violence, and growing radicalization on both sides has added to the frictions.[47] In December India introduced a controversial citizenship law that sparked protests across the country and clashes with security forces that left dozens dead.[48]

Pakistan's internal security threats

Intrastate violence involving various armed groups remained a major threat in Pakistan in 2019, especially in the Khyber Pakhtunkhwa province that borders Afghanistan, but also in the other three provinces. In May for example, the TEP claimed responsibility for a suicide attack in Lahore (Punjab province) that killed at least nine people.[49] Balochistan, the largest of Pakistan's four provinces, has faced several insurgencies from Baloch nationalists since 1948. The current phase of the insurgency (which started in 2003) has been at a relatively low level since 2012 and involves some militant Baloch nationalist groups, the most prominent being the Baloch Liberation Army.[50]

The risk of sectarian violence in Pakistan, mainly between Sunni and Shia groups, was also ongoing in 2019—especially by the Sunni fundamentalist group LEJ, which has been targeting the minority (and predominantly Shia) Hazara community.[51] On 12 April 2019 for example, a bomb attack on a market

---

[44] Author's analysis using the ACLED data export tool.

[45] Kishi, R. et al., *Year in Review* (ACLED: 2 Mar. 2020), pp. 19, 22–23, 75.

[46] Hart, M., 'Is India's Nagaland peace process nearing a breakthrough?' Geopolitical Monitor, 8 July 2019; *Times of India*, 'Centre holds dialogue with NSCN-IM; peace talks may continue beyond Oct 31', 28 Oct. 2019.

[47] See e.g. Misra, A., 'India's 500-year-old religious dispute', Asia Times, 20 Apr. 2019; and Malji, A., 'The rise of Hindu nationalism and its regional and global ramifications', *Asian Politics*, vol. 23, no. 1 (spring 2018).

[48] Ellis-Petersen, H., 'Violent clashes continue in India over new citizenship bill', *The Guardian*, 13 Dec. 2019.

[49] BBC, 'Pakistan Data Darbar: Bomber kills nine outside Sufi Shrine in Lahore', 8 May 2019.

[50] Bhattacherjee, K., 'Explained: The Baloch Liberation Army', *The Hindu*, 3 July 2019.

[51] Wani, S. A., 'Political indifference and state complicity: The travails of Hazaras in Balochistan', *Strategic Analysis*, vol. 43, no. 4 (2019), pp. 328–34.

Table 4.3. Estimated conflict-related fatalities in Pakistan, 2013–19

Event type	2013	2014	2015	2016	2017	2018	2019
Battles	1 428	1 754	1 951	1 175	891	479	620
Explosions/remote violence	2 087	2 826	1 953	805	669	410	185
Protests, riots and strategic developments	72	53	81	39	30	44	14
Violence against civilians	667	650	535	188	150	293	328
Total	**4 254**	**5 283**	**4 520**	**2 207**	**1 740**	**1 226**	**1 147**

Note: For definitions of event types, see Armed Conflict Location & Event Data Project (ACLED), 'ACLED definitions of political violence and protest', 11 Apr. 2019.

Source: ACLED, 'Data export tool', [n.d.].

in Quetta carried out by a faction of the TEP in collaboration with the LEJ killed at least 20 people, including eight members of the Hazara community.[52] However, overall battle-related fatalities and deaths from remote violence have declined considerably since the 2013–15 period (see table 4.3).

The Pakistani military and intelligence services are regularly criticized by Western diplomats for using militant proxies to destabilize Afghanistan and Kashmir. In 2018 the Financial Action Task Force (FATF), founded by the Group of Seven (G7) in 1989 to combat money laundering and later terrorism financing, placed Pakistan on a sanctions 'grey list'. The Pakistan foreign minister estimated that it could cost the country $10 billion annually if it remained on the list.[53] In addition, President Trump froze aid to Pakistan worth up to $1.6 billion in 2018.[54]

The arrest of Hafiz Saeed, founder of the LET armed group, by Pakistan police in July 2019 on terrorism-financing charges was in part aimed at appeasing the FATF and the USA. India accused Saeed of organizing the 2008 Mumbai attacks that killed at least 165 people, while LET has been responsible for attacks against Indian security forces in Kashmir.[55] China's consent to the inclusion in May 2019 of Masood Azhar, leader and founder of JEM, on the UN's list of individuals subject to sanctions under UN Security Council Resolution 2368 (2017) could also be seen as a supportive move towards Pakistan within the context of the FATF, as well as a reaction to the group's attack in Kashmir in February 2019.[56]

---

[52] Zafar, M., '20 martyred as blast rips through Quetta market', *Express Tribune*, 12 Apr. 2019.

[53] Ahmad, I., 'FATF could blacklist Pak due to "lobbying by India": Qureshi', *Hindustan Times*, 2 Apr. 2019.

[54] Tomlinson, H., 'Pakistan must prove it is fighting terrorism, warns US', *The Times*, 14 Oct. 2019.

[55] Hashim, A., 'Pakistan police arrest Lashkar-e-Taiba founder Hafiz Saeed', Al Jazeera, 17 July 2019.

[56] UN Security Council Resolution 2368 (2017), S/RES/2368 (2017), 20 July 2017; Tripathi, R., 'Pakistan has third highest number in UN proscribed list', *Economic Times*, 3 May 2019; and Abrams, C. and Shah, S., 'UN designates Pakistani as terrorist after China acquiesces', *Wall Street Journal*, 1 May 2019.

III. Armed conflict and peace processes in South East Asia

IAN DAVIS

South East Asia—comprising the states of Brunei Darussalam, Cambodia, Indonesia, Laos, Malaysia, Myanmar, the Philippines, Singapore, Thailand, Timor-Leste and Viet Nam—is mainly tropical and includes a wide range of ethnicities and religions. The many coastal communities in the island-studded region are highly vulnerable to the growing threats from climate change, with sea-level rises predicted to displace millions of people.[1] Another non-traditional security threat in 2019 was the rapid spread of African swine fever across the region, which threatened food security and the livelihoods of millions of households reliant on pig farming.[2] Some of Asia's most organized Islamist extremist groups are active in the region, most notably in Indonesia, Malaysia and the Philippines.[3] This section focuses on the four countries in the region with subnational armed conflicts: one high-intensity armed conflict (i.e. more than 1000 deaths) in Myanmar and two low-intensity armed conflicts in Indonesia and Thailand (i.e. less than 1000 deaths). In the Philippines, when fatalities from the 'war on drugs' are added to those from the subnational armed conflict, the number of conflict-related deaths rises to nearly 1700, making it also a high-intensity armed conflict.

Armed conflict in Indonesia

Indonesia is one of the world's major emerging economies. The country faces demands for independence in the two provinces on the island of Papua and increasing attacks by Islamist armed groups. In particular, the country has become one of the main focal points of the Islamic State in South East Asia.[4] However, in 2019 it was the long-simmering insurgency in Papua that was the

[1] Babson, E., 'Strained stability: Climate change and regional security in Southeast Asia', American Security Project, June 2018; and Nordqvist, P. and Krampe, F., 'Climate change and violent conflict: Sparse evidence from South Asia and South East Asia', SIPRI Insights on Peace and Security no. 2018/4, Sep. 2018.

[2] Normile, D., 'African swine fever keeps spreading in Asia, threatening food security', *Science Magazine*, 14 May 2019.

[3] Abuza, Z. and Clarke, C. P., 'The Islamic State meets Southeast Asia', *Foreign Affairs*, 16 Sep. 2019.

[4] On the rise of the Islamic State in Indonesia, see Schulze, K. E. and Liow, J. C., 'Making jihadis, waging jihad: Transnational and local dimensions of the ISIS phenomenon in Indonesia and Malaysia', *Asian Security*, vol. 15, no. 2 (2019), pp. 122–39; and Sheikh, M. K., 'Islamic State and al-Qaeda in a thriving Indonesian democracy', ed. Sheikh, M. K. et al., *Global Jihad in Southeast Asia: Examining the Expansion of the Islamic State and al-Qaeda* (Danish Institute for International Studies: 2019), pp. 39–58. On the role of social media in the rise of Islamist extremism in Indonesia, see Nuraniyah, N., 'The evolution of online violent extremism in Indonesia and the Philippines', Global Research Network on Terrorism and Technology, Paper no. 5, Royal United Services Institute for Defence and Security Studies and Institute for Policy Analysis of Conflict, July 2019. On attempts to reintegrate extremists, see Sumpter, C., 'Reintegration in Indonesia: Extremists, start-ups and occasional engagements', International Centre for Counter-Terrorism, 19 Feb. 2019.

Table 4.4. Estimated conflict-related fatalities in Myanmar, 2013–19

Event type	2013	2014	2015	2016	2017	2018	2019
Battles	300	358	1 078	155	196	118	1 238
Explosions/remote violence	45	53	27	35	30	31	85
Protests, riots and strategic developments	91	9	0	0	9	9	30
Violence against civilians	29	84	162	221	1 018	67	132
Total	**465**	**504**	**1 267**	**411**	**1 253**	**225**	**1 485**

Note: For definitions of event types, see Armed Conflict Location & Event Data Project (ACLED), 'ACLED definitions of political violence and protest', 11 Apr. 2019.

Source: ACLED, 'Data export tool', [n.d.].

focus of most of the combat-related armed violence in the country. In March 2019 for example, fighting between Indonesian Government forces and the West Papua National Liberation Army left at least 15 people dead.[5] Further deaths resulted from clashes between Indonesia's security forces and protesters in Wamena city and the provincial capital Jayapura in September.[6]

According to the Armed Conflict Location & Event Data Project (ACLED) there were 213 conflict-related deaths in Indonesia in 2019, with 61 of these being related to armed conflict (battles or explosions/remote violence). However, the ACLED data shows disorder on the rise in Indonesia in 2019, with 152 fatalities in 2019 attributed to protests, riots and violence against civilians.[7] This disorder was linked to growing intercommunal tensions (between religious minorities and the majority Muslim population) and growing political divisions.[8] It also raised concerns about the Indonesian armed forces' growing political influence and the risk of a return to authoritarian rule.[9]

Armed conflict in Myanmar

Insurgencies have persisted for much of the past seven decades in Myanmar's Chin, Kachin, Kayin, Mon, Rakhine and Shan states. Various armed insurgent groups have fought the country's armed forces, known as the Tatmadaw, over political control of territory, ethnic minority rights and access to natural resources.[10] Off-budget funding of the Tatmadaw has contributed to its ability to operate without civilian oversight in conducting counter-

---

[5] Associated Press, 'West Papua: Up to 15 feared dead as rebels and Indonesian soldiers clash', *The Guardian*, 8 Mar. 2019.

[6] Karmini, N., 'Death toll climbs in Indonesia's Papua protests', *The Diplomat*, 26 Sep. 2019.

[7] Bynum, E., 'Improving ACLED's Indonesia data (2015–2019)', ACLED infographic, 18 Dec. 2019; and ACLED, 'Data export tool', [n.d.].

[8] Lindsay, T., 'Jakarta riots reveal Indonesia's deep divisions on religion and politics', The Conversation, 27 May 2019.

[9] *The Economist*, 'Indonesian politicians are giving the armed forces a bigger role in government', 31 Oct. 2019.

[10] Hart, M., 'Myanmar's peace process on life support', Geopolitical Monitor, 10 Jan. 2019.

insurgency campaigns.[11] In Kachin and Shan states the ethnic conflict is also fuelled by a growing drugs trade, resource extraction (gems and timber) and money laundering.[12] The repercussions of the forcible displacement in 2017 of the Rohingya—members of a predominantly Sunni Muslim ethnic group—from Rakhine state continued into 2019.[13] An ongoing peace process, launched in 2015, made little headway during 2019 against a backdrop of rising violence especially in Rakhine state. According to ACLED there were over 1200 battle-related deaths in Myanmar in 2019 (up from just under 120 in 2018), which accounted for 83 per cent of all conflict-related fatalities in the year (see table 4.4).[14] The table also shows the huge change in the nature of the armed violence: from violence against civilians that dominated 2017 to predominantly battle-related fatalities in 2019.[15]

In the north-eastern states of Kachin and Shan over 120 000 people were displaced during 2011–18.[16] In August 2019 fighting escalated in Shan state, as the Brotherhood Alliance—an alliance of three ethnic armed groups: the Arakan Army (AA), the Ta'ang National Liberation Army (TNLA) and Myanmar National Democratic Alliance Army—launched coordinated attacks on military targets, including a military academy, killing about 15 people.[17] A four-month unilateral ceasefire declared by the military of Myanmar in December 2018 in Kachin and Shan states was extended three times during 2019, but ended on 21 September 2019.[18] However, the alliance of three ethnic armed groups announced its own unilateral ceasefire on 9 September 2019 for one month and then extended it to the end of the year.[19]

There were also increased clashes during 2019 in Rakhine state between the Myanmar military and the AA, an ethnic Rakhine armed group that is a participant in the Kachin conflict, but which has additional training camps in

[11] See chapter 8, section III, in this volume.

[12] International Crisis Group, *Fire and Ice: Conflict and Drugs in Myanmar's Shan State*, Asia Report no. 299 (International Crisis Group: Brussels, 8 Jan. 2019); and Walsh, J., 'Failing drug wars in northern Myanmar', East Asia Forum, 21 Sep. 2019.

[13] On the Rohingya crisis in 2017, see Davis, I., Ghiasy, R. and Su, F., 'Armed conflict in Asia and Oceania', *SIPRI Yearbook 2018*, pp. 49–52.

[14] On the methodological challenges for the recording of political violence amidst the complexity of the disorder in Myanmar, see ACLED, 'ACLED methodology and coding decisions around political violence in Myanmar', Nov. 2019.

[15] For a detailed analysis of Myanmar's conflict landscape in 2019, see Bynum, E., 'Dueling ceasefires: Myanmar's conflict landscape in 2019', ACLED, 12 Feb. 2020.

[16] Nickerson, J., 'The Kachin IDP crisis: Myanmar's other humanitarian disaster', Al Jazeera, 2 Dec. 2018; and International Rescue Committee, 'Beyond Rakhine, civilians at risk in Northern Shan and Kachin as violence continues in Myanmar', 30 Apr. 2018.

[17] *The Economist*, 'A Chinese development scheme complicates Myanmar's ethnic conflicts', 29 Aug. 2019; and International Crisis Group, 'Myanmar: A violent push to shake up ceasefire negotiations', Asia Briefing no. 158, 24 Sep. 2019.

[18] Weng, L., 'Renewed fighting in Shan and Rakhine as Myanmar military lets ceasefire expire', The Irrawaddy, 24 Sep. 2019.

[19] Nyein, N., 'Myanmar rebel armies extend truce but fighting continues', The Irrawaddy, 3 Jan. 2020.

Rakhine state. In January 2019 for example, the AA carried out attacks on four police stations, and in October the group abducted almost 60 police officers, soldiers and government workers in Rakhine state.[20] The upsurge in fighting in parts of Rakhine state led to further population displacement (over 30 000 people as at 1 November 2019) and reduced the already low prospects of voluntary repatriation of the Rohingya from camps in Bangladesh.[21]

The crisis in Rakhine state and referral to the International Criminal Court and International Court of Justice

At the beginning of 2019 more than 900 000 Rohingya remained in refugee camps in Cox's Bazar in southern Bangladesh after being driven out by the Tatmadaw in late 2017 and 2018.[22] Displacement continued in 2019, albeit at much lower rates, and Cox's Bazar remained the largest and densest refugee settlement in the world.[23] With no guarantees of citizenship and security if the Rohingya were to return to Myanmar, repatriation plans have been delayed indefinitely, and their future remains uncertain.[24]

The Independent International Fact-finding Mission (FFM) on Myanmar, established in March 2017 by the United Nations Human Rights Council to investigate allegations of human rights violations by military and security forces in Kachin, Rakhine and Shan states, concluded in its 2018 report that the Tatmadaw's actions constituted crimes against humanity, war crimes and possible genocide.[25] In September 2019 the FFM's final report stated that over 600 000 Rohingya remaining in Myanmar continued to face 'serious risk' of genocide and called for the situation to be referred to the International Criminal Court (ICC), or for the creation of a special mechanism, to prosecute

---

[20] International Crisis Group, 'A new dimension of violence in Myanmar's Rakhine state', Asia Briefing no. 154, 24 Jan. 2019; and Nang, S. and Ives, M., 'A daring helicopter rescue after rebels capture a ferry in Myanmar', *New York Times*, 28 Oct. 2019.

[21] Al Jazeera, 'Myanmar: UN "disturbed" over attacks against civilians in Rakhine', 5 Apr. 2019; and United Nations Office for the Coordination of Humanitarian Affairs and UN High Commissioner for Refugees, 'Myanmar: Conflict between the Arakan Army and the Myanmar Military, Update on humanitarian needs and response in Rakhine and Chin states', 1 Nov. 2019.

[22] On developments in 2018, see Davis, I., 'Armed conflict and peace processes in Asia and Oceania', *SIPRI Yearbook 2019*, pp. 66–68.

[23] Wake, C. et al., 'Rohingya refugees' perspectives on their displacement in Bangladesh: Uncertain futures', Humanitarian Policy Group Working Paper, Overseas Development Institute, June 2019. On the international humanitarian response, see UN Office for the Coordination of Humanitarian Affairs, *2019 Joint Response Plan for Rohingya Humanitarian Crisis, January-December* (UN Office for the Coordination of Humanitarian Affairs: 15 Feb. 2019). On the socio-economic impact on the host community, see UN Development Programme, 'Impacts of the Rohingya refugee influx on host communities', 27 July 2019.

[24] Ellis-Petersen, H., 'Myanmar and Bangladesh to start sending back thousands of Rohingya', *The Guardian*, 16 Aug. 2019; and International Crisis Group, *A Sustainable Policy for Rohingya Refugees in Bangladesh*, Asia Report no. 303 (International Crisis Group: Brussels, 27 Dec. 2019).

[25] UN Human Rights Council, 'Report of the detailed findings of the Independent International Fact-finding Mission on Myanmar', A/HRC/39/CRP.2, 17 Sep. 2018.

Tatmadaw generals.[26] In an August report the FFM focused on the continued use of sexual and gender-based violence by the Myanmar armed forces and allied militias in operations against Kachin, Shan and other ethnic minorities in northern Myanmar.[27]

The FFM's mandate ended in September when it transferred the information it collected about serious crimes under international law to the UN's new Independent Investigative Mechanism (IIM) for Myanmar. The IIM will build on this evidence and conduct its own investigations to support prosecutions in national, regional and international courts of perpetrators of atrocities in Myanmar.[28] The Government of Myanmar has continued to reject the FFM's findings. It established its own Independent Commission of Enquiry in August 2018 to investigate the Tatmadaw's conduct, and is expected to report its findings in early 2020. The government has also argued that any misconduct by individuals from the state security forces should be tried in military courts.[29]

In February 2019 UN Secretary-General António Guterres launched an investigation into UN conduct in Myanmar, following accusations it ignored warning signs of escalating violence ahead of the attacks on the Rohingya in 2017.[30]

Accountability and justice for alleged atrocities committed against the Rohingya people and other ethnic minorities in Myanmar remain elusive, despite legal efforts pending at both the ICC and International Court of Justice (ICJ). In March 2019 the Organisation of Islamic Cooperation (OIC) unanimously approved a measure establishing the legal rights of the Rohingya people before the ICJ. This paved the way for individuals to bring cases against the Government of Myanmar for crimes committed against them by state armed forces in Rakhine.[31] In October Yanghee Lee, the special rapporteur on human rights in Myanmar, reported no change in the situation, called for sanctions against military-run companies and commanders

---

[26] UN Human Rights Council, 'Detailed findings of the Independent International Fact-finding Mission on Myanmar', A/HRC/42/CRP.5, 16 Sep. 2019. For further details on the ICC, see annex B, section I, in this volume.

[27] UN Human Rights Council, 'Sexual and gender-based violence in Myanmar and the gendered impact of its ethnic conflicts', A/HRC/42/CRP.4, 22 Aug. 2019.

[28] UN Human Rights Council, 'UN fact-finding mission on Myanmar hands over to Independent Investigative Mechanism for Myanmar', Media advisory, 9 Sep. 2019.

[29] Independent Commission of Enquiry website; Reuters, 'Myanmar army chief denies systematic persecution of Rohingya', 15 Feb. 2019; and Reuters, 'Myanmar military court to probe Rohingya atrocity allegations', 18 Mar. 2019.

[30] Stoakes, E. and Ellis-Petersen, H., 'Rohingya crisis: UN investigates its "dysfunctional" conduct in Myanmar', *The Guardian*, 27 Feb. 2019.

[31] *Daily Star*, 'OIC okays legal action against Myanmar at ICJ', 4 Mar. 2019. For further details on the OIC and ICJ, see annex B, section I, in this volume.

responsible for serious violations and urged the UN Security Council to refer the situation to the ICC.[32]

In November, Gambia (on behalf of the OIC) filed a lawsuit at the ICJ in an attempt to have Myanmar's leadership tried for genocide, while the ICC approved a request from the prosecutor's office to mount its own investigation.[33] In December Aung San Suu Kyi, Myanmar's de facto leader (officially known as State Counsellor), appeared at the ICJ to respond to the initial charges.[34] While a decision on whether Myanmar acted with genocidal intent could take years to reach, a decision on provisional measures, including whether judges need to issue an emergency order to protect the Rohingya in Myanmar, is expected early in 2020.

The peace process

The Government of Myanmar has been attempting to push forward a complex peace process, the core of which is the 2015 Nationwide Ceasefire Agreement (NCA). The NCA includes a promise for political talks towards the creation of a federal union to guarantee future equality and autonomy for ethic nationalities.[35] China is a major stakeholder in the peace process, not least because of its economic and security interests: numerous Belt and Road Initiative corridors run through insurgent areas in Myanmar, while many of the insurgent groups hold territory along or close to the 2000-kilometre border that Myanmar shares with China.[36] At the end of 2018 progress in the peace process had stalled, with most of the country's most powerful militias (including the Kachin Independence Army and TNLA) still refusing to join the accord, and two key signatories (the Karen National Union/Karen National Liberation Army and the Restoration Council of Shan State/Shan State Army-South) suspending their participation in formal peace negotiations.[37]

---

[32] UN Human Rights Office of the High Commissioner, 'Myanmar: UN human rights expert calls for targeted sanctions', 23 Oct. 2019.

[33] Al Jazeera, 'ICC approves probe into Myanmar's alleged crimes against Rohingya', 15 Nov. 2019; and Simons, M., 'Myanmar genocide lawsuit is filed at United Nations court', New York Times, 11 Nov. 2019.

[34] Beech, H. and Nang, S., 'As Myanmar genocide hearing closes, focus is on trapped Rohingya', New York Times, 12 Dec. 2019, updated 23 Jan. 2020.

[35] On the history of questions of autonomy or self-determination in Myanmar, see Kipgen, N., 'The quest for federalism in Myanmar', Strategic Analysis, vol. 42, no. 6 (2018), pp. 612–26. On the role of civil society and peace movements in Myanmar, see Orjuela, C., 'Countering Buddhist radicalisation: Emerging peace movements in Myanmar and Sri Lanka', Third World Quarterly, vol. 41, no. 1 (2020), pp. 133–50.

[36] Sun, Y., 'Why China is sceptical about the peace process', Frontier, 3 Oct. 2019; and United States Institute of Peace, China's Role in Myanmar's Internal Conflicts, Senior Study Group Report no. 1 (US Institute of Peace: Washington DC, Sep. 2018).

[37] On the earlier rounds of peace talks in 2016–18, see Davis, Ghiasy and Su (note 13), pp. 48–50; SIPRI Yearbook 2019 (note 22), p. 68; The Mainichi, 'Myanmar peace conference reaches more agreements for future union', 17 July 2018; and Nyein, N., 'KNU reiterates hiatus in peace talks', The Irrawaddy, 12 Nov. 2018.

Several rounds of peace and reconciliation discussions in 2019 made no or little progress, although temporary and fragile bilateral ceasefires agreed with some individual armed groups helped localized de-escalation of some conflict. The prominent role of the military in politics and government with a set proportion of representation continues to be a major obstacle to constitutional reform.[38] At the end of the year the peace process remained burdened with division and uncertainty, with only 10 of the 21 ethnic armed organizations signed up to the NCA.[39]

Armed conflict in the Philippines

There were two main intrastate armed conflicts in the Philippines in 2019: the Moro insurgency in the southern Philippines and the New People's Army (NPA) insurgency. Although the insurgencies are two of Asia's longest and deadliest conflicts, the peace process in the southern Philippines made major progress in 2019, and it is the more recent war on drugs that appeared to produce the most fatalities during the year (see below).

An end to the Moro insurgency in the southern Philippines?

The establishment in March 2019 of a new autonomous region in the Mindanao region of the southern Philippines could mark the end of the almost 50-year Moro separatist conflict, although many challenges remain. Over the years, the web of Muslim-majority actors involved in this conflict coalesced into two main separatist groups: the Moro National Liberation Front and the Moro Islamic Liberation Front (MILF)—both signing peace agreements with the Philippine Government, in 1996 and 2014, respectively.[40] Pro-Islamic State groups also emerged in the region and were involved in a violent insurgency in the city of Marawi in 2017.[41] Since then tensions have remained high, and martial law was extended in Mindanao by President Rodrigo Duterte until the end of 2019.[42]

---

[38] Lintner, B., 'Peace march kicks up more war in Myanmar', Asia Times, 19 Mar. 2019; Aung, S. H., 'Four years after truce deal, peace remains a dream', *Myanmar Times*, 31 Oct. 2019; and International Crisis Group (note 17).

[39] Mon, S. L., 'Not a good year for peace process', *Myanmar Times*, 31 Dec. 2019.

[40] On Moro nationalism and Islamism, see Andersen, L. E., 'Transnational jihadism in the Philippines', ed. Sheikh, M. K. et al., *Global Jihad In Southeast Asia: Examining the Expansion of the Islamic State and al-Qaeda* (Danish Institute for International Studies: 2019), pp. 19–38. On the peace process with the MILF, see Svensson, I. and Lundgren, M., 'Mediation and peace agreements', *SIPRI Yearbook 2014*, pp. 51–52; and Vizcarra Tobia, I. N., 'Populism, politics and peace processes: Analysing the nexus between peacebuilding and the Philippines' Populist Politics', *Journal of Peacebuilding & Development*, vol. 13, no. 3 (2018), pp. 115–20.

[41] On the conflict in Marawi, see Davis, Ghiasy and Su (note 13), pp. 54–55; and Franco, J., 'Philippines: Addressing Islamist militancy after the battle for Marawi', International Crisis Group commentary, 17 July 2018.

[42] Reuters, 'Philippine Congress extends Mindanao martial law until end-2019', 12 Dec. 2018.

In July 2018 President Duterte signed the Bangsamoro Organic Law—a legal instrument deriving from the 2014 peace agreement. Among the prominent features of the law was the replacement of the current Autonomous Region in Muslim Mindanao (created in 1989) with the Bangsamoro Autonomous Region in Muslim Mindanao. The new law was overwhelmingly endorsed in a two-stage plebiscite in January and February 2019. The new autonomous region includes additional provinces, and its government will have greater devolved powers. An 80-member Bangsamoro Transition Authority (with 41 representatives nominated by the MILF and 39 selected by the national government) is now responsible for governing the region until 2022 when elections for a Bangsamoro Parliament and Government are due to take place.[43]

One of the main challenges still to be addressed is the decommissioning of the MILF's armed force: the Bangsamoro Islamic Armed Forces (BIAF). Under the 2014 peace agreement, 30 per cent of the BIAF was to be decommissioned after passage of the Bangsamoro Organic Law, and in March 2019 the MILF submitted a list of 12 000 combatants to the Independent Decommissioning Body (comprising representatives from Brunei Darussalam, Norway and Turkey), which is responsible for verifying and registering combatants and stockpile management of MILF weapons. Over 8000 of this first group of fighters had been decommissioned by the end of 2019, and two further decommissioning stages are due to be completed by the end of the transition phase in 2022. The benefits package promised to former combatants will be a crucial part of the decommissioning process.[44]

Over time these new autonomy and decommissioning arrangements could end the Moro insurgency and act as a dampener on militant Islamist recruitment. A small number of Islamist armed groups outside of the peace process with links to the Islamic State—principally the Abu Sayyaf Group, Bangsamoro Islamic Freedom Fighters and the Maute Group—pose the greatest ongoing threat, to state security forces and as potential spoilers of the peace process within local communities.[45] A few days after the plebiscite, for example, a cathedral bombing attributed to Abu Sayyaf/Islamic State in Sulu province killed at least 22 soldiers and civilians. A further twin bomb attack similarly attributed in the same province in June 2019 killed three

---

[43] International Crisis Group, *The Philippines: Militancy and the New Bangsamoro*, Asia Report no. 301 (International Crisis Group: Brussels, 27 June 2019).

[44] International Crisis Group (note 43), pp. 10–12; Felongco, G. P., 'Philippines: Demobilised Moro fighters to receive Dh70,784 each', *Gulf News*, 8 Sep. 2019; and Tomacruz, S., 'Over 8,000 MILF fighters decommissioned in 2019—OPAPP', Rappler, 19 Jan. 2020.

[45] International Crisis Group (note 43), pp. 14–19.

soldiers and three civilians.[46] However, the nature of transnational jihadism in the Philippines, which is mixed up with criminality, drug crime and political struggle, makes it difficult to evaluate and attribute such attacks.[47] The Philippine military confirmed in April 2019 that it killed the leader of the Maute Group, and self-proclaimed leader of the Islamic State in the country, Benito Marohombsar (known as Abu Dar), in clashes a month earlier.[48]

While a large part of the instability problems in Mindanao is due to the high number of non-state armed groups, there is also a blurring between some of those groups and state actors due to the activities of private militias and clan feuds.[49] Thus, the Mindanao conflict theatre is complex, and achieving a settlement with the MILF may not be sufficient to bring peace to the region.

The New People's Army insurgency

Equally elusive, despite sporadic peace talks, has been the goal of ending the 50-year-old insurgency by the NPA—the armed wing of the Communist Party of the Philippines and its political umbrella organization, the National Democratic Front.[50] Violence between the Philippine armed forces and the NPA continued throughout the year, despite fruitful negotiations between local rebel commands and government officials. Instead of negotiating with the NPA leadership, the government is trying to exploit the distinctly local qualities of the insurgency by holding a series of peace talks across the various regions with regional NPA representatives. This localized peace drive is designed to winnow the ranks of the NPA, which is now estimated at around 4000 fighters (down from a peak of 26 000 in the 1980s).[51]

The war on drugs and contested casualty statistics

While the number of civilians killed in the Philippines in 2019 is uncertain and disputed, indications are that the government's war on drugs, initiated when President Duterte took office in 2016, resulted in twice as many deaths as the

---

[46] *The Economist*, 'Jihadists bomb a church in the Philippines', 2 Feb. 2019; Hart, M., 'Abu Sayyaf is bringing more of ISIS' brutal tactics to the Philippines', World Politics Review, 22 July 2019; and Agence France Press, 'Philippines: Isis claims bombing that killed five on Jolo island', *The Guardian*, 29 June 2019.

[47] Andersen (note 40).

[48] Fonbuena, C., 'Leader of Isis in Philippines killed, DNA test confirm', *The Guardian*, 14 Apr. 2019.

[49] Herbert, S., 'Conflict analysis of The Philippines', K4D helpdesk service, UK Department for International Development, 29 July 2019.

[50] For further details on the peace talks, see GMA News Online, 'Timeline: The peace talks between the government and the CPP-NPA-NDF, 1986–present', 6 Dec. 2017. On the efforts to create a community-led peace zone in the Sagada region, see Macaspac, N. V., 'Insurgent peace: Community-led peacebuilding of indigenous peoples in Sagada, Philippines', *Geopolitics*, vol. 24, no. 4 (2019), pp. 839–77.

[51] Lischin, L., 'Think national, start local: Taming the Philippines communists', The Interpreter, 27 May 2019; Armas, S. G., 'Communist insurgency completes 50 years in Philippines with no end in sight', Agencia EFE, 29 Mar. 2019; and Santos, D. J., 'Philippine Defense chief rejects truce with NPA rebels', Benar News, 9 Dec. 2019.

Table 4.5. Estimated conflict-related fatalities in the Philippines, 2016–19

Event type	2016	2017	2018	2019
Battles	856	1 955	587	533
Explosions/remote violence	67	64	37	48
Protests, riots and strategic developments	10	2	0	4
Violence against civilians	3 269	2 067	1 161	1 108
Total	**4 202**	**4 088**	**1 785**	**1 693**

Notes: The first available year for data on the Philippines in the Armed Conflict Location & Data Project (ACLED) database is 2016. For definitions of event types, see ACLED, 'ACLED definitions of political violence and protest', 11 Apr. 2019.

Source: ACLED, 'Data export tool', [n.d.].

insurgencies (the latter are shown in table 4.5). According to the government the estimated death toll in the anti-drugs campaign between 1 July 2016 and 30 November 2019 was 5552, with 220 728 drug suspects arrested, although the release of conflicting official data raises questions over the reliability of these figures.[52] Human rights groups suggest that drug-war killings could be over 20 000.[53] ACLED estimated that about 75 per cent of the civilian deaths in the first half of 2019 was due to the war on drugs.[54]

There were also increasing allegations in 2019 that the war on drugs is being used to silence political opponents.[55] In February 2018 the ICC began an examination of whether the war on drugs involved crimes against humanity. However, the Philippines formally left the ICC on 17 March 2019, a year after the government deposited its withdrawal notice and despite two petitions to prevent the country's withdrawal still pending before the Supreme Court of the Philippines.[56]

Armed conflict in Thailand

The decades-old, low-intensity armed conflict in the south of Thailand among the military government and various secessionist groups continued

[52] Al Jazeera, 'Philippine authorities "getting away with murder" in drug war', 12 Dec. 2019; Tupas, E., 'Drug war death toll hits 6,847', Philippine Star, 16 Aug. 2019; and Associated Press, 'Roger Duterte hands over "war on drugs" to vice-president and critic', *The Guardian*, 7 Nov. 2019.

[53] Matar, L., 'UN needs to act now to end Philippines killings', Human Rights Watch, 24 June 2019; and Coronel, S. et al. and the Stabile Center for Investigative Journalism, 'The undocumented dead in Duterte's drug war', *The Atlantic*, 19 Aug. 2019. Also see Stabile Center for Investigative Journalism, 'Philippine drug war casualties', Dataset.

[54] Jones, S., 'Data confirm wave of targeted attacks in the Philippines', ACLED press release, 3 July 2019.

[55] De Lima, L., 'President Duterte's war on drugs is a pretense', *New York Times*, 22 July 2019; ASEAN Parliamentarians for Human Rights, *"In the Crosshairs of the Presidency": Attacks on Opposition Lawmakers in the Philippines* (ASEAN Parliamentarians for Human Rights: June 2019); and Aspinwall, N., 'Duterte turns death squads on political activists', Foreign Policy, 10 June 2019.

[56] Philstar, 'Philippines won't cooperate with ICC probe, says Panelo', 14 Mar. 2019; and Buan, L., 'PH out of ICC soon: Eyes on the Supreme Court to intervene', Rappler, 11 Mar. 2019.

in 2019.[57] More than 7000 people have been killed in the conflict since 2004, with little progress in Malaysian-brokered peace talks that started in 2015 between the government and Mara Patani, an umbrella organization of Thai Malay secessionists groups.[58] The most significant insurgent group, the National Revolutionary Front, continued to boycott the talks.[59] ACLED recorded less than 80 battle-related deaths in 2019.[60]

More broadly, despite a return to formal elections in March 2019 (the first since a military coup in 2014), the election was widely criticized for being heavily rigged in favour of the military junta.[61] Thus, the outcome of the election—coup-leader General Prayuth Chan-ocha forming a coalition government and continuing as prime minister—further exacerbated divisions in Thai society.[62]

[57] See e.g Agence France-Presse, 'Thailand: At least 15 killed in biggest attack in restive south in years', *The Guardian*, 6 Nov. 2019. On the history of the insurgency in southern Thailand, see Wilson, C. and Akhtar, S., 'Repression, co-optation and insurgency: Pakistan's FATA, southern Thailand and Papua, Indonesia', *Third World Quarterly*, vol. 40, no. 4 (2019), pp. 710–26.

[58] Hart, M., 'Southern Thailand's fractured peace process at a crossroads', Geopolitical Monitor, 15 Feb. 2019; and Wheeler, M., 'Behind the insurgent attack in southern Thailand', International Crisis Group Q&A, 8 Nov. 2019.

[59] Watcharasakwet, W. et al., 'Southern Thai peace talks: Malaysian broker says violence can end in 2 years', *Benar News*, 4 Jan. 2019; and International Crisis Group, *Southern Thailand's Peace Dialogue: Giving Substance to Form*, Asia Report no. 304 (International Crisis Group: Brussels, 21 Jan. 2020).

[60] ACLED, 'Data export tool', [n.d.].

[61] *The Economist*, 'Thailand's military junta gets its way in rigged vote', 24 Mar. 2019; and Suhartono, M. and Ramzy, A., 'Thailand's election results signal military's continued grip on power', *New York Times*, 9 May 2019.

[62] ASEAN Today, 'There's a boot on the neck of Thailand's democracy undermining its legitimacy', 25 Oct. 2019.

5. Armed conflict and peace processes in Europe

Overview

One armed conflict was active in Europe in 2019: the low-intensity internationalized, subnational armed conflict in Ukraine. Since April 2014 this armed conflict between Ukrainian Government forces and Russian-backed separatists has led to about 13 000 deaths (at least 3330 civilians and approximately 9670 combatants), but since 2018 combat-related deaths have been much lower: estimated at 405 in 2019, down from 886 in 2018.

Political changes in Ukraine during 2019, and especially the presidential victory by Volodymyr Zelensky and his acceptance of the so-called 'Steinmeier formula' for resolving the conflict, created a new opportunity for further negotiations. At the first Normandy Format leaders meeting for more than three years, the leaders of France, Germany, Russia and Ukraine endorsed the Steinmeier formula, agreed to implement a 'full and comprehensive' ceasefire by the end of the year and to hold further talks in four months. Despite this promising new opening, fundamental disagreements endured among the parties about the nature of the conflict and their involvement in it, as well as over the sequencing and implementation of the formula.

Although most of Europe has seemed peaceful for about two decades, various tensions remain, including: (a) persistent tensions between Russia and large parts of the rest of Europe; (b) long-standing conflicts that have not yet been resolved—especially in the post-Soviet space, the Western Balkans and Cyprus—in the latter, oil and gas discoveries, maritime border disputes and regional power rivalries added to tensions; and (c) the security response to problems on Europe's southern flank, which encompasses several European states' involvement in armed conflicts in Afghanistan, the Middle East and North Africa and sub-Saharan Africa. There were 18 multilateral peace operations active in Europe in 2019, all of which had been active in the previous year.

Two issues that have been at the forefront of European security thinking in recent years—irregular migration and terrorism—both have a strong connection to developments in the south. The European Union (EU) has been at the forefront of managing irregular migration to Europe, and it is an issue that has been a prominent driver in EU engagement with Libya and Turkey. Terrorism continued to constitute a significant threat to security in Europe in 2019, although the latest trend reports suggest that the risk is declining.

IAN DAVIS

I. Key general developments in the region

IAN DAVIS

One armed conflict was active in Europe in 2019: in Ukraine (see section II). Although most of Europe has seemed peaceful for about two decades, various tensions remain, such as: (*a*) persistent tensions between Russia and most of the rest of Europe; (*b*) long-standing conflicts that have not yet been resolved, especially in the post-Soviet space, the Western Balkans and Cyprus; and (*c*) the security challenges in Europe's southern flank, including several European states' involvement in armed conflicts in Afghanistan, the Middle East and North Africa (MENA) region and sub-Saharan Africa. These three issues are discussed briefly below.

There were 18 multilateral peace operations active in Europe in 2019, all of which had been active in the previous year. Many of these operations have been active for many years in former Soviet and Yugoslav republics that experienced conflict, often over disputed territory, following the break-up of the Soviet Union and Yugoslavia. The only peace operations in Europe established more recently were deployed in response to the outbreak of conflict in Ukraine in 2014. Most of these missions are strictly civilian and relatively small. The number of personnel deployed in peace operations in Europe is therefore relatively small compared to the number of operations deployed and to most other regions. The number of personnel serving in multilateral peace operations in Europe fell by 3.8 per cent during 2019, from 8126 to 7819.

One peace process that had positive developments and also setbacks in 2019 was the North Macedonia integration issue. In June 2018 the Former Yugoslav Republic of Macedonia (FYROM) reached agreement with Greece to change its name to the Republic of North Macedonia.[1] Following a referendum in FYROM in September 2018 the final steps to implement the agreement—ratification in the Greek and Macedonian parliaments—were taken in January 2019, thereby ending a 27-year dispute over the name of Macedonia.[2] While this has set North Macedonia on the path to eventual membership of the North Atlantic Treaty Organization (NATO), anticipated European Union (EU) accession talks were subsequently blocked by a few EU member states, led by France.[3]

---

[1] Kitsantonis, N., 'Macedonia agrees to change its name to resolve dispute with Greece', *New York Times*, 12 June 2018. Also see Davis, I., 'Armed conflict and peace processes in Europe', *SIPRI Yearbook 2019*, p. 76.

[2] Pardew, J., 'Something remarkable just happened in the Balkans', *The Hill*, 31 Jan. 2019; and *The Economist*, 'Macedonia gets a new name and a new start', 17 Jan. 2019.

[3] Rankin, J., 'EU failure to open membership talks with Albania and North Macedonia condemned', *The Guardian*, 18 Oct. 2019.

Tensions with Russia

Persistent tensions between Russia and large parts of the rest of Europe have led to several highly militarized and contested security contexts, such as those in the Black Sea region.[4] One manifestation is growing military spending, especially among NATO countries bordering Russia in Eastern Europe.[5] Moreover, measures intended to reduce the risk of the re-emergence of military confrontation in Europe are strained, with little prospect of new approaches to risk reduction being agreed.[6] Allegations of Russian non-compliance with the 1987 Intermediate-Range Nuclear Forces Treaty, for example, could not be resolved and led to the withdrawal of the United States from the treaty in August 2019.[7]

In the last decade Russia has been widely accused within Europe and North America of systematically undermining regional security.[8] In 2019 for example, it was reported that security officials from several Western countries had concluded that a series of past Russian operations in Europe formed a coordinated and ongoing destabilization campaign from a dedicated unit within the Russian intelligence system known as Unit 29155.[9] However, there were also a few signs and attempts at seeking a more pragmatic approach to Russia.[10] For example, French President Emmanuel Macron talked about the need to 'rebuild or build a new architecture of trust and security in Europe and clarify our relationship with Russia'.[11] In addition, despite Russian–US relations balancing on the edge of further deterioration throughout the

---

[4] Melvin, N. J., 'Rebuilding collective security in the Black Sea region', SIPRI Policy Paper no. 50, Dec. 2018; and Åtland, K. and Kabanenko, I., 'Russia and its western neighbours: A comparative study of the security situation in the Black, Baltic and Barents Sea regions', *Europe–Asia Studies*, vol. 72, no. 2 (2019), pp. 286–313.

[5] Tian, N. et al., 'Trends in world military expenditure, 2018', SIPRI Fact Sheet, Apr. 2019. On military spending in NATO, also see chapter 8, section II and III, in this volume.

[6] On the evolving strategic environment in Europe and opportunities for risk reduction, see Anthony, I., 'Reducing military risk in Europe', SIPRI Policy Paper no. 51, June 2019.

[7] On the Intermediate-Range Nuclear Forces Treaty, see chapter 11, section I, in this volume.

[8] On the deteriorating relationship between Russia and the USA, see Smith, D., 'International tensions and shifting dynamics of power', *SIPRI Yearbook 2018*, pp. 11–12; Smith, D., 'International tensions and the dynamics of power', *SIPRI Yearbook 2019*, pp. 18–19; and chapter 1 in this volume. For a comparative study of the official peace and war narratives of Russia and the USA as presented at the United Nations Security Council, see Bakalova, E. and Jüngling, K., 'Conflict over peace? The United States' and Russia's diverging conceptual approaches to peace and conflict settlement', *Europe–Asia Studies*, vol. 72, no. 2 (2019), pp. 155–79.

[9] Schwirtz, M., 'Top secret Russian unit seeks to destabilize Europe, security officials say', *New York Times*, 8 Oct. 2019.

[10] See e.g. Chazan, D., 'France says "time has come" to ease tensions with Russia', *The Telegraph*, 9 Sep. 2019; and Graham, T., 'Let Russia be Russia: The case for a more pragmatic approach to Moscow', *Foreign Affairs*, Nov./Dec. 2019.

[11] NATO, 'Joint press point with NATO Secretary General Jens Stoltenberg and the President of France Emmanuel Macron', 28 Nov. 2019.

year, US President Donald J. Trump repeatedly mentioned his intention to improve dialogue with Russia.[12]

Developments in the North Atlantic Treaty Organization

There have been growing intra-NATO political tensions in recent years, and some of these fissures deepened in 2019 over a range of issues, including trade, climate change, Iran and arms control. Internal divisions within NATO—especially those generated by the leaders of France, Turkey and the USA—led to a low-key leaders meeting in the United Kingdom in December.[13] However, despite this backdrop of transatlantic political anxiety there were at least four significant developments in NATO in 2019: (*a*) the latest element of the NATO readiness initiative, the Four Thirties—under which 30 mechanized battalions, 30 air squadrons and 30 combat ships are to be ready within 30 days—was achieved; (*b*) the 'out of area' discussion returned with the efforts of President Macron to focus NATO more on Africa, and several member states (most notably, Germany, Turkey and USA) suggesting a stronger focus on the Middle East; (*c*) finding a common approach to the rise of China became NATO business for the first time; and (*d*) NATO agreed to initiate a 'forward-looking reflection process' on how to strengthen its political dimension.[14]

Unresolved conflicts

Inactive armed conflicts in the post-Soviet space

In 2019 three armed conflicts in the post-Soviet space—Nagorno-Karabakh (Armenia and Azerbaijan), South Ossetia and Abkhazia (Georgia) and Trans-Dniester (Moldova)—remained relatively inactive (i.e. with fewer than 25 conflict-related deaths in the year). However, the socio-economic and political dimensions of the conflicts continued to evolve, and the armed forces of the various parties largely remained in a heightened state of readiness.[15] The conflicts are all tied to the wider European security framework because they represent a significant part of Russia's leverage in that discourse.

[12] See e.g. Wadhams, N. and Arkhipov, I., 'Secretary Pompeo to meet with Putin as President Trump seeks better Russia ties—again', *Time*, 11 May 2019.

[13] *The Economist*, 'NATO's Watford summit features a troublesome trio', 1 Dec. 2019.

[14] NATO, 'London Declaration issued by the heads of state and government participating in the meeting of the North Atlantic Council in London 3–4 December 2019', 4 Dec. 2019; Fiorenza, N., 'NATO improves force readiness', *Jane's Defence Weekly*, 4 Dec. 2019; and Mehta, A., 'NATO struggles with its China conundrum', *Defense News*, 3 Dec. 2019. On Turkish and US actions in Syria, see chapter 6, section II, in this volume. On Iranian–US tensions, see chapter 6, section I, in this volume. On France's role in the Sahel, see chapter 7, section II, in this volume.

[15] On developments in the conflicts in the post-Soviet space in 2018, see *SIPRI Yearbook 2019* (note 1), pp. 73–75. Also see Klimenko, E., 'Protracted armed conflicts in the post-Soviet space and their impact on Black Sea security', SIPRI Insights on Peace and Security no. 2018/8, Dec. 2018.

The Nagorno-Karabakh conflict—an interstate confrontation between Armenia and Azerbaijan over disputed territory—remained relatively calm in 2019. Ceasefire violations continued to take place along the line of contact but were fewer than in previous years.[16] There were also growing hopes for progress in the decades-long peace process being mediated by the Organization for Security and Co-operation in Europe (OSCE) Minsk Group.[17] In January 2019 the foreign ministers of Armenia and Azerbaijan agreed on the 'necessity of taking concrete measures to prepare the populations for peace'.[18] Armenian Prime Minister Nikol Pashinyan and Azerbaijani President Ilham Aliyev held their first official meeting about Nagorno-Karabakh in March, where they committed to strengthen the ceasefire, improve communications and implement humanitarian projects.[19]

However, the killing of four soldiers in the Nagorno-Karabakh conflict zone between 30 May and 13 June was a major setback for diplomacy, and by the end of the year the political process to reach a settlement appeared to have faltered.[20]

The Abkhazia and South Ossetia conflicts in Georgia remained unresolved in 2019, with little sign of a political breakthrough. Abkhazia and South Ossetia are recognized only by Russia and four other states (Nauru, Nicaragua, Syria and Venezuela), while the rest of the international community regards them as being parts of Georgia. There are regular calls (mainly by Western institutions) on Russia to fulfil the terms of the 2008 ceasefire agreement and withdraw its forces from the breakaway territories.[21] However, throughout the year Russia continued to voice support for the two breakaway regions and also announced that it would finance the modernization of Abkhazia's armed forces.[22]

---

[16] Shiriyev, Z., 'A listening tour of the Azerbaijani front lines', International Crisis Group, 17 Sep. 2019.

[17] Shiriyev, Z., 'Old conflict, new Armenia: The view from Baku', International Crisis Group commentary, 8 Feb. 2019. For a brief description and list of members of the OSCE Minsk Group, see annex B, section II, in this volume. Other peace proposals have included the peace initiative of Kazakhstan and Russia, the mediation efforts of Iran and Turkey, and the resolutions of the UN Security Council. Also see Gasparyan, A., 'Understanding the Nagorno-Karabakh conflict: Domestic politics and twenty-five years of fruitless negotiations 1994–2018', *Caucasus Survey*, vol. 7, no. 3 (2019), pp. 235–50.

[18] OSCE, Press statement by the co-chairs of the OSCE Minsk Group, Press release, 16 Jan. 2019.

[19] OSCE, Joint statement by the foreign ministers of Armenia and Azerbaijan and the co-chairs of the OSCE Minsk Group, Press statement, 29 Mar. 2019. On the humanitarian impact of the conflict, see Istrate, D., 'Nagorno Karabakh: An ongoing humanitarian crisis', Emerging Europe, 12 Sep. 2019.

[20] Kucera, J., 'Fatal frontline shootings heighten tensions between Armenia and Azerbaijan', Eurasianet, 3 June 2019; and International Crisis Group, *Digging out of Deadlock in Nagorno-Karabakh*, Europe Report no. 255 (International Crisis Group: Brussels, 20 Dec. 2019).

[21] See e.g. OSCE, 'OSCE Permanent Council no. 1236, Vienna, 18 July 2019, EU statement in reply to the address of Mr Lasha Darsalia, Deputy Foreign Minister of Georgia', PC.DEL/943/19, 22 July 2019.

[22] TASS Russian News Agency, 'Russia to finance modernization of Abkhazia's armed forces', 23 Aug. 2019.

In both of the breakaway regions there appeared to be growing discontent among some of the isolated ethnic Georgian populations living along the separation lines with limited movement into Georgian-controlled territory. In August for example, renewed fence building by Russian and South Ossetian border guards along the line between Georgia and South Ossetia—to which Georgia responded by building police stations in contested areas—led to rising tensions.[23] Mediators representing the EU, OSCE and United Nations criticized the closure of border crossings and called for all parties to engage more constructively.[24]

The main OSCE negotiation forum for tackling practical problems in the conflict zones is the Incident Prevention and Response Mechanism, which was created in 2009 and involves regular meetings of Abkhaz/South Ossetian, Georgian and Russian security officials, facilitated by international mediators. The EU Monitoring Mission in Georgia remains the only international presence on the ground, although it is unable to operate in contested areas. In September the foreign ministers of Georgia and Russia held talks for the first time since the outbreak of the 2008 war between the two countries.[25]

The Western Balkans

Areas of instability remain in the Western Balkans. For example, in Bosnia and Herzegovina the complex political arrangements established by the 1995 Dayton Accords have contributed towards political deadlock and economic stagnation. The situation in the country now resembles a frozen conflict, but one where ethnic nationalist sentiment is on the rise.[26] In March the International Criminal Tribunal for the former Yugoslavia increased former Bosnian Serb leader Radovan Karadžić's sentence from 40 years to life in prison during appeal proceedings on his 2016 conviction for war crimes committed during the 1995 Srebrenica massacre.[27]

Tensions between Kosovo Serbs and Kosovo Albanians continued in 2019, particularly in the Serb-majority northern part of Kosovo.[28] In May for example, a police raid on organized crime suspects in the northern part of Kosovo prompted Serbia to put its military on full combat alert.[29] A

---

[23] Vartanyan, O., 'Easing travel between Georgia and breakaway Abkhazia', International Crisis Group commentary, 5 Sep. 2019.

[24] OSCE, 'Press communiqué of the co-chairs of the Geneva International Discussions', Press release, 3 Apr. 2019.

[25] Istrate, D., 'EU, UN praise Georgia for first-high level talks with Russia since 2008', Emerging Europe, 27 Sep. 2019.

[26] Brezar, A., 'Bosnia is close to the edge. We need Europe's help', The Guardian, 29 May 2019.

[27] BBC, 'Radovan Karadzic sentence increased to life at UN tribunal', 20 Mar. 2019.

[28] On the lasting controversies, implications and legacy of NATO's intervention in 1999, see Brown, D. and Smith, M. A. et al., 'Twenty years after Kosovo and allied force: Controversies, implications and legacy', Special issue, Comparative Strategy, vol. 38, no. 5 (2019).

[29] Bytyci, F. and Vasovic, A., 'Serbia places forces on alert after Kosovo police operation in Serb-populated north', Reuters, 28 May 2019.

Table 5.1. Mediterranean refugee and migrant situation, 2014–19

Year	Arrivals	Dead and missing
2014	225 455	3 538
2015	1 032 408	3 771
2016	373 652	5 096
2017	185 139	3 139
2018	141 472	2 277
2019	125 472	1 327

Note: Arrivals include sea arrivals to Cyprus, Italy and Malta, and sea and land arrivals to Greece and Spain.

Source: United Nations High Commissioner for Refugees, 'Operational portal, Refugee situations, Mediterranean situation', [n.d.].

comprehensive agreement that was unofficially proposed in 2018 by Serbian President Aleksander Vučić and Kosovan President Hashim Thaçi—which included an ethnic element in proposed border adjustments—continued to be opposed by domestic constituencies and the EU.[30] In August five NATO states (France, Germany, Italy, UK and USA) urged Kosovo and Serbia to enter into dialogue to alleviate tensions in the region.[31] Twenty years after NATO ground troops first entered Kosovo, around 3500 alliance troops remained in the country as part of the Kosovo Force.[32]

Cyprus

UN diplomats have been trying to broker an agreement to reunify Cyprus for decades. The latest negotiations collapsed in 2017 due to a failure to reach agreement on security guarantees and power-sharing arrangements.[33] A political settlement to the Cyprus conflict remained elusive in 2019, with oil and gas discoveries, maritime border disputes and regional power rivalries—including in relation to armed conflicts in the MENA region—adding to tensions.[34] Turkey sent ships to drill for oil and gas in waters off the coast of Cyprus, effectively triggering a Turkish border dispute with the EU.[35] The EU subsequently imposed limited sanctions on Turkey.[36]

---

[30] Santora, M., 'Talk of ethnic partition of Kosovo revives old Balkan ghosts', *New York Times*, 19 Sep. 2018; and Wintour, P., 'Deal with Serbia possible this year, says Kosovan president', *The Guardian*, 15 Apr. 2019.

[31] Deutsche Welle, 'Serbia, Kosovo urged to ease tensions by NATO countries', 13 Aug. 2019.

[32] Sabbagh, D., '"Still needed": NATO marks 20 years in Kosovo', *The Guardian*, 12 June 2019.

[33] See Davis, I. and Anthony, I., 'Armed conflict in Europe', *SIPRI Yearbook 2018*, p. 62.

[34] On the armed conflicts in the MENA region, see chapter 6 in this volume.

[35] Al Jazeera, 'Cyprus calls Turkey gas exploration "provocative and aggressive"', 4 Oct. 2019.

[36] Sengül, E., 'EC adopts sanction framework for Turkish E.Med drilling', Anadolu Agency, 11 Nov. 2019.

The European response to security challenges in the south

Changes in the security dynamic linking South Eastern Europe, the eastern Mediterranean, MENA and other parts of Africa are exacerbating some unresolved conflicts, such as the one in Cyprus, and are also shaping broader European security responses in the south. For example, the NATO reflection process initiated in December 2019 is at least partly a response to the French call for more balance in thinking about the east and the south, including the fight against non-state groups in the Sahel.[37] Two issues at the forefront of European security thinking in recent years—migration and terrorism—both have a strong south dimension.

Managing irregular migration

While the number of refugees and migrants arriving in southern Europe continued to fall in 2019, as did the deaths of people crossing the Mediterranean from North Africa (see table 5.1), both remained issues of concern. Greece continued to be the recipient of the highest number of new arrivals, with over 74 000 in 2019.[38]

The EU has been at the forefront of managing irregular migration to Europe.[39] In 2019 the new president of the European Commission, Ursula von der Leyen, laid out political guidelines that ensure migration will continue to be among the EU top priorities in the future.[40] One specific EU policy response has been to expand the European Border and Coast Guard Agency, commonly known as Frontex, which is expected to increase from 1300 to some 10 000 border guards by 2021.[41]

One of the main tasks of the new EU leadership is to find a common approach to the EU internal policy framework on migration.[42] However, this is likely to be challenging given that the 2018 Global Compact for Safe, Orderly and Regular Migration (GCM) was a divisive topic within the EU:

[37] Wintour P. and McKernan, B., 'Macron defends "brain-dead NATO" remarks as summit approaches', *The Guardian*, 28 Nov. 2019.

[38] UN High Commissioner for Refugees, 'Operational portal', [n.d.]; and Smith, H., 'Greece says it's "reached limit" as arrivals of refugees show no sign of slowing', *The Guardian*, 16 Dec. 2019.

[39] Irregular migration is defined as 'Movement of persons that takes place outside the laws, regulations, or international agreements governing the entry into or exit from the State of origin, transit or destination'; see International Organization for Migration (IOM), *Glossary on Migration* (IOM: Geneva, 2019). On the initial EU policy response to the refugee crisis, see Grip, L., 'The global refugee crisis and its impact in Europe', *SIPRI Yearbook 2016*, pp. 439–52; and Grip, L., 'United Nations and regional responses to displacement crises', *SIPRI Yearbook 2017*, pp. 280–82.

[40] European Commission, 'Communication from the Commission to the European Parliament, the European Council and the Council, Progress report on the implementation of the European agenda on migration', COM(2019) 481 final, 16 Oct. 2019; and von der Leyen, U., 'A union that strives for more, my agenda for Europe: Political guidelines for the next European Commission 2019–2024', 16 July 2019.

[41] European Commission, 'EU delivers on stronger European Border and Coast Guard to support member states', Press release, 8 Nov. 2019.

[42] On the EU internal dimension to migration, see Kadysheva, O. et al., *Common Home: Migration and Development in Europe and Beyond* (Caritas Europa: Brussels, Nov. 2019).

at the UN General Assembly, three EU member states voted against it, five abstained and one did not vote.[43] Going forward supporters of the GCM will want to see elements of it included in EU decisions, while opponents will scrutinize any such proposals critically.

Irregular migration fears have also been a prominent driver in EU engagement with Turkey and Libya. In July 2019 Turkey suspended its 2016 readmission agreement with the EU in which Turkey agreed to accept the return of irregular migrants and asylum seekers who crossed from its territory to Greece after 20 March 2016.[44] In the past three years, only 1884 people were returned to Turkey under the agreement, and its suspension largely reflected Turkey's broader grievances with the EU, including the lack of progress on visa liberalization and EU sanctions related to oil drilling near Cyprus (see above).[45]

In October as a result of European criticism of Turkish military actions against Kurdish groups in Syria, Turkish President Recep Erdoğan threatened to 'open the gates' and send 3.6 million refugees to Europe.[46] While Turkey did not follow through with this threat, at the end of the year it warned of a potentially new wave of refugees from an escalation in the Syrian armed conflict.[47]

In Libya the EU has also sought to prevent irregular migration to Europe through two Common Security and Defence Policy (CSDP) missions, including assistance to the Libyan border and coast guard and other support for local migration management.[48] A Tripartite Taskforce on the Situation of Stranded Migrant and Refugees in Libya (established by the African Union, the EU and the UN) has facilitated the repatriation of more than 50 000 African migrants from Libya since it was created in November 2017.[49] However, aid and human rights groups have criticized Europe's outsourcing of migration controls to 'buffer' countries like Libya, Niger and Turkey for

[43] On the creation of the GCM, see *SIPRI Yearbook 2019*, pp. 39–40. Czechia, Hungary and Poland voted against it; Austria, Bulgaria, Italy, Latvia and Romania abstained; and Slovakia did not vote.

[44] On the 2016 EU–Turkey deal, see *SIPRI Yearbook 2017*, pp. 157, 158, 280, 281.

[45] *Daily Sabah*, 'Readmission agreement with EU no longer functional, Ankara says', 23 July 2019; and Euractiv, 'Turkey suspends deal with the EU on migrant readmission', 24 July 2019.

[46] Safi, M. and McKernan, B., 'US warns Turkey of red lines as Syria offensive death toll mounts', *The Guardian*, 11 Oct. 2019. On Turkey's role in the armed conflict in Syria, see chapter 6, section II, in this volume.

[47] Squires, N., 'Turkey warns refugee crisis could return with a vengeance in 2020 as Greece struggles with overcrowded camps', *The Telegraph*, 24 Dec. 2019.

[48] The two CSDP missions in Libya are EUNAVFOR MED Operation Sophia and EUBAM Libya. See EU External Action Service, 'EU–Libya relations', 25 Sep. 2019. On the armed conflict in Libya, see chapter 6, section IV, in this volume.

[49] EU External Action Service, 'Joint press release—Meeting of the Joint AU–EU–UN Taskforce to address the migrant and refugee situation in Libya', 25 Sep. 2019.

contributing to conflict dynamics and abuses in detention centres.[50] These criticisms extend to the broader trend of increased securitization of different aspects of migration policy.[51]

Counterterrorism

In recent years, some European states (including Belgium, Denmark, France, Germany, Italy, Netherlands, Norway, Poland, Russia, Spain, Sweden and UK) have been directly involved in conducting or assisting military action against non-state armed groups operating in Afghanistan (chapter 4), the MENA region (chapter 6) and parts of Africa (chapter 7). Several other European states have been involved in missions to train local security forces or assist countries in those regions to strengthen their counterterror capacity, often in close coordination with the USA.

Terrorism continued to constitute a significant threat to security in Europe in 2019, although the latest trend reports (covering periods to the end of 2018 only) indicate a declining risk. For example, the *Global Terrorism Index 2019* showed that the number of deaths from terrorism in Europe fell for the second successive year, from over 200 in 2017 to 62 in 2018.[52] Similarly, Europol (covering EU member states only) recorded a decline in militant Islamist attacks (as compared to 2017), and for the third year in a row an increase in arrests linked to right-wing terrorism. Overall however, the number of failed, foiled or completed terrorist attacks in the EU in 2018 remained low (129 in total), with ethnonationalist and separatist terrorist attacks (83 in total) greatly outnumbering other types of terrorist attacks.[53] How to deal with returning foreign fighters (individuals that have joined an armed conflict abroad) remained one of Europe's main counterterrorism challenges.[54] At least 450 suspected European foreign fighters were estimated to be detained in Iraq and Syria, together with about 700–750 European children.[55]

---

[50] See e.g. de Bellis, M., 'Europe's shameful failure to end the torture and abuse of refugees and migrants in Libya', Amnesty International, 7 Mar. 2019; Andersson, R. and Keen, D., *Partners in Crime? The Impacts of Europe's Outsourced Migration Controls on Peace Stability and Rights* (Saferworld: July 2019); and Medecins Sans Frontieres, 'Trading in suffering: Detention, exploitation and abuse in Libya', 23 Dec. 2019.

[51] See e.g. Mixed Migration Centre, 'The ever-rising securitisation of mixed migration', 17 Dec. 2019.

[52] Institute for Economics & Peace, *Global Terrorism Index 2019: Measuring the Impact of Terrorism* (Institute for Economics & Peace: Sydney, Nov. 2019), p. 3.

[53] Europol, *European Union Terrorism Situation and Trend Report 2019* (Europol: June 2019).

[54] See e.g. Renard, T. and Coolsaet, R., 'Losing control over returnees?', Lawfare, 13 Oct. 2019; and Metodieva, A., 'Europe's state of denial about Islamic State returnees', German Marshall Fund, 7 Nov. 2019.

[55] Coolsaet, R. and Renard, T., 'New figures on European nationals detained in Syria and Iraq', Egmont Institute Research Note, 15 Oct. 2019.

II. Armed conflict and the peace process in Ukraine

IAN DAVIS

Since the annexation of Crimea in March 2014 and the breakout of armed conflict in eastern Ukraine shortly thereafter, Ukraine has been the focus of Europe's main territorial conflict. The initial causes of this conflict and the extent to which it represents a civil war, with primarily domestic origins, or a foreign intervention by Russia remain intensely contested—although new evidence emerged in 2019 of Russia's military involvement and political subversion in Ukraine.[1] In November 2019 the International Court of Justice found unanimously that it has jurisdiction on the basis of antiterrorism and anti-discrimination treaties to hear a lawsuit filed by Ukraine against Russia for its support of pro-Russian separatists.[2] In this chapter, the status of the armed conflict in 2019 is defined as a low-intensity internationalized, subnational armed conflict.[3]

Since April 2014 the armed conflict between Ukrainian Government forces and Russian-backed separatists has led to about 13 000 deaths (at least 3330 civilians and approximately 9670 combatants).[4] Since 2018 battle-related deaths and civilian casualties in the Donbas region have been much lower than in earlier years: according to the Armed Conflict Location & Event Data Project (ACLED) there were 405 combat-related deaths in 2019 (down from 886 in 2018).[5] However, ACLED also recorded an increase of 12 per cent in the number of political violence events since 2018. Most of the 14 852 political violence events in 2019 (the second highest in the world after Syria), were clashes between the military forces of Ukraine and the United Armed Forces

---

[1] For a discussion on the initial causes of the conflict in Ukraine, and the extent to which it represented a civil war (now downgraded to a subnational armed conflict), with primarily domestic origins, or a foreign intervention by Russia, see Wilson, A., 'External intervention in the Ukraine conflict: Towards a frozen conflict in the Donbas', *SIPRI Yearbook 2016*, pp. 143–57; Clem, R. S., 'Clearing the fog of war: Public versus official sources and geopolitical storylines in the Russia–Ukraine conflict', *Eurasian Geography and Economics*, vol. 58, no. 6 (2017), pp. 592–612; Bowen, A. S., 'Coercive diplomacy and the Donbas: Explaining Russian strategy in eastern Ukraine', *Journal of Strategic Studies*, vol. 42, no. 3–4 (2019), pp. 312–43; and Freedman, L., *Ukraine and the Art of Strategy* (Oxford University Press: 2019). Also see Walker, S., 'New evidence emerges of Russian role in Ukraine conflict', *The Guardian*, 18 Aug. 2019; and Shandra, A. and Seely, R., 'The Surkov leaks: The inner workings of Russia's hybrid war in Ukraine', Royal United Services Institute Occasional Paper, July 2019.

[2] van den Berg, S., 'In Ukraine victory, top UN court rejects Moscow's bid to block case', Reuters, 8 Nov. 2019.

[3] For conflict definitions and typologies, see chapter 2, section I, in this volume.

[4] Office of the United Nations High Commissioner for Human Rights (OHCHR), *Report on the Human Rights Situation in Ukraine: 16 August to 15 November 2019* (OHCHR: 2019), p. 8; and OHCHR, *Report on the Human Rights Situation in Ukraine: 16 November 2018 to 15 February 2019* (OHCHR: 2019), p. 6.

[5] ACLED, 'Data export tool', [n.d.].

of Novorossiya (the militias and armed volunteer groups affiliated with the unrecognized political union called Novorossiya).[6]

In addition, during 2019 at least 5.2 million people continued to be caught up in a protracted humanitarian crisis in eastern Ukraine, of whom 3.5 million were in need of humanitarian assistance, and about 800 000 people were internally displaced.[7] Eastern Ukraine also has some of the world's worst landmine contamination.[8]

In November 2018 a new dimension to the conflict opened on the Sea of Azov, where a naval incident resulted in the Russian capture of 3 Ukrainian vessels and 24 crew members.[9] Maritime tensions continued to simmer in the region throughout 2019. In February 2019 the European Union imposed sanctions on eight Russians connected with the November incident, while in May 2019 the International Tribunal for the Law of the Sea ordered Russia to release the sailors and ships.[10] Although Russia did not recognize the tribunal's authority in this matter, it released the sailors as part of a prisoner exchange in September 2019 (see below) and the three vessels in November.[11]

In June 2019 four men, three suspected of having close ties to Russian military and intelligence agencies and one Ukrainian separatist fighter, were found responsible for the shooting down of Malaysian Airlines Flight 17 in 2014 and were charged in the Netherlands with murder. The trial is expected to begin in March 2020, but none of the accused are likely to be present, as Russia did not accept the findings of the Dutch-led investigation.[12]

The internationalized nature of the conflict

The conflict in Ukraine is driven by and also helps to drive the wider geopolitical confrontation between Russia and Western powers.[13] In March for example, Russia marked the five-year anniversary of its 'unification' with Crimea and announced plans to deploy nuclear-capable bombers to the

---

[6] Kishi, R. et al., *Year in Review* (ACLED: 2 Mar. 2020).

[7] UN Office for the Coordination of Humanitarian Affairs (UN OCHA), 'Ukraine, situation reports', [n.d.]; and Congressional Research Service, 'Ukraine: Background, conflict with Russia, and US policy', Report R45008, 19 Sep. 2019, p. 12.

[8] UN OCHA, 'Eastern Ukraine one of the areas most contaminated by landmines in the world', 4 Apr. 2019. On the impact of landmines, also see chapter 13, section I, in this volume.

[9] *The Economist*, 'Sea of troubles: Explaining the naval clash between Russia and Ukraine', 1 Dec. 2018. Also see *SIPRI Yearbook 2019*, pp. 78–79.

[10] International Tribunal for the Law of the Sea, 'Case concerning the detention of three Ukrainian naval vessels', 25 May 2019.

[11] BBC, 'Russia returns Ukrainian boats seized off Crimea', 18 Nov. 2019.

[12] Government of the Netherlands, 'Suspects to be prosecuted for the downing of flight 17', Press release, 19 June 2019; and Krammer, A. E., 'Four to face murder charges in downing of Malaysia airlines flight 17', *New York Times*, 19 June 2019.

[13] For a detailed analysis of the roles of external actors in and around Ukraine, see Wittke, C. and Rabinovych, M., 'Five years after: The role of international actors in the "Ukraine Crisis"', *East European Politics*, vol. 35, no. 3 (2019), pp. 259–63.

Black Sea peninsula, describing the deployment as a response to the United States Aegis Ashore missile defence system in Romania.[14] The Russian military build-up in Crimea included a naval base, aviation and air defence forces, and around 30 000 troops.[15]

The internationalized nature of the conflict is also exemplified by the supply of arms and military assistance to the two sides in eastern Ukraine. Ukraine claimed that Russian-backed separatist forces in the Donbas region have about 35 000 troops, including 'over 2,100 Russian regular military, mostly in key command and control positions'—a significant decline since the peak year US estimate of about 12 000 Russian troops in eastern Ukraine in 2015. A further 87 750 Russian military personnel were said to be based on the Russian side of the border.[16] Russia has consistently denied Ukrainian and Western accusations that it sends troops and weapons to fight Ukrainian forces in the region. However, several reports have identified weapons being used in the conflict that could have come only from Russia, and President Vladimir Putin has acknowledged the presence of Russian mercenaries.[17]

The Ukrainian Government in turn is receiving arms and training from the USA and some other member states of the North Atlantic Treaty Organization. The USA has supplied Ukraine with $1.5 billion in security assistance since 2014, plus an average of $320 million a year in non-military aid.[18] While the Obama administration refused to supply lethal military equipment, this policy changed under US President Donald J. Trump's administration, which has supplied Javelin anti-tank missiles and sniper rifles to Ukraine.[19] During 2019 US military aid to Ukraine became central to an impeachment inquiry into Trump's possible abuse of power for political gain. The inquiry focused

---

[14] Reuters, 'Russia decides to deploy nuclear-capable strategic bombers to Crimea: RIA', 18 Mar. 2019. On perceptions of legitimacy surrounding the annexation of Crimea, see O'Loughlin, J. and Toal, G., 'The Crimea conundrum: Legitimacy and public opinion after annexation', *Eurasian Geography and Economics*, vol. 60, no. 1 (2019), pp. 6–27.

[15] Kuimova, A. and Wezeman, S. T., 'Russia and Black Sea security', SIPRI Background Paper, Dec. 2018; Tucker, P., 'US intelligence officials and satellite photos detail Russian military buildup on Crimea', Defense One, 12 June 2019; and UNIAN Information Agency, 'Ukraine intel assesses size of Russia's military force amassed in occupied Crimea', 21 June 2019.

[16] Remarks by Ukraine's representative to the UN Security Council, 8461st meeting, S/PV.8461, 12 Feb. 2019, p. 23; and Reuters, 'Some 12,000 Russian soldiers in Ukraine supporting rebels: US commander', 3 Mar. 2015.

[17] Walker (note 1); Grove, T. and Strobel, W., 'Special report: Where Ukraine's separatists get their weapons', Reuters, 29 July 2014; and RBC, [Putin admitted to the presence of Russians "resolving military issues" in Donbas], 17 Dec. 2015 (in Russian).

[18] Congressional Research Service (note 7), pp. 30–32.

[19] Marzalik, P. J. and Toler, A., 'Lethal weapons to Ukraine: A primer', Atlantic Council, 26 Jan. 2018; and Sisk, R., 'NATO commander backs sending more Javelins to Ukraine', Military.com, 3 Oct. 2019. On arms transfers to Ukraine, also see chapter 9, section II, in this volume.

on a $400 million aid package (that includes $250 million for military aid), part of which was frozen in July before being released in September.[20]

Three training missions for the Ukrainian security forces have been operating since 2015: the Joint Multinational Training Group-Ukraine (Canada, Denmark, Lithuania, Poland, Sweden, United Kingdom and USA), Operation Orbital (UK) and Operation UNIFIER (Canada).[21]

Presidential and parliamentary elections

In the run-up to Ukrainian presidential elections in March and April, there were allegations of irregularities and warnings of Russian interference. However, according to international observers the elections were carried out in accordance with democratic standards and without major irregularities.[22] In the second round of the vote the opposition candidate, Volodymyr Zelensky, won a landslide victory and pledged to find a peaceful solution to the conflict in eastern Ukraine as well as outlining an ambitious reform programme.[23] In an early test for the Ukrainian president-elect, in April Russia introduced a policy making it easier for certain residents of separatist-controlled eastern Ukraine to obtain Russian passports, prompting Zelensky to call for more international sanctions against Russia. In July Russia expanded these procedures to cover all residents of Donetsk and Luhansk regions.[24]

Zelensky consolidated his presidential victory by winning snap parliamentary elections in July; his newly formed party, Servant of the People, won 60 per cent of the seats, making it the first party in independent Ukraine to win an outright majority.[25] The political changes in Ukraine also

[20] Zengerle, P., 'Trump administration reinstates military aid for Ukraine', Reuters, 12 Sep. 2019; *The Economist*, 'The backstory to impeachment: From Paul Manafort to Donald Trump's fateful phone call', 12 Oct. 2019; and US Government Accountability Office, 'Decision, Office of Management and Budget—withholding of Ukraine security assistance', 16 Jan. 2020.

[21] 7th Army Training Command, 'Joint Multinational Training Group-Ukraine', [n.d.]; Forces Network, 'UK to extend training mission in Ukraine', 5 Nov. 2019; and Government of Canada, 'Operation UNIFIER', [n.d.].

[22] Organization for Security and Co-operation in Europe (OSCE), 'Ukraine, Presidential election, 31 March 2019: Statement of preliminary findings and conclusions', 1 Apr. 2019; and Ukrainian Election Task Force, 'Foreign interference in Ukraine's democracy', May 2019.

[23] *Kyiv Post*, 'Quick wins, big promises: Zelensky's agenda for parliament, government', 6 Sep. 2019; and *The Economist*, 'Hope and fear: Can Volodymyr Zelensky live up to the expectations he has created?', 26 Sep. 2019. On the status of the reform programme in Ukraine, see Gressel, G., 'Guarding the guardians: Ukraine's security and judicial reforms under Zelensky', European Council for Foreign Relations Policy Brief, Aug. 2019.

[24] Korsunskaya, D. and Polityuk, P., 'Russia offers passports to east Ukraine, president-elect decries "aggressor state"', Reuters, 24 Apr. 2019; and RadioFreeEurope/RadioLiberty, 'Putin widens citizenship offer to all residents of Ukraine's Donetsk, Luhansk regions', 18 July 2019.

[25] Congressional Research Service (note 7); and Wilson, A., 'Shock to the sistema: Ukraine's youthful new government', European Council for Foreign Relations commentary, 4 Sep. 2019.

brought renewed expectations that it might be possible to break the deadlock in the Donbas region.[26]

The peace process

The peace process is structured around a set of measures known as the Minsk agreements, which were signed in 2014 and 2015 by Russia, Ukraine and the Organization for Security and Co-operation in Europe (OSCE)—known as the Trilateral Contact Group, which has four working groups (economic, humanitarian, political and security)—and representatives of the separatist-controlled areas of eastern Ukraine.[27] The Trilateral Contact Group meets every two weeks in Minsk, but with few concrete results. A broader international grouping, the Normandy Four (France, Germany, Russia and Ukraine), meets regularly at various levels (foreign ministers, diplomatic advisers, political directors etc.), but the meeting in December 2019 (see below) was the first at the level of heads of state since October 2016.

An important characteristic of the Trilateral Contact Group and the Normandy Four is the absence of the USA. In July 2017 the Trump administration appointed a special representative for Ukraine negotiations (Kurt Volker), which provided Ukraine with an important policy bridge to the USA. One of the damaging effects of drawing Ukraine into US domestic politics (via the impeachment inquiry) was the resignation of key US officials, including Volker, in September 2019.[28]

According to the OSCE Special Monitoring Mission to Ukraine—an unarmed civilian monitoring mission established in 2014—the peace deal and ceasefire reached in February 2015, as part of the Minsk II Agreement, was violated almost daily in 2019.[29] With no effective body to adjudicate and sanction non-compliance with the Minsk agreements, many of the most significant measures remain largely unfulfilled.[30] There have also been frequent discussions and suggestions to deploy a United Nations peacekeeping operation in eastern Ukraine as part of the process for breaking

[26] International Crisis Group, *Rebels Without a Cause: Russia's Proxies in Eastern Ukraine*, Europe Report no. 254 (International Crisis Group: Brussels, 16 July 2019).

[27] On the negotiation and implementation of the Minsk agreements, see Wittke, C., 'The Minsk agreements—more than "scraps of paper"?', *East European Politics*, vol. 35, no. 3 (2019), pp. 264–90; and Landwehr, J., 'No way out? Opportunities for mediation efforts in the Donbas region', *East European Politics*, vol. 35, no. 3 (2019), pp. 291–310.

[28] Baker, P., 'Kurt Volker, Trump's envoy for Ukraine, resigns', *New York Times*, 27 Sep. 2019; and Mackinnon, A. and Gramer, R., 'State department expected to scrap post of Special Envoy to Ukraine', *Foreign Policy*, 7 Nov. 2019.

[29] The Special Monitoring Mission to Ukraine makes weekly and ad hoc reports on the crisis in Ukraine; see <https://www.osce.org/ukrainecrisis>. On the conflict and crisis management in Ukraine, see *SIPRI Yearbook 2017*, pp. 137–138, 146–49; Wilson (note 1); and Anthony, I., Perlo-Freeman, S. and Wezeman, S., 'The Ukraine conflict and its implications', *SIPRI Yearbook 2015*, pp. 55–98.

[30] See e.g. Congressional Research Service (note 7), pp. 15–19.

the Minsk stalemate, but the UN Security Council and its permanent members have been divided on the scope of any mandate.[31]

At a meeting of the Trilateral Contact Group on 17 July 2019, parties committed to another ceasefire in eastern Ukraine. The Ukrainian Government also announced measures to facilitate transit to and from the separatist-controlled areas, including repair of the Stanytsia Luhanska bridge (the sole border crossing point in the Luhansk region).[32] However, as was the case in earlier ceasefires, it broke down almost immediately, with six Ukrainian military personnel killed within three weeks of the ceasefire.[33] Prisoner exchanges are also governed by the Minsk II Agreement. A major exchange took place in September when each side released 35 individuals, including the 24 Ukrainian sailors taken captive by Russia in November 2018.[34] Further prisoner exchanges took place at the end of the year.[35]

More substantially, on 1 October President Zelensky announced that his government had accepted the so-called 'Steinmeier formula' (named after German President Frank-Walter Steinmeier, who proposed a formula for implementing part of the Minsk agreements in 2016 while foreign minister of Germany). The formula entails eastern Ukraine holding local elections in separatist-controlled districts, and if OSCE observers recognize the voting process as free and fair, then a special self-governing status for the territories would be initiated, eventually enabling Ukraine to resume control of its eastern border with Russia.[36] While this formula continues to receive a mixed reaction in Ukraine, Zelensky's acceptance of it (and the prior endorsement by Russia) creates a new opportunity for further negotiations aimed at resolving the conflict.[37] However, several hurdles regarding

[31] Lawson, E., 'Considering a UN peacekeeping mission in the Donbas', Conference report, Royal United Services Institute, Feb. 2019.

[32] OSCE, 'OSCE Chair Lajčák welcomes new recommitment to ceasefire in eastern Ukraine and plans for urgently needed repairs to Stanytsia Luhanska bridge; urges sides to honour and implement them', Press release, 18 July 2019.

[33] Ukrinform, 'Six Ukrainian soldiers killed, nine wounded during "harvest ceasefire"', 7 Aug. 2019.

[34] Grytsenko, O., 'What we know about 35 Ukrainian political prisoners released from Russia', Kyiv Post, 7 Sep. 2019; and Bennets, M., 'Families reunite in Russia–Ukraine prisoner exchange', The Guardian, 7 Sep. 2019.

[35] Agence France-Presse, 'Ukraine and Russia-backed separatists exchange 200 prisoners', The Guardian, 29 Dec. 2019.

[36] On decentralization efforts in Ukraine more broadly, see Romanova, V. and Umland, A., 'Decentralising Ukraine: Geopolitical implications', Survival, vol. 61, no. 5 (2019), pp. 99–112.

[37] International Crisis Group, 'A possible step toward peace in eastern Ukraine', Statement, 9 Oct. 2019. On public attitudes to potential diplomatic solutions, see Haran, O. et al., 'Identity, war, and peace: Public attitudes in the Ukraine-controlled Donbas', Eurasian Geography and Economics, vol. 60, no. 6 (2019), pp. 684–708.

sequencing and implementation of the formula remain.[38] For example, prior to holding elections, bilateral disengagement of Ukrainian and Russian-backed separatist troops along the front line needs to occur. Despite both sides agreeing to do so, it remains to be seen how or if it will happen, although by the end of the year troops had been disengaged in three eastern towns: Petrivske, Stanytsia Luhanska and Zolote.[39]

A meeting of the leaders of France, Germany, Russia and Ukraine in Paris on 9 December 2019 provided further impetus—the first Normandy Format meeting at that level for more than three years. While a comprehensive path towards peace did not emerge, the leaders agreed to implement a 'full and comprehensive' ceasefire by the end of the year, to disengage military forces in three unspecified additional regions by the end of March 2020 and to hold further talks in four months.[40] The final communiqué also endorsed the Steinmeier formula.

Thus, at the end of 2019 despite the promising new opening following political change in Ukraine, fundamental disagreements endured among the parties about the nature of the conflict and their involvement in it, as well as the implementation of existing agreements. It remains to be seen if this pragmatic approach—where the two sides take small steps (prisoner release, disengagement in certain locations etc.) to test the good faith of the adversary—can overcome these fundamental disagreements in 2020.

[38] See e.g. the critique by Gressel, G., 'Ukraine prisoner swap: A sign of hope or desperation?', European Council on Foreign Relations commentary, 26 Sep. 2019; D'Anieri, P., 'War, state and society in Ukraine', *Eurasian Geography and Economics*, vol. 60, no. 6 (2019), pp. 647–55; and Melvin, N., 'Ukraine talks: A peaceful outcome or a peaceful sellout?', Royal United Services Institute commentary, 6 Dec. 2019.

[39] BBC, 'Ukraine and Russia agree to implement ceasefire', 10 Dec. 2019.

[40] President of Russia, 'Paris "Normandy" Summit common agreed conclusions', 9 Dec. 2019; Higgins, A., 'In first meeting with Putin, Zelensky plays to a draw despite a bad hand', *New York Times*, 9 Dec. 2019; and Utkin, S., 'Why the Normandy Summit was not a waste of time', Carnegie Moscow Center, 12 Dec. 2019.

6. Armed conflict and peace processes in the Middle East and North Africa

Overview

There were seven countries with active armed conflicts in the Middle East and North Africa in 2019 (the same as in 2018): Egypt (high-intensity, subnational armed conflict), Iraq (internationalized civil war), Israel (low-intensity, extrastate armed conflict), Libya (internationalized civil war), Syria (major internationalized civil war), Turkey (low-intensity, extrastate and subnational armed conflict) and Yemen (major internationalized civil war). All the armed conflicts had fewer fatalities than in 2018, except for Libya. Many of these conflicts, which have killed hundreds of thousands of people and displaced millions more, were interconnected and involved regional and international powers, as well as numerous non-state actors.

There are three cross-cutting issues that shape security dilemmas in the region: (a) ongoing regional interstate rivalries with a shifting network of external alliances and interests; (b) continuing threats from violent jihadist groups; and (c) increasing competition over water and growing climate change impacts (see section I). On several occasions during 2019 tensions between Iran and the United States (and its Gulf allies) threatened to escalate into a more serious interstate military conflict. Massive anti-government protests occurred in Algeria, Egypt, Iran, Iraq, Jordon, Lebanon, Morocco, the Palestinian territories and Tunisia. There were 14 multilateral peace operations in the MENA region in 2019, two more than in 2018.

The complex and interlinked armed conflicts in Iraq, Syria and Turkey are discussed in section II. Turkey continued its military operations in northern Iraq and carried out a new incursion of northern Syria, after an announced US withdrawal. Russia and Turkey subsequently created a 'safe zone' in north-eastern Syria in October 2019, while the Assad government consolidated its hold in most of the country and achieved further strategic gains. Iraq remained a fragile, largely post-conflict state—although available data suggests that combat-related fatalities remain at the level of a high-intensity armed conflict— with weak institutions and growing protests.

The Israeli–Palestinian conflict (section III) continued with rising instability in the Golan Heights and the West Bank adding to tensions in Gaza. The USA unveiled the economic part of its proposed Israeli–Palestinian peace plan, but at the end of 2019 there appeared to be little prospect of resolving the underlying conflict.

SIPRI Yearbook 2020: Armaments, Disarmament and International Security
www.sipriyearbook.org

In North Africa (section IV) there is a convergence of crises, which also puts the stability of neighbouring states in sub-Saharan Africa at risk. In Libya the fighting escalated between the two competing governments. There was also a deepening internationalization of the conflict—with Egypt, Russia, Saudi Arabia and the United Arab Emirates on one side and Qatar and Turkey on the other, and an array of foreign armed groups and mercenaries on both sides. In Libya the fighting escalated between the two competing governments. There was a deepening internationalization of the conflict—with Egypt, Russia, Saudi Arabia and the United Arab Emirates on one side and Qatar and Turkey on the other, and an array of foreign armed groups and mercenaries on both sides.

The humanitarian crisis in Yemen (section V) remained the worst in the world in 2019. While initial steps were taken to implement the December 2018 Stockholm Agreement, in Yemen's fractured south, fighting intensified and the rivalry within the anti-Houthi coalition risked escalating into a fully fledged civil war within a civil war, until a peace deal was concluded in Riyadh in November 2019. The Stockholm and Riyadh agreements provide a potential path towards a political settlement of the Yemen civil war, but many challenges remain with continued inter- and intra-coalition fighting.

IAN DAVIS

I. Key general developments in the region

IAN DAVIS

There were seven countries with active armed conflicts in the Middle East and North Africa (MENA) in 2019 (the same as in 2018): Egypt (high-intensity, subnational armed conflict), Iraq (internationalized civil war), Israel (low-intensity, extrastate armed conflict), Libya (internationalized civil war), Syria (major internationalized civil war), Turkey (low-intensity, extrastate and subnational armed conflict) and Yemen (major internationalized civil war).[1] All the armed conflicts had fewer fatalities than in 2018, except for Libya (which increased from nearly 12 000 fatalities in 2018 to nearly 21 000 in 2019).[2] Developments in each of the armed conflicts and any related peace processes are covered in subsequent sections: Iraq, Syria and Turkey (section II); the Israeli–Palestinian conflict (section III); Egypt and Libya (section IV); and Yemen (section V).

Many of these conflicts, which have killed hundreds of thousands of people and displaced millions more, were interconnected and involved regional and international powers, as well as numerous non-state actors. Massive anti-government protests have occurred in several states in the region since 2018, including Algeria, Egypt, Iran, Iraq, Jordon, Lebanon, Morocco, the Palestinian territories and Tunisia. Some are calling this the second or new Arab Spring.[3]

There were 14 multilateral peace operations in the MENA region in 2019, two more than in 2018. While most of the operations have been active for many years, one was new in 2019—the United Nations Mission to Support the Hodeidah Agreement (see section V)—while the European Union (EU) Border Assistance Mission in Libya also qualified as a multilateral peace operation under SIPRI's definition following the entry into force of its new mandate in December 2018.[4] One peace operation ended in 2019: the Temporary International Presence in Hebron (see section III). MENA was the only region in which there was an increase in the number of personnel that were deployed in peace operations in 2019: an increase of 5 per cent, from 14 408 on 31 December 2018 to 15 082 on 31 December 2019.[5]

---

[1] For conflict definitions and typologies, see chapter 2, section I, in this volume.

[2] Armed Conflict Location & Event Data Project (ACLED), 'Data export tool', [n.d.].

[3] *The Economist*, 'Protests are making a comeback in the Arab world', 21 Mar. 2019; England, A., 'In Algeria and Sudan, a second Arab spring is brewing', *Financial Times*, 11 Apr. 2019; and Hearst, D., 'The second Arab Spring? Egypt is the litmus test for revolution in the Middle East', Middle East Eye, 16 Apr. 2019.

[4] Council of the EU, 'EUBAM Libya becomes a fully-fledged civilian CSDP mission', Press release, 17 Dec. 2018.

[5] For global and regional trends in multilateral peace operations, see chapter 2, section II, in this volume.

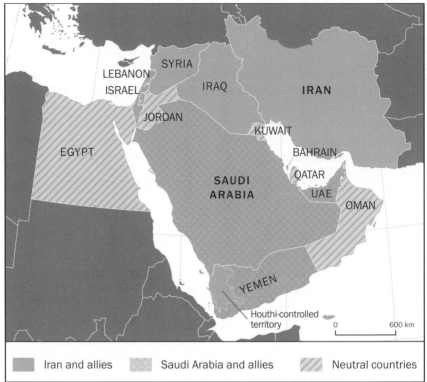

Figure 6.1. Regional rivalries in the Middle East and North Africa

UAE = United Arab Emirates.

Source: *The Economist*, 'Iran was not predestined to become a regional hegemon', 9 Feb. 2019.

There are three cross-cutting issues that shape security dilemmas in the region: (*a*) ongoing regional interstate rivalries with a shifting network of external alliances and interests; (*b*) continuing threats from violent jihadist groups; and (*c*) increasing competition over water and growing climate change impacts.[6] This section briefly examines how these three issues evolved in 2019, and pays particular attention to escalating Iranian–United States tensions.

Shifting alliances and rivalries: Escalating Iranian–US tensions

In the MENA region fault lines intersect in complex ways with shifting alliances and rivalries (see figure 6.1).[7] The most destabilizing and high-risk

---

[6] See Davis, I., 'Armed conflict and peace processes in the Middle East and North Africa', *SIPRI Yearbook 2019*, pp. 81–85.

[7] Malley, R., 'The unwanted wars: Why the Middle East is more combustible than ever', *Foreign Affairs*, Nov./Dec. 2019.

interstate rivalries in 2019 continued to be between Iran (and its allies in Iraq, Lebanon, Syria and Yemen) and an ad hoc group of four states: Israel, Saudi Arabia, the United Arab Emirates (UAE) and the USA.[8] Saudi Arabia—the country with the highest levels of military spending and arms imports in the region—and the UAE (and to a lesser extent some of the other Gulf states) have been actively opposing Iran in Iraq, Lebanon, Syria and Yemen, while Israeli opposition to Iran has been focused on Lebanon and Syria, as well as on the 2015 nuclear agreement (Joint Comprehensive Plan of Action, JCPOA).[9] As it did in 2018 Israel attacked Iranian and Iranian-aligned targets in Syria on several occasions in 2019, but also extended air strikes to Iranian-backed militias in Iraq and Hezbollah in Lebanon.[10] There was also an ongoing Sunni–Sunni rift, with Egypt, Saudi Arabia and the UAE competing with Qatar and Turkey (especially in the Horn of Africa and Libya), and the Islamic State carrying out predominantly Sunni-on-Sunni violence.[11] However, it was the action–reaction dynamic between Iran and the USA (and its Gulf allies) that came to the fore during the year, which on several occasions threatened to escalate from proxy war into a regional-wide interstate military conflict.[12] The geopolitical power struggle between Iran and the USA also complicated UN mediation in Yemen (see section V).

The 'maximum pressure' campaign of the United States

Iranian–US relations have been adversarial since the 1979 Islamic Revolution in Iran, which had its 40th anniversary in February 2019.[13] Relations have continued to deteriorate in recent years, with the US withdrawal from the

---

[8] For further details on the rivalries and how they played out in 2018, see *SIPRI Yearbook 2019* (note 6), pp. 82–84. On the role of geostrategic factors, see Ghoble, V. T., 'Saudi Arabia–Iran contention and the role of foreign actors', *Strategic Analysis*, vol. 43, no. 1 (2019), pp. 42–53. On the Saudi Arabian–UAE relationship, see Ziadah, R., 'The importance of the Saudi–UAE alliance: Notes on military intervention, aid and investment', *Conflict, Security & Development*, vol. 19, no. 3 (2019), pp. 295–300. On the Israeli–Saudi Arabian relationship, see Rynhold, J. and Yaari, M., 'The quiet revolution in Saudi–Israeli relations', *Mediterranean Politics*, Dec. 2019.

[9] Wezeman, P. and Kuimova, A., 'Military spending and arms imports by Iran, Saudi Arabia, Qatar and the UAE', SIPRI Fact Sheet, May 2019. On the JCPOA, see chapter 11, section III, in this volume.

[10] See e.g. Middle East Monitor, 'Satellite images show Iran missile factory in Syria destroyed by Israel air strikes', 15 Apr. 2019; Reuters, 'Israel says air strike in Syria sent "no immunity" message to Iran', 25 Aug. 2019; and Cohen, E. T. and Huggard, K., 'What can we learn from the escalating Israeli raids in Syria?', The Brookings Institution, 6 Dec. 2019.

[11] Agha, H. and Malley, R., 'The Middle East's great divide is not sectarianism', *New Yorker*, 11 Mar. 2019; and International Crisis Group, *Intra-Gulf Competition in Africa's Horn: Lessening the Impact*, Middle East Report no. 206 (International Crisis Group: Brussels, 19 Sep. 2019). On armed conflict in the Horn of Africa, see chapter 7, section IV, in this volume.

[12] See e.g. International Crisis Group, *Averting the Middle East's 1914 Moment*, Middle East Report no. 205 (International Crisis Group: Brussels, 1 Aug. 2019); and *The Economist*, 'The brewing conflict between America and Iran', 9 May 2019.

[13] Jahanpour, F., 'Iran at crossroads on 40th anniversary of its Islamic revolution', The Transnational, 11 Feb. 2019; and *The Economist*, 'Four decades after its revolution, Iran is still stuck in the past', 9 Feb. 2019. On the deep-rooted cultural and ideological dimensions of the conflict, see Chitsazian, M. R. and Taghavi, S. M. A., 'An Iranian perspective on Iran–US relations: Idealists versus materialists', *Strategic Analysis*, vol. 43, no. 1 (2019), pp. 28–41.

JCPOA in 2018, and also due to the US coercive policy of 'maximum pressure' by which the USA hoped to force Iran back to the negotiating table in a weaker position.[14] In turn, Iran seemed convinced that by securing 'forward deterrence' and threatening to resume its pre-JCPOA nuclear activities, the USA and its allies would be forced to reassess their policy options.[15] In an early sign of this action–reaction dynamic the USA designated the Islamic Revolutionary Guard Corps as a 'foreign terrorist organization', and Iran subsequently declared US Central Command and related forces in the Middle East to be terrorists.[16] However, it was the maritime confrontations in the Strait of Hormuz from May through to July 2019—including Iran shooting down a US surveillance drone in June and the US responding with cyberattacks against Iran—and a series of alleged Iranian attacks on Saudi Arabian oil facilities in September that raised the risk of a regional conflagration (see chapter 1, section I).[17]

Despite a further incident involving an Iranian oil tanker in the Red Sea in October, Iranian–US tensions eased somewhat in October and November, while Iran and Saudi Arabia were reported to be working through intermediaries to establish a dialogue.[18] However, despite an exchange of prisoners between Iran and the USA in early December, a series of military clashes in Iraq between Iran's allies and the USA later in the month (see section II) suggested further escalation would be likely in 2020.[19]

---

[14] Katzman, K. et al., *US–Iran Tensions and Implications for US Policy* (Congressional Research Service: 23 Sep. 2019), p. 1; and US Department of State, Office of the Spokesperson, 'Advancing the US maximum pressure campaign on Iran', Fact Sheet, 22 Apr. 2019. On the US withdrawal from the Iran nuclear deal, see Erästö, T., 'Implementation of the Joint Comprehensive Plan of Action', *SIPRI Yearbook 2019*, pp. 378–86.

[15] On Iran's forward deterrence posture and key foreign policy objectives, see Ahmadian, H. and Mohseni, P., 'Iran's Syria strategy: The evolution of deterrence', *International Affairs*, vol. 95, no. 2 (2019), pp. 341–64; and Watling, J., 'Iran's objectives and capabilities: Deterrence and subversion', Royal United Services Institute, Occasional Paper, Feb. 2019.

[16] US Department of State, Office of the Spokesperson, 'Designation of the Islamic Revolutionary Guard Corps', Fact Sheet, 8 Apr. 2019; and Galvin, C., 'A threat to Jus in Bello: Legal implications of Iran's designation of the US Central Command as a Terrorist Organization', Royal United Services Institute commentary, 15 May 2019.

[17] Landler, M. et al., 'US puts Iran on notice and weighs response to attack on oil tankers', *New York Times*, 14 June 2019; Deeks, A. and Andersen, S. R., 'Iran shoots down a US drone: Domestic and international legal implications', Lawfare, 20 June 2019; Shear, M. D. et al., 'Strikes on Iran approved by Trump, then abruptly pulled back', *New York Times*, 20 June 2019; Barnes, J. E. and Gibbons-Neff, T., 'US carried out cyberattacks on Iran', *New York Times*, 22 June 2019; Kirkpatrick, D. D. et al., 'Who was behind the Saudi oil attack? What the evidence shows', *New York Times*, 16 Sep. 2019; and International Crisis Group, 'After the Aramco attack: A Middle East one step closer to its "1914 moment"', Commentary, 20 Sep. 2019. On the proliferation of unmanned aerial vehicles in the Middle East, see *The Economist*, 'The growing appetite for armed drones in the Middle East', 9 Mar. 2019; and Balas, A., 'UAVs in the Middle East: Coming of age', Royal United Services Institute commentary, 10 July 2019.

[18] Fassihi, F. and Hubbard, B., 'Saudi Arabia and Iran make quiet openings to head off war', *New York Times*, 4 Oct. 2019.

[19] Crowley, M., 'In prisoner swap, Iran frees American held since 2016', *New York Times*, 7 Dec. 2019.

Violent jihadist groups

The Salafi–jihadist threat in the MENA region and globally has become fractured and localized, but with the Islamic State and/or al-Qaeda continuing to drive or influence a number of disparate groups.[20] The Islamic State lost its last territorial foothold in Iraq in December 2017 and in Syria in March 2019, and its caliph Abu Bakr al-Baghdadi was killed by US forces in Syria in October 2019.[21] Assessing the size of the remaining jihadi base in the region remains difficult, given its covert nature and a continuing significant component of 'foreign fighters' (individuals that have joined an armed conflict abroad).[22] One estimate puts the Islamic State's current strength in Iraq and Syria at around 18 000 fighters.[23] Despite its setbacks and visible weakening, the Islamic State remained active throughout 2019 in Iraq and Syria.

Water stress and other climate change impacts

Linkages among water scarcity, climate change and insecurity issues in the MENA region are 'complex, diverse and multi-directional'.[24] In several cases climate change and water stress have played direct or indirect roles in recent and ongoing conflicts in the region. The World Economic Forum's 2019 annual meeting in Davos, Switzerland, ranked the threat of a water crisis

---

[20] On the likely future direction of violent radical Islamism, see Clarke, C. P., *After the Caliphate* (Polity Press: Cambridge, 2019); Byman, D., 'Does Al Qaeda have a future?', *Washington Quarterly*, vol. 42, no. 3 (2019), pp. 65–75; and Almohammad, A., 'Seven years of terror: Jihadi organisation's strategies and future directions', International Centre for Counter-Terrorism Research Paper, Aug. 2019. On divisions and competition between al-Qaeda and Islamic State, see Bacon, T. and Grimm Arsenault, E., 'Al Qaeda and the Islamic State's break: Strategic strife or lackluster leadership?', *Studies in Conflict & Terrorism*, vol. 42, no. 3 (2019), pp. 229–63.

[21] *The Economist*, 'Islamic State after the death of Abu Bakr al-Baghdadi', 2 Nov. 2019; Chulov, M., 'Abu Bakr al-Baghdadi's death comes as new order takes shape in Middle East', *The Guardian*, 27 Oct. 2019; and White House, 'The United States and our global partners have liberated all ISIS-controlled territory', 23 Mar. 2019. On the Islamic State, its goals, operations and affiliates, and the international military campaign to defeat it, see Davis, I., 'The aims, objectives and modus operandi of the Islamic State and the international response', *SIPRI Yearbook 2016*, pp. 22–39; and Davis, I., 'The Islamic State in 2016: a failing 'caliphate' but a growing transnational threat?', *SIPRI Yearbook 2017*, pp. 89–104.

[22] No estimates were given e.g. in the UN secretary-general's ninth report on the Islamic State threat: UN Security Council, Ninth report of the Secretary-General on the threat posed by ISIL (Da'esh) to international peace and security and the range of United Nations efforts in support of member states in countering the threat, S/20197612, 31 July 2019. On the historical impact of foreign fighters, see Cragin, R. K. and Stipanovich, S., 'Metastases: Exploring the impact of foreign fighters in conflicts abroad', *Journal of Strategic Studies*, vol. 42, no. 3–4 (2019), pp. 395–424.

[23] Rogers, P., 'The ISIS comeback is happening—but the west isn't learning any lessons', openDemocracy, 22 Aug. 2019.

[24] Schaar, J., 'A confluence of crises on water, climate and security in the Middle East and North Africa', SIPRI Insights on Peace and Security no. 2019/4, July 2019.

as the biggest single risk facing the MENA region.[25] For example, in Libya during 2019 there were repeated attacks and interruptions to the water and energy infrastructure.[26] Large parts of the population in the Persian Gulf are dependent on desalination for their drinking water—there are 30 major desalination plants in Saudi Arabia and 70 in the UAE—and the desalination infrastructure would be highly vulnerable in an armed conflict.[27] In contrast in March and April 2019 half a million Iranians were temporarily displaced due to severe flooding.[28]

[25] Middle East Business Intelligence, 'How the GCC is tackling its looming water crisis', 28 Mar. 2019.

[26] Wintour, P., 'Water supply restored for millions in Libya, averting crisis', The Guardian, 21 May 2019.

[27] Salacanin, S., 'How drinking water has become a major conflict deterrence factor in the Gulf region', New Arab, 21 Aug. 2019.

[28] International Federation of Red Cross and Red Crescent Societies, 'Iran floods: Two million people in need of humanitarian aid', Press release, 15 Apr. 2019.

II. Armed conflict and peace processes in Iraq, Syria and Turkey

IAN DAVIS AND DYLAN O'DRISCOLL

This section reviews the complex and interlinked armed conflicts in Iraq, Syria and Turkey. During 2019 the Assad government consolidated its hold in Syria and achieved further strategic gains, while Iraq remained a fragile, largely post-conflict state with weak institutions and growing protests. In a sign of the growing normalization between the two countries, a border crossing that had been closed since 2012 was reopened in September 2019.[1] Iran remained an influential presence in both countries. In 2019 Turkey continued its military operations in northern Iraq and carried out a new incursion of northern Syria, after United States President Donald J. Trump announced a US withdrawal. An agreement by Russia and Turkey to create a 'safe zone' in north-eastern Syria in October 2019 cemented Russia's role as a key power broker in Syria, moved Turkey further away from its Western orbit and signified a diminished US influence in the region. Overall, the Kurds— an ethnic group of about 30 million people with populations living in Iran, Iraq, Syria and Turkey—were the main losers in a reordering of the regional balance of power during the year (despite some political gains in Iraq).[2]

Declining armed conflict but growing protests in Iraq

Iraq is scarred by decades of armed conflict.[3] But after the territorial defeat of the Islamic State in December 2017 Iraq appeared to be enjoying a period of relative stability. However, underlying sectarian tensions, a low-level Islamic State insurgency in remote northern parts of the country and huge post-war reconstruction, reconciliation and governance challenges remained.[4]

In another indication of the ongoing challenges, three main security actors continued to operate within the state: the Iraqi Security Forces (ISF), supported by the US-led Global Coalition Against Daesh and a North Atlantic Treaty Organization (NATO) training and capacity-building mission; the Kurdish Peshmerga; and the Hashd al-Shaabi, also known as the Popular

---

[1] Reuters, 'Iraq to open border-crossing with Syria on Monday', 28 Sep. 2019.

[2] On the history of the Kurdish struggle for a state, see Özel, S. and Yilmaz, A., 'The Kurds in the Middle East, 2015', *SIPRI Yearbook 2016*, pp. 53–71; and Barkey, H. J., 'The Kurdish awakening: Unity, betrayal, and the future of the Middle East', *Foreign Affairs*, Mar./Apr. 2019.

[3] See various earlier SIPRI Yearbooks. On the consequences for the health of the Iraqi people, see Lafta, R. K. and Al-Nuaimi, M. A., 'War or health: A four-decade armed conflict in Iraq', *Medicine, Conflict and Survival*, vol. 35, no. 3 (2019), pp. 209–26.

[4] O'Driscoll, D., 'Governing the "ungoverned": Suppressing the Islamic State's insurgency in Iraq', SIPRI commentary, 12 Apr. 2019; and International Organization for Migration, 'Iraq Mission, Displacement tracking matrix', Oct. 2019.

Table 6.1. Estimated conflict-related fatalities in Iraq, 2016–19

Event type	2016	2017	2018	2019
Battles	24 595	15 216	2 736	1 710
Explosions/remote violence	25 645	13 921	2 494	1 201
Protests, riots and strategic developments	319	58	57	469
Violence against civilians	5 755	2 823	311	225
Total	56 314	32 018	5 598	3 605

Notes: The first available year for data on Iraq in the Armed Conflict Location & Event Data Project (ACLED) database is 2016. For definitions of event types, see ACLED, 'ACLED definitions of political violence and protest', 11 Apr. 2019.

Source: ACLED, 'Data export tool', [n.d.].

Mobilization Forces (PMF)—an Iraqi state-sponsored umbrella organization composed of a number of predominantly Shia militias (some supported by Iran) and Christian, Shabak, Sunni, Turkmen and Yazidi militias.[5] Integrating the PMF into the ISF has been one of the goals of the Iraqi Government, but progress has been slow. In addition, a small European Union (EU) Advisory Mission in Iraq has been providing advice on civilian security sector reform since October 2017.[6]

In response to continuing Islamic State attacks, which included the new tactic of burning crops, the Iraqi Government launched several military and counterterrorism operations against the group during the year, some involving joint operations that included the ISF, PMF and US-led coalition air strikes.[7] Turkish military operations against the Kurdistan Workers' Party (Partiya Karkerên Kurdistanê, PKK) in northern Iraq also continued in 2019.[8]

Since early 2018 Iraq has often been described as being in a largely post-conflict period. However, while the available data suggests a steep decline in combat-related fatalities in 2018 and 2019 (see table 6.1), they remained at the level of a high-intensity armed conflict (i.e. above 1000 combat-related deaths in the year).[9] In addition, humanitarian conditions in the country remained challenging, with more than 1.4 million people internally displaced and 6.7 million in need of humanitarian assistance, as of December 2019.[10]

---

[5] International Crisis Group, *Iraq's Paramilitary Groups: The Challenge of Rebuilding a Functioning State*, Middle East Report no. 188 (International Crisis Group: Brussels, 30 July 2018). The Global Coalition Against Daesh maintains a website at <https://theglobalcoalition.org/en/>. Details on the NATO Mission Iraq can be found on the NATO website at <https://www.nato.int/cps/en/natohq/topics_166936.htm>.

[6] EU, 'EU Advisory Mission in support of security sector reform in Iraq', 18 Oct. 2018.

[7] Guerin, O., 'Isis in Iraq: Militants "getting stronger again"', BBC, 23 Dec. 2019.

[8] Al Jazeera, 'Turkey launches operation against PKK fighters in northern Iraq', 28 May 2019; and Starr, S., 'Turkey's military interventions in Iraq hardly achieve anything', *Arab Weekly*, 31 Aug. 2019.

[9] On definitions of armed conflicts, see chapter 2, section I, in this volume.

[10] UN Children's Fund, 'Iraq: 2019 humanitarian situation report, reporting period: 1 January 2019 to 31 December 2019', [n.d.].

The role of the United States in Iraq

The US administration has made Iraq one of the front lines in its largely political fight with Iran (see section I), demanding that the country disband several Shiite militias with close to ties to Iran.[11] The USA accused the militias of carrying out several rocket attacks during 2019 against US military (about 5000 US troops remain in the country at the invitation of the Iraqi Government), commercial and diplomatic assets in the country. Despite the prominent role Iran plays in key Iraqi institutions, the Iraqi Government has sought to remain neutral in the Iranian–US rivalry.[12] In December the Iranian–US conflict in Iraq heated up. Responding to a series of attacks on US assets, including one that killed a US contractor, the US launched air strikes on the Iranian-backed Kata'ib Hezbollah militia's base in Iraq, killing at least 25 fighters. Some militia members and their supporters then attacked the US embassy in Baghdad.[13]

Mass protests in the Shia south

In recent years uprisings in Sunni areas and separatist demands of the Kurds have challenged the Iraqi Government. The 2018 regional and national elections in Iraq resulted in a government led by Prime Minister Adil Abdul Mahdi, a former oil minister and Shia politician. Although this represented Iraq's fourth successive peaceful transfer of power, the government faced many economic and political challenges, including the Kurdish boundary question and the need to find a mutually acceptable formula for sharing Iraq's oil and gas revenues.[14] Prime Minister Mahdi managed to improve relations with the Kurds; however, he failed to implement any major changes and was unable to control the militias and their political wings. Correspondingly, his government was seen as a continuation of a political system where the elite divide Iraq's wealth, with little development in the country.[15]

As a result in the Shia south, major anti-government protests demanding economic and political reforms erupted in October 2019, the largest since the end of the US occupation in 2010. Starting in Baghdad on 1 October 2019

[11] Robinson, L., 'Winning the peace in Iraq', *Foreign Affairs*, Sep./Oct. 2019; and International Crisis Group, 'Iraq: Evading the gathering storm', Middle East Briefing no. 70, 29 Aug. 2019.

[12] Arango, T. et al., 'The Iran cables: Secret documents show how Tehran wields power in Iraq', *New York Times*, 18 Nov. 2019.

[13] Aboulenein, A. and Rasheed, A., 'Iraq condemns US air strikes as unacceptable and dangerous', Reuters, 30 Dec. 2019; and O'Driscoll, D., 'Tensions on Iraqi soil likely to overshadow anti-government protest demands', SIPRI commentary, 9 Jan. 2020.

[14] International Crisis Group, *After Iraqi Kurdistan's Thwarted Independence Bid*, Middle East Report no. 199 (International Crisis Group: Brussels, 27 Mar. 2019). On the potential for local peacebuilding in Kirkuk, see O'Driscoll, D., 'Building everyday peace in Kirkuk, Iraq: The potential of locally focused interventions', SIPRI Policy Paper no. 52, Sep. 2019.

[15] O'Driscoll (note 13).

Table 6.2. Estimated conflict-related fatalities in Syria, 2017–19

Event type	2017	2018	2019
Battles	26 577	16 001	8 296
Explosions/remote violence	25 244	11 802	5 752
Protests, riots and strategic developments	222	18	56
Violence against civilians	2 358	2 264	1 169
Total	54 401	30 085	15 273

Notes: The first available year for data on Syria in the Armed Conflict Location & Event Data Project (ACLED) database is 2017. For definitions of event types, see ACLED, 'ACLED definitions of political violence and protest', 11 Apr. 2019.

Source: ACLED, 'Data export tool', [n.d.].

they then spread across much of southern Iraq.[16] Security forces (thought to include a combination of government forces and Iran-aligned Shiite militias), using live ammunition, tear gas and stun grenades against mostly young, unarmed protesters, killed more than 110 people in the first seven days of the protests.[17] By the end of 2019 it was estimated that more than 460 people had been killed and around 25 000 injured in protest-related violence.[18]

At the end of October 2019 Prime Minister Mahdi offered to resign on the condition that a successor could be agreed. The Iraqi Parliament accepted his resignation at the beginning of December.[19] However, the largest bloc in parliament put forward two candidates that were rejected by the protesters and correspondingly were not endorsed by Iraqi President Barham Salih. As a result, Mahdi remained as acting prime minister, and the protest movement continued, with its demands remaining unanswered in 2019.[20]

Armed conflict in Syria

Since 2011 the political power of the Alawite elite in Syria has been contested in a multi-sided armed conflict that, while initially sparked by the Arab Spring, evolved into a complex war involving regional and international powers. Since 2018 there has been a clear de-escalation in the war due to the Syrian Government's consolidation of territorial control and the eventual territorial defeat

---

[16] *The Economist*, 'Iraq's government seems powerless to halt protests in the Shia heartland', 10 Oct. 2019; and Hassan, F. and Rubin, A. J., 'Iraq struggles to contain wave of deadly protests', *New York Times*, 4 Oct. 2019.

[17] Fantappie, M., 'Widespread protests point to Iraq's cycle of social crisis', International Crisis Group commentary, 10 Oct. 2019.

[18] Abdul-Ahad, G. and Graham-Harrison, E., 'Defiant protesters back in Baghdad square within an hour of slaughter', *The Guardian*, 7 Dec. 2019; and Al Jazeera, 'Iraq: Anti-government protesters denounce pro-Iran crowds', 2 Jan. 2020.

[19] BBC, 'Iraq protests: PM Adel Abdul Mahdi "will resign if replacement is found"', 31 Oct. 2019; and Chulov, M., 'Iraq risks breakup as tribes take on Iran's militias in "blood feud"', *The Guardian*, 30 Nov. 2019.

[20] O'Driscoll (note 13).

of the Islamic State in March 2019.[21] Nonetheless, Syria remained the most violent country in the world covered by the Armed Conflict Location & Event Data Project (ACLED) in 2019 and the most dangerous country for civilians. It had the highest number of political violence events in the world in 2019 (17 667 recorded events—19 per cent of the global total), the highest number of events with direct civilian targeting (3432 recorded events that resulted in the highest number of direct civilian fatalities: 4165) and the third-highest number of total reported fatalities (15 273, see table 6.2).[22]

By the end of 2019 the government of President Bashar al-Assad was in control of around 70 per cent of the country, with armed opposition focused on two areas: Idlib province in the north-west and the north-east partially ruled by Kurds. The armed conflict continued to attract a complex and changing cast of combatants, including regional and global powers: Russia and Turkey in the north-west; and Russia, Turkey and the USA in the north-east—where the civil war was pushed in new directions by a protracted and unclear US military withdrawal and Turkey's subsequent new cross-border military operations. In the south-west Iran retained an entrenched presence, and Israel continued with its campaign of air strikes on Iran-allied targets in an attempt to enforce a buffer between itself and the Iranian-backed Syrian Government.[23] Russia became a more influential player in Syria as a whole, while remnants of the Islamic State remained a threat.[24] Throughout 2019 there was also a risk of the Syrian conflict being widened either by the tangle of competing foreign militaries in Syria or the broader Iranian–US rivalry (see section I). There were also ongoing concerns about the Syrian Government possessing chemical weapons.[25]

The north-west: The battle for Idlib

In the north-west of Syria, following the recapture of the Damascus suburbs (eastern Ghouta) and the negotiated surrender of rebels in Homs in 2018, the focus of government forces (backed by Iran and Russia) in 2019 was on the remaining rebel-held province of Idlib—home to 3 million civilians (including 1 million internally displaced people from other parts of Syria)

---

[21] On the Syrian conflict in 2016–18 see Smith, D., 'The Middle East and North Africa: 2016 in perspective', *SIPRI Yearbook 2017*, pp. 77–82; Davis, I., 'Armed conflict in the Middle East and North Africa', *SIPRI Yearbook 2018*, pp. 76–79; and Davis, I., 'Armed conflict and peace processes in the Middle East and North Africa', *SIPRI Yearbook 2019*, pp. 98–107.

[22] Kishi, R. et al., *Year in Review* (ACLED: 2 Mar. 2020), pp. 19–20, 46–47.

[23] Reuters, 'Israel says air strike in Syria sent "no immunity" message to Iran', 25 Aug. 2019; and Specia, M., 'Israel launches airstrikes in Syria to target Iranian forces', *New York Times*, 20 Nov. 2019. On Iran's role in Syria, see Juneau, T., 'Iran's costly intervention in Syria: A pyrrhic victory', *Mediterranean Politics*, vol. 25, no. 1 (2020), pp. 26–44.

[24] See e.g. BBC, 'Syria war: "IS suicide bomber" kills US troops in Manbij', 16 Jan. 2019.

[25] Corder, M., 'Chemical weapons watchdog members voice concerns over Syria', Associated Press, 9 July 2019. Also see chapter 12, section I, in this volume.

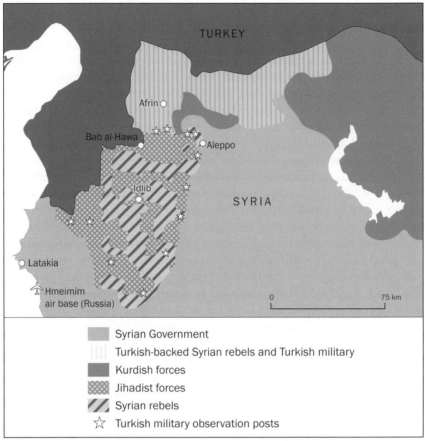

Figure 6.2. Territorial control in Idlib province, February 2019

Source: IHS Control Monitor, 25 Feb. 2019; and and BBC, cited in Sinjab, l., 'Syria war: Jihadist takeover in rebel-held Idlib sparks alarm', BBC, 26 Feb. 2019.

and an estimated 100 000 armed rebels and assorted jihadists.[26] An assault on Idlib seemed to have been averted in September 2018 by a Russian–Turkish agreement to establish and monitor a demilitarized buffer zone to protect civilians in the province.[27] However, armed militant groups—including the main jihadist group with roots in al-Qaeda, Hayat Tahrir al-Sham, with an

---

[26] Lederer, E. M., 'UN: Idlib offensive could spark worst humanitarian emergency', Associated Press, 28 Aug. 2018; *The Economist*, 'The battle for Syria's last rebel redoubt looms', 6 Sep. 2018; and International Crisis Group, 'Saving Idlib from destruction', Middle East Briefing no. 63, 3 Sep. 2018.

[27] International Crisis Group, 'Syria's Idlib wins welcome reprieve with Russia–Turkey deal', Statement, 18 Sep. 2018; and *The Economist*, 'Turkey and Russia cut a deal over Syria', 20 Sep. 2018.

estimated 20 000 fighters—failed to withdraw from the buffer zone and began to assert control in the province (see figure 6.2).[28]

Russian President Vladimir Putin held talks with Turkish President Recap Tayyip Erdoğan in January to discuss a new joint Russian–Turkish plan to stabilize the province. However, in February aerial and ground offensives by pro-government forces (mainly Syrian army troops and aircraft, Iranian-linked militias and Russian aircraft and 'advisers') to oust Hayat Tahrir al-Sham and affiliated armed groups escalated markedly.[29] Details about Russia's 'light footprint' strategy in Syria, including the presence of ground and special forces, remained sketchy.[30] A ceasefire agreement negotiated by Russia and Turkey in June failed to halt the fighting, which intensified again in July and August.[31] Extensive use of air strikes and artillery by pro-government forces led to rising numbers of civilian casualties, although attributing responsibility for some of the atrocities proved controversial.[32] However, the United Nations Independent International Commission of Inquiry on the Syrian Arab Republic reported that essential infrastructure, including hospitals, markets, educational facilities and agricultural resources, were destroyed in the offensive, which also displaced more than 330 000 civilians towards the Turkish border.[33]

On 27 August President Erdoğan and President Putin agreed to uphold their 2018 agreement, while remaining divided over the characterization of some of the key actors in Idlib and on whether the Syrian Government should regain control of the north-west.[34] In September the UN Security Council voted on competing draft resolutions on a cessation of hostilities in Idlib. Belgium, Germany and Kuwait proposed a draft demanding compliance with international law in all counterterrorism efforts, while a draft by China and

---

[28] Sinjab, L., 'Syria war: Jihadist takeover in rebel-held Idlib sparks alarm', BBC, 26 Feb. 2019; and International Crisis Group, *The Best of Bad Options for Syria's Idlib*, Middle East Report no. 197 (International Crisis Group: Brussels, 14 Mar. 2019).

[29] Astakhova, O., 'Russia and Turkey to act to stabilise Syria's Idlib province—Putin', Reuters, 23 Jan. 2019; and The Economist, 'Bashar al-Assad's ruinous campaign to retake Idlib from Syrian rebels', 6 June 2019.

[30] See e.g. Jones, S. G., 'Russia's battlefield success in Syria: Will it be a pyrrhic victory?', *CTC Sentinel*, vol. 12, no. 1 (Oct. 2019), pp. 1–9; Mardasov, A., 'What are Russian special operations forces doing in Idlib?', Al Jazeera, 29 Aug. 2019; and Al-Khalidi, S., 'Syrian rebels say Moscow deploys ground forces in Idlib campaign', Reuters, 18 July 2019. On Russian arms transfers to Syria, see chapter 9, section I, in this volume.

[31] Reuters, 'Russia and Turkey broker ceasefire in Syria's Idlib: Russian news agencies', 12 June 2019.

[32] See e.g. Karam, Z., 'Syrian activists say airstrikes kill 27 in rebel-held town', Associated Press, 22 July 2019; and Reuters, 'At least 544 civilians killed in Russian-led assault in Syria, rights group say', *The Guardian*, 7 July 2019.

[33] UN General Assembly, 'Report of the Independent International Commission of Inquiry on the Syrian Arab Republic', A/HRC/42/51, 15 Aug. 2019.

[34] Al Jazeera, 'Putin, Erdogan hail close defence ties as Idlib divisions remain', 27 Aug. 2019.

Russia aimed to exempt operations against armed non-state groups.[35] The UN Security Council failed to reach consensus on either resolution.[36]

In November and December Russian and Syrian forces intensified air strikes and started a ground offensive in the north-west, taking territory from rebel groups and creating a new wave of refugees. President Erdoğan vowed not to accept any of these latest Syrian refugees and called for an end to the violence.[37] As had been forecast earlier in 2019 Syria now faced potentially the 'worst humanitarian disaster' this century, with more than 235 000 people fleeing the latest fighting in the Idlib region.[38]

The north-east: A protracted United States withdrawal triggers a new Turkish offensive

At the end of 2018 the north-east of Syria was relatively if precariously stable under the control of the US-backed Syrian Democratic Forces (SDF), led primarily by a Kurdish-dominated armed group, the People's Protection Units (Yekîneyên Parastina Gel, YPG). However, Turkey regards the YPG as a terrorist organization due to its links to the PKK, which has waged an insurgency against Turkey since the 1980s. Turkish-backed Syrian rebels took control of the previously Kurdish-held Afrin province in March 2018, but throughout most of 2018 the main conflict was between the US-backed SDF and remnants of the Islamic State.[39] Under a June 2018 Turkish–US road map for governance and security arrangements in the city of Manbij, Turkey and the USA had commenced joint patrols in October 2018, and the US military had begun to establish observation posts to help Turkey secure its border.[40] However, in December 2018 President Trump announced the withdrawal of approximately 2000 US troops from Syria. Although this later turned out to be only a partial withdrawal, it left the 60 000-strong SDF/YPG potentially exposed to an attack either from Turkey and Turkish-backed Syrian forces

[35] UN Security Council, 'Belgium, Germany and Kuwait: Draft resolution', S/2019/756, 19 Sep. 2019; UN Security Council, 'China and Russian Federation: Draft resolution', S/2019/757, 19 Sep. 2019; and Nichols, M., 'UN Security Council to vote on rival calls for truce in Syria's Idlib', Reuters, 18 Sep. 2019.

[36] The draft resolution by Belgium, Germany and Kuwait received 12 out of 15 votes, while 9 members voted against the China–Russia draft resolution and 4 abstained: UN News, 'Security Council: Two draft resolutions, zero consensus on ceasefire in Syria's Idlib', 19 Sep. 2019.

[37] Gumrukcu, T., 'Erdogan says Turkey cannot handle new migrant wave from Syria, warns Europe', Reuters, 22 Dec. 2019; and Mckernan, B. and Akoush, H., 'Thousands flee north-west Syria amid fierce assault toy Assad', *The Guardian*, 24 Dec. 2019.

[38] Graham-Harrison, E. and Akoush, H., 'More than 235,000 people have fled Idlib region in Syria, says UN', *The Guardian*, 27 Dec. 2019; and France 24, 'UN warns "worst humanitarian disaster" of the century is unfolding in Syria's Idlib', 31 July 2019.

[39] Chulov, M., 'ISIS withdraws from last urban stronghold in Syria', *The Guardian*, 14 Dec. 2018.

[40] Rempfer, K., 'The US military is putting new observation posts in northern Syria', Military Times, 21 Nov. 2018.

or the Syrian Government.[41] Throughout 2019 the USA continued to send mixed messages about its role and commitment to allies in Syria.[42]

In January 2019 President Trump and President Erdoğan discussed the possibility of establishing a safe zone in north-eastern Syria, which might allow the return of many of the 3.6 million Syrian refugees residing in Turkey.[43] As the SDF/YPG closed in on the last pocket of Islamic State territory in eastern Syria in February, the USA announced it would leave 'a small peacekeeping group' of around 200 troops in the country.[44] France and the United Kingdom agreed to deploy additional forces to Syria to compensate for the US withdrawal.[45] In March, after capturing the last remaining Islamic State territory, the SDF called on the international community to establish an international court in north-east Syria to prosecute Islamic State detainees.[46]

With Turkey threatening to attack the YPG if Turkey and the USA failed to reach agreement, a preliminary deal was finally agreed on 7 August to establish a joint operations centre to coordinate and manage the setting up of a safe zone.[47] In September President Erdoğan threatened to force out at least a million Syrian refugees, either by moving them into the proposed safe zone or by sending them to Europe.[48] A few days later, in an effort to reduce tensions with Turkey, the US military announced it was setting up joint Turkish–US reconnaissance flights and ground patrols.[49]

In another major shift in US policy on 6 October President Trump announced the withdrawal of US troops from the area, but in a tweet the next day warned President Erdoğan that he would 'destroy and obliterate' the

---

[41] Landler, M. et al., 'Trump to withdraw US forces from Syria, declaring "We have won against ISIS"', *New York Times*, 19 Dec. 2018; 'The US withdrawal from Syria', *Strategic Comments*, vol. 25, no. 1 (2019), pp. i–iii; and International Crisis Group, *Squaring the Circles in Syria's North East*, Middle East Report no. 204 (International Crisis Group: Brussels, 31 July 2019).

[42] See e.g. Landler et al. (note 41); and Associated Press, 'Bolton: US troops will not leave Syria till ISIS beaten and Kurds protected', *The Guardian*, 6 Jan. 2019.

[43] Reuters, 'Trump, Erdogan discuss creation of secure zone in northern Syria—Turkish presidency', 14 Jan. 2019; and Al Jazeera, 'Erdogan: Safe zones in Syria will allow refugees to return home', 28 Jan. 2019.

[44] Karni, A. and Gibbons-Neff, T., '200 US troops to stay in Syria, White House says', *New York Times*, 21 Feb. 2019; and BBC, 'Islamic State group: Civilians evacuated from last Syria enclave', 20 Feb. 2019.

[45] Sabbagh, D., 'UK and France to send further forces to Syria in aid of US withdrawal', *The Guardian*, 9 July 2019.

[46] Kurdistan 24, 'SDF calls for creation of international court to prosecute ISIS members in Syria', 25 Mar. 2019.

[47] Reuters, 'Turkey will launch operation in Syria if safe zone not established: Minister', 22 July 2019; and Fox, T., 'Turkey, US agree to set up operation centre for Syria safe zone', Al Jazeera, 7 Aug. 2019.

[48] Gall, C., 'Turkey's radical plan: Send a million refugees back to Syria', *New York Times*, 10 Sep. 2019.

[49] Schmitt, E., 'US poised to send 150 troops to patrol northeastern Syria', *New York Times*, 12 Sep. 2019.

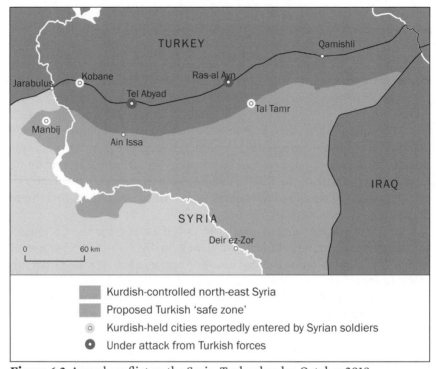

Figure 6.3. Armed conflict on the Syria–Turkey border, October 2019

Source: McKernan, B., 'Russian troops patrol between Turkish and Syrian forces on border', *The Guardian*, 15 Oct. 2019.

Turkish economy if any offensive went too far.[50] Nonetheless, on 9 October Turkey launched a major offensive against the Kurdish-led forces in the border area.[51] The next day, with tens of thousands of civilians fleeing the area, the UN Security Council met in an inconclusive emergency closed-door meeting to discuss the situation.[52] Several EU member states imposed restrictions on arms exports to Turkey.[53]

---

[50] Schmitt, E. et al., 'President endorses Turkish military operation in Syria, shifting US policy', *New York Times*, 7 Oct. 2019; Donald J. Trump (@realDonaldTrump), Twitter, 7 Oct. 2019; and Ford, W., 'Congress on US policy toward Syria and Turkey: An overview of recent hearings', Lawfare, 29 Oct. 2019.

[51] Recep Tayyip Erdoğan (@RTErdogan), Twitter, 9 Oct. 2019; *The Economist*, 'Turkey launches an attack on northern Syria', 10 Oct. 2019; and Koseoglu, S., 'Will Turkey succeed in creating a "safe zone" for Syrians?', Al Jazeera, 8 Oct. 2019.

[52] Rettman, A., 'EU stands alone against US and Russia on Syria', *EUobserver*, 11 Oct. 2019; and UN News, 'Civilians "must not be a target"', urges UNHCR, following military escalation in northern Syria', 10 Oct. 2019.

[53] Rettman, A., 'EU countries to halt arms sales to Turkey', *EUobserver*, 14 Oct. 2019. On attempts to impose an EU arms embargo on Turkey, see chapter 14, section II, in this volume. On arms transfers to Turkey, see chapter 9, sections I and II, in this volume.

In the wake of the US withdrawal announcement—criticized by the SDF as a 'stab in the back'—the Kurdish-led forces initiated talks with the Syrian Government for security support to counter the Turkish offensive.[54] In a deal brokered by Russia, the SDF/YPG agreed to surrender the border cities of Kobane and Manbij (where US forces were previously stationed) to Syrian Government forces, thereby potentially widening the conflict in north-east Syria (see figure 6.3). In an effort to prevent Syrian–Turkish clashes, Russian military police began patrolling the area around Manbij.[55] There were also reports of Islamic State supporters escaping from detention camps amidst the chaos.[56] Meanwhile, President Trump announced new sanctions on Turkish government agencies and officials in response to their 'heinous acts' in Syria, as well as suspending negotiations on a $100 billion trade deal with Turkey.[57] A second closed-door meeting of the UN Security Council on 16 October agreed a brief statement, but stopped short of calling for a ceasefire.[58]

A five-day ceasefire negotiated by US Vice President Michael Pence and President Erdoğan on 17 October was designed to allow the YPG to withdraw from the safe zone, but appeared to do little to prevent the fighting.[59] Reports also suggested that President Trump was now considering keeping about 200 US troops in Syria to secure the oil fields.[60] However, within days the Turkish–US deal was overtaken by events.

The Russian–Turkish Sochi agreement

Presidents Erdoğan and Putin, meeting in Sochi, Russia, on 22 October, after expiry of the US-brokered ceasefire, agreed their own arrangement for territorial control and a ceasefire in the north-eastern area once patrolled by the USA.[61] As a result of this ceasefire, which ostensibly ended Turkey's offensive, President Trump removed sanctions against Turkish officials.

---

[54] McKernan, B., 'Turkey–Syria offensive: Kurds reach deal with Damascus to stave off assault', *The Guardian*, 14 Oct. 2019; and Safi, M. and Mckernan, B., 'Syrian troops enter Kurdish fight against Turkish forces', *The Guardian*, 14 Oct. 2019.

[55] McKernan, B., 'Russian troops patrol between Turkish and Syrian forces on border', *The Guardian*, 15 Oct. 2019.

[56] McKernan, B., 'At least 750 ISIS affiliates escape Syria camp after Turkish shelling', *The Guardian*, 13 Oct. 2019.

[57] Rappeport, A. and Crowley, M., 'Trump imposes sanctions on Turkey as Syria conflict intensifies', *New York Times*, 14 Oct. 2019.

[58] UN Audiovisual Library, 'UN/Syria Security Council', 16 Oct. 2019.

[59] White House, 'The United States and Turkey agree to ceasefire in Northeast Syria', Statement, 17 Oct. 2019; and Khadder, K. et al., 'Kurds say Turkey is violating hours-old "ceasefire" in northern Syria', CNN, 18 Oct. 2019.

[60] Schmitt, E. and Haberman, M., 'Trump said to favor leaving a few hundred troops in eastern Syria', *New York Times*, 20 Oct. 2019; and Borger, J. and Chulov, M., 'US deploying more troops around Syria oil fields after killing of Isis leader', *The Guardian*, 28 Oct. 2019.

[61] Al Jazeera, 'Full text of Turkey, Russia agreement on northeast Syria', 22 Oct. 2019; Fraser, S. and Isachenkov, V., 'Russia, Turkey seal power in northeast Syria with new accord', Associated Press, 22 Oct. 2019; and *The Economist*, 'Russia and Turkey agree to carve up northern Syria', 24 Oct. 2019.

The Sochi agreement allows Turkish forces to retain seized territory while Russian and Syrian forces will control the remainder of the Syria–Turkey border. It remained unclear whether the deal would permit the resettlement of significant numbers of Syrian refugees and how much of the existing YPG self-government structures would be preserved as the presence of the Syrian Government increased. The USA was also considering new options in north-east Syria, including leaving about 500 troops and sending dozens of battle tanks to the area.[62]

By the end of October Kurdish fighters had withdrawn from the safe zone, clearing the way for Russia and Turkey to jointly secure the area.[63] In late November the remaining 500–600 US troops had reportedly resumed counterterrorism operations against the Islamic State in the area still controlled by the SDF/YPG.[64] At the end of 2019 a challenging but fragile stalemate had returned to north-eastern Syria, with the SDF/YPG-protected autonomous administration continuing to govern areas in most of the north-east not held by Turkey or its Syrian allies.

The humanitarian impact of the armed conflict

Despite the territorial focus of the armed conflict narrowing, it remains one of the most devastating in the world, with over half of the Syrian population still displaced at the end of 2019. After more than eight years of war, more than a third of Syria's infrastructure has been destroyed or damaged. Although there are no reliable casualty statistics, over 400 000 Syrians are thought to have died due to the fighting.[65] ACLED estimates that there were approximately 15 200 fatalities in 2019 (about half the number of 2018 and two thirds less than in 2017—see table 6.2).[66] In 2019 Syria also remained the country worst affected by explosive weapons such as large bombs and missiles, indirect fire weapons (mortars, rockets and artillery) and improvised explosive devices.[67]

---

[62] Lubold, G. and Youssef, N.A., 'US weighs leaving more troops, sending battle tanks to Syria', *Wall Street Journal*, 24 Oct. 2019.

[63] Rasmussen, S. E., 'Kurdish fighters withdraw from Syrian border area as cease-fire ends, Russia says', *Wall Street Journal*, 29 Oct. 2019; and International Crisis Group, 'Steadying the new status quo in Syria's north east', Middle East Briefing no. 72, 27 Nov. 2019.

[64] Schmitt, E., 'US resumes large-scale operations against ISIS in northern Syria', *New York Times*, 25 Nov. 2019; and Stewart, P., 'US military completes pullback from northeast Syria, Esper says', 5 Dec. 2019.

[65] International Crisis Group, *Ways out of Europe's Syria Reconstruction Conundrum*, Middle East Report no. 209 (International Crisis Group: Brussels, 25 Nov. 2019); and Humud, C. et al., 'Counting casualties in Syria and Iraq: Process and challenges', Congressional Research Service Insight, 12 Apr. 2016.

[66] ACLED, 'Data export tool', [n.d.].

[67] Action on Armed Violence, 'Explosive violence in 2019', 7 Jan. 2020. On the issue of explosive weapons in populated areas, also see chapter 13, section I, in this volume.

Clearance of landmines and remnants of other explosive weapons could take up to 50 years.[68]

Conflict continued to be the driver of humanitarian needs with over half the population still displaced. The latest report by the Independent International Commission of Inquiry on the Syrian Arab Republic, which was established by the UN Human Rights Council in 2011, highlighted how ongoing hostilities had increased the number of displaced Syrians to approximately 13 million, including 6.7 million refugees (up from 5.6 million in 2018), hosted mainly by Jordan, Lebanon and Turkey, and 6.2 internally displaced people (up from 6 million in 2018).[69] The commission also reported that up to 70 000 people, mainly women and children, remained interned in inhumane conditions at Al-Hol camp in the north-east, where SDF/YPG forces guard families of imprisoned Islamic State fighters.

At the end of 2019 about 11.1 million people (down from 13.1 million in 2018) required humanitarian assistance, 6.6 million were food insecure (6.7 million in 2018) and a further 2.6 million were at risk of acute food insecurity (4.5 million in 2018).[70] Of the $3.29 billion requested in the 2019 Humanitarian Response Plan for Syria, only $1.9 billion (58 per cent) had been funded.[71]

Actual or suspected war crimes have been reported at every stage of Syria's civil war, and potential war crimes continued to be committed in 2019.[72] There was also growing evidence of the scale of human rights abuses by the Syrian Government, including torture and enforced disappearances.[73]

The wider Syrian peace processes

The main peace efforts in Syria have included long-standing UN-mediated talks, regular discussions by the Astana Group (Iran, Russia and Turkey), an October 2018 Quartet Meeting (France, Germany, Russia and Turkey) and a fragile patchwork of localized de-escalation agreements and ceasefires.[74] The centrepiece of UN efforts—the creation of a committee to write a new

---

[68] Foreign & Commonwealth Office, 'Clearance of improvised explosive devices in the Middle East, Monday 22–Wednesday 24 May 2017', Wilton Park Report WP1548, June 2017.

[69] UN General Assembly, A/HRC/42/51 (note 33).

[70] World Food Programme, 'WFP Syria situation report no. 11, November 2019', Jan. 2020.

[71] United Nations Office for the Coordination of Humanitarian Affairs (OCHA), 'Humanitarian response plan, January–December 2019, Syrian Arab Republic', Aug. 2019; and OCHA, 'Humanitarian update, Syrian Arab Republic', no. 7, 23 Dec. 2019.

[72] See e.g. UN General Assembly, A/HRC/42/51 (note 33); Amnesty International, 'Syria: Damning evidence of war crimes and other violations by Turkish forces and their allies', 18 Oct. 2019; and Broches, E., 'An accountability update for crimes committed in Syria', Lawfare, 13 Jan. 2020.

[73] Barnard, A., 'Inside Syria's secret torture prisons: How Bashar al-Assad crushed dissent', New York Times, 11 May 2019.

[74] On the Syrian Government using ceasefires to forcibly reassert its authority, see Sosnowski, M., 'Ceasefires as violent state-building: Local truce and reconciliation agreements in the Syrian civil war', Conflict, Security & Development (2019).

Table 6.3. Estimated conflict-related fatalities in Turkey, 2016–19

Event type	2016	2017	2018	2019
Battles	3 648	2 294	1 640	742
Explosions/remote violence	1 365	526	255	165
Protests, riots and strategic developments	14	4	8	4
Violence against civilians	166	97	28	14
Total	**5 193**	**2 921**	**1 931**	**925**

Notes: The first available year for data on Turkey in the Armed Conflict Location & Event Data Project (ACLED) database is 2016. For definitions of event types, see ACLED, 'ACLED definitions of political violence and protest', 11 Apr. 2019.

Source: ACLED, 'Data export tool', [n.d.].

Syrian constitution—was still not in place at the end of the 2018, and there had been no significant progress in the Astana process.[75]

However, at the end of October 2019, 150 delegates (50 each from the government, opposition and civil society) met in Geneva, Switzerland, for the first time to begin drafting a new Syrian constitution—the first step in a political process that will lead to UN-supervised elections under UN Security Council Resolution 2254 adopted in 2015.[76] Almost 30 per cent of the delegates were women, and decisions have to be taken by consensus, where possible, or a majority of 75 per cent, so that no bloc can decide the outcomes.[77]

At the end of 2019 an outline of how the fighting might end was becoming clearer. An eventual Turkish withdrawal from the north-east will likely be facilitated by disarming the SDF/YPG and re-establishing Syrian Government authority in those areas. Similarly, some of the rebels in Idlib are likely to accept a deal with the Syrian Government, while the Salafi–jihadist groups are likely to disperse or be killed or captured. However, reconstruction will take a long time, and reconciliation among the various conflict parties is likely to be an even longer-term process.[78]

Armed conflict between Turkey and the Kurds

Turkish military action against Kurdish forces in northern Syria, and Turkey's sensitivity to proposals to strengthen Kurdish forces or support some degree of Kurdish political autonomy in either Iraq or Syria, have to be understood in the light of the conflict inside predominantly Kurdish

---

[75] On the key developments in the peace processes in 2018, see *SIPRI Yearbook 2019* (note 21), pp. 105–107.

[76] Bibbo, B., 'Long-awaited Syria constitutional committee meets for the first time', Al Jazeera, 30 Oct. 2019; and UN Security Council Resolution 2254, 18 Dec. 2015.

[77] BBC, 'Syria war: UN backed talks on new constitution begin in Geneva', 30 Oct. 2019.

[78] Samaha, N., 'Can Assad win the peace?', European Council on Foreign Relations policy brief, May 2019; and Barnes-Dacey, J., 'The geopolitics of reconstruction: Who will rebuild Syria', European Council on Foreign Relations commentary, 16 Sep. 2019.

south-eastern Turkey. This area has been the focus of an almost continuous armed confrontation between Turkish security forces and the PKK since 1984, punctuated by occasional ceasefires. The collapse in July 2015 of the Kurdish–Turkish peace process (also known as the resolution process) led to a new cycle of violence.[79]

The armed confrontation continued in 2019. Two independent sources gave differing estimates of fatalities in 2019: according to the International Crisis Group, 482 people were killed (27 civilians, 369 PKK militants and 86 state security forces), down from 563 in 2018, with nearly 4800 deaths in the conflict in total since July 2015, while ACLED estimated that there were 925 conflict-related fatalities in 2019 (representing a continuous decline in fatalities since 2016, as shown in table 6.3).[80]

Ending this conflict is inextricably linked to the creation of peaceful relations between Turkey and the YPG in Syria, but at the close of 2019 there was no prospect of peace talks between the parties.

---

[79] On the role of the Kurds in Turkish politics, see Özel and Yilmaz (note 2); and Christofis, N., 'The state of the Kurds in Erdoğan's "new" Turkey', *Journal of Balkan and Near Eastern Studies*, vol. 21, no. 3 (2019), pp. 251–59. On the transformation of Turkey under President Erdoğan, see Hakan Yavuz, M. and Erdi Öztürk, A., 'Turkish secularism and Islam under the reign of Erdoğan', *Southeast European and Black Sea Studies*, vol. 19, no. 1 (2019), pp. 1–9. On the collapse of the peace process, see Toktamış, K. F., '(Im)possibility of negotiating peace: 2005–2015 peace/reconciliation talks between the Turkish government and Kurdish politicians', *Journal of Balkan and Near Eastern Studies*, vol. 21, no. 3 (2019), pp. 286–303.

[80] International Crisis Group, 'Turkey's PKK conflict: A visual explainer', [n.d.]; and ACLED, 'Data export tool', [n.d.].

III. The Israeli–Palestinian conflict and peace process

IAN DAVIS

The history of Israel's occupation of the Gaza Strip, Golan Heights and West Bank—territories it captured in the 1967 Arab–Israeli War—is extensive and complex.[1] In 2018 the Israeli–Palestinian conflict returned to the centre of international attention when the ongoing civil unrest and armed conflict between Israel and Hamas and other Palestinian organizations in Gaza rose to its highest level since the 2014 Gaza–Israel War.[2] Israeli settlement expansion in the occupied territories continued, while a new study highlighted Israeli targeting of infrastructure and restrictions on development.[3] At the beginning of 2019 rising West Bank instability added to the tensions in Gaza.

In 2019 Israeli forces killed 135 Palestinians (108 in the Gaza Strip and 27 in the West Bank), with over 15 300 injured. (A total of 295 Palestinians had been killed and more than 29 000 injured by Israeli forces in 2018, mostly in the protests along the Gaza–Israel border.) In 2019 Palestinians killed 10 Israelis and injured at least 120 others.[4]

In February 2019 a commission of inquiry by the United Nations Human Rights Council reported evidence of Israeli forces committing crimes against humanity during the 2018 protests by targeting unarmed civilians, including children. The panel's report called on Israel to investigate 'every protest-related killing and injury in accordance with international standards' to determine whether war crimes or crimes against humanity had been committed.[5] Israel did not cooperate with the commission, accused it of bias and blamed Hamas for the violence.[6] In December 2019 the International Criminal Court, having commenced a preliminary investigation in 2015 into the 'situation in Palestine', concluded that there was sufficient evidence

---

[1] See e.g. Shlaim, A., *The Iron Wall: Israel and the Arab World* (W. W. Norton: New York, 2014); Thrall, N., *The Only Language they Understand: Forcing Compromise in Israel and Palestine* (Metropolitan Books: New York, 2017); and Anziska, S., *Preventing Palestine: A Political History from Camp David to Oslo* (Princeton University Press: Princeton, 2018).

[2] On developments in 2018, see Davis, I., 'Armed conflict and peace processes in the Middle East and North Africa', *SIPRI Yearbook 2019*, pp. 90–94.

[3] Al Jazeera, 'Israeli settlement activity surged in Trump era: Monitor group', 2 Jan. 2019; and Weinthal, E. and Sowers, J., 'Targeting infrastructure and livelihoods in the West Bank and Gaza', *International Affairs*, vol. 95, no. 2 (2019), pp. 319–40.

[4] United Nations Office for the Coordination of Humanitarian Affairs (OCHA), '2018: More casualties and food insecurity, less funding for humanitarian aid', 27 Dec. 2018; and OCHA, 'Humanitarian bulletin occupied Palestinian territory', Dec. 2019.

[5] UN Human Rights Council, 'Report of the detailed findings of the independent international Commission of inquiry on the protests in the Occupied Palestinian Territory', A/HRC/40/CRP.2, 18 Mar. 2019.

[6] Cumming-Bruce, N., 'Israelis may have committed crimes against humanity in Gaza protests, UN says', *New York Times*, 28 Feb. 2019.

to open a formal investigation into alleged war crimes in the occupied territories.[7]

The conflict in Gaza

Hamas—a Palestinian Sunni–Islamist organization, with a social service wing (Dawah) and a military wing (the Izz ad-Din al-Qassam Brigades)—has been the de facto governing authority of the Gaza Strip since the 2007 Fatah–Hamas conflict. The 2007 Fatah–Hamas conflict, also referred to as the Palestinian Civil War, was a conflict between the two main Palestinian political parties, Fatah and Hamas, after Hamas won the 2006 elections, resulting in the split of the Palestinian Authority in 2007. Fatah, under Palestinian President Mahmoud Abbas, retains control of the West Bank. Hamas and Israel fought asymmetric wars in 2008–2009, 2012 and 2014, which resulted in a high number of Palestinian civilian casualties. Gaza has also been subject to an Egyptian and Israeli blockade for over a decade, with huge economic and humanitarian consequences: 80 per cent of the population depend on foreign aid to meet daily living requirements.[8] In 2018 frequent military exchanges between Hamas (rockets fired into Israel) and Israel (air strikes in Gaza) threatened to escalate into a new full-scale confrontation, until another ceasefire was agreed in November 2018.[9]

The ceasefire became strained in March 2019 by further military exchanges between Hamas and Israel, before Hamas announced another ceasefire on 26 March, brokered by Egypt and the UN.[10] However, on 4 and 5 May a further round of cross-border exchanges between the two main Gaza groups (Hamas and the Islamic Jihad Movement in Palestine) and Israel resulted in further fatalities, before a new, tentative ceasefire was reached.[11]

After a period of relative calm, violence escalated again in November 2019. Israel killed Baha Abu al-Ata, a senior commander of Islamic Jihad in an air strike on 12 November. Islamic Jihad responded by firing about 450 rockets into Israel, with most landing in open areas or intercepted by

---

[7] International Criminal Court, 'Statement of ICC Prosecutor, Fatou Bensouda, on the conclusion of the preliminary examination of the situation in Palestine, and seeking a ruling on the scope of the Court's territorial jurisdiction', 20 Dec. 2019.

[8] Rankin, J., 'One million face hunger in Gaza after US cut to Palestine aid', *The Guardian*, 15 May 2019.

[9] Holmes, O. and Balousha, H., 'Israel and Hamas agree to Gaza ceasefire after intense violence', *The Guardian*, 13 Nov. 2018; and *The Economist*, 'The politics surrounding an assassination and its aftermath in Gaza', 14 Nov. 2019.

[10] Halbfinger, D. M., 'Israel strikes after rockets are fired from Gaza to Tel Aviv', *New York Times*, 14 Mar. 2019; Kershner, I., 'Gaza rockets sets off daylong battle between Hamas and Israel', *New York Times*, 25 Mar. 2019; Baconi, T., 'Stopping an unwanted war in Gaza', International Crisis Group Q&A, 26 Mar. 2019; and Associated Press, 'Hamas says cease-fire reached with Israel', 26 Mar. 2019.

[11] Kershner, I., 'Fragile cease-fire takes hold between Israel and Gaza after weekend attacks', *New York Times*, 6 May 2019; and *The Economist*, 'Israel and Hamas come close to war', 9 May 2019.

Israel's Iron Dome defence system. In turn, Israel increased its air strikes on Gaza, including on homes suspected of harbouring militants, killing at least 34 Palestinians.[12] An Egyptian-mediated ceasefire between Israel and Islamic Jihad forces appeared to be holding after two days of military exchanges.[13]

The conflicts in Golan Heights and the West Bank

In January 2019 Israel expelled a civilian observer mission, the Temporary International Presence in Hebron (TIPH), which was established in 1994 to protect residents in the Palestinian city of Hebron in the West Bank.[14] Norway (one of the six countries providing personnel for the TIPH) warned that the mission's withdrawal might violate the Oslo accords—a set of agreements between Israel and the Palestine Liberation Organization in 1993 and 1995.[15]

In March 2019 President Donald J. Trump called for United States recognition of Israel's sovereignty over the Golan Heights, a region captured from Syria in 1967 and formally annexed in 1981.[16] The decision reversed decades of US policy (akin to his December 2017 recognition of Jerusalem as Israel's capital) and defied international law. In addition, it was feared that it might also lead to Israel's future annexation of parts of the West Bank— something Prime Minister Benjamin Netanyahu promised if re-elected in the 9 April general election.[17] However, neither that election nor a second on 17 September were able to provide a clear path to a coalition government, and a third general election was due to take place in March 2020.[18]

A further barrier to Israel's annexation of Palestinian territory was removed on 18 November 2019, with a US announcement that it would no longer consider Israeli settlements in the West Bank a violation of international law.[19] The Israeli settlements are deemed illegal under the 1949

---

[12] Holmes, O., 'Israel strikes on Islamic Jihad chiefs prompt reprisal rocket attacks', *The Guardian*, 12 Nov. 2019; and Akram, F. and Federman, J., 'Amid Gaza fighting, Israel could face questions on tactics', Associated Press, 15 Nov. 2019.

[13] Al-Mughrabi, N. and Williams, D., 'Islamic Jihad offers Israel truce as Gaza toll hits 26', Reuters, 13 Nov. 2019.

[14] Landau, N. and Berger, Y., 'Israel to expel international monitoring force in Hebron after 20-year presence', Haaretz, 28 Jan. 2019.

[15] The other countries suppling observers were: Denmark, Italy, Sweden, Switzerland and Turkey. Middle East Monitor, 'PA calls on UN for protection after Israel expels international observers', 29 Jan. 2019; and *Times of Israel*, 'Norway says Israel's axing of Hebron observer force may violate Oslo accords', 30 Jan. 2019.

[16] Landler, M. and Wong, E., 'In Golan Heights, Trump bolsters Israel's Netanyahu but risks roiling Middle East', *New York Times*, 21 Mar. 2019.

[17] Halbfinger, D. M. and Kershner, I., 'Netanyahu says Golan Heights move "proves you can" keep occupied territories', *New York Times*, 26 Mar. 2019; and Associated Press, 'Netanyahu vows to annex West Bank settlements if re-elected', Politico, 7 Apr. 2019.

[18] Holmes, O., 'Israel heads for unprecedented third election in a year as stalemate continues', *The Guardian*, 11 Dec. 2019.

[19] Jakes, L. and Halbfinger, D. M., 'In shift, US says Israeli settlements in West Bank do not violate international law', *New York Times*, 18 Nov. 2019.

Geneva Convention relative to the Protection of Civilian Persons in Time of War, which states 'the occupying power shall not deport or transfer parts of its own civilian population into the territory it occupies'.

The peace process

Intermittent peace discussions have been held since the beginning of the conflict. Since 2003 the basis for an Israeli–Palestinian peace agreement has been a two-state solution: an independent state of Palestine alongside the state of Israel. The latest direct negotiations between the two sides collapsed in 2014.[20] In April 2019 UN Under-Secretary-General for Political and Peacekeeping Affairs Rosemary DiCarlo said that without any change in approach there would be more deterioration and radicalization on both sides, and noted the fading hope for a two-state solution in the face of the growing threats of annexation in the West Bank.[21]

Details of a new US peace initiative led by President Trump's son-in-law and US Middle East peace envoy, Jared Kushner, failed to materialize in 2018.[22] Unofficial reports in April 2019 suggested that the initiative contained practical improvements for the lives of Palestinians, but was likely to exclude the creation of a sovereign Palestinian state.[23] On 22 June 2019 the USA unveiled the economic part of the initiative, which included a pledge of $50 billion worth of investment in Palestine and neighbouring countries after a peace deal.[24] However, Palestinian leaders boycotted the Bahrain Peace to Prosperity workshop on 25 and 26 June at which the economic plan was discussed. Wider attendance reflected political allegiances in the Middle East and North Africa region (see section I), with Saudi Arabian–US allies attending and Iranian allies shunning the meeting.[25] At the end of 2019 there appeared to be no plan for resolving the underlying conflict, including Israel's occupation, in its various forms, and the schism between the Palestinian leaders in Gaza and the West Bank.

[20] National Public Radio, 'Former US envoy explains why Mideast peace talks collapsed in 2014', 8 June 2017.

[21] UN News, '"Continuing absence" of political solution to Israel–Palestine conflict "undermines and compounds" UN efforts to end wholesale crisis', 29 Apr. 2019; and Munayyer, Y., 'There will be a one-state solution', *Foreign Affairs*, Nov./Dec. 2019.

[22] Gardner, D., 'Trump's "deal of the century" offers nothing good to Palestinians', *Financial Times*, 5 Sep. 2018; and Miller, A., 'The Israeli–Palestine conflict is not a bankruptcy sale', Lawfare, 23 Jan. 2019.

[23] Al Jazeera, 'Palestinian state likely not in US proposed peace plan: Report', 15 Apr. 2019; and *The Economist*, 'Jared Kushner's peace plan is supposedly imminent', 11 May 2019.

[24] White House, *Peace to Prosperity. The Economic Plan: A New Vision for the Palestinian People* (White House: June 2019).

[25] *The Economist*, 'An underwhelming start to the "ultimate" Israel-Palestinian deal', 27 June 2019; and International Crisis Group, 'Bahrain workshop sets back Arab-Israeli rapprochement', Commentary, 26 June 2019.

IV. Armed conflict and peace processes in North Africa

IAN DAVIS

Less than a decade after the Arab Spring, North Africa—here comprising Algeria, Egypt, Libya, Morocco and Tunisia—is undergoing a convergence of crises, which also puts the stability of neighbouring states in sub-Saharan Africa at risk (see chapter 7).[1] The lone Arab Spring democracy in Tunisia is also at risk, sandwiched between Libya's civil war and an Algeria in transition. The protracted security breakdown in Libya has also spilled over into western Egypt, with cross-border weapons smuggling and infiltration from non-state armed groups exacerbating a complex interplay of human and internal security challenges in that country.[2] Returning 'foreign fighters' (individuals that have joined an armed conflict abroad) from the conflicts in Iraq, Libya and Syria, climate change and increasing water stress exacerbate underlying conflict dynamics.[3] Disputes over the Nile's waters, for example, have created long-term tensions among Egypt, Ethiopia and Sudan.[4] More than 7000 foreign fighters came from North Africa, and several states, particularly Egypt, Morocco and Tunisia, now face challenges of how to deal with returning jihadists and their families.[5]

Algeria

Tens of thousands of people peacefully protesting across Algeria since mid-February 2019 prompted President Abdelaziz Bouteflika—in power since 1999 and preparing to run for a fifth term—to resign on 2 April and postpone elections scheduled for 18 April.[6] The weekly Friday protest movement became known as the Revolution of Smiles or Hirak Movement.[7] An interim president was appointed in April, and his mandate was extended following the cancellation of July elections. In September the Algerian military took

---

[1] There is no single accepted definition of North Africa. Some definitions include Sudan in North Africa. The conflict in Sudan is discussed in chapter 7, section IV, in this volume.

[2] Kandeel, A., 'NATO countries should help Egypt mitigate security challenge near Libyan border', Atlantic Council, 29 Oct. 2019.

[3] Bryant, L., 'Climate change puts North Africa in a hot spot', Voice of America, 19 Nov. 2019. On the roots of Islamic radicalization in North Africa, see Neo, R., 'The Jihad post-Arab Spring: Contextualising Islamic radicalism in Egypt and Tunisia', *African Security Review*, vol. 28, no. 2 (2019), pp. 95–109.

[4] Palios, E., 'Nile Basin water wars: The never-ending struggle between Egypt, Ethiopia and Sudan', Geopolitical Monitor situation reports, 4 Nov. 2019.

[5] Renard, T. (ed.), 'Returnees in the Maghreb: Comparing policies on returning foreign terrorist fighters in Egypt, Morocco and Tunisia', Egmont Institute and the Konrad-Adenauer-Stiftung, Egmont Paper 107, Apr. 2019.

[6] International Crisis Group, 'Post-Bouteflika Algeria: Growing protests, signs of repression', Middle East and North Africa Briefing no. 68, 26 Apr. 2019.

[7] Algeria Press Service, '26th Friday protest marches reiterate main Hirak Movement's demands', 16 Aug. 2019; and Meddi, A., 'In Algiers, the "revolution of smiles" spreads everywhere', Middle East Eye, 19 Mar. 2019.

a harder line against the continuing demonstrations and increased arrests of protest leaders.[8] Presidential elections held on 12 December were won by former prime minister Abdelmadjid Tebboune, but with a low voter turnout following nationwide calls for a boycott.[9] At the end of 2019 the standoff between protesters and security forces continued.

Western Sahara

The mandate of the United Nations Mission for the Referendum in Western Sahara was extended in October 2019 for a further 12 months, but a second round of UN-mediated talks in March 2019 to resolve the 40-year conflict over Western Sahara between Morocco and the Popular Front for the Liberation of Saguia el Hamra and Río de Oro ended with no clear resolution.[10] A proposed third round of talks was put in doubt when the personal envoy of the UN secretary-general for Western Sahara, former German president Horst Köhler, resigned in May. At the end of 2019 a new personal envoy had yet to be appointed.

Armed conflict in Egypt

The Sinai insurgency (2011–present) is an armed conflict between Egyptian security forces and Islamist militants in the Sinai peninsula. After militants in Sinai embraced the Islamic State in 2014 (the local affiliate is Islamic State–Al Wilayat Sinai, or Islamic State–Sinai Province) there were large-scale attacks on civilian targets.[11] The Egyptian military claims to have killed over 7000 militants and arrested 27 000 since July 2013, while about 1000 security personnel have been killed in the region.[12] At the end of 2018 the situation had deteriorated, with Egypt facing the worst human rights conditions in decades and open civil war in Sinai.[13] A state of emergency has existed in northern Sinai since October 2014 and in the country as a whole since April 2017.[14] Repression of civil society and opposition voices continued in 2019.

---

[8] Al Jazeera, 'Thousands march in Algeria in first protest since election call', 20 Sep. 2019.

[9] *The Economist*, 'An Algerian general takes over from another general', 4 Jan. 2020.

[10] Guerraoui, S., 'Parties to Western Sahara conflict agree to convene for third round of talks', *Arab Weekly*, 24 Mar. 2019; and UN, 'Security Council extends mandate of United Nations Mission in Western Sahara, adopting Resolution 2494 (2019) by 13 votes in favour, 2 abstentions', SC/14003, 30 Oct. 2019.

[11] On the historical developments and sociopolitical causes leading to the rise of Sinai Province and its military build-up, see Ashour, O., 'Sinai's insurgency: Implications of enhanced guerrilla warfare', *Studies in Conflict & Terrorism*, vol. 42, no. 6 (2019), pp. 541–58.

[12] The Tahir Institute for Middle East Policy, *Five Years of Egypt's War on Terror* (The Tahir Institute for Middle East Policy: July 2018); and The Tahir Institute for Middle East Policy, 'Attacks against security forces continue in Egypt's North Sinai', 11 Sep. 2017.

[13] On developments in Egypt in 2018, see Davis, I., 'Armed conflict and peace processes in the Middle East and North Africa', *SIPRI Yearbook 2019*, pp. 87–88.

[14] Egyptian Streets, 'Egypt's state of emergency is extended for the tenth time', 4 Nov. 2019.

Table 6.4. Estimated conflict-related fatalities in Egypt, 2010–19

Event type	2010	2011	2012	2013	2014	2015	2016	2017	2018	2019
Battles	1	54	64	468	927	1 746	1 031	770	898	612
Explosions/ remote violence	1	29	44	89	178	660	575	347	164	346
Protests, riots and strategic developments	7	1 071	113	1 821	172	55	9	1	2	0
Violence against civilians	61	101	23	107	86	396	106	426	48	44
Total	**70**	**1 255**	**244**	**2 485**	**1 363**	**2 857**	**1 721**	**1 544**	**1 112**	**1 002**

Note: For definitions of event types, see Armed Conflict Location & Event Data Project (ACLED), 'ACLED definitions of political violence and protest', 11 Apr. 2019.

Source: ACLED, 'Data export tool', [n.d.].

In September 2019 anti-government protests broke out in Cairo, and the government responded with mass arrests and internet shutdowns.[15]

The changing pattern of the armed conflict over the past seven years is reflected in the Armed Conflict Location & Event Data Project fatalities data in table 6.4. With access to the region restricted, independent verification of events on the ground is difficult, but human rights groups have documented widespread abuse against civilians, mainly by the Egyptian security services, including allegations of war crimes.[16] The Egyptian military occasionally provides statements on its operations, claiming on 4 November 2019, for example, that it had killed 83 suspected fighters from undisclosed armed groups in the preceding month.[17] Overall, however, combat-related fatalities in 2019 fell to the lowest level since 2013.

Armed conflict in Libya

There has been armed conflict in Libya since an armed rebellion, with support of a Western military intervention, deposed its leader Muammar Gaddafi in 2011 (see table 6.5).[18] Under the UN-led 2015 Libyan Political Agreement (LPA), a unity government—the Government of National Accord (GNA)—was installed in Tripoli in 2016, headed by Prime Minister Fayez al-Sarraj. The GNA is supported by a loose alliance of militias in the capital and controls what remains of the Libyan state and its institutions in Tripoli. The GNA is opposed by a rival state institution, the Tobruk-based House of

---

[15] Younes, A. and Allahoum, R., 'Nearly 2,000 arrested as Egypt braces for anti-Sisi protests', Al Jazeera, 27 Sep. 2019; and *The Economist*, 'The authorities in Egypt raid Mada Masr—and reveal their fears', 28 Nov. 2019.

[16] Human Rights Watch, 'If you are afraid for your lives, leave Sinai!', 28 May 2019. On arms transfers to Egypt, see chapter 9, sections I and II, in this volume.

[17] Al Jazeera, 'Egypt forces kill 83 fighters in Sinai, military says', 4 Nov. 2019.

[18] Kuperman, A., 'Obama's Libya debacle: How a well-meaning intervention ended in failure', *Foreign Affairs*, Mar./Apr. 2015; and Hamid, S., 'Everyone says the Libya intervention was a failure. They're wrong', Brookings Institution, 12 Apr. 2016.

Table 6.5. Estimated conflict-related fatalities in Libya, 2010–19

Event type	2010[a]	2011	2012	2013	2014	2015	2016	2017	2018	2019
Battles	0	2 073	458	197	2 381	1 999	2 207	972	715	1 226
Explosions/ remote violence	0	2 150	27	83	468	647	797	464	350	751
Protests, riots and strategic developments	0	818	21	83	11	19	11	0	0	0
Violence against civilians	0	491	46	76	475	336	250	227	123	97
Total	**0**	**5 532**	**552**	**439**	**3 335**	**3 001**	**3 265**	**1 663**	**1 188**	**2 074**

Note: For definitions of event types, see Armed Conflict Location & Event Data Project (ACLED), 'ACLED definitions of political violence and protest', 11 Apr. 2019.

[a]There were no estimated conflict-related fatalities in 2010.

Source: ACLED, 'Data export tool', [n.d.].

Representatives in the east of the country, which has failed to ratify the LPA. Khalifa Haftar, head of the self-styled Libyan National Army (LNA), which is a mix of armed groups with a tribal or regional basis, supports the House of Representatives.

After Haftar announced that he would no longer abide by the LPA, new fighting broke out in mid-2018 in Libya's coastal areas and then spread to the capital. A tentative ceasefire was negotiated by the UN Support Mission in Libya (UNSMIL) on 12 September 2018. The power vacuum also allowed a resurgence of Islamist militant groups, including the Islamic State.[19] The armed conflict has resulted in large-scale forced displacement of civilians, across the border into Tunisia and also within Libya.[20] Meanwhile, in southern Libya, ethnic Toubou and Tuareg militias have been fighting for control amid general lawlessness, especially on the border with Chad.[21]

During 2019 there was a deepening internationalization of the conflict—with Egypt, Russia, Saudi Arabia and the United Arab Emirates (UAE) on one side and Qatar and Turkey on the other, and an array of foreign armed groups and mercenaries on both sides.[22] With the GNA and LNA receiving weapons and military support from third states, a December 2019 UN sanctions committee report concluded that the eight-year arms embargo was being systematically violated, with Jordan, Turkey and the UAE identified as the main suppliers of weapons. The presence of Chadian and Sudanese

[19] On the Libyan conflict in 2016–18, see Smith, D., 'The Middle East and North Africa: 2016 in perspective', *SIPRI Yearbook 2017*, pp. 83–84; Davis, I., 'Armed conflict in the Middle East and North Africa', *SIPRI Yearbook 2018*, pp. 74–75; and *SIPRI Yearbook 2019* (note 13), pp. 94–98.

[20] El Taraboulsi-McCarthy, S. et al., 'Protection of displaced Libyans: Risks, responses and border dynamics', Humanitarian Policy Group and Overseas Development Institute, HPG Working Paper, Aug. 2019.

[21] Tubiana, J. and Gramizzi, C., *Lost in Trans-nation: Tubu and Other Armed Groups and Smugglers along Libya's Southern Border* (Small Arms Survey: Dec. 2018).

[22] International Crisis Group, 'Averting a full-blown war in Libya', Alert, 10 Apr. 2019; and Megerisi, T., 'Libya's global civil war', European Council on Foreign Relations Policy Brief, June 2019.

armed groups (numbering over 3500 fighters in total) was also noted in the report—with the consequent risk of conflict spillover from Libya into Lake Chad, the Sahel and Sudan.[23] The head of UNSMIL and the UN secretary-general's special representative, Ghassan Salamé, described the UN arms embargo as a 'cynical joke'.[24]

Continuing violence in 2019

The four-month-old ceasefire in Tripoli broke down in January 2019 when clashes erupted among rival armed groups. Separately, Haftar's LNA consolidated its control over much of the south-west, including the oilfields. By the end of March 2019 the LNA controlled three quarters of the country and was preparing to attack Tripoli. About 50 000–70 000 LNA troops faced about 20 000–40 000 GNA-aligned militias and volunteers.[25] On 4 April Haftar's forces began advancing towards Tripoli, and the escalation of fighting between Libya's two competing governments led to the postponement of the UN-hosted national conference on Libya's political future that was scheduled to take place on 14 and 15 April.[26] Saudi Arabia reportedly helped to finance Haftar's military offensive, while the UN High Commissioner for Human Rights, Michelle Bachelet, warned that the attacks against civilians and civilian infrastructures might amount to war crimes.[27]

After initial successes by both sides, first by the LNA and then a counteroffensive by the GNA-aligned forces, a stalemate settled in from late April onwards.[28] In late June the GNA-aligned forces captured the city of Gharyan (80 kilometres south of Tripoli), the LNA's key supply base for

---

[23] UN Security Council, 'Final report of the Panel of Experts on Libya established pursuant to Security Council resolution 1973 (2011)', S/2019/914, 9 Dec. 2019. On the UN embargo on Libya, also see chapter 14, section II, in this volume. On the armed conflicts in the Sahel and Lake Chad, see chapter 7, section II, in this volume. On the armed conflict in Sudan, see chapter 7, section IV, in this volume.

[24] UNSMIL, Remarks of SRSG Ghassan Salamé to the United Nations Security Council on the Situation in Libya, 21 May 2019.

[25] 'Libya's conflict', *Strategic Comments*, vol. 25, no. 5 (2019), pp. x–xii. On the complex and changing make-up of the two forces, see Lacher, W., 'Who is fighting whom in Tripoli? How the 2019 civil war is transforming Libya's military landscape', Small Arms Survey Briefing Paper, Aug. 2019. On the influence of Madkhali–Salafis in the LNA and GNA, see International Crisis Group, *Addressing the Rise of Libya's Madkhali-Salafis*, Middle East and North Africa Report no. 200 (International Crisis Group: Brussels, 25 Apr. 2019).

[26] Elumami, A. and al-Warfalli, A., 'Battle rages for Libya's capital, airport bombed', Reuters, 8 Apr. 2019; Wintour, P., 'UN postpones Libya national conference amid fighting in Tripoli', *The Guardian*, 9 Apr. 2019; and *The Economist*, 'Khalifa Haftar, Libya's strongest warlord, makes a push for Tripoli', 13 Apr. 2019.

[27] Malsin, J. and Said, S., 'Saudi Arabia promised support to Libyan warlord in push to seize Tripoli', *Wall Street Journal*, 12 Apr. 2019; and UN Human Rights Office of the High Commissioner, 'Libya: Attacks against civilians and civilian infrastructure may amount to war crimes, Bachelet warns', 9 Apr. 2019.

[28] International Crisis Group, 'Stopping the war for Tripoli', Middle East and North Africa Briefing no. 69, 23 May 2019.

its Tripoli offensive.[29] The indiscriminate use of explosive ordnance by both sides has been routine and widespread, including an attack on a migrant detention facility outside the Libyan capital on 2 July.[30] The armed conflict also expanded into the world's first 'drone war', with the two sides conducting more than 800 drone strikes from early April to the end of October.[31]

In early November it was reported that about 200 Russian mercenaries had joined Haftar's forces (with some estimates suggesting there are 1400 Russian mercenaries in the country), as part of a broader effort by Russia to shape the outcome of the civil war, drawing parallels with its intervention in Syria.[32] For its part, Turkey signed an agreement in December with the Tripoli-based government on maritime border delimitations in the eastern Mediterranean. In exchange for recognizing its claims in the sea, Turkey renewed its military assistance to the GNA, including a new commitment to supply ground troops if requested by the GNA.[33]

The peace process

At least 26 peace agreements and transition documents were signed in Libya between 2011 and 2018, including national-level agreements (such as the LPA), intercommunal agreements and localized ceasefires.[34] An UNSMIL-mandated national conference process (NCP)—a series of public consultations focusing on priorities for the national government, security, governance and the electoral process—took place between April and July 2018.[35] In addition, France (closely aligned with Haftar) and Italy (more closely aligned with the GNA) have been vying to influence the peace process, and each country hosted a summit in 2018.[36] However, with no significant breakthroughs, at the end of 2018 there seemed little prospect of a political

---

[29] Wintour, P., 'Libyan government forces capture key town from warlord', *The Guardian*, 27 June 2019.

[30] UN Security Council, S/2019/914 (note 23), pp. 14–15, 120–32.

[31] UN Security Council, S/2019/914 (note 23), pp. 31–39; and UNSMIL, 'SRSG Ghassan Salamé briefing to the Security Council—18 November 2019', 18 Nov. 2019. On the wider proliferation of armed drones in the region, see the database: Royal United Services Institute, 'Armed drones in the Middle East, The proliferation of UAV technology and norms in the region', [n.d.].

[32] Kirkpatrick, D. D., 'Russian snipers, missiles and warplanes try to tilt Libyan war', *New York Times*, 5 Nov. 2019; and *The Economist*, 'Foreign powers are piling into Libya', 12 Dec. 2019.

[33] Wintour, P., 'Turkey renews military pledge to Libya as threat of Mediterranean war grows', *The Guardian*, 15 Dec. 2019; Bulos, N., 'Libya's battlefields, already saturated with fighters, are getting more', *Los Angeles Times*, 29 Dec. 2019; and Megerisi, T. and Aydintasbas, A., 'Turkey in Libya: Filling the European vacuum', European Council on Foreign Relations commentary, 17 Dec. 2019.

[34] Forster, R., *A Gender Analysis of Peace Agreements and Transitional Documents in Libya, 2011–2018*, PA-X Spotlight Series (UN Women: 2019).

[35] Alunni, A. and Tusa, F., 'In search of a negotiated solution in Libya', Aspenia online, 13 Sep. 2018. Reports of the NCP meetings are available in Arabic at <http://multaqawatani.ly>.

[36] *The Economist*, 'Libya's feuds cross the Mediterranean', 8 Nov. 2018. On Italy's policy aims in Libya, see Varvelli, A. and Villa, M., 'Italy's Libyan conundrum: The risks of short-term thinking', European Council on Foreign Relations commentary, 26 Nov. 2019.

settlement.[37] This was confirmed during 2019 as the escalating violence led to the postponement of the national conference scheduled for April 2019, as well as a proposed reconciliation conference hosted by the African Union in July 2019.[38]

At the grassroots level, UNSMIL has been supporting the development of a national network of mediators that will include tribal leaders, elders, civil society, youth and women activists, academics and businesspeople.[39] In July 2019 Salamé called for a truce, trust-building exercises and an international conference to push a bottom-up political process.[40] To cultivate consensus among external parties to the conflict, Germany was invited by Salamé to attempt to set the groundwork for such a process. Under this Berlin process monthly consultations took place from October among senior officials from the permanent members of the African Union, the European Union, the League of Arab States and the UN Security Council, as well as Egypt, Germany, Italy, Turkey and the UAE.[41] The aim was to agree a draft communiqué that outlines six baskets of activities for ending the conflict, including: a return to the Libyan-led political process and accompanying economic reform; a ceasefire, implementation of the arms embargo and security reform; and upholding international human rights and humanitarian law. A proposed Berlin summit in early 2020 is due to be followed by a UN-led intra-Libyan political dialogue.[42]

However, by the end of 2019 at least 1500 people had been killed (accounting for about three quarters of the total conflict-related fatalities in 2019, see table 6.5) and 120 000 displaced by the fighting around Tripoli. With the growing internationalization of the conflict, further escalation seems likely in 2020.

---

[37] Permanent Mission of France to the UN in New York, 'Political statement on Libya: Joint statement by Fayez al-Sarraj, Aguila Saleh, Khalid Meshri, Khalifa Haftar, Paris', 29 May 2018.

[38] Agence France-Presse, 'African Union to host Libya "reconciliation" conference', *Mail & Guardian*, 31 Mar. 2019; and Panafrican News Agency, 'AUC Chief cancels reconciliation conference on Libya because of continued fighting around Tripoli', 20 June 2019.

[39] UNSMIL (note 31).

[40] Alwasat, 'Salamé hopes to achieve Eid truce, calls for an international conference followed by a Libyan meeting', 9 Aug. 2019.

[41] Megerisi, T., 'Can Germany stop Libya becoming the new Syria?', European Council on Foreign Relations commentary, 24 Sep. 2019; and Wildangel, R. and Megerisi, T., 'Germany's quiet leadership on the Libyan war', European Council on Foreign Relations commentary, 20 Nov. 2019.

[42] UNSMIL (note 31).

V. Armed conflict and peace processes in Yemen

IAN DAVIS

The roots of the current conflict and humanitarian crisis in Yemen are complex and contested.[1] The Houthi insurgency began in 2004 when Hussein Badreddin al-Houthi, a leader of the Zaidi Shi'a, launched an uprising against the Yemeni Government. Al-Houthi was killed in that uprising, and the insurgents have been known as the Houthis since then (the official name is Ansar Allah).[2] In 2014 after several years of growing violence, the country descended into a new phase of civil war between the internationally recognized government of President Abdrabbuh Mansur Hadi and an uneasy alliance of Iran-backed Houthis and forces loyal to former president Ali Abdallah Saleh that controlled the capital, Sanaa, and large parts of the country.

Since March 2015 a coalition led by Saudi Arabia has been intervening militarily on the side of President Hadi, although the coalition itself is divided by conflicts and rivalries. In addition to the United Arab Emirates (UAE), the coalition has included Bahrain, Egypt, Jordan, Kuwait, Morocco, Qatar (until 2017), Senegal and Sudan, either supplying ground troops or carrying out air strikes.[3] The coalition has also received substantial international support. United States assistance has included intelligence, training and arms sales, while several European countries, including France and the United Kingdom, have also been key suppliers of major weapon systems to Saudi Arabia and the UAE.[4]

---

[1] See Davis, I. et al., 'Armed conflict in sub-Saharan Africa', *SIPRI Yearbook 2018*, pp. 80–82. See also e.g. Orkaby, A., 'Yemen's humanitarian nightmare: The real roots of the conflict', *Foreign Affairs*, Nov/ Dec. 2017.

[2] On the goals of and divisions within the Houthis, see Al-Hamdani, S., 'Understanding the Houthi faction in Yemen', Lawfare, 7 Apr. 2019.

[3] On the role played by the UAE, see Abdul-Ahad, G., 'Yemen on the brink: How the UAE is profiting from the chaos of civil war', *The Guardian*, 21 Dec. 2018. On Saudi Arabia's framing of the intervention, see Clausen, M., 'Justifying military intervention: Yemen as a failed state', *Third World Quarterly*, vol. 40, no. 3 (2019), pp. 488–502.

[4] On US and EU member states' assistance to the coalition, see International Crisis Group, *Ending the Quagmire: Lessons for Washington from Four Years of War*, US Report no. 3 (International Crisis Group: Brussels, 15 Apr. 2019); Bachman, J. S., 'A "synchronised attack" on life: The Saudi-led coalition's "hidden and holistic" genocide in Yemen and the shared responsibility of the US and UK', *Third World Quarterly*, vol. 40, no. 2 (2019), pp. 298–316; Cochrane, P., 'EU countries approve arms sales to Saudi, UAE worth 55 times aid to Yemen', Middle East Eye, 12 Nov. 2018; Merat, A., '"The Saudis couldn't do it without us": The UK's true role in Yemen's deadly war', *The Guardian*, 18 June 2019; and Made in France, 'Yemen papers', [n.d.]. On arms transfers to Saudi Arabia and the UAE, see also chapter 9, sections I and II, and chapter 14, section IV, in this volume. On the United Nation arms embargo on Yemen, see chapter 14, section II, in this volume.

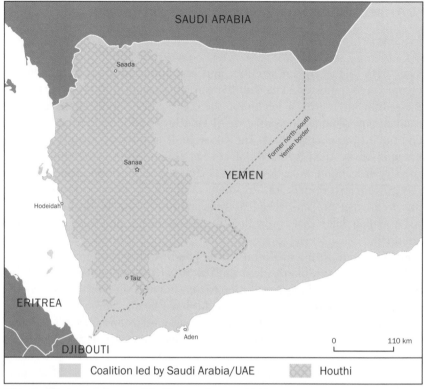

Figure 6.4. Areas of control in Yemen, August 2019

UAE = United Arab Emirates.

Source: *The Economist*, 'Southern separatists are tearing Yemen apart', 15 Aug. 2019.

Armed conflict in 2019 and allegations of war crimes

At the end of 2018 there were at least four separate but interlinked armed
conflicts in Yemen: (*a*) the main civil war, with a focus on the Red Sea coast,
where government forces backed by the UAE pushed up from the south
and threatened Hodeidah, the fourth largest city in Yemen and its principal port on the Red Sea for importing food—although a ceasefire brokered
by the United Nations centred on Hodeidah agreed on 13 December 2018
provided fresh grounds for optimism; (*b*) the Saudi Arabia–Yemen border,
including increased Houthi missile strikes targeting cities in Saudi Arabia
and retaliatory air strikes; (*c*) a secondary civil war within the coalition led
by Saudi Arabia and the UAE—between the central government (normally
based in the north) and the Southern Movement, a fragile coalition of
separatist groups operating in Aden, Hadramaut and Shebwa in the south,
and represented politically by the Southern Transitional Council (STC); and
(*d*) a US-led counterterrorism campaign against radical Islamist groups,

including al-Qaeda in the Arabian Peninsula (AQAP).[5] A UN panel of experts on Yemen concluded that many of the armed groups were trying to achieve two primary objectives: 'a monopoly over armed violence within the territory under their control and control over revenue streams'.[6] Figure 6.4 shows areas of control within Yemen in late 2019.

The main civil war between Houthi and government forces

While the Hodeidah-wide ceasefire agreed in Stockholm in December 2018 continued to hold and the warring parties took initial steps to implement the agreement (see the discussion on implementation of the Stockholm Agreement below), fighting occurred in other areas not covered by the agreement, including among supposed allies: in the north between Houthi rebels and the Hajour tribe and in the southern city of Taiz among nominally allied pro-government groups.[7] Factional clashes within the Houthi–Saleh alliance were a regular occurrence during 2019, especially in Ibb governorate.[8] The Houthis continued to suppress dissent in areas under their control.[9]

The Saudi Arabian–Yemeni air war

Houthi forces have been carrying out missile attacks on targets in Saudi Arabia since late 2016. Between June and September 2019 the pace of cross-border Houthi–Saudi Arabian attacks intensified. The Houthis launched multiple unmanned aerial vehicle and cruise missile attacks into Saudi Arabia, including against regional airports. In turn, the coalition intensified bombing of Houthi-controlled areas in Yemen, including Sanaa.[10] In September Yemen risked becoming further embroiled in the wider regional Iranian–Saudi Arabian/US conflict, when the Houthis claimed responsibility for an attack on Saudi Arabian oil facilities, which was more widely attributed to Iran.[11] In response, forces led by Saudi Arabia launched air strikes close to Hodeidah.[12] The situation de-escalated when the Houthis suspended cross-border attacks and the Saudi Arabians reduced air strikes in Yemen.[13]

---

[5] On developments in Yemen in 2018, see Davis, I., 'Armed conflict and peace processes in the Middle East and North Africa', *SIPRI Yearbook 2019*, pp. 108–14. On conflicts in Yemen in 2019, also see UN Security Council, 'Final report of the Panel of Experts on Yemen', S/2020/70, 27 Jan. 2020, pp. 6–8.

[6] UN Security Council, S/2020/70 (note 5), p. 6.

[7] International Crisis Group, 'Crisis Group Yemen update no. 7', Briefing note, 8 Mar. 2019; and al-Deen, M.S., 'The Houthi–Tribal conflict in Yemen', Carnegie Endowment for International Peace, 23 Apr. 2019.

[8] Carboni, A. and Nevola, L., 'Inside Ibb: A hotbed of infighting in Houthi-controlled Yemen', Armed Conflict Location & Event Data Project (ACLED), 3 Oct. 2019.

[9] UN Security Council, S/2020/70 (note 5), pp. 10–12.

[10] *Jane's Defence Weekly*, 'Yemeni rebels unveil cruise missile, long-range UAVs', 8, July 2019; and UN Security Council, S/2020/70 (note 5), pp. 19–21.

[11] See section I in this chapter and chapter 1, section I, in this volume.

[12] Wintour, P., 'Saudi-led forces launch airstrikes on Yemeni city of Hodeidah', *The Guardian*, 20 Sep. 2019.

[13] Reuters, 'Saudi-led coalition air strikes in Yemen down 80%: UN envoy', 22 Nov. 2019.

Yemen's fractured south

On 10 August after fighting that killed at least 40 people, UAE allies seized the city of Aden from the government of President Hadi that was backed by Saudi Arabia.[14] The rivalry within the anti-Houthi coalition risked escalating into a fully fledged civil war within a civil war.[15] However, in October, control of the city was handed back to the government after the withdrawal of UAE forces.[16] A peace deal was concluded between the two sides in November (see the discussion on the Riyadh Agreement below).

The counterterrorism campaign against radical Islamist groups

The USA has been carrying out regular air strikes against AQAP, or its antecedents, in Yemen since at least 2009.[17] From 2009 to 2019 the USA carried out more than 336 air strikes, causing between 174 and 225 civilian deaths.[18] A US air strike on 1 January 2019 reportedly killed Jamal al-Badawi, a Yemeni al-Qaeda operative accused of leading the 2000 attack on the USS *Cole* that killed 17 US sailors.[19] However, the frequency of US air strikes against AQAP decreased, with only nine reported in 2019.[20] In June Saudi Arabian special forces captured the Islamic State leader in Yemen, Abu Osama Al-Muhajir.[21]

Allegations of war crimes

All parties to the conflict have faced allegations of crimes under international law over the past four years, and fresh allegations surfaced in 2019.[22] In particular, the air strikes by the coalition led by Saudi Arabia have been repeatedly criticized for targeting civilian infrastructure, including hospitals and detention centres.[23] A report by the international Group of

---

[14] On the various patterns of political violence and the different actors in the south of Yemen, see Roy, E. and Nevola, L., 'Yemen's fractured South: Aden, Abyan, and Lahij', ACLED, 18 Dec. 2019.

[15] International Crisis Group, 'After Aden: Navigating Yemen's new political landscape', Middle East Briefing no. 71, 30 Aug. 2019; Bianco, C., 'Cracks in the Saudi–Emirati alliance?', European Council on Foreign Relations commentary, 13 Sep. 2019; and UN Security Council, S/2020/70 (note 5), pp. 14–15.

[16] Yaakoubi, A. E., 'Saudis take control of Yemen's Aden to end stand-off between allies', Reuters, 14 Oct. 2019.

[17] Kendall, E., 'Contemporary jihadi militancy in Yemen: How is the threat evolving?', Middle East Institute Policy Paper 2018-7, July 2018.

[18] Bureau of Investigative Journalism, 'Drone strikes in Yemen', [n.d.].

[19] Youssef, N. A. and Ballhaus, R., 'US kills al Qaeda figure accused of leading 2000 attack on USS Cole', *Wall Street Journal*, 6 Jan. 2019.

[20] Bureau of Investigative Journalism, 'Yemen: Reported US covert actions 2019', [n.d.].

[21] Al-Sulami, M., 'Revealed: How Saudi special forces captured Yemen's Daesh chief in daring 10-minute raid', *Arab News*, 27 June 2019. On other AQAP and Islamic State leaders arrested in 2019, see UN Security Council, S/2020/70 (note 5), p. 16.

[22] See e.g. Amnesty International, 'Yemen: Four years on, fears of further violations with no end in sight to brutal conflict', 25 Mar. 2019; and UN Security Council, S/2020/70 (note 5), pp. 36–44.

[23] See e.g. Fox, G., 'Seven killed in Saudi-led coalition airstrike on hospital in Yemen, says Save the Children', *Independent*, 27 Mar. 2019; and Agence France-Presse, 'Red Cross says more than 100 people killed in airstrike on Yemen prison', *The Guardian*, 1 Sep. 2019.

Eminent Experts on Yemen (created by the UN Human Rights Council in December 2017) detailed a wide range of possible war crimes committed by various parties to the conflict over the past five years, including air strikes, indiscriminate shelling, snipers, landmines, arbitrary killings and detention, torture, sexual and gender-based violence, and preventing access to humanitarian aid.[24] The group of experts also identified individuals involved in the conflict who may be responsible for international crimes.[25]

The humanitarian crisis

According to the UN the humanitarian crisis in Yemen remained the worst in the world in 2019.[26] The cholera epidemic—more than 1.36 million suspected cases between late 2016 and December 2018, and nearly 2800 associated deaths—continued into 2019, with more than 56 000 new cases reported in the first nine months of the year. Outbreaks of dengue fever and malaria were also reported.[27] In addition to endemic diseases an estimated 80 per cent of the population (24 million people) required some form of humanitarian or protection assistance, with 15.9 million people in urgent need of food and livelihood assistance at the beginning of 2019.[28] An estimated 4 million people remained displaced, including 375 000 during 2019.[29]

In February 2019 international donors (led by Saudi Arabia and the UAE), pledged $2.6 billion in funding towards the UN 2019 $4.2 billion humanitarian plan for Yemen—the single largest UN humanitarian appeal ever.[30] The distribution of humanitarian aid within Yemen is itself a component of the conflict, especially in areas controlled by the Houthis.[31]

At the end of October 2019 the Armed Conflict Location & Event Data Project (ACLED) estimated that over 100 000 people had been killed in the Yemeni war since 2015 (including over 12 000 civilian fatalities in direct

[24] UN General Assembly, Human Rights Council, 'Situation of human rights in Yemen, including violations and abuses since September 2014', A/HRC/42/17, 9 Aug. 2019.

[25] UN Human Rights Council, 'Yemen: Collective failure, collective responsibility—UN expert report', Press release, 3 Sep. 2019; and Wintour, P., 'UK, US and France may be complicit in Yemen war crimes—UN report', *The Guardian*, 3 Sep. 2019.

[26] UN News, 'Humanitarian crisis in Yemen remains the worst in the world, warns UN', 14 Feb. 2019. On the role of gender in humanitarian assistance in Yemen, see Christiansen, C. C., 'Gender, development and security in Yemen's transition process', *Journal of Intervention and Statebuilding*, vol. 13, no. 2 (2019), pp. 197–215.

[27] Al Jazeera, 'Red Cross: Yemen faces new outbreak of dengue fever', 26 Nov. 2019.

[28] UN Office for the Coordination of Humanitarian Affairs (OCHA), *Global Humanitarian Overview 2020* (OCHA: 10 Dec. 2019), p. 49.

[29] OCHA (note 28).

[30] Parker, B., 'Saudi Arabia and UAE in record pledge at Yemen aid conference', New Humanitarian, 26 Feb. 2019.

[31] *The Economist*, 'The Houthi rebels wrestle with the UN over food aid', 28 Nov. 2019.

Table 6.6. Estimated conflict-related fatalities in Yemen, 2015–19

Event type	2015	2016	2017	2018	2019
Battles	9 097	8 366	10 634	20 575	15 686
Explosions/remote violence	7 884	6 712	6 346	11 314	9 687
Protests, riots and strategic developments	77	21	17	47	188
Violence against civilians	207	242	199	416	329
Total	**17 265**	**15 341**	**17 196**	**32 352**	**25 890**

Notes: The first available year for data on Yemen in the Armed Conflict Location & Event Data Project (ACLED) database is 2015. For definitions of event types, see ACLED, 'ACLED definitions of political violence and protest', 11 Apr. 2019.

Source: ACLED, 'Data export tool', [n.d.].

attacks).[32] Over 25 800 people were killed in 2019 alone, making it the second most lethal year in a row (table 6.6). This estimate almost certainly undercounts the true extent of casualties and excludes deaths from disease, malnutrition and other consequences of the crisis. The UN Development Programme, for example, estimated that by the end of 2019 total conflict fatalities from fighting and indirect deaths (due to lack of food, health services and infrastructure) would be 233 000 (or 0.8 per cent of the country).[33]

Implementation of the Stockholm Agreement

The December 2018 Stockholm Agreement between the Houthis and the Yemeni Government included several confidence-building measures: a commitment to exchange almost 5000 prisoners, an immediate ceasefire across the governorate of Hodeidah, demilitarization of the Red Sea trade corridor, transfer of Hodeidah port to UN management and the reopening of a humanitarian corridor linking Hodeidah with Sanaa.[34] A Redeployment Coordination Committee (RCC)—a Houthi–Hadi working group—was formed to oversee the ceasefire, mine action operations and the 'mutual redeployment of forces', including the difficult question of the make-up of the 'local security forces' that would subsequently police the city and ports.[35] While implementation of the agreement in 2019 went through several ups and downs, especially in the first half of the year, significant progress was made.[36]

---

[32] ACLED, 'Over 100,000 reported killed in Yemen war', Press release, 31 Oct. 2019; and ACLED, 'Ten conflicts to worry about in 2020', Jan. 2020, p. 9.

[33] Moyer, J. D. et al., *Assessing the Impact of War on Development in Yemen* (UN Development Programme: 2019).

[34] Office of the Special Envoy of the Secretary-General for Yemen, 'Full text of the Stockholm Agreement', 13 Dec. 2018; and Walsh, D., 'Yemen peace talks begin with agreement to free 5,000 prisoners', *New York Times*, 6 Dec. 2018.

[35] International Crisis Group, 'Crisis Group Yemen update no. 9', Briefing note, 19 Apr. 2019.

[36] See e.g. International Crisis Group, *Saving the Stockholm Agreement and Averting a Regional Conflagration in Yemen*, Middle East Report no. 203 (International Crisis Group: Brussels, 18 July 2019).

On 16 January 2019 Houthi and government delegates met in Amman, Jordan, to discuss implementation of the prisoner exchange arrangements, but failed to reach agreement.[37] Thereafter, the issue remained unresolved, although the Houthis unilaterally released 290 prisoners on 30 September 2019, and the coalition forces released 128 Houthi prisoners in November 2019.[38]

The United Nations support mission and withdrawal of forces from Hodeidah

On 16 January 2019 the UN Security Council passed Resolution 2452 (2019) that established the UN Mission to Support the Hodeidah Agreement (UNMHA). On 31 January a Danish general, Michael Anker Lollesgaard, was appointed to head the newly constituted mission.[39] With an initial mandate of six months and an authorized personnel of up to 75 monitors as well as additional support staff, UNMHA will lead and support the RCC in monitoring compliance with the ceasefire and work with parties to ensure that security is assured by local security forces. In July the UNMHA mandate was extended for a further six months under UN Security Council Resolution 2481 (2019).[40] In September, a retired Indian general, Abhijit Guha, took over leadership of the mission.[41]

In the first quarter of 2019 the RCC worked to resolve technical disagreements over the redeployment of military forces from front-line positions in and around Hodeidah, and in mid-April UN Special Envoy for Yemen Martin Griffiths announced that a detailed plan for troop withdrawal had been agreed.[42] However, the issue of who would control the area after the withdrawal remained unresolved. On 11 May Houthi forces began withdrawing from Hodeidah in accordance with the plan, and in June they agreed a mechanism to allow UN inspection of ships entering the ports.[43] In early July the UAE announced a withdrawal of its forces from the city and a partial drawdown in other parts of the country.[44] In August 2019 Special

---

[37] Al-Khalidi, S., 'Yemen combatants start talks in Jordan on prisoner swap deal', Reuters, 16 Jan. 2019; and Al Jazeera, 'Yemen's warring sides fail to reach agreement on prisoner swap', 19 Jan. 2019.

[38] International Committee of the Red Cross, 'Yemen: 290 detainees released with facilitation of the ICRC', 30 Sep. 2019; and International Committee of the Red Cross, '128 detainees repatriated to Yemen from Saudi Arabia', 28 Nov. 2019.

[39] UN Security Council Resolution 2452 (2019), S/RES/2452 (2019), 16 Jan. 2019; and UNMHA website, <https://dppa.un.org/en/mission/unmha-hudaydah-agreement>.

[40] UN Security Council Resolution 2481 (2019), S/RES/2481 (2019), 15 July 2019.

[41] UN, 'Secretary-General appoints Lieutenant General Abhijit Guha of India to head United Nations Mission in support of Hudaydah Agreement', 12 Sep. 2019.

[42] UN News, 'Plan for troop pullback "now accepted" by rival forces around key Yemen port, but fighting intensifying elsewhere, Security Council warned', 15 Apr. 2019.

[43] BBC, 'Yemen war: Houthi withdrawal from Hudaydah as planned—UN', 12 May 2019; and Reuters, 'Yemen's Houthis to allow UN to inspect ships in Hodeidah: Sources', 18 June 2019.

[44] Wintour, P. and McKernan, B., 'Yemen: UAE confirms withdrawal from port city of Hodeidah', *The Guardian*, 9 July 2019; and *The Economist*, 'The UAE begins pulling out of Yemen', 4 July 2019.

Envoy Griffiths reported that there had been no major military operations in Hodeidah or in the surrounding area since the signing of the Stockholm Agreement. In September 2019 the RCC deployed monitoring teams in four locations on the front lines of the city as an initial step to sustain the ceasefire.[45]

The Riyadh Agreement

Extending the peace process to include the STC was a significant development during the year. On 5 November 2019 a deal was signed by the government (backed by Saudi Arabia) and the STC (backed by the UAE) in Riyadh, Saudi Arabia, after more than a month of negotiations. Saudi Arabia's crown prince, Mohammed bin Salman, said the deal—which stipulates the formation of a new, Aden-based, 24-member government comprising equal numbers of northern and southern ministers, integration of STC-affiliated forces into national military and security structures, and inclusion of the STC in government delegations to future UN-led talks with the Houthis over a political settlement to end the war—was a positive step on the path towards resolving the multifaceted conflict in Yemen.[46] However, the Houthis rejected the agreement; at the end of 2019 it had largely not been implemented and clashes were continuing.[47]

Conclusions

The combined Stockholm and Riyadh agreements provide a path towards national-level peace talks and a political settlement of the Yemen civil war. Saudi Arabia is likely to be pivotal in shaping any subsequent security and political arrangement, having taken over coalition command in the south from the UAE. Talks between the Houthis and Saudi Arabians aimed at ending cross-border attacks could be the prelude to the start of a national political process under UN auspices. While the Riyadh Agreement might provide a negotiating platform for the fragmented anti-Houthi bloc, there is also a risk of intra-coalition fighting during its implementation as parties strive for advantage on paper and on the ground.

---

[45] UN Office of the Special Envoy of the Secretary-General for Yemen, 'Briefing of the Special Envoy of the United Nations Secretary-General for Yemen to the open session of the Security Council', 20 Aug. 2019; and UN and RCC, 'The Sixth joint RCC meeting', Joint press statement, 9 Sep. 2019.

[46] Reuters, 'Yemen's Government signs peace deal with southern rebels', *New York Times*, 5 Nov. 2019; and Salisbury, P., 'The beginning of the end of Yemen's civil war?', International Crisis Group commentary, 5 Nov. 2019.

[47] ACLED, 'Ten conflicts to worry about in 2020' (note 32), p. 10; and UN Security Council, S/2020/70 (note 5), pp. 17–18.

7. Armed conflict and peace processes in sub-Saharan Africa

Overview

There were at least 15 countries with active armed conflicts in sub-Saharan Africa in 2019: Burkina Faso, Burundi, Cameroon, the Central African Republic (CAR), Chad, the Democratic Republic of the Congo (DRC), Ethiopia, Kenya, Mali, Mozambique, Niger, Nigeria, Somalia, South Sudan and Sudan. Eight were low-intensity, subnational armed conflicts, and seven were high-intensity armed conflicts (Nigeria, Somalia, the DRC, Burkina Faso, Mali, South Sudan and Cameroon). Almost all the armed conflicts were internationalized, including as a result of state actors (whether directly or through proxies) and the transnational activities of violent Islamist groups, other armed groups and criminal networks. The conflict dynamics and ethnic and religious tensions were often rooted in a combination of state weakness, corruption, ineffective delivery of basic services, competition over natural resources, inequality and a sense of marginalization. Two other cross-cutting issues continued to shape regional security: the continuing internationalization of counterterrorism activities, and water scarcity and the growing impact of climate change (see section I).

There were two new peace agreements in sub-Saharan Africa in 2019: in the CAR and in Mozambique. There were also 20 multilateral peace operations active in the region (two less than in 2018), including several large-scale operations in countries that were experiencing armed conflict such as CAR, DRC, Mali, Somalia and South Sudan. The number of personnel serving in those multilateral peace operations (97 519 on 31 December 2019) decreased for the fourth year in a row and reached the lowest point since 2012.

In the Sahel and Lake Chad regions (section II), all of the armed conflicts (in Burkina Faso, Cameroon, Chad, Mali, Niger and Nigeria) worsened in 2019. The security challenges are linked to the rise of violent extremism and the proliferation of armed non-state groups, such as Boko Haram, which has spread from Nigeria across the Lake Chad region. The violent extremist groups are interwoven with rural insurgent groups, feeding off intercommunal tensions and exploiting grievances of marginalized communities. Armed conflict fatalities increased significantly in Burkina Faso in 2019, due to a broadening of three interconnected layers of conflict: the government's conflict with heavily armed Islamist groups, increasing clashes between armed ethnic and Islamist groups, and intercommunal violence.

There were two main challenges in Central Africa in 2019 (section III): the implementation of a new peace agreement in the CAR between the government and armed groups, and a period of political transition in the DRC. In the former, the UN panel of experts on the CAR reported in December 2019 that the agreement's implementation 'remained limited', while the political changes in the latter were accompanied by an increase in insecurity and political violence in the eastern provinces and an ongoing health emergency from measles and Ebola outbreaks.

The Horn of Africa (section IV) contains some of the most fragile countries in the world, derived from a complex mix of limited or uneven access to natural resources, intergroup tensions, poverty and economic inequalities, and weak state institutions. Relatively peaceful transitions of power in Ethiopia (in 2018) and Sudan (in 2019) and the implementation of a 2018 peace agreement in South Sudan led to significant decreases in armed violence in these three states. However, the armed conflict in Somalia remained one of the deadliest in the world.

IAN DAVIS

I. Key general developments in the region

IAN DAVIS

There were at least 15 countries with active armed conflicts in sub-Saharan Africa in 2019: Burkina Faso, Burundi, Cameroon, the Central African Republic (CAR), Chad, the Democratic Republic of the Congo (DRC), Ethiopia, Kenya, Mali, Mozambique, Niger, Nigeria, Somalia, South Sudan and Sudan. Eight were low-intensity, subnational armed conflicts (i.e. with fewer than conflict-related 1000 deaths), and seven were high-intensity armed conflicts (with 1000–9999 deaths): Nigeria (5400), Somalia (4000), the DRC (3700), Burkina Faso (2200), Mali (1900), South Sudan (1800) and Cameroon (1200). Almost all of the armed conflicts were internationalized.[1]

Many of these armed conflicts overlapped across states and regions as a result of state actors, whether directly or through proxies, and/or the transnational activities of violent Islamist groups, other armed groups and criminal networks. While Islamist violence is not endemic to the region, many of the countries suffering from armed conflict are afflicted by extremist Islamist violence. With the continuation of the violence and the chaos it has created, a range of problems have followed or have been exacerbated, such as economic fragility, increased poverty and low resilience. The conflict dynamics and ethnic and religious tensions are often rooted in a combination of state weakness, corruption, ineffective delivery of basic services, competition over natural resources, inequality and a sense of marginalization.[2] Because of these overlaps and regional dimensions, developments in each of the armed conflicts in 2019 are discussed in more detail in subsequent subregional sections of this chapter: the Sahel and Lake Chad region (section II), Central Africa (section III) and the Horn of Africa (section IV)—except for the armed conflict in Mozambique, which is discussed briefly below.

While Southern Africa remains the most peaceful region in sub-Saharan Africa, it faces a number of evolving challenges, including high levels of inequality and growing socio-economic unrest. In Zimbabwe for example, the economic and humanitarian crisis deepened during the year. In August 2019 the United Nations World Food Programme warned that more than 2 million Zimbabweans were on the brink of starvation after a drought

---

[1] For conflict definitions and typologies, see chapter 2, section I, in this volume. For armed conflicts in North Africa, see chapter 6 in this volume.

[2] On the extent of cross-border state support to parties involved in intrastate armed conflict and its under-representation in Africa conflict data sets, see Twagiramungu, N. et al., 'Re-describing transnational conflict in Africa', *Journal of Modern African Studies*, vol. 57, no. 3 (2019), pp. 377–91. On child poverty in Africa, see Watkins, K. and Quattri, M., 'Child poverty in Africa: An SDG emergency in the making', Overseas Development Institute Briefing paper, Aug. 2019. On the factors that influence unrest in the region, see Adelaja, A. and George, J., 'Grievances, latent anger and unrest in Africa', *African Security*, vol. 12, no. 1 (2019), pp. 111–40.

destroyed more than half of the country's maize harvest. Protests and acts of repression by the security forces were a regular occurrence in the early part of the year.[3] There were also significant levels of political and criminal violence in South Africa during 2019.[4]

There were two new peace agreements in sub-Saharan Africa in 2019: in the CAR (see section III) and in Mozambique, where the former armed opposition group Mozambican National Resistance (Resistência Nacional Moçambicana, RENAMO) signed a peace agreement with the government on 6 August 2019 (having signed an initial deal on 1 August), formally ending decades of hostilities.[5] More than 5200 RENAMO fighters were expected to disarm under the agreement: some were due to be absorbed into the country's security forces, while others were to be reintegrated into civilian life. However, a RENAMO splinter group threatened to ignore the agreement, and tensions rose again in October 2019, as RENAMO rejected the 15 October general election results.[6]

In addition, there was an ongoing Islamist insurgency in Cabo Delgado province in the north of Mozambique. The main insurgent group was Ansar al-Sunna, a local extremist faction, but in June 2019 the Islamic State claimed its first attack against Mozambican security forces.[7] According to the Armed Conflict Location & Event Data Project (ACLED) there were 663 conflict-related fatalities in Mozambique in 2019, with the majority being in the categories 'violence against civilians' (383) and 'battles' (252)—the latter confirming that Mozambique met the threshold for a low-level armed conflict in 2019.[8]

In the Horn of Africa, relatively peaceful transitions of power in Ethiopia (in 2018) and Sudan (in 2019) and the implementation of a 2018 peace agreement in South Sudan led to significant decreases in armed violence in those three states (see section IV).

There were 20 multilateral peace operations active in sub-Saharan Africa in 2019, two less than in 2018 and six fewer than in 2014.[9] The UN Mission in Liberia and the Southern African Development Community Preventative

---

[3] BBC, 'Zimbabwe: A third of population faces food crisis, says UN', 7 Aug. 2019; *The Economist*, 'Zimbabwe faces its worst economic crisis in a decade', 15 Aug. 2019; and *The Economist*, 'Zimbabwe sees its worst state violence in a decade', 26 Jan. 2019.

[4] Campbell, J., 'What's behind South Africa's recent violence?', Council on Foreign Relations, 15 Nov. 2019.

[5] France 24, 'Mozambique's former civil war foes sign landmark peace deal', 1 Aug. 2019; and *Mail & Guardian*, 'Mozambique's rivals sign peace deal', 8 Aug. 2019. On the history of the armed conflict in Mozambique, see Gerety, R. M., *Go Tell the Crocodiles: Chasing Prosperity in Mozambique* (New Press: New York, 2018).

[6] Africa News, 'Mozambique's Renamo wants election results cancelled', 19 Oct. 2019; *East African*, 'Mozambique peace deal at risk over poll fraud claims', 3 Nov. 2019; and PSC Report, Institute for Security Studies, 'New threats to peace in Mozambique', 24 Nov. 2019.

[7] Weiss, C., 'Islamic State claims first attack in Mozambique', Long War Journal, 4 June 2019.

[8] ACLED, 'Data export tool', [n.d.].

[9] The peace operations were deployed across 10 countries, see chapter 2, section II, in this volume.

Mission in the Kingdom of Lesotho ended in 2018, and there were no new missions in the sub-Saharan Africa region in 2019. The peace operations included several large-scale operations in countries that were experiencing armed conflict such as the CAR, the DRC, Mali, Somalia and South Sudan. The number of personnel serving in multilateral peace operations in sub-Saharan Africa decreased by 6 per cent during 2019, from 103 528 on 31 December 2018 to 97 519 on 31 December 2019, mainly due to scaling down by the African Union (AU) Mission in Somalia, the UN–AU Hybrid Operation in Darfur, the UN Multidimensional Integrated Stabilization Mission in the CAR and the UN Organization Stabilization Mission in the DRC. The number of personnel deployed in the region decreased for the fourth year in a row and reached the lowest point since 2012. All large-scale peace operations in the region except for the UN Mission in South Sudan decreased in size during the year.[10] These developments notwithstanding, sub-Saharan Africa continued to host far more peace operations personnel in 2019 than any other region—on average 71 per cent of the global total.[11]

In February 2019 AU leaders held their annual summit in Addis Ababa, Ethiopia. Key points on the agenda included tariff liberalization in the African Continental Free Trade Area, institutional reform of the AU and progress on Agenda 2063 (a vision and action plan to build a 'prosperous and united Africa based on shared values and a common destiny').[12] Since its creation in 2002 the AU has taken on greater responsibility for upholding peace and security in Africa, including through peace support operations—often through regional bodies such as the Economic Community of West African States (ECOWAS). There have been long-standing tensions between the UN Security Council and the equivalent decision-making body within the AU, its Peace and Security Council, over which institution should have primacy in addressing the prevention, management and resolution of African conflicts.[13] These tensions continued in 2019 over the conflicts in Sudan (section IV in this chapter) and Libya (chapter 6), as well as over proposed changes to funding of AU-led peace operations.[14] However, AU–UN cooperation improved in other areas, including the Sahel (section II), the CAR (section III) and South Sudan (section IV).

---

[10] On the reasons for this decrease, see chapter 2, section II, in this volume.

[11] See figure 2.5 in chapter 2, section II, in this volume.

[12] Office of the Special Adviser on Africa, 'Agenda 2063'; and AU, 'Key decisions of the 32nd Ordinary Session of the Assembly of the African Union (January 2019)', 12 Feb. 2019. For further details and membership of the AU, see annex B in this volume.

[13] International Crisis Group, *A Tale of Two Councils: Strengthening AU–UN Cooperation*, Africa Report no. 279 (International Crisis Group: Brussels, 25 June 2019). For further details and membership of ECOWAS, see annex B in this volume.

[14] On the AU–UN burden-sharing debate in 2019, see International Crisis Group, *The Price of Peace: Securing UN Financing for AU Peace Operations*, Africa Report no. 286 (International Crisis Group: Brussels, 31 Jan. 2020).

Two additional cross-cutting issues shaped security dilemmas in sub-Saharan Africa in 2019: (*a*) the continuing internationalization of counter-terrorism activities and (*b*) water scarcity and the growing impact of climate change.[15] This section now briefly examines how these two issues evolved in 2019.

The internationalization of counterterrorism and security activities

Many of the global powers, such as the United States, China, several major West European powers and Russia, have significant security and economic interests in sub-Saharan Africa, which is being increasingly treated as an arena for great power competition in a process that has been dubbed the new or third 'scramble' for Africa.[16] In the Horn of Africa for example, an even wider variety of international security actors—from Asia, Europe, the Middle East and North Africa, and North America—operate in the region, largely driven by geopolitical, commercial and military competition.[17]

However, largely separate from this geopolitical competition, the USA and European states in particular are also centrally involved in the fight against transnational jihadist groups in the area, albeit rarely directly. In the case of European states this fight also extends to criminal networks and irregular migration. Most Western forces train and build capacity in local forces, including the two subregional counterterrorism task forces: the Multinational Joint Task Force in the Lake Chad region and the Joint Force of the Group of Five for the Sahel (discussed in section II).[18] The threat from transnational jihadism is particularly pronounced in the Sahel and Lake Chad region (section II) and in the Horn of Africa, from where Islamist and criminal violence is spreading into East Africa (section IV).[19] Despite the loss

---

[15] As identified in Davis, I. and Melvin, N., 'Armed conflict and peace processes in sub-Saharan Africa', *SIPRI Yearbook 2019*, pp. 115–21.

[16] The first 'scramble' was during the 19th century colonial period and the second during the cold war. *The Economist*, 'The new scramble for Africa', 7 Mar. 2019; Devermont, J., 'Haven't we done this before? Lessons from and recommendations for strategic competition in sub-Saharan Africa', Lawfare, 15 Apr. 2019; and *The Economist*, 'Africa is attracting ever more interest from powers elsewhere', 7 Mar. 2019.

[17] Melvin, N. J., 'The foreign military presence in the Horn of Africa region', SIPRI Background Paper, Apr. 2019; and Melvin, N. J., 'The new external security politics of the Horn of Africa region', SIPRI Insights on Peace and Security no. 2019/2, Apr. 2019. Also see section IV in this chapter.

[18] *The Economist*, 'The West's new front against Jihadism is in the Sahel', 2 May 2019. On US counterterrorism policy in the region, see Guido, J., 'The American way of war in Africa: The case of Niger', *Small Wars & Insurgencies*, vol. 30, no. 1 (2019), pp. 176–99.

[19] On the targeting of civilians in the region by violent Islamist groups, see Dowd, C., 'Fragmentation, conflict, and competition: Islamist anti-civilian violence in sub-Saharan Africa', *Terrorism and Political Violence*, vol. 31, no. 3 (2019), pp. 433–53.

of its territories in Iraq and Syria, the Islamic State and its affiliates appeared to be inspiring some jihadist groups in sub-Saharan Africa to link up with it.[20]

The USA continued to adjust its regional deployments as part of its 2018 move away from counterterrorism operations around the world towards a focus on competition among major state powers. In 2018 these included an announced 10 per cent cut of its 7200 personnel deployed in Africa, but also a build-up of forces in Somalia. A first tranche of 'roughly 300' US military personnel are expected to be removed by June 2020, although it remains to be seen whether further cuts will be implemented.[21] Armed unmanned aerial vehicles became operational at a US airbase in Niger during 2019. There were about 500–600 US military personnel in Somalia where US air strikes targeting the al-Shabab group became more frequent in 2019 (than in any year since the initial US air strikes in Somalia in 2007).[22]

As expected regional and European partners took on a slightly larger share of crisis management and counterterrorism, especially France, which has 4700 military personnel in West and Central Africa under Operation Barkhane.[23] In turn, France appealed in June 2019 to other European states to assist their forces in Africa and join a new special forces task force.[24] European Union (EU) member states already collectively dedicate significant political, financial and military resources to the Sahel region, as part of one of the EU's central foreign policy pillars—driven partly by concerns about refugees and irregular migrants from the region coming to Europe.[25] Germany and Italy each have about 1000 soldiers in Africa.[26] The United Kingdom's military engagement in 40 Africa countries focuses on security sector reform and defence engagement, including the provision of specialist training for

[20] Burke, J., 'ISIS claims sub-Saharan attacks in a sign of African ambitions', *The Guardian*, 6 June 2019.

[21] General Thomas Waldhauser, Testimony before the House Armed Services Committee, 'National security challenges and US military activities in the Greater Middle East and Africa', 7 Mar. 2019; Alexis Arieff, Statement before the Committee on Oversight and Reform, Subcommittee on National Security, US House of Representatives, Hearing on 'US counterterrorism priorities and challenges in Africa', Congressional Research Service Testimony, 16 Dec. 2019; and Cooper, H. et al., 'Pentagon eyes Africa drawdown as first step in global troop shift', *New York Times*, 24 Dec. 2019.

[22] Correll, D. S., 'Armed drones to fly out of Niger air base now operational after delayed completion', *Air Force Times*, 1 Nov. 2019; and Browne, R., 'US military mission in Somalia could take seven years to complete', CNN, 13 Apr. 2019.

[23] SIPRI Multilateral Peace Operations Database, <http://www.sipri.org/databases/pko/>; de Hoop Scheffer, A. and Quencez, M., 'US "burden-shifting" strategy in Africa validates France's ambition for greater European strategic autonomy', German Marshall Fund of the United States, Transatlantic take, 23 Jan. 2019; *Africa Confidential*, 'In search of allies', 19 Dec. 2019; and Associated Press, 'French forces kill 33 Islamic extremists in Mali, says Macron', *The Guardian*, 21 Dec. 2019.

[24] Intelligence Online, 'Special forces in Africa: French armed forces minister Florence Parly appeals to European allies', issue 833, 26 June 2019. Also see chapter 2, section II, in this volume.

[25] European Commission, 'The European Union's partnership with the G5 Sahel countries', 6 Dec. 2018; and Dörrie, P., 'Europe has spent years trying to prevent "chaos" in the Sahel. It failed', *World Politics Review*, 25 June 2019.

[26] *The Economist* (note 18).

Nigerian troops fighting Boko Haram, three helicopters and about 90 troops to support French counterterrorism activities in Mali and training in Kenya of AU peacekeepers deployed in Somalia.[27]

China's increasing military footprint is partly linked to its growing economic presence in Africa, including securing its Belt and Road Initiative facilities.[28] Out of the five permanent members of the UN Security Council, it is the leading supplier of UN peacekeepers in the region, mostly in the DRC, Mali, South Sudan and Sudan.[29] Russia's increasing security activities on the continent also have a strong economic and geostrategic dimension.[30] In 2018 and 2019 Russia supplied arms and advisers to the CAR (section III). In October 2019 Russia and more than 40 heads of state gathered in Sochi, Russia, for the first ever Russia–Africa summit, during which President Vladimir Putin announced that Russia has written off African debt worth more than \$20 billion and called for trade with African countries to double in the next five years.[31] In addition, Russia and China are the largest arms exporters to sub-Saharan Africa.[32]

Water scarcity and climate change

While Africa is responsible for only 4 per cent of global carbon dioxide emissions, it is particularly vulnerable to the double burden of climate-related factors and political fragility. Of the 21 countries facing the highest risk from this double burden, 12 are in sub-Saharan Africa: Angola, Cameroon, Chad, Côte d'Ivoire, the DRC, Ethiopia, Guinea, Nigeria, Sierra Leone, South Sudan, Sudan and Uganda.[33] The *African Peace and Security Architecture Roadmap 2016–2020* highlights climate change as one of the cross-cutting issues

---

[27] UK Foreign and Commonwealth Office, *Conflict, Stability and Security Fund: Annual Report 2017/18* (Foreign and Commonwealth Office: July 2018); UK Government, 'PM's speech in Cape Town', 28 Aug. 2018; and UK Joint Committee on the National Security Strategy, *Revisiting the UK's National Security Strategy: The National Security Capability Review and the Modernising Defence Programme* (House of Commons: 21 July 2019).

[28] Kovrig, M., 'China expands its peace and security footprint in Africa', International Crisis Group commentary, 24 Oct. 2018; Cabestan, J.-P., 'China's military base in Djibouti: A microcosm of China's growing competition with the United States and new bipolarity', *Journal of Contemporary China* (2019); and Walsh, B., 'China's pervasive yet forgotten regional security role in Africa', *Journal of Contemporary China*, vol. 28, no. 120 (2019), pp. 965–83.

[29] *The Economist*, 'Africa is attracting ever more interest from powers elsewhere' (note 16).

[30] Marten, K., 'Russia's back in Africa: Is the cold war returning?', *Washington Quarterly*, vol. 42, no. 4 (2019), pp. 155–70; and Besenyő, J., 'The Africa policy of Russia', *Terrorism and Political Violence*, vol. 31, no. 1 (2019), pp. 132–53.

[31] Roscongress, 'Declaration of the First Russia–Africa Summit', 24 Oct. 2019; *Moscow Times*, 'Russia vows to forgive Ethiopia's debt amid growing push for influence in Africa', 22 Oct. 2019; and *The Economist*, 'Vladimir Putin flaunts Russia's increasing influence in Africa', 24 Oct. 2019.

[32] On arms transfers to sub-Saharan Africa, see chapter 9, section II, in this volume.

[33] Moran, A. et al., *The Intersection of Global Fragility and Climate Risks* (US Agency for International Development: Sep. 2018), pp. 11–13; and Ritchie, H., 'Global inequalities in CO_2 emissions', Our World in Data, 16 Oct. 2018.

affecting peace and security.[34] A 2019 study shows how climate change has amplified existing challenges and strengthened radical groups in Somalia.[35]

There is always a direct or decisive link between climate change and increased insecurity. However, economic opportunity and political considerations are just as important factors behind increased insecurity. Nonetheless, the context is set in part by frequent and severe droughts, famines and flash floods in sub-Saharan Africa that have displaced millions and contributed to high levels of migration: in 2018, 6 of the 10 largest flooding events globally that triggered displacement were in the region, and urban areas were the worst hit.[36] In Zambia an estimated 2.3 million people were in urgent need of food assistance in 2019 as a result of recurring and prolonged droughts, with seasonal rainfalls in southern and western Zambia recorded at their lowest levels since 1981.[37] It is broadly accepted that water management and infrastructure will need to improve to reduce climate vulnerability in the region.[38]

[34] African Union Commission, *African Peace and Security Architecture, APSA Roadmap 2016–2020* (African Union Commission, Peace and Security Department: Addis Ababa, Dec. 2015), pp. 20–21. On the framing and understanding of climate-related security risks in AU policy frameworks, see Aminga, V., 'Policy responses to climate-related security risks: The African Union', SIPRI Background Paper, May 2020

[35] Eklöw, K. and Krampe, F., 'Climate-related security risks and peacebuilding in Somalia', SIPRI Policy Paper no. 53, Oct. 2019.

[36] Internal Displacement Monitoring Centre and Norwegian Refugee Council, *Global Report on Internal Displacement 2019*, p. 12.

[37] IPC, 'IPC acute food insecurity analysis Zambia, May 2019–March 2020', Aug. 2019; and European Commission, 'ECHO daily flash archive, Zambia', 31 Aug. 2019.

[38] Mason, N. et al., 'Climate change is hurting Africa's water sector, but investing in water can pay off', World Resources Institute, 7 Oct. 2019.

II. Armed conflict and peace processes in the Sahel and Lake Chad region

IAN DAVIS

For the purpose of this section the Sahel and Lake Chad region comprises 12 countries: Burkina Faso, Cameroon, Chad, Côte d'Ivoire, Gambia, Ghana, Guinea, Mali, Mauritania, Niger, Nigeria and Senegal. At least half of them (Burkina Faso, Cameroon, Chad, Mali, Niger and Nigeria) were involved in armed conflicts in 2019, all of which worsened in terms of conflict-related fatalities (compared with 2018).

The region faces acute security challenges linked to weakness of the states, corruption and non-inclusive governance, which have added to or exacerbated a range of existing problems, including extreme poverty, economic fragility and low resilience. This economic fragility (Niger is at the bottom of the United Nations Development Programme 2019 human development index, while Burkina Faso, Chad and Mali are near the bottom) and the impact of climate change in a region where more than 80 per cent of the population relies essentially on agriculture and pastoral activities have led to increased food insecurity and heightened intercommunal conflict.[1] The conflict dynamics also include irregular migration, illicit trafficking and transnational organized crime, especially where there are weak governmental institutions. The rising violence has also led to schools being targeted by armed groups and increasing numbers of school closures in the region. Between April 2017 and June 2019 for example, the three countries of the central Sahel (Burkina Faso, Mali and Niger) witnessed a sixfold increase in school closures due to violence, from 512 to 3005.[2]

These security challenges have been increasingly linked to the rise of violent extremism and the proliferation of armed non-state groups, with some important differences between the Sahel and Lake Chad regions. In the latter for example, the main insurgent group, Boko Haram, has spread from Nigeria (see below) across the Lake Chad region, causing a massive humanitarian crisis and increasing internal and cross-border displacement of people.[3] Prior to 2019 the other three main violent extremist groups—Group to Support Islam and Muslims (Jama'a Nusrat ul-Islam wa al-Muslimin, JNIM), Ansarul Islam and Islamic State in the Greater Sahara (ISGS) (see box 7.1)—were mostly confined to the Sahel: Mali, northern Burkina Faso and western Niger, respectively. However, in 2019 following the deterioration in

---

[1] UN Development Programme, '2019 human development index ranking', [n.d.]; and World Food Programme, 'Emergency dashboard, Central Sahel', Sep. 2019.

[2] UNICEF, 'Education under threat in West and Central Africa', Aug. 2019.

[3] On the historical processes that produced Boko Haram, see MacEachern, S., *Searching for Boko Haram: A History of Violence in Central Africa* (Oxford University Press: Oxford, 2018).

Box 7.1. Groups with a Salafist jihadism ideology in the Sahel and Lake Chad region

Ansarul Islam (Defender of Islam)

Ansarul Islam began in 2016 as a localized insurgency in the northern provinces of Burkina Faso. The group is allied to Group to Support Islam and Muslims (Jama'a Nusrat ul-Islam wa al-Muslimin, JNIM), and is led by Abdoul Salam Dicko (although he was reportedly killed in October 2019). Today, it is composed largely of Fulani fighters and also operates increasingly in the tri-border area with Mali and Niger known as the Liptako-Gourma region.

Boko Haram/Islamic State West Africa Province

Boko Haram emerged in Nigeria in 2002 and began its violent uprising in 2009 under the leadership of Abubakar Shekau. The group is allied to the Islamic State. It is based in north-eastern Nigeria, but the group is also active in other countries in the Lake Chad region, including northern Cameroon, Chad and Niger. It split into two factions in 2016: Islamic State West Africa Province (ISWAP) led by Abu-Musab al-Barnawi; and People Committed to the Propagation of the Prophet's Teachings and Jihad (Jama'tu Ahlis Sunna Lidda'awati wal-Jihad, JAS, but still commonly known as Boko Haram) led by Shekau. Abu Abdallah al-Barnawi became the new leader of ISWAP in March 2019. ISWAP is thought to have 3500–5000 fighters and Boko Haram 1500–2000 fighters.

Jama'a Nusrat ul-Islam wa al-Muslimin (Group to Support Islam and Muslims)

JNIM was formed in 2017 from four jihadist groups: al-Mourabitoun, al-Qaeda in the Islamic Maghreb, Ansar Dine and Katiba Macina. JNIM acts as the official branch of al-Qaeda in Mali and increasingly operates in Burkina Faso and Niger. It is estimated to have between 1000 and 2000 fighters. The group is led by former Ansar Dine leader Iyad Ag Ghaly.

Islamic State in the Greater Sahara

Islamic State in the Greater Sahara (ISGS) operates in the tri-border area of Burkina Faso, Mali and Niger. It was formed in 2015 as a result of a split in the militant group al-Mourabitoun and is estimated to have about 200–400 fighters. It is led by Abou Walid al-Sahraoui.

Sources: Center for Strategic & International Studies, 'Jama'at Nasr al-Islam wal Muslimin (JNIM)', Backgrounder, 25 Sep. 2018; Warner, J., 'Sub-Saharan Africa's three "new" Islamic State affiliates', *CTC Sentinel*, vol. 10, no. 1 (Jan. 2017), pp. 28–32; International Crisis Group, *Facing the Challenge of the Islamic State in West Africa Province*, Africa Report no. 273 (International Crisis Group: Brussels, 16 May 2019); Le Roux, P., 'Exploiting borders in the Sahel: The Islamic State in the Greater Sahara', Africa Center for Strategic Studies, 10 June 2019; Tobie, A. and Sangaré, B., *The Impact of Armed Groups on the Populations of Central and Northern Mali: Necessary Adaptations of the Strategies for Re-establishing Peace* (SIPRI and Ministry for Foreign Affairs of Finland: Oct. 2019); and BBC, 'Burkina Faso's war against militant Islamists', 30 May 2019.

the security situation in Burkina Faso (see below), there was a heightened risk that they might spread to coastal West African states, such as Benin, Ghana and Togo.[4] Some of the jihadist groups have been adept at exploiting the grievances of marginalized communities and intercommunal tensions to recruit members. According to one study for example, 'Lack of economic

---

[4] International Crisis Group, 'The risk of jihadist contagion in West Africa', Africa Briefing no. 149, 20 Dec. 2019.

Table 7.1. External national and multilateral peace and counterterrorism operations in the Sahel and Lake Chad region

Launched or established	Name	Contributing countries/ organizations	Force level	Country of deployment
2012	European Union (EU) Capability Mission Sahel Niger	EU member states	115 police and civilians	Niger
2013	Multidimensional Integrated Stabilization Mission in Mali	United Nations (mainly African countries, Bangladesh, Egypt, China and Germany)	14 438 troops, police and civilians	Mali
2013	EU Training Mission in Mali	EU member states	697 troops and 3 civilians	Mali
2014[a]	Multinational Joint Task Force	Benin, Cameroon, Chad, Niger and Nigeria	10 746 troops	Cameroon, Chad, Niger and Nigeria
2014[b]	Operation Barkhane	France	4 700 troops	Burkina Faso, Chad, Mali and Niger
2015	EU Capability Mission Sahel Mali	EU member states	127 police and civilians	Mali
2017	Joint Force of the Group of Five for the Sahel	Burkina Faso, Chad, Mali, Mauritania and Niger	5 000 troops	Burkina Faso, Chad, Mali, Mauritania and Niger

[a] Initiated as a solely Nigerian force in 1994; expanded to include Chad and Niger in 1998.
[b] Succeeded Operation Serval, which was launched in January 2013 and ended in July 2014.

Sources: SIPRI Multilateral Peace Operations Database, <http://www.sipri.org/databases/pko/>; van der Lijn, J., 'Multilateral non-peace operations', *SIPRI Yearbook 2018*, pp. 141–42; Dieng, M., 'The Multi-National Joint Task Force and the G5 Sahel Joint Force: The limits of military capacity-building efforts', *Contemporary Security Policy*, vol. 40, no. 4 (2019), pp. 481–501; French Ministry of Defence, 'Operation Barkhane', Press Pack (French Ministry of Defence: Feb. 2020); and EU Capacity Building Mission in Niger (EU External Action Service), 'Partnership for security in the Sahel', Fact Sheet, 2019.

opportunities, a sense of diminished social status, and the need for protection against cattle theft' were factors that apparently influenced the decision of local people to join ISGS.[5]

---

[5] Le Roux, P., 'Exploiting borders in the Sahel: The Islamic State in the Greater Sahara', Africa Center for Strategic Studies, 10 June 2019.

Table 7.2. Estimated conflict-related fatalities in Burkina Faso, 2013–19

Event type	2013	2014	2015	2016	2017	2018	2019
Battles	1	7	9	36	40	95	782
Explosions/remote violence	0	0	0	0	3	32	109
Protests, riots and strategic developments	2	28	13	7	7	3	12
Violence against civilians	5	1	1	38	66	173	1 295
Total	**8**	**36**	**23**	**81**	**116**	**303**	**2 198**

Note: For definitions of event types, see Armed Conflict Location & Event Data Project (ACLED), 'ACLED definitions of political violence and protest', 11 Apr. 2019.

Source: ACLED, 'Data export tool', [n.d.].

To combat these groups and to prevent them spreading to more countries in the region and beyond, several multilateral peace and counterterrorism operations have been established (see table 7.1).

Burkina Faso

Ansarul Islam has been waging a low-level insurgency in Burkina Faso since 2016, but in 2019 the country became the focal point of the Sahel jihadi crisis, with JNIM and to a lesser extent ISGS significantly expanding their operations in the country.[6] Armed conflict fatalities increased significantly in Burkina Faso in 2019 (see table 7.2). However, attributing responsibility for the armed violence is complex due to several interconnected layers of conflict, including: (*a*) the government's conflict with the heavily armed jihadists, mainly along the northern border with Mali—a spillover from the Mali crisis and retaliation for Burkina Faso's participation in the UN Multidimensional Integrated Stabilization Mission in Mali (MINUSMA)—and in the east towards the border with Niger, (*b*) increasing clashes between local self-defence groups (ethnic and village militias) and jihadist groups and (*c*) other sources of violence, such as banditry, farmer–herder competition and land disputes.

After 27 years of uninterrupted, semi-authoritarian rule, public protests in 2014 resulted in the country's first ever civilian-led political transition, including peaceful elections in 2015. However, the government's failure to curb the violence forced the resignation of Prime Minister Paul Kaba Thieba and his entire cabinet in January 2019. The successor government is led by Christophe Dabiré.[7]

As the violence spread to the Boucle du Mouhoun, Centre-Nord, Est and Nord regions, the Islamist extremist groups were able to exploit divisions among the numerous ethnic groups in Burkina Faso. ISGS and JNIM have

---

[6] 'Burkina Faso and jihadism in West Africa', *Strategic Comments*, vol. 25, no. 6 (2019), pp. viii–x.
[7] Africa News, 'Burkina Faso: Christophe Joseph Marie Dabiré is new PM', 21 Jan. 2019.

Table 7.3. Estimated conflict-related fatalities in Cameroon, 2013–19

Event type	2013	2014	2015	2016	2017	2018	2019
Battles	17	1 223	959	340	269	983	640
Explosions/remote violence	0	33	202	175	217	31	20
Protests, riots and strategic developments	1	0	0	11	46	7	2
Violence against civilians	14	110	278	195	183	492	543
Total	**32**	**1 366**	**1 439**	**721**	**715**	**1 513**	**1 205**

Note: For definitions of event types, see Armed Conflict Location & Event Data Project (ACLED), 'ACLED definitions of political violence and protest', 11 Apr. 2019.

Source: ACLED, 'Data export tool', [n.d.].

recruited broadly among the Fulani community, for example.[8] In addition, as has been the case in Mali, self-defence groups and vigilantes have become increasingly involved in counter-militancy efforts, triggering intercommunal violence among jihadi groups and the self-defence groups and militias.[9]

Security continued to deteriorate throughout the year as suspected jihadists increased attacks on civilians and security forces, especially in the north and east. In May for example, six people were killed in an attack on a church in the country's north, following months of rising violence targeting schools and public services.[10] In November at least 37 people were killed in an attack on a Canadian mining company's convoy in the east, where the identity of the combatants was unknown, as has increasingly been the case in many of the attacks.[11]

The violence has triggered a sudden humanitarian crisis in the country, with about half a million people (out of a population of 20 million) being internally displaced, lacking healthcare and experiencing food insecurity.[12] Around 1.5 million people in Burkina Faso needed humanitarian aid—protection, food and livelihoods assistance—in 2019, and this is expected to rise to 2.2 million in 2020.[13]

---

[8] Kishi, R. et al., *Year in Review* (Armed Conflict Location & Event Data Project, ACLED: 2 Mar. 2020), p. 40.

[9] Human Rights Watch, 'Burkina Faso: Armed Islamist atrocities surge', 6 Jan. 2020; *The Economist*, 'States in the Sahel have unleashed ethnic gangs with guns', 2 May 2019; and Kleinfeld, P., 'Burkina Faso, part 2: Communities buckle as conflict ripples through the Sahel', New Humanitarian, 18 Apr. 2019.

[10] BBC, 'Burkina Faso church attack: Priest among six killed', 12 May 2019.

[11] Austen, I., 'Gunmen in Burkina Faso attack Canadian Mining Company convoy, killing 37', *New York Times*, 6 Nov. 2019; and *The Economist*, 'How West Africa's gold rush is funding jihadists', 14 Nov. 2019.

[12] UN Office for the Coordination of Humanitarian Affairs (OCHA), 'Stronger international support needed as Burkina Faso humanitarian emergency deepens', Press release, 11 Oct. 2019; and OCHA, 'Situation report, Burkina Faso', 29 Oct. 2019.

[13] OCHA, *Global Humanitarian Overview 2020* (OCHA: Geneva, Dec. 2019), p. 51.

Cameroon

There were two main unrelated armed conflicts in Cameroon in 2019: the anglophone crisis in the west and the Boko Haram insurgency in the north. In June for example, 16 soldiers and 8 civilians were killed in a Boko Haram attack, the deadliest attack against security forces since 2016.[14] However, the highest levels of violence took place in the west as government forces continued efforts to defeat the anglophone separatist insurgency. Conflict-related fatalities in 2019 were at a slightly lower level than in 2018, although violence against civilians increased to the highest levels in the 2013–19 period (see table 7.3).

The conflict in anglophone Cameroon

The origins of the anglophone crisis began almost a century ago. Between 1922 and 1960 France administered most of Cameroon, but the North-west and South-west regions were ruled as a British protectorate. Today, 5 million people in those two regions—about one fifth of the country's population—speak mainly English and have their own legal and educational systems. Long-standing tensions in this part of the country—the anglophone demand for an autonomous republic called Ambazonia, because of a sense of marginalization by the French-speaking majority, dates back to at least 1985—turned violent in October 2017.[15] The confrontation, which started as protests by anglophone teachers and lawyers against the use of French in anglophone schools and courts, was transformed into an armed insurgency by separatist militias after the protests were harshly repressed by the government.

In 2019 violence continued in the anglophone regions, and more than 486 000 people were displaced, with about 105 000 fleeing to Nigeria.[16] The conflict has turned into a significant and complex humanitarian emergency, with about 2.3 million people in need at the end of 2019, an increase of 80 per cent compared with the beginning of 2019 and an almost 15-fold increase since 2018. Attacks on medical staff and infrastructure became a frequent occurrence, and more than 80 per cent of government-run health facilities were closed in the two anglophone regions.[17] In addition, almost 90 per cent of children in the two regions have not gone to school for three years,

---

[14] Al Jazeera, 'Dozens killed in major Boko Haram attack on Cameroon island', 12 June 2019.

[15] International Crisis Group (ICG), *Cameroon's Anglophone Crisis at the Crossroads*, Africa Report no. 250 (ICG: Brussels, 2 Aug. 2017). On developments in 2018, see Davis, I. and Melvin, N., 'Armed conflict and peace processes in sub-Saharan Africa', *SIPRI Yearbook 2019*, pp. 124–25.

[16] OCHA (note 13), p. 52.

[17] OCHA (note 13), p. 52.

because of forced displacements and the enforcement of a boycott called for by separatists.[18]

Human rights abuses and violations continued to be reported during 2019, including torture, arbitrary arrest, detention and forced disappearances. Many of the attacks were attributed to government forces, and especially members of the Rapid Intervention Battalion.[19] Increasing violence and the lack of progress towards political solutions to the crisis suggests that further displacement and increased humanitarian needs will continue in 2020.

In 2018 it was hoped that a proposed anglophone general conference organized by religious leaders would be a first step towards a national dialogue and mediation process. However, the conference was postponed twice during that year, with no clear indication as to when the government might permit it to proceed.[20] On 10 September 2019 President Paul Biya proposed a national dialogue aimed at resolving the crisis, but it was reportedly unlikely to include separatists or other important English-speaking constituencies.[21] The national dialogue event took place from 30 September to 4 October in the capital Yaoundé. Opinion was divided as to whether it offered grounds for optimism or was a facade. Although several separatist leaders pulled out, calling instead for international mediation, a series of concessions and proposals emerged from the dialogue, including a special status for anglophone regions and more regional autonomy. President Biya also released more than 300 separatist fighters and opposition leader Maurice Kamto.[22] However, it seemed unlikely that the concessions would be sufficient to satisfy separatist groups and end the fighting.

Chad

Chad has been an important partner for the international community in the fight against jihadist groups in the Sahel.[23] In 2019 the security situation continued to deteriorate in the country, with a sharp increase in attacks by

---

[18] *The Economist*, 'A war of words: English-speaking villages are burning in Cameroon', 7 Nov. 2019; and Maclean, R., 'Stay home or risk being shot: Cameroon's back-to-school crisis', *The Guardian*, 3 Sep. 2019.

[19] Human Rights Watch, 'Cameroon: New attacks on civilians by troops, separatists', 28 Mar. 2019; and Human Rights Watch, 'Cameroon: Government forces attack village', 10 Apr. 2019.

[20] International Crisis Group, 'Cameroon: Proposed anglophone general conference deserves national and international support', Statement, 17 Sep. 2018; and *Cameroon Daily Journal*, 'Ambazonia war: Cameroon misses a golden opportunity to pull out of the anglophone crisis', 23 Nov. 2018.

[21] Ndi, N. E., 'Hope for Western Cameroon as Biya finally talks peace', *East African*, 14 May 2019; and International Crisis Group, 'Cameroon's anglophone dialogue: A work in progress', Statement, 26 Sep. 2019.

[22] Al Jazeera, 'Cameroon dialogue starts as anglophone separatists pull out', 30 Sep. 2019; and Chimtom, N. K., 'Cameroon's conflict: Will the national dialogue make any difference?', BBC, 5 Oct. 2019.

[23] International Crisis Group, *Chad: Between Ambition and Fragility*, Africa Report no. 233 (International Crisis Group: Brussels, 30 Mar. 2016).

Boko Haram, other Chadian armed groups and intercommunal violence—particularly between Arab and non-Arab communities in eastern Chad.[24] These conflicts flowed partly from farmer–herder competition, but also from deeper identity-based rivalries over land and political power. There were over 560 conflict-related fatalities in 2019 (and 450 were combat related), which is the highest level since 2015 (when there were nearly 430 conflict-related deaths).[25] In early February Chadian rebels based in southern Libya launched an incursion into north-east Chad. At the government's request, French air strikes halted their advance—the first direct French military intervention in Chad since 2008.[26] Incidents involving Boko Haram in 2019 included an assault by the group on a Chadian military position in the south-west in March that killed 23 soldiers, and an attack on a Lake Chad fishing village in the country's western region in December that killed over 14 people.[27] In August after dozens of people were killed in communal violence in eastern Chad, the government imposed a six-month state of emergency.[28]

More than 50 000 people were displaced by the deteriorating security environment in 2019, bringing the number of internally displaced in Chad to 175 000. In addition, the country hosted 468 000 refugees from the Central African Republic, Nigeria and Sudan. Legislative elections, originally scheduled for 2015, continued to be postponed, and the country faced many economic challenges, including declining oil revenues and the closure of borders. Food insecurity affected nearly 3.8 million people.[29]

Mali

Since 2015 Mali's central regions of Mopti and Ségou have become the focus of interconnected challenges of governance, development and security. Security in central Mali continued to deteriorate in 2019, whereas the situation in the north (Gao, Kidal, Ménaka, Taoudénit and Timbuktu) generally remained

---

[24] International Crisis Group, *Avoiding the Resurgence of Inter-communal Violence in Eastern Chad*, Africa Report no. 284 (International Crisis Group: Brussels, 30 Dec. 2019).

[25] ACLED, 'Data export tool', [n.d.].

[26] International Crisis Group, 'Rebel incursion exposes Chad's weaknesses', Q&A, 13 Feb. 2019; and Corey-Boulet, R., 'Threatened by rebels, Chad's Deby leans on firepower from France', *World Politics Review*, 8 Feb. 2019.

[27] Reuters, 'Boko Haram militants kill 23 Chad soldiers: Security sources', 22 Mar. 2019; and New Arab, 'Boko Haram launches deadly attack on Chad fishing village', 19 Dec. 2019.

[28] France 24, 'Chad declares emergency in east after dozens die in ethnic violence', 18 Aug. 2019.

[29] OCHA (note 13), p. 54.

Table 7.4. Estimated conflict-related fatalities in Mali, 2013–19

Event type	2013	2014	2015	2016	2017	2018	2019
Battles	547	301	316	210	563	759	831
Explosions/remote violence	191	39	27	32	144	177	234
Protests, riots and strategic developments	7	1	5	7	3	28	4
Violence against civilians	138	41	80	71	237	783	818
Total	**883**	**382**	**428**	**320**	**947**	**1 747**	**1 887**

Note: For definitions of event types, see Armed Conflict Location & Event Data Project (ACLED), 'ACLED definitions of political violence and protest', 11 Apr. 2019.

Source: ACLED, 'Data export tool', [n.d.].

stable. However, the security situation remained complex throughout the country.[30]

The situation in northern Mali

The instability in the north has its roots in a long-running Tuareg rebellion and, in 2012, an opportunistic alliance of Tuareg separatists and Islamist militants that seized control of northern cities. International intervention and a 2015 peace accord helped to quell, but not end, the armed conflict in the north, which is now multidimensional and includes three coalitions of armed groups that signed the 2015 peace accord or were included in the subsequent process—Coordination of Azawad Movements, Coordination of Entente Movements and Platform of Movements of 14 June 2014 of Algiers—a network of jihadist groups (mainly JNIM) and various self-defence groups.[31] According to a UN expert panel on Mali, the connections among the various armed groups 'are mainly opportunistic, either motivated by the local political dynamics and balance of power or by criminal interests'.[32] The UN reported in December 2019 that 'the security situation in the north has deteriorated and become increasingly more complex', and highlighted 'increased terrorist activity' in the Ménaka region.[33]

---

[30] On the evolution and complexity of the conflict in Mali, see Dal Santo, E. and van der Heide, E. J., 'Escalating complexity in regional conflicts: Connecting geopolitics to individual pathways to terrorism in Mali', *African Security*, vol. 11, no. 3 (2018), pp. 274–91; and Sköns, E., 'The implementation of the peace process in Mali: A complex case of peacebuilding', *SIPRI Yearbook 2016*, pp. 155–88. On developments in Mali in 2018, see *SIPRI Yearbook 2019* (note 15), pp. 127–29. On the relationship between religion and Malian society, see Lebovich, A., 'Sacred struggles: How Islam shapes politics in Mali', European Council on Foreign Relations, Policy Brief, Nov. 2019. On the role of gender in the conflict, see Gorman, Z. and Chauzal, G., '"Hand in hand": A study of insecurity and gender in Mali', SIPRI Insights on Peace and Security no. 2019/6, Dec. 2019.

[31] On the political and social dimensions of these armed groups, see Tobie, A. and Sangaré, B., *The Impact of Armed Groups on the Populations of Central and Northern Mali: Necessary Adaptations of the Strategies for Re-establishing Peace* (SIPRI and Ministry for Foreign Affairs of Finland: Oct. 2019).

[32] UN Security Council, 'Final report of the Panel of Experts established pursuant to resolution 2374 (2017) on Mali and extended pursuant to resolution 2432 (2018)', S/2019/636, 7 Aug. 2019, p. 19.

[33] UN Security Council, 'Situation in Mali', Report of the Secretary-General, S/2019/983, 30 Dec. 2019, p. 8.

The situation in central Mali

Since 2015 the centre has experienced a growing rise in social unrest, banditry and intercommunal violence—among the Fulani, Bambara and Dogon ethnic groups in the Mopti and Ségou regions.[34] The dynamics of the conflict in this region are multidimensional, often rooted in conflicts over land use and natural resources. The jihadist groups have been adept at mobilizing support by exploiting local grievances and social fractures. Their spread into the centre and the government's increasing reliance on some ethnically based self-defence groups to fight them has led to increased retributive violence. On 23 March 2019 for example, a Dogon militia attacked the village of Ogossagou and killed at least 157 Fulani civilians, while on 9 and 17 June armed attacks on Dogon-inhabited villages killed almost an equal number of civilians.[35]

Some of the counterterrorism operations of the Malian security and defences forces, which are supported by French forces (Operation Barkhane) and the Joint Force of the Group of Five for the Sahel (JF-G5S), appear to have exacerbated the intercommunal violence. Human rights abuses have been widespread and armed groups and local militias have proliferated, while root causes (such as the lack of public services and a weak governance) remain unaddressed.[36]

The humanitarian impact

In all the regions of Mali affected by armed conflict in 2019, essential services, including schools and health centres, were interrupted or halted. Conflict-related fatalities, including violence against civilians continued to rise in 2019, as shown in table 7.4. There were also heavy casualties in the armed conflict between government and international forces and jihadist groups. In November 2019 for example, ISGS militants killed 53 Malian soldiers and one civilian in an attack on an army base near the Mali–Niger border.[37]

The growing insecurity has also led to a large rise in internally displaced people—from 77 000 in September 2018 to 187 000 in September 2019—and increased food insecurity. The number of children with severe acute malnutrition increased by 20 per cent in the first half of 2019: from 160 000 in January to 190 000 in July.[38]

---

[34] Tobie, A., 'Central Mali: Violence, local perspectives and diverging narratives', SIPRI Insights on Peace and Security no. 2017/5, Dec. 2017; Matfess, H., 'What explains the rise of communal violence in Mali, Nigeria and Ethiopia?', *World Politics Review*, 11 Sep. 2019; and Bodian, M. et al., 'The challenges of governance, security and development in the central regions of Mali', SIPRI Background Paper no. 2020/4, Mar. 2020.

[35] International Crisis Group, 'Central Mali: Putting a stop to ethnic cleansing', Q&A, 25 Mar. 2019; UN Security Council, S/2019/636 (note 32), p. 7; and BBC, 'Mali attack: "100 killed" in ethnic Dogon village', 10 June 2019.

[36] International Crisis Group, *Speaking with the 'Bad Guys': Toward Dialogue with Central Mali's Jihadists*, Africa Report no. 276 (International Crisis Group: Brussels, 28 May 2019).

[37] Al Jazeera, 'Mali: Dozens of troops killed in military outpost attack', 3 Nov. 2019.

[38] OCHA (note 13), p. 56.

The peace process and international stabilization efforts

A peace deal signed in 2015 between the government and some armed groups is supported by MINUSMA and international donors. As part of a road map adopted in March 2018 (to implement the 2015 peace agreement) and following the re-election of President Ibrahim Boubacar Keïta a few months later, the Malian Government embarked on ambitious political and institutional reforms. An October 2018 Pact for Peace in Mali between the Malian Government and the UN was meant to accelerate the implementation of the road map. A disarmament, demobilization and reintegration (DDR) process was launched a month later.[39] In 2019 however, the relevance of these agreements continued to be undermined by the worsening security situation in central Mali, the dire humanitarian situation and the limited implementation of the peace agreement. According to a UN panel of experts on Mali constitutional reforms were delayed and the electoral calendar was scrapped pending an 'inclusive political dialogue'—although there appeared to be limited opportunities for dialogue among the conflicting parties.[40] The expert panel also noted delays to the DDR process, although 63 000 combatants had been registered by mid-March 2019.[41]

The international stabilization effort also appeared to be at a crossroads. Despite years of training and assistance French officials acknowledged that government security forces remained incapable of bearing the anti-jihadist fight.[42] By the end of 2019 the effectiveness and wisdom of the French military mission, Operation Barkhane, was being increasingly questioned in the region and also in France—particularly following the rise of anti-French sentiment in the Sahel.[43] Similarly, the JF-G5S has been criticized for its military-centric approach, poor coordination among partner countries and disagreements over its precise mandate.[44] As noted above, far from stem-

---

[39] UN Security Council, Report of the Secretary-General on the situation in Mali, S/2018/1174, 28 Dec. 2018.

[40] International Crisis Group (note 36).

[41] UN Security Council, S/2019/636 (note 32), pp. 14–15.

[42] Mules, I., 'Anti-French sentiment on the rise in West Africa as security situation deteriorates', *Deutsche Welle*, 12 Dec. 2019. Also see Tull, D. M., 'Rebuilding Mali's army: The dissonant relationship between Mali and its international partners', *International Affairs*, vol. 95, no. 2 (2019), pp. 405–22.

[43] BBC, 'Helicopter collision kills 13 French troops in Mali', 26 Nov. 2019; 'In search of allies', *Africa Confidential*, vol. 60, no. 25, 19 Dec. 2019; and Louet, S. and Diallo, T., 'As France mourns 13 soldiers, top general says full victory in Africa impossible', Reuters, 27 Nov. 2019.

[44] Dieng, M., 'The Multi-National Joint Task Force and the G5 Sahel Joint Force: The limits of military capacity-building efforts', *Contemporary Security Policy*, vol. 40. no. 4 (2019), pp. 481–501; and Rupesinghe, N., 'The Joint Force of the G5 Sahel: An appropriate response to combat terrorism?', African Centre for the Constructive Resolution of Disputes, 18 Sep. 2018.

ming the violence, international engagement and the actions of state security forces often appeared to be exacerbating instability.[45]

There have also been questions over the effectiveness of MINUSMA's efforts to help stabilize the country and protect civilians.[46] It is by far the deadliest UN peace operation and continued to suffer more casualties than any other UN mission in 2019.[47] Resolution 2480, adopted by the UN Security Council on 28 June 2019, renewed MINUSMA's mandate for the fifth time, extending it to 30 June 2020. The Security Council decided that the mission's 'second strategic priority', after support for implementation of the 2015 accord, would be to 'facilitate' a future Malian-led strategy to protect civilians, reduce intercommunal violence and re-establish state authority in the centre of the country.[48] Without effective implementation of the 2015 peace agreement and the return of the rule of law and essential services throughout the country, armed attacks and communal violence are likely to continue in 2020.

Niger

Niger has been a key transit point for armed criminal and extremist Islamist groups operating in the Sahel region. Since 2015 the Nigerien army has been subject to increased attacks by such groups: by Boko Haram on the eastern part of the country, and since 2017 by groups near the borders with Burkina Faso and Mali.[49] French Operation Barkhane and United States forces support the Nigerien armed forces in counterterrorism operations inside the country.[50] Armed violence by non-state armed groups in neighbouring countries—Mali and Nigeria in particular—continued to spill across the border in 2019, and insecurity and attacks severely disrupted essential social services, exacerbated food insecurity and led to significant displacement. As

---

[45] See e.g. Watson, A. and Karlshøj-Pedersen, M., *Fusion Doctrine in Five Steps: Lessons Learned from Remote Warfare in Africa* (Oxford Research Group: Nov. 2019); Raineri, L., *If Victims Become Perpetrators: Factors Contributing to Vulnerability and Resilience to Violent Extremism in the Central Sahel* (International Alert: June 2018); Hickendorff, A., 'Civil Society White Book on Peace and Security in Mali', English summary, SIPRI, July 2019; and Dörrie, P., 'Europe has spent years trying to prevent "chaos" in the Sahel. It failed', *World Politics Review*, 25 June 2019.

[46] van der Lijn, J. et al., *Assessing the Effectiveness of the United Nations Mission in Mali/MINUSMA* (Norwegian Institute of International Affairs: Oslo, 2019).

[47] See chapter 2, section II, in this volume.

[48] UN Security Council Resolution 2480, 28 June 2019. On the role of MINUSMA, also see Smit, T. 'Regional trends and developments in peace operations', *SIPRI Yearbook 2019*, pp. 163–64.

[49] On the role of the illicit economy and trafficking in fuelling violence in Niger, see International Crisis Group, *Managing Trafficking in Northern Niger*, Africa Report no. 285 (International Crisis Group: Brussels, 6 Jan. 2020).

[50] Kelly, F., 'Joint France-Niger air and ground operation near Tongo Tongo kills 15 "terrorists"', Defense Post, 30 Dec. 2018; and Correll, D. S., 'Armed drones to fly out of Niger air base now operational after delayed completion', *Air Force Times*, 1 Nov. 2019.

Table 7.5. Estimated conflict-related fatalities in Nigeria, 2013–19

Event type	2013	2014	2015	2016	2017	2018	2019
Battles	2 326	4 031	3 329	2 191	1 779	2 470	2 484
Explosions/remote violence	255	1 311	1 938	681	1 424	759	770
Protests, riots and strategic developments	66	252	366	138	144	161	110
Violence against civilians	2 039	5 794	5 285	1 886	1 599	2 853	2 075
Total	**4 686**	**11 388**	**10 918**	**4 896**	**4 946**	**6 243**	**5 439**

Note: For definitions of event types, see Armed Conflict Location & Event Data Project (ACLED), 'ACLED definitions of political violence and protest', 11 Apr. 2019.

Source: ACLED, 'Data export tool', [n.d.].

of October 2019 at least 440 000 people had been internally displaced and were living in vulnerable conditions across the country.[51]

In December 2019 at least 71 Nigerien soldiers were killed in an attack by an unknown jihadist group in the west near the Malian border, the deadliest single attack against security forces in the country's history.[52] Conflict-related fatalities in Niger increased to over 700 in 2019 (including nearly 490 combat-related deaths), the highest level since 2015.[53] There was also increased use of improvised explosive devices (IEDs) by armed groups, especially ISGS, in western Niger.[54]

Nigeria

The conflict dynamic involving government forces, Boko Haram and other non-state armed groups have devastated communities in north-east Nigeria, and the resulting humanitarian crisis remains one of the most severe in the world. Armed conflict, forced displacement and grave human rights violations, including killings, sexual violence, abduction and recruitment of child soldiers, have been widespread in Adamawa, Borno and Yobe states over the last decade.[55] Insecurity in Nigeria is also fuelled by other complex security challenges, including separatist aspirations in eastern Nigeria, violence between sedentary farmers and nomadic herders in the country's Middle Belt (an area that stretches across the middle third of the country

---

[51] OCHA (note 13), p. 57.

[52] Armstrong, H., 'Behind the Jihadist attack in Inates', International Crisis Group Q&A, 13 Dec. 2019; and BBC, 'Niger army base attack leaves at least 71 soldiers dead', 12 Dec. 2019.

[53] ACLED (note 25).

[54] Pavlik, M. et al., 'Explosive developments: The growing threat of IEDs in Western Niger', ACLED, 19 June 2019. On the efforts to address the IED threat, see chapter 13, section I, in this volume.

[55] On the gender question in the Boko Haram insurgency, see Okoli, A. C. and Nnaemeka Azom, S., 'Boko Haram insurgency and gendered victimhood: Women as corporal victims and objects of war', *Small Wars & Insurgencies*, vol. 30, no. 6–7 (2019), pp. 1214–32; Okolie-Osemene, J. and Okolie-Osemene, R. I., 'Nigerian women and the trends of kidnapping in the era of Boko Haram insurgency: Patterns and evolution', *Small Wars & Insurgencies*, vol. 30, no. 6–7 (2019), pp. 1151–68; and International Crisis Group, *Returning from the Land of Jihad: The Fate of Women Associated with Boko Haram*, Africa Report no. 275 (International Crisis Group: Brussels, 21 May 2019).

from east to west) and the re-emergence of armed militant groups in the Niger Delta.[56] The threat landscape in Nigeria may also be evolving with a burgeoning Shia inspired group, the Islamic Movement in Nigeria.[57] In February 2019 election-related violence occurred around Nigeria's presidential election, leaving at least 40 dead. President Muhammadu Buhari won a second term, but his main challenger Atiku Abubakar rejected the result.[58]

As of August 2019 nearly 2 million people were internally displaced, and another 240 000 were refugees in neighbouring countries. At the end of 2019 an estimated 7.7 million people were in need of humanitarian assistance, an 8 per cent increase from the end of 2018. An estimated 3 million people were food insecure as of September 2019, an increase from 2.7 million people since October 2018.[59] In 2019 conflict-related fatalities in Nigeria were the fourth highest in the world at 5439 (see table 7.5), with the highest number of fatalities attributed to armed conflict (battles) between the Nigerian military and Boko Haram and the Islamic State West Africa Province (ISWAP, a Boko Haram splinter group).[60]

Insurgency in the north-east

Although territory controlled by Boko Haram was recaptured by the Nigerian armed forces during 2015–16, and President Buhari has repeatedly claimed that the group has been defeated, it remained a serious threat in 2019.[61] ISWAP was particularly active with several military successes, deepening roots in the civilian population and a growing membership (estimated at 3500–5000 fighters).[62] In 2019 Borno state continued to be the epicentre of the conflict.

---

[56] Beaumont, P. and Abrak, I., 'Oil-rich Nigeria outstrips India as country with most people in poverty', *The Guardian*, 16 July 2018.

[57] Gray, S. and Adeakin, I., 'Nigeria's Shi'a Islamic Movement and evolving Islamist threat landscape: Old, new and future generators of radicalization', *African Security*, vol. 12, no. 2 (2019), pp. 174–99.

[58] Searcey, D., 'Dozens dead in Nigeria as election results are delayed', *New York Times*, 25 Feb. 2019; and *The Economist*, 'Nigeria's President Muhammadu Buhari wins a second term', 28 Feb. 2019.

[59] OCHA (note 13), p. 58.

[60] Kishi et al. (note 8), p. 20.

[61] On developments within the Boko Haram insurgency in 2017–18, see Davis, I. et al., 'Armed conflict in sub-Saharan Africa', *SIPRI Yearbook 2018*, pp. 95–96; and *SIPRI Yearbook 2019* (note 15), pp. 121–23. On Nigeria's failure to defeat Boko Haram, see Banini, D. K., 'Security sector corruption and military effectiveness: The influence of corruption on countermeasures against Boko Haram in Nigeria', *Small Wars & Insurgencies*, vol. 31, no. 1 (2020), pp. 131–58; Mickler, D. et al., '"Weak state", regional power, global player: Nigeria and the response to Boko Haram', *African Security*, vol. 12, no. 3–4 (2019), pp. 272–99; Chidubem Iwuoha, V., 'Clash of counterterrorism-assistance-seeking states and their super power sponsors: Implications on the war against Boko Haram', *African Security Review*, vol. 28, no. 1 (2019), pp. 38–55; and Botha, A. and Abdile, M., 'Reality versus perception: Toward understanding Boko Haram in Nigeria', *Studies in Conflict & Terrorism*, vol. 42, no. 5 (2019), pp. 493–519.

[62] International Crisis Group, *Facing the Challenge of the Islamic State in West Africa Province*, Africa Report no. 273 (International Crisis Group: Brussels, 16 May 2019). On the political–military character of ISWAP, see Stoddard, E., 'Revolutionary warfare? Assessing the character of competing factions within the Boko Haram insurgency', *African Security*, vol. 12, no. 3–4 (2019), pp. 300–29. On the splintering of Boko Haram, see Zenn, J. 'Boko Haram's factional feuds: Internal extremism and external interventions', *Terrorism and Political Violence* (2019).

For example, at least a dozen soldiers were killed in an assault on an army base by ISWAP in June 2019, and the group carried out a series of attacks on the Nigerian army in northern Borno throughout September.[63] In July a Boko Haram attack on a funeral and villages near Maiduguri in north-east Nigeria killed over 70 people.[64] To end the insurgency the International Crisis Group suggested that the Nigerian Government will need to supplement its military campaign with measures that address the factors that contribute to the insurgency, including weak governance and a lack of basic services.[65] Corruption and political misuse of Nigeria's security sector will also need to be addressed.[66]

Communal violence and resource conflicts

Communal violence in Nigeria involves numerous actors and occurs across the country. In particular, conflicts over how to manage natural resources have spiralled into attacks on civilians by ethnic militias. In the Niger Delta region there is a conflict between militants and federal government over the control of petroleum resources. In the Middle Belt region and part of the north-west armed conflicts have occurred between mostly Christian farmers and predominantly Muslim herders, who have been migrating southward because of desertification, insecurity and the loss of grazing land to expanding settlements.[67]

[63] New Arab, 'Militants kill 15 soldiers, raid Nigerian military base', 19 June 2019; and Kelly, F., 'Nigeria: Islamic State claims "tens" of military casualties in 2 Borno attacks', Defense Post, 11 Sep. 2019.

[64] Sawab, I. et al., 'Nigerians flee after men on motorbikes shoot down mourners', *New York Times*, 29 July 2019.

[65] International Crisis Group (note 62).

[66] Page, M., 'Nigeria's struggles with security sector reform', Chatham House, 2 Apr. 2019.

[67] Ajodo-Adebanjoko, A., 'Political economy and national security implications of resource-based conflicts in Nigeria', *African Security Review*, vol. 28, no. 1 (2019), pp. 56–71.

III. Armed conflict and peace processes in Central Africa

IAN DAVIS

The African Development Bank defines Central Africa as Cameroon, the Central African Republic (CAR), Chad, the Democratic Republic of the Congo (DRC), the Republic of the Congo, Equatorial Guinea and Gabon.[1] For the purpose of this chapter Burundi is also considered to be part of Central Africa. Although five Central African states were involved in armed conflicts in 2019—Burundi, Cameroon, the CAR, Chad and the DRC—the armed conflicts in Cameroon and Chad were discussed in section II as part of the Lake Chad region. In this section the focus is on the long-running armed conflicts in the CAR and the DRC. In the CAR the main challenge was in implementing a new February 2019 peace agreement between the government and armed groups, while in the DRC a period of political transition was accompanied by increasing insecurity and political violence in the eastern provinces and an ongoing health emergency from the measles and Ebola outbreaks.

Burundi

Burundi is one of the world's poorest nations and the scene of one of Africa's most intractable ethnic-based civil wars (1993–2005). A new wave of violence, political unrest and human rights violations commenced in 2015 (resulting in over 1100 fatalities) when President Pierre Nkurunziza announced he was running for a third term (at odds with the constitution's two-term limit). Government security forces and a pro-government militia (the Imbonerakure) began targeting suspected dissidents.[2] Several armed groups were formed and some, like RED-Tabara, began operating out of eastern DRC.[3] In 2019 the civil unrest and armed violence left nearly 300 people dead, including over 100 battle-related fatalities and over 160 from violence against civilians.[4] The Imbonerakure continued to be one of the most active perpetrators of violence targeting civilians, especially in the context of the approaching 2020 presidential elections.[5]

---

[1] African Development Bank, 'Central Africa'.

[2] Mayanja, N. E., 'Burundi's enduring legacy of ethnic violence and political conflict', Rosa Luxemburg Stiftung, Feb. 2019.

[3] Defense Post, 'Several killed in clashes between Burundi security forces and RED-Tabara rebels', 23 Oct. 2019; and Defense Post, 'Gunmen ambush Burundi soldiers near Rwanda border, defense ministry says', 19 Nov. 2019.

[4] Armed Conflict Location & Event Data Project (ACLED), 'Data export tool', [n.d.].

[5] Kishi, R. et al., *Year in Review* (ACLED, 2 Mar. 2020), p. 55.

Table 7.6. Estimated conflict-related fatalities in the Central African Republic, 2013–19

Event type	2013	2014	2015	2016	2017	2018	2019
Battles	1 223	1 144	191	443	1 250	624	280
Explosions/remote violence	4	105	12	1	10	2	3
Protests, riots and strategic developments	122	105	56	8	14	25	4
Violence against civilians	1 210	2 265	266	287	555	520	286
Total	**2 559**	**3 619**	**525**	**739**	**1 829**	**1 171**	**573**

Note: For definitions of event types, see Armed Conflict Location & Event Data Project (ACLED), 'ACLED definitions of political violence and protest', 11 Apr. 2019.

Source: ACLED, 'Data export tool', [n.d.].

The Central African Republic

Almost the entire territory of the CAR has been affected by conflict and violence among shifting alliances of armed groups that have displaced 25 per cent of the population. The armed conflict began in December 2012 between the mainly Muslim Séléka armed group (which seized power in 2013) and the mainly Christian Anti-balaka armed group. Although the Séléka handed power to a transitional government in 2014, violence continued, and the country was effectively partitioned despite the presence of a United Nations peace operation, the UN Multidimensional Integrated Stabilization Mission in the CAR (MINUSCA). Since then both groups have splintered into smaller factions, and despite a June 2017 peace agreement between the government and 13 of the 14 armed groups, violence soon resumed.[6] In July 2017 the African Union (AU) and partners produced a new road map for peace and reconciliation in the CAR, but the situation continued to deteriorate in 2018 with neither MINUSCA nor the fledgling national army, trained by the European Union (EU) and Russian advisers, able to constrain the fighting.[7]

However, in 2019 the number of attacks targeting civilians and clashes among armed groups decreased (largely as a result of a new peace agreement and ceasefire, see below), resulting in the lowest level of conflict-related fatalities since 2015, see table 7.6. Nonetheless, a UN panel of experts on the CAR concluded that displacement figures—at the end of September 2019 more than 600 000 people remained internally displaced, while the number of CAR refugees had risen to 607 000 (mostly in Cameroon, Chad and

---

[6] Centraafrique-presse, 'Accord politique pour la paix en République centrafricaine' [Political agreement for peace in the Central African Republic], Blog post, 19 June 2017. On the historical and contemporary roots of conflict in CAR, see Olayiwola, O. A., 'A leadership perspective for sustainable peace in the Central African Republic', African Centre for the Constructive Resolution of Disputes, 2 Sep. 2019.
[7] On developments in the CAR in 2017–18, see *SIPRI Yearbook 2018*, pp. 87–88; and *SIPRI Yearbook 2019*, pp. 129–31. On MINUSCA's role in 2018, see *SIPRI Yearbook 2019*, pp. 166–67. On local and international stakeholders views on security sector reform in the CAR, see Glawion, T. et al., 'Securing legitimate stability in CAR: External assumptions and local perspectives', SIPRI Policy Study, Sep. 2019.

the DRC)—indicated little change in the security situation.[8] There were also continued reports of violations of human rights and international humanitarian law, and about 2.6 million people (more than half of the population) remained in need of humanitarian assistance, with about 41 per cent of the population being severely food insecure.[9]

A new peace agreement in 2019

On 6 February 2019, following months of negotiations, the government and 14 armed groups reached a new peace agreement, the Political Agreement for Peace and Reconciliation in the Central African Republic, following talks in Sudan facilitated by Russia—the eighth such agreement since the outbreak of conflict in 2013.[10] Representatives from armed groups were granted ministerial positions in a new inclusive government as part of the peace deal. The agreement began to fray almost immediately, with the withdrawal of some of the signatories, but following further discussions under AU auspices in Addis Ababa, Ethiopia, on 18–20 March 2019, the government agreed to increase the number of ministerial posts given to armed groups, and the deal appeared to be back on track.[11]

The UN panel of experts on the CAR reported in December 2019 that the agreement's implementation 'remained limited'.[12] One of the main provisions of the agreement was to establish by April 2019 three joint government-armed group security units, known as special mixed security units (unités spéciales mixtes de sécurité, USMS), which were designed to encourage armed groups 'to protect the populations instead of committing racketeering crimes', according to AU spokesperson, Francis Che.[13] However, training and operationalization of the joint security units were delayed, and only one (covering the west of the country) was close to being operational at the end of

---

[8] UN Security Council, 'Final report of the Panel of Experts on the Central African Republic extended pursuant to Security Council resolution 2454 (2019)', S/2019/930, 14 Dec. 2019, p. 8.

[9] UN Office for the Coordination of Humanitarian Affairs (OCHA), *Aperçu des Besoins Humanitaires: République Centrafricaine 2020* [*Humanitarian Needs Overview: Central African Republic 2020*], Oct. 2019, (in French); IPC, 'IPC acute food insecurity analysis 2019, Central African Republic', June 2019; UN Security Council, S/2019/930 (note 8), pp. 20–35; UN General Assembly, Human Rights Council, 'Human rights situation in the Central African Republic', A/HRC/42/61, 9 Aug. 2019; and OCHA, 'Central African Republic, Overview of population movements', 25 Oct. 2019.

[10] The agreement is annexed to the UN Security Council, Letter dated 14 February 2019 from the Secretary-General addressed to the President of the Security Council, S/2019/145, 15 Feb. 2019.

[11] Hilton, K., 'CAR peace accord: Efforts continue to save deal', *Cameroon Tribune*, 21 Mar. 2019; and Institute for Security Studies, 'The AU has stepped in to save the February peace deal in the Central African Republic, but it remains fragile', 23 Apr. 2019.

[12] UN Security Council, S/2019/930 (note 8). Also see Diatta, M. M., 'Can the Central African Republic's peace deal be saved?', Institute for Security Studies, 7 Oct. 2019.

[13] Cited in Surprenant, A., 'In Central African Republic, rebels fight on as peace deal falters', New Humanitarian, 4 Nov. 2019.

Table 7.7. Estimated conflict-related fatalities in the Democratic Republic of the Congo, 2013–19

Event type	2013	2014	2015	2016	2017	2018	2019
Battles	1 093	603	749	899	1 364	1 744	1 970
Explosions/remote violence	77	10	13	4	108	9	15
Protests, riots and strategic developments	16	38	65	145	79	56	119
Violence against civilians	789	579	936	693	1 659	1 286	1 564
Total	**1 975**	**1 230**	**1 763**	**1 741**	**3 210**	**3 095**	**3 668**

Note: For definitions of event types, see Armed Conflict Location & Event Data Project (ACLED), 'ACLED definitions of political violence and protest', 11 Apr. 2019.

Source: ACLED, 'Data export tool', [n.d.].

2019.[14] Disagreements over the units' command structures and the reluctance of some armed groups to commit fighters to longer-term disarmament has hindered formation of the USMS.[15]

After receiving training from the EU and Russian military advisers, the national army has now been deployed across most of the country, but continued to face operational challenges, despite the easing of the UN arms embargo in September 2019.[16] Implementation of the national disarmament, demobilization, reintegration and repatriation programme gathered pace: since its launch on 17 December 2018, 1321 combatants, including 81 women, have been disarmed and demobilized, and 802 weapons of war, 1239 unexploded ordnances and 67 281 rounds of ammunition collected. Despite this progress, the UN secretary-general reported that the disarmament and demobilization timelines were not being met—the process was scheduled to end in January 2020—mainly due to some armed groups failing to commit to disarmament.[17]

The government, with the support of MINUSCA, has had some success with dialogue and reconciliation efforts at the local level, and established 29 local peace and reconciliation committees across the country during 2019.[18] In November 2019 the mandate of MINUSCA was extended for a further 12 months until 15 November 2020.[19] At the end of 2019 the peace agreement remained fragile. Presidential and legislative elections sched-

[14] UN Security Council, 'Central African Republic', Report of the Secretary-General, S/2020/124, 14 Feb. 2020; and UN Security Council, S/2019/930 (note 8), pp. 10–12.

[15] International Crisis Group, *Making the Central African Republic's Latest Peace Agreement Stick*, Africa Report no. 277 (International Crisis Group: 18 June 2019); and UN Security Council, S/2019/930 (note 8), pp. 10–12.

[16] UN Security Council, S/2019/930 (note 8), pp. 32–35. On changes to the UN arms embargo on the CAR, see chapter 14, section II, in this volume.

[17] UN Security Council, Letter dated 31 December 2019 from the Secretary-General addressed to the President of the Security Council, S/2019/1008, 31 Dec. 2019.

[18] UN Security Council, 'Central African Republic', Report of the Secretary-General, S/2019/822, 15 Oct. 2019.

[19] UN Security Council Resolution 2499, 15 Nov. 2019.

uled for December 2020 could lead to further instability, especially as the commitment of some of the signatory armed groups to implement the peace agreement remained in question.[20]

The Democratic Republic of the Congo

The DRC—the second-largest country in Africa with a population of about 80 million—is suffering from one of the longest and most complex crises in the world, where armed conflict, epidemics and natural disasters combine with high levels of poverty, weak public infrastructure and services. Competition over land and mineral resources are also part of the conflict dynamic.[21] Since the end of the 1998–2003 Second Congo War conflict has persisted in the eastern DRC, where there are still dozens of armed groups and a major UN peacekeeping force, the UN Organization Stabilization Mission in the DRC (MONUSCO), has been deployed since 1999.[22]

The election held on 31 December 2018 resulted in the first peaceful transfer of power to an opposition party in the country's history. Although the results of the election were disputed and challenged by some observers and candidates, Félix Tshisekedi was declared the new president in early January.[23] He promised reforms and immediately released over 700 political prisoners.[24] He also prioritized improving relations with the country's neighbours—Burundi, Rwanda and Uganda—with the goal of establishing a new framework for regional cooperation against armed groups within the DRC.[25] While most of the DRC's 26 provinces were stable in 2019, 6 of the eastern provinces (particularly Ituri, North Kivu and South Kivu) faced continued attacks by armed groups and a resurgence of intercommunal violence.

The overall scale of violence remained high, as reflected in the conflict-related fatalities for 2019 being the highest recorded in the 2013–19 period (see table 7.7). Ongoing insurgencies in the eastern provinces by nearly 20 armed groups contributed to the rise in overall fatalities.[26] The Armed

---

[20] Surprenant (note 13).

[21] For detailed analysis of the armed conflict, see the various reports of the group of experts on the DRC, e.g. UN Security Council, 'Midterm report of the Group of Experts on the Democratic Republic of the Congo', S/2019/974, 20 Dec. 2019.

[22] The UN Organization Mission in the DRC was deployed in 1999 and renamed MONUSCO in 2010.

[23] Salihu, N., 'Elections in the Democratic Republic of the Congo', African Centre for the Constructive Resolution of Disputes, 2 Sep. 2019; and Wilson, T. et al., 'Congo voting data reveal huge fraud in poll to replace Kabila', *Financial Times*, 15 Jan. 2019.

[24] UN Security Council, 'United Nations Organization Stabilization Mission in the Democratic Republic of the Congo', Report of the Secretary-General, S/2019/575, 17 July 2019; and Al Jazeera, 'DRC President Tshisekedi pardons about 700 political prisoners', 14 Mar. 2019.

[25] International Crisis Group, 'A new approach to the UN to stabilise the DR Congo', Africa Briefing no. 148, 4 Dec. 2019.

[26] For details of the armed groups, see Africa Intelligence, 'Felix Tshisekedi a hostage to armed groups', *West Africa Newsletter*, issue 798, 10 Apr. 2019; and UN Security Council, S/2019/974 (note 21).

Conflict Location & Event Data Project recorded over 900 events with direct targeting of civilians, including a significant rise in political violence by anonymous or unidentified armed groups.[27] A former militia leader in the DRC, Bosco Ntaganda, was convicted in July 2019 by the International Criminal Court (ICC) of war crimes committed in 2002–2003, and was sentenced to 30 years in prison, the longest the ICC has ever handed down.[28] Four other militia leaders are being tried by the ICC, while others are being tried in national courts.[29]

With more than 940 000 people displaced in 2019, the DRC hosted the largest internally displaced population in Africa (5.01 million displaced people), as well as some 517 000 refugees from neighbouring countries. Almost 16 million people faced severe acute food insecurity—the second-highest number of acutely food-insecure people worldwide.[30] Enduring health epidemics further added to the severity of the crisis. The Ebola virus disease outbreak that began in August 2018 is the second-largest recorded outbreak in global history, and as of 31 December 2019, 2232 people had died from it.[31] Efforts to combat the Ebola outbreak were hampered by attacks on health workers and treatment centres.[32] The DRC also experienced its worst measles epidemic, with more than 6000 deaths during 2018–19, and outbreaks of cholera also remained a major concern.[33] The number of people in need of humanitarian assistance in the DRC is expected to rise to 15.9 million in 2020 (20 per cent of the population), with at least 4 million people expected to be at emergency levels of food insecurity.[34]

The future of the United Nations Organization Stabilization Mission in the Democratic Republic of the Congo

The focus of MONUSCO's mandate has generally been the protection of civilians and the extension of state authority in eastern DRC. Since 2013 this has included a Force Intervention Brigade authorized by the UN Security Council to 'neutralize and disarm' armed groups, including via offensive operations. However, the scope of these interventions has been

---

[27] Kishi et al. (note 5), pp. 28, 34, 36; and *The Economist*, 'Killings in Congo's north-east spark fears of a return to war', 13 July 2019.

[28] BBC, 'Bosco Ntaganda sentenced to 30 years for crimes in DR Congo', 7 Nov. 2019.

[29] *The Economist*, 'A warlord's trial aims to end impunity in Congo', 18 Dec. 2019.

[30] OCHA, *Global Humanitarian Overview 2020* (OCHA: Geneva, Dec. 2019), p. 55.

[31] World Health Organization, 'Ebola virus disease—Democratic Republic of the Congo', Disease outbreak news: Update, 2 Jan. 2020.

[32] Goldstein, J., 'Fighting Ebola when mourners fight the responders', *New York Times*, 19 May 2019; and Burke, J., 'Ebola health workers killed and injured by rebel attack in Congo', *The Guardian*, 28 Nov. 2019.

[33] World Health Organization, 'Deaths from Democratic Republic of Congo measles outbreak top 6000', 7 Jan. 2020; and World Health Organization, 'Major cholera vaccination campaign begins in North Kivu in the Democratic Republic of the Congo', 27 May 2019.

[34] OCHA (note 30).

limited by, among other things, a lack of capacity and political will among troop contributors.[35] Since 2018 MONUSCO has also been providing logistical support to the Ebola response. In March 2019 the UN Security Council extended MONUSCO's mandate for nine months, and called for an independent strategic review of the mission, including consideration of an exit strategy.[36] The review, published in October 2019, concluded that a successful, gradual transition and a responsible exit of MONUSCO would take an 'absolute minimum' of three years, but would have to remain flexible based on the ongoing security situation in the DRC. The review envisaged a progressive transfer of MONUSCO's tasks to the Government of the DRC.[37] In December 2019 MONUSCO's mandate and troop ceiling was extended until 20 December 2020.[38]

MONUSCO's footprint has reduced in recent years, not least because former president Joseph Kabila was hostile to it. The new president is more supportive and has enabled its continuation largely unchanged.[39] It remains too early to assess whether the recent democratic transition can provide an enabling environment for sustainable peace, including bringing to an end the armed conflict in eastern DRC, that would also permit the anticipated drawdown of MONUSCO.

---

[35] International Crisis Group (note 25); and Sweet, R., 'Militarizing the peace: UN intervention against Congo's "terrorist" rebels', Lawfare, 2 June 2019.

[36] UN Security Council Resolution 2463, 29 Mar. 2019.

[37] UN Security Council, 'Transitioning from stabilization to peace: An independent strategic review of the United Nations Organization Stabilization Mission in the Democratic Republic of the Congo', S/2019/842, 25 Oct. 2019.

[38] UN Security Council Resolution 2502, 19 Dec. 2019.

[39] Afrique Panorama, 'Félix Tshisekedi at the UN: "The DRC still needs MONUSCO"', 27 Sep. 2019.

IV. Armed conflict and peace processes in the Horn of Africa

IAN DAVIS

In this section the Horn of Africa is defined as the eight member states of the Intergovernmental Authority on Development (IGAD)—Djibouti, Eritrea, Ethiopia, Kenya, Somalia, South Sudan, Sudan and Uganda. These states are 'listed among the thirty-five most fragile countries in the World'.[1] The state fragility is derived from a complex mix of limited or uneven access to natural resources, intergroup tensions (on regional, religious and ethnic lines), poverty and economic inequalities, and weak state institutions.[2] This 'state fragility–conflict dynamic nexus' shapes the security environment of all countries in the region.[3] In 2019 only three of those states—Djibouti, Eritrea and Uganda—were free from armed conflicts. The armed conflicts in the other five states are discussed below. Relatively peaceful transitions of power in Ethiopia (in 2018) and Sudan (in 2019) and the implementation of a 2018 peace agreement in South Sudan led to significant decreases in armed violence in those three states. The armed conflict in Somalia remained one of the worst in the world.

Counterterrorism and anti-piracy efforts have been priorities in the region for a growing number of external actors over the last decade. This has created a crowded playing field that includes China, India, the United States and other Western powers (France, Germany, Italy, Japan, Spain and the United Kingdom) and several Middle Eastern countries (Egypt, Qatar, Saudi Arabia, Turkey and the United Arab Emirates, UAE)—with growing geopolitical tensions, rivalries and risk of destabilizing proxy conflicts.[4]

The Horn of Africa also has a long history of interstate disputes, cross-border violent incidents and border conflicts, such as the Kenya–Somalia maritime border dispute.[5] Disputes over resource allocation and access have also been significant in the region. For example, the dispute over the sharing of the eastern Nile waters, involving Egypt, Ethiopia and Sudan, remained

---

[1] IGAD, *IGAD Regional Strategy: Volume 1, The Framework* (IGAD: Djibouti, Jan. 2019), p. 15.

[2] IGAD (note 1), pp. 8–10.

[3] Adeto, Y. A., 'State fragility and conflict nexus: Contemporary security issues in the Horn of Africa', African Centre for Constructive Resolution of Disputes, 22 July 2019.

[4] See Melvin, N., 'The new external security politics of the Horn of Africa region', SIPRI Insights on Peace and Security no. 2019/2, Apr. 2019; Melvin, N., 'The foreign military presence in the Horn of Africa region', SIPRI Background Paper, Apr. 2019; and International Crisis Group, *Intra-Gulf Competition in Africa's Horn: Lessening the Impact*, Middle East Report no. 206 (International Crisis Group: Brussels, 19 Sep. 2019). On geopolitical tensions in the Middle East and North Africa, see chapter 6, section I, in this volume.

[5] Quartz Africa, 'Why the US, UK, France and Norway are taking sides in Kenya's maritime row with Somalia', 7 Nov. 2019; and Wabuke, E., 'The Kenya–Somalia maritime dispute and its potential national security costs', Lawfare, 15 May 2019.

deadlocked in 2019.[6] Many of the region's social, political and economic challenges are compounded by the impacts of climate change, including droughts and floods. These impacts are local and transnational in character, and add to the risks of political tensions and violent conflict within and among states in the Horn of Africa.[7]

Ethiopia

The relatively peaceful transition of power in Ethiopia in 2018 and a series of reforms initiated by Prime Minister Abiy Ahmed led to an opening of the domestic political space and the signing of a Joint Declaration on Peace and Friendship with Eritrea.[8] The 2018 peace agreement formally ended the Eritrean–Ethiopian war (1998–2000) and border conflict (2000–18) and restored full diplomatic relations between the two countries.[9] Abiy was awarded the 2019 Nobel Peace Prize for resolving the border conflict with Eritrea and promoting peace and reconciliation in his own country and the region.[10] Confidence has also been growing in the country's macroeconomic outlook—Ethiopia's annual growth rate of 7.4 per cent placed it among the 10 fastest-growing world economies in 2019, and the country has attracted a considerable amount of foreign direct investment—although structural challenges remain.[11]

However, in 2019 while internal armed resistance against the Ethiopian Government decreased—battle-related fatalities in 2019 were the lowest for the 2013–19 period (see table 7.8)—ethnic-based violence increased amidst a breakdown in social cohesion in some areas.[12] The border area with Eritrea also remained tense.[13] Conflict, displacement and disease outbreaks, as well

---

[6] Palios, E., 'Nile Basin water wars: The never-ending struggle between Egypt, Ethiopia, and Sudan', Geopolitical Monitor, 4 Nov. 2019; and International Crisis Group, *Bridging the Gap in the Nile Waters Dispute*, Africa Report no. 271 (International Crisis Group: Brussels, 20 Mar. 2019).

[7] For a regional analysis of environment, peace and security linkages in the region with specific focus on water security and governance, see Krampe, F. et al., 'Water security and governance in the Horn of Africa', SIPRI Policy Paper no. 54, Mar. 2020.

[8] On developments within Ethiopia in 2018 and the Eritrea–Ethiopia peace agreement, see *SIPRI Yearbook 2019*, pp. 134–37.

[9] Gebrekidan, S., 'Ethiopia and Eritrea declare an end to their war', *New York Times*, 9 July 2018; and Ylönen, A., 'From demonisation to rapprochement: Abiy Ahmed's early reforms and implications of the coming together of Ethiopia and Eritrea', *Global Change, Peace & Security*, vol. 31, no. 3 (2019), pp. 341–49.

[10] BBC, 'Nobel Peace Prize: Ethiopia PM Abiy Ahmed wins', 11 Oct. 2019.

[11] African Development Bank, *African Economic Outlook 2020: Developing Africa's Workforce for the Future* (African Development Bank: 30 Jan. 2020); Sidhu, A., 'FDI in Ethiopia: Is "Abiymania" enough?', Geopolitical Monitor, 31 July 2019; and Oqubay, A., 'Will the 2020s be the decade of Africa's economic transformation?', Overseas Development Institute, 14 Jan. 2020.

[12] International Crisis Group, *Keeping Ethiopia's Transition on the Rails*, Africa Report no. 283 (International Crisis Group: Brussels, 16 Dec. 2019).

[13] Plaut, M., 'How the glow of the historic accord between Ethiopia and Eritrea has faded', *Mail & Guardian*, 8 July 2019.

Table 7.8. Estimated conflict-related fatalities in Ethiopia, 2013–19

Event type	2013	2014	2015	2016	2017	2018	2019
Battles	418	237	568	1 065	875	718	193
Explosions/remote violence	48	2	16	15	4	22	17
Protests, riots and strategic developments	33	53	177	677	132	241	169
Violence against civilians	85	43	49	755	341	572	286
Total	**584**	**335**	**810**	**2 512**	**1 352**	**1 553**	**665**

Note: For definitions of event types, see Armed Conflict Location & Event Data Project (ACLED), 'ACLED definitions of political violence and protest', 11 Apr. 2019.

Source: ACLED, 'Data export tool', [n.d.].

as flooding in some parts of the country and rainfall shortages in others, remained key drivers of humanitarian needs in Ethiopia during 2019. At least 8 million people were projected to require humanitarian assistance in 2020.[14]

Challenges to consolidating the political transition

Ethiopia is made up of 10 semi-autonomous ethnically based federal states (one of which was added in 2019, see below). With the opening up of the political space the competition among them has increased, and people living outside of their own ethnic regions have faced increasing attacks.[15] Armed violence between ethnonationalist groups and those supporting the central government also took place within some regions during the year, especially attacks by splinter factions of the Oromo Liberation Front in western Oromia in October 2019.[16] Similar violence in the Amhara region in June 2019 resulted in the assassination of Amhara's regional leader and also the chief of staff of Ethiopia's military.[17]

There were frequent political protests during 2019, many in support or opposition to the prime minister's reform agenda. The creation of a new pan-Ethiopian political grouping, the Prosperity Party, to replace the former ruling Ethiopian People's Revolutionary Democratic Front—a coalition of four ethnic parties that has controlled all tiers of government since 1991—ahead of elections in 2020 was particularly controversial. While seen by some of Ethiopia's ethnic groups as an attempt by Abiy to fashion a more unified national identity, it was perceived by others as a further setback to their claims for political autonomy and cultural justice.[18] One ethnic group administered

[14] United Nations Office for the Coordination of Humanitarian Affairs (OCHA), *Global Humanitarian Overview 2020* (OCHA: Geneva, Dec. 2019), p. 37.

[15] BBC, 'Abiy Ahmed's reforms in Ethiopia lift the lid on ethnic tensions', 29 June 2019; Associated Press, '67 killed in days of unrest in Ethiopia, police say', 26 Oct. 2019; and Reuters, 'Ethiopia deploys police in universities to stop ethic violence', 10 Dec. 2019.

[16] *The Economist*, 'Ethnic violence threatens to tear Ethiopia apart', 2 Nov. 2019.

[17] International Crisis Group, 'Restoring calm in Ethiopia after high-profile assassinations', Statement, 25 June 2019.

[18] Allo, A. K., 'Why Abiy Ahmed's Prosperity Party could be bad news for Ethiopia', Al Jazeera, 5 Dec. 2019.

under Ethiopia's Southern Nations, Nationalities, and People's Region made a successful bid for federal statehood: Sidama became Ethiopia's 10th semi-autonomous regional state in November 2019, after protests and a successful referendum.[19] The referendum could fuel similar demands by other ethnic regions in southern Ethiopia, particularly those of Wolayta, while separatist movements are growing in other parts of the country, especially in Tigray.[20]

Pivotal elections scheduled for May 2020 will be delayed because of the coronavirus disease 2019 (COVID-19) pandemic. Despite having a popular leader Ethiopia's system of ethnic federalism is at risk of increased fragmentation due to the spread of ethnic violence, while significant regional challenges also remain.[21]

Kenya

The main threat to peace and security in Kenya comes from al-Shabab, the Somalia-based group that is affiliated with al-Qaeda.[22] Since 2015 the group has conducted over 100 small-scale assaults in the north-east of Kenya, killing dozens of security forces, mostly by roadside bombs.[23] An attack by al-Shabab in Kenya's capital on 15 January 2019 killed at least 21 civilians and brought back memories of the 2013 attack on a shopping centre that killed 67 people.[24] According to the Armed Conflict Location & Event Data Project (ACLED), Kenya had 61 battle-related fatalities in 2019, down from 156 in 2018 (out of a total of 268 conflict-related fatalities for the year, compared with 406 in 2018).[25]

Somalia

Following the overthrow of the military regime of President Siad Barre in 1991 Somalia disintegrated into rival clan-based armed groups. An internationally backed unity government formed in 2000 failed to establish control, and the two relatively peaceful northern regions of Somaliland and Puntland sought to break away from Somalia: although both remain inter-

[19] Sileshi, E., 'Sidama becomes Ethiopia's 10th regional state', *Addis Standard*, 23 Nov. 2019; and International Crisis Group, 'Time for Ethiopia to bargain with Sidama over statehood', Africa Briefing no. 146, 4 July 2019.

[20] Temare, G. G., 'The Republic of Tigray? Aydeln, yekenyeley!', Ethiopia Insight, 28 Sep. 2019.

[21] Mosley, J., 'Ethiopia's transition: Implications for the Horn of Africa and Red Sea region', SIPRI Insights on Peace and Security no. 2020/5, Mar. 2020.

[22] On al-Shabab recruitment in Kenya, see Speckhard, A. and Shajkovci, A., 'The Jihad in Kenya: Understanding Al-Shabaab recruitment and terrorist activity inside Kenya—in their own words', *African Security*, vol. 12, no. 1 (2019), pp. 3–61.

[23] Abdille, A., 'The hidden cost of al-Shabaab's campaign in north-eastern Kenya', International Crisis Group commentary, 4 Apr. 2019.

[24] *The Economist*, 'Another terrorist outrage in Nairobi', 17 Jan. 2019.

[25] ACLED, 'Data export tool', [n.d.].

Table 7.9. Estimated conflict-related fatalities in Somalia, 2013–19

Event type	2013	2014	2015	2016	2017	2018	2019
Battles	1 985	2 894	2 786	3 731	2 686	3 034	2 154
Explosions/remote violence	529	953	750	1 215	2 188	1 446	1 221
Protests, riots and strategic developments	15	19	8	27	74	48	23
Violence against civilians	628	602	561	676	887	573	640
Total	**3 157**	**4 468**	**4 105**	**5 649**	**5 835**	**5 101**	**4 038**

Note: For definitions of event types, see Armed Conflict Location & Event Data Project (ACLED), 'ACLED definitions of political violence and protest', 11 Apr. 2019.

Source: ACLED, 'Data export tool', [n.d.].

nationally recognized as autonomous regions of Somalia.[26] The seizure of the capital Mogadishu and much of the country's south by the Islamic Courts Union (ICU) in 2006 prompted an intervention by Ethiopia, and in 2007 by the African Union Mission in Somalia (AMISOM). The ICU subsequently splintered into more radical groups, including the al-Shabab group, which is aligned with al-Qaeda. Since 2012 the main armed conflict has been between the Somali Government, backed by AMISOM and US forces, and al-Shabab insurgents.[27] In 2018 AMISOM adopted a security transition plan for the gradual transfer of security responsibilities to Somali forces, with final withdrawal of the mission by 2021.[28]

In 2019 despite continued AMISOM operations and increased US air strikes, al-Shabab remained a major threat to Somali society and President Mohamed Abdullahi Farmajo's government. According to ACLED continued expansion by al-Shabab made Somalia the country with the third-highest level of Islamist activity in 2019.[29] Improvised explosive devices continued to be the 'weapon of choice'.[30] In addition, Somalia's rural populations continued to suffer from clan-based violence, with weak state security forces unable to prevent clashes over water and pasture resources. Thus, although there was a small decrease in the total number of conflict-related fatalities in 2019 compared with the previous three years—and battle-related fatalities were at their lowest since 2013 (see table 7.9)—the armed conflict remained one of the worst in the world.

[26] On the tensions between Somalia and Somaliland in 2019, see International Crisis Group, *Somalia–Somaliland: The Perils of Delaying New Talks*, Africa Report no. 280 (International Crisis Group: Brussels, 12 July 2019.

[27] On developments in Somalia in 2018, see *SIPRI Yearbook 2019*, pp. 137–40.

[28] Oluoch, F., 'Amisom ready to withdraw', *East African*, 12 Nov. 2018. On developments within AMISOM in 2018, see *SIPRI Yearbook 2019*, pp. 169–71.

[29] Kishi, R. et al., *Year in Review* (ACLED: 2 Mar. 2020), p. 54. On the role of women in the insurgency, see International Crisis Group, 'Women and al-Shabaab's insurgency', Africa Briefing no. 145, 27 June 2019.

[30] UN Security Council, 'Final report of the Panel of Experts on Somalia', S/2019/858, 1 Nov. 2019, pp. 5 and 9–12.

The persistent insecurity was compounded by weather extremes (below-average rainfall, but severe flooding from heavy rains in November 2019) and the poorest harvest since detailed record-keeping began in 1995. These conditions drove an additional 1 million people in Somalia into humanitarian need, and nearly 302 000 people were newly displaced in 2019, joining more than 2.6 million existing internally displaced persons. It was projected that an estimated 6.3 million people will be food insecure, and 1 million children under the age of five are likely to be acutely malnourished in 2020.[31]

The fight against al-Shabab and drawdown of the African Union Mission in Somalia

The USA increased its engagement in Somalia in 2019—conducting 63 air strikes against al-Shabab targets (compared to 45 in 2018, 35 in 2017, 14 in 2016, 11 in 2015 and 11 during 2007–14)—as part of an effort to weaken the insurgency prior to the planned handover of security operations from AMISOM to the Somali armed forces in 2021.[32] According to independent reports the air strikes continued to involve civilian casualties not acknowledged by the US military.[33]

In May 2019, following a joint African Union (AU)–United Nations technical review of AMISOM, the UN Security Council renewed AMISOM's mandate until 31 May 2020 and reduced personnel by 1000 to a maximum level of 19 626 by 28 February 2020.[34] However, al-Shabab remained resilient in the face of this increased military pressure from Somali and international military forces, and continued to carry out armed attacks on those forces and civilian targets.[35] These attacks intensified towards the end of 2019: an attack on a checkpoint in Mogadishu on 28 December 2019, for example, killed 81 people.[36] A national Defector Rehabilitation Programme aimed at helping al-Shabab members to disengage, rehabilitate and reintegrate has also failed to weaken the group.[37]

---

[31] OCHA (note 14), p. 38. On the impact of climate-related change in livelihood options and migration in Somalia, see also Eklöw, K. and Krampe, F., 'Climate-related security risks and peacebuilding in Somalia', SIPRI Policy Paper no. 53, Oct. 2019; and Hujale, M., 'Mogadishu left reeling as conflict and climate shocks spark rush to capital', *The Guardian*, 27 Jan. 2020.

[32] Bureau of Investigative Journalism, 'Somalia: Reported US actions 2019', [n.d.]; and Schmitt, E. and Savage, C., 'Trump administration steps up air war in Somalia', *New York Times*, 10 Mar. 2019.

[33] Dewan, K. and Dahir, A. H., '"We heard it coming": US lethal operations in Somalia', TRT World Research Centre, Sep. 2019; and Amnesty International, 'The hidden US war in Somalia: Civilian casualties from air strikes in Lower Shabelle', Mar. 2019.

[34] UN Security Council, 'Security Council extends mandate of African Union Mission in Somalia, authorizes troop reduction, unanimously adopting resolution 2472 (2019)', SC/13828, 31 May 2019. The joint AU–UN review is contained in UN Security Council, Letter dated 10 May 2019 from the Secretary-General addressed to the President of the Security Council, S/2019/388, 13 May 2019.

[35] See e.g. Al Jazeera, 'US special forces base, Italian army convoy attacked in Somalia', 30 Sep. 2019.

[36] AFP, 'Death toll in Somalia bombing climbs to 81: Govt', News 24, 30 Dec. 2019.

[37] Gjelsvik, I. M., 'Disengaging from violent extremism: The case of al-Shabaab in Somalia', African Centre for the Constructive Resolution of Disputes, 24 June 2019.

Political fragmentation and Somalia's federalism

Reflecting the fragmented nature of Somali politics after nearly three decades of civil war, the country is organized as a federal republic, with a central authority (the federal government) and six federal member states, which are divided into 18 administrative regions. Power-sharing arrangements along the main clan lines are common in all levels of Somali governance. In 2018 the council of ministers of the federal government endorsed a road map for inclusive politics, designed to counter the political fragmentation in the country, paving the way for elections in 2020.[38] However, in 2019 there were continuing disagreements between the federal government and federal states over power and resources.[39] These disagreements also hampered the counter-insurgency effort. In July and August for example, during heightened political tensions arising from a disputed presidential electoral process in Jubaland, al-Shabab carried out its first attack in the city of Kismayo, resulting in 26 fatalities.[40]

Further political destabilization in Somalia has occurred as a result of the Gulf rivalry. Qatar and Turkey for example, are important supporters of President Farmajo's federal government, while the UAE has supported Somaliland, effectively undermining the federal government's authority.[41]

Somalia is scheduled to hold a 'universal suffrage' election in 2020 (to replace the existing clan-based, power-sharing model) for the first time since the outbreak of the civil war in 1992. With al-Shabab undefeated and Somalia's Gulf allies likely to increase their efforts to secure political influences ahead of the general election, 2020 will be a pivotal year for Somalia.[42] The proposed AMISOM withdrawal adds a further layer of uncertainty.

South Sudan

South Sudan gained independence from Sudan on 9 July 2011 after a 2005 agreement that ended one of Africa's longest-running civil wars. A UN peacekeeping mission, the UN Mission in South Sudan (UNMISS), was established on 8 July 2011. Although a post-independence civil war (2013–15) was curtailed by a 2015 peace agreement, the legacy of violence continued in the form of an armed conflict waged primarily between two groups—the Government of South Sudan and its allies, led by President Salva Kiir (an

---

[38] UN Security Council, 'Report of the Secretary-General on Somalia', S/2018/411, 2 May 2018.

[39] UN Security Council, S/2019/858 (note 30), pp. 21–24.

[40] UN Security Council, S/2019/858 (note 30), p. 23; and UN Security Council, 'Security Council press statement on terrorist attack in Kismayo, Somalia', SC/13883, 15 July 2019.

[41] Southern, N. P., 'UAE's relations with Somalia flounder over Qatar', Global Risk Insights, 1 Feb. 2019; and Bergman, R. and Kirkpatrick, D. D., 'With guns, cash and terrorism, Gulf States vie for power in Somalia', *New York Times*, 22 July 2019.

[42] Associated Press, 'Somali official: 2020 could see first election in 50 years', 22 Nov. 2019.

ethnic Dinka), and the Sudan People's Liberation Army-in-Opposition and the Nuer White Army, led by former vice president Riek Machar (an ethnic Nuer). Although the main division in the subsequent conflict has been between the Dinka and Nuer ethnic groups, underlying conflict dynamics are primarily political and vary considerably across the country. Opposition groups have become more fractured and localized.

In September 2018 Kiir and Machar signed a new peace deal, the Revitalized Agreement on the Resolution of the Conflict in South Sudan.[43] However, at the end of 2018 it remained contested and partial, and required further negotiations to form a unity government, transitional security arrangements and a unified national army. Limited and localized, clashes among some of the armed groups associated with the signatories were also continuing.[44]

Implementation of the 2018 peace agreement

According to UN reports, implementation of the agreement remained selective and significantly behind schedule during 2019. In particular, the planned formation of a new unity government, delayed from May to mid-November 2019, was in question because concerns about the accord's transitional security arrangements, the reunification of the army, and the number of states and their boundaries remained unaddressed.[45] Just before the 12 November deadline the pre-transitional period was extended by a further 100 days.[46] A UN panel of experts on South Sudan also noted inconsistent support for the agreement among IGAD and neighbouring states, specifically Ethiopia, Kenya, Sudan and Uganda.[47]

More promising was the reduction in fighting in most parts of the country as a result of the 2018 ceasefire—as reflected in the lower battle-related fatalities in 2019 (see table 7.10). Nonetheless, intercommunal violence and clashes between the government and opposition forces continued in some areas, mainly in the Central and Western Equatoria and the Upper Nile

---

[43] IGAD, *Revitalized Agreement on the Resolution of the Conflict in the Republic of South Sudan* (IGAD: Addis Ababa, 12 Sep. 2018); and Vhumbunu, C. H., 'Reviving peace in South Sudan through the Revitalised Peace Agreement: Understanding the enablers and possible obstacles', African Centre for the Constructive Resolution of Disputes, 11 Feb. 2019. On developments in South Sudan in 2017–18, see *SIPRI Yearbook 2018*, pp. 99–100; and *SIPRI Yearbook 2019*, pp. 140–43.

[44] UN Security Council, 'Report of the Secretary-General on South Sudan (covering the period from 2 September to 30 November 2018)', S/2018/1103, 10 Dec. 2018.

[45] UN Security Council, 'Interim report of the Panel of Experts on South Sudan submitted pursuant to resolution 2471 (2019)', S/2019/897, 22 Nov. 2019, pp. 8–12; UN Security Council, 'Situation in South Sudan', Report of the Secretary-General, S/2020/145, 26 Feb. 2020, pp. 2–3; and UN Security Council, 'Situation in South Sudan', Report of the Secretary-General, S/2019/936, 11 Dec. 2019, pp. 1–3. Also see Tombe, S., 'Revitalising the peace in South Sudan: Assessing the state of the pre-transitional phase', African Centre for the Constructive Resolution of Disputes, 24 June 2019.

[46] UN Security Council, 'Security Council press statement on South Sudan', SC/14033, 22 Nov. 2019.

[47] UN Security Council, S/2019/897 (note 45), p. 12.

Table 7.10. Estimated conflict-related fatalities in South Sudan, 2013–19

Event type	2013	2014	2015	2016	2017	2018	2019
Battles	1 300	4 473	2 309	2 541	3 356	1 134	823
Explosions/remote violence	18	61	61	46	18	30	10
Protests, riots and strategic developments	0	11	24	1	4	5	4
Violence against civilians	3 075	1 849	1 206	960	1 416	530	963
Total	**4 393**	**6 394**	**3 600**	**3 548**	**4 794**	**1 699**	**1 800**

Note: For definitions of event types, see Armed Conflict Location & Event Data Project (ACLED), 'ACLED definitions of political violence and protest', 11 Apr. 2019.

Source: ACLED, 'Data export tool', [n.d.].

regions.[48] The UN also documented 'the continued use of conflict-related sexual violence by the parties to the conflict', targeted attacks on civilians and an increase in the recruitment of child soldiers.[49]

The UN Security Council extended the mandate of UNMISS on 15 March 2019, maintaining an authorized strength of 17 000 military personnel, including a 4000-strong Regional Protection Force and 2101 police.[50] However, as was the case in 2018 UNMISS did not achieve this strength in 2019: as of 31 December 2019 UNMISS deployed 14 962 military personnel and 1799 police officers.[51]

The humanitarian situation

As a result of years of persistent armed conflict, enduring vulnerabilities and weak basic services, humanitarian needs in South Sudan remained exceptionally high in 2019. More than two thirds of the population (about 7.5 million people) were in need of humanitarian assistance, while nearly 4 million South Sudanese remained displaced (about 1.7 million internally displaced and the remainder as refugees outside the country). Unusually heavy seasonal flooding in 2019 affected more than 900 000 people and deepened the humanitarian crisis. Food insecurity reached record levels during 2019.[52]

---

[48] On the conflict in the Upper Nile, see Crace, J., *Displaced and Immiserated: The Shilluk of Upper Nile in South Sudan's Civil War, 2014–19* (Small Arms Survey: Sep. 2019).

[49] UN Security Council, S/2019/936 (note 45), pp. 7–13; UN General Assembly, 'Report of the Commission on Human Rights in South Sudan', A/HRC/43/56, 31 Jan. 2020; and Austin, R., 'Rise in children forced to joint militias raises fresh fears over South Sudan', *The Guardian*, 18 Sep. 2019. On gender commitments and requirements for women's representation under the 2018 peace agreement, see UN Security Council, 'Summary of the meeting of the Informal Expert Group on Women and Peace and Security on the situation in South Sudan, held on 28 February 2019', S/2019/232, 13 Mar. 2019.

[50] UN Security Council Resolution 2459, 15 Mar. 2019.

[51] UN Security Council, S/2019/936 (note 45), p. 15. On developments within UNMISS in 2018, see *SIPRI Yearbook 2019*, pp. 167–68. On developments within peace operations more generally, see chapter 2, section II, in this volume.

[52] OCHA (note 14), p. 39.

At the end of 2019 South Sudan was at a critical juncture, with the peace process seemingly deadlocked.[53] The delay in the formation of a coalition government brought uncertainty and doubt about the full implementation of the peace agreement and concern over the potential recurrence of high levels of violence.

Sudan

A major transition of power occurred in Sudan in 2019. Towards the end of 2018 President Omar al-Bashir, who came to power in a military coup in 1989, faced widespread economic-related protests.[54] On 11 April 2019 following months of protest—led by an alliance of civil society groups, the Sudanese Professionals Association and political parties known as the Forces for Freedom and Change—the president was removed from power by the Sudanese army, which subsequently dissolved the government, suspended the constitution and declared a state of emergency.[55] As demonstrations continued, on 15 April the AU called on state forces to transfer power to a civilian government within 15 days, or face suspension from the regional organization; a further 60-day deadline was announced by the AU on 1 May.[56]

Dialogue between military and civilian leaders took place amidst increasing violence, with paramilitary forces reportedly killing over 120 protesters on 3 June 2019.[57] In June Sudan was temporarily suspended from the AU. In July a power-sharing agreement was finally reached between the Sudanese Military Transition Council and a coalition of opposition and protest groups. Under the agreement Sudan will hold elections following an approximately three-year period of shared rule between the military and civilian groups.[58] On 17 August 2019 the parties signed a landmark constitutional declaration and power-sharing accord, and formed a transitional government.[59] The

[53] 'Peace deal wheelspin', *Africa Confidential*, vol. 60, no. 25 (19 Dec. 2019); and International Crisis Group, 'A short window to resuscitate South Sudan's ailing peace deal', Statement, 2 Dec. 2019. On the 'trust deficit' among the parties, see Onapa, S. A., 'South Sudan power-sharing agreement R-ARCSS: The same thing expecting different results', *African Security Review*, vol. 28, no. 2 (2019), pp. 75–94.

[54] International Crisis Group, 'Improving prospects for a peaceful transition in Sudan', Africa Briefing no. 143, 14 Jan. 2019; and 'The protests in Sudan', *Strategic Comments*, vol. 25, no. 1 (2019), pp. iv–vi.

[55] Walsh, D. and Goldstein, J., 'Sudan's President Omar Hassan al-Bashir is ousted, but not his regime', *New York Times*, 11 Apr. 2019; Beaumont, P. and Salih, Z. M., 'Fall of Bashir risks leaving Sudan prey to rival regional powers', *The Guardian*, 27 Apr. 2019.

[56] Al Jazeera, 'African Union gives Sudan military further 60 days to cede power', 1 May 2019.

[57] Walsh, D., 'Sudan talks collapse amid clashes in Khartoum', *New York Times*, 15 May 2019; Matfess, H., 'The Rapid Support Forces and the escalation of violence in Sudan', ACLED, 2 July 2019; and *The Economist*, 'Pro-democracy protesters are slaughtered in Khartoum', 8 June 2019.

[58] Burke, J. and Salih, Z. M., 'Sudanese military and protesters sign power-sharing accord', *The Guardian*, 17 July 2019.

[59] Magdy, S., 'Sudanese protesters sign final power-sharing deal with army', Associated Press, 17 Aug. 2019; and BBC, 'Sudan crisis: What you need to know', 16 Aug. 2019.

Sudanese Professionals Association took on an independent oversight role in the new government. In September 2019 the AU lifted its suspension of Sudan following the announcement of a new cabinet by new Prime Minister Abdalla Hamdok.[60] On 14 December 2019 a Sudanese court sentenced former president al-Bashir to two years in prison for money laundering and corruption.[61]

The new administration inherited a deepening economic crisis and significantly increased food insecurity in 2019—at least 17.7 million people (42 per cent of the population) suffered from some level of food insecurity— and weakened public services, including health, water and education. Nearly one quarter of the population (about 9.3 million people) needed humanitarian assistance. Some 1.9 million people were internally displaced, and more than 1.1 million refugees and asylum seekers were living in camps, out-of-camp settlements and urban areas across Sudan, including about 895 000 South Sudanese refugees.[62] Hamdok has estimated that the country will need foreign investment of about $10 billion over the next two years.[63]

Sudan has been affected by conflict for most of its recent history. Long-standing insurgencies remained extant in Darfur and in the southern border states of Blue Nile and South Kordofan in 2019, and involved a fragmented mosaic of armed groups. In Darfur the main armed group was the Sudan Liberation Army, led by Abdul Wahid al Nur, as well as various Arab militias. There were also various armed groups from Darfur present in Libya as mercenaries.[64] Although the new government declared a ceasefire with all armed groups, the insurgent commanders refused to endorse the power-sharing agreement.

Armed conflict in Darfur and the drawdown of the United Nations–African Union Hybrid Operation in Darfur

The power-sharing deal was criticized by the Sudan Revolutionary Front, an alliance of the largest armed groups in Darfur, and other armed groups for not giving sufficient attention to achieving peace in Sudan.[65] The deal calls for the newly established Sudanese transitional government to reach a peace agreement with the armed groups in Darfur and other states within

---

[60] Al Jazeera, 'African Union lifts suspension of Sudan', 7 Sep. 2019.

[61] Ahmed, N. and Magdy, S., 'Ex-Sudan strongman al-Bashir gets 2 years for corruption', Associated Press, 14 Dec. 2019.

[62] OCHA (note 14), p. 40.

[63] International Crisis Group, *Safeguarding Sudan's Revolution*, Africa Report no. 281 (International Crisis Group: Brussels, 21 Oct. 2019).

[64] For details of the various armed groups in Sudan (as well as Darfurian armed groups in Libya), see UN Security Council, 'Final report of the Panel of Experts on the Sudan', S/2020/36, 14 Jan. 2020, pp. 15–28.

[65] UN Security Council, 'Special report of the Chairperson of the African Union Commission and the Secretary-General of the United Nations on the African Union-United Nations Hybrid Operation in Darfur', S/2019/816, 15 Oct. 2019, p. 2.

six months. The first round of meetings took place in Juba, South Sudan, in October 2019.[66] A second round of talks began on 10 December and a framework agreement on the issues to be discussed in future direct talks was reached between the government and some of the armed groups on 28 December 2019.[67]

Since 2014 the UN Security Council has reconfigured and gradually reduced the activities of the joint UN–AU Hybrid Operation in Darfur (UNAMID), which has been deployed in the region since 2007. Under pressure from Sudan's government for an exit strategy, the UN Security Council approved further troop reductions in 2017 and 2018, and refocused the mission on the protection of civilians in the Jebel Marra region of Darfur. A tentative exit strategy was set under Resolution 2429 (2018) for 30 June 2020, contingent on the security situation and progress on specified benchmarks.[68]

In April 2019 the UN described the security situation in Darfur as 'relatively stable', except in Jebel Marra, where clashes continued.[69] Similarly, in May 2019 a joint AU–UN assessment team, while noting a spike in violence in several camps for internally displaced persons, suggested that Darfur had generally 'evolved into a post-conflict setting' and that the proposed drawdown could proceed, albeit gradually.[70] However, in June 2019 UN human rights officials and human rights groups reported a deterioration in human rights in Darfur, with increased reports of killing, abduction, sexual violence and other abuses.[71] This led the AU Peace and Security Council to call for the remaining AU–UN peacekeepers to be consolidated until the situation stabilized.[72]

On 27 June 2019 the UN Security Council voted to pause the drawdown until 31 October 2019, pending a fresh AU–UN assessment of the situation.[73] In its October 2019 report the assessment team found that the security situation in Darfur remained volatile, but largely unchanged from the May

[66] UN Security Council, S/2020/36 (note 64), pp. 7–8.
[67] Sudan Tribune, 'Sudan, armed groups sign framework agreement for peace in Darfur', 29 Dec. 2019.
[68] For UNAMID-related developments in 2018, see *SIPRI Yearbook 2019*, pp. 168–69.
[69] UN Security Council, 'African Union–United Nations Hybrid Operation in Darfur', Report of the Secretary-General, S/2019/305, 10 Apr. 2019, p. 1.
[70] UN Security Council, 'Special report of the Chairperson of the African Union Commission and the Secretary-General of the United Nations on the strategic assessment of the African Union–United Nations Hybrid Operation in Darfur', S/2019/445, 30 May 2019, pp. 2, 17.
[71] OCHA, 'Briefing to the Security Council on Sudan by Andrew Gilmour, Assistant Secretary-General for Human Rights, New York, 14 June 2019', 14 June 2019; Amnesty International, 'Sudan: Fresh evidence of government-sponsored crimes in Darfur shows drawdown of peacekeepers premature and reckless', 11 June 2019; and Henry, J., 'Sudan's transition hasn't ended abuses in Darfur', Human Rights Watch, 8 May 2019.
[72] AU, 'Communiqué adopted by the Peace and Security Council at its 856th meeting held on 13 June 2019, on the activities of the African Union–United Nations Hybrid Operation in Darfur (UNAMID) and the situation in Darfur', 13 June 2019.
[73] UN Security Council Resolution 2479, 27 June 2019.

Table 7.11. Estimated conflict-related fatalities in Sudan, 2013–19

Event type	2013	2014	2015	2016	2017	2018	2019
Battles	5 595	3 049	2 440	2 939	851	700	314
Explosions/remote violence	479	263	263	294	33	28	17
Protests, riots and strategic developments	342	15	9	27	34	37	213
Violence against civilians	380	831	754	639	373	289	223
Total	**6 796**	**4 158**	**3 466**	**3 899**	**1 291**	**1 054**	**767**

Note: For definitions of event types, see Armed Conflict Location & Event Data Project (ACLED), 'ACLED definitions of political violence and protest', 11 Apr. 2019.

Source: ACLED, 'Data export tool', [n.d.].

report. While armed conflict between government forces and armed opposition movements had subsided, the report concluded that some of the major grievances underlying the Darfur crisis, including intercommunal conflicts, remained fundamentally unaddressed.[74] On the basis of this assessment, the UN Security Council renewed UNAMID's mandate until 31 October 2020, with current troop and police ceilings (4050 and 2500, respectively) maintained until at least 31 March 2020.[75]

The predominance of mainly localized security incidents in Darfur and other conflict-affected regions in 2019 is reflected in the continuing fall in battle-related fatalities in Sudan (see table 7.11). However, it is difficult to predict how the political transition in Sudan may evolve in 2020. It faces numerous obstacles, including resistance by elements of the old military regime—the fractured security establishment comprises the Sudanese Armed Forces, the Rapid Support Forces (a paramilitary group formed from the remnants of the Janjaweed militia in Darfur), the intelligence services and allied militias—as well as unresolved local insurgencies and the competing agendas of external powers.[76]

[74] UN Security Council, S/2019/816 (note 65), pp. 3, 5.

[75] UN Security Council Resolution 2495, 31 Oct. 2019; and UNAMID, 'UNAMID facts and figures, as of January 2020', Jan. 2020.

[76] Downie, R., 'From the Gulf to Egypt, foreign powers are playing with fire in Sudan', *World Politics Review*, 6 Aug. 2019; and International Crisis Group (note 63).

Part II. Military spending and armaments, 2019

Chapter 8.   Military expenditure

Chapter 9.   International arms transfers and developments in arms production

Chapter 10. World nuclear forces

8. Military expenditure

Overview

World military expenditure is estimated to have been US$1917 billion in 2019— the highest level since SIPRI started estimating total world military expenditure (see section I). It accounted for 2.2 per cent of world gross domestic product (GDP) or $249 per person. Spending in 2019 was 3.6 per cent higher than in 2018 and 7.2 per cent higher than 2010.

The increase in total global military spending in 2019 was the fifth consecutive annual increase and the largest increase of the period 2010–19, surpassing the 2.6 per cent increase in 2018. Military expenditure also increased in at least four of the world's five regions: by 5.0 per cent in Europe, 4.8 per cent in Asia and Oceania, 4.7 per cent in the Americas, and 1.5 per cent in Africa.

The growth in total spending in 2019 was largely influenced by expenditure patterns in the United States and China, which together account for over half of the world's military spending. The USA increased its spending for the second straight year to reach $732 billion in 2019. This was 2.7 times larger than the $261 billion spent by China, the world's next highest spender. China's total was 5.1 per cent higher than in 2018 and 85 per cent higher than in 2010.

With a 16 per cent decrease in its spending, Saudi Arabia fell from being the third-largest spender in 2018 to fifth position in 2019. India's spending of $71.1 billion ranked it as the third-largest spender for the first time, while Russia's increase of 4.5 per cent moved it up from fifth to fourth.

Among states in Western Europe, France continued to spend the most, with military expenditure of $50.1 billion in 2019. However, the largest increase in spending among the top 15 military spenders in 2019 was made by Germany: its military spending rose by 10 per cent to $49.3 billion.

Military expenditure in Europe totalled $356 billion in 2019, accounting for 19 per cent of global spending (see section II). This was behind spending by states in the Americas, at $815 billion (43 per cent of the world total), and Asia and Oceania, at $523 billion (27 per cent of world spending). Spending in the Middle East is estimated to have been 9.4 per cent of the world total. The $41.2 billion spent by African countries was the lowest of all the regions, at only 2.1 per cent of global military expenditure.

Following the annexation of Crimea by Russia and the rise of the Islamic State in 2014, the level of threat perceived by European members of the North Atlantic Treaty Organization (NATO) was substantially heightened. To address these perceived threats, at their summit meeting in September 2014 NATO members pledged to increase their military expenditure as a share of GDP to 2 per cent and to spend at least 20 per cent of their military expenditure on equipment (see section III). The number of European NATO countries allocating 20 per cent or more of their military expenditure to equipment increased from 5 at the time of the 2014 summit to 14 in 2019. The five with the highest relative increase in equipment spending as a share of total military expenditure—Bulgaria, Hungary, Lithuania, Romania and Slovakia—are all in Central Europe. While their sharp increases were driven by numerous factors—such as the need to modernize their weaponry or to decrease their dependence on Russia for maintenance of existing weapon systems—the primary reason was perceptions of heightened threat from Russia. Among other European members of NATO, increases in equipment spending as a share of military expenditure have been more moderate. Responses to NATO's equipment spending guideline have varied significantly based on the extent to which countries are affected by the identified threats and the technical conditions and size of their existing military arsenals.

Tracking countries' military spending requires transparency. At the international level such transparency remains a concern as the rate of reporting to military expenditure reporting mechanisms continues to decrease (see section IV). The decline in responses to the United Nations Report on Military Expenditures continued in 2019 and the number of states exchanging spending figures in the Organization for Security and Co-operation in Europe (OSCE) also decreased. Moreover, reporting to the South American Defense Expenditure Registry of the Union of South American Nations (Unión de Naciones Suramericanas, UNASUR) seems to have ended entirely. In contrast, at the national level, of the 169 countries for which SIPRI attempted to collect military expenditure information for 2019, data was found for 150, including in 147 cases from official government documents.

Among these 169 countries, the level of transparency varies widely. In some states, military expenditure is funded outside the government budget or has been in the past. Often these states are or have been ruled by military regimes, with weak parliamentary oversight of the armed forces. While democracy has been known to improve levels of transparency, transparency in military spending may take a long time to fully develop. In Myanmar, a 2019 UN report details how the armed forces have relied on off-budget allocations to secure a large degree of financial autonomy. Despite the political reforms introduced since 2015, the military still maintains control over its budget. The case of Myanmar underscores how off-budget funding mechanisms and opacity in military expenditure can allow the military to act unchecked and to perpetrate crimes against minorities.

NAN TIAN

I. Global developments in military expenditure, 2019

NAN TIAN, PIETER D. WEZEMAN, DIEGO LOPES DA SILVA,
SIEMON T. WEZEMAN AND ALEXANDRA KUIMOVA

World military expenditure in 2019 is estimated to have been more than US$1.9 trillion, the highest level since SIPRI started estimating total world military expenditure.[1] It was 3.6 per cent higher in real terms than in 2018 and 7.2 per cent higher than in 2010 (see table 8.1 and figure 8.1).[2] World military spending rose in each of the five years from 2015, having decreased almost steadily from 2011 until 2014 following the global financial and economic crisis. The world military burden—global military expenditure as a share of global gross domestic product (GDP)—was 2.2 per cent in 2019, after a minor increase from 2018.[3] Military spending per capita increased from $243 in 2018 to $249 in 2019 as the growth in military spending surpassed world population growth (1.1 per cent).

In at least four of the world's five regions, military expenditure increased in 2019 (see figure 8.1 and section II). The rate of increase was highest in Europe, at 5.0 per cent, taking the regional total to $356 billion. This was followed by an increase of 4.8 per cent in Asia and Oceania to $523 billion, a 4.7 per cent rise in the Americas to $815 billion, and growth of 1.5 per cent in Africa to $41.2 billion. The countries with the highest absolute increase in each of these regions were Germany in Europe, China in Asia and Oceania, the United States in the Americas, and Algeria in Africa.

For the fifth successive year, SIPRI cannot provide an estimate of total spending in the Middle East.[4] Missing data from two large spenders in the region (Qatar and the United Arab Emirates) and from two countries affected by conflict (Syria and Yemen) mean that no reliable estimate can be provided for this region. Of the 11 countries in the Middle East for which data is available, the combined military expenditure fell by 7.5 per cent to

---

[1] Of the 169 countries for which SIPRI attempted to estimate military expenditure in 2019, relevant data was found for 150. See the notes in table 8.1 for more details on estimates in world and regional totals.

[2] All figures for spending in 2019 are quoted in current 2019 US dollars. Except where otherwise stated, figures for increases or decreases in military spending are expressed in constant 2018 US dollars, often described as changes in 'real terms' or adjusted for inflation.

All SIPRI's military expenditure data is freely available in the SIPRI Military Expenditure Database. The sources and methods used to produce the data discussed here are also presented on the SIPRI website.

[3] The world military burden increased slightly (by 1.3%) in 2019, but this change is concealed by the conventions of rounding. See table 8.1. GDP estimates are from International Monetary Fund (IMF), International Financial Statistics Database, Sep. 2019.

[4] The estimate of total world military expenditure includes a rough estimate of total spending in the Middle East.

Table 8.1. Military expenditure and the military burden by region, 2010–19

Figures for 2010–19 are in US$ b. at constant (2018) prices and exchange rates. Figures for 2019 in the right-most column, marked *, are in current US$ b.

	2010	2011	2012	2013	2014	2015	2016	2017	2018	2019	2019*
World total	1 793	1 799	1 783	1 756	1 750	1 776	1 785	1 807	1 855	1 922	1 917
Geographical regions											
Africa	(35.5)	(39.2)	40.4	45.1	46.4	(44.3)	(43.3)	(42.5)	(41.0)	(41.6)	(41.2)
North Africa	(14.0)	(17.3)	18.9	22.2	22.9	(23.3)	(23.4)	(22.9)	(22.3)	(23.4)	(23.5)
Sub-Saharan Africa	(21.5)	(21.8)	(21.5)	22.9	23.4	20.9	19.9	19.6	18.6	18.2	17.7
Americas	924	914	868	808	764	750	747	746	768	805	815
Central America and the Caribbean	5.7	6.1	6.5	6.9	7.2	7.0	7.7	7.2	7.9	8.5	8.7
North America	867	858	810	748	703	690	688	685	705	741	754
South America	50.8	50.1	51.3	53.4	54.0	53.4	51.0	53.9	55.2	55.3	52.8
Asia and Oceania	352	366	381	400	423	446	467	489	507	531	523
Central Asia	1.3	1.4	1.6	1.8	1.9	1.9	1.7	1.6	1.8	2.1	2.2
East Asia	234	246	260	276	294	310	323	337	354	370	363
Oceania	24.5	24.1	23.3	23.1	25.0	27.3	29.8	29.9	29.5	30.6	29.0
South Asia	63.1	64.1	64.3	64.2	67.8	69.0	74.9	80.7	83.8	89.1	88.1
South East Asia	29.7	30.4	31.3	34.4	34.1	37.2	37.9	39.6	38.0	39.6	40.5
Europe	336	330	331	326	328	337	351	342	348	365	356
Central Europe	20.2	19.7	19.3	19.1	20.4	23.1	23.4	25.2	28.5	32.6	31.5
Eastern Europe	53.6	57.6	66.4	69.5	74.8	80.9	85.5	70.2	68.9	72.3	74.0
Western Europe	262	252	246	238	233	233	243	247	251	261	251
Middle East	146	149	161	176	188	..	..	..	..	..	..
World military spending per capita (current US$)	237	248	245	242	239	226	239	240	243	249	

Military burden (i.e. world military spending as a % of world gross domestic product, both measured in current US$)[a]

World	2.5	2.4	2.3	2.2	2.4	2.4	2.2	2.3	2.3	2.2	2.2
Africa	1.7	1.7	1.8	2.2	1.9	1.9	2.2	2.0	1.8	1.6	1.6
Americas	1.5	1.5	1.5	1.4	1.4	1.4	1.4	1.5	1.4	1.4	1.4
Asia and Oceania	1.7	1.6	1.6	1.7	1.7	1.7	1.7	1.6	1.7	1.6	1.7
Europe	1.6	1.5	1.5	1.5	1.6	1.5	1.5	1.5	1.5	1.6	1.7
Middle East	4.3	4.3	4.6	4.8	5.4	5.2	4.8	4.7	5.0	4.7	4.5

( ) = total based on country data accounting for less than 90% of the regional total; .. = estimate not provided due to unusually high levels of uncertainty and missing data.

Notes: The totals for the world and regions are estimates, based on data from the SIPRI Military Expenditure Database. When military expenditure data for a country is missing for a few years, estimates are made, most often on the assumption that the rate of change in that country's military expenditure is the same as that for the region to which it belongs. When no estimates can be made, countries are excluded from the totals. The countries excluded from all totals here are Cuba, Djibouti, Eritrea, Myanmar, North Korea, Somalia, Syria, Turkmenistan and Uzbekistan. Totals for regions cover the same groups of countries for all years. The SIPRI military expenditure figures are presented on a calendar-year basis, calculated on the assumption of an even rate of expenditure throughout the financial year. Rough estimates for the Middle East are included in the world totals for 2015–19. Further detail on sources and methods can be found on the SIPRI website.

[a] The military burden of a region is the average military burden for countries in the region for which data is available.

Sources: SIPRI Military Expenditure Database, Apr. 2020; International Monetary Fund, World Economic Outlook Database, Oct. 2019; International Monetary Fund, International Financial Statistics Database, Sep. 2019; and United Nations Department of Economic and Social Affairs, Population Division, 'World population prospects 2019', Aug. 2019.

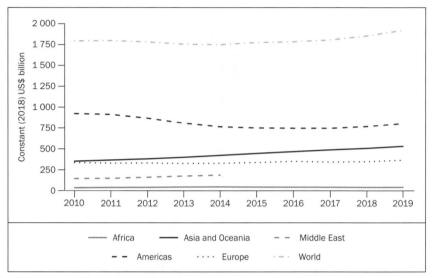

Figure 8.1. Military expenditure by region, 2010–19

Note: No estimate of military expenditure in the Middle East for 2015–19 is given since the data is highly uncertain. However, a rough estimate for the Middle East is included in the estimated world total.

Source: SIPRI Military Expenditure Database, Apr. 2020.

$147 billion in 2019. This overall fall was caused by decreases in spending in 7 of these 11 countries, most notably Saudi Arabia.

The rise in world military spending in 2019 can be illustrated by comparing the scale of the largest absolute increases with that of the largest absolute decreases. In 2018 constant US dollars, the five largest increases in military spending were $36.2 billion by the USA, $13.0 billion by China, $4.7 billion by Germany, $4.5 billion by India and $3.2 billion by the Republic of Korea (South Korea). In contrast, the largest decreases were substantially smaller: the largest decrease was $11.9 billion by Saudi Arabia, followed by $1.6 billion by Iran, $889 million by Oman, $451 million by Canada and $330 million by Lebanon.

This section continues by describing global trends in military expenditure over the period 2010–19. It then identifies the 15 states with the highest military spending in 2019, with a focus on the top 2: the USA and China. Regional trends are described in section II.

Trends in military expenditure, 2010–19

The 3.6 per cent increase in total global military spending in 2019 was the largest annual increase of the period 2010–19, surpassing the 2.6 per cent increase in 2018. Military spending over the 2010s rose by 7.2 per cent, but with the trend varying across three periods: a small increase between 2010 and 2011, decreases in 2012–14 and continuous increases in 2015–19 (see table 8.1).

The USA and China—which together spend almost $1 trillion—account for over half of the world's military spending and so any change in their spending will have a substantial influence on the trend in the global total. India, Russia and Saudi Arabia have also contributed—albeit to a lesser extent—to changes in the world total. For example, the withdrawal of US troops from Iraq in 2010 and Afghanistan in 2011 led to substantial decreases in US military spending, which greatly affected global military spending. The fall in world spending between 2011 and 2014 was roughly a quarter of the drop in US spending. The decrease in world spending would have been far larger if the US fall had not been counteracted by major increases in Chinese, Russian and Saudi Arabian military spending. By 2015 the USA had withdrawn most of its troops from Afghanistan and the steep falls in US spending ended.[5] As a result, US military spending decreased at a slower rate than before, falling by an annual average of 1.2 per cent between 2015 and 2017 compared with the average annual decrease of 5.1 per cent in 2011–14. It was also during 2015–17 that global military spending increased for the first time since 2011, albeit at a slow rate. However, this time the minor rise was due to increases in military spending by China and India. While Saudi Arabia's military spending fell by 13 per cent between 2017 and 2019, this decrease was counteracted by spending increases by the USA, China, India and Russia. As a result, global military spending rose by 2.6 per cent in 2018 and by 3.6 per cent in 2019, the highest annual increases since 2009.

Over the decade 2010–19 regional total military spending decreased in only the Americas (–13 per cent), while it increased in Africa (17 per cent), Asia and Oceania (51 per cent), Europe (8.8 per cent) and for countries in the Middle East (21 per cent) for which data is available (see table 8.2). Among the 13 subregions, spending fell over the decade in only 3: sub-Saharan Africa (–15 per cent), North America (–15 per cent) and Western Europe (–0.6 per cent). In all other subregions, military spending grew. The five largest increases were in North Africa (67 per cent), Central Asia (63 per cent), Central Europe (61 per cent), East Asia (58 per cent), and Central America and the Caribbean (49 per cent).

The decline in military spending in sub-Saharan Africa from 2010 was the result of spending decreases by three of the four countries with the largest military expenditure in the subregion: Angola, Nigeria and Sudan. In North America (i.e. Canada and the USA), the decrease was solely because of changes by the USA. Following the USA-initiated 'global war on terrorism' in

---

[5] Chandrasekaran, R., 'The Afghan surge is over', *Foreign Policy*, 25 Sep. 2012; and Landler, M., 'US troops to leave Afghanistan by end of 2016', *New York Times*, 28 May 2014.

Table 8.2. Key military expenditure statistics by region and subregion, 2019

Expenditure figures are in US$, at current prices and exchange rates. Changes are in real terms, based on constant (2018) US$.

Region/ subregion	Military expenditure, 2019 (US$ b.)	Change (%) 2018–19	Change (%) 2010–19	Major changes, 2018–19 (%)[a] Increases		Major changes, 2018–19 (%)[a] Decreases	
World	**1 917**	**3.6**	**7.2**				
Africa[b]	(41.2)	*1.5*	*17*	Togo	*70*	Zimbabwe	*–50*
North Africa	(23.5)	*4.6*	*67*	Uganda	*52*	Mozambique	*–22*
Sub-Saharan Africa[b]	17.7	*–2.2*	*–15*	Burkina Faso	*22*	Benin	*–20*
				DRC	*16*	Niger	*–20*
Americas[c]	815	*4.7*	*–13*	Guatemala	*24*	Argentina	*–9.2*
Central America and Caribbean[c]	8.7	*8.1*	*49*	Jamaica	*20*	Bolivia	*–5.0*
				Mexico	*7.9*	Uruguay	*–4.0*
North America	754	*5.1*	*–15*	Paraguay	*7.7*	Ecuador	*–3.6*
South America	52.8	*0.2*	*8.9*				
Asia and Oceania[d]	523	*4.8*	*51*	Afghanistan	*20*	Kyrgyzstan	*–2.4*
Central Asia[e]	2.2	*16*	*63*	New Zealand	*19*	Indonesia	*–2.3*
East Asia[f]	363	*4.6*	*58*	Kazakhstan	*19*	Nepal	*–2.2*
Oceania	29.0	*3.5*	*25*	Brunei Darussalam	*17*	Japan	*–0.1*
South Asia	88.1	*6.4*	*41*				
South East Asia[g]	40.5	*4.2*	*34*				
Europe	356	*5.0*	*8.8*	Bulgaria	*127*	Cyprus	*–5.6*
Central Europe	31.5	*14*	*61*	Slovakia	*48*	Austria	*–0.8*
Eastern Europe	74.0	*4.9*	*35*	Serbia	*43*	Greece	*–0.4*
Western Europe	251	*3.9*	*–0.6*	N. Macedonia	*30*		
Middle East[h]	..	..	..	Iraq	*21*	Saudi Arabia	*–16*
				Turkey	*5.8*	Iran	*–15*
				Kuwait	*4.7*	Lebanon	*–12*

( ) = uncertain estimate; . . = not available; DRC = Democratic Republic of the Congo.

[a] These lists show the countries with the largest increases or decreases for each region as a whole, rather than by subregion. Countries with a military expenditure in 2019 of less than $100 million, or $50 million in Africa, are excluded.

[b] Figures exclude Djibouti, Eritrea and Somalia.

[c] Figures exclude Cuba.

[d] Figures exclude North Korea, Myanmar, Turkmenistan and Uzbekistan.

[e] Figures exclude Turkmenistan and Uzbekistan.

[f] Figures exclude North Korea.

[g] Figures exclude Myanmar.

[h] No SIPRI estimates for the Middle East are available for 2015–19. A rough estimate for the Middle East (excluding Syria) is included in the world total.

Source: SIPRI Military Expenditure Database, Apr. 2020.

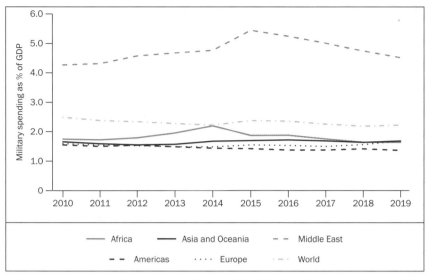

Figure 8.2. Military burden, by region, 2010–19

Note: The military burden is military expenditure as a share of gross domestic product (GDP). The military burden of a region is the average military burden of the countries in the region for which data is available.

Source: SIPRI Military Expenditure Database, Apr. 2020.

2001, US military spending peaked in 2010, then fell, with seven consecutive years of decrease in 2011–17.

In contrast, the growth in North Africa was the result of higher spending by all countries for which data is available. In Central Asia the increase can be attributed to higher spending by Kazakhstan, the subregion's largest spender. The increase in Central Europe was driven by states' perceptions of a growing threat from Russia and the need to modernize and replace old military equipment (see section III).[6] The growth in East Asia was largely due to continued increases in Chinese military spending, albeit with a lower annual increase in 2019 than in 2010. In Central America and the Caribbean the rise was principally the result of Mexico's ongoing drug war (see section II).

At 2.2 per cent, the world military burden in 2019 was 0.3 percentage points lower than in 2010 (see table 8.1 and figure 8.2). The world military burden followed a declining trend in 2010–19, decreasing every year except for 2015 and 2019, despite the 7.2 per cent increase in military spending. The increase in military burden in 2015 was the result of a fall in world GDP, the first since 2009, while in 2019 the 3.6 per cent increase in world military spending was roughly 1.6 percentage points more than the growth in world GDP.

[6] On the modernization and replacement of major arms see also chapter 9, section II, in this volume.

Table 8.3. The 15 countries with the highest military expenditure in 2019

Expenditure figures and GDP are in US$, at current prices and exchange rates. Changes are in real terms, based on constant (2018) US$.

Rank			Military expenditure,	Change (%)		Military expenditure as a share of GDP (%)[b]		Share of world military expenditure,
2019	2018[a]	Country	2019 ($ b.)	2018–19	2010–19	2019	2010	2019 (%)
1	1	USA	732	5.3	–15	3.4	4.9	38
2	2	China	[261]	5.1	85	[1.9]	[1.9]	[14]
3	4	India	71.1	6.8	37	2.4	2.7	3.7
4	5	Russia	65.1	4.5	30	3.9	3.6	3.4
5	3	Saudi Arabia	[61.9]	–16	14	[8.0]	8.6	[3.2]
Subtotal top 5			**1 191**	..	..	..	..	62
6	6	France	50.1	1.6	3.5	1.9	2.0	2.6
7	9	Germany	49.3	10	15	1.3	1.3	2.6
8	7	UK[c]	48.7	0.0	–15	1.7	2.4	2.5
9	8	Japan	47.6	–0.1	2.0	0.9	1.0	2.5
10	10	South Korea	43.9	7.5	36	2.7	2.5	2.3
Subtotal top 10			**1 430**	..	..	..	..	75
11	11	Brazil	26.9	–0.5	6.1	1.5	1.5	1.4
12	12	Italy	26.8	0.8	–11	1.4	1.5	1.4
13	13	Australia	25.9	2.1	23	1.9	1.9	1.3
14	14	Canada	22.2	–2.0	27	1.3	1.2	1.2
15	15	Israel	20.5	1.7	30	5.3	5.9	1.1
Subtotal top 15			**1 553**	..	..	..	..	81
World			**1 917**	3.6	7.2	2.2	2.5	100

[ ] = estimated figure; GDP = gross domestic product.

[a] Rankings for 2018 are based on updated military expenditure figures for 2018 in the current edition of the SIPRI Military Expenditure Database. They may therefore differ from the rankings for 2018 given in *SIPRI Yearbook 2019* and in other SIPRI publications in 2019.

[b] These figures are based on GDP estimates from International Monetary Fund, World Economic Outlook Database, Oct. 2019; and International Monetary Fund, International Financial Statistics Database, Sep. 2019.

[c] Spending in the UK increased by 0.047% in 2019, but due to conventions of rounding the increase appears in the table as 0.0.

Source: SIPRI Military Expenditure Database, Apr. 2020.

There is substantial variation in the average military burden of each region. The average military burdens for countries in Africa and for countries in the Americas decreased, while in European and Middle Eastern countries they increased and in Asia and Oceania it remained unchanged. In 2019, on average, states in the Americas had the lowest military burden, at 1.4 per cent of GDP. For African states the average was slightly higher, at 1.6 per cent, and in both Asia and Oceania and Europe it was 1.7 per cent. The highest average, 4.5 per cent, was for the states in the Middle East for which data is available.

The largest military spenders in 2019

The top 15 military spenders in the world in 2019 were the same as in 2018, but there were some significant changes in the rankings among the highest spenders (see table 8.3).[7] Most notably, India ranked as the third-largest spender in 2019 for the first time.

Military spending by the top 15 countries was $1553 billion in 2019, accounting for 81 per cent of global expenditure. The USA (38 per cent) and China (14 per cent) remained the two largest spenders, together accounting for more than half of world spending. The gap between the military spending of China and that of the USA increased in 2019 for the first time since 2003 because the USA increased spending by almost three times more than China.

A moderate increase in India's military spending (6.8 per cent) together with a significant fall in Saudi Arabia's spending (–16 per cent) meant that India ranked third in 2019 for the first time. Saudi Arabia's decrease and the increase in Russia's spending (4.5 per cent) meant that Russia moved up one place in the rankings, from fifth to fourth, while Saudi Arabia fell from third to fifth position.

France increased its spending only slightly in 2019 but remained the biggest spender in Western Europe. The 10 per cent increase in Germany's spending was the highest increase of any top 15 spender in 2019. It meant that Germany moved up two places in the rankings, from ninth to seventh, while Japan and the United Kingdom each moved down one place.

The top 15 countries can be divided into four groups according to the scale of their military expenditure. The USA and China are the largest spenders— together they spent almost 1.8 times more than the other 13 countries combined. Next are three countries—India, Russia and Saudi Arabia—that spent approximately $60–75 billion on their militaries in 2019. The third group consists of France, Germany, the UK, Japan and South Korea, with spending in the range $40–55 billion in 2019. The fourth group includes five countries— Brazil, Italy, Australia, Canada and Israel—that each spent $20–30 billion.

All but three countries in the top 15 had higher military expenditure in 2019 than in 2010. The exceptions were the USA (–15 per cent), the UK (–15 per cent) and Italy (–11 per cent). China's increase (85 per cent) was by far the largest among the top 15. There were more moderate increases (i.e. 10–39 per cent) in the spending of Australia, Canada, Germany, India, Israel, Russia, Saudi Arabia and South Korea, and minor increases (i.e. less than 10 per cent) by Brazil, France and Japan.

Among the top 15 military spenders in 2019, Japan had the lowest military burden: it devoted only 0.9 per cent of its GDP to military expenditure. Saudi

---

[7] The United Arab Emirates (UAE) would probably rank as one of the 15 largest spenders, most likely in the range 11–15, but a lack of data since 2014 means that no reasonable estimate of its military spending can be made and thus it has been omitted from the top 15 ranking.

Table 8.4. Components of US military expenditure, financial years 2015–19

Figures are in US$ b. at current prices unless otherwise stated. Years are US financial years, which start on 1 Oct. of the previous year.

	2015	2016	2017	2018	2019[a]
Department of Defense	562	566	569	604	652
Military personnel	145	148	145	146	157
O&M	247	243	245	257	276
Procurement	101	103	104	113	123
RDT&E	64.1	64.9	68.1	80.0	85.3
Other DOD military	4.6	6.8	6.8	8.6	11.2
Department of Energy	27.2	28.0	29.8	30.4	32.4
Atomic energy, 'defence'	18.7	19.4	20.5	20.9	23.6
Other, 'defence' related	8.5	8.6	9.3	9.5	8.8
National Intelligence Program, military related	[37.7]	[39.8]	[41.0]	[44.6]	[45.2]
Department of State, international security assistance	6.4	6.7	7.1	6.8	5.7
Transfers to fund border wall construction	..	..	..	..	–3.6
Total	**634**	**640**	**647**	**686**	**732**
As a share (%) of GDP	*3.5*	*3.4*	*3.3*	*3.3*	*3.4*

[ ] = estimated figure; DOD = US Department of Defense; GDP = gross domestic product; O&M = operations and maintenance; RDT&E = research, development, test and evaluation.

[a] Figures for financial year 2019 are estimates.

Source: US Department of Defense (DOD), Office of the Undersecretary of Defense (Comptroller), *National Defense Budget Estimates for FY2019* (DOD: Washington, DC, Apr. 2018).

Arabia had the highest, 8.0 per cent. Among the top 15, the military burdens of Israel (5.3 per cent), Russia (3.9 per cent), the USA (3.4 per cent), South Korea (2.7 per cent) and India (2.4 per cent) were also higher than the global military burden of 2.2 per cent.

The United States

US military expenditure was $732 billion in 2019, an increase of 5.3 per cent compared with 2018 (see table 8.4). This was the second year of growth in US military spending following seven years of continuous real-terms decline— between 2010 and 2017 spending fell by 22 per cent. The USA remained by far the largest spender in the world in 2019, spending 2.8 times more than the second-largest military spender, China.

During his 2016 campaign for the US presidency, Donald J. Trump promised to rebuild what he considered a 'depleted' US military.[8] Following his election, both President Trump and the US Congress championed a

---

[8] Lewis, N., 'Trump's claim that "they just kept cutting, cutting, cutting the military" until it was "depleted"', *Washington Post*, 5 Dec. 2017.

'military rebuild'.[9] The rebuilding of the US military was to have two central factors. The first was an increase in personnel costs, mainly attributed to the recruitment of 16 000 more military personnel.[10] The second factor was arms-acquisition programmes involving both conventional and nuclear weapon modernization.[11] However, in 2019 President Trump diverted $3.6 billion from the military budget to pay for the building of a wall along the border between the USA and Mexico.[12] The cumulative effect of all these changes was an 8.5 per cent increase in total US military expenditure between 2017 and 2019.

The increase in the US military budget to pay for the rebuild meant removing the automatic mechanism—known as the sequester—that reduces levels of expenditure under previously agreed budget caps. The caps were established by the 2011 Budgetary Control Act (BCA), which was designed to reduce the US Government's large financial deficit.[13] However, sequestration was last implemented in the early 2010s: the spending caps imposed by the BCA were commonly circumvented by adding more funding to the overseas contingency operations (OCO) category as the BCA did not limit OCO funding. In 2019 OCO spending was $69 billion, accounting for almost 10 per cent of total US military spending.

In July 2019 the Congress approved raising the existing BCA spending caps, following which there was a move to change how US spending will be allocated in the future.[14] Starting in 2020, an average of $45 billion per year that previously fell under the OCO budget will be moved to base budget of the US Department of Defense (DOD).[15]

SIPRI's estimate of US military spending is comprised of expenditure from four areas of government (see table 8.4): the DOD, the Department of Energy, the Department of State and the National Intelligence Program (NIP). DOD expenditure covers military personnel, operations and maintenance, procurement, and research and development (R&D). In 2019 it accounted for 89 per cent of total US military spending. Spending from the Department of Energy includes nuclear weapon activities and some other military-related

[9] Bratels, F., 'Trump and Congress just gave the military a big boost', Heritage Foundation Commentary, 28 Sep. 2018.

[10] McGarry, B. W., 'The FY2019 defense budget request: An overview', In Focus, US Congress, Congressional Research Service, 9 May 2018.

[11] On the nuclear weapon modernization programme see chapter 10, section I, in this volume.

[12] Grisales, C., 'These are the military projects losing funding to Trump's border wall', All Things Considered, National Public Radio, 4 Sep. 2019.

[13] Sköns, E. and Perlo-Freeman, S., 'The United States' military spending and the 2011 budget crisis', SIPRI Yearbook 2012, pp. 162–66; and Heniff, B., Rybicki, E. and Mahan, S. M., The Budget Control Act of 2011, Congressional Research Service (CRS) Report for Congress R41965 (US Congress, CRS: Washington, DC, 19 Aug. 2011).

[14] Gould, J., 'Divided Senate passes 2-year budget deal with military boost', Defense News, 1 Aug. 2019.

[15] Woodward, F. M., Funding for Overseas Contingency Operations and Its Impact on Defense Spending (Congressional Budget Office: Washington, DC, Oct. 2018).

Box 8.1. Revised estimates for the military expenditure of the United States

The United States intelligence community is made up of two independent programmes, the Military Intelligence Program (MIP) and National Intelligence Program (NIP). Spending on the NIP is now included as a fourth category in the SIPRI estimate of US military spending.

MIP activities are conducted exclusively for the Department of Defense (DOD) and expenditure on the MIP is included in the DOD budget—thus, SIPRI has always included it as part of total US military spending. In contrast, the NIP provides both military and non-military services. Including NIP expenditure in total US military spending thus requires an estimate of the NIP's military-related activities and the corresponding expenditure. A newly acquired consistent time series of figures dating back to 1965 allows estimation of the proportion of total spending on the NIP that can be considered military related.[a]

In general, the NIP is divided into eight DOD components and nine non-DOD components.[b] The eight DOD components are the Defense Intelligence Agency (DIA), the National Geospatial-Intelligence Agency (NGA), the National Reconnaissance Office (NRO), the National Security Agency (NSA), US Air Force Intelligence, US Army Intelligence, US Marine Corps Intelligence and US Navy Intelligence. All of these are included in estimating the military-related activities of the NIP. Two of the nine non-DOD components of the NIP are also military related: the Office of the Director of National Intelligence (ODNI) and the Central Intelligence Agency (CIA). The other seven non-DOD components are part of the departments of Energy, Homeland Security, Justice, State and Treasury.

Total NIP spending in 2019 was an estimated $60.2 billion.[c] SIPRI estimates that 75 per cent of this total is military related. This adds $45.2 billion (in current prices) to US military spending in 2019 (see table 8.4), making it 6.6 per cent higher than the total excluding intelligence spending.

[a] Available information on intelligence spending has been obtained through the US Freedom of Information Act. This information has been published by both the Office of the Director of National Intelligence and other organizations, including the Federation of American Scientists (FAS). Federation of American Scientists, Intelligence Resource Program, 'Intelligence budget data'.

[b] DeVine, M. E., *Intelligence Community Spending: Trends and Issues*, Congressional Research Service (CRS) Report for Congress R44381 (US Congress, CRS: Washington, DC, 6 Nov. 2019).

[c] DeVine (note b).

---

activities, which together make up around 4 per cent of US military spending. Spending on international military aid by the Department of State accounts for about 1 per cent of the total. This includes peacekeeping operations, military aid, and international military education and training. The remaining 6 per cent is spending on the NIP, which can now be included in the SIPRI total estimate of US military spending (see box 8.1).

China

In 2019 China's military expenditure is estimated to have totalled $261 billion, representing 14 per cent of global military spending. Spending in 2019 was 5.1 per cent higher than in 2018 and 85 per cent higher than in 2010 (see table 8.5). Indeed, military spending in China has now increased for 25 consecutive years, the longest streak of uninterrupted increase by any country

Table 8.5. Components of China's military expenditure, 2015–19

Figures are in yuan b. at current prices unless otherwise stated.

	2015	2016	2017	2018	2019^a
National defence budget (central and local)	909	977	1 044	1 128	1 213
People's Armed Police (central and local)	164	178	192	206	225
Payments to demobilized and retired soldiers	76.3	85.5	93.4	104	112
Additional military RDT&E spending	[122]	[132]	[139]	[153]	[174]
Additional military construction spending	[52.0]	[55.6]	[59.5]	[64.3]	[69.4]
Arms imports	[11.6]	[10.9]	[16.4]	[20.6]	[10.0]
Total (yuan b.)	1 335	1 438	1 545	1 676	1 803
Total (US$ b.)	214	216	228	253	261

[ ] = estimated figure; RDT&E = research, development, test and evaluation.

Source: SIPRI Military Expenditure Database, Apr. 2020; and Chinese Ministry of Finance, Budget Division.

in the SIPRI Military Expenditure Database. Since the last decrease, in 1994, Chinese military spending has increased tenfold. The growth in China's military spending has closely matched the country's economic growth. Between 2010 and 2019, China's military burden remained almost unchanged, at 1.9 per cent of its GDP.

SIPRI's military expenditure figures for China differ from the official Chinese figures. SIPRI's estimate is almost 50 per cent higher than the figure that the Chinese Government publishes in its national defence budget: 1.2 trillion yuan ($178 billion) in 2019.[16] In estimating Chinese military expenditure, SIPRI seeks to account for significant elements of military-related spending that are outside the official budget for the Ministry of National Defense (see table 8.5).[17]

Official information is available for three categories of expenditure: the national defence budget, the budget of the People's Armed Police, and payments to demobilized and retired soldiers. These three items accounted for 86 per cent of total spending in 2019. The remaining 14 per cent of the total came from three further expenditure items that need to be estimated: additional funding for military research, development, testing and evaluation (RDT&E) outside the national defence budget (9.6 per cent of the total), additional military construction expenses (3.8 per cent), and arms imports (0.6 per cent).

In 2019 China released a new defence white paper, *China's National Defense in the New Era*, which offers insight into its long-term plan for mili-

---

[16] Olsen, K., 'China's defense spending is growing more slowly. But that doesn't mean military tensions are easing', CNBC, 5 Mar. 2019.

[17] SIPRI's estimate of China's military spending is based on a methodology adopted in 1999. Wang, S., 'The military expenditure of China, 1989–98', *SIPRI Yearbook 1999*, pp. 334–49. The original methodology included 8 expenditure categories, 2 of which (commercial earnings of the PLA and subsidies to the arms industry) are now redundant.

tary development and modernization.[18] The three-step plan aims to achieve 'mechanization' and 'enhanced informationization' by 2020, complete the modernization of the military by 2035 and fully transform China's armed forces—the People's Liberation Army (PLA)—into a 'world-class force' by the middle of the century. It is ambitious and indicates that modernizing the PLA continues to be a priority.[19] The white paper also states the need to narrow the gap between the PLA and 'the world's leading militaries', which probably refers to the USA.[20] In addition, it outlines a 'demand-oriented' approach to planning and funding. Thus, unless there is a severe political or economic change, Chinese military spending can be expected to continue to increase in the coming years.

[18] Chinese Ministry of National Defense (MND), *China's National Defense in the New Era* (MND: Beijing, 24 July 2019).

[19] Bitzinger, R. A., 'Modernising the Chinese military in an age of information', *East Asia Forum*, 10 Sep. 2019.

[20] Chinese Ministry of National Defense (note 18), chapter V.

II. Regional developments in military expenditure, 2019

The global total military expenditure of US$1917 billion in 2019 was not evenly distributed among the world's regions.[1] One region—the Americas—accounted for more than two-fifths (43 per cent) of the world total. This was followed by Asia and Oceania with 27 per cent and Europe with 19 per cent. The Middle East is estimated to have accounted for about 9.4 per cent of the total.[2] Spending by African countries was the lowest of all the regions, with only 2.1 per cent of global military expenditure in 2019.

This section reviews military expenditure developments in each of the world's five regions in turn. It describes how the spending decisions of individual countries affect the subregional and regional trends. On the impact on global trends see section I.

Africa

In 2019 military expenditure in Africa increased marginally, by 1.5 per cent to an estimated $41.2 billion.[3] This, the first increase in Africa for five years, was the smallest relative increase by a region in 2019 (see table 8.2 in section I). Over the period 2010–19 African military spending first increased in 2010–14, followed by decreases in 2015–18 and the minor increase in 2019 to give overall growth of 17 per cent (see table 8.1 in section I).

North Africa

Military spending by countries in North Africa is estimated to have totalled $23.5 billion in 2019, representing 57 per cent of the total for Africa. Amid long-standing tensions between Algeria and Morocco, domestic insurgencies and continuing civil war in Libya, military spending in the subregion was 4.6 per cent higher than in 2018 and 67 per cent higher than in 2010 (see figure 8.3).[4]

Algeria's military expenditure of $10.3 billion in 2019 was the highest in North Africa (and, indeed, Africa), accounting for 44 per cent of the subregional total. Spending in 2019 was 7.8 per cent higher than in 2018.

---

[1] All figures for spending in 2019 are quoted in current 2019 US dollars. Except where otherwise stated, figures for increases or decreases in military spending are expressed in constant 2018 US dollars, often described as changes in 'real terms' or adjusted for inflation. All SIPRI's military expenditure data is freely available in the SIPRI Military Expenditure Database. The sources and methods used to produce the data discussed here are also presented on the SIPRI website.

[2] This regional share is based on rough estimates for Qatar and the United Arab Emirates, for which accurate spending figures are unavailable.

[3] This regional total excludes Djibouti, Eritrea and Somalia, for which no reliable series of estimates could be made. SIPRI has no military spending data for Djibouti since 2009 and for Eritrea since 2003. While Somalia has a military budget in US dollars, there is no GDP or inflation data, so it is not possible to include the country in estimates of regional or world totals.

[4] On the armed conflict in Libya see chapter 6, section IV, in this volume.

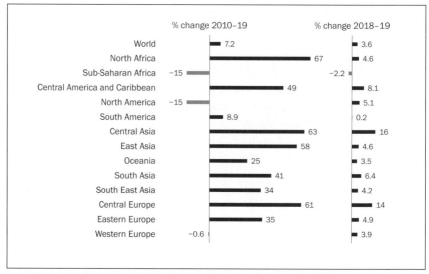

Figure 8.3. Changes in military expenditure by subregion, 2010–19 and 2018–19

Note: No estimate of change in military expenditure in the Middle East is given since data for 2015–19 is highly uncertain. However, a rough estimate for the Middle East is included in the estimated world total.

Source: SIPRI Military Expenditure Database, Apr. 2020.

Algeria's military spending has risen almost continuously over the past two decades, and particularly in the period 2004–16, when expenditure grew for 13 consecutive years and reached an all-time high in 2016. This was followed by two years of decline in real terms in 2017 and 2018. Since 2004 Algeria has procured a wide-range of major arms as part of a general force-improvement effort in response to growing perceived security threats in the region.[5] At 6.0 per cent of its gross domestic product (GDP), Algeria's military burden was the highest in Africa.

Morocco's military spending of $3.7 billion in 2019 was about one-third of Algeria's. Its spending was 1.7 per cent higher than in 2018, mostly as a result of increased spending on personnel.[6] The increase in military spending is likely to continue in the coming years as Morocco has announced plans to place several large orders for advanced equipment from France and the United States.[7]

[5] Ghanem-Yazbeck, D., 'The Algerian army: Cooperation, not intervention', Commentary, Italian Institute for Political Studies, 7 Dec. 2017. See also chapter 9, section II, in this volume.
[6] Loi de finances no. 18-80 pour l'année budgetaire 2019 [Finance act no. 18-80 for the financial year 2019], *Bulletin Officiel* (Rabat), no. 6736 bis, 21 Dec. 2018, pp. 1961–2066.
[7] E.g. Moroccan Defense Network, 'Morocco buys French CAESAR howitzer and surface to air VL-MICA missiles', 21 Jan. 2021; and US Defense Security Cooperation Agency, 'Morocco—F-16 Block 72 new purchase', News Release no. 19-09, 25 Mar. 2019. See also chapter 9, section II, in this volume.

Sub-Saharan Africa

Military spending in sub-Saharan Africa fell by 2.2 per cent in 2019 to reach $17.7 billion, which was 15 per cent lower than in 2010. Of the 42 countries in the subregion for which data is available, 19—that is, almost half—increased their military spending, while the remainder decreased spending. Sub-Saharan Africa has both the largest number of countries of any subregion and the lowest average military spending per country ($402 million).[8] However, actual national spending ranged from $9.7 million by Cabo Verde to $3.5 billion by South Africa.

In recent years spending on the military by sub-Saharan African states has been volatile. Of the 19 countries that increased military spending in 2019, 8 had decreased spending in 2018. Similarly, 13 of the 23 countries that lowered spending in 2019 had raised spending in 2018. This means that in 21 of the 42 countries in sub-Saharan Africa for which data is available, the trend in changes reversed in 2019. This high proportion of countries with volatility in spending is unique to sub-Saharan Africa. Economic fluctuation, political instability and armed conflict (persistent and new) remain the most immediate factors influencing military expenditure in the subregion.[9]

Unlike in previous years, the drop in total military expenditure in sub-Saharan Africa was caused by numerous small absolute decreases combined with lower spending by the largest spenders (i.e. South Africa, Nigeria and Angola) that together offset the many small increases by other states.

The four largest relative decreases in military spending in 2019 occurred in Zimbabwe (–50 per cent), Mozambique (–22 per cent), Benin (–20 per cent) and Niger (–20 per cent). Although Zimbabwe's military spending halved in real terms, it rose by 30 per cent in nominal terms (i.e. without accounting for inflation and changes in exchange rates). The real-terms contraction was a result of a sharp increase in inflation, from single digits in early 2019 to over 200 per cent in November 2019.[10]

The four countries with the biggest relative increases in sub-Saharan Africa were Togo (70 per cent), Uganda (52 per cent), Burkina Faso (22 per cent) and the Democratic Republic of the Congo (DRC, 16 per cent). The increase in Togolese military spending was entirely due to the substantial increase (278 per cent) in spending on acquisition of goods and services (a category

---

[8] The total for sub-Saharan Africa excludes the Comoros and Sao Tome and Principe—as the SIPRI Military Expenditure Database excludes small states low expenditure—and Djibouti, Eritrea and Somalia (see note 3).

[9] African Development Bank Group (ADB), *African Economic Outlook 2019* (ADB: Abidjan, 2019), pp. 1–49; and Melina, G. and Portillo, R., *Economic Fluctuations in Sub-Saharan Africa*, International Monetary Fund (IMF) Working Paper no. WP18/40 (IMF: Washington, DC, Mar. 2018).

[10] African Development Bank Group (note 9), p. 189.

that includes military operations).[11] As a response to the growing threat of jihadist groups in the neighbourhood, Togo participated in numerous military operations in 2019, such as Operation Otapuanu in Burkina Faso and Operation Koudalgou III in Togo and Ghana.[12]

Armed conflict is a major driver of military spending in sub-Saharan Africa. Zones of conflict can be grouped into three rough geographic areas: Central Africa, the Horn of Africa, and the Sahel and Lake Chad regions.[13]

The main countries involved in conflict in Central Africa are the Central African Republic (CAR), the DRC, South Sudan and Uganda. In CAR, military spending increased by 8.7 per cent in 2019, despite the February peace deal between rebels and the government.[14] The DRC's military expenditure increased for the first time since 2016, by 16 per cent to $353 million in 2019. This may have been a reaction to an escalation in violence in 2018 following contentious elections.[15] To the DRC's east, Uganda increased its military spending by 52 per cent in 2019 as it continued to fight an insurgency by the Allied Democratic Forces (ADF).[16] Expenditure on equipment, which increased by 320 per cent, accounted for all of the increase.[17] In South Sudan, despite the 2018 peace agreement, armed conflict and violence have continued to plague the country.[18] In 2018 its actual military spending was almost four times larger than the original budget. This was because of additional procurement contracts for equipment for the South Sudanese Army that were not in the 2018 budget.[19] Military spending was down 7.5 per cent

---

[11] Togolese Ministry of the Economy and Finances, 'Loi de finances rectificative—gestion 2018—depenses' [Supplementary finance act—2018 period—expenditure], pp. 123–41; and Togolese Ministry of the Economy and Finances, 'Loi de finances rectificative, gestion 2019: Tableau des depense' [Supplementary finance act, 2019 period: Expenditure table].

[12] International Crisis Group (ICG), *The Risk of Jihadist Contagion in West Africa*, ICG Briefing no. 149 (ICG: Brussels, 20 Dec. 2019), pp. 4–10.

[13] Based on Armed Conflict Location & Event Data Project (ACLED), conflict event by location database. On the armed conflicts in these areas see chapter 7, sections II–IV, in this volume.

[14] Van Eyssen, B., 'Central African Republic peace deal—violated and fragile', Deutsche Welle, 15 Aug. 2019. On the armed conflict and peace process in CAR see chapter 7, section III, in this volume.

[15] Armed Conflict Location & Event Data Project (ACLED), 'Conflict in the DRC', ACLED Fact Sheet, 25 July 2019; and Weber, L., 'Election chaos is making history's second-largest Ebola outbreak worse', HuffPost, 5 Jan. 2019. On the armed conflict in the DRC see chapter 7, section III, in this volume.

[16] Nantulya, P., 'The ever-adaptive Allied Democratic Forces insurgency', Africa Center for Strategic Studies, 8 Feb. 2019.

[17] Ugandan Government, *Draft Estimates of Revenue and Expenditure (Recurrent and Development) FY 2019/20*, vol. 1, *Central Government Votes for the Year Ending on the 30th June 2020* (Republic of Uganda: Kampala, [2019]), pp. 117–27.

[18] Marsden, R., 'Will South Sudan's new peace deal stick?', Chatham House, 26 Nov. 2018; and Kishi, R. (ed.), *Ten Conflicts to Worry About in 2019: Mid-year Update* (Armed Conflict Location & Event Data Project: Madison, WI, Aug. 2019), p. 12. On the armed conflict and peace process in South Sudan see chapter 7, section IV, in this volume.

[19] United Nations, Security Council, Final report of the Panel of Experts on South Sudan submitted pursuant to Resolution 2428 (2018), S/2019/301, 9 Apr. 2019, pp. 27–32; and South Sudanese Ministry of Finance and Economic Planning (MOFEP), *FY: 2019/2020 Approved Budget Book* (MOFEP: Juba, [2019]), pp. 664–65.

in 2019 as the shrinking economy put pressure on all forms of government expenditure.[20]

In the Horn of Africa, fighting against al-Shabab continued in Ethiopia, Kenya and Somalia. Only incomplete data is available for Somalia itself.[21] In 2019 Ethiopia's military spending fell by 1.6 per cent and Kenya's by 1.7 per cent. These falls in spending were not indicative of any new developments in the Horn of Africa: Kenya's spending had increased for each of the previous four years and Ethiopia's for each of the previous five years. Over the period 2010–19, military spending increased by 25 per cent in Kenya and by 12 per cent in Ethiopia.

In the Sahel and Lake Chad regions, Burkina Faso, Cameroon, Chad, Mali and Nigeria are among the countries that have recently been involved in armed conflicts against Boko Haram, Islamic State West Africa Province and rebel forces.[22] Military spending by Burkina Faso has risen by 130 per cent since 2014, when the ousting of long-term Burkinabe President Blaise Compaoré was followed by the spread of Islamist extremism. With continued fighting against numerous armed groups, spending rose for the fourth consecutive year in 2019, by 22 per cent.[23] Despite the armed conflicts around the Lake Chad Basin, military spending by Chad itself fell by 5.1 per cent in 2019.[24] Chad's military expenditure has been extremely volatile over the past 10 years, with decreases in six years and increases in four. The changes almost always alternated between an increase and a decrease. This may reflect Chad's instability—both economic and security—as a result of the armed conflict. Despite Cameroon's declaration of war against Boko Haram in 2014, its military spending only increased slightly, up by 16 per cent in 2014–19 and by 1.4 per cent in 2018–19.[25] At $474 million, Mali's military spending was 3.6 per cent higher in 2019 than in 2018. Its military expenditure has increased by 253 per cent since fighting against militant jihadist groups began in 2012.[26] To support the fight against Islamist extremism, France has provided substantial military support since 2013, with over 4500 soldiers deployed in the Sahel.[27] In 2019 Nigeria, sub-Saharan Africa's second-largest spender, reduced its

[20] African Development Bank Group (note 9), p. 177.

[21] SIPRI has military expenditure information for Somalia in current US dollars, but without inflation data real changes cannot be calculated. In 2019 Somalia military spending rose by 2.3% in nominal terms. On the armed conflicts in the Horn of Africa see chapter 7, section IV, in this volume.

[22] On the armed conflicts in the Sahel and Lake Chad regions see chapter 7, section II, in this volume.

[23] Mbogori, A., 'Conflict, violence in Burkina Faso displaces nearly half a million people', United Nations High Commissioner for Refugees, 11 Oct. 2019; and Mednick, S., 'Islamic extremism wracks Burkina Faso, spreading east', Associated Press, 10 Jan. 2020.

[24] United Nations Office for the Coordination of Humanitarian Affairs (OCHA), *Lake Chad Basin: Crisis Update* (OCHA: New York, June 2019).

[25] BBC, 'Africa leaders declare "war" on Nigeria Boko Haram', 17 May 2014.

[26] Chauzal, G. and van Damme, T., *The Roots of Mali's Conflict: Moving Beyond the 2012 Crisis* (Netherlands Institute of International Relations Clingendael: The Hague, Mar. 2015), pp. 10–13.

[27] French Ministry of the Armed Forces, *Defence Key Figures*, 2019 edn (Ministère des Armées: Paris, 2019), p. 24. On France's role in the Sahel see chapter 7, sections I and II, in this volume.

military spending by 8.2 per cent to $1.9 billion. However, there is continued insecurity as a result of, among other things, activities by Boko Haram militants.[28] This raises doubts about the accuracy of Nigeria's official military spending figures. Off-budget military expenditure in the form of undisclosed 'security votes' suggests that actual military spending in Nigeria may be far higher than the official figures.[29]

The Americas

Military expenditure in the Americas reached $815 billion in 2019— 4.7 per cent higher than in 2018. Over the decade 2010–19, however, military expenditure decreased by 13 per cent (see tables 8.1 and 8.2). North American countries (i.e. the United States and Canada) are by far the largest spenders in the region, accounting for 92 per cent of the total, followed by South America with 6.5 per cent and Central America and the Caribbean with 1.1 per cent.

North America

North America's military expenditure grew by 5.1 per cent in 2019 (see figure 8.3), the second consecutive year of increase, to reach $754 billion. Spending was 15 per cent lower than in 2010, when it reached its highest level since the end of the cold war. Nearly all of the subregion's spending is accounted for by the USA (see section I).

Central America and the Caribbean

Military expenditure in Central America and the Caribbean had the largest relative increase in the Americas in 2019: it grew by 8.1 per cent to reach $8.7 billion.

Mexico's spending accounted for 75 per cent of the subregional total. At $6.5 billion, it was 7.9 per cent higher than in 2018. The growth is largely due to the strategy of President Andrés Manuel López Obrador to combat drug cartels.[30] In 2019 the Mexican Government created a new police force, the National Guard, with the aim of curbing the growing violence in Mexico.[31] Its budget for 2020 is approximately $114 million.[32] Although the National

---

[28] On the conflict in Nigeria see chapter 7, section II, in this volume.

[29] Lopes da Silva, D. and Tian, N., 'Ending off-budget military funding: Lessons from Chile', SIPRI Backgrounder, 16 Dec. 2019; and Anderson, E. and Page, M. T., *Weaponising Transparency: Defence Procurement Reform as a Counterterrorism Strategy in Nigeria* (Transparency International: London, May 2017), pp. 8, 17.

[30] On the armed conflict in Mexico see chapter 3, section III, in this volume.

[31] Cacelín, J., 'Con más de 17,000 asesinatos, el primer semestre de 2019 se convierte en el más violento en la historia de México' [With more than 17 000 murders, the first half of 2019 becomes the most violent in the history of Mexico], Univision, 24 July 2019.

[32] Cruz Vargas, J. C., 'Presupuesto para seguridad en 2020 se eleva 6.3%; 2.2 mmdp serán para la Guardia Nacional' [Security budget in 2020 rises 6.3%; 2.2 billion pesos will go to the National Guard], *Proceso*, 8 Sep. 2019.

Guard is formally a civilian police force, its operations are militarized: it is composed of military, naval and federal police personnel and its training is provided by the Secretariat of National Defence and the Secretariat of the Navy. Thus, most of its costs will be counted as military expenditure according to SIPRI's definition.[33]

South America

South America's military expenditure was relatively unchanged in 2019, at $52.8 billion, up 0.2 per cent from 2018. This growth, albeit minor, continued an upward trend in military expenditure over the decade: between 2010 and 2019, spending grew by 8.9 per cent.

Brazil alone is responsible for over half (51 per cent) of South America's total military spending. Following two consecutive years of growth (totalling 13 per cent), Brazilian military expenditure fell slightly in 2019, by 0.5 per cent, to reach $26.9 billion. While the level of military expenditure remained relatively unaltered in 2019, important changes took place in spending categories. Personnel costs had the largest increase in over a decade, as part of a plan to boost military salaries.[34] Conversely, there was a significant cut in capital investment. If the government had not increased the capital of Empresa Gerencial de Projetos Navais (EMGEPRON), a state-owned company involved in Brazil's nuclear submarine programme, investment spending would have been at the lowest level since 2009.[35]

At $5.2 billion, Chile's military expenditure remained relatively unchanged in 2019, with a minor increase of 0.3 per cent compared with 2018. Chile implemented substantial changes in its military funding system in 2019 by repealing the 1958 Restricted Law on Copper.[36] This law had transferred funds directly from the state-owned National Copper Corporation (Corporación Nacional del Cobre, Codelco) to the armed forces for acquisitions and maintenance of arms. As of September 2019, the Chilean Congress must approve any allocations. Despite the change, military spending is not likely to decrease in the coming years since, over a transition period of 12 years, allocations must not fall below a baseline based on the average contribution over the final 6 years of the Copper Law.[37]

---

[33] Pérez Correa, C., 'México necesita una Guardia Nacional realmente civil' [Mexico needs a truly civilian National Guard], *New York Times*, 8 Aug. 2019. For SIPRI's definition of military expenditure see the SIPRI website.

[34] Brazilian Ministry of Defence, 'Senado aprova reajuste de salário para militares da ativa, inativo e pensionista' [Senate approves salary adjustment for active, inactive and retired military personnel], 12 July 2016.

[35] Gielow, I. and Patu, G., 'Defesa tem maior gasto com pessoal da década, e investimento militar cai' [Largest defence spending on personnel of the decade, and military investment drops], *Folha da S. Paulo*, 21 Apr. 2019.

[36] Ley Reservada del Cobre [Restricted Law on Copper], Law no. 13 196 of 29 Oct. 1958, Repealed by Law no. 21 174 of 26 Sep. 2019.

[37] Lopes da Silva and Tian (note 29).

The largest relative decrease in the Americas in 2019 was in Argentina, where military expenditure fell by 9.2 per cent to $3.1 billion. This followed an 11 per cent fall in 2018. The reductions were made in the context of a debate in Argentina on how the armed forces should be funded.[38] The argument attracted increased attention with the sinking of the submarine ARA *San Juan* in 2017, which was largely attributed to a lack of funds for maintenance.[39] While the Argentinian Government acknowledges the need for more resources, an acute financial crisis has severely restrained its capacity to invest.[40] In 2019 the country's inflation soared and in 2018 external debt had reached 56 per cent of its gross national income (GNI).[41]

Asia and Oceania

Military spending in Asia and Oceania totalled $523 billion in 2019. Five of the top 15 global spenders in 2019 are in Asia and Oceania (see table 8.3, in section I): China (rank 2), India (rank 3), Japan (rank 9), the Republic of Korea (South Korea, rank 10) and Australia (rank 13). Military spending by states in Asia and Oceania was 4.8 per cent higher in 2019 than in 2018, continuing an uninterrupted upward trend dating back to at least 1989. Asia and Oceania is the only region with continuous growth since 1989 and the growth of 51 per cent over the decade 2010–19 was by far the largest of any region (see tables 8.1 and 8.2).[42] The increase was due primarily to the rise in Chinese military spending, which in 2019 accounted for 50 per cent of total spending in the region, up from 36 per cent in 2010 (see section I).

There were substantial increases in all five subregions of Asia and Oceania between 2018 and 2019 and over the decade 2010–19 (see figure 8.3). Over both periods, the highest rate of increase was in Central Asia (63 per cent in 2010–19 and 16 per cent in 2018–19).

All but two states in Asia and Oceania for which data is available increased their military spending between 2010 and 2019. The largest relative increase was made by Cambodia (168 per cent). There were other high increases

[38] Battaglino, J., 'Auge, caída y retorno de la defensa en Argentina' [The rise, fall and return of defence in Argentina], *Foreign Affairs Latinoamérica*, vol. 13, no. 1 (Mar. 2013), pp. 32–39.

[39] Pardo, D., 'Por qué Argentina es el país que menos gasta en defensa en Sudamérica y cómo pudo eso afectar al submarino desaparecido ARA San Juan' [Why Argentina is the country that spends the least on defence in South America and how this could affect the missing submarine ARA San Juan], BBC, 28 Nov. 2017.

[40] Molina, F. R. and Centenera, M., 'El FMI inicia en Buenos Aires las negociaciones por la deuda argentina' [The IMF begins negotiations on Argentina's debt in Buenos Aires], *El País* (Madrid), 13 Feb. 2019.

[41] World Bank, *International Debt Statistics 2020* (World Bank: Washington, DC, 2019), p. 28.

[42] No data is available for North Korea, Turkmenistan or Uzbekistan for 2010–19 and they are not included in the totals for Asia and Oceania. Data for Viet Nam is not available for many of the years 2010–19. For Myanmar official data on the military budget is available for most years but is not used as there is significant spending outside the official budget (see section IV). Incomplete data for Tajikistan, which indicates an increase, is included in the total.

(40–100 per cent) by China (85 per cent), Bangladesh (81 per cent), Mongolia (75 per cent), Pakistan (70 per cent), Indonesia (67 per cent), Kazakhstan (62 per cent), Kyrgyzstan (56 per cent) and New Zealand (45 per cent). With the exceptions of Afghanistan and Timor-Leste, which decreased their spending, the other states in Asia and Oceania increased their spending by between 1.9 and 39 per cent.

South Asia

Military spending in South Asia increased by 41 per cent between 2010 and 2019, including an increase of 6.4 per cent in 2019, to reach $88.1 billion. This continued a trend of consistent growth since 1993.

India has the largest military budget in South Asia and in 2019 it became the third-largest spender globally, with expenditure of $71.1 billion. This includes spending on the Ministry of Defence (MOD), the armed forces, military pensions and several large paramilitary forces under the Ministry of Home Affairs (see table 8.6). Most of the MOD budget is currently spent on salaries for the 1.4 million active personnel. Another growing element is spending on pensions for military pensioners (currently 3.1 million).[43]

India's spending was 6.8 per cent higher in 2019 than in 2018. In the six consecutive years of growth starting in 2014, spending grew 37 per cent overall. Over the 30-year period 1990–2019, India's spending grew in 24 years and total growth was 259 per cent. However, as GDP grew faster than military spending, the military burden dropped from 3.1 per cent of GDP in 1990 to 2.4 per cent in 2019. This was one of the lowest levels since the early 1960s, only matched in 2006 and 2007.

Tensions and rivalry with Pakistan and China are major drivers for India's increased military spending. In early 2019 India took the unprecedented step of attacking what it called 'terrorist camps' in Pakistan, leading to small but intense clashes with Pakistani forces.[44] In late 2019 the newly appointed chief of the Indian Army Staff, General Manoj Mukund Naravane, called such strikes the 'new normal' for India, marking a shift in India's military doctrine towards more offensive action.[45] India already planned to acquire large volumes of new equipment to enhance the capabilities of its armed forces and a more aggressive policy will probably lead to more demand for equipment.[46] However, capital spending in recent years has been substantially below the levels necessary for India's stated acquisition plans—and even below the level

---

[43] Behera, L. K., *India's Defence Budget 2019–20*, Institute for Defence Studies and Analyses (IDSA) Issue Brief (IDSA: New Delhi, 8 July 2019); and Misra, S. N., 'India's defence budget for 2019–20: The disturbing trends', *Indian Defence Review*, 11 June 2019.

[44] On the territorial conflict between India and Pakistan over Kashmir and other armed conflicts in India see chapter 1, section I, and chapter 4, section II, in this volume.

[45] Press Trust of India, 'New army chief warns Pakistan, says India reserves right to "preemptively strike" at sources of terror', *Economic Times*, 1 Jan. 2020.

[46] On India's arms acquisitions from abroad see chapter 9, section II, in this volume.

Table 8.6. Components of India's military expenditure, 2015/16–19/20

Figures are in rupees b. at current prices unless otherwise stated. Years are Indian financial years, which start on 1 Apr.

	2015/16	2016/17	2017/18	2018/19	2019/20
Ministry of Defence	2 939	3 516	3 797	4 045	4 488
Ministry of Defence (civil)	323	150	151	109	147
Military pensions	602	878	920	1 018	1 178
Salaries and operational costs of the armed forces	1 297	1 624	1 821	1 956	2 059
Capital outlay of the armed forces	717	864	904	962	1 104
Paramilitary forces[a]	384	451	493	574	650
Total (rupee b.)	**3 323**	**3 967**	**4 290**	**4 619**	**5 138**
Total (US$ b.)	**51.8**	**59.0**	**65.8**	**67.6**	**73.0**

[a] These are the Central Reserve Police Force, the Border Security Force, the Indo-Tibetan Border Police, the Assam Rifles and the Shashastra Seema Bal (armed border force), which form part of the Central Armed Police Forces in the budget of the Ministry of Home Affairs.

Source: Indian Ministry of Finance, 'Union budget 2020–21', Feb. 2020.

needed to cover agreed acquisitions. There has been constant pressure from many directions, including the armed forces, to increase the MOD budget to at least 3 per cent of GDP.[47]

Pakistan's military spending in 2019 was $10.3 billion. Its spending has increased every year since 2009: between 2010 and 2019 expenditure rose by 70 per cent, including an increase of 1.8 per cent between 2018 and 2019. Pakistan's military burden was 4.0 per cent in 2019, up from 3.4 per cent in 2010.

East Asia

Military spending in East Asia increased by 4.6 per cent in 2019 to reach $363 billion, continuing the consistent trend of growth since 1995. Over the decade 2010–19 spending increased by 58 per cent. China accounts for most of the spending in East Asia (see section I), but Japan and South Korea also rank among the world's top 15 military spenders.

Military spending by Japan was $47.6 billion in 2019, 0.1 per cent lower than in 2018.[48] Between 2010 and 2019 spending increased by 2.0 per cent. A similar or slightly higher level of spending is planned for the period 2020–23.[49] In 2019 Japan's military burden was 0.9 per cent, remaining below the threshold of 1 per cent of GDP that has been the policy or guideline since 1976.[50] How-

---

[47] Misra (note 43).

[48] The SIPRI figures for Japan do not include spending by the MOD on the large coastguard, which is considered a civilian police force.

[49] Japanese Ministry of Defense, 'Medium term defense program (FY 2019–FY 2023)', 18 Dec. 2018; and Reuters, 'Japan government approves 8th straight defence spending hike to record high', Channel News Asia, 20 Dec. 2019.

[50] Pryor, C. and Le, T., 'Looking beyond 1 percent: Japan's security expenditures', The Diplomat, 3 Apr. 2018; and Bosack, M. M., 'What to make of the record defense budget', *Japan Times*, 20 Feb. 2020.

ever, pressure from the USA to increase Japan's contribution to the cost of US troops based in Japan (see below) and growing perceived security threats, mainly from China and the Democratic People's Republic of Korea (DPRK, or North Korea), are factors that could lead to increased spending in the coming years.[51] While under the current plans for 2020–23 spending will not cross the threshold of 1 per cent of GDP, there is a discussion in Japan about more substantial increases.[52] However, suggestions in Japan and the USA that Japan should increase spending to the guideline of 2 per cent of GDP set by the North Atlantic Treaty Organization (NATO) for its members have been rejected by the Japanese Government.[53] The government also points out that, under the NATO definition, it already spends 1.1–1.3 per cent of GDP on national security.[54]

In South Korea the upward trend in military spending since 2000 continued. In 2019 its military spending reached $43.9 billion, an increase of 7.5 per cent since 2018 and of 36 per cent since 2010. South Korea plans to increase spending by its Ministry of National Defense by an average of 7.5 per cent annually in 2019–23, with a high proportion of the increase (35 per cent) used for procurement and research and development (R&D).[55]

The military spending figures for Japan and South Korea include payments to the USA as a direct contribution to the cost of the US troops stationed in each country. In 2019 Japan paid $1.7–2.0 billion for the US troops based there (approximately 54 000 troops) and South Korea paid almost $1 billion for the US troops stationed there (approximately 28 500).[56] However, US President Donald J. Trump highlighted these payments as part of his 2016 election campaign and threatened to withdraw US troops if the full costs are not covered by the host states.[57] For 2020 Trump has demanded that Japan pays $8 billion and that South Korea pays $4.7 billion.[58] This would be more

---

[51] Japanese Ministry of Defense, 'National defense program guidelines for FY 2019 and beyond', 18 Dec. 2018.

[52] Kato, M., 'New Japan defense chief calls 2% spending target "inappropriate"', *Nikkei Asian Review*, 5 Oct. 2018; and Bosack (note 50).

[53] Kato (note 52). On this guideline see section III in this chapter.

[54] Harding, R., 'Japan seeks to resist US pressure on military spending', *Financial Times*, 9 Apr. 2019.

[55] Grevatt, J., 'Seoul proposes a further 8% boost to defence spending', *Jane's Defence Weekly*, 26 June 2019, p. 21. This increase refers only to MOD spending. SIPRI also includes South Korea's separate spending on military pensions in the total military expenditure figure.

[56] Seligman, L. and Gramer, R., 'Trump asks Tokyo to quadruple payments for US troops in Japan', *Foreign Policy*, 15 Nov. 2019; Corell, D. S., 'Esper says South Korea, which paid 90 percent of costs for Camp Humphreys, needs to increase "burden-sharing" to keep US troops in South Korea', *Military Times*, 15 Nov. 2019; and Flynn, M. E., Matinez Machain, C. and Allen, M. A., 'Why does the US pay so much for the defense of its allies? 5 questions answered', The Conversation, 2 Dec. 2019.

[57] *The Mainichi*, 'News navigator: How much does Japan pay to host US military forces?', 30 May 2016; Gaouette, N., 'Trump hikes price tag for US forces in Korea almost 400% as Seoul questions alliance', CNN, 15 Nov. 2019; and Correll, D. S., 'Demanding South Korea pay more for US presence drives wedge between allies, House leaders say', *Military Times*, 3 Dec. 2019.

[58] Seligman and Gramer (note 56); Corell (note 56); and Flynn, Matinez Machain and Allen (note 56).

than the actual cost to the USA: for 2021 the US Department of Defense has budgeted a total of $5.7 billion to pay for US troops based in Japan and $4.5 billion for those in South Korea. Moreover, it is estimated that if the forces stationed in South Korea were returned to the USA, the basing cost would be about $2 billion less.[59] The demands have raised concerns in South Korea, Japan and the USA about the USA's commitment to the security of Japan and South Korea and its reliability as an ally.[60]

Oceania

Total military spending in Oceania increased by 3.5 per cent in 2019 to reach $29.0 billion. Spending increased by 25 per cent over the decade 2010–19.

Australia's military expenditure in 2019 was $25.9 billion. This was 2.1 per cent higher than in 2018 and 23 per cent higher than in 2010. Australia perceives heightened military threats in its neighbourhood, including from China, and globally.[61] A large majority in the Australian Parliament has in recent years supported higher military spending to increase the capabilities of the Australian armed forces, with the aim of pushing the military burden up from 1.9 per cent of GDP in 2019 to 2.0 per cent in 2020, with further additional increases planned.[62] Australia's spending includes approximately $350 million over 2019–22 to pay for the construction of 21 patrol craft for donation to Pacific island states and Timor-Leste.[63]

New Zealand's military spending increased by 45 per cent between 2010 and 2019 to reach $2.9 billion. Most of the increase was in 2018 and 2019, with the 19 per cent increase in 2019 being one of the highest year-on-year increases in Asia and Oceania. The increase in 2019 was largely due to acquisitions of new equipment and other capital spending.[64]

South East Asia

Military spending in South East Asia increased by 4.2 per cent in 2019 to reach $40.5 billion, after a 4.1 per cent drop in 2018.[65] Over the decade 2010–19 spending increased by 34 per cent.

---

[59] Moran, M., 'What Trump gets right about alliances', *Foreign Policy*, 5 Dec. 2019.

[60] *The Mainichi* (note 57); Gaouette (note 57) ; Correll (note 57); and Seligman and Gramer (note 56).

[61] Reynolds, L., Australian Minister for Defence, '2019 ministerial statement on defence operations', Australian Department of Defence, 5 Dec. 2019; and Packham, B., 'Out-of-date strategies in defence white paper', *The Australian*, 8 Oct. 2019.

[62] Lowy Institute, 'Australian election 2019: Where the parties stand—defence spending', accessed 10 Feb. 2020; Australian Department of Defence, 'A safer Australia—Budget 2019-20—Defence overview', 2 Apr. 2019; and Hellyer, M., 'Boring is the new black: Defence budget 2019-20', The Strategist, Australian Strategic Policy Institute, 3 Apr. 2019.

[63] Australian Department of Defence (note 62).

[64] New Zealand Government, *The Estimates of Appropriations for the Government of New Zealand for the Year Ending 30 June 2020*, vol. 4, *External Sector* (Treasury: Wellington, 30 May 2019), pp. 27–44 and pp. 45–92.

[65] The estimated subregional total for South East Asia excludes Myanmar.

The largest spenders in the subregion in 2019 were Singapore (28 per cent of the total), Indonesia (19 per cent) and Thailand (18 per cent). For several states—including Indonesia, Malaysia and the Philippines—the increases in the past decade are partly to pay for expansion of the capabilities of their armed forces, especially in the maritime domain, as a reaction to Chinese claims and activities in the South China Sea.[66] In turn, several other states in the region—including Singapore—reacted at least partly to their neighbours' expansion.

Europe

Total military spending in Europe in 2019 was $356 billion, 5.0 per cent higher than in 2018 and 8.8 per cent higher than in 2010 (see tables 8.1 and 8.2). Five of the world's 15 largest military spenders are in Europe: Russia (rank 4), France (rank 6), Germany (rank 7), the United Kingdom (rank 8) and Italy (rank 12).

Nearly all the countries in Western Europe and Central Europe cooperate in the military frameworks of NATO or the European Union (EU). Taken together, the military spending of the states in these subregions totalled $282 billion in 2019. This was 79 per cent of total European spending, and was up by 5.0 per cent from 2018 and by 3.8 per cent from 2010. Of the 39 states in Western Europe and Central Europe (excluding microstates), only 3 decreased their military spending in 2019: Greece (−0.4 per cent), Austria (−0.8 per cent) and Cyprus (−5.6 per cent). Seventeen increased their military spending by 10 per cent or more in 2019.

Western Europe

Military spending in Western Europe in 2019 was $251 billion—up by 3.9 per cent from 2018 but down by 0.6 per cent from 2010 (see figure 8.3). The main contributors to the increase in 2019 were Germany, which accounted for 48 per cent of the increase, and the Netherlands, which accounted for 13 per cent.

France's military spending rose by 1.6 per cent in 2019 to reach $50.1 billion (see box 8.2). Over the decade 2010–19 France's military spending increased by 3.5 per cent. The rise in 2019 followed the adoption of the Military Planning Law for 2019–25, a seven-year plan aimed at reaching the NATO guideline of

---

[66] On these dynamics see Wezeman, S. T., *Arms Flows to South East Asia* (SIPRI: Stockholm, Dec. 2019).

Box 8.2. Revised estimates for the military expenditure of France

In 2019 SIPRI's figures for France's military spending were revised to reflect more accurately the activities carried out by the Gendarmerie—France's paramilitary force for the maintenance of public order.

Disaggregated data on the Gendarmerie indicates that a much smaller share of its resources is allocated to military tasks than previously assumed. Based on the budget figures, SIPRI's new estimates suggest that, on average, only 2.3 per cent of the tasks of the Gendarmerie are military. In 2019 an estimated $220 million of spending for the Gendarmerie should be included as part of France's military expenditure (0.4 per cent of total military expenditure).

After this revision, French military spending was 16 per cent lower than it would have been under the previous methodology.

spending 2 per cent of GDP on the military by 2025.[67] The French Government plans to increase military spending annually by €1.7 billion ($1.9 billion) until 2022, and then by €3.0 billion ($3.4 billion) in subsequent years. Overall, the Military Planning Law allocates a total of €295 billion ($330 billion) to the armed forces between 2019 and 2025, excluding pensions.

The military spending of the other two large powers in Western Europe—Germany and the UK—is at a similar level to that of France (but see box 8.3).

In 2019 Germany raised its military spending by 10 per cent to $49.3 billion, equivalent to 1.3 per cent of its GDP. Its military expenditure was 15 per cent higher than in 2010, when it was also 1.3 per cent of GDP. Indeed, spending in 2019 was at the highest level since 1993, when the military burden was 1.7 per cent of GDP. German military spending reached its lowest point since the end of the cold war in 2006, after which it increased again until 2012, dropped in 2013–14 to just above the 2006 level, and then increased each year. In 2016 Germany adopted the long-term aim of reaching the NATO guideline of spending 2 per cent of GDP on the military.[68] However, it did not then set an explicit timeline. In 2019 the German minister of defence, Annegret Kramp-Karrenbauer, declared a commitment to spend 1.5 per cent of GDP on the military by 2024 and 2.0 per cent by 2031.[69] However, political discussions about the need to reach the 2 per cent guideline continued in 2019.[70]

---

[67] Loi no. 2018-607 du 13 juillet 2018 relative à la programmation militaire pour les années 2019 à 2025 et portant diverses dispositions intéressant la défense (1) [Law no. 2018-607 of 13 July 2018 on military planning for the years 2019 to 2025 and on various provisions relating to defence (1)], *Journal Officiel de la République Française*, 14 July 2018. See also French Ministry of the Armed Forces, 'Draft Military Planning Law 2019/2025: Synopsis—a MPL based on renewal', Feb. 2018.

[68] German Ministry of Defence (MOD), *Weissbuch 2016 zur Sicherheitspolitik und zur Zukunft der Bundeswehr* [White book 2016 on security policy and the future of the Bundeswehr] (MOD: Berlin, June 2016), p. 67. On this guideline see also section III of this chapter.

[69] *Die Zeit*, 'Verteidigungsetat könnte auf mehr als 50 Milliarden Euro steigen' [Defence budget could increase to over 50 billion euro], 16 Oct. 2019.

[70] Deutscher Bundestag, '45,05 Milliarden Euro für das Bundesministerium der Verteidigung' [45.05 billion euro the for Ministry of Defence], 29 Nov. 2019.

At $48.7 billion, the United Kingdom's military expenditure was unchanged in 2019 but was 15 per cent lower than in 2010. British military spending has remained stable since 2015. In 2019 the British Government committed itself to increasing the military budget by 2.6 per cent in real terms in 2020, a substantial shift from the previous target of real annual increases of 0.5 per cent since 2015.[71] The increased spending is an attempt to bridge the funding gap in the UK's 10-year equipment plan and ease concerns about the UK's ability to fund its long-term programme to modernize its arsenals.[72]

Central Europe

The rate of increase in military spending in 2010–19 in Central Europe was much higher than in Western Europe (see also section III). Spending in the subregion in 2019 was $31.5 billion, 14 per cent higher than in 2018 and 61 per cent higher than in 2010. Four countries in Central Europe increased military spending by more than 150 per cent between 2010 and 2019: Lithuania (232 per cent), Latvia (176 per cent), Bulgaria (165 per cent) and Romania (154 per cent). Poland, which accounted for 38 per cent of the total for Central Europe in 2019, increased its military spending by 51 per cent between 2010 and 2019.

Eastern Europe

In 2019 military expenditure in Eastern Europe totalled $74.0 billion. This was 35 per cent higher than in 2010 and 4.9 per cent higher than in 2018. All seven countries in Eastern Europe increased their military spending in 2019, five of them—Armenia, Azerbaijan, Belarus, Moldova and Ukraine—by more than 5 per cent (ranging from 6.2 per cent to 17 per cent). The largest relative increases in military spending over the decade 2010–19 were made by Ukraine (132 per cent), Moldova (105 per cent), Azerbaijan (70 per cent) and Armenia (69 per cent).

Ukraine's military expenditure in 2019 was $5.2 billion, an increase of 9.3 per cent compared with 2018. This was the second consecutive year of increase after a minor decrease, of 0.1 per cent, in 2017. The 2019 increase brought the military burden up from 3.2 per cent of GDP in 2018 to 3.4 per cent in 2019—the highest level since 1993.[73]

At $1.9 billion in 2019, military expenditure by Azerbaijan was almost three times higher than Armenia's military spending of $673 million. Azerbaijan's spending in 2019 was 7.9 per cent higher than in 2018 and Armenia's was 8.1 per cent higher. As noted above, over the 10-year period 2010–19, both

---

[71] British Treasury, *Spending Round 2019* (Her Majesty's Stationery Office: London, Sep. 2019), p. 13.

[72] Chambers, M., 'The end of defence austerity? The 2019 spending round and the UK defence budget', Commentary, Royal United Services Institute, 30 Sep. 2019; and Chuter, A., 'UK MOD gets budget boost of more than $1B with three programs in mind', *Defense News*, 29 Oct. 2018.

[73] On the armed conflict in Ukraine see chapter 5, section II, in this volume.

Box 8.3. Estimating the military expenditure of Germany and the United Kingdom

Since countries use different definitions when reporting on military expenditure, SIPRI has adopted a standard definition as a guideline.[a] This means that there can be differences between SIPRI's estimates and the official data reported by countries. For example, SIPRI's annual estimates of military spending for Germany and the United Kingdom are significantly lower than the 'defence expenditure' figures that they report to the North Atlantic Treaty Organization (NATO).[b] The gap between the SIPRI estimates for these countries and their NATO data has widened in recent years.

SIPRI's estimate of German military expenditure in 2019 is $3.3 billion lower than the 'defence expenditure' figure that Germany reported to NATO for that year. This is explained by the fact that the SIPRI total only includes spending by the German Ministry of Defence (MOD) and some minor spending on military activities by other ministries. In its 'defence expenditure' figure for NATO, Germany also includes spending on non-military efforts linked to sustaining peace and security, such as humanitarian and development aid in the context of crisis and peacebuilding and conflict-resolution activities.[c] However, full details of the German submission to NATO are confidential.[d] It is therefore impossible to assess how much of the NATO figure is accounted for by these activities or if other activities of a military nature are included in the total.

SIPRI's estimate of British military expenditure in 2019 is $11.2 billion lower than the British figure for NATO 'defence expenditure'.[e] The SIPRI figure is based on public data on expenditure by the British MOD. The British Government has not published an explanation of what is included in its submission to NATO.[f] Other sources, including an assessment for 2017 by the House of Commons (the lower house of the British Parliament), indicate that $3–4 billion of the NATO figure might be attributable to military pension payments that are in addition to the reported expenditure by the MOD.[g] These are not included in the SIPRI estimate because consistent spending data for the pension scheme is not available for the entire data series. Other spending items that might be part of the UK's submission to NATO include the British contribution to United Nations peace operations and the cost of military operations not covered by the MOD budget. However, these additional expenditure items do not fully bridge the $11.2 billion gap. Questions thus remain about what the British Government reports to NATO on its military expenditure.

[a] SIPRI Military Expenditure Database, 'Sources and methods'.

[b] NATO, 'Defence expenditure of NATO countries (2013–2019)', Press Release no. PR/CP(2019)123, 29 Nov. 2019.

[c] German Ministry of Defence, Communication with author, 18 Mar. 2020.

[d] Deutscher Bundestag, 'Antwort der Bundesregierung, Rüstungsauasgaben in der Bundesrepublik Deutschland von 1945 bis heute' [Military expenditures in the German Federal Republic from 1945 to today], 20 Aug. 2019, Drucksache 19/12780.

[e] NATO (note b).

[f] British Ministry of Defence, Defence Resources Secretariat, Freedom of information request no. FOI2019/00481, 7 Feb. 2019; Perlo-Freeman, S., *Fighting the Wrong Battles: How Obsession with Military Power Diverts Resources from the Climate Crisis* (Campaign Against the Arms Trade: London, Feb. 2020), pp. 36–38; and United Nations, Department of Peace Operations, 'How we are funded', [n.d.].

[g] British House of Commons, Defence Committee, *Shifting the Goalposts? Defence Expenditure and the 2% Pledge*, 2nd report of 2015/16 (House of Commons: London, 21 Apr. 2016).

countries increased military spending by roughly 70 per cent. The unresolved armed conflict over Nagorno-Karabakh remains the main driver of increased military spending.[74] Both countries are trying to improve their military capabilities by financing modernization of their armed forces, including procurement of advanced weapons.[75]

Russia's military spending accounted for 88 per cent of the subregional total in 2019. At $65.1 billion, its spending was 4.5 per cent higher than in 2018, while its military burden rose from 3.7 per cent to 3.9 per cent. Russian military expenditure has grown significantly over the past two decades: by 2019, it was 30 per cent higher than in 2010 and 175 per cent higher than in 2000.

The growth in Russian spending in 2019 was due primarily to increased spending in three of the five main components of Russian military expenditure (see table 8.7). The largest component, 'National defence' (i.e. mainly the armed forces), increased by 5.9 per cent in nominal terms in 2019, while spending on paramilitary forces (the National Guard and the Border Service of the Federal Security Service) increased by 7.9 per cent in nominal terms. However, the component with the largest relative increase was 'Other MOD expenditure', which rose by 52 per cent in 2019. Disaggregating this category showed that spending on military housing increased 25-fold in 2019 and social support was up by 34 per cent.[76]

Russia plans to gradually increase its military spending in the next few of years.[77] According to the proposed budget for 2020–22, growth in military expenditure will be mostly driven by increased spending on the Russian armed forces, including arms procurement and applied military R&D, and on the paramilitary forces.[78]

The Middle East

SIPRI has not provided an estimate for total Middle Eastern military expenditure since 2014 because of a lack of data for four countries: Qatar, Syria, the United Arab Emirates (UAE) and Yemen. Qatar and the UAE are assessed to have significant levels of military spending based on their large

---

[74] On the armed conflict in Nagorno-Karabakh see chapter 5, section I, in this volume.

[75] See chapter 9, section II, in this volume.

[76] Cooper, J., 'Military expenditure in Russia in 2019 and in the amended federal budget for 2020–22', Unpublished paper, 20 Feb. 2020.

[77] Cooper, J., 'Military spending in Russia in 2019 and in the three-year budget 2020–22', Unpublished paper, Dec. 2019; [Federal law no. 380-FZ of 02.12.2019 'On the federal budget for 2020 and the planning period 2021 and 2022'], 2 Dec. 2019 (in Russian); and [Federal law no. 389-FZ of 02.12.2019 'On amendments to the Federal law "On the federal budget for 2019 and the planning period 2020 and 2021"'], 2 Dec. 2019 (in Russian).

[78] Cooper (note 77).

Table 8.7. Components of Russia's military expenditure, 2015–19

Figures are in roubles b. at current prices unless otherwise stated. Years are calendar years, which correspond to the financial year.

	2015	2016	2017	2018	2019
National defence[a]	3 181	3 776	2 852	2 826	2 992
Military pensions	306	328	339	345	347
Paramilitary forces[b]	257	246	340	353	381
Other MOD expenditure[c]	292	283	338	316	479
Additional subsidies for Rosatom and the Baikonur Space Centre	10.9	11.1	10.7	10.5	11.1
Total (rouble b.)	**4 048**	**4 644**	**3 880**	**3 850**	**4 210**
Total (US$ b.)	**66.4**	**69.2**	**66.5**	**61.4**	**65.1**

MOD = Ministry of Defence.

[a] 'National defence' includes expenditure on the Russian armed forces, mobilization and training of reserve forces, the nuclear weapons complex, international military-technical cooperation, applied military research and development, and some other military-related activities.

[b] These are the National Guard and the Border Service of the Federal Security Service.

[c] This includes expenditure on social support, housing, education, health, culture etc.

Sources: Cooper, J., 'Military expenditure in Russia in 2019 and in the amended federal budget for 2020–22', Unpublished report, 20 Feb. 2020; Russian Ministry of Finance, [Preliminary assessment of execution of the federal budget for January–December 2019], 13 Jan. 2019, appendix 3 (in Russian); and Russian Federal Treasury, [Report on federal budget execution as of 01.01.2020], 17 Feb. 2020 (in Russian).

arms acquisitions in the past decade and the levels of their military spending in years for which data is available.[79]

Data is available for 11 of the 15 countries in the region. The combined total military expenditure in 2019 of these countries was $147 billion.[80] Two of the top 15 global spenders in 2019 are in the Middle East: Saudi Arabia (rank 5) and Israel (rank 15).[81] In addition, 6 of the 10 countries with the highest military burden are in the Middle East: Oman, which spent 8.8 per cent of its GDP on the military (the highest level in the world), Saudi Arabia at 8.0 per cent, Kuwait at 5.6 per cent, Israel at 5.3 per cent, Jordan at 4.7 per cent and Lebanon at 4.2 per cent.

Saudi Arabia is by far the largest military spender in the region, with an estimated total of $61.9 billion in 2019 (see table 8.3). After military spending peaked at an all-time high in 2015, when Saudi Arabia was the third-largest military spender in the world, it dropped by 28 per cent in 2016, climbed by

[79] On their arms acquisitions see e.g. chapter 9, section II, in this volume.

[80] The 11 countries included in the estimate are Bahrain, Egypt, Iran, Iraq, Israel, Jordan, Kuwait, Lebanon, Oman, Turkey and Saudi Arabia. In 2014 these 11 countries accounted for 87% of the regional total.

[81] If data were available, the UAE would probably also have ranked in the top 15 in 2019. The most recent available estimate for military spending by the UAE is $22.8 billion (in current US dollars) in 2014, when it was the second-largest military spender in the region.

15 per cent between 2016 and 2018, but decreased again in 2019, by 16 per cent. The fall in 2016 appears to have been caused by a drop in government revenue after a steep decline in oil prices.[82] However, the fall in 2019 did not coincide with similar dramatic developments in the Saudi Arabian economy, even though growth in Saudi Arabian GDP slowed in 2019.[83] The drop in military spending in 2019 was also unexpected as Saudi Arabia continued its military operations in Yemen and, after a missile attack caused significant damage to its oil industry in September 2019, tensions with Iran increased.[84]

The drop in 2019 may also be smaller than available data indicates. The figure for 2019 is an estimate and experience from previous years shows that actual Saudi Arabian military spending tends to be higher than implied by the government budget or the estimates of actual government spending made at the end of each year. For example, data on estimated government spending available at the end of 2018 led to military spending being estimated as $68.1 billion (in current US dollars) in that year, whereas data available at the end of 2019 on actual government spending in 2018 resulted in the estimate being revised up to $74.4 billion.[85]

Military spending by Israel was $20.5 billion in 2019—a slight increase of 1.7 per cent compared with 2018. In addition, Israel receives military aid from the USA, which in 2019 was $3.8 billion.[86] Between 2010 and 2019, Israeli military spending increased steadily, and in 2019 it was 30 per cent higher than in 2010. However, Israel's economy grew faster than its military spending: in 2010 Israel spent 5.9 per cent of its GDP on the military, while in 2019 the military burden was 5.3 per cent. In August 2018 the Israeli prime minister, Benjamin Netanyahu, announced a '2030 Security Concept', which aims for an annual growth in military spending of 3–4 per cent until Israel's GNI reaches $500 billion, at which point the annual increase in military spending would be re-examined.[87] Netanyahu has continued to seek increases higher than the 1.7 per cent increase of 2019. In October 2019 he stated that military spending needed to grow by $1.1 billion per year, equivalent to 5.4 per cent of

[82] Tian, N. and Lopes da Silva, D., 'Debt, oil and military expenditure', *SIPRI Yearbook 2018*, pp. 175–78.

[83] World Bank, *Middle East and North Africa: Macro Poverty Outlook* (World Bank Group: Washington, DC, Oct. 2019), pp. 174–75.

[84] On the attacks on Saudi oil facilities see chapter 1, section I, and chapter 6, section I, in this volume; and on the armed conflict in Yemen see chapter 6, section V, in this volume.

[85] Saudi Arabian Ministry of Finance (MOF), *Budget Statement: Fiscal Year 2019* (MOF: Riyadh, Dec. 2018); and Saudi Arabian Ministry of Finance, *Budget Statement: Fiscal Year 2020* (MOF: Riyadh, Dec. 2019).

[86] Sharp, J. M., *US Foreign Aid to Israel*, Congressional Research Service (CRS) Report to Congress RL33222 (US Congress, CRS: Washington, DC, 7 Aug. 2019), p. 2. SIPRI does not include military aid in the military expenditure of the recipient country.

[87] Israeli Ministry of Foreign Affairs, 'PM Netanyahu presents "2030 Security Concept" to the Cabinet', 15 Aug. 2018. Israel's GNI in 2018 was $371 billion. In the period 2014–18 annual GNI growth was in the range 2–5.5%. World Bank Open Data, accessed 17 Feb. 2020.

Israeli military spending in 2019.[88] However, the Israeli Ministry of Finance questioned whether it would be possible to fund the plan.

Between 2010 and 2019 Turkish military expenditure increased by 86 per cent to reach $20.4 billion. There was a particularly steep increase in Turkish military spending between 2017 and 2018, of 27 per cent, while the increase between 2018 and 2019 was 5.8 per cent. The increases in military spending in 2018 and 2019 coincided with an intensification of Turkish military operations against Kurdish armed groups in Syria.[89] In addition, since 2015 Turkey has significantly increased its spending on equipment, which was 54 per cent higher in 2019 than in 2015.[90] One of the key components of Turkish military procurement planning was the acquisition of up to 100 F-35 combat aircraft from the USA, 30 of which had been ordered by 2018 and 6 were scheduled to be delivered in 2019. However, after Turkey ordered S-400 surface-to-air missile (SAM) systems from Russia, the USA cancelled the F-35 deal and stopped all deliveries in 2019 and Turkey demanded a refund of the $1.25 billion it had already paid for the F-35 programme.[91] While the effect of the cancellation on Turkish military spending in 2019 is unclear, the size of the deal and the amount demanded by Turkey show that it may have been substantial.

Over the period 2010–19 Iranian military spending first increased to a high point in 2017, when Iran's economy grew significantly following the lifting of international sanctions.[92] However, in 2018 military spending decreased by 23 per cent and in 2019 it fell by 15 per cent to $12.6 billion. This coincided with the USA's reinstatement of economic sanctions in early 2018 and a decrease in Iranian GDP in 2018.[93] The decrease in military spending in 2019 occurred despite the further deterioration in Iran's relations with Saudi Arabia and the USA.[94]

At $3.7 billion in 2019, military expenditure by Egypt was almost unchanged from 2018 (down by 0.5 per cent) but was 20 per cent lower than in 2010. Between 2010 and 2013 Egyptian military expenditure decreased by 6.3 per cent, followed by two years of growth: 9.1 per cent in 2014 and 6.0 per cent in 2015. Four consecutive years of decline that started in 2016 resulted in the lowest level of Egyptian military spending since 1999. In 2019

---

[88] Azulai, Y., 'IDF's future vision mired in budgetary uncertainty', *Globes*, 7 Oct. 2019.

[89] On Turkey's role in the conflict in Syria and its conflict with the Kurds see chapter 6, section II, in this volume.

[90] NATO, 'Defence expenditure of NATO countries (2013–2019)', Press Release no. PR/CP(2019)123, 29 Nov. 2019, p. 13. See also Wezeman, S. T. and Kuimova, A., 'Turkey and Black Sea security', SIPRI Background Paper, Dec. 2018; and chapter 9, section II, in this volume.

[91] Ahval, 'Erdoğan says Turkey will ask US to return F-35 payments if it halts delivery', 27 June 2019. For full details see chapter 9, sections I and II, in this volume.

[92] See chapter 11, section III, in this volume.

[93] BBC, 'Six charts that show how hard US sanctions have hit Iran', 9 Dec. 2019.

[94] On the tensions in the Gulf region see chapter 1, section I, and chapter 6, section I, in this volume.

Egypt had one of the smallest military budgets in the region. This may be due to the significant military aid that it receives each year: about $1.3 billion for arms procurement from the USA.[95] In addition, there are claims that Egypt has significant off-budget military spending based on the revenue from military-owned civilian businesses.[96] The Egyptian military owns and operates a wide range of businesses in different sectors of the Egyptian economy, such as infrastructure, mining, food production, fish farms and holiday resorts.[97] However, there is little specific information available on the revenue and profits of these businesses and it remains unclear if and how much of the profits are used to fund military spending.

[95] Sharp, J. M., *Egypt: Background and US Relations*, Congressional Research Service (CRS) Report to Congress RL33003 (US Congress, CRS: Washington, DC, 12 Mar. 2019), p. 20.

[96] Abul-Magd, Z., 'Egypt's adaptable officers. business, nationalism, and discontent', eds Z. Abul-Magd and E. Grawert, *Businessmen in Arms: How the Military and Other Armed Groups Profit in the MENA Region* (Rowman and Littlefield: Lanham, MD, 2016).

[97] Sayigh, Y., *Owners of the Republic: An Anatomy of Egypt's Military Economy* (Carnegie Endowment for International Peace: Beirut, 2019); and Abul-Magd (note 96).

III. Spending on military equipment by European members of the North Atlantic Treaty Organization

NAN TIAN, DIEGO LOPES DA SILVA AND PIETER D. WEZEMAN

The annexation of Crimea by the Russian Federation and the rise of the Islamic State in 2014 was a pivotal moment for the security environment of the European members of the North Atlantic Treaty Organization (NATO). It significantly heightened the level of threat perceived by NATO members and led them to reinforce the military element of their security policies.[1]

As one of the actions to address these perceived threats, NATO members included a pledge to increase their military burdens—that is, military expenditure as a share of gross domestic product (GDP)—to 2 per cent in the summit declaration after their summit meeting in Newport, Wales, in September 2014. Although this guideline had been discussed since 2002, inclusion in a summit declaration was unprecedented.[2] At the Wales summit, NATO members also publicly pledged to spend at least 20 per cent of their military expenditure on equipment.[3] Since then, numerous discussions have focused on the 2 per cent military burden guideline.[4] However, there has been limited discourse on the 20 per cent equipment spending pledge.[5] This section thus maps and assesses the trends in both military burden sharing and equipment spending as a share of total military expenditure in European NATO members since the 2014 Wales summit.

The section first summarizes NATO's threat perceptions in order to identify official rationales for the two military expenditure guidelines. It then provides an overview of trends in the military expenditure of European NATO members and the 2 per cent guideline. It continues by mapping the changes in spending on equipment as a share of total military expenditure for European NATO members. The focus is on the five member states with the

---

[1] NATO, *The Secretary General's Annual Report 2014* (NATO: Brussels, 2015), p. 3.

[2] Dowdy, J., 'More tooth, less tail: Getting beyond NATO's 2 percent rule', eds N. Burns, L. Bitounis and J. Price, *The World Turned Upside Down: Maintaining American Leadership in a Dangerous Age* (Aspen Institute: Washington, DC, 2017), pp. 151–65.

[3] North Atlantic Council, Wales summit declaration, 5 Sep. 2014, para. 14; and Mesterhazy, A. (rapporteur), *Burden Sharing: New Commitments in a New Era*, NATO Parliamentary Assembly, Defence and Security Committee, Sub-committee on Transatlantic Defence and Security Cooperation (NATO Parliamentary Assembly: Brussels, 17 Nov. 2018), pp. 2–4.

[4] E.g. Blum, J. and Potrafke, N., 'Does a change of government influence compliance with international agreements? Empirical evidence for the NATO two percent target', *Defence and Peace Economics*, published online 5 Feb. 2019; Kim, W. and Sandler T., 'NATO at 70: Pledges, free riding, and benefit-burden concordance', *Defence and Peace Economics*, published online 10 July 2019; and Richter, A., 'Sharing the burden? US allies, defense spending, and the future of NATO', *Comparative Strategy*, vol. 35, no. 4 (2016), pp. 298–314.

[5] E.g. Béraud-Sudreau, L. and Giegerich, B., 'NATO defence spending and European threat perceptions', *Survival*, vol. 60, no. 4 (Aug.–Sep. 2018), pp. 53–74.

highest relative increases, with explanations of their changing expenditure decisions. The section closes by drawing conclusions.

NATO's threat perceptions and military expenditure guidelines

The European security environment changed fundamentally over the decade 2010–19, in particular after Russia's annexation of Crimea and the rise of the Islamic State in 2014.[6] The threats and risks stemming from these shifts were reviewed at successive NATO summits in 2014 and 2016–19. The final declarations of these summits highlight two key areas of growing instability: to the east and to the south.[7] The instability to the east is attributed mainly to Russia's 'aggressive actions', including in Ukraine, interference in election processes in European countries, and cyber and hybrid attacks. To the south the instability arises from the armed conflicts in Afghanistan, the Middle East and North Africa, the increased threat from Islamist militant groups, and their spillover into the refugee and migrant crisis.

Preceding these changes, there was a long-standing debate on burden-sharing within NATO, the essence of which is that European military spending is proportionately less than that of the United States.[8] The intention to spend at least 2 per cent of GDP on the military dates back to 2002, when NATO members discussed the guideline as a non-binding target.[9] They restated their willingness to work towards the 2 per cent guideline at the 2006 Riga summit.[10] The changes in perceived threats and the US pressure on burden sharing came together in the Defence Investment Pledge made at the 2014 Wales summit.[11] This was a joint effort to reverse the declining trend in military expenditure among members and to increase their spending to 2 per cent of GDP (or maintain it at that level if it had already been achieved). This pledge included the aim of spending at least 20 per cent of military expenditure on major new equipment, including research and development, by 2024. The pledge has been reaffirmed at all subsequent summits, and at the 2017 summit the NATO leaders agreed to submit annual national action plans setting out how they intend to meet the pledge.[12]

---

[6] On the armed conflict in Ukraine and tensions between NATO and Russia see chapter 5, section II, in this volume.

[7] E.g. North Atlantic Council, Brussels summit declaration, 11 July 2018.

[8] Cooper, C. A. and Zycher, B. *Perceptions of NATO Burden-Sharing* (Rand Corp.: Santa Monica, CA, June 1989); Mesterhazy (note 3), pp. 2–4; and North Atlantic Council (note 3).

[9] Dowdy (note 2).

[10] E.g. NATO, Meeting of the North Atlantic Council at the level of Defence Ministers, Press briefing, 8 June 2006.

[11] North Atlantic Council (note 3).

[12] NATO, 'NATO leaders agree to do more to fight terrorism and ensure fairer burden sharing', 25 May 2017.

Table 8.8. Trends in military spending by European members of the North Atlantic Treaty Organization, 2010–19

Expenditure figures are in US$, at current prices and exchange rates. Changes are in real terms, based on constant (2018) US$. GDP estimates are from the International Monetary Fund's World Economic Outlook database.

State	Military expenditure, 2019 ($ m.)	Change in military expenditure (%)			Military expenditure as a share of GDP, 2019 (%)
		2010–19	2010–14	2014–19	
Central Europe	29 880	*64*	*2.1*	*61*	*1.8*
Albania	198	*–6.0*	*–11*	*5.7*	*1.3*
Bulgaria	2 127	*165*	*–16*	*216*	*3.2*
Croatia	1 009	*8.8*	*1.5*	*7.2*	*1.7*
Czechia	2 910	*20*	*–18*	*46*	*1.2*
Estonia	656	*91*	*37*	*39*	*2.1*
Hungary	1 904	*62*	*–10*	*80*	*1.2*
Latvia	710	*176*	*5.9*	*161*	*2.0*
Lithuania	1 084	*232*	*20*	*176*	*2.0*
Poland	11 903	*51*	*13*	*33*	*2.0*
Romania	4 945	*154*	*18*	*115*	*2.0*
Slovakia	1 865	*68*	*–20*	*110*	*1.8*
Slovenia	569	*–22*	*–41*	*33*	*1.1*
Western Europe	230 865	*–1.6*	*–12*	*11*	*1.5*
Belgium	4 818	*–7.3*	*–8.5*	*1.4*	*0.9*
Denmark	4 557	*8.1*	*–16*	*28*	*1.3*
France	50 119	*3.5*	*–3.4*	*7.1*	*1.9*
Germany	49 277	*15*	*–7.7*	*25*	*1.3*
Greece	5 472	*–23*	*–34*	*17*	*2.6*
Italy	26 790	*–11*	*–20*	*11*	*1.4*
Luxembourg	429	*61*	*–6.5*	*72*	*0.6*
Netherlands	12 060	*9.8*	*–15*	*30*	*1.3*
Norway	7 003	*30*	*11*	*17*	*1.7*
Portugal	4 513	*1.7*	*–18*	*24*	*1.9*
Spain	17 177	*–7.1*	*–18*	*14*	*1.2*
United Kingdom	48 650	*–15*	*–16*	*–2.1*	*1.7[a]*
Total	**260 745**	**3.1**	**–11**	**16**	**1.7**

GDP = gross domestic product.

[a] According to NATO's own expenditure data, the UK has achieved the 2% guideline. The SIPRI figure of 1.7% is based on the net cash requirements figures provided by the British Ministry of Defence (MOD). NATO reports figures that include numerous items that are not in the MOD budget. This has been noted by a parliamentary report as inflating military expenditure as a means for the UK to meet the 2% target. See British House of Commons, Defence Committee, *Shifting the Goalposts? Defence Expenditure and the 2% Pledge*, 2nd report of 2015/16 (House of Commons: London, 21 Apr. 2016); and Perlo-Freeman, S., *Fighting the Wrong Battles: How Obsession with Military Power Diverts Resources from the Climate Crisis* (Campaign Against the Arms Trade: London, Feb. 2020).

Sources: SIPRI Military Expenditure Database, Apr. 2020; and International Monetary Fund World Economic Outlook Database, Oct. 2019.

Towards the 2 per cent guideline

While all but seven European NATO member states had decreased their military expenditure between 2010 and 2014, all but one (the United Kingdom) increased their spending following the Wales summit (see table 8.8). Between 2014 and 2019, the military expenditure of the 24 European NATO states assessed here increased by 16 per cent in real terms, to $261 billion.[13] However, the increases in military expenditure were not uniform across sub-regions: the increases were particularly strong in the Central European NATO states. The combined military expenditure of these 12 NATO states increased by 61 per cent between 2014 and 2019 to $29.9 billion. Most notable are the substantial increases by Bulgaria (216 per cent), Lithuania (176 per cent), Latvia (161 per cent), Romania (115 per cent) and Slovakia (110 per cent) in this five-year period.

The average military burden of European NATO states followed a similar pattern to overall expenditure: it increased from 1.3 per cent of GDP in 2014 to 1.7 per cent by 2019.[14] Among Central European NATO states, the rise in military burden was even greater: from 1.3 per cent in 2014 to 1.8 per cent in 2019. Overall, the number of NATO countries that spent 2 per cent or more of their GDPs on the military rose from one in 2014 to seven in 2019—and six of the latter are in Central Europe.

During the period 2014–19, as military expenditure increased, most countries in Europe had also recovered from the financial and economic crisis that started in 2008.[15] The improved national finances allowed European NATO states to increase their military expenditure in order to move towards the 2 per cent guideline.[16] Thus, the rise in military burden was the result of increases in military expenditure outpacing economic growth, rather than being caused by static military spending in a shrinking economy.

Trends in equipment spending as a share of military expenditure

European NATO members have also taken steps to increase their equipment spending as a share of military expenditure. From 2014, the number of European NATO countries that spent more than 20 per cent of their military

---

[13] Of the 29 NATO member states, 26 are in Europe. Two of these—Iceland and Montenegro—are excluded from this study since the former has no military expenditure and the latter only joined NATO on 5 June 2017. Two NATO members—Canada and the United States—are in North America, and Turkey is in the Middle East.

[14] All averages calculated in the text are based on arithmetic mean.

[15] Szczepanski, M., 'A decade on from the crisis: Main responses and remaining challenges', European Parliament, European Parliamentary Research Service, Oct. 2019.

[16] E.g. Christie, E. H., 'The demand for military expenditure in Europe: The role of fiscal space in the context of a resurgent Russia', *Defence and Peace Economics*, vol. 30, no. 1 (2019), pp. 72–99.

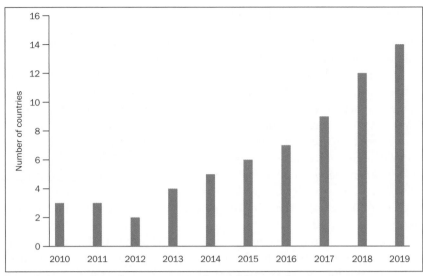

Figure 8.4. Number of European members of the North Atlantic Treaty Organization that reached the equipment spending guideline, 2010–19

Note: The bar chart shows the number of states (excluding Iceland and Montenegro) that spent more than 20 per cent of their military expenditure on equipment.

Source: NATO, 'Defence expenditure of NATO countries', Press release, Various editions, 2010–19.

expenditure on equipment increased at a fast pace: from 5 of the 24 European member states in 2014 to 14 in 2019 (see figure 8.4).

Twenty of the 24 European NATO countries increased both their total military spending and equipment spending as a share of their military expenditure between 2014 and 2019. Average spending on equipment as a share of total military spending rose from 12 per cent in 2014 to 23 per cent in 2019 (see figure 8.5). Equipment spending as a share of total military expenditure declined between 2014 and 2019 in four countries: Albania, Estonia, France and the UK. However, France and the UK both remained well above the 20 per cent NATO guideline in 2019, at 24 per cent and 22 per cent, respectively.

The highest increases in equipment spending as a share of military expenditure occurred in five Central European states: Bulgaria, Lithuania, Romania and Slovakia all more than doubled the share between 2010 and 2019, while Hungary's share almost doubled. Notably, this cluster of countries is in close geographical proximity to Russia, which has featured most prominently in NATO's threat assessments since 2014 (see figure 8.6). Underlying the upward trend in spending on equipment of these five countries were variations in the pace and extent of the increases (see figure 8.7). These five

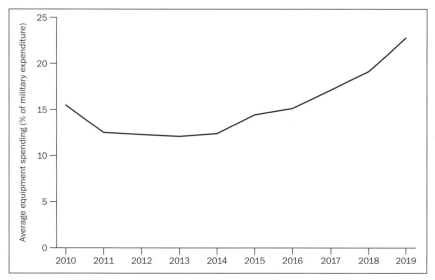

Figure 8.5. Average spending on equipment as a share of total military expenditure by European members of the North Atlantic Treaty Organization

Source: NATO, 'Defence expenditure of NATO countries', Press release, Various editions, 2010–19.

cases are described in detail below to explore possible explanations for their increases and the differences in the trends.

According to Bulgaria's 2015 armed forces development programme, the instability along NATO's eastern and southern flanks calls for the implementation of the decisions made at the 2014 Wales summit.[17] Alongside the 'fundamentally changed security environment' and the NATO guidelines, Bulgaria's plan to increase its military burden to 2 per cent emphasizes the urgent need to modernize the equipment of the armed forces.[18] Although the original plan aimed for a gradual increase over seven years, in 2019 Bulgarian military spending increased sharply—by 127 per cent—to reach $2.1 billion. Similarly, while equipment spending as a share of military expenditure in the years 2010–18 was 6.8 per cent on average, it jumped from 9.7 per cent of total military spending in 2018 to 59 per cent in 2019. Both of these spikes were due to an acceleration in the $1.2 billion procurement of eight new combat aircraft, which were ordered in June 2019 for delivery in 2024. Full payment for these was made in August 2019.[19] Paying arms contracts upfront years

[17] Bulgarian Council of Ministers, *Programme for the Development of the Defence Capabilities of the Bulgarian Armed Forces 2020* (Council of Ministers: Sofia, 30 Sep. 2015); p. 2. On developments in Bulgarian defence policy see Wezeman, S. T. and Kuimova, A., 'Bulgaria and Black Sea security', SIPRI Background Paper, Dec. 2018.

[18] Bulgarian Council of Ministers, *National Plan for Increasing the Defense Spending to 2% of the Gross Domestic Product until 2024* (Council of Ministers: Sofia, 2017), p. 2.

[19] Fiorenza. N., 'Bulgaria makes F-16 payment', *Jane's Defence Weekly*, 14 Aug. 2019.

Figure 8.6. Per cent change in equipment spending as a share of military expenditure by European members of the North Atlantic Treaty Organization, 2010–19

Note: The figure shows European NATO countries, other than Iceland and Montenegro, as of 31 Dec. 2019.

Source: NATO, 'Defence expenditure of NATO countries', Press release, Various editions, 2010–19.

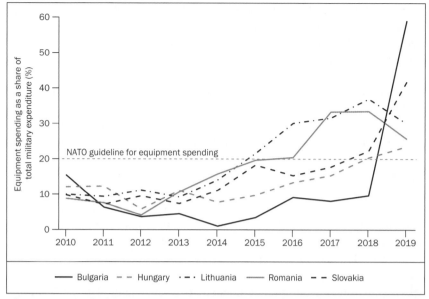

Figure 8.7. The five largest increases in spending on equipment as a share of total military expenditure by European members of the North Atlantic Treaty Organization, 2010–19

Source: NATO, 'Defence expenditure of NATO countries', Press release, Various editions, 2010–19.

before delivery is exceptional, as countries generally spread out payments over several years. It is therefore likely that Bulgaria's total military spending and its equipment spending will decrease substantially in 2020.

While Lithuania echoes the overall NATO security assessment, the first and foremost threat that it perceives is Russia's 'growing aggressiveness' and 'growing military capabilities'.[20] The country's military expenditure increased by 232 per cent in 2010–19. Equipment spending increased from 10 per cent of the military budget to 30 per cent in the same period. For Lithuania, arms procurement has been less about replacing old equipment—as it had little to start with—and more about building up military capability. The largest orders during 2014–19 were for 86 infantry fighting vehicles for $435 million and two air defence systems for $89.3 million.[21]

Romania's 2015 national defence strategy was also aligned to NATO's threat assessments.[22] Romanian military expenditure increased by 154 per cent

---

[20] Lithuanian Ministry of National Defence (MND), *Lithuanian Defence Policy 2017*, White paper (MND: Vilnius, 2017), pp. 7, 13.

[21] SIPRI Arms Transfers Database, Mar. 2019.

[22] Romanian Presidential Administration, *National Defense Strategy 2015–2019: A Strong Romania within Europe and the World* (Presidential Administration: Bucharest, 2015). On developments in Romanian defence policy see Wezeman, S. T. and Kuimova, A., 'Romania and Black Sea security', SIPRI Background Paper, Dec. 2018.

between 2010 and 2019, while spending on equipment in 2019 was 193 per cent higher than in 2010. The increase in equipment spending has been particularly steep since 2013. The Romanian armed forces still operate equipment largely acquired before the end of the cold war. The 2015 national defence strategy and later policy documents emphasize the need for acquisition of new equipment, continuing the efforts to replace old and partly Soviet-origin equipment with equipment from Romania's NATO or European Union (EU) partners. A $4.6 billion order for air defence systems from the USA in 2017 is probably the main reason for the significant increase in equipment spending in that year.[23]

Slovakia's spending on equipment as a share of total military expenditure rose from 9.8 per cent in 2010 to 42 per cent in 2019. Its overall military expenditure rose by 68 per cent in the same period. The increase in military spending has been justified by a national security assessment that is generally in line with that of NATO.[24] To justify the increase in spending on equipment, the Slovak defence white paper of 2016 cites a need to replace outdated equipment.[25] In addition, replacement of Slovakia's arsenal of mainly Soviet- or Russian-sourced equipment needed to be accelerated because of EU restrictions on arms imports from Russia imposed following the annexation of Crimea.[26] The Slovak Ministry of Defence notes in particular the need for the replacement of Russian-supplied combat aircraft and Soviet-supplied air defence systems to reduce military technological dependence on Russia. This echoes the NATO goal formulated after 2014 to address dependencies on Russian-sourced military equipment.[27] The largest Slovak military procurement project in 2014–19 was a $1.8 billion order in 2018 for 14 combat aircraft from the USA for delivery from 2023.[28] It is plausible that the steep increase in Slovak equipment spending in 2019 is related to this project.

As well as perceived threats from Russia, Hungary's security assessment has also been dominated by what its government considers a 'refugee and migrant crisis'. It argues that this requires that the military be used to guard borders and deployed in the Middle East and North Africa to 'manage problems at the root'.[29] Hungary's military expenditure increased by 62 per cent between 2010 and 2019 and its equipment spending increased by 94 per cent.

---

[23] Army Recognition, 'Raytheon to deliver Patriot Configuration 3+ air defense systems to Romania', 17 May 2018; and US Defense Security Cooperation Agency, 'Romania: Patriot air defense system and related support and equipment', News Release no. 17-35, 11 July 2017.

[24] Slovak Ministry of Defence (MOD), *White Paper on Defence of the Slovak Republic* (MOD: Bratislava, 28 Sep. 2016), pp. 6.

[25] Slovak Ministry of Defence (note 24), pp. 10, 25.

[26] On the EU's arms embargo on Russia see chapter 14, section II, in this volume.

[27] E.g. North Atlantic Council (note 7), para. 31.

[28] SIPRI Arms Transfers Database (note 21).

[29] Balogh, O., 'The importance of the Zrínyi 2026 defence and military development program', *Vojenské rozhledy*, vol. 28, no. 3 (Sep. 2019), pp. 55–70; and MTI, 'Defence minister warns of new military threats', Hungary Today, 3 June 2019.

Hungary had already started to replace Russian-sourced equipment in the mid-2000s when it acquired Swedish combat aircraft. The next round of major procurement started in late 2018 and included the acquisition of 46 tanks and 24 self-propelled guns from Germany for $565 million.[30]

Conclusions

The decrease in military expenditure by NATO member states following the 2008 financial and economic crisis started to reverse in the mid-2010s. Threat perceptions became more pronounced, in particular from Russia after its annexation of Crimea, but also in relation to the rise of the Islamic State and the refugee and migrant crisis. These perceptions led NATO members to officially confirm their shared objective to spend 2 per cent of GDP on the military and a minimum of 20 per cent of military expenditure on equipment. At the same time, national economies and public finances recovered, which permitted increased spending.

Since the NATO summit in 2014, the number of NATO countries that allocate 20 per cent or more of their military expenditure to equipment has increased. Growth has been more significant among Central European members of NATO, driven by a combination of factors. Chief among these is perceptions of heightened threat from Russia. In addition, a large share of the equipment used by Central European NATO countries was outdated, and in many cases had been supplied by Russia in the 1990s or by the Soviet Union. Thus, as these states sought to modernize their weaponry, they also sought to decrease their dependence on Russia for maintenance of the existing major equipment.

Among other European members of NATO, however, increases in equipment spending as a share of military expenditure have been more moderate. Their responses to NATO's equipment spending guideline have varied significantly based on the extent to which they are affected by the identified threats and the technical conditions and size of their existing military arsenals.

While the European members of NATO have made progress towards meeting the NATO guideline of spending 20 per cent of military expenditure on equipment, there are still questions as to whether they are now more prepared to deal with the perceived threats. Spending more on equipment does not necessarily result in better military capability or preparedness. The focus on military spending guidelines risks simplifying the response to a multifaceted and unstable array of threats to security.

---

[30] SIPRI Arms Transfers Database (note 21).

IV. Transparency in military expenditure

PIETER D. WEZEMAN AND SIEMON T. WEZEMAN

Government transparency in military expenditure fulfils a number of functions. At the international level it is a tool for confidence building in the area of security. At the national level it is a key element of good governance, adequate management of military expenditure and government accountability.[1]

This section first describes the declining participation in 2019 in two international transparency mechanisms: the United Nations Report on Military Expenditures and reporting to the Organization for Security and Co-operation in Europe (OSCE). The apparent end of a third international mechanism, the South American Defense Expenditure Registry of the Union of South American Nations (Unión de Naciones Suramericanas, UNASUR), is also briefly described. The section then looks, at the national level, at how many governments publish data on their military expenditure and how that data varies. As a case study, it examines Myanmar and the role of income from military-controlled businesses in providing off-budget military expenditure. The section also highlights the difficulties in not only identifying that such practices exist but also changing or ending them.

Reporting at the international level

Reporting to two international instruments that aim for transparency in military expenditure—the UN Report on Military Expenditures and the OSCE Vienna Document 2011 on Confidence- and Security-Building Measures— continued in 2019. These instruments aim to build confidence among states in the political-military sphere and to reduce the level of suspicion between states regarding each other's intentions and military capabilities.

In 1980 the UN General Assembly agreed to establish an annual report in which all UN member states could voluntarily provide data on their military expenditure in the previous year.[2] The report specifically aims to enhance transparency in military matters, increase predictability of military activities, reduce risk of military conflict and raise public awareness of disarmament

---

[1] E.g. Bromley, M. and Solmirano, C., *Transparency in Military Spending and Arms Acquisition in Latin America and the Caribbean*, SIPRI Policy Paper no. 31 (SIPRI: Stockholm, Jan. 2012), pp. 1–5; and Tian, N., Wezeman, P. D. and Yun, Y., *Military Expenditure Transparency in Sub-Saharan Africa*, SIPRI Policy Paper no. 48 (SIPRI: Stockholm, Nov. 2018), pp. 1–3.

[2] UN General Assembly Resolution 35/142 B, 'Reduction of military budgets', A/RES/35/142, 12 Dec. 1980; and United Nations, General Assembly, Report of the Group of Governmental Experts to Review the Operation and Further Development of the United Nations Report on Military Expenditures, A/72/293, 4 Aug. 2017, p. 8.

matters.[3] Interest in the report, which is now known as the UN Report on Military Expenditures, has waned over the years.

Participation in the report was at its highest in 2002, when 81 states participated, but has since declined to a low level.[4] In 2018 only 36 of the 193 UN member states submitted information on their military spending in 2017, and in 2019 the number that reported on spending in 2018 declined to 30 states.[5] Of these 30, 3 are in Asia and Oceania, 1 in the Americas, 2 in the Middle East, 24 in Europe and 0 in Africa. Of the five largest military spenders in the world—the United States, China, India, Russia and Saudi Arabia—only India submitted a report in 2019. However, the USA and China did submit national reports in 2015 and 2017, respectively. Seven of the top 15 largest military spenders in the world in 2019 submitted information: Australia, Canada, France, Germany, India, Italy and Japan. Based on SIPRI military expenditure figures, the 30 countries that reported in 2019 accounted for 19 per cent of total world spending in 2018.[6]

The UN General Assembly adopts every second year a resolution that calls on member states to provide the secretary-general with a report on their military expenditure. The most recent such resolution was adopted in December 2019.[7] In the previous resolution, of December 2017, the General Assembly tasked the UN Office for Disarmament Affairs with sending a questionnaire to states aimed at identifying their priorities regarding transparency in military expenditure, the reasons for non-reporting to the UN report and ways to improve reporting.[8] By July 2019, 13 countries had replied to the questionnaire.[9] However, the content of the replies has not been published and there is no public report that indicates whether the answers have provided the substantial insight that is needed to revive the UN military spending report.

The Vienna Document 2011 requires the OSCE participating states to annually exchange information on military budgets and expenditure in

---

[3] United Nations, A/72/293 (note 2), para. 2.

[4] United Nations, General Assembly, Report of the Group of Governmental Experts on the Operation and Further Development of the United Nations Standardized Instrument for Reporting Military Expenditures, A/66/89, 14 June 2011, p. 26.

[5] Tian, N., Lopes da Silva, D. and Wezeman, P. D., 'Transparency in military expenditure data', *SIPRI Yearbook 2019*, pp. 214–15; and United Nations, General Assembly, 'Objective information on military matters, including transparency of military expenditures', Report of the Secretary-General, A/74/155, 12 July 2019. This report lists 28 submissions. In addition 2 reports that had been submitted after the deadline for inclusion in this annual report are included in the UNARM database.

[6] SIPRI Military Expenditure Database, Apr. 2020.

[7] UN General Assembly Resolution 74/24, 'Objective information on military matters, including transparency of military expenditures', 12 Dec. 2019, A/RES/74/24, 18 Dec. 2019.

[8] UN General Assembly Resolution 72/20, 'Objective information on military matters, including transparency of military expenditures', 4 Dec. 2017, A/RES/72/20, 11 Dec. 2017, para. 8(c). The questionnaire was taken from United Nations, A/72/293 (note 2), annex I.

[9] United Nations, A/74/155 (note 5), para. 7.

the preceding year, using the categories of the UN Report on Military Expenditures.[10] However, these reports are not made publicly available. Of the 57 OSCE participating states, 41 states reported in 2019, down from 46 in 2018.[11]

UNASUR established the South American Defense Expenditure Registry in 2011 as a confidence- and security-building measure.[12] The latest year for which data from the registry has been published was 2015.[13] During 2019 a majority of UNASUR's member states either left the organization or started the withdrawal process.[14]

Transparency at the national level

At the national level, transparency in military spending is usually achieved through the publication of national budgets or expenditure reports and is connected to wider domestic concerns about achieving budgetary transparency and the effective use of resources.[15] This disclosure of information to civil society helps to strengthen good governance, acts as a means of assessing expenditure management and makes accountability possible. Moreover, the military sector has been shown to be prone to corruption, and information transparency is a tool to help to identify possible cases of corruption.[16]

Of the 169 countries for which SIPRI attempted to estimate military expenditure in 2019, relevant data was found for 150.[17] For 147 of these, the data came from official government documents. For the three countries for which official government reports could not be found, data was obtained

---

[10] Vienna Document 2011, paras 15.3–15.4, as updated by OSCE, Forum for Security Cooperation, Decision no. 2/13, 3 Mar. 2013. On the Vienna Document see annex A, section II, in this volume; and OSCE, 'Ensuring military transparency—the Vienna Document', [n.d.]. For a brief description and list of participating states of the OSCE see annex B, section II, in this volume.

[11] OSCE, Communication with author, 11 Feb. 2020.

[12] Bromley and Solmirano (note 1), p. 18. For a brief description and list of member states of UNASUR see annex B, section II, in this volume.

[13] Vega, J. M. and Comini, N., *Registro Suramericano de Gastos de Defensa: El legado de UNASUR* [South American Defense Expenditure Registry: The legacy of UNASUR], Instituto Español de Estudios Estratégicos (IEEE) Documento Opinión no. 129/2017 (IEEE: Madrid, 22 Dec 2017), p. 15.

[14] Deutsche Welle, 'South America leaders form Prosur to replace defunct Unasur bloc', 23 Mar. 2019.

[15] Perlo-Freeman, S., 'Measuring transparency in military expenditure: The case of China', University of California San Diego, Defense Transparency Project, Policy Brief no. 2011-4, Oct. 2011.

[16] Perlo-Freeman, S., 'Transparency and accountability in military spending', SIPRI Commentary, 3 Aug. 2016.

[17] The 19 states for which SIPRI could not find information on military spending in 2019 are Cuba, Djibouti, Equatorial Guinea, Eritrea, Guinea-Bissau, North Korea, Laos, Libya, Myanmar, Qatar, Somalia (partial), Syria, Tajikistan, Turkmenistan, the United Arab Emirates, Uzbekistan, Venezuela, Viet Nam and Yemen. Among the 150 countries with data, 3 had no military spending: Costa Rica, Iceland and Panama. For practical reasons, SIPRI does not collect military expenditure data for some of the smallest states.

from other sources such as reports by the International Monetary Fund (IMF) or media reports that quote government information.[18]

For the 169 countries for which SIPRI collects military expenditure information, the level of transparency varies widely. In particular, in some states military expenditure is funded outside the government budget or has been in the past. Most of this off-budget funding comes from business activities of the armed force. It may not be common, but in the past it has been identified for several states (e.g. Chile, China and Indonesia) and suspected in some others (e.g. Egypt and Viet Nam).[19] Often these states are or have been ruled by military regimes, with weak parliamentary oversight of the armed forces. While democracy has been known to improve levels of transparency, transparency in military spending may take a long time to fully develop.[20] For example, in the case of Myanmar, despite a transition to a democratically elected government, transparency and accountability in the military sector remain a concern.

Myanmar

Between 1962 and 2016 Myanmar was ruled by military regimes. Until 2012 there was either no official or semi-official publication or statement on the budget of the Ministry of Defence (MOD), or inconsistent information. Starting in 2012, when internal protests and external pressure forced the armed forces (known as the Tatmadaw) into a political reform process, Myanmar has published the budget of the MOD in official budget documents and statements. However, four elements of Myanmar's military spending have been omitted from the published government budgets. Two of these are funded from government revenue. The 2011 Special Fund Law allows the Tatmadaw to draw on additional government funds outside the normal budget and parliamentary oversight.[21] Similar funding specifically for arms procurement has also been reported.[22] The two other elements are completely outside government revenue streams or government oversight. The largest is income from trade and industries owned or controlled by the

---

[18] These 3 countries are Brunei Darussalam, Cambodia and Ethiopia.

[19] Lopes da Silva, D. and Tian, N., 'Ending off-budget military funding: Lessons from Chile', SIPRI Commentary, 16 Dec. 2019; Human Rights Watch (HRW), *Too High a Price: The Human Rights Cost of the Indonesian Military's Economic Activities* (HRW: New York, June 2006); Marpaung, J. V., 'TNI's gold mine: Corruption and military-owned businesses in Indonesia', Global Anticorruption Blog, 17 June 2016; and Abuza, Z. and Nhat Anh, N., 'Vietnam's military modernization', The Diplomat, 28 Oct. 2016. On Egypt see also section I in this chapter.

[20] Hollyer, J. R., Rosendorff, B. P. and Vreeland, J. R., 'Democracy and transparency', *Journal of Politics*, vol. 73, no. 4 (Oct. 2011), pp. 1191–205.

[21] The Special Fund Relating to Necessary Expenditures for Perpetuation of the State Sovereignty Law, State Peace and Development Council Law No. 10/2011, 27 Jan. 2011.

[22] Grevatt, J., 'Myanmar proposes a 2017 defence budget of $2.1 billion', *Jane's Defence Industry*, 2 Mar. 2017.

Tatmadaw. The other is 'donations' solicited by the Tatmadaw from private companies. While these second two elements had been reported by media and researchers for many years, in 2019 they were extensively documented in a report by the UN's Independent International Fact-finding Mission on Myanmar (IIFFMM), an independent group of experts established in 2017 by the UN General Assembly's Human Rights Council.[23]

The IIFFMM found two Tatmadaw-owned holding companies, Myanmar Economic Holding Limited (MEHL) and Myanmar Economic Corporation (MEC), through which the military controls or owns at least 106 companies and 27 'affiliated' companies in almost all sectors of production and services.[24] While neither holding company publishes financial reports, the IIFFMM concluded that the two companies and their subsidiaries 'generate revenue that dwarfs that of any civilian-owned company' in Myanmar.[25]

MEHL officially has largely non-military objectives: welfare of military and veteran families, the welfare of the general public, and general economic development.[26] Evidence found by the IIFFMM 'suggests' that its income is properly declared in military budgets, but the IIFFMM's report does not reach a final conclusion on that.[27] MEC, in contrast, is more secretive and its goals are much more military, including 'reducing defence spending' and 'fulfilling the needs of the Tatmadaw'.[28] Its income is not declared in the budget and 'reducing defence spending' seems to mean reducing the official military budget, not total military spending.

The IIFFMM could not determine the total size of the off-budget income from the Tatmadaw-owned companies. However, it estimates that the profit of the businesses may total billions of US dollars each year.[29] Tax data, although found to be inconsistent, indicates that the two holding companies and some of their subsidiaries are among the largest taxpayers in Myanmar, but the report notes that more company revenue goes to the Tatmadaw than is paid in tax and that it seems to be directly funding the Tatmadaw's operations.[30] The income from the solicited donations—intended for Tatmadaw operations against the Rohingya minority—is even more hidden but is likely

---

[23] United Nations, General Assembly, Human Rights Council, Independent International Fact-finding Mission on Myanmar, 'The economic interests of the Myanmar military', 5 Aug. 2019, A/HRC/42/CRP.3. The IIFFMM was established in 2017 to investigate human rights violations by the Tatmadaw, especially against the Rohingya minority. Its original report was submitted in 2018 and published on 5 Aug. 2019. A few updates were published in 'Update from the UN Independent International Fact-finding Mission on Myanmar on its report on "The economic interests of Myanmar's military"', 9 Aug. 2019. For the earlier reporting see e.g. Fullbrook, D., 'Burma's generals on a buying spree', Asia Sentinel, 18 Dec. 2006.

[24] United Nations, A/HRC/42/CRP.3 (note 23), para. 6(a).

[25] United Nations, A/HRC/42/CRP.3 (note 23), para. 48.

[26] United Nations, A/HRC/42/CRP.3 (note 23), para. 50.

[27] United Nations, A/HRC/42/CRP.3 (note 23), para. 46fn.

[28] United Nations, A/HRC/42/CRP.3 (note 23), para. 51.

[29] United Nations, A/HRC/42/CRP.3 (note 23), para. 56.

[30] United Nations, A/HRC/42/CRP.3 (note 23), para. 58.

to be much smaller. For one month in 2017, the IIFFMM found that these donations totalled US$6.15 million.[31]

The lack of information makes assessing the importance of hidden spending difficult. Together, the four types of off-budget military spending probably formed a substantial part, possibly the majority, of Myanmar's total military spending until at least 2018. A possible indication of the size of the two non-regular government funds—the Special Fund and the fund for procurement—could be given by the MOD budget request for the 2017/18 financial year. This was the first budget request that was to be determined by a government and a parliament (the Assembly of the Union) in which the armed forces were in a minority. The MOD requested 3.90 trillion kyats ($2.8 billion), significantly more than the official budget in 2016/17. However, the military budget proposed in the Assembly was only 2.9 trillion kyats ($2.1 billion) and the final approved budget was 3.0 trillion kyats ($2.2 billion).[32] There are two possible explanations for the high request by the MOD. It could have been due to a perceived need for significantly more funds to deal with new developments such as the increased operations against the Rohingya and rebel groups in other parts of the country or to fund large arms-procurement programmes that were underway or planned.[33] But the high request could also have been a way to normalize one or both of the two non-regular government funds by including them in the regular budget.

The IIFFMM's report notes that the independent income of the Tatmadaw has contributed to its ability to operate without civilian oversight and to continue its operations against the Rohingya and other minorities.[34] After 2018 the Tatmadaw seems to have continued its operations and arms acquisitions at the same level as before and has not been drastically reduced in size. At the same time, the official military budget for 2018/19 was 3.3 trillion kyats ($2.2 billion) and the requested budget for 2019/20 was 3.4 trillion kyats ($2.2 billion)—both in absolute value and as a share of government spending, these are not much higher than in earlier years and in real terms are probably a decrease.[35] This

---

[31] United Nations, A/HRC/42/CRP.3 (note 23), para. 6(c).

[32] Grevatt (note 22); and Parameswaran, P., 'What does Myanmar's new defense budget mean?', The Diplomat, 3 Mar. 2017. Until 2017/18 Myanmar's financial year ran from 1 Apr. to 31 Mar. Since 2018/19 it has run from 1 Oct. to 30 Sep. Because of the uncertain but probably large hidden military spending, SIPRI does not use the official defence budget of Myanmar or an estimate of total military spending by Myanmar in regional and subregional military spending estimates.

[33] On the arms-procurement plans see Wezeman, S. T., *Arms Flows to South East Asia* (SIPRI: Stockholm, Dec. 2019); and SIPRI Arms Transfers Database, Mar 2020.

[34] United Nations, A/HRC/42/CRP.3 (note 23), paras 1–2, 60. On the armed conflict in Myanmar, see also chapter 4, section III, in this volume.

[35] Thura, M., 'Bigger budget request is due to inflation: Tatmadaw', *Myanmar Times*, 24 July 2019; Lwin, N., 'Myanmar military proposes larger budget for "stronger" armed forces', *The Irrawaddy*, 22 July 2019; and Lwin, N., 'Tracking the Myanmar Govt's income sources and spending', *The Irrawaddy*, 22 Oct. 2019.

strongly suggests that the size of the undisclosed military spending has not diminished.

As in several other cases where democratically elected civilian governments have come to power after a long period of military rule, dealing with the lack of transparency and oversight may be a difficult and long process for the government.[36] In Myanmar, non-military parties, led by the National League for Democracy (NLD), gained a majority in the Assembly in 2015 for the first time since 1962, and since April 2016 they have formed a largely non-military government. However, under the 2008 Constitution, the Tatmadaw retains 25 per cent of the seats in the Assembly and control of the three security ministries: the MOD, the Ministry of Home Affairs and the Ministry of Border Affairs.[37] The Constitution also gives the Assembly almost no control over the Tatmadaw or its budget.[38]

The NLD-led government considers improving budget transparency and efficiency to be priorities.[39] However, it will have to tackle a culture of secrecy and an uncontrolled military resulting from more than 50 years of military rule. While a parliament existed during some of those years, it did not have full insight into the military budget or any other control and oversight of the Tatmadaw. This has not yet completely changed.

Conclusions

The trend in international transparency in military expenditure differs significantly from the trend at the national level. At the international level reporting to the UN has dropped to a low point and the South American Defense Expenditure Registry has come to a de facto end. In Europe, while participation in the OSCE mechanism remains high, there was a marked decline in 2019. In contrast, at the national level most governments actively report their military budgets in official public documents. However, there remain cases where a country's lack of transparency can have implications that reach far beyond accountability, civilian control and the effective use of resources.

In Myanmar the opacity of the military budget and its off-budget funding system enable the persecution of the Rohingya and other minorities. The Tatmadaw has relied on off-budget allocations to secure a large degree of financial autonomy. Despite the political reforms introduced since 2015, the military still maintains control over its budget. The NLD-led government has proposed improvements to transparency and efficiency in public expendi-

---

[36] Similar cases include Chile and Indonesia. Lopes da Silva and Tian (note 19); Human Rights Watch (note 19); and Marpaung (note 19).
[37] United Nations, A/HRC/42/CRP.3 (note 23), para. 4.
[38] United Nations, A/HRC/42/CRP.3 (note 23), para. 4.
[39] Lwin, 'Tracking the Myanmar Govt's income sources and spending' (note 35).

ture; yet, it is still unclear whether it will be successful. The IIFFMM's report highlights the extent to which Myanmar's reported military spending is underestimated. The case of Myanmar underscores how opacity in military expenditure, as well as off-budget funding mechanisms, can contribute to the military perpetrating crimes against minorities and acting unchecked.

9. International arms transfers and developments in arms production

Overview

The volume of international transfers of major arms grew by 5.5 per cent between 2010–14 and 2015–19, reaching its highest level since the end of the cold war (see figure 9.1). This growth is a continuation of the steady upward trend that began in the early 2000s. However, the total volume for 2015–19 was still 33 per cent lower than the total for 1980–84, when arms transfers peaked. While SIPRI data on arms transfers does not represent their financial value, many arms-exporting states do publish figures on the financial value of their arms exports (see section IV). Based on this data, SIPRI estimates that the total value of the global arms trade was at least $95 billion in 2017 (the most recent year for which data is available).

The five largest suppliers in 2015–19—the United States, Russia, France, Germany and China—accounted for 76 per cent of the total volume of exports. Since 1950 the USA and Russia (or the Soviet Union before 1992) have consistently been by far the largest suppliers (see section I). In 2015–19 US arms exports accounted for 36 per cent of the global total and were 23 per cent higher than in 2010–14. In contrast, Russia's arms exports decreased by 18 per cent and its share of the global total dropped from 27 per cent in 2010–14 to 21 per cent in 2015–19. Exports by the three other largest suppliers all grew between 2010–14 and 2015–19: France's by 72 per cent, Germany's by 17 per cent and China's by 6.3 per cent.

SIPRI identified 160 states as importers of major arms in 2015–19. The five largest arms importers were Saudi Arabia, India, Egypt, Australia and China, which together accounted for 36 per cent of total arms imports (see section II). The region that received the largest volume of major arms supplies in 2015–19 was Asia and Oceania, accounting for 41 per cent of the total, followed by the Middle East, which received 35 per cent—a higher share than in any of the 13 consecutive five-year periods since 1950–54. The flow of arms to two regions increased between 2010–14 and 2015–19—the Middle East (by 61 per cent) and Europe (by 3.2 per cent, the first increase since 1990–94)—while flows to the other three regions decreased—the Americas (by 40 per cent), Africa (by 16 per cent) and Asia and Oceania (by 7.9 per cent).

The total arms sales of the 100 largest arms producers and military services companies in the world (excluding China)—the SIPRI Top 100—amounted to

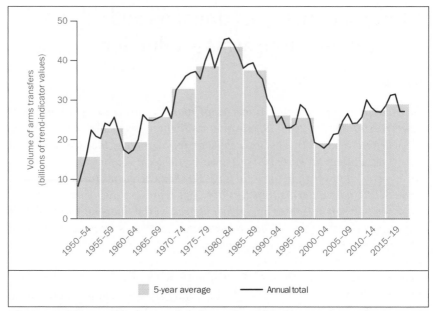

Figure 9.1. The trend in international transfers of major arms, 1950–2019

Note: Since year-on-year deliveries can fluctuate, SIPRI compares consecutive multi-year periods—normally five-year periods. This provides a more stable measure of trends in transfers of major arms. See box 9.1 in section I for an explanation of the SIPRI trend-indicator value.

Source: SIPRI Arms Transfers Database, Mar. 2020.

$420 billion in 2018 (see section V). This represented an increase of 4.6 per cent on the previous year.

Following the trend of recent years, there were few positive developments in official public transparency in arms transfers in 2019 (see section III). The number of states reporting their arms exports and imports to the United Nations Register of Conventional Arms (UNROCA) remained at a low level and no major changes occurred in the various national and regional reporting instruments. The number of states fulfilling their treaty obligation under the 2013 Arms Trade Treaty (ATT) to report arms exports and imports has grown: from 53 for 2016 to 61 for 2018. However, as more states have ratified the ATT, the proportion of states parties submitting a report has fallen: from 71 per cent for 2016 to 66 per cent for 2018.

SIEMON T. WEZEMAN

I. Developments among the suppliers of major arms, 2015–19

SIEMON T. WEZEMAN, ALEXANDRA KUIMOVA, DIEGO LOPES DA SILVA, NAN TIAN AND PIETER D. WEZEMAN

SIPRI has identified 68 states as exporters of major arms in the five-year period 2015–19.[1] The five largest suppliers of arms during that period—the United States, Russia, France, Germany and China—accounted for 76 per cent of all arms exports (see table 9.1). The top five in 2015–19 were the same as in 2010–14 but the combined total of their exports of major arms was 9.5 per cent higher. The exports of four of these five increased—those of France at the greatest rate (72 per cent)—while Russia's arms exports fell.

The top 25 arms exporters accounted for 99 per cent of the world's major arms exports in 2015–19. Of these 25 states, 16 are in North America and Europe, 4 are in Asia and Oceania, 3 are in the Middle East, 1 is in Africa and 1 is in South America (see table 9.2). States in North America and Europe (including Russia) accounted for 87 per cent of all arms exports. This concentration of suppliers in the Euro-Atlantic region has been a feature of the entire period covered by the SIPRI Arms Transfers Database (1950–2019). Many of the states listed in the top 25 for 2015–19 have also appeared in this list in previous periods. However, for the first time in two decades a state that has never previously appeared in the top 10 entered this group in 2015–19: the Republic of Korea (South Korea) was the 10th-largest supplier over the period.

This section reviews the arms exports and arms export policies of the world's main arms suppliers in 2015–19. It starts with the two largest suppliers, the USA and Russia, which together have long dominated the international supply of arms. It then looks at the arms supplies of members of the European Union (EU), in particular France, Germany and the United Kingdom. It ends by looking at the three largest suppliers outside Europe and North America: China, which is by far the largest, Israel and South Korea.

The United States

The USA was the largest exporter of major arms in the five-year period 2015–19, a position that it has occupied since the end of the cold war. The volume of US arms exports grew by 23 per cent between 2010–14 and 2015–19

---

[1] Except where indicated, the information on the arms deliveries and orders referred to in this section is taken from the SIPRI Arms Transfers Database. For a definition of 'major arms' and a description of how the volume of transfers is measured see box 9.1 in this section. The sources and methods used to produce the data discussed here are also presented on the SIPRI website. The figures here may differ from those in previous editions of the SIPRI Yearbook because the Arms Transfers Database is updated annually.

Box 9.1. Definitions and methodology for SIPRI data on international arms transfers

The SIPRI Arms Transfers Database contains information on deliveries of major arms to states, international organizations and non-state armed (i.e. rebel) groups from 1950 to 2019. A new set of data is published annually, replacing the data in earlier editions of the SIPRI Yearbook or other SIPRI publications.

Definitions

SIPRI's definition of 'transfer' includes sales, manufacturing licences, aid, gifts, and most loans or leases. The item must have a military purpose: the recipient must be the armed forces or paramilitary forces or intelligence agency of another country, a non-state armed group, or an international organization.

The SIPRI Arms Transfers Database only includes 'major arms', which are defined as (*a*) most aircraft, including unmanned aerial vehicles; (*b*) air defence missile systems and larger air defence guns; (*c*) air refuelling systems; (*d*) most armoured vehicles; (*e*) artillery over 100 millimetres in calibre; (*f*) engines for combat-capable aircraft and other larger aircraft, for combat ships and larger support ships, and for armoured vehicles; (*g*) guided missiles, torpedoes, bombs and shells; (*h*) sensors (radars, sonars and many passive electronic sensors); (*i*) most ships; (*j*) ship-borne weapons (naval guns, missile launch systems and anti-submarine weapons); (*k*) reconnaissance satellites; and (*l*) most gun or missile-armed turrets for armoured vehicles.

In cases where an air refuelling system, engine, sensor, naval gun or other ship-borne system, or turret (items c, f, h, j and l) is fitted on a platform (vehicle, aircraft or ship), the transfer only appears as a separate entry in the database if the item comes from a different supplier from that of the platform.

The SIPRI trend-indicator value

SIPRI has developed a unique system for measuring the volume of transfers of major arms using a common unit, the trend-indicator value (TIV). The TIV is intended to represent the transfer of military resources. Each weapon has its own specific TIV. Second-hand and second-hand but significantly modernized arms are given a reduced TIV. SIPRI calculates the volume of transfers by multiplying the weapon-specific TIV with the number of arms delivered in a given year. SIPRI TIV figures do not represent the financial values of arms transfers.

---

and the USA's share of total global arms exports rose from 31 per cent to 36 per cent (see table 9.1). The gap between the total arms exports of the USA and those of Russia—the second-largest exporter—has grown rapidly: in 2010–14, US exports of major arms were 17 per cent higher than those of Russia, whereas in 2015–19 they were 76 per cent higher. In 2015–19 the USA delivered major arms to at least 96 states, a far higher number of destinations for arms exports than any other supplier. The USA also delivered a few armoured vehicles and anti-tank missiles to rebel groups in Syria.

States in the Middle East received 51 per cent of total US arms exports in 2015–19 (see table 9.3). The volume of US arms exports to the region increased by 79 per cent between 2010–14 and 2015–19, partly to meet demand arising from the conflict in Yemen (see below).

Arms exports to states in Asia and Oceania accounted for 30 per cent of total US arms exports in 2015–19. US arms exports to this region were 20 per cent lower than in 2010–14 as a result of decreases in arms exports to India (–51 per cent), Pakistan (–92 per cent), Singapore (–60 per cent), South Korea (–34 per cent) and Taiwan (–38 per cent). These decreases were partly offset by increases in US arms exports to Australia, which rose by 41 per cent (making Australia the second-largest importer of US arms in 2015–19), and to Japan, which rose by 85 per cent.

Arms exports to states in Europe accounted for 13 per cent of US arms exports in 2015–19, an increase of 45 per cent on 2010–14. US arms exports to Africa increased by 10 per cent between 2010–14 and 2015–19, while those to the Americas decreased by 20 per cent.

US arms exports to Saudi Arabia and the conflict in Yemen

By far the largest recipient of US arms in 2015–19 was Saudi Arabia. It received 25 per cent of US arms exports (see table 9.2), up from 7.4 per cent in 2010–14.

In recent years, there have been discussions in the US Congress and elsewhere about halting or restricting US deliveries of major arms to the Middle East. These discussions intensified after 2015 when a coalition of Middle Eastern states, led by Saudi Arabia, started a military intervention in the armed conflict in Yemen.[2] Although the discussions in the Congress at that time did not result in an outright block on arms exports, in 2016 the US administration placed restrictions on arms transfers to Saudi Arabia, including on large transfers of guided bombs.[3] In 2018–19 the US Congress discussed the possibility of placing further restrictions on arms exports to Saudi Arabia and considered restrictions on arms exports to the United Arab Emirates (UAE) based on concerns not only about alleged violations of international humanitarian law by Saudi Arabian and Emirati forces in Yemen, but also about the human rights situation in Saudi Arabia itself.[4]

However, the US administration resisted calls to impose additional restrictions, and arms exports to Saudi Arabia continued in 2019. For example, the USA delivered 30 of the 154 F-15SA combat aircraft ordered by Saudi Arabia in 2011. The US administration also controversially authorized the sale to Saudi Arabia of an estimated 59 000 guided bombs and other ammunition and military equipment.[5] To complete the deal, the administration broke

---

[2] On the conflict in Yemen see chapter 6, section V, in this volume.

[3] Blanchard, C. M., *Saudi Arabia: Background and US Relations*, Congressional Research Service (CRS) Report for Congress RL33533 (US Congress, CRS: Washington, DC, 18 Feb. 2020), p. 25.

[4] Blanchard (note 3), pp. 2–26; Kerr, P. K., *Arms Sales: Congressional Review Process*, Congressional Research Service (CRS) Report for Congress RL31675 (US Congress, CRS: Washington, DC, 3 Mar. 2020), pp. 6–7; and Abramson, J., 'Senate bucks Trump's Saudi approach', *Arms Control Today*, vol. 49, no. 1 (Jan./Feb. 2019).

[5] Blanchard (note 3), p. 53; and Mehta, A., 'Revealed: Trump's $110 billion weapons list for the Saudis', *Defense News*, 8 June 2017.

Table 9.1. The 50 largest suppliers of major arms, 2015–19

The table lists states, international organizations and non-state actors that exported major arms in the 5-year period 2015–19. Figures for volume of exports are SIPRI trend-indicator values (TIV).

Rank			Volume of exports (TIV, millions)		Share (%),	Change in volume (%), compared
2015–19	2010–14[a]	Supplier	2019	2015–19	2015–19	with 2010–14
1	1	United States	10 752	53 034	36	23
2	2	Russia	4 718	30 069	21	–18
3	5	France	3 368	11 544	7.9	72
4	4	Germany	1 185	8 518	5.8	17
5	3	China	1 423	8 080	5.5	6.3
6	6	United Kingdom	972	5 451	3.7	–15
7	7	Spain	1 061	4 539	3.1	13
8	12	Israel	369	4 331	3.0	77
9	9	Italy	491	3 134	2.1	–17
10	14	South Korea	688	3 085	2.1	143
11	10	Netherlands	285	2 703	1.9	–2.8
12	8	Ukraine	91	1 422	1.0	–63
13	13	Switzerland	254	1 346	0.9	2.6
14	19	Turkey	245	1 160	0.8	86
15	11	Sweden	206	883	0.6	–65
16	15	Canada	188	837	0.6	–33
17	16	Norway	32	575	0.4	–30
18	23	UAE	104	537	0.4	86
19	20	Australia	148	505	0.3	11
20	18	Belarus	115	504	0.3	–23
21	34	Czechia	13	487	0.3	453
22	17	South Africa	145	419	0.3	–36
23	39	India	115	300	0.2	426
24	24	Brazil	10	299	0.2	6.8
25	46	Portugal	3	241	0.2	1 239
26	52	Indonesia	8	204	0.1	2 450
27	25	Jordan	86	200	0.1	–28
28	39	Bulgaria	–	175	0.1	230
29	22	Finland	24	153	0.1	–59
30	32	Denmark	4	103	0.1	6.2
31	21	Uzbekistan	–	102	0.1	–76
32	31	Singapore	–	95	0.1	–19
33	28	Belgium	42	89	0.1	–58
34	36	Serbia	–	88	0.1	33
35	..	Lithuania	–	60	<0.05	..
36	30	Austria	3	56	<0.05	–67
37	49	Slovakia	–	55	<0.05	323
38	26	Poland	–	44	<0.05	–81
39	29	Iran	–	40	<0.05	–81
40	..	Greece	–	30	<0.05	..
41	53	Egypt	2	24	<0.05	243

Rank			Volume of exports (TIV, millions)		Share (%),	Change in volume (%), compared
2015–19	2010–14[a]	Supplier	2019	2015–19	2015–19	with 2010–14
42	60	Colombia	10	20	<0.05	..
43	35	New Zealand	–	17	<0.05	–77
44	..	Kyrgyzstan	–	14	<0.05	..
45	59	Qatar	11	14	<0.05	..
46	..	Georgia	–	13	<0.05	..
47	43	Brunei Darussalam	–	12	<0.05	–50
48	56	Taiwan	2	8	<0.05	300
49	..	Oman	–	7	<0.05	..
50	..	Pakistan	1	7	<0.05	..
..	..	19 others	2	35	<0.05	..
..	..	Unknown supplier(s)	22	106	0.1	29
		Total	**27 194**	**145 776**	..	**5.5**

.. = not available or not applicable; – = no deliveries, <0.05 = between 0 and 0.05; UAE = United Arab Emirates.

Note: The SIPRI TIV is an indicator of the volume of arms transfers and not their financial value. The method for calculating the TIV is described in box 9.1.

[a] The rank order for suppliers in 2010–14 differs from that published in *SIPRI Yearbook 2015* because of subsequent revision of figures for these years.

Source: SIPRI Arms Transfers Database, Mar. 2020.

from the normal practice of seeking approval from the Congress by invoking an emergency authority under the 1976 Arms Export Control Act to authorize the sale.[6] The authorization was granted despite protests by a majority in both houses of the Congress that this procedure undermined its role in arms export decision making.[7] The administration argued that it needed to use the emergency authority because 'regional volatility' in the Middle East had increased and the arms sales would support US allies to deter and defend themselves against Iran.[8]

US arms exports policy as a tool to counter Russia

The USA has attempted to use its position as the world's largest arms exporter—in terms of both total sales and the number of states that acquire US military technology—as a tool in its efforts to limit Russia's global influence and as part of its sanctions regime against Russia. For this purpose,

[6] Arms Export Control Act of 1976, US Public Law 90–629, as amended up to US Public Law 115–232, Enacted 13 Aug. 2018.

[7] Blanchard, C. M., Sharp, J. M. and Thomas, C., 'Emergency arms sales to the Middle East: Context and legislative history', Memorandum, US Congress, Congressional Research Service, 7 June 2019; Blanchard (note 3), pp. 22, 26; Kerr (note 4), pp. 5–6; and Abramson (note 4).

[8] Pompeo, M. R., US Secretary of State, 'Emergency notification of arms sales to Jordan, the United Arab Emirates, and Saudi Arabia', Press statement, 24 May 2019. On Iranian–US relations in 2019 see chapter 6, section I, in this volume.

Table 9.2. The 25 largest suppliers of major arms and their three main recipients, 2015–19

Rank 2015–19	Supplier	Main recipients (share of supplier's total exports, %), 2015–19		
		1st	2nd	3rd
1	United States	Saudi Arabia (25)	Australia (9.1)	UAE (6.4)
2	Russia	India (25)	China (16)	Algeria (14)
3	France	Egypt (26)	Qatar (14)	India (14)
4	Germany	South Korea (18)	Greece (10)	Algeria (8.1)
5	China	Pakistan (35)	Bangladesh (20)	Algeria (9.9)
6	United Kingdom	Saudi Arabia (41)	Oman (14)	USA (9.1)
7	Spain	Australia (33)	Singapore (13)	Turkey (11)
8	Israel	India (45)	Azerbaijan (17)	Viet Nam (8.5)
9	Italy	Turkey (20)	Pakistan (7.5)	Saudi Arabia (7.2)
10	South Korea	UK (17)	Iraq (14)	Indonesia (13)
11	Netherlands	Indonesia (17)	USA (14)	Jordan (13)
12	Ukraine	China (31)	Russia (20)	Thailand (17)
13	Switzerland	Australia (18)	China (14)	Saudi Arabia (14)
14	Turkey	Turkmenistan (25)	Oman (12)	Pakistan (12)
15	Sweden	USA (22)	Algeria (12)	UAE (9.9)
16	Canada	Saudi Arabia (34)	India (11)	UAE (10)
17	Norway	Oman (35)	USA (20)	Finland (14)
18	UAE	Egypt (41)	Algeria (13)	Unknown recipient (12)
19	Australia	USA (42)	Indonesia (18)	Canada (18)
20	Belarus	Viet Nam (31)	Sudan (16)	Serbia (15)
21	Czechia	Iraq (39)	USA (17)	Ukraine (9.0)
22	South Africa	USA (23)	UAE (20)	Malaysia (11)
23	India	Myanmar (46)	Sri Lanka (25)	Mauritius (14)
24	Brazil	Afghanistan (38)	Indonesia (17)	Lebanon (11)
25	Portugal	Romania (95)	Uruguay (2.9)	Cabo Verde (1.2)

UAE = United Arab Emirates.

Source: SIPRI Arms Transfers Database, Mar. 2020.

in 2017 the US Congress passed the Countering America's Adversaries Through Sanctions Act (CAATSA).[9] Among other things, the act gives the US Government the authority to deny US arms exports to states that buy arms from Russia and to impose other sanctions on states, companies or persons. In several cases, CAATSA has been used to put pressure on states that are seen as strategic partners by the USA but that have acquired or planned to acquire arms from Russia. For example, the USA has invoked procedures

[9] Countering America's Adversaries Through Sanctions Act, US Public Law 115–44, signed into law 2 Aug. 2017. See also US Department of the Treasury, 'Resource center: Countering America's Adversaries Through Sanctions Act', updated 21 May 2019; US Department of State, Bureau of International Security and Nonproliferation, 'Section 231 of the Countering America's Adversaries Through Sanctions Act of 2017', [n.d.]; and Wezeman, S. T. et al., 'Supplier developments, 2018', *SIPRI Yearbook 2019*, pp. 235–39.

under CAATSA against Egypt, India and Turkey. (On the case of India see section II.)

The most important development in this area in 2019 involved Turkey—a long-term ally of the USA and a member of the North Atlantic Treaty Organization (NATO). In late 2017 Turkey ordered S-400 surface-to-air missile (SAM) systems from Russia, having rejected offers from the USA and China and a combined offer from France and Italy. In response to the order, the USA completely removed Turkey from the F-35 programme in mid-2019 after the first S-400 systems were delivered.[10] Turkey had by that time ordered 30 F-35s and planned to acquire up to 70 more. The USA's decision was not based on CAATSA; instead, it was based on US concerns that Russia's access to the Turkish S-400 systems could possibly have allowed it to gather intelligence on the capabilities of the F-35 aircraft supplied to Turkey.[11] Later in 2019 the US Congress invoked CAATSA to apply pressure on the US administration to take further steps and implement sanctions against Turkey for not yielding to US demands to remove the S-400 systems from its arsenal.[12]

The USA has supplied Egypt with large volumes of major arms since 1978 as aid, making the USA one of the top arms suppliers to Egypt. However, from around 2015 Egypt started to turn to Russia to fulfil several major arms procurement programmes, including deals for combat aircraft and combat helicopters (see section II). Egypt placed these orders before CAATSA was introduced. However, in 2019 Egypt reportedly signed a deal for 20 Su-35 combat aircraft from Russia. In response, the US Government signalled that the deal would 'complicate' US military aid to Egypt and would put Egypt at risk of sanctions under CAATSA.[13] By the end of 2019 it remained unclear whether the pressure applied by the USA had had an impact on the deal.

Russia

Russian arms exports accounted for 21 per cent of total world arms exports in 2015–19. However, the volume of Russia's exports was 18 per cent lower than in 2010–14 (see table 9.1). In 2015–19 Russia delivered major arms to 47 states, with 55 per cent of its arms exports going to its three main recipients: India, China and Algeria (see table 9.2). Although India remained the main recipient of Russian arms in 2015–19, accounting for 25 per cent of the total, the

[10] White House, 'Statement by the Press Secretary', 17 July 2019.

[11] Mehta, A., 'Turkey officially kicked out of F-35 program, costing US half a billion dollars', *Defense News*, 17 July 2019; and Roque, A. and Herschelman, K., 'Washington to cut ties with Turkey on F-35 programme and shift supply chain to US', *Jane's Defence Weekly*, 24 July 2019, p. 5.

[12] Seligman, L., 'US lawmakers move to punish Turkey for buying Russian missile system', *Foreign Policy*, 10 Dec. 2019.

[13] Sharp, J. M., *Egypt: Background and US Relations*, Congressional Research Service (CRS) Report for Congress RL33003 (US Congress, CRS: Washington, DC, 21 Nov. 2019), pp. 21–23.

Table 9.3. The 10 largest suppliers of major arms and their destinations, by region and subregion, 2015–19

Figures are the percentage shares of the supplier's total volume of exports delivered to each recipient region or subregion in the 5-year period 2015–19.

Recipient region	Supplier									
	USA	Russia	France	Germany	China	UK	Spain	Israel	Italy	South Korea
Africa	2.7	17	3.5	8.3	16	1.5	0.9	1.0	7.4	–
North Africa	2.4	14	1.7	8.2	9.9	1.4	–	–	3.7	–
Sub-Saharan Africa	0.3	3.3	1.8	0.1	6.4	0.2	0.9	1.0	3.7	–
Americas	3.5	0.8	7.5	11	2.6	12	6.2	11	8.2	9.5
Central America and the Caribbean	1.1	0.4	0.6	0.1	0.2	–	2.5	1.2	0.4	–
North America	1.4	–	3.1	8.3	–	9.1	1.9	6.4	0.2	–
South America	1.0	0.4	3.8	2.5	2.4	3.1	1.7	3.0	7.6	9.5
Asia and Oceania	30	57	30	30	74	23	66	61	23	50
Central Asia	0.1	5.2	0.9	0.6	4.7	–	2.1	0.1	1.1	–
East Asia	12	16	5.3	18	–	8.1	8.6	2.3	5.1	–
Oceania	9.3	–	2.3	1.2	–	0.4	33	–	–	7.0
South Asia	4.9	27	14	3.0	56	8.1	0.3	45	9.3	7.0
South East Asia	3.5	8.8	7.3	6.8	13	6.3	22	14	7.2	43
Europe	13	5.7	6.6	26	0.2	7.6	0.8	25	15	24
Central Europe	0.9	0.5	0.5	3.5	0.2	1.3	–	1.6	5.0	1.9
Eastern Europe	0.1	5.2	0.4	–	<0.05	0.1	0.3	17	–	–
Western Europe	12	–	5.6	23	..	6.1	0.5	6.4	9.8	22
European Union	10	–	5.9	26	0.2	7.4	0.5	8.0	11	20
Middle East	51	19	52	24	6.7	56	26	1.5	47	17
Other	<0.05	–	–	–	–	–	0.6	0.2	<0.05	–

.. = not available or not applicable; – = nil; <0.05 = between 0 and 0.05.

Note: 'Other' refers to international organizations (or some non-state actors) that are not based in a single region, as well as unidentified recipients that cannot be linked to a specific region.

Source: SIPRI Arms Transfers Database, Mar. 2020.

volume of Russian arms exports to India fell by 47 per cent between 2010–14 and 2015–19.

At the regional level, the largest share of Russia's arms exports (57 per cent) went to states in Asia and Oceania (see table 9.3), but China and India alone accounted for nearly three-quarters of this (41 per cent of the total). Similarly, Algeria's large share of Russian exports (14 per cent) meant that the third-largest share of Russian exports (17 per cent) went to states in Africa.

The second-largest share of Russian exports of major arms went to states in the Middle East (19 per cent). The volume of Russia's exports to this region increased by 30 per cent between 2010–14 and 2015–19. Egypt and Iraq were the main recipients of Russian arms exports to the Middle East in 2015–19. Deliveries to Egypt rose by 191 per cent between 2010–14 and 2015–19 to account for 49 per cent of Russian deliveries to the region. Similarly, exports to Iraq rose by 212 per cent to account for 29 per cent of Russian deliveries to the Middle East. Although Russian forces have been operating in Syria since 2015 in support of the Syrian Government, the volume of Russian arms deliveries to Syria (including as aid) fell by 87 per cent between 2010–14 and 2015–19.[14] They accounted for only 3.9 per cent of Russian arms exports to the Middle East and 0.7 per cent of total Russian arms exports in 2015–19.

In 2015–19 Russia continued to be the main arms supplier to many states of the former Soviet Union. The exports are an important part of the military cooperation between Russia and the recipient states, and they are often provided as aid or on preferential terms.[15] The volume of Russian arms exports to several of these states increased significantly between 2010–14 and 2015–19. Kazakhstan became the largest recipient of Russian arms among the former Soviet states, accounting for 5.0 per cent of all Russian arms exports in 2015–19, after a fivefold increase. Deliveries included 16 Su-30 combat aircraft and 5 S-300 SAM systems. In 2015–19 the volume of Russian arms exports to Belarus was three times higher than in 2010–14. Exports included S-300 SAM systems and Yak-130 trainer/combat aircraft. Russia was also the main supplier of major arms to Armenia and the second-largest supplier to Azerbaijan, as the armed conflict between the two countries continued (see section II).

Arms suppliers in the European Union

The top 25 arms exporters in 2015–19 included 9 members of the European Union (see table 9.2).[16] The five largest of these exporters—France, Germany,

---

[14] On Russia's role in the conflict in Syria see chapter 6, section II, in this volume.

[15] E.g. Russian Embassy in Belarus, [Military and military-technical cooperation], [n.d.] (in Russian); and Putz, C., 'Kazakhstan takes delivery of (free) Russian S-300 defense systems', The Diplomat, 9 June 2016.

[16] The UK was a member of the EU until Jan. 2020 and is included as such here.

the UK, Spain and Italy—together accounted for 23 per cent of global arms exports in 2015–19, compared with 20 per cent in 2010–14. The volume of French, German and Spanish arms exports increased between the two periods, while British and Italian arms exports decreased.

The combined arms exports by all 28 EU member states were 9.0 per cent higher than in 2010–14 and they accounted for 26 per cent of the global total in 2015–19. Intra-EU transfers of arms remained at a relatively low level: only 12 per cent of the exports by EU member states in 2015–19 were to other EU member states. Among the five largest EU exporters, only two delivered more than 10 per cent of their total arms exports to other EU states: Germany (26 per cent) and Italy (11 per cent). However, because the volume of arms imported by EU member states is relatively low (only 7.8 per cent of the global total), deliveries from other EU member states accounted for 41 per cent of all arms imports by EU member states.

France

France was the third-largest supplier of major arms in 2015–19, accounting for 7.9 per cent of the global total (see table 9.1). In 2015–19 French arms exports reached their highest level for any five-year period since 1990. After a fall of 31 per cent between 2005–2009 and 2010–14, French arms exports rose by 72 per cent between 2010–14 and 2015–19. The volume of French arms exports to states in the Middle East was 363 per cent higher than in 2010–14. The region accounted for the largest share—52 per cent—of French arms exports in 2015–19, followed by Asia and Oceania with 30 per cent (see table 9.3).

Although France delivered major arms to 75 states in 2015–19, a large proportion of its arms exports tends to be concentrated among a small number of recipients. In 2010–14 France's three main recipients—Morocco, China and the UAE—together received 39 per cent of French arms exports, while its three main recipients in 2015–19—Egypt, Qatar and India—together received 54 per cent (see table 9.2). The five-year period 2015–19 was the first in which Egypt, Qatar and India had been among the main recipients of French arms since the 1980s. Deliveries of a total of 49 Rafale combat aircraft to these three countries accounted for nearly a quarter of French arms exports in 2015–19.

At the end of 2019 there were outstanding orders for a wide range of French major arms, including orders for 43 Rafales (from India and Qatar), 8 submarines (from Brazil and India) and 15 frigates (from Egypt, Malaysia, Romania and the UAE). Most of these are planned to be delivered in the next five years, indicating that France's arms exports will remain at a relatively high level.

France officially claims that its arms industry is a necessary foundation of its strategic autonomy and independent foreign policy.[17] However, while France procures significant numbers of major arms for its armed forces in all categories from its own arms industry, the French Government assesses that domestic demand is insufficient to sustain many of its key arms development and production programmes.[18] In order to maintain a viable arms industry, the French Government has taken an assertive approach to arms exports in recent years. For example, it has frequently offered advantageous credit facilities and technology transfers to prospective clients. It has even been willing to fast-track deliveries by exporting major arms that were originally ordered and put into production for the French armed forces.[19]

This assertive approach continued in 2015–19. The French Government pressed ahead with exports of major arms to certain countries, including Egypt and states involved in the Saudi Arabia-led military intervention in Yemen. This was despite allegations that these countries had used French arms in human rights violations or infringements of international humanitarian law.[20] In particular, according to official French documents leaked in 2019, French major arms supplied to Saudi Arabia and the UAE have been used against civilian targets in Yemen.[21] While some of these arms (e.g. Mirage 2000-9 combat aircraft) were delivered over a decade ago, some (e.g. Aravis armoured vehicles and targeting pods for combat aircraft) were delivered after the intervention in Yemen started in 2015.[22] Despite criticism from some non-governmental organizations (NGOs) and opposition parliamentarians, France's policy on exports of arms to countries involved in the conflict in Yemen remained unchanged.

Germany

Germany was the world's fourth-largest supplier of major arms in 2015–19, with 5.8 per cent of the global total. The volume of its exports was 17 per cent higher than in 2010–14 (see table 9.1). The largest share of its exports

[17] French National Assembly, Commission for National Defence and the Armed Forces, 'Audition de Mme Florence Parly, ministre des Armées, sur les opérations en cours et les exportations d'armement' [Hearing of Florence Parly, Minister for the Armed Forces, on current operations and arms exports], 7 May 2019. On the largest French arms-producing companies see section V in this chapter.

[18] French Ministry of the Armed Forces (MAF), *Rapport au Parlement sur les exportations d'armements de la France 2019* [Report to Parliament on French arms exports 2019] (MAF: Paris, June 2019), p. 18.

[19] Béraud-Sudreau, L., *La politique française de soutien à l'export de defense: Raison et limites d'un succès* [French defence export support policy: The reasons for and limits to success], Focus stratégique no 73 (Institut français des relations internationales: Paris, June 2017).

[20] Houry, N. and Jeannerod, B., '« Les armes françaises favorisent les abus en Egypte »' ['French weapons facilitate abuses in Egypt'], *Le Monde*, 28 Jan. 2019; and Human Rights Watch (HRW), *World Report 2020* (HRW: New York, 2019), pp. 487–94.

[21] Dodman, B., 'France under pressure to come clean over arms exports in Yemen war', France 24, 20 Apr. 2019.

[22] Human Rights Watch (note 20); and Disclose, 'Made in France: The Yemen papers', 15 Apr. 2019.

Table 9.4. Deliveries by arms category by the 10 largest suppliers of major arms, 2015–19

Figures are the percentage share of each category of major arms in the exports of the 10 largest suppliers in 2015–19.

	Aircraft	Air defence systems	Armoured vehicles	Artillery	Engines	Missiles	Sensors	Ships	Other
USA	56	6.1	12	0.3	3.2	17	2.5	1.6	0.3
Russia	51	7.6	9.9	0.2	9.2	13	1.8	6.5	1.5
France	42	2.1	3.6	0.9	4.1	13	9.9	22	1.9
Germany	12	0.9	13	2.1	9.4	7.9	4.5	49	–
China	27	9.0	15	2.0	<0.05	17	2.5	27	0.3
UK	60	0.9	0.4	1.7	11	9.5	2.0	6.9	7.7
Spain	62	–	0.9	0.7	–	–	4.2	33	–
Israel	4.7	25	1.3	0.9		33	21	11	3.3
Italy	58	–	6.9	2.1	<0.05	3.9	14	8.5	6.3
South Korea	26	–	1.2	9.7	–	0.9	–	62	–
World	**45**	**5.9**	**10**	**1.1**	**5.0**	**13**	**4.6**	**13**	**1.3**

– = no deliveries; <0.05 = between 0 and 0.05.

Notes: 'Other' includes naval weapons, satellites, gun turrets for armoured vehicles, and air refuelling systems. On SIPRI's categories of major arms see box 9.1.

Source: SIPRI Arms Transfers Database, Mar. 2020.

(30 per cent) went to states in Asia and Oceania (see table 9.3), but it also exported large shares to other states in Europe (26 per cent) and to states in the Middle East (24 per cent).

Germany delivered major arms to 55 countries in 2015–19. South Korea was by far the largest recipient, accounting for 18 per cent of German arms exports. Ships made up almost half of the volume of major arms exported by Germany (see table 9.4). Most of these were submarines (39 per cent of the total): Germany delivered four to South Korea, three each to Egypt and Greece, two each to Colombia and Italy, and one to Israel. Among the new large export deals that Germany agreed in 2019 were deals for 4 frigates each for Brazil and Egypt and for 508 armoured vehicles for the UK.

In 2018–19 the German Government suspended some arms exports to Saudi Arabia and Turkey, both of which were among the largest arms importers in 2015–19. The suspension of some arms exports to Saudi Arabia in 2018 was in response to its military operations in Yemen and its involvement in the murder of the journalist Jamal Khashoggi in Istanbul in October 2018.[23] The suspension was formalized in March 2019 and in September 2019 was extended to March 2020. The main direct effect of the suspension on German arms exports in 2019 was a block on the delivery of 20 patrol boats

[23] Deutsche Welle, 'German arms export freeze on Saudi Arabia extended', 18 Sep. 2019. See also chapter 14, section IV, in this volume.

from an order for 35 made by Saudi Arabia in 2014. In 2019 Germany also announced that it would stop issuing new licences for exports of arms to Turkey that could be used in the conflict between Turkey and Kurdish rebel groups in Syria.[24] However, these restrictions did not apply to the export of naval equipment and will therefore not affect the delivery of six submarines to Turkey planned for 2022–27.[25]

The United Kingdom

The UK was the world's sixth-largest arms exporter in 2015–19, with 3.7 per cent of the total volume of arms exports. More than half (56 per cent) of British exports of major arms went to states in the Middle East (see table 9.3), mainly to Saudi Arabia (41 per cent of the total) and Oman (14 per cent).

British arms exports fell by 15 per cent between 2010–14 and 2015–19 (see table 9.1). This was primarily caused by decreases in arms exports to three of the UK's four largest recipients: India (–48 per cent), the USA (–27 per cent) and Saudi Arabia (–13 per cent). In contrast, exports to Oman rose by 77 per cent between 2010–14 and 2015–19, mainly as a result of the delivery of 12 Typhoon combat aircraft in 2017–18.

In 2015–19 the British Government came under pressure from parliamentarians, NGOs and the general public to place restrictions on arms exports to the Middle East, in particular to Saudi Arabia. The pressure increased in the light of allegations that arms supplied by the UK had been used in breaches of international humanitarian law by the Saudi Arabia-led coalition in its military intervention in Yemen.[26] In a court action against the British Government, a group of NGOs argued that the government had failed to properly assess Saudi Arabia's application of international humanitarian law, as it was obliged to do under British arms export licensing law. In June 2019 the Court of Appeal in London ordered the British Government to make the required assessments for both past and future export licences.[27] As a result, the government suspended the issuance of new licences for export

---

[24] Deutsche Presse-Agentur, 'Kein kompletter Stopp deutscher Rüstungsexporte für die Türkei' [No complete stop of German arms exports to Turkey], *Süddeutsche Zeitung*, 19 Oct. 2019; and Nußbaum, U., 'Schriftliche Frage an die Bundesregeirung im Monat Oktober 2019, Fragen Nt. 109' [Written question to the Federal Government in October 2019, Question no. 109], German Ministry for Economic Affairs and Energy, 18 Oct. 2019.

[25] Muller, N., 'German arms exports to Turkey at highest level since 2005', Deutsche Welle, 17 Oct. 2019.

[26] Maletta, G., 'Legal challenges to EU member states' arms exports to Saudi Arabia: Current status and potential implications', SIPRI Commentary, 28 June 2019.

[27] Court of Appeal of England and Wales, The Queen (on the application of Campaign Against Arms Trade) v. Secretary of State for International Trade and others, Case no. T3/2017/2079, Judgement, 20 June 2019; Cable, V., British Secretary of State for Business, Innovation and Skills, 'Consolidated EU and national arms export licensing criteria', Written statement, British House of Commons, *Hansard*, 25 Mar. 2014, column 9WS; and Isbister, R., 'The UK's arms-to-Saudi quagmire: From tragedy to farce', Saferworld, 20 Sep. 2019.

to Saudi Arabia and its coalition partners of arms that might be used in the conflict in Yemen.[28]

Arms suppliers outside Europe and North America

Countries outside Europe and North America play a relatively small role in exports of major arms: they accounted for just 13 per cent of total exports in 2015–19 and 11 per cent in 2010–14. Only nine of the top 25 arms-exporting countries in 2015–19 were outside Europe or North America: China, Israel, South Korea, Turkey, the UAE, Australia, South Africa, India and Brazil (see table 9.2). Of these countries, only China, Israel and South Korea were among the top 10 exporters of major arms.

China

China was the world's fifth-largest arms exporter in 2015–19, with a 5.5 per cent share of the total volume of arms exports (see table 9.1). After an increase of 133 per cent between 2005–2009 and 2010–14, Chinese arms exports grew by only 6.3 per cent between 2010–14 and 2015–19.

The number of countries to which China delivers arms has grown significantly: from 40 in 2010–14 to 53 in 2015–19. Nearly all of China's arms exports in 2015–19 were to developing states, and it has now clearly emerged as a competitor to Russia and Western arms exporters in selling arms to such states.[29]

Pakistan was the main recipient of Chinese arms exports in 2015–19 (receiving 35 per cent of the total), as it has been for all five-year periods since 1991. Overall, nearly three-quarters (74 per cent) of China's exports in 2015–19 went to a total of 16 other states in Asia and Oceania (see table 9.3).

In 2015–19, 16 per cent of China's exports of major arms went to states in Africa. China exported to 22 states in Africa—more than any other arms exporter. China also exported to eight states in the Middle East (accounting for 6.7 per cent of its exports) and to five states in the Americas (2.6 per cent).

Some of the world's largest arms importers in 2015–19—including Australia, India, Japan, South Korea, the USA and almost all European states—have not bought arms from China and are unlikely to do so in the near future. Unless there is a major political shift, it appears that China's arms exports are close to reaching a ceiling.

---

[28] Brooke-Holland, L., *UK Arms Exports to Saudi Arabia: Q&A*, Briefing Paper no. 08425 (House of Commons Library: London, 11 July 2019). See also chapter 14, section IV, in this volume.

[29] Raska, M. and Bitzinger, R. A., 'Strategic contours of China's arms transfers', *Strategic Studies Quarterly*, vol. 14, no. 1 (spring 2020), pp. 91–116.

Israel

Israel was the eighth-largest arms supplier in 2015–19. Its arms exports accounted for 3.0 per cent of the global total and were 77 per cent higher than in 2010–14 (see table 9.1). Although Israel has ranked higher than eighth in some earlier five-year periods, the volume of its arms exports in 2015–19 was at its highest level ever.

Israel exported major arms to 39 countries in 2015–19. India was the main recipient, receiving 45 per cent of Israeli arms exports (see table 9.2). Exports of air defence systems, missiles and sensors accounted for 79 per cent of Israeli exports of major arms in 2015–19 (see table 9.4).

South Korea

South Korea was the 10th-largest arms exporter in 2015–19, with a 2.1 per cent share of the global total. Its arms exports increased by 143 per cent between 2010–14 and 2015–19, the highest level of increase among exporters in the top 10 (see table 9.1).

The number of countries to which South Korea delivered arms rose from 7 in 2010–14 to 17 in 2015–19. Unlike in 2005–2009 and 2010–14, when well over half of South Korean arms exports went to just one state (Turkey), in 2015–19 the distribution of South Korean arms exports was far wider. Half of the volume went to other states in Asia and Oceania, 24 per cent to Europe and 17 per cent to the Middle East (see table 9.3), while the largest recipient (the UK) accounted for only 17 per cent of South Korean arms exports.

South Korea sees its arms industry as a 'growth engine' of the national economy and strongly promotes arms exports for economic reasons.[30] However, in 2015–19 its arms imports remained substantially higher than its arms exports.

---

[30] Grevatt, J., 'South Korea launches military export agency', *Jane's Defence Industry*, Nov. 2018. On South Korea's largest arms-producing companies see section V in this chapter.

II. Developments among the recipients of major arms, 2015–19

SIEMON T. WEZEMAN, ALEXANDRA KUIMOVA, DIEGO LOPES DA SILVA, NAN TIAN AND PIETER D. WEZEMAN

SIPRI has identified 160 states as importers of major arms in the five-year period 2015–19.[1] The top five arms importers—Saudi Arabia, India, Egypt, Australia and China—accounted for 36 per cent of the total volume of arms imports in 2015–19 (see tables 9.5 and 9.6). Of these, Saudi Arabia, India and China were also among the top five importers in 2010–14. The top five arms importers in 2015–19 are all in the two regions—Asia and Oceania and the Middle East—that received by far the greatest volume of imports in 2015–19 (see table 9.7). States in Europe, Africa and the Americas imported much lower overall volumes of major arms. This section reviews significant developments among the main recipients of arms in each region in turn.

Africa

Arms imports by states in Africa decreased by 16 per cent between 2010–14 and 2015–19 (see table 9.7). The three largest importers were Algeria (which received 58 per cent of arms transfers to Africa), Morocco (12 per cent) and Angola (7.0 per cent). Russia accounted for 49 per cent of arms exports to the region, the United States for 14 per cent and China for 13 per cent.

North Africa

Nearly three-quarters of the arms imported by African states in 2015–19 went to the four states in North Africa—Algeria, Libya, Morocco and Tunisia. The total volume of their arms imports increased by 8.5 per cent between 2010–14 and 2015–19 (see table 9.7).

Algeria alone accounted for 79 per cent of the subregion's arms imports in 2015–19. Its arms imports were 71 per cent higher than in 2010–14, making it the sixth-largest arms importer in the world in 2015–19 (see table 9.5). The increase occurred in the context of Algeria's long-standing tensions with its neighbour Morocco, internal tensions, and the conflicts in neighbouring Mali and Libya. As in 2010–14, Russia was the largest arms supplier to Algeria in 2015–19, providing 67 per cent of Algerian arms imports (see tables 9.6

---

[1] Except where indicated, the information on the arms deliveries and orders referred to in this section is taken from the SIPRI Arms Transfers Database. For a definition of 'major arms' and a description of how the volume of transfers is measured see box 9.1 in section I. The sources and methods used to produce the data discussed here are also presented on the SIPRI website. The figures here may differ from those in previous editions of the SIPRI Yearbook because the Arms Transfers Database is updated annually.

and 9.8). Algeria's arms imports from Russia, including 203 T-90 tanks and 14 Su-30 combat aircraft, were 40 per cent higher than in 2010–14.

Algeria appears to have been pursuing a policy of diversifying its arms suppliers in recent years and has signed contracts for large arms deals with China (for 3 frigates) and Germany (for almost 1000 armoured vehicles and 2 frigates). It received the bulk of deliveries related to these deals in 2015–19: 13 per cent of Algeria's arms imports in this period came from China, and the volume of these was nine times higher than in 2010–14; and 11 per cent came from Germany, and the volume of these was 30 times higher. However, while there are no known outstanding deliveries of Chinese arms to Algeria, there were unconfirmed reports in 2019 of new orders from Russia, including for tanks and around 30 combat aircraft.[2]

The volume of Morocco's imports of major arms in 2015–19 was 62 per cent lower than in 2010–14 (see table 9.5). France was the main arms supplier to Morocco in 2010–14, largely due to the delivery of combat aircraft and ships. As the contracts were completed, France's share fell to 8.9 per cent in 2015–19. Because deliveries from the USA (mainly combat and other aircraft, tanks and other armoured vehicles, and artillery) were much more stable, the US share increased to 91 per cent (up from 29 per cent in 2010–14). Morocco's arms imports are likely to grow in the coming years: in 2019 it announced plans to place large orders for advanced military equipment, including 25 combat aircraft and 24–36 combat helicopters from the USA and surface-to-air missile (SAM) systems from France.[3]

Arms transfers and the conflict in Libya

The civil war between Libya's internationally recognized Government of National Accord (GNA) and the self-described Libyan National Army (LNA) that started in 2014 continued in 2019.[4] Both sides have received arms from abroad in violation of the arms embargo imposed on Libya by the United Nations Security Council in 2011, but no country has been sanctioned for this.[5]

Details about these arms deliveries are scarce and the volume cannot be estimated. For example, in 2019 the GNA received an unknown number of armoured vehicles and armed unmanned aerial vehicles (UAVs) from Turkey. In 2015–19 the LNA received armoured vehicles from Jordan and the United

---

[2] Safronov, I., [Algeria bought Russian fighters for about $2 billion], *Vedomosti*, 9 Sep. 2019 (in Russian); and *Military Watch*, 'Finest armour in Africa: Algerian Army receives new batch of T-90SA battle tanks', 12 Jan. 2020.

[3] US Defense Security Cooperation Agency, 'Morocco—F-16 Block-72 new purchase', News Release no. 19-09, 25 Mar. 2019; US Defense Security Cooperation Agency, 'Morocco—AH-64E helicopters', News Release no. 19-63, 20 Nov. 2019; and Moroccan Defense Network, 'Morocco buys French CAESAR howitzer and surface to air VL-MICA missiles', 21 Jan. 2020.

[4] On the conflict in Libya see chapter 6, section IV, in this volume.

[5] See chapter 14, section II, in this volume.

Table 9.5. The 50 largest recipients of major arms, 2015–19

The table lists states, international organizations and non-state actors that imported major arms in the 5-year period 2015–19. Figures for volume of imports are SIPRI trend-indicator values (TIV).

Rank			Volume of imports (TIV, millions)		Share (%),	Change in volume (%), compared
2015–19	2010–14[a]	Recipient	2019	2015–19	2015–19	with 2010–14
1	2	Saudi Arabia	3 673	17 694	12	130
2	1	India	2 964	13 412	9.2	−32
3	14	Egypt	1 193	8 396	5.8	212
4	6	Australia	1 399	7 133	4.9	40
5	5	China	887	6 300	4.3	3.3
6	10	Algeria	140	6 150	4.2	71
7	8	South Korea	1 510	5 004	3.4	3.3
8	4	UAE	644	4 982	3.4	−18
9	17	Iraq	175	4 960	3.4	98
10	46	Qatar	2 258	4 943	3.4	631
11	3	Pakistan	561	3 830	2.6	−39
12	11	Viet Nam	161	3 212	2.2	−9.3
13	9	United States	1 048	2 925	2.0	−37
14	33	Israel	507	2 873	2.0	181
15	7	Turkey	833	2 621	1.8	−48
16	23	Japan	891	2 574	1.8	72
17	15	Indonesia	219	2 553	1.8	−4.6
18	19	United Kingdom	377	2 503	1.7	17
19	12	Singapore	614	2 411	1.7	−29
20	28	Bangladesh	743	2 289	1.6	93
21	40	Italy	186	2 246	1.5	175
22	31	Thailand	301	1 741	1.2	67
23	26	Oman	105	1 710	1.2	24
24	35	Norway	443	1 628	1.1	67
25	55	Kazakhstan	312	1 523	1.0	238
26	18	Taiwan	51	1 379	0.9	−41
27	27	Canada	200	1 332	0.9	4.2
28	36	Greece	165	1 328	0.9	39
29	20	Afghanistan	391	1 296	0.9	−38
30	21	Azerbaijan	25	1 231	0.8	−40
31	13	Morocco	26	1 231	0.8	−62
32	41	Jordan	85	1 156	0.8	54
33	24	Myanmar	252	1 006	0.7	−32
34	25	Brazil	169	869	0.6	−37
35	75	Philippines	187	866	0.6	403
36	43	Mexico	3	863	0.6	17
37	63	Belarus	331	831	0.6	186
38	32	Netherlands	490	811	0.6	−21
39	34	Kuwait	70	778	0.5	−22
40	39	Poland	308	761	0.5	−14
41	45	Finland	70	734	0.5	8.3

Rank			Volume of imports (TIV, millions)		Share (%),	Change in volume (%), compared
2015–19	2010–14[a]	Recipient	2019	2015–19	2015–19	with 2010–14
42	109	Angola	166	734	0.5	2 124
43	48	Malaysia	70	729	0.5	18
44	52	Turkmenistan	–	692	0.5	33
45	62	Peru	–	591	0.4	102
46	37	Spain	56	502	0.3	–47
47	58	France	102	450	0.3	23
48	65	Iran	3	437	0.3	61
49	67	Romania	61	378	0.3	65
50	89	Armenia	248	377	0.3	416
..	..	Unknown recipient(s)	41	134	0.1	84
..	..	118 others	1 488	8 669	5.9	..
		Total	**27 194**	**145 776**	**100**	**5.5**

.. = not available or not applicable; – = nil; UAE = United Arab Emirates.

Note: The SIPRI TIV is an indicator of the volume of arms transfers and not their financial value. The method for calculating the TIV is described in box 9.1 in section I.

[a] The rank order for recipients in 2010–14 differs from that published in *SIPRI Yearbook 2015* because of subsequent revision of figures for these years.

Source: SIPRI Arms Transfers Database, Mar. 2020.

Arab Emirates (UAE), combat helicopters from Belarus, supplied via the UAE, and combat aircraft from Egypt. Combat aircraft and armed UAVs originating from the UAE have been used in the fighting, including in 2019.[6] It is unclear whether they were operated by the UAE or whether the UAE had supplied them to the LNA.[7]

The UAE's involvement in Libya is part of its assertive foreign policy, which also includes its military intervention in Yemen.[8] In 2015–19 the UAE accounted for 3.4 per cent of global arms imports. It received major arms from a total of 17 countries in 2015–19 but the bulk (68 per cent) came from the USA (see tables 9.6 and 9.8). In 2019 the UN Security Council called on states not to intervene in the conflict in Libya.[9] In the same year the UAE had major arms import deals ongoing with Australia, Brazil, Canada, China, France, Russia, South Africa, Spain, Sweden, Turkey, the United Kingdom and the USA.

[6] United Nations, Security Council, Final report of the panel of experts on Libya established pursuant to Security Council Resolution 1973 (2011), 29 Nov. 2019, S/2019/914, 9 Dec. 2019, paras 108–10 and annex 15, paras 14–16.

[7] United Nations, S/2019/914 (note 6), para. 108 and annex 15, paras 12–16.

[8] See e.g. United Nations, Security Council, Final report of the Panel of Experts on Yemen, S/2020/70, 27 Jan. 2020.

[9] United Nations, Security Council, Press statement on Libya, SC/13873, 5 July 2019; and UN Security Council Resolution 2486, 12 Sep. 2019, para. 4.

Table 9.6. The 40 largest recipients of major arms and their three main suppliers, 2015–19

Rank 2015–19	Recipient	Main suppliers (share of recipient's total imports, %), 2015–19		
		1st	2nd	3rd
1	Saudi Arabia	USA (73)	UK (13)	France (4.3)
2	India	Russia (56)	Israel (14)	France (12)
3	Egypt	France (35)	Russia (34)	USA (15)
4	Australia	USA (68)	Spain (21)	France (3.6)
5	China	Russia (76)	France (8.8)	Ukraine (6.9)
6	Algeria	Russia (67)	China (13)	Germany (11)
7	South Korea	USA (55)	Germany (30)	Spain (7.8)
8	UAE	USA (68)	France (11)	Netherlands (3.4)
9	Iraq	USA (45)	Russia (34)	South Korea (8.6)
10	Qatar	USA (50)	France (34)	Germany (9.2)
11	Pakistan	China (73)	Russia (6.6)	Italy (6.1)
12	Viet Nam	Russia (74)	Israel (12)	Belarus (4.9)
13	United States	Germany (21)	UK (17)	Netherlands (13)
14	Israel	USA (78)	Germany (16)	Italy (6.2)
15	Turkey	USA (38)	Italy (24)	Spain (19)
16	Japan	USA (96)	UK (2.4)	Sweden (1.6)
17	Indonesia	USA (20)	Netherlands (18)	South Korea (16)
18	United Kingdom	USA (67)	South Korea (21)	Germany (4.7)
19	Singapore	USA (37)	Spain (24)	France (18)
20	Bangladesh	China (72)	Russia (15)	UK (2.4)
21	Italy	USA (62)	Germany (25)	Israel (6.5)
22	Thailand	South Korea (21)	China (21)	Ukraine (14)
23	Oman	UK (45)	USA (13)	Norway (12)
24	Norway	USA (77)	Italy (7.9)	South Korea (7.2)
25	Kazakhstan	Russia (90)	Spain (3.2)	China (2.1)
26	Taiwan	USA (100)	–	–
27	Canada	USA (56)	Netherlands (11)	Israel (9.6)
28	Greece	Germany (64)	USA (19)	UK (7.5)
29	Afghanistan	USA (87)	Brazil (8.8)	Canada (1.2)
30	Azerbaijan	Israel (60)	Russia (31)	Turkey (3.2)
31	Morocco	USA (91)	France (8.9)	UK (0.3)
32	Jordan	USA (30)	Netherlands (30)	Russia (10)
33	Myanmar	China (49)	Russia (16)	India (14)
34	Brazil	France (26)	USA (20)	UK (17)
35	Philippines	South Korea (32)	Indonesia (21)	USA (19)
36	Mexico	USA (64)	Spain (9.5)	France (8.5)
37	Belarus	Russia (98)	Ukraine (1.2)	China (0.5)
38	Netherlands	USA (76)	Germany (13)	Italy (7.6)
39	Kuwait	USA (70)	France (9.5)	Switzerland (7.1)
40	Poland	USA (29)	Germany (18)	Italy (14)

UAE = United Arab Emirates.

Source: SIPRI Arms Transfers Database, Mar. 2020.

Table 9.7. Imports of major arms, by region and subregion, 2010–14 and 2015–19

Figures for volume of imports are SIPRI trend-indicator values (TIV).

Recipient region	Volume of imports (TIV)		Change in volume from 2010–14 to 2015–19 (%)	Share of total imports (%)	
	2010–14	2015–19		2010–14	2015–19
Africa	12 502	10 528	−16	9.0	7.2
North Africa	7 183	7 793	8.5	5.2	5.3
Sub-Saharan Africa	5 318	2 720	−49	3.8	1.9
Americas	13 729	8 292	−40	9.9	5.7
Central America and the Caribbean	998	1 228	23	0.7	0.8
North America	5 907	4 257	−2.5	4.3	2.9
South America	6 825	2 770	−59	4.9	1.9
Asia and Oceania	64 103	59 041	−7.9	46	41
Central Asia	1 019	2 629	158	0.7	1.8
East Asia	14 896	15 347	3.0	11	11
Oceania	5 321	7 287	37	3.9	5.0
South Asia	29 237	21 079	−28	21	14
South East Asia	13 627	12 698	−6.8	9.9	8.7
Europe	15 876	16 389	3.2	11	11
Central Europe	1 703	2 036	20	1.2	1.4
Eastern Europe	3 020	2 944	−2.5	2.2	2.0
Western Europe	11 153	11 409	2.3	8.1	7.8
Middle East	31 867	51 261	61	23	35
Other	126	273	117	0.1	0.2

Note: The SIPRI TIV is an indicator of the volume of arms transfers and not their financial value. The method for calculating the TIV is described in box 9.1 in section I.

Source: SIPRI Arms Transfers Database, Mar. 2020.

Sub-Saharan Africa

States in sub-Saharan Africa accounted for 26 per cent of African arms imports in 2015–19. The total volume of arms imported by states in the subregion was 49 per cent lower than in 2010–14 (see table 9.7) and was at its lowest level since 1995–99. In 2015–19 Russia supplied 36 per cent of the arms imported by states in the subregion, China 19 per cent and France 7.6 per cent. The five largest arms importers in sub-Saharan Africa—Angola, Nigeria, Senegal, Sudan and Zambia—accounted for 63 per cent of all arms imports into the subregion. There were falls in the volumes of arms imported by Nigeria (−33 per cent) and Sudan (−48 per cent) between 2010–14 and 2015–19, while there were increases in those of Angola (2124 per cent), Senegal (306 per cent) and Zambia (107 per cent).

Angola accounted for 27 per cent of arms imports into sub-Saharan Africa and it was the 42nd-largest arms importer globally in 2015–19 (see table 9.5). Even though Angola's economy was in recession and its military spending fell in each year of the five-year period, its arms imports were 22 times higher than in 2010–14.[10] The increase can largely be attributed to deliveries from Russia, which supplied 68 per cent of Angola's imports in 2015–19. The Russian deliveries included 12 Su-30 combat aircraft, 12 Mi-24 combat helicopters and 12 Mi-17 transport helicopters.

For four of the top five importers in sub-Saharan Africa, China was either the largest (in the cases of Sudan and Zambia) or second-largest (in the cases of Nigeria and Senegal) arms supplier in 2015–19. This is perhaps evidence of China's growing willingness to engage with African countries in a peace and security role. China's ambitions in this area were also in evidence at the first China–Africa Defense and Security Forum in 2018 and the first China–Africa Peace and Security Forum in 2019, both organized by the Chinese Ministry of National Defense.[11] China is not alone in attempting to secure greater influence in Africa through arms exports. The USA, Russia and France are also among the largest suppliers to Africa and each has a military presence in Africa.[12] All these suppliers seem to have the aim of winning influence both in specific countries and the region as a whole.[13]

South Africa was the largest arms importer in sub-Saharan Africa in 2005–2009, mainly as a result of deliveries of frigates and submarines from Germany and combat aircraft from Sweden. In 2010–14 the volume of its arms imports fell by 78 per cent and in 2015–19 it nearly reached zero. This sharp decrease was partly a result of South Africa's severe economic problems, which led to several rounds of cuts to the military budget.[14] In 2018–19 there were reports that the South African armed forces were encountering both technical and financial problems in the operation of the frigates and submarines supplied by Germany and that it had received only 40 per cent of the funding needed for the South African Air Force.[15] The financial and operational challenges raise questions about the long-term viability of South Africa's policy of procuring expensive major arms.

[10] SIPRI Military Expenditure Database.

[11] Kovrig, M., 'China expands its peace and security footprint in Africa', International Crisis Group, 24 Oct. 2018; Grieger, G., 'China's growing role as a security actor in Africa', Briefing, European Parliamentary Research Service, Oct. 2019; and Chen, L. et al., 'Overview of 1st China–Africa Peace and Security Forum', Chinese Ministry of National Defense, 17 July 2019. See also Huang, C. and Ismail, O., 'China', eds O. Ismail and E. Sköns, SIPRI, Security Activities of External Actors in Africa (Oxford University Press: Oxford, 2014), pp. 15–37.

[12] eds Ismail and Sköns (note 11).

[13] The Economist, 'The new scramble for Africa', 7 Mar. 2019.

[14] Wingrin, D., 'Defence minister sounds budget alarm bells', DefenceWeb, 18 July 2019.

[15] Wingrin, D., 'SA Navy in danger of losing frigate and submarine capabilities due to declining budget', DefenceWeb, 19 Sep. 2019; Badri-Maharaj, S., 'South Africa boosts naval capabilities: But can it afford an expansion?', Manohar Parrikar Institute for Defence Studies and Analyses, 5 Feb. 2018; and Wingrin, D., 'Parliament hears of parlous state of the Air Force', DefenceWeb, 16 Sep. 2018.

The Americas

Imports of major arms by states in the Americas decreased by 40 per cent between 2010–14 and 2015–19 (see table 9.7).

The USA was the largest importer of major arms in the region in 2015–19, receiving 35 per cent of all deliveries. The main exporters to the USA were Germany (21 per cent), the UK (17 per cent) and the Netherlands (13 per cent; see table 9.6). The USA was also the largest supplier to states in the Americas: it supplied 23 per cent of all arms imports by states in the region in 2015–19, up from 17 per cent in 2010–14.

While Russia was among the largest arms suppliers to the Americas in 2010–14, supplying 16 per cent of the total volume, its share decreased sharply in 2015–19 to just 3.0 per cent. The fall was mainly because Venezuela—the main importer of Russian arms in the region in 2010–14—did not import major arms from Russia in 2015–19 as a result of an ongoing economic crisis (see below).

Central America and the Caribbean

Arms imports by states in Central America and the Caribbean increased by 23 per cent between 2010–14 and 2015–19 (see table 9.7). Mexico received 70 per cent of all arms imported into the subregion in 2015–19. The volume of Mexico's arms imports increased by 17 per cent between 2010–14 and 2015–19 (see table 9.5) in part because of acquisitions of major arms such as helicopters and armoured vehicles for its ongoing military operations against drug cartels.[16] The USA was Mexico's largest arms supplier by far, accounting for 64 per cent of its arms imports in 2015–19 (see table 9.6).

South America

Arms imports by states in South America fell by 15 per cent between 2005–2009 and 2010–14, and by a further 59 per cent between 2010–14 and 2015–19 (see table 9.7). The USA accounted for 19 per cent of the subregion's arms imports in 2015–19, France for 16 per cent and Italy for 8.6 per cent.

Venezuela was the largest arms importer in South America in 2010–14, when it was re-equipping with mainly Russian arms. However, Venezuela's arms imports in 2015–19 were 88 per cent lower than in 2010–14, with no deliveries at all recorded in 2017–19, as it continued to be affected by a severe economic crisis.[17] China was the largest arms supplier to Venezuela in 2015–19, accounting for 58 per cent of imports, followed by Ukraine with a 38 per cent share.

---

[16] On the impact of the operations against drug cartels on Mexico's military expenditure see chapter 8, section II, in this volume.

[17] Ribando Seelke, C. et al., *Venezuela: Background and US Relations*, Congressional Research Service (CRS) Report for Congress R44841 (US Congress, CRS: Washington, DC, 12 Mar. 2020).

Although the volume of Brazil's arms imports in 2015–19 was 37 per cent lower than in 2010–14 (see table 9.5), it was the largest arms importer in South America and accounted for 31 per cent of the subregion's arms imports. France became Brazil's largest arms supplier in 2015–19, providing 26 per cent of its imports (see table 9.6), mainly due to the delivery of 23 helicopters and a second-hand amphibious assault ship. In 2010–14 it had been only the fourth-largest arms supplier to Brazil (with a 9.7 per cent share), behind Germany (31 per cent), the USA (22 per cent) and Russia (12 per cent). By the end of 2019 Brazil had the largest volume of outstanding orders for arms of any state in South America, including orders for combat aircraft from Sweden and submarines from France.

Asia and Oceania

Arms imports by states in Asia and Oceania decreased by 7.9 per cent between 2010–14 and 2015–19 (see table 9.7). States in the region received 41 per cent of the total global volume of arms imports in 2015–19, compared with 46 per cent in 2010–14. Of the 10 largest importers in 2015–19, four are in Asia and Oceania: India, Australia, China and South Korea. Russia accounted for 29 per cent of arms imports by states in the region, the USA for 27 per cent and China for 10 per cent.

The decrease in the regional total disguises wide variations in subregional trends. Between 2010–14 and 2015–19 there were increases in arms transfers to Central Asia (158 per cent), Oceania (37 per cent) and East Asia (3.0 per cent), while there were decreases in transfers to South Asia (–28 per cent) and South East Asia (–6.8 per cent).[18] Overall, the large absolute decrease in imports into South Asia—in particular India and Pakistan—had the greatest influence on the regional trend.

India and Pakistan

In 2010–14 India was the largest and Pakistan the third-largest importer of major arms globally. Between 2010–14 and 2015–19 arms imports by India decreased by 32 per cent and those by Pakistan fell by 39 per cent, making India the second-largest arms importer and Pakistan the 11th-largest in 2015–19 (see table 9.5). India accounted for 9.2 per cent of global imports of major arms, about 3.5 times Pakistan's share of 2.6 per cent. Although both countries produce major arms, they remain largely dependent on imports and have substantial outstanding orders and plans for imports of all types of major arms.

---

[18] On arms imports by South East Asian states see Wezeman, S. T., *Arms Flows to South East Asia* (SIPRI: Stockholm, Dec. 2019).

Russia was the largest supplier to India in both 2010–14 and 2015–19, but its deliveries fell by 47 per cent and its share of total Indian arms imports fell from 72 to 56 per cent (see tables 9.6 and 9.8). The USA became the second-largest arms supplier to India in 2010–14 as the security relationship between the two countries developed into a strategic partnership.[19] However, the new closer relationship did not lead to a continued increase in US arms sales to India. On the contrary, in 2015–19 Indian arms imports from the USA were 51 per cent lower than in 2010–14, and the USA was only the fourth-largest supplier of major arms to India. This was partly because lengthy negotiations on planned acquisitions had reached an impasse due to India's insistence on including technology transfers as part of the deals and the USA's reluctance to agree to this.[20] There was a breakthrough in the negotiations in December 2019 when the two states signed an agreement on technology transfers.[21] This paved the way for new US sales of advanced major arms to India.[22] There is, nonetheless, still a risk that the USA might invoke its 2017 Countering America's Adversaries Through Sanctions Act (CAATSA) to block future deals with India.[23] CAATSA allows the US Government to deny arms exports to states that buy arms from Russia—and India has ordered, among other things, S-400 SAM systems from Russia. In June 2019 a senior official of the US Department of State stated that the USA had informed India that at some point 'a strategic choice has to be made about partnerships and a strategic choice about what weapons systems and platforms . . . to adopt'.[24]

Another reason why the developing strategic partnership between the USA and India might not lead to an immediate rise in arms imports from the USA is that India appears to be maintaining its long-standing policy of supplier diversification.[25] In 2015–19 India's arms imports from Israel increased by 175 per cent (mainly land-based and naval air defence systems) and those from France increased by 715 per cent (including the first 2 of 6 Scorpene submarines and the first 4 of 36 Rafale combat aircraft). This made Israel the second-largest and France the third-largest supplier of major arms to India in the period, ahead of the USA.

[19] Council on Foreign Relations, 'US–India relations 1947–2020', 2020.

[20] Rej, A., 'Dalliance no more: How India–US defence trade relationship matures over years', News18, 24 Feb. 2020.

[21] Indo-Asian News Service (IANS), 'India, US sign defence tech transfer pact, pledge to boost strategic ties at 2+2', Economic Times, 19 Dec. 2019.

[22] Sink, J. et al., 'US and India to sign $3 billion in defense deals, Trump says', Fortune, 24 Feb. 2020.

[23] Countering America's Adversaries Through Sanctions Act, US Public Law 115–44, signed into law 2 Aug. 2017. On CAATSA see also section I in this chapter; and Wezeman, S. T. et al., 'Supplier developments, 2018', SIPRI Yearbook 2019, pp. 235–39.

[24] Wells, A., US Acting Assistant Secretary of State for South and Central Asia, quoted in Rajghatta, C., 'US cautions India over S-400 deal with Russia, cites strategic partnership choices', Times of India, 15 June 2019.

[25] Kapoor, N., India–Russia Ties in a Changing World Order: In Pursuit of a 'Special Strategic Partnership', Observer Research Foundation (ORF) Occasional Paper no. 218 (ORF: New Dehli, 22 Oct. 2019).

Table 9.8. The 10 largest recipients of major arms and their suppliers, 2015–19

Figures are the percentage shares of the recipient's total volume of imports received from each supplier. Only suppliers with a share of 1 per cent or more of total imports of any of the 10 largest recipients are included in the table. Smaller suppliers are grouped together under 'Others'.

Supplier	Recipient									
	Saudi Arabia	India	Egypt	Australia	China	Algeria	South Korea	UAE	Iraq	Qatar
Bulgaria	0.1	–	–	–	–	–	–	–	2.2	–
Canada	1.6	0.7	0.3	0.6	–	–	–	1.7	–	0.3
China	0.9	–	0.5	–	..	13	–	2.5	1.1	2.4
Czechia	–	–	–	–	..	–	–	–	3.8	–
France	4.3	12	35	3.6	8.8	1.3	1.1	11	–	34
Germany	1.6	1.5	7.6	1.4	0.7	11	30	1.2	0.5	9.2
Israel	–	14	–	–	–	–	2.0	–	–	–
Italy	1.3	0.1	0.1	2.2	–	1.9	–	2.2	3.4	0.8
Netherlands	0.1	0.1	0.5	–	–	0.6	–	3.4	–	–
Russia	<0.05	56	34	–	76	67	–	2.4	34	0.2
South Africa	0.1	0.3	0.7	–	–	0.3	–	1.7	<0.05	–
South Korea	–	1.6	–	–	–	–	..	–	8.6	–
Spain	1.7	–	1.7	21	–	–	7.8	1.2	0.6	–
Sweden	–	–	–	–	–	1.7	0.2	1.8	–	–
Switzerland	1.1	0.1	–	3.4	3.1	–	–	–	–	1.8
Turkey	–	–	–	–	–	1.2	–	2.4	–	1.3
UAE	–	–	2.6	–	–	–	–	..	–	–
Ukraine	–	0.8	–	–	6.9	–	–	–	–	0.5
United Kingdom	13	2.7	–	0.3	3.3	1.2	3.4	0.3	–	–
United States	73	9.1	15	68	–	0.4	55	68	45	50
Uzbekistan	–	–	–	–	1.6	–	–	–	–	–
Others	0.5	0.3	1.6	<0.05	–	0.1	–	0.4	1.0	<0.05

.. = not available or not applicable; – = nil; <0.05 = between 0 and 0.05; UAE = United Arab Emirates.

Source: SIPRI Arms Transfers Database, Mar. 2020.

The decrease of 39 per cent in Pakistan's arms imports in 2015–19 was linked to the reduction in arms supplied as military aid from the USA since around 2011. This culminated in an almost complete halt in aid in 2017.[26] As a consequence, the USA's share of Pakistan's arms imports fell from 30 per cent in 2010–14 to only 4.1 per cent in 2015–19. In an attempt to meet its ongoing demand for major arms, Pakistan turned increasingly to China: the latter's share of Pakistan's arms imports rose from 51 per cent in 2010–14 to 73 per cent in 2015–19 (see table 9.6). Pakistan also continued to import major arms from European states in 2015–19 (in particular Russia and Italy) and strengthened its arms import relations with Turkey with orders for 30 combat helicopters and 4 frigates in 2018.

Cross-border attacks between India and Pakistan intensified in early 2019.[27] Pakistan reportedly used JF-17 combat aircraft imported from China, equipped with Russian engines, and F-16 combat aircraft from the USA supported by Saab-2000 airborne early warning and control (AEW&C) aircraft from Sweden.[28] India reportedly used Mirage-2000 combat aircraft imported from France, MiG-21 combat aircraft from Russia, SPICE guided bombs from Israel and FH-77 artillery from Sweden.[29] Some of these major arms, such as the SPICE guided bombs and JF-17 aircraft, were recent deliveries but some, such as the MiG-21 aircraft and the FH-77 artillery, were supplied decades ago. This shows that exported arms can play a major role in an armed conflict many years after delivery.

East Asia

Arms imports by East Asian states increased by 3.0 per cent between 2010–14 and 2015–19 (see table 9.7). Together, states in East Asia imported 11 per cent of all arms transfers in 2015–19.

China, which accounted for 4.3 per cent of global arms imports in 2015–19, was the largest arms importer in East Asia and the fifth largest in the world (see table 9.5). Although China has developed an advanced arms industry, it remains reliant on imports for certain arms technologies. Its arms imports increased by 3.3 per cent between 2010–14 and 2015–19, largely due to deliveries in 2018–19 from Russia. These included the engines for most combat and large transport aircraft produced in China and S-400 SAM systems. China also continued to acquire some engines for large military

---

[26] Kronstadt, K. A., 'Pakistan–US relations', In Focus, US Congress, Congressional Research Service (CRS), 15 July 2019.

[27] On the conflict between India and Pakistan see chapter 4, section II, in this volume

[28] Seligman, L., 'India's dogfight loss could be a win for US weapons-makers', *Foreign Policy*, 5 Mar. 2019; and Press Trust of India, 'JF-17 used to shoot down Indian aircraft, says Pakistan military', *Economic Times*, 25 Mar. 2019.

[29] Frantzman, S. J. and Ahronheim, A., 'If India and Pakistan go to war, Israeli weapons could be decisive', *Jerusalem Post*, 1 Mar. 2019; Seligman (note 28); and Gurung, S. K., 'Army uses Bofors guns to respond to border shelling by Pakistan', *Economic Times* (New Delhi), 7 Mar. 2019.

ships from France and Ukraine or to produce them under licence in 2015–19. In addition, it continued to produce helicopters of French design under licence. However, China's need to rely on arms imports is rapidly diminishing as its arms industry is mastering the design and production of indigenous alternatives. For example, the latest versions of Chinese combat aircraft reportedly use Chinese engines instead of Russian engines.[30]

Taiwan imports all of its major arms from the USA (see table 9.6). Its arms imports in 2015–19 were 41 per cent lower than in 2010–14 (see table 9.5). However, in 2019 it placed orders for 66 F-16V combat aircraft and 108 tanks from the USA. The USA had initially been reluctant to agree to these transfers because of the damage that previous arms sales to Taiwan had caused to Chinese–US relations.[31] These relations were especially sensitive in 2019 as China and the USA were negotiating a trade agreement.[32] The sales appear to be in line with the USA's perception that China is the major potential military threat to the USA and its allies in Asia and Oceania and with its policy of creating a network of allies and friendly states in the region. China objected to the arms deal and announced that it would impose sanctions on the US companies involved, some of which have growing civilian markets in China.[33] While the US sales will increase Taiwan's arms imports in the coming years, they are relatively minor compared with China's new arms acquisitions (mainly from Chinese domestic production).

The volume of arms imported by Japan increased by 72 per cent between 2010–14 and 2015–19 (see table 9.5). It mainly imports major arms from the USA, which accounted for 89 per cent of Japan's imports in 2010–14 and 96 per cent in 2015–19. Japan's imports and the high US share are both likely to continue to rise based on new orders for arms from the USA, including an order in 2019 for 105 F-35 combat aircraft.

---

[30] Rupprecht, A. and Ju, J., 'Images suggest China has begun fitting indigenous WS10 engine into J-10C fighters', *Jane's Defence Weekly*, 5 Mar. 2020.

[31] Gady, F.-S., 'US administration accused of delaying F-16 fighter jets sale to Taiwan', The Diplomat, 31 July 2019; and Wong, E., 'Trump administration approves F-16 fighter jet sales to Taiwan', *New York Times*, 16 Aug. 2019.

[32] US Department of Defense (DOD), Office of the Secretary of Defense, *Military and Security Developments Involving the People's Republic of China 2019*, Annual Report to Congress (DOD: Arlington, VA, May 2019); US Defense Intelligence Agency (DIA), *China Military Power: Modernizing a Force to Fight and Win* (DIA: Washington, DC, 2019); US Department of State, *A Free and Open Indo-Pacific: Advancing a Shared Vision* (Department of State: Washington, DC, 4 Nov. 2019); and Dotson, J., 'Arms sales and high-level visits signal closer US relations with Taiwan', *China Brief*, vol. 19, no. 14 (31 July 2019).

[33] E.g. Zhou, C., 'US defence giant Honeywell distances itself from Taiwan under threat of China sanctions over arms deal', *South China Morning Post*, 16 July 2019.

Europe

Imports of major arms by states in Europe fell by 37 per cent between 2005–2009 and 2010–14. However, this downward trend reversed in 2015–19: the volume of arms imports by European states was 3.2 per cent higher than in 2010–14 and accounted for 11 per cent of the global total (see table 9.7). The USA supplied 41 per cent of the region's arms imports in 2015–19, Germany 14 per cent and Russia 10 per cent.

Arms transfers and armed conflict in Europe

Major arms were used in conflicts in Europe in 2015–19: in eastern Ukraine and in skirmishes between Armenia and Azerbaijan.[34]

The volume of arms imported by Ukraine was low in 2015–19, despite the armed conflict there, mainly because it had inherited large inventories of major arms from the Soviet Union and has a substantial local arms industry.[35] Its largest imports of major arms included 50 second-hand armoured vehicles from Czechia and 210 anti-tank missiles from the USA.

Armenia's arms imports increased by 416 per cent between 2010–14 and 2015–19 (see table 9.5). Nearly all (94 per cent) of its arms imports in 2015–19 came from Russia. Despite a fall of 40 per cent between 2010–14 and 2015–19, the volume of arms imported by Azerbaijan in 2015–19 was over three times higher than that of Armenia. Israel supplied 60 per cent and Russia 31 per cent of Azerbaijan's arms imports in 2015–19 (see table 9.6). In 2018 Azerbaijan received LORA surface-to-surface missiles (SSMs) from Israel, probably in response to Armenia's acquisition of Iskander SSMs from Russia in 2016. With these acquisitions, each state is now capable of attacking key targets deep inside the other's territory.

Re-equipping European air forces

In many West and Central European states, growing tensions with Russia and involvement in military air operations in the Middle East have contributed to a growing demand for new combat aircraft.[36] In 2015–19 states in Western and Central Europe imported a total of 59 new combat aircraft. At the end of 2019, these states had outstanding orders for imports of 380 new combat aircraft (356 F-35s and 24 F-16s), most for delivery in 2020–29.

All of these aircraft will be supplied by the USA. In most cases, they were selected over rival offers from a French company (the Rafale), a Swedish company (the Gripen) or a consortium of British, German, Italian and Spanish

---

[34] On these armed conflicts see chapter 5, sections I and II, in this volume.

[35] Wezeman, S. T. and Kuimova, A., 'Ukraine and Black Sea security', SIPRI Background Paper, Dec. 2018.

[36] On spending on military equipment by European members of the North Atlantic Treaty Organization (NATO) see chapter 8, section III, in this volume.

companies (the Typhoon) supported by their respective governments. For example, in 2019 Bulgaria selected the F-16V combat aircraft over the Typhoon and the Gripen.[37] Similarly, Poland selected the F-35A over European alternatives on the basis that it wanted to procure a fifth-generation, multi-role combat aircraft.[38] West and Central European suppliers have been more successful in selling other categories of major arms to their European neighbours. For example, in 2015–19 all warships and all tanks imported or ordered for import by European states came from suppliers in Europe.

The Middle East

The volume of arms imported by states in the Middle East was 61 per cent higher in 2015–19 than in 2010–14 (see table 9.7). Five of the world's top 10 arms-importing countries in 2015–19 are in the Middle East: Saudi Arabia (which received 35 per cent of arms transfers to the region), Egypt (16 per cent), the UAE (9.7 per cent), Iraq (9.7 per cent) and Qatar (9.6 per cent). Israel and Turkey also imported significant volumes of arms (see table 9.5). The USA supplied 53 per cent of total arms transfers to the region, France 12 per cent and Russia 11 per cent.

Saudi Arabia

Saudi Arabia was the world's largest arms importer in 2015–19, accounting for 12 per cent of all imports of major arms (see table 9.5). The volume of its arms imports was 130 per cent higher in 2015–19 than in 2010–14. The USA is by far the largest arms supplier to Saudi Arabia—in 2015–19 it accounted for 73 per cent of Saudi Arabian arms imports (see tables 9.6 and 9.8), followed by the UK (13 per cent).

Discussions in the USA, Canada and many West European states about restrictions on arms exports to Saudi Arabia continued in 2019 based on concerns that the Saudi Arabian-led military intervention in Yemen involved violations of international humanitarian law and was prolonging the civil war there (see section I).[39] However, Saudi Arabia continued to import arms from some of these states in 2019, including 30 F-15SA combat aircraft and large numbers of missiles and guided bombs from the USA, armoured vehicles from Canada, armoured vehicles and patrol boats from France, and missiles

---

[37] Adamowski, J., 'Bulgaria approves draft deals to buy F-16s in record defense procurement', *Defense News*, 10 July 2019; and Radio Free Europe/Radio Liberty, 'Bulgaria gives final green light to biggest military acquisition since fall of communism', 31 July 2019.

[38] Jarocki, M., 'Poland's billion-dollar-procurement programmes', European Security & Defence, 7 May 2019.

[39] On control on exports to Saudi Arabia see also chapter 14, section IV, in this volume; and e.g. Russell, A., 'Experts dispute Canada's claim of no link between Saudi arms sales and human rights abuses', Global News, 22 Nov. 2019. On the armed conflict in Yemen see chapter 6, section V, in this volume.

and trainer aircraft from the UK. Unlike the other European suppliers among the top 10 arms exporters in 2015–19, Germany suspended the bulk of its—already limited—arms exports to Saudi Arabia (see section I).

China and Russia each supplied less than 1 per cent of Saudi Arabia's arms imports in 2015–19 (see table 9.8). China has supplied armed UAVs to Saudi Arabia since 2014. In 2019 Russia exported major arms to Saudi Arabia for the first time; however, the transfer was for only a limited number of specialized rocket launchers of a type not available from other suppliers.

Egypt

The volume of Egypt's arms imports was 212 per cent higher in 2015–19 than in 2010–14, and it rose from 14th place to be the third-largest arms importer in the world (see table 9.5). Its arms imports accounted for 5.8 per cent of the global total. The upward trend in Egypt's arms imports coincided with its military involvement in Libya and in Yemen and fighting with rebel groups in the Sinai peninsula.[40] It might also be linked to Egypt's concerns over the security of its natural gas fields in the Mediterranean Sea and its water supply from the Nile Basin.[41]

The USA, which has supplied large volumes of major arms to Egypt since 1978 as aid, was the largest arms supplier to Egypt in all five-year periods between 1980 and 2014. Although the volume of US arms exports to Egypt remained largely unchanged in 2015–19, the USA was only the third-largest arms supplier to Egypt in this period: it accounted for 15 per cent of Egypt's arms imports, down from 47 per cent in 2010–14 (see tables 9.6 and 9.8). Notable deliveries from the USA in 2015–19 included 125 M-1A1 Abrams tanks, 12 F-16C combat aircraft, 10 AH-64 combat helicopters and 1 corvette. Most of these were delivered in 2015. Because of frictions with the USA related to the military coup in Egypt in 2013, Egypt has intensified its efforts to become less dependent on the USA and procure more arms from other suppliers.[42] In 2015–19 France became the largest arms supplier to Egypt, supplying 35 per cent of imports, up from 2.3 per cent in 2010–14. Deliveries from France in 2015–19 included 24 Rafale combat aircraft, 2 Mistral amphibious assault ships, a FREMM frigate and cruise missiles. Russia remained Egypt's second-largest arms supplier, supplying 34 per cent of Egyptian arms imports in 2015–19. Its deliveries in 2015–19 included 39 MiG-29 combat aircraft, 48 Ka-52 combat helicopters and 3 S-300V SAM systems.

[40] On the armed conflict in Egypt see chapter 6, section IV, in this volume.
[41] Sharp, J. M., *Egypt: Background and US Relations*, Congressional Research Service (CRS) Report for Congress RL33003 (US Congress, CRS: Washington, DC, 21 Nov. 2019), p. 16.
[42] Sharpe (note 41), p. 16.

Qatar

Qatar's arms imports in 2015–19 were 631 per cent higher than in 2010–14 and it entered the top 10 group of arms recipients for the first time (see table 9.5). The increase in Qatari arms imports was mainly due to the delivery of 21 Rafale combat aircraft from France in 2019.

Qatar has several outstanding orders for major arms, including 15 more Rafale combat aircraft from France, 24 Typhoon combat aircraft from the UK, 36 F-15QA combat aircraft from the USA, and 4 frigates and a landing ship from Italy. All these major arms are to be delivered in 2020–25 and will increase the volume of Qatar's arms imports significantly.

Turkey

In 1995–99 Turkey was the third-largest arms importer in the world; by 2005–2009 it was the ninth largest and in 2015–19 it ranked 15th. The volume of Turkey's arms imports in 2015–19 was 48 per cent lower than in 2010–14, even though its armed forces were fighting the Kurdistan Workers' Party (Partiya Karkerên Kurdistanê, PKK) rebel group and were involved in the conflicts in Libya and Syria.[43] The decrease was partly due to delays in the production of submarines ordered from Germany, which were originally planned for delivery in 2015–19.[44] An additional factor was the increase in procurement from Turkey's domestic arms industry of warships and armoured vehicles, which in the past Turkey has mostly imported.

The volume of Turkish arms imports in 2015–19 was also affected by restrictions imposed in 2018 and 2019 by arms suppliers. In 2019 the USA blocked the sale of up to 100 F-35 combat aircraft to Turkey, including the delivery of the first batch planned for 2019 (see section I).[45] In addition, Turkey's attack on Kurdish groups in Syria led to several European states restricting their arms sales to Turkey in 2019.[46]

---

[43] On Turkey's role in the conflicts in Syria and Libya see chapter 6, sections II and IV, respectively, in this volume. See also Wezeman, S. T. and Kuimove, A., 'Turkey and Black Sea security', SIPRI Background Paper, Dec. 2018.

[44] Naval Today, 'Turkish 1st type 214 class submarine launched', 23 Dec. 2019.

[45] White House, 'Statement by the Press Secretary', 17 July 2019; and Roque, A. and Herschelman, K., 'Washington to cut ties with Turkey on F-35 programme and shift supply chain to US', *Jane's Defence Weekly*, 24 July 2019, p. 5.

[46] See chapter 14, section II, in this volume.

III. Transparency in arms transfers

MARK BROMLEY AND SIEMON T. WEZEMAN

Official and publicly accessible data on arms transfers—both exports and imports—is important for assessing states' policies on arms exports, arms procurement and defence. At some point in the past 25 years, 170 states have published information on their arms exports and imports in the form of national reports on arms exports or through their participation in regional or international reporting instruments (although in many cases the information covers only one or a few years).[1]

The main international reporting instruments in the field of international arms transfers are the United Nations Register of Conventional Arms (UNROCA) and the 2013 Arms Trade Treaty (ATT) reporting instrument. This section analyses the current status of these two instruments after a brief review of national and regional reporting.

National reports and regional reporting mechanisms

As of 31 December 2019, 37 states had published at least one national report on arms exports in the past 25 years.[2] As in 2015–18, no state produced a national report on arms exports in 2019 that had not done so previously, and there were no significant developments in either the types of data included or the level of detail provided. Some states that do not publish a national report on their arms exports release data on the overall financial value of their arms exports. These states include India, Israel, Pakistan and Russia (see section IV).

In addition, a number of regional reporting instruments have been mandated or established since the early 1990s. The main such instruments are (a) the instrument created under the 2006 Economic Community of West African States (ECOWAS) Convention on Small Arms and Light Weapons, Their Ammunition and Other Related Materials; (b) instruments created by the Organization of American States (OAS); (c) information exchanges in the Organization for Security and Co-operation in Europe (OSCE); and (d) the European Union (EU) annual report.[3] No significant developments relating to these instruments took place in 2019.

---

[1] This section covers only public reporting instruments in the field of arms transfers. Confidential exchanges of information, such as those that occur within the Wassenaar Arrangement on Export Controls for Conventional Arms and Dual-Use Goods and Technologies, are not addressed.

[2] SIPRI collects all published national reports on arms transfers and makes them available in its National Reports Database.

[3] On these regional reporting instruments see Bromley, M. and Wezeman, S. T., 'Transparency in arms transfers', *SIPRI Yearbook 2016*, pp. 595–603. For a summary and other details of the ECOWAS SALW Convention see annex A, section II, in this volume.

Table 9.9. Reports submitted to the United Nations Register of Conventional Arms (UNROCA), by region, 2014–18

Years are year of transfer, not year of reporting. Regions are as defined on p. xxiv. Percentages are the percentage per region of UN members that have reported for each year.

Region (no. of UN members)	2014	2015	2016	2017	2018
Africa (53)	– (–)	2 (3.8%)	1 (1.9%)	2 (3.8%)	1 (1.9%)
Americas (35)	8 (23%)	8 (23%)	5 (14%)	5 (14%)	5 (14%)
Asia and Oceania (43)	9 (21%)	12 (28%)	5 (12%)	6 (14%)	5 (12%)
Europe (47)	37 (79%)	32 (68%)	32 (68%)	36 (77%)	23 (49%)
Middle East (15)	2 (13%)	1 (6.7%)	3 (20%)	2 (13%)	1 (6.7%)
Total (193)	**56 (29%)**	**55 (28%)**	**46 (24%)**	**51 (26%)**	**35 (18%)**

Sources: UNROCA database; and reports on UNROCA by the UN Secretary-General to the UN General Assembly, various years.

The United Nations Register of Conventional Arms

UNROCA was established in 1991 and reporting started in 1993 (for transfers in 1992). It aims to build confidence between states and 'to prevent the excessive and destabilizing accumulation of arms'.[4] Each year, all UN member states are 'requested' to report, on a voluntary basis, information on their exports and imports in the previous year of seven categories of weapon, specifically those that are deemed to be 'the most lethal' or 'indispensable for offensive operations': (*a*) battle tanks, (*b*) armoured combat vehicles, (*c*) large-calibre artillery systems, (*d*) combat aircraft, (*e*) attack helicopters, (*f*) warships, and (*g*) missiles and missile launchers.[5] States are also invited to provide additional background information on holdings of weapons and on procurement from national production. In addition, since 2003, states have been invited to provide background information on exports and imports of small arms and light weapons (SALW).

Reporting levels have decreased since the mid-2000s: over 100 states reported annually in the early 2000s compared with 46–56 annually for 2014–17 and only 35 for 2018 (see table 9.9). As in most years since 1993, the level of reporting for 2018 by states in Africa and the Middle East was low. As of 31 December 2019, only 1 of the 53 states in Africa and 1 of the 15 states in the Middle East had submitted a report for 2018.[6] The rate of reporting by states in Europe, at 49 per cent, was the highest of any region but significantly below the levels of 2014–17 (see below).

---

[4] UN General Assembly Resolution 46/36 L, 'Transparency in armaments', 6 Dec. 1991, A/46/41 (Vol. I), Aug. 1992, para. 2.

[5] The reports are made publicly available in the UNROCA database.

[6] United Nations, General Assembly, 'United Nations Register of Conventional Arms', Report of the Secretary-General, A/74/201, 19 July 2019; and UNROCA database (note 5). In previous years, it has been common for some states to report late; it is likely, therefore, that the final figures will be slightly higher than those stated here as late reports for transfers in 2018 are submitted.

Eight of the top 10 exporters of major arms in 2015–19 (see section I) reported to UNROCA for 2018, including the two largest (the United States and Russia). The two exceptions are Israel and France, although they did report for almost every other year since 1992.[7] In contrast, most of the world's largest arms importers in 2015–19 did not report for 2018. There were reports for 2018 from only three of the top 10 importers (see section II): Australia, China and South Korea.

The low level of participation by states is the main obstacle faced by UNROCA; however, there are also serious problems with the quality of the reporting. For example, there have been numerous cases where a state has reported a transfer elsewhere (e.g. in an official national report) but did not report the transfer to UNROCA. In some cases, the discrepancy can be explained by variations in a state's interpretation of weapon categories or types of transfer covered by a specific reporting instrument. In other cases, the state has simply failed to report a transfer that was also clearly covered by UNROCA.[8]

UNROCA reporting by OSCE participating states

The UN General Assembly resolution that established UNROCA called on states to 'cooperate at a regional and subregional level . . . with a view to enhancing and coordinating international efforts aimed at increased openness and transparency in armaments'.[9] The OSCE has been particularly active in raising the profile of UNROCA and in seeking to increase levels of participation among OSCE participating states.[10] For example, since 1997 the OSCE participating states—which include states from North America and Central Asia as well as Europe—have agreed to share their annual submissions to UNROCA with each other and to do so no later than 30 June each year.[11]

Initially, the exchange was confidential, but in 2016 the OSCE participating states agreed to make their UNROCA exchanges publicly available.[12] Thus, reports submitted for 2016, 2017 and 2018 are available on the OSCE website.

---

[7] In addition, Italy's report for 2018 did not follow UNROCA's standard reporting format and did not identify the importers of Italy's exports.

[8] For qualitative analysis of the content of the reports see Wezeman, S. T., 'Reporting to the United Nations Register of Conventional Arms for 2017', SIPRI Background Paper, June 2019.

[9] UN General Assembly Resolution 46/36 L (note 4), para. 17.

[10] For a list of participating states and other details of the OSCE see annex B, section II, in this volume.

[11] OSCE, Forum for Security Co-operation, 'Further transparency in arms transfers', Decision no. 13/97, FSC.DEC/13/97, 16 July 1997.

[12] OSCE, Forum for Security Co-operation, 'Enabling the publication of information exchanges in the field of small arms and light weapons, conventional arms transfers and anti-personnel mines', Decision no. 4/16, FSC.DEC/4/16/Corr.1, 21 Sep. 2016.

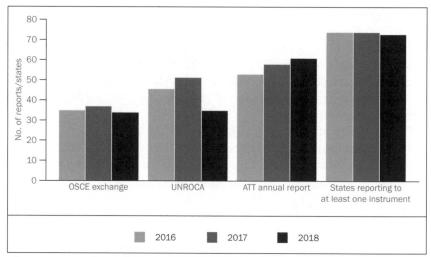

Figure 9.2. Numbers of reports submitted to the international reporting instruments on arms transfers, 2016–18

ATT = Arms Trade Treaty, OSCE = Organization for Security and Co-operation in Europe, UNROCA = United Nations Register of Conventional Arms.

Sources: ATT Secretariat, 'Annual reports'; United Nations, General Assembly, 'United Nations Register of Conventional Arms', Report of the Secretary-General, A/74/201, 19 July 2019, A/73/185, 18 July 2018, and A/72/331, 14 Aug. 2017; UNROCA database; and OSCE, Forum for Security Co-operation, 'Information exchange on conventional arms transfer'. All data as of 15 Mar. 2020.

Of the 57 OSCE participating states, 35 made their UNROCA submissions for 2016 available via the OSCE information exchange. The figure rose to 37 for 2017 but fell to 34 for 2018 (see figure 9.2).[13]

The Arms Trade Treaty report on arms transfers

Article 13 of the Arms Trade Treaty obliges each state party to provide the ATT Secretariat with an annual report on arms exports and imports during the previous calendar year.[14] The number of states complying with their reporting obligations and submitting a report has remained relatively stable in recent years: 53 for 2016, 58 for 2017 and 61 for 2018 (see figure 9.2). However, as the number of states parties has increased, the proportion fulfilling their

[13] OSCE, Forum for Security Co-operation, 'Information exchange on conventional arms transfer', accessed 15 Mar. 2020. These figures do not include reports submitted by the Holy See, which is not a member of the UN and so is not requested to make a submission to UNROCA.

[14] Arms Trade Treaty, Article 13(3). For a summary and other details of the Arms Trade Treaty see annex A, section I, in this volume.

reporting obligations has decreased—from 71 per cent for 2016 (53 of the 75 states parties) to 66 per cent for 2018 (61 of the 92 states parties). Moreover, fewer than half of the states parties had submitted their report on arms transfers in 2018 by the deadline of 31 May 2019.[15]

Perhaps most concerning from a public transparency perspective is the increase in the number of states choosing to make their reports accessible only to other states parties: it rose from 1 for 2015 (Slovakia) to 3 for 2016 (Liberia, Panama and Senegal), 4 for 2017 (Argentina, Cyprus, Greece and Madagascar) and 10 for 2018 (Cyprus, Georgia, Greece, Honduras, Liberia, Lithuania, Madagascar, Mauritius, Nigeria and Senegal). Five of the states parties that kept their 2018 reports private had previously released public reports (Georgia, Greece, Liberia, Lithuania and Mauritius).[16]

Levels of reporting to the international instruments

A comparison of the levels of reporting to UNROCA, the OSCE information exchange and the ATT annual report shows that there is a significant lack of consistency in states' reporting practices. For example, while Cyprus, Greece and Lithuania made their annual reports to the ATT for 2018 available only to other states parties, they also submitted publicly available reports on arms transfers to both UNROCA and the OSCE information exchange. Similarly, Mauritius made its annual reports to the ATT available only to other states parties but submitted a publicly available report to UNROCA.

In addition, while the reporting requirements are in essence the same, many states did not submit reports to all the instruments in which they are required or requested to participate. For 2018, 73 states that were invited or required to do so submitted a report to at least one of these three instruments. However, only 26 states submitted reports to all of the instruments. A further 19 submitted to two instruments and 28 submitted to just one. For example, 17 of the 34 OSCE participating states that shared their UNROCA submission via the OSCE exchange did not submit it to UNROCA itself. Conversely, 9 of the 26 OSCE participating states that submitted a report to UNROCA did not submit it to the OSCE exchange. Likewise, 33 states that made submissions to the ATT annual report for 2018 did not make a submission to UNROCA.

---

[15] Arms Trade Treaty, Working Group on Transparency and Reporting (WGTR), Co-chairs' draft report to CSP5, ATT/CSP5.WGTR/2019/CHAIR/533/Conf.Rep.Rev1, 29 Aug. 2019, para. 36(a).

[16] ATT Secretariat, 'Annual reports', accessed 15 Mar. 2020. On the ATT and its other reporting obligations see chapter 14, section I, in this volume.

While rates of reporting have fallen for individual instruments, the number of states that have submitted a report to at least one of them has remained steady in recent years (see figure 9.2). This indicates that persuading states to make a report submitted to one instrument available to all of the other instruments could help to reverse the falling reporting rates of individual instruments. This process could be facilitated by improving the channels of communication between the bodies responsible for these reporting instruments: the ATT Secretariat, the OSCE and the UN Office for Disarmament Affairs.

IV. The financial value of states' arms exports

PIETER D. WEZEMAN AND MARK BROMLEY

Official data on the financial value of states' arms exports in the years 2009–18 is presented in table 9.10. The data is taken from reports by—or direct quotes from—national governments. The stated data coverage reflects the language used by the original source. National practices in this area vary, but the term 'arms exports' generally refers to the financial value of the arms actually delivered; 'arms export licences' generally refers to the financial value of the licences for arms exports issued by the national export licensing authority; and 'arms export agreements' or 'arms export orders' refers to the financial value of contracts or other agreements signed for arms exports.

The arms export data for the states in table 9.10 is based on national definitions and methodologies and is thus not necessarily comparable. There is no internationally agreed definition of what constitutes 'arms' and governments use different lists when collecting and reporting data on the financial value of their arms exports. In addition, there is no standardized methodology concerning how to collect and report such data, with some states reporting on export licences issued or used and other states using data collected from customs agencies.

According to the SIPRI Arms Transfers Database, countries that produce official data on the financial value of their arms exports accounted for over 90 per cent of the total volume of deliveries of major arms. By adding together the data in table 9.10 it is therefore usually possible to attain a rough estimate of the financial value of the global arms trade. There are significant limitations in using this data to make such an estimate. First, as noted above, the data sets used are not directly comparable. Second, several states (e.g. the United Kingdom) do not release data on arms exports but only on arms export licences, while other states (e.g. China) do not release any data on either exports, licences, agreements or orders. Nonetheless, by adding together the data that states have made available on the financial value of their arms exports, as well as estimates for those that only provide data on arms export licences, agreements or orders—for earlier years when the latest data is not available—it is possible to estimate the total value of the global arms trade.

For 2018, part of the data for the United States, which generally accounts for around 25 per cent of the overall figure, had not been published at the time of writing. An estimate for 2018 is thus not possible. The estimate of the financial value of the global arms trade for 2017, the latest year for which US data is available, was at least $95 billion.[1] However, the true figure is likely to be higher.

---

[1] For a full description of the methodology used to calculate this figure see the 'Financial value of the global arms trade' page of the SIPRI website.

Table 9.10. The financial value of states' arms exports according to national government and industry sources, 2009–18

Figures are in constant (2018) US$ m. Conversion to constant US dollars is made using the market exchange rates of the reporting year and the US consumer price index (CPI). Years are calendar years unless otherwise stated.

State	2009	2010	2011	2012	2013	2014	2015	2016	2017	2018	Explanation of data
Austria	566	569	667	639	753	755	395	739	437	352	Arms exports
Belgium	3 658	2 697	2 533	2 184	3 398	1 271	1 274	4 606	2 306	1 788	Arms export licences
	1 792	1 530	1 296	1 362	877	6 351	1 310	1 445	852	1 374	Arms export licences
Bosnia and Herzegovina	37	15	64	58	56	94	123	120	120	..	Arms exports
	75	43	88	65	160	182	270	353	340	..	Arms export licences
Brazil	116	..	..	..	..	..	..	..	..	..	Arms exports
Bulgaria	236	393	358	308	336	568	1 647	1 174	1 401	903	Arms exports
	514	451	346	490	703	1 165	751	1 457	1 597	1 237	Arms export licences
Canada[a]	555	456	715	1 141	713	764	560	567	813	1 595	Arms exports
Croatia	..	82	54	72	123	100	46	86	78	116	Arms exports
Czechia	364	679	237	334	1 019	678	449	439	521	451	Arms export licences
	285	331	284	385	412	602	661	797	659	644	Arms exports
	634	688	537	372	469	704	872	398	585	460	Arms export licences
Denmark	..	..	..	..	33	63	90	130	105	97	Arms expots
	410	573	368	312	1 119	207	157	235	236	314	Arms export licences
Estonia	5	<1	5	<1	1	4	5	5	2	<1	Arms exports
	13	3	543	4	4	6	16	10	74	44	Arms export licences
Finland	141	90	151	82	319	314	115	153	121	151	Arms export licences
	304	93	286	166	492	319	425	113	225	208	Arms exports
France	5 159	5 683	5 871	5 309	4 836	5 692	7 287	8 239	7 737	8 222	Arms exports
	13 275	7 806	10 113	6 769	9 838	11 565	19 882	16 133	7 978	10 762	Arms export licences
Germany	2 177	3 232	1 994	1 329	1 335	2 565	1 827	2 895	3 048	910	Arms exports[b]
	11 445	8 375	16 752	12 473	11 936	9 174	15 062	7 992	7 548	5 712	Arms export licences[c]
Greece	369	450	351	478	..	..	..	..	..	157	Arms export licences
Hungary	28	29	28	38	46	47	54	22	51	44	Arms exports
	207	210	242	379	734	609	1 507	681	671	467	Arms export licences
India[d]	80	..	..	94	126	173	340	233	736	1 572	Arms exports

Ireland	73	37	42	66	89	121	51	73	29	39	Arms export licences
Israel	8 076	8 291	7 814	8 170	..	..	..	..	..	..	Arms exports
	8 661	>8 406	6 497	..	7 050	6 004	6 039	6 801	9 425	7 500	Arms export agreements
Italy	3 585	940	1 588	4 230	3 967	4 686	3 776	3 303	3 310	2 900	Arms exports
	10 883	4 958	8 167	5 846	3 076	3 731	9 262	16 937	10 935	5 641	Arms export licences
Korea, South	1 365	1 368	2 659	2 573	3 682	3 831	3 752	2 676	3 196	..	Arms export agreements
Lithuania	72	23	74	27	23	27	32	47	82	112	Arms exports
	128	35	79	28	31	22	69	106	69	53	Arms export licences
Montenegro	13	9	..	4	4	13	5	1	7	..	Arms exports
	13	15	6	7	9	15	13	9	10	..	Arms export licences
The Netherlands	922	1 031	1 198	1 155	362	352	696	655	764	675	Arms exports
	2 138	1 392	646	1 322	1 378	2 906	1 026	1 638	925	759	Arms export licences
Norway	838	699	712	729	605	495	429	446	663	584	Arms exports
Pakistan[e]	16	20	11	14	14	18	64	32	59	212	Arms exports
Poland	..	..	..	..	481	556	495	443	543	575	Arms exports
	2 262	697	1 318	890	1 228	1 294	1 491	1 420	1 243	1 838	Arms export licences
Portugal	26	31	39	44	252	221	224	691	186	248	Arms exports
	46	32	48	73	209	358	80	282	68	203	Arms export licences
Romania	115	142	146	91	191	169	171	189	198	195	Arms exports
	193	175	205	196	319	264	233	252	270	204	Arms export licences
Russia	9 949	11 516	15 294	16 624	16 923	16 547	15 362	15 694	>15 366	16 000	Arms exports
Serbia	164	221	194	205	187	332	410	471	282	..	Arms exports
	528	869	442	490	876	850	859	967	836	..	Arms export licences
Slovakia	72	23	16	35	44	51	67	69	79	110	Arms exports
	174	88	47	103	175	377	333	241	263	223	Arms export licences
Slovenia	8	9	14	6	4	13	13	19	26	14	Arms exports
	20	17	19	13	13	4	36	50	59	77	Arms export licences
South Africa	1 079	1 310	1 412	1 412	352	291	228	296	264	357	Arms export licences
Spain	2 190	1 720	3 773	2 744	5 593	4 507	4 371	4 688	4 996	4 392	Arms exports
	5 192	3 413	4 455	10 813	6 184	5 159	12 545	6 422	24 235	13 460	Arms export licences
Sweden	2 074	2 196	2 392	1 576	1 976	1 230	937	1 342	1 346	1 308	Arms exports
	1 698	2 113	1 874	1 281	1 626	693	622	7 558	974	974	Arms export licences
Switzerland	783	708	1 097	816	536	653	492	437	465	522	Arms exports

State	2009	2010	2011	2012	2013	2014	2015	2016	2017	2018	Explanation of data
Turkey	784	730	912	1 312	1 498	1 747	1 753	1 756	1 781	2 035	Arms exports
United Kingdom	13 221	10 372	9 658	15 195	16 514	14 846	12 463	8 329	11 823	18 676	Arms export orders[f]
	5 629	4 327	10 868	3 744	7 488	3 639	9 422	4 571	8 677	3 731	Arms export licences
Ukraine	936	1 102	1 121	1 120	1 078	..	604	806	..	..	Arms exports
United States[g]	25 103	20 953	21 814	19 192	21 912	20 603	22 438	22 087	31 310	..	Arms exports[h]
	33 911	24 417	28 845	68 591	25 311	33 285	47 549	28 789	50 577	..	Arms export agreements[i]
	42 105	39 251	48 978	36 717	22 417	66 860	78 346	52 145	52 838	63 432	Arms export licences[j]

.. = not available.

Note: The states included in this table are those that provide official data on the financial value of either 'arms exports', 'contracts signed for arms exports', 'arms export orders placed' or 'licences for arms exports' and where the average of the values given in at least 1 of the data sets exceeds $10 million. The arms export data for the different states in this table is not necessarily comparable and may be based on significantly different definitions and methodologies.

[a] Figures for Canada exclude exports to the USA.

[b] These figures only include exports of 'war weapons' as defined under German legislation.

[c] These figures include arms export licences for international collaborative projects.

[d] Figures for India cover the period 1 Apr.–31 Mar. (e.g. the figure for 2018 covers the period 1 Apr. 2018–31 Mar. 2019). The figure for 2009 covers the period 1 Apr. 2009–31 Dec. 2009.

[e] Figures for Pakistan for 2009–17 cover the period 1 Apr.–31 Mar. (e.g. the figure for 2017 covers the period 1 Apr. 2017–31 Mar. 2018). The figure for 2018 covers the period 1 Aug. 2018–31 July 2019.

[f] These figures cover defence equipment and additional aerospace equipment and services.

[g] US figures are for the period 1 Oct.–30 Sep. (e.g. the available figures for 2018 cover the period 1 Oct. 2017–30 Sep. 2018).

[h] These figures include items sold under the government-to-government Foreign Military Sales programme and sales by US industry direct to foreign governments as Direct Commercial Sales.

[i] These figures only include items sold under the government-to-government Foreign Military Sales programme.

[j] These figures only include sales by US industry direct to foreign governments as Direct Commercial Sales.

Sources: Reports by—or direct quotes from—national governments. For a full list of sources and all available financial data on arms exports see the 'Financial value of the global arms trade' page of the SIPRI website.

V. The 100 largest arms-producing and military services companies, 2018

AUDE FLEURANT, ALEXANDRA KUIMOVA, DIEGO LOPES DA SILVA,
NAN TIAN, PIETER D. WEZEMAN AND SIEMON T. WEZEMAN

Developments in the Top 100[1]

Table 9.11 lists the SIPRI Top 100—the world's largest arms producers and military services companies (excluding those in China)—ranked by their arms sales in 2018. The arms sales of the Top 100 totalled $420 billion in 2018—an increase of 4.6 per cent compared with 2017 and 47 per cent higher than in 2002.

As has been the case every year since 2002, the vast majority of companies listed in the Top 100 in 2018 were based in the USA, Europe and Russia.[2] A total of 70 companies based in the USA and Europe are listed in 2018, accounting for $348 billion (or 83 per cent) of total Top 100 arms sales. Their total arms sales in 2018 were 5.2 per cent higher than in 2017. Companies based in eight other countries were listed in the Top 100 in 2018: six in Japan, three each in Israel, India and South Korea, two in Turkey and one each in Australia, Canada and Singapore. Together, they accounted for $36.2 billion of the total Top 100 arms sales in 2018, representing an 8.6 per cent share of the total.

The United States

In 2018, for the first time since 2002, the top 5 in the Top 100 consisted solely of companies based in the USA. Taken together, the arms sales of the top 5 were $148 billion, representing 35 per cent of total Top 100 arms sales. The combined arms sales of the 43 companies based in the USA listed in the Top 100 were $246 billion in 2018—an increase of 7.2 per cent on 2017. The USA's share of total Top 100 arms sales was 59 per cent in 2018.

Lockheed Martin is, by far, the largest arms producer in the world: in 2018 its share of total Top 100 arms sales was 11 per cent and its arms sales grew by 5.2 per cent. It has occupied the first position in the Top 100 every year since 2009. Northrop Grumman's arms sales grew by 14 per cent in 2018, to $26.2 billion, making it the third-largest arms producer. The $3.3 billion growth in its arms sales was the largest absolute increase of any company listed in the Top 100 for 2018 and was driven by its acquisition of Orbital-ATK and strong domestic and international demand for its weapons.

---

[1] For a more detailed analysis see Fleurant, A., 'The SIPRI Top 100 arms-producing and military services companies, 2018', SIPRI Fact Sheet, Dec. 2019.

[2] Developments relating to companies based in Russia are assessed separately from the regional discussion on Europe in this analysis.

Europe and Russia

There were 27 companies based in Europe in the Top 100 for 2018. Their combined arms sales of $102 billion accounted for 24 per cent of total Top 100 arms sales in 2018. Eight of the companies were based in the UK, six in France, four in Germany, two in Italy and one each in Poland, Spain, Sweden, Switzerland and Ukraine. Two of the 27 companies—Airbus Group and MBDA—are categorized as 'trans-European' because their ownership and control structures are located in more than one European country.

The combined arms sales of the 10 companies based in Russia listed in the Top 100 were $36.2 billion in 2018, accounting for 8.6 per cent of the overall total. Russia's largest arms producer, Almaz-Antey, was the only Russian company ranked in the top 10 (at 9th position) and accounted for 27 per cent of the total arms sales of Russian companies in the Top 100. Its arms sales rose by 18 per cent in 2018, to $9.6 billion.

Methodology

Except where indicated, the information and data in this section is from the SIPRI Arms Industry Database. The data starts in 2002 because this is the first year for which SIPRI has sufficient data to include Russian companies. SIPRI estimates that several Chinese companies have large enough arms sales to rank in the Top 100. However, Chinese companies are not included in the database because of a lack of data on which to make a reasonable or consistent estimate of arms sales dating back to 2002.

The data for all years is revised annually based on new information. This section focuses on developments in 2018 (rather than 2019) because this is the latest year for which consistent data on arms sales of companies in the SIPRI Top 100 is available.

Unless otherwise specified, all changes are expressed in real terms. All changes between 2017 and 2018 are based on the list of companies ranked in 2018 (i.e. the annual comparison is between the same set of companies). Longer-term comparisons (e.g. between 2002 and 2018) are based on the sets of companies listed in the respective year (i.e. the comparison is between a different set of companies).

Definition of 'arms sales'

Sales of arms and military services (or 'arms sales' for short) are defined as sales of military goods and services to military customers domestically and abroad; sales are only for those companies ranked.[3]

---

[3] For a full definition and more detail on methodology see the Arms Industry Database on the SIPRI website.

Table 9.11. The SIPRI Top 100 arms-producing and military services companies in the world excluding China, 2018[a]

Figures for arms sales and total sales are in millions of US dollars.

Rank[b] 2018	Rank[b] 2017	Company[c]	Country[d]	Arms sales, 2018 (US$ m.)	Arms sales, 2017 (constant 2018 US$ m.)[e]	Change in arms sales, 2017–18 (%)	Total sales, 2018 (US$ m.)	Arms sales as a % of total sales, 2018
1	1	Lockheed Martin Corp.	United States	47 260	44 935	5.2	53 762	88
2	2	Boeing	United States	29 150	27 577	5.7	101 126	29
3	3	Northrop Grumman Corp.	United States	26 190	22 908	14	30 095	87
4	4	Raytheon	United States	23 440	22 570	3.9	27 058	87
5	6	General Dynamics Corp.	United States	22 000	19 969	10	36 193	61
6	5	BAE Systems	United Kingdom	21 210	22 384	-5.2	22 428	95
7	7	Airbus Group	Trans-European[f]	11 650	10 691	9.0	75 195	15
8	9	Leonardo	Italy	9 820	9 403	4.4	14 447	68
9	10	Almaz-Antey	Russia	9 640	8 195	18	9 872	98
10	8	Thales	France	9 470	9 601	-1.4	18 767	50
11	11	United Technologies Corp.	United States	9 310	7 967	17	66 501	14
12	12	L3 Technologies	United States	8 250	7 936	4.0	10 244	81
13	13	Huntington Ingalls Industries	United States	7 200	6 626	8.7	8 176	88
14	16	Honeywell International	United States	5 430	4 567	19	41 802	13
15	14	United Aircraft Corp.[g]	Russia	5 420	6 168	-12	6 563	83
16	19	Leidos	United States	5 000	4 485	11	10 194	49
17	17	Harris Corp.	United States	4 970	4 557	9.1	6 801	73
18	15	United Shipbuilding Corp.	Russia	4 700	4 762	-1.3	5 565	84
19	20	Booz Allen Hamilton	United States	4 680	4 424	5.8	6 704	70

Rank[b] 2018	2017	Company[c]	Country[d]	Arms sales, 2018 (US$ m.)	Arms sales, 2017 (constant 2018 US$ m.)[e]	Change in arms sales, 2017–18 (%)	Total sales, 2018 (US$ m.)	Arms sales as a % of total sales, 2018
20	18	Rolls-Royce	United Kingdom	4 680	4 714	-0.7	20 972	22
21	21	Naval Group	France	4 220	4 404	-4.2	4 259	99
22	26	Rheinmetall	Germany	3 800	3 652	4.1	7 257	52
23	27	MBDA	Trans-European[f]	3 780	3 621	4.4	3 777	100
24	23	General Electric	United States	3 650	3 922	-6.9	121 615	3.0
25	25	Mitsubishi Heavy Industries[g]	Japan	3 620	3 669	-1.3	36 947	10
26	24	Tactical Missiles Corp.	Russia	3 600	3 443	4.6	3 668	98
27	22	Textron	United States	3 500	4 199	-17	13 972	25
28	29	Elbit Systems	Israel	3 500	3 263	7.3	3 684	95
29	33	CACI International	United States	3 490	3 052	14	4 986	70
30	31	Saab	Sweden	3 240	3 092	4.8	3 814	85
31	34	Safran	France	3 240	3 107	4.3	24 846	13
32	28	Babcock International Group	United Kingdom	3 180	3 445	-7.7	6 881	46
33	32	United Engine Corp.	Russia	2 950	2 926	0.8	3 904	76
34	51	Dassault Aviation Groupe	France	2 930	2 250	30	6 001	49
35	36	Science Applications International Corp.	United States	2 800	2 826	-0.9	4 659	60
36	52	AECOM	United States	2 770	2 120	31	20 156	14
37	45	General Atomics[g]	United States	2 750	2 273	21	..	..
38	38	Hindustan Aeronautics	India	2 740	2 647	3.5	2 883	95
39	40	Israel Aerospace Industries	Israel	2 650	2 500	6.0	3 682	72

		Company	Country					
40	35	High Precision Systems[g]	Russia	2 630	2 706	-2.8	2 711	97
41	42	Rockwell Collins	United States	2 630	2 355	12	8 665	30
42	56	KBR	United States	2 600	1 792	45	4 913	53
43	–	Perspecta[h]	United States	2 590	2 183	19	4 030	64
44	47	Rafael	Israel	2 540	2 236	14	2 595	98
45	43	Russian Electronics	Russia	2 330	2 171	7.3	2 668	87
46	50	Hanwha Aerospace	South Korea	2 320	2 219	4.6	4 047	57
47	48	CEA	France	2 300	2 314	-0.6	6 226	37
48	49	Kawasaki Heavy Industries[g]	Japan	2 260	2 199	2.8	14 456	16
49	30	Bechtel Corp.[g]	United States	2 000	3 226	-38	25 500	7.8
50	59	Fincantieri	Italy	1 900	1 759	8.0	6 461	29
51	55	Oshkosh Corp.	United States	1 850	1 884	-1.8	7 705	24
52	37	Russian Helicopters	Russia	1 810	2 601	-30	3 006	60
53	46	KRET	Russia	1 770	2 113	-16	1 931	92
54	62	ASELSAN	Turkey	1 740	1 237	41	1 866	93
55	58	Krauss-Maffei Wegmann[g]	Germany	1 680	1 767	-4.9	1 770	95
56	44	Indian Ordnance Factories	India	1 650	2 258	-27	1 682	98
57	54	ThyssenKrupp	Germany	1 650	2 046	-19	50 400	3.3
58	60	Cobham	United Kingdom	1 590	1 685	-5.6	2 484	64
59	63	DynCorp International	United States	1 560	1 454	7.3	2 148	73
60	100	Korea Aerospace Industries	South Korea	1 550	900	72	2 532	61
61	57	ST Engineering	Singapore	1 540	1 731	-11	4 965	31
62	66	Bharat Electronics[g]	India	1 460	1 379	5.9	1 725	85
63	67	ManTech International Corp.	United States	1 430	1 393	2.7	1 959	73

Rank[b]		Company[c]	Country[d]	Arms sales, 2018 (US$ m.)	Arms sales, 2017 (constant 2018 US$ m.)[e]	Change in arms sales, 2017–18 (%)	Total sales, 2018 (US$ m.)	Arms sales as a % of total sales, 2018
2018	2017							
64	68	UralVagonZavod	Russia	1 370	1 281	6.9	2 209	62
65	90	Jacobs Engineering Group	United States	1 370	922	49	14 985	9.1
66	88	Fluor Corp.	United States	1 350	952	42	19 166	7.0
67	61	LIG Nex1	South Korea	1 340	1 622	–17	1 343	100
68	74	TransDigm Group	United States	1 330	1 219	9.1	3 811	35
69	64	Melrose Industries[i]	United Kingdom	1 320	1 504	–12	16 329	8.1
70	53	United Launch Alliance[g]	United States	1 320	1 997	–34	1 800	73
71	83	UkrOboronProm[g]	Ukraine	1 300	1 101	18	1 378	95
72	78	Fujitsu[g]	Japan	1 270	1 151	10	35 806	3.5
73	71	Serco Group	United Kingdom	1 260	1 333	–5.5	4 283	29
74	75	PGZ	Poland	1 250	1 273	–1.8	1 385	90
75	99	Teledyne Technologies	United States	1 240	881	41	2 902	43
76	89	Navantia	Spain	1 240	975	27	1 307	95
77	76	Hensoldt	Germany	1 240	1 232	0.7	1 298	95
78	79	Vectrus	United States	1 230	1 147	7.2	1 279	96
79	73	Aerojet Rocketdyne	United States	1 220	1 249	–2.3	1 896	64
80	82	Austal	Australia	1 140	1 015	12	1 383	82
81	81	Sierra Nevada Corp.[g]	United States	1 100	1 045	5.3	1 690	65
82	80	IHI Corp.[g]	Japan	1 090	1 100	–0.9	13 439	8.1
83	85	Nexter[g]	France	1 080	1 029	5.0	1 135	95
84	72	Turkish Aerospace Industries	Turkey	1 070	1 065	0.5	1 248	86

85	70	BWX Technologies	United States	1 070	1 331	–20	1 800	59
86	69	Engility	United States	1 070	1 331	–20	1 605	67
87	102	CAE	Canada	1 010	851	19	2 546	40
88	97	MIT	United States	980	891	10	3 627	27
89	95	Meggitt	United Kingdom	970	938	3.4	2 775	35
90	94	Curtiss-Wright Corp.	United States	970	911	6.4	2 412	40
91	93	The Aerospace Corp.	United States	970	911	6.4	1 054	92
92	115	Ball Corp.[g]	United States	930	686	36	11 635	8.0
93	98	Moog	United States	920	881	4.5	2 709	34
94	104	QinetiQ	United Kingdom	910	874	4.1	1 215	75
95	96	RUAG	Switzerland	900	885	1.7	2 043	44
96	111	ViaSat	United States	860	717	20	2 068	42
97	103	Mitsubishi Electric Corp.[g]	Japan	860	853	0.8	40 947	2.1
98	128	Arconic	United States	840	533	58	14 014	6.0
99	101	NEC Corp.[g]	Japan	840	863	–2.7	26 394	3.2
100	109	Amphenol Corp.	United States	820	717	14	8 202	10

.. = data not available; Corp. = Corporation.

[a] Although several Chinese arms-producing companies are large enough to rank among the SIPRI Top 100, it has not been possible to include them because of a lack of comparable and sufficiently accurate data.

[b] Companies are ranked according to the value of their arms sales at the end of what SIPRI considers to be their financial year. A dash (–) indicates that the company did not rank among the SIPRI Top 100 for 2017. Company names and structures are listed as they were at the end of their financial year. Information about subsequent changes is provided in these notes. Rankings for 2017 are based on the updated arms-production figures in the 2018 company list in the SIPRI Arms Industry Database. They may differ from those published in any earlier SIPRI publication and elsewhere owing to continual revision of data, most often because of changes reported by the company itself and sometimes because of improved estimations. Major revisions are explained in these notes.

[c] Holding and investment companies with no direct operational activities are not treated as arms-producing companies, and companies owned by them are listed and ranked as if they were parent companies.

[d] Country refers to the country in which the ownership and control structures of the company are located.

[e] To allow comparison with arms sales in 2018, figures for arms sales in 2017 are given in constant 2018 US dollars.

[f] Trans-European refers to companies whose ownership and control structures are located in more than one European country.

[g] The arms sales figure for this company is an estimate with a high degree of uncertainty.

[h] Perspecta is the result of a merger between DXC, Vencore and Keypoint. Its arms sales figure for 2017 is 'pro forma', i.e. it is the combined 2017 arms sales of DXC and Vencore. Keypoint was not an arms company.

[i] Melrose Industries acquired GKN in 2018. The rank and sales for Melrose Industries for 2017 refer to those of GKN.

Source: SIPRI Arms Industry Database, Dec. 2019.

10. World nuclear forces

Overview

At the start of 2020, nine states—the United States, Russia, the United Kingdom, France, China, India, Pakistan, Israel and the Democratic People's Republic of Korea (DPRK, or North Korea)—possessed approximately 13 400 nuclear weapons, of which 3720 were deployed with operational forces (see table 10.1). Approximately 1800 of these are kept in a state of high operational alert.

Overall, inventories of nuclear warheads continue to decline. This is primarily due to the USA and Russia dismantling retired warheads. At the same time, both the USA and Russia have extensive and expensive programmes under way to replace and modernize their nuclear warheads, missile and aircraft delivery systems, and nuclear weapon production facilities (see sections I and II).

The nuclear arsenals of the other nuclear-armed states are considerably smaller (see sections III–IX), but all are either developing or deploying new weapon systems or have announced their intention to do so. China is in the middle of a significant modernization and expansion of its nuclear arsenal, and India and Pakistan are also thought to be increasing the size of their arsenals. North Korea continues to prioritize its military nuclear programme as a central element of its national security strategy, although in 2019 it adhered to its self-declared moratoria on the testing of nuclear weapons and long-range ballistic missile delivery systems.

The availability of reliable information on the status of the nuclear arsenals and capabilities of the nuclear-armed states varies considerably. The USA has disclosed important information about its stockpile and nuclear capabilities, but in 2019 the administration of President Donald J. Trump ended the practice of disclosing the size of the US stockpile. The UK and France have also declared some information. Russia refuses to publicly disclose the detailed breakdown of its forces counted under the 2010 Treaty on Measures for the Further Reduction and Limitation of Strategic Offensive Arms (New START), even though it shares the information with the USA. China now publicly displays its nuclear forces more frequently than in the past but releases little information about force numbers or future development plans. The governments of India and Pakistan make statements about some of their missile tests but provide no information about the status or size of their arsenals. North Korea has acknowledged conducting nuclear weapon and missile tests but provides no information about its nuclear weapon capabilities. Israel has a long-standing policy of not commenting on its nuclear arsenal.

Table 10.1. World nuclear forces, January 2020

All figures are approximate. The estimates presented here are based on public information and contain some uncertainties, as reflected in the notes to tables 10.1–10.10.

Country	Year of first nuclear test	Deployed warheads[a]	Stored warheads[b]	Other warheads	Total inventory
United States	1945	1 750[c]	2 050[d]	2 000[e]	5 800
Russia	1949	1 570[f]	2 745[g]	2 060[e]	6 375
United Kingdom	1952	120	95	–	215[h]
France	1960	280	10	..	290
China	1964	–	320	–	320
India	1974	–	150	..	150
Pakistan	1998	–	160	..	160
Israel	..	–	90	..	90
North Korea	2006	–	..	[30–40]	[30–40][i]
Total[j]		3 720	5 620	4 060	13 400

.. = not applicable or not available; – = zero; [] = uncertain figure.

Note: SIPRI revises its world nuclear forces data each year based on new information and updates to earlier assessments. The data for Jan. 2020 replaces all previously published SIPRI data on world nuclear forces.

[a] These are warheads placed on missiles or located on bases with operational forces.

[b] These are warheads in central storage that would require some preparation (e.g. transport and loading on to launchers) before they could become fully operationally available.

[c] This figure includes approximately 1600 strategic warheads (about 1300 on ballistic missiles and nearly 300 on bomber bases), as well as c. 150 non-strategic (tactical) nuclear bombs deployed outside the USA for delivery by US and other North Atlantic Treaty Organization aircraft.

[d] This figure includes c. 80 non-strategic nuclear bombs stored in the USA.

[e] This figure is for retired warheads awaiting dismantlement.

[f] This figure includes approximately 1370 strategic warheads on ballistic missiles and about 200 deployed at heavy bomber bases.

[g] This figure includes c. 870 warheads for strategic bombers and nuclear-powered ballistic missile submarines (SSBNs) in overhaul and c. 1875 non-strategic nuclear weapons for use by short-range air, air defence and naval forces.

[h] The British Government has stated that the process to reduce the stockpile to 180 warheads is under way. Although some sources suggest that the stockpile remains at 215 warheads, it is possible that, under this process, the stockpile may have already been reduced to 195 warheads.

[i] There is no publicly available evidence that North Korea has produced an operational nuclear warhead for delivery by an intercontinental-range ballistic missile.

[j] Totals do not include figures for North Korea.

The raw material for nuclear weapons is fissile material, either highly enriched uranium (HEU) or separated plutonium. China, France, Russia, the UK and the USA have produced both HEU and plutonium for use in their nuclear weapons; India and Israel have produced mainly plutonium; and Pakistan has produced mainly HEU but is increasing its ability to produce plutonium. North Korea has produced plutonium for use in nuclear weapons but may have produced HEU as well. All states with a civilian nuclear industry are capable of producing fissile materials (see section X).

SHANNON N. KILE AND HANS M. KRISTENSEN

I. US nuclear forces

HANS M. KRISTENSEN

As of January 2020, the United States maintained a military stockpile of approximately 3800 nuclear warheads, roughly the same number as in January 2019. The stockpile included approximately 1750 deployed nuclear warheads, consisting of about 1600 strategic and 150 non-strategic (or tactical) warheads. In addition, about 2050 warheads were held in reserve and around 2000 retired warheads were awaiting dismantlement (385 fewer than the estimate for January 2019), giving a total inventory of approximately 5800 nuclear warheads (see table 10.2).

The USA reached compliance with the final warhead limits prescribed by the 2010 Treaty on Measures for the Further Reduction and Limitation of Strategic Offensive Arms (New START) by the specified deadline of 5 February 2018, at which point it was reported to have 1393 deployed warheads attributed to 660 deployed strategic launchers—that is, deployed intercontinental ballistic missiles (ICBMs), deployed submarine-launched ballistic missiles (SLBMs) and deployed heavy bombers.[1] As of September 2019, the New START aggregate numbers showed the USA deploying 1376 warheads attributed to 668 deployed strategic launchers.[2] The number of deployed warheads reported under New START differs from the estimate presented here because the treaty attributes one weapon to each deployed bomber—even though bombers do not carry weapons under normal circumstances—and does not count warheads stored at bomber bases.

Nuclear modernization

In 2019 the administration of President Donald J. Trump continued to implement the 2018 Nuclear Posture Review (NPR).[3] The NPR recommended maintaining the comprehensive nuclear weapon modernization programme decided by the previous administration but with several new nuclear weapons and an increase in the production of plutonium cores for nuclear weapons. Specifically, the NPR outlined plans to introduce a new class (Columbia) of nuclear-powered ballistic missile submarine (SSBN); a new nuclear-capable strategic bomber (B-21 Raider); a new long-range

---

[1] US Department of State, Office of the Spokesperson, 'Key facts about New START implementation', Fact Sheet, 5 Feb. 2018. For a summary and other details of New START see annex A, section III, and chapter 11, section I, in this volume.

[2] US Department of State, Bureau of Arms Control, Verification and Compliance, 'New START Treaty aggregate numbers of strategic offensive arms', Fact Sheet, 1 Sep. 2019.

[3] US Department of Defense (DOD), *Nuclear Posture Review 2018* (DOD: Arlington, VA, Feb. 2018). For a summary and other details of the Nuclear Posture Review see Kristensen, H. M., 'US nuclear forces', *SIPRI Yearbook 2019*, pp. 289–94.

Table 10.2. US nuclear forces, January 2020

All figures are approximate and some are based on assessments by the author. Totals for strategic and non-strategic forces are rounded up to the nearest 5 warheads.

Type	Designation	No. of launchers	Year first deployed	Range (km)[a]	Warheads x yield	No. of warheads[b]
Strategic forces						3 570
Bombers		60/107[c]				848[d]
B-52H	Stratofortress	42/87	1961	16 000	20 x ALCMs 5–150 kt[e]	528
B-2A	Spirit	18/20	1994	11 000	16 x B61-7, -11, B83-1 bombs[f]	320
ICBMs		400				800[g]
LGM-30G	Minuteman III					
	Mk-12A	200	1979	13 000	1–3 x W78 335 kt	600[h]
	Mk-21 SERV	200	2006	13 000	1 x W87 300 kt	200[i]
SSBNs/SLBMs		240[j]				1 920[k]
UGM-133A	Trident II (D5/D5LE)					
	Mk-4	..	1992	>12 000	1–8 x W76-0 100 kt	..[l]
	Mk-4A	..	2008	>12 000	1–8 x W76-1 90 kt	1 511
	Mk-4A	..	2019	>12 000	1 x W76-2 8 kt	25[m]
	Mk-5	..	1990	>12 000	1–8 x W88 455 kt	384
Non-strategic forces						230[n]
F-15E	Strike Eagle	..	1988	3 840	5 x B61-3, -4[o]	80
F-16C/D	Falcon	..	1987	3 200[p]	2 x B61-3, -4	70
F-16MLU	Falcon (NATO)	..	1985	3 200	2 x B61-3, -4	40
PA-200	Tornado (NATO)	..	1983	2 400	2 x B61-3, -4	40
Total stockpile						3 800[q]
Deployed warheads						1 750[r]
Reserve warheads						2 050
Retired warheads awaiting dismantlement[s]						2 000
Total inventory						5 800[t]

.. = not available or not applicable; ALCM = air-launched cruise missile; ICBM = intercontinental ballistic missile; kt = kiloton; NATO = North Atlantic Treaty Organization; SERV = security-enhanced re-entry vehicle; SLBM = submarine-launched ballistic missile; SSBN = nuclear-powered ballistic missile submarine.

[a] Maximum unrefuelled range. All nuclear-equipped aircraft can be refuelled in the air. Actual mission range will vary according to flight profile and weapon loading.

[b] The number shows the total number of warheads assigned to nuclear-capable delivery systems. Only some of these warheads are deployed on missiles and at aircraft bases.

[c] Bombers have two numbers: the first is the number assigned to the nuclear mission; the second is the total inventory. The US Air Force has 66 nuclear-capable bombers (20 B-2As and 46 B-52Hs) of which no more than 60 will be deployed at any given time.

[d] Of the bomber weapons, c. 300 (200 ALCMs and 100 bombs) are deployed at the bomber bases; all the rest are in central storage. Many of the gravity bombs are no longer fully active and are slated for retirement after the B61-12 is fielded in the early 2020s.

[e] The B-52H is no longer configured to carry nuclear gravity bombs.

[f] Strategic gravity bombs are only assigned to B-2A bombers. The maximum yields of strategic bombs are: B61-7 (360 kt), B61-11 (400 kt), B83-1 (1200 kt). However, they also have lower yields. Most B83-1s have been moved to the inactive stockpile and B-2As rarely exercise with the B83-1. The administration of President Barack Obama decided that the B83-1 would be retired once the

B61-12 was deployed, but the administration of President Donald J. Trump has indicated that it might retain the B83-1 for a longer period.

^{g} Of these ICBM warheads, only 400 are deployed on the missiles. The remaining warheads are in central storage.

^{h} Only 200 of these W78 warheads are deployed; all the rest are in central storage.

^{i} Another 340 W87s are possibly in long-term storage outside the stockpile for planned use in the W78 replacement warhead (W87-1).

^{j} Of the 14 SSBNs, 2 are normally undergoing refuelling overhaul at any given time. They are not assigned weapons. Another 2 or more submarines may be undergoing maintenance at any given time and may not be carrying missiles. The number of deployable missiles has been reduced to 240 to meet the 2010 Treaty on Measures for the Further Reduction and Limitation of Strategic Offensive Arms (New START) limit on deployed strategic missile launchers.

^{k} Of these warheads, only about 930 are deployed on submarines; all the rest are in central storage. Although each D5 missile was counted under the 1991 Strategic Arms Reduction Treaty as carrying 8 warheads and the missile was initially flight tested with 14, the US Navy has downloaded each missile to an average of 4–5 warheads. D5 missiles equipped with the new low-yield W76-2 carry only 1 warhead.

^{l} It is assumed here that all W76-0 warheads have been replaced by the W76-1.

^{m} According to US military officials, the new low-yield W76-2 warhead will normally be deployed on at least 2 of the SSBNs on patrol in the Atlantic and Pacific oceans.

^{n} Approximately 150 of the tactical bombs are thought to be deployed across 6 NATO airbases outside the USA. The remaining bombs are in central storage in the USA. Older B61 versions will be returned to the USA once the B61-12 is deployed.

^{o} The maximum yields of tactical bombs are: B61-3 (170 kt) and B61-4 (50 kt). All have selective lower yields. The B61-10 was retired in 2016.

^{p} Most sources list 2400 km unrefuelled ferry range but Lockheed Martin, which produces the F-16, lists 3200 km.

^{q} Of these weapons, approximately 1750 are deployed on ballistic missiles, at bomber bases in the USA and at 6 NATO airbases outside the USA; all the rest are in central storage.

^{r} The deployed warhead number in this table differs from the number declared under New START because the treaty attributes 1 warhead per deployed bomber—even though bombers do not carry warheads under normal circumstances—and does not count warheads stored at bomber bases.

^{s} Up until 2018, the US Government published the number of warheads dismantled each year, but the Trump administration ended this practice. Based on previous performance and the completion of the W76-1 life-extension programme, it is estimated here that approximately 385 retired warheads were dismantled during 2019.

^{t} In addition to these intact warheads, there are more than 20 000 plutonium pits stored at the Pantex Plant, Texas, and perhaps 4000 uranium secondaries stored at the Y-12 facility at Oak Ridge, Tennessee.

Sources: US Department of Defense, various budget reports and plans, press releases and documents obtained under the Freedom of Information Act; US Department of Energy, various budget reports and plans; US Air Force, US Navy and US Department of Energy, personal communications; *Bulletin of the Atomic Scientists*, 'Nuclear notebook', various issues; and author's estimates.

air-launched cruise missile (ALCM), known as the long-range standoff weapon (LRSO); a new intercontinental ballistic missile (Ground Based Strategic Deterrent, GBSD); and a new nuclear-capable, tactical fighter-bomber (F-35A). The programme also aims to upgrade the command and control systems at the US Department of Defense (DOD), and the nuclear warheads and their supporting infrastructure at the US Department of Energy's National Nuclear Security Administration (NNSA).

According to an estimate published in January 2019 by the US Congressional Budget Office (CBO), modernizing and operating the US nuclear arsenal and the facilities that support it will cost around $494 billion for the period 2019–28, $94 billion more than the CBO's 2017 estimate for the period 2017–26. The rise partly reflects the expected increase in costs based on the progression of the modernization programme as well as the 2018 NPR's addition of new nuclear weapons.[4] The nuclear modernization (and maintenance) programme will continue well beyond 2028 and, based on the CBO's estimate, will cost $1.2 trillion over the next three decades. Notably, although the CBO estimate accounts for inflation, other estimates forecast that the total cost will be closer to $1.7 trillion.[5] The NPR acknowledged that cost estimates of the modernization programme vary but stated that the programme is 'an affordable priority' and emphasized that the total cost represented only a small portion of the overall defence budget.[6] There is little doubt, however, that limited resources, competing nuclear and conventional modernization programmes, and the rapidly growing federal budget deficit will present significant challenges for the nuclear modernization programme in the years ahead.

Bombers

The US Air Force (USAF) currently operates a fleet of 169 heavy bombers: 62 B-1Bs, 20 B-2As and 87 B-52Hs. Of these, 66 (20 B-2As and 46 B-52Hs) are nuclear capable, although only 60 (18 B-2As and 42 B-52Hs) are thought to be assigned nuclear delivery roles. It is estimated here that there are nearly 850 warheads assigned to strategic bombers, of which about 300 are deployed at bomber bases.

Both the B-2As and B-52Hs are undergoing modernization intended to improve their ability to receive and transmit secure nuclear mission data. This includes the ability to communicate with the Advanced Extreme High Frequency satellite network used by the US president and military leadership to transmit launch orders and manage nuclear operations.[7]

The development of the next-generation long-range strike bomber, known as the B-21 Raider, is well under way with the first test aircraft under

---

[4] US Congressional Budget Office, 'Projected costs of US nuclear forces, 2019 to 2028', Jan. 2019, p. 1.
[5] See e.g. Reif, K., 'US nuclear modernization programs', Arms Control Association, Fact Sheet, updated Aug. 2018.
[6] US Department of Defense (note 3), pp. XI, 51–52.
[7] US Department of Defense (DOD), *Fiscal Year (FY) 2020 Budget Estimates, Air Force, Justification Book Volume 3a of 3: Research, Development, Test & Evaluation, Air Force, Vol–III Part 1* (DOD: Arlington, VA, Mar. 2019).

construction.[8] The B-21 will be capable of delivering B61-12 guided nuclear gravity bombs, which are currently in development, and LRSO cruise missiles. The USAF plans to acquire 1000 LRSO missiles, of which about half will be nuclear armed and the rest used for spares and test launches.[9] The new bomber is scheduled to enter service in the mid-2020s.[10] The B-21 will replace the B-1B and B-2A bombers at Dyess Air Force Base (AFB) in Texas, Ellsworth AFB in South Dakota, and Whiteman AFB in Missouri.[11] The USAF plans to acquire at least 100 B-21s but the final order may be significantly higher.[12]

Land-based ballistic missiles

As of January 2020, the USA deployed 400 Minuteman III ICBMs in 450 silos across three missile wings. Fifty of the 450 silos are empty but kept in a state of readiness and can be reloaded with stored missiles if necessary.[13]

Each Minuteman III ICBM is armed with one warhead: either a 335-kiloton W78/Mk12A or a 300-kt W87/Mk21. Missiles carrying the W78 can be uploaded with up to two more warheads for a maximum of three multiple independently targetable re-entry vehicles (MIRVs). It is estimated here that there are 800 warheads assigned to the ICBM force, of which 400 are deployed on the missiles.

The USAF has begun development of a next-generation ICBM, the above-mentioned GBSD, which is scheduled to begin replacing the Minuteman III in 2028 and achieve full operational capability in 2036.[14] The plan is to buy 642 missiles, of which 400 would be deployed, 50 stored and the rest used for test launches and as spares.[15] Development and production of the GBSD will go on well into the mid-2030s. The projected cost of the programme continues to increase. It rose from $62.5 billion projected in 2015 to around $100 billion in 2017.[16] In 2019 the CBO estimated that the cost for the 10-year

---

[8] US Air Force, Secretary of the Air Force Public Affairs, 'Acting SecAF Donovan announces B-21 manufacturing, testing locations', 16 Sep. 2019.

[9] Rand, R. (Gen.), Commander, Air Force Global Strike Command, 'FY19 posture for Department of Defense nuclear forces', Presentation to the Strategic Forces Subcommittee, Armed Services Committee, US House of Representatives, 11 Apr. 2018, p. 13.

[10] Gertler, J., *Air Force B-21 Raider Long-Range Strike Bomber*, Congressional Research Service (CRS), Report for Congress R44463 (US Congress, CRS: Washington, DC, updated 13 Nov. 2019), p. 10.

[11] US Air Force, Secretary of the Air Force Public Affairs, 'Air force selects locations for B-21 aircraft', 2 May 2018.

[12] Clark, C., 'More B-21s likely: B-1s to carry up to 8 hypersonic weapons', Breaking Defense, 17 Sep. 2019.

[13] Air Force Technology, 'USAF removes last of 50 Minuteman III ICBMs and meets NST requirements', 3 July 2017.

[14] Richard, C. A., Commander, US Strategic Command, Statement before the Committee on Armed Services, US Senate, 13 Feb. 2020, p. 9.

[15] Reif, K., 'Air Force drafts plan for follow-on ICBM', *Arms Control Today*, 8 July 2015.

[16] Reif, K., 'New ICBM replacement cost revealed', *Arms Control Today*, Mar. 2017.

period 2019–28 alone would be $61 billion, $18 billion higher than the 2017 estimate for 2017–26.[17] In late 2019 the USAF confirmed that Northrop Grumman will produce the GBSD. The expectation is that the contract will be signed in the second half of 2020.[18]

The USAF is modernizing the nuclear warheads that will be used to arm the GBSD. These will also be used to arm the Minuteman III for the remainder of its service life. The W87/Mk21 warhead is being upgraded with a new fuze (arming, fuzing and firing unit). The W78/Mk12A will be replaced entirely. The replacement warhead was formerly known as the Interoperable Warhead 1 (IW1) but in 2018 it was given the designation W87-1 to reflect that it will use a W87 plutonium pit with insensitive high explosives instead of the conventional high explosives used in the W78.[19] The projected cost of the W87-1 programme is between $10.6 billion and $13.2 billion.[20]

During 2019, the USAF Global Strike Command carried out four operational and developmental test launches of the Minuteman III ICBM weapon system. The missiles were launched from Vandenberg AFB in California with the payload impacting at the Ronald Reagan Ballistic Missile Defense Test Site in the Kwajalein Atoll in the Marshall Islands.[21]

Ballistic missile submarines

The US Navy operates a fleet of 14 Ohio class SSBNs, of which 12 are normally considered to be operational and 2 are typically undergoing refuelling overhaul at any given time.

All of the 14 Ohio class SSBNs—8 of which are based at Naval Submarine Base Kitsap in Washington State and 6 at Naval Submarine Base Kings Bay in Georgia—can carry up to 20 Trident II D5 SLBMs. To meet the New START limit on deployed launchers, 4 missile tubes on each submarine have been deactivated so that the 12 deployable SSBNs can carry no more than 240 missiles.[22]

---

[17] US Congressional Budget Office (note 4), p. 9.

[18] Erwin, S., 'Northrop Grumman wins competition to build future ICBM, by default', *Space News*, 14 Dec. 2019.

[19] Padilla, M., 'Sandia on target for first Mk21 Fuze flight test in 2018', *Sandia Lab News*, vol. 70, no. 6 (16 Mar. 2018); and US Department of Energy, National Nuclear Security Administration (NNSA), *W78 Replacement Program (W87-1): Cost Estimates and Use of Insensitive High Explosives*, Report to Congress (NNSA: Washington, DC, Dec. 2018), pp. III, 7.

[20] US Department of Energy, National Nuclear Security Administration (NNSA), *Fiscal Year 2020 Stockpile Stewardship and Management Plan*, Report to Congress (NNSA: Washington, DC, July 2019), pp. 8–41.

[21] Murray, D., 'Air Force Global Strike Command year in review: 2019', US Air Force Global Strike Command Air Forces Strategic-Air, 3 Jan. 2020.

[22] US Navy, 'Fleet ballistic missile submarines: SSBN', United States Navy Fact File, 29 Jan. 2019.

Around 8 to 10 SSBNs are normally at sea, of which 4 or 5 are on alert in their designated patrol areas and ready to fire their missiles within 15 minutes of receiving the launch order.

Since 2017, the navy has been replacing its Trident II D5 SLBMs with an enhanced version known as the D5LE (LE for 'life extended'). Another 24 were deployed in 2018 (and possibly in 2019) and the upgrade is scheduled to be completed in 2024.[23] The D5LE is equipped with the new Mk-6 guidance system. The D5LE will arm Ohio class SSBNs for the remainder of their service lives (up to 2042) and will also be deployed on British Trident submarines (see section III). The D5LE will initially also arm the new Columbia class SSBN, the first of which—the *USS Columbia* (SSBN-826)—is scheduled to start patrols in 2031, but will eventually be replaced with a new SLBM, currently named the SWS (Strategic Weapon System) 534 or D5LE2.[24] The 2018 NPR stated that the navy 'will begin studies in 2020 to define a cost-effective, credible, and effective SLBM that . . . [can be deployed] throughout the service life of the COLUMBIA SSBN'.[25]

The Trident SLBMs carry two basic warhead types: either the 455-kt W88 or the 90-kt W76-1 (the older W76-0 version has been, or remains in the process of being, retired). The W76-1 is equipped with a new fuze that improves its targeting effectiveness.[26] It is estimated here that around 1920 warheads are assigned to the SSBN fleet, of which about 930 are deployed on missiles.[27] Each SLBM can carry up to eight warheads but normally carries an average of four to five.

In late 2019 the navy started to deploy a new low-yield warhead on some of its SSBNs.[28] The new warhead is the W76-2, which is a modification of the W76-1 and is estimated to have an explosive yield of about 8 kt.[29] The 2018 NPR claimed that the warhead is needed to deter Russian first use of low-yield tactical nuclear weapons.[30] The first SSBN to deploy with the W76-2 was the *USS Tennessee* (SSBN-734), which left the Kings Bay base at the end of 2019 for a deterrent patrol in the Atlantic Ocean.[31] According to US

---

[23] Wolfe, J., Director, Strategic Systems Programs, Statement before the Subcommittee on Strategic Forces, Armed Services Committee, US Senate, 23 Mar. 2019, p. 4.

[24] Peterson, J., 'Navy strategic missile boss starting concept development for new missile', *Seapower*, 24 May 2017.

[25] US Department of Defense (note 3), p. 49.

[26] Kristensen, H. M., McKinzie, M. and Postol, T. A., 'How US nuclear forces modernization is undermining strategic stability: The burst-height compensating super-fuze', *Bulletin of the Atomic Scientists*, 1 Mar. 2017.

[27] US Department of State (note 2).

[28] Arkin, W. M. and Kristensen, H. M., 'US deploys new low-yield nuclear submarine warhead', FAS Strategic Security Blog, Federation of American Scientists, 29 Jan. 2020; and US Department of Defense, 'Statement on the fielding of the W76-2 low-yield submarine-launched ballistic missile warhead', Press release, 4 Feb. 2020.

[29] US military officials, Private communications with the author, 2019–20.

[30] US Department of Defense (note 3), p. 55

[31] Arkin and Kristensen (note 28); and US Department of Defense (note 28).

military officials, the W76-2 has also been deployed in the Pacific Ocean and it is believed that at least two of the SSBNs on patrol in each of these oceans will normally carry one or two D5 missiles, each with one W76-2.[32]

Non-strategic nuclear weapons

The USA has one basic type of non-strategic (tactical) weapon in its stockpile—the B61 gravity bomb, which exists in two versions: B61-3 and B61-4.[33] An estimated 230 tactical B61 bombs remain in the stockpile.

Approximately 150 of the bombs are thought to be deployed for potential use by fighter-bomber aircraft at six North Atlantic Treaty Organization (NATO) airbases in five countries: Aviano and Ghedi, Italy; Büchel, Germany; Incirlik, Turkey; Kleine Brogel, Belgium; and Volkel, the Netherlands.[34] In 2019 the debate on whether the USA should continue to store nuclear weapons in Turkey intensified after incursions by Turkey into northern Syria, and there were reports that the US military was reviewing evacuation plans for the weapons.[35]

The 80 other B61 bombs are stored at bases in the continental USA for potential use by US aircraft in support of allies outside Europe, including in East Asia.

The USA is close to completing the development of the B61-12 guided nuclear bomb, which will replace all existing versions of the B61. Delivery was scheduled to start in 2020 but production problems in 2019 caused delays and delivery is now expected to take place in late 2021.[36] The new version is equipped with a guided tail kit that enables it to hit targets more accurately, meaning that it could be used with a lower yield and potentially produce less radioactive fallout.[37]

Integration of the B61-12 on existing USAF and NATO aircraft continued in 2019. The USAF plans to integrate the B61-12 on seven types of aircraft: the B-2A, the B-21, the F-15E, the F-16C/D, the F-16 MLU, the F-35A and the PA-200 (Tornado).[38] To ensure that Germany can continue to participate in

---

[32] US military officials, Private communications with the author, 2019–20.

[33] A third version, the B61-10, was retired in Sep. 2016. US Department of Energy, National Nuclear Security Administration (NNSA), *Fiscal Year 2018 Stockpile Stewardship Management Plan*, Report to Congress (NNSA: Washington, DC, Nov. 2017), figure 1–7, pp. 1–13.

[34] For a detailed overview of the dual-capable aircraft programmes of the USA and its NATO allies see Kristensen, H. M., 'US nuclear forces', *SIPRI Yearbook 2019*, pp. 299–300; and Andreasen, S. et al., Nuclear Threat Initiative (NTI), *Building a Safe, Secure, and Credible NATO Nuclear Posture* (NTI: Washington, DC, Jan. 2018).

[35] Sanger, D. E., 'Trump followed his gut on Syria. Calamity came fast', *New York Times*, 14 Oct. 2019.

[36] Gould, J. and Mehta, A., 'Nuclear gravity bomb and warhead upgrades face new delays', *Defense News*, 4 Sep. 2019.

[37] Kristensen, H. M. and McKinzie, M., 'Video shows earth-penetrating capability of B61-12 nuclear bomb', FAS Strategic Security Blog, Federation of American Scientists, 14 Jan. 2016.

[38] US Air Force (USAF), *United States Air Force Acquisition, Annual Report, Fiscal Year 2018: Cost-effective Modernization* (USAF: Arlington, VA, [2019]), p. 24.

the NATO nuclear strike mission after it has completed the planned replace-ment of its Tornados with either Eurofighter or F/A-18 aircraft, some of the new aircraft would also need to undergo integration with the B61-12.[39]

During 2019, the US Navy began an 'analysis of alternatives' study for the new nuclear-armed sea-launched cruise missile called for by the 2018 NPR.[40] The development of the weapon would mark a significant change in approach by the US Navy, which completely eliminated all non-strategic naval nuclear weapons after the end of the cold war.[41] If funded by the US Congress, the new missile could be deployed on attack submarines or surface ships by the end of the 2020s and could potentially result in the first increase in the size of the US nuclear weapon stockpile since 1996.

---

[39] Shalal, A., 'Germany drops F-35 from fighter tender; Boeing F/A-18 and Eurofighter to battle on', Reuters, 31 Jan. 2019.

[40] Burgess, R. R., 'Navy's Trident missile director: Planning for sea-launched nuclear cruise missile set for 2019', *Seapower*, 22 Mar. 2018. See also Kristensen, H. M., 'US nuclear forces', *SIPRI Yearbook 2019*, pp. 292–94.

[41] Kristensen, H. M., 'Declassified: US nuclear weapons at sea', FAS Strategic Security Blog, Federation of American Scientists, 3 Feb. 2016.

II. Russian nuclear forces

HANS M. KRISTENSEN

As of January 2020, Russia maintained a military stockpile of approximately 4315 nuclear warheads—around 15 fewer than the estimate for January 2019.[1] About 2440 of these were offensive strategic warheads, of which roughly 1570 were deployed on land- and sea-based ballistic missiles and at bomber bases. Russia also possessed approximately 1875 non-strategic (tactical) nuclear warheads—a slight increase compared with the estimate for January 2019 due to the fielding of dual-capable non-strategic weapons. All of the non-strategic warheads were in central storage sites.[2] An estimated additional 2060 retired warheads were awaiting dismantlement (110 fewer than the estimate for January 2019), giving a total inventory of approximately 6375 warheads (see table 10.3). As of September 2019, Russia was reported, under the 2010 Treaty on Measures for the Further Reduction and Limitation of Strategic Offensive Arms (New START), to have 1426 deployed warheads attributed to 513 deployed strategic launchers—that is, deployed intercontinental ballistic missiles (ICBMs) deployed submarine-launched ballistic missiles (SLBMs) and deployed heavy bombers.[3] The number of deployed warheads reported under New START differs from the estimate presented here because the treaty attributes one weapon to each deployed bomber—even though bombers do not carry weapons under normal circumstances—and does not count warheads stored at bomber bases.

Strategic bombers

Russia's Long-range Aviation Command operates a fleet of approximately 13 Tu-160 (Blackjack) and 55 Tu-95MS (Bear) bombers.[4] Not all of these are fully operational and some are undergoing various upgrades. The maximum possible loading on the bombers is nearly 750 nuclear weapons but, since only some of the bombers are fully operational, it is estimated that the number of assigned weapons is lower—around 580—of which approximately 200 might be stored at the two strategic bomber bases: Engels in the Saratov oblast and

---

[1] The data presented in this section is based on assessments by the author.

[2] For a recent overview of Russia's nuclear weapon storage facilities see Podvig, P. and Serrat, J., *Lock Them Up: Zero-deployed Non-strategic Nuclear Weapons in Europe* (United Nations Institute for Disarmament Research: Geneva, 2017).

[3] US Department of State, Bureau of Arms Control, Verification and Compliance, 'New START Treaty aggregate numbers of strategic offensive arms', Fact Sheet, 1 Sep. 2019. For a summary and other details of New START see annex A, section III, and chapter 11, section I, in this volume.

[4] The Tu-95MS exists in 2 versions: the Tu-95MS16 (Bear-H16) and the Tu-95MS6 (Bear-H6).

Ukrainka in the Amur oblast.[5] An upgrade of the nuclear weapon storage site at Engels is under way.[6]

Modernization of the bombers, which includes upgrades to their avionics suites, engines and long-range nuclear and conventional cruise missiles, is progressing, but at a slower pace than anticipated.[7] The upgraded Tu-95MS is known as the Tu-95MSM and the upgraded Tu-160 is known as the Tu-160M. The upgraded bombers are capable of carrying the new Kh-102 (AS-23B) nuclear air-launched cruise missile (ALCM). Six Tu-95MSMs were delivered in 2019.[8] It seems likely that all of the Tu-160s and most of the Tu-95s will be upgraded to maintain a bomber force of perhaps 50–60 operational aircraft.

The Russian Government has also announced plans to resume production of the Tu-160 to produce up to 50 Tu-160M2s, with serial production starting in the early 2020s.[9] These and the other modernized bombers mentioned above are intended to be only a temporary bridge to Russia's next-generation bomber: the PAK-DA, a subsonic aircraft that looks similar to the flying-wing design of the United States' B-2 bomber. The serial production of the PAK-DA has been delayed and is scheduled to begin in 2027.[10] The PAK-DA will eventually replace all Tu-95s and Tu-160s as well as the Tu-22s that are deployed with non-strategic forces (see below).[11]

Russian strategic bombers carried out operations over the Baltic Sea and the Arctic, Atlantic and Pacific oceans in 2019. The Pacific operations included a joint Russian–Chinese exercise, which led to a serious incident in July involving South Korea. South Korean aircraft fired warning shots when a surveillance aircraft, operating together with Tu-95 bombers, allegedly violated South Korean airspace over islands in the Sea of Japan that are the subject of a territorial dispute.[12] Russian bomber operations in 2019 also included the first-ever visit by two Tu-160s to South Africa.[13]

[5] Podvig, P., 'Strategic aviation', Russian Strategic Nuclear Forces, accessed Jan. 2020.

[6] Kristensen, H. M. and Korda, M., 'Nuclear upgrade at Russian bomber base and storage site', FAS Strategic Security Blog, Federation of American Scientists, 25 Feb. 2019.

[7] Trevithick, J., 'Russia rolls out new Tu-160M2, but are Moscow's bomber ambitions realistic?', The Drive, 16. Nov. 2017.

[8] O'Shaughnessy, T. J. (Gen.), Commander, United States Northern Command and North American Aerospace Defense Command, Statement before the Armed Services Committee, US Senate, 13 Feb. 2020, p. 4.

[9] TASS, [The Russian military will receive four Tu-160M2 bombers by 2023], 30 Jan. 2019 (in Russian).

[10] Lavrov, A., Kretsul, R. and Ramm, A., [Batch agreement: The latest bomber assigned a deadline for production], Izvestia, 14 Jan. 2020 (in Russian).

[11] TASS, [Russia to test next-generation stealth strategic bomber], 2 Aug. 2019 (in Russian).

[12] BBC, 'Russia and South Korea spar over airspace "intrusion"', 24 July 2019.

[13] Moscow Times, 'Russia sends nuclear-bombers to South Africa in "friendly" visit', 23 Oct. 2019.

Table 10.3. Russian nuclear forces, January 2020

All figures are approximate and are estimates based on assessments by the author. Totals for strategic and non-strategic forces are rounded up to the nearest 5 warheads.

Type/ Russian designation (NATO designation)	No. of launchers	Year first deployed	Range (km)[a]	Warhead loading	No. of warheads[b]
Strategic offensive forces					**2 440**[c]
Bombers	*50/68*[d]				*580*[e]
Tu-95MS/M (Bear-H)[f]	39/55	1981	6 500– 10 500	6–16 x AS-15A or AS-23B ALCMs	448
Tu-160/M (Blackjack)	11/13	1987	10 500– 13 200	12 x AS-15B or AS-23B ALCMs, bombs	132
ICBMs	*302*				*1 136*[g]
RS-20V (SS-18 Satan)	46	1992	11 000– 15 000	10 x 500–800 kt	460
RS-18 (SS-19 Stiletto)	..	1980	10 000	6 x 400 kt	..[h]
Avangard (SS-19 Mod 4)[i]	2	2019	10 000	1 x HGV [400 kt]	2
RS-12M Topol (SS-25 Sickle)	36	1985	10 500	1 x 800 kt	36
RS-12M2 Topol-M (SS-27 Mod 1/silo)	60	1997	10 500	1 x 800 kt	60
RS-12M1 Topol-M (SS-27 Mod 1/mobile)	18	2006	10 500	1 x [800 kt]	18
RS-24 Yars (SS-27 Mod 2/ mobile)	126	2010	10 500	4 x [100 kt]	504
RS-24 Yars (SS-27 Mod 2/silo)	14	2014	10 500	4 x [100 kt]	56
RS-28 Sarmat (SS-X-29)	..	[2021]	10 000+	MIRV [.. kt]	..
SLBMs	*10/160*[j]				*720*[j]
RSM-50 Volna (SS-N-18 M1 Stingray)	1/16	1978	6 500	3 x 50 kt	48
RSM-54 Sineva (SS-N-23 M1)	6/96	1986/2007	9 000	4 x 100 kt	384
RSM-56 Bulava (SS-N-32)	3/48	2014	>8 050	6 x [100 kt]	288
Non-strategic forces					**1 875**[k]
ABM, air/coastal defence	*1 124*				*382*
53T6 (SH-08, Gazelle)	68	1986	30	1 x 10 kt	68
S-300/400 (SA-20/21)	1 000[l]	1992/2007	..	1 x low kt	290
3M-55 Yakhont (SS-N-26)	48	[2014]	400+	1 x [.. kt]	20
SSC-1B (Sepal)	8	1973	500	1 x 350 kt	4
Air force weapons[m]	*315*				*495*
Tu-22M3 (Backfire-C)	90	1974	..	3 x ASMs, bombs	270
Su-24M/M2 (Fencer-D)	90	1974	..	2 x bombs	90[n]
Su-34 (Fullback)	125	2006	..	2 x bombs	125[n]
Su-57 (Felon)	..	[2020]	..	[bombs, ASM?]	..
MiG-31K (Foxhound)	10	2018	..	1 x ALBM	10
Army weapons	*164*				*90*
Iskander-M (SS-26 Stone)	144	2005	350[o]	[1 x 10–100 kt]	70[p]
9M729 (SSC-8)	20	2016	2 350	1 x [.. kt]	20

Type/ Russian designation (NATO designation)	No. of launchers	Year first deployed	Range (km)[a]	Warhead loading	No. of warheads[b]
Navy weapons					*905*
Submarines/surface ships/air		LACMs, SLCMs, ASWs, SAMs, depth bombs, torpedoes[q]			
Total stockpile					**4 315**
Deployed warheads					1 570[r]
Reserve warheads					2 745[s]
Retired warheads awaiting dismantlement					**2 060**
Total inventory					**6 375**

. . = not available or not applicable; [ ] = uncertain figure; ABM = anti-ballistic missile; ALBM = air-launched ballistic missile; ALCM = air-launched cruise missile; ASM = air-to-surface missile; ASW = anti-submarine weapon; HGV = hypersonic glide vehicle; ICBM = intercontinental ballistic missile; kt = kiloton; LACM = land-attack cruise missile; MIRV = multiple independently targetable re-entry vehicle; NATO = North Atlantic Treaty Organization; SAM = surface-to-air missile; SLBM = submarine-launched ballistic missile; SLCM = sea-launched cruise missile.

Note: The table lists the total number of warheads estimated to be available for the delivery systems. Only some of these are deployed and they do not necessarily correspond to the 2010 Treaty on Measures for the Further Reduction and Limitation of Strategic Offensive Arms (New START) data counting rules.

[a] Aircraft range is for illustrative purposes only; actual mission range will vary according to flight profile and weapon loading.

[b] The number shows the total number of available warheads, both deployed and in storage, assigned to the delivery systems.

[c] Approximately 1570 of these strategic warheads are deployed on land- and sea-based ballistic missiles and at bomber bases. The remaining warheads are in central storage.

[d] The first number is the number of bombers estimated to be counted as deployed under New START; the second number is the total number of bombers in the inventory. Because of ongoing bomber modernization, there is considerable uncertainty about how many bombers are operational.

[e] The maximum possible loading on the bombers is nearly 750 nuclear weapons but, since only some of the bombers are fully operational, it is assumed here that only 580 weapons are assigned to the long-range bomber force, of which approximately 200 might be stored at the 2 strategic bomber bases. The remaining weapons are in central storage facilities.

[f] There are 2 types of Tu-95MS aircraft: the Tu-95MS6, which can carry 6 AS-15A missiles internally; and the Tu-95MS16, which can carry an additional 10 AS-15A missiles externally, for a total of 16 missiles. Both types are being modernized. The modernized aircraft (Tu-95MSM) can carry 8 AS-23B missiles externally and possibly 6 internally, for a total of 14 missiles.

[g] These ICBMs can carry a total of 1136 warheads but it is estimated here that they have been downloaded to carry just over 810 warheads, with the remaining warheads in storage.

[h] It is possible that the remaining RS-18s have been retired.

[i] The missile uses a modified RS-18 (SS-19) ICBM booster with an HGV payload.

[j] The Russian Navy has a fleet of 10 operational nuclear-armed nuclear-powered ballistic missile submarines (SSBNs): 6 Delfin class (Delta IV), 1 Kalmar class (Delta III) and 3 Borei class. One or two of the Delta SSBNs are in overhaul at any given time and do not carry their assigned nuclear missiles and warheads. It is estimated here that only about 560 of the 720 warheads are deployed.

[k] According to the Russian Government, non-strategic nuclear warheads are not deployed with their delivery systems but are kept in a central storage facility. Some storage facilities are near operational bases.

[l] There are at least 80 S-300/400 sites across Russia, each with an average of 12 launchers, each with 2–4 interceptors. Each launcher has several reloads.

[m] The subtotal is based on an estimate of the total number of nuclear-capable aircraft. However, only some of them are thought to have nuclear missions. Most can carry more than 1 nuclear weapon. Other potential nuclear-capable aircraft include the Su-25 Frogfoot and the Su-30MK.

[n] The estimate assumes that half of the aircraft have a nuclear role.

[o] Although many unofficial sources and news media reports state that the Iskander-M (SS-26) has a range of nearly 500 km, the US Air Force National Air and Space Intelligence Center (NASIC) lists the range as 350 km.

[p] The estimate assumes that half of the dual-capable launchers have a secondary nuclear role.

[q] Only submarines are thought to be assigned nuclear torpedoes.

[r] The deployed warhead number in this table differs from the number declared under New START because the treaty attributes 1 warhead per deployed bomber—even though bombers do not carry warheads under normal circumstances—and does not count warheads stored at bomber bases.

[s] Reserve warheads include the 1875 non-strategic warheads in central storage (see note k).

Sources: Russian Ministry of Defence, various press releases; US Department of State, START Treaty Memoranda of Understanding, 1990–July 2009; New START aggregate data releases, various years; US Air Force, National Air and Space Intelligence Center (NASIC), *Ballistic and Cruise Missile Threat* (NASIC: Wright-Patterson Air Force Base, OH, July 2017); US Department of Defense (DOD), *Nuclear Posture Review 2018* (DOD: Arlington, VA, Feb. 2018); US DOD, *Missile Defense Review 2019* (DOD: Arlington, VA, 2019); US Department of Defense, Office of the Deputy Assistant Secretary of Defense for Nuclear Matters (ODASDNM), *Nuclear Matters Handbook 2020* (ODASDNM: Arlington, VA, Mar. 2020); US DOD, various Congressional testimonies; BBC Monitoring; Russian news media; Russian Strategic Nuclear Forces website; International Institute for Strategic Studies, *The Military Balance* (Routledge: London, various issues); Cochran, T. B. et al., *Nuclear Weapons Databook*, vol. 4, Soviet Nuclear Weapons (Harper & Row: New York, 1989); *IHS Jane's Strategic Weapon Systems*, various issues; *Proceedings*, US Naval Institute, various issues; *Bulletin of the Atomic Scientists*, 'Nuclear notebook', various issues; and author's estimates.

Land-based ballistic missiles

As of January 2020, Russia's Strategic Rocket Forces—the branch of the armed forces that controls land-based ICBMs—consisted of 12 missile divisions grouped into 3 armies and deploying an estimated 302 ICBMs of different types and variations (see table 10.3). These ICBMs can carry a total of about 1136 warheads but it is estimated here that they have been downloaded to carry around 810 warheads, approximately 52 per cent of Russia's deployed strategic warheads. This is a slight reduction compared with the estimate for January 2019 and appears to confirm the US Air Force National Intelligence and Space Center's (NASIC) projection from 2017 that 'the number of missiles in the Russian ICBM force will continue to decrease because of arms control agreements, aging missiles, and resource constraints'.[14] It should be noted that, unless Russia and the USA agree to extend or renegotiate New

---

[14] US Air Force, National Air and Space Intelligence Center (NASIC), *Ballistic and Cruise Missile Threat* (NASIC: Wright-Patterson Air Force Base, OH, July 2017), p. 27.

START before February 2021, the treaty will expire and the limit on deployed warheads will no longer apply. Should this happen, both Russia and the USA could significantly increase the number of warheads deployed on their ICBMs.[15]

Russia's ICBM force is two-thirds through a significant modernization programme to replace all Soviet-era missiles with new types, albeit not on a one-for-one basis. The modernization also involves substantial reconstruction of silos, launch control centres, garrisons and support facilities.[16] The missile modernization programme, which started two decades ago, appears to be progressing more slowly than previously envisioned. According to Sergey Shoygu, the Russian defence minister, over 76 per cent of the ICBM force had been modernized by the end of 2019.[17] This is significantly lower than the 97 per cent modernization by the end of 2020 planned for in 2014.[18] In January 2020 Colonel General Sergey Karakaev, commander of the Strategic Rocket Forces, stated that the last Soviet-era ICBM would be phased out by 2024.[19] However, this seems unlikely based on an assessment of the probable time frame for replacing the RS-20V (SS-18; see below).

Russia's ICBM modernization is focused on the multiple-warhead version of the RS-12, known as RS-24 Yars (SS-27 Mod 2). Five of seven mobile divisions have already been completed (Irkutsk, Novosibirsk, Tagil, Teykovo and Yoshkar-Ola), with two more in progress (Barnaul and Vypolzovo— sometimes referred to as Bologovsky).[20] The first silo-based RS-24s have been installed at Kozelsk; one regiment of 10 silos is complete and 4 silos of the second regiment are operational, with 6 more under construction as of late 2019.[21] It is possible that a third regiment will be installed at Kozelsk and that at least some of the former RS-18 (SS-19) silos at the Tatishchevo division might also be upgraded to the RS-24.

In December 2019 two missiles equipped with the Avangard hypersonic glide vehicle (HGV) system were installed in former RS-20V silos of the 621st Regiment at Dombarovsky.[22] This missile type uses former RS-18 boosters and has been designated as the SS-19 Mod 4 by the North

---

[15] For more detail on this issue see chapter 11, section I, in this volume.

[16] See e.g. Kristensen, H. M., 'Russian ICBM upgrade at Kozelsk', FAS Strategic Security Blog, Federation of American Scientists, 5 Sep. 2018.

[17] President of Russia, 'Defence Ministry Board meeting', 24 Dec. 2019.

[18] TRK Petersburg Channel 5, 'Russian TV show announces new ICBM to enter service soon', 21 Apr. 2014, Translation from Russian, BBC Monitoring.

[19] TASS, [What equipment will the Russian army receive in 2020?], 14 Jan. 2020 (in Russian).

[20] Tikhonov, A., [You won't catch them by surprise], *Krasnaya Zvezda*, 28 May 2018 (in Russian); and RIA Novosti, [The commander of the Strategic Missile Forces announced the completion of the rearmament of the Tagil connection], 29 Mar. 2018 (in Russian).

[21] Author's assessment based on observation of satellite imagery.

[22] TASS, 'Russia's 1st two Avangard hypersonic missile systems to assume combat duty—source', 13 Nov. 2019.

Atlantic Treaty Organization (NATO).[23] Russia plans to install a total of two regiments, each with six missiles, at Dombarovsky by 2027.[24]

Russia is also developing a new 'heavy' liquid-fuelled, silo-based ICBM, known as the RS-28 Sarmat (SS-X-29), as a replacement for the RS-20V. Like its predecessor, the RS-28 is expected to carry a large number of multiple independently targetable re-entry vehicles (possibly as many as 10) but some might be equipped with one or a few Avangard HGVs. After much delay, full-scale flight testing of the RS-28 is scheduled to begin in 2020, with possible first entry into service in 2021—although this would be dependent on a successful flight-test programme.[25] Once cleared for service, deployment of the RS-28 will begin at the Dombarovsky and Uzhur missile divisions where replacement of the RS-20V will probably take most of the 2020s.

Russia normally conducts several large-scale exercises with road-mobile and silo-based ICBMs each year. These include combat patrols for road-mobile regiments, simulated launch exercises for silo-based regiments, and participation in command staff exercises. During 2019, the ICBM forces conducted more than 200 tactical and command staff exercises.[26] Russia carried out five ICBM test launches in 2019.[27]

Ballistic missile submarines and sea-launched ballistic missiles

The Russian Navy has a fleet of 10 operational nuclear-armed nuclear-powered ballistic missile submarines (SSBNs). The fleet includes 6 Soviet-era Delfin class (Project 667BDRM, or Delta IV NATO designation) submarines, 1 Kalmar class (Project 667BDR, or Delta III) submarine, and 3 (of a planned total of 10) Borei class (Project 955/A) submarines. A former Project 941 (Typhoon) SSBN has been converted to a test-launch platform for SLBMs but it is not thought to be nuclear armed.[28]

Two of the Borei class SSBNs are operational with the Pacific Fleet and one with the Northern Fleet. The first of an improved design, known as Borei-A (Project 955A), is fitting out. A further four are under construction and

---

[23] US Department of Defense (DOD), *Nuclear Posture Review 2018* (DOD: Arlington, VA, Feb. 2018), p. 8; and Kristensen, H. M. and Korda, M., 'Russian nuclear forces, 2019', *Bulletin of the Atomic Scientists*, vol. 75, no. 2 (2019), p. 78.

[24] TASS, [Source: The first Avangard complexes will be on duty in 2019], 29 Oct. 2018 (in Russian).

[25] Safronov, I. and Nikolsky, A., [Tests of the latest Russian nuclear missile start at the beginning of the year], *Vedomosti*, 29 Oct. 2019 (in Russian).

[26] Russian Ministry of Defence, [In 2020, strategic rocketeers plan to conduct more than 200 exercises], 3 Jan. 2020 (in Russian).

[27] Russian Ministry of Defence (note 26).

[28] Saranov, V., [Decommissioning 'Akula': Why Russia abandons the biggest submarines], RIA Novosti, 24 Jan. 2018 (in Russian).

expected to enter service over the next decade.[29] It is likely that Russia aims to maintain an SSBN fleet similar in size to that of the USA.

Each SSBN type is equipped with 16 ballistic missiles and the Russian fleet can carry a total of 720 warheads. However, one or two SSBNs are normally undergoing repairs and maintenance at any given time and are not armed. It is also possible that the warhead loading on some missiles has been reduced to meet the total warhead limit under New START. As a result, it is estimated here that only about 560 of the 720 warheads are deployed.

Non-strategic nuclear weapons

As of January 2020, Russia had an estimated 1875 warheads assigned for potential use by non-strategic forces. These include warheads for ships and submarines, various types of aircraft, air- and missile-defence systems, and army missiles. The US military estimates that 'Russia's overall nuclear stockpile is likely to grow significantly over the next decade—growth driven primarily by a projected increase in Russia's non-strategic nuclear weapons'.[30]

Russia's non-strategic nuclear weapons chiefly serve to compensate for perceived weaknesses in its conventional forces. There has been considerable debate about the role that non-strategic nuclear weapons have in Russian nuclear strategy, including potential first use.[31]

Navy weapons

The Russian military service assigned the highest number of non-strategic nuclear weapons is the navy, with about 905 warheads for use by land-attack cruise missiles, anti-ship cruise missiles, anti-submarine rockets, depth bombs, and torpedoes delivered by ships, submarines and naval aviation. Among these weapons, perhaps the most significant is the nuclear version of the long-range, land-attack Kalibr sea-launched cruise missile (SLCM), known as the 3M-14 (SS-N-30A), which has been deployed on numerous

---

[29] TASS, 'Russia to complete Borei and Yasen series of nuclear-powered submarines in 2023–2024', 27 June 2019.

[30] Richard, C. A., Commander, US Strategic Command, Statement before the Committee on Armed Services, US Senate, 13 Feb. 2020, p. 5.

[31] On the debate about the role of Russian non-strategic nuclear weapons see e.g. US Department of Defense (note 23), p. 30; Oliker, O., 'Moscow's nuclear enigma: What is Russia's arsenal really for?', *Foreign Affairs*, vol. 97, no. 6 (Nov./Dec. 2018); Stowe-Thurston, A., Korda, M., Kristensen, H. M., 'Putin deepens confusion about Russian nuclear policy', Russia Matters, 25 Oct. 2018; Tertrais, B., 'Russia's nuclear policy: Worrying for the wrong reasons', *Survival*, vol. 60, no. 2 (Apr. 2018), pp. 33–44; and Ven Bruusgaard, K., 'The myths of Russia's lowered nuclear threshold', War on the Rocks, 22 Sep. 2017.

types of surface ship and attack submarine.[32] Other notable navy weapons include the 3M-55 (SS-N-26) SLCM and the 3M-22 Tsirkon (SS-NX-33) hypersonic anti-ship missile, which is undergoing final test launches.[33] The navy is also developing the Poseidon (Status-6, or Kanyon NATO designation), a long-range nuclear-powered torpedo, for future deployment on modified submarines.[34]

Air force weapons

The Russian Air Force has nearly 500 nuclear warheads for use by Tu-22M3 (Backfire-C) intermediate-range bombers, Su-24M (Fencer-D) fighter-bombers, Su-34 (Fullback) fighter-bombers and MiG-31K (Foxhound) attack aircraft. The new Su-57 (Felon), also known as PAK-FA, which is in production and scheduled to be deployed in 2020, is also dual capable.[35] The MiG-31K is equipped with the new Kh-47M2 Kinzhal air-launched ballistic missile, and a test launch took place in the Arctic in November 2019.[36] Russia is also developing a new nuclear-capable air-to-surface missile (Kh-32) to replace the Kh-22N (AS-4) used on the Tu-22M3.[37]

Air, coastal and missile defence

The Russian air-, coastal- and missile-defence forces are estimated to have around 380 nuclear warheads for use by dual-capable S-300 and S-400 air-defence forces, the Moscow A-135 missile defence system and coastal defence units (although only a small number of warheads are assigned to the coastal defence units). Russia is also developing the S-500 air-defence system that might potentially be dual capable, but there is no publicly available authoritative information confirming a nuclear role.[38]

Army weapons

The Russian Army is thought to have approximately 90 warheads to arm short-range ballistic missiles (SRBMs) and ground-launched cruise missiles (GLCMs). The dual-capable Iskander-M (SS-26) SRBM has now completely

---

[32] There is considerable confusion about the designation of what is commonly referred to as the Kalibr missile. The Kalibr designation actually refers not to a specific missile but to a family of weapons that, in addition to the 3M-14 (SS-N-30/A) land-attack versions, includes the 3M-54 (SS-N-27) anti-ship cruise missile and the 91R anti-submarine missile. For further detail see US Navy, Office of Naval Intelligence (ONI), *The Russian Navy: A Historic Transition* (ONI: Washington, DC, Dec. 2015), pp. 34–35; and US Air Force, National Air and Space Intelligence Center (note 14), p. 37.

[33] TASS, 'Russia plans new trials of Tsirkon hypersonic missile before yearend: Source', 22 Nov. 2019.

[34] Sutton, H. I., 'Poseidon torpedo', Covert Shores, 22 Feb. 2019.

[35] US Department of Defense, Office of the Deputy Assistant Secretary of Defense for Nuclear Matters (ODASDNM), *Nuclear Matters Handbook 2020* (ODASDNM: Arlington, VA, Mar. 2020), p. 3.

[36] TASS, [Sources: Dagger hypersonic missile tests first conducted in Arctic], 30 Nov. 2019 (in Russian).

[37] US Department of Defense (note 23), p. 8.

[38] Podvig, P., 'Missile defense in Russia', Working paper, Federation of American Scientists Project on Nuclear Dynamics in a Multipolar Strategic BMD [ballistic missile defence] World, May 2017.

replaced the Tochka (SS-21) SRBM in 12 missile brigades.[39] The other army dual-capable missile is the 9M729 (SSC-8) GLCM that the USA cited as its main reason for withdrawing from the 1987 Treaty on the Elimination of Intermediate-Range and Shorter-Range Missiles (INF Treaty) in August 2019.[40] It is estimated that five 9M729 battalions have so far been co-deployed with five of the Iskander-M brigades. In 2019 there were press reports that the 9M729 had been deployed to Kamyshlov (Sverdlovsk oblast), Kapustin Yar (Astrakhan oblast), Mozdok (North Ossetia), Shuya (Ivanovo oblast) and Leningrad oblast, presumably at the base in Luga.[41]

[39] Author's assessment based on observation of satellite imagery.

[40] US Department of State, Bureau of Arms Control, Verification and Compliance, 'INF Treaty: At a glance', Fact Sheet, 8 Dec. 2017, p. 1. For a summary and other details of the INF Treaty see annex A, section III, in this volume. See also chapter 11, section I, in this volume; and Kile, S. N., 'Russian–US nuclear arms control and disarmament', *SIPRI Yearbook 2018*, pp. 321–24.

[41] Gutschker, T., 'Russland verfügt über mehr Raketen als bislang bekannt' [America is not planning an arms race], 10 Feb. 2019; and RIA Novosti, [Electronic launches of 9M729 missiles took place in the Leningrad region], 8 Feb. 2019 (in Russian).

III. British nuclear forces

SHANNON N. KILE AND HANS M. KRISTENSEN

As of January 2020, the British nuclear stockpile consisted of approximately 195–215 warheads (see table 10.4). In its 2015 Strategic Defence and Security Review (SDSR), the British Government reaffirmed its plans to cut the size of the nuclear arsenal. The number of operationally available nuclear warheads has been reduced to no more than 120. The overall size of the nuclear stockpile, including non-deployed warheads, will decrease to no more than 180 by the mid-2020s.[1]

The British nuclear deterrent consists exclusively of a sea-based component: four Vanguard class Trident nuclear-powered ballistic missile submarines (SSBNs).[2] The United Kingdom is the only nuclear weapon state that operates a single deterrent capability. In a posture known as continuous at-sea deterrence (CASD), which began in 1969, one British SSBN is on patrol at all times.[3] While the second and third SSBNs can be put to sea rapidly, the fourth would take longer because of the cycle of extensive overhaul and maintenance.

The Vanguard class SSBNs can each be armed with up to 16 UGM-133 Trident II D5 submarine-launched ballistic missiles (SLBMs). The UK does not own the missiles but leases them from a pool of 58 Trident SLBMs shared with the United States Navy at the US Strategic Weapons Facility in Kings Bay, Georgia.[4] Under limits set out in the 2010 SDSR, when on patrol, the submarines are armed with no more than 8 operational missiles with a total of 40 nuclear warheads.[5] The missiles are kept in a 'detargeted' mode, meaning that target data would need to be loaded into the guidance system before launch, and have a reduced alert status (i.e. several days' notice would be required to fire the missiles).[6]

---

[1] British Government, *National Security Strategy and Strategic Defence and Security Review 2015: A Secure and Prosperous United Kingdom*, Cm 9161 (Stationery Office: London, Nov. 2015), para. 4.66.

[2] HMS *Vanguard* entered service in Dec. 1994, while the last submarine in the class, HMS *Vengeance*, entered service in Feb. 2001. Mills, C., 'Replacing the UK's strategic nuclear deterrent: Progress of the Dreadnought class', Commons Briefing Paper CBP-8010, House of Commons Library, 11 Feb. 2020, p. 9.

[3] British Ministry of Defence, 'Continuous at sea deterrent 50: What you need to know', 3 May 2019.

[4] Allison, G., 'No, America doesn't control Britain's nuclear weapons', UK Defence Journal, 20 July 2017.

[5] British Ministry of Defence, *Securing Britain in an Age of Uncertainty: The Strategic Defence and Security Review*, Cm 7948 (Stationery Office: London, Oct. 2010), pp. 5, 38.

[6] British Government (note 1), para. 4.78.

The Trident submarine successor programme

In 2016 the House of Commons approved by a large majority a motion supporting the government's commitment to a replacement of the Vanguard class SSBNs with four new ballistic missile submarines.[7] The new submarine class, which has been named Dreadnought, will have a missile compartment that holds 12 launch tubes—a reduction from the 16 carried by the Vanguard class. As a cost-saving measure, a Common Missile Compartment is being designed in cooperation with the US Navy that will also equip the latter's new Columbia class SSBNs. During 2019, programme contractors continued to work to resolve technical problems with the manufacturing of the missile launch tubes to be used in the compartment.[8]

The Dreadnought submarines were originally expected to begin to enter into service by 2028 but this has been delayed until the early 2030s. The delay was part of the extended development and acquisition programme announced in the 2015 SDSR. The service life of the Vanguard class SSBNs was commensurately extended.[9]

The replacement of the Trident II D5 missile is not part of the Dreadnought development and acquisition programme. Instead, the UK is participating in the US Navy's current programme to extend the service life of the Trident II D5 (D5LE) missile to the early 2060s.[10]

The 2015 SDSR reaffirmed that the replacement of the current British-manufactured warhead, known as Holbrook, for the Trident II missiles would not be required at least until the 2030s. A decision on a new warhead is to be taken by the current parliament, and work continues on developing replacement options.[11] The work includes cooperation between the UK and the USA on warhead safety, security, and manufacturing technologies under the Joint Technology Demonstrator project.[12]

In the meantime, the British Atomic Weapons Establishment (AWE) has begun a programme to improve the performance and extend the life of the Trident Holbrook warhead—which is modelled on the US W76-1 warhead and incorporated into the USA-produced Mk4A re-entry vehicle—in collaboration with US nuclear weapon laboratories.[13]

---

[7] British Parliament, House of Commons, 'UK's nuclear deterrent', House of Commons Hansard, col. 559, vol. 613, 18 July 2016.

[8] British Ministry of Defence, 'The United Kingdom's future nuclear deterrent: 2019 update to Parliament', 20 Dec. 2019, pp. 1–2.

[9] British Government (note 1), para. 4.65.

[10] Mills (note 2), p. 7.

[11] British Ministry of Defence (note 8), p. 2.

[12] British Ministry of Defence (note 8).

[13] British Ministry of Defence (note 8), p. 3; and Kristensen, H. M., 'British submarines to receive upgraded US nuclear warhead', FAS Strategic Security Blog, Federation of American Scientists, 1 Apr. 2011.

Table 10.4. British nuclear forces, January 2020

Type	Designation	No. deployed	Year first deployed	Range (km)[a]	Warheads x yield	No. of warheads
Submarine-launched ballistic missiles[b]						
D5	Trident II	48	1994	>7 400	1–8 x 100 kt[c]	195–215[d]

kt = kilotons.

[a] Range is for illustrative purposes only; actual mission range will vary according to flight profile and weapon loading.

[b] The Vanguard class Trident nuclear-powered ballistic missile submarines (SSBNs) carry a reduced loading of no more than 8 Trident II missiles and 40 nuclear warheads. One submarine is on patrol at any given time.

[c] The British warhead is called the Holbrook, a modified version of the United States' W76-1 warhead, with a lower-yield option.

[d] The British Government has stated that the process to reduce the stockpile to 180 warheads is under way. Although some sources suggest that the stockpile remains at 215 warheads, it is possible that, under this process, the stockpile may have already been reduced to 195 warheads. Of the total warheads in the stockpile, 120 are operationally available.

Sources: British Ministry of Defence, white papers, press releases and website; British House of Commons, *Hansard*, various issues; *Bulletin of the Atomic Scientists*, 'Nuclear notebook', various issues; and authors' estimates.

The cost of the Dreadnought programme has been a source of concern and controversy since its inception. In 2015 the British Ministry of Defence (MOD) estimated the total cost of the programme to be £31 billion ($47.4 billion). It set aside a contingency of £10 billion ($15.3 billion) to cover possible increases.[14] In 2018 the UK's National Audit Office (NAO) reported that the MOD was facing an 'affordability gap' of £2.9 billion ($3.9 billion) in its military nuclear programmes between 2018 and 2028.[15] The MOD's budget for 2018–19 received an additional £600 million ($800 million) from the contingency fund to keep the Dreadnought programme on schedule.[16] In its annual update to parliament in December 2019, the MOD reported that a total of £7 billion ($8.9 billion) had been spent on the programme's development, design and early manufacturing phases.[17]

In January 2020 the NAO reported that three key nuclear-regulated infrastructure projects in the UK's nuclear weapon programme faced delays of between one and six years, with costs increasing by over £1.3 billion ($1.7 billion) to a forecasted total of £2.5 billion ($3.2 billion).[18] Specifically,

[14] British Government (note 1), para. 4.76.

[15] British National Audit Office (NAO), *The Defence Nuclear Enterprise: A Landscape Review*, Report by the Comptroller and Auditor General, HC 1003, Session 2017–2019 (NAO: London, 22 May 2018). Spending on defence nuclear programmes was estimated to account for *c.* 14% of the total 2018–19 defence budget.

[16] Mehta, A. and Chuter, A., 'UK releases extra funding, but military relevancy challenges remain', *Defense News*, 29 Mar. 2018.

[17] British Ministry of Defence (note 8), p. 3.

[18] British National Audit Office, *Managing Infrastructure Projects on Nuclear-regulated Sites*, Report by the Comptroller and Auditor General (NAO: London, 10 Jan. 2020), pp. 5–6.

the report identified the work under way to enhance or replace existing facilities at the shipyard in Barrow-in-Furness in Cumbria, where the four Dreadnought class SSBNs are being built. The other projects involved the development of cores for a new generation of nuclear reactors to power the Dreadnought submarines and the construction of a new warhead assembly and disassembly facility (MENSA) in Berkshire to be operated by the AWE. The NAO report attributed the rising costs and delays to poor project management and insufficient oversight by the MOD.[19] It set out a series of recommendations to address identified shortcomings. However, the report also noted that some of the increased costs reflected the need for the MOD to comply with stricter security and safety regulations for the nuclear industry.[20]

[19] British National Audit Office (note 18), p. 8.
[20] British National Audit Office (note 18), p. 13.

IV. French nuclear forces

SHANNON N. KILE AND HANS M. KRISTENSEN

France's nuclear arsenal consists of approximately 290 warheads. The warheads are earmarked for delivery by 48 submarine-launched ballistic missiles (SLBMs) and 50 air-launched cruise missiles (ALCMs) produced for land- and carrier-based aircraft (see table 10.5). France considers all of its nuclear weapons to be strategic, even though the weapons carried by the airborne component of its nuclear forces have characteristics (i.e. a limited range and yield) that other nuclear-armed states consider to be tactical.[1]

The main component of France's nuclear forces is the Strategic Oceanic Force (Force Océanique Stratégique, FOST). It consists of four Triomphant class nuclear-powered ballistic missile submarines (SSBNs) based on the Île Longue peninsula near Brest. Each of the SSBNs is capable of carrying 16 SLBMs. However, one SSBN is out of service for overhaul and maintenance work at any given time and is not armed. The submarines began to enter operational service in 1997, replacing six older Redoubtable class SSBNs.[2] The French Navy has maintained a continuous at-sea deterrent posture, whereby one SSBN is on patrol at all times, since the establishment of the FOST in 1972.[3]

France continues to modernize its SLBMs and associated warheads. In 2018 the French Navy completed work to modify the Triomphant class submarines to carry the M51 SLBM, which replaced the M45 missile.[4] The M51 is currently deployed in two versions. The M51.1 is capable of carrying up to six multiple independently targetable re-entry vehicle (MIRV) TN-75 warheads, each with an explosive yield of 100 kilotons. It is being replaced by an upgraded version known as M51.2, which has greater range and improved accuracy. The M51.2 is designed to carry the new, stealthier oceanic nuclear warhead (tête nucléaire océanique, TNO), which has a reported yield of up to 100 kilotons.[5] The number of warheads on some of the missiles has been

---

[1] Hollande, F., French President, 'Discours sur la dissuasion nucléaire : Déplacement auprès des forces aériennes stratégiques' [Speech on nuclear deterrence: Visit to the strategic air forces], Istres, 25 Feb. 2015.

[2] Le Triomphant entered active service in July 1997, while the fourth and final submarine in the class, Le Terrible, entered service in Sep. 2010. Tertrais, B., French Nuclear Deterrence Policy, Forces and Future, Recherches & Documents no. 01/2019 (Fondation pour la Recherche Stratégique: Paris, Jan. 2019), p. 61.

[3] French Ministry of the Armed Forces, '500e patrouille d'un sous-marin nucléaire lanceur dengins' [500th patrol of a nuclear-powered ballistic missile submarine], 12 Oct. 2018.

[4] Navy Recognition, 'Final French Navy SSBN "Le Temeraire" upgraded for M51 SLBM', 18 Aug. 2018. Le Terrible was equipped with launch tubes for the M51 missile during its construction.

[5] Groizeleau, V., 'Dissuasion : 25 milliards en cinq ans pour le renouvellement des deux composantes' [Deterrence: 25 billion in five years for the renewal of the two components], Mer et Marine, 2 Oct. 2019; and Groizeleau, V., 'Dissuasion : F. Hollande détaille sa vision et l'arsenal français' [Deterrence: F. Hollande outlines his vision and the French arsenal], Mer et Marine, 20 Feb. 2015.

reduced in order to improve targeting flexibility.[6] France has commenced design work on a new M51.3 SLBM with improved accuracy. It is scheduled to replace the M51.2 and become operational in 2025.[7]

France has also begun preliminary design work on a third-generation SSBN, designated the SNLE 3G, which will eventually be equipped with a new modification of the M51 (M51.4) SLBM.[8] The construction of the first of four submarines in the class is scheduled to begin in 2023.[9] The aim is to have an operational successor to the Triomphant class submarine in service by the early 2030s.[10]

The airborne component of the French nuclear forces consists of land- and carrier-based aircraft. The French Air Force has 40 deployed land-based nuclear-capable Rafale BF3 aircraft. It retired the last of its nuclear-capable Mirage 2000N aircraft in 2018.[11] All the Rafale BF3s are normally based at Saint-Dizier Air Base. The year 2019 marked 55 years of continuous nuclear alert by the French Air Force.[12]

The French Naval Nuclear Air Force (Force Aéronavale Nucléaire, FANu) consists of a squadron of 10 Rafale MF3 aircraft aboard the aircraft carrier the *Charles de Gaulle*. The ship returned to operational service in early 2019 after completing a mid-life refit that included refuelling its two nuclear reactors. Its first deployment following the refit was to Singapore and lasted from March to July.[13] The year 2019 marked the 40th anniversary of the FANu.[14]

The Rafale aircraft are equipped with medium-range air-to-surface cruise missiles (air-sol moyenne portée-améliorée, ASMP-A), which entered service in 2009. France produced 54 ASMP-As, including test missiles.[15] A mid-life refurbishment programme for the ASMP-A that began in 2016 will

---

[6] Tertrais (note 2), p. 63.

[7] French Ministry of the Armed Forces, 'Missiles balistiques stratégiques (MSBS)' [Strategic ballistic missiles], 28 Jan. 2020; and French Ministry of the Armed Forces, 'Discours de Florence Parly, ministre des Armées prononcé à l'usine des Mureaux, ArianeGroup, le 14 décembre 2017' [Speech by Florence Parly, Minister of the Armed Forces, presented at the Mureaux factory, ArianeGroup], 14 Dec. 2017.

[8] Tertrais (note 2), pp. 63, 67.

[9] Groizeleau, 'Deterrence: 25 billion in five years for the renewal of the two components' (note 5).

[10] Hollande (note 1); and Le Drian, J. Y., French Minister of Defence, 'Discours de clôture du colloque pour les 50 ans de la dissuasion' [Conference closing speech on the 50th anniversary of deterrence], French Ministry of Defence, Paris, 20 Nov. 2014.

[11] French Ministry of the Armed Forces, 'La dissuasion aéroportée passe au tout Rafale' [Airborne deterrence goes to the Rafale], 5 Sep. 2018; and Huberdeau, E., 'L'Adieu au Mirage 2000N' [Farewell to the Mirage 2000N], *Air & Cosmos*, 22 June 2018.

[12] French Ministry of the Armed Forces, 'Les FAS à l'honneur dans le nouveau numéro d'Air actualités' [FAS in the spotlight in the new issue of Air actualités], 18 Oct. 2019.

[13] French Ministry of the Armed Forces, 'CLEMENCEAU: Fin de mission pour le groupe aéronaval' [CLEMENCEAU: End of mission for the Carrier Strike Group], 9 July 2019.

[14] French Ministry of the Armed Forces, 'Fin des travaux de refonte à mi-vie du porte-avions : La ministre des Armées sur le Charles de Gaulle' [Completion of the mid-life refit of the aircraft carrier: The minister of defence on the Charles de Gaulle], 9 Nov. 2018.

[15] Hollande (note 1); Tertrais (note 2), p. 65.

Table 10.5. French nuclear forces, January 2020

Type	No. deployed	Year first deployed	Range (km)[a]	Warheads x yield	No. of warheads
Land-based aircraft					
Rafale BF3[b]	40	2010–11	2 000	1 x [up to 300 kt] TNA[c]	40
Carrier-based aircraft					
Rafale MF3[b]	10	2010–11	2 000	1 x [up to 300 kt] TNA[c]	10
Submarine-launched ballistic missiles[d]					
M51.1	16	2010	>6 000	4–6 x 100 kt TN-75	80[e]
M51.2	32[f]	2017	>9 000[g]	4–6 x 100 kt TNO	160
M51.3[h]	0	[2025]	>[9 000]	[up to 6 x 100 kt] TNO	0
Total					**290[i]**

[] = uncertain figure; kt = kiloton; TNA = tête nucléaire aéroportée (airborne nuclear warhead); TNO = tête nucléaire océanique (oceanic nuclear warhead).

[a] Aircraft range is for illustrative purposes only; actual mission range will vary according to flight profile and weapon loading.

[b] The Rafale BF3s and MF3s carry the ASMP-A air-launched cruise missile (ALCM). Most sources report that the ASMP-A has a range of 500–600 km, although some suggest that it might be over 600 km.

[c] The TNA has a reported maximum yield of 300 kt but lower-yield options are thought to be available.

[d] France has only produced enough submarine-launched ballistic missiles (SLBMs) to equip 3 operational nuclear-powered ballistic missile submarines (SSBNs); the fourth SSBN is out of service for overhaul and maintenance work at any given time.

[e] Although the M51 SLBM can carry up to 6 warheads, the number of warheads is believed to have been reduced on some of the missiles in order to improve targeting flexibility.

[f] The French Navy is transitioning from the M51.1 to the M51.2. The last M51.1 missiles will be replaced in 2020.

[g] The M51.2 has a 'much greater range' than the M51.1, according to the French Ministry of the Armed Forces.

[h] The M51.3 is under development and has not yet been deployed.

[i] In a speech in Feb. 2020, President Emmanuel Macron reaffirmed that the arsenal 'is currently under 300 nuclear weapons'. A small number of stockpiled warheads are undergoing maintenance and surveillance at factories.

Sources: Macron, E., French President, 'Discours du Président Emmanuel Macron sur la stratégie de défense et de dissuasion devant les stagiaires de la 27ème promotion de l'école de guerre' [Speech by President Emmanuel Macron on strategic defence and deterrence to officers of the 27th graduation of the military academy], Paris, 7 Feb. 2020; French Ministry of the Armed Forces, 'Discours de Florence Parly, ministre des Armées prononcé à l'usine des Mureaux, ArianeGroup, le 14 décembre 2017' [Speech by Florence Parly, Minister of the Armed Forces, presented at the Mureaux factory, ArianeGroup], 14 Dec. 2017; Hollande, F., French President, 'Discours sur la dissuasion nucléaire: Déplacement auprès des forces aériennes stratégiques' [Speech on nuclear deterrence: Visit to the strategic air forces], Istres, 25 Feb. 2015; Sarkozy, N., French President, Speech on defence and national security, Porte de Versailles, 17 June 2008; Sarkozy, N., French President, 'Presentation of SSBM "Le Terrible"', Speech, Cherbourg, 21 Mar. 2008; Chirac, J., French President, Speech during visit to the Strategic Forces, Landivisiau, L'Île Longue, Brest, 19 Jan. 2006; French Ministry of Defence/Ministry of the Armed Forces, various publications; French National Assembly, various defence bills; *Air Actualités*, various issues; *Aviation Week & Space Technology*, various issues; *Bulletin of the Atomic Scientists*, 'Nuclear notebook', various issues; Tertrais, B., *French Nuclear Deterrence Policy, Forces and Future*, Recherches & Documents no. 01/2019 (Fondation pour la Recherche Stratégique: Paris, Jan. 2019); and authors' estimates.

deliver the first upgraded missiles in 2022 or 2023.[16] The missiles are armed with a nuclear warhead (tête nucléaire aéroportée, TNA) that has a reported yield of up to 300 kt.[17] The French Ministry of the Armed Forces has initiated research on a successor missile—air-sol nucléaire (air-to-surface nuclear), fourth-generation (ASN4G)—with enhanced stealth and manoeuvrability to counter potential technological improvements in air defences.[18] The ASN4G is scheduled to replace the ASMP-A in 2035.[19]

French President Emmanuel Macron has reaffirmed the government's commitment to the long-term modernization of France's air- and sea-based nuclear deterrent forces.[20] In 2018 he signed the law on military planning for 2019–25 following its approval by the French parliament.[21] Among other provisions, the law allocated €37 billion ($43.7 billion) to maintain and modernize France's nuclear forces and infrastructure.[22] This marked a significant increase on the €23 billion ($27.1 billion) allocated to nuclear forces and associated infrastructure in the law on military planning for 2014–19.[23] The Ministry of the Armed Forces' budget for 2020 allocated €4.7 billion ($5.3 billion) for the modernization of nuclear forces.[24]

[16] French Ministry of the Armed Forces, 'Projet de loi de programmation militaire, 2019–2025' [Law on military planning, 2019–2025], Dossier de presse [Press kit], Feb. 2018, p. 42; and Medeiros, J., '"Faire FAS" : 55 ans de dissuasion nucléaire aéroportée' ['Go FAS' : 55 years of airborne nuclear deterrence], *Air Actualités*, Oct. 2019, p. 36; and Tertrais (note 2), p. 67.

[17] Groizeleau, 'Deterrence: F. Hollande outlines his vision and the French arsenal' (note 5).

[18] French Ministry of the Armed Forces, 'La dissuasion nucléaire: Synthèse du point-presse du Ministère des Armées' [Nuclear deterrence: Summary of the press briefing by the Ministry of the Armed Forces], Actu Défense, 14 June 2018, p. 1; and Tran, P., 'France studies nuclear missile replacement', *Defense News*, 29 Nov. 2014.

[19] Medeiros (note 16).

[20] Macron, E., French President, 'Déclaration de M. Emmanuel Macron, Président de la République, sur les défis et priorités de la politique de défense' [Statement by Emmanuel Macron, President of the Republic, on the challenges and priorities of defense policy], Toulon, 19 Jan. 2018.

[21] AFP, 'Macron promulgue la loi de programmation militaire 2019–2025' [Macron signs the law on military programming 2019–2025], *Le Figaro*, 13 July 2018.

[22] AFP, 'France to spend 37 bn euros on upgrading nuclear arsenal', France24, 8 Feb. 2018. The total defence budget approved for the 7-year period was €295 billion ($348 billion).

[23] Loi relative à la programmation militaire pour les années 2014 à 2019 [Law on military planning for the years 2014 to 2019], French Law no. 2013-1168 of 18 Dec. 2013.

[24] Groizeleau, 'Deterrence: 25 billion in five years for the renewal of the two components' (note 5); and Rose, M., 'Amid arms race, Macron offers Europe French nuclear wargames insight', Reuters, 7 Feb. 2020.

V. Chinese nuclear forces

SHANNON N. KILE AND HANS M. KRISTENSEN

China has been slowly increasing the size of its nuclear weapon stockpile over the past decade. The pace of growth has increased in recent years with the fielding of new weapon systems. As of January 2020, China maintained an estimated total stockpile of about 320 nuclear warheads, compared with an estimated total of 260 warheads in 2015.[1] Around 240 warheads are assigned to China's operational land- and sea-based ballistic missiles and to nuclear-configured aircraft (see table 10.6). The remainder are assigned to non-operational forces, such as new systems in development, operational systems that may increase in number in the future, and reserves.

China is modernizing and diversifying its nuclear forces as part of a long-term programme to develop a more survivable and robust deterrence posture consistent with its nuclear strategy of assured retaliation.[2] The Chinese Government's declared aim is to maintain its nuclear capabilities at the minimum level required for safeguarding national security. China has adopted a nuclear strategy of self-defence, the goal of which is 'deterring other countries from using or threatening to use nuclear weapons' against it.[3] In this context, China has prioritized building an operational triad of land-, sea- and air-based nuclear forces to strengthen its nuclear deterrence and counterstrike capabilities in response to the evolving nuclear strategies of other countries.[4]

Despite the continuing growth in its nuclear arsenal, China's ongoing modernization programmes do not appear to portend changes to its long-standing nuclear policies. In 2019 the Chinese Government reaffirmed its commitment to 'a nuclear policy of no first use of nuclear weapons at any time and under any circumstances and not using or threatening to use nuclear weapons against non-nuclear-weapon states or nuclear-weapon-free zones unconditionally'.[5] In its 2019 annual report to the United States Congress on Chinese military developments, the US Department of Defense (DOD) stated that while there has been some debate in China about the conditions

---

[1] See Schell, P. P. and Kristensen, H. M., 'Chinese nuclear forces', *SIPRI Yearbook 2015*, pp. 491–95.

[2] Cunningham, F. and Fravel, T., 'Assuring assured retaliation: China's nuclear posture and US–China strategic stability', *International Security*, vol. 40, no. 2 (Oct. 2015), pp. 7–50. Assured retaliation is the ability to survive an initial attack and retaliate with nuclear strikes that inflict unacceptable damage on the attacker.

[3] Chinese State Council, *China's Military Strategy*, Defence White Paper (Information Office of the State Council: Beijing, July 2019), section 2.

[4] Fabey, M., 'China on faster pace to develop nuclear triad, according to Pentagon, analysts', *Jane's Navy International*, 3 May 2019; and Reuters, 'Chinese military paper urges increase in nuclear deterrence capabilities', 30 Jan. 2018.

[5] Chinese State Council (note 3). See also Pan, Z., 'A study of China's no-first-use policy on nuclear weapons', *Journal for Peace and Nuclear Disarmament*, vol. 1, no. 1 (2018), pp. 115–36.

for the application of its no-first-use policy, there 'has been no indication that national leaders are willing to attach such nuances and caveats' to China's existing policy.[6] Although the Chinese military is working to increase the overall readiness of its missile forces, Chinese nuclear warheads are believed to be 'de-mated' from their delivery vehicles—that is, stored separately and not available for immediate use.[7]

As part of the Chinese Government's move to restructure and modernize the military under a streamlined command system, it established the People's Liberation Army (PLA) Rocket Force (PLARF) in 2016 as the fourth service in China's armed forces.[8] As the 'core force of strategic deterrence', the PLARF has assumed command responsibility for all of China's nuclear forces, and exercises custodial and operational control over the country's nuclear warheads.[9] In addition, the PLARF has been put in charge of conventional missiles and support forces and tasked with strengthening China's medium- and long-range strike capabilities in accordance with the requirements of 'full-area war deterrence'.[10]

Land-based ballistic missiles

China's nuclear-capable land-based ballistic missile arsenal is undergoing gradual modernization as China replaces ageing silo-based, liquid-fuelled missiles with new mobile solid-fuelled models and increases the number of road-mobile missile launchers. China's shift towards more survivable mobile missiles has been motivated by concerns that US advances in intelligence, surveillance and reconnaissance (ISR) capabilities and in precision-guided conventional weapons pose a pre-emptive threat to fixed missile launch sites and supporting infrastructure.[11]

Intercontinental ballistic missiles

In its 2019 annual report on Chinese military developments, the US DOD estimated that China had deployed a total of 90 intercontinental ballistic

---

[6] US Department of Defense (DOD), Office of the Secretary of Defense, *Military and Security Developments Involving the People's Republic of China 2019*, Annual Report to Congress (DOD: Arlington, VA, May 2019), pp. 65–67.

[7] Stokes, M. A., *China's Nuclear Warhead Storage and Handling System* (Project 2049 Institute: Arlington, VA, 12 Mar. 2010), p. 8; and Bin, L., 'China's potential to contribute to multilateral nuclear disarmament', *Arms Control Today*, vol. 41, no. 2 (Mar. 2011), pp. 17–21.

[8] Chinese Ministry of National Defense, 'China establishes Rocket Force and Strategic Support Force', 1 Jan. 2016. The PLARF replaced the PLA Second Artillery Corps.

[9] Gill, B. and Ni, A., 'The People's Liberation Army Rocket Force: Reshaping China's approach to strategic deterrence', *Australian Journal of International Affairs*, vol. 73, no. 2 (Jan. 2019), p. 163.

[10] Gill and Ni (note 9), p. 164.

[11] O'Connor, S., 'Sharpened Fengs: China's ICBM modernisation alters threat profile', *Jane's Intelligence Review*, vol. 27, no. 12 (Dec. 2015), pp. 44–49.

Table 10.6. Chinese nuclear forces, January 2020

Type/Chinese designation (US designation)	Launchers deployed	Year first deployed	Range (km)[a]	Warheads x yield	No. of warheads[b]
Land-based ballistic missiles[c]	188[d]				172
DF-4 (CSS-3)	..[e]	1980	5 500	1 x 3.3 Mt	..
DF-5A (CSS-4 Mod 1)	10	1981	12 000+	1 x 4–5 Mt	10
DF-5B (CSS-4 Mod 2)	10	2015	12 000	3 x 200–300 kt MIRV	30
DF-5C (CSS-4 Mod 3)	..	..	..	MIRV	..
DF-15 (CCS-6 Mod 1)	..	1994	600	[1 x 10–50 kt]	.[f]
DF-21 (CSS-5 Mod 2/6)[g]	40	1996/2017	2 100	1 x 200–300 kt	40
DF-26 (CSS-..)	72	2017	>4 000	1 x 200–300 kt	36
DF-31 (CSS-10 Mod 1)	8	2006	>7 000	1 x 200–300 kt	8
DF-31A/AG (CSS-10 Mod 2)	48	2007/2018	>11 200	1 x 200–300 kt	48
DF-41 (CSS-X-20)	..	[2020][h]	>12 000	3 x 200–300 kt MIRV	..
Sea-based ballistic missiles[i]	48				48[j]
JL-2 (CSS-NX-14)	48	2016	>7 000	1 x 200–300 kt	48
Aircraft[k]	20				20
H-6K (B-6)	20	2009	3 100	1 x bomb	20
H-6N (B-6)	..	[2025]	..	1 x ALBM	..
H-20 (B-20)	..	[2020s]	..	..	..
Cruise missiles[l]	..	..	..	..	..
Other stored warheads[m]					80
Total	**256**				**320[m]**

.. = not available or not applicable; [ ] = uncertain figure; ALBM = air-launched ballistic missile; kt = kiloton; Mt = megaton; MIRV = multiple independently targetable re-entry vehicle.

[a] Aircraft range is for illustrative purposes only; actual mission range will vary according to flight profile and weapon loading.

[b] Figures are based on estimates of 1 warhead per nuclear-capable launcher, except the MIRVed DF-5B, which is estimated to have 3 warheads. The DF-26 is a dual capable launcher. It is estimated that half of the dual-capable missiles are assigned nuclear warheads. Only 1 missile load is assumed for nuclear missiles. The warheads are not thought to be deployed on launchers under normal circumstances but kept in storage facilities. All estimates are approximate.

[c] China defines missile ranges as short-range, <1000 km; medium-range, 1000–3000 km; long-range, 3000–8000 km; and intercontinental range, >8000 km.

[d] The estimate only counts nuclear launchers. Some launchers with non-nuclear capability (for medium or intermediate-range ballistic missiles) might have 1 or more reloads of missiles.

[e] It is thought that the DF-4 has been withdrawn from service or is in the process of being retired.

[f] The US Central Intelligence Agency concluded in 1993 that China had 'almost certainly' developed a warhead for the DF-15, although it is unclear whether the capability was ever fielded.

[g] The range of the nuclear-armed DF-21 variants (CSS-5 Mods 2 and 6) is thought to be greater than the 1750 km reported for the original CSS-5 Mod 1, which has been retired. In 2017 the US Air Force National Air and Space Intelligence Center (NASIC) reported that China had 'fewer than 50' Mod 2 launchers. The Mod 6 is thought to be a replacement for the Mod 2.

[h] The DF-41 was publicly displayed for the first time in 2019 but has not yet been declared operational.

[i] China has 4 operational Type 094 nuclear-powered ballistic missile submarines (SSBNs), each of which can carry up to 12 sea-launched ballistic missiles (SLBMs), giving a total of 48 launchers. Two additional Type 094 SSBNs are in development but are not yet operational.

[j] There is no authoritative information that Chinese SLBMs are armed with nuclear warheads under normal circumstances.

[k] The US Department of Defense (DOD) reported in 2018 that the People's Liberation Army Air Force has been reassigned a nuclear mission. H-6 bombers were used to deliver nuclear weapons during China's nuclear weapon testing programme (one test used a fighter) and models of nuclear bombs are displayed in military museums. It is thought (but uncertain) that a small number of H-6K bombers might have been assigned a nuclear mission. The new H-20 is expected to be nuclear capable.

[l] Official US Government documents are inconsistent and contradictory about possible Chinese nuclear cruise missiles. US Air Force Global Strike Command in 2013 listed the CJ-20 as nuclear capable. In 2013 NASIC listed the CJ-10 as 'conventional or nuclear' but in 2017 it listed the CJ-10 as conventional. A US DOD fact sheet from 2018 listed both an air-launched cruise missile (ALCM) and a sea-launched cruise missile (SLCM). No estimate is provided here because of the very high degree of uncertainty.

[m] In addition to the *c.* 240 warheads estimated to be assigned to operational forces, an additional *c.* 80 warheads are thought to have been produced (or be in production) to arm China's new DF-41s (*c.* 56 warheads) and additional JL-2s (*c.* 24 warheads), for a total estimated stockpile of *c.* 320 warheads. China's inventory is expected to continue to increase.

Sources: US Air Force, National Air and Space Intelligence Center (NASIC), *Ballistic and Cruise Missile Threat*, various years; US Air Force Global Strike Command, various documents; US Central Intelligence Agency, various documents; US Defense Intelligence Agency, various documents; US Department of Defense, *Military and Security Developments Involving the People's Republic of China*, various years; Kristensen, H. M., Norris, R. S. and McKinzie, M. G., *Chinese Nuclear Forces and US Nuclear War Planning* (Federation of American Scientists/Natural Resources Defense Council: Washington, DC, Nov. 2006); *Bulletin of the Atomic Scientists*, 'Nuclear notebook', various issues; Google Earth; and authors' estimates.

missiles (ICBMs).[12] The silo-based, liquid-fuelled, two-stage Dong Feng-5 (DF-5 or CSS-4) family of missiles are currently China's longest-range ICBMs. Along with the road-mobile, solid-fuelled, three-stage DF-31A/AG (CSS-10 Mod 2) ICBM, they are the only operational missiles in China's arsenal capable of targeting all of the continental USA.[13]

The PLARF has been developing a longer-range ICBM, the road-mobile, solid-fuelled, three-stage DF-41 (CSS-X-20), since the late 1990s. With an estimated range in excess of 12 000 kilometres, the DF-41 will have a range similar to that of the older DF-5. Rail-mobile and silo-based versions of the missile are believed to be under development.[14] Open-source imagery in 2019 indicated that the PLARF was building a new type of silo at a missile training area near Jilantai in northern China, possibly for the DF-41, and new silo construction might have started in Henan Province in 2017.[15]

[12] US Department of Defense (note 6), pp. 44, 66.

[13] US Department of Defense (note 6), p. 46.

[14] US Department of Defense (note 6), p. 45.

[15] Kristensen, H. M., 'New missile silo and DF-41 launchers seen in Chinese nuclear missile training area', FAS Strategic Security Blog, Federation of American Scientists, 3 Sep. 2019; and LaFoy, S. and Eveleth, D., 'Possible ICBM modernization underway at Sundian', Arms Control Wonk, 5 Feb. 2020.

There have been 10 known flight tests of the DF-41 since 2012.[16] In January 2019 the DF-41 might have been part of a simulated second-strike exercise conducted by the PLARF.[17] DF-41 launchers operated at the Jilantai training area in April–May 2019 and were publicly displayed for the first time during the annual National Day parade held in Beijing on 1 October 2019.[18] While there has been speculation that the missile has completed its development and testing cycle and achieved an initial operational capability, it had not entered into service by the end of 2019.[19]

After many years of research and development, China has modified a small number of ICBMs to deliver nuclear warheads in multiple independently targetable re-entry vehicles (MIRVs). China has prioritized the deployment of MIRVs in order to improve its warhead penetration capabilities in response to advances in US and, to a lesser extent, Russian (and Indian) missile defences.[20] It has modified the liquid-fuelled, silo-based DF-5A (CSS-4 Mod 1) ICBM, which first went into service in the early 1980s, to carry multiple warheads.[21] One variant of the missile, the DF-5B (CSS-4 Mod 2), is assessed to carry up to three MIRVed warheads.[22] A second variant under development, the DF-5C (CSS-4 Mod 3), can reportedly also carry MIRVed warheads. Some US media reports have suggested that it might be capable of carrying up to 10 warheads, but it seems more likely that it will carry a number similar to the DF-5B version.[23] The deployment of MIRVs on the ageing DF-5 missiles may have been an interim arrangement necessitated by delays in the development of the DF-41 mobile ICBM.[24] There has been speculation that the DF-41 is able to carry 6–10 MIRVed warheads, but there is significant uncertainty about the actual capability.[25]

Intermediate- and medium-range ballistic missiles

In 2018 the PLARF began the deployment of the new dual-capable DF-26 intermediate-range ballistic missile, which has an estimated maximum range exceeding 4000 km and can reach targets in the western Pacific Ocean,

---

[16] Gertz, B., 'China flight tests new multi-warhead ICBM', Washington Free Beacon, 6 June 2018.

[17] Liu, X., 'China's rocket force conducts mock ICBM strike exercise', *Global Times*, 22 Jan. 2019.

[18] Kristensen (note 15); and Yang, S. and Liu, X., 'China debuts most advanced ICBM DF-41 at parade', *Global Times*, 1 Oct. 2019.

[19] US Department of Defense, Office of the Deputy Assistant Secretary of Defense for Nuclear Matters (ODASDNM), *Nuclear Matters Handbook 2020* (ODASDNM: Arlington, VA, Mar. 2020), p. 3.

[20] US Department of Defense (note 6), p. 65; and Lewis, J., 'China's belated embrace of MIRVs', eds M. Krepon, T. Wheeler and S. Mason, *The Lure and Pitfalls of MIRVs: From the First to the Second Nuclear Age* (Stimson Center: Washington, DC, May 2016), pp. 95–99.

[21] US Department of Defense (note 6), p. 44.

[22] O'Halloran, J. (ed.), 'DF-5', *IHS Jane's Weapons: Strategic, 2015–16* (IHS Jane's: Coulsdon, 2015), pp. 7–8.

[23] Gertz, B., 'China tests missile with 10 warheads', Washington Free Beacon, 31 Jan. 2017.

[24] Minnick, W., 'Chinese parade proves Xi in charge', *Defense News*, 6 Sep. 2015.

[25] O'Halloran, ed. (note 22), pp. 21–22; and Gertz, B., 'China flight tests new multiple-warhead missile', Washington Free Beacon, 16 Apr. 2016.

including Guam.[26] The missile is equipped with a manoeuvrable re-entry vehicle (MaRV) warhead that is capable of precision conventional or nuclear strikes against ground targets, as well as conventional strikes against naval targets.[27] A flight test of a DF-26 was carried out on 27 January 2019.[28] China appears to be producing the DF-26 in significant numbers and there were sightings of the missile at several brigade bases during 2019.[29]

The PLARF currently possesses one nuclear-capable medium-range ballistic missile (MRBM). The DF-21 (CSS-5) is a two-stage, solid-fuelled mobile missile that was first deployed in 1991. An upgraded variant, the DF-21A (SSC-5 Mod 2), was first deployed in 1996 and an enhanced version (SSC-5 Mod 6) was fielded in 2017.[30] Two other versions of the missile (DF-21C and DF-21D) were designed for conventional anti-ship and anti-access/area-denial (A2/AD) missions.

Ballistic missile submarines

China continues to pursue its long-standing strategic goal of developing and deploying a sea-based nuclear deterrent. According to the US DOD's 2019 annual report on Chinese military developments, the PLA Navy (PLAN) has commissioned four Type 094 nuclear-powered ballistic missile submarines (SSBNs).[31] Two additional submarines are being outfitted at a shipyard in Huludao.[32] The DOD report assessed that the four operational Type 094 SSBNs represent China's 'first credible, sea-based nuclear deterrent'.[33]

The Type 094 submarine can carry up to 12 three-stage, solid-fuelled Julang-2 (JL-2) submarine-launched ballistic missiles (SLBMs). The JL-2 is a sea-based variant of the DF-31 ICBM. It has an estimated maximum range in excess of 7000 km and is believed to carry a single nuclear warhead. The JL-2 SLBM has been deployed on China's four operational Type 094 SSBNs.[34]

[26] US Department of Defense (note 19), pp. 31, 49; and *Global Times*, 'China deploys Dongfeng-26 ballistic missile with PLA Rocket Force', 27 Apr. 2018.

[27] Tate, A., 'China touts ASBM capabilities of DF-26', *Jane's Defence Weekly*, 6 Feb. 2019, p. 6; and *Global Times* (note 26).

[28] Liu, X., 'Missile launch shows China's DF-26 able to adjust position mid-flight, attack moving aircraft carriers: Expert', *Global Times*, 27 Jan. 2019.

[29] Kristensen, H. M., 'China's new DF-26 missile shows up at base in eastern China', FAS Strategic Security Blog, Federation of American Scientists, 21 Jan. 2020.

[30] O'Halloran, ed. (note 22), pp. 15–17; and US Department of Defense (note 6), p. 66.

[31] US Department of Defense (note 6), p. 36. The Type 094 SSBN is designated the Jin class by the United States and the North Atlantic Treaty Organization.

[32] Dill, C., 'Counting Type 094 Jin-Class SSBNs with planet imagery', Arms Control Wonk, 21 Nov. 2018; and Tate, A., 'Satellite imagery shows two Chinese SSBNs in Huludao', *Jane's Defence Weekly*, 5 Dec. 2018.

[33] US Department of Defense (note 6), p. 36.

[34] US Department of Defense (note 6), p. 36.

There has been considerable speculation about when a Type 094 SSBN carrying nuclear-armed JL-2 SLBMs will begin deterrence patrols. Although there were media reports in 2016 that China would soon commence patrols, there was no evidence in 2019 to suggest that they had begun.[35] In its 2014 report on Chinese military developments, the US DOD predicted that China would commence submarine deterrence patrols imminently. Some of the subsequent reports have made the same claim but the 2019 report did not refer to the issue. The routine deployment by China of nuclear weapons on its SSBNs would constitute a significant change to the country's long-held practice of keeping nuclear warheads in central storage in peacetime and would pose operational challenges for its nuclear command and control arrangements.[36]

The PLAN is developing its next-generation SSBN, the Type 096. In 2019 the US DOD assessed that construction would probably begin in the early 2020s.[37] Reports vary widely on the design parameters, but the new submarine is expected to be larger and quieter than the Type 094 and might be equipped with more missile launch tubes. Given the expected lifespans of both the current Type 094 and the next-generation Type 096 submarines, the PLAN will probably operate both types of SSBN concurrently.[38]

The Type 096 will be armed with a successor to the JL-2: the JL-3 SLBM.[39] The new missile is thought to use technologies from the land-based DF-41 ICBM and have a longer range than the JL-2. It might also be MIRV capable. On 2 June 2019 the PLAN reportedly conducted the second flight test of the JL-3 SLBM from a modified conventional submarine in the Bohai Sea, following an initial test in November 2018.[40] The Chinese Government did not officially confirm the tests. It has yet to reveal publicly the number of missiles to be carried by the Type 096 or how many submarines will be built.

Aircraft and cruise missiles

According to the US DOD's 2018 annual report on Chinese military developments, the PLA Air Force (PLAAF) had been 're-assigned a nuclear mission'.[41]

---

[35] See e.g. Borger, J., 'China to send nuclear-armed submarines into Pacific amid tensions with US', *The Guardian*, 26 May 2016.

[36] Center for Strategic and International Studies, 'Does China have an effective sea-based nuclear deterrent?', China Power, updated Mar. 2020.

[37] US Department of Defense (note 6), p. 36.

[38] US Department of Defense (note 6), p. 66.

[39] US Department of Defense (note 6), p. 36.

[40] Tate, A., 'China conducts probable test launch of JL-3 SLBM', *Jane's Defence Weekly*, 3 June 2019.

[41] US Department of Defense (DOD), Office of the Secretary of Defense, *Military and Security Developments Involving the People's Republic of China 2018*, Annual Report to Congress (DOD: Arlington, VA, Aug. 2018), p. 75. Medium-range combat aircraft were China's earliest means of delivering nuclear weapons and were used to conduct more than 12 atmospheric nuclear tests in the 1960s and 1970s.

The previous year's DOD report had stated that the PLAAF 'does not currently have a nuclear mission'.[42]

China possesses a small number of H-6K bombers that may have been given a nuclear weapon delivery role as an interim measure until a new bomber is available.[43] The PLAAF is currently developing its first long-range strategic bomber known as the H-20. The aircraft, which may have a range of up to 8500 km, reportedly will have stealth characteristics similar to those of the US B-2 bomber.[44] The H-20 will be able to deliver both conventional and nuclear weapons and is expected to be fielded sometime in the 2020s.[45]

The US Defense Intelligence Agency reported in 2018 that China was developing two new air-launched ballistic missiles, 'one of which may include a nuclear payload'.[46] The missiles may be variants of the DF-21 MRBM for delivery by a modified H-6N bomber.[47] The H-6N was displayed at the National Day parade in Beijing in October 2019 but there was no reference to a possible future nuclear capability.[48]

The PLA currently deploys several types of ground-, sea- and air-launched cruise missiles, but there is considerable uncertainty about whether these may have nuclear delivery roles. For example, in its 2017 assessment of ballistic missile and cruise missile threats, the US Air Force National Air and Space Intelligence Center (NASIC) did not list any Chinese cruise missile as being nuclear capable.[49] In its previous assessment, published in 2013, NASIC had listed the ground-launched Donghai-10 (DH-10, also designated Changjian-10, CJ-10) as a 'conventional or nuclear' (dual-capable) system.[50]

---

[42] US Department of Defense (DOD), Office of the Secretary of Defense, *Military and Security Developments Involving the People's Republic of China 2017*, Annual Report to Congress (DOD: Arlington, VA, May 2017), p. 61.

[43] US Department of Defense (note 6), p 41; and Military-Today, 'H-6K: Long-range strategic bomber', [n.d.].

[44] US Department of Defense (note 6), p 61; Yeo, M., 'In first, China confirms "new long-range strategic bomber" designation', *Defense News*, 11 Oct. 2018; and Tate, A., 'Details emerge about requirement for China's new strategic bomber', *Jane's Defence Weekly*, 4 Jan. 2017, p. 4.

[45] US Department of Defense (note 6), p. 61.

[46] Ashley, R., Director, Defense Intelligence Agency, Statement for the Record: Worldwide Threat Assessment, Armed Services Committee, US Senate, 6 Mar. 2018, p. 8. See also US Department of Defense (note 6), p. 67.

[47] Panda, A., 'Revealed: China's nuclear-capable air-launched ballistic missile', The Diplomat, 10 Apr. 2018.

[48] Yang, S. and Liu, X., 'China unveils new H-6N bomber with extended range, extra capabilities', *Global Times*, 1 Oct. 2019.

[49] US Air Force, National Air and Space Intelligence Center (NASIC), *Ballistic and Cruise Missile Threat* (NASIC: Wright-Patterson Air Force Base, OH, July 2017), p. 37.

[50] US Air Force, National Air and Space Intelligence Center (NASIC), *Ballistic and Cruise Missile Threat* (NASIC: Wright-Patterson Air Force Base, OH, 2013), p. 29.

VI. Indian nuclear forces

HANS M. KRISTENSEN AND SHANNON N. KILE

As of January 2020, India was estimated to have a growing arsenal of approximately 150 nuclear weapons (see table 10.7). This figure is based on calculations of India's inventory of weapon-grade plutonium and the number of operational nuclear-capable delivery systems. India is expanding the size of its nuclear weapon stockpile as well as its infrastructure for producing nuclear warheads.

Indian nuclear doctrine

During 2019, there was renewed speculation that India was considering modifying or scrapping the no-first-use nuclear doctrine that it adopted in 1998.[1] On 16 August, Indian defence minister Rajnath Singh posted on Twitter that 'India has strictly adhered to this doctrine. What happens in future depends on the circumstances'.[2] Singh's statement added to a growing number of similar statements by Indian defence officials issued over the past decade.[3] It cast further doubt on India's commitment to no-first-use and revived discussions both inside and outside India about the scope and limits of the doctrine and whether India would continue to maintain it.[4] Singh's statement was particularly noteworthy because it followed on the heels of a debate about whether India's modernization of its nuclear weapons was gradually moving the country closer to a more aggressive nuclear policy similar to the counterforce strategy (the capability for pre-emptive or retaliatory strikes on targets of military value) of many other nuclear-armed states.[5]

---

[1] Although India publicly stated in 2003 that the no-first-use doctrine would not prevent it from responding with nuclear weapons to chemical and biological attacks, it remained fairly clear that the doctrine covered nuclear scenarios. For further detail see e.g. Boyd, K., 'India established formal nuclear command structure', *Arms Control Today*, Jan. 2003.

[2] Rajnath Singh (@rajnathsingh), 'Pokhran is the area which witnessed Atal Ji's firm resolve to make India a nuclear power and yet remain firmly committed to the doctrine of "No First Use". India has strictly adhered to this doctrine. What happens in future depends on the circumstances', Twitter, 16 Aug. 2019.

[3] For examples of earlier statements by Indian defence officials see e.g. Chaudhury, D. R., 'Why bind ourselves to "no first use policy", says Manahar Parrika on India's nuke doctrine', *Economic Times*, 11 Nov. 2016.

[4] See e.g. *The Hindu*, 'Unclear doctrine: On "no first use" nuclear policy', 19 Aug. 2019; and Panda, A., 'If India rethinks nuclear no first use, it won't surprise Pakistan or China', The Diplomat, 26 Aug. 2019.

[5] Clary, C. and Narang, V., 'India's counterforce temptations: Strategic dilemmas, doctrine, and capabilities', *International Security*, vol. 43, no. 3 (winter 2018), pp. 7–52; and Sundaram, K. and Ramana, M. V., 'India and the nuclear policy of no first use of nuclear weapons', *Journal for Peace and Nuclear Disarmament*, vol. 1, no. 1 (2018), pp. 152–68.

Military fissile material production

India's nuclear weapons are believed to be single-stage plutonium-based implosion designs. The plutonium was produced at the Bhabha Atomic Research Centre (BARC) in Trombay, Mumbai, by the 40-megawatt-thermal (MW(t)) heavy water CIRUS reactor, which was shut down at the end of 2010, and the 100-MW(t) Dhruva heavy water reactor. India reportedly has plans to build a new 100 MW(t) reactor near Visakhapatnam, Andhra Pradesh.[6] To extract the plutonium, India operates a plutonium reprocessing plant for military purposes at the BARC as well as three dual-use plants elsewhere.[7]

The Indian Department of Atomic Energy has proposed plans to build six fast breeder reactors—at three sites with twin reactor units—by 2039.[8] This would significantly increase India's capacity to produce plutonium that could be used for building weapons.[9] The unsafeguarded 500-megawatt-electric (MW(e)) prototype fast breeder reactor (PFBR) at the Indira Gandhi Centre for Atomic Research complex at Kalpakkam, Tamil Nadu, was expected to achieve criticality in 2019 following a series of technical delays, but by the end of that year it remained unclear whether this had happened.[10] A new reprocessing plant is also under construction at Kalpakkam to reprocess spent fuel from the PFBR and future fast breeder reactors. The plant is scheduled to be commissioned by 2022.[11]

India is also increasing its uranium enrichment capabilities and continues to produce enriched uranium at the expanded gas centrifuge facility at the Rattehalli Rare Materials Plant near Mysore, Karnataka, for highly enriched uranium (HEU) for use as naval reactor fuel.[12] India is building a new industrial-scale centrifuge enrichment plant, the Special Material Enrichment Facility, near Challakere, Karnataka. This will be a dual-use facility that produces HEU for both military and civilian purposes.[13] India's expanding centrifuge enrichment capacity is motivated by plans to build new

---

[6] International Panel on Fissile Materials, 'Countries: India', 12 Feb. 2018.

[7] International Panel on Fissile Materials (note 6).

[8] Indian Government, Department of Atomic Energy, 'Statement referred to in reply to Lok Sabha starred question no. 2 due for answer on 18.07.2018 by Shri Rahul Shewale regarding nuclear power plants', [n.d.], p. 2.

[9] Sharma, R., 'India to have six fast breeder reactors by 2039; first to become operational in 2018', Nuclear Asia, 8 Nov. 2017; and Ramana, M. V., 'A fast reactor at any cost: The perverse pursuit of breeder reactors in India', Bulletin of the Atomic Scientists, 3 Nov. 2016.

[10] Press Trust of India (PTI), 'Kalpakkam fast breeder reactor may achieve criticality in 2019', Times of India, 20 Sep. 2018.

[11] The Hindu, 'HCC to construct fuel processing facility at Kalpakkam', 7 Aug. 2017; and World Nuclear News, 'India awards contract for fast reactor fuel cycle facility', 8 Aug. 2017.

[12] International Panel on Fissile Materials (note 6); and Naval Technology, 'India builds reactors to power nuclear submarines', 8 Sep. 2010.

[13] Albright, D. and Kelleher-Vergantini, S., India's Stocks of Civil and Military Plutonium and Highly Enriched Uranium, End 2014 (Institute for Science and International Security: Washington, DC, 2 Nov. 2015).

Table 10.7. Indian nuclear forces, January 2020

Type (US/Indian designation)	Launchers deployed	Year first deployed	Range (km)[a]	Warheads x yield[b]	No. of warheads[c]
Aircraft[d]	48				48
Mirage 2000H	32	1985	1 850	1 x bomb	32
Jaguar IS	16	1981	1 600	1 x bomb	16
Land-based ballistic missiles	70				70
Prithvi-II	30	2003	250[e]	1 x 12 kt	30
Agni-I	20	2007	>700	1 x 10–40 kt	20
Agni-II	12	2011	>2 000	1 x 10–40 kt	12
Agni-III	8	[2014]	>3 200	1 x 10–40 kt	8
Agni-IV	0	[2020]	>3 500	1 x 10–40 kt	0
Agni-V	0	[2025]	>5 000	1 x 10–40 kt	0
Sea-based ballistic missiles	14				16
Dhanush	2	2013	400	1 x 12 kt	4[f]
K-15 (B05)[g]	1/12[h]	2018	700	1 x 12 kt	12
K-4	..[i]	..	3 000	1 x 10–40 kt	..
Cruise missiles[j]	..	..	..	..	..
Other stored warheads[k]					16
Total					**150[k]**

.. = not available or not applicable; [ ] = uncertain figure; kt = kiloton.

[a] Aircraft range is for illustrative purposes only; actual mission range will vary according to flight profile and weapon loading. Missile payloads may have to be reduced in order to achieve maximum range.

[b] The yields of India's nuclear warheads are not known. The 1998 nuclear tests demonstrated yields of up to 12 kt. Since then, it is possible that boosted warheads have been introduced with a higher yield, perhaps up to 40 kt. There is no open-source evidence that India has developed two-stage thermonuclear warheads.

[c] Aircraft and several missile types are dual capable. This estimate counts an average of 1 warhead per launcher. Warheads are not deployed on launchers but kept in separate storage facilities. All estimates are approximate.

[d] Other aircraft that could potentially have a secondary nuclear role include the Su-30MKI.

[e] The Prithvi-II's range is often reported as 350 km. However, the US Air Force, National Air and Space Intelligence Center (NASIC) sets the range at 250 km.

[f] Each Dhanush-equipped ship is thought to have possibly 1 reload.

[g] Some sources have referred to the K-15 missile as Sagarika, which was the name of the missile development project.

[h] The first figure is the number of operational nuclear-powered ballistic missile submarines (SSBNs); the second is the number of missiles they can carry. Only 1 of India's 2 SSBNs—*INS Arihant*—is believed to be operational and probably has only limited capability. The other SSBN—*INS Arighat*—is fitting out. The SSBNs have 4 missile tubes, each of which can carry 3 K-15 submarine-launched ballistic missiles (SLBMs), for a total of 12 missiles per SSBN.

[i] Each missile tube will be able to carry 1 K-4 SLBM once it becomes operational.

[j] There have been reports suggesting that the Nirbhay cruise missile might be nuclear capable but no official sources have confirmed this.

[k] In addition to the c. 134 warheads estimated to be assigned to operational forces, an additional c. 16 warheads are thought to have been produced (or be in production) to arm additional Agni and K-15 missiles, for a total estimated stockpile of c. 150 warheads. India's inventory is expected to continue to increase.

Sources: Indian Ministry of Defence, annual reports and press releases; International Institute for Strategic Studies, *The Military Balance 2019* (Routledge: London, 2019); US Air Force, National Air and Space Intelligence Center (NASIC), *Ballistic and Cruise Missile Threat* (NASIC: Wright-Patterson Air Force Base, OH, July 2017); Indian news media reports; *Bulletin of the Atomic Scientists*, 'Nuclear notebook', various issues; and authors' estimates.

naval propulsion reactors. However, the HEU produced at the plants could also hypothetically be used to manufacture thermonuclear or boosted-fission nuclear weapons.[14]

Aircraft

Aircraft are the most mature component of India's nuclear strike capabilities. It is estimated here that there are approximately 48 nuclear bombs assigned to aircraft.

The Indian Air Force (IAF) has reportedly certified its Mirage 2000H fighter-bombers for delivery of nuclear gravity bombs.[15] It is widely speculated that the IAF's Jaguar IS fighter-bombers may also have a nuclear delivery role.[16]

India is acquiring a planned total of 36 Rafale aircraft from France. The majority of the aircraft are scheduled for delivery in 2021–22.[17] The French Air Force uses the Rafale in a nuclear strike role. The Rafale aircraft could therefore potentially replace India's Jaguar IS fighter-bomber in that role. However, as of January 2020, there had been no official confirmation of this. According to the Indian Ministry of Defence, the 'Rafale will provide IAF the strategic deterrence and requisite capability cum technological edge'.[18]

Land-based missiles

Other than occasional parade displays and announcements about missile flight tests, the Indian Government does not provide much public information about the status of its nuclear-capable, land-based ballistic missiles. The Indian Army's Strategic Forces Command operates four types of mobile nuclear-capable ballistic missile: the short-range Prithvi-II (250 kilometres) and Agni-I (700 km); the medium-range Agni-II (2000+ km); and the

---

[14] Levy, A., 'India is building a top-secret nuclear city to produce thermonuclear weapons, experts say', *Foreign Policy*, 16 Dec. 2015.

[15] Kampani, G., 'New Delhi's long nuclear journey: How secrecy and institutional roadblocks delayed India's weaponization', *International Security*, vol. 38, no. 4 (spring 2014), pp. 94, 97–98.

[16] Cohen, S. and Dasgupta, S., *Arming Without Aiming: India's Military Modernization* (Brookings Institution Press: Washington, DC, 2010), pp. 77–78; and India Defence Update, 'SEPECAT Jaguar is India's only tactical nuclear carrying and ground attack aircraft', 13 Dec. 2016.

[17] Rajnath Singh (@rajnathsingh), Video footage, Twitter, 8 Oct. 2019; and Indian Ministry of Defence, Press Information Bureau, 'Rafale Jet', 20 Nov. 2019. For further detail see chapter 9, section II, in this volume.

[18] Indian Ministry of Defence (MOD), *Annual Report 2018–19* (MOD: New Delhi, 2019), p. 43.

intermediate-range Agni-III (3200+ km).[19] It is estimated here that India has approximately 70 nuclear warheads for its land-based ballistic missiles.

Two new and longer-range land-based ballistic missiles are in development: the Agni-IV (3500+ km) and the Agni-V (5000+ km). A variant with an even longer range, the Agni-VI (6000 km), is in the design stage of development.[20] Unlike the other Agni missiles, the Agni-V is designed to be stored in and launched from a new mobile canister system—an arrangement that, among other things, increases operational readiness by reducing the time required to place the missiles on alert in a crisis.[21]

India reportedly carried out at least six test launches of ballistic missiles in 2019. The known launches included flight tests of four Prithvi-II missiles, one Agni-II, and one Agni-III, which failed.[22]

India is pursuing a technology development programme for multiple independently targetable re-entry vehicles (MIRVs). However, there have been conflicting views among defence planners and officials about how to proceed with the programme, in particular, about whether MIRVs should be initially deployed on the Agni-V or on the longer-range Agni-VI, which will have a heavier payload capacity.[23]

Sea-based missiles

With the aim of creating an assured second-strike capability, India continues to develop the naval component of its triad of nuclear forces and is building a fleet of four to six nuclear-powered ballistic missile submarines (SSBNs).[24] The first of the four SSBNs, the *INS Arihant*, was launched in 2009 and formally commissioned in 2016.[25] It is estimated here that 12 nuclear warheads have been delivered for potential deployment by the *Arihant* and more are in production.

---

[19] The Prithvi-II's range is often reported as 350 km. However, the US Air Force, National Air and Space Intelligence Center (NASIC) sets the range at 250 km. NASIC, *Ballistic and Cruise Missile Threat* (NASIC: Wright-Patterson Air Force Base, OH, July 2017), p. 17.

[20] Vikas, S., 'Why India may not test Agni 6 even if DRDO is ready with technology', OneIndia, 10 July 2019.

[21] Aroor, S., 'New chief of India's military research complex reveals brave new mandate', *India Today*, 13 July 2013.

[22] Press Trust of India (PTI), 'Nuclear-capable Prithvi II successfully test-fired', *Times of India*, 27 June 2019; PTI, 'DRDO successfully conducts Agni II missile's night trial for first time', *The Hindu*, 16 Nov. 2019; Asian News International (ANI), 'India successfully carries out night-time tests of Prithvi ballistic missile off Odisha coast', *Economic Times*, 20 Nov. 2019; Rout, H. K., 'Nuclear capable Agni-III missile fails in maiden night trial', *New Indian Express*, 1 Dec. 2019; and PTI, 'India conducts another night trial of Prithvi-II missile', *India Today*, 4 Dec. 2019.

[23] Basrur, R. and Sankaran, J., 'India's slow and unstoppable move to MIRV', eds M. Krepon, T. Wheeler and S. Mason, *The Lure and Pitfalls of MIRVs: From the First to the Second Nuclear Age* (Stimson Center: Washington, DC, May 2016), pp. 149–76.

[24] Davenport, K., 'Indian submarine completes first patrol', *Arms Control Today*, Dec. 2018.

[25] Dinakar, P., 'Now, India has a nuclear triad', *The Hindu*, 18 Oct. 2016.

In November 2018 the Indian Government announced that the *Arihant* had completed its first 'deterrence patrol'.[26] However, it is doubtful that the submarine's missiles carried nuclear warheads during the patrol.[27] The *Arihant* is assessed here to have only a limited operational capability.

A second SSBN, the *INS Arighat*, was launched in November 2017 and is fitting out at the naval base near Visakhapatnam.[28] Construction work has reportedly begun on a third and fourth submarine, with expected launch dates in 2020 and 2022, respectively.[29]

India seems to be developing a new SSBN class that would be able to carry more missiles than the *Arihant* and *Arighat*, which are each equipped with a four-tube vertical launch system and can carry up to 12 two-stage, 700-km range K-15 (also known as B05) submarine-launched ballistic missiles (SLBMs). After a visit to the Defence Research and Development Organization's (DRDO) Naval Science and Technological Laboratory, the Indian Vice President, Muppavarapu Venkaiah Naidu, posted a photograph on his Twitter account that appeared to show part of a model of a new SSBN.[30] The missile compartment looked wider and taller than on the *Arihant*, leading to speculation that the compartment might be able to carry eight or more SLBMs.[31]

The DRDO is developing a two-stage, 3500-km range SLBM, known as the K-4, which will eventually replace the K-15.[32] It has also started to develop extended-range versions: the K-5 SLBM, which reportedly will have a range in excess of 5000 km, and the K-6, which will have an even longer range.[33]

India's first naval nuclear weapon was the Dhanush missile, a version of the Prithvi-II that can be launched from a surface ship. Two Sukanya class coastal patrol ships based at the Karwar naval base on India's east coast have been converted to launch the Dhanush. The missile reportedly can carry a 500-kg warhead to a maximum range of 400 km and is designed to be able

[26] Indian Government, Prime Minister's Office, Press Information Bureau, 'Prime Minister felicitates crew of INS Arihant on completion of Nuclear Triad', 5 Nov. 2018; and Davenport (note 24).

[27] Joshi, Y., 'Angels and dangles: Arihant and the dilemma of India's undersea nuclear weapons', War on the Rocks, 14 Jan. 2019.

[28] Unnithan, S., 'A peek into India's top secret and costliest defence project, nuclear submarines', *India Today*, 10 Dec. 2017. The submarine was originally assumed to be named *INS Aridhaman*, but when launched it was named *INS Arighat*.

[29] Unnithan (note 28).

[30] Vice President of India (@VPSecretariat), 'Went around an exhibition displaying Naval Weapons and Systems at Naval Science & Technological Laboratory (NSTL), DRDO at Vizag, Andhra Pradesh today. I am here to participate in the Golden Jubilee Celebrations of NSTL', Twitter, 28 Aug. 2019.

[31] Sutton, H. I., 'Tweet may have inadvertently revealed India's next-Gen nuclear weapons platform with global reach', *Forbes*, 8 Sep. 2019.

[32] Jha, S., 'India's undersea deterrent', The Diplomat, 30 Mar. 2016; and the US Air Force, National Air and Space Intelligence Center (note 19), p. 25.

[33] Rout (note 22); and Unnithan (note 28).

to hit both sea- and shore-based targets.[34] The last known test launch was in November 2018.[35]

Cruise missiles

There have been unconfirmed reports that the Nirbhay long-range subsonic cruise missile is nuclear capable.[36] However, neither the Indian Government nor the United States' intelligence sources have stated that the Nirbhay is a nuclear-capable system.

[34] Indian Defence Research and Development Organization, 'Successful launch of Dhanush and Prithvi missiles', Press release, 11 Mar. 2011; and *New Indian Express*, 'Nuke-capable Dhanush and Prithvi-II launched', 12 Mar. 2011.

[35] Indian Ministry of Defence (note 18), p. 100.

[36] Pandit, R., 'India successfully tests its first nuclear-capable cruise missile', *Times of India*, 8 Nov. 2017; and Gady, F. S., 'India successfully test fires indigenous nuclear-capable cruise missile', The Diplomat, 8 Nov. 2017.

VII. Pakistani nuclear forces

HANS M. KRISTENSEN AND SHANNON N. KILE

Pakistan continues to prioritize the development and deployment of new nuclear weapons and delivery systems as part of its 'full spectrum deterrence posture' vis-à-vis India.[1] It is estimated that Pakistan possessed approximately 160 nuclear warheads as of January 2020 (see table 10.8). Pakistan's nuclear weapon arsenal is likely to continue to expand over the next decade, although projections vary considerably.[2]

Pakistan is believed to be gradually increasing its military fissile material holdings, which include both weapon-grade plutonium and highly enriched uranium (see section X).[3]

Aircraft

The aircraft that are most likely to have a nuclear delivery role are the Pakistan Air Force's (PAF) Mirage III and Mirage V aircraft. The Mirage III has been used for developmental test flights of the nuclear-capable Ra'ad (Hatf-8) air-launched cruise missile (ALCM; see below), while the Mirage V is believed to have been given a strike role with nuclear gravity bombs.[4] The PAF currently operates about 160 Mirage aircraft, of which approximately 120 are fighter-bombers.[5] According to reports in 2019, Pakistan plans to buy an additional 36 Mirage V aircraft from Egypt.[6]

The nuclear capability of Pakistan's F-16 fighter-bombers is unclear but many analysts continue to assign a potential nuclear role to the aircraft (see box 10.1).[7] In the light of this, the table in this edition of the Yearbook has been updated: Pakistan's F-16s are listed as having a potential nuclear role but the nuclear weapons carried by airborne nuclear forces are assigned to Mirage aircraft.

---

[1] For a detailed assessment of Pakistan's nuclear posture see Tasleem, S. and Dalton, T., 'Nuclear emulation: Pakistan's nuclear trajectory', *Washington Quarterly*, vol. 41, no. 4 (winter 2019), pp. 135–55.

[2] See e.g. Sundaresan, L. and Ashok, K., 'Uranium constraints in Pakistan: How many nuclear weapons does Pakistan have?', *Current Science*, vol. 115, no. 6 (25 Sep. 2018); and Salik, N., 'Pakistan's nuclear force structure in 2025', Carnegie Endowment for International Peace, Regional Insight, 30 June 2016.

[3] For further detail on Pakistan's plutonium production and uranium enrichment facilities see Kile, S. N. and Kristensen, H. M., 'Pakistani nuclear forces', *SIPRI Yearbook 2019*, pp. 332–33.

[4] Kerr, P. and Nikitin, M. B., *Pakistan's Nuclear Weapons*, Congressional Research Service (CRS) Report for Congress RL3248 (US Congress, CRS: Washington, DC, 1 Aug. 2016), p. 7.

[5] International Institute for Strategic Studies, *The Military Balance 2019* (Routledge: London, 2019), pp. 298–99.

[6] *News International*, 'Pakistan to buy 36 Mirage V jets from Egypt', 5 Sep. 2019.

[7] See e.g. International Institute for Strategic Studies (note 5), p. 297.

Box 10.1. The uncertain nuclear capability of Pakistan's F-16s

Pakistan procured 40 F-16A/B aircraft from the United States between 1983 and 1987. In 1989 the US Department of Defense assured the US Congress that Pakistan did not have the capability to convert the aircraft to deliver nuclear weapons, even though experts at US nuclear weapon laboratories and the Central Intelligence Agency reportedly concluded that the F-16s could carry a nuclear payload with relatively minor modifications that were well within the capabilities of Pakistani technicians. In 1990 the USA cancelled the sales of additional F-16s to Pakistan in response to Pakistan's ongoing development of nuclear weapons. At the time, Western intelligence sources stated that Pakistan, 'in violation of agreements with Washington, is busily converting US-supplied F-16 fighter planes ... into potential nuclear-weapons carriers'.[a] In 1993 the US National Security Council informed the US Congress that 'Currently, Pakistan probably would rely on its F-16 fighters, and possibly Mirage III and V aircraft' for a nuclear mission.[b]

In 2006 the USA controversially decided to restart sales of F-16s to Pakistan, apparently under tightened use requirements. During a congressional hearing in 2006, the US State Department gave an assurance that 'The F-16s we are giving them ... will not be nuclear capable'.[c] In response to concerns that it might be possible for Pakistan to equip the F-16s with its own technology to deliver Pakistani nuclear weapons, the US State Department stated that a new security programme involving US personnel on the ground in Pakistan would make it difficult for Pakistan to convert the aircraft in secret. Extension of the onsite security programme was most recently authorized by the US State Department in July 2019.

The mechanisms under the security programme were triggered in 2019 after India complained that Pakistan had used an F-16 to shoot down one of its aircraft during a border dispute. The US Government subsequently reprimanded Pakistan for violating the conditions of use, which are to operate the F-16s and their USA-produced air-defence missiles at the Mushaf and Shahbaz air bases only for counterterror operations. It is unclear whether the restrictions also cover the original 40 F-16s acquired by Pakistan in the 1980s, but the aircraft have since been upgraded and might therefore be covered.

Whether the restrictions make it impossible for Pakistan to use some of the F-16s in a nuclear role is uncertain. However, it is possible that they might have prompted Pakistan to focus the nuclear mission on its Mirage aircraft, which do not appear to be subject to similar user restrictions.

[a] US Senate, Congressional Record, 20 Sep. 1995, p. S 13966.

[b] US National Security Council, 'Report to Congress on status of China, India and Pakistan nuclear and ballistic missile programs', July 1993, p. 7.

[c] US House of Representatives, Committee on International Relations, 'Proposed sale of F-16 aircraft and weapons systems to Pakistan', Serial no. 109–220, 20 July 2006, p. 41.

Sources: US National Security Council, 'Report to Congress on status of China, India and Pakistan nuclear and ballistic missile programs', July 1993; US Senate, Congressional Record, 20 Sep. 1995; US House of Representatives, Committee on International Relations, 'Proposed sale of F-16 aircraft and weapons systems to Pakistan', Serial no. 109–220, 20 July 2006; Frantz, D. and Collins, C., *The Nuclear Jihadist: The True Story of the Man Who Sold the World's Most Dangerous Secrets ... and How We Could Have Stopped Him* (Hachette Book Group: New York, 2007), pp. 162–80; US Department of Defense, Defense Security Cooperation Agency, 'Pakistan: Technical Security Team (TST) in continued support of F-16 program', News Release no. 19-29, 26 July 2019; and Shinkman, P. D., 'State Department reprimanded Pakistan for misusing F-16s, document shows', US News and World Report, 11 Dec. 2019.

Pakistan is acquiring a significant number of JF-17 aircraft, jointly developed with China, to replace the ageing Mirage aircraft. Pakistan currently operates about 100 JF-17s in four to six squadrons, with upgraded aircraft being added.[8] Initial reports on upgrades to the JF-17 suggested that the PAF aimed to integrate the dual-capable Ra'ad ALCM onto the aircraft, but more recent reports on upgrades have not mentioned the weapon.[9]

The Ra'ad ALCM is intended to provide the PAF's fighter-bombers with a standoff nuclear capability. It has been flight tested seven times since 2007. The last reported flight test was in 2016.[10] An improved version, the Ra'ad-II, was displayed for the first time in 2017 and is reported to have a range of 600 kilometres. The Ra'ad-II appears to have new engine air-intake and tail-wing configurations.[11]

Land-based missiles

Pakistan is expanding its nuclear-capable ballistic missile arsenal, which consists of short- and medium-range systems (see table 10.8). It currently deploys the Abdali (also designated Hatf-2), the Ghaznavi (Hatf-3), Shaheen-I (Hatf-4) and Nasr (Hatf-9) solid-fuelled, road-mobile short-range ballistic missiles. An extended-range version of the Shaheen-I, the Shaheen-IA, is still in development. The Ghaznavi, Nasr and Shaheen-I were all test launched in 2019.[12]

The arsenal currently includes two types of medium-range ballistic missile: the liquid-fuelled, road-mobile Ghauri (Hatf-5), with a range of 1250 km; and the two-stage, solid-fuelled, road-mobile Shaheen-II (Hatf-6) with a range of 2000 km.[13] The Shaheen-II was test launched in May 2019.[14] A longer-range variant, the Shaheen-III, is currently in development but

[8] Khan, B., 'Pakistan inches closer to inducting the JF-17 Block 3', Quwa Defence News and Analysis Group, 1 July 2019; Waldron. G., 'Paris: JK-17 Block III to have first flight by year-end', Flight Global, 20 June 2019; and International Institute for Strategic Studies (note 5), pp. 298–99.

[9] Fisher, R., 'JF-17 Block II advances with new refuelling probe', Jane's Defence Weekly, 27 Jan. 2016.

[10] Pakistan Inter Services Public Relations, Press Release PR-16/2016-ISPR, 19 Jan. 2016.

[11] Pakistan Inter Services Public Relations, 'Pakistan conducted successful flight test of air launched cruise missile "Ra'ad-II"', Press Release PR-27/2020-ISPR, 18 Feb. 2020.

[12] Pakistan Inter Services Public Relations, 'Pakistan today conducted another successful launch of short range surface to surface ballistic missile "Nasr"', Press Release PR-37/2019-ISPR, 31 Jan. 2019; Pakistan Inter Services Public Relations, 'Pakistan successfully carried out night training launch of surface to surface ballistic missile Ghaznavi, capable of delivering multiple types of warheads up to a range of 290 kilometers', Press Release PR-156/2019-ISPR, 29 Aug. 2019; and Pakistan Inter Services Public Relations, 'Pakistan today successfully conducted training launch of surface to surface ballistic missile Shaheen-1', Press Release PR-194/2019-ISPR, 18 Nov. 2019.

[13] US Air Force, National Air and Space Intelligence Center (NASIC), Ballistic and Cruise Missile Threat (NASIC: Wright-Patterson Air Force Base, OH, July 2017), p. 25.

[14] Pakistan Inter Services Public Relations, 'Pakistan conducted successful training launch of surface to surface ballistic missile Shaheen-II', Press Release PR-104/2019-ISPR, 23 May 2019.

Table 10.8. Pakistani nuclear forces, January 2020

Type (US/Pakistani designation)	Launchers deployed	Year first deployed	Range (km)[a]	Warheads x yield[b]	No. of warheads[c]
Aircraft	36				36
F-16A/B[d]	..	1998	1 600	1 x bomb	..
Mirage III/V	36	1998	2 100	1 x bomb or Ra'ad ALCM[e]	36
Land-based missiles	120[f]				120
Abdali (Hatf-2)	10	2015	200	1 x 5–12 kt	10
Ghaznavi (Hatf-3)	16	2004	300	1 x 5–12 kt	16
Shaheen-I (Hatf-4)	16	2003	750	1 x 5–12 kt	16
Shaheen-IA (Hatf-4)[g]	..	[2020]	900	1 x 5–12 kt	..
Shaheen-II (Hatf-6)	18	2014	2 000	1 x 10–40 kt	18
Shaheen-III (Hatf-..)[h]	..	[2022]	2 750	1 x 10–40 kt	..
Ghauri (Hatf-5)	24	2003	1 250	1 x 10–40 kt	24
Nasr (Hatf-9)	24	2013	70	1 x 5–12 kt	24
Ababeel (Hatf-..)	..	..	2 200	MIRV or MRV	..[i]
Babur GLCM (Hatf-7)	12	2014	350[j]	1 x 5–12 kt	12
Babur-2 GLCM (Hatf-..)	..	..[k]	700	1 x 5–12 kt	..
Sea-based missiles					
Babur-3 SLCM (Hatf-..)	0	..[l]	450	1 x 5–12 kt	0
Other stored warheads[m]					4
Total	**156**				**160[m]**

.. = not available or not applicable; [ ] = uncertain figure; ALCM = air-launched cruise missile; GLCM = ground-launched cruise missile; kt = kiloton; MIRV = multiple independently targetable re-entry vehicle; MRV = multiple re-entry vehicle; SLCM = sea-launched cruise missile.

[a] Aircraft range is for illustrative purposes only; actual mission range will vary according to flight profile and weapon loading. Missile payloads may have to be reduced in order to achieve maximum range.

[b] The yields of Pakistan's nuclear warheads are not known. The 1998 nuclear tests demonstrated a yield of up to 12 kt. Since then, it is possible that boosted warheads have been introduced with higher yields. There is no open-source evidence that Pakistan has developed two-stage thermonuclear warheads.

[c] Aircraft and several missile types are dual capable. Cruise missile launchers carry more than 1 missile. This estimate counts an average of 1 warhead per launcher. Warheads are not deployed on launchers but kept in separate storage facilities.

[d] There are unconfirmed reports that some of the 40 F-16 aircraft procured from the USA in the 1980s were modified by Pakistan for a nuclear weapon delivery role (see box 10.1). However, it is assumed here that the nuclear weapons carried by airborne nuclear forces are assigned to Mirage aircraft.

[e] The Ra'ad (Hatf-8) ALCM has a declared range of 350 km and an estimated yield of 5–12 kt. However, there is no available evidence to suggest that the Ra'ad has been deployed. In 2017 the Pakistani military displayed a Ra'ad-II variant with a reported range of 600 km. It is estimated here that the new version might be deployed in around 2021 in place of the original version.

[f] Some launchers might have 1 or more reloads of missiles.

[g] It is unclear whether the Shaheen-IA has the same designation as the Shaheen-I.

[h] The designation for the Shaheen-III is unknown.

[i] According to the Pakistani military, the missile is 'capable of delivering multiple warheads', using MIRV technology.

j The Pakistani Government claims the range is 700 km, double the range reported by the US Air Force National Air and Space Intelligence Center (NASIC).

k The Babur-2, which was first test launched on 14 Dec. 2016, is an improved version of the original Babur GLCM and will probably replace it.

l The first test launch of a Babur-3 SLCM was carried out from an underwater platform on 9 Jan. 2017.

m In addition to the *c.* 156 warheads estimated to be assigned to operational forces, a small number of additional warheads are thought to have been produced (or be in production) to arm future Shaheen-III and cruise missiles, for a total estimated stockpile of *c.* 160 warheads. Pakistan's warhead inventory is expected to continue to increase.

Sources: Pakistani Ministry of Defence; various documents; US Air Force, National Air and Space Intelligence Center (NASIC), *Ballistic and Cruise Missile Threat* (NASIC: Wright-Patterson Air Force Base, OH, July 2017); International Institute for Strategic Studies, *The Military Balance 2019* (Routledge: London, 2019); *Bulletin of the Atomic Scientists*, 'Nuclear notebook', various issues; and authors' estimates.

has been test launched once—in 2015.[15] The missile has a declared range of 2750 km, making it the longest-range system to be tested by Pakistan to date. A variant of the Shaheen-III, the Ababeel, which is possibly equipped with multiple independently targetable re-entry vehicle (MIRV) technology, is also in development. It was last test launched in 2017.[16]

In addition to expanding its arsenal of land-based ballistic missiles, Pakistan continues to develop the nuclear-capable Babur (Hatf-7) ground-launched cruise missile. The Babur has been test launched at least 12 times since 2005 and has been used in army field training since 2011. An extended-range version, which is known as Babur-2 and sometimes referred to as Babur Weapon System-1 (B), has a claimed range of 700 km, as against the 350-km range of the original version. It was first test launched in 2016 and was tested for a second time in 2018.[17]

Sea-based missiles

As part of its efforts to achieve a secure second-strike capability, Pakistan is seeking to create a nuclear triad by developing a sea-based nuclear force. The Babur-3 submarine-launched cruise missile (SLCM) appears to be intended to develop a nuclear capability for the Pakistan Navy's three diesel-electric

[15] Pakistan Inter Services Public Relations, 'Shaheen 3 missile test', Press Release PR-61/2015-ISPR, 9 Mar. 2015.

[16] For further detail on the Ababeel see Kile and Kristensen (note 3), p. 335.

[17] Pakistan Inter Services Public Relations, 'Pakistan today conducted a successful test of an enhanced range version of the indigenously developed Babur cruise missile', Press Release PR-142/2018-ISPR, 14 Apr. 2018.

Agosta class submarines.[18] The Babur-3 was first test launched in 2017 and was tested for a second time in 2018.[19]

Pakistan has ordered eight air-independent propulsion-powered conventional submarines from China, the first of which is expected to be delivered in 2022. It is possible that these submarines, known as the Hangor class, might also be given a nuclear role with the Babur-3 SLCM.[20]

[18] Panda, A. and Narang, V., 'Pakistan tests new sub-launched nuclear-capable cruise missile. What now?', The Diplomat, 10 Jan. 2017.

[19] Pakistan Inter Services Public Relations, 'Pakistan conducted another successful test fire of indigenously developed submarine launched cruise missile Babur having a range of 450 kms', Press Release PR-125/2018-ISPR, 29 Mar. 2018.

Reports of a ship-launched cruise missile test in 2019 might have been for a different missile. Gady, F. S., 'Pakistan's navy test fires indigenous anti-ship/land-attack cruise missile', The Diplomat, 24 Apr. 2019.

[20] Khan, B., 'Profile: Pakistan's new Hangor submarine', Quwa Defence News and Analysis Group, 11 Nov. 2019.

VIII. Israeli nuclear forces

SHANNON N. KILE AND HANS M. KRISTENSEN

Israel continues to maintain its long-standing policy of nuclear opacity: it neither officially confirms nor denies that it possesses nuclear weapons.[1] Like India and Pakistan, Israel has never been a party to the 1968 Treaty on the Non-Proliferation of Nuclear Weapons (Non-Proliferation Treaty, NPT).[2]

Declassified government documents (from Israel and the United States) indicate that Israel began building a stockpile of nuclear weapons in the early 1960s, using plutonium produced by the Israel Research Reactor 2 (IRR-2) at the Negev Nuclear Research Center near Dimona.[3] There is little publicly available information about the operating history and power capacity of the unsafeguarded IRR-2, which was commissioned in 1963.[4] It may now be operated primarily to produce tritium.[5] The ageing heavy water reactor, which was originally scheduled to be shut down in 2003, remains in operation despite the existence of a number of identified structural problems in its core.[6] The reactor is due to be shut down in 2023, but the Israeli Atomic Energy Commission is reportedly examining ways to extend its service life until the 2040s.[7]

It is estimated that Israel has approximately 90 operational nuclear weapons (see table 10.9). The locations of the storage sites for the warheads, which are thought to be stored partially unassembled, are unknown. Approximately 30 of the weapons are believed to be gravity bombs for delivery by F-16I aircraft. It is possible that some of Israel's F-15 aircraft may also serve a nuclear strike role, but this is unconfirmed.

Up to 50 warheads are thought to be for delivery by land-based Jericho ballistic missiles. However, the Israeli Government has never publicly confirmed that it possesses the Jericho missiles.

Israel's arsenal probably still includes solid-fuelled, two-stage Jericho II medium-range ballistic missiles, which are believed to be based, along with

---

[1] On the role of this policy in Israel's national security decision making see Cohen, A., 'Israel', eds H. Born, B. Gill and H. Hänggi, SIPRI, *Governing the Bomb: Civilian Control and Democratic Accountability of Nuclear Weapons* (Oxford University Press: Oxford, 2010), pp. 152–70.

[2] For a summary and other details of the NPT see annex A, section I, in this volume.

[3] For a history of Israel's nuclear weapon programme see Cohen, A., *The Worst-kept Secret: Israel's Bargain with the Bomb* (Columbia University Press: New York, 2010).

[4] Glaser, A. and Miller, M., 'Estimating plutonium production at Israel's Dimona reactor', Science, Technology and Global Security Working Group, Massachusetts Institute of Technology, 2011.

[5] Kelley, R. and Dewey, K., 'Assessing replacement options for Israel's ageing Dimona reactor', *Jane's Intelligence Review*, 20 Nov. 2018; and International Panel on Fissile Material (IPFM), 'Countries: Israel', 12 Feb. 2018.

[6] Levinson, C., 'Israel's Dimona nuclear reactor plagued by 1,537 defects, scientists say', *Haaretz*, 16 Apr. 2016.

[7] Bob, Y. J., 'Experts agree Dimona nuke reactor can exceed original life expectancy', *Jerusalem Post*, 12 July 2019.

Table 10.9. Israeli nuclear forces, January 2020

Type	Range (km)^a	Payload (kg)	Status	No. of warheads
Aircraft^b				..
F-16I	1 600	5 400	98 aircraft in the inventory; a small number (1–2 squadrons) is believed to be equipped for nuclear weapon delivery.	30
Land-based ballistic missiles^c				..
Jericho II	1 500– 1 800	750– 1 000	c. 50 missiles; first deployed in 1990.	25
Jericho III^d	>4 000	1 000– 1 300	Became operational in 2011–15 and is gradually replacing Jericho II.	25
Cruise missiles				..
..	..	..	Unconfirmed reports suggest that Dolphin class diesel-electric submarines have been equipped with nuclear-armed SLCMs; Israeli officials have declined to comment publicly on the reports.	10
Total				**90**^{e}

.. = not available or not applicable; SLCM = sea-launched cruise missile.

^{a} Aircraft range is for illustrative purposes only; actual mission range will vary. Weapon payloads may have to be reduced in order to achieve maximum range.

^{b} It is assumed here that only the I-version of the F-16 is used in the nuclear role. It is possible that some of Israel's F-15 aircraft may also serve a nuclear strike role, but this is unconfirmed.

^{c} The Israeli Government has never publicly acknowledged that it possesses Jericho missiles.

^{d} A longer-range version of the missile with a new rocket motor may be under development.

^{e} SIPRI's estimate, which is approximate, is that Israel has c. 90 stored nuclear warheads. There is significant uncertainty about the size of Israel's nuclear arsenal and its warhead capabilities.

Sources: Cohen, A., *The Worst-kept Secret: Israel's Bargain with the Bomb* (Columbia University Press: New York, 2010); Cohen, A. and Burr, W., 'Israel crosses the threshold', *Bulletin of the Atomic Scientists*, vol. 62, no. 3 (May/June 2006); Cohen, A., *Israel and the Bomb* (Columbia University Press: New York, 1998); Albright, D., Berkhout, F. and Walker, W., SIPRI, *Plutonium and Highly Enriched Uranium 1996: World Inventories, Capabilities and Policies* (Oxford University Press: Oxford, 1997); International Institute for Strategic Studies, *The Military Balance 2019* (Routledge: London, 2019); IHS Jane's *Strategic Weapon Systems*, various issues; Fetter, S., 'Israeli ballistic missile capabilities', *Physics and Society*, vol. 19, no. 3 (July 1990); *Bulletin of the Atomic Scientists*, 'Nuclear notebook', various issues; and authors' estimates.

their mobile transporter-erector-launchers (TELs), in caves at a base near Zekharia, about 25 kilometres west of Jerusalem.[8] Israel's Shavit space-launch vehicle, which carried a military satellite into orbit on its maiden flight in 1988, is based on the Jericho II.[9]

---

[8] O'Halloran, J. (ed.), 'Jericho missiles', *IHS Jane's Weapons: Strategic, 2015–16* (IHS Jane's: Coulsdon, 2015), p. 53.

[9] Graham, W., 'Israel launches Ofek spy satellite: Officials confirm malfunctions', NASASpaceflight. com, 13 Sep. 2016.

A three-stage Jericho III intermediate-range ballistic missile, with a range exceeding 4000 km, was declared operational in 2011 and might be replacing (or might possibly have already replaced) the Jericho II.[10] In 2013 Israel tested a Jericho III missile, possibly designated the Jericho IIIA, with a new motor that some sources believe may give the missile an intercontinental range—that is, a range exceeding 5500 km.[11] On 6 December 2019 the Israeli Ministry of Defense announced that it had conducted a test launch of an unspecified rocket propulsion system from a military base in central Israel, but it did not identify the missile that was used.[12] According to unconfirmed reports, the base was the Palmachim Air Base, which is located on Israel's Mediterranean coast and used as a test launch site for Jericho missiles.[13] The launch led to renewed speculation that Israel might be developing a new Jericho IV missile.[14]

Israel currently operates five German-built Dolphin and Dolphin-2 class diesel-electric submarines.[15] There have been numerous unconfirmed reports that Israel has modified some or all of the submarines to carry indigenously produced nuclear-armed sea-launched cruise missiles (SLCMs), giving it a sea-based second-strike capability.[16] Israeli officials have consistently declined to comment publicly on the reports. If they are true, the naval arsenal might include about 10 warheads, assuming a couple of warheads per submarine.

[10] O'Halloran, ed. (note 8).

[11] Ben David, A., 'Israel tests Jericho III missile', *Aviation Week & Space Technology*, 22 July 2013.

[12] Gross, J. A., 'Defense ministry conducts missile test over central Israel', *Times of Israel*, 6 Dec. 2019; and Melman, Y., 'Why would Israel reportedly have missiles that reach beyond Iran', *Haaretz*, 11 Dec. 2019.

[13] Trevithick, J., 'Did Israel just conduct a ballistic missile test from a base on its Mediterranean coast?', The Drive, 6 Dec. 2019.

[14] Ahronheim, A., 'IDF tests rocket propulsion system', *Jerusalem Post*, 7 Dec. 2019.

[15] Naval Today, 'Israel changes name of sixth Dolphin submarine', 11 Jan. 2019. A 6th submarine is scheduled to be delivered to Israel in 2020.

[16] See e.g. Cohen (note 3), p. 83; Bergman, R. et al., 'Israel's deployment of nuclear missiles on subs from Germany', *Der Spiegel*, 4 June 2012; and Frantz, D., 'Israel's arsenal is point of contention', *Los Angeles Times*, 12 Oct. 2003.

IX. North Korea's military nuclear capabilities

SHANNON N. KILE AND HANS M. KRISTENSEN

The Democratic People's Republic of Korea (DPRK, or North Korea) maintains an active but highly opaque nuclear weapon programme. As of January 2020, it is estimated that North Korea possessed approximately 30–40 nuclear weapons (see table 10.10). This is based on calculations of the amount of fissile material—plutonium and highly enriched uranium (HEU)—that North Korea is estimated to have produced for use in nuclear weapons (see section X) and on assumptions about its weapon design and fabrication skills.[1]

In 2019 North Korea continued to adhere to the moratoria on nuclear explosive tests and flight tests of long-range ballistic missiles that had been announced by North Korean leader Kim Jong Un in April 2018.[2] North Korea did, however, conduct multiple tests of guided artillery rocket systems and several new types of short-range ballistic missile (SRBM) in 2019. It also conducted the first flight test of a new submarine-launched ballistic missile (SLBM).

Fissile material production

North Korea's plutonium production and separation capabilities for manufacturing nuclear weapons are located at the Yongbyon Nuclear Scientific Research Centre (YNSRC).[3] In 2019 some of the nuclear facilities located there appeared not to be operating. In August the International Atomic Energy Agency (IAEA) reported that its analysis of satellite imagery and remote-sensor data showed no indications that the ageing 5 megawatt-electric (MW(e)) graphite-moderated research reactor located at the YNSCR had been in operation since the end of 2018.[4] In addition, the IAEA reported that there were no indications that reprocessing activities were under way at the adjacent Radiochemical Laboratory used to separate plutonium from

---

[1] For a discussion of US intelligence and other assessments of North Korea's nuclear warhead status see Kile, S. N. and Kristensen, H. M., 'North Korea's military nuclear capabilities', *SIPRI Yearbook 2019*, pp. 343–44.

[2] Korean Central News Agency, 'Third Plenary Meeting of Seventh CC, WPK held in presence of Kim Jong Un', 21 Apr. 2018. North Korea conducted underground nuclear test explosions in Oct. 2006, May 2009, Feb. 2013, Jan. and Sep. 2016, and Sep. 2017. The estimated explosive yields of the tests progressively increased.

[3] For an assessment of North Korea's nuclear weapon production facilities and infrastructure see Hecker, S. S., Carlin, R. L. and Serbin, E. A., 'A comprehensive history of North Korea's nuclear program: 2018 update', Center for International Security and Cooperation, Stanford University, 11 Feb. 2019, p. 3.

[4] International Atomic Energy Agency, 'Application of safeguards in the Democratic People's Republic of Korea', Report to the Board of Governors by the Acting Director General, GOV/2019/33-GC(63)/20, 19 Aug. 2019, p. 4; and Pabian, F. V., Liu, J. and Makowsky, P., 'North Korea's Yongbyon Nuclear Complex: No sign of operations', 38 North, 15 Mar. 2019.

the 5-MW(e) reactor's spent fuel rods.[5] In November 2019 commercial satellite imagery analysed by non-governmental experts indicated that the Experimental Light Water Reactor (ELWR) under construction at Yongbyon, which is also capable of producing plutonium for nuclear weapons, was undergoing system tests but had not yet commenced operation.[6]

There is considerable uncertainty about North Korea's uranium enrichment capabilities and its stock of HEU. It is widely believed that North Korea has focused on the production of HEU for use in nuclear warheads to overcome its limited capacity to produce weapon-grade plutonium. In 2019 satellite imagery analysis indicated that North Korea continued to operate the gas centrifuge enrichment plant located at the Yongbyon complex that it had declared in 2010.[7] Using commercial satellite imagery, several non-governmental researchers have identified a suspected covert uranium enrichment plant located at Kangsong, to the south-west of Pyongyang.[8] However, analysts cautioned that without access to the plant it was not possible to confirm the nature and purpose of the activities being conducted there.[9] A US intelligence assessment in 2018 reportedly concluded that North Korea probably had more than one covert uranium enrichment plant and that the country was seeking to conceal the types and numbers of production facilities in its nuclear weapon programme.[10]

Land-based ballistic missiles

North Korea is expanding and modernizing its ballistic missile force, which consists of indigenously produced short-, medium- and long-range missile systems that are either deployed or under development.[11] In recent years it has pursued the serial development of several missile systems with progressively longer ranges and increasingly sophisticated delivery capabilities.[12]

---

[5] International Atomic Energy Agency (note 4). The plutonium separated from the reactor's spent fuel can be used for the production of nuclear weapons.

[6] Serbin, E. and Puccioni, A., 'North Korea's Experimental Light Water Reactor: Possible testing of cooling system', 38 North, 6 Dec. 2019.

[7] Pabian, F. V. and Liu, J., 'North Korea's Yongbyon nuclear facilities: Well-maintained but showing limited operations', 38 North, 9 Jan. 2019; and Hecker, Carlin and Serbin (note 3), pp. 3–4.

[8] Panda, A., 'Exclusive: Revealing Kangson, North Korea's first covert uranium enrichment site', The Diplomat, 13 July 2018; and Albright, D., 'Kangsong: A suspect uranium enrichment plant', Imagery Brief, Institute for Science and International Security, 2 Oct. 2018.

[9] Hecker, Carlin and Serbin (note 3), p. 4; and Madden, M., 'Much ado about Kangson', 38 North, 3 Aug. 2018.

[10] Kube, C., Dilanian, K. and Lee, C. E, 'North Korea has increased nuclear production at secret sites, say US officials', NBC News, 1 July 2018; and Nakashima, E. and Warrick, J., 'North Korea working to conceal key aspects of its nuclear program, US officials say', Washington Post, 30 June 2018.

[11] Center for Strategic and International Studies Missile Defence Project, 'Missiles of North Korea', Missile Threat, accessed Jan. 2020.

[12] James Martin Center for Nonproliferation Studies (CNS), CNS North Korea Missile Test Database, accessed Jan. 2020. North Korea conducted 20 known tests of such missiles in 2017.

Table 10.10. North Korean forces with potential nuclear capability, January 2020

Type[a]	Range (km)	Payload (kg)	Status	No. of warheads
Land-based ballistic missiles				..
Hwasong-7 (Nodong)	>1 200	1 000	Single-stage, liquid-fuel missile. Fewer than 100 launchers; first deployed in 1990.	
Hwasong-9 (Scud-ER)	1 000	500	Scud missile variant, lengthened to carry additional fuel.	
Bukkeukseong-2 (KN-15)	1 000	..	Single-stage, solid-fuel missile under development launched from canister TEL. Land-based version of Bukkeukseong-1 SLBM; test launched in 2017.	
Hwasong-10 (BM-25, Musudan)	>3 000	[1 000]	Single-stage, liquid-fuel missile under development; several failed tests in 2016.	
Hwasong-12 (KN-17)	>3 000	1 000	Single-stage, liquid-fuel missile under development.	
Hwasong-13 (KN-08)[b]	>5 500	..	Three-stage, liquid-fuel missile with potential intercontinental range under development; no known test launches.	
Hwasong-14 (KN-20)	6 700– 10 400	500– 1 000	Two-stage, liquid-fuel missile under development; tested in 2017.	
Hwasong-15 (KN-22)	13 000	1 000– 1 500	Two-stage, liquid-fuel missile under development; two tests in 2017.	
Taepodong-2[c]	12 000	..	Under development; three-stage space launch vehicle variant placed satellites in orbit in Dec. 2012 and Feb. 2016.	
Submarine-launched ballistic missiles				..
Bukkeukseong-3	[1 900]	..	Two-stage, solid-fuel SLBM under development, replacing earlier Bukkeukseong-1 version. First flight tested in Oct. 2019.	
Total				**[30–40]**[d]

.. = not available or not applicable; [ ] = uncertain figure; SLBM = submarine-launched ballistic missile; TEL = transporter-erector-launcher.

[a] This table lists the ballistic missiles that could potentially have a nuclear capability. There is no publicly available evidence that North Korea has produced an operational nuclear warhead for delivery by an intercontinental-range ballistic missile.

[b] A two-stage variant, the KN-14, is under development but has yet to be test launched.

[c] A two-stage Taepodong-1 missile was unsuccessfully flight tested in 1998.

[d] SIPRI's estimate is that North Korea may have enough fissile material to build between 30 and 40 nuclear warheads. It is unknown how many warheads may have been assembled.

Sources: US Department of Defense (DOD), Office of the Secretary of Defense, *Missile Defense Review 2019* (DOD: Arlington, VA, 2019); US Air Force, National Air and Space Intelligence Center (NASIC), *Ballistic and Cruise Missile Threat* (NASIC: Wright-Patterson Air Force Base, OH, July 2017); *IHS Jane's Strategic Weapon Systems*, various issues; *Bulletin of the Atomic Scientists*, 'Nuclear notebook', various issues; and authors' estimates.

However, the flight tests were stopped in 2018, and the United States' Department of Defense (DOD) reported in January 2019 that none of the new longer-range ballistic missiles (Hwasong-10/12/13/14/15 or Bukkeokseong-1/2) had been deployed.[13]

In December 2019 North Korea conducted two sustained static firings of rocket engines at the Sohae Vertical Engine Test Stand.[14] Some analysts suggested that North Korea had ground tested a large, solid-fuel rocket motor designed for a new long-range ballistic missile.[15] However, others suggested that it was more likely that the test involved either a new, unknown liquid-fuel engine or an existing one.[16]

Short-range ballistic missiles

In 2019 North Korea conducted the initial launches of at least three new types of solid-fuelled SRBM.[17] One missile, designated by the US DOD as the KN-23, externally resembles the Russian Iskander-M SRBM.[18] The missile has an estimated maximum range exceeding 600 kilometres and was flight tested four times in 2019.[19] A second missile, designated by the US DOD as the KN-25, uses a large-calibre, multiple-launch rocket system and has a demonstrated range of 380 km.[20] A third missile, the KN-24, resembles an enlarged version of the US Army Tactical Missile System (ATACMS).[21] It was tested twice in 2019 and has an estimated range of 400 km.[22]

There is very little open-source information about the technical dimensions of the new SRBMs, including their ranges, accuracy and missile defence penetration capabilities. In 2019 some analysts speculated that the

---

[13] US Department of Defense (DOD), Office of the Secretary of Defense, *Missile Defense Review 2019* (DOD: Arlington, VA, 2019), p. 7.

[14] Warrick, J., 'North Korea never halted efforts to build powerful new weapons, experts say', *Washington Post*, 24 Dec. 2019.

[15] Ankit Panda (@nktpnd), 'Also, given the "very important" test that's set to improve their "strategic position"—and now Kim Yong Chol talking about surprises—we have more reason to expect the demonstration of a *qualitatively new* capability that we haven't seen before. Solid-fuel ICBM/ IRBM looks likely', Twitter, 9 Dec. 2019.

[16] Elleman, M., 'North Korea's rocket engine test: What we know and don't know', 38 North, 10 Dec. 2019.

[17] Center for Strategic and International Studies Missile Defence Project, 'North Korean missile launches & nuclear tests: 1984-present', Missile Threat, 25 Mar. 2020.

[18] Lewis, J., 'Preliminary analysis: KN-23 SRBM', Middlebury Institute of International Studies at Monterey, James Martin Center for Nonproliferation Studies, 5 June 2019.

[19] Center for Strategic and International Studies Missile Defence Project, 'KN-23', Missile Threat, accessed Jan. 2020.

[20] Center for Strategic and International Studies Missile Defence Project, 'KN-25', Missile Threat, accessed Jan. 2020; and Byrne, L., 'North Korea tests "super-large" multiple rocket launch system: KCNA', NK News, 24 Aug. 2019.

[21] Elleman, M., 'North Korea's new short-range missiles: A technical evaluation', 38 North, 9 Oct. 2019; and Panda, A., 'North Korea tests new type of short-range ballistic missile', The Diplomat, 12 Aug. 2019.

[22] Center for Strategic and International Studies Missile Defence Project, 'KN-24', Missile Threat, accessed Jan. 2020.

KN-23 and perhaps the KN-24 missiles might be so-called dual-capable systems—that is, assigned delivery roles for both conventional and nuclear warheads.[23] They raised concerns that such a capability could create a 'new level of unpredictability' in military decision making because neither the USA nor South Korea would be able to ascertain whether an incoming missile of one of these types was nuclear armed and they might therefore respond disproportionately.[24] However, while older inaccurate SRBMs might have been developed with dual capability, there is no publicly available authoritative information confirming a nuclear delivery role for the more accurate KN-23 (or KN-24).[25]

Medium- and intermediate-range ballistic missiles

Assuming that North Korea is able to produce a sufficiently compact warhead, some observers assess that the size, range and operational status of the Hwasong-7 or Nodong (also transliterated as Rodong) medium-range missile make it the system most likely to be given a nuclear delivery role.[26] Based on a Soviet-era Scud missile design, the Nodong is a single-stage, liquid-fuelled ballistic missile with an estimated range exceeding 1200 km. In addition, North Korea has developed the single-stage, liquid-fuelled Hwasong-9 or Scud-ER (extended-range), which may also be a nuclear-capable delivery system. Based on the Hwasong-6 (Scud C variant) missile with a lengthened fuselage to carry additional fuel, the Scud-ER has an estimated range of 1000 km.[27]

The Hwasong-10 missile, also designated the Musudan or BM-25, is a single-stage, liquid-fuelled missile with an estimated range exceeding 3000 km. The Musudan was first unveiled at a military parade in 2010. Flight testing began in 2016, with multiple failures.[28] No flight tests of the Musudan are known to have been conducted since 2016–17, and the status of the missile development programme is unclear.

The Hwasong-12 (also referred to by the US DOD designation KN-17) is a single-stage, intermediate-range missile that is believed to have a new

[23] Denyer, S., 'Fast, low and hard to stop: North Korea's missile tests crank up the threat level', *Washington Post*, 15 Aug. 2019; and Lewis (note 18).

[24] Kim, D. and Hanham, M., 'North Korean missiles: Size does not matter', *Bulletin of the Atomic Scientists*, 15 May 2019.

[25] For an unofficial technical assessment that did not assign nuclear capability to the KN-23 see Elleman (note 21).

[26] See e.g. Fitzpatrick, M., 'North Korea nuclear test on hold?', Shangri-La Voices, International Institute for Strategic Studies, 27 May 2014; and Albright, D., 'North Korean miniaturization', 38 North, 13 Feb. 2013.

[27] US Air Force, National Air and Space Intelligence Center (NASIC), *Ballistic and Cruise Missile Threat* (NASIC: Wright-Patterson Air Force Base, OH, July 2017), pp. 18, 25.

[28] Savelsberg, R. and Kiessling, J., 'North Korea's Musudan missile: A performance assessment', 38 North, 20 Dec. 2016. In 2016 North Korea conducted 8 flight tests of the Musudan system. Only 1 of the tests was judged to have been successful. In the other tests, the missiles exploded on launch or shortly thereafter.

liquid-propellant booster engine as well as design features that may serve as a technology test bed for a future intercontinental-range ballistic missile (ICBM).[29] Some analysts have speculated that the missile carries a small post-boost vehicle that, in addition to increasing its maximum range, can be used to improve warhead accuracy.[30] The missile, which has an estimated range of more than 3000 km, was last test launched in 2017 but has not been deployed.[31]

North Korea is developing the Bukkeukseong-2 missile (US DOD designation, KN-15), which is a land-based variant of the Bukkeukseong-1 SLBM. The two-stage, solid-fuelled missile has an estimated range of approximately 1000 km.[32] It was flight tested twice in 2017. Some analysts have noted that North Korea's development of the Bukkeukseong-2 was probably part of an effort to improve the survivability of its nuclear-capable ballistic missile systems. Solid-fuelled missiles can be fired more quickly than liquid-fuelled systems and require fewer support vehicles that might give away their position to overhead surveillance.[33]

Intercontinental-range ballistic missiles

North Korea is widely believed to have prioritized building and deploying an ICBM that could potentially deliver a nuclear warhead to targets in the continental USA. However, there has remained considerable uncertainty in assessments of North Korea's current long-range missile capabilities.[34]

The Hwasong-13 (US DOD designation, KN-08) was first presented by North Korea as a road-mobile, three-stage missile with intercontinental range at a military parade in April 2012, although some non-governmental analysts have argued that the missiles displayed were only mock-ups.[35] Estimates of the range and payload capabilities of the missile are highly speculative. As of 2019, it had not been flight tested.

North Korea has developed the Hwasong-14 (US DOD designation, KN-20), a prototype ICBM that first appeared in 2015 at a military parade in Pyongyang.[36] The two-stage missile appears to use the same high-energy

---

[29] Yi, Y., 'Hwasong-12 a stepping-stone in North Korea's ICBM development', *The Hankyoreh*, 16 May 2017; and Savelsberg, R., 'A quick technical analysis of the Hwasong-12 missile', 38 North, 19 May 2017.

[30] Elleman, M., 'North Korea's Hwasong-12 launch: A disturbing development', 38 North, 30 Aug. 2017.

[31] Panda, A., 'North Korea shows increased operational confidence in the Hwasong-12 IRBM', The Diplomat, 17 Sep. 2017; and US Department of Defense (note 13).

[32] US Air Force, National Air and Space Intelligence Center (note 27), p. 25.

[33] Panda, A., 'It wasn't an ICBM, but North Korea's first missile test of 2017 is a big deal', The Diplomat, 14 Feb. 2017.

[34] Albert, E., 'North Korea's military capabilities', Council on Foreign Relations, updated 20 Dec. 2019.

[35] Schiller, M. and Kelley, R., 'Evolving threat: North Korea's quest for an ICBM', *Jane's Defence Weekly*, 18 Jan. 2017, p. 24.

[36] Schiller and Kelley (note 35).

liquid-propellant booster engine as the single-stage Hwasong-12.[37] Based on a flight test conducted in 2017, analysts have estimated that the missile's range was unlikely to exceed 8000 km when carrying a 500 kilogram payload, which is thought to be around the weight of a nuclear warhead. This meant that the missile could not reach targets in the USA beyond the West Coast when launched from North Korea.[38]

North Korea is developing a new two-stage ICBM, the Hwasong-15 (US DOD designation, KN-22), which has a significantly larger second stage and more powerful booster engines than the Hwasong-14. The first flight test was conducted in 2017, when a Hwasong-15 was launched on an elevated trajectory and flew higher and for a longer duration than any previous North Korean missile. One estimate put the theoretical maximum range of the Hwasong-15 on a normal trajectory at up to 13 000 km—sufficient to reach Washington, DC, and other targets on the East Coast of the USA.[39] The missile was assessed to be carrying a light payload, however, and the range would be significantly reduced if it were carrying a heavier payload such as a nuclear warhead.[40]

While North Korea has made important progress towards building a nuclear-armed ICBM capable of credibly threatening the USA, it has yet to validate the performance and reliability of the missile systems under development.[41] In particular, defence analysts have pointed out that North Korea has not demonstrated a mastery of the technology for building a reliable atmospheric re-entry vehicle or for terminal-stage guidance and warhead activation.[42] The US DOD's 2019 *Missile Defense Review* indicated that North Korea had deployed one ICBM, the Taepodong-2.[43] However, other official US sources list the missile as a space-launch vehicle that would need reconfiguration to be used as an ICBM.[44]

Submarine-launched ballistic missiles

North Korea continues to pursue the development of an SLBM system as part of an effort to improve the survivability of its nuclear-capable ballistic missile

[37] According to one non-governmental analyst, North Korea probably acquired the engine through illicit channels operating in Russia, Ukraine or both. Elleman, M., 'The secret to North Korea's ICBM success', IISS Voices blog, International Institute for Strategic Studies, 14 Aug. 2017.

[38] Elleman, M., 'North Korea's Hwasong-14 ICBM: New data indicates shorter range than many thought', 38 North, 29 Nov. 2018.

[39] Wright, D., 'Re-entry of North Korea's Hwasong-15 missile', All Things Nuclear blog, Union of Concerned Scientists, 7 Dec. 2017.

[40] Elleman, M., 'North Korea's third ICBM launch', 38 North, 29 Nov. 2017.

[41] Acton, J., 'Assessing North Korea's progress in developing a nuclear-armed ICBM', Carnegie Endowment for International Peace, 4 May 2018.

[42] Wright (note 39); and Elleman (note 40). See also Ali, I., 'US general says North Korea not demonstrated all components of ICBM', Reuters, 30 Jan. 2018.

[43] US Department of Defense (note 13), p. 7.

[44] See e.g. US Defense Intelligence Agency (DIA), *Global Nuclear Landscape 2018* (DIA: Washington, DC, 2018), p. 22.

systems. In October 2019 North Korea announced that it had test launched 'a new type' of SLBM called the Bukkeukseong-3 (also transliterated as Pukguk-song-3).[45] The test was conducted from a towed underwater platform in the waters off North Korea's east coast. The missile was a two-stage, solid-fuelled design, but it was unclear whether it used the same booster engine as the Bukkeukseong-1 SLBM that preceded it. With an estimated maximum range of 1900 km, the Bukkeukseong-3 would be the longest-range, solid-fuelled missile in the North Korean inventory.[46]

During 2019, North Korea demonstrated that it had made progress towards achieving its goal of designing, building and eventually deploying an operational ballistic missile submarine. Currently, North Korea has one Sinpo class experimental submarine in service, which can hold and launch one SLBM. A visit by North Korean leader Kim Jong Un to the Sinpo South Shipyard in July 2019 revealed circumstantial evidence that North Korea was building a new ballistic missile submarine.[47] The vessel appeared to be based on a modified Romeo class diesel-electric submarine and fitted with three missile-launch canisters.[48] According to the state-run Korean Central News Agency, the submarine's operational deployment was 'near at hand'.[49]

[45] Korean Central News Agency, 'DPRK succeeds in test-firing new-type submarine-launched ballistic missile', 2 Oct. 2019; Lee, J., 'North Korea says it successfully tested new submarine-launched ballistic missile', Reuters, 2 Oct. 2019; and Ji, D., 'Pukguksong-3 SLBM test-launch is "powerful blow" to hostile forces: Rodong Sinmun', NK News, 4 Oct. 2019.

[46] Panda, A., 'North Korea finally unveils the Pukguksong-3 SLBM: First takeaways', The Diplomat, 3 Oct. 2019; and Center for Strategic and International Studies Missile Defence Project (note 11).

[47] Bermudez, J. and Cha, V., 'Sinpo South Shipyard: Construction of a new ballistic missile submarine?', Beyond Parallel, Centre for Strategic and International Studies, 28 Aug. 2019.

[48] Liu, J. and Town, J., 'North Korea's Sinpo South shipyard: Recent activity', 38 North, 26 Sep. 2019; and Hotham, O., 'New North Korean submarine capable of carrying three SLBMs: South Korean MND', NK News, 31 July 2019.

[49] Yonhap News Agency, 'NK leader inspects new submarine to be deployed in East Sea: State media', 23 July 2019.

X. Global stocks and production of fissile materials, 2019

MORITZ KÜTT, ZIA MIAN AND PAVEL PODVIG
INTERNATIONAL PANEL ON FISSILE MATERIALS

Materials that can sustain an explosive fission chain reaction are essential for all types of nuclear explosives, from first-generation fission weapons to advanced thermonuclear weapons. The most common of these fissile materials are highly enriched uranium (HEU) and plutonium. This section gives details of military and civilian stocks, as of the beginning of 2019, of HEU (table 10.11) and separated plutonium (table 10.12), including in weapons, and details of the current capacity to produce these materials (tables 10.13 and 10.14, respectively). The information in the tables is based on estimates prepared for the International Panel on Fissile Materials (IPFM). The most recent annual declarations (INFCIRC/549 declarations) on civilian plutonium and HEU stocks to the International Atomic Energy Agency (IAEA) were released in 2019 and give data for 31 December 2018, and so are taken here to be applicable for the start of 2019.

The production of both HEU and plutonium starts with natural uranium. Natural uranium consists almost entirely of the non-chain-reacting isotope uranium-238 (U-238) and is only about 0.7 per cent uranium-235 (U-235). The concentration of U-235, however, can be increased through enrichment—typically using gas centrifuges. Uranium that has been enriched to less than 20 per cent U-235 (typically, 3–5 per cent)—known as low-enriched uranium—is suitable for use in power reactors. Uranium that has been enriched to contain at least 20 per cent U-235—known as HEU—is generally taken to be the lowest concentration practicable for use in weapons. However, in order to minimize the mass of the nuclear explosive, weapon-grade uranium is usually enriched to over 90 per cent U-235. Plutonium is produced in nuclear reactors when U-238 is exposed to neutrons. The plutonium is subsequently chemically separated from spent fuel in a reprocessing operation. Plutonium comes in a variety of isotopic mixtures, most of which are weapon-usable. Weapon designers prefer to work with a mixture that predominantly consists of plutonium-239 (Pu-239) because of its relatively low rate of spontaneous emission of neutrons and gamma rays and the low level of heat generation from radioactive alpha decay. Weapon-grade plutonium typically contains more than 90 per cent of the isotope Pu-239. The plutonium in typical spent fuel from power reactors (reactor-grade plutonium) contains 50–60 per cent Pu-239 but is weapon-usable, even in a first-generation weapon design.

All states with a civil nuclear industry have some capability to produce fissile materials that could be used for weapons.

Table 10.11. Global stocks of highly enriched uranium, 2019

State	National stockpile (tonnes)[a]	Production status	Comments
China	14 ± 3	Stopped 1987–89	
France[b]	30 ± 6	Stopped 1996	Includes 5.1 tonnes declared civilian[c]
India[d]	4.4 ± 1.6	Continuing	Includes HEU in naval reactor cores
Israel[e]	0.3	–	
Korea, North[f]	Uncertain	Uncertain	
Pakistan	3.7 ± 0.4	Continuing	
Russia[g]	679 ± 120	Stopped 1987–88	Includes about 6 tonnes in use in research applications
UK[h]	22.6	Stopped 1962	Includes 0.7 tonnes declared civilian[c]
USA[i]	565 (85 not available for military purposes)	Stopped 1992	Includes HEU in a naval reserve
Other states[j]	~15		
Total[k]	**~1 335**		

HEU = highly enriched uranium.

[a] Most of this material is 90–93% enriched uranium-235 (U-235), which is typically considered weapon-grade. The estimates are for the end of 2018 and treated as applicable for the start of 2019. Important exceptions are noted.

[b] The uncertainty in the estimate applies only to the military stockpile of about 25 tonnes and does not apply to the declared civilian stock. A 2014 analysis offers grounds for a significantly lower estimate of the stockpile of weapon-grade HEU (as high as 10 ± 2 tonnes or as low as 6 ± 2 tonnes), based on evidence that the Pierrelatte enrichment plant may have had both a much shorter effective period of operation and a smaller weapon-grade HEU production capacity than previously assumed.

[c] INFCIRC/549 declaration to the International Atomic Energy Agency (IAEA) for the end of 2018 and treated as applicable for the start of 2019.

[d] It is believed that India is producing HEU (enriched to 30–45%) for use as naval reactor fuel. The estimate is for HEU enriched to 30%.

[e] Israel may have acquired illicitly about 300 kg of weapon-grade HEU from the USA in or before 1965.

[f] North Korea is known to have a uranium enrichment plant at Yongbyon and possibly others elsewhere. Independent estimates of uranium enrichment capability and possible HEU production extrapolated to the end of 2018 suggest an accumulated HEU stockpile range of 180–850 kg.

[g] This estimate may understate the amount of HEU in Russia since it assumes that it ceased production of all HEU in 1988. However, Russia may have continued producing HEU for civilian and non-weapon military uses after that date. The material in discharged naval cores is not included in the current stock since the enrichment of uranium in these cores is believed to be less than 20% U-235.

[h] The estimate reflects a UK declaration of 21.9 tonnes of military HEU as of 31 Mar. 2002, the average enrichment of which was not given. As the UK continues to use HEU in naval reactors, the value contains an increasing fraction of spent naval fuel. In 2018 about 500 kg of HEU from the UK were transferred to the USA for downblending into low-enriched uranium.

[i] The amount of US HEU is given in actual tonnes, not 93%-enriched equivalent. In 2016 the USA declared that, as of 30 Sep. 2013, its HEU inventory was 585.6 tonnes, of which 499.4 tonnes was declared to be for 'national security or non-national security programs including nuclear

weapons, naval propulsion, nuclear energy, and science'. The remaining 86.2 tonnes was composed of 41.6 tonnes 'available for potential down-blend to low enriched uranium or, if not possible, disposal as low-level waste', and 44.6 tonnes in spent reactor fuel. As of the end of Sep. 2018, another 17 tonnes had been downblended or shipped for blending down. The amount available for use had been reduced to about 480 tonnes, mostly by consumption in naval reactors. The 85 tonnes declared excess includes the remaining about 69 tonnes as well as 16 tonnes of the 20 tonnes originally reserved for HEU fuel for research reactors.

[j] The 2018 IAEA Annual Report lists 160 significant quantities of HEU under comprehensive safeguards in non-nuclear weapon states as of the end of 2018. In order to reflect the uncertainty in the enrichment levels of this material, mostly in research reactor fuel, a total of 15 tonnes of HEU is assumed. About 10 tonnes of this is in Kazakhstan and has been irradiated; it was initially slightly higher than 20%-enriched fuel. It is possible that this material is no longer HEU.

In INFCIRC/912 (from 2017) more than 20 states committed to reducing civilian HEU stocks and providing regular reports. So far, only Norway has reported under this scheme. At the end of 2018, it held less than 4 kg of HEU for civilian purposes.

[k] Totals are rounded to the nearest 5 tonnes.

Sources: International Panel on Fissile Materials (IPFM), *Global Fissile Material Report 2015: Nuclear Weapon and Fissile Material Stockpiles and Production* (IPFM: Princeton, NJ, Dec. 2015). China: Zhang, H., *China's Fissile Material Production and Stockpile* (IPFM: Princeton, NJ, Dec. 2017). France: International Atomic Energy Agency (IAEA), Communication Received from France Concerning its Policies Regarding the Management of Plutonium, INFCIRC/549/Add.5-21, 29 Sep. 2017; and Philippe, S. and Glaser, A., 'Nuclear archaeology for gaseous diffusion enrichment plants', *Science & Global Security*, vol. 22, no. 1 (2014), pp. 27–49. Israel: Myers, H., 'The real source of Israel's first fissile material', *Arms Control Today*, vol. 37, no. 8 (Oct. 2007), p. 56; and Gilinsky, V. and Mattson, R. J., 'Revisiting the NUMEC affair', *Bulletin of the Atomic Scientists*, vol. 66, no. 2 (Mar./Apr. 2010). North Korea: Hecker, S. S., Braun, C. and Lawrence, C., 'North Korea's stockpiles of fissile material', *Korea Observer*, vol 47, no. 4 (winter 2016), pp. 721–49. Russia: Podvig, P. (ed.), *The Use of Highly-Enriched Uranium as Fuel in Russia* (IPFM: Washington, DC, Sep. 2017). UK: British Ministry of Defence, 'Historical accounting for UK defence highly enriched uranium', Mar. 2006; and IAEA, Communications Received from the United Kingdom of Great Britain and Northern Ireland Concerning its Policies Regarding the Management of Plutonium, INFCIRC/549/Add.8-22, 23 Oct. 2019. USA: US Department of Energy (DOE), *Highly Enriched Uranium, Striking a Balance: A Historical Report on the United States Highly Enriched Uranium Production, Acquisition, and Utilization Activities from 1945 through September 30, 1996* (DOE: Washington, DC, 2001); Personal communication, US DOE, Office of Fissile Material Disposition, National Nuclear Security Administration; White House, Office of the Press Secretary, 'Fact sheet: Transparency in the US highly enriched uranium inventory', 31 Mar. 2016; US DOE, *FY 2019 Congressional Budget Request* (DOE: Washington, DC, Mar. 2018), p. 474; and US DOE, *Tritium and Enriched Uranium Management Plan through 2060*, Report to Congress (DOE: Washington, DC, Oct. 2015). Non-nuclear weapon states: IAEA, *IAEA Annual Report 2018* (IAEA: Vienna, 2018), Annex, Table A4, p. 129.

Table 10.12. Global stocks of separated plutonium, 2019

State	Military stocks (tonnes)	Military production status	Civilian stocks (tonnes)[a]
China	2.9 ± 0.6	Stopped in 1991	0.04[b]
France	6 ± 1.0	Stopped in 1992	67.7 (excludes foreign owned)
India[c]	0.6 ± 0.15	Continuing	6.9 ± 3.7 (includes 0.4 under safeguards)
Israel[d]	0.96 ± 0.13	Continuing	–
Japan	–	–	45.7 (includes 36.7 in France and UK)
Korea, North[e]	0.04	Continuing	–
Pakistan[f]	0.37 ± 0.1	Continuing	–
Russia[g]	128 ± 8 (40 not available for weapons)	Stopped in 2010	61.3
UK	3.2	Stopped in 1995	115.8 (excludes 23.1 foreign owned)[b]
USA[h]	79.7 (41.3 not available for weapons)	Stopped in 1988	8[i]
Other states[j]	–	–	1.9
Totals[k]	**~220 (81 not available for weapons)**		**~300**

– = nil or negligible figure.

[a] The data for France, Japan, Russia, the UK and the USA is for the end of 2018, reflecting their most recent INFCIRC/549 declaration. Some countries with civilian plutonium stocks do not submit an INFCIRC/549 declaration to the International Atomic Energy Agency (IAEA). Of these countries, Italy, the Netherlands, Spain and Sweden store their plutonium abroad.

[b] As of Mar. 2020, China had not submitted IAEA INFCIRC/549 declarations for the end of 2017, nor for the end of 2018. The number is based on the 2016 declaration.

[c] As part of the 2005 Indian–US Civil Nuclear Cooperation Initiative, India has included in the military sector much of the plutonium separated from its spent power-reactor fuel. While it is labelled civilian here since it is intended for breeder reactor fuel, this plutonium was not placed under safeguards in the 'India-specific' safeguards agreement signed by the Indian Government and the IAEA on 2 Feb. 2009. India does not submit an IAEA INFCIRC/549 declaration.

[d] Israel is believed to still be operating the Dimona plutonium production reactor but may be using it primarily for tritium production. The estimate is for the end of 2018.

[e] North Korea reportedly declared a plutonium stock of 37 kg in June 2008. It resumed plutonium production in 2009 but has probably expended some material in the nuclear tests that were conducted since then. It is believed to have separated up to 8 kg of plutonium in 2016. An additional 10–14 kg of plutonium may be in irradiated fuel unloaded in Dec. 2018 and is not included here.

[f] As of the end of 2018, Pakistan was operating 4 plutonium production reactors at its Khushab site. This estimate assumes that Pakistan is separating plutonium from the cooled spent fuel from all 4 reactors.

[g] The 40 tonnes of plutonium not available for weapons comprises 25 tonnes of weapon-origin plutonium stored at the Mayak Fissile Material Storage Facility and about 15 tonnes of weapon-grade plutonium produced between 1 Jan. 1995 and 15 Apr. 2010, when the last plutonium production reactor was shut down. The post-1994 plutonium, which is currently stored at Zheleznogorsk, cannot be used for weapon purposes under the terms of the US–Russian agreement on plutonium production reactors signed in 1997. Russia made a commitment to eliminate 34 tonnes of that material (including all 25 tonnes of plutonium stored at Mayak) as part of the US–Russian Plutonium Management and Disposition Agreement concluded in 2000.

Russia does not include the plutonium that is not available for weapons in its INFCIRC/549 declaration; nor does it make the plutonium it reports as civilian available to IAEA safeguards.

[h] In 2012 the USA declared a government-owned plutonium inventory of 95.4 tonnes as of 30 Sep. 2009. In its 2019 IAEA INFCIRC/549 declaration, the most recent submitted, the USA declared 49.3 tonnes of unirradiated plutonium (both separated and in mixed oxide, MOX) as part of the stock that was identified as excess for military purposes. Since most of this material is stored in classified form, it is considered military stock. The USA considers a total of 61.5 tonnes of plutonium as declared excess to national security needs.

[i] The USA placed about 3 tonnes of its excess plutonium, stored at the K-Area Material Storage facility at the Savannah River Plant, under IAEA safeguards. In addition, it reported that 4.6 tonnes of plutonium was contained in unirradiated MOX fuel, and also declared 0.4 tonnes of plutonium that was brought to the USA in 2016 from Japan, Germany and Switzerland (331 kg, 30 kg and 18 kg, respectively). All this material is considered civilian.

[j] This is estimated by reconciling the amounts of plutonium declared as 'held in locations in other countries' and 'belonging to foreign bodies' in the INFCIRC/549 declarations.

[k] Totals are rounded to the nearest 5 tonnes.

Sources: International Panel on Fissile Materials (IPFM), Global Fissile Material Report 2015: Nuclear Weapon and Fissile Material Stockpiles and Production (IPFM: Princeton, NJ, Dec. 2015). Civilian stocks (except for India): declarations by countries to the International Atomic Energy Agency (IAEA) under INFCIRC/549. China: Zhang, H., China's Fissile Material Production and Stockpile (IPFM: Princeton, NJ, Dec. 2017). North Korea: Kessler, G., 'Message to US preceded nuclear declaration by North Korea', Washington Post, 2 July 2008; Hecker, S. S., Braun, C. and Lawrence, C., 'North Korea's stockpiles of fissile material', Korea Observer, vol 47, no. 4 (winter 2016), pp. 721–49; and IAEA, Board of Governors, General Conference, 'Application of safeguards in the Democratic People's Republic of Korea', Report by the Acting Director General, GOV/2019/33-GC(63)/20, 19 Aug. 2019. Russia: Agreement Concerning the Management and Disposition of Plutonium Designated as No Longer Required for Defense Purposes and Related Cooperation (Russian–US Plutonium Management and Disposition Agreement), signed 29 Aug. and 1 Sep. 2000, amended Apr. 2010, entered into force July 2011. USA: National Nuclear Security Administration (NNSA), The United States Plutonium Balance, 1944–2009 (NNSA: Washington, DC, June 2012); and Gunter, A., 'US DOE, Office of Environmental Management, K-Area Overview/Update', 28 July 2015.

Table 10.13. Significant uranium enrichment facilities and capacity worldwide, 2019

State	Facility name or location	Type	Status	Enrichment process[a]	Capacity (thousands SWU/yr)[b]
Argentina[c]	Pilcaniyeu	Civilian	Uncertain	GD	20
Brazil	Resende Enrichment	Civilian	Expanding capacity	GC	35
China[d]	Lanzhou	Civilian	Operational	GC	2 600
	Hanzhong (Shaanxi)	Civilian	Operational	GC	2 000
	Emeishan	Civilian	Operational	GC	1 050
	Heping	Dual-use	Operational	GD	230
France	Georges Besse II	Civilian	Operational	GC	7 500
Germany	Urenco Gronau	Civilian	Operational	GC	3 900
India	Rattehalli	Military	Operational	GC	15–30
Iran[e]	Natanz	Civilian	Limited operation	GC	3.5–5
	Qom (Fordow)	Civilian	Limited operation	GC	..
Japan	Rokkasho[f]	Civilian	Resuming operation	GC	75
Korea, North	Yongbyon[g]	Uncertain	Operational	GC	8
Netherlands	Urenco Almelo	Civilian	Operational	GC	5 200
Pakistan	Gadwal	Military	Operational	GC	..
	Kahuta	Military	Operational	GC	15–45
Russia	Angarsk	Civilian	Operational	GC	4 000
	Novouralsk	Civilian	Operational	GC	13 300
	Seversk	Civilian	Operational	GC	3 800
	Zelenogorsk[h]	Civilian	Operational	GC	7 900
UK	Capenhurst	Civilian	Operational	GC	4 600
USA	Urenco Eunice	Civilian	Operational	GC	4 900

[a] The gas centrifuge (GC) is the main isotope-separation technology used to increase the percentage of uranium-235 (U-235) in uranium, but a few facilities continue to use gaseous diffusion (GD).

[b] SWU/yr = Separative work units per year, a measure of the effort required in an enrichment facility to separate uranium of a given content of U-235 into two components, one with a higher and one with a lower percentage of U-235. Where a range of capacities is shown, the capacity is uncertain or the facility is expanding its capacity.

[c] In Dec. 2015 Argentina announced resumption of production at its Pilcaniyeu GD uranium enrichment plant, which was shut down in the 1990s. There is no evidence of actual production.

[d] Assessments of China's enrichment capacity in 2015 and 2017 identified new enrichment sites and suggested a much larger total capacity than had previously been estimated.

[e] In July 2015 Iran agreed a Joint Comprehensive Plan of Action (JCPOA) that ended uranium enrichment at Fordow but kept centrifuges operating, and limited the enrichment capacity at Natanz to 5060 IR-1 centrifuges (equivalent to 3500–5000 SWU/yr) for 10 years. In Nov. 2019, following the USA's withdrawal from the JCPOA, Iran announced a limited restart of enrichment at Natanz and Fordow.

[f] The Rokkasho centrifuge plant has been in the process of being refitted with new centrifuge technology since 2011. Production since the start of retrofitting has been negligible.

[g] North Korea revealed its Yongbyon enrichment facility in 2010. It appears to be operational as of 2019. It is believed that North Korea is operating at least one other enrichment facility located elsewhere.

[h] Zelenogorsk operates a cascade for highly enriched uranium production for fast reactor and research reactor fuel.

Sources: Indo-Asian News Service, 'Argentina president inaugurates enriched uranium plant', *Business Standard*, 1 Dec. 2015; Zhang, H., 'China's uranium enrichment complex', *Science & Global Security*, vol. 23, no. 3 (2015), pp. 171–90; Zhang, H., *China's Fissile Material Production and Stockpile* (International Panel on Fissile Materials, IPFM: Princeton, NJ, Dec. 2017); Hecker, S. S., Carlin, R. L. and Serbin, E. A., 'A comprehensive history of North Korea's nuclear program', Center for International Security and Cooperation, accessed Feb. 2019; Pabian, F. V., Liu, J. and Town, J., 'North Korea's Yongbyon Nuclear Center: Continuing activity at the Uranium Enrichment Plant', 38 North, 5 June 2019; and Wolgelenter, M. and Sanger, D. E., 'Iran steps further from nuclear deal with move on centrifuges', *New York Times*, 5 Nov. 2019. Enrichment capacity data is based on International Atomic Energy Agency, Integrated Nuclear Fuel Cycle Information Systems (INFCIS); Urenco, *Annual Report and Accounts 2018* (Urenco: Stoke Poges, 2018); and IPFM, *Global Fissile Material Report 2015: Nuclear Weapons and Fissile Material Stockpile and Production* (IPFM: Princeton, NJ, Dec. 2015).

Table 10.14. Significant reprocessing facilities worldwide, as of 2019

All facilities process light water reactor (LWR) fuel, except where indicated.

State	Facility name or location	Type	Status	Design capacity (tHM/yr)[a]
China[b]	Jiuquan pilot plant	Civilian	Operational	50
France	La Hague UP2	Civilian	Operational	1 000
	La Hague UP3	Civilian	Operational	1 000
India[c]	Kalpakkam (HWR fuel)	Dual-use	Operational	100
	Tarapur (HWR fuel)	Dual-use	Operational	100
	Tarapur-II (HWR fuel)	Dual-use	Operational	100
	Trombay (HWR fuel)	Military	Operational	50
Israel	Dimona (HWR fuel)	Military	Operational	40–100
Japan	JNC Tokai	Civilian	Reprocessing shut down[d]	(was 200)
	Rokkasho	Civilian	Start planned for 2021	800
Korea, North	Yongbyon	Military	Operational	100–150
Pakistan	Chashma (HWR fuel)	Military	Starting up	50–100
	Nilore (HWR fuel)	Military	Operational	20–40
Russia[e]	Mayak RT-1, Ozersk	Civilian	Operational	400
	EDC, Zheleznogorsk	Civilian	Starting up	5
UK	BNFL B205 (Magnox fuel)	Civilian	To be shut down 2020	1 500
	BNFL Thorp, Sellafield	Civilian	Shut down in 2018	(was 1 200)
USA	H-canyon, Savannah River Site	Civilian	Operational	15

HWR = heavy water reactor.

[a] Design capacity refers to the highest amount of spent fuel the plant is designed to process and is measured in tonnes of heavy metal per year (tHM/yr), tHM being a measure of the amount of heavy metal—uranium in these cases—that is in the spent fuel. Actual throughput is often a small fraction of the design capacity. LWR spent fuel contains about 1% plutonium, and heavy water- and graphite-moderated reactor fuel about 0.4%.

[b] China is building a pilot reprocessing facility near Jinta in Gansu province with a capacity of 200 tHM/yr, to be commissioned in 2025.

[c] As part of the 2005 Indian–US Civil Nuclear Cooperation Initiative, India has decided that none of its reprocessing plants will be opened for International Atomic Energy Agency safeguards inspections.

[d] In 2014 the Japan Atomic Energy Agency announced the planned closure of the head-end of its Tokai reprocessing plant, effectively ending further plutonium separation activity. In 2018 the Japanese Nuclear Regulation Authority approved a plan to decommission the plant.

[e] A 250 tHM/yr Pilot Experimental Centre is under construction in Zheleznogorsk. A pilot reprocessing line with the capacity of 5 tHM/yr was launched in June 2018. A second pilot line is expected to be completed in 2020.

Sources: Kyodo News, 'Japan approves 70-year plan to scrap nuclear reprocessing plant', 13 June 2018; and RIA Novosti, [Rosatom is ready to start 'green' processing of spent nuclear fuel], Rosatom, 29 May 2018 (in Russian). Data on design capacity is based on International Atomic Energy Agency (IAEA), Integrated Nuclear Fuel Cycle Information Systems (INFCIS); and International Panel on Fissile Materials (IPFM), *Global Fissile Material Report 2015: Nuclear Weapon and Fissile Material Stockpiles and Production* (IPFM: Princeton, NJ, Dec. 2015).

Part III. Non-proliferation, arms control and disarmament, 2019

Chapter 11. Nuclear disarmament, arms control and non-proliferation

Chapter 12. Chemical and biological security threats

Chapter 13. Conventional arms control and new weapon technologies

Chapter 14. Dual-use and arms trade controls

11. Nuclear disarmament, arms control and non-proliferation

Overview

In 2019 the prospects for sustaining the achievements made in Russian–United States nuclear arms control appeared to be increasingly remote. During the year, the long-running dispute between the USA and Russia over a seminal cold war-era arms control treaty, the 1987 Soviet–US Treaty on the Elimination of Intermediate-Range and Shorter-Range Missiles (INF Treaty), culminated with the collapse of the treaty (see section I). The USA alleged that Russia had developed and deployed a mobile ground-launched cruise missile that had a flight range prohibited under the treaty—an allegation that Russia consistently dismissed as baseless. In August the USA confirmed its withdrawal from the INF Treaty in light of Russia's failure to address US compliance concerns. The decision marked the effective demise of the treaty, which raised concern among European members of the North Atlantic Treaty Organization (NATO) about the risk of new nuclear weapons in Europe.

Also during the year, Russia and the USA made no progress towards extending the sole remaining nuclear arms control agreement between them— the 2010 Treaty on Measures for the Further Reduction and Limitation of Strategic Offensive Arms (New START). The two countries had achieved the final New START force reduction limits by the specified deadline the previous year. However, the treaty will lapse if there is no agreement between the two parties to extend it by February 2021, along with its notification and inspection regime. The impasse over New START came against the background of tensions between Russia and the USA over missile defences, advanced weapon delivery systems and increases in Chinese strategic capabilities, which have underscored differences in their respective goals and priorities for nuclear arms control.

Tensions persisted in 2019 between the USA and the Democratic People's Republic of Korea (DPRK, or North Korea) over the latter's ongoing pro-grammes to develop nuclear weapons and ballistic missile delivery systems (see section II). The two countries remained locked in a diplomatic stalemate over the commitments made by their respective leaders during a summit meeting the previous year to work towards establishing peaceful relations and achieving the denuclearization of the Korean peninsula. A second summit meeting between the leaders held in February ended with no concrete results. In addition, while North Korea continued to adhere to its self-declared moratorium on the testing of nuclear weapons and long-range ballistic missiles, during the year it conducted multiple flight tests of shorter-range ballistic missiles, including several new types of systems.

In 2019 there continued to be controversy over the implementation of the 2015 Joint Comprehensive Plan of Action (JCPOA), an eight-party agreement designed to limit Iran's proliferation-sensitive nuclear activities and to build international confidence about the exclusively peaceful nature of its nuclear programme (see section III). During the year, Iran announced that it would incrementally scale back its compliance with the limits set out by the agreement, in response to the USA's reimposition of sanctions against it following the US withdrawal from the JCPOA in 2018. The Iranian Government appealed to the other signatories, particularly the European Union, to provide guarantees that at least some degree of sanctions relief—one of Iran's principal benefits under the JCPOA—could be provided despite the extraterritorial impact of the US sanctions in order for Iran to stay in the deal. Against the background of growing political tensions, the International Atomic Energy Agency (IAEA) confirmed that Iran continued to facilitate inspection and monitoring activities by the agency pursuant to the JCPOA.

There were various developments and activities during 2019 in relation to multilateral treaties and initiatives on nuclear disarmament, arms control and non-proliferation (see section IV). In the framework of the 1968 Treaty on the Non-proliferation of Nuclear Weapons (Non-Proliferation Treaty, NPT), the third and final session of the preparatory committee for the 2020 NPT Review Conference was convened in New York in April and May. There was also a steadily increasing number of signatures and ratifications for the Treaty on the Prohibition of Nuclear Weapons (TPNW), which is the first treaty establishing a comprehensive ban on nuclear weapons, including their development, deployment, possession, use and threat of use. In December, the United Nations General Assembly adopted a resolution calling on all states that had not yet done so to 'sign, ratify, accept, approve or accede to the Treaty at the earliest possible date'.

There were also events during the year connected with two long-running items on the multilateral nuclear disarmament and non-proliferation agenda. In September, the 11th biannual Conference on Facilitating the Entry into Force of the 1996 Comprehensive Nuclear-Test-Ban Treaty (CTBT) was convened in New York. The conference took place against the background of US allegations that Russia was violating its commitments under the CTBT. In November, a Conference on the Establishment of a Middle East Zone Free of Nuclear Weapons and Other Weapons of Mass Destruction held its first session at the UN in New York. While the decision to hold the conference was made by the UN General Assembly in December 2018, calls to establish a nuclear weapon-free zone in the Middle East date back to 1974.

TYTTI ERÄSTÖ, SHANNON N. KILE AND PETR TOPYCHKANOV

I. Russian–United States nuclear arms control and disarmament

PETR TOPYCHKANOV AND IAN DAVIS

Events in 2019 clearly showed that bilateral nuclear arms control between Russia and the United States was failing. On 2 August the USA formally withdrew from the 1987 Treaty on the Elimination of Intermediate-range and Shorter-range Missiles (INF Treaty) due principally to alleged non-compliance by Russia, leading to the treaty's demise.[1] In addition, there was no agreement to extend the only remaining nuclear arms control agreement between Russia and the USA—the 2010 Treaty on Measures for the Further Reduction and Limitation of Strategic Offensive Arms (New START)—which, if not extended before February 2021, will also lapse.[2] With these two decisions, Russian–US arms control faced the most significant crisis since 2002, when the USA withdrew from the bilateral 1972 Anti-Ballistic Missile Treaty (ABM Treaty).[3]

As bilateral efforts stalled, there were some limited and conflicting efforts to move the debates into a trilateral format including China or a multilateral format including other nuclear weapon states. However, the prospects for replacing bilateral Russian–US agreements with a new multilateral architecture that includes China were not promising. Instead, the post-INF Treaty world was already seeing the first signs of further missile proliferation, with the USA test-firing two missiles that would not have been allowed under the treaty.

This section reviews the key developments in 2019 in the INF and New START treaties and concludes by arguing that the era of bilateral nuclear arms control treaties between the two countries appears to be coming to a close.

The collapse of the Intermediate-range Nuclear Forces Treaty

By the end of 2018, the INF Treaty dispute between Russia and the USA (along with its allies in the North Atlantic Treaty Organization, NATO) had reached a point where the possibility of salvaging the treaty had become extremely unlikely.[4] On 4 December 2018 the US Department of State and

---

[1] For a summary and other details of the INF Treaty see annex A, section III, in this volume.

[2] For a summary and other details of New START see annex A, section III, in this volume.

[3] For a summary and other details of the ABM Treaty see annex A, section III, in this volume. On its demise see Kile, S. N., 'Ballistic missile defence and nuclear arms control', *SIPRI Yearbook 2002*, pp. 500–11; and Kile, S. N., 'Nuclear arms control, non-proliferation and ballistic missile defence', *SIPRI Yearbook 2003*, pp. 603–604.

[4] For developments related to the INF Treaty in 2018 see Topychkanov, P., Kile, S. N. and Davis, I., 'US–Russian nuclear arms control and disarmament', *SIPRI Yearbook 2019*, pp. 369–77.

Box 11.1. The 9M729 missile system and the 1987 Intermediate-range Nuclear Forces Treaty

The 1987 Intermediate-range Nuclear Forces (INF) Treaty banned Russia, the United States and its other parties from possessing, producing or testing ground-launched ballistic and cruise missiles with a range of 500–5500 kilometres.[a] The treaty permitted testing of a missile from a fixed ground launcher to a prohibited range if the missile was intended to be sea- or air-launched once deployed. The USA alleges that Russia first tested a new missile, designated 9M729 (or SSC-8 by NATO), from a fixed launcher to a prohibited range and then from a mobile launcher to a permitted range (below 500 km). By combining these test results, it was able to develop a prohibited ground-launched missile.[b] Russia denies this.[c]

There are few open source technical specifications on the 9M729 missile system. Independent experts consider that the Russian Navy's 3M-14 Kalibr sea-launched cruise missile (NATO designation SS-N-30A) could have served as the basic model for the missile.[d] It is also suggested that the 9M729 missile could be used with the Iskander-M launcher.[e] Although this launcher is not directly banned by the INF Treaty, its use with a banned system would mean that it must be destroyed along with the prohibited missiles.

[a] For a summary and other details of the Treaty on the Elimination of Intermediate-range and Shorter-range Missiles see annex A, section III, in this volume.

[b] US Office of the Director of National Intelligence, 'Director of National Intelligence Daniel Coats on Russia's Intermediate-range Nuclear Forces (INF) Treaty violation', 30 Nov. 2018.

[c] US Department of State, 'Timeline of highlighted US diplomacy regarding the INF Treaty since 2013', Fact sheet, 30 July 2019; and 'US fails to rectify INF violations, senior Russian diplomat says', TASS, 5 Aug. 2019.

[d] Podvig, P., 'The INF Treaty culprit identified. Now what?', Russian Strategic Nuclear Forces, 5 Dec. 2017.

[e] Podvig (note d).

---

the foreign ministers of NATO members made simultaneous statements alleging Russia's 'material breach' of the INF Treaty.[5] The allegations, which date back to 2013, centred on Russia's 9M729 mobile ground-launched cruise missile (GLCM), which was alleged to have a flight range prohibited by the treaty (see box 11.1). Russia has consistently denied these allegations.

After the USA was persuaded by European NATO members to give Russia a 60-day grace period until early February 2019, the NATO secretary general, Jens Stoltenberg, warned Russia that it had a 'last chance' to comply with the INF Treaty.[6] For the USA and NATO, compliance meant the verifiable destruction of the 9M729 missiles, its launchers and related equipment. If this did not happen, the USA would suspend its commitments under the treaty and give the required six-month notice of withdrawal.

---

[5] US Department of States, 'Russia's violation of the Intermediate-Range Nuclear Forces (INF) Treaty', Fact sheet, 4 Dec. 2018; and NATO, Statement on the Intermediate-Range Nuclear Forces (INF) Treaty, Press Release no. (2018) 162, 4 Dec. 2018.

[6] NATO, 'Press conference by NATO Secretary General Jens Stoltenberg following the meeting of the North Atlantic Council in Foreign Ministers' session', 4 Dec. 2018.

January 2019: The grace period expires

Russia continued to refute the alleged treaty violation and described the allegations as a pretext for the USA to withdraw from the treaty.[7] The Russian response combined legal, military and diplomatic arguments. First, the deputy foreign minister, Sergey Ryabkov, argued that it was not legally possible to suspend the treaty, and that Russia would see any attempts by the USA to develop, produce and test banned missiles during any period of suspension as a violation of the treaty.[8] Second, Russia threatened to enhance its military capabilities and to target any US missiles deployed to Europe following a US withdrawal from the treaty.[9] Third, Russia engaged in diplomatic efforts to prevent the suspension and potential US withdrawal.[10]

On 15 January 2019, Russia and the USA held consultations in Geneva. Ryabkov and the US under secretary of state for arms control and international security, Andrea Thompson, led the respective delegations. However, the two sides were unable to move beyond mutual recriminations, with the USA continuing to insist on the dismantlement of the disputed missile.[11] The INF Treaty's dispute mechanism, the Special Verification Commission (SVC), did not meet in 2019.[12]

On 23 January 2019, the Russian Ministry of Defence allowed foreign observers to inspect the Iskander-M mobile launcher and a separate missile container, but it is unclear whether either actually contained the 9M729 missile. In any case, the USA and most of its NATO allies refused to attend the inspection event.[13] Later, the USA criticized the demonstration as 'completely controlled' by Russia and argued that it did not change the fact

---

[7] 'Lavrov points out US showed no proof that Russia breached INF with new missile's tests', TASS, 18 Jan. 2019.

[8] 'INF Treaty cannot be suspended, it can only be violated, says senior Russian diplomat', TASS, 18 Dec. 2018.

[9] 'Russia eyes beefing up armed forces amid US plans to quit INF, says defense chief', TASS, 4 Dec. 2018; and 'Russia to target any US missiles deployed in Europe after INF Treaty terminated—Kremlin', TASS, 20 Dec. 2018.

[10] E.g. the foreign ministers of the members of the Collective Security Treaty Organization (CSTO) issued a statement in support of the INF Treaty. Organization for Security and Co-Operation in Europe (OSCE), Ministerial Council, Joint statement by the ministers for foreign affairs of the Republic of Armenia, the Republic of Belarus, the Republic of Kazakhstan, the Kyrgyz Republic, the Russian Federation and the Republic of Tajikistan at the Twenty-Fifth Meeting of the OSCE Ministerial Council, MC.DEL/21/18, 6 Dec. 2018.

[11] 'Russia, US fail to save missile treaty, Washington to pull out', Reuters, 16 Jan. 2019.

[12] The SVC met 31 times, with the final meeting taking place on 14 Dec. 2017.

[13] Russian Ministry of Defence, 'Russian Defence Ministry briefs military attaches with presentation of 9M729 missile of Iskander-M complex', 23 Jan. 2019; 'US mobilizes allies to blame Russia for dismantling INF Treaty—Lavrov', TASS, 16 Feb. 2019; Reevell, P., 'Russia exhibits missile US cites as reason for leaving key arms treaty', ABC News, 24 Jan. 2019; and Pifer, S., 'The blame game begins over the INF Treaty's demise, and Washington is losing', Brookings Institution, 25 Jan. 2019.

that Russia had already tested the 9M729 missile to ranges prohibited by the INF Treaty.[14]

February–August 2019: Withdrawal from the treaty

Since Russia did not destroy the 9M729 missile, its launchers and associated equipment in the 60-day grace period, on 1 February 2019 US President Donald J. Trump initiated the process of withdrawal from the treaty and suspended the USA's obligations under it.[15] The suspension came into force the next day and the six-month notice of withdrawal started. In a statement, NATO supported the US decision and attributed full responsibility for the possible demise of the INF Treaty to Russia.[16] The USA and the other members of NATO also reiterated that the treaty would survive if Russia dismantled the concerned missile system in a verifiable way—otherwise the USA would formally withdraw on 2 August.

Russia initially responded by announcing that it would be developing a new land-based intermediate-range hypersonic missile to mirror what it viewed as similar developments by the USA.[17] On 2 February 2019, for example, the Russian Ministry of Defence accused the USA of expanding a missile programme that initially started in 2017 to produce missiles with ranges banned by the INF Treaty.[18]

Between 2 February and 2 August there were several efforts to reach a compromise to save the treaty. On 4 March the chief of the Russian General Staff, General Valery Gerasimov, and the chairman of the US Joint Chiefs of Staff, General Joseph Dunford, met in Vienna to discuss the INF Treaty and strategic stability.[19] There was no breakthrough in the talks and on the same day Russian President Vladimir V. Putin officially suspended Russia's compliance with the treaty.[20] On 14–15 May the US secretary of state, Michael R. Pompeo, held talks in Sochi, southern Russia, with President Putin, the Russian foreign minister, Sergey Lavrov, and other Russian officials; and on 12 June Ryabkov and Thompson met again in Prague to 'build

---

[14] US Department of State, 'INF myth busters: Pushing back on Russian propaganda regarding the INF Treaty', Fact sheet, 30 July 2019.

[15] White House, Statement from the President regarding the Intermediate-Range Nuclear Forces (INF) Treaty, 1 Feb. 2019; and US Department of State, 'INF Treaty: US intent to withdraw from the INF Treaty', Diplomatic note, 2 Feb. 2019.

[16] NATO, North Atlantic Council, Statement on Russia's failure to comply with the Intermediate-Range Nuclear Forces (INF) Treaty, Press Release no. (2019) 015, 1 Feb. 2019.

[17] 'Russia starts developing land-based hypersonic missile with intermediate range, says Putin', TASS, 2 Feb. 2019.

[18] Russian Ministry of Defence, 'Russian Defence Ministry: US started production of intermediate-range missiles two years before it accused Russia of violating the INF Treaty', 2 Feb. 2019.

[19] 'Russian, US top military brass hash over missile defense, INF, New START', TASS, 4 Mar. 2019.

[20] President of Russia, Executive Order suspending Russia's compliance with the USSR–US INF Treaty, 4 Mar. 2019.

on' the previous bilateral talks.[21] Neither of these meetings was able to make any progress.

The risk of the treaty's demise became a topic of significant concern around the globe. The United Nations secretary-general, António Guterres, repeatedly called on Russia and the USA to preserve the treaty. On 25 February 2019, for example, during a regular session of the Conference on Disarmament, he highlighted the risks of nuclear competition in Europe that would be provoked by the end of the treaty.[22] Several states also urged Russia and the USA to prevent the treaty's collapse. Among them were China, France, Germany and Japan, reflecting the fact that the end of the INF Treaty would probably have the greatest impacts in Europe and North East Asia.[23] In contrast, Ukraine (a state party to the INF Treaty) announced that it now had the right to develop intermediate-range missiles, although the technical and financial challenges associated with doing so made this unlikely.[24]

The end of the INF Treaty: What next?

On the expiry of the six-month period of notice, the USA formally withdrew from the INF Treaty on 2 August 2019.[25] NATO repeated its support for the US decision.[26]

Russia responded by making a voluntary commitment not to deploy ground-launched intermediate- and shorter-range missiles, but only in the regions where there would be no US deployment of missiles of similar ranges.[27] On 19 September President Putin invited NATO member states to match this

---

[21] US Department of State, Remarks to traveling press, 14 May 2019; and US Department of State, 'Under Secretary Andrea Thompson continues discussions with Russian Deputy Foreign Minister Ryabkov in Prague', 12 June 2019.

[22] United Nations, Secretary-General, Remarks to the Conference on Disarmament, 25 Feb. 2019.

[23] German Federal Foreign Office, 'Außenminister Heiko Maas zu Gesprächen in Moskau und Kiew' [Foreign minister Heiko Maas for talks in Moscow and Kiev], 18 Jan. 2019; Élysée, 'Entretien téléphonique du Président de la République avec le Président des Etats-Unis d'Amérique Donald Trump' [Telephone conversation between the President of the Republic and the President of the United States of America Donald Trump], Press release, 22 Oct. 2018; Chinese Ministry of Foreign Affairs, 'Ambassador Liu Xiaoming contributes an article to the Financial Times entitled The US's wrong-headed decision to pull out of the nuclear arms treaty', 6 May 2019; and Japanese Ministry of Foreign Affairs, 'Press conference by foreign minister Taro Kono', 23 Oct. 2018.

[24] Ukrainian Ministry of Foreign Affairs, 'Comment of the MFA of Ukraine in connection with the Intermediate-Range Nuclear Forces Treaty', 7 Mar. 2019; and Sinovets, P and Odessa Center for Nonproliferation (ODCNP), *Responses to the INF Treaty Crisis: The European Dimension* (Odessa I. I. Mechnikov National University: Odessa, 3 May 2019). With the dissolution of the Soviet Union in 1991, the membership of the bilateral Soviet–US INF Treaty expanded to include Russia and 3 other successor states of the Soviet Union—Belarus, Kazakhstan and Ukraine—that had inspectable facilities on their territories.

[25] Pompeo, M. R., 'US withdrawal from the INF Treaty on August 2, 2019', Press statement, US Department of State, 2 Aug. 2019.

[26] NATO, Statement by the North Atlantic Council on the Intermediate-Range Nuclear Forces Treaty, 2 Aug. 2019.

[27] Russian Ministry of Foreign Affairs, 'Foreign Ministry statement on the withdrawal of the United States from the INF Treaty and its termination', 2 Aug. 2019.

non-deployment commitment.[28] While NATO rejected this proposal as not being credible due to the alleged deployment of 9M729 missiles, some member states, including France, saw it as a potential basis for discussion.[29] The short declaration issued by the NATO Leaders' Meeting in London in December 2019 referred in general terms to the alliance's openness to dialogue with Russia 'when Russia's actions make that possible', but it did not specify any diplomatic effort or confidence-building measure to address the post-INF Treaty challenges.[30]

French President Emmanuel Macron elaborated on his vision for the European dimension of post-INF Treaty talks during a meeting with President Trump on 3 December. Macron argued that, due to the increased risks faced by European countries after the treaty's demise, the European component should be 'part of the future negotiations of such a new INF Treaty'.[31] However, this French position was not reflected in the declaration issued at the 2019 NATO Leaders' Meeting.

In the run-up to and following its withdrawal from the INF Treaty, the USA raised concerns about China's growing nuclear and conventional missile inventory, which is mostly composed of systems in the range that was prohibited by the Russian–US treaty.[32] NATO supported this view at its 2019 Leaders' Meeting. According to Jens Stoltenberg of NATO, the alliance had started a debate on engaging China on arms control issues, but he did not disclose any specific details about what kind of arms control arrangement would be sought with China.[33] To date, China has expressed no interest in joining the INF Treaty or a replacement treaty.[34] The Russian statement on the US withdrawal from the INF Treaty also referenced the 'third countries' issue (without explicitly mentioning China), but highlighted that such countries were 'not ready to assume the relevant treaty obligations'.[35] Thus, while Russia appears to be interested in engaging other countries on this

[28] Chernenko, E. and Soloviev, V., 'Rakety srednei i men'shei mirnosti' [Missiles of medium and shorter peacefulness], *Kommersant*, 25 Sep. 2019.

[29] Peel, M. and Foy, H., 'NATO rejects Russian offer on nuclear missiles freeze', *Financial Times*, 26 Sep. 2019; and NATO, 'Joint press point with NATO Secretary General Jens Stoltenberg and the President of France Emmanuel Macron', 28 Nov. 2019.

[30] NATO, London Declaration issued by the heads of state and Government participating in the meeting of the North Atlantic Council in London 3–4 December 2019, Press Release no. (2019) 115, 4 Dec. 2019.

[31] White House, Remarks by President Trump and President Macron of France before bilateral meeting, 3 Dec. 2019.

[32] Ghoshal, D., 'China and the INF Treaty', *Comparative Strategy*, vol. 35, no. 5 (2016), pp. 363–70; Taylor, A., 'How China plays into Trump's decision to pull-out of INF Treaty with Russia', *Washington Post*, 23 Oct. 2018; and United Nations, General Assembly, First Committee, Statement by the United States, 10 Oct. 2019. On China's nuclear forces see chapter 10, section V, in this volume.

[33] NATO, 'Press conference by NATO Secretary General Jens Stoltenberg following the meeting of the North Atlantic Council at the level of heads of state and/or government', 4 Dec. 2019.

[34] Chinese Ministry of Foreign Affairs, Remarks by HE Ambassador Li Song at the CD on the US withdrawal from the INF Treaty, 6 Aug. 2019.

[35] Russian Ministry of Foreign Affairs (note 27).

issue—including France and the United Kingdom as well as China—it is seemingly opposed to replacing Russian–US arms control with a process that has no clear future.

With little appetite elsewhere to replace the INF Treaty with a multilateral framework, it seems likely that the treaty's demise will lead to further missile proliferation, as well as, over time, new deployments of anti-missile defences, especially in Europe and Asia.[36] While Russia itself did not test any missiles in 2019 that would have been prohibited under the treaty, this new era seemed to be presaged by the USA testing a GLCM on 18 August 2019 and a ground-launched ballistic missile on 12 December 2019.[37]

New START

The INF Treaty crisis also cast a shadow over the future of the one remaining bilateral Russian–US nuclear arms control agreement: New START. Mutual recriminations in the fields of arms control, security and political affairs have created an atmosphere of mistrust between the two countries, with misperceptions extending to each other's nuclear doctrines and capabilities. Notwithstanding this climate of mistrust, both parties fulfilled their obligations under New START. However, they take different approaches to the future of arms control, which have so far prevented the treaty from being extended or renegotiated. The treaty is due to expire in 2021.

Implementation of the treaty

Under the treaty, the parties are required to exchange data on the numbers of nuclear warheads and their delivery vehicles twice a year. The data for 2019 confirmed that Russia and the USA remained within the final treaty limits (see table 11.1). Meetings of the treaty's Bilateral Consultative Commission took place in April and November 2019, and in July the Russian and US delegations also met in Geneva for strategic stability consultations.

In 2019 the USA was generally satisfied with Russia's compliance with its New START obligations. The main Russian concerns about US compliance were related to the conversion of nuclear delivery systems into conventional ones. Russia complained that it could not verify that 56 launchers for

---

[36] On the links between missile proliferation and missile defences, see e.g. O'Rourke, R., *Navy Aegis Ballistic Missile Defense (BMD) Program: Background and Issues for Congress*, Congressional Research Service (CRS) Report for Congress RL33745 (US Congress, CRS: Washington, DC, 17 Dec. 2019); and Lombardi, C., 'Recent exercises demonstrate importance of layered integrated air and missile defence to counter advanced threats', Euractiv, 3 Oct. 2019.

[37] 'US test-fires cruise missile after INF treaty pullout', Deutsche Welle, 19 Aug. 2019; Mehta, A., 'Watch the Pentagon test a previously banned ballistic missile', *Defense News*, 12 Dec. 2019; 'Going ballistic: Missile-testing', *The Economist*, 18 Dec. 2019; and Safronov, I., 'Putin ob'yavil nazvanie novoi rakety srednei dal'nosti' [Putin has announced the name of a new medium-range missile], *Vedomosti*, 24 Dec. 2019.

Table 11.1. Russian and United States aggregate numbers of strategic offensive arms under New START, as of 5 February 2011, 1 March 2019 and 1 September 2019

Category	Treaty limits	Russia			United States		
		Feb. 2011	Mar. 2019	Sep. 2019	Feb. 2011	Sep. 2018	Sep. 2019
Deployed ICBMs, SLBMs and heavy bombers	700	521	524	513	882	656	668
Warheads on deployed ICBMs, SLBMs and heavy bombers[a]	1 550	1 537	1 461	1 426	1 800	1 365	1 376
Deployed and non-deployed launchers of ICBMs, SLBMs and heavy bombers	800	865	760	757	1 124	800	800

ICBM = intercontinental ballistic missile; SLBM = submarine-launched ballistic missile.

Note: The treaty entered into force on 5 Feb. 2011. The treaty limits had to be reached by 5 Feb. 2018.

[a] Each heavy bomber, whether equipped with cruise missiles or gravity bombs, is counted as carrying only 1 warhead, even though the aircraft can carry larger weapon payloads.

Source: US Department of State, Bureau of Arms Control, Verification and Compliance, 'New START Treaty aggregate numbers of strategic offensive arms', Fact sheets, 1 June 2011; 1 Mar. 2019; and 1 Sep. 2019.

submarine-launched ballistic missiles and 41 heavy bombers that the USA had converted to non-nuclear missions—and exempted from the treaty's provisions—could not be reconverted to a nuclear role. Russia also complained about its inability to inspect four so-called training silos that are not specifically covered by New START.[38]

Prospects for extension or replacement of the treaty

Russian diplomats indicated that their concerns about US compliance with New START would need to be addressed before extending the treaty, but also showed a willingness to continue dialogue with the USA on strategic issues.[39] During the strategic stability discussions in July, for example,

[38] Russian Ministry of Foreign Affairs, 'Comment by the Russian Ministry of Foreign Affairs on the US report on adherence to and compliance with arms control, nonproliferation, and disarmament agreements and commitments (ACNPD) (to be added to the comment by the Russian Ministry of Foreign Affairs of May 5, 2019)', 20 Sep. 2019.

[39] Russian Ministry of Foreign Affairs, 'Director of the Foreign Ministry Department on Non-Proliferation and Arms Control Vladimir Yermakov answers media questions', 4 July 2019.

Russia proposed including new types of nuclear-capable weapon under the existing New START, notably its Sarmat silo-based intercontinental ballistic missile (ICBM) and its Avangard boost-glide system.[40] Russia exhibited the latter system, which it said would became operational in December 2019, for US inspectors during their treaty verification visit on 24–26 November.[41] Furthermore, on 5 December 2019 President Putin suggested that Russia would be ready to extend the treaty immediately, without any preconditions.[42] Lavrov, the Russian foreign minister, repeated Putin's offer on 10 December while in Washington, DC, and during a TV debate in December reiterated that the Sarmat and Avangard missiles were covered by the treaty and so would also be included once it was extended.[43]

The USA did not formally respond to these offers. However, US officials have raised several questions that, while not being directly about New START-related systems, could nonetheless influence the US decision on whether to agree to an extension of the treaty. For example, the USA expressed concerns about the destabilizing nature of several new weapons that Russia had recently demonstrated, including the Burevestnik nuclear-powered GLCM, the Poseidon nuclear-powered unmanned underwater vehicle, the Kinzhal nuclear-capable air-launched ballistic missile, and the above-mentioned Sarmat and Avangard.[44] The US defence secretary, Mark Esper, argued that if New START were to be extended, then it should cover all of these new weapons, not just the two systems offered by Russia.[45]

As with the INF Treaty, the USA has indicated an interest in negotiating new nuclear arms control arrangements that include China. For example, in a statement in a meeting of the First Committee of the UN General Assembly in October 2019, the US delegation said 'we need a new era of arms control, one in which Russia and China are at the negotiating table and willing to reduce nuclear risks rather than heighten them'.[46] Similarly, in October President Trump also indicated that he intended to work with both China and Russia

---

[40] 'Russia proposes viewing new types of arms as part of New START', TASS, 17 July 2019.

[41] 'Russia demonstrates Avangard hypersonic missile system to US', TASS, 26 Nov. 2019; and 'Russia's Avangard hypersonic missile system to go on combat alert in December—top brass', TASS, 26 Nov. 2019.

[42] President of Russia, 'Meeting with Defence Ministry leadership and heads of defence industry enterprises', 5 Dec. 2019.

[43] Wong, E. and Crowley, M., 'Trump and Pompeo spoke to Russian official about US elections. Did only one deliver a warning?', New York Times, 10 Dec. 2019; and Russian Ministry of Foreign Affairs, 'Foreign Minister Sergey Lavrov's answers to questions in The Great Game show on Channel One, Moscow, December 22, 2019', 22 Dec. 2019.

[44] United Nations (note 32). On the autonomous capabilities of the Poseidon system, see Topychkanov, P., 'Autonomy in Russian nuclear forces', ed. V. Boulanin, The Impact of Artificial Intelligence on Strategic Stability and Nuclear Risk, vol. I, Euro–Atlantic Perspectives (SIPRI: Stockholm, May 2019), pp. 74–75.

[45] Leon, M. and Griffin, J., 'Pentagon "very carefully" watching China, it's [sic] "no. 1 priority", Defense Secretary Mark Esper tells Fox News', Fox News, 22 Aug. 2019.

[46] United Nations (note 32).

on nuclear arms control.[47] However, China has clearly stated that it has no interest in participating in trilateral nuclear arms reduction negotiations with the USA and Russia.[48]

Conclusions

The almost complete breakdown of Russian–US nuclear arms control reflects the deterioration of the broader bilateral relationship and a growing difference in approaches to the issue by the two states. For example, during 2019 there were further disagreements on nuclear-related arms control in the contexts of two multilateral treaties: the 1996 Comprehensive Nuclear-Test-Ban Treaty (CTBT) and the 1992 Treaty on Open Skies.[49] The USA accused Russia of breaching the nuclear testing moratorium with very low-yield tests, which Russia (and some experts) dispute.[50] Similarly, Russia and the USA each accused the other of violating the Open Skies Treaty by applying restrictions on certain observation overflights, and the USA is said to be considering withdrawal.[51]

Essentially, the two states' different approaches to nuclear arms control can be characterized as follows. Russia is largely committed to business as usual, meaning arms control focused on reductions in the numbers of nuclear weapons, but with linkages to limits on US missile defences. In contrast, the current US administration sees no benefit in bilateral arrangements with Russia and wants to move to trilateral or even multilateral arrangements that also include China. The statement by Pompeo, the US secretary of state, on the US withdrawal from the INF Treaty sums up the principles that underpin current US thinking:

The United States remains committed to effective arms control that advances US, allied, and partner security; is verifiable and enforceable; and includes partners that comply responsibly with their obligations. President Trump has charged this Administration with beginning a new chapter by seeking a new era of arms control that moves beyond the bilateral treaties of the past. Going forward, the United States calls upon Russia and China to join us in this opportunity to deliver real security results to our nations and the entire world.[52]

---

[47] Bugos, S. and Reif, K., 'US seeks "new era of arms control"', *Arms Control Today*, vol. 49, no. 9 (Nov. 2019).

[48] E.g. Chinese Ministry of Foreign Affairs, 'Briefing by Mr FU Cong, Director General of the Department of Arms Control and Disarmament of Ministry of Foreign Affairs', 6 Aug. 2019.

[49] For summaries and other details of the CTBT and the Treaty on Open Skies, see annex A, sections I and II respectively, in this volume.

[50] See section IV of this chapter.

[51] Gordon, M. R. and Salama, V., 'Trump moves closer to ending another post-cold war treaty', *Wall Street Journal*, 27 Oct. 2019; 'The Open Skies Treaty', *Strategic Comments*, vol. 25, no. 10 (Dec. 2019), pp. vii–ix; and Gould, J. and Mehta, A., 'US to Europe: Fix Open Skies Treaty or we quit', *Defense News*, 21 Nov. 2019.

[52] Pompeo (note 25).

Despite such statements, there appears to be no active US engagement with China or Russia (or any other nuclear weapon state) to this end, nor any practical proposals for doing so. Given this apparent lack of groundwork and the complexity of undertaking trilateral arms control negotiations, it seems likely that, at best, only some limited form of strategic trilateral dialogue could take place before New START expires.

Furthermore, these mismatches between Russian and US arms control principles and objectives, combined with wider political, economic and strategic differences between the two states, suggest that the era of bilateral nuclear arms control agreements between the two counties might be coming to an end. Future political changes on either side may alter the balance once again, especially since support for arms control remains strong among segments of the policy community on both sides.[53] However, in a seemingly new era of strategic competition between the major powers, their commitment to any form of nuclear arms control is beginning to appear illusionary.[54]

---

[53] E.g. Edelman, E. and Miller, F. C., 'Russia is beefing up its nuclear arsenal. Here's what the US needs to do', Politico, 31 Dec. 2019; and 'US–Russian dialogue on arms control: Does it have a future?', 8th meeting in the US–Russia Dialogue series, co-organized by the James Martin Center for Nonproliferation Studies, Monterey, CA, and the Center for Energy and Security Studies, Moscow, 7 Nov. 2019—especially the conclusions and discussion papers.

[54] On this strategic competition see chapter 1, section II, in this volume.

II. North Korean–United States nuclear diplomacy

SHANNON N. KILE

In 2019 tensions persisted between the Democratic People's Republic of Korea (DPRK, or North Korea) and the United States over the former's ongoing programmes to develop nuclear weapons and ballistic missile delivery systems. North Korea had dismantled its nuclear test site at Pyunggye-ri in 2018 and it continued to adhere to the moratorium on the testing of nuclear weapons and long-range ballistic missiles declared by its supreme leader, Kim Jong Un, in April 2018.[1] However, during 2019 North Korea conducted multiple flight tests of short-range ballistic missiles in contravention of a United Nations Security Council resolution demanding that it halt all missile tests.[2] At the same time, North Korea and the USA remained locked in a diplomatic stalemate over their political commitments made the previous year to work towards establishing peaceful relations and achieving the denuclearization of the Korean peninsula. The impasse coincided with the breakdown of peace and reconciliation efforts between North Korea and the Republic of Korea (South Korea) initiated in 2018.[3]

This section reviews developments in North Korean–US nuclear diplomacy in 2019. It first describes developments at the bilateral summit in Hanoi in February and then looks at the aftermath of the meeting.

The second North Korean–US summit meeting

The outcome of the Singapore summit meeting

The year 2019 began with no tangible progress towards implementing the commitments made by Kim Jong Un and US President Donald J. Trump at the June 2018 summit meeting in Singapore—the first ever between a sitting US president and a North Korean leader.[4] At the end of the meeting, the two leaders had issued a joint declaration in which, among other things, Trump committed to provide security guarantees to North Korea and to normalize bilateral relations, while Kim reaffirmed his 'firm and unwavering commitment to complete denuclearization of the Korean Peninsula'.[5] The two leaders pledged to hold follow-on negotiations 'at the earliest possible date' and to work jointly 'to build a lasting and stable peace regime' on the peninsula.

---

[1] Korean Central News Agency (KCNA), 'Third plenary meeting of seventh CC, WPK held in presence of Kim Jong Un', 21 Apr. 2018.

[2] UN Security Council Resolution 1718, 14 Oct. 2006, paras 5, 7.

[3] On North Korean–South Korean dialogue see chapter 4, section I, in this volume.

[4] See Kile, S. N., 'North Korean–US nuclear diplomacy', *SIPRI Yearbook 2019*, pp. 363–65.

[5] North Korean–US Singapore Summit Meeting, Joint statement, 12 June 2018.

The Singapore joint declaration did not address long-standing disagreements between North Korea and the USA over the definition of denuclearization and the scope and sequencing of steps for achieving that goal. US officials, led by the secretary of state, Michael R. Pompeo, and the national security advisor, John R. Bolton, continued to insist that North Korea provide a detailed, written disclosure of its nuclear weapon stockpile, its nuclear fuel cycle and related production facilities, and its ballistic missile delivery systems at the beginning of a denuclearization process. However, Kim Jong Un had repeatedly rejected the idea of his country making any such disclosures in the absence of a permanent peace treaty, arguing that doing so would be tantamount to giving an enemy a list of targets.[6]

A related obstacle was the USA's insistence that all international sanctions on North Korea remain in place until it had completely, verifiably and irreversibly dismantled its nuclear weapon and ballistic missile programmes. For its part, North Korea continued to insist that the USA agree to a phased lifting of international sanctions as part of a step-by-step approach to denuclearization.

In his New Year's Day speech on 1 January 2019, Kim stated that he was prepared to have a second summit meeting with President Trump 'anytime' to discuss denuclearization.[7] However, he warned that he would seek an unspecified 'new way' if the USA persisted with its policy of sanctions and pressure against his country. Kim also reiterated a list of steps to be taken by the USA before North Korea would proceed with denuclearization measures. These included the halting of joint military training between the USA and South Korea, the withdrawal of US nuclear forces based on or near the Korean peninsula, and the conclusion of a peace treaty formally ending the 1950–53 Korean War.[8]

On 18 January the White House announced that President Trump would have a second summit meeting with the North Korean leader before the end of February. The location of the meeting was not identified.[9]

Following the announcement, an informal working-level meeting between North Korean, South Korean and US special envoys was convened near Stockholm, Sweden, on 20–22 January.[10] The purpose was to consider measures for implementing the commitments agreed by Kim and Trump in

[6] Cole, B., 'Kim Jong Un won't tell Trump where weapons are as it gives US a "list of targets for attacks"', *Newsweek*, 11 July 2018.

[7] Korean Central News Agency (KCNA), 'New Year address of Supreme Leader Kim Jong Un', 1 Jan. 2019.

[8] Korean Central News Agency (KCNA) (note 7); and Sanger, D. E., 'Kim and Trump back at square 1: If US keeps sanctions, North will keep nuclear program', *New York Times*, 1 Jan. 2019.

[9] Nakamura, D., Hudson, J. and Gearan, A. 'Trump to meet with North Korean leader Kim Jong Un in late February, White House says', *Washington Post*, 18 Jan. 2019.

[10] Tanner, J., 'US, South Korean diplomats attending NKorea talks in Sweden', Associated Press, 20 Jan. 2019. The meeting was co-organized by the Swedish Government and SIPRI.

the Singapore joint declaration. Afterwards, the lead South Korean negotiator said that the trilateral discussions had proceeded smoothly and set the stage for diplomatic advances at the upcoming summit meeting.[11] In an apparent easing of US demands, the US special representative for North Korea, Stephen E. Biegun, indicated that North Korea's submission of the detailed disclosure of its nuclear weapon and ballistic programmes demanded by the US side would be acceptable 'at some point' in the denuclearization process and not necessarily at the outset.[12]

The Hanoi summit meeting

On 27 February 2019 Kim and Trump, accompanied by their respective national delegations, gathered in Hanoi, Viet Nam, for the second summit meeting.[13] This came against the background of mounting speculation about whether the two leaders could agree on concrete steps for implementing the denuclearization and peacebuilding commitments made in Singapore.[14] However, the meeting ended abruptly on 28 February, with the two delegations departing without issuing an expected concluding communiqué or joint declaration.

The primary cause of the meeting's breakdown was a disagreement over sanctions relief for North Korea.[15] There were contradictory accounts about the nature of the disagreement. During a news conference, President Trump said that North Korea had demanded the lifting of all sanctions against it in return for shutting down and dismantling its main nuclear material production facility, located at Yongbyon. Trump noted that such a deal would have left untouched North Korea's arsenal of nuclear warheads and ballistic missile delivery systems.[16] Pompeo cautioned that, in addition to the Yongbyon plant, there were a number of suspected undisclosed nuclear fuel production sites around the country.[17]

In contrast, the North Korean minister of foreign affairs, Ri Yong Ho, explained that his country had in fact sought the 'partial' removal of sanctions in return for dismantling its Yongbyon nuclear site.[18] Specifically, North Korea

---

[11] Yonhap News Agency, 'S. Korea's chief nuclear envoy sees "rapid progress" for future US–NK talks', 23 Jan. 2019.

[12] Johnson, J., 'US envoy to North Korea warns of "Asia-Pacific nuclear weapons challenge" but softens demand for list of arsenal', *Japan Times*, 1 Feb. 2019.

[13] 'Trump and Kim start Vietnam summit with dinner', BBC, 27 Feb. 2019.

[14] Denyer, S., 'The grand bargain in Hanoi takes shape, but can Trump and Kim close the deal?', *Washington Post*, 25 Feb. 2019; and Choe, S., 'Trump and Kim may declare end of war at summit, South Korea says', *New York Times*, 25 Feb. 2019.

[15] Lemire, J., Riechmann, D. and Klug, F., 'Trump, Kim end summit with standoff over easing US sanctions', Associated Press, 28 Feb. 2019.

[16] Rucker, P., Denyer, S. and Nakamura, D., 'North Korea's foreign minister says country seeks only partial sanctions relief, contradicting Trump', *Washington Post*, 1 Mar. 2019.

[17] Associated Press, 'North Korea disputes Trump's account of talks breakdown', *Asahi Shimbun*, 1 Mar. 2019.

[18] 'DPRK FM Ri Yong Ho disputes Trump reason for summit collapse', *People's Daily*, 1 Mar. 2019.

had requested the lifting of five UN Security Council sanctions resolutions passed in 2016 and 2017.[19] The sanctions targeted North Korea's mineral and food exports as well as its fuel imports and, according to Ri, were damaging the livelihoods of the North Korean people.[20] In return, North Korea would permanently dismantle all of the nuclear material production facilities at Yongbyon, including for plutonium and uranium, with the participation of US experts.[21] Ri emphasized that North Korea was seeking an incremental approach that exchanged North Korean steps on denuclearization for US action to lift sanctions against North Korea and address its security concerns.[22]

Developments after the Hanoi summit meeting

North Korea's deadline for a new US approach

The immediate public reactions of both Donald Trump and Kim Jong Un to the collapse of the Hanoi summit meeting were restrained. They emphasized their cordial personal relations while seeking to minimize the persisting differences in the countries' respective approaches to denuclearization.[23]

Kim subsequently expressed growing frustration over the alleged unwillingness of the USA to consider the relaxation of sanctions against North Korea as part of an incipient denuclearization process. Trump had described international sanctions against North Korea as being at a 'fair level'.[24] Speaking before the Supreme People's Assembly (the North Korean Parliament) on 13 April, Kim stated that is was 'essential for the US to quit its current calculation method and approach us with new one' if it were genuinely interested in pursuing denuclearization talks.[25] Kim said that he was open to having another summit meeting with Trump, but he set the end of 2019 as a deadline for the US administration to offer mutually acceptable terms for an agreement to continue talks.

---

[19] On the 9 UN Security Council sanctions resolutions on North Korea's nuclear weapon and ballistic missile activities, see Kile, S. N., 'International non-proliferation sanctions against North Korea', *SIPRI Yearbook 2018*, pp. 386–88.

[20] 'DPRK FM Ri Yong Ho disputes Trump reason for summit collapse' (note 18).

[21] For a non-governmental assessment of the implications of dismantling the Yongbyon facilities, see Samore, G., 'How significant is the dismantlement of Yongbyon?', 38 North, 11 Mar. 2019.

[22] 'DPRK FM Ri Yong Ho disputes Trump reason for summit collapse' (note 18).

[23] Associated Press (note 17); and Yonhap News Agency, 'N. Korea refrains from criticism of US despite breakdown of Trump summit', 5 Mar. 2019.

[24] Cohen, Z., 'Trump says sanctions on North Korea are at a "fair level"', CNN, 12 Apr. 2019.

[25] Korean Central News Agency (KCNA), 'Supreme Leader Kim Jong Un makes policy speech at first session of 14th SPA', 13 Apr. 2019; and Smith, J. and Lee, J., 'North Korea's Kim Jong Un gives US to year-end to become more flexible', Reuters, 13 Apr. 2019.

On 4 May, North Korea test-launched a new type of solid-fuel short-range ballistic missile as well as two multiple-launch rocket systems.[26] The launches marked North Korea's first ballistic missile test since 2017. There were conflicting assessments among analysts about North Korea's motivations for resuming the tests, with some speculating that it was seeking to force a breakthrough in the stalled negotiations with the USA.[27] During 2019, North Korea conducted multiple tests of short-range missiles and artillery rocket systems, including several new types.[28]

A breakdown of renewed talks

The prospects for renewed North Korean–US nuclear diplomacy improved in mid-2019. While on a visit to Seoul hosted by South Korean President Moon Jae-in, President Trump accepted an invitation from Kim Jong Un to have an impromptu meeting in the demilitarized zone (DMZ) along the intra-Korean border.[29] During the meeting, Trump became the first sitting US president to cross into North Korean territory. The two leaders said afterwards that they had agreed that their negotiators would meet within the next few weeks to resume discussions about implementing the commitments made in the Singapore joint declaration. They did not indicate whether they had discussed specific steps and measures.[30]

Following protracted diplomatic exchanges, on 4–5 October North Korean and US negotiators held a working-level meeting in Stockholm hosted by the Swedish Government.[31] The two sides came away with sharply diverging assessments of the talks. According to a spokesperson of the US Department of State, there had been 'good' discussions at the meeting.[32] He said that the US negotiating team had brought new proposals to address the goals laid out in the Singapore joint declaration.

However, North Korea's chief nuclear negotiator, Kim Myong Gil, declared that the talks had 'not fulfilled our expectations'. They had, in fact, broken down 'entirely' because the US side had not 'discarded its old stance and attitude' towards the denuclearization of the Korean peninsula and had come to the negotiating table with an 'empty hand'.[33] Kim stated that the two coun-

---

[26] Kim, D. and Hanham, M., 'North Korean missiles: Size does not matter', *Bulletin of the Atomic Scientists*, 15 May 2019. See also chapter 10, section IX, in this volume.

[27] Panda, A. and Narang, V., 'Why North Korea is testing missiles again', *Foreign Affairs*, 16 May 2019.

[28] CNS North Korea Missile Test Database, Nuclear Threat Initiative (NTI), 31 Mar. 2020.

[29] BBC, 'Trump in North Korea: KCNA hails "amazing" visit', 1 July 2019

[30] Crowley, M. and Sanger, D. E., 'In new talks, US may settle for a nuclear freeze by North Korea', *New York Times*, 30 June 2019.

[31] Hotham, O., 'North Korea, US to begin high-stakes preliminary working-level talks in Sweden', *NK News*, 4 Oct. 2019.

[32] Ortagus, M., 'North Korea talks', Press statement, US Department of State, 5 Oct. 2019.

[33] Tanner, J. and Lee, M., 'North Korea decries breakdown of talks US says were "good"', Associated Press, 6 Oct. 2019. See also Hotham, O., 'North Korea–US talks in Sweden fail to reach a deal, chief DPRK negotiator says', *NK News*, 5 Oct. 2019.

tries could discuss the next denuclearization steps only if the USA 'sincerely responds' to the steps that North Korea had taken in good faith to improve bilateral relations, in particular, the halting of its nuclear and long-range missile tests and the dismantling of its nuclear test site at Pyunggye-ri.[34] He did not mention specific steps that the USA should take to move forward with denuclearization talks.

The negotiator's remarks were followed on 10 October by a statement from the North Korean Ministry of Foreign Affairs warning that the country was prepared to resume long-range missile tests in the light of the USA's failure to respond with concrete proposals.[35] It accused the USA of having instigated a joint statement issued by the five European members of the UN Security Council—Belgium, France, Germany, Poland and the United Kingdom.[36] In response to North Korea's recent test of a new submarine-launched ballistic missile, the European states had condemned the test and a series of short-range ballistic missile launches in the previous weeks as violations of Security Council resolutions and called on North Korea to abandon its nuclear and missile programmes.[37]

On 3 December, a North Korean vice-foreign minister issued a statement warning that, if the US administration did not offer a more constructive proposal for relaxing sanctions and scaling down confrontation by the year-end deadline, it could expect an unwelcome 'Christmas gift'.[38] This was widely interpreted by analysts and US government officials as a euphemism for a long-range missile test or possibly another nuclear weapon test by North Korea.[39]

The meeting of the Central Committee of the Korean Worker's Party

Against the background of the rising tensions between North Korea and the USA, a plenary meeting of the Central Committee of the ruling Korean Worker's Party (KWP) was held in Pyongyang on 28–31 December 2019 under the chairmanship of the party's leader, Kim Jong Un.[40] The four-day meeting adopted new policy guidance on a range of military, economic and internal

[34] Tanner and Lee (note 33).

[35] North Korean Ministry of Foreign Affairs, 'Spokesperson for DPRK Foreign Ministry denounces US moves against DPRK', 10 Oct. 2019.

[36] Kim, H., 'N. Korea threatens to resume nuke, long-range missile tests', Associated Press, 10 Oct. 2019.

[37] 'Condemnation of North Korea's nuclear missile tests', Joint statement by Belgium, Estonia, France, Germany, Poland and the UK, 8 Oct. 2019; and Panda, A., 'European States on UN Security Council issue statement on North Korean missile tests', *The Diplomat*, 9 Oct. 2019.

[38] North Korean Ministry of Foreign Affairs, 'DPRK Vice Foreign Minister for US Affairs issues statement', 3 Dec. 2019.

[39] Denyer, S., 'North Korea warns United States of an unwelcome "Christmas gift"', *Washington Post*, 3 Dec. 2019.

[40] Korean Central News Agency (KCNA), 'Fifth plenary meeting of seventh Central Committee of Workers' Party of Korea held', 1 Jan. 2019.

administration issues. It also set out a 'new path' for 2020, which included a de facto return to the country's *byungjin* policy line, which prioritizes the simultaneous development of nuclear weapon capabilities and the domestic economy.[41]

In a report of the meeting carried by state news media, Kim emphasized the urgent need to take 'offensive measures to reliably ensure the sovereignty and security of our state' and to 'shift to a shocking actual action' in response to the USA's continued hostile policy towards it.[42] The measures included placing the country's nuclear deterrent on 'constant alert' and continuing to develop its nuclear arsenal. Kim said that North Korea would reveal a new strategic weapon 'in the near future'.

Kim also called into question his commitment to North Korea's self-declared moratorium on tests of nuclear weapons and long-range missiles. He warned that, having halted the tests while receiving only perceived provocations from the USA, 'there is no ground for us to get unilaterally bound to the commitment any longer'.[43] However, Kim appeared to moderate his message by not formally declaring the end of the moratorium. He said instead that a decision to do so depended on the USA's 'future attitude' towards North Korea.[44]

In addition, Kim left open the possibility for further negotiations with the US administration over peacebuilding and denuclearization issues. He emphasized that this could happen only if the USA 'rolls back its hostile policy towards [North Korea]' and a 'lasting and durable peace-keeping mechanism' is built on the peninsula.[45] At the same time, he indicated that he was prepared for a protracted stalemate with the USA, as the latter showed no willingness to abandon its 'provocative political, military and economic maneuvers to completely strangle and stifle [North Korea]' despite its professed interest in a diplomatic dialogue.[46]

The initial reactions to Kim's speech from President Trump and other senior US officials were restrained. According to the US national security advisor, Robert C. O'Brien, the administration had 'reached out to the North

---

[41] The *byungjin* policy line adopted in Apr. 2013 had been replaced by a 'new strategic line' focused solely on economic development at the Apr. 2018 plenary meeting of the Central Committee. Korean Central News Agency (KCNA), 'Third plenary meeting of seventh C.C., WPK held in presence of Kim Jong Un', 21 Apr. 2018.

[42] Korean Central News Agency (KCNA), 'Report on 5th plenary meeting of 7th C.C., WPK', 1 Jan. 2020.

[43] Korean Central News Agency (KCNA) (note 42).

[44] Korean Central News Agency (KCNA) (note 42).

[45] Korean Central News Agency (KCNA) (note 42).

[46] Korean Central News Agency (KCNA) (note 42); and Scott, B. and Lee, J., 'Kim Jong Un gives up on Trump, prepares to endure US sanctions', Bloomberg, 2 Jan. 2020.

Koreans' to request the resumption of diplomatic negotiations to reach a denuclearization agreement.[47]

Conclusions

In 2019, North Korean–United States negotiations made no progress towards implementing the commitments to denuclearization and peacebuilding agreed by President Trump and Kim Jong Un the previous year. There was, however, a shift in the negotiations as the two sides began to move the talks from the head-of-state level to a working-group process. The latter involved small-format meetings intended to allow the negotiating teams to discuss specific measures that could then be adopted by the two leaders during a summit meeting. However, the negotiations remained stalled by the unwillingness of either side to adjust their positions on the scope and sequencing of steps for denuclearization, in particular, on the lifting of international sanctions against North Korea as part of the process.

Rather than a single grand bargain on denuclearization, a series of small agreements might allow the declared goal to be reached incrementally. However, as the year ended, there were few indications that North Korea and the USA were prepared to move away from their respective demands in order to allow such agreements.

[47] Swan, J., Talev, M. and Treene, A., 'Exclusive: Trump tells Kim Jong-un he wants to resume talks', Axios, 12 Jan. 2020.

III. Implementation of the Joint Comprehensive Plan of Action

TYTTI ERÄSTÖ

The Joint Comprehensive Plan of Action (JCPOA) is a landmark agreement concluded on 14 July 2015 by Iran and the E3/EU+3—France, Germany and the United Kingdom (E3); China, Russia and the United States (+3); and facilitated by the European Union (EU). The JCPOA appeared to resolve the international crisis over Iran's nuclear programme, which had started in 2002 and escalated over a dispute regarding Iran's right to uranium enrichment. The agreement was based on a compromise whereby Iran accepted limits on and strict monitoring of its proliferation-sensitive activities in return for the lifting of international sanctions.[1]

Despite Iran's verified compliance with what was widely considered to be 'the most robust verification system in existence anywhere in the world', the US Government withdrew from the JCPOA in May 2018.[2] The USA later reimposed all the nuclear-related sanctions on Iran that had been waived under the agreement, as well as additional sanctions on the country. While critical of this policy, other JCPOA parties were unable to prevent US sanctions from crippling the Iranian economy: the sanctions, notably the oil and banking sanctions, contributed to various socio-economic problems, such as high inflation and unemployment, and even jeopardized food security and access to medicines in the country.[3] The dire economic situation led to growing domestic discontent with both the JCPOA and more broadly with Iranian President Hassan Rouhani's administration.[4]

This section details Iran's compliance with the JCPOA, as well as the Iranian decision in May 2019 to gradually reduce its commitments under the agreement in response to US sanctions. It also describes new sanctions imposed by the USA, and the responses by other JCPOA parties to both US and Iranian actions. Furthermore, although not directly related to the JCPOA, the section touches on other issues that contributed to the escalation of Iranian–US tensions, notably the controversy over Iran's missile programme.

---

[1] Joint Comprehensive Plan of Action (JCPOA), 14 July 2015, Vienna, reproduced as Annex A of UN Security Council Resolution 2231, 20 July 2015. For background information see Erästö, T., 'Implementation of the Joint Comprehensive Plan of Action', *SIPRI Yearbook 2019*, pp. 378–86.

[2] Amano, Y., Speech on Iran, the JCPOA and the IAEA at the Belfer Center for Science and International Affairs, Harvard Kennedy School, 14 Nov. 2017.

[3] United Nations, General Assembly, 'Situation of human rights in the Islamic Republic of Iran', Report of the Special Rapporteur on the situation of human rights in the Islamic Republic of Iran, A/74/188, 18 July 2019, <https://undocs.org/en/A/74/188>.

[4] Erästö (note 1).

Iran's compliance with its JCPOA commitments

The JCPOA aims to prevent the production of weapon-grade fissile materials by limiting Iran's uranium enrichment activities, cutting its enriched uranium stockpiles and minimizing the amount of plutonium produced by the Arak heavy water reactor. Sensitive materials—excess stockpiles of enriched uranium and heavy water, as well as spent nuclear fuel—are to be shipped abroad under the agreement. Iran also accepted additional inspections under the Model Additional Protocol to its Comprehensive Safeguards Agreement with the International Atomic Energy Agency (IAEA), applying it provisionally pending parliamentary ratification, which it agreed to seek by 2023.

On 8 May 2019 Iran's leadership announced that the country would gradually reduce its commitments under the JCPOA every 60 days, unless the remaining parties managed to compensate for the US sanctions.[5] In this context, it referred to JCPOA articles 26 and 36, which state that Iran can 'cease performing its commitments . . . in whole or in part' in response to a reimposition of nuclear-related sanctions, and that 'significant non-performance' by others may provide grounds for another to 'cease performing its commitments' under the agreement.[6] It also mentioned the withdrawal from the 1968 Treaty on the Non-Proliferation of Nuclear Weapons (NPT) as a remaining option in responding to US sanctions.[7]

Following its May announcement, Iran ceased to observe the agreed limits on enriched uranium and heavy water stocks.[8] It renounced limits on enrichment levels in July, and on centrifuge research and development (R&D) in September.[9] In November, Iran stopped observing the ban on enrichment activities at the underground nuclear facility in Fordow. Iran argues that all of these measures are reversible, meaning that it is ready to return to full compliance with the JCPOA when the other parties do the same.[10] As well as its standard quarterly reports on Iran's compliance with the JCPOA, the IAEA documented these Iranian steps in several additional reports, discussed in more detail below.

---

[5] Supreme National Security Council, Statement addressing nuclear deal parties, official website of the President of the Islamic Republic of Iran, 8 May 2019.

[6] JCPOA (note 1), articles 26 and 36.

[7] Reuters, 'Iran says leaving nuclear treaty one of many options after US sanctions move', 28 Apr. 2019.

[8] Supreme National Security Council (note 5).

[9] Wintour, P., 'Iran nuclear deal in jeopardy after latest enrichment breach', *The Guardian*, 7 July 2019; and Hafezi, P. and Arshad, M., 'Iran to develop centrifuges for faster uranium enrichment', Reuters, 4 Sep. 2019.

[10] Fars News, 'Iran undertakes 4th step in scaling down n. commitments', 5 Nov. 2019.

Activities related to heavy water and reprocessing

As part of the JCPOA, Iran agreed to redesign the Arak heavy water reactor to minimize the amount of plutonium in the spent nuclear fuel it produced. Despite Iran's announcement in May 2019 that it would no longer abide by the JCPOA limit on heavy water reserves, all IAEA reports until November 2019 confirmed Iran's continued compliance with related obligations. Iran had not pursued the construction of the Arak reactor based on its original design; the natural uranium pellets, fuel pins and assemblies related to that design remained in storage, and the heavy water stock remained under the agreed limit of 130 metric tonnes.[11] However, on 18 November the IAEA reported that Iran had slightly exceeded the heavy water stock limit, maintaining a reserve of 131.5 metric tonnes.[12]

Activities related to enrichment and fuel

Under the JCPOA, Iran agreed not to enrich uranium above 3.67 per cent, to maintain its enriched uranium stockpiles below 300 kilograms and to conduct all enrichment activities at the Fuel Enrichment Plant (FEP) in Natanz. These limits were to apply until 2030. Iran also agreed to keep the number of its operating centrifuges at the FEP below 5060, while all non-operational centrifuges would remain in storage—a restriction that was to be in place until 2025. The Fordow Fuel Enrichment Plant (FFEP) was to be converted into a nuclear, physics and technology centre.

In its February and May reports, the IAEA confirmed that Iran continued to meet all of the above commitments, including allowing the IAEA regular access to all relevant facilities in Natanz and Fordow.[13] In July 2019, however, the IAEA verified that Iran had exceeded the agreed level of enrichment at the FEP, enriching to about 4.5 per cent, and that its total enriched uranium stockpile was beyond the 300-kg limit.[14] In November 2019 the IAEA reported that Iran had resumed enrichment activities at the FFEP, after having transferred nuclear material from Natanz to Fordow.[15]

---

[11] After the commissioning of the new reactor, the heavy water stock limit would be reduced to 90 metric tonnes. See JCPOA (note 1), annex I.

[12] IAEA, 'Verification and monitoring in the Islamic Republic of Iran in light of United Nations Security Council Resolution 2231 (2015)', Report by the Acting Director General, GOV/INF/2019/17, 18 Nov. 2019.

[13] IAEA, 'Verification and monitoring in the Islamic Republic of Iran in light of United Nations Security Council Resolution 2231 (2015)', Reports by the Director General, GOV/2019/10, 22 Feb. 2019 and GOV/2019/21, 31 May 2019.

[14] Noting that the 300-kg limit on uranium hexafluoride (UF6) corresponds to 202.8 kg of uranium, the IAEA report on 1 July stated that the Iranian stockpile was at 205 kg; IAEA, Report by the Director General, GOV/INF/2019/8, 1 July 2019. In Aug. and Nov. 2019 the stockpile was 241.6 kg and 372.3 kg, respectively; see IAEA, Reports by the Acting Director General, GOV/2019/32, 30 Aug. 2019 and GOV/2019/55, 11 Nov. 2019.

[15] IAEA, GOV/2019/55 (note 14).

Centrifuge research and development, manufacturing and inventory

Under the JCPOA, Iran's operational uranium enrichment centrifuges should only include the so-called first generation type (IR-1). However, the agreement allows limited enrichment R&D activities on more advanced centrifuges (IR-4, IR-5, IR-6 and IR-8), as long as enriched uranium is not accumulated. The permitted R&D also allows mechanical testing (typically not involving uranium) on up to two single centrifuges of other types.[16] The limits on centrifuge R&D were intended to be in place until 2025.[17]

Following Iran's decision to stop observing the limits on centrifuge R&D, the IAEA's report on 8 September 2019 verified that Iran had installed, or was in the process of installing, advanced centrifuges of the type IR-4, IR-5, IR-6 and IR-6s at the Pilot Fuel Enrichment Plant (PFEP) in Natanz.[18] On 26 September the IAEA noted that some of the centrifuge cascades at the PFEP were 'accumulating, or had been prepared to accumulate, enriched uranium'.[19] Iran had also begun to manufacture centrifuge rotor tubes using carbon fibre that was not subject to continuous containment and surveillance measures by the IAEA.[20]

In November the IAEA verified that several centrifuges—including types not mentioned in the JCPOA—were 'installed and being tested with UF6' at the PFEP. According to information provided to the IAEA by Iran, the centrifuges would be 'used to accumulate enriched uranium'.[21] The new centrifuge types are more effective than the old IR-1 model, which Iran had previously planned to replace only after the expiry of JCPOA limits.[22]

Transparency, the Additional Protocol and other issues

In 2019 the IAEA confirmed that Iran was continuing to apply the Additional Protocol and facilitating the IAEA's inspection and monitoring. As in previous years, the 2019 reports noted that the IAEA had, under the Additional Protocol, gained complementary access to all the Iranian sites and locations it needed to visit, and that it continued to evaluate Iran's declarations under

---

[16] In addition to IR-4, IR-5, IR-6 and IR-8, mechanical testing could be done on the IR-2m, IR-6s and IR-7 centrifuges. See JCPOA (note 1), annex I.

[17] See JCPOA (note 1), annex I.

[18] IAEA, Report by the Acting Director General, GOV/INF/2019/10, 8 Sep. 2019.

[19] IAEA, Report by the Acting Director General, GOV/INF/2019/12, 26 Sep. 2019.

[20] IAEA, GOV/INF/2019/12 (note 19).

[21] The centrifuge types included IR-2m, IR-3, IR-4, IR-5, IR-6 and IR-6s, IR-6m, IR-6sm, IR-7, IR-8, IR-8s, IR-8B, IR-9 and IR-s centrifuges. See IAEA, GOV/2019/55 (note 14).

[22] Atomic Energy Organization of Iran, 'AEOI deputy elaborates on the JCPOA commitment reduction, third step details', 21 Nov. 2019; and Hafezi, P., 'Iran launches more advanced machines to speed up nuclear enrichment: Official', Reuters, 4 Nov. 2019.

the protocol. The August report, however contained language that implied cooperation could be better.[23]

In November, the quarterly report by the IAEA's acting director general referred to a confidential report earlier that month, which stated that the IAEA had 'detected natural uranium particles of anthropogenic origin at a location in Iran not declared to the Agency'. The quarterly report added that 'It is essential for Iran to continue interactions with the Agency to resolve the matter as soon as possible'.[24] This apparently referred to a reported IAEA visit to what Israel claimed was a 'secret atomic warehouse' in Tehran, containing archives and equipment related to the pre-2003 Iranian nuclear weapon programme.[25] According to press reports, IAEA inspectors had taken environmental samples at the site earlier in 2019.[26] On 7 November, one of the inspectors was reportedly denied access to the Natanz facility and briefly detained.[27]

US sanctions on Iran

After the US withdrawal from the JCPOA, the administration of US President Donald J. Trump adopted a policy of 'maximum pressure' on Iran, which focused on depriving the country of its oil revenues and ending all uranium enrichment there.[28] On 2 May 2019 the policy was taken even further, as the US Government revoked the remaining sanctions waivers to eight countries that were importing Iranian oil.[29] Other unprecedented additional measures included the designation of the Islamic Revolutionary Guard Corps (IRGC) as a terrorist organization in April and imposing sanctions on Iran's supreme leader, Ayatollah Ali Khamenei, and foreign minister, Javad Zarif, in June.[30]

In May, the USA also revoked the waivers that had allowed Iran to ship excess stocks of heavy water and enriched uranium abroad to meet its

---

[23] The report stated that 'Ongoing interactions between the Agency and Iran relating to Iran's implementation of its Safeguards Agreement and Additional Protocol require full and timely cooperation by Iran. The Agency continues to pursue this objective with Iran'. IAEA, GOV/2019/32 (note 14).

[24] IAEA, GOV/2019/55 (note 14).

[25] Netanyahu, B., Statement at the United Nations General Assembly, 27 Sep. 2018; Arnold, A. et al., 'The Iran nuclear archive: Impressions and implications', Report, Belfer Center for Science and International Affairs, Harvard Kennedy School, Apr. 2019; and BBC, 'Iran nuclear deal: IAEA finds uranium particles at undeclared site', 11 Nov. 2019.

[26] BBC (note 25).

[27] BBC, 'Iran cancels accreditation of IAEA nuclear inspector', 7 Nov. 2019.

[28] Erästö (note 1); and White House, Statement from the Press Secretary, 1 July 2019. On US–Iran tensions during 2019, also see chapter 6, section I, in this volume.

[29] Katzman, K., 'Iran sanctions', Congressional Research Service report, updated 15 Nov. 2019; and Wong, E., 'US punishes Chinese company over Iranian oil', New York Times, 22 July 2019.

[30] White House, Statement from the President on the designation of the Islamic Revolutionary Guard Corps as a foreign terrorist organization, 8 Apr. 2009; and New York Times, 'Trump imposes new sanctions on Iran, adding to tensions', 24 June 2019.

JCPOA commitments.[31] The United Nations secretary-general described that decision, as well as sanctions on Iranian oil exports, as contrary to UN Security Council Resolution 2231.[32] The issue was raised at the June meeting of the Joint Commission of the JCPOA, which 'tasked experts to look into practical solutions in particular for the export of low enriched uranium (LEU) and heavy water under appropriate arrangements'.[33] In November, responding to Iran's announcement that it would resume enrichment at the FFEP, the USA decided not to extend the waiver on the conversion of the Fordow facility in December.[34] The waiver allowing the conversion of the Arak reactor nevertheless remained in place.[35]

The role of other JCPOA parties

Other parties continued to stress their commitment to the JCPOA in 2019, but had little leverage in countering or compensating for the economic damage caused by the reimposed US sanctions on Iran.[36] Expectations of Europe's ability to safeguard the JCPOA therefore fell further during the year. The E3 established the Instrument in Support of Trade Exchanges (INSTEX) in January, but its scope was reduced to non-dollar transactions and trade in non-sanctioned goods, such as food and medicine—in contrast to previous plans for facilitating oil exports from Iran. In addition, INSTEX did not become operational in 2019, in spite of the E3's announcement to the contrary on 28 June.[37]

In response to Iran's reduction of its JCPOA commitments, the E3 and the High Representative of the EU for Foreign Affairs and Security Policy urged Iran to 'refrain from any escalatory steps' in May, and stressed that their 'commitment to the nuclear deal depends on full compliance by Iran' in July.[38] In September, the E3 stated that 'the time has come for Iran to accept

---

[31] Katzman (note 29); and Davenport, K., 'Timeline of nuclear diplomacy with Iran', Arms Control Association, updated Nov. 2019.

[32] United Nations, Security Council, 'Implementation of Security Council Resolution 2231 (2015)', Report of the Secretary-General, S/2019/492, 13 June 2019.

[33] European External Action Service, Chair's statement following the 28 June 2019 meeting of the Joint Commission of the Joint Comprehensive Plan of Action, 28 June 2019.

[34] Pompeo, M. R., Remarks to the press, 18 Nov. 2019.

[35] It seems that the waivers allowing the removal of spent fuel from the Bushehr nuclear reactor and the delivery of 20% enriched uranium fuel for the Tehran nuclear reactor also remained in place, although this was not explicitly stated by the administration. Psaledakis, D., 'US to no longer waive sanctions on Iranian nuclear site', Reuters, 18 Nov. 2019; and Davenport (note 31).

[36] See Erästö (note 1).

[37] European External Action Service (note 33); and Irish, J. and Pennetier, M., 'No trade mechanism until Iran passes terrorism financing laws: French diplomat', Reuters, 4 Sep. 2019.

[38] European External Action Service, Joint statement by High Representative of the European Union and the foreign ministers of France, Germany and the United Kingdom on the JCPOA, 9 May 2019; and European External Action Service, The foreign ministers of France, Germany, the UK and the High Representative of the European Union on Iran/JCPOA, 2 July 2019.

negotiation on a long-term framework for its nuclear programme as well as on issues related to regional security, including its missile programme and other means of delivery'.[39] While the E3 had previously aligned its views with the USA on Iran's missiles and its regional role, this statement diverged from the previous European position, which opposed US calls for renegotiating the JCPOA as a broader agreement. In November, following Iran's decision to transgress the R&D limits, the E3 and the High Representative threatened to trigger the JCPOA dispute resolution mechanism.[40] The mechanism could lead to the reimposition of previous UN Security Council sanctions on Iran.[41]

France sought to mediate between the Trump administration and Iran in the context of a heightened threat of Iranian–US military confrontation following attacks on oil tankers in the Persian Gulf in May and the downing by Iran of a US surveillance drone in June.[42] France suggested a credit line in exchange for Iran's full compliance with the JCPOA and negotiations on longer-term nuclear arrangements and regional issues. The aim was to compensate Iran for its lost oil revenues, thus making room for diplomacy in the absence of sanctions lifting. However, this would have reportedly required a US waiver, which the Trump administration was unwilling to grant.[43]

Both Russia and China clearly placed the responsibility for the erosion of the JCPOA on US policy, which the former called a 'thoughtless political campaign against the nuclear deal' and the latter 'the root cause of the current crisis'.[44] Russia condemned, in particular, the US Government's return to a zero-enrichment policy and its decision to sanction the Fordow conversion project. Determined to continue the project, Russia called for the Joint Commission of the JCPOA to 'issue a meaningful response' and for Europe to 'defend the JCPOA in cooperation with Russia and China'.[45] China called for the USA to end its 'wrong behavior to make room for diplomatic efforts and create conditions for de-escalation' and for other parties to exercise

[39] British Prime Minister's Office, Joint statement by the heads of state and government of France, Germany and the United Kingdom, 23 Sep. 2019 (updated 24 Sep. 2019).

[40] European External Action Service, Joint statement by the foreign ministers of France, Germany and the United Kingdom and the EU High Representative on the JCPOA, 11 Nov. 2019.

[41] JCPOA (note 1).

[42] Both US and Israeli intelligence attributed the sabotage of the oil tankers to Iran, but Iran denied involvement. Halbfinger, D. M., 'Mossad chief bluntly blames Iran for tanker attacks', New York Times, 1 July 2019; Shear, M. D. et al., 'Strikes on Iran approved by Trump, then abruptly pulled back', New York Times, 20 June 2019; and see chapter 6, section I, in this volume.

[43] Kimball, D. G. and Masterson, J., 'French proposal on hold as tensions mount,' P4+1 and Iran Nuclear Deal Alert, Arms Control Association, 24 Sep. 2019.

[44] Russian Ministry of Foreign Affairs, Comment by the Information and Press Department on yet another series of US verbal attacks on the Joint Comprehensive Plan of Action (JCPOA) for Iran's nuclear programme, 19 Nov. 2019; and Chinese Ministry of Foreign Affairs, Foreign Ministry Spokesperson Geng Shuang's regular press conference, 12 Nov. 2019.

[45] Russian Ministry of Foreign Affairs (note 44).

restraint.[46] China strongly rejected the US sanctions against Iran's oil exports after a Chinese company was targeted by them in July.[47]

Controversy over Iran's missiles and United Nations Resolution 2231

While the JCPOA does not cover missiles, the Annex of UN Security Council Resolution 2231—which endorsed the agreement in July 2015—calls on Iran 'not to undertake any activity related to ballistic missiles designed to be capable of delivering nuclear weapons' until 2023.[48] The same annex also imposes an arms embargo on Iran until October 2020, constituting, together with Resolution 2216, the legal basis against Iran's short-range missile transfers in the region.[49]

The Iranian position is that its missiles are conventional and not designed to carry nuclear weapons. The USA, in contrast, regards Iran's continuing missile tests and satellite launches as a breach of Resolution 2231—an argument that was part of the US Government's withdrawal from the JCPOA in 2018. The E3, for its part, maintains that Iran's missile activities are 'inconsistent' with Resolution 2231, without however defining them as a violation of that resolution.[50]

The continuing controversy over Iran's missiles in 2019 was captured by the UN secretary-general's December report on the implementation of Resolution 2231. The report referred to US and E3 claims that Iran's Shahab-3 ballistic missile is 'designed to be capable of delivering nuclear weapons', based on the Missile Technology Control Regime (MTRC) definition. As noted, Iran and Russia denied the relevance of that definition for interpreting Resolution 2231, which makes no reference to the MTCR.[51]

The report also recounted allegations of Iranian transfers of missiles to its allies in the Middle East, including its alleged role in the drone and cruise missile attacks against Saudi Arabian oil facilities on 14 September. The UN secretary-general was 'unable to independently corroborate' claims that the components recovered from the site in Saudi Arabia 'are of Iranian origin and were transferred from the Islamic Republic of Iran in a manner inconsistent

---

[46] Chinese Ministry of Foreign Affairs (note 44).

[47] Williams, A., Sheppard, D. and Liu, X., 'China condemns US sanctions over Iran crude oil', *Financial Times*, 23 July 2019.

[48] UN Security Council Resolution 2231, 20 July 2015.

[49] UN Security Council Resolution 2231 (note 48); and UN Security Council Resolution 2216, 14 Apr. 2015.

[50] See BBC, 'Iran developing nuclear-capable missiles, European powers warn UN,' 5 Dec. 2019; and Erästö, T., 'Dissecting international concerns about Iran's missiles', SIPRI Backgrounder, 15 Nov. 2018.

[51] According to the Missile Technology Control Regime (MTCR), all missiles that exceed a 300-km range and are able to carry a 500-kg payload are nuclear-capable. See Davenport, K., 'The Missile Technology Control Regime at a glance', Arms Control Association, update July 2017; and United Nations, Security Council, 'Implementation of Security Council Resolution 2231 (2015)', Report of the Secretary-General, S/2019/934, 10 Dec. 2019.

with Resolution 2231'.[52] Although not directly connected to the JCPOA, the issue of Iranian missile transfers did play a part in the escalation of Iranian–US tensions and, together with the incidents against oil tankers, it arguably contributed to the hardening of the E3's position on Iran.

The outlook for 2020

The already dim prospects for maintaining the JCPOA began to look increasingly difficult in 2019. The Trump administration's policy of maximum pressure on Iran left Europe little room for manoeuvre in order to compensate for the economic harm done by US sanctions. At the same time, the EU/E3 position on Iran hardened following Iranian steps to reduce its JCPOA commitments, as well as Iran's regional responses to US policy. In this context, Iran might see little benefit in remaining in the JCPOA. Assuming that the agreement does not collapse before the end of 2020, the single most important factor determining the JCPOA's future might be the US presidential elections, as several Democratic candidates have stated their intention to rejoin the agreement.[53]

[52] United Nations (note 51).

[53] Toosi, N., 'Democrats want to rejoin the Iran nuclear deal: It's not that simple', Politico, 20 July 2019.

IV. Multilateral nuclear arms control, disarmament and non-proliferation treaties and initiatives

TYTTI ERÄSTÖ AND SHANNON N. KILE

This section reviews the developments and negotiations that took place in 2019 in four multilateral nuclear arms control, disarmament and non-proliferation treaties and initiatives: the 1996 Comprehensive Test Ban Treaty (CTBT); preparations for the 2020 Review Conference for the 1968 Treaty on the Non-Proliferation of Nuclear Weapons (Non-Proliferation Treaty, NPT); the 2019 conference on the establishment of a zone free of weapons of mass destruction (WMD) in the Middle East; and developments in the 2017 Treaty on the Prohibition of Nuclear Weapons (TPNW). Developments in the Joint Comprehensive Plan of Action (JCPOA) are covered in section III.

Developments related to the Comprehensive Nuclear-Test-Ban Treaty

The Comprehensive Nuclear-Test-Ban Treaty would prohibit its states parties from conducting 'any nuclear weapon test explosion or any other nuclear explosion' anywhere in the world.[1] As of 31 December 2019 the CTBT had been ratified by 168 states and signed by an additional 16 states.[2] However, the treaty cannot enter into force until all 44 of the states listed in its Annex 2 have ratified it, and 8 of these states—China, Egypt, India, Iran, Israel, the Democratic People's Republic of Korea (DPRK, or North Korea), Pakistan and the United States—had yet to do so.[3]

The Preparatory Commission for the Comprehensive Nuclear-Test-Ban Treaty Organization (CTBTO) was established in 1996 to prepare for the entry into force of the treaty. In particular, this involves building the International Monitoring System (IMS), consisting of 321 seismic, hydroacoustic, infrasound and radionuclide monitoring stations and 16 laboratories to detect evidence of nuclear explosions, and the International Data Centre (IDC) to process and analyse the data registered by the monitoring stations and transmit it to member states.

Conference on entry into force

Until the CTBT enters into force, the states that have ratified it may periodically call a conference on facilitating the entry into force (a so-called Article XIV conference).[4] The 11th such conference was held at the United

---

[1] CTBT, Article 1(1). For a summary of the CTBT see annex A, section I, in this volume.
[2] In Feb. 2019 Zimbabwe became the 168th state to ratify the treaty.
[3] The 44 states listed in annex 2 all had nuclear power or research reactors on their territories when the treaty was opened for signature in Sep. 1996.
[4] CTBT (note 1), Article XIV(2).

Nations headquarters in New York on 25 September 2019, attended by representatives from 81 states signatories, with Pakistan participating as an observer.[5] During the conference, many states emphasized the importance of bringing the CTBT into force on an expedited basis.[6] The proceedings largely followed the pattern of previous Article XIV conferences. What distinguished the 2019 conference was the absence of the USA, which declined to participate for the first time.

The final declaration of the conference reaffirms 'that a universal and effectively verifiable Treaty constitutes a fundamental instrument in the field of nuclear disarmament and non-proliferation'.[7] It outlines a number of steps and measures to promote the early entry into force and universalization of the treaty. These focus on education, training and public outreach initiatives. They also involve support for the continuing work of the CTBTO in building the IMS and developing enhanced on-site inspection capabilities to verify whether a nuclear explosion has taken place.[8]

US allegations of Russian nuclear tests

The US decision not to attend the Article XIV conference came against a background of allegations that Russia was conducting nuclear tests and domestic partisan calls for US President Donald J. Trump to 'unsign' the CTBT.[9] The allegations had gained public attention following a statement made by the director of the US Defense Intelligence Agency (DIA), Robert P. Ashley, on 29 May. Ashley stated that the USA believed that Russia 'probably is not adhering to the nuclear testing moratorium in a manner consistent with the zero-yield standard' codified in the CTBT.[10] Two weeks later, the DIA released a statement clarifying that the US Government had 'assessed that Russia has conducted nuclear weapons tests that have created nuclear yield'.[11] This would violate its obligations as a state signatory to the CTBT.

However, US officials provided no evidence that Russia had conducted nuclear explosive tests that violated the treaty's zero-yield limit. This led some sceptical experts in Washington to suggest that the Trump administration was seeking to free the USA of any constraints on its own nuclear weapon development effort, and, indirectly, to try to undermine the CTBT itself.[12]

---

[5] Conference on Facilitating the Entry into Force of the CTBT, Report of the Conference, CTBT-Art. XIV/2019/6, 9 Oct. 2019, paras 3–4.

[6] Bugos, S., 'Frustrations surface at CTBT conference', *Arms Control Today*, vol. 49, no. 9 (Nov. 2019).

[7] Conference on Facilitating the Entry into Force of the CTBT (note 5), Final declaration, para. 1.

[8] Conference on Facilitating the Entry into Force of the CTBT (note 5), Final declaration, paras 8, 10.

[9] Andreasen, S., 'Trump is quietly leading us closer to nuclear disaster', *Washington Post*, 26 June 2019.

[10] Ashley, R. P. (Lt Gen.), 'The arms control landscape', Keynote remarks, Hudson Institute, 29 May 2019, 7:30–7:40.

[11] US Defense Intelligence Agency (DIA), DIA statement on Lt. Gen. Ashley's remarks at Hudson Institute, 13 June 2019.

[12] Kimball, D. G., 'US claims of illegal Russian nuclear testing: Myths, realities, and next steps', Policy white paper, Arms Control Association, 21 Aug. 2019, p. 5.

The Russian Government promptly dismissed the claim as groundless.[13] The deputy foreign minister, Sergey Ryabkov, had earlier stated that Russia, unlike the USA, had ratified the CTBT and that it was acting in 'full and absolute accordance' with the treaty and Russia's unilateral moratorium on nuclear tests.[14]

Status of monitoring stations in Russia

The CTBTO's IMS became the focus of international scrutiny after an accident on 8 August 2019 at the Nenoksa missile test site on the White Sea coast of Russia set off an explosion and release of radioactivity. Amid conflicting media accounts, a US intelligence assessment reportedly concluded that the accident occurred during Russia's attempted recovery of the on-board nuclear reactor from a Burevestnik missile that had crashed in the sea after a failed test.[15]

The 80 planned or operational radionuclide stations in the IMS monitor for airborne radioactive particles that are by-products of nuclear explosions. Seven of these operational stations are in Russia. The CTBTO reported that two days after the accident the two radionuclide stations in Russia closest to the explosion had suddenly halted transmissions of data.[16] Russian officials told the CTBTO that the stations were experiencing 'communication and network issues'.[17] By 13 August a further two radionuclide stations in Russia had ceased transmissions to the IDC, and a fifth subsequently went offline. This led to speculation that Russia had deliberately shut them down to avoid transmissions of data about the radioactive isotopes detected following the accident. Such data could help other CTBT signatories to understand the nature of the weapon under development.[18] According to the CTBTO, the two stations furthest from Nenoksa resumed operations on 20 August and were backfilling data to the IDC.[19]

In response to the reports from the CTBTO, Ryabkov, the Russian deputy foreign minister, stated that the accident involving the nuclear reactor at Nenoksa 'should have no connection' to CTBTO activities since the

---

[13] Russian Ministry of Foreign Affairs, 'Comment by the Information and Press Department regarding unacceptable US allegations of Russia exceeding the "zero-yield" standard', 17 June 2019.

[14] Kimball (note 12).

[15] Macias, A., 'US intel report says mysterious Russian explosion was triggered by recovery mission of nuclear-powered missile, not a test', CNBC, 29 Aug. 2019; and United Nations, General Assembly, First Committee, Remarks by Thomas Dinanno, US Deputy Assistant Secretary of Defense, 10 Oct. 2019. See also chapter 10, section II, in this volume.

[16] Murphy, F., 'Global network's nuclear sensors in Russia went offline after mystery blast stations', Reuters, 19 Aug. 2019.

[17] Murphy (note 16); and Lassina Zerbo (@SinaZerbo), CTBTO executive secretary, Twitter, 18 Aug. 2019.

[18] Webb, G., 'Russian weapons accident raises nuclear concerns', Arms Control Today, vol. 49, no. 7 (Sep. 2019).

[19] Murphy, F., 'Some Russian radiation sensors back online–global network operator', Reuters, 20 Aug. 2019.

organization's mandate does not extend to weapon development.[20] He also complained about the CTBTO's sharing of information with the public, adding that the transmission of data from national stations which are part of the IMS 'is entirely voluntary for any country'.[21] Indeed, according to the CTBT, 'Each State Party shall have the right to take measures to protect sensitive installations and to prevent disclosure of confidential information and data not related to this Treaty'.[22]

Preparations for the 2020 Non-Proliferation Treaty Review Conference

Every five years, the states parties to the Non-Proliferation Treaty meet in a conference to review the operation of the treaty.[23] These review conferences are preceded by meetings of a preparatory committee, which considers procedural and substantive issues and makes recommendations for the upcoming review conference. The preparatory committee for the 2020 Review Conference held its third and final session in New York from 29 April to 10 May. The session was chaired by Ambassador Mohamad Hasrin Aidid of Malaysia.

As in earlier sessions, the discussions were overshadowed by the lack of progress on nuclear disarmament by the nuclear weapon states.[24] Several non-nuclear weapon states expressed concern over the uneven implementation of the NPT's three pillars—nuclear non-proliferation, nuclear disarmament and the peaceful use of nuclear energy. For example, the Non-Aligned Movement (NAM) argued that 'pursuing non-proliferation alone while ignoring nuclear disarmament obligations is both counterproductive and unsustainable'.[25] States parties also expressed concern over backward steps, such as the erosion of the Russian–US arms control architecture and the modernization of nuclear arsenals.[26]

The five nuclear weapon states defined by the NPT—China, France, Russia, the United Kingdom and the USA (collectively known as the P5)—viewed further progress in disarmament as being impeded by current circumstances,

[20] Osborn, A. and Kiseleyova, M., 'Russia to nuclear test ban monitor: Test accident not your business', Reuters, 20 Aug. 2019; and Webb (note 18).

[21] Osborn and Kiseleyova (note 20); and Interfax, [The Russian MFA called data transfer from radiation monitoring stations voluntary], 20 Aug. 2019 (in Russian).

[22] CTBT (note 1), Article IV(7).

[23] For a summary and other details of the NPT see annex A, section I, in this volume.

[24] The NPT defines a nuclear weapon state to be a state that manufactured and exploded a nuclear explosive device prior to 1 Jan. 1967. There are only 5 such states. All other states are defined as non-nuclear weapon states. NPT (note 23), Article IX(3).

[25] Preparatory Committee for the 2020 NPT Review Conference, Third Session, Statement by Venezuela on behalf of the Non-Aligned Movement, 29 Apr. 2019, para. 4. For a description and list of members of the NAM see annex B, section I, in this volume.

[26] See e.g. Preparatory Committee for the 2020 NPT Review Conference, Third Session, Statement by the European Union, 1 May 2019. On Russia–US arms control see section I of this chapter. On modernization of nuclear arsenals see chapter 10 in this volume.

although they held different views as to what constituted the main obstacles.[27] In an apparent effort to hedge against criticism about imposing preconditions to the fulfilment of its NPT obligations, the USA renamed its 'creating the conditions for nuclear disarmament' approach as 'creating an environment for nuclear disarmament' (CEND).[28] It also presented a plan to operationalize CEND by inviting selected countries to 'identify a list of issues or questions relating to the international security environment affecting disarmament prospects'.[29]

Some non-nuclear weapon states were sympathetic to the view that progress toward nuclear disarmament was conditional on addressing challenges in the international security environment.[30] Others rejected that logic. For example, the New Agenda Coalition—a group of six states that tries to build a consensus on steps towards nuclear disarmament—argued that NPT commitments 'are not to be reinterpreted, rolled back, or conditioned in any form'.[31] Sweden presented its own 'stepping stone' initiative, which sought to remove blockages to disarmament diplomacy while taking into account different perspectives and to build 'political support for pragmatic, short-term, achievable demonstrations of commitment to the global disarmament regime'.[32] Several countries expressed support for disarmament education and for promoting the gender perspective within the NPT process.[33]

As in 2018, fiery 'right of reply' exchanges took place between the USA and three other countries—Iran, Russia and Syria. Yet Russia and the USA presented a united front as part of the P5. This reflected the success of

---

[27] Erästö, T., '50 years of the NPT—cause for celebration or commemoration?', Commentary, SIPRI, 23 May 2019.

[28] Erästö, T. et al., 'Other developments related to multilateral treaties and initiatives on nuclear arms control, disarmament and non-proliferation', *SIPRI Yearbook 2019*, pp. 391–93; and Burford, L., Meier, O. and Ritchie, N., 'Sidetrack or kickstart? How to respond to the US proposal on nuclear disarmament', *Bulletin of the Atomic Scientists*, 19 Apr. 2019.

[29] Erästö, T. et al. (note 28); and Preparatory Committee for the 2020 NPT Review Conference, Third Session, 'Operationalizing the creating an environment for nuclear disarmament (CEND) initiative', Working paper submitted by the United States, NPT/CONF.2020/PC.III/WP.43, 26 Apr. 2019.

[30] E.g. Preparatory Committee for the 2020 NPT Review Conference, Third Session, Statement by Latvia, 29 Apr. 2019.

[31] Preparatory Committee for the 2020 NPT Review Conference, Third Session, Statement by Brazil on behalf of the New Agenda Coalition, 29 Apr. 2019. The 6 members of the New Agenda Coalition are Brazil, Egypt, Ireland, Mexico, New Zealand and South Africa.

[32] Preparatory Committee for the 2020 NPT Review Conference, Third Session, 'Unlocking disarmament diplomacy through a "stepping stone" approach', Working paper submitted by Sweden, NPT/CONF.2020/PC.III/WP.33, 25 Apr. 2019, p. 3.

[33] E.g. Preparatory Committee for the 2020 NPT Review Conference, Third Session, 'Disarmament and non-proliferation education', Working paper submitted by the members of the Non-Proliferation and Disarmament Initiative (Australia, Canada, Chile, Germany, Japan, Mexico, the Netherlands, Nigeria, Philippines, Poland, Turkey and the United Arab Emirates), NPT/CONF.2020/PC.III/WP.26, 18 Apr. 2019; and Preparatory Committee for the 2020 NPT Review Conference, Third Session, 'Integrating gender perspectives in the implementation of the Treaty on the Non-Proliferation of Nuclear Weapons', Working paper submitted by Australia, Canada, Ireland, Namibia, Sweden and the United Nations Institute for Disarmament Research, NPT/CONF.2020/PC.III/WP.27, 18 Apr. 2019.

China's efforts to build a consensus at a P5 conference that it hosted in Beijing in February 2019.[34] The P5 announced some modest steps—such as a plan to organize a side event on nuclear policies and doctrines at the 2020 Review Conference—in an apparent attempt to address the widespread criticism over the lack of disarmament.[35]

Several countries expressed their support for the 2015 Joint Comprehensive Plan of Action (JCPOA)—a landmark nuclear agreement between Iran and China, France, Germany, the UK, Russia and the USA. Reflecting concern over the future of the agreement following US withdrawal from it in 2018, they called for Iran's continued compliance.[36] However, the committee session coincided with Iran's announcement that it would reduce its JCPOA commitments in response to the USA's withdrawal from the agreement.[37]

Many delegations also expressed their support for the decision of the UN General Assembly to convene a UN conference on the establishment of a zone free of nuclear weapons and other WMD in the Middle East (see below). While welcoming that decision, the NAM explained that this new process would not replace previous commitments made in the context of the NPT, including the 1995 Resolution on the Middle East.[38] Given their divisions on several issues—including the TPNW and its compatibility with the NPT (see below)—the preparatory committee was unable to agree on joint recommendations for the 2020 Review Conference, and instead produced a more informal working paper.[39]

The preparatory committee initially chose Ambassador Rafael Grossi of Argentina as the chair of the 2020 Review Conference.[40] However, Grossi was subsequently elected as the new director general of the International Atomic Energy Agency (IAEA) in October. The post of review conference chair thus remained empty at the end of 2019, but Gustavo Zlauvinen, the deputy foreign minister of Argentina, was nominated in January 2020.[41]

---

[34] Conference on Disarmament, 'Chair's summary of the P5 Beijing conference 30 January 2019, Beijing', 7 Feb. 2019, CD/2156, 3 May 2019.

[35] Preparatory Committee for the 2020 NPT Review Conference, Third Session, Statement by China on behalf of the P5 states, 1 May 2019.

[36] Joint Comprehensive Plan of Action (JCPOA), 14 July 2015, Vienna, reproduced as annex A of UN Security Council Resolution 2231, 20 July 2015.

[37] For further background and recent developments in the JCPOA see section III in this chapter.

[38] Preparatory Committee for the 2020 NPT Review Conference, Statement by Venezuela (note 25); and 1995 NPT Review and Extension Conference, Resolution on the Middle East, NPT/CONF.1995/32 (Part I), 1995, annex.

[39] Preparatory Committee for the 2020 NPT Review Conference, Third Session, 'Recommendations by the chair to the 2020 Review Conference', Chair's working paper, NPT/CONF.2020/PC.III/WP.49, 10 May 2019.

[40] Preparatory Committee for the 2020 NPT Review Conference, Third Session, 'Election of the President and other officers', NPT/CONF.2020/PC.III/DEC.1, 8 May 2019.

[41] Webb, G. and Kimball, D. G., 'Argentine selected to lead IAEA', *Arms Control Today*, vol. 49, no. 9 (Nov. 2019); and 2020 NPT Review Conference, 'The Tenth Review Conference of the Parties to the Treaty on the Non-Proliferation of Nuclear Weapons', Press release, Jan 2020.

Persistent divisions among the NPT membership are likely to make it difficult for the parties to agree on a final consensus document at the 2020 Review Conference. Against the background of the previous such failure at the 2015 Review Conference, this raises concerns about the viability of the NPT as the cornerstone of the global nuclear disarmament and non-proliferation regime.

The conference on the establishment of a weapons of mass destruction-free zone in the Middle East

The Conference on the Establishment of a Middle East Zone Free of Nuclear Weapons and Other Weapons of Mass Destruction held its first session on 18–22 November 2019 at the UN in New York. The conference was convened by UN Secretary-General António Guterres and presided over by Ambassador Sima Bahous of Jordan.

The decision to hold the conference had been made by the UN General Assembly on 22 December 2018, based on a draft proposed in the First Committee by a group of Arab states.[42] However, calls in the UN General Assembly to free the Middle East of nuclear weapons date back to 1974. In 1990 Egypt had proposed broadening the agenda to cover all WMD, and the 1995 NPT Review Conference adopted the Resolution on the Middle East, whereby states parties agreed to promote the establishment of a WMD-free zone in the region.[43] However, efforts to promote that goal through the NPT review process were ineffectual over the 1990s and 2000s.[44] The first attempt towards the practical implementation of the 1995 resolution was made in 2010, when the NPT review conference agreed to hold a conference on the establishment of a Middle East WMD-free zone by 2012.[45] That this decision was not subsequently implemented can be seen as the single most important factor behind the failure of the 2015 NPT Review Conference.[46]

The 1995 Resolution on the Middle East eventually provided the terms of reference for the 2019 conference. All Middle Eastern states were invited to participate in the conference and the five NPT nuclear weapon states were

---

[42] United Nations, General Assembly, 'Convening a conference on the establishment of a Middle East zone free of nuclear weapons and other weapons of mass destruction', Decision 73/546, 22 Dec. 2018, p. 23; and Erästö et al. (note 28), p. 392.

[43] 1995 NPT Review and Extension Conference (note 38).

[44] Erästö, T., 'The lack of disarmament in the Middle East: A thorn in the side of the NPT', SIPRI Insights on Peace and Security no. 2019/1, Jan. 2019; and Cserveny, V. et al., *Building a Weapons of Mass Destruction Free Zone in the Middle East: Global Non-Proliferation Regimes and Regional Experiences* (United Nations Institute for Disarmament Research: Geneva, 2004).

[45] Kile, S. N., 'Nuclear arms control and non-proliferation', *SIPRI Yearbook 2011*, 363–87.

[46] Erästö (note 44); and Rauf, T., 'The 2015 Non-Proliferation Treaty Review Conference', *SIPRI Yearbook 2016*, p. 699.

invited to observe it. All but two invitees—Israel and the USA—participated.[47] The themes debated included the principles and objectives, general obligations regarding nuclear weapons and other WMD, peaceful uses and international cooperation, and institutional arrangements. It was agreed that representatives from existing nuclear weapon-free zones would be invited to the second session of the conference—planned for 16–20 November 2020—to share good practices and lessons on treaty implementation.[48]

The conference adopted a political declaration in which participating states declared their

commitment to pursue, in accordance with relevant international resolutions, and in an open and inclusive manner with all invited States, the elaboration of a legally binding treaty to establish a Middle East zone free of nuclear weapons and other weapons of mass destruction, on the basis of arrangements freely arrived at by consensus by the States of the region.[49]

The conference will be held every year until its objective of a legally binding treaty creating the planned zone is achieved.[50] According to observers, the general tone of the discussions was positive and constructive. However, the UK reportedly regretted the convening of the conference, which prompted critical responses from some Middle Eastern participants.[51]

The conference did not achieve immediate results, which was expected due to the absence of the region's only nuclear-armed state, Israel. However, it can be seen to have laid the basis for sustained multilateral efforts towards WMD disarmament in the Middle East. As the president of the conference noted, the conference was the beginning of a process. As such, it also might relieve some of the pressure on the NPT review process that the lack of implementation of the 1995 Resolution on the Middle East has created.

Treaty on the Prohibition of Nuclear Weapons

The Treaty on the Prohibition of Nuclear Weapons is the first multilateral treaty establishing a comprehensive ban on nuclear weapons, including

---

[47] For a list of the 22 participants, 4 observers and other organizations see United Nations, General Assembly, Conference on the Establishment of a Middle East Zone Free of Nuclear Weapons and Other Weapons of Mass Destruction, First session, List of participants, A/CONF.236/INF/3, 22 Nov. 2019.

[48] United Nations, General Assembly, Conference on the Establishment of a Middle East Zone Free of Nuclear Weapons and Other Weapons of Mass Destruction, First session, Report of the conference on the work of its first session, A/CONF.236/6, 22 Nov. 2019, para. 13.

[49] United Nations A/CONF.236/6 (note 48), Political declaration.

[50] United Nations, General Assembly, Decision 73/546 (note 42), para. d.

[51] Dolev, S., Kiyaei, E. and Saadallah, D., 'Achieving the possible: A WMD-free zone in the Middle East', Reaching Critical Will, Nov. 2019.

their development, deployment, possession, use and threat of use.[52] As of 31 December 2019, 34 states had ratified or acceded to the TPNW and a further 47 states had signed but not yet ratified it.[53] It will enter into force 90 days after 50 states have either ratified or acceded to it. Several states that had not yet ratified the treaty reported that their domestic ratification processes were ongoing.[54]

In 2019 the TPNW continued to be subject to contradictory interpretations. During the 2019 meeting of the Preparatory Committee for the 2020 NPT Review Conference, supporters argued that the TPNW complements and strengthens the NPT.[55] Critics stated the opposite.[56] China—whose position towards the TPNW has generally been more positive than the other nuclear weapon states—also joined the criticism in the joint P5 statement, according to which 'the TPNW contradicts, and risks undermining the NPT'.[57] Reflecting the majority view, the idea of the TPNW's 'complementarity with the Non-Proliferation Treaty' was nevertheless incorporated into the informal working paper produced by the chair of the preparatory committee.[58]

The meeting of the First Committee of the UN General Assembly in October adopted a draft resolution supportive of the TPNW, which was sponsored by 49 states.[59] This resolution, which was adopted by the General Assembly on 12 December, calls on 'all States that have not yet done so to sign, ratify, accept, approve or accede to the Treaty at the earliest possible date'.[60] Given the broad support for the treaty, the prospect of its entry into force seems increasingly likely in the coming years.

---

[52] For a summary and other details of the TPNW see annex A, section I, in this volume. For background see Kile, S. N., 'Treaty on the Prohibition of Nuclear Weapons, *SIPRI Yearbook 2018*, pp. 307–18; and Erästö, T., 'Treaty on the Prohibition of Nuclear Weapons, *SIPRI Yearbook 2019*, pp. 387–90.

[53] For a list of these states see annex A, section I, in this volume.

[54] International Campaign to Abolish Nuclear Weapons (ICAN), 'First Committee foreshadows disarmament fights at 2020 NPT Review Conference', 12 Nov. 2019.

[55] E.g. Preparatory Committee for the 2020 NPT Review Conference, Third Session, 'Joint statement on the Treaty on the Prohibition of Nuclear Weapons (TPNW)', Statement by Austria, Brazil, Costa Rica, Ireland, Indonesia, Mexico, New Zealand, Nigeria, South Africa and Thailand, 2 May 2019.

[56] E.g. Preparatory Committee for the 2020 NPT Review Conference, Third Session, 'Nuclear disarmament', Statement by France, 2 May 2019.

[57] Preparatory Committee for the 2020 NPT Review Conference, Statement by China on behalf of the P5 states (note 35).

[58] Preparatory Committee for the 2020 NPT Review Conference, NPT/CONF.2020/PC.III/WP.49 (note 39).

[59] United Nations, General Assembly, First Committee, 74th session, 'Treaty on the Prohibition of Nuclear Weapons', 21 Oct. 2019, A/C.1/74/L.12.

[60] UN General Assembly Resolution 74/41, 'Treaty on the Prohibition of Nuclear Weapons', 12 Dec. 2019, A/RES/74/41.

12. Chemical and biological security threats

Overview

Allegations of chemical weapons use by Syria continued to be investigated by the Organisation for the Prohibition of Chemical Weapons (OPCW) in 2019. The Declaration Assessment Team continued its work to resolve gaps, inconsistencies and discrepancies in Syria's initial declaration, and the Fact-finding Mission (FFM) in Syria continued to collect and analyse information in relation to allegations of use. The FFM reported in March 2019 that there were 'reasonable grounds' for believing that a chemical weapon attack occurred in Douma in April 2018. Some of the report's findings proved controversial and were challenged by a few states.

Outside of Syria, investigations were ongoing into the use of a toxic chemical from the novichok nerve agent family in the UK in March 2018. In January 2019, the European Union placed the two Russian nationals charged with carrying out the attack on a European sanctions list. The head and deputy head of the GRU, the Main Intelligence Directorate of the Armed Forces of the Russian Federation, were also included on the list. In March, the UK announced that the specialist decontamination work at the 12 sites across Salisbury and Amesbury had been completed.

Continued divisions among states parties over the decision adopted at the June 2018 Special Session, placed high levels of institutional stress on the OPCW during 2019. In particular, a small number of states parties continued to regard the decision to establish an Investigation and Identification Team (IIT) as illegitimate. Nonetheless, the IIT, which is responsible for identifying the perpetrators of the use of chemical weapons in Syria, became fully operational in March 2019 and is focusing on nine incidents of use. The political divisions played out in OPCW Executive Council meetings and at the main conference of the year, the 24th Session of the Conference of States Parties (CSP) to the Chemical Weapons Convention. However, the CSP did manage to adopt two decisions by consensus to amend for the first time the Annex on Chemicals to the Convention to include novichok agents.

As of 31 October 2019, 97.3 per cent of declared Category 1 chemical weapons had been destroyed under international verification. The USA remains the only declared possessor state party with CWs yet to be destroyed, but is expected to complete its remaining destruction activities within the current timelines.

In 2019, Tanzania became the 183rd state party to ratify the principal legal instrument against biological warfare: the 1972 Biological and Toxin Weapons Convention (BWC). Key biological disarmament and non-proliferation activities in 2019 were carried out in connection with the second set of 2018–20 BWC intersessional Meetings of Experts (MXs)—MX1 focused on cooperation and assistance; MX2 on science and technology; MX3 on national implementation; MX4 on assistance, response and preparedness; and MX5 on institutional strengthening—the First Committee of the United Nations General Assembly and the BWC Meeting of States Parties (MSP).

Reviewing the financial situation of the BWC formed a central focus for the 2019 MSP meeting. The meeting also considered the reports of each MX, but as in 2018 the MSP report simply noted that 'no consensus was reached on the deliberations including any possible outcomes of the Meetings of Experts'. However, the chair proposed and initiated a new process to circumvent the reporting impasse and feed substantive work of the MXs into the MSPs and the 2021 Review Conference. The process also encourages states parties to establish continuity between the work of the three intersessional years, to synthesize the work and identify areas of convergence, and to avoid a confrontational approach. In particular, disagreements between the USA and Russia seem set to continue.

One of the developing trends in the field is the rise of civil society as a major contributor to shaping global dialogues around biological threats and appropriate responses to them. This is reflected in greater numbers of NGO participants attending BWC meetings and organizing side events, but also in civil society organizations convening global initiatives, workshops and events related to biosecurity. A new development in 2019 was the growing recognition of the topic of 'gender and disarmament' within the BWC community.

CAITRÍONA MCLEISH AND FILIPPA LENTZOS

I. Allegations of use of chemical weapons in Syria

CAITRÍONA MCLEISH

In 2019 the conflict in Syria entered its eighth year and, as in previous years, there were continued allegations of use and preparations for use of chemical weapons. This included an allegation that the Syrian Arab Republic used chlorine in Kabanah, north-west Syria, on 19 May.[1] Director-general of the Organisation for the Prohibition of Chemical Weapons (OPCW), Fernando Árias, later reported that the OPCW Fact-finding Mission (FFM) was analysing and investigating this allegation.[2] The FFM also continued its work investigating earlier allegations. Between 5 and 15 January the FFM deployed a team to Syria to conduct interviews and visit hospitals in Aleppo and to receive samples from the Syrian authorities in connection with an alleged use of toxic chemicals in Aleppo on 24 November 2018.[3] The team deployed at least three other times, at the end of September and during both October and December. In the last of these deployments, the team interviewed witnesses and collected further information regarding incidents that had taken place in Yarmouk, Damascus, on 22 October 2017; in Khirbat Masasinah on 7 July 2017 and 4 August 2017; in Qalib Al-Thawr, Al-Salamiyah, on 9 August 2017; and in Al-Balil, Souran, on 8 November 2017.[4] The OPCW Technical Secretariat (the Secretariat) is analysing the collected information.

The OPCW Declaration Assessment Team (DAT) also continued its efforts to clarify and resolve all of the identified gaps, inconsistencies and discrepancies in the initial declaration submitted by the Syrian Arab Republic in 2013. Between 4 and 8 February, the Secretariat and a delegation of the Syrian Arab Republic met in Beirut, Lebanon, to review the implementation of various activities, including those of the DAT. During these discussions, both parties reviewed the status of all outstanding issues pertaining to the 2013 initial declaration, regrouped them and created an action plan for each

---

[1] Ortagus, M., Spokesperson for US Department of State, 'Alleged use of chemical weapons by the Assad Regime in northwest Syria', 21 May 2019.

[2] OPCW Executive Council, 'Opening statement by the Director-General to the Ninety-second Session of the Executive Council (full version)', EC-92/DG.34, 8 Oct. 2019, para. 8.

[3] OPCW Executive Council, 'Progress in the elimination of the Syrian chemical weapons programme', Report by the Director-General, EC-92/DG.6, 23 Aug 2019, para. 18.

[4] OPCW Executive Council, 'Progress in the elimination of the Syrian chemical weapons programme', Note by the Director-General, EC-93/DG.5, 24 Dec. 2019, para. 15. A previous report on FFM activities relating to these incidents noted that the 'evolving' security situation was impacting upon FFM activities: OPCW Technical Secretariat, 'Summary update of the activities carried out by the OPCW Fact-finding Mission in Syria', Note by the Technical Secretariat, S/1677/2018, 10 Oct. 2018, para 11; while another report described the FFM as 'awaiting sample analysis results from the last deployments, [and] planning further deployments': OPCW Executive Council, 'Opening statement by the Director-General to the Ninety-second Session of the Executive Council', EC-92/DG.33, 8 Oct. 2019, para 8.

issue based on the activities that could be conducted to resolve it.[5] As part of the newly agreed structured dialogue, three further rounds of consultation took place, the first from 18 to 21 March 2019 in The Hague and the second and third in Syria from 10 to 17 April 2019 and 14 to 23 October respectively. These were, respectively, the 20th, 21st and 22nd rounds of such consultations. During the 21st round of consultations in Syria, the DAT conducted one interview, collected 33 samples from field visits to five sites, and received new information and documents.[6] In relation to one outstanding issue—indicators of undeclared chemical warfare agents which had been found in samples collected by the DAT in 2016—the Syrian authorities 'acknowledged research and development activities'.[7]

In June 2019, the OPCW Executive Council learned that a Schedule 2.B.04 chemical had been detected in a sample taken at the Barzah facility during the third round of inspections of the Barzah and Jamrayah facilities conducted in November 2018. The report from the designated laboratory suggested the chemical, later identified as ethyl ethylphosphonate, 'could be the primary hydrolysis product of a Schedule 1.A.01 or 1.A.03 chemical'.[8] The Syrian Arab Republic offered the Secretariat an explanation as to its presence in a note verbale dated 7 November 2019. The director-general noted in his December progress report that the Secretariat was analysing the explanation.[9]

In September, the 92nd Session of the Executive Council noted the director-general's report of the work of the DAT, which concluded that 'the Secretariat remains unable to resolve all of the identified gaps, inconsistencies, and discrepancies in the Syrian Arab Republic's declaration', and so 'cannot fully verify that the Syrian Arab Republic has submitted a declaration that can be considered accurate and complete'.[10]

At the beginning of November, Director-General Árias addressed the United Nations Security Council in a private session. This was 'a departure from the norm' and is the first time since the adoption of Resolution 2118 in 2013 that the Security Council has held a private meeting to receive the OPCW monthly briefing. It was still a formal session of the Security Council

---

[5] OPCW Executive Council, 'Outcome of consultations with the Syrian Arab Republic regarding its chemical weapons declaration', Note by the Director-General, EC-91/DG.23, 5 July 2019, para. 3.

[6] OPCW Executive Council, EC-91/DG.23 (note 5) para. 5.

[7] OPCW Executive Council, EC-91/DG.23 (note 5) para. 6.

[8] OPCW Executive Council, 'Progress in the elimination of the Syrian chemical weapons programme', Note by the Director-General, EC-91/DG.14, 24 June 2019, para. 13; and OPCW Executive Council, 'Progress in the elimination of the Syrian chemical weapons programme', Note by the Director-General, EC-92/DG.1, 24 July 2019, para. 12.

[9] OPCW Executive Council, 'Progress in the elimination of the Syrian chemical weapons programme', Note by the Director General, EC-93/DG.3, 25 Nov. 2019, para. 11.

[10] OPCW Executive Council, Report of the Ninety-second Session of the Executive Council, EC-92/5, 11 Oct. 2019, para. 7.21; and OPCW Executive Council, 'Progress in the elimination of the Syrian chemical weapons programme', Note by the Director-General, EC-93/DG.5, 24 Dec. 2019, para. 9.

and as such open to 'persons other than Council members and Secretariat officials' to attend.[11] The meeting communiqué records that representatives of several member states made initial statements—the United States, the Russian Federation, Kuwait, Poland, Côte d'Ivoire, Peru, China, South Africa, Indonesia, France, Belgium, the Dominican Republic, Germany, Equatorial Guinea and the United Kingdom—and the Russian Federation made a further statement. The Security Council also heard from the representative of the Syrian Arab Republic.[12]

In a presidential statement presented by the British Ambassador to the United Nations, Karen Pierce,[13] at the end of November, the Security Council condemned the use of chemical weapons anywhere, at any time, by anyone; reaffirmed that chemical weapons are a threat to international peace and security; and reaffirmed its strong support for the 1993 Chemical Weapons Convention (CWC).[14]

OPCW Fact-finding Mission final report on Douma incident

On 1 March 2019 the FFM issued its 106-page final report into the April 2018 alleged use of toxic chemicals in Douma (Douma Final Report), having finished the evaluation and analysis of all of the information gathered during its investigation, and having received all the results of the analysis by the designated laboratories of the prioritized samples.[15] The Douma Final Report records that there are 'reasonable grounds that the use of a toxic chemical as a weapon took place. This toxic chemical contained reactive chlorine.'[16]

The FFM found, among other things, that 'the objects from which the samples were taken at both locations had been in contact with one or more substances containing reactive chlorine'; that 'No organophosphorous nerve agents, their degradation products or synthesis impurities were detected either in environmental samples . . . or in plasma samples from alleged casualties'; and that 'there was no indication' that either the warehouse or

---

[11] Security Council Report, 'Syria chemical weapons: Private meeting with the OPCW Director-General', *What's in Blue: Insights on the Work of the UN Security Council*, 4 Nov. 2019.

[12] United Nations Security Council, Official communiqué of the 8659th (closed) meeting of the Security Council, S/PV.8659, 6 Nov. 2019.

[13] The UK held the presidency of the Security Council for Nov. 2019. See UN Security Council, Statement by the President of the Security Council, S/PRST/2019/14, 22 Nov. 2019.

[14] For a summary and other details of the 1993 Convention on the Prohibition of the Development, Production, Stockpiling and Use of Chemical Weapons and on their Destruction, see annex A, section I, in this volume.

[15] OPCW Technical Secretariat, 'Report of Fact-finding Mission regarding an incident of alleged toxic chemical use as a weapon in Douma, Syrian Arab Republic, on 7 Apr 2018', Note by the Technical Secretariat, S/1731/2019, 1 Mar. 2019.

[16] OPCW Technical Secretariat, S/1731/2019 (note 15), para. 2.17.

facilities suspected by the Syrian authorities of producing chemical weapons had been involved in their manufacture.[17]

On the matter of the two yellow industrial cylinders which the FFM observed at two separate locations (Locations 2 and 4), and which proved highly controversial (see next subsection), the Douma Final Report states:

The team analysed the available material and consulted independent experts in mechanical engineering, ballistics and metallurgy who utilised specialised computer modelling techniques to provide qualified and competent assessments of the trajectory and damage to the cylinders . . .

The analyses indicated that the structural damage to the rebar-reinforced concrete terrace at Location 2 was caused by an impacting object with a geometrically symmetric shape and sufficient kinetic energy to cause the observed damage. The analyses indicate that the damage observed on the cylinder found on the roof-top terrace, the aperture, the balcony, the surrounding rooms, the rooms underneath and the structure above, is consistent with the creation of the aperture observed in the terrace by the cylinder found in that location.

At Location 4, the results of the studies indicated that the shape of the aperture produced in the modulation matched the shape and damage observed by the team. The studies further indicated that, after passing through the ceiling and impacting the floor at lower speed, the cylinder continued an altered trajectory, until reaching the position in which it was found . . .

Based on the analysis results of the samples taken by the FFM from the cylinders, their proximity at both locations, as well as the analysis results of the samples . . . it is possible that the cylinders were the source of the substances containing reactive chlorine.[18]

Reactions to the release of the Douma Final Report

The 90th Session of the Executive Council opened on 12 March, 11 days after the release of the Douma Final Report. Several delegations noted their concerns about the findings, with Canada stating that it 'expect[s] that the FFM's work on the Douma case will be referred to the Investigation and Identification Team [IIT], once it begins its activities'.[19] Other delegations commended the FFM: Romania on behalf of the European Union noted the professionalism of the FFM;[20] the United States commended the FFM 'for its independent and impartial work undertaken in difficult and dangerous

[17] OPCW Technical Secretariat, S/1731/2019 (note 15), paras 2.6, 2.7 and 2.9.

[18] OPCW Technical Secretariat, S/1731/2019 (note 15), paras 2.13–2.16.

[19] OPCW Executive Council, Canada, 'Statement by HE Ambassador Sabine Nölke, Permanent Representative of Canada to the OPCW, at the Ninetieth Session of the Executive Council', EC-90/NAT.14, 12 Mar. 2019, p. 1.

[20] OPCW Executive Council, Romania, 'Statement on behalf of the European Union delivered by HE Ambassador Brandusa Predescu, Permanent Representative of Romania to the OPCW, at the Ninetieth Session of the Executive Council', EC-90/NAT.9, 12 Mar. 2019, p. 1.

circumstances';[21] and Denmark stated that it 'firmly rejects recent attempts to discredit and undermine the Technical Secretariat and its work'.[22]

However, other delegations expressed dissatisfaction with the report. For example, Iran expressed continued dissatisfaction with the FFM's 'work methodology' and with the fact that the Final Report was issued 'nearly one year after the incident on 7 April 2018'.[23] After the session, on 26 April the Russian Federation requested, via note verbale, that its commentary on the Douma Final Report be circulated as an official document of the 90th Session.[24] The Russian commentary takes particular issue with the report's findings about the two cylinders and suggests that 'the parameters, characteristics and exterior of the cylinders, as well as the data obtained from the locations of those incidents, are not consistent with the argument that they were dropped from an aircraft'.[25] The Syrian Arab Republic also sent a note verbale on the Douma Final Report to the OPCW on 11 March. The Technical Secretariat responded to both on 21 May.[26]

In the months that followed, controversy about the findings of the report intensified, particularly after the disclosure outside the OPCW of an internal report from a Technical Secretariat staff member who held a dissenting view. Director-General Árias told states parties during a briefing on 28 May that he received the first indication that an internal document 'could have been disclosed outside of the Secretariat' in March.[27] The staff member was described as 'a liaison officer at [the OPCW] Command Post Office in Damascus . . . tasked with temporarily assisting the FFM with information collection at some sites in Douma'.[28] Reassuring states parties that 'the Secretariat encourages serious and professional debates' and that 'all views, analysis, information and opinions are considered', the director-general continued, 'The document produced by this staff member pointed at possible attribution, which is outside of the mandate of the FFM . . . Therefore, I

---

[21] OPCW Executive Council, United States of America, 'United States statement regarding the OPCW Fact-finding Mission report on investigation into chemical weapons use in Douma, Syria', EC-90/NAT.16, 13 Mar. 2019, p. 1.

[22] OPCW Executive Council, Denmark, 'Statement by HE Ambassador Jens-Otto Horslund, Permanent Representative of Denmark to the OPCW, at the Ninetieth Session of the Executive Council', EC-90/NAT.21, 12 Mar. 2019, p. 2.

[23] OPCW Executive Council, Islamic Republic of Iran, 'Statement by HE Ambassador Reza Najafi, Director General for International Peace and Security, Ministry of Foreign Affairs, at the Ninetieth Session of the Executive Council', EC-90/NAT.23, 13 Mar. 2019, p. 2.

[24] OPCW Executive Council, Russian Federation, 'Request for circulation of a document', EC-90/NAT.41, 26 Apr 2019. The commentary is in the annex (pp. 3–11) to the request: Russian Federation, 'Commentaries on the conclusion of the report of the Fact-finding Mission on the use of chemical weapons in Syria regarding the alleged use of chemical weapons in Douma on 7 April 2018'.

[25] Russian Federation, annex (note 24), p. 10.

[26] OPCW Technical Secretariat, 'Update on the OPCW Fact-finding Mission in Syria', Note by the Technical Secretariat, S/1755/2019, 21 May 2019.

[27] Árias, F., OPCW Director-General, Remarks of the Director-General at the briefing for states parties on Syrian Arab Republic: Update on IIT-FFM-SSRC-DAT, 28 May 2019, p. 3.

[28] Árias (note 27), p. 3.

instructed that, beyond the copy that would exclusively be kept by the FFM, the staff member be advised to submit his assessment to the IIT, which he did, so that this document could later be used by the IIT.'[29]

He also informed states parties that he had authorized an investigation into the sharing of the document and that they would be informed of the outcome.[30] The Secretariat published the findings of the investigation on 6 February 2020.[31]

At the 91st Session of the Executive Council in July 2019, the director-general informed states parties that the investigation 'does not have any bearing on the findings of the Douma report'.[32] He continued:

Since an internal working document was disclosed outside the Technical Secretariat, the Office of Confidentiality and Security has been collecting, preserving, and analysing information in order to understand how this document was disclosed. I have informed the Permanent Representative of the Syrian Arab Republic and the Chairperson of the Executive Council that I have authorised a full confidentiality investigation. In order to protect the integrity of the investigation and the due process rights of anyone involved, and in accordance with normal practice in respect of ongoing investigations, no further information about the investigation is available at this time.[33]

At the 24th Conference of States Parties (CSP) in November, the director-general repeated his view that the overall conclusions of the FFM inquiry were 'based on the preponderance of objective facts', noting that 'it is in the nature of any thorough inquiry for individuals in a team to express subjective views'.[34] He continued: 'While some of these diverse views continue to circulate in certain public discussion fora, I would like to reiterate that I stand by the impartial and professional conclusions reached by the FFM.'[35]

This restatement was timely as the month before, on 15 October, another Technical Secretariat staff member reportedly presented dissenting views about the Douma Final Report to a panel of individuals in Brussels. Convened by the Courage Foundation (which describes itself as 'an international organisation that supports those who risk life or liberty to make significant contributions to the historical record'[36]), the panel included the first director-general of the OPCW Technical Secretariat, Ambassador José

---

[29] Árias (note 27), p. 3.

[30] Árias (note 27), p. 3.

[31] OPCW Technical Secretariat, 'Report of the investigation into possible breaches of confidentiality', Note by the Technical Secretariat, S/1839/2020, 6 Feb 2020.

[32] OPCW Executive Council, 'Opening statement by the Director-General to the Ninety-first Session of the Executive Council (full version)', EC-91/DG.25, 9 July 2019, para. 24.

[33] OPCW Executive Council, EC-91/DG.25 (note 32), para. 25.

[34] OPCW, Conference of the States Parties, 'Opening Statement by the Director-General to the Conference of the States Parties at its Twenty-fourth Session (full version)', C-24/DG.21, 25 Nov. 2019, para. 16.

[35] OPCW Conference of the States Parties, C-24/DG.21 (note 34), para. 17.

[36] Courage Foundation, 'About Courage', [n.d.].

Bustani of Brazil.[37] After the meeting, the panel issued a statement which, among other things, called on the OPCW to 'permit all inspectors who took part in the Douma investigation to come forward and report their differing observations in an appropriate forum' of states parties. The panel presented these criticisms 'with the expectation' that the OPCW would 'revisit' its investigation.[38]

One week before the opening of the CSP, states parties received an open letter signed by the panel members and 16 other prominent individuals.[39] The letter drew attention to the deliberations of the panel and asked states parties for their 'support in taking action . . . aimed at restoring the integrity of the OPCW and regaining public trust'.[40] This letter was mentioned during some interventions at the CSP, especially in the closing stages of the meeting.[41]

[37] Courage Foundation, 'Panel criticizes "unacceptable practices" in the OPCW's investigation of the alleged chemical attack in Douma, Syria on April 7th 2018', Press release, 23 Oct. 2019.

[38] Courage Foundation, Press release (note 37).

[39] Courage Foundation, Open letter to Permanent Representatives to the OPCW, 18 Nov. 2019.

[40] Courage Foundation, Open letter (note 39), p. 1.

[41] Speaking on this issue under agenda item 24 (any other business) were Syria, Russia, Iran, China, USA, Venezuela, Belgium, Nicaragua and the United Kingdom. See OPCW, Webcast CSP-24, 'Day 5—Morning', 0:59.46–1:07.55, 1:15.36–1:39.16 and 1:41.11–2:00.37.

II. Use of novichok agents

CAITRÍONA MCLEISH

The Skripal case: Update on the assassination attempt in the United Kingdom using a toxic chemical

After 10 months of recuperation, Wiltshire police officer Detective Sergeant Nick Bailey returned to active duty on 15 January 2019. Bailey and another police officer had come into contact with a toxic chemical that was later identified as a member of the novichok family when they searched the Salisbury home of Sergey Skripal in March 2018.[1]

About a week after Bailey's return to duty, on 21 January 2019 the European Union placed the two Russian nationals charged with carrying out the attack, known by their aliases Alexander Petrov and Ruslan Boshirov, on a European sanctions list.[2] The list also included Igor Olegovich Kostyukov and Vladimir Stepanovich Alexseyev, the head and deputy head, respectively, of the GRU, the Main Intelligence Directorate of the Armed Forces of the Russian Federation. This was the first set of listings under the new EU sanctions regime focusing on chemical weapons since its adoption in October 2018.[3]

Continuing its investigation of the Skripal poisonings, Bellingcat—an investigative research network that uses open sources and social media—linked a third Russian military intelligence officer to the attack.[4] He was identified as Denis Sergeyev, who Bellingcat suggested 'was likely in charge of coordinating the Salisbury operation'.[5] This claim led to media reports that the Skripal poisoning was 'part of a coordinated and ongoing campaign to destabilize Europe, executed by an elite unit inside the Russian intelligence system skilled in subversion, sabotage and assassination'.[6]

Shortly before the one-year anniversary of the Skripal attack, on 1 March the British Department for Environment, Food and Rural Affairs announced the completion of Operation Morlop, the specialist decontamination work at the 12 sites across Salisbury and Amesbury.[7] During the operation, military

---

[1] Wiltshire Police, 'Update: Latest on the Counter Terrorism Policing investigation into Novichok poisonings', [n.d.].

[2] Council of the European Union, 'Chemical weapons: The EU places nine persons and one entity under new sanctions regime', Press release, 21 Jan. 2019.

[3] Council of the European Union, 'Chemical weapons: The Council adopts a new sanctions regime', Press release, 15 Oct. 2018.

[4] Rakuszitzky, M., 'Third suspect in Skripal poisoning identified as Denis Sergeyev, high-ranking GRU officer', Bellingcat news, 14 Feb. 2019.

[5] Bellingcat Investigation Team, 'The GRU globetrotters: Mission London', Bellingcat news, 28 June 2019.

[6] Schwirtz, M., 'Top secret Russian unit seeks to destabilize Europe, security officials say', New York Times, 8 Oct. 2019.

[7] British Department of Environment, Food and Rural Affairs (DEFRA), 'Clean-up work completed in Salisbury', Press release, 1 Mar. 2019.

personnel, including the Joint Chemical, Biological, Radiological and Nuclear Task Force, and specialist contractors worked for '13 000 hours in protective clothing' and collected 'around 5000 samples—ranging from samples taken from ambulances and cars to chairs and pieces of plaster', which were then analysed at the Defence Science and Technology Laboratory at Porton Down.[8] The approach taken was 'precautionary'.[9]

Two days later on 3 March, the eve of the anniversary of the poisonings, the then British Defence Secretary Gavin Williamson announced 11 million pounds of additional funding for measures to bolster the UK's response to chemical attacks.[10] The range of measures included: 'developing plans to deploy drones and robots into potentially hazardous areas'; 'boosting the Defence Science and Technology Laboratory's ability to analyse substances, by investing in new technical capabilities'; and 'keeping the UK at the forefront of medical advances to combat the effects of chemical agents'.[11]

The then prime minister, Theresa May, visited Salisbury the following day to mark the first anniversary of the attack. Her visit included meeting the father of Dawn Sturgess (the deceased Amesbury victim) and her partner Charlie Rowley (the other Amesbury victim). Sturgess's father told *The Guardian* newspaper that 'it was the first time that someone from the government had spoken directly to the family', adding: 'She couldn't give me any more information about what happened but it was reassuring that people [at] that level are thinking of us.'[12]

Also marking the first anniversary, Deputy Assistant Commissioner Dean Haydon, the Senior National Coordinator for Counter Terrorism Policing, said that the investigation into the poisoning was continuing.[13] Haydon used the occasion to appeal for any further information, especially in relation to the perfume box and bottle that had been recovered from Rowley's address. He commented that the police could not 'account for the whereabouts of the bottle, nozzle or box between the attack on the Skripals on 4 March and when Charlie Rowley said he found it on Wednesday, 27 June'.[14]

The following month, on 6 April, Rowley met with the Russian ambassador to the United Kingdom, Alexander Yakovenko.[15] Despite Yakovenko outlining 'in detail the Russian view on what had happened in Salisbury and

[8] Haynes, D., 'Novichok attack: Skripal house to be brought back as home', *Sky News*, 1 Mar. 2019.

[9] DEFRA (note 7).

[10] British Ministry of Defence, 'Defence Secretary announces £11 million boost to chemical defences', Press release, 3 Mar. 2019.

[11] British Ministry of Defence (note 10).

[12] Morris, S. and Bannock, C., 'PM meets father of novichok victim Dawn Sturgess', *The Guardian*, 5 Mar 2019.

[13] Haydon, D., 'Salisbury: Investigation continues one year on', Update on Salisbury and Amesbury Investigation, British Counter Terrorism Policing, Mar. 2019.

[14] Haydon (note 13).

[15] Russian Embassy in the UK, 'Ambassador Yakovenko meets Charlie Rowley', Photo report, 7 Apr. 2019.

Amesbury', Rowley later told the press that the meeting 'had not changed his view on Russia's involvement'.[16]

The following month, on 21 June, Rowley revealed in an interview additional details about how Sturgess was exposed to the novichok agent. He described the bottle and pump as being 'packaged separately in hard plastic':

'It was a thick plastic. You couldn't tear it. It was tough. I remember having to use a kitchen knife.' As he attached the pump to the bottle, Rowley pressed the nozzle down. 'It released on to me. I rinsed it off. It had an oily texture and next to no smell. I did mention [the lack of smell] to Dawn. She just carried on and gave it a spray, thinking nothing of it.'[17]

The Pre-Inquest Review into the death of Dawn Sturgess was listed to begin on 16 January 2019. Following two requests from the Crown Prosecution Service to relist the date, on the basis that there was 'an ongoing criminal investigation and that a person(s) may be charged with a homicide offence', the senior coroner for Wiltshire and Swindon, David Ridley, set a new date of 18 October 2019.[18] Michael Mansfield QC, representing the Sturgess family, had urged the coroner to hold the inquest under the terms of Article 2 of the European Convention on Human Rights which would allow the scope of the inquest to be widened to consider 'how and in what circumstances' Sturgess died. The coroner released his preliminary view on this issue in September, in a letter which set out the scope and provisional agenda for the inquest, including that he did not consider Article 2 was engaged.[19] The provisional agenda and scope were not accepted by all interested parties.[20] At the time of writing, the Pre-Inquest Review is adjourned to allow for a judicial review of the scope.[21]

Technical change to the schedules to the Chemical Weapons Convention

On 14 January 2019, the 62nd Meeting of the Executive Council of the Organisation for the Prohibition of Chemical Weapons (OPCW) considered

---

[16] Rowley states, 'I liked the ambassador but I thought some of what he said trying to justify Russia not being responsible was ridiculous. I'm glad I met him and feel I did find out some things I didn't know before. But I still think Russia carried out the attack.' See Quinn, B., 'Man poisoned after novichok attack meets Russian ambassador', *The Guardian*, 7 Apr 2019.

[17] Morris, S. and Bannock, C., 'Novichok victim: "We're being kept in the dark"', *The Guardian*, 21 June 2019.

[18] Wiltshire and Swindon Coroner's Court, News updates: Coroner's decision, 'Ruling in relation to the application of Article 2, European Convention on Human Rights and Scope', Case no. 1380/18, 20 Dec. 2019, para. 2.

[19] Wiltshire and Swindon Coroner's Court (note 18), para. 3.

[20] Wiltshire and Swindon Coroner's Court (note 18) para. 5.

[21] Griffin, K., 'Inquest hearing into death of Novichok victim Dawn Sturgess pushed back', *Salisbury Journal*, 30 Jan. 2020.

the joint proposal made by Canada, the Netherlands and the United States on 16 October 2018. The proposal was designed to ensure that novichok agents, including the one used in the Salisbury incident, were listed in Schedule 1 (as chemical warfare agents) to the Chemical Weapons Convention (CWC).[22]

The OPCW director-general delivered his report on the potential financial, administrative and budget implications of the decision, if it were to be adopted, to states parties on 10 January, four days before the 62nd meeting.[23] The report stated that the OPCW Technical Secretariat (the Secretariat) did not expect a significant increase of inspections at Schedule 1 facilities as a result of adoption, although additional requirements might be needed for training and capacity building for relevant Secretariat staff and to incorporate the relevant information into OPCW support programmes.[24]

Taking the floor on the matter, Ambassador Paul van den Ijssel of the Netherlands (the host country) affirmed the importance of the credibility of the CWC and the OPCW, before arguing that adding the two proposed chemical families—which he described as 'military-grade, extremely toxic chemicals' with 'no known use for purposes not prohibited'—'strongly reinforces' that credibility.[25] Romania on behalf of the European Union concurred, welcoming the 'timely submission' of the proposal and encouraging its recommendation.[26]

However, Ambassador Alexander Shulgin of the Russian Federation noted in his statement his disappointment that the technical change was 'limited to just two families' despite Russia having 'submitted extensive material (over 300 pages) specifying several hundreds of chemical compounds'.[27] He suggested that the 'additional information' submitted by Russia was 'not

[22] OPCW, Fourth Review Conference, United States, 'Statement by HE Ambassador Kenneth D. Ward, Permanent Representative of the United States of America to the OPCW, at the Fourth Special Session of the Conference of the States Parties to Review the Operation of the Chemical Weapons Convention', RC-4/NAT.7, 22 Nov. 2018, p. 3; and OPCW, Fourth Review Conference, Canada, 'Statement of Canada to the Fourth Review Conference, Delivered by Ambassador Sabine Nölke, Permanent Representative', 22 Nov. 2018. For a summary and other details of the Convention on the Prohibition of the Development, Production, Stockpiling and Use of Chemical Weapons and on their Destruction (Chemical Weapons Convention, CWC), see annex A, section I, in this volume.

[23] OPCW Executive Council, 'Financial, administrative and programme and budget implementation of the follow-up activities related to the adoption of the Joint proposal under item 3 of the provisional agenda of the 62nd Meeting of the Executive Council', Report by the Director-General, EC-M-62/DG.2, 10 Jan. 2019.

[24] OPCW Executive Council, EC-M-62/DG.2 (note 23), paras 5–6.

[25] OPCW Executive Council, the Netherlands, 'Statement by HE Ambassador Paul van den Ijssel, Permanent Representative of the Kingdom of the Netherlands to the OPCW, at the Sixty-second Meeting of the Executive Council', EC-M-62/Nat.3, 14 Jan. 2019, p. 1.

[26] OPCW Executive Council, Romania, 'Statement by the European Union concerning the "Joint Proposal by Canada, the Netherlands, and the United States of American for a Technical Change to Schedule 1 of the Annex on Chemicals to the Chemical Weapons Convention" (S/1682/2018, dated 25 October 2019)', EC-M-62/Nat.1, 14 Jan. 2019.

[27] OPCW Executive Council, Russian Federation, 'Statement by HE Ambassador A. V. Shulgin, Permanent Representative of the Russian Federation to the OPCW, at the Sixty-second Meeting of the Executive Council', EC-M-62/NAT.4, 14 Jan. 2019, p. 1.

taken into account by the Technical Secretariat' and therefore considered 'this limited initiative to be politically motivated'.[28]

The meeting 'considered and adopted, by consensus' the decision to recommend a change to Schedule 1 as per the proposal by Canada, the Netherlands and the United States. The Russian Federation disassociated itself from that consensus.[29]

With regard to the series of five proposals submitted by the Russian Federation for a technical change to Schedule 1 (received on 30 November 2018), the Secretariat issued its evaluation on 29 January 2019, followed quickly by two corrigenda.[30] On 18 February 2019, the director-general issued a note on the financial, administrative, programme and budget implications of the follow-up activities related to the adoption of the proposal.[31]

The Executive Council convened on 25 February to consider the Russian proposals. Speaking at the meeting, the deputy permanent representative of the United Kingdom commented that the structures of the first two groups of chemicals proposed were the same as some of those in the joint proposal and so they had 'no substantive objection to their inclusion'.[32] The UK also concurred with the Secretariat with regard to groups 3 and 4 (while noting that group 4 'is entirely unrelated to the toxic chemical used in Salisbury') and the view of the Secretariat that group 5 chemicals did not meet the criteria for inclusion in Schedule 1.[33] Ambassador Brandusa Predescu of Romania, speaking on behalf of the European Union, expressed similar views about the group 5 chemicals.[34]

While there is no publicly available report of the 63rd Meeting of the Executive Council to confirm the outcome, it subsequently became known that the Executive Council did not recommend the adoption of the Russian proposals 'due to disagreements' on whether the chemicals in group 5 were consistent with the guidelines for Schedule 1A.[35] In a press conference the

---

[28] OPCW Executive Council, EC-M-62/NAT.4 (note 27), p. 1.

[29] OPCW Executive Council, Report of the Sixty-second Meeting of the Executive Council, EC-M-62/2, 14 Jan. 2019, paras 3.10 and 3.11. This was the first time that an Executive Council state party disassociated itself from a consensus decision. However, this is a more common occurrence in other policy-making fora. A state will do this to express its disagreement with the text but will not challenge it by calling for a vote. As a result, the action is largely symbolic.

[30] OPCW Executive Council, Opening remarks of the Director-General at the Sixty-third Meeting of the Executive Council (EC-M-63), 25 Feb. 2019.

[31] OPCW Executive Council, Opening remarks (note 30), p. 1.

[32] OPCW Executive Council, United Kingdom, 'Statement by Nicola Stewart, Deputy Permanent Representative of the United Kingdom of Great Britain and Northern Ireland to the OPCW, at the Sixty-third Meeting of the Executive Council (EC-M-63)', 25 Feb. 2019, p. 1.

[33] OPCW Executive Council, United Kingdom (note 32), p. 2.

[34] See OPCW Executive Council, Romania, 'Statement on behalf of the European Union delivered by HE Ambassador Brandusa Predescu, Permanent Representative of Romania to the OPCW, at the Sixty-third Meeting of the Executive Council', EC-M-63/NAT.2, 25 Feb. 2019.

[35] OPCW Scientific Advisory Board, 'Summary of the Third Meeting of the Scientific Advisory Board Temporary Working Group on Investigative Science and Technology', SAB-28/WP.3, 4 June 2019, para. 6.10.

day after the 63rd Meeting of the Executive Council, Ambassador Shulgin suggested that the reason the Russian proposals had been rejected was because 'the US and its closest allies . . . research prohibited chemicals in NATO's specialized centres'.[36] Ambassador Sabine Nölke of Canada rejected this suggestion, stating at the next session of the Executive Council that 'Through extensive direct consultations with the Russian delegation, we made clear that there was a path to consensus. Instead, the Russian Federation chose to proceed with a decision that it knew would fail.'[37] In accordance with Article XV subparagraph 5(d) of the CWC, the decision relating to the Canada–Netherlands–USA proposal opened a 90-day window during which a state party could object to the decision. On 9 April Russia lodged an objection. With regard to the decision not to adopt the Russian proposals, Article XV subparagraph 5(e) states that it shall be taken as a matter of substance by the Conference at its next session. On 9 April Burundi lodged an objection to the Executive Council decision not to recommend the Russian proposal for adoption.[38] That meant that the two amendment proposals would be addressed by the 24th Session of the Conference of States Parties in November (see section III, this chapter).

---

[36] Russian Embassy in NL(@rusembassynl), Twitter, 26 Feb. 2019.

[37] OPCW Executive Council, Canada, 'Statement by HE Ambassador Sabine Nölke, Permanent Representative of Canada to the OPCW, at the Ninetieth Session of the Executive Council', EC-90/Nat.14, 12 Mar. 2019, p. 1.

[38] OPCW Scientific Advisory Board, SAB-28/WP.3 (note 35), para. 6.10.

III. Chemical arms control and disarmament

CAITRÍONA MCLEISH

As of December 2019, there are 193 states parties to the 1993 Chemical Weapons Convention (CWC), the principal international legal instrument against chemical warfare; one state has signed but not ratified it; and three states have neither signed nor ratified the convention.[1] No state joined the treaty in 2019.

On 14 January 2019 Ambassador Odette Melono of the Republic of Cameroon joined the Technical Secretariat as the deputy director-general of the Organisation for the Prohibition of Chemical Weapons (OPCW). She is the fourth person to hold this office and succeeds Ambassador Hamid Ali Rao of India.

In February 2019, the OPCW fulfilled its first commitment for the International Gender Champions Initiative with the appointment of 10 OPCW Gender Focal Points. In his opening remarks to the 24th Session of the Conference of States Parties (CSP) in November 2019, the OPCW director-general, Ambassador Fernando Árias, also announced that the Technical Secretariat had 'achieved 50–50 gender balance in the 10 top management structure positions of the Secretariat'.[2]

In August, the Secretariat released the 2019 versions of the Handbook on Chemicals and Online Scheduled Chemicals Database, with each now including those scheduled chemicals newly declared and those registered by the Chemical Abstracts Service between 2014 and 2017.[3] The director-general informed the CSP that the new Electronic Declarations Information System, which will make the preparation and submission of electronic declarations (including declarations on riot control agents) more efficient, 'will be released before the end of 2019'.[4]

OPCW developments

Throughout 2019, work related to responding to allegations of use of chemical weapons continued to dominate the agenda of the OPCW Technical Secretariat. A particular focus was implementing the decision adopted by states parties at the June 2018 Special Session, C-SS-4/DEC.3 (the June

---

[1] For a summary and other details of the Convention on the Prohibition of the Development, Production, Stockpiling and Use of Chemical Weapons and on their Destruction (Chemical Weapons Convention, CWC), see annex A, section I, in this volume.

[2] OPCW Conference of the States Parties (CSP), 'Opening Statement by the Director-General to the Conference of the States Parties at its Twenty-fourth Session (full version)', C-24/DG.21, 25 Nov. 2019, para. 137.

[3] OPCW, *Handbook on Chemicals*, 2019 (OPCW: The Hague, 2019).

[4] OPCW CSP, C-24/DG.21 (note 2), para. 57.

decision).[5] The continued divisions among states parties over this decision placed high levels of institutional stress on the OPCW. This played out in Executive Council meetings and at the main conference of the year, the 24th Session of the Conference of States Parties.

Implementing the June decision

During 2019, the OPCW Executive Council received four progress reports on the activities of the Investigation and Identification Team (IIT): two from the director-general on the status of implementation as of March and September, and two from the Technical Secretariat on the work of the IIT as at June and October.[6] The first report from the IIT itself is expected in early 2020.

At the 90th Session of the Executive Council in March, the director-general informed states parties that the recruitment process for the members of the team was under way and that the IIT would become 'fully operational in the coming weeks'.[7] A stated goal of the Secretariat was to build sustainable capabilities within the IIT, and so a key activity during the post-recruitment period would be to establish 'training to further build investigative capabilities in areas such as crime scene management, witness interviews, evidence collection, and forensics'.[8]

The June progress report concentrated on IIT working methods and personnel.[9] The recruitment process for IIT personnel and support staff, in which due regard was had to both gender balance and representation of all geographical regions, hired a number of 'experienced investigators and analysts with relevant qualifications and experience in complex investigations, analysis and forensics, as well as an expert in information systems, an administrative assistant, and a legal adviser'.[10] On the basis of 'a preliminary assessment of relevant incidents', the IIT was focusing its work on nine incidents: Al-Tamanah, 12 April 2014; Kafr-Zita, 18 April 2014; Al-Tamanah, 18 April 2014; Marea, 1 September 2015; Ltamenah, 24 March 2017; Ltamenah, 25 March 2017; Ltamenah, 30 March 2017; Saraqib,

[5] OPCW CSP, Fourth Special Session of the Conference of the States Parties, 'Addressing the threat from chemical weapons use', Decision, C-SS-4/DEC.3, 27 June 2018; and OPCW CSP, 'Report of the Fourth Special Session of the Conference of the States Parties', C-SS-4/3, 27 June 2018, para. 3.15.

[6] OPCW Executive Council, 'Progress in the implementation of Decision C-SS-4/Dec.3 on addressing the threat from chemical weapons', Report by the Director-General, EC-90/DG.14, 7 Mar. 2019; OPCW Executive Council, 'Work of the Investigation and Implementation Team established by C-SS-4/Dec.3 (dated 27 June 2018)', Note by the Technical Secretariat, EC-91/S/3, 28 June 2019; OPCW Executive Council, 'Progress in the implementation of Decision C-SS-4/Dec.3 on addressing the threat from chemical weapons', Report by the Director-General, EC-92/DG.26, 27 Sep. 2019; and OPCW Executive Council, 'Work of the Investigation and Implementation Team established by C-SS-4/Dec.3 (dated 27 June 2018)', Note by the Technical Secretariat, EC-92/S/8, 3 Oct. 2019.

[7] OPCW Executive Council, 'Opening statement by the Director-General to the Ninetieth Session of the Executive Council', Note by the Director-General, EC-90/DG.16, 12 Mar. 2019, para. 11.

[8] OPCW Executive Council, EC-90/DG.14 (note 6), para. 14.

[9] OPCW Executive Council, EC-91/S/3 (note 6), annex 1.

[10] OPCW Executive Council, EC-91/S/3 (note 6), annex 1.

4 February 2018; and Douma, 7 April 2018.[11] The report noted that the IIT was 'in the process' of establishing contact with member states and other actors, including at the regional and local levels, 'to gather information and conduct investigations and analysis, as it considers necessary and appropriate'.[12]

By the 92nd Session of the Executive Council in October 2019, the €1.3 million voluntary funding requirements specified in the 2019 budget as being needed to support the IIT had been met.[13] The Technical Secretariat's October report informed the Executive Council that the IIT had 'further developed internal work practices', especially in regard to 'information management, investigations and evidence collection, documentation, and chain of custody'.[14] Specific practices include that access to information within the IIT is on a 'need-to-know basis'; that the IIT's information management system and its file storage system can be accessed only through designated terminals which are 'air-gapped' (i.e. physically isolated from unsecured networks); that chain of custody is properly ensured through its registry procedures; and that, to prevent records from being deleted or lost, 'only pre-authorised IIT personnel are able to delete records' and there are 'audit trails that cannot be modified or removed'.[15]

Continued dissatisfaction about the June decision

Despite this progress, a small number of states parties continued to regard the decision to establish the IIT as illegitimate. At the 91st Session of the Executive Council in July 2019—some months after the IIT began operating—Russia re-stated its position that the June decision 'is illegitimate and is a direct violation of the prerogatives of the United Nations Security Council, and reaches far beyond the framework of the Convention and the mandate of the Organisation'.[16] Iran also expressed its discontent, stating that the decision had 'diverted the Organisation from its very technical nature'.[17] Syria continued with its position that the decision lacked 'international legitimacy', ran 'contrary to the provisions of the Convention, and was adopted in a manner widely departing from the OPCW tradition of

---

[11] OPCW Executive Council, EC-91/S/3 (note 6), annex 2.

[12] OPCW Executive Council, EC-91/S/3 (note 6), para. 9.

[13] Contributions and pledges came from Australia, Canada, Denmark, Germany, New Zealand, Norway, Slovenia, Sweden, Switzerland, the United Kingdom and the European Union. See OPCW Executive Council, EC-92/DG.26 (note 6), para. 10.

[14] OPCW Executive Council, EC-92/S/8 (note 6), para. 8.

[15] OPCW Executive Council, EC-92/S/8 (note 6), paras 9, 11, 12 and 14.

[16] OPCW Executive Council, Russian Federation, 'Statement by HE Ambassador A. V. Shulgin, Permanent Representative of the Russian Federation to the OPCW, at the Ninety-First Session of the Executive Council', EC-91/NAT.44, 9 July 2019, p. 1.

[17] OPCW Executive Council, Islamic Republic of Iran, 'Statement by HE Ambassador Dr Alireza Kazemi Abadi, Permanent Representative of the Islamic Republic of Iran, to the OPCW at the Ninety-First Session of the Executive Council', EC-91/NAT.27, 10 July 2019, p. 3.

consensus, which is the keystone for all its decisions'.[18] As a consequence of Syria's position, on 23 April 2019 the deputy minister of foreign affairs of the Syrian Arab Republic, Faisal Mekdad, informed the director-general through note verbale that 'the Syrian Arab Republic would not issue a visa to the Coordinator of the IIT to visit Damascus'.[19] At the time of writing this remains the case.

Follow-up to the Fourth Review Conference

Expressing their deep regret that a Final Report was not adopted at the Fourth Review Conference, the Non-Aligned Movement of states parties and China, at the 90th Session of the Executive Council, issued a joint position paper proposing the establishment of an open-ended working group (OEWG) 'to identify those items contained in the Chairperson's Report of the Proceedings of the Fourth Review Conference on which consensus is achievable and to determine the prioritisation of implementation of the identified items'.[20] The nominated co-facilitators of the process were Ambassador Agustín Vásquez Gómez of El Salvador, who had been chair of the Fourth Review Conference, and Ambassador I Gusti Agung Wesaka Puja of Indonesia, who had been the chair of the OEWG for the preparation of the Fourth Review Conference.

At the 91st session of the Executive Council in July, co-facilitators Gómez and Puja reported that they had held six rounds of consultation: in March; on 21 and 28 June; and on 3, 5 and 8 July.[21] During the June consultations, states parties exchanged views on a Secretariat non-paper entitled 'Ensuring Diverse and Qualified Workforce of the Technical Secretariat', which contained a number of proposals about the future of the Secretariat. This discussion resulted in a proposal to establish an OEWG on the topics contained within the non-paper.[22] A revised version of this proposal was issued in July but did not enjoy consensus primarily due to disagreement about identifying topics for the OEWG to consider.[23] Although the co-facilitators noted a continued 'absence of viable common ground' on the proposal to establish an OEWG, they observed that there is a 'strong sense that the current facilitations could

---

[18] OPCW Executive Council, Syrian Arab Republic, 'Statement by HE Ambassador Bassam Sabbagh, Permanent Representative of the Syrian Arab Republic, to the OPCW at the Ninety-First Session of the Executive Council', EC-91/NAT.41, 10 July 2019, p. 1.

[19] OPCW Executive Council, EC-91/DG.14 (note 8), para. 15.

[20] OPCW Executive Council, 'Joint position paper by the member states of the non-aligned movement that are states parties to the Chemical Weapons Convention and China: A follow up to the Fourth Special Session of the Conference of the States Parties to review the operation of the Chemical Weapons Convention', EC-90/Nat.4, 7 Mar. 2019, para. 1.

[21] OPCW Executive Council, 'Report by HE Ambassador Agustín Vásquez Gómez and HE Ambassador I Gusti Agung Wesaka Puja, co-facilitators nominated by the Ninetieth Session of the Executive Council', EC-91/WP.1, 10 July 2019, paras 5–12.

[22] OPCW Executive Council, EC-91/WP.1 (note 21), paras 9 and 10.

[23] OPCW Executive Council, EC-91/WP.1 (note 21), para. 11.

Table 12.1. Voting record for the adoption of the Draft Programme and Budget of the OPCW for 2020, 92nd session 11 Oct. 2019

Voting record	State
For the decision (30 votes)	Argentina, Brazil, Bulgaria, Cameroon, Canada, Chile, Czech Republic, Denmark, France, Germany, Ghana, Guatemala, Indonesia, Italy, Japan, Malta, Mexico, Morocco, the Netherlands, Nigeria, Panama, Peru, Portugal, Republic of Korea, Romania, Saudi Arabia, Senegal, Ukraine, United Kingdom, United States
Against the decision (3 votes)	China, Iran, Russia
Abstentions (8 votes)	Algeria, Bangladesh, India, Iraq, Kenya, Pakistan, South Africa, Sudan

Source: OPCW Executive Council, 'Report of the Ninety-Second Session of the Executive Council', EC-92/5, 11 Oct. 2019, para. 11.19.

benefit from a revitalising impulse'.[24] The Executive Council requested that the co-facilitators continue their work.[25]

Reporting to the 92nd Session of the Executive Council in October, co-facilitators Gómez and Puja noted that their proposed structure for further deliberations was reflected in 'the Chair's non-paper on the revitalisation of the facilitation framework, enhancing coordination and addressing issues on which progress is sought by States Parties in a non-discriminatory and effective manner'.[26] Reactions to their proposal were mixed, leading the co-facilitators to conclude that although their proposal had 'come as close to the "golden middle ground" as is possible', the divergent approaches among states could not be ignored.[27] They reported that they felt 'the need to take a realistic approach and leave it to others to take over from now on',[28] and that 'The OPCW cannot freeze in the past, it needs to evolve with times and adapt to the changing external environment. We need to make sure that our working methods adequately reflect this evolution and changes.'[29]

The chair of the Executive Council requested that co-facilitators Gómez and Puja 'make an extra and final effort for a period of one month' to conduct additional consultations to find a proposal which enjoyed consensus.[30] The

---

[24] OPCW Executive Council, EC-91/WP.1 (note 21), paras 12 and 13.
[25] OPCW Executive Council, 'Report by HE Ambassador Agustín Vásquez Gómez and HE Ambassador I Gusti Agung Wesaka Puja, co-facilitators nominated by the Ninetieth Session of the Executive Council', EC-92/WP.1, 9 Oct. 2019, para. 3.
[26] OPCW Executive Council, EC-92/WP.1 (note 25), para. 3.
[27] OPCW Executive Council, EC-92/WP.1 (note 25), para. 7.
[28] OPCW Executive Council, EC-92/WP.1 (note 25), para. 9.
[29] OPCW Executive Council, EC-92/WP.1 (note 25), para. 11.
[30] OPCW Executive Council, 'Report of the Ninety-Second Session of the Executive Council', EC-92/5, 11 Oct. 2019, para. 5.3.

co-facilitators circulated a further proposal on 12 November 2019, which was welcomed by some states parties at the 24th Session of the CSP.[31]

Build-up to the 24th Session of the Conference of States Parties

At the 92nd Session of the Executive Council held on 8–11 October, states parties considered a number of matters, including the Draft Programme and Budget for 2020 and 'key strategic financing proposals' to 'bolster the Organisation's programmatic and financial strength and address the issue of future programme and budgets at zero real growth', such as transitioning from an annual to biennial programme and budget cycle.[32]

The publicly available national statements from the 92nd Session indicate division among the states parties along similar lines drawn in 2018 with regard to allocating budget towards implementation of the IIT according to the June decision.[33] Russia, for example, found the idea of an 'omnibus decision bundle' to be particularly objectionable.[34] The representative of the United States described those countries objecting to the omnibus format as 'attempting to hold the 2020 budget hostage'.[35] According to the report of the 92nd Session, a vote to adopt the Draft Programme and Budget resulted in 30 in favour, 3 against and 8 abstentions (table 12.1). The result meant that the Executive Council adopted the Draft Programme and Budget and transmitted it to the CSP with a recommendation for approval.[36]

The 24th Session of the Conference of the States Parties

The 24th Session of the CSP was held between 25 and 29 November 2019 with Ambassador Krassimir Kostov of Bulgaria as chair. As well as considering the proposals to amend the CWC Schedules, the CSP was tasked, among other things, with making decisions on matters related to the Programme and

---

[31] See e.g. OPCW CSP, Azerbaijan, 'Statement on behalf of the members of the non-aligned movement that are states parties to the Chemical Weapons Convention and China, delivered by HE Ambassador Jafar Huseynzada, Acting Director of the Department for Political-Military Affairs, Ministry of Foreign Affairs of the Republic of Azerbaijan, at the Twenty-Fourth Session of the Conference of States Parties', C-24/Nat.7, 25 Nov. 2019, p. 2; and OPCW CSP, Finland, 'Statement of the European Union, delivered by HE Ambassador Mika-Markus Leinonen, EU Liaison Officer to The Hague, at the Twenty-fourth Session of the Conference of States Parties', C-24/NAT.48, 25 Nov. 2019, p. 3.

[32] OPCW Executive Council, 'Opening statement by the Director-General to the Ninety-second Session of the Executive Council (full version)', EC-92/DG.34, 8 Oct. 2019, para. 4.

[33] See e.g. OPCW Executive Council, Iran, 'Statement by HE Ambassador Dr Alireza Kazemi Abadi, Permanent Representative of the Islamic Republic of Iran, to the OPCW at the Ninety-second Session of the Executive Council', EC-92/Nat.9, 8 Oct. 2019, p. 3.

[34] OPCW Executive Council, Russian Federation, 'Statement by HE Ambassador A. V. Shulgin, Permanent Representative of the Russian Federation, to the OPCW at the Ninety-second Session of the Executive Council', EC-92/Nat.26, 8 Oct. 2019, pp. 2–3.

[35] OPCW Executive Council, United States, 'Statement by HE Ambassador Kenneth D. Ward, Permanent Representative of the United States of America, to the OPCW at the Ninety-second Session of the Executive Council', EC-92/Nat.13, 8 Oct. 2019, p. 2.

[36] OPCW Executive Council, EC-92/5 (note 30), para. 11.19.

Table 12.2. Voting record for the adoption of the Draft Programme and Budget of the OPCW for 2020, 24th session, 29 Nov. 2019

Voting record	State
For the decision (106 votes)	Afghanistan, Albania, Andorra, Argentina, Australia, Austria, Azerbaijan, Bahrain, Bangladesh, Belgium, Benin, Bhutan, Bosnia and Herzegovina, Botswana, Brazil, Brunei Darussalam, Bulgaria, Cameroon, Canada, Chile, Colombia, Costa Rica, Côte d'Ivoire, Croatia, Cyprus, Czech Republic, Denmark, Ecuador, El Salvador, Estonia, Eswatini, Fiji, Finland, France, Georgia, Germany, Ghana, Greece, Guatemala, Guyana, Holy See, Honduras, Hungary, Iceland, Indonesia, Ireland, Italy, Jamaica, Japan, Kuwait, Latvia, Liberia, Liechtenstein, Lithuania, Luxembourg, Malawi, Malaysia, Maldives, Malta, Mauritius, Mexico, Monaco, Montenegro, Morocco, Namibia, the Netherlands, New Zealand, Nigeria, North Macedonia, Norway, Oman, Panama, Paraguay, Peru, the Philippines, Poland, Portugal, Qatar, Republic of Korea, Republic of Moldova, Romania, Saint Lucia, Saint Vincent and the Grenadines, San Marino, Saudi Arabia, Senegal, Singapore, Slovakia, Slovenia, Solomon Islands, South Africa, Spain, Sweden, Switzerland, Thailand, Togo, Tunisia, Turkey, Ukraine, United Arab Emirates, United Kingdom, United States, Uruguay, Vanuatu, Viet Nam, Zambia
Against the decision (19 votes)	Armenia, Belarus, China, Cuba, Iran, Kazakhstan, Kyrgyzstan, Laos, Mongolia, Myanmar, Nicaragua, Palestine, Russia, Sudan, Syrian Arab Republic, Tajikistan, Uzbekistan, Venezuela, Zimbabwe
Abstentions (17 votes)	Algeria, Angola, Bolivia, Burkina Faso, Cambodia, Ethiopia, India, Iraq, Jordan, Kenya, Lebanon, Mozambique, Nepal, Pakistan, Rwanda, Sri Lanka, Uganda

Source: OPCW Conference of States Parties, 'Report of the Twenty-Fourth Session of the Conference of States Parties, 25–29 November 2019', C-24/5, 29 Nov. 2019, para. 14.4.

Budget of the OPCW for 2020, on which no consensus had been reached in the Executive Council.

Two months before the session, on 24 September 2019 Russia submitted a modification to its proposal to change Schedule 1 (see section II in this chapter), by dropping group 5 from the proposal.[37] This modification paved the way for many states parties at the 24th Session to express support in their national statements for the adoption, by consensus, of both the Canada–Netherlands–USA proposed change and the Russian modified proposal. The CSP considered both proposals together under agenda item 10 and adopted

---

[37] OPCW CSP, 'Report of the Twenty-Fourth Session of the Conference of States Parties, 25–29 November 2019', C-24/5, 29 Nov. 2019, para. 10.2.

them in parallel and by consensus.[38] This resulted in 'a spontaneous round of applause'.[39] In his response to the adoption of these changes to the CWC schedules, the director-general informed states parties that the Secretariat would issue a note before the end of the year to provide guidance regarding the implementation of the decisions.[40]

The moment of consensus among states parties quickly gave way to discord. By way of an explanation for the lack of consensus in the Executive Council on the Programme and Budget of Work for 2020 (agenda item 14), Ambassador Alexander Shulgin of the Russian Federation suggested there had been 'dogged attempts to push through not only the regular budget but also other provisions which have nothing to do with the objectives set forth in the CWC'.[41] Echoing Russia's dissatisfaction with the omnibus format, China outlined its concerns with 'the format and content' and also suggested that 'a couple of countries' had 'forcefully pushed' the draft decision to a vote and 'rushed' to submit it to the CSP.[42] Russia and China also raised the funding required to implement the June decision, which they opposed.

Taking the floor immediately after their interventions, Ambassador Kenneth Ward of the United States said that the objections of Russia and China were 'a refusal on their part to support the implementation by the Technical Secretariat of a valid decision' and requested a roll-call vote.[43] After a 24-hour delay, as required by the Rules of Procedures, voting to adopt the OPCW Draft Programme and Budget for 2020 took place. The result was 106 in favour, 19 against and 17 abstentions (table 12.2).[44] The votes fulfilled the requirement of two-thirds of the states parties present and voting in favour to adopt the budget.

Eleven delegations (Algeria, China, Cuba, India, Iran, Pakistan, Malaysia, Russia, South Africa, Syria and Venezuela) took the floor to explain their vote.[45] The predominant themes in these explanations were 'a call for consensus and a questioning of the legitimacy' of the June decision.[46]

---

[38] See OPCW CSP, 'Technical change to Schedule 1(a) of the Annex on Chemicals to the Chemical Weapons Convention', Decision, C-24/Dec.4, 27 Nov. 2019; and OPCW CSP, 'Changes to Schedule 1 of the Annex on Chemicals to the Chemical Weapons Convention', Decision, C-24/Dec.5, 27 Nov 2019.

[39] Guthrie, R., *'Conclusion of the general debate and the Schedule amendment decision(s)'*, Report of the Twenty-Fourth Session of the Conference of the States Parties, CWC-CSP-24 Report no. 4, 28 Nov. 2019, p. 1.

[40] OPCW CSP, 'Statement by the Director-General in response to the adoption of two decisions under Article XV of the Chemical Weapons Convention to amend the Annex on Chemicals', C-24/DG.20, 27 Nov. 2019, para. 7.

[41] OPCW, Webcast CSP-24, 'Day 3—Afternoon', 1:06:17–1:14.49.

[42] OPCW, Webcast CSP-24 (note 41), 1:14:55–1:20:38.

[43] OPCW, Webcast CSP-24 (note 41), 1:20:44–1:23:57.

[44] OPCW CSP, C-24/5 (note 37), para. 14.4.

[45] OPCW CSP, C-24/5 (note 37), para. 14.5.

[46] Guthrie, R., *'CW destruction, attribution, a vote on the budget and EC membership'*, Report of the Twenty-Fourth Session of the Conference of the States Parties, CWC-CSP-24 Report no. 5, 29 Nov. 2019, p. 2.

A joint statement issued by 45 states parties during the CSP noted that the accreditation of some non-governmental organizations (NGOs) to that meeting had been blocked.[47] Some states had expressed their concern about this in advance of the CSP, especially their concern in relation to those NGOs who had previously been approved.[48] In responding to the joint statement, Russia expressed its concern about particular NGOs 'bringing in unjustified politicisation to what is primarily technical activity', making particular reference to the Syrian Civil Defence and White Helmets.[49] In the same statement, Russia confirmed its full support for the participation of civil society in the work of the main body of the OPCW, describing their participation as 'an imperative'.

Other developments in 2019

The destruction of chemical weapons

As of 31 October 2019, 97.3 per cent of declared Category 1 chemical weapons (CWs) had been destroyed under international verification.[50] The USA remains the only declared possessor state party with CWs yet to be destroyed. In April 2019, the OPCW director-general and chair of the Executive Council, together with a delegation of Executive Council members, visited the Pueblo Chemical Agent-Destruction Pilot Plant (PCAPP) in Colorado and also held meetings in Washington, DC.[51] As well as engaging with officials, the delegation met with the Colorado Citizens Advisory Commission. The chair reported to the Executive Council that the delegation was 'confident' that the United States could complete its remaining destruction activities 'within the current timelines'.[52] During a detailed presentation on the status of the chemical demilitarization programme at the 24th Session of the CSP, the USA affirmed its commitment to destroy its CWs as quickly as practicable and that it was on track to meet the planned completion date, noting that to

---

[47] OPCW CSP, 'Joint statement concerning accreditation of non-governmental organisations for the Twenty-fourth Session of the Conference of the States Parties', C-24/NAT.26, 25 Nov. 2019.

[48] See e.g. OPCW Executive Council, Australia, 'Statement by Michelle McKendry, Deputy Permanent Representative of Australia to the OPCW at the Ninety-second Session of the Executive Council', EC-92/NAT.20, 8 Oct. 2019, p. 2.

[49] OPCW CSP, Russia, 'Statement by HE Ambassador A. V. Shulgin, Deputy Head of the Delegation of the Russian Federation, Permanent Representative of the Russian Federation to the OPCW at the Twenty-fourth Session of the Conference of the States Parties, in response to a statement by a group of countries on NGO participation', C-24/Nat.39, 25 Nov. 2019.

[50] OPCW, CSP, 'Opening statement by the Director-General to the Conference of States Parties at its Twenty-fourth Session', C24/DG.19, 25 Nov. 2019, para. 33.

[51] OPCW, 'OPCW Executive Council and Director-General visit the United States', Press release, 15 Apr. 2019.

[52] OPCW Executive Council, 'Visit by the Chairperson of the Executive Council, the Director-General and representatives of the Executive Council to the Pueblo chemical agent-destruction pilot plant, Colorado, United States of America, 6–11 April 2019', EC-91/2, 14 June 2019, para. 66.

date it had safely destroyed more than 93.26 per cent of its CW stockpiles at a cost of $31.6 billion.[53]

Destruction of CWs abandoned by Japan on Chinese territory continued in 2019. In September, the director-general, the chair and representatives of the Executive Council visited the Haerbaling Abandoned Chemical Weapons Destruction Site 'to better understand the technical and administrative issues associated with recovery identification and destruction' of the abandoned CWs.[54]

During 2019, the Secretariat conducted twelve related inspections in China, as well as eight inspections of old CWs in seven states parties (Belgium, France, Germany, Italy, Japan, the Netherlands and the UK).[55]

The Centre for Chemistry and Technology

Work continues on the Centre for Chemistry and Technology project, for which the principal objective is to provide increased and enhanced space and capabilities for the OPCW Laboratory, Equipment Store and training facilities, currently in Rijswijk.[56] The latest publicly available report on the project noted that the design tender was planned for completion in the fourth quarter of 2019 and that the purchase agreement for the plot was expected to be concluded by the end of December 2019.[57] The land purchase agreement and deed of transfer were signed on 19 December, as planned, and work on the design of the building was scheduled to begin in January 2020.[58] As of December 2019, 28 countries and the European Union had made or pledged financial contributions to the project.[59] At the 24th Session of the CSP, the director-general renewed his appeal to all states parties to 'pledge financial support for this project, regardless of the amount'.[60]

The OPCW Scientific Advisory Board

In 2019 the OPCW Scientific Advisory Board (SAB) produced four reports and continued its 'Science for Diplomats' initiative. Included in the report of the 28th Session of the SAB was a recommendation that the appointment

---

[53] OPCW, Webcast CSP-24, 'Day 4—Morning', 2:10–15:07.

[54] OPCW, 'Executive Council and Director-General review progress on destruction of abandoned chemical weapons in China', Press release, 9 Sep. 2019.

[55] OPCW CSP, C-24/DG.21 (note 2), paras 36 and 38.

[56] OPCW Technical Secretariat, 'Progress in the project to upgrade the OPCW Laboratory and Equipment Store to a Centre for Chemistry and Technology', Note by the Technical Secretariat, S/1769/2019, 9 July 2019, para. 3.

[57] OPCW Technical Secretariat, S/1769/2019 (note 56), paras 128–29.

[58] OPCW, 'OPCW and municipality of Pijnacker-Nootdorp sign location agreement for new Centre for Chemistry and Technology', Press release, 19 Dec. 2019.

[59] The 28 countries are Bangladesh, Belgium, Canada, Chile, China, Czech Republic, Estonia, Finland, France, Hungary, Ireland, Italy, Japan, Kazakhstan, Luxembourg, the Netherlands, New Zealand, Pakistan, Poland, Portugal, Republic of Korea, Slovakia, Slovenia, Spain, Turkey, UK, United Arab Emirates and USA. See OPCW, Press release, 19 Dec. 2019 (note 58).

[60] OPCW CSP, C-24/DG.21 (note 2), para. 30.

of a forensic adviser with broad experience in forensic science and international law be considered to provide advice to the director-general and the OPCW.[61] In his reply to the report, the director-general said that the Secretariat 'is exploring the modalities of how such an advisory role might be operationalised'.[62] More recommendations can be expected in the Final Report of the Temporary Working Group (TWG) on Investigative Science and Technology. This TWG considered a range of new technologies relevant to CW investigations, including geospatial verification of weapons of mass destruction (WMD), crowdsourcing WMD verification, remote verification techniques, robotics and artificial intelligence support to investigations in hazardous environments, forensic biometrics in conflict zones, forensic big data analysis, and a generic integrated forensic toolbox.[63] The TWG held its final meeting in Helsinki in November 2019 and its Final Report is due before its mandate ends in February 2020. At the time of writing, this report has not appeared on the public website of the OPCW.

SAB members maintained their engagement with the Biological Weapons Convention[64] community by sharing relevant experiences about the provision of scientific advice to disarmament decision makers and the development of The Hague Ethical Guidelines.[65] The practice of increasing the visibility of the work of the SAB with the scientific community also continued. Two pieces of SAB advice, co-authored by all members, on medical care and treatment of injuries from nerve agents were published in peer-reviewed journals in 2019, alongside other peer-reviewed publications, including papers on investigative science and technology and on the role of green and sustainable chemistry in disarmament.[66]

[61] OPCW Scientific Advisory Board (SAB), 'Report of the Scientific Advisory Board at its Twenty-Eighth Session, 10–14 June 2019', SAB-28/1, 14 June 2019, para. 1.3(a).

[62] OPCW Executive Council, 'Response to the report of the Twenty-Eighth Session of the Scientific Advisory Board, 10–14 June 2019', Note by the Director-General, EC-92/DG.12, 9 Sep. 2019, para 10(a).

[63] OPCW SAB, 'Summary of the Third Meeting of the Scientific Advisory Board Temporary Working Group on Investigative Science and Technology', SAB-28/WP.3, 4 June 2019, paras 8.1–8.18.

[64] For a summary and other details of the Convention on the 1972 Prohibition of the Development, Production and Stockpiling of Bacteriological (Biological) and Toxin Weapons and on their Destruction (Biological Weapons Convention, BWC), see annex A, section I, in this volume.

[65] See Biological Weapons Convention, 2019 BWC Meeting of Experts, 'Provisional agenda for the 2019 Meeting of Experts on review of developments in the field of science and technology related to the Convention', BWC/MSP/2019/MX.2/1, 21 May 2019, agenda items 6 and 7; and OPCW, 'Statement by the OPCW at the 2019 Meeting of States Parties to the Biological and Toxins Weapons Convention', 4 Dec. 2019.

[66] See Timperley, C. et al., 'Advice on assistance and protection provided by the Scientific Advisory Board of the Organisation for the Prohibition of Chemical Weapons: Part 1. On medical care and treatment of injuries from nerve agents', *Toxicology*, vol. 415 (Mar. 2019); Timperley, C. et al., 'Advice on assistance and protection by the Scientific Advisory Board of the Organisation for the Prohibition of Chemical Weapons: Part 2. On preventing and treating health effects from acute, prolonged, and repeated nerve agent exposure, and the identification of medical countermeasures able to reduce or eliminate the longer term health effects of nerve agents', *Toxicology*, vol. 413 (Feb. 2019); Borrett, V. et al., 'Investigative science and technology supporting the Organization for the Prohibition of Chemical Weapons (OPCW)', *Australian Journal of Forensic Sciences*, vol. 51, no. 6 (2019); and Forman, J. and

The terms of office for six SAB members ended in 2019, including that of the chair of the SAB, Dr Cheng Tang, and chair of the TWG on Investigative Science and Technology, Dr Veronica Borrett. In addition, at the end of 2019 the OPCW's Science Policy Adviser, Jonathan Forman, left as required by the OPCW tenure policy. New SAB members began their terms on 1 January 2020, with a new Science Policy Adviser joining later in 2020.

The Advisory Board on Education and Outreach

During 2019, the Advisory Board on Education and Outreach (ABEO) convened twice—from 26 to 28 February and from 20 to 22 August—and welcomed eight new members from Argentina, Australia, Guatemala, India, Japan, Kazakhstan, Malaysia and Pakistan. At its session in August, ABEO members elected Dr Jo Husbands and Dr Adriana Bernacchi as chair and vice-chair, respectively, for 2020.

To facilitate its work, the ABEO established four intersessional working groups to undertake several projects, including an exploration of using the history of CW use as a possible educational tool and preparation of new education and outreach (E&O) material.[67] During the Eighth Session of the ABEO, the director-general expressed his support for its initiative on e-learning, noting 'the Organisation's need to strengthen its E&O capacity online' and that 'an enhanced e-learning offering will increase the ability to engage with a broader spectrum of audiences, particularly younger generations, to better prepare key stakeholders for the more traditional training formats the Secretariat offers'.[68]

To that end, the development of online courses and a MOOC (massive open online course) are e-learning priorities for the ABEO during 2020 and 2021.[69]

OPCW–The Hague Award

On 20 November 2019 the OPCW–The Hague Award Committee announced its decision to honour Dr Robert Mikulak, Dr Tang and the International Union of Pure and Applied Chemistry as the joint recipients of the 2019 OPCW–The Hague Award. On 25 November, the first day of the 24th Session of the CSP, each award recipient received a medal, a certificate of recognition and a share of the €90,000 prize.

Timperley, C., 'Is there a role for green and sustainable chemistry in chemical disarmament and nonproliferation?' *Current Opinion in Green and Sustainable Chemistry*, vol. 15 (Feb. 2019).

[67] OPCW Advisory Board on Education and Outreach (ABEO), 'Report of the Seventh Session of the Advisory Board on Education and Outreach', ABEO-7/1, 28 Feb. 2019, para. 8.6.

[68] OPCW ABEO, 'Report of the Eighth Session of the Advisory Board on Education and Outreach', ABEO-8/1, 22 Aug. 2019, para. 3.2.

[69] OPCW ABEO (note 68), annex 2.

Central nervous system acting chemicals

There have been ongoing discussions within the OPCW, dating back to the First Review Conference in 2003, about the possible use for law enforcement purposes of aerosolized opioids (such as fentanyl or homologues) or other chemicals that act on the central nervous system (CNS), some of which have been previously but inaccurately referred to as 'incapacitants'. The SAB has also considered scientific aspects of CNS-acting chemicals in a comprehensive manner.[70]

During the 24th Session of the CSP, the general debate included numerous statements supporting Australian, Swiss and US efforts to prepare a draft decision that would result in a statement declaring that aerosolized use of CNS-acting chemicals was inconsistent with law enforcement purposes as a 'purpose not prohibited' under the CWC.[71] There was also a well-attended side-event co-hosted by Australia, Switzerland and the USA on this issue.

Activities in cooperation with other international agencies

The OPCW continued its partnership with other international organizations in areas of common interest and benefit, including by serving as a vice-chair of the UN Working Group on Emerging Threats and Critical Infrastructure Protection, along with the United Nations Office for Disarmament Affairs (UNODA) and the United Nations Interregional Crime and Justice Research Institute. The United Nations Office for the Coordination of Humanitarian Affairs, the World Health Organization, INTERPOL and the Biological Weapons Convention Implementation Support Unit jointly developed a proposal for the next phase of a project to enhance inter-agency interoperability and public communications in the event of a chemical or biological attack. The proposal is pending acceptance by the UN Office of Counter-Terrorism.[72] On 16 October the Technical Secretariat and the Polish Ministry of Foreign Affairs co-organized a presentation entitled 'Addressing the challenge posed by chemical terrorism: OPCW capacity building for states parties' in the margins of the UN General Assembly First Committee. The presentation highlighted the successful outcomes of the Critical Incident Preparedness for Hospitals (HOSPREP) programme in Bangladesh which had been held in July.[73]

---

[70] OPCW SAB, 'Central nervous system acting chemicals—considerations from the OPCW Scientific Advisory Board', Conference of States Parties (CSP-22), 28 Nov. 2017.

[71] See Guthrie, R., 'Conclusion of the general debate and the Schedule amendment decision(s)', CBW Events–CWC Reports, CSP-24 Report no. 4, 28 Nov. 2019, p. 2.

[72] OPCW CSP, C-24/DG.21 (note 2), para. 76.

[73] OPCW, 'OPCW programmes for addressing chemical terrorism showcased at UN General Assembly side-event', Press release, 21 Oct. 2019.

The United Nations agenda for disarmament and chemical weapons

Action 9 of the UN agenda for disarmament concerns restoring respect for the global norm against chemical weapons.[74] The objectives of this action are to provide the UN Security Council 'with food for thought on how it can fulfill its responsibilities' and to undertake 'a lessons-learned process on the OPCW–United Nations Joint Investigative Mechanism'.[75] Over the course of 2019, the UNODA web page for Action 9 listed Canada and France as 'champions' of this item, and the European Union, Sweden and Finland as 'supporters'.[76] The live implementation plan on this page showed, at the time of writing, that the first two activities—funding and scoping the issues to be examined by the lessons-learned process, and recruiting a new staff member to carry out the substantive and administrative tasks related to implementing the lessons-learned process—had been 'completed'. The third activity— convening four workshops to take place in 2019—was, at the time of writing, 'in progress'; while the final activity (a report) was 'not yet initiated'.[77]

Related and relevant areas proposed in the UN agenda for disarmament include encouraging responsible innovation of science and technology (Action 28), supported by India, and societal engagement (Action 39), including identifying applicable models for access and engagement (step 1).[78] On the latter issue, the agenda notes: 'Disarmament initiatives have been most successful when they involve effective partnerships between Governments, the expert community and civil society.'[79]

---

[74] United Nations Office for Disarmament Affairs (UNODA), *Securing Our Common Future: An Agenda for Disarmament* (UNODA: New York, 2018), p. 25.

[75] UNODA, 'Ensuring respect for norms against chemical and biological weapons', Objectives.

[76] UNODA (note 75), Change Log.

[77] UNODA (note 75), 'Steps and activities' and Change Log.

[78] UNODA, 'Encouraging responsible innovation and application of new technologies'; and UNODA, 'Enhancing participation by civil society and engagement by the private sector', Action 39 and 'Steps and activities'.

[79] UNODA, *Securing Our Common Future* (note 74), p. xi.

IV. Biological weapon disarmament and non-proliferation

FILIPPA LENTZOS

The principal legal instrument against biological warfare is the 1972 Biological and Toxin Weapons Convention (BWC).[1] In 2019, the United Republic of Tanzania ratified the convention, becoming the 183rd state party.[2] A further 4 states have signed but not ratified the convention, and 10 states have neither signed nor ratified the convention.[3]

Key biological disarmament and non-proliferation activities in 2019 were carried out in connection with the second set of 2018–20 BWC intersessional Meetings of Experts (MXs), the First Committee of the United Nations General Assembly and the BWC Meeting of States Parties (MSP). One of the developing trends in the field is the rise of civil society as a major contributor to shaping global dialogues around biological threats and appropriate responses to them.

The 2019 Meetings of Experts

The second set of the five 2018–20 BWC intersessional MXs took place from 29 July to 8 August 2019.[4] MX1 focused on cooperation and assistance; MX2 on science and technology; MX3 on national implementation; MX4 on assistance, response and preparedness; and MX5 on institutional strengthening—as agreed in 2017.[5] In advance of each MX, the BWC Implementation Support Unit (ISU) produced a general background document on the topic under consideration.[6] Since the 2018 chairs' papers providing reflections and proposals for possible outcomes after the 2018 MXs proved contentious, the MX chairs did not produce such papers for the 2019 meetings.

Meeting of Experts 1

MX1 met on 29–30 July 2019 and was chaired by Ambassador Victor Dolidze of Georgia. The purpose of the meeting was to discuss and promote common understanding and effective action on cooperation and assistance, with a particular focus on strengthening cooperation and assistance on peaceful

---

[1] For a summary and other details of the Convention on the Prohibition of the Development, Production and Stockpiling of Bacteriological (Biological) and Toxin Weapons and on their Destruction, see annex A, section I, in this volume.

[2] BWC, 'Report on universalization activities', BWC/MSP/2019/3, 8 Oct. 2019, para. 1.

[3] BWC, BWC/MSP/2019/3 (note 2), para. 1.

[4] For a discussion of the first set of meetings, see Lentzos, F., 'Biological weapon disarmament and non-proliferation', *SIPRI Yearbook 2019*, pp. 434–39.

[5] BWC, 'Report of the Meeting of States Parties', BWC/MSP/2017/6, 19 Dec. 2017, para. 19.

[6] For background documents, along with all working papers, technical briefing presentations, side event details and the joint NGO position paper, see BWC, '2019 Meetings of Experts (29 July–8 Aug. 2019)', Meetings and documents.

uses of the life sciences and associated technologies (Article X of the BWC).[7] States parties submitted six working papers (half the number submitted to the meeting in 2018). There was diverse input to the meeting, including two technical briefings presented by independent experts and a joint non-governmental organization (NGO) position paper submitted to all five MXs setting out a collective NGO view on key action points for the meetings. China and Russia hosted two side events.[8]

The meeting had seven substantive topics for discussion (agenda items 4–10).[9] Under the first, on consideration of national reports on Article X implementation, states parties emphasized the value of these reports, and discussed how to further encourage and facilitate voluntary reporting in order to raise the low number of reports submitted. Several states parties provided examples of their activities supporting the aims and objectives of Article X, and recipients of assistance reported on supported activities. Under the second topic, on the assistance and cooperation database established by the Seventh Review Conference and commonly known as the Article X database, states parties welcomed operational enhancements undertaken by the ISU and funded by Ireland, as well as the increased number of offers and requests listed, but highlighted that use of the database remains low. States parties discussed ways of mobilizing resources to support the database, along with measures to strengthen its operationalization.

States parties continued sharing views on challenges and obstacles to developing and deepening international cooperation between developed and developing countries (the third substantive topic). Under the fourth topic, they considered mobilizing resources, including financial resources, on a voluntary basis to address gaps and needs effectively, as well as the guidelines and procedures for that mobilization. Several states supported the idea of a potential voluntary trust fund to support cooperation and assistance activities. Some states also supported a new ISU post of Cooperation and Assistance Officer.

For the fifth topic, on education, training, exchange and twinning programmes, states parties considered existing international and regional platforms to support human resource development in the field of biological sciences. States parties also noted important leading events, and the numerous university-based programmes and technology exchanges involving scientists and academia among developing and developed states. States parties shared views, under the sixth topic, on promoting capacity building

---

[7] BWC, 'Report of the 2019 Meeting of Experts on cooperation and assistance, with a particular focus on strengthening cooperation and assistance under Article X', BWC/MSP/2019/MX.1/2, 26 Sep. 2019, para. 4.

[8] BWC, '2019 Meetings of Experts', [n.d.].

[9] BWC, BWC/MSP/2019/MX.1/2 (note 7), paras 16–24 and annex 1, paras 4–33.

through international cooperation and also considered best practices when implementing sustainable cooperation activities.

Under the final item, on collaboration with international organizations, states parties reiterated the merits of continued coordination and collaboration with international organizations and networks related to combating infectious disease, as a means of implementing Article X. The meeting also considered regional and subregional cooperation fora that can contribute to engaging international stakeholders on issues such as international preparedness or biosafety and biosecurity.

One commentator on MX1 noted that 'there was improved interactive discussion over the year before, which itself had been a great improvement on previous practice in this regard.'[10]

Meeting of Experts 2

MX2 met on 31 July and 2 August 2019 and was chaired by Yury Nikolaichik of Belarus. The purpose of the meeting was to discuss and promote common understanding and effective action on developments in the fields of science and technology related to the BWC.[11] States parties submitted seven working papers, compared with twelve in 2018. There were five technical briefings and eight side events—twice the number of side events in 2018.[12]

The meeting had four substantive topics for discussion (agenda items 4–7).[13] The first was a review of relevant science and technology developments. States parties highlighted rapid advances, particularly in synthetic biology, genome editing, gene drive techniques and metabolic engineering; considered examples of scientific research for possible dual-use application and technologies with the potential to reduce biological risks; and noted the growing 'do-it-yourself bio' community. States parties exchanged views on features of a systematic and structured science and technology review process; suggestions included incorporating a standing science and technology advisory function in the ISU and more regular sharing of information on relevant events and the work that international academics and states parties undertake.

Under the second topic, on biological risk assessment and management, states parties noted the difficulty of adequately anticipating future advances and assessing related risks and benefits; emphasized the need to further improve assessment methodologies; and discussed various approaches to risk assessment, with several states providing information about their existing

---

[10] Guthrie, R., 'Conclusion of MX1 and a look forward to MX2: Science and technology', MX Report no. 3, 31 July 2019, Daily Reports from BWC Meetings, BioWeapons Prevention Project, p. 1.

[11] BWC, 'Report of the 2019 Meeting of Experts on review of developments in the field of science and technology related to the Convention', BWC/MSP/2019/MX.2/2, 8 Oct. 2019, para. 4.

[12] BWC, '2019 Meetings of Experts' (note 8).

[13] BWC, BWC/MSP/2019/MX.2/2 (note 11), paras 16–20 and annex 1, paras 4–24.

practices. Other points raised included the challenges of assessing benefits and of addressing intangible aspects of technology in risk–benefit assessments and convergence with other technologies. States parties 'stressed the need for a holistic approach towards bio-risk assessment and management' that cuts 'across scientific disciplines and involve[s] stakeholders from a variety of backgrounds'.[14]

The development of a voluntary model code of conduct for biological scientists and all relevant personnel was the focus of the third topic. In the exchange of views, states parties noted that there was no code that could cover all contexts and that some states parties in favour of codes would prefer professional and learned societies to draft their own codes, rather than have the BWC impose a code. Several states parties and international organizations presented examples of codes of conduct and highlighted the benefits of these instruments. States parties also noted that they saw awareness-raising and education as complementary to codes and crucially important.

Under the last topic, on other science and technology developments of relevance, states parties noted in particular the convergence between cybertechnologies, artificial intelligence and biotechnologies, recognizing that 'convergence' can mean more than just overlap; for instance, some convergences between the biological and cyber spheres are 'game changers' that will impact upon the world both positively and negatively.[15] The states parties also noted the widespread availability and accessibility of new technologies and information, including intangible information, and stressed the need for closer collaboration among experts and between relevant international organizations.[16]

The MX2 discussion was generally interactive and detailed. At the start of the meeting the chair reordered the agenda items 'so that delegations could receive the freshest information about events in other platforms and about the potential trends that could be discussed in the BWC'.[17] This move, one commentator noted, 'was not without controversy'.[18] More substantively, MX2 demonstrated, 'broad agreement and much common ground on a need for effective review of scientific and technological developments, but divergences on what might be the best method. Most delegations expressed an interest in some form of new meeting format or dedicated body; a notable exception was Iran which expressed scepticism in relation to anything new.'[19]

---

[14] BWC, BWC/MSP/2019/MX.2/2 (note 11), annex 1, para. 13.

[15] Guthrie, R., 'MX2: Future developments, science advice and codes of conduct', MX Report no. 4, 2 Aug. 2019, Daily Reports from BWC Meetings, BioWeapons Prevention Project, p. 1.

[16] BWC, BWC/MSP/2019/MX.2/2 (note 11), annex 1, paras 21–22.

[17] Guthrie, MX Report no. 4 (note 15), p. 2.

[18] Guthrie, MX Report no. 4 (note 15), p. 1.

[19] Guthrie, R., 'The conclusion of MX2 and a look to MX3 on national implementation', MX Report no. 5, 5 Aug. 2019, Daily Reports from BWC Meetings, BioWeapons Prevention Project, pp. 1–2.

Differences remain on the mandate, composition, chair, funding, name and relationship to other BWC meetings. Several delegations encouraged further work to develop a substantive proposal that might achieve consensus at the Ninth Review Conference.

Meeting of Experts 3

MX3 met on 5 August 2019 and was chaired by Lebogang Phihlela of South Africa. The purpose of the meeting was to discuss and promote common understanding and effective action on strengthening national implementation.[20] States parties submitted six working papers, compared to nine on this topic in 2018. The Organisation for the Prohibition of Chemical Weapons (OPCW) and one independent expert provided technical briefings to the meeting. Canada, Malaysia, the Netherlands and Uganda jointly hosted one side event and France hosted another.[21]

The meeting had five substantive topics for discussion (agenda items 4–8).[22] The first, on national measures to implement the BWC, included consideration of biosafety, biosecurity, outbreak control and outreach activities. States parties highlighted the value of a single, coordinated framework to address the range of biological threats (naturally occurring; accidental or deliberate; domestic or international; affecting humans, animals or plants); and also emphasized the value of sharing best practices and experiences, including challenges, and the importance of assistance and cooperation in capacity building.

Under the second topic, on confidence-building measures (CBMs), states parties emphasized the importance of strengthening CBMs in terms of quantity and quality. Some states continue to view the CBMs as voluntary, rather than politically binding. Although the CBMs are not derived directly from the text of the BWC, the Second Review Conference resulted in a consensus decision that states parties were 'to implement [the CBMs] on the basis of mutual co-operation'.[23] This decision means that participation in the CBMs is a politically binding requirement for all BWC states parties. The states parties also discussed the new electronic CBM platform, which the ISU developed and Germany and the European Union funded, to simplify the compilation and submission of CBMs. The ISU indicated that nine states parties made submissions via the platform and that it had received a total

---

[20] BWC, 'Report of the 2019 Meeting of Experts on strengthening national implementation', BWC/MSP/2019/MX.3/2, 1 Nov. 2019, para. 4.

[21] BWC, '2019 Meetings of Experts' (note 8).

[22] BWC, BWC/MSP/2019/MX.3/2 (note 20), paras 16–19 and annex 1, paras 4–28.

[23] BWC, 'Second Review Conference of the Parties to the Convention on the Prohibition of the Development, Production and Stockpiling of Bacteriological (Biological) and Toxin Weapons and on their Destruction (final document)', BWC/CONF.II/13, 30 Sep. 1986, p. 6.

of 75 submissions so far in 2019.[24] States parties made further proposals to continue enhancing the utility and use of the CBMs, including a step-by-step approach to CBM submission and the establishment of cooperative networks of relevant domestic agencies.[25]

The ambitious meeting agenda combined with active state party interventions meant the one-day meeting ran out of time and states parties were unable to complete their consideration of the remaining three agenda items. Many states parties expressed regret that the meeting ran out of time, but the meeting decided to move straight to the adoption of the report in English rather than continuing to discuss substantive items with the limitations and disadvantages of having no interpretation.[26] One commentator noted that despite Phihlela's capable chairing, there was little that could be done to push through the uncompleted agenda items—not least because of the range and number of related activities that states parties were committed to pursuing (e.g. presentations, statements and interventions)— and that it is evident there needs to be a reduction in the MX3 workload.[27]

Meeting of Experts 4

MX4 met on 6–7 August 2019 and was chaired by Usman Iqbal Jadoon of Pakistan. The purpose of the meeting was to discuss and promote common understanding and effective action on assistance, response and preparedness.[28] States parties submitted seven working papers, compared with eleven in 2018. There were four technical briefings and six side events.[29]

The meeting had six substantive topics of discussion (agenda items 4–9).[30] The first focused on practical challenges and possible solutions for implementing Article VII, which obliges states parties to provide assistance to any state party that has been exposed to danger as a result of a violation of the BWC. The discussion focused particularly on the question of leadership and coordination in the international response to a deliberate biological event. Divergent views were evident among states parties, especially on the question of the focal point for preparations for Article VII responses: many Western states were of the view that this should be the United Nations secretary-general while other states, in particular Iran and Russia, held that this should

---

[24] Guthrie, R., 'MX3 has more substance than time, and a look to MX4 assistance and response', MX Report no. 6, 6 Aug. 2019, Daily Reports from BWC Meetings, BioWeapons Prevention Project, p. 1.

[25] BWC, BWC/MSP/2019/MX.3/2 (note 20), annex 1, para. 14.

[26] BWC, BWC/MSP/2019/MX.3/2 (note 20), annex 1, paras 3 and 19.

[27] Guthrie, MX Report no. 6 (note 24) p. 2.

[28] BWC, 'Report of the 2019 Meeting of Experts on assistance, response and preparedness', BWC/MSP/2019/MX.4/2, 8 Oct. 2019, para. 4.

[29] BWC, '2019 Meetings of Experts' (note 8).

[30] BWC, BWC/MSP/2019/MX.4/2 (note 28), paras 16–22 and annex 1, paras 4–25.

be BWC states parties and ultimately the UN Security Council.[31] Russia's position, as elaborated later to the UN General Assembly First Committee on 11 October 2019, was that it is 'unacceptable to create alternative BTWC verification mechanisms in contravention of the UNSC and the provisions of the Convention' and that 'any disarmament and arms control mechanisms should be discussed and adopted by states parties' consensus at specialized international fora, in this case, the BTWC'.[32] More positively, the meeting reaffirmed the importance of national preparedness, particularly by having access to new technologies and equipment for detection of and response to emerging biological threats against humans, animals and plants.[33]

Under the second substantive topic, on guidelines and formats for assistance under Article VII, there appeared to be broad support for the guidelines outlined in the South African working paper submitted to MX4 in 2018 (and in 2014 in an earlier incarnation). Under the third topic, the meeting further discussed a database to facilitate assistance under the framework of Article VII, as supported by the Eighth Review Conference, as well as a proposal to establish a fund for assistance.[34] States parties considered, under the fourth topic, mobile biomedical units which Russia had promoted to BWC states parties for a number of years.[35] While delegates generally recognized that mobile labs would contribute to any response effort, opinions diverged widely on whether mobile labs should be a BWC activity with associated costs managed centrally, or whether they should be added to a roster of units offered by various countries to be deployed in relevant circumstances.[36]

The meeting explored strengthening international response capabilities for both natural and deliberate infectious disease outbreaks, under the fifth topic item. States parties shared national experiences of strengthening national health systems and national response capabilities, including by means of national response plans, specialized response units, and regular tabletop and field exercises.[37] They also highlighted the importance of 'a consistent and flexible communication strategy in an incident'; stressed the importance of 'well-equipped' national laboratories; and presented information on efforts to strengthen the roster of designated laboratories under the UN Secretary-

---

[31] BWC, BWC/MSP/2019/MX.4/2 (note 28), annex 1, paras 5–6; Guthrie, MX Report no. 6 (note 24), p. 2; and Guthrie, R., 'The first day of MX4: Challenges, guidelines and a database', MX Report no. 7, 7 Aug. 2019, Daily Reports from BWC Meetings, BioWeapons Prevention Project, p. 2.

[32] Yermakov, V., 'Statement by Mr Vladimir Yermakov, Head of Delegation of the Russian Federation to the First Committee of the 74th UNGA session, Director of the Department for Nonproliferation and Arms Control of the Ministry of Foreign Affairs of the Russian Federation, within the General Debate', United Nations, General Assembly First Committee, New York, 11 Oct. 2019, p. 6.

[33] BWC, BWC/MSP/2019/MX.4/2 (note 28), annex 1, para. 8.

[34] BWC, BWC/MSP/2019/MX.4/2 (note 28), annex 1, paras 9–15.

[35] BWC, BWC/MSP/2019/MX.4/2 (note 28), annex 1, paras 16–18.

[36] Guthrie, MX Report no. 7 (note 31), p. 2.

[37] BWC, BWC/MSP/2019/MX.4/2 (note 28), annex 1, para. 19.

General's Mechanism, including the conduct of a larger capstone field exercise in 2020.[38]

The final substantive item considered deliberate attacks against agriculture, livestock and the natural environment, and was discussed in more depth than in 2018. Suggestions for areas to focus on in future included practical measures such as sharing best practices for attack preparation and response, and developing procedures for facilitating preparation and response coordination.[39] The UN General Assembly has declared 2020 as the International Year of Plant Health, and some states parties proposed to devote particular focus to plant health issues at the 2020 MX4.[40]

In his summary report, the chair acknowledged the many challenges to implementing Article VII, but also highlighted the emergence of broad support in some areas.[41] In a workshop panel discussion on MX4 in November 2019, he indicated that these broad areas of convergence included establishing guidelines to submit assistance requests, developing an assistance database, compiling a roster of mobile biomedical units, the value of training and exercises, and overlaps and links between Articles VII and X.[42] In the same discussion he also noted that the stumbling block to consensus will likely be finding agreement on the roles of the UN secretary-general, the UN Security Council and individual states parties in any investigations of a deliberate biological event.

Meeting of Experts 5

MX5 met on 8 August 2019 and was chaired by Laurent Masmejean of Switzerland. The purpose of the meeting was to discuss and promote common understanding and effective action on institutional strengthening of the BWC.[43] States parties submitted four working papers, the same number as in 2018. There were two technical briefings and one side event.[44]

The meeting had only one substantive agenda item: consideration of the full range of approaches and options to further strengthen the BWC and its functioning through possible additional legal measures or other measures in the framework of the convention. Divergent views within the BWC have historically been most pronounced when it comes to the best ways of

---

[38] BWC, BWC/MSP/2019/MX.4/2 (note 28), annex 1, paras 19 and 20.

[39] BWC, BWC/MSP/2019/MX.4/2 (note 28), annex 1, para. 22.

[40] BWC, BWC/MSP/2019/MX.4/2 (note 28), annex 1, para. 24.

[41] BWC, BWC/MSP/2019/MX.4/2 (note 28), annex 1, para. 3.

[42] Jadoon, U. I., Comments at a panel discussion on MX4 during a workshop jointly organized by the UN Office for Disarmament Affairs (UNODA), Japan and the Geneva Centre for Security Policy, 'Taking stock of deliberations on assistance, response and preparedness under the current intersessional programme', Geneva, 19 Nov. 2019.

[43] BWC, 'Report of the 2019 Meeting of Experts on institutional strengthening of the Convention', BWC/MSP/2019/MX.5/2, 4 Oct. 2019, para. 4.

[44] BWC, '2019 Meetings of Experts' (note 8).

strengthening the convention, the most significant point of disagreement being whether to pursue objectives through a new legally-binding agreement.[45] These differences in view were clear at the meeting.

States parties seeking to find middle ground between those pushing for a return to the failed negotiations of 2001 for a legally-binding agreement, and those arguing verification in the BWC context is impossible, counselled pursuing 'a pragmatic, incremental approach' of adopting individual measures to strengthen the convention's existing provisions and suggested 'a broad range of possible measures with a view to strengthening the BWC institutionally'.[46] These measures included strengthening the consultative provisions of Article V; improving and expanding the scope of the CBMs; analysing the content of CBM submissions to reinforce their utility; transparency initiatives such as voluntary peer review exercises and voluntary visits; bolstering capacities to investigate the alleged use of biological weapons; enhancing the operationalization of Article VII; and establishing a more structured approach to science and technology review.[47]

Many states parties also emphasized that the BWC needs a solid and sustainable financial foundation to ensure it, the ISU and the intersessional process function effectively. While delegates welcomed the Working Capital Fund (WCF) established at the 2018 MSP, several states parties reiterated that the WCF aims to ensure adequate cash flow, and that it is not a long-term solution and cannot resolve structural problems or late and non-payments, reminding all states parties of the need to abide by their financial obligations by paying in full and on time.[48]

The First Committee of the UN General Assembly

Resolution A/C.1/74/L.44 on the BWC was adopted in the First Committee of the UN General Assembly on 4 November 2019 without a vote.[49] Unlike the First Committee resolution on the Chemical Weapons Convention (CWC), where several highly politicized elements have hampered consensus, the BWC resolution continues to achieve unanimous support, reflecting the international community's undisputed norm against this particular kind of weapon.[50]

---

[45] Lentzos, F., *Compliance and Enforcement in the Biological Weapons Regime* (UNIDIR: Geneva, 2019).

[46] BWC, BWC/MSP/2019/MX.5/2 (note 43, annex 1, paras 11 and 12.

[47] BWC, BWC/MSP/2019/MX.5/2 (note 43), annex 1, paras 13–20.

[48] BWC, BWC/MSP/2019/MX.5/2, (note 43) annex 1, para 24.

[49] United Nations, General Assembly, First Committee, Convention on the Prohibition of the Development, Production and Stockpiling of Bacteriological (Biological) and Toxin Weapons and on Their Destruction, A/RES/74/79, 12 Dec. 2019.

[50] United Nations, General Assembly, First Committee, 'Implementation of the Convention on the Prohibition of the Development, Production, Stockpiling and Use of Chemical Weapons and on Their

The resolution welcomed the increase in ratifications of, and accessions to, the BWC, while underscoring the continuing need to achieve universalization.[51]

The resolution reaffirmed the importance of national measures in implementing the BWC and called on all states parties to participate in the implementation of Review Conference recommendations, including the exchange of data under the CBMs.[52] It recognized the importance of ongoing efforts to enhance international cooperation and assistance, and encouraged states parties to submit requests for, and offers of, cooperation and assistance, as well as to provide information on their implementation of Article X of the BWC.[53]

The resolution reiterated decisions of the Eighth Review Conference, noted ongoing intersessional activities and encouraged preparations for the Ninth Review Conference in 2021. For the first time, the resolution introduced new language encouraging equitable participation of women and men in the framework of the BWC.[54]

The resolution gave considerable attention to the detrimental financial situation of the BWC, and called upon states parties to tackle its financial deficit as a matter of urgency.[55]

A call for action on the adverse financial situation also featured in a statement[56] delivered to the First Committee by the chair of the 2019 BWC MSP, Ambassador Yann Hwang of France, who gave the statement on behalf of the chairs of the four disarmament conventions hosted by the United Nations Office at Geneva.[57] He stressed how the serious financial difficulties experienced across the four conventions compromise the progress of work and the credibility of the disarmament conventions:

over the years, meetings approved by all states parties have been cut short due to lack of funds, and several unacceptable cost-cutting measures, including the sacrifice of

---

Destruction', A/RES/74/40, 19 Dec. 2019. For a summary and other details of the 1993 Convention on the Prohibition of the Development, Production, Stockpiling and Use of Chemical Weapons and on their Destruction, see annex A, section I, in this volume.

[51] United Nations, General Assembly, A/RES/74/79 (note 49), Preamble, p. 1.

[52] United Nations, General Assembly, A/RES/74/79 (note 49), Preamble, p. 2 and Article 4.

[53] United Nations, General Assembly, A/RES/74/79 (note 49), Preamble, p. 2 and Article 6.

[54] United Nations, General Assembly, A/RES/74/79 (note 49), Preamble, p. 2.

[55] United Nations, General Assembly, A/RES/74/79 (note 49), Articles 11 and 12.

[56] Hwang, Y., 'Intervention de M. Yann Hwang, Ambassadeur, Representant permanent de la France auprès de la Conference du Desarmement, Chef de la delegation français' [Statement by Mr Yann Hwang, Ambassador, Permanent representative of France to the Conference on Disarmament, Head of the French delegation], 74th UN General Assembly First Committee, 30 Oct. 2019. English translation: United Nations, 'First Committee, 19th meeting—General Assembly, 74th session', 30 Oct. 2019, UN Web TV.

[57] Convention on the Prohibition of the Use, Stockpiling, Production and Transfer of Anti-Personnel Mines and on Their Destruction, APLC; BWC; Convention on Cluster Munitions, CCM; and Convention on Certain Conventional Weapons, CCW. For a summary and other details of these conventions, see annex A, section I, in this volume.

the interpretation of our meetings and the translation of official documents, have been taken. In addition, the precarious financial situation also threatens the very existence of certain support units for implementation, which are essential for the implementation and strengthening of the conventions it serves.[58]

The joint statement appealed to the respective states parties to consider additional measures to tackle non-payment beyond those already introduced.[59]

While there was unanimous support for the BWC resolution, clear differences in views were apparent from statements made to the First Committee. The United States, for instance, firmly pushed back on the 'small number of States Parties repeatedly blocking action' to strengthen the BWC by 'insisting' the only way forward is resuming multilateral negotiations on a non-discriminatory legally binding Protocol.[60]

The 2019 Meeting of States Parties

The 2019 MSP was convened from 3 to 6 December 2019, chaired by Ambassador Yann Hwang of France, with Ambassador Adrian Vierita of Romania and Ambassador Andreano Erwin of Indonesia serving as vice-chairs. The MSPs are responsible for managing the intersessional programme, through consideration of MX reports, and for taking the necessary measures with respect to budgetary and financial matters. The chair of the 2019 MSP produced a report on universalization activities in advance of the meeting.[61] Upon request from the 2018 MSP, the chair also produced, for the 2019 MSP to consider, a report on the financial situation of the BWC and the implementation of the financial measures adopted in 2018.[62] The ISU produced an annual report on its activities.[63] States parties submitted 5 working papers, considerably less than the 11 produced for the 2018 MSP. In the general debate, 63 states parties made statements (one fewer than in 2018).[64] There were 15 side events, notably up on the 9 side events of the 2018 MSP.[65]

[58] Hwang (note 56), p. 1.

[59] Hwang (note 56), p. 2.

[60] Wood, R., 'Statement by HE Ambassador Robert Wood, Permanent Representative of the United States to the Conference on Disarmament', 74th United Nations, General Assembly First Committee, 23 Oct. 2019, p. 2.

[61] BWC, BWC/MSP/2019/3 (note 2).

[62] BWC, 'Report on the overall financial situation of the Biological Weapons Convention', BWC/MSP/2019/5, 28 Nov. 2019.

[63] BWC, 'Annual report of the Implementation Support Unit', BWC/MSP/2019/4, 8 Oct. 2019.

[64] BWC, 'Report of the 2019 Meeting of States Parties', BWC/MSP/2019/7, 11 Dec. 2019, para. 15; and BWC, 'Report of the 2018 Meeting of States Parties', BWC/MSP/2018/6, 11 Dec. 2018, para. 15.

[65] BWC, '2019 Meeting of States Parties', [n.d.].

The financial situation of the Convention

Reviewing the financial situation of the BWC formed a central focus for the meeting. The chair's financial report informed states parties that as of 27 November 2019, the WCF had received a total of $276 855.04 in voluntary contributions from China, France, Germany, Russia and the United Kingdom.[66] The report stated that no withdrawals had at that time been made from the WCF, but noted that because WCF funds were available at the time that ISU staff contracts were due for renewal, the ISU could extend the contracts for a longer period than would otherwise have been possible. The WCF acted as a guarantee covering the contract extensions, but the ISU did not use the funds in the end because it received additional contributions in time to cover the payroll charges.[67]

The financial report noted that while the measures adopted by the 2018 MSP 'effectively addressed liquidity issues and structural problems', the problem of outstanding contributions from activities prior to 2018 remained; these amounted to almost $76 000 as of 31 October 2019.[68] During the discussion, none of the countries significantly in arrears took the floor.[69] The report concluded that although it was too soon to assess the full impact of the financial measures adopted at the 2018 MSP, the initial impact was positive, 'providing much-needed predictability and stability for the intersessional programme and also preventing the continued accumulation of financial liabilities by the United Nations'.[70] States parties requested the chair of the 2020 MSP to provide a similar report to review the financial situation in a year's time.[71]

Issues considered

In addition to the financial deliberations, the meeting considered universalization, the annual report of the ISU, and arrangements for the 2020 meetings, as well as initial arrangements for the 2021 Review Conference and its Preparatory Committee. The meeting approved the Non-Aligned Movement (NAM) nomination of Ambassador Aliyar Lebbe Abdul Azeez of Sri Lanka as chair of the 2020 MSP. The 2020 MXs are scheduled for 25 August to 3 September, and the 2020 MSP for 8–11 December 2020. The Ninth Review Conference will be held in November 2021, with exact dates to be decided at the 2020 MSP.[72]

[66] BWC, BWC/MSP/2019/5 (note 62), para. 10.
[67] BWC, BWC/MSP/2019/5 (note 62), para. 11.
[68] BWC, BWC/MSP/2019/5 (note 62), para. 16.
[69] Guthrie, R., 'Three MXs, preparations for the Review Conference and annual reports', MSP Report no. 4, 6 Dec. 2019, Daily Reports from BWC Meetings, BioWeapons Prevention Project, p. 2.
[70] BWC, BWC/MSP/2019/5 (note 62), para. 17.
[71] BWC, BWC/MSP/2019/7 (note 64), para. 23.
[72] BWC, BWC/MSP/2019/7 (note 64), paras 28–32.

More substantively, the meeting considered the reports of each MX. Regrettably, as in 2018, the outcome was minimal. Unlike the 2018 MSP report, the 2019 MSP report did express gratitude to the MX chairs, acknowledging the reports of the MXs and noting the value of both the work and the discussions of the MXs.[73] However, in terms of real substance, the report simply contained the same one-line sentence on the MXs as the 2018 MSP report: 'No consensus was reached on the deliberations including any possible outcomes of the Meetings of Experts.'[74] This was despite several states parties having expressed regret at the lack of a substantive MSP outcome document in 2018, at the MXs, in the First Committee of the UN General Assembly, and at the MSP itself. Russia, for instance, had announced in the First Committee that it would purse the adoption of a 'meaningful' final MSP document.[75] Following through on its announcement, on the second day of the MSP Russia circulated draft text for the MSP report that included proposed paragraphs relating to each of the MXs. One commentator noted:

This was interpreted by many in the room as an attempt to get substantive issues reflected in the final report, which has in the past been opposed by Iran. There were suggestions from some delegations that Russia should circulate the text as an MSP working paper as there was little remaining time in the MSP for discussion. The US delegation stated that there would be nothing they could agree to that could come out of discussion of the Russian text.[76]

A novel initiative by the 2019 MSP chair provides an opportunity to circumvent the reporting impasse on substantive issues. At the MSP, the chair circulated a paper outlining a proposed process for feeding the substantive work of the MXs into the MSPs and the 2021 Review Conference.[77] Noting that 'the financial cost and environmental footprint . . . would be outrageous if the MSP was to prove unproductive in substance',[78] he suggested the MX chairs and the MSP chair produce an overview of proposals expressed by experts at the MXs in an *aide memoire* that could then be updated following the 2020 meetings and be made available for the Ninth Review Conference.[79] He also suggested that the outgoing MSP chair transmit a letter to the incoming MSP chair, copied to all states parties, reporting on work undertaken and highlighting key proposals most likely to garner consensus.[80] The paper

---

[73] BWC, BWC/MSP/2019/7 (note 64) para. 26.

[74] BWC, BWC/MSP/2019/7 (note 64), para. 25.

[75] Yermakov (note 32), p. 6.

[76] Guthrie, R., 'The closing day of the Meeting of States Parties and some reflections', MSP Report no. 5, 31 Dec. 2019, Daily Reports from BWC Meetings, BioWeapons Prevention Project, p. 2.

[77] BWC, Communications from the MSP Chair at the 2019 MSP, 'Consideration by the Chair of the 2019 Meeting of States Parties on methodological issues in view of the Ninth Review Conference', 4 Dec. 2019.

[78] BWC, Communications from the MSP Chair (note 77), para. 1, fourth item.

[79] BWC, Communications from the MSP Chair (note 77), para. 2, first item.

[80] BWC Communications from the MSP Chair (note 77), para. 2, third item.

encouraged states parties to establish continuity between the work of the three intersessional years, to synthesize the work and identify areas of convergence, and to avoid a confrontational approach.[81]

Disagreements between the United States and Russia

While a full-blown confrontation is not yet apparent, a frosty relationship between the two major BWC states parties, Russia and the USA, certainly is, which often has adverse consequences for the entire BWC community. In response to the US dismissal of the Russian draft text for the MSP report, Russia objected to a paragraph in the final version referencing the *aide memoire* circulated by the MSP chair, with the result that all such references were deleted from the report. One commentator noted: 'No objection to the paragraph had been made while the Russian proposal for new text was up for discussion.'[82]

Disputes between the two states parties seem set to continue. At an early 2020 press conference reflecting on Russian diplomacy in 2019, Russian Acting Foreign Minister Sergey Lavrov characterized the USA as blocking inclusive dialogue that could enable a consensus in the BWC, by taking international security issues into its own hands. Referring to multilateral negotiations on a legally binding Protocol to the BWC, Lavrov said, 'The Americans basically unilaterally block this solution and seek to promote their own interests through secretariats of various international organizations, including the UN Secretariat, through their non-transparent, murky, back-door bilateral contacts that push their agendas.'[83]

Lavrov also reiterated Russia's key BWC-related allegation from 2018, that the USA is setting up biological laboratories in post-Soviet territories.[84]

Areas of agreement

While significant differences remain among states parties on how best to strengthen the BWC, some areas engendering broad agreement are becoming apparent (even if there are different views on the details). The Article X database is generally seen as valuable, even though it is widely recognized that there is some room for improvement. Establishing an analogous database on Article VII issues seems generally supported, as do guidelines to help a country request humanitarian assistance within the framework of Article VII. There is cross-regional support for a cooperation officer post

---

[81] BWC, Communications from the MSP Chair (note 77), para. 1, first, second and third items.

[82] Guthrie, MSP Report no. 5 (note 76), p. 1.

[83] TASS, 'Lavrov castigated US for reluctance to speak openly about bioweapons with other nations', 17 Jan. 2020.

[84] Lentzos, F., 'The Russian disinformation attack that poses a biological danger', *Bulletin of the Atomic Scientists*, 19 Nov. 2018; and Lentzos, F., 'Biological weapon disarmament and non-proliferation', *SIPRI Yearbook 2019*, pp. 444–45.

within the ISU, potentially with an equivalent science and technology officer post. There is broad agreement on the need for some form of science and technology review. Codes of conduct are broadly recognized as valuable. The need to review the CBM modalities is widely acknowledged, and there is wide support for a CBM assistance network.

Gender and disarmament

A new development in 2019 was the growing recognition of the topic of 'gender and disarmament' within the BWC community. In 2018, no states parties referred to gender and disarmament. At the 2019 MXs, three delegations raised the issue, and at the 2019 MSP twelve delegates spoke to the topic.[85] The statements called for greater gender diversity, better analysis of the gendered impacts of biological weapons and respective policy processes, and broader inclusion of gender perspectives in BWC processes. The 2019 MXs featured the first-ever side event on gender in the BWC context, discussing possible differences in effects of biological weapons on women and men and the significance for assistance, response and preparedness.[86] Shortly thereafter, the United Nations Institute for Disarmament Affairs (UNIDIR) published a study emphasizing that sex- and gender-disaggregated data, as well as knowledge of gender perspectives, can contribute to state preparedness and enhance the effectiveness of assistance under the BWC.[87]

Dialogues beyond Geneva and New York

The high volume of BWC-related workshops in 2018 continued in 2019.[88] The EU funded two regional universalization workshops, both organized by the ISU and the UN Office for Disarmament Affairs (UNODA), one in Ethiopia for African states not party to the BWC and the other in New Zealand for Pacific non-party states.[89] Australia funded a second ISU/UNODA-organized universalization workshop in Fiji for Pacific non-party states.[90] Japan funded three ISU/UNODA-organized workshops in Thailand, Kyrgyzstan and Malaysia on regional capacity building in Central and South East Asia.[91]

---

[85] Reaching Critical Will (RCW), '2019 Biological Weapons Convention Meeting of States Parties', Latest news from RCW, 11 Dec. 2019.

[86] United Nations Institute for Disarmament Research (UNIDIR) and Norway, 'Gender-responsive BWC? Understanding gender-related impacts of biological weapons and implications for assistance, response and preparedness', Interactive meeting on the margins of the 2019 BWC MX4, Palais des Nations, Geneva, 7 Aug. 2019.

[87] Dalaqua, R. H. et al., *Missing Links: Understanding Sex- and Gender-related Impacts of Chemical and Biological Weapons* (UNIDIR: Geneva, 2019).

[88] Lentzos, 'Biological weapon disarmament and non-proliferation' (note 84), p. 443.

[89] BWC, BWC/MSP/2019/3 (note 2), para. 2.

[90] BWC, BWC/MSP/2019/3 (note 2), para. 2.

[91] BWC, BWC/MSP/2019/4 (note 63), para. 7.

France funded an ISU/UNODA-organized tabletop exercise on Article VII held in Togo for Francophone states parties in West Africa.[92]

One of the major trends becoming apparent in the biological disarmament field is the rise of civil society as a significant contributor to shaping dialogues around biological threats and appropriate responses to these threats. This is reflected in greater numbers of NGO participants attending BWC meetings and organizing side events, but also in civil society organizations convening global initiatives, workshops and events related to biosecurity.[93] Traditionally, civil society engagement with the BWC has been mostly expert-based and highly technical, marked by quiet lobbying and supportive partnerships with national delegations on a variety of issues. The individuals involved have tended to have long-term personal commitments to the BWC and long histories of BWC engagement (and often also CWC engagement). Contemporary civil society engagement is becoming much more diverse. Significant new actors have come in, with different backgrounds, affiliations, agendas and strategies. By these measures, BWC civil society is becoming more heterogeneous. Yet, by other measures, BWC civil society remains fairly homogeneous. The vast majority of representatives are white, Western and from the global north. Many are now also funded through the same funder, the Open Philanthropy Project (Open Phil), which focuses on a very particular aspect of biosecurity risk: global catastrophic biological risks.[94] This could have significant implications for the direction of the biological disarmament and non-proliferation field in the years to come.[95]

---

[92] BWC, BWC/MSP/2019/4 (note 63), para. 7.
[93] See e.g. the initiatives and events convened by NTI | bio, the Johns Hopkins Center for Health Security, and the Center for Global Health Science and Security at Georgetown University.
[94] Lentzos, F., 'Will splashy philanthropy cause the biosecurity field to focus on the wrong risks?', *Bulletin of the Atomic Scientists*, 25 Apr. 2019.
[95] See Lentzos (note 94).

13. Conventional arms control and new weapon technologies

Overview

Conventional arms control by states usually falls within one of two broad approaches: limiting and/or prohibiting weapons considered to be inhumane or indiscriminate; or regulating and managing weapons procurement, production, transfers and trade, with a view to preventing their destabilizing accumulation, diversion and/or misuse. Section I reviews the developments and negotiations that took place in 2019 in three of the main global instruments for regulating the production, trade and use of conventional weapons: the 1981 Convention on Prohibitions or Restrictions on the Use of Certain Conventional Weapons which may be Deemed to be Excessively Injurious or to have Indiscriminate Effects (the CCW Convention); the 1997 Convention on the Prohibition of the Use, Stockpiling, Production and Transfer of Anti-Personnel Mines and on their Destruction (the APM Convention); and the 2008 Convention on Cluster Munitions (CCM). The 2013 Arms Trade Treaty (ATT), another major instrument, is discussed in chapter 14.

Despite growing international concern over the use of incendiary weapons and explosive weapons in populated areas (EWIPA), including the use of improvised explosive devices (IEDs) by non-state armed groups, discussions in the CCW failed to generate new concrete outcomes. The lack of progress within the CCW is leading some states to explore the creation of new arms control instruments. Ireland convened the first of a series of open consultations on a political declaration on EWIPA in Geneva in November 2019, with a view to finalizing and adopting a declaration in 2020.

International differences on the development of norms of responsible state behaviour in cyberspace led to two parallel processes starting in 2019: an Open-ended Working Group and a new Group of Governmental Experts. However, in the absence of consensus, a binding agreement within either seems unlikely in the near future.

While new uses of APMs by states are now extremely rare, their use by non-state armed groups in conflicts is a growing problem, especially their use of victim-activated IEDs. APMs were used by such groups in at least six states between mid-2018 and October 2019: Afghanistan, India, Myanmar, Nigeria, Pakistan and Yemen. The non-state armed group Polisario Front of Western Sahara completed the destruction of its stockpiled landmines in 2019. The Maldives and the Philippines became states parties to the CCM in 2018, taking the total number of states parties to 107. There was continued use of cluster munitions in Syria in 2019.

Section II look at efforts to regulate lethal autonomous weapon systems (LAWS). As was the case in 2017–18, the discussions on LAWS took place in the format of a group of governmental experts (GGE) within the framework of the CCW Convention. While a consensus has emerged among states that autonomy in weapon systems cannot be unlimited, there is still disagreement on whether additional regulation is needed. In 2019 the GGE adopted 11 guiding principles (10 of which had been proposed in 2018) and agreed to meet again in 2020 and 2021 to continue discussions. A majority of states would like the GGE to present substantial and politically ambitious recommendations at the 2021 CCW Review Conference, but a handful of technology advanced military powers continue to impede progress.

Section III discusses developments related to the United Nations agenda item: the Prevention of an Arms Race in Outer Space (PAROS). Since 2017, some states, most notably the United States, have openly declared space to be a domain of war or an area for both offensive and defensive military operations. Others, including France, India and Japan, announced new dedicated military space units in 2019, and in March 2019 India tested an anti-satellite weapon. The North Atlantic Treaty Organization also announced in 2019 that outer space is now a domain of operation. Despite the growing risk of a conflict in outer space, international discussions on both security and safety aspects of space activities, including PAROS, remained blocked.

IAN DAVIS

I. Global instruments for conventional arms control

IAN DAVIS

Introduction

Conventional arms control by states usually falls within one of two broad approaches: limiting and/or prohibiting weapons considered to be inhumane or indiscriminate; or regulating and managing weapons procurement, production, transfers and trade, with a view to preventing their destabilizing accumulation, diversion and/or misuse. There are five main global instruments for regulating the production, trade and/or use of conventional weapons: (*a*) the 1981 Convention on Prohibitions or Restrictions on the Use of Certain Conventional Weapons which may be Deemed to be Excessively Injurious or to have Indiscriminate Effects (the CCW Convention); (*b*) the 1997 Convention on the Prohibition of the Use, Stockpiling, Production and Transfer of Anti-Personnel Mines and on their Destruction (the APM Convention); (*c*) the 2001 United Nations Programme of Action to Prevent, Combat and Eradicate the Illicit Trade in Small Arms and Light Weapons in All its Aspects (the UN POA); (*d*) the 2008 Convention on Cluster Munitions (CCM); and (*e*) the 2013 Arms Trade Treaty (ATT).

This section reviews the key developments and negotiations that took place in four of these instruments in 2019. The ATT is discussed in chapter 14. This section also reviews efforts to create new global instruments governing cyberspace and the use of explosive weapons in populated areas (EWIPA). The two other sections in this chapter provide more detailed discussions on efforts to regulate lethal autonomous weapon systems (LAWS, section II) and prevent an arms race in outer space (section III).

The CCW Convention

The CCW Convention and its five protocols ban or restrict the use of specific types of weapon that are considered to cause unnecessary or unjustifiable suffering to combatants or to affect civilians indiscriminately.[1] It is a so-called umbrella treaty, to which specific agreements can be added in the form of protocols (see box 13.1). As of the end of December 2019 there were 125 states parties to the original convention and its protocols. No new states joined the CCW in 2019. Not all the states parties have ratified all the amended or additional protocols.[2]

---

[1] For a summary of the CCW Convention see annex A, section I, in this volume.
[2] For details of the states parties that have ratified the amended or additional protocols see annex A, section I, in this volume

---

Box 13.1. The Certain Conventional Weapons Convention

The Certain Conventional Weapons (CCW) Convention originally contained three protocols: prohibiting the use of weapons that employ fragments not detectable in the human body by X ray (Protocol I); regulating the use of landmines, booby traps and similar devices (Protocol II); and limiting the use of incendiary weapons (Protocol III). In subsequent years, states added two protocols: Protocol IV prohibiting the use and transfer of blinding laser weapons was added in 1995; and Protocol V on explosive remnants of war (ERW)—landmines, unexploded ordnance and abandoned explosive ordnance—in 2003. In addition, amendments have expanded and strengthened the convention. Amended Protocol II, for example, places further constraints on the use of anti-personnel mines (APMs), while the scope of the convention was expanded in 2001 to situations of intra state armed conflict. Because Amended Protocol II fell short of a ban on the use of landmines, a parallel process outside of the CCW Convention led to the creation of the APM Convention.

The CCW Convention is also important for addressing the challenges posed by the development or use of new types of weapons and their systems with respect to international humanitarian law (IHL). Many of the contemporary debates on conventional arms control are shaped by the concept of 'humanitarian disarmament', which prioritizes the protection, security and well-being of people as opposed to states. In particular, this approach strives to increase the protection of civilians by reducing the human and environmental impacts of arms.[3] In recent years, however, there have been increasing tensions between the prioritization of humanitarian demands and the perceived military needs of certain states, with the result that many of the discussions on the convention have become deadlocked.[4]

Meetings of states parties

The states parties to the CCW Convention meet regularly at an annual Meeting of the High Contracting Parties and at a Review Conference, which takes place every fifth year. These meetings also consider the work of the Group of Governmental Experts (GGE) established in 2001, which has been convened in various formats since then. Amended Protocol II and Protocol V have their own implementation processes, which function in parallel with the CCW Convention. There were seven CCW-related meetings in 2019 (see table 13.1).

---

[3] See the discussions on humanitarian disarmament in Anthony, I., 'International humanitarian law: ICRC guidance and its application in urban warfare', *SIPRI Yearbook 2017*, pp. 545–53; and Davis, I. and Verbruggen, M., 'The Convention on Certain Conventional Weapons', *SIPRI Yearbook 2018*, p. 381. See also International Committee of the Red Cross, *International Humanitarian Law and the Challenges of Contemporary Armed Conflicts: Recommitting to Protection in Armed Conflict on the 70th Anniversary of the Geneva Conventions* (ICRC: Geneva, Oct. 2019).

[4] See the discussion on the 2016 CCW Review Conference in Davis, I. et al., 'Humanitarian arms control regimes: Key developments in 2016', *SIPRI Yearbook 2017*, pp. 554–61; and on developments in 2017 and 2018 in Davis and Verbruggen (note 3), pp. 381–92 and Boulanin, V., Davis, I. and Verbruggen, M., 'The Convention on Certain Conventional Weapons and lethal autonomous weapon systems', *SIPRI Yearbook 2019*, pp. 449–61.

The Thirteenth Annual Conference of the High Contracting Parties to Protocol V discussed the report of the June 2018 meeting of experts, which focused on universalization of the protocol, national reporting, clearance of ERW, victim assistance and the practical implementation of Article 4 of Protocol V on the recording, retaining and transmission of information.[5] There were no significant new proposals and the conference agreed to continue to focus its work on these topics in 2020.[6]

The Twenty-first Annual Conference of the High Contracting Parties to Amended Protocol II reviewed the status and operation of the protocol and considered matters arising from the national annual reports of states parties.[7] As was the case in 2018, the meeting also issued an appeal for the universalization of the protocol and considered a report by the group of experts on improvised explosive devices (IEDs).[8] Despite the increasing saliency of the IED threat (see below on the APM Convention and EWIPA), no significant new measures were agreed. Instead, the focus remained on voluntary information exchange on national measures and best practices regarding identification, humanitarian clearance and civilian protection from IEDs.

The 2019 Meeting of the High Contracting Parties was held in Geneva on 13–15 November 2019, chaired by Pakistan. The meeting reviewed compliance with and progress towards the universalization of the CCW Convention. The three substantive issues on the agenda were: (a) LAWS (see section II); (b) incendiary weapons; and (c) mines other than anti-personnel mines (MOTAPM). Some limited discussions also took place on EWIPA but because certain governments have prevented it from being a formal agenda item, the main impetus on that issue has shifted to a new political process begun outside of the CCW by Austria and Ireland (see below). The states parties endorsed the guiding principles affirmed by the GGE on LAWS and

---

[5] United Nations, Thirteenth Conference of the High Contracting Parties to Protocol V on Explosive Remnants of War to the Convention on Prohibitions or Restrictions on the Use of Certain Conventional Weapons which May be Deemed to be Excessively Injurious or to have Indiscriminate Effects, 11 Nov. 2019, 'Report on the 2019 Meeting of Experts of the High Contracting Parties to Protocol V', CCW/P.V/CONF/2019/2, 7 Oct. 2019.

[6] United Nations, Thirteenth Conference of the High Contracting Parties to Protocol V on Explosive Remnants of War to the Convention on Prohibitions or Restrictions on the Use of Certain Conventional Weapons which may be Deemed to be Excessively Injurious or to have Indiscriminate Effects, 19 Nov. 2019, 'Final document', CCW/P.V/CONF/2019/5, 11 Nov. 2019.

[7] United Nations, Twenty-first Annual Conference of the High Contracting Parties to Amended Protocol II to the Convention on Prohibitions or Restrictions on the Use of Certain Conventional Weapons which may be Deemed to be Excessively Injurious or to have Indiscriminate Effects, 'Final Document', 12 Nov. 2019.

[8] United Nations, Twenty-first Annual Conference of the High Contracting Parties to Amended Protocol II to the Convention on Prohibitions or Restrictions on the Use of Certain Conventional Weapons which may be Deemed to be Excessively Injurious or to have Indiscriminate Effects, 'Report on improvised explosive devices', 26 Sep. 2019. See also the discussion on IEDs in Davis and Verbruggen (note 3), pp. 387–88.

Table 13.1. The Certain Conventional Weapons Convention meetings in 2019

Dates	Meeting
25–29 March	GGE on LAWS
20–21 August	GGE on LAWS
22 August	Amended Protocol II Group of Experts
23 August	Protocol V meeting of experts
11 November	13th Annual Conference of the HCP to Protocol V
12 November	21st Annual Conference of the HCP on Amended Protocol II
13–15 November	Meeting of the High Contracting Parties

GGE = Governmental Group of Experts; HCP = High Contracting Parties; LAWS = Lethal Autonomous Weapon Systems.

Note: All meetings took place in Geneva.

agreed the group's schedule of meetings for 2020–21. As in 2017 and 2018, the meeting also agreed to place 'emerging issues in the context of the objectives and purposes of the Convention' on the agenda of its next meeting, with an open invitation to states parties to submit relevant working papers.[9]

While no meetings were cancelled for financial reasons in 2019, as had been the case in 2017, the CCW's continuing funding problems were a key theme of discussions. Following proposals from the chair to address structural and cash flow-related issues, including funding of the CCW Implementation Support Unit, the states parties agreed several financial measures, including the creation of a voluntary Working Capital Fund to provide liquidity during the financial year.[10]

Overall, as in recent years, there was little progress due to the lack of consensus, and a handful of states obstructed advances in most of the CCW agenda. Despite the fact that the CCW has traditionally operated in an inclusive and transparent manner, the 2019 final report was negotiated behind closed doors.[11] The Sixth Review Conference of the CCW will take place on 13–17 December 2021.

Incendiary weapons

Protocol III to the CCW Convention prohibits the use of any incendiary weapons on civilian objects and the use of air-dropped incendiary weapons on military objects in residential areas. However, its restrictions have

---

[9] Meeting of the High Contracting Parties to the Convention on Prohibitions or Restrictions on the Use of Certain Conventional Weapons which may be Deemed to be Excessively Injurious or to have Indiscriminate Effects, Geneva, Final report, CCW/MSP/2019/9, 13 Dec. 2019

[10] Meeting of the High Contracting Parties to the Convention on Prohibitions or Restrictions on the Use of Certain Conventional Weapons which may be Deemed to be Excessively Injurious or to have Indiscriminate Effects, Geneva, 13–15 Nov. 2019, 'Further suggested measures that could be considered to improve the stability of the Secretariat's support to the Convention and on financial issues related to the Convention and its annexed Protocols', 12 Nov. 2019, CCW/MSP/2019/CRP.1. See also Geyer, K., 'Financial issues', *CCW Report*, vol. 7, no. 8, Reaching Critical Will (17 Nov. 2019).

[11] Acheson, R., 'The CCW is still standing, but to what end?', *CCW Report*, vol. 7, no. 8, Reaching Critical Will (17 Nov. 2019).

failed to prevent civilian harm from such use in recent years, notably in Syria, Ukraine and Yemen. The protocol has two major loopholes: weaker regulation of ground-launched incendiary weapons in comparison with air-dropped models; and inadequate wording on multipurpose munitions that can be used for several purposes on the battlefield, such as those containing white phosphorus which can be used as an obscurant or smokescreen, for signalling and marking, but also as an incendiary weapon.

Syria is not a state party to Protocol III and is therefore not bound by its restrictions. The Syrian Government has been using Russian-made or Soviet-era incendiary weapons since 2012. Incendiary weapon attacks in Syria became more frequent after Russia, which is a state party to the protocol, began joint operations with Syria in 2015.[12] In 2019 Human Rights Watch (HRW) documented the continued use of incendiary weapons in or near civilian areas in Syria in joint military operations by the Syrian-Russian military alliance. In May–June 2019, for example, incendiary weapons were used at least 27 times, mostly in Idlib governorate. Since November 2012, HRW has identified about 150 incendiary weapon attacks in Syria, but the total number is likely to be higher.[13] HRW is also looking into allegations that white phosphorus was used in Syria by Turkey and its allies in October 2019.[14]

Discussions on incendiary weapons in the CCW began in the wake of Israel's use of white phosphorus in Gaza in 2009.[15] Several states, along with the International Committee of the Red Cross (ICRC), the UN secretary-general and many non-governmental organizations (NGOs), have condemned more recent incendiary weapon attacks and called for Protocol III to be revisited and strengthened.[16] It was an agenda item at the 2017 and 2018 CCW meetings but at the latter meeting, Russia, with some backing from China and Cuba, blocked proposals to keep it as a separate agenda item for the 2019 meeting.[17] Nonetheless, at least 14 states parties condemned or expressed concern about the use of incendiary weapons during the meeting, and reiterated their calls for dedicated CCW discussions to strengthen the protocol. However, states parties failed to reinstate this as an agenda item for 2020 because two—Russia and the United States—publicly opposed it. The

---

[12] For more information on the use of incendiary weapons in Syria, see Human Rights Watch and International Human Rights Clinic, 'An overdue review: Addressing incendiary weapons in the contemporary context', Memorandum to delegates at the Meeting of States Parties to the Convention on Conventional Weapons, Nov. 2017, pp. 14–18. On the armed conflict in Syria, see chapter 6, section II, in this volume.

[13] Human Rights Watch, 'Standing firm against incendiary weapons: Memorandum to delegates of the Meeting of States Parties to the Convention on Conventional Weapons', Nov. 2019.

[14] 'Kurds accuse Turkey of using napalm and white phosphorus', France 24, 24 Oct. 2019.

[15] Human Rights Watch, 'Rain of fire: Israel's unlawful use of white phosphorous in Gaza', 25 Mar. 2009.

[16] See the discussion on incendiary weapons in Davis et al. (note 4), pp. 556–57; and Davis and Verbruggen (note 4), pp. 388–89.

[17] On developments in 2018, see Boulanin, Davis and Verbruggen (note 3), pp. 460–61.

final report reflected both the widespread concern over use of incendiary weapons and the divisions over how to proceed.[18]

Mines other than anti-personnel mines

Discussions on MOTAPM were focused on anti-vehicle mines (AVMs), which include anti-tank mines. The most recent data indicate an 18 per cent increase in AVM incidents in 2018, leading to 569 reported casualties, 53 per cent of them civilian, in 23 states.[19] It is a topic that has been discussed within the CCW Convention for over a decade, but without any consensus among states parties on how to move the debate forward. Two informal open consultation meetings in 2018 were unable to bridge the differences, although the chair's report recommended the continuation of informal consultations in 2019.[20] As was the case with incendiary weapons, however, while the majority of states participating in the 2019 discussions on MOTAPM expressed concern at the humanitarian impact of their indiscriminate and disproportionate use, two states—Russia and Belarus—argued against any further restrictions.[21] Indeed, the final CCW report failed to even mention MOTAPM.

The Anti-Personnel Mines Convention

In 2019, the APM Convention celebrated the 20th anniversary of its entry into force on 1 March 1999 and held its Fourth Review Conference. The convention prohibits, among other things, the use, development, production and transfer of APMs. These are mines that detonate on human contact, that is they are 'victim-activated', and therefore encompass IEDs that act as APMs, also known as 'improvised mines'.[22] At the Third Review Conference in 2014, states parties set a target of fully eliminating APMs and addressing the consequences of past use by 2025.

While compliance with the APM Convention has generally been good, it continues to be undermined by the refusal of some states, such as China, Iran, Israel, the Democratic People's Republic of Korea (DPRK, North Korea), Russia, Saudi Arabia and the USA, to sign it. There are currently 164 states parties to the APM Convention. These include all the European Union (EU)

---

[18] Docherty, B., 'Incendiary weapons', *CCW Report*, vol. 7, no. 8, Reaching Critical Will (17 Nov. 2019); and Meeting of the High Contracting Parties to the CCW Convention, Final report (note 9).

[19] Hofmann, U. et al., 'Global mapping and analysis of anti-vehicle mine incidents in 2018', Geneva International Centre for Humanitarian Demining and SIPRI, June 2019.

[20] Meeting of the High Contracting Parties to the Convention on Prohibitions or Restrictions on the Use of Certain Conventional Weapons Which may be Deemed to be Excessively Injurious or to have Indiscriminate Effects, Geneva, 'Mines other than Anti-Personnel Mines', report of the Chairperson-elect, 2 Nov. 2018, CW/MSP/2018/3.

[21] Geyer, K., 'Mines other than anti-personnel mines', *CCW Report*, vol. 7, no. 8, Reaching Critical Will (17 Nov. 2019).

[22] IEDs are also discussed in the CCW Convention, see above, and in the UN General Assembly First Committee, including through the submission of resolutions.

member states, every state in sub-Saharan Africa and every state in the Americas apart from Cuba and the USA. Only 33 states remain outside the treaty.[23] No new states joined in 2019.

Production and use of APMs in 2019

New uses of APMs by states are now extremely rare. According to *Landmine Monitor, 2019*, only Myanmar—a state outside the treaty—is recorded as having used APMs in the period October 2017 to October 2019, and has been deploying them for the past 20 years.[24] More than 50 states have produced APMs in the past, but only 11 are currently identified as producers by the International Campaign to Ban Landmines (ICBL) and only three of those (India, Myanmar and Pakistan) are thought likely to be actively producing.[25] While there is a de facto moratorium on the production and use of the weapon among most states in the world, the use of APMs, including victim-activated IEDs, by non-state armed groups in conflicts is a growing problem. APMs were used by such groups in at least six states between mid-2018 and October 2019: Afghanistan, India, Myanmar, Nigeria, Pakistan and Yemen. There were also unconfirmed allegations of use by non-state armed groups in seven other states: Cameroon, Colombia, Libya, Mali, the Philippines, Somalia and Tunisia.[26]

In 2018, the last year for which data is available, the ICBL recorded 6897 casualties linked to mines/ERW, of which at least 3059 were fatal and the majority (71 per cent) were civilian. This marked a fourth successive year of exceptionally high casualties, albeit lower than in 2016 and 2017. It was also the third year in a row in which the highest number of annual casualties was caused by improvised mines, and 2018 was the year with the most improvised mine casualties recorded to date (3789 casualties). The three states with the most casualties in 2018 were Afghanistan (2234), Syria (1465) and Yemen (596). The three states with the most casualties in the 20-year period 1999–2018 were Afghanistan (27 670), Colombia (10 869) and Cambodia (8802).[27]

---

[23] For a summary of the APM Convention see annex A, section I, in this volume.

[24] International Campaign to Ban Landmines–Cluster Munition Coalition (ICBL–CMC), *Landmine Monitor, 2019* (ICBL–CMC: Geneva, Nov. 2019), pp. 1, 8–10. The report focuses on the calendar year 2018 with information included up to Nov. 2019 wherever possible.

[25] The other 8 listed producers are: China, Cuba, Iran, North Korea, Russia, Singapore, South Korea and Viet Nam. International Campaign to Ban Landmines–Cluster Munition Coalition (note 24), pp. 15–16.

[26] International Campaign to Ban Landmines–Cluster Munition Coalition (note 24), pp. 1, 8–14.

[27] International Campaign to Ban Landmines–Cluster Munition Coalition (note 24), pp. 2, 53–64. In Afghanistan, the problem spans several decades, see Fiederlein, S. and Rzegocki, S., 'The human and financial costs of the Explosive Remnants of War in Afghanistan', Costs of War Project, Brown University, 19 Sep. 2019.

Clearance and destruction measures

In 2018 nearly $700 million was contributed by donors and affected states to international support for mine action—the clearance of landmines and other ERW in order to release land back to the community. This is the second-highest amount in more than two decades. The top five mine action donors—the USA, the EU, the United Kingdom, Norway and Germany—contributed 71 per cent of all international funding in 2018.[28]

In the five-year period 2014–18, an estimated 800 square kilometres of land was cleared of landmines and at least 661 491 landmines were destroyed. Since the APM Convention entered into force, 33 states and areas have completed clearance of all APMs from their territory. Among the 59 states and other areas that are known to have mine contamination, 33 are states parties to the APM Convention. These include some of the most mine-affected states in the world: Afghanistan, Angola, Bosnia and Herzegovina, Cambodia, Chad, Croatia, Iraq, Thailand, Turkey and Yemen. As of October 2019, 29 of the 33 states parties had deadlines to meet their mine clearance obligations before 2025, although Yemen (current deadline March 2023) and Bosnia and Herzegovina (current deadline March 2021) have both requested interim extensions to enable them to better define their remaining contamination. Four states parties had deadlines after 2025: Croatia (2026), Iraq (2028), Palestine (2028) and Sri Lanka (2028).[29]

Collectively, states parties have destroyed more than 55 million stockpiled APMs. More than 1.4 million were destroyed in 2018. Only three states parties have remaining stockpile destruction obligations: Greece, Sri Lanka and Ukraine. On 6 January 2019, following its eighth and final destruction, of 2485 stockpiled APMs, the non-state armed group Polisario Front of Western Sahara destroyed the last of its 20 493 stockpiled mines.[30]

The total remaining global stockpile of APMs is estimated to be less than 50 million, down from about 160 million in 1999. With the exception of Ukraine, the largest stockpilers are non-signatories: Russia (26.5 million), Pakistan (6 million), India (4–5 million), China (5 million), Ukraine (3.5 million) and the USA (3 million).[31]

The Fourth Review Conference of the APM Convention

The Fourth Review Conference of the APM Convention was held in Oslo on 25–29 November 2019, following two preparatory meetings on 24 May 2019

---

[28] International Campaign to Ban Landmines–Cluster Munition Coalition (note 24), pp. 2–3, 83–96.

[29] International Campaign to Ban Landmines–Cluster Munition Coalition (note 24), pp. 3–4, 25–52.

[30] Geneva Call, 'Final destruction of 2,485 stockpiled anti-personnel mines in Western Sahara', Press release, 22 Jan. 2019.

[31] International Campaign to Ban Landmines–Cluster Munition Coalition (note 24), pp. 4–5, 17–18.

and 18 September 2019.[32] The review conference assessed existing progress in all areas and adopted the Oslo Political Declaration and Oslo Action Plan, 2020–24 to guide efforts for the next five years to achieve a mine-free world. The plan adopts a gender perspective, advances mine risk education to prevent new casualties and challenges states parties to increase the pace of mine clearance.[33] Seven states parties—Argentina, Cambodia, Chad, Eritrea, Ethiopia, Tajikistan and Yemen—requested and were granted extensions to their mine clearance deadlines that all fell within the global 2025 mine-free target.[34]

The Convention on Cluster Munitions

The 2008 Convention on Cluster Munitions (CCM) is an international treaty of more than 100 states, among which are former major producers and users as well as affected states. It addresses the humanitarian consequences of, and unacceptable harm to civilians caused by, cluster munitions—air-dropped or ground-launched weapons that release a number of smaller submunitions intended to kill enemy personnel or destroy vehicles. There are three main criticisms of cluster munitions: they disperse large numbers of submunitions imprecisely over an extended area; they frequently fail to detonate and are difficult to detect; and unexploded submunitions can remain explosive hazards for many decades.[35] The CCM establishes an unconditional prohibition and a framework for action.[36] It also requires the destruction of stockpiles within eight years, the clearance of areas contaminated by cluster munition remnants within 10 years and the provision of assistance for victims of such weapons.

In 2019, the CCM gained two additional member states: the Philippines ratified the convention on 3 January 2019 and the Maldives acceded on 27 September 2019. As of 31 December 2019, the CCM had 107 states parties and 14 signatory states. In December 2019, 144 states, including 32 non-signatories to the convention, voted to adopt the fifth UN General Assembly resolution supporting the CCM.[37] The resolution provides states outside of the CCM with an important opportunity to indicate their sup-

---

[32] For details of the proceedings, documents and statements by states parties, see Anti-Personnel Mine Ban Convention, Fourth Review Conference, Oslo, 25–29 Nov. 2019.

[33] Fourth Review Conference of the States Parties to the Convention on the Prohibition of the Use, Stockpiling, Production and Transfer of Anti-Personnel Mines and on Their Destruction, Oslo, 26–29 Nov. 2019, 'Final document', APLC/CONF/2019/5, 9 Dec. 2019.

[34] For details of each of the requests, additional information submitted by the state party, analysis and decisions, see Fourth Review Conference (note 33).

[35] Congressional Research Service (CRS), *Cluster Munitions: Background and Issues for Congress*, CRS Report to Congress RS22907 (CRS: Washington, DC, 2019).

[36] For a summary of the Convention on Cluster Munitions see annex A, section I, in this volume.

[37] UN General Assembly Resolution 74/62, General and complete disarmament: Implementation of the Convention on Cluster Munitions, 12 Dec. 2019.

port for the humanitarian rationale behind the treaty and the objective of its universalization. For the fifth consecutive year, Zimbabwe was the only state to vote against the resolution, while 38 other states abstained (as was the case in 2018).[38]

Use and production of cluster munitions in 2019

No state party has used cluster munitions since the CCM was adopted and most of the states still outside of the convention abide de facto by the ban on the use and production of the weapon. Despite international condemnation, however, there was continued use of cluster munitions in Syria in 2019, albeit at decreasing levels. According to *Cluster Munition Monitor, 2019* there were at least 38 cluster munition attacks in the 12 months to June 2019, mostly carried out by the armed forces of the Syrian Government, and at least 674 cluster munition attacks were reported between July 2012 and June 2019.[39] There were also unverified allegations of cluster munition use in Libya.[40]

Sixteen states, none of which are states parties to the CCM Convention, are listed as producers of cluster munitions, although a lack of transparency means that it is unclear whether any of them were actively producing munitions in 2019.[41]

Destruction and clearance measures

As of July 2019, 35 of the 41 states parties that possessed stockpiles had completed the destruction of their stockpiles. This destruction of nearly 1.5 million stockpiled cluster munitions containing 178 million submunitions represents the destruction of 99 per cent of all the cluster munitions and submunitions declared as stockpiled under the CCM. Six states parties— Bulgaria, Guinea, Guinea-Bissau, Peru, Slovakia and South Africa—still have a combined total of nearly 12 000 stockpiled cluster munitions to destroy. Botswana and Switzerland were the most recent states parties to complete destruction of their stockpiled cluster munitions, in September 2018 and March 2019 respectively.[42] Guinea-Bissau failed to meet its stockpile destruction deadline of 1 May 2019 and is now in violation of the convention.

---

[38] Convention on Cluster Munitions, '2019 UNGA resolution on the implementation of the Convention on Cluster Munitions', [n.d.] For a summary of the debates on the CCM in the General Assembly First Committee, see Vićentić, J., 'Cluster munitions', *First Committee Monitor*, vol. 17, no. 6, Reaching Critical Will (9 Nov. 2019), p. 14.

[39] *Cluster Munition Monitor, 2019* focuses on calendar year 2018, with information included to August 2019 where possible. International Campaign to Ban Landmines–Cluster Munition Coalition (ICBL–CMC), *Cluster Munition Monitor, 2019* (ICBL–CMC: Geneva, Aug. 2019), pp. 12–15. On the conflict in Syria, see chapter 6, section II, in this volume.

[40] International Campaign to Ban Landmines–Cluster Munition Coalition (note 39), pp. 14–15.

[41] The countries are: Brazil, China, Egypt, Greece, India, Iran, Israel, North Korea, South Korea, Pakistan, Poland, Romania, Russia, Singapore, Turkey and the USA. International Campaign to Ban Landmines–Cluster Munition Coalition (note 39), pp. 16–17.

[42] International Campaign to Ban Landmines–Cluster Munition Coalition (note 39), pp. 18–25.

Bulgaria submitted a request to extend its stockpile destruction deadline by 18 months to 1 April 2021. It is the first state party to make such a request.[43] It is not possible to provide a global estimate of the quantity of cluster munitions currently stockpiled by non-signatories to the CCM as too few have disclosed information on the types and quantities they possess.

Conflict and insecurity made the clearance of cluster munitions more challenging in several states in 2019. An accurate estimate of the total size of the contaminated area is not possible because the extent of contamination and the progress of clearance are difficult to identify in many states, especially non-signatory states. At least 26 states and three other areas remain contaminated by cluster munitions.[44] Eight states parties have so far completed clearance of areas declared contaminated under the CCM.[45] For the first time, two states parties requested five-year extensions (to August 2025) to their clearance deadlines: Germany, to clear a former military training area; and Laos, which is one of the countries in the world most contaminated by cluster munitions.[46]

Ninth Meeting of States Parties to the CCM

The Ninth Meeting of States Parties to the CCM was due to take place in Geneva on 2–4 September 2019 under the presidency of Sri Lanka, but was shortened to two days due to a lack of funds.[47] It was the fourth formal meeting since the adoption of the 2015 Dubrovnik Action Plan, a five-year plan that provides a roadmap for states to implement and universalize the

---

[43] Convention on Cluster Munitions, Article 3 extension request by the Republic of Bulgaria, 24 Apr. 2019.

[44] The states parties with cluster munition remnants are: Afghanistan, Bosnia and Herzegovina, Chad, Chile, Croatia, Germany, Iraq, Laos, Lebanon, Montenegro, Somalia and the United Kingdom; signatory: Angola; non-signatories: Azerbaijan, Cambodia, Georgia, Iran, Libya, Serbia, South Sudan, Sudan, Syria, Tajikistan, Ukraine, Viet Nam and Yemen; other areas: Kosovo, Nagorno-Karabakh and Western Sahara. International Campaign to Ban Landmines–Cluster Munition Coalition (note 39), pp. 37–41.

[45] Albania, the Democratic Republic of the Congo, Grenada, Guinea-Bissau, Mauritania, Mozambique, Norway and Zambia. International Campaign to Ban Landmines–Cluster Munition Coalition (note 39), p. 38.

[46] Convention on Cluster Munitions, Extension request of the Federal Republic of Germany in the context of its obligations under Article 4 of the Convention on Cluster Munitions, Former Soviet military training area Wittstock, Jan. 2019; Convention on Cluster Munition Article 4 Extension Request, Executive summary, 26 Feb. 2019; and Convention on Cluster Munitions, 'Extension requests to be considered at the 9MSP', [n.d.].

[47] Convention on Cluster Munitions, Letter from the President of the Ninth Meeting of the States Parties to the Convention on Cluster Munitions (CCM) to the States Parties, 28 June 2019; and Convention on Cluster Munitions, 'Draft Provisional Annotated Programme of Work', 3 July 2019.

CCM.[48] In the final report of the meeting, as was the case in the previous year, states parties 'expressed their strong concern regarding recent incidents and evidence of use of cluster munitions in different parts of the world' and 'condemned any use by any actor'. They also expressed satisfaction at the progress made with the implementation of the Dubrovnik Action Plan. The meeting approved Bulgaria's request for an extension of its destruction deadline, but for 12 months rather than the 18 months requested; and the requests by Germany and Laos for a five-year extension to their clearance deadlines.[49] Concerns about the financial status of the CCM were also discussed, but action was deferred until the Second Review Conference in 2020.[50]

Efforts to create new global instruments

In addition to the existing global frameworks for conventional arms control discussed above, there are also a number of other processes and political instruments at various stages of development. Two efforts are highlighted below: the development of a political declaration on EWIPA; and international discussions to develop 'rules of the road' for state activity in the fifth domain of warfare: cyberspace.[51]

Towards a political declaration on explosive weapons in populated areas

After many years of seeking to address EWIPA issues within the framework of the CCW Convention, a separate process gathered momentum in 2019 with the aim of developing a political declaration to reinforce existing commitments under IHL.[52] Such a declaration would aim to set new international standards on the use of explosive weapons in towns and cities,

---

[48] The Dubrovnik Action Plan was adopted at the First Review Conference of the Convention on Cluster Munitions, Dubrovnik, Croatia, on 11 Sep. 2015. For the text of the plan see http://www.clusterconvention.org/wp-content/uploads/2016/04/The-Dubrovnik-Action-Plan.pdf. For an update on progress, see Convention on Cluster Munitions, Ninth Meeting of States Parties, 'Progress report monitoring progress in implementing the Dubrovnik Action Plan', Submitted by the President of the Ninth Meeting of States Parties, CCM/MSP/2019/11, 5 July 2019.

[49] Convention on Cluster Munitions, Final Report, CCM/MSP/2019/13, 18 Sep. 2019. See also the coverage of the meeting on the website of the CCM Implementation Support Unit, 'The Ninth Meeting of States Parties', [n.d.].

[50] Convention on Cluster Munitions, 'Possible measures to address financial predictability and sustainability of the Convention on Cluster Munitions', CCM/MSP/2019/5, 1 July 2019.

[51] In 2010, *The Economist* declared that 'warfare has entered the fifth domain: cyberspace'. 'Cyberwar: War in the fifth domain', *The Economist*, 1 July 2010. The other four domains are land, sea, air and space. See also Clarke, R. A. and Knake, R. K., *The Fifth Domain: Defending Our Country, Our Companies, and Ourselves in the Age of Cyber Threats* (Penguin Press: New York, 2019).

[52] For earlier discussions on EWIPA in the CCW Convention, see Anthony, I., 'A relaunch of conventional arms control in Europe', *SIPRI Yearbook 2017*, pp. 557–58; Davis and Verbruggen (note 3); and Boulanin, Davis and Verbruggen (note 4).

which could in turn drive changes in military practice at the policy and operational levels.

The use of EWIPA—and especially the use of explosive weapons with a large destructive radius, an inaccurate delivery system or the capacity to deliver multiple munitions over a wide area—has frequently led to situations in which over 90 per cent of casualties are civilian rather than combatants.[53] According to Action on Armed Violence (AOAV), there were 6478 civilian deaths and 12 908 injuries linked to explosive weapons in 2019—a reduction in civilian deaths compared to 2018 (9615), but an increase in the total number injured (12 720 in 2018). The vast majority of casualties occurred when explosive weapons were used in populated areas and the highest numbers were recorded in Syria, Afghanistan, Yemen, Somalia and Libya.[54] The continuing use of explosive weapons in the eight-year-long Syrian war, for example, has led to massive ERW contamination and devastating humanitarian impacts, as well as acute challenges with regard to access to health care, and social and economic deprivation.[55]

The International Network on Explosive Weapons (INEW), an NGO partnership formed in 2011, was the first to articulate this as an issue that demanded attention, and its efforts led to calls from an increasing number of states, successive UN secretary-generals, international bodies and other NGOs for measures to provide better protection for civilians and to prevent such harm.[56] One of the three principal themes of the UN secretary-general's May 2018 disarmament agenda was a new focus on 'disarmament that saves lives'. This included efforts to 'rein in' the use of EWIPA with wide-area impacts by supporting 'the efforts of Member States to develop a political declaration, as well as appropriate limitations, common standards and operational policies in conformity with international humanitarian law'.[57]

These calls for action continued in 2019. UN Secretary-General António Guterres raised the issue again in his protection of civilians report published on 7 May 2019, and it was discussed in the annual open debate on the

---

[53] International Committee of the Red Cross, 'Explosive weapons in populated areas', Factsheet, 14 June 2016; and International Network on Explosive Weapons (INEW), 'Protecting civilians from the use of explosive weapons in populated areas', Oct. 2019.

[54] Action on Armed Violence, 'Explosive violence in 2019', 7 Jan. 2020; and AOAV database, 2019, <http://www.explosiveviolencedata.com/>.

[55] O'Reilly, C. et al., 'The waiting list: Addressing the immediate and long-term needs of victims of explosive weapons in Syria', Humanity & Inclusion, Sep. 2019. On the armed conflict in Syria, see chapter 6, section II, in this volume.

[56] See e.g. International Committee of the Red Cross (note 53); and Article 36, 'Effects of explosive weapons', Working paper on explosive weapons in populated areas, Dec. 2019. For a list of the 109 states and territories and 6 state groupings that have publicly acknowledged the harm caused by EWIPA in statements, see 'Political response', on the International Network on Explosive Weapons (INEW) website.

[57] United Nations, Office for Disarmament Affairs, *Securing Our Common Future: An Agenda for Disarmament* (Office for Disarmament Affairs: New York, May 2018), pp. x, 36.

protection of civilians in the UN Security Council on 23 May 2019.[58] The debate marked the 20th anniversary of the adoption of the first UN Security Council resolution on the protection of civilians in armed conflict.[59] In July, the African Union Peace and Security Council issued a statement indicating its support for a political declaration to stop the use of EWIPA.[60] In September 2019, a joint appeal from the president of the ICRC and the UN secretary-general expressed alarm at 'the devastating humanitarian consequences of urban warfare'.[61] On 1–2 October 2019, Austria convened the Vienna Conference on the Protection of Civilians in Urban Warfare.[62] There were participants from 133 states, several international organizations and a number of NGOs. Most made substantive and practical proposals on the development of a political declaration on EWIPA.[63] At the 2019 meeting of the UN General Assembly First Committee on Disarmament and International Security in October 2019, a joint statement on the issue coordinated by Ireland was endorsed by 71 member states.[64]

As a result of this increasing international political pressure, Ireland convened the first of a series of open consultations on a political declaration on EWIPA in Geneva on 18 November 2019, with a view to finalizing and adopting a declaration in 2020.[65] The first meeting provided an opportunity for government delegates to share views on what they thought should be in such a political declaration. Most delegations called for the declaration to acknowledge the humanitarian impact of explosive weapons with wide-area effects and supported the idea of it encouraging the sharing of best practices and policies on the protection of civilians in urban conflict settings, and on the provision of victim assistance. Views differed, however, on how it should relate to IHL and on whether it should seek to prohibit or limit specific types

---

[58] United Nations, Security Council, Report of the Secretary-General, 'Protection of civilians in armed conflict', S/2019/373, 7 May 2019; UN Secretary-General, 'Secretary-general's remarks to the Security Council on the protection of civilians in armed conflict', 23 May 2019; and Hamid, Z., 'Security Council open debate: Protection of civilians in armed conflict, May 2019', Peace Women, 23 May 2019.

[59] United Nations Security Council Resolution 1265, 17 Sep. 1999.

[60] African Union, Peace and Security Council (PSC), 'Press Statement of the 859th meeting of the PSC, held on 17 July 2019, dedicated to an open session on the theme: "Protection of Civilians from the Use of Explosive Weapons in Populated Areas (EWIPA)"', Addis Ababa, 24 July 2019.

[61] United Nations, Secretary-General, 'Joint appeal by the UN secretary-general and the president of the International Committee of the Red Cross on the use of explosive weapons in cities', Note to correspondents, 18 Sep. 2019.

[62] Federal Ministry, Austria, 'Vienna Conference on Protecting Civilians in Urban Warfare', Vienna, 1–2 Oct. 2019.

[63] Federal Ministry, Austria, 'Vienna Conference on Protecting Civilians in Urban Warfare: Summary of the conference', Vienna, 1–2 Oct. 2019; Article 36, 'Vienna Conference marks turning point as states support negotiation of an international political declaration on explosive weapons', 2 Oct. 2019; and Pytlak, A., 'States commit to take political action on explosive weapons at Vienna conference', *First Committee Monitor*, vol. 17, no. 1, Reaching Critical Will (7 Oct. 2019), pp. 10–14.

[64] United Nations General Assembly, First Committee, 'Joint statement on explosive weapons in populated areas', New York, 24 Oct. 2019.

[65] Irish Department of Foreign Affairs and Trade, 'Protecting civilians in urban warfare', [n.d.].

of weapons. Some delegations argued that existing IHL is sufficient, while others said that the objective of the declaration should be to strengthen IHL. Ireland asked for written contributions on possible elements of a political declaration by 6 December 2019 and committed to publish a first draft text reflecting areas of convergence and divergence in mid-January 2020.[66] The next consultations will take place in mid-February and early April 2020.

Governing state behaviour in cyberspace

Cyberattacks and their consequences are a major international concern. The exploitation of cyber vulnerabilities in critical civilian infrastructure, for example, has become a particularly pervasive security threat.[67] By one estimate, the world experienced almost 100 significant cyber incidents in the first 11 months of 2019.[68] These involved a wide spectrum of activities and actors, including cybercrime by non-state actors and state or state-sponsored cyber operations that often occurred in legal grey areas below the threshold of armed conflict.[69] However, the use of cyber operations during armed conflicts is also a growing concern, and many states have developed or are developing digital operations within their military doctrines and strategies.[70]

Despite two decades of international discussions within the UN on the development of norms of responsible state behaviour in cyberspace, there is little common ground between states on the nature of the threat and the measures needed to address it. Member states are now polarized around one of two positions. The first, which is mainly the position of Western states, regards the proliferation of information and communications technologies (ICTs) as a positive tendency and considers existing international law sufficient for guiding state behaviour in cyberspace. Another key element of this position is that human rights apply online as well as offline, including rights related to privacy. The other position, adopted by a group of states led by China and Russia, regards digitalization as a threat and would prefer new

---

[66] For a summary of the issues discussed, see Reaching Critical Will, 'Towards a political declaration on the use of explosive weapons in populated areas: States need to ensure that expressed commitments translate into real impacts on the ground', [n.d.]. See also Reaching Critical Will, 'Statements from the political declaration process on explosive weapons in populated areas', 18 Nov. 2019.

[67] See e.g. Gisel, L. and Olejnik, L., 'The potential human cost of cyber operations', International Committee of the Red Cross, Report of Expert Meeting, 14–16 Nov. 2018.

[68] 'Significant cyber incidents' are defined as cyberattacks on government agencies or defence-related and high-tech companies, or economic crimes involving losses of more than US$ 1 million. See 'Significant cyber incidents', Center for Strategic and International Studies, [n.d.].

[69] Moynihan, H., *The Application of International Law to State Cyberattacks: Sovereignty and Non-intervention*, Chatham House Research Paper (Royal Institute of International Affairs: London, Dec. 2019).

[70] See e.g. Laudrain, A. P. B., 'France's new offensive cyber doctrine', Lawfare, 26 Feb. 2019; Brent, L., 'NATO's role in cyberspace', NATO Review, 12 Feb. 2019; and US Department of Defense, 'Summary, Cyber Strategy, 2018'.

normative guidance on state use and development of ICTs, and preferably a new legal instrument in the form of a treaty.[71]

Some developing countries, especially those with digital priorities that are different from those of more networked states, fall between these two groups and have noted that the cyber norms discussed previously do not include their perspectives. This politicization of the issue into two rival camps continued in 2019 with the adoption of two First Committee resolutions on cybersecurity and ICTs: one tabled by Russia and the other by the USA.[72]

These different perspectives have prevented international consensus on a way forward. Instead, in December 2018 the UN General Assembly established two processes—an Open-ended Working Group (OEWG) and a new Group of Governmental Experts (GGE)—to replace earlier GGEs convened by the UN in this area. A key difference between the two processes is their level of openness—all UN member states can participate in the OEWG, whereas only 25 states are permitted to attend the GGE.[73]

The OEWG held a first substantive session in September 2019 and an informal multi-stakeholder intersessional meeting in December 2019. The OEWG session on 9–13 September 2019 focused on six subjects: existing and potential threats; international law; rules, norms and principles; institutional dialogue; confidence-building measures; and capacity building.[74] The meeting identified several practical next steps, although states continued to have differences over the applicability of IHL and human rights to cyberspace, and the extent to which the activities of non-state actors are relevant to the OEWG discussions.[75]

Although much was made of how the OEWG would be accessible for civil society, in reality many NGOs were barred from attending the first substantive session and their level of access to future meetings is unclear. While the 2–4 December 2019 meeting was significant for its inclusion of civil society,

[71] See Tikk, E., 'Cyber arms control and resilience', *SIPRI Yearbook 2019*, pp. 479–99; and Lété, B., 'Shaping inclusive governance in cyberspace', *German Marshall Fund Policy Paper*, no. 23 (Sep. 2019).

[72] UN First Committee Resolution L.49/Rev.1, 'Advancing responsible state behaviour in cyberspace in the context of international security' was introduced by the USA as its main sponsor and adopted by a vote of 161 in favour and 10 against with 8 abstentions; Resolution L.50/Rev.1, 'Developments in the field of information and telecommunications in the context of international security' was tabled by Russia and adopted by a vote of 124 in favour and 6 against with 48 abstentions. See United Nations, 'First Committee defers action on text proposing move to Geneva, while approving 9 draft resolutions', Press release, 6 Nov. 2019; and Reaching Critical Will, *First Committee Monitor*, vol. 17, no. 6 (9 Nov. 2019).

[73] For documents and information related to the meetings held by these two groups see United Nations, Group of Governmental Experts; and United Nations, Open-ended Working Group. For further analysis and discussion, see Reaching Critical Will, 'Information and communications technology (ICT)', [n.d.].

[74] United Nations, General Assembly, Open-ended Working Group, 'Organization of work of the first substantive session', A/AC.290/2019/2, 25 July 2019.

[75] Samler, D. and Pytlak. A., 'News in brief', *Cyber Peace & Security Monitor*, vol. 1, no. 3 (Sep. 2019).

it was the only opportunity for non-governmental stakeholder input into the OEWG process in 2019.[76]

The GGE held several regional consultations and an informal consultation with all UN member states on 5–6 December 2019, before starting its formal work on 9–13 December 2019.[77]

In the absence of consensus, a binding agreement within either the OEWG or the GGE process seems unlikely in the near future. Instead, states will continue to operate independently in cyberspace to promote and protect their strategic interests.

Conclusions

Some analysts see the world as in a state of flux and cooperative security policies as modest exceptions to the rule of unilateral, competitive arms build-ups and the unravelling of the arms control architecture.[78] While most of the focus of this undoing of arms control and disarmament agreements has been on nuclear, biological and chemical weapons, the processes for finding solutions to the significant challenges related to conventional weapons and international security have also become more unpredictable.

Many of the discussions within the global instruments for conventional arms control can be characterized by competing positions, repetitive debates and a discernible absence of progress—and, in some cases, even a lack of funding for treaty meetings. The CCW Convention in particular is treading water and forcing states to pursue alternative arms control arrangements, largely through fledgling political 'declarations of the willing' that bypass its consensus rule.

---

[76] United Nations, Informal intersessional consultative meeting of the OEWG with industry, non-governmental organizations and academia, 2–4 Dec. 2019.

[77] United Nations, 'Chair's summary: Informal consultative meeting of the Group of Governmental Experts (GGE) on advancing responsible state behaviour in cyberspace in the context of international security', 5–6 Dec. 2019. For collated summaries of the regional consultations see 'Regional consultations series of the Group of Governmental Experts on advancing responsible state behaviour in cyberspace in the context of international security', [n.d.].

[78] See e.g. Lodgaard, S., 'Arms control and world order', *Journal for Peace and Nuclear Disarmament*, vol. 2, no. 1 (2019), pp. 1–18; and chapter 1 in this volume.

II. The group of governmental experts on lethal autonomous weapon systems

MOA PELDÁN CARLSSON AND VINCENT BOULANIN

The legal, ethical and security challenges posed by lethal autonomous weapon systems (LAWS) have been the subject of intergovernmental discussions within the framework of the 1981 Convention on Certain Conventional Weapons (CCW Convention) since 2014.[1] Over the years this process under the auspices of the United Nations has become the focal point of the expert and intergovernmental discussions on the military applications of recent advances in artificial intelligence (AI) and autonomous systems.[2] Since 2017 the discussions have been led by an open-ended group of governmental experts (GGE), which has a mandate to 'explore and agree on possible recommendations on options related to emerging technologies in the area of LAWS, in the context of the objectives and purposes of the Convention, taking into account all proposals—past, present and future'.[3]

The mandate, which was agreed in 2016, was purposefully left broad and exploratory given that the states parties still had at the time—even after three years of informal discussions—very different views of the scope and nature of the problems posed by LAWS and consequently of the types of policy response that could be appropriate to govern the development of technology in these areas.

Between 2017 and 2019, the GGE made significant progress on the substantial side: a consensus has emerged among states that autonomy in weapon systems cannot be unlimited. On the political side, there is still disagreement on whether additional regulation is needed. This section reports on the activities of the GGE in 2019. It describes the guiding principles adopted by the group and then looks in turn at the other issues discussed and the way ahead for the GGE on LAWS.

---

[1] For earlier discussions of the regulation of LAWS see Anthony, I. and Holland, C., 'The governance of autonomous weapon systems', *SIPRI Yearbook 2014*, pp. 423–31; Davis, I. et al., 'Humanitarian arms control regimes: Key development in 2016', *SIPRI Yearbook 2017*, pp. 559–61; Davis, I. and Verbruggen, M., 'The Convention on Certain Conventional Weapons', *SIPRI Yearbook 2018*, pp. 383–86; Boulanin, V., Davis, I. and Verbruggen, M., 'The Convention on Certain Conventional Weapons and lethal autonomous weapon systems', *SIPRI Yearbook 2019*, pp. 452–57. For other developments in the CCW framework in 2019 see section I of this chapter. For a summary and other details of the CCW Convention see annex A, section I, in this volume.

[2] 'Autonomous weapons and the new laws of war', *The Economist*, 19 Jan. 2019; and 'Artificial intelligence is changing every aspect of war', *The Economist*, 7 Sep. 2019.

[3] Certain Conventional Weapons Convention, Fifth Review Conference, Report of the 2016 informal meeting of experts on lethal autonomous weapons systems, CCW/CONF.V/2, 10 June 2016, annex, para. 3. The GGE is open-ended in the sense that its membership is open: all CCW states parties, other states that participate as observers, international organizations and non-governmental organizations may participate. In contrast, GGEs established under the UN General Assembly are open only to UN member states. Certain Conventional Weapons Convention, Fifth Review Conference, Draft rules of procedure, CCW/CONF.V/4, 28 Sep. 2016, rules 46–49.

The guiding principles

The 2019 meetings of the GGE were chaired by Ljupčo Jivan Gjorgjinski of North Macedonia. According to the decision of the 2018 meeting of CCW state parties that established the 2019 GGE, the group was supposed to meet for a total of seven days, which was three days fewer than in previous years. However, the group eventually met for 10 days in total, as the chair convened three days of informal sessions over the course of the year. As in previous years, the GGE included wide participation from both states and civil society. Seven working papers were submitted by states and other participants before the meetings, which was half the number submitted in 2018.[4] The working papers differed in character and varied in focus, but all had a clear objective of trying to assist the GGE to reach common understanding about how to deal with the issue of LAWS.

The starting point of discussions in 2019 was a list of 10 possible guiding principles that the GGE had agreed in 2018.[5] This list encompassed the points of convergence in the discussions over the years. Among these were the understanding that international humanitarian law fully applies to LAWS; that humans must continue to exercise responsibility for decisions on the use of weapon systems; and that states should not only conduct the required legal reviews of new weapons, means and methods of warfare (known as Article 36 reviews), but should also consider safeguards to deal with the risk of their acquisition by terrorist groups and the risk of proliferation.[6] In 2019 the GGE agreed to recommend removal of the qualifier 'possible' and adoption of the 10 guiding principles in full along with an additional 11th principle, guiding principle c, on human–machine interaction (see box 13.2). This new principle reflected the increased focus that the issue of human control over LAWS has received over the years. These recommendations were subsequently adopted by the meeting of states parties in November 2019.[7]

The principles guided the discussions at the GGE meetings in 2019 and prompted the five agenda items for the group's meeting: potential challenges posed by LAWS to international humanitarian law; characterization of the systems to promote a common understanding on concepts; the human element in the use of lethal force; review of potential military applications of related technologies; and possible options for addressing challenges to

---

[4] United Nations Office at Geneva (UNOG), '2019 group of governmental experts on lethal autonomous weapons systems (LAWS)'.

[5] Certain Conventional Weapons Convention, Group of Governmental Experts on Emerging Technologies in the Area of Lethal Autonomous Weapons Systems, Report of the 2018 session, CCW/GGE.1/2018/3, 23 Oct. 2018, para. 21.

[6] Such legal reviews are a requirement of Article 36 of the 1977 Protocol I Additional to the 1949 Geneva Conventions, and Relating to the Protection of Victims of International Armed Conflicts. For a summary and other details of the protocol see annex A, section I, in this volume.

[7] Certain Conventional Weapons Convention, Meeting of States Parties, Final report, CCW/MSP/2019/9, 13 Dec. 2019.

Box 13.2. Guiding Principles agreed in 2019 by the Group of Governmental Experts on Lethal Autonomous Weapon Systems

[The group] affirmed that international law, in particular the United Nations Charter and International Humanitarian Law (IHL) as well as relevant ethical perspectives, should guide the continued work of the Group. Noting the potential challenges posed by emerging technologies in the area of lethal autonomous weapons systems to IHL, the following were affirmed, without prejudice to the result of future discussions:

(a) International humanitarian law continues to apply fully to all weapons systems, including the potential development and use of lethal autonomous weapons systems;

(b) Human responsibility for decisions on the use of weapons systems must be retained since accountability cannot be transferred to machines. This should be considered across the entire life cycle of the weapons system;

(c) Human–machine interaction, which may take various forms and be implemented at various stages of the life cycle of a weapon, should ensure that the potential use of weapons systems based on emerging technologies in the area of lethal autonomous weapons systems is in compliance with applicable international law, in particular IHL. In determining the quality and extent of human–machine interaction, a range of factors should be considered including the operational context, and the characteristics and capabilities of the weapons system as a whole;

(d) Accountability for developing, deploying and using any emerging weapons system in the framework of the CCW must be ensured in accordance with applicable international law, including through the operation of such systems within a responsible chain of human command and control;

(e) In accordance with States' obligations under international law, in the study, development, acquisition, or adoption of a new weapon, means or method of warfare, determination must be made whether its employment would, in some or all circumstances, be prohibited by international law;

(f) When developing or acquiring new weapons systems based on emerging technologies in the area of lethal autonomous weapons systems, physical security, appropriate non-physical safeguards (including cyber-security against hacking or data spoofing), the risk of acquisition by terrorist groups and the risk of proliferation should be considered;

(g) Risk assessments and mitigation measures should be part of the design, development, testing and deployment cycle of emerging technologies in any weapons systems;

(h) Consideration should be given to the use of emerging technologies in the area of lethal autonomous weapons systems in upholding compliance with IHL and other applicable international legal obligations;

(i) In crafting potential policy measures, emerging technologies in the area of lethal autonomous weapons systems should not be anthropomorphized;

(j) Discussions and any potential policy measures taken within the context of the CCW should not hamper progress in or access to peaceful uses of intelligent autonomous technologies;

(k) The CCW offers an appropriate framework for dealing with the issue of emerging technologies in the area of lethal autonomous weapons systems within the context of the objectives and purposes of the Convention, which seeks to strike a balance between military necessity and humanitarian considerations.

Source: Quoted from Certain Conventional Weapons Convention, Group of Governmental Experts on Emerging Technologies in the Area of Lethal Autonomous Weapons Systems, Report of the 2019 session of the Group of Governmental Experts on Emerging Technologies in the Area of Lethal Autonomous Weapons Systems, CCW/GGE.1/2019/3, 25 Sep. 2019, <https://undocs.org/CCW/GGE.1/2019/3>, annex IV.

humanitarian and international security.[8] The following five subsections address each of these in turn.

Potential challenges posed by LAWS to international humanitarian law

The agenda item on potential challenges to international humanitarian law arises from the introduction to the agreed guiding principles. As in previous years, states agreed that international humanitarian law continues to apply to all weapon systems, including LAWS; that it is humans, not machines, that are accountable for complying with this law; and that human responsibility for the use of force needs therefore to be retained. However, states continued to disagree on whether international humanitarian law is sufficiently clear on the issue of LAWS, or whether there is instead a need for a completely new framework to deal with the possible humanitarian risks posed by these weapon systems.

During the discussions in 2019, many states argued that Article 36 reviews could be a valuable method for ensuring that LAWS comply with international humanitarian law. Some delegations (e.g. the European Union and the Netherlands) argued for increasing transparency in Article 36 reviews and sharing of best practices to help other states to better comply with international humanitarian law.[9] However, several delegations (e.g. Austria) claimed that legal reviews alone might not be sufficient.[10] Some participants (notably the International Panel on the Regulation of Autonomous Weapons, IPRAW, an international group of scientists) went further to argue that the unique nature of LAWS poses challenges to the process of legal reviews as it can be difficult to review components of the weapon systems, such as functions enabled by machine learning.[11] Others (e.g. Austria) also noted that Article 36 reviews are national procedures conducted at the discretion of each state and therefore do not contribute to the development of international standards.

There were also discussions about the impact of LAWS on the implementation of international humanitarian law. Some states (e.g. Russia and the United States) argued that LAWS could essentially improve the implementation of international humanitarian law—for example, by allowing

---

[8] Certain Conventional Weapons Convention, Group of Governmental Experts on Emerging Technologies in the Area of Lethal Autonomous Weapons Systems, Provisional agenda, 8 Mar. 2019, CCW/GGE.1/2019/1.

[9] Certain Conventional Weapons Convention, Group of Governmental Experts on Emerging Technologies in the Area of Lethal Autonomous Weapons Systems, 'An exploration of the potential challenges posed by emerging technologies in the area of lethal autonomous weapons systems to international humanitarian law', Statement by the European Union, 25–29 Mar. 2019; and Certain Conventional Weapons Convention, Group of Governmental Experts on Emerging Technologies in the Area of Lethal Autonomous Weapons Systems, 'Agenda item 5(a): An exploration of the potential challenges posed by emerging technologies in the area of lethal autonomous weapons systems to international humanitarian law', Statement by the Netherlands, 26 Apr. 2019.

[10] Pytlak, A. and Geyer, K., 'News in brief', *CCW Report*, vol. 7, no. 3 (29 Mar. 2019), pp. 4–10.

[11] Pytlak and Geyer (note 10).

armed force to be applied with greater precision. Conversely, many other states (e.g. Brazil, Chile and Pakistan) and non-governmental organizations (NGOs) argued that LAWS risk undermining it—for Brazil, the use of LAWS would 'risk a [dilution] of the very concept of accountability as legal answerability over one's actions and choices'.[12] In addition, Human Rights Watch—an NGO—underscored that LAWS would be incompatible with 'the principles of humanity and the dictates of the public conscience' and would thus breach what is known as the Martens Clause, an accepted element of customary international law.[13]

Promoting a common understanding on concepts

In 2019 states continued to have difficulties reaching a common understanding of the characteristics of LAWS. To support the GGE's work on that matter, the chair proposed several questions for states to consider.[14]

The initial question was whether autonomy is an attribute of a weapon system as a whole, or whether it should be attached to the different tasks of weapon systems. States generally agreed that the focus of the discussion should be on autonomy in target selection and engagement—two critical functions. They were also able to agree that autonomy should be seen as a spectrum, and that it is difficult to identify a clear dividing line between semi- and fully autonomous weapon systems. However, at a late-night session in August 2019, the Russian delegation firmly and repeatedly asserted that autonomy is not a key characteristic of LAWS as autonomy is not necessarily problematic and is already a characteristic found in many existing weapon systems. This created frustration among other delegations.[15] Similarly, in 2018 Russia had argued that the GGE should be concerned with 'the elaboration of general understanding of what the future LAWS could be

---

[12] Pytlak and Geyer (note 10); and Certain Conventional Weapons Convention, Group of Governmental Experts on Emerging Technologies in the Area of Lethal Autonomous Weapons Systems, 'Challenge to IHL—Item 5(a)', Statement by Brazil, 25–29 Mar. 2019.

[13] Certain Conventional Weapons Convention, Group of Governmental Experts on Emerging Technologies in the Area of Lethal Autonomous Weapons Systems, 'Agenda item 5(a) regarding challenged posed to international humanitarian law', Statement by Human Rights Watch, 26 Mar. 2019. A form of the Martens Clause appears as Article 1(2) of the 1977 Additional Protocol I (note 6) and in the preamble of the 1977 Additional Protocol II, among other treaties and conventions.

[14] Certain Conventional Weapons Convention, Group of Governmental Experts on Emerging Technologies in the Area of Lethal Autonomous Weapons Systems, Provisional programme of work submitted by the chairperson, CCW/GGE.1/2019/2, 19 Mar. 2019, p. 2.

[15] Acheson, R., 'While a few countries control the CCW, we risk losing control over weapons', *CCW Report*, vol. 7, no. 7 (22 Aug. 2019), pp. 1–4.

with the "advanced" level of "artificial intelligence'", rather than discussing 'existing operational systems with a high autonomy/automation degree'.[16]

With regard to the question of what characteristics are important from the perspective of compliance with international humanitarian law, views were more divided. Some states (e.g. India) suggested that the capability to self-learn or to redefine a mission or objective independently should be considered as a key characteristic of LAWS.[17] However, several other states (e.g. Costa Rica and Peru) found this characterization to be too restrictive.[18] The question of whether the discussion should focus on the use of LAWS against people rather than against material was also raised, although again some delegations (e.g. Ireland) believed that this distinction was not relevant.[19]

In the light of the definitional questions, many states called for a 'technology-neutral approach'. They argued that, in order to move the debate forward, it would be more productive to focus on the human element in the use of force rather than detailed discussion about technical characteristics of LAWS.[20]

The human element in the use of lethal force

The agenda item on the human element in the use of lethal force arises from guiding principle b (see box 13.2). Under this agenda item, the GGE considered the need to maintain human responsibility for decisions on the use of weapon systems. The discussions focused on the type and degree of human–machine interaction that should be required in order to comply with international humanitarian law.

As reflected by the adoption of the 11th guiding principle, states agreed that human–machine interaction may take various forms and be implemented at

---

[16] Certain Conventional Weapons Convention, Group of Governmental Experts on Emerging Technologies in the Area of Lethal Autonomous Weapons Systems, 'Russia's approaches to the elaboration of a working definition and basic functions of lethal autonomous weapons systems in the context of the purposes and objectives of the Convention', Working Paper submitted by Russia, CCW/GGE.1/2018/WP.6, 4 Apr. 2018, para. 3.

[17] Certain Conventional Weapons Convention, Group of Governmental Experts on Emerging Technologies in the Area of Lethal Autonomous Weapons Systems, 'Characterisation of the systems under consideration in order to promote a common understanding on concepts and characteristics relevant to the objectives and purposes of the convention', Statement by India, 25 Mar. 2019.

[18] Pytlak and Geyer (note 10).

[19] Certain Conventional Weapons Convention, Group of Governmental Experts on Emerging Technologies in the Area of Lethal Autonomous Weapons Systems, 'Characterization of the systems under consideration in order to promote a common understanding on concepts and characteristics relevant to the objectives and purposes of the convention', Statement by Ireland, 25 Mar. 2019.

[20] Certain Conventional Weapons Convention, Group of Governmental Experts in the Area of Lethal Autonomous Weapons Systems, Chair's summary of the discussion of the 2019 Group of Governmental Experts on emerging technologies in the area of lethal autonomous weapons systems, CCW/GGE.1/2019/3/Add.1, 8 Nov. 2019, para. 14.

various stages of the life cycle of a weapon. However, they could not agree on the types and degree of control that would be required in the different stages of a weapon's life cycle. In the debate, some states (e.g. Austria, Brazil and Mexico) expressed concerns about the lack of ethical considerations.[21] For them, the determination about human–machine interaction should not only be guided by legal and military considerations, but also moral consideration. In their view, ethics require direct human agency in decisions about the use of force.

States' divergent views on the necessary form of human–machine inter-action was further reflected in the debate about the terminology and phrasing that would most suitably convey the need for a human to exercise responsibility for the use of LAWS. The majority of states continued to use the term 'human control', the term that has been the most frequently used since the start of the LAWS debate. Several delegations (in particular Australia and the USA) continued to be critical of the term, pointing out that the very term 'control' could be interpreted in different—if not contradictory—ways. Australia presented in a working paper the concept of 'system of control', a comprehensive system that Australia implements to ensure that its military processes and capabilities are directed by humans at all stages of their design, development, training and use and are compliant with international and domestic law.[22] The USA, as in 2018, continued to argue that the term 'human judgement' would be more meaningful than 'human control'.[23] The US Department of Defense uses the alternative term in its directive on autonomy in weapon systems, which requires that 'Autonomous and semi-autonomous weapon systems shall be designed to allow commanders and operators to exercise appropriate levels of human judgment over the use of force'.[24]

In the spirit of compromise, several states (e.g. Belgium, Ireland, Luxembourg and the United Kingdom) proposed alternate terminology in their working papers and statements: human responsibility, human

---

[21] Pytlak and Geyer (note 10).

[22] Certain Conventional Weapons Convention, Group of Governmental Experts on Emerging Technologies in the Area of Lethal Autonomous Weapons Systems, 'Australia's system of control and applications for autonomous weapon systems', Working paper submitted by Australia, CCW/GGE.1/2019/WP.2, 20 Mar. 2019, paras 7–9.

[23] Certain Conventional Weapons Convention, Group of Governmental Experts on Emerging Technologies in the Area of Lethal Autonomous Weapons Systems, 'Human–machine interaction in the development, deployment and use of emerging technologies in the area of lethal autonomous weapons systems', Working paper submitted by the United States, CCW/GGE.2/2018/WP.4, 28 Aug. 2018.

[24] Certain Conventional Weapons Convention, CCW/GGE.2/2018/WP.4 (note 23), paras 9–13; and US Department of Defense, 'Autonomy in weapon systems', Directive no. 3000.09, 8 May 2017.

intervention, human supervision, human involvement, human authority, and type and degree of human–machine interaction.[25]

Eventually, the term 'human control', which had been used in previous GGE reports, was removed as a stand-alone phrase from the final report of the 2019 GGE at the insistence of the US delegation.[26] This decision was criticized by a number of delegations, notably Brazil and Costa Rica. In the discussions and in several working papers, many states referred to the different stages of human–machine interaction explored by the 2018 GGE.[27] This led to the term 'human–machine interaction' being used in the 2019 final report as an overarching concept in discussions on which 'elements of control and judgement' can be considered the human element in the use of force.[28]

Review of potential military applications of related technologies

The agenda item on potential military applications of autonomous technologies considered guiding principle k, which recalls that the debate on LAWS should 'strike a balance between military necessity and humanitarian considerations'. The GGE discussed how militaries might adopt and use autonomous technologies and the potential risks of doing so. States agreed that civilian casualties and injuries must always be considered but disagreed as to whether autonomy would increase or decrease the risk to civilians. Notably, the USA argued that autonomy in weapon systems could lead to increased security for civilians through, for example, better accuracy in target selection and engagement, and could therefore increase compliance with international humanitarian law.[29] Further, some states highlighted that autonomy in weapon systems could make military personnel operate more efficiently and with reduced risk of harm.[30]

---

[25] Certain Conventional Weapons Convention, Group of Governmental Experts on Emerging Technologies in the Area of Lethal Autonomous Weapons Systems, 'Food for thought paper', Working paper submitted by Belgium, Ireland and Luxembourg, CCW/GGE.1/2019/WP.4, 28 Mar. 2019; and Certain Conventional Weapons Convention, Group of Governmental Experts on Emerging Technologies in the Area of Lethal Autonomous Weapons Systems, 'Agenda item 5(d): Further consideration of the human element in the use of lethal force; aspect of human-machine interaction in the development, deployment and use of emerging technologies in the area of lethal autonomous weapon systems', Statement by the United Kingdom, 25–29 Mar. 2019.

[26] Certain Conventional Weapons Convention, Group of Governmental Experts on Emerging Technologies in the Area of Lethal Autonomous Weapons Systems, Report of the 2019 session of the Group of Governmental Experts on Emerging Technologies in the Area of Lethal Autonomous Weapons Systems, CCW/GGE.1/2019/3, 25 Sep. 2019.

[27] Certain Conventional Weapons Convention, CCW/GGE.1/2018/3 (note 5).

[28] Certain Conventional Weapons Convention, CCW/GGE.1/2019/3 (note 26), paras 21–22.

[29] Certain Conventional Weapons Convention, Group of Governmental Experts on Emerging Technologies in the Area of Lethal Autonomous Weapons Systems, 'Implementing international humanitarian law in the use of autonomy in weapon systems', Working paper submitted by the United States, CCW/GGE.1/2019/WP.5, 28 Aug. 2018

[30] Pytlak and Geyer (note 10).

In contrast, as in previous years, a majority of states expressed serious concern about whether LAWS would perform as expected in complex environments and be capable of being used in accordance with the requirements of international humanitarian law.[31]

Options for addressing challenges

The eventual policy outcome of the GGE process has been a contentious issue since the GGE was formed in 2017. The policy options on the table for discussion in 2019 were more or less the same as in 2018: these range from a full prohibition to no action at all.

By the end of 2019, many states had called for the negotiation of a legally binding instrument—in the form of a protocol to the CCW Convention or an independent treaty—that would prohibit or regulate LAWS or impose obligations on their use.[32] France and Germany called for the negotiation of a political declaration containing politically, but not legally, binding commitments, which would possibly lead to a code of conduct based on the guiding principles.[33] Several states (e.g. Argentina) called for Article 36 reviews to be improved and for states to increase information sharing on these reviews.[34] Other states (e.g. Australia, Israel, Russia and the USA) claimed that there is no need for further legal measures because existing international humanitarian law is fully applicable to the challenges posed by LAWS.[35]

A new proposal was made—by Portugal—in 2019: a review of existing applicable international law.[36] This would be comparable to the 2008 Montreux Document, which describes how existing international law

---

[31] Certain Conventional Weapons Convention, CCW/GGE.1/2019/3/Add.1 (note 20); and Certain Conventional Weapons Convention, Group of Governmental Experts on Emerging Technologies in the Area of Lethal Autonomous Weapons Systems, 'Possible options for addressing LAWS—Agenda Item 5(e)', Statement by Brazil, 25 Mar. 2019.

[32] For a list of these states—which is more or less the same as in previous years—see Campaign to Stop Killer Robots, 'Country views on killer robots', 25 Oct. 2019. On the existing CCW protocols see annex A, section I, in this volume.

[33] Certain Conventional Weapons Convention, Group of Governmental Experts on Emerging Technologies in the Area of Lethal Autonomous Weapons Systems, 'On agenda item 5(e) possible options for addressing the humanitarian and international security challenges posed by emerging technologies in the area of lethal autonomous weapons systems in the context of the objectives and purposes of the Convention without prejudicing policy outcomes and taking into account past, present and future proposals', Statement by Germany, 27 Mar. 2019.

[34] Certain Conventional Weapons Convention, Group of Governmental Experts on Emerging Technologies in the Area of Lethal Autonomous Weapons Systems, 'Questionnaire on the legal review mechanism of new weapons, means and methods of warfare', Working paper submitted by Argentina, CCW/GGE.1/2019/WP.6, 29 Mar. 2019.

[35] E.g. Certain Conventional Weapons Convention, CCW/GGE.1/2018/WP.6 (note 16).

[36] Certain Conventional Weapons Convention, CCW/GGE.1/2019/3/Add.1 (note 20), para. 30.

applies to the participation of private military companies in armed conflict.[37] Portugal's proposal was considered to be similar to the proposed code of conduct in that it would be a non-legally binding, technical outcome.[38]

As no significant progress was made in reaching consensus on how to address the challenges posed by LAWS, states called for working groups of technical, military and legal experts from the GGE to discuss the issues further and to provide input on and further elaboration of the guiding principles.[39] States also noted that, regardless of the type of instrument, there is a need for further clarification of how to define the type and degree of human responsibility, judgement or control required.[40]

The way ahead

According to the chair's summary of the 2019 meetings, the GGE aims to reach consensus on how to address the legal, ethical and security challenges posed by the use of autonomy in weapon systems by 2021. The chair therefore recommended that in 2020 the GGE should focus on legal, ethical, technological and military work aspects, and in 2021 on the 'consideration, clarification, and development of aspects of the normative and operational framework' on emerging technologies in the area of LAWS.[41] This would allow the GGE to deliver concrete recommendations for the 2021 Review Conference of the CCW Convention. The recommendations were formulated in purposefully broad terms to accommodate the range of views on the way ahead. Nonetheless, lengthy discussions followed on the group's mandate and the number of days for upcoming GGE meetings. These discussions carried over from the August meeting of the GGE to the November meeting of CCW Convention states parties, where there was a protracted struggle to reach agreement.

Many delegations called for a programme of work to advance a negotiating mandate for a legally or politically binding regulation on LAWS. For example, France and Germany argued that it was high time to start operationalizing the findings from the GGE meetings and suggested that the guiding principle could form a useful basis for the adoption of their suggested political declaration.[42] The Campaign to Stop Killer Robots—a coalition of NGOs—also asserted that, if the 2019 meeting did not deliver a clear negotiating mandate,

---

[37] Swiss Federal Department of Foreign Affairs and International Committee of the Red Cross (ICRC), *The Montreux Document on Pertinent International Legal Obligations and Good Practices for States Related to Operations of Private Military and Security Companies during Armed Conflict* (ICRC: Geneva, Aug. 2009).

[38] Certain Conventional Weapons Convention, CCW/GGE.1/2019/3/Add.1 (note 20), para. 30.

[39] Certain Conventional Weapons Convention, CCW/GGE.1/2019/3/Add.1 (note 20), para. 26(d).

[40] Certain Conventional Weapons Convention, CCW/GGE.1/2019/3 (note 26), para 22(b).

[41] Certain Conventional Weapons Convention, CCW/GGE.1/2019/3/Add.1 (note 20), para. 40.

[42] Certain Conventional Weapons Convention, Statement by Germany (note 33).

then it would be time to move the negotiations elsewhere, for instance to the First Committee of the UN General Assembly.[43]

The chair and many states argued for the GGE's mandate to be expanded from merely the 'clarification' and 'consideration' of aspects of the normative and operational framework of LAWS to also include the 'development' of those aspects.[44] Opposing this, Russia claimed that the GGE did not have the right to change its own mandate and that this was to be decided at the 2021 Review Conference. However, in the end, the meeting of states parties included 'development' in the phrasing of the mandate of the 2020 and 2021 GGEs.[45]

There was further extensive discussion about the number of meeting days in the coming years. Almost all states agreed that the GGE should meet for 30 days over 2020 and 2021 since they believed that the 2019 meetings had been too short, resulting in too many informal sessions. Some delegations, notably France, complained that the informal sessions were held outside the official agenda with no language support, contributing to unequal opportunity for delegations to attend and to express themselves in their preferred language. Russia was the only opponent of an increased number of meeting days in the upcoming years. It argued that the GGE should only meet for 20 days due to the worrying financial situation of the CCW regime and that 10 days each year would be sufficient time to make progress.[46] The consensus decision reached was that the GGE should meet for 10 days in 2020 and for between 10 and 20 days in 2021, with the final duration to be decided at the meeting of state parties in 2020. The chair of the GGE in 2020 will be Jānis Kārkliņš of Latvia.

In the discussions over the number of days and the wording of the mandate, there was a clear divide between a handful of technology advanced military powers and the other CCW states parties. The Campaign to Stop Killer Robots and a number of delegations have invoked the possibility that, if no major progress in achieved by 2021, it will be time to take the discussion up in another forum such as the UN General Assembly or even in a separate process comparable to the Oslo process that led to the 2008 Convention on Cluster Munitions (CCM).[47] However, for such a process to be successful, it would have to be politically and financial driven by a champion state and it remains unclear at this stage which state that could be. None of the technology advanced military powers that are keen to see progress in the CCW framework have expressed a clear interest in starting a separate process at this stage.

[43] Pytlak and Geyer (note 10).

[44] Certain Conventional Weapons Convention, CCW/GGE.1/2019/3/Add.1 (note 20), paras 36, 40.

[45] Certain Conventional Weapons Convention, CCW/MSP/2019/9 (note 7), para. 31.

[46] Certain Conventional Weapons Convention, CCW/MSP/2019/9 (note 7), para. 18.

[47] For a summary and other details of the CCM see annex A, section I, in this volume. On the implementation of the CCM in 2019 see section I in this chapter.

III. Creeping towards an arms race in outer space

DANIEL PORRAS

The year 2019 was an eventful one for space security, with numerous developments related directly to the United Nations agenda item on the prevention of an arms race in outer space (PAROS). Some states openly declared space to be a domain of war or an area for both offensive and defensive military operations, others announced new dedicated military space units, and another gave a live-fire demonstration of an anti-satellite (ASAT) weapon. All these developments lead to a central question for the international community: Is there already an arms race in outer space?

This question is particularly pertinent given the world's increasing reliance on space capabilities for everyday uses such as weather forecasting, communication, mapping and navigation. This reliance is especially true of modern military forces: satellites are critical for providing telecommunications for troops, reconnaissance and early warning information, and missile targeting capabilities. There is also a trend towards the development of 'counterspace capabilities'; that is, the ability to deny the use and benefits of space systems to an adversary. As relations between major geopolitical rivals are increasingly strained today, the acquisition of tools that deny space services to an opponent are becoming increasingly attractive. Indeed, as the ASAT demonstrations of 2019 indicated (see below), counterspace capabilities are now considered to be a vital part of modern military forces in some states.

While the interest in counterspace capabilities is becoming clearer, the consequences are not. The use of weapons in space could have negative impacts for military rivals—especially those armed with nuclear weapons—but also for everyday civilian uses of space systems. Moreover, the introduction of counterspace capabilities raises concern over the vulnerability of strategic systems. Under certain circumstances, this might prompt some states to think it is more advantageous to strike first.[1] Lack of clarity can lead to misperceptions and miscalculations, which in turn can lead to strategic escalation. In such a case, the consequences of counterspace capabilities could be much more dire on Earth than in orbit.

Against this backdrop, the UN engaged in numerous dialogues throughout 2019 in the hope of finding ways to slow the current trend towards the weaponization of outer space. Unfortunately, political tensions and lack of consensus meant these dialogues had limited outcomes, leaving any progress on preventing an arms race in outer space for 2020 and beyond.

---

[1] See Arbatov, A., 'Arms control in outer space: The Russian angle, and a possible way forward', *Bulletin of Atomic Scientists*, Special Issue, vol. 75, no. 4 (2019).

2019: A year for anti-satellite demonstrations

Two high-profile events involving the use of counterspace capabilities brought the issue of a possible arms race in space into the spotlight in 2019. In March, the Indian Defence Research and Development Organisation used a ballistic missile interceptor to destroy an Indian satellite in low Earth orbit (roughly 280 kilometres in altitude).[2] This mission, entitled Mission Shakti, demonstrated India's capability to target and strike an object in space. Prime Minister Narendra Modi hailed the mission as an achievement, labelling it as a purely 'defensive' measure that was not directed at any other country.[3] Nevertheless, many experts saw this demonstration as sending a message to China, which has endured strained relations with India in recent years.[4]

The demonstration also showed the difficulty in predicting the behaviour of debris resulting from the use of ASAT weapons. While the Indian authorities predicted that the debris would 'vanish' in 45 days or possibly 'within weeks', almost a year later, 30 per cent of the debris remains, with some debris orbiting at the same altitude as the International Space Station.[5] This debris, which can remain in orbit for years traveling faster than a bullet, puts all resident space objects at risk of collision.

Another activity that received considerable public attention in 2019 involved close-proximity operations by a Russian co-orbital satellite.[6] While the type of satellite is unconfirmed, observers believe it was a small, highly manoeuvrable satellite (drone). Some have speculated it can be used in non-benign ways, including the inspection of other satellites and conduct of espionage operations.[7] Throughout 2019, one of these Russian satellites was observed moving close to commercial and military satellites.[8] While there is no official confirmation or proof that the Russian satellite posed any threat, several countries, including the United States and France, apparently perceived this as a threat from Russia.[9] The result of this perceived threat, as

---

[2] Indian Government, Ministry of External Affairs, 'Frequently asked questions on Mission Shakti, India's anti-satellite missile test conducted on 27 March, 2019', Press release, 27 Mar. 2019.

[3] Modi', N., 'Address on the successful test of the Anti-Satellite (ASAT) Missile', YouTube, 26 Mar. 2019.

[4] Swami, P., 'India's A-SAT programme born in response to China's growing space capabilities: Understanding Mission Shakti', Firstpost, 8 May 2019; and Rajagopalan, R. P., 'Having tested its ASAT capability, India should help shape global space norms', Observer Research Foundation commentaries, 29 Mar. 2019.

[6] Strout, N., 'Russian satellite creeps up to Intelsat satellite—again', C4ISRNET, 3 Sep. 2019; and Hennigan, W. J., 'Exclusive: Strange Russian spacecraft shadowing US spy satellite, general says', *TIME*, 10 Feb. 2020.

[7] Weedon, B. and Samson, V. (eds), 'Russian co-orbital ASAT', *Global Counterspace Capabilities: An Open Source Assessment* (Secure World Foundation: Washington, DC, Apr. 2019), section 2.1.

[8] Analytical Graphics, 'Episode 14: LUCH space activities', YouTube, 26 June 2019.

[9] Parly, F., French Defence Minister, 'Présentation de la stratégie spatiale de défense' [Presentation of the strategy spatial defence], Airbase 942, Lyon, 25 July 2019; and US Mission to International Organizations in Geneva, 'Statement by Assistant Secretary Poblete at the Conference on Disarmament', 19 Mar. 2019.

well as others, is that several countries are preparing for conflict in space. Importantly, the use of co-orbital satellites is not restricted to Russia.[10] The USA, for example, also possesses these capabilities. However, US satellites did not receive the same attention throughout 2019 as the Russian drones. This is partly because US co-orbital satellites are not listed in the US catalogue of space objects. Moreover, the companies able to publicly release information about Russian proximity operations involving drones are US companies and make it a policy not to track unlisted US objects.[11]

New policies on military space operations

While the operations mentioned above drew considerable attention to the threat of arms in space, the issues surrounding PAROS became even more visible to the public eye after some major states revised their national policies on space. This trend began in 2017, when US President Donald J. Trump first proposed a Space Force: a dedicated military unit whose sole function is to ensure the integrity of US military space systems. The US Space Force (USSF) was officially established in December 2019, 'within the Department of the Air Force, meaning the Secretary of the Air Force has overall responsibility for the USSF, under the guidance and direction of the Secretary of Defense'.[12] While the functions of the USSF are not radically different from earlier iterations that existed within the US Air Force, the geopolitical signalling was not lost on rivals and adversaries in space. Russia, for example, stated that it needed to develop its own space forces further in response.[13] The strong reactions by rival countries, however, may have more to do with President Trump's rhetoric accompanying the establishment of the Space Force— described as being to 'safeguard American dominance in space'—as opposed to the actual mandates of the unit.[14] Nonetheless, this step combined with the establishment of the Pentagon's Space Development Agency, whose main function is to find new military space capabilities, also raises some concerns

[10] Weedon and Samson (note 7), 'Chinese co-orbital ASAT', section 1.1, and 'US co-orbital ASAT', section 3.1.

[11] Hall, B., Analytical Graphics, Presentation at the UNIDIR event 'Navigating space: Charting a course for a sustainable space environment', United Nations, New York, 28 Oct. 2019.

[12] US Space Force, 'US Space Force fact sheet', 20 Dec. 2019; and Erwin, S., 'Trump signs defense bill establishing US Space Force: What comes next', *SpaceNews*, 20 Dec. 2019.

[13] BBC, Reality Check Team, 'Russian president warns over expansion of US space force', 4 Dec. 2019; and Associated Press, 'China attacks US Space Force as threat to peace', Air Force Times, 23 Dec. 2019.

[14] White House, 'President Donald J. Trump is launching America's Space Force', Fact sheet, 23 Oct. 2018; and White House, 'Donald Trump signs Space Force directive in the Oval Office', Remarks, 19 Feb. 2019.

that the USA is pursuing new weapons for space, including for offensive purposes.[15]

Other countries also began a process of changing their military postures in space. For example, not long after Mission Shakti, in April 2019 India formally established its Defence Space Agency and in June 2019 it announced a Defence Space Research Organisation, with a mandate to protect India's space capabilities and to act as a deterrent against foreign interference.[16]

Both France and Japan reacted to the activities of the Russian co-orbital drone described above by announcing their own changes to posture in space. In July 2019, French President Emmanuel Macron announced that France would adopt a new space doctrine and establish its own space command within the French Air Force.[17] The purpose of this new policy was to develop four areas of French activity in space: 'space service support, situational awareness, operations support and active space defence'.[18] On the last point, France also declared its intention to explore mounting 'defensive' measures on certain military satellites, including high-energy lasers.[19] Such lasers could be used on a co-orbital satellite encroaching on a sensitive French military satellite. Similarly, the Japanese Government announced that it would be establishing a space unit in its Self Defense Forces, with plans to deploy 'guardian drones' to engage other hostile space objects. [20]

These policy announcements were not restricted to national governments. The North Atlantic Treaty Organization (NATO) announced that outer space is now a domain of operations, and that an 'attack' on a satellite belonging to an allied state would be considered sufficient to trigger collective defence under Article 5 of the Washington Treaty.[21] NATO stressed that it did not have plans to weaponize space and that this policy shift was intended to protect space services for NATO military missions. However, NATO did not offer any clarity on what it considered to be an 'attack' on a satellite, although jamming and physical harm appear to constitute one. Indeed, there does not appear to be any consensus among NATO states, let alone non-NATO states, as to what constitutes an 'attack' on a space object.

All these developments put space activities, and specifically space security, much more in the public eye than in years past. This attention comes with the growing concern that it is only a matter of time before open conflict

---

[15] Mehta, A., and Insinna, V., 'Pentagon officially stands up Space Development Agency, names first director', *Defense News*, 13 Mar. 2019.

[16] Raghuvanshi, V., 'India to launch a defense-based space research agency', *DefenseNews*, 12 June 2019; and Lele, A., 'India's growing clamour is space and why the country needs a separate Space Force', *Financial Express*, 2 Aug. 2019.

[17] Reuters, 'France to create space command within air force: Macron', 13 July 2019.

[18] French Ministry for the Armed Forces, *Space Defence Strategy: Report of the 'Space' Working Group* (French Government Publishing Office: Paris, 2019), p. 10.

[19] Parly (note 9).

[20] *Japan News*, 'SDF space unit set to launch in FY20', 5 Aug. 2019.

[21] Banks, M., 'NATO names space as an "operational domain," but without plans to weaponize it', *DefenseNews*, 20 Nov. 2019.

emerges in space. Moreover, the physical properties of space are such that the consequences of a conflict could affect all users of space services. For example, the surge in resident space objects in low Earth orbit and the constant addition of new space activities in 2019 means the potential impact of space debris could be considerable. That makes 2019 a particularly worrying year for space security.

Recent efforts at the multilateral level and the challenges ahead

Member states of the UN held numerous talks, on both security and safety aspects of space activities, with a view to finding paths towards new measures (or the strengthening of existing ones) to minimize the likelihood of open conflict in outer space.

The Conference on Disarmament (CD), the international negotiating body on arms control and disarmament, sought to re-establish subsidiary bodies on individual agenda items. This approach, previously adopted in 2018, is a means of moving beyond the blockage that has prevented the CD from adopting a programme of work for nearly 20 years. In 2018, Subsidiary Body 3 looked at PAROS and was able to produce a report that outlined areas of convergence where the international community might be able to work.[22] Unfortunately, external political reasons meant that the CD was unable to reach a decision in 2019 to reconstitute the subsidiary bodies; as a consequence, no substantive work was done throughout 2019 in relation to PAROS.

Another initiative that began in 2018 and concluded in 2019 was the Group of Governmental Experts (GGE) on further practical measures for PAROS. This GGE first met for a two-week session in August 2018 and again for an intersessional meeting in New York on 31 January 2019, at which the Chair of the GGE presented a report on his findings thus far.[23] This report laid out two distinct approaches under discussion: one focusing on the prohibition of technology and the other on the prohibition of behaviours. It also presented several scenarios that served to highlight the types of threats that might disrupt the space environment, such as co-orbital vehicles and ASAT missiles. The GGE continued its work at its second two-week session in March 2019 but, despite considerable efforts, was unable to reach consensus on a final report. The draft of the report was released, however, when the Africa Group made it publicly available in a statement to the UN Disarmament Committee (UNDC) in April 2019.[24]

---

[22] United Nations Conference on Disarmament (CD), 'Report of Subsidiary Body 3: Prevention of an arms race in outer space', CD/2140, 11 Sep. 2018.

[23] Group of Government Experts on PAROS, 'Report by the Chair of the Group of governmental experts on further practical measures for the prevention of an arms race in outer space', 31 Jan. 2019.

[24] United Nations Disarmament Committee, Nigeria (on behalf of the African Group), 'Recommendations to promote the practical implementation of transparency and confidence-building measures in outer space activities', Working paper, A/CN.10/2019/WP.1, 25 Apr. 2019.

Finally, in 2017 the UNDC established a Working Group in accordance with its three-year work programme, which includes voluntary measures such as 'transparency and confidence building measures' (TCBMs) for space activities. This Working Group was unable to meet formally in 2019 due to political issues. However, it did manage to hold a brief informal session, during which the Africa Group issued the above-mentioned statement. It is unclear if the UNDC will be able to meet in 2020.

The difficult relations between certain UN member states were also evident from the resolutions adopted by the 74th Session of the UN General Assembly. The resolution on TCBMs (usually adopted without a vote) was adopted by vote for the second year in a row, with the USA and Israel both voting against.[25] The USA also voted against Resolution 74/32 on PAROS, although in the past it has abstained.[26] Most notable, however, was Resolution 74/34 on 'Further practical measures for the prevention of an arms race in outer space', which now includes a new reference to one of the key sources of concern related to PAROS: '*Expressing serious concern* over the plans declared by certain States that include the placement of weapons, in particular strike combat systems, in outer space'.[27] Resolution 74/34 was adopted by a considerable majority, although with more abstentions than other space-related resolutions. This resolution is also significant because it calls on the CD to take into account the work of the GGE on PAROS, in the form of the draft report that was never agreed to by consensus. It remains to be seen if a new GGE will continue working on PAROS.

Following the developments of 2019, it is not clear how UN member states can achieve consensus on the issues around PAROS. While the CD remains the most likely venue for discussions, the political deadlock makes progress on any issue difficult. Meanwhile, there are clear indications that the major military powers will continue to seek counterspace capabilities where feasible, anticipating that no diplomatic solutions will emerge to protect space objects. Although it is not yet inevitable that open conflict will emerge in space, the signs are becoming more obvious that there is an arms race underway among major geopolitical rivals, and that space will play a considerable role in this arms race. The challenge is to find ways to dampen an arms race that targets space objects and systems, and to mitigate the harmful effects on non-rival parties. If a solution is not found, space may become a source of strategic unpredictability, with destabilizing consequences on earth.

[25] United Nations, General Assembly, Resolution 74/67, 12 Dec. 2019. Votes were 173–2–6 (for–against–abstentions).

[26] United Nations, General Assembly, Resolution 74/32, 12 Dec. 2019. Votes were 183–2–0.

[27] United Nations, General Assembly, Resolution 74/34, 12 Dec. 2019, Preamble. Votes were 131–6–45 (for–against–abstentions).

14. Dual-use and arms trade controls

Overview

Global, multilateral and regional efforts continued in 2019 to strengthen controls on the trade in conventional arms and in dual-use items connected with conventional, biological, chemical and nuclear weapons and their delivery systems. Membership of the different international and multilateral instruments that seek to establish and promote agreed standards for the trade in arms and dual-use items remained stable. At the same time, there were growing signs that the strength of these instruments is being increasingly tested by stretched national resources and broader geopolitical tensions. This could be seen in the shortfalls in compliance with mandated reporting and funding obligations under the 2013 Arms Trade Treaty (ATT), the various reported violations of United Nations arms embargoes, and differences both within and among groups of states about how the obligations generated by these different instruments should be implemented. At the same time, states continued to make substantive progress on reaching agreement on expanding and developing many of the technical aspects of these agreements. For example, states continued to outline in more detail how key obligations under the ATT should be implemented and made a number of additions to the set of good practice documents and control lists connecting the various export control regimes.

The Fifth Conference of States Parties (CSP) to the ATT took place in Geneva in August 2019 (see section I). Despite tensions and disputes, CSP5 made progress on articulating how the treaty's provisions should be implemented, particularly those on gender-based violence (GBV). The ATT remains the only international agreement in the field of arms or arms transfer controls that includes explicit provisions on GBV, and states' attempts to specify what they mean in practice could have significance for other instruments. Perhaps the most important developments in terms of the long-term health of the ATT took place outside of the CSP. During 2019 the United States announced its intention to 'unsign' the ATT while China stated that it was taking steps towards acceding to the treaty. These contrasting moves will no doubt have implications for efforts to expand the membership of the ATT but the way in which this will happen remains hard to predict.

During 2019 13 UN embargoes were in force, 21 European Union (EU) embargoes and 1 League of Arab States embargo (see section II). No new embargo was imposed and none was lifted. Ten of the EU arms embargoes matched the scope of ones imposed by the UN, three were broader in terms of duration, geographical scope or the types of weapon covered, and eight had no

UN counterpart. The single Arab League arms embargo, on Syria, had no UN counterpart. As in previous years, investigations by the UN revealed numerous reported cases of violations of varying significance. Particular problems were noted in connection with the implementation of the UN arms embargo on Libya, which has done little to halt the flow of arms into the conflict. During 2019 some instances of arms transfers raised questions about which types of activities and goods are covered by EU arms embargoes, and also highlighted the potential need for improved mechanisms of national reporting and independent monitoring.

Each of the four multilateral export control regimes—the Australia Group (on chemical and biological weapons), the Missile Technology Control Regime (MTCR), the Nuclear Suppliers Group and the Wassenaar Arrangement on Export Controls for Conventional Arms and Dual-use Goods and Technologies—reviewed its respective control lists and guidelines in 2019 (see section III). None of the four regimes admitted any new participating states (or partners) during 2019, despite a number of pending applications in several regimes. Geopolitical tensions continued to affect the work of the regimes, particularly work of a politically sensitive nature, such as information sharing on procurement efforts. In contrast, progress continued on the more technical aspects of the regimes' work, such as control list amendments, including ones on cyber-surveillance and cyber-warfare tools by the Wassenaar Arrangement. Several regimes engaged more substantially with each other on specific overlaps in control lists and potential overlaps in coverage of emerging technologies.

To implement these four regimes in its common market, the EU has established a common legal basis for controls on the export, brokering, transit and trans-shipment of dual-use items and, to a certain degree, military items (see section IV). The EU is the only regional organization to have developed such a framework. During 2019 the EU's two main instruments in this area—the EU Common Position on Arms Exports and the EU Dual-use Regulation—were the subject of review processes. The process of reviewing the EU Common Position was completed in September 2019 and led to limited changes to both the text of the instrument and its accompanying User's Guide. However, the review of the EU Dual-use Regulation, begun in 2011, was still ongoing at the end of 2019. While substantive progress was made in 2019, the discussions also highlighted differences among the parties—the European Commission, European Parliament and the Council of the EU—about the overall purpose of the regulation.

MARK BROMLEY

I. The Arms Trade Treaty

GIOVANNA MALETTA AND MARK BROMLEY

The 2013 Arms Trade Treaty (ATT) is the first legally binding international agreement to establish standards for regulating the international trade in conventional arms and preventing illicit arms transfers.[1] As of 31 December 2019, 105 states were party to the ATT and 33 had signed but not yet ratified it.[2] There were five new ATT states parties in 2019—Botswana, Canada, Lebanon, Maldives and Palau—a decrease compared to 2018 when six states ratified the treaty.[3] During 2019, President Donald J. Trump announced that the United States would withdraw its signature from the ATT.[4] In contrast, China—which has been sceptical of the ATT and has not signed it—announced its intention to join the treaty.[5]

Following two sets of preparatory sessions and meetings of the Working Groups on Treaty Universalization (WGTU), Effective Treaty Implementation (WGETI) and Transparency and Reporting (WGTR), the Fifth Conference of States Parties (CSP5) to the ATT was held in Geneva on 26–30 August 2019 under the presidency of Ambassador Jānis Kārkliņš of Latvia. CSP5 was attended by 106 states and 47 regional and international organizations, non-governmental organizations (NGOs), research institutes, industry associations and national implementing agencies.[6] The proceedings covered seven areas: (*a*) treaty implementation; (*b*) transparency and reporting; (*c*) treaty universalization; (*d*) international assistance; (*e*) the work of the ATT Secretariat; (*f*) the status of financial contributions to the ATT budget and how the financial situation might be improved; and

---

[1] For a summary and other details of the Arms Trade Treaty see annex A, section I, in this volume. The 2001 UN Firearms Protocol is also legally binding but only covers controls on the trade in firearms. United Nations, General Assembly, Resolution 55/255, Protocol against the Illicit Manufacturing of and Trafficking in Firearms, their Parts and Components and Ammunition, supplementing the UN Convention against Transnational Organized Crime (UN Firearms Protocol), adopted 31 May 2001, entered into force 3 July 2005.

[2] Arms Trade Treaty, 'Treaty status', [n.d.].

[3] Lebanon and Palau ratified the ATT in May and April 2019, respectively, Botswana and Canada in June 2019 and Maldives in Sep. 2019. See United Nations, United Nations Treaty Collection, Status of Treaties, ch. XXVI Disarmament: 8. Arms Trade Treaty; Arms Trade Treaty, 'Treaty status' (note 2).

[4] Smith, D., 'Trump withdraws from UN arms treaty as NRA crowd cheers in delight', *The Guardian*, 26 Apr. 2019.

[5] Stavrianakis, A. and Yun, H., *China and the Arms Trade Treaty: Prospects and Challenges*, (Saferworld: London, May 2014); and AFP/Reuters, 'China advances plans to join Arms Trade Treaty spurned by Trump', *Deutsche Welle*, 28 Sep. 2019.

[6] CSP5 was attended by 86 states parties of the then 102 states parties and 15 of the then 33 signatories. In addition, Botswana and Canada, which by then had acceded to the ATT, also participated in the work of the conference. Finally, three states (China, Fiji and Tonga) participated as observers. See Arms Trade Treaty, 5th Conference of States Parties (CSP5), Final Report, ATT/CSP5/2019/SEC/536/Conf.FinRep.Rev1, 30 Aug. 2019.

Table 14.1. Arms Trade Treaty ratifications, accessions and signatories, by region[a]

Region	No. of states	No. of parties	No. of signatories	No. of non-signatories
Africa	53	26	14	13
Americas	35	27	3[b]	5
Asia	29	4	7	18
Europe	48[c]	41	2	5[c]
Middle East	16[d]	2[c]	4	10
Oceania	14	5	3	6
Total	195	105	33	57

[a] The treaty was open for signature until it entered into force in Dec. 2014. Existing signatories may accept, approve or ratify the treaty in order to become a state party. A non-signatory state must now directly accede to the treaty in order to become a state party.

[b] This figure includes the United States. On 18 July 2019, the USA notified the ATT of its intention not to become a state party to the treaty.

[c] This figure includes the Holy See.

[d] This figure includes Palestine.

Source: United Nations, United Nations Treaty Collection, Status of Treaties, ch. XXVI Disarmament: 8. Arms Trade Treaty.

(*g*) preparations for CSP6.[7] The first day of the conference also featured a discussion on gender and gender-based violence (GBV), which Latvia chose as the official theme of CSP5.[8]

Discussion of these areas briefly gave way to exchanges between Japan and the Republic of Korea (South Korea) over Japan's imposition in July 2019 of restrictions on the export to South Korea of certain dual-use goods, namely chemicals used in the production of smartphone displays and semi-conductors. Japan cited national security concerns as the reason for the restrictions, prompting protests from South Korea in several international fora, including the World Trade Organization.[9] During the CSP5 plenary, South Korean officials claimed that the measures were politically motivated and undermined the credibility of the ATT.[10] The final day of CSP5 also saw disagreements about the potential adoption of measures aimed at persuading states to make their assessed financial contributions to support the functioning of the ATT (see below under the heading 'Financial contributions').

Despite these tensions and disputes, CSP5 reached consensus on the adoption of a final report and made progress with establishing language on how key aspects of the treaty should be implemented. This section summarizes

[7] Arms Trade Treaty, CSP5, 'CSP5 Provisional Annotated Programme of Work', ATT/CSP5/2019/SEC/525/Conf.AnnPoW, 26 July 2019.

[8] Arms Trade Treaty, CSP5, 'CSP5 Provisional Annotated Programme of Work' (note 7); Arms Trade Treaty, 'Gender and gender based violence', Working paper presented by the president of the Fifth Conference of State Parties to the ATT, ATT/CSP5/2019/PRES/410/PM1.GenderGBV, 15 Jan. 2019.

[9] Johnson, K., 'Why are Japan and South Korea at each other's throats?', *Foreign Policy*, 15 July 2019.

[10] Republic of Korea, 'Arms Trade Treaty CSP5', Statement, 26 Aug. 2019, p.4 .

key ATT-related developments and debates during 2019 and at CSP5, including during working group and preparatory meetings. It looks at the status of treaty universalization and the provision of international assistance; treaty implementation and the focus on gender and GBV; and issues related to the functioning of the treaty, focusing in particular on noncompliance with national reporting obligations and shortfalls in financial contributions.

Treaty universalization and international assistance

Treaty universalization

Achieving universalization remains a key priority for the ATT. Although the treaty currently counts more than 100 states parties, geographical representation in ATT participation remains unbalanced, with states from Asia and the Middle East being particularly under-represented in terms of signatories and states parties (table 14.1).[11] In the run-up to and during CSP5, the WGTU discussed ways and proposed measures to enhance universalization, including the development of the ATT Universalization Toolkit and a 'Welcome pack for new States Parties to the ATT', both of which CSP5 adopted.[12] In line with the suggestions of the WGTU co-chairs, CSP5 also encouraged stakeholders to translate these documents into other languages (including non-UN official languages) and South Korea offered to take on this task.[13] The WGTU also stressed the role of the ATT Voluntary Trust Fund (VTF) in promoting universalization through its outreach activities and the need to have regular exchanges among the CSP president, the WGTU, the VTF chair and civil society.[14]

In 2019, the two developments with the potentially most significant impact on the universalization of the ATT were the US decision to stop the process of joining the treaty and the Chinese announcement of its intention to accede to it. The USA took an active role in negotiating the ATT—which it signed in September 2013—and many of the treaty's key provisions directly reflect the views and positions of the US government of the time.[15] However, given the need for a two-thirds majority of the US Senate to approve, ratification was

---

[11] Bromley, M., Brockmann, K. and Maletta, G., 'The Arms Trade Treaty', *SIPRI Yearbook 2019*, pp. 503–10; Bromley, M. and Brockmann, K., 'The Arms Trade Treaty', *SIPRI Yearbook 2018*, pp. 405–12; and Acheson, R. and Kerins, A., 'News in Brief', *ATT Monitor*, vol 12. no 7, 29 Aug. 2019, pp. 10–11.

[12] Arms Trade Treaty, CSP5, Final Report (note 6), para. 28; Arms Trade Treaty, Working Group on Treaty Universalization (WGTU), Co-chairs' draft report to CSP5, ATT/CSP5.WGTU/2019/CHAIR/532/Conf.Rep, 26 July 2019, annex A and annex B.

[13] Arms Trade Treaty, CSP5, Final Report (note 6), para. 28(b); Arms Trade Treaty, WGTU (note 12), para. 13(b).

[14] Arms Trade Treaty, WGTU (note 12), para. 13(e).

[15] See German Government, 'Memorandum of the Federal Government on the Arms Trade Treaty', 1 Mar. 2014. As a signatory of the ATT the USA is required to 'refrain from acts which would defeat the object and purpose of a treaty': Vienna Convention on the Law of Treaties 1969, Article 18.

unlikely, even under the Administration of President Barack Obama, and then became impossible under that of President Trump, which strongly opposes the treaty. In March 2019 Trump announced in a speech at a National Rifle Association of America (NRA) event that the USA was 'taking its signature back'.[16] However, while the ATT contains provisions detailing how a state that has joined the treaty can withdraw, it does not lay out procedures for how a state that has not yet joined can withdraw its signature. In July 2019, the US Government informed the United Nations secretary-general that the USA 'does not intend to become a party' to the ATT and so 'no legal obligation' arises from its signature.[17]

China also took an active role in the ATT negotiations and influenced key aspects of its text.[18] However, China abstained from the UN General Assembly vote adopting the draft ATT in April 2013 and chose not to sign the treaty. China stated that its opposition was based on the fact that the ATT was a multilateral arms control treaty adopted through a majority vote in the General Assembly rather than on the basis of consensus.[19] In September 2019 China announced at the 74th Session of the UN General Assembly that it had 'initiated the domestic legal procedures to join the Arms Trade Treaty'.[20] It portrayed the move as evidence of its commitment to multilateral arms control and contrasted its positions on these issues with those of the USA.[21] China was the world's fifth largest arms exporter during 2015–19 and its decision to join the ATT could boost the credibility of the instrument, particularly in Asia where several states were reportedly waiting to see whether key arms suppliers—including China—would join the treaty before doing so themselves.[22] However, the decision of the world's largest arms supplier, the USA, to stop the process of joining the treaty may have more influence over states that are not members of the ATT, including other major arms exporters.[23] The US announcement could also have implications for the financial health of the ATT (see 'Financial contributions' below).

[16] Weaver, C., 'Donald Trump to withdraw US from UN Arms Trade Treaty', *Financial Times*, 27 Apr. 2019; Smith (note 4).

[17] United Nations (note 3).

[18] Bromley, M., Duchâtel, M. and Holtom, P., *China's Exports of Small Arms and Light Weapons*, SIPRI Policy Paper no. 38 (SIPRI: Stockholm, Oct. 2013), pp. 9–11.

[19] Bromley, Duchâtel and Holtom (note 18), pp. 9–11.

[20] Wang Yi (Chinese Minister of Foreign Affairs), 'China today: A proud member of the global community', Statement at the 74th Session of the United Nations General Assembly, 27 Sep. 2019, pp. 6–7.

[21] Fu, C. (Director-General, Department of Arms Control, Chinese Ministry of Foreign Affairs), Statement at the 74th Session of the United Nations General Assembly, 12 Oct. 2019.

[22] Bromley and Brockmann (note 11), pp. 405–12, Wezeman, P. D. et al., 'Trends in international arms transfers, 2019', SIPRI Factsheet, Mar. 2020.

[23] Stohl, R., 'Trump unsigns the Arms Trade Treaty: How did we get here?', *War on the Rocks*, 3 May 2019.

International assistance

CSP5 also discussed international assistance in the form of financial support through the VTF, and its role in supporting ATT universalization and implementation. Within this framework, the ATT Secretariat reported on VTF activities over the last year and noted that, since its establishment in 2016, the VTF has received more than $8 million in voluntary contributions.[24] The funds provide a solid financial basis for the activities of the VTF, in contrast to the shortfall in funding for the treaty's infrastructure (see 'Financial contributions' below). Since 2016, the VTF has either provided funding or had plans to provide funding for 44 projects (the majority in African countries); the VTF Selection Committee approved 20 of these under the 2019 project cycle.[25] The VTF Selection Committee issued a new call for applications for the 2020 project cycle in October 2019.[26]

The VTF is not the only instrument providing ATT-related assistance. The European Union Partner-to-Partner (P2P) export control programme implements a significant number of assistance activities aimed at improving ATT implementation. The UN Trust Facility Supporting Cooperation on Arms Regulation (UNSCAR) also provides financial support for this type of assistance.[27] These projects and activities have a certain degree of geographical and functional overlap.[28] As part of its mandate as VTF administrator, the ATT Secretariat continued to seek cooperation with the EU and its member states and the UN in order to avoid overlaps and duplication of efforts.[29] During CSP5 the ATT Secretariat also highlighted the continued need for better coordination among implementing organizations and donors.[30]

As mandated by CSP4, the VTF Selection Committee, supported by the ATT Secretariat, also developed the document 'Guidance for VTF Project Evaluation', to support assessment of completed projects and ensure

---

[24] Arms Trade Treaty, Voluntary Trust Fund (VTF), 'Report on the work of the ATT Voluntary Trust Fund (VTF) for the period August 2018 to August 2019', ATT/VTF/2019/CHAIR/531/Conf.Rep, 26 July 2019, para. 7.

[25] The other 24 projects are: 17 selected for the first project cycle (2017) but 2 beneficiaries withdrew, leaving 15 projects; and 10 selected for the second project cycle (2018) but one beneficiary withdrew, leaving 9. See Arms Trade Treaty, VTF (note 24), paras 11, 12 and 15, and annex F.

[26] Arms Trade Treaty, VTF (note 24), para. 17.

[27] European Commission, 'EU P2P export control programme for arms—ATT', 3 Oct. 2019; and United Nations Office for Disarmament Affairs (UNODA), 'UNSCAR: UN Trust Facility Supporting Cooperation on Arms Regulation', [n.d.].

[28] Maletta, G., 'Coordinating arms transfer and SALW control assistance: What role for the Arms Trade Treaty?', SIPRI WritePeace Blog, 27 Mar. 2019.

[29] ATT Secretariat, 'Terms of reference of the ATT Voluntary Trust Fund', ATT/VTF18/2018/SEC/251/ToR.Cons.Dr.v1.Rev1, Aug. 2016, Attachment, para. 7; Arms Trade Treaty, VTF (note 24), para. 24; and Maletta, 'Coordinating arms transfer and SALW control assistance: What role for the Arms Trade Treaty?' (note 28).

[30] Arms Trade Treaty, VTF (note 24), para. 24; Maletta, 'Coordinating arms transfer and SALW control assistance: What role for the Arms Trade Treaty?' (note 28); Geyer, K., Pytlak, A. and Kerins, A., 'News in Brief', *ATT Monitor*, vol. 12, no. 6 (28 Aug. 2019), p. 6.

transparency and accountability in their management.[31] CSP5 noted this guidance document and welcomed further outreach activities to promote the VTF.[32] The CSP5 also discussed proposals on how to improve the reach and effectiveness of the VTF. The United Kingdom, for example, called for the establishment of a mechanism providing 'in-depth feedback' to applications that were rejected in order to improve the quality of submitted proposals.[33] Representatives from NGOs proposed to open the VTF to projects led only by civil society organizations and called for a general review of the VTF reporting requirements that could better ensure transparency.[34]

Treaty implementation

Gender and gender-based violence

Article 7(4) of the ATT requires states parties, when conducting an export assessment in line with the provisions contained in Article 7(1), to 'take into account' the risk that the export items may be used to commit or facilitate serious acts of GBV or violence against women and children. GBV can be understood as violence targeting a person on the basis of gender and sex that, although also perpetrated against men and boys, disproportionately affects women and girls—especially in the context of armed conflicts.[35] A number of organizations, in several contexts, have stressed the role of the illicit pro-liferation and misuse of conventional arms, especially small arms and light weapons (SALW), in facilitating these forms of violence.[36] However, the ATT is the first legally binding international agreement which both recognizes the

---

[31] Arms Trade Treaty, 'Report on the ATT Secretariat's work for the period 2018/2019', ATT/CSP5/2019/SEC/526/Conf.SecRep, 26 July 2019, para. 10(j); Arms Trade Treaty, VTF (note 24), annex H.

[32] Arms Trade Treaty, CSP5, Final Report (note 6), para. 24.

[33] Geyer, Pytlak and Kerins (note 30), p. 5.

[34] Geyer, Pytlak and Kerins (note 30), p. 6; Control Arms, 'Summary of CSP5 Day 2', 27 Aug. 2019, p. 1.

[35] Control Arms, *How to Use the Arms Trade Treaty to Address Gender-based Violence: A Practical Guide for Risk Assessment*, Control Arms Practical Guide (Control Arms: New York, Aug. 2018); Lindsey, C., *Women Facing War: ICRC Study on the Impact of Armed Conflict on Women* (International Committee of the Red Cross: Geneva, Oct. 2001); United Nations Security Council Resolution 1325 (2000) [on women and peace and security], 31 Oct. 2000. On the definition of violence against women see e.g. UN General Assembly Resolution A/RES/48/104, 20 Dec. 1993; UN Committee on the Elimination of Discrimination Against Women (CEDAW), General Recommendation 19 of CEDAW on Violence Against Women (llth session, 1992), A/47/38; and United Nations Commission on the Status of Women (CSW), 'Agreed conclusions on the elimination and prevention of all forms of violence against women and girls', *Report on the Fifty-seventh Session (4–15 March 2013)*, E/CN.6/2013/11, (United Nations: New York, 2 Apr. 2013), ch. 1 part A, paras 10–11.

[36] See e.g. UN CSW (note 35), para. 25; UN Secretary-General, *Securing Our Common Future: An Agenda for Disarmament* (UNODA: New York, 2018), pp. 39–40; UNODA, Third Review Conference of the UN Programme of Action on SALW, Final Report, A/CONF.192/2018/RC/3, 6 July 2018, paras 73–79; United Nations, Sustainable Development Goals Knowledge Platform, 'Sustainable Development Goal 16', [n.d.].

link between the proliferation of arms and GBV, and requires states parties to take preventive steps in response.

The inclusion of GBV within the operative provisions of the ATT was largely a result of the campaigning work by NGOs with support from a group of states that championed this issue.[37] Issues related to the practical implementation of Article 7(4), its relation to other ATT articles (including Article 6 on prohibitions) and the interpretation of key terms, emerged during the intersessional meetings of the WGETI.[38] However, these discussions highlighted a general lack of expertise among states parties on how to properly operationalize Article 7(4). In particular, no states parties appear to have a well-developed risk assessment for GBV in their national systems and none has denied a licence on the basis of this provision.[39] Some commentators see the lack of interest among some countries in discussing GBV-related issues, and the higher priority some of them attach to other implementation matters, as a potential obstacle for GBV-related risks being properly considered in arms transfer decisions.[40]

Having taken note of these issues, the CSP5 president developed a list of policy recommendations which CSP5 considered for adoption. These recommendations went beyond the application of GBV-related risk assessment to cover measures such as gender-balanced representation in ATT-related decision-making processes and facilitating states parties' understanding of the gendered impact of armed violence and conflict.[41] CSP5 adopted most of these recommendations along with related measures, such as inviting states to be represented in ATT events and bodies by gender-balanced delegations; considering gender-related criteria in the sponsorship programme and as part of the selection process of the VTF; and encouraging states to collect and publish gender-disaggregated data as part of their national statistics on crime and health, including on victims of violence.[42] CSP5 also adopted a series of measures directly impacting the future work of the WGETI, including developing a voluntary GBV-training guide; encouraging discussions on the interpretation of key terms in the treaty's text that broadly apply to Article 7, such as 'serious', 'facilitate' and 'overriding' risk; and facilitating exchanges on national practices with reference to

---

[37] These states were originally Finland, Iceland, Kenya, Malawi, Norway, and Trinidad and Tobago. See Green, C. et al., 'Gender-based violence and the Arms Trade Treaty: Reflections from a campaigning and legal perspective', *Gender & Development*, vol. 21, no. 3 (2013), pp. 555–56.

[38] Arms Trade Treaty, WGETI, 'Chair's draft report to CSP5', ATT/CSP5.WGETI/2019/CHAIR/529/Conf.Rep, 26 July 2019, para. 10.

[39] Arms Trade Treaty, WGETI (note 38), para. 10; Alvarado Cóbar, J. F. and Maletta, G., 'The inclusion of gender-based violence concerns in arms transfers decisions: The case of the Arms Trade Treaty', SIPRI WritePeace Blog, 23 Aug. 2019.

[40] Alvarado Cóbar and Maletta (note 39).

[41] Arms Trade Treaty, CSP5 president, 'Draft decision of the CSP on gender and gender based violence', ATT/CSP5/2019/PRES/528/Conf.GenderGBV, 26 July 2019, paras 1.1–1.5 and 2.1–2.4.

[42] Arms Trade Treaty, CSP5, Final Report (note 6), para. 22(a)–(b).

'mitigating measures'.[43] Although modest, these achievements are significant given the original resistance of some states parties to including a GBV-related provision in the treaty and proved, once again, the strong influence civil society can have in initiating certain debates.[44]

Other implementation issues

While the work of the WGETI sub-working group on Article 6 (Prohibitions) and Article 7 (Export and Export Assessment) largely focused on GBV, the sub-working groups on Article 5 and Article 11 continued to address issues related to, respectively, general implementation and diversion.[45] More specifically, the sub-working group on Article 5 made progress in elaborating initial sections for a 'Voluntary Basic Guide to establishing a National Control System'.[46] The WGETI chair recommended that the work of the sub-working group on Article 5 'could be temporarily discontinued to start addressing other ATT articles', particularly Article 9 (Transit and transshipment).[47] CSP5 accepted this recommendation.[48]

Discussions on diversion continued within the sub-working group on Article 11, particularly highlighting the 'the lack of shared understanding on terminology for end-use and end-user documentation' and reaching consensus on developing a voluntary guide that would serve as a 'repository of key terms used by states'.[49] In conclusion the sub-working group agreed that more work on diversion is still needed and proposed a multi-year work plan for Article 11; CSP5 adopted this proposal.[50] Discussion of diversion also took place within the framework of the WGTR meetings which—in consultation with the WGETI chair, the facilitator on diversion and the ATT Secretariat—organized the first informal meeting in the margins of CSP5 to discuss concrete cases of diversion.[51]

Issues related to the functioning of the treaty

Reporting obligations

The ATT Secretariat and states parties carried out substantial work to assist states with fulfilling their reporting obligations under the ATT. For example, the WGTR has produced guidance documents, one focusing on systemic

[43] Arms Trade Treaty, CSP5, Final Report (note 6), para. 22(c).
[44] See Green et al. (note 37).
[45] Arms Trade Treaty, WGETI (note 38).
[46] Arms Trade Treaty, WGETI (note 38), para. 31(a) and annex A.
[47] Arms Trade Treaty, WGETI (note 38), para. 31(a).
[48] Arms Trade Treaty, CSP5, Final Report (note 6), para. 25.
[49] Arms Trade Treaty, WGETI (note 38).
[50] Arms Trade Treaty, CSP5, Final Report (note 6), annex D.
[51] Pytlak, A., 'What will—and won't—be discussed at CSP5', *ATT Monitor*, vol. 12, no. 4 (26 Aug. 2019), p. 2; Arms Trade Treaty, Working Group on Transparency and Reporting (WGTR), Co-chairs' draft report to CSP5, ATT/CSP5.WGTR/2019/CHAIR/533/Conf.Rev1, 29 Aug. 2019, para. 11.

issues that hamper national reporting and another on 'Reporting authorized or actual exports and imports of conventional arms under the ATT'; the WGTR revised and updated the latter during 2019.[52] Despite these efforts, rates of compliance with the ATT's reporting instruments are either stagnant or in decline.

Within one year of ratification, each state party is obliged to provide the ATT Secretariat with an initial report detailing the 'measures undertaken in order to implement this Treaty'.[53] As of 31 December 2019, 26 per cent of the states that were due to submit an initial report had failed to do so, the joint highest proportion at this point in the reporting year since the treaty entered into force (figure 14.1). Promoting 'transparency' in the international arms trade is listed as one of the objects and purposes of the treaty. Nonetheless, of the 72 states that have submitted their initial report, 12 (Benin, Burkina Faso, Cyprus, Greece, Honduras, Kazakhstan, Madagascar, Mauritius, Nigeria, Senegal, Palestine and Tuvalu) chose to only allow their reports to be seen by other ATT states parties.[54]

States parties to the ATT are also required to submit an annual report on their arms imports and exports during the previous calendar year.[55] The percentage of states fulfilling this reporting obligation has decreased—from 80 per cent for 2015 to 66 per cent for 2018—meaning that while the number of treaty members has increased, the number of submitted reports on arms transfers has not increased at the same level (figure 14.2). Moreover, fewer than half of the state parties had submitted their report on arms transfers in 2018 by the deadline of 31 May 2019.[56]

Financial contributions

All ATT states parties and signatories, as well as states attending CSPs as observers, are required to make financial contributions to cover the costs of organizing the CSPs and the work of the ATT Secretariat.[57] However, a significant number of states are failing to pay their assessed contributions. As of 20 December 2019, 52 of the 147 states that have been obliged to make contributions since 2015 were behind with their payments, creating an accumulated deficit of $345 673.[58] The final report of CSP5 again highlighted 'the risks that the ATT process and its essential activities . . . will face if the

---

[52] Arms Trade Treaty, WGTR (note 51), annex B.

[53] Arms Trade Treaty (note 1), Article 13(1).

[54] Arms Trade Treaty, ATT Secretariat, 'Annual reports'.

[55] Arms Trade Treaty (note 1), Article 13(1).

[56] Arms Trade Treaty, WGTR (note 51) para. 36(a). On states' reports on arms transfers under the ATT and other international instruments, see chapter 9, section III, in this volume.

[57] Arms Trade Treaty, First Conference of States Parties (CSP1), 'Financial rules for the Conferences of States Parties and the Secretariat', ATT/CSP1/CONF/2, 25 Aug. 2015, Rules 5.1 and 5.2.

[58] Arms Trade Treaty, ATT Secretariat, 'Status of contributions to ATT budgets (as at 20 December 2019)'.

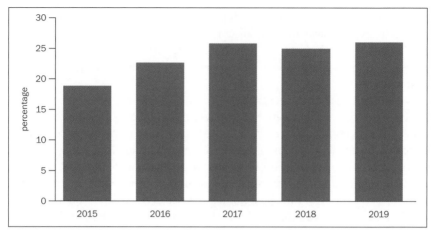

Figure 14.1. Number of Arms Trade Treaty states parties submitting annual reports, 2015–17

Source: Arms Trade Treaty, ATT Secretariat, 'Annual reports'.

situation is not addressed'.[59] The decision of the US government to stop the process of joining the ATT may increase these challenges. As is the case in most areas where the UN standards of assessed contributions are applied, US support for the running of the ATT has been the highest of all states and the USA provided 13 per cent of all budgetary contributions made during 2019.[60] If the US decision leads it to end financial support for the treaty, that would create a significant challenge for the treaty's long-term health.

Several disarmament and arms control instruments are facing similar challenges in ensuring that states provide the financial support they require.[61] As has occurred in the context of these other instruments, ATT states parties sought to introduce measures in 2019 to improve financial liquidity. During CSP5 a group of European states and Australia sought to promote the full application of Rule 8.1(d) of the 'Financial Rules for the Conferences of States Parties and the Secretariat', which have been largely ignored to date.[62] Applying Rule 8.1(d) in full would entail suspending the voting rights and other prerogatives within CSP bodies for states that have not paid their financial contributions for two or more years. The move was strongly opposed by African and Latin American states. The final report of CSP5

[59] Arms Trade Treaty, CSP5, 'Final Report' (note 6), para. 34.

[60] Arms Trade Treaty, ATT Secretariat (note 58).

[61] These include the Biological Weapons Convention, the Anti-Personnel Mines Convention, the Convention on Cluster Munitions, and the Convention on Certain Conventional Weapons (CCW)—see annex A, section I, in this volume for details of these treaties. On financial hardship, see Boulanin, V. et al., 'The Convention on Certain Conventional Weapons and lethal autonomous weapons systems', *SIPRI Yearbook 2019*, pp. 449–57; and LeGrone, O., 'As 2020 dawns, disarmament treaties face financial hardship', *Arms Control Now*, 17 Jan. 2020.

[62] Arms Trade Treaty, CSP1 (note 57), Rule 8.1(d).

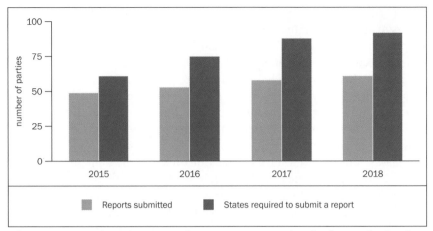

Figure 14.2. Number of Arms Trade Treaty states parties that have submitted required annual reports, 2015–18

Source: ATT Secretariat, 'Annual Reports'.

delayed a final resolution of the issue by requesting that the Management Committee prepare guidelines on how to address the topic for discussion at CSP6.[63] Efforts to persuade states to comply with their financial obligations also affected discussions about the work of the VTF. In the run-up to CSP5 the VTF Selection Committee proposed that for the 2020 project cycle, applications from states that are in arrears with their financial contributions be 'unlikely' to receive 'positive consideration'.[64] Members of civil society organizations and representatives of less resourced states argued that the countries that benefit the most from the VTF and other assistance instruments (e.g. the sponsorship programme) are also the ones encountering particular challenges in complying with their financial obligations.[65] The final report of CSP5 noted that for the time being 'no State shall be prejudiced' in applying for support from the VTF until CSP6, 'when this matter will be considered'.[66]

Conclusions

As in previous years, CSP and working group meetings largely focused on administrative and technical issues related to the functioning of the ATT, such as the fulfilment of states' reporting and financial commitments. For

---

[63] Arms Trade Treaty, CSP5, Final Report (note 6), para. 35; Acheson, R. and Pytlak, A., 'Turning from the final report to implementation, let's make the ATT a treaty that saves lives', *ATT Monitor*, vol. 12, no. 9 (30 Aug. 2019), pp. 2–3.

[64] Arms Trade Treaty, Voluntary Trust Fund (VTF) (note 24), para. 18; Arms Trade Treaty, CSP1 (note 57), Rule 8.

[65] Acheson, R, 'A fight for the moral and political credibility of the ATT', *ATT Monitor*, vol. 12, no. 8 (30 Aug. 2019).

[66] Arms Trade Treaty, CSP5, 'Final Report' (note 6), para. 36.

their part, NGOs continued to stress the importance of making use of these events to address what has been described as the 'rhetoric–compliance' gap in treaty implementation.[67] In this regard, they noted that while the CSPs widely discuss non-compliance with reporting or financial contributions obligations, there is still a reluctance to address the possible non-compliance of particular arms transfers with treaty provisions (e.g. Article 6 and Article 7), including those transfers whose legality the national courts of some states have called into question.[68] States parties have often responded to this argument by noting that the ATT does not set absolute standards and leaves interpretation of its obligations up to individual governments. However, this discrepancy—and a perceived CSP focus 'to "do" arms trading better'—may increase doubts about the long-term ability of the treaty to truly fulfil its humanitarian purpose of 'reducing human suffering'.[69]

[67] Acheson (note 65), p. 1.

[68] Pytlak, A, 'The meaning of implementation', *ATT Monitor*, vol. 12, no. 7 (29 Aug. 2019), p. 2; Maletta G., 'Legal challenges to EU member states' arms exports to Saudi Arabia: Current status and potential implications', SIPRI Topical Backgrounder, 28 June 2019.

[69] Pytlak, A., 'New opportunities to reduce human suffering', *ATT Monitor*, vol. 13, no. 1 (3 Feb. 2020), p. 3.

II. Multilateral arms embargoes

MARK BROMLEY AND PIETER D. WEZEMAN

The United Nations Security Council uses its powers under Chapter 7 of the UN Charter to impose arms embargoes—that is, restrictions on transfers of arms and, in certain cases, dual-use items—that are binding for all UN member states, which form part of what the UN generally refers to as 'sanctions measures'.[1] During 2019, 13 UN arms embargoes were in force (table 14.2). The European Union also imposes arms embargoes under its Common Foreign and Security Policy (CFSP) that are binding for EU member states, which form part of what the EU generally refers to as 'restrictive measures'.[2] During 2019, 21 EU arms embargoes were in force. Of these EU embargoes, 10 matched the coverage of a UN arms embargo; 3 (on Iran, South Sudan and Sudan) were broader in duration, geographical scope or the types of arms covered; while 8 had no UN counterpart. The Arab League had one arms embargo in place (on Syria) that also had no UN counterpart.[3] No new multilateral arms embargo was imposed in 2019 and none was lifted. The European Council discussed a possible EU arms embargo on Turkey but did not impose one.

Multilateral arms embargoes varied in type of materiel covered. Most covered arms and military materiel. However, the UN and EU arms embargoes on the Democratic People's Republic of Korea (DPRK, North Korea), Iran and Somalia, and the EU arms embargoes on Russia, also covered certain exports or imports of dual-use items—goods and technologies that can be used for both civilian purposes and to produce, maintain or operate conventional, biological, chemical or nuclear weapons.[4] Certain EU arms embargoes also covered equipment that might be used for internal repression and certain types of communications surveillance equipment. Multilateral arms embargoes also varied in the types of restrictions imposed and recipients targeted. Some placed a ban on all transfers to the state in question, while others banned transfers to a non-state actor or group of non-state actors. Certain UN arms embargoes were 'partial', in that they allowed

---

[1] United Nations, Security Council, 'Sanctions', [n.d.].

[2] European Council, 'Sanctions: How and when the EU adopts restrictive measures', [n.d.].

[3] In addition, one voluntary multilateral embargo was in force: The Conference on Security and Co-operation in Europe (now renamed the Organization for Security and Co-operation in Europe) requests that all participating states impose an embargo on arms deliveries to Armenian and Azerbaijani forces engaged in combat in the Nagorno-Karabakh area. Conference on Security and Co-operation in Europe, Committee of Senior Officials, Statement, annex 1 to Journal no. 2 of the 7th Meeting of the Committee, Prague, 27–28 Feb. 1992.

[4] The UN and EU embargoes on Iran and North Korea apply to dual-use items on the control lists of the Nuclear Suppliers Group (NSG) and the Missile Technology Control Regime (MTCR). The UN and EU embargoes on Somalia apply to certain dual-use items on the control lists of the Wassenaar Arrangement that can be used to produce, maintain and operate improvised explosive devices. The EU embargo on Russia applies to transfers to military end-users of all items on the EU's dual-use list.

Table 14.2. Multilateral arms embargoes in force during 2019

Target (entities or territory covered)[a]	Date embargo first imposed (duration type)	Materiel covered[a]	Key developments, 2019
United Nations arms embargoes			
Afghanistan (Taliban: NGF)	16 Jan. 2002 (OE)	Arms and related materiel and services	
Central African Republic (government: PT; NGF)	5 Dec. 2013 (TL)	Arms and military materiel (small arms exempted for government)	Extended until 31 Jan. 2020 Government allowed to acquire small arms without advance approval from UN sanctions committee
Democratic Republic of the Congo (government: PT; NGF)	28 July 2003 (TL)	Arms and military materiel	Extended until 1 July 2020
Iran (whole country: PT)	23 Dec. 2006 (TL)	Major arms, with some exceptions; Items related to nuclear weapon delivery systems; Items used in the nuclear fuel cycle	
Iraq (NGF)	6 Aug. 1990 (OE)	Arms and military materiel	
ISIL (Da'esh), al-Qaeda and associated individuals and entities (NGF)	16 Jan. 2002 (OE)	Arms and military materiel	
Korea, North (whole country)	15 July 2006 (OE)	Arms and military materiel; Items relevant to nuclear, ballistic missiles and other weapons of mass destruction related programmes.	
Lebanon (NGF)	11 Aug. 2006 (OE)	Arms and military materiel	
Libya (government: PT; NGF)	26 Feb. 2011 (OE)	Arms and military materiel	
Somalia (government: PT; NGF)	23 Jan. 1992 (TL)	Arms and military materiel; Components for improvised explosive devices	Extended until 15 Nov. 2020
South Sudan (whole country)	13 July 2018 (TL)	Arms and military materiel	Extended until 31May 2020
Sudan (Darfur: PT)	30 July 2004 (OE)	Arms and military materiel	
Yemen (NGF)	14 Apr. 2015 (OE)	Arms and military materiel	

Target (entities or territory covered)[a]	Date embargo first imposed (duration type)	Materiel covered[a]	Key developments, 2019
European Union arms embargoes[b]			
Belarus (whole country)	20 June 2011 (OE)	Arms and military materiel	Extended until 28 Feb. 2020
China[c] (whole country)	27 June 1989 (OE)	Arms	
Egypt[c] (whole country)	21 Aug. 2013 (OE)	Equipment which might be used for internal repression	
Iran (whole country)	27 Feb. 2007 (TL)	Equipment which might be used for internal repression; Communication surveillance equipment	
Myanmar (whole country)	29 July 1991 (TL)	Arms and military materiel; Communication surveillance equipment	Extended until 30 April 2020
Russia (whole country)	31 July 2014 (TL)	Arms and military materiel; Dual-use materiel for military use or military end-user	Extended until 31 Jan. 2020
South Sudan (whole country)	18 July 2011 (OE)	Arms and military materiel	
Sudan (whole country)	15 Mar. 1994 (OE)	Arms and military materiel	
Syria (whole country)	9 May 2011 (OE)	Equipment which might be used for internal repression; Communication surveillance equipment	
Venezuela (whole country)	13 Nov. 2017 (OE)	Arms and equipment which might be used for internal repression; Communication surveillance equipment	
Zimbabwe (whole country)	18 Feb. 2002 (OE)	Arms and military materiel	Extended until 20 Feb. 2020
League of Arab States arms embargoes			
Syria (whole country)	3 Dec. 2011 (OE)	Arms	

ISIL = Islamic State in Iraq and the Levant; NGF = Non-governmental forces; OE = open-ended; PT = partial, i.e. embargo allows transfers to the state in question provided the supplier or recipient state has received permission from, or notified, the relevant UN Sanctions Committee or the UN Security Council; TL = time-limited.

[a] The target, entities and territory, and materiel covered may have changed since the first imposition of the embargo. The target, entities and material stated in this table are as of the end of 2019.

[b] EU embargoes that had no UN counterpart or had a broader scope than UN embargoes on the same target.

[c] The EU embargoes on China and Egypt are political declarations whereas the other embargoes are legal acts imposed by EU Council Decisions and EU Council Regulations.

Sources: UN Security Council, 'Sanctions'. The SIPRI Arms Embargo Archive, <https://www.sipri.org/databases/embargoes>, provides a detailed overview of most multilateral arms embargoes that have been in force since 1950 along with the principle instruments establishing or amending the embargoes.

transfers to the state in question provided the supplier or recipient state had received permission from, or notified, the relevant UN Sanctions Committee or UN Security Council. In certain cases, these partial arms embargoes also required or encouraged the recipient state to put in place improved standards for stockpile management to help prevent the diversion of weapons delivered.

During 2019 the various UN investigations on the implementation of UN arms embargoes highlighted challenges of varying scope and significance. In particular, the UN investigations on the arms embargoes on Libya and Yemen noted that they were ineffective in both preventing transfers to the warring groups and helping to halt the ongoing armed conflict. Unlike the UN, the EU and Arab League do not have systematic mechanisms in place for monitoring compliance with their arms embargoes.

This section reviews significant developments and implementation challenges in UN and EU arms embargoes in 2019. In particular, it highlights cases where amendments to embargoes were implemented, debated or demanded and gives examples of actual or alleged violations.

United Nations arms embargoes: Developments and contraventions

During 2019 the UN introduced no new UN arms embargoes, but amended the embargo on Central African Republic (CAR) in response to demands from the national government and regional organizations (see below). The UN panels and groups of experts that monitor UN arms embargoes reported mainly on two types of violations in 2019. First, cases of varying size and significance occurred where the delivery of arms directly violated an arms embargo—namely the embargo on transfers to and from North Korea, and the embargoes on transfers to non-governmental forces in Afghanistan, CAR, Libya, Sudan (Darfur) and Yemen. Second, there were cases where arms were delivered without prior approval from the relevant UN sanctions committee or the UN Security Council. This occurred in relation to the embargo on Libya, which received arms without the required approval of the relevant UN sanctions committee; allegedly occurred in relation to the embargo on exports from Iran, which was accused of exporting arms without the required approval of the UN Security Council; and occurred in respect of Sudan, which moved weapons into the region of Darfur. In both types of cases, the UN did not impose sanctions on any of the countries reportedly involved in the violations. This subsection provides details of developments in relation to eight embargoes where examples of these types of violations took place.

Afghanistan (Taliban)

The UN arms embargo on Afghanistan bans transfers to the Taliban and other groups that threaten the peace, stability and security of Afghanistan.[5] Through various UN resolutions the list of such groups has expanded to include al-Qaeda and Islamic State in Iraq and the Levant (ISIL). Despite the embargo, the UN monitoring team for Afghanistan reported that in 2019 the Taliban continued to 'enjoy robust supplies of weapons, ammunition, funding and manpower'.[6] They also reported claims of Afghan officials that the Taliban continued to receive arms and ammunition through states in the region.[7] However, the monitoring team could not verify these claims, in part because many of the weapons shown to them had their serial and batch manufacturing marks removed. The monitoring team also documented the continued and probably increasing supply of commercial and military night-vision equipment to the Taliban. Previous reports have stated that the origin of these items likely includes both the capture of goods from Afghan military forces and the open commercial market.[8]

Central African Republic

The UN arms embargo on CAR bans transfers to non-state armed groups but permits deliveries to the government's security forces, provided that they have been approved in advance by the relevant UN sanctions committee. The CAR Government, with support from the Economic Community of West African States and the Economic Community of Central African States, argued in 2018, as in previous years, that the requirement for advanced approval by the relevant UN sanctions committee for arms supplies to government forces posed a barrier to solving the country's security crisis.[9] In February 2019 the CAR Government signed a peace agreement with 14 non-state armed groups operating in the country.[10] Citing the agreement, the UN Security Council voted unanimously in September 2019 to amend the embargo by lifting the requirement for advance approval of supplies of weapons and ammunition

---

[5] On the armed conflict in Afghanistan, see chapter 4, section II, in this volume.

[6] UN Security Council, Afghanistan Analytical Support and Sanctions Monitoring Team, Tenth report of the Analytical Support and Sanctions Monitoring Team submitted pursuant to resolution 2255 (2015) concerning the Taliban and other associated individuals and entities constituting a threat to the peace, stability and security of Afghanistan, S/2019/481, 13 June 2019, p. 3.

[7] UN Security Council, Afghanistan Analytical Support and Sanctions Monitoring Team, S/2019/481 (note 6), pp. 20–21.

[8] UN Security Council, Afghanistan Analytical Support and Sanctions Monitoring Team, Ninth report of the Analytical Support and Sanctions Monitoring Team submitted pursuant to resolution 2255 (2015) concerning the Taliban and other associated individuals and entities constituting a threat to the peace, stability and security of Afghanistan, S/2018/466, 30 May 2018, p. 21.

[9] Bromley, M. and Wezeman, P. D., 'Multilateral embargoes on arms and dual-use items', SIPRI Yearbook 2019, p. 516.

[10] On the armed conflict and peace agreement in CAR, see chapter 7, section III, in this volume. See also 'Central African Republic: UN chief hails signing of new peace agreement', UN News, 6 Feb. 2019.

to CAR security forces with a caliber of 14.5 millimetres or less. Instead, the UN sanctions committee has to receive an advance notification that details the types and numbers of the weapons being supplied, their purpose, the destination unit in CAR security forces and the intended place of storage.[11]

In December 2019 the panel of experts on the CAR arms embargo reported that implementation of the February 2019 peace agreement had been 'limited' and that armed groups—including the Movement of Central African Liberators for Justice (Mouvement des libérateurs centrafricains pour la justice, MLCJ) and the Popular Front for the Rebirth of the Central African Republic (Front populaire pour la renaissance de la Centrafrique, FPRC), both of which signed the February agreement—continued to acquire arms, including from groups based in Sudan.[12] The panel also reported that the CAR Government did not believe that the amendments made to the embargo in September were sufficient and was pushing for the lifting of all remaining reporting requirements.[13]

Iran

The UN arms embargo on Iran prohibits transfers of most types of major arms to Iran (until 18 October 2020), the transfer of all arms from Iran (also until 18 October 2020), and the transfer to and from Iran of items that could contribute to the development of nuclear weapon delivery systems (until 18 October 2023) unless these items have been approved in advance by the UN Security Council. The embargo also places equivalent approval requirements on transfers to Iran of items that could contribute to Iran's activities related to uranium enrichment, nuclear fuel reprocessing or heavy water (until 18 October 2025).[14]

The lifting of prohibitions on transfers of major arms to and all arms from Iran scheduled for 18 October 2020 will only occur if Iran continues to comply with the terms of the Joint Comprehensive Programme of Action (JCPOA).[15] In May 2019, one year after the United States withdrew from the JCPOA, Iran began to reduce its commitments under the agreement.[16] Viewing Iran's actions as inconsistent with the terms of the JCPOA, in late 2019 France, Germany, the United Kingdom and the EU—four of the seven states parties to the agreement—signalled that they might respond by triggering 'all mechanisms in the JCPOA, including the dispute resolution

---

[11] UN Security Council Resolution 2488, 12 Sep. 2019.

[12] UN Security Council, 'Final report of the Panel of Experts on the Central African Republic extended pursuant to Security Council resolution 2454 (2019)', S/2019/930, 14 Dec. 2019, pp. 19–20.

[13] UN Security Council, S/2019/930 (note 12), p. 30.

[14] This differs from other UN arms embargoes where responsibility for issuing such approvals devolves to the relevant UN sanctions committee.

[15] UN Security Council Resolution 2231 (2015) [on Iran nuclear issue], 20 July 2015, annex A.

[16] On the developments regarding the JCPOA, see chapter 11, section III, in this volume.

mechanism'.[17] The activation of the mechanism would be the first step in a process that could lead to finding Iran in non-compliance with the JCPOA and re-imposition of the pre-JCPOA UN sanctions, including the previous arms embargo on Iran. Separately, the United States has stated that it would seek to keep all aspects of the current arms embargo in place after October 2020.[18] However, such a move would require a fresh UN Security Council resolution. Russia—which would be able to veto any such decision—has indicated that it will not support an extension of the embargo beyond the time-frame of the current agreement.[19]

Since 2015 no panel of experts has been appointed to monitor the UN arms embargo on Iran. Instead, both the UN secretary-general and the Security Council facilitator for the implementation of Resolution 2231 (2015) have published short reports every six months. In 2019 these reports included allegations about Iranian exports of military materiel in contravention of the UN arms embargo. Israel alleged that Iran had moved a missile to Syria and fired it at the Golan Heights, transferred technology for the production of unmanned aerial vehicles (UAVs) to Iraq and supplied technology for the production of precision-guided munitions to Hezbollah.[20] Saudi Arabia alleged that Iran had supplied weapons to the Houthi rebels in Yemen.[21] France, Germany and the United Kingdom reported that the Houthi forces in Yemen were using ballistic missiles, which they concluded were possibly supplied by Iran.[22] However, the UN reports only listed these allegations and did not present any conclusions about whether Iran had been in breach of the UN arms embargo.

Libya

The UN arms embargo on Libya bans transfers to non-state armed groups but permits deliveries to the internationally recognized Government of National Accord (GNA), provided that the transfers have been approved in advance by the UN sanctions committee for Libya. Throughout 2019 there were rising tensions and open conflict between forces under the control of the GNA and

---

[17] European Union External Action Service (EEAS), 'Joint statement by the foreign ministers of France, Germany and the United Kingdom and the EU High Representative on the JCPOA', 11 Nov. 2019.

[18] 'Iran sees lifting of UN arms embargo in 2020 as "huge political goal"', Reuters, 11 Nov. 2019; and Lazaroff, T., 'UN must renew its arms embargo against Iran, Pompeo says in Israel', *Jerusalem Post*, 20 Oct. 2019.

[19] Russian Ministry of Foreign Affairs, 'Deputy Foreign Minister Sergey Ryabkov's interview with Interfax news agency', 26 Dec. 2019.

[20] UN Security Council, Seventh six-month report of the facilitator on the implementation of Security Council resolution 2231 (2015), S/2019/514, 21 June 2019, para. 35; UN Security Council, 'Implementation of Security Council Resolution 2231 (2015)', Eighth report of the Secretary-General, S/2019/934, 10 Dec. 2019, para. 23.

[21] UN Security Council, S/2019/514 (note 20), para. 37. On the armed conflict in Yemen, also see chapter 6, section V, in this volume.

[22] UN Security Council, S/2019/934 (note 20), para. 25.

the main non-state armed group in Libya, the Libyan National Army (LNA) (also known as the Haftar Armed Forces).[23] Since the imposition of the embargo in 2011, the associated UN panel of experts has reported on multiple cases of alleged violations.[24] At the end of 2019 the panel was particularly explicit in its conclusions that the arms embargo had been ineffective during 2019 and that this had contributed to increased violence, and that the GNA and LNA had 'routinely and sometimes blatantly' received weapons and other military support in violation of the arms embargo.[25] The panel assessed that Jordan and the United Arab Emirates (UAE) had been the main suppliers of weapons such as armoured vehicles and UAVs to the LNA in contravention of the arms embargo. It also named Turkey as the main supplier of arms to the GNA and noted that these transfers also contravened the arms embargo since Turkey had not requested advance approval from the UN sanctions committee.[26] In November 2019 the Security Council discussed the situation in Libya, with several states calling for an end to foreign interference in Libya and strict adherence to the arms embargo.[27] However, the Security Council did not undertake any action towards Jordan, Turkey or the UAE. In December 2019, at an address to the Italian Senate, UN Secretary-General António Guterres declared his frustration that armed actors in Libya and several UN member states were not respecting the arms embargo.[28]

North Korea

The UN arms embargo on North Korea prohibits transfers to North Korea of arms and military materiel as well as items that can directly contribute to the development of the capability of North Korea's armed forces or that are relevant to the development of nuclear or ballistic missiles or any programmes related to weapons of mass destruction. It also bans states from receiving from North Korea arms and military materiel as well as any related police, military or paramilitary training. The UN panel of experts on North Korea released two reports in 2019, both of which documented cases of illegal transfers of dual-use items to North Korea and, in particular, transfers of arms from North Korea. The May 2019 report documented allegations of attempts to supply arms to a range of end-users, including Houthi rebels in

---

[23] On the armed conflict in Libya, see chapter 6, section IV, in this volume.

[24] Bromley and Wezeman (note 9), pp. 516–17. See also equivalent chapters in the SIPRI Yearbook from 2012 through 2018 editions.

[25] UN Security Council, 'Final report of the Panel of Experts on Libya established pursuant to Security Council Resolution 1973 (2011)', S/2019/914, 9 Dec. 2019, p. 2.

[26] UN Security Council, S/2019/914 (note 25), p. 2 and paras 60–62.

[27] United Nations, 'Foreign involvement in Libya must be stopped, top official tells Security Council, describing "race against time" to reach peaceful solution, spare lives', Press Release SC/14023, 18 Nov. 2019.

[28] UN Secretary-General, Remarks on multilateral solutions to global challenges at the Italian Senate, Statement, Rome, 18 Dec. 2019.

Yemen, armed groups in Libya and the armed forces of Sudan and Syria.[29] However, it is unclear how many of these contacts resulted in significant arms transfers. The contacts between North Korea and Libya consisted of an exchange of letters, in 2015, between the then chief of the Libyan Supreme Council of Defence and deputy to the prime minister, Khalifa al-Ghwail, and North Korean officials; it is unclear if any deals were signed.[30] After denying any sales had taken place, Sudan admitted in early 2019 that contracts had been in place for the development of '122mm [weapons] and aerial bombs' and the repair of air-defence systems but that these had all been cancelled.[31] Indeed, the September 2019 report noted that 'instances of military cooperation appear to have been declining as more Member States have complied with resolutions'.[32] However, the panel did provide evidence of ongoing cooperation between North Korea and Syria, which included the supply of weapons to the Syrian armed forces and the involvement of Syrian nationals in brokering the supply of North Korean weapons to armed groups in Libya and Yemen.[33]

Somalia

The UN arms embargo on Somalia prohibits transfers to non-state armed groups but permits deliveries to the government's security forces.[34] However, the UN Security Council requires the Somali Government to notify the UN sanctions committee for Somalia of any transfers in advance of delivery and to submit a post-delivery report. In addition, the Security Council requests the Somali Government to report to the UN sanctions committee every six months on its stockpile management standards and practices. In 2019 the UN panel of experts on Somalia noted an improvement in the quality of the Somali Government notifications.[35] The panel also called for the UN arms embargo to hinder al-Shabab, the main armed group against which the arms embargo is aimed, from acquiring the components and materials used in improvised explosive devices (IEDs).[36] In response the UN Security Council decided to explicitly require that states prevent the supply to Somalia of a list of specified explosive materials, explosives precursors, explosive-related equipment and related technology, if there is sufficient evidence that these

---

[29] UN Security Council, 'Report of the Panel of Experts established pursuant to Resolution 1874 (2009)', S/2019/171, 5 Mar. 2019, p. 4.

[30] UN Security Council, S/2019/171 (note 29), para. 73.

[31] UN Security Council, S/2019/171 (note 29), para. 84.

[32] UN Security Council, 'Report of the Panel of Experts established pursuant to Resolution 1874 (2009)', S/2019/691, 30 Aug. 2019, para. 32.

[33] UN Security Council, S/2019/171 (note 29), para. 90.

[34] On the armed conflict in Somalia, see chapter 7, section IV, in this volume.

[35] UN Security Council, Letter dated 27 September 2019 from the Panel of Experts on Somalia addressed to the Chair of the Security Council Committee pursuant to Resolution 751 (1992) concerning Somalia, S/2019/858, 1 Nov. 2019, p. 5 and para. 109.

[36] UN Security Council, S/2019/858 (note 35), p. 5 and para. 24.

will be used, or a significant risk they may be used, in the manufacture of IEDs.[37] This is the first time this category of item has been included in the materiels coverage of a UN arms embargo.

Sudan (Darfur)

The UN arms embargo on Sudan prohibits transfers to the Sudanese region of Darfur. The Sudanese Government can move arms to Darfur if it has received prior approval from the UN Sudan sanctions committee. As in previous years the UN panel of experts on the Sudan reported that in 2019 the Government of Sudan 'routinely' violated the embargo by transferring arms to Darfur.[38] It also reported on the cooperation between several Darfurian rebel groups and the LNA. For example, it reported that the Sudanese Liberation Army/Minni Minawi (SLA/MM) has been fighting as mercenaries for the LNA in Libya for several years and had received financing and equipment in return. This included the supply of several armoured vehicles in 2016, which the SLA/MM used in Darfur in 2017, followed by more deliveries in 2018.[39]

Yemen

The UN arms embargo on Yemen prohibits transfers to non-state actors in Yemen.[40] Allegations and investigations regarding the violation of the embargo have focused on reports about arms supplies from Iran to the Houthi rebels, which controlled large parts of the north of Yemen.[41] The UN panel of experts on Yemen concluded that commercially available parts, such as engines, servo actuators and electronics, are exported from several countries through a network of intermediaries to the Houthis, where they are used to produce UAVs and IEDs. It also concluded that—as in previous years—the Houthi forces continued to receive small arms and light weapons (SALW) and cruise missiles. While the panel did not explicitly conclude that these weapons came from Iran, it did note that they had technical characteristics similar to weapons made in Iran.[42]

Of particular importance for regional security were accusations concerning the origin of the cruise missiles and UAVs that had been used in attacks on oil facilities in Saudi Arabia in May and September 2019 and on a Saudi airport in June and August 2019.[43] The September attack caused significant disruptions in Saudi oil production and raised major concerns about possible escalation

---

[37] UN Security Council Resolution 2498, 15 Nov. 2019.

[38] UN Security Council, 'Final report of the Panel of Experts on the Sudan', S/2020/36, 14 Jan. 2020, p. 2.

[39] UN Security Council, S/2020/36 (note 38), paras. 79–84.

[40] On the armed conflict in Yemen, see chapter 6, section V, in this volume.

[41] See, e.g, UN Security Council, S/2019/514 (note 20), para. 37; and UN Security Council, S/2019/171 (note 29), p. 4.

[42] UN Security Council, 'Final report of the Panel of Experts on Yemen', S/2020/70, 27 Jan. 2020, p. 2.

[43] On the attacks on Saudi oil facilities and the regional tensions, see chapter 6, section I, in this volume.

of the tensions between the USA and Saudi Arabia on one side and Iran on the other. The Houthi rebels claimed responsibility for these attacks. However, Saudi Arabia and the USA stated that the weapons originated from Iran, while France, Germany and the UK also concluded that Iran bore responsibility for the attack.[44] The UN panel of experts on Yemen concluded that the Houthi forces did not launch the attacks in September 2019.[45]

EU arms embargoes: Developments and implementation challenges

During 2019 the EU made no significant modifications to any existing EU arms embargoes and did not introduce any new embargoes. Both within and among EU member states and in the European Parliament there have been continuous discussions since 2015 about the imposition of restrictions on arms supplies to Saudi Arabia in response to concerns about Saudi military operations in Yemen. In February 2016, October 2017 and in October 2018 the European Parliament adopted resolutions calling for an arms embargo on Saudi Arabia.[46] However, the European Parliament did not adopt a resolution on the matter in 2019, despite individual EU member states imposing or continuing restrictions on arms exports to Saudi Arabia in 2019.[47] The closest the EU came to imposing a new arms embargo was on Turkey (see below). Unlike the UN, the EU has no systematic mechanisms in place for monitoring compliance with its arms embargoes, although the need to create such measures has been highlighted in the update of the EU SALW strategy (see below). However, as in previous years, during 2019 there were cases of arms transfers that raised questions about the types of activities and goods covered by particular EU arms embargoes. These cases, in relation to Belarus and Myanmar (see below), underscore the potential need for more effective monitoring of embargo implementation.

Turkey

In October 2019 Turkey launched a large military operation in northern Syria aimed at pushing the armed Kurdish People's Protection Units (YPG) away from the border between Syria and Turkey.[48] Although armed conflict between the Turkish Government and armed Kurdish groups started in the 1980s, this particular offensive led to strong reactions among many EU member states, in particular because of the major role the YPG played in defeating ISIL. As

---

[44] British Prime Minister's Office, 'Joint statement by the heads of state and government of France, Germany and the United Kingdom: New York, 23 September 2019', 23 Sep. 2019.

[45] UN Security Council, S/2020/70 (note 42), para. 19.

[46] Bromley and Wezeman (note 9), pp. 519–20.

[47] On individual EU member states' restrictions on exports to Saudi Arabia see section IV in this chapter.

[48] On Turkey's military operation in Syria, see chapter 6, section II, in this volume.

an immediate response, several of those states imposed major restrictions on arms exports to Turkey; these states included France, Germany and Italy, which had been major suppliers of arms to Turkey in recent years.[49] On 14 October Sweden proposed imposing an EU arms embargo on Turkey during a meeting of the Council of the EU.[50] However, though the Council condemned Turkey's military action as seriously undermining stability and security in northern Syria and noted that several EU member states had imposed restrictions, it did not impose an EU arms embargo.[51]

Monitoring the implementation of EU arms embargoes

Unlike in the case of UN arms embargoes, there are no mechanisms through which independent experts are appointed to monitor the implementation of EU arms embargoes and produce reports on possible violations. However, the EU has provided funding to support the work of organizations that investigate and map the origins and supply routes of weapons used in armed conflicts, including those subject to EU arms embargoes.[52] The update of the EU SALW strategy, published in July 2018, stated that the European Council would 'explore modalities to improve the monitoring and enforcement of EU arms embargoes'.[53] However, it is unclear what measures have since been taken to implement this commitment. As for UN arms embargoes, states are required to report on the steps taken at the national level to implement EU arms embargoes. For example, the EU Council Regulation concerning the sanctions on Iran requires EU member states to share information on 'violations and enforcement problems and judgments issued by national courts'.[54] Equivalent language is included in most other EU sanctions currently in place.[55] However, the steps EU member states are taking to comply with this requirement, if any, are unclear. If any states are producing reports on embargo implementation, they are not being made public, as is the case with reports on the implementation of UN arms embargoes.

---

[49] Emmott, R., 'EU governments limit arms sales to Turkey but avoid embargo', Reuters, 14 Oct. 2019.

[50] 'Sverige vill se vapenembargo mot Turkiet' [Sweden wants arms embargo against Turkey], *Dagens Nyheter*, 11 Oct. 2019.

[51] Council of the European Union, 3720th meeting, 'Outcome of the Council meeting', 13066/19, 14 Oct. 2019, pp. 3–4.

[52] In particular, the EU has provided funding to support Conflict Armament Research's iTrace project. See Conflict Armament Research, 'iTrace'.

[53] Council of the European Union, 'Council conclusions on the adoption of an EU strategy against illicit firearms, small arms & light weapons & their ammunition', 13581/18, 19 Nov. 2018, p. 24.

[54] Council Regulation 267/2012 of 23 Mar. 2012 concerning restrictive measures against Iran and repealing Regulation 961/2010, *Official Journal of the European Union*, L88, 24 Mar. 2012, p. 17, Article 44(1)(b).

[55] EU guidelines on the implementation of EU sanctions recommend that relevant legal instruments should require member states to provide 'regular reporting on the implementing measures and enforcement actions' they have taken. See Council of the European Union, 'Guidelines on implementation and evaluation of restrictive measures (sanctions) in the framework of the EU Common Foreign and Security Policy', 5664/19, 4 May 2018, p. 45.

During 2019 two instances of arms transfers highlighted the potential utility of creating strengthened mechanisms of reporting on and monitoring of the implementation of EU arms embargoes. The first case, in Bulgaria, concerned an apparent difference of opinion between different branches of the government about whether the modernization of SU-25 combat aircraft in Belarus would constitute a breach of the EU arms embargo on Belarus.[56] The modernization deal with Belarus was signed in late 2018 but its implementation was delayed by the Bulgarian Ministry of Economy out of concern that its implementation would violate the EU arms embargo. In 2019 the Bulgarian Government transferred responsibility for issuing licences for military repair work from the Ministry of Economy to the Ministry of Defence, which was willing to approve the deal.[57] The second case, in Austria, concerned claims by a UN expert that the transfer of helicopter mini-UAVs from Austria to Myanmar during 2019 constituted a violation of the EU arms embargo on Myanmar.[58] In response, the Austrian government stated that its licensing procedures comply 'with the requirements of the European Union and the applicable international legal provisions'.[59] The Austrian company concerned stated that the drones were for 'the modernisation of the country's infrastructure and transport system as well as for monitoring and mapping in mining and road construction'.[60] However, a budget document of the Myanmar Ministry of Defence had mentioned the acquisition in November 2018 and during 2019 the drones were seen in service with the Myanmar military.[61]

Conclusions

As in previous years, the various investigative mechanisms attached to UN arms embargoes documented a wide range of reported cases of violations of varying size and significance in 2019. Particular noteworthy were problems in connection with the implementation of the UN arms embargo on Libya, which appears to have done little to halt the flow of arms into the conflict. However, these reports have generated little in the way of a concrete response from the international community. None of the states named as having supplied arms in violation of the embargo faced any censure from the UN Security Council.

---

[56] 'Bulgaria', *Scramble*, no. 484 (Sep. 2019), pp. 65–66.

[57] 'NATO country changes law to repair aircraft in Belarus', 21 Aug. 2019, Belsat; and 'Bulgaria sends first of eight Su-25 aircraft to Belarus for overhaul', *Sofia Globe*, 29 Aug. 2019.

[58] 'UN expert calls for EU investigation into Austrian firm that sold drones to Myanmar', *Myanmar Now*, 10 Aug. 2019.

[59] *Myanmar Now* (note 58).

[60] *Myanmar Now* (note 58).

[61] UN Human Rights Council, Independent International Fact-finding Mission on Myanmar, 'The economic interests of the Myanmar military', A/HRC/42/CRP.3, 5 Aug. 2019, p. 110; and *Myanmar Now* (note 58).

The ability of arms embargoes to influence the direction of conflicts was also highlighted by the case of the Central African Republic. Amendments to the embargo, which were partly aimed at supporting the peace deal signed in February 2019, appear to have done little to prevent poor implementation of the agreement. Unlike with UN arms embargoes there are no mechanisms in place for monitoring national implementation of EU embargoes. The need for such measures has been highlighted in official EU policy documents but no measures have been taken to date, even though discussions around two cases of arms transfers in 2019 underlined the importance of their creation.

III. The multilateral export control regimes

KOLJA BROCKMANN

The four main multilateral export control regimes—the Australia Group (AG), the Missile Technology Control Regime (MTCR), the Nuclear Suppliers Group (NSG) and the Wassenaar Arrangement on Export Controls for Conventional Arms and Dual-use Goods and Technologies (Wassenaar Arrangement, WA)—are informal groups of states which coordinate trade controls on goods and technologies that have uses in connection with chemical, biological, nuclear and conventional weapons (table 14.3).[1] The four regimes take all decisions by consensus and are politically rather than legally binding. Their participating states implement the controls prescribed by the regimes through national laws. The regimes also have an important norm-setting function beyond their membership.[2] In particular, many non-participating states have voluntarily decided to adhere to regime guidelines, adopt regime control lists and follow regime-issued guidance. The regimes also serve an important information-exchange function. The participating states share information on export licence denials and licences granted, and provide a framework in which policy, licensing, enforcement, technical and intelligence officers can meet and discuss implementation and proliferation challenges.

None of the four regimes admitted any new participating states (or partners) during 2019, despite a number of pending applications in several regimes. This reflects the inherent difficulty of balancing competing aims: universalizing the export control standards, maintaining functionality and confidentiality, and ensuring that decision-making procedures remain manageable. Many of the long-participating states have thought to achieve this balance by limiting admissions of additional states, which in all cases must be approved by consensus. However, there have also been cases in which participating states have blocked applications for membership due to political disputes that lie beyond the scope of the regime's objectives.[3]

As in previous years, common challenges faced by the regimes included keeping pace with technical developments, maintaining effective operations, and identifying and combating illicit procurement efforts. Geopolitical tensions continued to adversely affect the work of the regimes, particularly

---

[1] For brief descriptions and lists of the participating states in each of these regimes see annex B, section III, in this volume.

[2] Bauer, S., 'Main developments and discussions in the export control regimes', Literature Review for the Policy and Operations Evaluations Department of the Dutch Ministry of Foreign Affairs: Final Report (SIPRI: Stockholm, Aug. 2017), p. 62.

[3] Bauer, S. and Maletta, G., 'Dual-use and arms trade controls', *SIPRI Yearbook 2017*, pp. 603–604; and Stewart, I. J., 'Export controls at the crossroads', *Bulletin of the Atomic Scientists*, Analysis, 15 Oct. 2015.

Table 14.3. The four multilateral export control regimes

Region (year established)	Scope	No. of participants [a]	2019 plenary chair	2019 plenary
Australia Group (1985)	Equipment, materials, technology and software that could contribute to chemical and biological weapons activities	43	Australia	3–7 June, Paris, France
Missile Technology Control Regime (1987)	Unmanned aerial vehicles capable of delivering weapons of mass destruction	35	New Zealand	7–11 Oct., Auckland, New Zealand
Nuclear Suppliers Group (1974)	Nuclear and nuclear related materials, software and technology	48[b]	Kazakhstan	17–21 June, Nur-Sultan, Kazakhstan
Wassenaar Arrangement (1996)	Conventional arms and dual-use items and technologies	42	Greece	4–5 Dec., Vienna, Austria

[a] Participant numbers are as of 31 December 2019.

[b] In addition, the European Union and the chair of the Zangger Committee are permanent observers of the Nuclear Suppliers Group.

Sources: Australia Group; Missile Technology Control Regime; Nuclear Suppliers Group; and Wassenaar Arrangement on Export Controls for Conventional Arms and Dual-use Goods and Technologies.

activities of a politically sensitive nature, such as the sharing of intelligence-based information on procurement efforts. In contrast, progress continued on the more technical aspects of the regimes' work, such as control list amendments. During the last several years, some of the regimes engaged more substantially with each other on specific overlaps in control lists and potential overlaps in coverage of emerging technologies.[4] Engagement in these more formalized technical dialogue meetings has demonstrated a number of challenges, including resistance from certain members that have sought to maintain the principle that regime matters cannot be discussed with non-members. However, many participating states have also appreciated such engagement as a valuable tool to address rapid technological developments with cross-regime relevance.[5] The MTCR—by means of its Technical Experts Meeting—was the first and only regime to develop a more structured process for arranging inter-regime informal meetings of experts.[6]

[4] Brockmann, K., *Challenges to Multilateral Export Controls: The Case for Inter-Regime Dialogue and Coordination* (SIPRI: Stockholm, Dec. 2019).

[5] Brockmann (note 4), pp. 22–23.

[6] National regime delegate, Correspondence with the author, 25 Sep. 2019.

The Australia Group

The AG seeks to 'minimise the risk' of participating states contributing to the proliferation of chemical and biological weapons (CBW) by coordinating and harmonizing national export controls.[7] Australia chairs the AG on a permanent basis. The AG was established in 1985 in response to the findings of a United Nations investigation into the use of chemical weapons in the 1980–88 Iran–Iraq War, which revealed extensive procurement by Iraq of precursor chemicals and materials from several Western states.[8] The AG has since expanded its coverage from chemical weapons and associated production equipment and technology, to include biological weapons and equipment, materials and technology relevant to their development, production and use.[9] The AG's control lists defining these items are continuously updated through consensus decisions of the participating states. Since its creation the number of participants in the AG has grown from 18 to 43, including the European Union. No new participating states were admitted to the AG in 2019, with several applications still pending. The AG participants continued to encourage voluntary declarations of adherence by as many states as possible.[10] The AG affords adherents increased access to information and support from AG participants to assist them in implementing the AG guidelines and control lists. Despite this offer, Kazakhstan remains the only officially declared adherent to have submitted to the AG chair a notification of political commitment to adherence to the guidelines and control lists of the AG.[11]

In 2019, there were noteworthy developments in three key functional areas of the AG's work: responding to chemical weapons proliferation and use cases; assessing and addressing technological developments; and conducting AG outreach to non-members and expert communities.

During the AG plenary in June 2019 in Paris, the participating states shared their concerns about efforts to 'discredit' the investigative work of the Organisation for the Prohibition of Chemical Weapons (OPCW) and expressed their support for the OPCW's director-general, Technical Secretariat and the Investigation and Identification Team (IIT).[12] The AG

---

[7] Australia Group, 'The Australia Group: An introduction', [n.d.]; and Australia Group, 'Objectives of the Group', [n.d.].

[8] Australia Group, 'The origins of the Australia Group', [n.d.].

[9] Australia Group, 'The origins of the Australia Group' (note 8).

[10] Australia Group, 'Statement by the chair of the 2019 Australia Group plenary', 15 July 2019.

[11] Australia Group, 'Australia Group adherents', [n.d.].

[12] Australia Group, 'Statement by the chair of the 2019 Australia Group plenary' (note 10).

participants called on all states to fulfil their obligations under the 1992 Chemical Weapons Convention (CWC).[13]

The AG continued its technical discussions during the plenary. As in 2018, the AG had detailed discussions on the potential addition of novichoks precursors to its control lists.[14] While the AG did not adopt list changes in this regard by the end of 2019, the OPCW for the first time amended Schedule 1 of the Annex on Chemicals to the CWC by adding agents of the novichok family in November 2019.[15] The AG is not bound by the CWC schedules of chemicals, but the participants regard the work of the AG as 'an effective means of implementing . . . key obligations in the CWC'.[16] The AG participants identified the discussion of the potential listing of novichoks precursors as a priority for the coming year and welcomed the Slovak Republic's offer to host an intersessional meeting in early 2020 that would address the possible listing of novichoks precursors and 'more effective implementation of catch-all controls'.[17]

Participating states also shared approaches regarding intangible technology transfers, proliferation financing, procurement, trans-shipment and broader proliferation networks. Noting the rapid pace of new technological and scientific developments as well as the value of outreach to industry and academia, the AG Secretariat invited several guest speakers to address the plenary on relevant proliferation and technology development topics.[18]

During 2019, the AG further strengthened its outreach efforts to non-members and engagement with non-governmental experts. Following the dialogue meetings with Latin American states in 2017 and with African states in 2018, the AG organized a regional dialogue meeting for Middle Eastern states in Malta in March 2019.[19] The AG participants agreed to increase follow-up with dialogue participants from previous meetings and reiterated the call for states to adopt the AG's guidelines and control lists and to use them as a model of international best practice.[20]

---

[13] For a summary and other details of the Convention on the Prohibition of the Development, Production, Stockpiling and Use of Chemical Weapons and on their Destruction (Chemical Weapons Convention or CWC) see annex A, section I, in this volume.

[14] Australia Group, 'Statement by the chair of the 2019 Australia Group plenary' (note 10).

[15] On the addition of novichoks see chapter 12, section II, in this volume; see also Costanzi, S. and Koblentz, G. D., 'Controlling novichoks after Salisbury: Revising the Chemical Weapons Convention schedules', *Nonproliferation Review*, Viewpoint (online 30 Sep. 2019).

[16] Australia Group, 'Relationship with the Chemical Weapons Convention', [n.d.].

[17] Australia Group, 'Statement by the chair of the 2019 Australia Group plenary' (note 10).

[18] Researchers from King's College London and from SIPRI provided presentations on proliferation challenges associated with cloud laboratories and additive manufacturing, and on countering proliferation financing. Australia Group, 'Statement by the chair of the 2019 Australia Group plenary' (note 10); Brockmann, K., 'Advances in 3D printing technology: Increasing biological weapon proliferation risks?', SIPRI WritePeace Blog, 29 July 2019; Lentzos, F. and Invernizzi, C., 'Laboratories in the cloud', *Bulletin of the Atomic Scientists*, 2 July 2019.

[19] Australia Group, 'Statement by the chair of the 2019 Australia Group plenary' (note 10); Australia Group, 'Statement by the chair of the 2018 Australia Group plenary', 8 June 2018.

[20] Australia Group, 'Statement by the chair of the 2019 Australia Group plenary' (note 10).

The Missile Technology Control Regime

The MTCR seeks to prevent the proliferation of missiles and other unmanned delivery systems capable of delivering chemical, biological or nuclear (CBN) weapons. The largest industrialized states—known as the Group of Seven (G7)—originally created the MTCR in 1987 to help prevent the proliferation of nuclear weapons by controlling the export of goods and technologies related to missiles capable of carrying nuclear weapons.[21] The scope of controls subsequently expanded to include ballistic and cruise missiles and all unmanned aerial vehicles (UAVs) capable of delivering CBN weapons.[22] The MTCR covers any such system 'capable of delivering a payload of at least 500 kg to a range of at least 300 km', or destined to be used to deliver CBN weapons.[23] Since its creation by the G7, the MTCR's membership has grown from 7 to 35 states (the partners). No additional partners were admitted to the MTCR in 2019. Three states—Estonia, Kazakhstan and Latvia—have unilaterally declared their adherence to the guidelines and control lists of the MTCR.[24]

In 2019, the MTCR resumed holding an annual plenary (no partner had volunteered to chair and host a plenary in 2018). New Zealand assumed the chair of the MTCR for the period 2019/20 and hosted the plenary in October 2019 in Auckland. Ambassador Dell Higgie of New Zealand is the first female chair of the MTCR.[25] In light of the absence of a chair for the previous period, the MTCR partners discussed a range of internal operational issues, including its system for appointing a chair. To prevent a repeat of the issue, three states have already volunteered to assume the chair several years into the future. Austria will assume the chair of the MTCR at the next plenary for the period 2020/21.[26] The partners also supported Russia's intention to assume the chair in 2021/22 and approved Switzerland's offer to assume the chair for the period 2022/23.[27]

The MTCR Technical Experts Meeting (TEM), Information Exchange Meeting (IEM) and the Licencing and Enforcement Experts Meeting (LEEM) each met during the plenary week in Auckland. The TEM reviewed the MTCR control list and agreed on a small number of changes, including to the description of thrust vector control subsystems and to the accuracy

---

[21] Missile Technology Control Regime, 'Frequently asked questions (FAQs)', [n.d.]. The G7 states are Canada, France, Germany, Italy, Japan, the United Kingdom and the United States.

[22] Missile Technology Control Regime, 'Frequently asked questions (FAQs)' (note 21).

[23] Missile Technology Control Regime, 'MTCR Guidelines and the Equipment, Software and Technology Annex', [n.d.].

[24] Missile Technology Control Regime, 'Partners', [n.d.].

[25] Missile Technology Control Regime, 'Report by the MTCR chair: Auckland plenary meeting Oct. 2019', 1 Nov. 2019.

[26] Missile Technology Control Regime, 'Public statement from the Plenary Meeting of the Missile Technology Control Regime, Auckland, 11 Oct. 2019' ('Public statement'), 18 Oct. 2019.

[27] Missile Technology Control Regime, 'Public statement' (note 26).

parameters used for missile guidance and navigation systems.[28] The IEM and LEEM discussed rapid technological developments and changes in proliferator procurement practices.[29] Discussions focused on ballistic missile developments and tests, proliferation trends and procurement activities, strategies of programmes for means of delivery for CBN weapons, intangible technology transfers, catch-all controls, transit and trans-shipment, outreach to industry and export control enforcement.[30] The IEM, LEEM and TEM also held a joint meeting in which the MTCR partners discussed the evolution of procurement strategies and challenges to the effective implementation of export controls.[31]

One of the main impacts of the failure to find a plenary chair for the period 2018/19 was the absence in 2019 of outreach visits to non-members, which are commonly undertaken by the chair, and of representation of the MTCR at international conferences and events. France continued acting as the point of contact (POC) of the MTCR and organized two reinforced point of contact (RPOC) meetings in Paris in 2019.[32]

The Hague Code of Conduct against Ballistic Missile Proliferation

The Hague Code of Conduct against Ballistic Missile Proliferation (HCOC) complements the MTCR, having originated within the MTCR in 2002 and since developing into an independent politically binding transparency and confidence-building instrument concerning ballistic missile proliferation.[33] In contrast to the export control regimes, which admit participating states by consensus decision, any state can subscribe to the HCOC by submitting its subscription to the Austrian Ministry for Foreign Affairs, which serves as the Immediate Central Contact for the HCOC. Subscribing states commit to implementing a limited range of transparency and confidence-building measures. In particular, they agree to provide annual declarations about national ballistic missile and space launch programmes and policies, and to exchange pre-launch notifications (PLNs) on launches and test flights of their ballistic missiles and space launch vehicles.[34]

The 18th annual regular meeting of the HCOC took place in Vienna on 3–4 June 2019, with delegations from 74 of the 140 subscribing states in

---

[28] Missile Technology Control Regime, 'Report by the chair of the Technical Experts Meeting: Update of MTCR Annex', 18 Oct. 2019; and Missile Technology Control Regime, 'Equipment, Software and Technology Annex', 18 Oct. 2019 (for the changes, see 'Changes from previous version: (Shown in track changes)').

[29] Missile Technology Control Regime, 'Report by the MTCR chair' (note 25).

[30] Missile Technology Control Regime, 'Public statement' (note 26).

[31] Missile Technology Control Regime, 'Public statement' (note 26).

[32] Missile Technology Control Regime, 'Public statement' (note 26).

[33] Hague Code of Conduct, 'What is HCOC?', Jan. 2019.

[34] Hague Code of Conduct, 'How to join HCOC', Nov. 2018.

attendance—a slight increase from the previous year's attendance.[35] Togo subscribed to the HCOC shortly before the regular meeting, becoming its 140th subscribing state.[36] The subscribing states discussed a range of developments in missile proliferation, such as the then impending demise of the Intermediate-range Nuclear Forces (INF) Treaty, and developments in the missile activities of the Democratic People's Republic of Korea (DPRK, North Korea).[37] Germany reported to the regular meeting that, according to its assessment, the implementation rate of PLNs increased to 73.1% in 2018 from 66.9% in 2017.[38] It further reported 74 launches—29 ballistic missile launches and 43 space launches—by non-subscribing states in 2018.[39] A German proposal to enter into an open-ended discussion among subscribing states to clarify the threshold for when to issue PLNs received mixed reactions and did not find consensus in the meeting. In addition to the regular meeting, an extraordinary 'informal expert meeting' on 24 January 2019 provided another opportunity to exchange views.[40]

Norway assumed the chair for the period 2019/20, taking over from Sweden.[41] The subscribing states agreed for Switzerland to assume the chair for the 2020/21 period. The incoming Norwegian chair outlined the main objectives for the chair as being universalization and further implementation of the HCOC, and expansion of the HCOC's relationship with the UN and 'other non-proliferation mechanisms' such as the Treaty on the Non-Proliferation of Nuclear Weapons (Non-Proliferation Treaty, NPT) of 1968.[42]

Several outreach activities took place during Sweden's tenure as chair, including regional seminars in the Caribbean region in November 2018, in South Asia in January 2019 and in West Africa in February 2019.[43] The chair made bilateral efforts towards universalization of the HCOC with several non-subscribing states, including leading an expert mission to Malaysia to discuss benefits of becoming a subscribing state.[44]

---

[35] Hague Code of Conduct, '18th regular meeting of the subscribing states to the Hague Code of Conduct against Ballistic Missile Proliferation', Press release, June 2019, p. 1; and Hague Code of Conduct, '17th regular meeting of the subscribing states to the Hague Code of Conduct against Ballistic Missile Proliferation', Press release, June 2018, p. 1.

[36] Hague Code of Conduct, '18th regular meeting of the subscribing states to the Hague Code of Conduct against Ballistic Missile Proliferation' (note 35), p. 1.

[37] Hague Code of Conduct, Immediate Central Contact (ICC), '18th HCOC Annual Regular Meeting: Chairperson's summary/plenary decisions', HCOC(19)016, 4 June 2019, para. 25.

[38] Hague Code of Conduct, ICC (note 37), para. 25.

[39] Hague Code of Conduct, ICC (note 37), para. 25.

[40] Hague Code of Conduct, ICC (note 37), para. 25.

[41] Norwegian Ministry of Foreign Affairs, 'Norway assumes chairmanship of the Hague Code of Conduct against Ballistic Missile Proliferation', Press release, 4 June 2019.

[42] Hague Code of Conduct, ICC (note 37), para. 4.

[43] Hague Code of Conduct, ICC (note 37), para. 2.

[44] Hague Code of Conduct, ICC (note 37), para. 2.

The Nuclear Suppliers Group

The NSG aims to prevent the proliferation of nuclear weapons by controlling transfers of nuclear and nuclear-related material, equipment, software and technology. The NSG was established in 1974 following India's first nuclear test—the first explosion of a nuclear weapon since the establishment of the NPT by a state not recognized as a nuclear-weapon state under the treaty. The number of participating states in the NSG has increased from an initial 7 at its inception to 48.[45] In 2019 the NSG participating states continued discussions on states' applications to participate in the NSG but did not find consensus on admitting any additional states. On the issue of the potential participation in the NSG of non-members to the 1968 NPT, the participating states continued their discussions on technical, legal and political aspects.[46] This involved discussion of the implementation of the 2008 Statement on Civil Nuclear Cooperation with India. The wider debate on this issue has received particular attention ever since the 2016 NSG plenary, after India and Pakistan submitted membership applications in that year.[47] The NSG made no decision to admit or reject the applications of either state in 2019.

Kazakhstan assumed the chair of the NSG in 2019 and hosted the plenary in Nur-Sultan on 20–21 June. At the plenary, Germany took over as chair of the Consultative Group, while Sweden continued to chair the Technical Experts Group and the USA continued to chair the Information Exchange Meeting.[48] The 2019 plenary continued to discuss developments in relation to North Korean nuclear activities and participating states expressed their support for ongoing diplomatic processes.[49] They reconfirmed their commitment to 'full and comprehensive implementation' of the nuclear weapon-related UN Security Council resolutions on North Korea.[50] They also noted the continued obligations under UN Security Council Resolution 2231 of 2015 concerning the Iranian nuclear programme, and the Joint Comprehensive Plan of Action (JCPOA), which set up a dedicated 'procurement channel' for the transfer of items, materials, equipment, goods and technology required

[45] Nuclear Suppliers Group, 'Participants', [n.d.].

[46] Nuclear Suppliers Group, 'Public statement of the 2019 NSG plenary', Nur-Sultan, Kazakhstan, 21 June 2019.

[47] For details on the export control exceptions afforded to India by the USA and India's efforts to build diplomatic support for membership, see Maletta, G. et al., 'The export control regimes', *SIPRI Yearbook 2019*, pp. 528–29; Bauer, S. et al., 'The export control regimes', *SIPRI Yearbook 2018*, pp. 431–33; Bauer, S. and Maletta, G., 'The export control regimes', *SIPRI Yearbook 2017*, pp. 600–601.

[48] Nuclear Suppliers Group, 'Public statement of the 2019 NSG plenary' (note 46).

[49] Nuclear Suppliers Group, 'Public statement of the 2019 NSG plenary' (note 46); On North Korean nuclear activities see chapter 9, section 2, in this volume.

[50] Most recently, UN Security Council resolutions 2371, 5 Aug. 2017; 2375, 11 Sep 2017; and 2397, 22 Dec. 2017. No UN Security Council sanctions-related resolution on North Korea has been added since 2017. For a summary of UN Security Council sanctions resolutions in response to North Korea's nuclear and ballistic missile tests, see Kile, S. N., 'International non-proliferation sanctions against North Korea', *SIPRI Yearbook 2018*, pp. 386–88.

for Iran's JCPOA-compliant nuclear activities.[51] Despite the US withdrawal from the JCPOA, the NSG continued to receive briefings on the procurement channel and requested further such briefings.[52]

During the plenary, participating states agreed on several changes to the NSG control lists, as part of the regular review to keep the NSG control lists up to date with technological developments.[53] In 2019 the NSG chair conducted an outreach programme with several nuclear industry organizations and non-participating states. At one such outreach event in April 2019, representatives from nuclear industry discussed issues including 'technology and industry developments in the context of NSG Guidelines and control lists'.[54] The NSG also convened another meeting with representation from nuclear industry in the June 2019 plenary week in Nur-Sultan. With a view to the next NPT Review Conference taking place in 2020, the participating states agreed to conduct an exercise to reach out to interested states on the margins of the Review Conference, 'to enhance understanding of the NSG and its Guidelines'.[55]

In 2019, the participating states continued to consider both positive opportunities created by technological developments and the proliferation challenges created by new technologies in a variety of forums, both internally and during Track 1.5 workshops and conferences. NSG chairs and participating states discussed proliferation challenges posed by a number of technological advances and so-called emerging technologies, including additive manufacturing, cloud computing and advanced reactor design. Informal discussions also took place within the NSG and in other forums on how certain technologies, such as blockchain and artificial intelligence, could be used to improve the effectiveness of export controls.[56]

The Wassenaar Arrangement

The WA seeks to increase transparency and responsibility in the transfers of conventional weapons and dual-use goods and technologies and to prevent such transfers from contributing to 'destabilising accumulations' of such weapons and technologies—including transfers to terrorists—that would endanger international and regional security and stability.[57] The WA was established on the basis of the 'Initial Elements' in 1996, as the successor to the Cold War era Co-ordinating Committee for Multilateral Export Controls

---

[51] UN Security Council Resolution 2231 (2015), 20 July 2015, annex A. For more on the JCPOA see chapter 9, section III in this volume.

[52] Nuclear Suppliers Group, 'Public statement of the 2019 NSG plenary' (note 46), p. 2.

[53] Nuclear Suppliers Group, 'NSG Part 1 and Part 2 Control Lists updated'.

[54] Nuclear Suppliers Group, 'Public statement of the 2019 NSG plenary' (note 46), p. 3.

[55] Nuclear Suppliers Group, 'Public statement of the 2019 NSG plenary' (note 46), p. 1.

[56] The author participated in several of these meetings as a presenter and moderator.

[57] Wassenaar Arrangement, 'About us', Updated 9 Aug. 2019.

(COCOM).[58] The WA's membership has expanded from 33 founding states to 42 participating states. India was the last state to be admitted in 2017. No new members were admitted in 2019.[59]

The WA held its annual plenary on 4–5 December 2019 in Vienna, Austria, chaired by Greece.[60] Croatia assumed the chair on 1 January 2020 while Ukraine assumed the chair of the General Working Group and Italy assumed the chair of the Licensing and Enforcement Officers Meeting.[61] Latvia continues to chair the Experts Group in 2020.

The participating states adopted a set of new control list items to the WA control lists.[62] These included two new sets of controls on certain types of cyber-surveillance technologies that are used by intelligence agencies and law-enforcement agencies to monitor, retain and analyse communications data. Specifically, controls were added on 'communications monitoring equipment', which covers certain types of 'monitoring centres' that are used to collect, store and analyse data from multiple sources.[63] Controls were also added on 'digital investigative tools/forensic systems', which cover certain types of tools used to retrieve and analyse data stored on networks, computers and mobile devices.[64] The additions mean that five types of cyber-surveillance technologies are included in the Wassenaar Arrangement's dual-use list.[65] Controls were also added on 'cyber-warfare software, . . . sub-orbital aerospace vehicles, technology for the production of substrates for high-end integrated circuits, hybrid machine tools, and lithography equipment and technology'.[66] The participating states also amended existing control list items to clarify controls on 'ballistic protection, optical sensors, ball bearings, and inorganic fibrous and filamentary materials'.[67] They also reduced controls on some list items, including controls on 'certain laminates and commercial components with embedded cryptography'.[68]

---

[58] Wassenaar Arrangement, 'About us' (note 57).

[59] Griffiths, P., 'Updates from the Wassenaar Arrangement', SMi 14th Annual Conference, Defence Exports, 2019, Amsterdam, 25–26 Sep. 2019, p. 2.

[60] Wassenaar Arrangement, 'Statement issued by the plenary chair on 2019 outcomes of the Wassenaar Arrangement on Export Controls for Conventional Arms and Dual-Use Goods and Technologies', Vienna, 5 Dec. 2019, p. 1.

[61] Wassenaar Arrangement (note 60), p. 2.

[62] Wassenaar Arrangement (note 60), p. 1.

[63] Wassenaar Arrangement (note 60), p. 1; and 'Monitoring centres: Force multipliers from the surveillance industry', *Privacy International*, 29 Apr. 2014.

[64] Wassenaar Arrangement (note 60), p. 1; and Fruhlinger, J., 'What is digital forensics? And how to land a job in this hot field', *CSO*, 25 Jan. 2019.

[65] Controls on 'Mobile telecommunications interception equipment' were added in 2012 and controls on 'Internet protocol (IP) network surveillance systems' and 'Intrusion software' were added in 2013. For more information, see Bromley, M., Export Controls, Human Security and Cyber-surveillance Technology: Examining the Proposed Changes to the EU Dual-use Regulation (SIPRI: Stockholm, Dec. 2017).

[66] Wassenaar Arrangement (note 60), p. 1.

[67] Wassenaar Arrangement (note 60), p. 1.

[68] Wassenaar Arrangement (note 60), p. 1.

The so-called emerging technologies of security concern that the WA continues to consider include intrusion software, UAV jamming systems, additive manufacturing equipment and novel spacecraft.[69] The participating states acknowledge and seek to address the challenge posed by 'intertwined development of both civilian and military applications of these technologies' and the 'balancing act' this requires.[70] Informal technical dialogues with the MTCR and the NSG will continue on the topic of additive manufacturing (3D printing) and other specific control list items 'to avoid duplication'.[71]

As part of the 2019 WA plenary, the participating states also updated the guidance on 'Best Practices for Exports of Small Arms and Light Weapons', which was last updated in 2007. They also updated its guidance on 'Best Practices for Disposal of Surplus/Demilitarised Military Equipment' from 2000. The regular review cycle continued and identified other guidance for appropriate updating in 2020.[72]

In 2019 the WA secretariat participated in a range of outreach activities, including international conferences, events and education initiatives. The secretariat participated in the Disarmament and International Security Affairs Fellowship programme in New Delhi, the 26th Asian Export Control Seminar in Tokyo, an OSCE-UNODA Scholarship for Peace and Security Training Programme, the 6th International Defense Technology Security Conference in Seoul, a World Trade Organization Capacity Building Workshop, the Fifth Conference of States Parties to the Arms Trade Treaty (ATT), and the UN Disarmament Fellows Programme.[73] In addition to the secretariat's efforts, the Greek chair, the expert group chairs and several participating states participated in a technical outreach mission to Israel.[74]

Conclusions

The four multilateral export control regimes continued to review their respective export control lists and guidelines in 2019, resulting in a number of control list amendments in each regime. Most significantly, the AG continued its consultations on the potential addition of novichoks precursors to its control lists and the WA added several types of cyber-surveillance technologies and a list item covering cyber-warfare software to its control

---

[69] Griffiths, P., 'Multilateral export control regimes—the Wassenaar Arrangement', Address to the 26th Asian Export Control Seminar, 26–28 Feb. 2019, Tokyo, p. 6.

[70] Griffiths (note 69), p. 6.

[71] Griffiths (note 69), p. 9.

[72] Griffiths (note 69), p. 9.

[73] Wassenaar Arrangement (note 60), p. 2. See e.g. Griffiths, P., 'The Wassenaar Arrangement's role for effective defence technology security and export control', Defence Acquisition Programme Administration (DAPA) 6th International Defence Technology Security Conference, 20 June 2019, Seoul.

[74] Wassenaar Arrangement (note 60), p. 2.

lists. The regimes did not admit any new participating states (or partners) during 2019, despite a number of pending applications. Geopolitical tensions continued to affect the work of the regimes, particularly work of a politically sensitive nature, such as information sharing on procurement efforts. The NSG continued strengthening engagement with industry and consultation processes on emerging technologies. Several regimes engaged more substantially with each other on specific overlaps in control lists and potential overlaps in coverage of emerging technologies. Despite some concerns expressed by participating states, most of them appreciated such engagement as a valuable tool to address rapid technological developments with cross-regime relevance. The development of a more structured process for arranging inter-regime informal meetings of experts by the Technical Experts Meeting of the MTCR in 2019 was a significant first step towards improving inter-regime dialogue on technical issues.

IV. Developments in the European Union's dual-use and arms trade controls

MARK BROMLEY AND GIOVANNA MALETTA

The European Union (EU) is currently the only regional organization with a common legal framework for controls on the export, brokering, transit and trans-shipment of dual-use items and, to a certain extent, also military items. The key elements of this legal framework are EU arms embargoes, the EU Dual-use Regulation, the EU Common Position on Arms Exports (EU Common Position), the Intra-Community Transfers Directive and the Anti-Torture Regulation.[1] Developments in EU arms embargoes are addressed in section II of this chapter. This section focuses on developments with regard to the EU Dual-use Regulation and the EU Common Position, which were both the subject of review processes in 2019. The EU member states and the European External Action Service (EEAS) completed the process of reviewing the EU Common Position in September 2019. However, the review of the EU Dual-use Regulation was ongoing at the end of 2019.

Review of the Dual-use Regulation

The EU Dual-use Regulation covers controls on the export, transit, trans-shipment and brokering of dual-use goods, software and technology. The regulation is directly applicable law in EU member states but is implemented and enforced via their national control systems. As mandated in Article 25 of the Dual-use Regulation, the instrument has been under review since 2011. As part of this process, the European Commission published a 'recast' proposal in the form of a draft of a new version of the regulation in September 2016.[2] The European Parliament published its proposed amendments to the Commission proposal in January 2018 and the Council of the EU

---

[1] Council Regulation 428/2009 of 5 May 2009 setting up a Community regime for the control of exports, transfer, brokering and transit of dual-use items, *Official Journal of the European Union*, L134, 29 May 2009; Council Common Position 2008/944/CFSP of 8 Dec. 2008 defining common rules governing control of exports of military technology and equipment, *Official Journal of the European Union*, L335, 8 Dec. 2008; Directive 2009/43/EC of the European Parliament and of the Council of 6 May 2009 simplifying terms and conditions of transfers of defence-related products within the Community, *Official Journal of the European Union*, L146, 10 June 2009; and Regulation (EU) 2016/2134 of the European Parliament and of the Council of 23 Nov. 2016 amending Council Regulation (EC) 1236/2005 concerning trade in certain goods which could be used for capital punishment, torture or other cruel, inhuman or degrading treatment or punishment, *Official Journal of the European Union*, L338, 13 Dec. 2016.

[2] European Commission, 'Proposal for a Regulation of the European Parliament and of the Council setting up a Union regime for the control of exports, transfer, brokering, technical assistance and transit of dual-use items (recast)', COM(2016) 616 final, 28 Sep. 2016. See also Bauer, S. and Bromley, M., 'Developments in EU dual-use and arms trade controls', *SIPRI Yearbook 2017*, pp. 612–15.

published its own negotiating mandate in June 2019.[3] Unlike the Parliament's amendments—which largely endorsed or expanded on the Commission's proposal—the Council's mandate pushes back on many parts of the Commission's text and seeks to keep large sections of the existing regulation intact.[4]

One key area where the Council's mandate differs from the positions taken by the Commission and the Parliament regards the creation of an 'autonomous' EU control list for items not covered by the lists of the multilateral export control regimes (see section III of this chapter). The creation of an autonomous list was proposed by the Commission and endorsed by the Parliament, primarily as a means of creating EU controls on exports of cyber-surveillance technologies that were not controlled by the Wassenaar Arrangement on Export Controls for Conventional Arms and Dual-use Goods and Technologies. The Commission has since indicated that the autonomous list could also be a mechanism through which the EU could keep pace with efforts by the United States to create new controls on exports of so-called 'emerging technologies'.[5] During the negotiations that led to the adoption of their negotiating mandate, EU member states appear to have been divided over whether to endorse the creation of an autonomous EU list. In January 2018 a group of 11 EU member states issued a working paper that gave qualified support for the proposal.[6] However, in May 2018 a group of nine other EU member states issued a second working paper that rejected it, arguing that it would place EU-based companies at a disadvantage and limit the value of the existing EU dual-use list as a composite of those drawn up in the regimes.[7] The Council's negotiating mandate omits all references to the creation of an autonomous list.

---

[3] European Parliament, 'Amendments adopted by the European Parliament on 17 Jan. 2018 on the proposal for a regulation of the European Parliament and of the Council setting up a Union regime for the control of exports, transfer, brokering, technical assistance and transit of dual-use items (recast) (COM(2016)0616—C8-0393/2016—2016/0295(COD))', 17 Jan. 2018; and Council of the European Union, 'Proposal for a for a regulation of the European Parliament and of the Council setting up a Union regime for the control of exports, brokering, technical assistance, transit and transfer of dual-use items (recast)—Mandate for negotiations with the European Parliament (2016/0295(COD))', 5 June 2019.

[4] For a more detailed overview of the European Commission's proposal and the European Parliament's amendments, see Bromley, M. and Maletta G., 'Developments in the European Union's dual-use and arms trade controls', *SIPRI Yearbook 2019*, pp. 532–37.

[5] See European Commission, *Progress Report on the Implementation of the EU–US Joint Statement of 25 July 2018*, 25 July 2019, pp. 25–26. For more information on the US steps towards adopting expanded national controls on emerging technology, see Bromley, M. and Brockmann, K., 'Controlling technology transfers and foreign direct investment: The limits of export controls', *SIPRI Yearbook 2019*, pp. 538–45.

[6] Council of the European Union, General Secretariat, 'EU export control: Recast of the Regulation 428/2009', Working paper WK 1019/2018 INIT, 29 Jan. 2018.

[7] Council of the European Union, 'Paper for discussion: For adoption of an improved EU Export Control Regulation 428/2009 and for cyber-surveillance controls promoting human rights and international humanitarian law', Working paper WK5755/2018 INIT, 15 May 2018.

Other areas where the Commission, Parliament and Council positions differ include the creation of new EU General Export Authorisations (EUGEAs) to facilitate 'low risk' exports; the insertion of language on human rights and international humanitarian law (IHL) into the text of the Dual-use Regulation; making changes to the definition of brokering; reducing controls on items that employ cryptography; and creating greater harmonization in the penalties states impose for export control violations. In all areas the Council's negotiating mandate rejects the changes that were put forward in the Commission's proposal and which were either endorsed or expanded on in the Parliament's amendments.[8]

In accordance with EU legislative procedures for adopting a final version, during the second half of 2019 the Commission's proposal began to go through a process of 'trilogue' involving the Commission, the Parliament and the Council (represented by Finland, which held the Council presidency until the end of 2019). The parties to the trilogue were unable to reach a final agreement.[9] The process will therefore continue during 2020 with Croatia, which holds the Council presidency from the start of 2020, replacing Finland in representing the Council.

At the time of writing it is unclear if the trilogue process will result in a new version of the regulation to which all parties agree. As it stands, the differences between the positions adopted by the Commission, the Parliament and the Council are substantial. Indeed, they point to divergent views about the overall purpose of the Dual-use Regulation and the extent to which the EU can and should go beyond the norms established multilaterally when determining content and focus of EU export controls. Nonetheless, the failure to conclude the review process did not prevent the taking of other steps to promote a more harmonized implementation of the existing regulation. For example, in July 2019 the EU published a set of non-binding guidelines aimed at companies, providing information on how to set up and implement internal compliance programmes to help them meet the requirements of the Dual-use Regulation.[10] The Commission and EU member states also continued work on the development of an additional set of compliance guidelines aimed at the research sector.[11]

---

[8] For a summary, see Akin Gump, 'EU trade update: Council issues negotiating mandate for recast Dual Use Regulation', Press release, 11 June 2019; and Bromley, M. and Gerharz, P., 'Revising the EU Dual-use Regulation: Challenges and opportunities for the trilogue process', SIPRI Topical backgrounder, 7 Oct. 2019.

[9] Chardon, S., 'EU export controls: 2019 update', Paper presented at the Export Control Forum 2019, 13 Dec. 2019, p. 4.

[10] Commission Recommendation (EU) 2019/1318 of 30 July 2019 on internal compliance programmes for dual-use trade controls under Council Regulation (EC) No 428/2009, *Official Journal of the European Union*, L205, 5 Aug. 2019.

[11] Chardon (note 9), p. 8s.

Box 14.1. The eight criteria of the European Union Common Position on arms exports

1. Respect for the international obligations and commitments of member states, in particular the sanctions adopted by the United Nations Security Council or the European Union, agreements on non-proliferation and other subjects, as well as other international obligations.

2. Respect for human rights in the country of final destination as well as respect by that country of international humanitarian law.

3. Internal situation in the country of final destination, as a function of the existence of tensions or armed conflicts.

4. Preservation of regional peace, security and stability.

5. National security of member states and of territories whose external relations are the responsibility of a member state as well as that of friendly and allied countries.

6. Behaviour of the buyer country with regard to the international community, in particular its attitude to terrorism, the nature of its alliances and its respect for international law.

7. Existence of a risk that the military technology or equipment will be diverted within the buyer country or re-exported under undesirable conditions.

8. Compatibility of the exports of the military technology or equipment with the technical and economic capacity of the recipient country, taking into account the desirability that states should meet their legitimate security and defence needs with the least diversion of human and economic resources for armaments.

Source: Council Common Position 2008/944/CFSP of 8 Dec. 2008 defining common rules governing control of exports of military technology and equipment, *Official Journal of the European Union*, L335, 8 Dec. 2008.

Review of the EU Common Position on Arms Exports

At the beginning of 2018, as mandated by the Council of the EU in 2015, the EEAS and the EU member states initiated a process of review of the EU Common Position with the goal of assessing its implementation and 'the fulfilment of its objectives'.[12] After almost two years, this process was completed in September 2019 with the adoption of a new Council Decision amending the text of the EU Common Position.[13] The User's Guide to the EU Common Position, which provides guidance on how this instrument should be applied, was also subject to some modifications.[14] In contrast, the previous and first review of the EU Common Position between 2011 and 2015 left the

---

[12] Council of the European Union, 'Council conclusions relating to the review of Common Position 2008/944/CFSP on arms exports and the implementation of the Arms Trade treaty (ATT)', 20 July 2015.

[13] Council of the European Union, 'Control of arms export: Council adopts conclusions, new decision updating the EU's common rules and a revised user's guide', Press release, 16 Sep. 2019.

[14] Council of the European Union, 'User's Guide to Council Common Position 2008/944/CFSP (as amended by Council decision (CFSP) 2019/1560) defining common rules governing the control of exports of military technology and equipment', 12189/19, 16 Sep. 2019.

language of the main document unchanged and focused amendments only on the User's Guide.[15]

The changes implemented in the text of the EU Common Position were mostly limited to some formal adjustments. The language of the eight criteria that states are obliged to consider when assessing arms exports (box 14.1) remains substantially untouched. The only substantive change made was in criterion one, which covers states' international obligations, to expand the list of relevant international instruments.[16] A change to the Preamble was the addition of references to the 2013 Arms Trade Treaty (ATT), the United Nations 2030 Agenda for Sustainable Development and the 2018 EU strategy against illicit firearms, small arms and light weapons (SALW).[17] No further adjustments have been made to the text of the criteria, despite calls from non-governmental organizations (NGOs) to better align certain sections with the language of the ATT.[18]

By contrast, changes to the User's Guide have aligned the EU Common Position and the ATT, by expanding existing references to states' obligation to assess the risk of exported weapons being used to commit acts of gender-based violence (GBV) and providing guidance on how to conduct this process as part of implementing criterion 2; and by including further guidance on implementing criterion 7.[19]

Other amendments to the text of the EU Common Position affected operational provisions such as reporting obligations. To limit delays in the publication of the EU Annual Report on arms exports—often noted as one of the flaws in the implementation of the EU Common Position—the deadline for member states to submit information feeding into the report is now 30 June of each year.[20] In addition, following the recommendations often

[15] On the outcome of the first review process of the EU Common Position, see Bauer, S. and Bromley, M., 'European Union export control developments', section IV in 'Dual-use and arms trade controls, *SIPRI Yearbook 2016*, pp. 768–69.

[16] The EU Common Position now explicitly references the Arms Trade Treaty (ATT), the Convention on Certain Conventional Weapons (CCW) and their relevant Protocols, the Ottawa Convention and the UN Programme of Action on Small Arms and Light Weapons (UNPOA) as international instruments whose obligations must be taken into account by member states while assessing arms export authorizations. See Council of the European Union, 'Council Decision (CFSP) 2019/1560 of 16 Sep. 2019 amending Common Position 2008/944/CFSP defining common rules governing control of exports of military technology and equipment', L239, 17 Sep. 2019.

[17] For a summary and other details of the Arms Trade Treaty see annex A, section I, in this volume. For the 2030 Agenda for Sustainable Development, see United Nations, *Transforming our World: The 2020 Agenda for Sustainable Development*, A/Res/70/1. For the EU SALW strategy, see Council of the European Union, 'Council conclusions on the adoption of an EU strategy against illicit firearms, small arms & light weapons and their ammunition', 1351/18, 19 Nov. 2018, annex.

[18] Saferworld, 'Notes from civil society–COARM workshop on the review of Common Position 2008/944/CFSP', Nov. 2018.

[19] Council of the European Union, 12189/19 (note 14).

[20] Council of the European Union, L239 (note 16); Bauer, S., et al., *The Further Development of the Common Position 944/2008/CFSP on Arms Exports Control* (European Parliament, Directorate-General for External Policies, Policy Department: Brussels, July 2018), p. 24.

formulated by think tanks, NGOs and EU parliamentarians to improve the user-friendliness of the EU Annual Report, it was decided that the Report will also become a 'searchable online database' to make the presentation of the data more accessible and, thus, transparent.[21] The User's Guide now also contains additional information on how to comply with reporting obligations, such as clarifications on the terms 'export', 'export licence' and 'actual exports' under these provisions.[22] Additionally, the review of the EU Common Position will now occur every five years instead of three. Other amendments included more elaborated instructions on the role and use of the Council Working Party on Conventional Arms Exports (COARM) online system.[23] Finally, the Council conclusions on the review process also called on COARM to 'consider a decision on end-user certificates' for the export of SALW and their ammunitions, an issue that was also mentioned in the 2018 EU SALW strategy.[24]

Amendments to Article 7 of the EU Common Position call on member states to identify 'possible measures to further increase convergence'.[25] However, among EU member states there seems to be significant resistance to taking concrete steps towards promoting substantive convergence, as well as significant differences over the implementation of the EU Common Position. During this review process, these differences have been particularly evident in the different approaches that EU governments have taken in relation to arms exports to members of the coalition led by Saudi Arabia militarily engaged in Yemen since 2015.[26]

Divergences in European Union arms exports policies towards Saudi Arabia

Concerns that members of the Saudi-led coalition might have violated IHL in the conduct of their war operations in Yemen—as alleged in reports produced by UN bodies and international NGOs—have sparked national debates throughout the EU about whether arms exports to these states are in line with the criteria of the EU Common Position and the obligations set

---

[21] Council of the European Union, L239 (note 16), p. 3; Bauer et al. (note 20), p. 24; Saferworld (note 18); and European Parliament, 'Report on arms exports: Implementation of Common Position 2008/944/CFSP (2018/2157(INI))', A8-0335/2018, 16 Oct. 2018, para. 7(e).

[22] Council of the European Union, 12189/19 (note 14).

[23] The Council Working Party on Conventional Arms Exports (COARM) handles work concerning export controls for conventional arms. COARM also deals with engagement in outreach activities, establishment of political dialogue with non-EU countries and participation in the UN process concerning the ATT.

[24] Council of the European Union, 'Council conclusions on the review of Council Common Position 2008/944/CFSP of 8 Dec. 2008 on the control of arms exports', 12195/19, 16 Sep. 2019, para. 13. See also Council of the European Union, 1351/18 (note 17), annex, pp. 12, 15.

[25] Council of the European Union, 12195/19 (note 24), annex, para. 1.

[26] On the armed conflict in Yemen, see chapter 6, section V, in this volume.

out in the ATT.[27] Partly as a result, some EU member states—including the Netherlands, Germany and Sweden, among others—have decided to halt or suspend some of their arms exports to some members of the Arab coalition and, in particular, Saudi Arabia.[28] The murder in October 2018 of the Saudi journalist Jamal Khashoggi in the Saudi Arabian consulate in Istanbul has also influenced the decision of some of these EU member states to adopt more restrictive arms export policies towards Saudi Arabia.[29] In contrast, other member states—such as the United Kingdom, France and, until July 2019, Italy—have resisted public pressure and continued with their supplies. In response, civil society organizations and NGOs in these countries have sought to challenge the legality of their arms export decisions in court, with varying levels of success.[30]

In the UK, the Court of Appeal recognized in June 2019 that the process adopted by the British Government to assess the presence of a clear risk of IHL being violated by Saudi Arabia was 'wrong in law'.[31] In response, the British Government announced that it would appeal the ruling, but in the meantime would suspend the issuing of new export licences for transfer of arms to Saudi Arabia and 'other coalition partners' that might be used in the conflict in Yemen.[32] In Italy, a criminal complaint against both the Italian export licensing authority (Unita' per le autorizzazioni dei materiali d'armamento, UAMA) and the arms manufacturer RWM Italia was dismissed in October 2019 by the public prosecutor.[33] The claimants originally called for the prosecutor to investigate the criminal liability of UAMA and RWM for the export of aircraft bombs allegedly used in a Saudi-led coalition airstrike against civilians in October 2016. The claimants also alleged the

[27] In addition to Saudi Arabia, the states are Bahrain, Egypt, Jordan, Kuwait, Senegal, Sudan and the United Arab Emirates; Qatar participated until June 2017 and Morocco until Feb. 2019. For examples of the debates, see United Nations, Security Council, 'Final report of the Panel of Experts in accordance with paragraph 6 of Resolution 2402 (2018)', S/2019/83, 25 Jan. 2019, pp. 47–51; Human Rights Watch (HRW), 'Yemen', *World Report 2019: Events of 2018* (HRW: New York, 2019), p. 663; and Amnesty International, 'Yemen', *Human Rights in the Middle East and North Africa: Review of 2018* (Amnesty International: London, 26 Feb. 2019), p. 70.

[28] Bromley and Maletta, 'Developments in the European Union's dual-use and arms trade controls' (note 4), pp. 535–37; Bromley, M. and Maletta, G., 'The conflict in Yemen and [the] EU's arms export controls: Highlighting the flaws in the current regime', SIPRI Essay, 16 Mar. 2018.

[29] Bromley, M. and Maletta, G., 'Developments in the European Union's dual-use and arms trade controls' (note 4), pp. 535–37.

[30] Maletta, G., 'Legal challenges to EU member states' arms exports to Saudi Arabia: Current status and potential implications', SIPRI Topical backgrounder, 28 June 2019.

[31] British Courts and Tribunals Judiciary, Press summary of *The Queen (on the application of Campaign Against Arms Trade) v The Secretary of State for International Trade* [2019] EWCA Civ 1020, 20 June 2019, p. 1. For all documents concerning the case, see Campaign Against Arms Trade (CAAT), 'Saudi Arabia—Legal challenge', Updated 20 Sep. 2019.

[32] Fox, L. (British Secretary of State for International Trade, Department for International Trade), Letter to Graham Jones MP, Chair of the Committees on Arms Export Controls House of Commons, 24 June 2019.

[33] European Center for Constitutional and Human Rights (ECCHR), 'European responsibility for war crimes in Yemen', [n.d.].

Italian Government failed to comply with both national and international law regulating arms exports. The Italian Government had already announced in the summer of 2019 its intention to suspend all exports of aircraft bombs and their components to Saudi Arabia and the United Arab Emirates but it is unclear if the legal challenge influenced this decision. In France, the administrative court in Paris rejected a claim in July 2019 that French arms exports to Saudi Arabia should be suspended in view of their incompatibility with France's obligation as a state party to the ATT, a decision which was confirmed by the administrative court of appeal in September 2019.[34] In November 2019 the NGOs involved announced their intention to bring their case to the French Council of State.[35]

Conversely, in at least one case, defence companies have challenged the decisions of their governments to restrict exports towards Saudi Arabia. In December 2019, in Germany, the Frankfurt Administrative Court annulled a defacto ban on the export by a subsidiary of the Rheinmetall group of military trucks to Saudi Arabia. The court argued that the decision of the German Government to suspend previously granted export licences was formally flawed as it did not meet the necessary legal requirements to suspend the validity of the licences. The court went further and stated that foreign and security policy interests did not exempt the government from upholding these requirements in the notices they issue. However, the judgment is not legally binding yet and the German Government can appeal the decision.[36]

The divisions between EU member states over the export of arms to the Saudi-led coalition, according to some commentators, possibly affects not only the ability of the EU to speak with a common voice on issues related to international and regional security, but also the credibility and relevance of the EU Common Position itself.[37] In addition, these divergent positions are also likely to impact the ongoing efforts to strengthen European defence cooperation through the establishment of a European Defence Fund (EDF). The EDF is meant to achieve this goal by supporting cooperative military research and development projects, and, therefore, joint production of

[34] Paris Administrative Court, Judgement no. 1807203 of 8 July 2019; Action Sécurité Ethique Républicaines (ASER), 'Le tribunal administratif de Paris se déclare compétent pour juger de la légalité des ventes d'armes de la France dans la guerre au Yémen mais valide celles-ci' [The Paris Administrative Court declares itself competent to judge the legality of arms sales from France in the war in Yemen but validates them], 9 July 2019; and Paris Administrative Court of Appeal, Ordinance no. 19 PA02929 of 26 Sep. 2019.

[35] 'Yémen: Des ONG tentent un nouveau recours contre les ventes d'armes françaises' [Yemen: NGOs attempt a new claim against the French arms sales], Reuters, 19 Nov. 2019.

[36] Hessen Administrative Court, 'Verwaltungsgericht hebt faktisches Ausfuhrverbot wegen formeller Fehler auf' [Administrative court abolishes defacto export ban due to formal errors], Press release, 3 Dec. 2019.

[37] Cops, D. and Duquet, N., 'Reviewing the EU Common Position on arms exports: Whither EU arms transfer controls?', Flemish Peace Institute (FPI) report (FPI: Brussels, 3 Dec. 2019); Bromley and Maletta, 'The conflict in Yemen and [the] EU's arms export controls: Highlighting the flaws in the current regime' (note 28).

weapon systems. However, considering the reliance of the European defence industry on exports, the divergence in the application of export control criteria could potentially represent a challenge to the long-term sustainability of this project.[38]

Conclusions

The review processes connected to the EU Dual-use Regulation and the EU Common Position were conducted through different legal frameworks and involved different institutional actors. Nonetheless, developments during 2019 point to certain common patterns that may have certain wider implications for the EU's export control system. In both cases, EU member states appeared to resist implementing major amendments to the texts of the instruments and took diverging positions from the EU institutions—and, to some extent, civil society organizations—on the goals the instruments should seek to achieve. The differences between the positions adopted by the European Commission, the European Parliament and the Council of the EU in the review of the Dual-use Regulation were such that this process was not concluded by the end of 2019. At the same time, EU member states themselves diverged in their implementation of these instruments—as their arms export policies towards Saudi Arabia showed—and in their views on what their scope should be, as reflected in the lengthy process of elaborating the Council's negotiating mandate for the Commission's proposed recast of the regulation. These differences raise questions over the long-term relevance of these instruments and their ability to respond to emerging security challenges.

---

[38] Cops, D. and Buytaert, A., 'Sustainable EU funding of European defence cooperation? Accountable and transparent coordination of arms export policies needed', FPI report (FPI: Brussels, 3 Dec. 2019).

Annexes

Annex A. Arms control and disarmament agreements

Annex B. International security cooperation bodies

Annex C. Chronology 2019

Annex A. Arms control and disarmament agreements

This annex lists multi- and bilateral treaties, conventions, protocols and agreements relating to arms control and disarmament. Unless otherwise stated, the status of agreements and of their parties and signatories is as of 1 January 2020. On the International security cooperation bodies mentioned here, see annex B.

Notes

1. The agreements are divided into universal treaties (i.e. multilateral treaties open to all states, in section I), regional treaties (i.e. multilateral treaties open to states of a particular region, in section II) and bilateral treaties (in section III). Within each section, the agreements are listed in the order of the date on which they were adopted, signed or opened for signature (multilateral agreements) or signed (bilateral agreements). The date on which they entered into force and the depositary for multilateral treaties are also given.

2. The main source of information is the lists of signatories and parties provided by the depositaries of the treaties. In lists of parties and signatories, states whose name appears in italics ratified, acceded or succeeded to, or signed the agreement during 2019.

3. States and organizations listed as parties had ratified, acceded to or succeeded to the agreements by 1 January 2020. Since many agreements delay the entry into force for a state for a certain period after ratification or accession, when that occurred late in 2019 the agreement may not have fully entered into force for that state by 1 January 2020.

4. Former non-self-governing territories, upon attaining statehood, sometimes make general statements of continuity to all agreements concluded by the former governing power. This annex lists as parties only those new states that have made an uncontested declaration on continuity or have notified the depositary of their succession. The Russian Federation continues the international obligations of the Soviet Union.

5. Unless stated otherwise, the multilateral agreements listed in this annex are open to all states, to all states in the respective zone or region, or to all members of a certain international organization for signature, ratification, accession or succession. Not all the signatories and parties are United Nations members. Taiwan, while not recognized as a sovereign state by many countries, is listed as a party to the agreements that it has ratified.

6. Where possible, the location (in a printed publication or online) of an accurate copy of the treaty text is given. This may be provided by a treaty depositary, an agency or secretariat connected with the treaty, or in the *United Nations Treaty Series* (available online at <https://treaties.un.org/>).

I. Universal treaties

Protocol for the Prohibition of the Use in War of Asphyxiating, Poisonous or Other Gases, and of Bacteriological Methods of Warfare (1925 Geneva Protocol)

Signed at Geneva on 17 June 1925; entered into force on 8 February 1928; depositary French Government

The protocol prohibits the use in war of asphyxiating, poisonous or other gases and of bacteriological methods of warfare. The protocol remains a fundamental basis of the international prohibition against chemical and biological warfare, and its principles, objectives and obligations are explicitly supported by the 1972 Biological and Toxin Weapons Convention and the 1993 Chemical Weapons Convention.

Parties (143): Afghanistan, Albania, Algeria, Angola, Antigua and Barbuda, Argentina, Armenia, Australia, Austria, Bahrain, Bangladesh, Barbados, Belgium, Benin, Bhutan, Bolivia, Brazil, Bulgaria, Burkina Faso, Cabo Verde, Cambodia, Cameroon, Canada, Central African Republic, Chile, China, Colombia, Costa Rica, Côte d'Ivoire, Croatia, Cuba, Cyprus, Czechia, Denmark, Dominican Republic, Ecuador, Egypt, El Salvador, Equatorial Guinea, Estonia, Eswatini, Ethiopia, Fiji, Finland, France, Gambia, Germany, Ghana, Greece, Grenada, Guatemala, Guinea-Bissau, Holy See, Hungary, Iceland, India, Indonesia, Iran, Iraq, Ireland, Israel, Italy, Jamaica, Japan, Jordan, Kenya, Korea (North), Korea (South), Kuwait, Laos, Latvia, Lebanon, Lesotho, Liberia, Libya, Liechtenstein, Lithuania, Luxembourg, Madagascar, Malawi, Malaysia, Maldives, Malta, Mauritius, Mexico, Moldova, Monaco, Mongolia, Morocco, Nepal, Netherlands, New Zealand, Nicaragua, Niger, Nigeria, North Macedonia, Norway, Pakistan, Palestine, Panama, Papua New Guinea, Paraguay, Peru, Philippines, Poland, Portugal, Qatar, Romania, Russia, Rwanda, Saint Kitts and Nevis, Saint Lucia, Saint Vincent and the Grenadines, Saudi Arabia, Senegal, Serbia, Sierra Leone, Slovakia, Slovenia, Solomon Islands, South Africa, Spain, Sri Lanka, Sudan, Sweden, Switzerland, Syria, Taiwan, Tanzania, Thailand, Togo, Tonga, Trinidad and Tobago, Tunisia, Turkey, Uganda, UK, Ukraine, Uruguay, USA, Venezuela, Viet Nam, Yemen

Notes: On joining the protocol, some states entered reservations which upheld their right to employ chemical or biological weapons against non-parties to the protocol, against coalitions which included non-parties or in response to the use of these weapons by a violating party. Many of these states have withdrawn these reservations, particularly after the conclusion of the 1972 Biological and Toxin Weapons Convention and the 1993 Chemical Weapons Convention since the reservations are incompatible with their obligation under the conventions.

In addition to these, 'explicit', reservations, a number of states that made a declaration of succession to the protocol on gaining independence inherited 'implicit' reservations from their respective predecessor states. For example, these implicit reservations apply to the states that gained independence from France and the UK before the latter states withdrew or amended their reservations. States that acceded (rather than succeeded) to the protocol did not inherit reservations in this way.

Protocol text: League of Nations, *Treaty Series*, vol. 94 (1929), pp. 65–74, <https://treaties.un.org/doc/Publication/UNTS/LON/Volume 94/v94.pdf>

Convention on the Prevention and Punishment of the Crime of Genocide (Genocide Convention)

Opened for signature at Paris on 9 December 1948; entered into force on 12 January 1951; depositary UN Secretary-General

Under the convention any commission of acts intended to destroy, in whole or in part, a national, ethnic, racial or religious group as such is declared to be a crime punishable under international law.

Parties (152): Afghanistan, Albania*, Algeria*, Andorra, Antigua and Barbuda, Argentina*, Armenia, Australia, Austria, Azerbaijan, Bahamas, Bahrain*, Bangladesh*, Barbados, Belarus*, Belgium, Belize, Benin, Bolivia, Bosnia and Herzegovina, Brazil, Bulgaria*, Burkina Faso, Burundi, Cabo Verde, Cambodia, Canada, Chile, China*, Colombia, Comoros, Congo (Democratic Republic of the), Costa Rica, Côte d'Ivoire, Croatia, Cuba, Cyprus, Czechia, Denmark, *Dominica*, Ecuador, Egypt, El Salvador, Estonia, Ethiopia, Fiji, Finland, France, Gabon, Gambia, Georgia, Germany, Ghana, Greece, Guatemala, Guinea, Guinea-Bissau, Haiti, Honduras, Hungary*, Iceland, India*, Iran, Iraq, Ireland, Israel, Italy, Jamaica, Jordan, Kazakhstan, Korea (North), Korea (South), Kuwait, Kyrgyzstan, Laos, Latvia, Lebanon, Lesotho, Liberia, Libya, Liechtenstein, Lithuania, Luxembourg, Malawi, Malaysia*, Maldives, Mali, Malta, *Mauritius*, Mexico, Moldova, Monaco, Mongolia*, Montenegro*, Morocco*, Mozambique, Myanmar*, Namibia, Nepal, Netherlands, New Zealand, Nicaragua, Nigeria, North Macedonia, Norway, Pakistan, Palestine, Panama, Papua New Guinea, Paraguay, Peru, Philippines*, Poland*, Portugal, Romania*, Russia*, Rwanda, Saint Vincent and the Grenadines, San Marino, Saudi Arabia, Senegal, Serbia*, Seychelles, Singapore*, Slovakia, Slovenia, South Africa, Spain, Sri Lanka, Sudan, Sweden, Switzerland, Syria, Tajikistan, Tanzania, Togo, Tonga, Trinidad and Tobago, Tunisia, Turkey, Turkmenistan, Uganda, UK, Ukraine*, United Arab Emirates*, Uruguay, USA*, Uzbekistan, Venezuela*, Viet Nam*, Yemen*, Zimbabwe

* With reservation and/or declaration.

Signed but not ratified (1): Dominican Republic

Convention text: United Nations Treaty Collection, <https://treaties.un.org/doc/Treaties/1951 /01/19510112 08-12 PM/Ch_IV_1p.pdf>

Geneva Convention (IV) Relative to the Protection of Civilian Persons in Time of War

Opened for signature at Geneva on 12 August 1949; entered into force on 21 October 1950; depositary Swiss Federal Council

The Geneva Convention (IV) establishes rules for the protection of civilians in areas covered by war and in occupied territories. Three other conventions were formulated at the same time, at a diplomatic conference held from 21 April to 12 August 1949: Convention (I) for the Amelioration of the Condition of the Wounded and Sick in Armed Forces in the Field; Convention (II) for the Amelioration of the Condition of the Wounded, Sick and Shipwrecked Members of Armed Forces at Sea; and Convention (III) Relative to the Treatment of Prisoners of War.

A party may withdraw from the convention, having given one year's notice. But if the party is involved in an armed conflict at that time, the withdrawal will not take effect until peace has been concluded and that party's obligations under the convention fulfilled.

Parties (196): Afghanistan, Albania*, Algeria, Andorra, Angola*, Antigua and Barbuda, Argentina, Armenia, Australia*, Austria, Azerbaijan, Bahamas, Bahrain, Bangladesh*, Barbados*, Belarus, Belgium, Belize, Benin, Bhutan, Bolivia, Bosnia and Herzegovina, Botswana, Brazil, Brunei Darussalam, Bulgaria, Burkina Faso, Burundi, Cabo Verde, Cambodia, Cameroon, Canada, Central African Republic, Chad, Chile, China*, Colombia, Comoros, Congo (Democratic Republic of the), Congo (Republic of the), Cook Islands, Costa Rica, Côte d'Ivoire, Croatia, Cuba, Cyprus, Czechia*, Denmark, Djibouti, Dominica, Dominican Republic, Ecuador, Egypt, El Salvador, Equatorial Guinea, Estonia, Eritrea, Eswatini, Ethiopia, Fiji, Finland, France, Gabon, Gambia, Georgia, Germany*, Ghana, Greece, Grenada, Guatemala, Guinea, Guinea-Bissau*, Guyana, Haiti, Holy See, Honduras, Hungary, Iceland, India, Indonesia, Iran*, Iraq, Ireland, Israel*, Italy, Jamaica, Japan, Jordan, Kazakhstan, Kenya, Kiribati, Korea (North)*, Korea (South)*, Kuwait*, Kyrgyzstan, Laos, Latvia, Lebanon, Lesotho, Liberia, Libya, Liechtenstein, Lithuania, Luxembourg, Madagascar, Malawi, Malaysia, Maldives, Mali, Malta, Marshall Islands, Mauritania, Mauritius, Mexico, Micronesia, Moldova, Monaco, Mongolia, Montenegro, Morocco, Mozambique, Myanmar, Namibia, Nauru, Nepal, Netherlands, New Zealand*, Nicaragua, Niger, Nigeria, North Macedonia*, Norway, Oman, Pakistan*, Palau, Palestine, Panama, Papua New Guinea, Paraguay, Peru, Philippines, Poland, Portugal*, Qatar, Romania, Russia*, Rwanda, Saint Kitts and Nevis, Saint Lucia, Saint Vincent and the Grenadines, Samoa, San Marino, Sao Tome and Principe, Saudi Arabia, Senegal, Serbia, Seychelles, Sierra Leone, Singapore, Slovakia, Slovenia, Solomon Islands, Somalia, South Africa, South Sudan, Spain, Sri Lanka, Sudan, Suriname*, Sweden, Switzerland, Syria, Tajikistan, Tanzania, Thailand, Timor-Leste, Togo, Tonga, Trinidad and Tobago, Tunisia, Turkey, Turkmenistan, Tuvalu, Uganda, UK*, Ukraine*, United Arab Emirates, Uruguay*, USA*, Uzbekistan, Vanuatu, Venezuela, Viet Nam*, Yemen*, Zambia, Zimbabwe

* With reservation and/or declaration.

Convention text: Swiss Federal Department of Foreign Affairs, <https://www.fdfa.admin.ch/dam/eda/fr/documents/aussenpolitik/voelkerrecht/geneve/070116-conv4_e.pdf>

Protocol I Additional to the 1949 Geneva Conventions, and Relating to the Protection of Victims of International Armed Conflicts

Protocol II Additional to the 1949 Geneva Conventions, and Relating to the Protection of Victims of Non-International Armed Conflicts

Opened for signature at Bern on 12 December 1977; entered into force on 7 December 1978; depositary Swiss Federal Council

The protocols confirm that the right of parties that are engaged in international or non-international armed conflicts to choose methods or means of warfare is not unlimited and that the use of weapons or means of warfare that cause superfluous injury or unnecessary suffering is prohibited.

Article 36 of Protocol I requires a state party, when developing or acquiring a new weapon, to determine whether its use could be prohibited by international law.

Parties to Protocol I (174) and Protocol II (169): Afghanistan, Albania*, Algeria*, Angola*, Antigua and Barbuda, Argentina*, Armenia, Australia*, Austria*, Bahamas,

Bahrain, Bangladesh, Barbados, Belarus*, Belgium*, Belize, Benin, Bolivia*, Bosnia and Herzegovina*, Botswana, Brazil*, Brunei Darussalam, Bulgaria*, Burkina Faso*, Burundi, Cabo Verde*, Cambodia, Cameroon, Canada*, Central African Republic, Chad, Chile*, China*, Colombia*, Comoros, Congo (Democratic Republic of the)*, Congo (Republic of the), Cook Islands*, Costa Rica*, Côte d'Ivoire, Croatia*, Cuba, Cyprus*, Czechia*, Denmark*, Djibouti, Dominica, Dominican Republic, Ecuador, Egypt*, El Salvador, Equatorial Guinea, Estonia*, Eswatini, Ethiopia, Fiji, Finland*, France*, Gabon, Gambia, Georgia, Germany*, Ghana, Greece*, Grenada, Guatemala, Guinea*, Guinea-Bissau, Guyana, Haiti, Holy See*, Honduras, Hungary*, Iceland*, Iraq[1], Ireland*, Italy*, Jamaica, Japan*, Jordan, Kazakhstan, Kenya, Korea (North)[1], Korea (South)*, Kuwait*, Kyrgyzstan, Laos*, Latvia, Lebanon, Lesotho*, Liberia, Libya, Liechtenstein*, Lithuania*, Luxembourg*, Madagascar*, Malawi*, Maldives, Mali*, Malta*, Mauritania, Mauritius*, Mexico[1], Micronesia, Moldova, Monaco*, Mongolia*, Montenegro*, Morocco, Mozambique, Namibia*, Nauru, Netherlands*, New Zealand*, Nicaragua, Niger, Nigeria, North Macedonia*, Norway*, Oman*, Palau, Palestine, Panama*, Paraguay*, Peru, Philippines*, Poland*, Portugal*, Qatar*, Romania*, Russia*, Rwanda*, Saint Kitts and Nevis*, Saint Lucia, Saint Vincent and the Grenadines*, Samoa, San Marino, Sao Tome and Principe, Saudi Arabia*, Senegal, Serbia*, Seychelles*, Sierra Leone, Slovakia*, Slovenia*, Solomon Islands, South Africa, South Sudan, Spain*, Sudan, Suriname, Sweden*, Switzerland*, Syria*[1], Tajikistan*, Tanzania, Timor-Leste, Togo*, Tonga*, Trinidad and Tobago*, Tunisia, Turkmenistan, Uganda, UK*, Ukraine*, United Arab Emirates*, Uruguay*, Uzbekistan, Vanuatu, Venezuela, Viet Nam[1], Yemen, Zambia, Zimbabwe

* With reservation and/or declaration.
[1] Party only to Protocol I.

Signed but not ratified Protocols I and II (3): Iran, Pakistan, USA

Protocol I text: Swiss Federal Department of Foreign Affairs, <https://www.fdfa.admin.ch/dam/eda/fr/documents/aussenpolitik/voelkerrecht/geneve/77prot1_en.pdf>

Protocol II text: Swiss Federal Department of Foreign Affairs, <https://www.fdfa.admin.ch/dam/eda/fr/documents/aussenpolitik/voelkerrecht/geneve/77prot2_en.pdf>

Antarctic Treaty

Signed by the 12 original parties at Washington, DC, on 1 December 1959; entered into force on 23 June 1961; depositary US Government

The treaty declares the Antarctic an area to be used exclusively for peaceful purposes. It prohibits any measure of a military nature in the Antarctic, such as the establishment of military bases and fortifications, and the carrying out of military manoeuvres or the testing of any type of weapon. The treaty bans any nuclear explosion as well as the disposal of radioactive waste material in Antarctica.

States that demonstrate their interest in Antarctica by conducting substantial scientific research activity there, such as the establishment of a scientific station or the dispatch of a scientific expedition, are entitled to become consultative parties. Consultative parties meet at regular intervals to exchange information and hold consultations on matters pertaining to Antarctica, as well as to recommend to their governments measures in furtherance of the principles and objectives of the treaty. Consultative parties have a right to inspect any station or installation in Antarctica to ensure compliance with the treaty's provisions.

Parties (54): Argentina*, Australia*, Austria, Belarus, Belgium*, Brazil*, Bulgaria*, Canada, Chile*, China*, Colombia, Cuba, Czechia*, Denmark, Ecuador*, Estonia, Finland*, France*, Germany*, Greece, Guatemala, Hungary, Iceland, India*, Italy*, Japan*, Kazakhstan, Korea (North), Korea (South)*, Malaysia, Monaco, Mongolia, Netherlands*, New Zealand*, Norway*, Pakistan, Papua New Guinea, Peru*, Poland*, Portugal, Romania, Russia*, Slovakia, *Slovenia*, South Africa*, Spain*, Sweden*, Switzerland, Turkey, UK*, Ukraine*, Uruguay*, USA*, Venezuela

   * Consultative party (29) under Article IX of the treaty.

Treaty text: Secretariat of the Antarctic Treaty, <https://www.ats.aq/documents/ats/treaty_original.pdf>

The Protocol on Environmental Protection (**1991 Madrid Protocol**) was opened for signature on 4 October 1991 and entered into force on 14 January 1998. It designated Antarctica as a natural reserve, devoted to peace and science.

Protocol text: Secretariat of the Antarctic Treaty, <https://www.ats.aq/documents/recatt/Att006_e.pdf>

Treaty Banning Nuclear Weapon Tests in the Atmosphere, in Outer Space and Under Water (Partial Test-Ban Treaty, PTBT)

Signed by three original parties at Moscow on 5 August 1963 and opened for signature by other states at London, Moscow and Washington, DC, on 8 August 1963; entered into force on 10 October 1963; depositaries British, Russian and US governments

The treaty prohibits the carrying out of any nuclear weapon test explosion or any other nuclear explosion (*a*) in the atmosphere, beyond its limits, including outer space, or under water, including territorial waters or high seas; and (*b*) in any other environment if such explosion causes radioactive debris to be present outside the territorial limits of the state under whose jurisdiction or control the explosion is conducted.

A party may withdraw from the treaty, having given three months' notice, if it decides that its supreme interests have been jeopardized by extraordinary events related to the treaty's subject matter.

Parties (126): Afghanistan, Antigua and Barbuda, Argentina, Armenia, Australia, Austria, Bahamas, Bangladesh, Belarus, Belgium, Benin, Bhutan, Bolivia, Bosnia and Herzegovina, Botswana, Brazil, Bulgaria, Cabo Verde, Canada, Central African Republic, Chad, Chile, Colombia, Congo (Democratic Republic of the), Costa Rica, Côte d'Ivoire, Croatia, Cyprus, Czechia, Denmark, Dominican Republic, Ecuador, Egypt, El Salvador, Equatorial Guinea, Eswatini, Fiji, Finland, Gabon, Gambia, Germany, Ghana, Greece, Guatemala, Guinea-Bissau, Honduras, Hungary, Iceland, India, Indonesia, Iran, Iraq, Ireland, Israel, Italy, Jamaica, Japan, Jordan, Kenya, Korea (South), Kuwait, Laos, Lebanon, Liberia, Libya, Luxembourg, Madagascar, Malawi, Malaysia, Malta, Mauritania, Mauritius, Mexico, Mongolia, Montenegro, Morocco, Myanmar, Nepal, Netherlands, New Zealand, Nicaragua, Niger, Nigeria, Norway, Pakistan, Panama, Papua New Guinea, Peru, Philippines, Poland, Romania, Russia, Rwanda, Samoa, San Marino, Senegal, Serbia, Seychelles, Sierra Leone, Singapore, Slovakia, Slovenia, South Africa, Spain, Sri Lanka, Sudan, Suriname, Sweden, Switzerland, Syria, Taiwan, Tanzania, Thailand, Togo, Tonga, Trinidad and Tobago, Tunisia, Turkey, Uganda, UK, Ukraine, Uruguay, USA, Venezuela, Yemen, Zambia

Signed but not ratified (10): Algeria, Burkina Faso, Burundi, Cameroon, Ethiopia, Haiti, Mali, Paraguay, Portugal, Somalia

Treaty text: Russian Ministry of Foreign Affairs, <https://mddoc.mid.ru/api/ia/download/?uuid=561590f5-ed1a-4e2a-a04e-f715bccb16ad>

Treaty on Principles Governing the Activities of States in the Exploration and Use of Outer Space, Including the Moon and Other Celestial Bodies (Outer Space Treaty)

Opened for signature at London, Moscow and Washington, DC, on 27 January 1967; entered into force on 10 October 1967; depositaries British, Russian and US governments

The treaty prohibits the placing into orbit around the earth of any object carrying nuclear weapons or any other kind of weapon of mass destruction, the installation of such weapons on celestial bodies, or the stationing of them in outer space in any other manner. The establishment of military bases, installations and fortifications, the testing of any type of weapon and the conducting of military manoeuvres on celestial bodies are also forbidden.

A party may withdraw from the treaty having given one year's notice.

Parties (110): Afghanistan, Algeria, Antigua and Barbuda, Argentina, Armenia, Australia, Austria, Azerbaijan, Bahamas, Bangladesh, Barbados, Belarus, Belgium, Benin, Brazil, Bulgaria, Burkina Faso, Canada, Chile, China, Cuba, Cyprus, Czechia, Denmark, Dominican Republic, Ecuador, Egypt, El Salvador, Equatorial Guinea, Estonia, Fiji, Finland, France, Germany, Greece, Guinea-Bissau, Hungary, Iceland, India, Indonesia, Iraq, Ireland, Israel, Italy, Jamaica, Japan, Kazakhstan, Kenya, Korea (North), Korea (South), Kuwait, Laos, Lebanon, Libya, Lithuania, Luxembourg, Madagascar, Mali, Malta, Mauritius, Mexico, Mongolia, Morocco, Myanmar, Nepal, Netherlands, New Zealand, Nicaragua, Niger, Nigeria, Norway, Pakistan, Papua New Guinea, Paraguay, Peru, Poland, Portugal, Qatar, Romania, Russia, Saint Vincent and the Grenadines, San Marino, Saudi Arabia, Seychelles, Sierra Leone, Singapore, Slovakia, *Slovenia*, South Africa, Spain, Sri Lanka, Sweden, Switzerland, Syria, Taiwan, Thailand, Togo, Tonga, Tunisia, Turkey, Uganda, UK, Ukraine, United Arab Emirates, Uruguay, USA, Venezuela, Viet Nam, Yemen, Zambia

Signed but not ratified (25): Bolivia, Botswana, Burundi, Cameroon, Central African Republic, Colombia, Congo (Democratic Republic of the), Ethiopia, Gambia, Ghana, Guyana, Haiti, Holy See, Honduras, Iran, Jordan, Lesotho, Malaysia, Montenegro, Panama, Philippines, Rwanda, Serbia, Somalia, Trinidad and Tobago

Treaty text: British Foreign and Commonwealth Office, Treaty Series no. 10 (1968), <https://assets.publishing.service.gov.uk/government/uploads/system/uploads/attachment_data/file/270006/Treaty_Principles_Activities_Outer_Space.pdf>

Treaty on the Non-Proliferation of Nuclear Weapons (Non-Proliferation Treaty, NPT)

Opened for signature at London, Moscow and Washington, DC, on 1 July 1968; entered into force on 5 March 1970; depositaries British, Russian and US governments

The treaty defines a nuclear weapon state to be a state that manufactured and exploded a nuclear weapon or other nuclear explosive device prior to 1 January 1967. According to this definition, there are five nuclear weapon states: China, France, Russia, the United Kingdom and the United States. All other states are defined as non-nuclear weapon states.

The treaty prohibits the nuclear weapon states from transferring nuclear weapons or other nuclear explosive devices or control over them to any recipient and prohibits them from assisting, encouraging or inducing any non-nuclear weapon state to manufacture or otherwise acquire such a weapon or device. It also prohibits non-nuclear weapon states parties from receiving nuclear weapons or other nuclear explosive devices from any source, from manufacturing them, or from acquiring them in any other way.

The parties undertake to facilitate the exchange of equipment, materials and scientific and technological information for the peaceful uses of nuclear energy and to ensure that potential benefits from peaceful applications of nuclear explo-sions will be made available to non-nuclear weapon states party to the treaty. They also undertake to pursue negotiations in good faith on effective measures relating to cessation of the nuclear arms race at an early date and to nuclear disarmament, and on a treaty on general and complete disarmament.

Non-nuclear weapon states parties undertake to conclude safeguard agreements with the International Atomic Energy Agency (IAEA) with a view to preventing diversion of nuclear energy from peaceful uses to nuclear weapons or other nuclear explosive devices. A Model Protocol Additional to the Safeguards Agreements, strengthening the measures, was approved in 1997; additional safeguards protocols are signed by states individually with the IAEA.

A review and extension conference, convened in 1995 in accordance with the treaty, decided that the treaty should remain in force indefinitely. A party may withdraw from the treaty, having given three months' notice, if it decides that its supreme interests have been jeopardized by extraordinary events related to the treaty's subject matter.

Parties (192): Afghanistan*, Albania*, Algeria*, Andorra*, Angola*, Antigua and Barbuda*, Argentina*, Armenia*, Australia*, Austria*, Azerbaijan*, Bahamas*, Bahrain*, Bangladesh*, Barbados*, Belarus*, Belgium*, Belize*, Benin*, Bhutan*, Bolivia*, Bosnia and Herzegovina*, Botswana*, Brazil*, Brunei Darussalam*, Bulgaria*, Burkina Faso*, Burundi*, Cabo Verde, Cambodia*, Cameroon*, Canada*, Central African Republic*, Chad*, Chile*, China*[†], Colombia*, Comoros*, Congo (Democratic Republic of the)*, Congo (Republic of the)*, Costa Rica*, Côte d'Ivoire*, Croatia*, Cuba*, Cyprus*, Czechia*, Denmark*, Djibouti*, Dominica*, Dominican Republic*, Ecuador*, Egypt*, El Salvador*, Equatorial Guinea, Eritrea, Estonia*, Eswatini*, Ethiopia*, Fiji*, Finland*, France*[†], Gabon*, Gambia*, Georgia*, Germany*, Ghana*, Greece*, Grenada*, Guatemala*, Guinea, Guinea-Bissau, Guyana*, Haiti*, Holy See*, Honduras*, Hungary*, Iceland*, Indonesia*, Iran*, Iraq*, Ireland*, Italy*, Jamaica*, Japan*, Jordan*, Kazakhstan*, Kenya*, Kiribati*, Korea (South)*, Korea (North)[‡], Kuwait*,

Kyrgyzstan*, Laos*, Latvia*, Lebanon*, Lesotho*, Liberia*, Libya*, Liechtenstein*, Lithuania*, Luxembourg*, Madagascar*, Malawi*, Malaysia*, Maldives*, Mali*, Malta*, Marshall Islands*, Mauritania*, Mauritius*, Mexico*, Micronesia, Moldova*, Monaco*, Mongolia*, Montenegro*, Morocco*, Mozambique*, Myanmar*, Namibia*, Nauru*, Nepal*, Netherlands*, New Zealand*, Nicaragua*, Niger*, Nigeria*, North Macedonia*, Norway*, Oman*, Palau*, Palestine, Panama*, Papua New Guinea*, Paraguay*, Peru*, Philippines*, Poland*, Portugal*, Qatar*, Romania*, Russia*[†], Rwanda*, Saint Kitts and Nevis*, Saint Lucia*, Saint Vincent and the Grenadines*, Samoa*, San Marino*, Sao Tome and Principe, Saudi Arabia*, Senegal*, Serbia*, Seychelles*, Sierra Leone*, Singapore*, Slovakia*, Slovenia*, Solomon Islands*, Somalia, South Africa*, Spain*, Sri Lanka*, Sudan*, Suriname*, Sweden*, Switzerland*, Syria*, Taiwan*, Tajikistan*, Tanzania*, Thailand*, Timor-Leste, Togo*, Tonga*, Trinidad and Tobago*, Tunisia*, Turkey*, Turkmenistan*, Tuvalu*, Uganda*, UK*[†], Ukraine*, United Arab Emirates*, Uruguay*, USA*[†], Uzbekistan*, Vanuatu*, Venezuela*, Viet Nam*, Yemen*, Zambia*, Zimbabwe*

* Party (181) with safeguards agreements in force with the IAEA, as required by the treaty, or concluded by a nuclear weapon state on a voluntary basis. In addition to these 181 states, as of 1 Jan. 2020 Cabo Verde, Guinea, Guinea-Bissau, Micronesia, Palestine, Timor-Leste had each signed a safeguards agreement that had not yet entered into force.

[†] Nuclear weapon state as defined by the treaty.

[‡] On 12 Mar. 1993 North Korea announced its withdrawal from the NPT with effect from 12 June 1993. It decided to 'suspend' the withdrawal on 11 June. On 10 Jan. 2003 North Korea announced its 'immediate' withdrawal from the NPT. A safeguards agreement was in force at that time. The current status of North Korea is disputed by the other parties.

Treaty text: International Atomic Energy Agency, INFCIRC/140, 22 Apr. 1970, <https://www.iaea.org/sites/default/files/publications/documents/infcircs/1970/infcirc140.pdf>

Additional safeguards protocols in force (137): Afghanistan, Albania, Andorra, Angola, Antigua and Barbuda, Armenia, Australia, Austria, Azerbaijan, Bahrain, Bangladesh, Belgium, *Benin*, Bosnia and Herzegovina, Botswana, Bulgaria, Burkina Faso, Burundi, Cambodia, Cameroon, Canada, Central African Republic, Chad, Chile, China, Colombia, Comoros, Congo (Democratic Republic of the), Congo (Republic of), Costa Rica, Côte d'Ivoire, Croatia, Cuba, Cyprus, Czechia, Denmark[1], Djibouti, Dominican Republic, Ecuador, El Salvador, Estonia, Eswatini, *Ethiopia*, Euratom, Fiji, Finland, France, Gabon, Gambia, Georgia, Germany, Ghana, Greece, Guatemala, Haiti, Holy See, Honduras, Hungary, Iceland, India, Indonesia, Iraq, Ireland, Italy, Jamaica, Japan, Jordan, Kazakhstan, Kenya, Korea (South), Kuwait, Kyrgyzstan, Latvia, Lesotho, Liberia, Libya, Liechtenstein, Lithuania, Luxembourg, Madagascar, Malawi, Mali, Malta, Marshall Islands, Mauritania, Mauritius, Mexico, Moldova, Monaco, Mongolia, Montenegro, Morocco, Mozambique, Namibia, Netherlands, New Zealand, Nicaragua, Niger, Nigeria, North Macedonia, Norway, Palau, Panama, Paraguay, Peru, Philippines, Poland, Portugal, Romania, Russia, Rwanda, Saint Kitts and Nevis, Senegal, Serbia, Seychelles, Singapore, Slovakia, Slovenia, South Africa, Spain, Sweden, Switzerland, Tajikistan, Tanzania, Thailand, Togo, Turkey, Turkmenistan, Uganda, UK, Ukraine, United Arab Emirates, Uruguay, USA, Uzbekistan, Vanuatu, Viet Nam

[1] A separate additional protocol is also in force for the Danish territory of Greenland.

Note: Taiwan has agreed to apply the measures contained in the Model Additional Protocol.

Additional safeguards protocols signed but not yet in force (14): Algeria, Belarus, *Bolivia*, Cabo Verde, Guinea, Guinea-Bissau, Iran*, Kiribati, Laos, Malaysia, Myanmar, Timor-Leste, Tunisia, Zambia

* Iran notified the IAEA that as of 16 Jan. 2016 it would provisionally apply the Additional Protocol that it signed in 2003 but has not yet ratified.

Model Additional Safeguards Protocol text: International Atomic Energy Agency, INFCIRC/540 (corrected), Sep. 1997, <https://www.iaea.org/sites/default/files/infcirc540c.pdf>

Treaty on the Prohibition of the Emplacement of Nuclear Weapons and other Weapons of Mass Destruction on the Seabed and the Ocean Floor and in the Subsoil thereof (Seabed Treaty)

Opened for signature at London, Moscow and Washington, DC, on 11 February 1971; entered into force on 18 May 1972; depositaries British, Russian and US governments

The treaty prohibits implanting or emplacing on the seabed and the ocean floor and in the subsoil thereof beyond the outer limit of a 12-nautical mile (22-kilometre) seabed zone any nuclear weapon or any other type of weapon of mass destruction as well as structures, launching installations or any other facilities specifically designed for storing, testing or using such weapons.

A party may withdraw from the treaty, having given three months' notice, if it decides that its supreme interests have been jeopardized by extraordinary events related to the treaty's subject matter.

Parties (95): Afghanistan, Algeria, Antigua and Barbuda, Argentina, Australia, Austria, Bahamas, Belarus, Belgium, Benin, Bosnia and Herzegovina, Botswana, Brazil*, Bulgaria, Canada*, Cabo Verde, Central African Republic, China, Congo (Republic of the), Côte d'Ivoire, Cuba, Cyprus, Czechia, Denmark, Dominican Republic, Eswatini, Ethiopia, Finland, Germany, Ghana, Greece, Guatemala, Guinea-Bissau, Hungary, Iceland, India*, Iran, Iraq, Ireland, Italy*, Jamaica, Japan, Jordan, Korea (South), Laos, Latvia, Lesotho, Libya, Liechtenstein, Luxembourg, Malaysia, Malta, Mauritius, Mexico*, Mongolia, Montenegro, Morocco, Nepal, Netherlands, New Zealand, Nicaragua, Niger, Norway, Panama, Philippines, Poland, Portugal, Qatar, Romania, Russia, Rwanda, Saint Kitts and Nevis, Saint Vincent and the Grenadines, Sao Tome and Principe, Saudi Arabia, Serbia*, Seychelles, Singapore, Slovakia, Slovenia, Solomon Islands, South Africa, Spain, Sweden, Switzerland, Taiwan, Togo, Tunisia, Turkey*, UK, Ukraine, USA, Viet Nam*, Yemen, Zambia

   * With reservation and/or declaration.

Signed but not ratified (21): Bolivia, Burundi, Cambodia, Cameroon, Colombia, Costa Rica, Equatorial Guinea, Gambia, Guinea, Honduras, Lebanon, Liberia, Madagascar, Mali, Myanmar, Paraguay, Senegal, Sierra Leone, Sudan, Tanzania, Uruguay

Treaty text: British Foreign and Commonwealth Office, Treaty Series no. 13 (1973), <https://assets.publishing.service.gov.uk/government/uploads/system/uploads/attachment_data/file/269694/Treaty_Prohib_Nuclear_Sea-Bed.pdf>

Convention on the Prohibition of the Development, Production and Stockpiling of Bacteriological (Biological) and Toxin Weapons and on their Destruction (Biological and Toxin Weapons Convention, BWC)

Opened for signature at London, Moscow and Washington, DC, on 10 April 1972; entered into force on 26 March 1975; depositaries British, Russian and US governments

The convention prohibits the development, production, stockpiling or acquisition by other means or retention of microbial or other biological agents or toxins (whatever their origin or method of production) of types and in quantities that have no justification of prophylactic, protective or other peaceful purposes. It also prohibits weapons, equipment or means of delivery designed to use such agents or toxins for hostile purposes or in armed conflict. The destruction of the agents, toxins, weapons, equipment and means of delivery in the possession of the parties, or their diversion to peaceful purposes, should be completed not later than nine months after the entry into force of the convention for each country.

The parties hold annual political and technical meetings to strengthen implementation of the convention. A three-person Implementation Support Unit (ISU), based in Geneva, was established in 2007 to support the parties in implementing the treaty, including facilitating the collection and distribution of annual confidence-building measures and supporting their efforts to achieve universal membership.

A party may withdraw from the convention, having given three months' notice, if it decides that its supreme interests have been jeopardized by extraordinary events related to the treaty's subject matter.

Parties (184): Afghanistan, Albania, Algeria, Andorra, Angola, Antigua and Barbuda, Argentina, Armenia, Australia, Austria*, Azerbaijan, Bahamas, Bahrain*, Bangladesh, Barbados, Belarus, Belgium, Belize, Benin, Bhutan, Bolivia, Bosnia and Herzegovina, Botswana, Brazil, Brunei Darussalam, Bulgaria, Burkina Faso, Burundi, Cabo Verde, Cambodia, Cameroon, Canada, Central African Republic, Chile, China*, Colombia, Congo (Democratic Republic of the), Congo (Republic of the), Cook Islands, Costa Rica, Côte d'Ivoire, Croatia, Cuba, Cyprus, Czechia*, Denmark, Dominica, Dominican Republic, Ecuador, El Salvador, Equatorial Guinea, Estonia, Eswatini, Ethiopia, Fiji, Finland, France, Gabon, Gambia, Georgia, Germany, Ghana, Greece, Grenada, Guatemala, Guinea, Guinea-Bissau, Guyana, Holy See, Honduras, Hungary, Iceland, India*, Indonesia, Iran, Iraq, Ireland*, Italy, Jamaica, Japan, Jordan, Kazakhstan, Kenya, Korea (North), Korea (South)*, Kuwait*, Kyrgyzstan, Laos, Latvia, Lebanon, Lesotho, Liberia, Libya, Liechtenstein, Lithuania, Luxembourg, Madagascar, Malawi, Malaysia*, Maldives, Mali, Malta, Marshall Islands, Mauritania, Mauritius, Mexico*, Moldova, Monaco, Mongolia, Montenegro, Morocco, Mozambique, Myanmar, Nauru, Nepal, Netherlands, New Zealand, Nicaragua, Niger, Nigeria, Niue, North Macedonia, Norway, Oman, Pakistan, Palau, Palestine, Panama, Papua New Guinea, Paraguay, Peru, Philippines, Poland, Portugal, Qatar, Romania, Russia, Rwanda, Saint Kitts and Nevis, Saint Lucia, Saint Vincent and the Grenadines, Samoa, San Marino, Sao Tome and Principe, Saudi Arabia, Senegal, Serbia, Seychelles, Sierra Leone, Singapore, Slovakia*, Slovenia, Solomon Islands, South Africa, Spain, Sri Lanka, Sudan, Suriname, Sweden, Switzerland*, Taiwan, Tajikistan, *Tanzania*, Thailand, Timor-Leste, Togo, Tonga, Trinidad and Tobago, Tunisia, Turkey, Turkmenistan, Uganda, UK*, Ukraine, United Arab Emirates, Uruguay, USA, Uzbekistan, Vanuatu, Venezuela, Viet Nam, Yemen, Zambia, Zimbabwe

* With reservation and/or declaration.

Signed but not ratified (4): Egypt, Haiti, Somalia, Syria

Treaty text: British Foreign and Commonwealth Office, Treaty Series no. 11 (1976), <https://assets.publishing.service.gov.uk/government/uploads/system/uploads/attachment_data/file/269698/Convention_Prohibition_Stock_Bacterio.pdf>

Convention on the Prohibition of Military or Any Other Hostile Use of Environmental Modification Techniques (Enmod Convention)

Opened for signature at Geneva on 18 May 1977; entered into force on 5 October 1978; depositary UN Secretary-General

The convention prohibits military or any other hostile use of environmental modification techniques that have widespread, long-lasting or severe effects as the means of destruction, damage or injury to states parties. The term 'environmental modification techniques' refers to any technique for changing—through the deliberate manipulation of natural processes—the dynamics, composition or structure of the earth, including its biota, lithosphere, hydrosphere and atmosphere, or of outer space. Understandings reached during the negotiations, but not written into the convention, define the terms 'widespread', 'long-lasting' and 'severe'.

Parties (78): Afghanistan, Algeria, Antigua and Barbuda, Argentina*, Armenia, Australia, Austria*, Bangladesh, Belarus, Belgium, Benin, Brazil, Bulgaria, Cabo Verde, Cameroon, Canada, Chile, China, Costa Rica, Cuba, Cyprus, Czechia, Denmark, Dominica, Egypt, Estonia, Finland, Germany, Ghana, Greece, Guatemala*, Honduras, Hungary, India, Ireland, Italy, Japan, Kazakhstan, Korea (North), Korea (South)*, Kuwait*, Kyrgyzstan, Lithuania, Laos, Malawi, Mauritius, Mongolia, Netherlands*, New Zealand*, Nicaragua, Niger, Norway, Pakistan, Palestine, Panama, Papua New Guinea, Poland, Romania, Russia, Saint Lucia, Saint Vincent and the Grenadines, Sao Tome and Principe, Slovakia, Slovenia, Solomon Islands, Spain, Sri Lanka, Sweden, Switzerland*, Tajikistan, Tunisia, UK, Ukraine, Uruguay, USA, Uzbekistan, Viet Nam, Yemen

* With reservation and/or declaration.

Signed but not ratified (16): Bolivia, Congo (Democratic Republic of the), Ethiopia, Holy See, Iceland, Iran, Iraq, Lebanon, Liberia, Luxembourg, Morocco, Portugal, Sierra Leone, Syria, Turkey, Uganda

Convention text: United Nations Treaty Collection, <https://treaties.un.org/doc/Treaties/1978/10/19781005 00-39 AM/Ch_XXVI_01p.pdf>

Convention on the Physical Protection of Nuclear Material and Nuclear Facilities

Original convention opened for signature at New York and Vienna on 3 March 1980; entered into force on 8 February 1987; amendments adopted on 8 July 2005; amended convention entered into force for its ratifying states on 8 May 2016; depositary IAEA Director General

The original convention—named the **Convention on the Physical Protection of Nuclear Material**—obligates its parties to protect nuclear material for peaceful purposes while in international transport.

The convention as amended and renamed also obligates its parties to protect nuclear facilities and material used for peaceful purposes while in storage.

A party may withdraw from the convention, having given 180 days' notice.

Parties to the original convention (160): Afghanistan, Albania, Algeria*, Andorra, Antigua and Barbuda, Argentina*, Armenia, Australia*, Austria*, Azerbaijan*, Bahamas*, Bahrain*, Bangladesh, Belarus*, Belgium*, *Benin*, Bolivia, Bosnia and Herzegovina, Botswana, Brazil,

Bulgaria, Burkina Faso, Cabo Verde, Cambodia, Cameroon, Canada*, Central African Republic, *Chad*, Chile, China*, Colombia, Comoros, Congo (Democratic Republic of the), Costa Rica, Côte d'Ivoire, Croatia, Cuba*, Cyprus*, Czechia, Denmark, Djibouti, Dominica, Dominican Republic, Ecuador, El Salvador*, Equatorial Guinea, Estonia, Eswatini, Euratom*, Fiji, Finland*, France*, Gabon, Georgia, Germany*, Ghana, Greece*, Grenada, Guatemala*, Guinea, Guinea-Bissau, Guyana, Honduras, Hungary, Iceland, India*, Indonesia*, Iraq, Ireland*, Israel*, Italy*, Jamaica, Japan, Jordan*, Kazakhstan, Kenya, Korea (South)*, Kuwait*, Kyrgyzstan, Laos*, Latvia, Lebanon, Lesotho, Libya, Liechtenstein, Lithuania, Luxembourg*, Madagascar, Malawi, Mali, Malta, Marshall Islands, Mauritania, Mexico, Moldova, Monaco, Mongolia, Montenegro, Morocco, Mozambique*, Myanmar*, Namibia, Nauru, Netherlands*, New Zealand, Nicaragua, Niger, Nigeria, Niue, North Macedonia, Norway*, Oman*, Pakistan*, Palau, Palestine, Panama, Paraguay, Peru*, Philippines, Poland, Portugal*, Qatar*, Romania*, Russia, Rwanda, Saint Kitts and Nevis, Saint Lucia*, San Marino, Saudi Arabia*, Senegal, Serbia, Seychelles, Singapore*, Slovakia, Slovenia, South Africa*, Spain*, Sudan, Sweden*, Switzerland*, *Syria*, Tajikistan, Tanzania, Thailand, Togo, Tonga, Trinidad and Tobago, Tunisia, Turkey*, Turkmenistan, Uganda, UK*, Ukraine, United Arab Emirates, Uruguay, USA*, Uzbekistan, Viet Nam*, Yemen, Zambia

* With reservation and/or declaration.

Signed but not ratified (1): Haiti

Note: In addition to the 160 parties as of 1 Jan. 2020, Eritrea acceded to the convention on 13 Mar. 2020.

Convention text: International Atomic Energy Agency, INFCIRC/274, Nov. 1979, <https://www.iaea.org/sites/default/files/infcirc274.pdf>

Parties to the amended convention (123): Albania, Algeria, Antigua and Barbuda, Argentina, Armenia*, Australia, Austria, Azerbaijan*, Bahrain, Bangladesh, Belgium*, *Benin*, Bolivia, Bosnia and Herzegovina, Botswana, Bulgaria, Burkina Faso, Cameroon, Canada*, *Chad*, Chile, China*, Colombia, *Comoros*, Costa Rica, Côte d'Ivoire, Croatia, Cuba, Cyprus, Czechia, Denmark, Djibouti, Dominican Republic, Ecuador, El Salvador, Estonia, Eswatini, Euratom*, Fiji, Finland, France, Gabon, Georgia, Germany, Ghana, Greece, Hungary, Iceland, India, Indonesia, Ireland, Israel*, Italy, Jamaica, Japan, Jordan, Kazakhstan, Kenya, Korea (South), Kuwait, Kyrgyzstan, Latvia, Lesotho, Libya, Liechtenstein, Lithuania, Luxembourg, Madagascar, Mali, Malta, Marshall Islands, Mauritania, Mexico, Moldova, Monaco, Montenegro, Morocco, Myanmar*, Namibia, Nauru, Netherlands, New Zealand, Nicaragua, Niger, Nigeria, North Macedonia, Norway, Pakistan*, Palestine, Panama, Paraguay, Peru, Poland, Portugal, Qatar, Romania, Russia, *Saint Kitts and Nevis*, Saint Lucia, San Marino, Saudi Arabia, Senegal, Serbia, Seychelles, Singapore*, Slovakia, Slovenia, Spain, Sweden, Switzerland, *Syria*, Tajikistan, Thailand, Tunisia, Turkey*, Turkmenistan, UK, Ukraine, United Arab Emirates, Uruguay, USA*, Uzbekistan, Viet Nam

* With reservation and/or declaration.

Note: In addition to the 123 parties as of 1 Jan. 2020, Eritrea accepted the amended convention on 13 Mar. 2020.

Amendment text and consolidated text of amended convention: International Atomic Energy Agency, INFCIRC/274/Rev.1/Mod.1, 9 May 2016, <https://www.iaea.org/sites/default/files/infcirc274r1m1.pdf>

Convention on Prohibitions or Restrictions on the Use of Certain Conventional Weapons which may be Deemed to be Excessively Injurious or to have Indiscriminate Effects (CCW Convention, or 'Inhumane Weapons' Convention)

Opened for signature with protocols I, II and III at New York on 10 April 1981; entered into force on 2 December 1983; depositary UN Secretary-General

The convention is an 'umbrella treaty', under which specific agreements can be concluded in the form of protocols. In order to become a party to the convention a state must ratify at least two of the protocols.

The amendment to Article I of the original convention was opened for signature at Geneva on 21 November 2001. It expands the scope of application to non-international armed conflicts. The amended convention entered into force on 18 May 2004.

Protocol I prohibits the use of weapons intended to injure using fragments that are not detectable in the human body by X-rays.

Protocol II prohibits or restricts the use of mines, booby-traps and other devices. *Amended Protocol II*, which entered into force on 3 December 1998, reinforces the constraints regarding anti-personnel mines.

Protocol III restricts the use of incendiary weapons.

Protocol IV, which entered into force on 30 July 1998, prohibits the employment of laser weapons specifically designed to cause permanent blindness to unenhanced vision.

Protocol V, which entered into force on 12 November 2006, recognizes the need for measures of a generic nature to minimize the risks and effects of explosive remnants of war.

A party may withdraw from the convention and its protocols, having given one year's notice. But if the party is involved in an armed conflict or occupation at that time, the withdrawal will not take effect until the conflict or occupation has ended and that party's obligations fulfilled.

Parties to the original convention and protocols (125): Afghanistan[2,] Algeria[2], Albania, Antigua and Barbuda[1], Argentina*, Australia, Austria, Bahrain[5], Bangladesh, Belarus, Belgium, Benin[2], Bolivia, Bosnia and Herzegovina, Brazil, Bulgaria, Burkina Faso, Burundi[4], Cabo Verde, Cambodia, Cameroon, Canada*, Chile[2], China*, Colombia, Costa Rica, Côte d'Ivoire[4], Croatia, Cuba, Cyprus*, Czechia, Denmark, Djibouti, Dominican Republic, Ecuador, El Salvador, Estonia[2], Finland, France*, Gabon[2], Georgia, Germany, Greece, Grenada[2], Guatemala, Guinea-Bissau, Holy See*, Honduras, Hungary, Iceland, India, Iraq, Ireland, Israel*[1], Italy*, Jamaica[2], Japan, Jordan[2], Kazakhstan[2], Korea (South)[3], Kuwait[2], Laos, Latvia, Lebanon[2], Lesotho, Liberia, Liechtenstein, Lithuania[2], Luxembourg, Madagascar, Maldives[2], Mali, Malta, Mauritius, Mexico, Moldova, Monaco[3], Mongolia, Montenegro, Morocco[4], Nauru, Netherlands*, New Zealand, Nicaragua[2], Niger, North Macedonia, Norway, Pakistan, Palestine[2], Panama, Paraguay, Peru[2], Philippines, Poland, Portugal, Qatar[2], Romania*, Russia, Saint Vincent and the Grenadines[1], Saudi Arabia[2], Senegal[5], Serbia, Seychelles, Sierra Leone[2], Slovakia, Slovenia, South Africa, Spain, Sri Lanka, Sweden, Switzerland, Tajikistan, Togo, Tunisia, Turkey*[3], Turkmenistan[1], Uganda, UK*, Ukraine, United Arab Emirates[2], Uruguay, USA*, Uzbekistan, Venezuela, Zambia

* With reservation and/or declaration.
[1] Party only to 1981 protocols I and II.
[2] Party only to 1981 protocols I and III.

[3] Party only to 1981 Protocol I.
[4] Party only to 1981 Protocol II.
[5] Party only to 1981 Protocol III.

Signed but not ratified the original convention and protocols (4): Egypt, Nigeria, Sudan, Viet Nam

Parties to the amended convention and original protocols (86): Afghanistan, Algeria, Albania, Argentina, Australia, Austria, Bangladesh, Belarus, Belgium, Benin, Bosnia and Herzegovina, Brazil, Bulgaria, Burkina Faso, Canada, Chile, China, Colombia, Costa Rica, Croatia, Cuba, Czechia, Denmark, Dominican Republic, Ecuador, El Salvador, Estonia, Finland, France, Georgia, Germany, Greece, Grenada, Guatemala, Guinea-Bissau, Holy See*, Hungary, Iceland, India, Iraq, Ireland, Italy, Jamaica, Japan, Korea (South), Kuwait, Latvia, Lebanon, Lesotho, Liberia, Liechtenstein, Lithuania, Luxembourg, Malta, Mexico*, Moldova, Montenegro, Netherlands, New Zealand, Nicaragua, Niger, North Macedonia, Norway, Panama, Paraguay, Peru, Poland, Portugal, Romania, Russia, Serbia, Sierra Leone, Slovakia, Slovenia, South Africa, Spain, Sri Lanka, Sweden, Switzerland, Tunisia, Turkey, UK, Ukraine, Uruguay, USA, Zambia

* With reservation and/or declaration.

Parties to Amended Protocol II (106): Afghanistan, Albania, Argentina, Australia, Austria*, Bangladesh, Belarus*, Belgium*, *Benin*, Bolivia, Bosnia and Herzegovina, Brazil, Bulgaria, Burkina Faso, Cabo Verde, Cambodia, Cameroon, Canada*, Chile, China*, Colombia, Costa Rica, Croatia, Cyprus, Czechia, Denmark*, Dominican Republic, Ecuador, El Salvador, Estonia, Finland*, France*, Gabon, Georgia, Germany*, Greece*, Grenada, Guatemala, Guinea-Bissau, Holy See, Honduras, Hungary*, Iceland, India, Iraq, Ireland*, Israel*, Italy*, Jamaica, Japan, Jordan, Korea (South)*, Kuwait, Latvia, Lebanon, Liberia, Liechtenstein*, Lithuania, Luxembourg, Madagascar, Maldives, Mali, Malta, Mauritius, Moldova, Monaco, Montenegro, Morocco, Nauru, Netherlands*, New Zealand, Nicaragua, Niger, North Macedonia, Norway, Pakistan*, Panama, Paraguay, Peru, Philippines, Poland, Portugal, Romania, Russia*, Saint Vincent and the Grenadines, Senegal, Serbia, Seychelles, Sierra Leone, Slovakia, Slovenia, South Africa*, Spain, Sri Lanka, Sweden*, Switzerland*, Tajikistan, Tunisia, Turkey, Turkmenistan, UK*, Ukraine*, Uruguay, USA*, Venezuela, Zambia

* With reservation and/or declaration

Parties to Protocol IV (109): Afghanistan, Algeria, Albania, Antigua and Barbuda, Argentina, Australia*, Austria*, Bahrain, Bangladesh, Belarus, Belgium*, *Benin*, Bolivia, Bosnia and Herzegovina, Brazil, Bulgaria, Burkina Faso, Cabo Verde, Cambodia, Cameroon, Canada*, Chile, China, Colombia, Costa Rica, Croatia, Cuba, Cyprus, Czechia, Denmark, Dominican Republic, Ecuador, El Salvador, Estonia, Finland, France, Gabon, Georgia, Germany*, Greece*, Grenada, Guatemala, Guinea-Bissau, Holy See, Honduras, Hungary, Iceland, India, Iraq, Ireland*, Israel*, Italy*, Jamaica, Japan, Kazakhstan, Kuwait, Latvia, Lesotho, Liberia, Liechtenstein*, Lithuania, Luxembourg, Madagascar, Maldives, Mali, Malta, Mauritius, Mexico, Moldova, Mongolia, Montenegro, Morocco, Nauru, Netherlands*, New Zealand, Nicaragua, Niger, North Macedonia, Norway, Pakistan, Panama, Paraguay, Peru, Philippines, Poland*, Portugal, Qatar, Romania, Russia, Saint Vincent and the Grenadines, Saudi Arabia, Serbia, Seychelles, Sierra Leone, Slovakia, Slovenia, South Africa*, Spain, Sri Lanka, Sweden*, Switzerland*, Tajikistan, Tunisia, Turkey, UK*, Ukraine, Uruguay, USA*, Uzbekistan

* With reservation and/or declaration.

Parties to Protocol V (96): Afghanistan, Albania, Argentina*, Australia, Austria, Bahrain, Bangladesh, Belarus, Belgium, *Benin*, Bosnia and Herzegovina, Brazil, Bulgaria, Burkina Faso, Burundi, Cameroon, Canada, Chile, China, Costa Rica, Côte d'Ivoire, Croatia, Cuba, Cyprus, Czechia, Denmark, Dominican Republic, Ecuador, El Salvador, Estonia, Finland, France, Gabon, Georgia, Germany, Greece, Grenada, Guatemala, Guinea-Bissau, Holy See*, Honduras, Hungary, Iceland, India, Iraq, Ireland, Italy, Jamaica, Korea (South), Kuwait, Laos,

Latvia, Lesotho, Liberia, Liechtenstein, Lithuania, Luxembourg, Madagascar, Mali, Malta, Mauritius, Moldova, Montenegro, Netherlands, New Zealand, Nicaragua, North Macedonia, Norway, Pakistan, Palestine, Panama, Paraguay, Peru, Poland, Portugal, Qatar, Romania, Russia, Saint Vincent and the Grenadines, Saudi Arabia, Senegal, Sierra Leone, Slovakia, Slovenia, South Africa, Spain, Sweden, Switzerland, Tajikistan, Tunisia, Turkmenistan, Ukraine, United Arab Emirates, Uruguay, USA*, Zambia

* With reservation and/or declaration.

Original convention and protocol text: United Nations Treaty Collection, <https://treaties.un.org/doc/Treaties/1983/12/19831202 01-19 AM/XXVI-2-revised.pdf>

Convention amendment text: United Nations Treaty Collection, <https://treaties.un.org/doc/Treaties/2001/12/20011221 01-23 AM/Ch_XXVI_02_cp.pdf>

Amended Protocol II text: United Nations Treaty Collection, <https://treaties.un.org/doc/Treaties/1996/05/19960503 01-38 AM/Ch_XXVI_02_bp.pdf>

Protocol IV text: United Nations Treaty Collection, <https://treaties.un.org/doc/Treaties/1995/10/19951013 01-30 AM/Ch_XXVI_02_ap.pdf>

Protocol V text: United Nations Treaty Collection, <https://treaties.un.org/doc/Treaties/2003/11/20031128 01-19 AM/Ch_XXVI_02_dp.pdf>

Convention on the Prohibition of the Development, Production, Stockpiling and Use of Chemical Weapons and on their Destruction (Chemical Weapons Convention, CWC)

Opened for signature at Paris on 13 January 1993; entered into force on 29 April 1997; depositary UN Secretary-General

The convention prohibits the development, production, acquisition, transfer, stockpiling and use of chemical weapons. The CWC regime consists of four 'pillars': disarmament, non-proliferation, assistance and protection against chemical weapons, and international cooperation on the peaceful uses of chemistry. The convention established the Organisation for the Prohibition of Chemical Weapons (OPCW) as its implementing body.

Each party undertook to destroy its chemical weapon stockpiles by 29 April 2012. Of the seven parties that had declared stocks of chemical weapons by that date, three had destroyed them (Albania, India and South Korea). Libya and Russia completed the destruction of their stockpiles in 2017 and Iraq did so in 2018, while the USA continues to destroy its stocks. The stockpile of chemical weapons that Syria declared when it acceded to the CWC in 2013 was destroyed in 2016, although gaps, inconsistencies and discrepancies in the 2013 declaration continue to be investigated. Old and abandoned chemical weapons will continue to be destroyed as they are uncovered from, for example, former battlefields.

A party may withdraw from the convention, having given 90 days' notice, if it decides that its supreme interests have been jeopardized by extraordinary events related to the treaty's subject matter.

Parties (193): Afghanistan, Albania, Algeria, Andorra, Angola, Antigua and Barbuda, Argentina, Armenia, Australia, Austria*, Azerbaijan, Bahamas, Bahrain, Bangladesh, Barbados, Belarus, Belgium*, Belize, Benin, Bhutan, Bolivia, Bosnia and Herzegovina, Botswana, Brazil, Brunei Darussalam, Bulgaria, Burkina Faso, Burundi, Cabo Verde, Cambodia, Cameroon, Canada,

Central African Republic, Chad, Chile, China*, Colombia, Comoros, Congo (Democratic Republic of the), Congo (Republic of the), Cook Islands, Costa Rica, Côte d'Ivoire, Croatia, Cuba*, Cyprus, Czechia, Denmark*, Djibouti, Dominica, Dominican Republic, Ecuador, El Salvador, Equatorial Guinea, Eritrea, Estonia, Eswatini, Ethiopia, Fiji, Finland, France*, Gabon, Gambia, Georgia, Germany*, Ghana, Greece*, Grenada, Guatemala, Guinea, Guinea-Bissau, Guyana, Haiti, Holy See*, Honduras, Hungary, Iceland, India, Indonesia, Iran*, Iraq, Ireland*, Italy*, Jamaica, Japan, Jordan, Kazakhstan, Kenya, Kiribati, Korea (South), Kuwait, Kyrgyzstan, Laos, Latvia, Lebanon, Lesotho, Liberia, Libya, Liechtenstein, Lithuania, Luxembourg*, Madagascar, Malawi, Malaysia, Maldives, Mali, Malta, Marshall Islands, Mauritania, Mauritius, Mexico, Micronesia, Moldova, Monaco, Mongolia, Montenegro, Morocco, Mozambique, Myanmar, Namibia, Nauru, Nepal, Netherlands*, New Zealand, Nicaragua, Niger, Nigeria, Niue, North Macedonia, Norway, Oman, Pakistan*, Palau, Palestine, Panama, Papua New Guinea, Paraguay, Peru, Philippines, Poland, Portugal*, Qatar, Romania, Russia, Rwanda, Saint Kitts and Nevis, Saint Lucia, Saint Vincent and the Grenadines, Samoa, San Marino, Sao Tome and Principe, Saudi Arabia, Senegal, Serbia, Seychelles, Sierra Leone, Singapore, Slovakia, Slovenia, Solomon Islands, Somalia, South Africa, Spain*, Sri Lanka, Sudan*, Suriname, Sweden, Switzerland, Syria*, Tajikistan, Tanzania, Thailand, Timor-Leste, Togo, Tonga, Trinidad and Tobago, Tunisia, Turkey, Turkmenistan, Tuvalu, Uganda, UK*, Ukraine, United Arab Emirates, Uruguay, USA*, Uzbekistan, Vanuatu, Venezuela, Viet Nam, Yemen, Zambia, Zimbabwe

* With reservation and/or declaration.

Signed but not ratified (1): Israel

Convention text: United Nations Treaty Collection, <https://treaties.un.org/doc/Treaties/1997/04/19970429 07-52 PM/CTC-XXVI_03_ocred.pdf>

Comprehensive Nuclear-Test-Ban Treaty (CTBT)

Opened for signature at New York on 24 September 1996; not in force; depositary UN Secretary-General

The treaty would prohibit the carrying out of any nuclear weapon test explosion or any other nuclear explosion and urges each party to prevent any such nuclear explosion at any place under its jurisdiction or control and refrain from causing, encouraging or in any way participating in the carrying out of any nuclear weapon test explosion or any other nuclear explosion.

The verification regime established by the treaty will consist of an International Monitoring System (IMS) to detect signs of nuclear explosions, an International Data Centre to collect and distribute data from the IMS, and the right to on-site inspection to determine whether an explosion has taken place. Work under the treaty will be implemented by the Comprehensive Nuclear-Test-Ban Treaty Organization (CTBTO).

The treaty will enter into force 180 days after the date that all of the 44 states listed in an annex to the treaty have deposited their instruments of ratification. All 44 states possess nuclear power reactors or nuclear research reactors. Pending entry into force, a Preparatory Commission is preparing for the treaty's implementation and the establishment of the CTBTO and the IMS.

After entry into force, a party will be able to withdraw from the treaty, having given six months' notice, if it decides that its supreme interests have been jeopardized by extraordinary events related to the treaty's subject matter.

States whose ratification is required for entry into force (44): Algeria, Argentina, Australia, Austria, Bangladesh, Belgium, Brazil, Bulgaria, Canada, Chile, China*, Colombia, Congo (Democratic Republic of the), Egypt*, Finland, France, Germany, Hungary, India*, Indonesia, Iran*, Israel*, Italy, Japan, Korea (North)*, Korea (South), Mexico, Netherlands, Norway, Pakistan*, Peru, Poland, Romania, Russia, Slovakia, South Africa, Spain, Sweden, Switzerland, Turkey, UK, Ukraine, USA*, Viet Nam

   * Has not ratified the treaty.

Ratifications deposited (168): Afghanistan, Albania, Algeria, Andorra, Angola, Antigua and Barbuda, Argentina, Armenia, Australia, Austria, Azerbaijan, Bahamas, Bahrain, Bangladesh, Barbados, Belarus, Belgium, Belize, Benin, Bolivia, Bosnia and Herzegovina, Botswana, Brazil, Brunei Darussalam, Bulgaria, Burkina Faso, Burundi, Cabo Verde, Cambodia, Cameroon, Canada, Central African Republic, Chad, Chile, Colombia, Congo (Democratic Republic of the), Cook Islands, Costa Rica, Côte d'Ivoire, Congo (Republic of the), Croatia, Cyprus, Czechia, Denmark, Djibouti, Dominican Republic, Ecuador, El Salvador, Eritrea, Estonia, Eswatini, Ethiopia, Fiji, Finland, France, Gabon, Georgia, Germany, Ghana, Greece, Grenada, Guatemala, Guinea, Guinea-Bissau, Guyana, Haiti, Holy See, Honduras, Hungary, Iceland, Indonesia, Iraq, Ireland, Italy, Jamaica, Japan, Jordan, Kazakhstan, Kenya, Kiribati, Korea (South), Kuwait, Kyrgyzstan, Laos, Latvia, Lebanon, Lesotho, Liberia, Libya, Liechtenstein, Lithuania, Luxembourg, Madagascar, Malawi, Malaysia, Maldives, Mali, Malta, Marshall Islands, Mauritania, Mexico, Micronesia, Moldova, Monaco, Mongolia, Montenegro, Morocco, Mozambique, Myanmar, Namibia, Nauru, Netherlands, New Zealand, Nicaragua, Niger, Nigeria, Niue, North Macedonia, Norway, Oman, Palau, Panama, Paraguay, Peru, Philippines, Poland, Portugal, Qatar, Romania, Russia, Rwanda, Saint Kitts and Nevis, Saint Lucia, Saint Vincent and the Grenadines, Samoa, San Marino, Senegal, Serbia, Seychelles, Sierra Leone, Singapore, Slovakia, Slovenia, South Africa, Spain, Sudan, Suriname, Sweden, Switzerland, Tajikistan, Tanzania, Thailand, Togo, Trinidad and Tobago, Tunisia, Turkey, Turkmenistan, Uganda, UK, Ukraine, United Arab Emirates, Uruguay, Uzbekistan, Vanuatu, Venezuela, Viet Nam, Zambia, *Zimbabwe*

Signed but not ratified (16): China, Comoros, Egypt, Equatorial Guinea, Gambia, Iran, Israel, Nepal, Papua New Guinea, Sao Tome and Principe, Solomon Islands, Sri Lanka, Timor-Leste, Tuvalu, USA, Yemen

Treaty text: United Nations Treaty Collection, <https://treaties.un.org/doc/Treaties/1997/09/19970910 07-37 AM/Ch_XXVI_04p.pdf>

Convention on the Prohibition of the Use, Stockpiling, Production and Transfer of Anti-Personnel Mines and on their Destruction (APM Convention)

Opened for signature at Ottawa on 3–4 December 1997 and at New York on 5 December 1997; entered into force on 1 March 1999; depositary UN Secretary-General

The convention prohibits anti-personnel mines (APMs), which are defined as mines designed to be exploded by the presence, proximity or contact of a person and which will incapacitate, injure or kill one or more persons.

Each party undertakes to destroy all of its stockpiled APMs as soon as possible but not later than four years after the entry into force of the convention for that state party. Each party also undertakes to destroy all APMs in mined areas under its jurisdiction or control not later than 10 years after the entry into force of the convention for that state party. Of the 164 parties, 161 no longer have stockpiles of APMs and 31 of the 64 parties that reported areas containing APMs have cleared them.

A party may withdraw from the convention, having given six months' notice. But if the party is involved in an armed conflict at that time, the withdrawal will not take effect until that conflict has ended.

Parties (164): Afghanistan, Albania, Algeria, Andorra, Angola, Antigua and Barbuda, Argentina*, Australia*, Austria, Bahamas, Bangladesh, Barbados, Belarus, Belgium, Belize, Benin, Bhutan, Bolivia, Bosnia and Herzegovina, Botswana, Brazil, Brunei Darussalam, Bulgaria, Burkina Faso, Burundi, Cabo Verde, Cambodia, Cameroon, Canada*, Central African Republic, Chad, Chile*, Colombia, Comoros, Congo (Democratic Republic of the), Congo (Republic of the), Cook Islands, Costa Rica, Côte d'Ivoire, Croatia, Cyprus, Czechia*, Denmark, Djibouti, Dominica, Dominican Republic, Ecuador, El Salvador, Equatorial Guinea, Eritrea, Estonia, Eswatini, Ethiopia, Fiji, Finland, France, Gabon, Gambia, Germany, Ghana, Greece*, Grenada, Guatemala, Guinea, Guinea-Bissau, Guyana, Haiti, Holy See, Honduras, Hungary, Iceland, Indonesia, Iraq, Ireland, Italy, Jamaica, Japan, Jordan, Kenya, Kiribati, Kuwait, Latvia, Lesotho, Liberia, Liechtenstein, Lithuania*, Luxembourg, Madagascar, Malawi, Malaysia, Maldives, Mali, Malta, Mauritania, Mauritius, Mexico, Moldova, Monaco, Montenegro*, Mozambique, Namibia, Nauru, Netherlands, New Zealand, Nicaragua, Niger, Nigeria, Niue, North Macedonia, Norway, Oman, Palau, Palestine, Panama, Papua New Guinea, Paraguay, Peru, Philippines, Poland*, Portugal, Qatar, Romania, Rwanda, Saint Kitts and Nevis, Saint Lucia, Saint Vincent and the Grenadines, Samoa, San Marino, Sao Tome and Principe, Senegal, Serbia*, Seychelles, Sierra Leone, Slovakia, Slovenia, Solomon Islands, Somalia, South Africa, South Sudan, Spain, Sri Lanka, Sudan, Suriname, Sweden, Switzerland, Tajikistan, Tanzania, Thailand, Timor-Leste, Togo, Trinidad and Tobago, Tunisia, Turkey, Turkmenistan, Tuvalu, Uganda, UK*, Ukraine, Uruguay, Vanuatu, Venezuela, Yemen, Zambia, Zimbabwe

* With reservation and/or declaration.

Signed but not ratified (1): Marshall Islands

Convention text: United Nations Treaty Collection, <https://treaties.un.org/doc/Treaties/1997/09/19970918 07-53 AM/Ch_XXVI_05p.pdf>

Rome Statute of the International Criminal Court

Opened for signature at Rome on 17 July 1998 and at New York on 18 October 1998; entered into force on 1 July 2002; depositary UN Secretary-General

The Rome Statute established the International Criminal Court (ICC), a permanent international court dealing with accusations of genocide, crimes against humanity, war crimes and the crime of aggression. The ICC can investigate and prosecute an alleged crime that takes place on the territory of a state party, is committed by a state party or is referred to it by the UN Security Council. The ICC may only prosecute a crime if the domestic courts are unwilling or unable to do so.

The Amendment to Article 8 adopted on 10 June 2010 makes it a war crime to use chemical weapons and expanding bullets in non-international conflicts. A series of *Amendments to Article 8 adopted on 14 December 2017* make it a war crime to use weapons which use microbial or other biological agents, or toxins; weapons the primary effect of which is to injure by fragments undetectable by x-rays in the human body; and blinding laser weapons. Amendments to Article 8 enter

into force for the parties that have accepted them one year after that acceptance.
The Amendments adopted on 11 June 2010 define the crime of aggression. The
ICC's jurisdiction over the crime of aggression was activated on 17 July 2018.
From that date, an apparent act of aggression may be referred to the ICC by the
UN Security Council regardless of whether it involves parties or non-parties to
the statute.

A state may withdraw from the statute and the ICC by giving 12 months' notice.

Parties to the Rome Statute (123): Afghanistan, Albania, Andorra, Antigua and Barbuda,
Argentina*, Australia*, Austria, Bangladesh, Barbados, Belgium, Belize, Benin, Bolivia,
Bosnia and Herzegovina, Botswana, Brazil, Bulgaria, Burkina Faso, Cabo Verde, Cambodia,
Canada, Central African Republic, Chad, Chile, Colombia*, Comoros, Congo (Democratic
Republic of the), Congo (Republic of the), Cook Islands, Costa Rica, Côte d'Ivoire, Croatia,
Cyprus, Czechia, Denmark, Djibouti, Dominica, Dominican Republic, Ecuador, El Salvador,
Estonia, Fiji, Finland, France*, Gabon, Gambia, Georgia, Germany, Ghana, Greece,
Grenada, Guatemala, Guinea, Guyana, Honduras, Hungary, Iceland, Ireland, Italy, Japan,
Jordan*, Kenya, *Kiribati*, Korea (South), Latvia, Lesotho, Liberia, Liechtenstein, Lithuania,
Luxembourg, Madagascar, Malawi, Maldives, Mali, Malta*, Marshall Islands, Mauritius,
Mexico, Moldova, Mongolia, Montenegro, Namibia, Nauru, Netherlands, New Zealand*,
Niger, Nigeria, North Macedonia, Norway, Palestine, Panama, Paraguay, Peru, Poland,
Portugal*, Romania, Saint Kitts and Nevis, Saint Lucia, Saint Vincent and the Grenadines,
Samoa, San Marino, Senegal, Serbia, Seychelles, Sierra Leone, Slovakia, Slovenia, South
Africa, Spain, Suriname, Sweden*, Switzerland, Tajikistan, Tanzania, Timor-Leste, Trinidad
and Tobago, Tunisia, Uganda, UK*, Uruguay, Vanuatu, Venezuela, Zambia

* With reservation and/or declaration.

Signed but not ratified (31): Algeria, Angola, Armenia, Bahamas, Bahrain, Cameroon, Egypt,
Eritrea, Guinea-Bissau, Haiti, Iran, Israel*, Jamaica, Kuwait, Kyrgyzstan, Monaco, Morocco,
Mozambique, Oman, Russia*, Sao Tome and Principe, Solomon Islands, Sudan*, Syria,
Thailand, Ukraine†, United Arab Emirates, USA*, Uzbekistan, Yemen, Zimbabwe

* These states have declared that they no longer intend to become parties to the statute.
† Ukraine has accepted the jurisdiction of the ICC with respect to alleged crimes committed on
its territory since 21 Nov. 2013.

Notes: Burundi withdrew from the statute and the ICC on 27 Oct. 2017 and the Philippines
withdrew on 17 Mar. 2019. Gambia and South Africa, which had declared in 2016 that they would
withdraw, rescinded those declarations in 2017.

Parties to the Amendment to Article 8 of 10 June 2010 (38): Andorra, Argentina, Austria,
Belgium, Botswana, Chile, Costa Rica, Croatia, Cyprus, Czechia, El Salvador, Estonia,
Finland, Georgia, Germany, Guyana, Latvia, Liechtenstein, Lithuania, Luxembourg, Malta,
Mauritius, Netherlands, North Macedonia, Norway, Palestine, Panama, *Paraguay*, Poland,
Portugal, Samoa, San Marino, Slovakia, Slovenia, Spain, Switzerland, Trinidad and Tobago,
Uruguay

Parties to the Amendments of 11 June 2010 defining the crime of aggression (39): Andorra,
Argentina, Austria, Belgium, Botswana, Chile, Costa Rica, Croatia, Cyprus, Czechia,
Ecuador, El Salvador, Estonia, Finland, Georgia, Germany, Guyana, Iceland, Ireland, Latvia,
Liechtenstein, Lithuania, Luxembourg, Malta, Netherlands, North Macedonia, Palestine,
Panama, *Paraguay*, Poland, Portugal, Samoa, San Marino, Slovakia, Slovenia, Spain,
Switzerland, Trinidad and Tobago, Uruguay

*Parties to the Amendment to Article 8 of 14 December 2017 on weapons which use microbial or
other biological agents, or toxins (2)*: Luxembourg, Slovakia

Parties to the Amendment to Article 8 of 14 December 2017 on weapons the primary effect of which is to injure by fragments undetectable by x-rays in the human body (2): Luxembourg, Slovakia

Parties to the Amendment to Article 8 of 14 December 2017 on blinding laser weapons (2): Luxembourg, Slovakia

Statute text: United Nations Treaty Collection, <https://treaties.un.org/doc/Treaties/1998/07/19980717 06-33 PM/Ch_XVIII_10p.pdf>

Text of the Amendment to Article 8 of 10 June 2010: United Nations Treaty Collection, <https://treaties.un.org/doc/Treaties/2010/10/20101011 05-46 PM/CN.533.2010.pdf>

Text of the Amendments of 11 June 2010 defining the crime of aggression: United Nations Treaty Collection, <https://treaties.un.org/doc/Treaties/2010/06/20100611 05-56 PM/CN.651.2010.pdf>

Text of the Amendment to Article 8 of 14 December 2017 on weapons which use microbial or other biological agents or toxins: United Nations Treaty Collection, <https://treaties.un.org/doc/Publication/CN/2018/CN.116.2018-Eng.pdf>

Text of the Amendment to Article 8 of 14 December 2017 on weapons the primary effect of which is to injure by fragments undetectable by x-rays in the human body: United Nations Treaty Collection, <https://treaties.un.org/doc/Publication/CN/2018/CN.125.2018-Eng.pdf>

Text of the Amendment to Article 8 of 14 December 2017 on blinding laser weapons: United Nations Treaty Collection, <https://treaties.un.org/doc/Publication/CN/2018/CN.126.2018-Eng.pdf>

Convention on Cluster Munitions

Opened for signature at Oslo on 3 December 2008; entered into force on 1 August 2010; depositary UN Secretary-General

The convention's objectives are to prohibit the use, production, transfer and stockpiling of cluster munitions that cause unacceptable harm to civilians. It also establishes a framework for cooperation and assistance to ensure adequate provision of care and rehabilitation for victims, clearance of contaminated areas, risk reduction education and destruction of stockpiles. The convention does not apply to mines.

Each party undertakes to destroy all of its stockpiled cluster munitions as soon as possible but not later than eight years after the entry into force of the convention for that state party. The first deadlines for stockpile destruction were in 2018. Each party also undertakes to clear and destroy all cluster munitions in contaminated areas under its jurisdiction or control not later than 10 years after the entry into force of the convention for that state party. The first deadlines for clearance are in 2020.

A three-person Implementation Support Unit (ISU), based in Geneva, was established in 2015 to, among other things, provide advice and technical support to the parties.

A party may withdraw from the convention, having given six months' notice. But if the party is involved in an armed conflict at that time, the withdrawal will not take effect until that conflict has ended.

Parties (107): Afghanistan, Albania, Andorra, Antigua and Barbuda, Australia, Austria, Belgium, Belize, Benin, Bolivia, Bosnia and Herzegovina, Botswana, Bulgaria, Burkina Faso, Burundi, Cabo Verde, Cameroon, Canada, Chad, Chile, Colombia*, Comoros, Cook Islands, Congo (Republic of the), Costa Rica, Côte d'Ivoire, Croatia, Cuba, Czechia, Denmark, Dominican Republic, Ecuador, El Salvador*, Eswatini, Fiji, France, Gambia, Germany, Ghana, Grenada, Guatemala, Guinea, Guinea-Bissau, Guyana, Holy See*, Honduras, Hungary, Iceland, Iraq, Ireland, Italy, Japan, Laos, Lebanon, Lesotho, Liechtenstein, Lithuania, Luxembourg, Madagascar, Malawi, *Maldives*, Mali, Malta, Mauritania, Mauritius, Mexico, Moldova, Monaco, Montenegro, Mozambique, Namibia, Nauru, Netherlands, New Zealand, Nicaragua, Niger, North Macedonia, Norway, Palestine, Palau, Panama, Paraguay, Peru, *Philippines*, Portugal, Rwanda, Samoa, Saint Kitts and Nevis, Saint Vincent and the Grenadines, San Marino, Senegal, Seychelles, Sierra Leone, Slovakia, Slovenia, Somalia, South Africa, Spain, Sri Lanka, Sweden, Switzerland, Togo, Trinidad and Tobago, Tunisia, UK, Uruguay, Zambia

* With reservation and/or declaration.

Signed but not ratified (14): Angola, Central African Republic, Congo (Democratic Republic of the), Cyprus, Djibouti, Haiti, Indonesia, Jamaica, Kenya, Liberia, Nigeria, Sao Tome and Principe, Tanzania, Uganda

Note: In addition to the 107 parties as of 1 Jan. 2020, Sao Tome and Principe ratified the convention on 27 Jan. 2020.

Convention text: United Nations Treaty Collection, <https://treaties.un.org/doc/Publication/CTC/26-6.pdf>

Arms Trade Treaty (ATT)

Opened for signature at New York on 3 June 2013; entered into force on 24 December 2014; depositary UN Secretary-General

The object of the treaty is to establish the highest possible common international standards for regulating the international trade in conventional arms; and to prevent and eradicate the illicit trade in conventional arms and prevent their diversion.

Among other things, the treaty prohibits a state party from authorizing a transfer of arms if they are to be used in the commission of genocide, crimes against humanity or war crimes. The treaty also requires the exporting state to assess the potential for any arms proposed for export to undermine peace and security or be used to commit serious violations of international humanitarian law or international human rights law.

Each party must submit an annual report on its authorized or actual exports and imports of conventional arms.

The treaty established the ATT Secretariat, based in Geneva, to support the parties in its implementation. Among other tasks, it collects the annual reports submitted by each party on imports and exports of conventional arms.

A party may withdraw from the treaty, having given 90 days' notice.

Parties (105): Albania, Antigua and Barbuda, Argentina, Australia, Austria, Bahamas, Barbados, Belgium, Belize, Benin, Bosnia and Herzegovina, *Botswana*, Brazil, Bulgaria, Burkina Faso, Cabo Verde, Cameroon, *Canada*, Central African Republic, Chad, Chile, Costa Rica, Côte d'Ivoire, Croatia, Cyprus, Czechia, Denmark, Dominica, Dominican Republic, El Salvador, Estonia, Finland, France, Georgia, Germany, Ghana, Greece, Grenada, Guatemala, Guinea, Guinea-Bissau, Guyana, Honduras, Hungary, Iceland, Ireland, Italy, Jamaica, Japan,

Kazakhstan*, Korea (South), Latvia, *Lebanon*, Lesotho, Liberia, Liechtenstein*, Lithuania, Luxembourg, Madagascar, *Maldives*, Mali, Malta, Mauritania, Mauritius, Mexico, Moldova, Monaco, Montenegro, Mozambique, Netherlands, New Zealand*, Niger, Nigeria, North Macedonia, Norway, *Palau*, Palestine, Panama, Paraguay, Peru, Poland, Portugal, Romania, Saint Kitts and Nevis, Saint Lucia, Saint Vincent and the Grenadines, Samoa, San Marino, Senegal, Serbia, Seychelles, Sierra Leone, Slovakia, Slovenia, South Africa, Spain, Suriname, Sweden, Switzerland*, Togo, Trinidad and Tobago, Tuvalu, UK, Uruguay, Zambia

* With reservation and/or declaration.

Signed but not ratified (33): Andorra, Angola, Bahrain, Bangladesh, Burundi, Cambodia, Colombia, Comoros, Congo (Republic of the), Djibouti, Eswatini, Gabon, Haiti, Israel, Kiribati, Libya, Malawi, Malaysia, Mongolia, Namibia, Nauru, Philippines, Rwanda, Sao Tome and Principe, Singapore, Tanzania, Thailand, Turkey, Ukraine, United Arab Emirates, USA*, Vanuatu, Zimbabwe

* This state has declared that it no longer intends to become a party to the treaty.

Treaty text: United Nations Treaty Collection, <https://treaties.un.org/doc/Treaties/2013/04/20130410 12-01 PM/Ch_XXVI_08.pdf>

Treaty on the Prohibition of Nuclear Weapons (TPNW)

Opened for signature at New York on 20 September 2017; not in force; depositary UN Secretary-General

In its preamble, the treaty cites the catastrophic humanitarian and environmental consequences of the use of nuclear weapons and invokes the principles of international humanitarian law and the rules of international law applicable in armed conflict. The treaty prohibits parties from developing, testing, producing, manufacturing, acquiring, possessing or stockpiling nuclear weapons or other nuclear explosive devices. Parties are prohibited from using or threatening to use nuclear weapons and other nuclear explosive devices. Finally, parties cannot allow the stationing, installation or deployment of nuclear weapons and other nuclear explosive devices in their territory.

The treaty outlines procedures for eliminating the nuclear weapons of any party that owned, possessed or controlled them after 7 July 2017, to be supervised by a 'competent international authority or authorities' to be designated by the states parties. Each party is required to maintain its existing safeguards agreements with the IAEA and must, at a minimum, conclude and bring into force a comprehensive safeguards agreement with the agency. The treaty also contains provisions on assisting the victims of the testing or use of nuclear weapons and taking necessary and appropriate measures for the environmental remediation of contaminated areas.

The treaty will enter into force 90 days after the deposit of the 50th instrument of ratification. Membership of the treaty does not prejudice the parties' other, compatible international obligations (such as the NPT and the CTBT). After entry into force, a party will be able to withdraw from the treaty, having given 12 months' notice, if it decides that its supreme interests have been jeopardized by extraordinary events related to the treaty's subject matter. But if the party is involved in an armed conflict at that time, the withdrawal will not take effect until it is no longer party to an armed conflict.

Ratifications deposited (34): Antigua and Barbuda, Austria, *Bangladesh, Bolivia*, Cook Islands*, Costa Rica, Cuba*, *Dominica, Ecuador, El Salvador*, Gambia, Guyana, Holy See, *Kazakhstan, Kiribati, Laos, Maldives*, Mexico, New Zealand*, Nicaragua, Palau, Palestine, *Panama, Saint Lucia, Saint Vincent and the Grenadines*, Samoa, San Marino, *South Africa*, Thailand, *Trinidad and Tobago*, Uruguay, Vanuatu, Venezuela, Viet Nam

* With reservation and/or declaration.

Signed but not ratified (47): Algeria, Angola, Benin, *Botswana*, Brazil, Brunei Darussalam, Cabo Verde, *Cambodia*, Central African Republic, Chile, Colombia, Comoros, Congo (Democratic Republic of the), Congo (Republic of the), Côte d'Ivoire, Dominican Republic, Fiji, Ghana, *Grenada*, Guatemala, Guinea-Bissau, Honduras, Indonesia, Ireland, Jamaica, *Lesotho*, Libya, Liechtenstein, Madagascar, Malawi, Malaysia, Myanmar, Namibia, *Nauru*, Nepal, Nigeria, Paraguay, Peru, Philippines, *Saint Kitts and Nevis*, Sao Tome and Principe, Seychelles, *Tanzania*, Timor-Leste, Togo, Tuvalu, *Zambia*

Note: In addition to the 34 states that had ratified the treaty as of 1 Jan. 2020, Paraguay ratified it on 23 Jan. 2020 and Namibia on 20 Mar. 2020. In addition to the 47 states that had signed but not ratified the treaty as of 1 Jan. 2020, Belize signed it on 6 Feb. 2020.

Treaty text: United Nations Treaty Collection, <https://treaties.un.org/doc/Treaties/2017/07/20170707 03-42 PM/Ch_XXVI_9.pdf>

II. Regional treaties

Treaty for the Prohibition of Nuclear Weapons in Latin America and the Caribbean (Treaty of Tlatelolco)

Original treaty opened for signature at Mexico City on 14 February 1967; entered into force on 22 April 1968; treaty amended in 1990, 1991 and 1992; depositary Mexican Government

The treaty prohibits the testing, use, manufacture, production or acquisition by any means, as well as the receipt, storage, installation, deployment and any form of possession of any nuclear weapons by any country of Latin America and the Caribbean and in the surrounding seas.

The parties should conclude agreements individually with the IAEA for the application of safeguards to their nuclear activities. The IAEA has the exclusive power to carry out special inspections. The treaty also established the Agency for the Prohibition of Nuclear Weapons in Latin America and the Caribbean (Organismo para la Proscripción de las Armas Nucleares en la América Latina y el Caribe, OPANAL) to ensure compliance with the treaty.

The treaty is open for signature by all the independent states of Latin America and the Caribbean. A party may withdraw from the treaty, having given three months' notice, if it decides that its supreme interests or the peace and security of another party or parties have been jeopardized by new circumstances related to the treaty's content.

Under *Additional Protocol I* states with territories within the zone—France, the Netherlands, the UK and the USA—undertake to apply the statute of military denuclearization to these territories.

Under *Additional Protocol II* the recognized nuclear weapon states—China, France, Russia, the UK and the USA—undertake to respect the military denuclearization of Latin America and the Caribbean and not to contribute to acts involving a violation of the treaty, nor to use or threaten to use nuclear weapons against the parties to the treaty.

Parties to the original treaty (33): Antigua and Barbuda[1], Argentina[1], Bahamas, Barbados[1], Belize[2], Bolivia, Brazil[1], Chile[1], Colombia[1], Costa Rica[1], Cuba, Dominica, Dominican Republic[3], Ecuador[1], El Salvador[1], Grenada[1], Guatemala[1], Guyana[3], Haiti, Honduras[1], Jamaica[1], Mexico[1], Nicaragua[3], Panama[1], Paraguay[1], Peru[1], Saint Kitts and Nevis[1], Saint Lucia[1], Saint Vincent and the Grenadines[4], Suriname[1], Trinidad and Tobago[1], Uruguay[1], Venezuela[1]

[1] Has ratified the amendments of 1990, 1991 and 1992.
[2] Has ratified the amendments of 1990 and 1992 only.
[3] Has ratified the amendment of 1992 only.
[4] Has ratified the amendments of 1991 and 1992 only.

Parties to Additional Protocol I (4): France*, Netherlands*, UK*, USA*

Parties to Additional Protocol II (5): China*, France*, Russia*, UK*, USA*

* With reservation and/or declaration.

Original treaty text: *United Nations Treaty Series*, vol. 634 (1968), <https://treaties.un.org/doc/Publication/UNTS/Volume 634/v634.pdf>

Amended treaty text: Agency for the Prohibition of Nuclear Weapons in Latin America and the Caribbean, Inf.11/2018, 5 June 2018, <https://www.opanal.org/wp-content/uploads/2019/10/Inf_11_2018_Treaty_Tlatelolco.pdf>

South Pacific Nuclear Free Zone Treaty (Treaty of Rarotonga)

Opened for signature at Rarotonga on 6 August 1985; entered into force on 11 December 1986; depositary Secretary General of the Pacific Islands Forum Secretariat

The South Pacific Nuclear Free Zone is defined as the area between the zone of application of the Treaty of Tlatelolco in the east and the west coast of Australia and the western border of Papua New Guinea and between the zone of application of the Antarctic Treaty in the south and, approximately, the equator in the north.

The treaty prohibits the manufacture or acquisition of any nuclear explosive device, as well as possession or control over such device by the parties anywhere inside or outside the zone. The parties also undertake not to supply nuclear material or equipment, unless subject to IAEA safeguards, and to prevent in their territories the stationing or testing of any nuclear explosive device and undertake not to dump, and to prevent the dumping of, radioactive waste and other radioactive matter at sea anywhere within the zone. Each party remains free to allow visits, as well as transit, by foreign ships and aircraft.

The treaty is open for signature by the members of the Pacific Islands Forum. If any party violates an essential provision or the spirit of the treaty, every other party may withdraw from the treaty, having given 12 months' notice.

Under *Protocol 1* France, the UK and the USA undertake to apply the treaty prohibitions relating to the manufacture, stationing and testing of nuclear explosive devices in the territories situated within the zone for which they are internationally responsible.

Under *Protocol 2* China, France, Russia, the UK and the USA undertake not to use or threaten to use a nuclear explosive device against the parties to the treaty or against any territory within the zone for which a party to Protocol 1 is internationally responsible.

Under *Protocol 3* China, France, Russia, the UK and the USA undertake not to test any nuclear explosive device anywhere within the zone.

Parties (13): Australia, Cook Islands, Fiji, Kiribati, Nauru, New Zealand, Niue, Papua New Guinea, Samoa, Solomon Islands, Tonga, Tuvalu, Vanuatu

Parties to Protocol 1 (2): France*, UK*; *signed but not ratified (1)*: USA

Parties to Protocol 2 (4): China*, France*, Russia*, UK*; *signed but not ratified (1)*: USA

Parties to Protocol 3 (4): China*, France*, Russia*, UK*; *signed but not ratified (1)*: USA

 * With reservation and/or declaration.

Treaty text: Pacific Islands Forum Secretariat, <https://www.forumsec.org/wp-content/uploads/2018/02/South-Pacific-Nuclear-Zone-Treaty-Raratonga-Treaty-1.pdf>

Protocol texts: Pacific Islands Forum Secretariat, <https://www.forumsec.org/wp-content/uploads/2018/02/South-Pacific-Nuclear-Zone-Treaty-Protocols-1.pdf>

Treaty on Conventional Armed Forces in Europe (CFE Treaty)

Original treaty signed by the 16 member states of the North Atlantic Treaty Organization (NATO) and the 6 member states of the Warsaw Treaty Organization (WTO) at Paris on 19 November 1990; entered into force on 9 November 1992; depositary Dutch Government

The treaty sets ceilings on five categories of treaty-limited equipment (TLE)—battle tanks, armoured combat vehicles, artillery of at least 100-mm calibre, combat aircraft and attack helicopters—in an area stretching from the Atlantic Ocean to the Ural Mountains (the Atlantic-to-the-Urals, ATTU). The treaty established the Joint Consultative Group (JCG) to promote its objectives and implementation.

The treaty was negotiated by the member states of the WTO and NATO within the framework of the Conference on Security and Co-operation in Europe (from 1995 the Organization for Security and Co-operation in Europe, OSCE).

The **1992 Tashkent Agreement**, adopted by the former Soviet republics with territories within the ATTU area of application (with the exception of Estonia, Latvia and Lithuania) and the **1992 Oslo Document** (Final Document of the Extraordinary Conference of the States Parties to the CFE Treaty) introduced modifications to the treaty required because of the emergence of new states after the break-up of the USSR.

A party may withdraw from the treaty, having given 150 days' notice, if it decides that its supreme interests have been jeopardized by extraordinary events related to the treaty's subject matter.

Parties (30): Armenia, Azerbaijan, Belarus, Belgium[2], Bulgaria[2], Canada[2], Czechia[2], Denmark[2], France, Georgia, Germany[2], Greece, Hungary[2], Iceland[2], Italy[2], Kazakhstan, Luxembourg[2], Moldova[2], Netherlands[2], Norway, Poland, Portugal[2], Romania, Russia[1], Slovakia[2], Spain, Turkey[2], UK[2], Ukraine, USA[2]

[1] On 14 July 2007 Russia declared its intention to suspend its participation in the CFE Treaty and associated documents and agreements, which took effect on 12 Dec. 2007. In Mar. 2015 Russia announced that it had decided to completely halt its participation in the treaty, including the JCG.

[2] In Nov.–Dec. 2011 these countries notified the depositary or the JCG that they would cease to perform their obligations under the treaty with regard to Russia.

The first review conference of the CFE Treaty adopted the **1996 Flank Document**, which reorganized the flank areas geographically and numerically, allowing Russia and Ukraine to deploy TLE in a less constraining manner.

Original (1990) treaty text: Dutch Ministry of Foreign Affairs, <https://treatydatabase. overheid.nl/en/Verdrag/Details/004285/004285_Gewaarmerkt_0.pdf>

Consolidated (1993) treaty text: Dutch Ministry of Foreign Affairs, <https://wetten.overheid.nl/ BWBV0002009/>

Flank Document text: Organization for Security and Co-operation in Europe, <https://www. osce.org/library/14099?download=true>, annex A

Concluding Act of the Negotiation on Personnel Strength of Conventional Armed Forces in Europe (CFE-1A Agreement)

Signed by the parties to the CFE Treaty at Helsinki on 10 July 1992; entered into force simultaneously with the CFE Treaty; depositary Dutch Government

This politically binding agreement sets ceilings on the number of personnel of the conventional land-based armed forces of the parties within the ATTU area.

Agreement text: Organization for Security and Co-operation in Europe, <https:// www.osce.org/library/14093?download=true>

Agreement on Adaptation of the Treaty on Conventional Armed Forces in Europe

Signed by the parties to the CFE Treaty at Istanbul on 19 November 1999; not in force; depositary Dutch Government

With the dissolution of the WTO and the accession of some former members to NATO, this agreement would have replaced the CFE Treaty's bloc-to-bloc military balance with a regional balance, established individual state limits on TLE holdings, and provided for a new structure of limitations and new military flexibility mechanisms, flank sub-limits and enhanced transparency. It would have opened the CFE regime to all other European states. It would have entered into force when ratified by all of the signatories.

The **1999 Final Act of the Conference of the CFE States Parties**, with annexes, contains politically binding arrangements with regard to Georgia, Moldova and Central Europe and to withdrawals of armed forces from foreign territories (known as the Istanbul commitments). Many signatories of the Agreement on Adaptation made their ratification contingent on the implementation of these political commitments.

Ratifications deposited (3): Belarus, Kazakhstan, Russia*[1]

    * With reservation and/or declaration.

Signed but not ratified (27): Armenia, Azerbaijan, Belgium, Bulgaria, Canada, Czechia, Denmark, France, Germany, Georgia, Greece, Hungary, Iceland, Italy, Luxembourg, Moldavia, Netherlands, Norway, Poland, Portugal, Romania, Slovakia, Spain, Turkey, Ukraine[2], UK, USA

    [1] On 14 July 2007 Russia declared its intention to suspend its participation in the CFE Treaty and associated documents and agreements, which took effect on 12 Dec. 2007. In Mar. 2015 Russia announced that it had decided to completely halt its participation in the treaty, including the JCG.
    [2] Ukraine ratified the Agreement on Adaptation on 21 Sep. 2000 but did not deposited its instrument with the depositary.

Agreement text: Dutch Ministry of Foreign Affairs, <https://treatydatabase.overheid.nl/en/Verdrag/Details/009241/009241_Gewaarmerkt_0.pdf>

Treaty text as amended by 1999 agreement: SIPRI Yearbook 2000, <https://www.sipri.org/sites/default/files/SIPRI Yearbook 2000.pdf>, appendix 10B, pp. 627–42

Final Act text: Organization for Security and Co-operation in Europe, <https://www.osce.org/library/14114?download=true>

Treaty on Open Skies

Opened for signature at Helsinki on 24 March 1992; entered into force on 1 January 2002; depositaries Canadian and Hungarian governments

The treaty obligates the parties to submit their territories to short-notice unarmed surveillance flights. The area of application stretches from Vancouver, Canada, eastward to Vladivostok, Russia.

    The treaty was negotiated between the member states of the WTO and NATO. Since 1 July 2002 any state can apply to accede to the treaty. A party may withdraw from the treaty, having given six months' notice.

Parties (34): Belarus, Belgium, Bosnia and Herzegovina, Bulgaria, Canada*, Croatia, Czechia, Denmark, Estonia, Finland, France, Georgia, Germany, Greece, Hungary, Iceland, Italy, Latvia, Lithuania, Luxembourg, Netherlands, Norway, Poland, Portugal, Romania, Russia, Slovakia, Slovenia, Spain*, Sweden*, Turkey, UK, Ukraine, USA*

    * With reservation and/or declaration.

Signed but not ratified (1): Kyrgyzstan

Treaty text: Canada Treaty Information, <https://www.treaty-accord.gc.ca/text-texte.aspx?id=102747>

Treaty on the Southeast Asia Nuclear Weapon-Free Zone (Treaty of Bangkok)

Signed by the 10 member states of the Association of Southeast Asian Nations (ASEAN) at Bangkok on 15 December 1995; entered into force on 27 March 1997; depositary Thai Government

The South East Asia Nuclear Weapon-Free Zone includes the territories, the continental shelves and the exclusive economic zones of the states parties. The treaty prohibits the development, manufacture, acquisition or testing of nuclear weapons inside or outside the zone as well as the stationing and transport of nuclear weapons in or through the zone. Each state party may decide for itself whether to allow visits and transit by foreign ships and aircraft. The parties undertake not to dump at sea or discharge into the atmosphere anywhere within the zone any radioactive material or waste or dispose of radioactive material on land. The parties should conclude an agreement with the IAEA for the application of full-scope safeguards to their peaceful nuclear activities.

The treaty is open for accession by all states of South East Asia. If any party breaches an essential provision of the treaty, every other party may withdraw from the treaty.

Under a *Protocol* to the treaty, China, France, Russia, the UK and the USA are to undertake not to use or threaten to use nuclear weapons against any state party to the treaty. They should further undertake not to use nuclear weapons within the zone. The protocol will enter into force for each state party on the date of its deposit of the instrument of ratification.

Parties (10): Brunei Darussalam, Cambodia, Indonesia, Laos, Malaysia, Myanmar, Philippines, Singapore, Thailand, Viet Nam

Protocol (0): no signatures, no parties

Treaty text: ASEAN Secretariat, <https://asean.org/?static_post=treaty-on-the-southeast-asia-nuclear-weapon-free-zone>

Protocol text: ASEAN Secretariat, <https://asean.org/?static_post=protocol-to-the-treaty-on-the-southeeast-asia-nuclear-weapon-free-zone>

African Nuclear-Weapon-Free Zone Treaty (Treaty of Pelindaba)

Opened for signature at Cairo on 11 April 1996; entered into force on 15 July 2009; depositary Secretary-General of the African Union

The African Nuclear Weapon-Free Zone includes the territory of the continent of Africa, island states members of the African Union (AU) and all islands considered by the AU to be part of Africa.

The treaty prohibits the research, development, manufacture and acquisition of nuclear explosive devices and the testing or stationing of any nuclear explosive device in the zone. Each party remains free to allow visits and transit by foreign ships and aircraft. The treaty also prohibits any attack against nuclear installations. The parties undertake not to dump or permit the dumping of radioactive waste and other radioactive matter anywhere within the zone. Each party should individually conclude an agreement with the IAEA for the application of comprehensive safeguards to their peaceful nuclear activities. The treaty also established the African Commission on Nuclear Energy (AFCONE) to ensure compliance with the treaty.

The treaty is open for accession by all the states of Africa. A party may withdraw from the treaty, having given 12 months' notice, if it decides that its supreme interests have been jeopardized by extraordinary events related to the treaty's subject matter.

Under *Protocol I* China, France, Russia, the UK and the USA undertake not to use or threaten to use a nuclear explosive device against the parties to the treaty.

Under *Protocol II* China, France, Russia, the UK and the USA undertake not to test nuclear explosive devices within the zone.

Under *Protocol III* France and Spain are to undertake to observe certain provisions of the treaty with respect to the territories within the zone for which they are internationally responsible.

Parties (41): Algeria, Angola, Benin, Botswana, Burkina Faso, Burundi, Cameroon, Chad, Comoros, Congo (Republic of the), Côte d'Ivoire, Equatorial Guinea, Eswatini, Ethiopia, Gabon, Gambia, Ghana, Guinea, Guinea-Bissau, Kenya, Lesotho, Libya, Madagascar, Malawi, Mali, Mauritania, Mauritius, Mozambique, Namibia, Niger, Nigeria, Rwanda, Sahrawi Arab Democratic Republic (Western Sahara), Seychelles, Senegal, South Africa, Tanzania, Togo, Tunisia, Zambia, Zimbabwe

Signed but not ratified (13): Cabo Verde, Central African Republic, Congo (Democratic Republic of the), Djibouti, Egypt, Eritrea, Liberia, Morocco, Sao Tome and Principe, Sierra Leone, Somalia, Sudan, Uganda

Parties to Protocol I (4): China, France*, Russia*, UK*; *signed but not ratified (1)*: USA*

Parties to Protocol II (4): China, France*, Russia*, UK*; *signed but not ratified (1)*: USA*

Parties to Protocol III (1): France*

* With reservation and/or declaration.

Treaty text: African Union, <https://au.int/sites/default/files/treaties/37288-treaty-0018_-_the_african_nuclear-weapon-free_zone_treaty_the_treaty_of_pelindaba_e.pdf>

Agreement on Sub-Regional Arms Control (Florence Agreement)

Adopted by the 5 original parties at Florence and entered into force on 14 June 1996

The agreement was negotiated under the auspices of the OSCE in accordance with the mandate in Article IV of Annex 1-B of the 1995 General Framework Agreement for Peace in Bosnia and Herzegovina (Dayton Agreement). It sets numerical ceilings on armaments of the former warring parties. Five categories of heavy conventional weapons are included: battle tanks, armoured combat vehicles, heavy artillery (75 mm and above), combat aircraft and attack helicopters. The limits were reached by 31 October 1997; by that date 6580 weapon items, or 46 per cent of pre-June 1996 holdings, had been destroyed. By 2014 a further 3489 items had been destroyed voluntarily.

The implementation of the agreement was monitored and assisted by the OSCE's Personal Representative of the Chairman-in-Office and the Contact Group (France, Germany, Italy, Russia, the UK and the USA) and supported by other OSCE states. Under a two-phase action plan agreed in November 2009, responsibility for the implementation of the agreement was transferred to the parties on 5 December 2014, following the signing of a new set of amendments to the agreement.

Parties (4): Bosnia and Herzegovina, Croatia, Montenegro, Serbia

Agreement text: Croatian Ministry of Defence, <https://www.racviac.org/downloads/treaties_agreements/aIV.pdf>

Inter-American Convention Against the Illicit Manufacturing of and Trafficking in Firearms, Ammunition, Explosives, and Other Related Materials (CIFTA)

Opened for signature by the member states of the Organization of American States (OAS) at Washington, DC, on 14 November 1997; entered into force on 1 July 1998; depositary General Secretariat of the OAS

The purpose of the convention is to prevent, combat and eradicate the illicit manufacturing of and the trafficking in firearms, ammunition, explosives and other related materials; and to promote and facilitate cooperation and the exchange of information and experience among the parties. A party may withdraw from the convention, having given six months' notice.

Parties (31): Antigua and Barbuda, Argentina*, Bahamas, Barbados, Belize, Bolivia, Brazil, Chile, Colombia, Costa Rica, Dominica, Dominican Republic, Ecuador, El Salvador, Grenada, Guatemala, Guyana, Haiti, Honduras, Mexico, Nicaragua, Panama, Paraguay, Peru, Saint Kitts and Nevis, Saint Lucia, Saint Vincent and the Grenadines, Suriname, Trinidad and Tobago, Uruguay, Venezuela

* With reservation.

Signed but not ratified (3): Canada, Jamaica, USA

Convention text: OAS, <https://www.oas.org/en/sla/dil/inter_american_treaties_A-63_illicit_manufacturing_trafficking_firearms_ammunition_explosives.asp>

Inter-American Convention on Transparency in Conventional Weapons Acquisitions

Opened for signature by the member states of the OAS at Guatemala City on 7 June 1999; entered into force on 21 November 2002; depositary General Secretariat of the OAS

The objective of the convention is to contribute more fully to regional openness and transparency in the acquisition of conventional weapons by exchanging information regarding such acquisitions, for the purpose of promoting confidence among states in the Americas. A party may withdraw from the convention, having given 12 months' notice.

Parties (17): Argentina, Barbados, Brazil, Canada, Chile, Costa Rica, Dominican Republic, Ecuador, El Salvador, Guatemala, Mexico, Nicaragua, Panama, Paraguay, Peru, Uruguay, Venezuela

Signed but not ratified (6): Bolivia, Colombia, Dominica, Haiti, Honduras, USA

Convention text: OAS, <https://www.oas.org/en/sla/dil/inter_american_treaties_A-64_transparency_conventional_weapons_adquisitions.asp>

Protocol on the Control of Firearms, Ammunition and other related Materials in the Southern African Development Community (SADC) Region

Opened for signature by the members states of SADC at Blantyre on 14 August 2001; entered into force on 8 November 2004; depositary SADC Executive Secretary

The objectives of the protocol include the prevention, combating and eradication of the illicit manufacturing of firearms, ammunition and other related materials, and the prevention of their excessive and destabilizing accumulation, trafficking, possession and use in the region. A party may withdraw from the protocol, having given 12 months' notice.

Parties (11): Botswana, Eswatini, Lesotho, Malawi, Mauritius, Mozambique, Namibia, South Africa, Tanzania, Zambia, Zimbabwe

Signed but not ratified (2):* Congo (Democratic Republic of the), Seychelles[†]

* Three member states of SADC—Angola, the Comoros and Madagascar—have neither signed nor ratified the protocol.

[†] Seychelles signed the protocol in 2001 but did not ratify it before withdrawing from SADC in 2004. It rejoined SADC in 2008.

Protocol text: SADC, <https://www.sadc.int/files/8613/5292/8361/Protocol_on_the_Control_of_Firearms_Ammunition2001.pdf>

Nairobi Protocol for the Prevention, Control and Reduction of Small Arms and Light Weapons in the Great Lakes Region and the Horn of Africa

Signed by the 10 member states of the Nairobi Secretariat on Small Arms and Light Weapons and the Seychelles at Nairobi on 21 April 2004; entered into force on 5 May 2006; depositary Regional Centre on Small Arms in the Great Lakes Region, the Horn of Africa and Bordering States (RECSA)

The objectives of the protocol include the prevention, combating and eradication of the illicit manufacture of, trafficking in, possession and use of small arms and light weapons (SALW) in the subregion. Its implementation is overseen by RECSA.

Parties (12): Burundi, Central African Republic, Congo (Democratic Republic of the), Congo (Republic of the), Djibouti, Eritrea, Ethiopia, Kenya, Rwanda, South Sudan, Sudan, Uganda

Signed but not ratified (3):* Seychelles, Somalia, Tanzania

* The accuracy of this list is uncertain. Some or all of these 3 states may have ratified the treaty.

Protocol text: RECSA, <https://www.recsasec.org/wp-content/uploads/2018/08/Nairobi-Protocol.pdf>

ECOWAS Convention on Small Arms and Light Weapons, their Ammunition and Other Related Materials

Adopted by the 15 member states of the Economic Community of West African States (ECOWAS) at Abuja, on 14 June 2006; entered into force on 29 September 2009; depositary President of the ECOWAS Commission

The convention obligates the parties to prevent and combat the excessive and destabilizing accumulation of SALW in the ECOWAS member states. The convention bans the transfer of SALW into, through or from the territories of the parties. The ECOWAS member states may, by consensus, grant a party an exemption for national defence and security needs or for use in multilateral peace operations. Possession of light weapons by civilians is banned and their possession of small arms must be regulated. Each party must also control the manufacture of SALW, establish registers of SALW and establish a national commission to implement the convention.

A party may withdraw from the treaty, having given 12 months' notice, if it decides that its supreme interests have been jeopardized by extraordinary events related to the treaty's subject matter.

Parties (14): Benin, Burkina Faso, Cabo Verde, Côte d'Ivoire, Ghana, Guinea, Guinea-Bissau, Liberia, Mali, Niger, Nigeria, Senegal, Sierra Leone, Togo

Signed but not ratified (1): Gambia

Convention text: ECOWAS Commission, <https://documentation.ecowas.int/download/en/publications/Convention on Small Arms.pdf>

Treaty on a Nuclear-Weapon-Free Zone in Central Asia (Treaty of Semipalatinsk)

Signed by the 5 Central Asian states at Semipalatinsk on 8 September 2006; entered into force on 21 March 2009; depositary Kyrgyz Government

The Central Asian Nuclear Weapon-Free Zone is defined as the territories of Kazakhstan, Kyrgyzstan, Tajikistan, Turkmenistan, Uzbekistan. The treaty obligates the parties not to conduct research on, develop, manufacture, stockpile or otherwise acquire, possess or have control over nuclear weapons or any other nuclear explosive device by any means anywhere. A party may withdraw from the treaty, having given 12 months' notice, if it decides that its supreme interests have been jeopardized by extraordinary events related to the treaty's subject matter.

Under a *Protocol* China, France, Russia, the UK and the USA undertake not to use or threaten to use a nuclear explosive device against the parties to the treaty.

Parties (5): Kazakhstan, Kyrgyzstan, Tajikistan, Turkmenistan, Uzbekistan

Parties to the protocol (4): China, France*, Russia, UK*; *signed but not ratified (1)*: USA

* With reservations and/or declaration.

Treaty and protocol text: United Nations Treaty Collection, <https://treaties.un.org/doc/Publication/UNTS/No Volume/51633/Part/I-51633-080000028023b006.pdf>

Central African Convention for the Control of Small Arms and Light Weapons, Their Ammunition and All Parts and Components That Can Be Used for Their Manufacture, Repair and Assembly (Kinshasa Convention)

Opened for signature by the 10 member states of the Communauté économique d'États de l'Afrique Centrale (CEEAC, Economic Community of Central African States) and Rwanda at Brazzaville on 19 November 2010; entered into force on 8 March 2017; depositary UN Secretary-General

The objectives of the convention are to prevent, combat and eradicate illicit trade and trafficking in SALW in Central Africa (defined to be the territory of the members of CEEAC and Rwanda); to strengthen the control in the region of the manufacture, trade, transfer and use of SALW; to combat armed violence and ease the human suffering in the region caused by SALW; and to foster cooperation and confidence among the states parties.

A party may withdraw from the treaty, having given 12 months' notice.

Parties (8): Angola, Cameroon, Central African Republic, Chad, Congo (Republic of the), *Equatorial Guinea*, Gabon, Sao Tome and Principe

Signed but not ratified (3): Burundi, Congo (Democratic Republic of the), Rwanda

Treaty text: United Nations Treaty Collection, <https://treaties.un.org/doc/Treaties/2010/04/20100430 01-12 PM/Ch_xxvi-7.pdf>

Vienna Document 2011 on Confidence- and Security-Building Measures

Adopted by the participating states of the Organization for Security and Co-operation in Europe at Vienna on 30 November 2011; entered into force on 1 December 2011

The Vienna Document 2011 builds on the 1986 Stockholm Document on Confidence- and Security-Building Measures (CSBMs) and Disarmament in Europe and previous Vienna Documents (1990, 1992, 1994 and 1999). The Vienna Document 1990 provided for annual exchange of military information, military budget exchange, risk reduction procedures, a communication network and an annual CSBM implementation assessment. The Vienna Document 1992 and the Vienna Document 1994 extended the area of application and introduced new mechanisms and parameters for military activities, defence planning and military contacts. The Vienna Document 1999 introduced regional measures aimed at increasing transparency and confidence in a bilateral, multilateral and regional context and some improvements, in particular regarding the constraining measures.

The Vienna Document 2011 incorporates revisions on such matters as the timing of verification activities and demonstrations of new types of weapon and equipment system. It also establishes a procedure for updating the Vienna Document every five years. The reissue due in 2016 did not occur.

Participating states of the OSCE (57): See annex B

Document text: Organization for Security and Co-operation in Europe, <https://www.osce.org/fsc/86597?download=true>

III. Bilateral treaties

Treaty on the Limitation of Anti-Ballistic Missile Systems (ABM Treaty)

Signed by the USA and the USSR at Moscow on 26 May 1972; entered into force on 3 October 1972; not in force from 13 June 2002

The parties—Russia and the USA—undertook not to build nationwide defences against ballistic missile attack and to limit the development and deployment of permitted strategic missile defences. The treaty prohibited the parties from giving air defence missiles, radars or launchers the technical ability to counter strategic ballistic missiles and from testing them in a strategic ABM mode. It also established a standing consultative commission to promote its objectives and implementation. The **1974 Protocol** to the ABM Treaty introduced further numerical restrictions on permitted ballistic missile defences.

In 1997 Belarus, Kazakhstan, Russia, Ukraine and the USA signed a memorandum of understanding that would have made Belarus, Kazakhstan and Ukraine parties to the treaty along with Russia as successor states of the USSR and a set of agreed statements that would specify the demarcation line between strategic missile defences (which are not permitted under the treaty) and non-strategic or theatre missile defences (which are permitted under the treaty). The 1997 agreements were ratified by Russia in April 2000, but the USA did not ratify them and they did not enter into force.

On 13 December 2001 the USA notified Russia that it had decided to withdraw from the treaty, citing the ballistic missile threat to its territory from other states; the withdrawal came into effect six months later, on 13 June 2002.

Treaty text: *United Nations Treaty Series*, vol. 944 (1974), <https://treaties.un.org/doc/Publication/UNTS/Volume 944/v944.pdf>, pp. 13–17

Protocol text: US Department of State, <https://2009-2017.state.gov/t/avc/trty/101888.htm #protocolabm>

Treaty on the Limitation of Underground Nuclear Weapon Tests (Threshold Test-Ban Treaty, TTBT)

Signed by the USA and the USSR at Moscow on 3 July 1974; entered into force on 11 December 1990

The parties—Russia and the USA—undertake not to carry out any underground nuclear weapon test having a yield exceeding 150 kilotons. The 1974 verification protocol was replaced in 1990 with a new protocol.

Either party may withdraw from the treaty, having given the other 12 months' notice, if it decides that its supreme interests have been jeopardized by extraordinary events related to the treaty's subject matter.

Treaty and protocol texts: *United Nations Treaty Series*, vol. 1714 (1993), <https://treaties.un.org/doc/Publication/UNTS/Volume 1714/v1714.pdf>, pp. 217–301

Treaty on Underground Nuclear Explosions for Peaceful Purposes (Peaceful Nuclear Explosions Treaty, PNET)

Signed by the USA and the USSR at Moscow and Washington, DC, on 28 May 1976; entered into force simultaneously with the TTBT, on 11 December 1990

The parties—Russia and the USA—undertake not to carry out any individual underground nuclear explosion for peaceful purposes having a yield exceeding 150 kilotons or any group explosion having an aggregate yield exceeding 150 kilotons; and not to carry out any group explosion having an aggregate yield exceeding 1500 kilotons unless the individual explosions in the group could be identified and measured by agreed verification procedures. The treaty established a joint consultative commission to promote its objectives and implementation. The 1976 verification protocol was replaced in 1990 with a new protocol.

The treaty cannot be terminated while the TTBT is in force. If the TTBT is terminated, then either party may withdraw from this treaty at any time.

Treaty and protocol texts: United Nations Treaty Series, vol. 1714 (1993), <https://treaties.un.org/doc/Publication/UNTS/Volume 1714/v1714.pdf>, pp. 432–72

Treaty on the Elimination of Intermediate-Range and Shorter-Range Missiles (INF Treaty)

Signed by the USA and the USSR at Washington, DC, on 8 December 1987; entered into force on 1 June 1988; not in force from 2 August 2019

The treaty obligated the original parties—the USA and the USSR—to destroy all ground-launched ballistic and cruise missiles with a range of 500–5500 kilometres (intermediate-range, 1000–5500 km; and shorter-range, 500–1000 km) and their launchers by 1 June 1991. The treaty established a special verification commission (SVC) to promote its objectives and implementation.

A total of 2692 missiles were eliminated by May 1991. For 10 years after 1 June 1991 on-site inspections were conducted to verify compliance. The use of surveillance satellites for data collection continued after the end of on-site inspections on 31 May 2001.

In 1994 treaty membership was expanded to include Belarus, Kazakhstan and Ukraine.

On 2 February 2019 the USA notified the other parties that it would withdraw from the treaty in six months, citing the alleged deployment by Russia of a missile in breach of the treaty's limits. The USA and then Russia also suspended their obligations under the treaty. The withdrawal came into effect on 2 August 2019.

Treaty text: United Nations Treaty Series, vol. 1657 (1991), <https://treaties.un.org/doc/Publication/UNTS/Volume 1657/v1657.pdf>, pp. 4–167

Treaty on the Reduction and Limitation of Strategic Offensive Arms (START I)

Signed by the USA and the USSR at Moscow on 31 July 1991; entered into force on 5 December 1994; expired on 5 December 2009

The treaty obligated the original parties—the USA and the USSR—to make phased reductions in their offensive strategic nuclear forces over a seven-year period. It set numerical limits on deployed strategic nuclear delivery vehicles (SNDVs)—intercontinental ballistic missiles (ICBMs), submarine-launched ballistic missiles (SLBMs) and heavy bombers—and the nuclear warheads they carry.

In the Protocol to Facilitate the Implementation of START (**1992 Lisbon Protocol**), which entered into force on 5 December 1994, Belarus, Kazakhstan and Ukraine also assumed the obligations of the former USSR under the treaty alongside Russia.

Treaty and protocol texts: US Department of State, <https://2009-2017.state.gov/t/avc/trty/146007.htm>

Treaty on Further Reduction and Limitation of Strategic Offensive Arms (START II)

Signed by Russia and the USA at Moscow on 3 January 1993; not in force

The treaty would have obligated the parties to eliminate their ICBMs with multiple independently targeted re-entry vehicles (MIRVs) and reduce the number of their deployed strategic nuclear warheads to no more than 3000–3500 each (of which no more than 1750 were to be deployed on SLBMs) by 1 January 2003. On 26 September 1997 the two parties signed a *Protocol* to the treaty providing for the extension until the end of 2007 of the period of implementation of the treaty.

The two signatories ratified the treaty but never exchanged the instruments of ratification. The treaty thus never entered into force. On 14 June 2002, as a response to the taking effect on 13 June of the USA's withdrawal from the ABM Treaty, Russia declared that it would no longer be bound by START II.

Treaty and protocol texts: US Department of State, <https://2009-2017.state.gov/t/avc/trty/102887.htm>

Treaty on Strategic Offensive Reductions (SORT, Moscow Treaty)

Signed by Russia and the USA at Moscow on 24 May 2002; entered into force on 1 June 2003; not in force from 5 February 2011

The treaty obligated the parties to reduce the number of their operationally deployed strategic nuclear warheads so that the aggregate numbers did not exceed 1700–2200 for each party by 31 December 2012. The treaty was superseded by New START on 5 February 2011.

Treaty text: United Nations Treaty Series, vol. 2350 (2005), <https://treaties.un.org/doc/Publication/UNTS/Volume 2350/v2350.pdf>

Treaty on Measures for the Further Reduction and Limitation of Strategic Offensive Arms (New START, Prague Treaty)

Signed by Russia and the USA at Prague on 8 April 2010; entered into force on 5 February 2011

The treaty obligates the parties—Russia and the USA—to each reduce their number of (*a*) deployed ICBMs, SLBMs and heavy bombers to 700; (*b*) warheads on deployed ICBMs and SLBMs and warheads counted for deployed heavy bombers to 1550; and (*c*) deployed and non-deployed ICBM launchers, SLBM launchers and heavy bombers to 800. The reductions were achieved by 5 February 2018, as required by the treaty.

The treaty established a bilateral consultative commission (BCC) to resolve questions about compliance and other implementation issues. A protocol to the treaty contains verifications mechanisms.

The treaty followed on from START I and superseded SORT. It will remain in force for 10 years unless superseded earlier by a subsequent agreement. If both parties agree, it can be extended for 5 years, but no more. Either party may also withdraw from the treaty, having given the other three months' notice, if it decides that its supreme interests have been jeopardized by extraordinary events related to the treaty's subject matter.

Treaty and protocol texts: US Department of State, <https://2009-2017.state.gov/t/avc/newstart/c44126.htm>

Annex B. International security cooperation bodies

This annex describes the main international organizations, intergovernmental bodies, treaty-implementing bodies and transfer control regimes whose aims include the promotion of security, stability, peace or arms control and lists their members or participants as of 1 January 2020. The bodies are divided into three categories: those with a global focus or membership (section I), those with a regional focus or membership (section II) and those that aim to control strategic trade (section III).

The member states of the United Nations and organs within the UN system are listed first, followed by all other bodies in alphabetical order. Not all members or participants of these bodies are UN member states. States that joined or first participated in the body during 2019 are shown in italics. The address of an Internet site with information about each organization is provided where available. On the arms control and disarmament agreements mentioned here, see annex A.

I. Bodies with a global focus or membership

United Nations (UN)

The UN, the world intergovernmental organization, was founded in 1945 through the adoption of its Charter. Its headquarters are in New York, USA. The six principal UN organs are the General Assembly, the Security Council, the Economic and Social Council (ECOSOC), the Trusteeship Council (which suspended operation in 1994), the International Court of Justice (ICJ) and the Secretariat.

The General Assembly has six main committees. The First Committee (Disarmament and International Security Committee) deals with disarmament and related international security questions. The Fourth Committee (Special Political and Decolonization Committee) deals with a variety of subjects including decolonization, Palestinian refugees and human rights, peacekeeping, mine action, outer space, public information, atomic radiation and the University for Peace.

The UN Office for Disarmament Affairs (UNODA), a department of the UN Secretariat, promotes disarmament of nuclear, biological, chemical and conventional weapons. The UN also has a large number of specialized agencies and other autonomous bodies.

UN member states (193) and year of membership

Afghanistan, 1946
Albania, 1955
Algeria, 1962
Andorra, 1993
Angola, 1976
Antigua and Barbuda, 1981
Argentina, 1945
Armenia, 1992
Australia, 1945
Austria, 1955
Azerbaijan, 1992
Bahamas, 1973
Bahrain, 1971
Bangladesh, 1974
Barbados, 1966
Belarus, 1945
Belgium, 1945
Belize, 1981
Benin, 1960
Bhutan, 1971
Bolivia, 1945
Bosnia and Herzegovina, 1992
Botswana, 1966
Brazil, 1945
Brunei Darussalam, 1984
Bulgaria, 1955
Burkina Faso, 1960
Burundi, 1962
Cabo Verde, 1975
Cambodia, 1955
Cameroon, 1960
Canada, 1945
Central African Republic,
   1960
Chad, 1960
Chile, 1945
China, 1945
Colombia, 1945
Comoros, 1975
Congo, Democratic Republic
   of the, 1960
Congo, Republic of the, 1960
Costa Rica, 1945
Côte d'Ivoire, 1960
Croatia, 1992
Cuba, 1945
Cyprus, 1960
Czechia, 1993
Denmark, 1945
Djibouti, 1977
Dominica, 1978
Dominican Republic, 1945

Ecuador, 1945
Egypt, 1945
El Salvador, 1945
Equatorial Guinea, 1968
Eritrea, 1993
Estonia, 1991
Eswatini, 1968
Ethiopia, 1945
Fiji, 1970
Finland, 1955
France, 1945
Gabon, 1960
Gambia, 1965
Georgia, 1992
Germany, 1973
Ghana, 1957
Greece, 1945
Grenada, 1974
Guatemala, 1945
Guinea, 1958
Guinea-Bissau, 1974
Guyana, 1966
Haiti, 1945
Honduras, 1945
Hungary, 1955
Iceland, 1946
India, 1945
Indonesia, 1950
Iran, 1945
Iraq, 1945
Ireland, 1955
Israel, 1949
Italy, 1955
Jamaica, 1962
Japan, 1956
Jordan, 1955
Kazakhstan, 1992
Kenya, 1963
Kiribati, 1999
Korea, Democratic People's
   Republic of (North Korea),
   1991
Korea, Republic of (South
   Korea), 1991
Kuwait, 1963
Kyrgyzstan, 1992
Laos, 1955
Latvia, 1991
Lebanon, 1945
Lesotho, 1966
Liberia, 1945
Libya, 1955

Liechtenstein, 1990
Lithuania, 1991
Luxembourg, 1945
Madagascar, 1960
Malawi, 1964
Malaysia, 1957
Maldives, 1965
Mali, 1960
Malta, 1964
Marshall Islands, 1991
Mauritania, 1961
Mauritius, 1968
Mexico, 1945
Micronesia, 1991
Moldova, 1992
Monaco, 1993
Mongolia, 1961
Montenegro, 2006
Morocco, 1956
Mozambique, 1975
Myanmar, 1948
Namibia, 1990
Nauru, 1999
Nepal, 1955
Netherlands, 1945
New Zealand, 1945
Nicaragua, 1945
Niger, 1960
Nigeria, 1960
North Macedonia, 1993
Norway, 1945
Oman, 1971
Pakistan, 1947
Palau, 1994
Panama, 1945
Papua New Guinea, 1975
Paraguay, 1945
Peru, 1945
Philippines, 1945
Poland, 1945
Portugal, 1955
Qatar, 1971
Romania, 1955
Russia, 1945
Rwanda, 1962
Saint Kitts and Nevis, 1983
Saint Lucia, 1979
Saint Vincent and the
   Grenadines, 1980
Samoa, 1976
San Marino, 1992
Sao Tome and Principe, 1975

Saudi Arabia, 1945	Suriname, 1975	Tuvalu, 2000
Senegal, 1960 Serbia, 2000	Sweden, 1946	Uganda, 1962
Seychelles, 1976	Switzerland, 2002	UK, 1945
Sierra Leone, 1961	Syria, 1945	Ukraine, 1945
Singapore, 1965	Tajikistan, 1992	United Arab Emirates, 1971
Slovakia, 1993	Tanzania, 1961	Uruguay, 1945
Slovenia, 1992	Thailand, 1946	USA, 1945
Solomon Islands, 1978	Timor-Leste, 2002	Uzbekistan, 1992
Somalia, 1960	Togo, 1960	Vanuatu, 1981
South Africa, 1945	Tonga, 1999	Venezuela, 1945
South Sudan, 2011	Trinidad and Tobago, 1962	Viet Nam, 1977
Spain, 1955	Tunisia, 1956	Yemen, 1947
Sri Lanka, 1955	Turkey, 1945	Zambia, 1964
Sudan, 1956	Turkmenistan, 1992	Zimbabwe, 1980

Non-member observer states (2): Holy See, Palestine

Website: <https://www.un.org/>

UN Security Council

The Security Council has responsibility for the maintenance of international peace and security. All UN members states must comply with its decisions. It has 5 permanent members, which can each exercise a veto on the Council's decisions, and 10 non-permanent members elected by the UN General Assembly for two-year terms.

Permanent members (the P5): China, France, Russia, UK, USA

Non-permanent members (10): Belgium*, Dominican Republic*, Estonia[†], Germany*, Indonesia*, Niger[†], Saint Vincent and the Grenadines[†], South Africa*, Tunisia[†], Viet Nam[†]

 * Member in 2019–20.
 [†] Member in 2020–21.

Website: <https://www.un.org/securitycouncil/>

Conference on Disarmament (CD)

The CD is intended to be the single multilateral arms control and disarmament negotiating forum of the international community. It has been enlarged and renamed several times since 1960. It is not a UN body but reports to the UN General Assembly. It is based in Geneva, Switzerland.

Members (65): Algeria, Argentina, Australia, Austria, Bangladesh, Belarus, Belgium, Brazil, Bulgaria, Cameroon, Canada, Chile, China, Colombia, Congo (Democratic Republic of the), Cuba, Ecuador, Egypt, Ethiopia, Finland, France, Germany, Hungary, India, Indonesia, Iran, Iraq, Ireland, Israel, Italy, Japan, Kazakhstan, Kenya, Korea (North), Korea (South), Malaysia, Mexico, Mongolia, Morocco, Myanmar, Netherlands, New Zealand, Nigeria, Norway, Pakistan, Peru, Poland, Romania, Russia, Senegal, Slovakia, South Africa, Spain, Sri Lanka, Sweden, Switzerland, Syria, Tunisia, Turkey, UK, Ukraine, USA, Venezuela, Viet Nam, Zimbabwe

Website: <https://www.unog.ch/cd>

UN Disarmament Commission (UNDC)

The UNDC in its original form was established in 1952. After changes of name and format, it became the Conference on Disarmament in 1978. In that year, the UN General Assembly re-established the UNDC in its current form. It meets for three weeks each year in New York to consider a small number of disarmament issues—currently two substantive items per session—and formulate consensus principles, guidelines and recommendations. It was unable to reach agreement on any such outcome in 2000–16, but in 2017 adopted consensus recommendations on 'Practical confidence-building measures in the field of conventional weapons'.

Members (193): The UN member states

Website: <https://www.un.org/disarmament/institutions/disarmament-commission/>

UN Peacebuilding Commission (PBC)

The PBC was established in 2005 by the General Assembly and the Security Council to advise them on post-conflict peacebuilding and recovery, to marshal resources and to propose integrated strategies.

The General Assembly, the Security Council and ECOSOC each elect seven members of the PBC for two-year terms; the remaining members are the top five providers of military personnel and civilian police to UN missions and the top five contributors of funds to the UN. Additional states and organizations participate in country-specific meetings on countries on the PBC agenda.

Members (30): Bangladesh*$^{||}$, Brazil*§, Canada*$^#$, China*‡, Colombia*§, Dominican Republic*‡, Egypt*†, Ethiopia*$^{||}$, France*‡, Germany*$^#$, Guatemala*†, India*$^{||}$, Iran*§, Ireland*§, Japan*$^#$, Kenya*†, Korea (South)*§, Mali*§, Mexico*†, Nepal*†, Niger*‡, Norway*$^#$, Pakistan*$^{||}$, Peru**†, Slovakia**†, Russia*‡, Rwanda*$^{||}$, Sweden*$^#$, UK*‡, USA*‡

  * Member until 31 Dec. 2020.
  ** Member until 31 Dec. 2021.
  † Elected by the General Assembly.
  ‡ Elected by the Security Council.
  § Elected by ECOSOC.
  $^{||}$ Top 5 contributor of personnel.
  $^#$ Top 5 contributor of funds.

Note: The full membership of the PBC is 31. Romania had been elected by ECOSOC for a two-year term ending on 31 Dec. 2020, but its membership lapsed when it ceased to be a member of ECOSOC on 31 Dec. 2019. ECOSOC will fill this vacancy during 2020.

Website: <https://www.un.org/peacebuilding/commission/>

International Atomic Energy Agency (IAEA)

The IAEA is an intergovernmental organization within the UN system. It is mandated by its Statute, which entered into force in 1957, to promote the peaceful uses of atomic energy and ensure that nuclear activities are not used to further any military purpose. Under the 1968 Non-Proliferation Treaty and the nuclear weapon-free zone treaties, non-nuclear weapon states must accept IAEA nuclear safeguards to demonstrate the fulfilment of their obligation not to manufacture nuclear weapons. Its headquarters are in Vienna, Austria.

Members (171): Afghanistan, Albania, Algeria, Angola, Antigua and Barbuda, Argentina, Armenia, Australia, Austria, Azerbaijan, Bahamas, Bahrain, Bangladesh, Barbados, Belarus, Belgium, Belize, Benin, Bolivia, Bosnia and Herzegovina, Botswana, Brazil, Brunei Darussalam, Bulgaria, Burkina Faso, Burundi, Cambodia, Cameroon, Canada, Central African Republic, Chad, Chile, China, Colombia, Congo (Democratic Republic of the), Congo (Republic of the), Costa Rica, Côte d'Ivoire, Croatia, Cuba, Cyprus, Czechia, Denmark, Djibouti, Dominica, Dominican Republic, Ecuador, Egypt, El Salvador, Eritrea, Estonia, Eswatini, Ethiopia, Fiji, Finland, France, Gabon, Georgia, Germany, Ghana, Greece, Grenada, Guatemala, Guyana, Haiti, Holy See, Honduras, Hungary, Iceland, India, Indonesia, Iran, Iraq, Ireland, Israel, Italy, Jamaica, Japan, Jordan, Kazakhstan, Kenya, Korea (South), Kuwait, Kyrgyzstan, Laos, Latvia, Lebanon, Lesotho, Liberia, Libya, Liechtenstein, Lithuania, Luxembourg, Madagascar, Malawi, Malaysia, Mali, Malta, Marshall Islands, Mauritania, Mauritius, Mexico, Moldova, Monaco, Mongolia, Montenegro, Morocco, Mozambique, Myanmar, Namibia, Nepal, Netherlands, New Zealand, Nicaragua, Niger, Nigeria, North Macedonia, Norway, Oman, Pakistan, Palau, Panama, Papua New Guinea, Paraguay, Peru, Philippines, Poland, Portugal, Qatar, Rwanda, Romania, Russia, *Saint Lucia*, Saint Vincent and the Grenadines, San Marino, Saudi Arabia, Senegal, Serbia, Seychelles, Sierra Leone, Singapore, Slovakia, Slovenia, South Africa, Spain, Sri Lanka, Sudan, Sweden, Switzerland, Syria, Tajikistan, Tanzania, Thailand, Togo, Trinidad and Tobago, Tunisia, Turkey, Turkmenistan, Uganda, UK, Ukraine, United Arab Emirates, Uruguay, USA, Uzbekistan, Vanuatu, Venezuela, Viet Nam, Yemen, Zambia, Zimbabwe

Notes: North Korea was a member of the IAEA until June 1994. In addition to the 171 members as of 1 Jan. 2020, the IAEA General Conference had also approved the membership of Cabo Verde, Comoros, Gambia and Tonga; it will take effect once the state deposits the necessary legal instruments with the IAEA.

Website: <https://www.iaea.org/>

International Court of Justice (ICJ)

The ICJ was established in 1945 by the UN Charter and is the principal judicial organ of the UN. The court's role is to settle legal disputes submitted to it by states and to give advisory opinions on legal questions referred to it by authorized UN organs and specialized agencies. The Court is composed of 15 judges, who are elected for terms of office of nine years by the UN General Assembly and the Security Council. Its seat is at The Hague, the Netherlands.

Website: <https://www.icj-cij.org/>

Bilateral Consultative Commission (BCC)

The BCC is a forum established under the 2010 Russian–US Treaty on Measures for the Further Reduction and Limitation of Strategic Offensive Arms (New START, Prague Treaty) to discuss issues related to the treaty's implementation. It replaced the joint compliance and inspection commission (JCIC) of the 1991 START treaty. The BCC is required to meet at least twice each year in Geneva, Switzerland, unless the parties agree otherwise. Its work is confidential.

Website: US Department of Defense, Under Secretary of Defense for Acquisition and Sustainment, <https://www.acq.osd.mil/tc/nst/NSTtoc.htm>

Commonwealth of Nations

Established in its current form in 1949, the Commonwealth is an organization of developed and developing countries whose aim is to advance democracy, human rights, and sustainable economic and social development within its member states and beyond. It adopted a charter reaffirming its core values and principles in 2012. The members' leaders meet in the biennial Commonwealth Heads of Government Meetings (CHOGMs). Its secretariat is in London, UK.

Members (53): Antigua and Barbuda, Australia, Bahamas, Bangladesh, Barbados, Belize, Botswana, Brunei Darussalam, Cameroon, Canada, Cyprus, Dominica, Eswatini, Fiji, Gambia, Ghana, Grenada, Guyana, India, Jamaica, Kenya, Kiribati, Lesotho, Malawi, Malaysia, Malta, Mauritius, Mozambique, Namibia, Nauru, New Zealand, Nigeria, Pakistan, Papua New Guinea, Rwanda[†], Saint Kitts and Nevis, Saint Lucia, Saint Vincent and the Grenadines, Samoa, Seychelles, Sierra Leone, Singapore, Solomon Islands, South Africa, Sri Lanka, Tanzania, Tonga, Trinidad and Tobago, Tuvalu, Uganda, UK[*], Vanuatu, Zambia

 [*] CHOGM host in 2018 and Chair-in-Office in 2018–20.
 [†] CHOGM host in 2020 and Chair-in-Office in 2020–22.

Note: In addition to the 53 members as of 1 Jan. 2020, the Maldives (which withdrew in 2016) rejoined on 1 Feb. Dec. 2020. Zimbabwe (which withdrew in 2013) applied to rejoin the Commonwealth in May 2018.

Website: <https://www.thecommonwealth.org/>

Comprehensive Nuclear-Test-Ban Treaty Organization (CTBTO)

The CTBTO will become operational when the 1996 Comprehensive Nuclear-Test-Ban Treaty (CTBT) has entered into force. It will resolve questions of compliance with the treaty and act as a forum for consultation and cooperation among the states parties. A Preparatory Commission and provisional Technical Secretariat are preparing for the work of the CTBTO, in particular by establishing the International Monitoring System, consisting of seismic, hydro-acoustic, infrasound and radionuclide stations from which data is transmitted to the CTBTO International Data Centre. Their headquarters are in Vienna, Austria.

Signatories to the CTBT (184): See annex A

Website: <https://www.ctbto.org/>

Financial Action Task Force (FATF)

The FATF is an intergovernmental policymaking body whose purpose is to establish international standards and develop and promote policies, at both national and international levels. It was established in 1989 by the Group of Seven (G7), initially to examine and develop measures to combat money laundering; its mandate was expanded in 2001 to incorporate efforts to combat terrorist financing and again in 2008 to include the financing of weapon of mass destruction (WMD) proliferation efforts. It published revised recommendations in 2012. Its secretariat is in Paris, France.

Members (39): Argentina, Australia, Austria, Belgium, Brazil, Canada, China, Denmark, European Commission, Finland, France, Germany, Greece, Gulf Cooperation Council, Hong Kong (China), Iceland, India, Ireland, Israel, Italy, Japan, Korea (South), Luxembourg, Malaysia, Mexico, Netherlands, New Zealand, Norway, Portugal, Russia, *Saudi Arabia*, Singapore, South Africa, Spain, Sweden, Switzerland, Turkey, UK, USA

Website: <https://www.fatf-gafi.org/>

Global Initiative to Combat Nuclear Terrorism (GICNT)

The GICNT was established in 2006 as a voluntary international partnership of states and international organizations that are committed to strengthening global capacity to prevent, detect and respond to nuclear terrorism. The GICNT works towards this goal by conducting multilateral activities that strengthen the plans, policies, procedures and interoperability of its partner. The partners meet at biennial plenaries. Russia and the USA act as co-chairs.

Partners (89): Afghanistan, Albania, Algeria, Argentina, Armenia, Australia, Austria, Azerbaijan, Bahrain, Belarus, Belgium, Bosnia and Herzegovina, Bulgaria, Cabo Verde, Cambodia, Canada, Chile, China, Côte d'Ivoire, Croatia, Cyprus, Czechia, Denmark, Estonia, Finland, France, Georgia, Germany, Greece, Hungary, Iceland, India, Iraq, Ireland, Israel, Italy, Japan, Jordan, Kazakhstan, Korea (South), Kyrgyzstan, Latvia, Libya, Lithuania, Luxembourg, Madagascar, Malaysia, Malta, Mauritius, Mexico, *Moldova*, Montenegro, Morocco, Nepal, Netherlands, New Zealand, Nigeria, North Macedonia, Norway, Pakistan, Palau, Panama, Paraguay, Philippines, Poland, Portugal, Romania, Russia, Saudi Arabia, Serbia, Seychelles, Singapore, Slovakia, Slovenia, Spain, Sri Lanka, Sweden, Switzerland, Tajikistan, Thailand, Turkey, Turkmenistan, UK, Ukraine, United Arab Emirates, USA, Uzbekistan, Viet Nam, Zambia

Official observers (6): European Union, International Atomic Energy Agency, International Criminal Police Organization (INTERPOL), UN Interregional Crime and Justice Research Institute, UN Office on Drugs and Crime, UN Office of Counter-Terrorism

Website: <https://gicnt.org/>

Group of Seven (G7)

The G7 is a group of leading industrialized countries that have met informally, at the level of head of state or government, since the 1970s. The presidents of the European Council and the European Commission represent the European Union at summits.

Between 1997 and 2013 the G7 members and Russia met together as the Group of Eight (G8). Following Russia's annexation of Crimea, the G7 states decided in March 2014 to meet without Russia until further notice.

Members (7): Canada, France*, Germany, Italy, Japan, UK‡, USA†

* Summit host in 2019.
† Summit host in 2020.
‡ Summit host in 2021.

Website: <https://g7.gc.ca/en/>

Global Partnership against the Spread of Weapons and Materials of Mass Destruction

The Global Partnership was launched in 2002 by the G8 to address non-proliferation, disarmament, counterterrorism and nuclear safety issues. The members meet twice each year, hosted by the state holding the G7 presidency, with the main goal of launching specific projects to tackle the abuse of weapons and materials of mass destruction and reduce chemical, biological, radioactive and nuclear risks. The Global Partnership was extended for an unspecified period in May 2011.

Members (31): Australia, Belgium, Canada, Chile, Czechia, Denmark, European Union, Finland, France, Georgia, Germany, Hungary, Ireland, Italy, Japan, Jordan, Kazakhstan, Korea (South), Mexico, Netherlands, New Zealand, Norway, Philippines, Poland, Portugal, Spain, Sweden, Switzerland, UK, Ukraine, USA

Note: Russia was a founding partner of the Global Partnership, but it ceased to be a partner following its exclusion from the G8.

Website: <https://www.gpwmd.com/>

International Criminal Court (ICC)

The ICC is a permanent international court dealing with the crime of genocide, crimes against humanity, war crimes and the crime of aggression. Its seat is at The Hague, the Netherlands, and it has field offices in the Central African Republic, Côte d'Ivoire, the Democratic Republic of the Congo, Kenya and Uganda. The court has 18 judges and an independent prosecutor, elected by the assembly of states parties for nine-year terms.

The court's powers and jurisdiction are defined by the 1998 Rome Statute and its amendments. While the ICC is independent of the UN, the Rome Statute grants the UN Security Council certain powers of referral and deferral.

Parties to the Rome Statute (123) and its amendments: See annex A

Website: <https://www.icc-cpi.int/>

Non-Aligned Movement (NAM)

NAM was established in 1961 as a forum for non-aligned states to consult on political, economic and arms control issues and coordinate their positions in the UN.

Members (120): Afghanistan, Algeria, Angola, Antigua and Barbuda, Azerbaijan*, Bahamas, Bahrain, Bangladesh, Barbados, Belarus, Belize, Benin, Bhutan, Bolivia, Botswana, Brunei Darussalam, Burkina Faso, Burundi, Cabo Verde, Cambodia, Cameroon, Central African Republic, Chad, Chile, Colombia, Comoros, Congo (Democratic Republic of the), Congo (Republic of the), Côte d'Ivoire, Cuba, Djibouti, Dominica, Dominican Republic, Ecuador, Egypt, Equatorial Guinea, Eritrea, Eswatini, Ethiopia, Fiji, Gabon, Gambia, Ghana, Grenada, Guatemala, Guinea, Guinea-Bissau, Guyana, Haiti, Honduras, India, Indonesia, Iran, Iraq, Jamaica, Jordan, Kenya, Korea (North), Kuwait, Laos, Lebanon, Lesotho, Liberia, Libya, Madagascar, Malawi, Malaysia, Maldives, Mali, Mauritania, Mauritius, Mongolia, Morocco, Mozambique, Myanmar, Namibia, Nepal, Nicaragua, Niger, Nigeria, Oman, Pakistan, Palestine Liberation Organization, Panama, Papua New Guinea, Peru, Philippines, Qatar, Rwanda, Saint Kitts and Nevis, Saint Lucia, Saint Vincent and the Grenadines, Sao Tome and Principe, Saudi Arabia, Senegal, Seychelles, Sierra Leone, Singapore, Somalia, South Africa, Sri Lanka, Sudan, Suriname, Syria, Tanzania, Thailand, Timor-Leste, Togo, Trinidad and Tobago, Tunisia, Turkmenistan, Uganda[†], United Arab Emirates, Uzbekistan, Vanuatu, Venezuela, Viet Nam, Yemen, Zambia, Zimbabwe

* NAM chair in 2019–22 and summit host in 2019.
[†] NAM chair in 2022–25 and summit host in 2022.

Website: <https://www.mnoal.org/>

Organisation for Economic Co-operation and Development (OECD)

Established in 1961, the OECD's objectives are to promote economic and social welfare by coordinating policies among the member states. Its headquarters are in Paris, France.

Members (36): Australia, Austria, Belgium, Canada, Chile, Czechia, Denmark, Estonia, Finland, France, Germany, Greece, Hungary, Iceland, Ireland, Israel, Italy, Japan, Korea (South), Latvia, Lithuania, Luxembourg, Mexico, Netherlands, New Zealand, Norway, Poland, Portugal, Slovakia, Slovenia, Spain, Sweden, Switzerland, Turkey, UK, USA

Note: In addition to the 36 members as of 1 Jan. 2020, Colombia signed an accession agreement with the OECD on 30 May 2018 and will become a member once that agreement has been ratified.

Website: <https://www.oecd.org/>

Organisation for the Prohibition of Chemical Weapons (OPCW)

The OPCW implements the 1993 Chemical Weapons Convention (CWC). Among other things, it oversees the destruction of chemical weapon stockpiles and associated infrastructure, implements a verification regime to ensure that such weapons do not re-emerge, provides assistance and protection to states parties threatened by such weapons, and facilitates and engages in international cooperation to strengthen treaty compliance and to promote the peaceful uses of chemistry. In addition to the responsibility to investigate alleged use of chemical weapons, in 2018 the OPCW gained the power to attribute responsibility for any chemical weapon use.

The work of the OPCW and its Technical Secretariat is overseen by the Executive Council, whose 41 members are elected for two-year terms by the Conference of States Parties. It is based in The Hague, the Netherlands.

Parties to the Chemical Weapons Convention (193): See annex A

Website: <https://www.opcw.org/>

Organisation of Islamic Cooperation (OIC)

The OIC (formerly the Organization of the Islamic Conference) was established in 1969 by Islamic states to promote cooperation among the members and to support peace, security and the struggle of the people of Palestine and all Muslim people. Among its organs are the Independent Permanent Human Rights Commission (IPHRC) and the Islamic Development Bank (IDB). Its secretariat is in Jeddah, Saudi Arabia.

Members (57): Afghanistan, Albania, Algeria, Azerbaijan, Bahrain, Bangladesh, Benin, Brunei Darussalam, Burkina Faso, Cameroon, Chad, Comoros, Côte d'Ivoire, Djibouti, Egypt, Gabon, Gambia, Guinea, Guinea-Bissau, Guyana, Indonesia, Iran, Iraq, Jordan, Kazakhstan, Kuwait, Kyrgyzstan, Lebanon, Libya, Malaysia, Maldives, Mali, Mauritania, Morocco, Mozambique, Niger, Nigeria, Oman, Pakistan, Palestine, Qatar, Saudi Arabia, Senegal, Sierra Leone, Somalia, Sudan, Suriname, Syria, Tajikistan, Togo, Tunisia, Turkey, Turkmenistan, Uganda, United Arab Emirates, Uzbekistan, Yemen

Website: <https://www.oic-oci.org/>

Special Verification Commission (SVC)

The SVC was established by the 1987 Soviet–US Treaty on the Elimination of Intermediate-Range and Shorter-Range Missiles (INF Treaty) as a forum to resolve compliance questions and measures necessary to improve the viability and effectiveness of the treaty. The SVC, which had not met since 2000, met in November 2016 and in December 2017.

On 2 August 2019 the USA withdrew from the INF Treaty, which is now no longer in force, and the SVC ceased to exist.

Former parties to the INF Treaty (5): See annex A

II. Bodies with a regional focus or membership

African Commission on Nuclear Energy (AFCONE)

AFCONE was established by the 1996 Treaty of Pelindaba to ensure compliance with the treaty and to advance the peaceful application of nuclear science and technology in Africa. Its seat is in Pretoria, South Africa.

Parties to the Treaty of Pelindaba (41): See annex A

Website: <http://www.afcone.peaceau.org/>

African Union (AU)

The AU was formally established in 2001 and launched in 2002. It replaced the Organization for African Unity (OAU), which had been established in 1963. Membership is open to all African states. The AU promotes unity, security and conflict resolution, democracy, human rights, and political, social and economic integration in Africa. Its main organs include the Assembly (the supreme body, consisting of heads of state and government), the Executive Council (made up of designated national ministers), the Commission (the secretariat), the Pan-African Parliament and the Peace and Security Council. The AU's headquarters are in Addis Ababa, Ethiopia.

Members (55): Algeria, Angola, Benin, Botswana, Burkina Faso, Burundi, Cabo Verde, Cameroon, Central African Republic, Chad, Comoros, Congo (Democratic Republic of the), Congo (Republic of the), Côte d'Ivoire, Djibouti, Egypt, Equatorial Guinea, Eritrea, Eswatini, Ethiopia, Gabon, Gambia, Ghana, Guinea, Guinea-Bissau, Kenya, Lesotho, Liberia, Libya, Madagascar, Malawi, Mali, Mauritania, Mauritius, Morocco, Mozambique, Namibia, Niger, Nigeria, Rwanda, Sahrawi Arab Democratic Republic (Western Sahara), Sao Tome and Principe, Senegal, Seychelles, Sierra Leone, Somalia, South Africa, South Sudan, Sudan*, Tanzania, Togo, Tunisia, Uganda, Zambia, Zimbabwe

* Sudan was suspended from the AU on 6 June 2019 after violent repression of anti-government protests. The suspension was lifted on 6 Sep. 2019 after the formation of a civilian-led government.

Website: <https://www.au.int/>

Peace and Security Council (PSC)

The PSC is the AU's standing decision-making organ for the prevention, management and resolution of conflicts. Its 15 members are elected by the Executive Council subject to endorsement by the Assembly. It is the main pillar of the African Peace and Security Architecture (APSA).

Members for a 3-year term 1 Apr. 2019–31 Mar. 2022 (5): Algeria, Burundi, Kenya, Lesotho, Nigeria

Members for a 2-year term 1 Apr. 2018–31 Mar. 2020 (10): Angola, Djibouti, Equatorial Guinea, Gabon, Liberia, Morocco, Rwanda, Sierra Leone, Togo, Zimbabwe

Website: <http://www.peaceau.org/>

Asia–Pacific Economic Cooperation (APEC)

APEC was established in 1989 as a regional economic forum to enhance open trade and economic prosperity in the Asia–Pacific region. Security and political issues—including combating terrorism, non-proliferation of WMD and effective transfer control systems—have been increasingly discussed in this forum since the mid-1990s. The APEC Secretariat is based in Singapore.

Member economies (21): Australia, Brunei Darussalam, Canada, Chile*, China, Hong Kong, Indonesia, Japan, Korea (South), Malaysia†, Mexico, New Zealand‡, Papua New Guinea, Peru, Philippines, Russia, Singapore, Taiwan, Thailand, USA, Viet Nam

* Host of APEC Economic Leaders' Meeting in 2019.
† Host of APEC Economic Leaders' Meeting in 2020.
‡ Host of APEC Economic Leaders' Meeting in 2021.

Website: <https://www.apec.org/>

Association of Southeast Asian Nations (ASEAN)

ASEAN was established in 1967 to promote economic, social and cultural development as well as regional peace and security in South East Asia. Development
of the ASEAN Political–Security Community is one of the three pillars (along
with the Economic and Sociocultural communities) of the ASEAN Community,
which was launched in 2015. The ASEAN Secretariat is in Jakarta, Indonesia.

Members (10): Brunei Darussalam, Cambodia, Indonesia, Laos, Malaysia, Myanmar,
Philippines, Singapore, Thailand, Viet Nam

Website: <https://www.asean.org/>

ASEAN Regional Forum (ARF)

The ARF was established in 1994 to foster constructive dialogue and
consultation on political and security issues and to contribute to
confidence-building and preventive diplomacy in the Asia-Pacific region.

Participants (27): The ASEAN member states and Australia, Bangladesh, Canada,
China, European Union, India, Japan, Korea (North), Korea (South), Mongolia, New
Zealand, Pakistan, Papua New Guinea, Russia, Sri Lanka, Timor-Leste, USA

Website: <https://aseanregionalforum.asean.org/>

ASEAN Plus Three (APT)

The APT cooperation began in 1997, in the wake of the Asian financial
crisis, and was institutionalized in 1999. It aims to foster economic,
political and security cooperation and financial stability among its
participants.

Participants (13): The ASEAN member states and China, Japan, Korea (South)

Website: <https://www.asean.org/asean/external-relations/asean-3>

East Asia Summit (EAS)

The East Asia Summit started in 2005 as a regional forum for dialogue on
strategic, political and economic issues with the aim of promoting peace,
stability and economic prosperity in East Asia. The annual meetings are
held in connection with the ASEAN summits.

Participants (18): The ASEAN member states and Australia, China, India, Japan,
Korea (South), New Zealand, Russia, USA

Website: <https://www.asean.org/asean/external-relations/east-asia-summit-eas/>

Collective Security Treaty Organization (CSTO)

The CSTO was formally established in 2002–2003 by six signatories of the 1992 Collective Security Treaty. It aims to promote military and political cooperation among its members. Under Article 4 of the 1992 treaty, aggression against one member state is considered to be aggression against them all. An objective of the CSTO is to provide a more efficient response to strategic problems such as terrorism and narcotics trafficking. Its seat is in Moscow, Russia.

Members (6): Armenia, Belarus, Kazakhstan, Kyrgyzstan, Russia, Tajikistan

Website: <https://odkb-csto.org/>

Commonwealth of Independent States (CIS)

The CIS was established in 1991 as a framework for multilateral cooperation among former republics of the Soviet Union. The institutions of the CIS, including the Council of Defence Ministers, were established by the 1993 Charter. Their headquarters are in Minsk, Belarus.

Members (11): Armenia, Azerbaijan, Belarus, Kazakhstan, Kyrgyzstan, Moldova, Russia, Tajikistan, Turkmenistan*, Ukraine[†], Uzbekistan

 * Turkmenistan has not ratified the 1993 CIS Charter but since 26 Aug. 2005 has participated in CIS activities as an associate member.
 [†] Although Ukraine did not ratify the CIS Charter, it was an unofficial associate member from 1993. Ukraine decided to end its participation in CIS institutions in May 2018; it completed the process of withdrawing from the CIS coordination bodies in Feb. 2019. It continues to withdraw from CIS agreements.

Website: <http://www.cis.minsk.by/>

Communauté économique des États de l'Afrique Centrale (CEEAC, Economic Community of Central African States, ECCAS)

CEEAC was established in 1983 to promote political dialogue, create a customs union and establish common policies in Central Africa. It also coordinates activities under the 2010 Central African Convention for the Control of Small Arms and Light Weapons, Their Ammunition and All Parts and Components That Can Be Used for Their Manufacture, Repair and Assembly (Kinshasa Convention). Its secretariat is in Libreville, Gabon.

The **Council for Peace and Security in Central Africa (Conseil de paix et de sécurité de l'Afrique Centrale, COPAX)** is a mechanism for promoting joint political and military strategies for conflict prevention, management and resolution in Central Africa.

Members (11): Angola, Burundi, Cameroon, Central African Republic, Chad, Congo (Democratic Republic of the), Congo (Republic of the), Equatorial Guinea, Gabon, Rwanda, Sao Tome and Principe

Website: <http://www.ceeac-eccas.org/>

Conference on Interaction and Confidence-building Measures in Asia (CICA)

Initiated in 1992, CICA was formally established in 1999 as a forum to enhance security cooperation and confidence-building measures among the member states. It also promotes economic, social and cultural cooperation. Its secretariat is in Astana, Kazakhstan.

Members (27): Afghanistan, Azerbaijan, Bahrain, Bangladesh, Cambodia, China, Egypt, India, Iran, Iraq, Israel, Jordan, Kazakhstan, Korea (South), Kyrgyzstan, Mongolia, Pakistan, Palestine, Qatar, Russia, Sri Lanka, Tajikistan*, Thailand, Turkey, United Arab Emirates, Uzbekistan, Viet Nam

* Chair in 2018–20.

Website: <http://www.s-cica.org/>

Council of Europe (COE)

The Council was established in 1949. Membership is open to all European states that accept the principle of the rule of law and guarantee their citizens' human rights and fundamental freedoms. Its seat is in Strasbourg, France. Among its organs are the Council of Ministers, the Parliamentary Assembly, the European Court of Human Rights and the Council of Europe Development Bank.

Members (47): Albania, Andorra, Armenia, Austria, Azerbaijan, Belgium, Bosnia and Herzegovina, Bulgaria, Croatia, Cyprus, Czechia, Denmark, Estonia, Finland, France, Georgia, Germany, Greece, Hungary, Iceland, Ireland, Italy, Latvia, Liechtenstein, Lithuania, Luxembourg, Malta, Moldova, Monaco, Montenegro, Netherlands, North Macedonia, Norway, Poland, Portugal, Romania, Russia*, San Marino, Serbia, Slovakia, Slovenia, Spain, Sweden, Switzerland, Turkey, UK, Ukraine

* The Parliamentary Assembly suspended Russia's voting rights on 10 Apr. 2014 following its annexation of Crimea. These rights were restored on 17 May 2019.

Website: <https://www.coe.int/>

Council of the Baltic Sea States (CBSS)

The CBSS was established in 1992 as a regional intergovernmental organization for cooperation among the states of the Baltic Sea region. Its secretariat is in Stockholm, Sweden.

Members (12): Denmark, Estonia, European Union, Finland, Germany, Iceland, Latvia, Lithuania, Norway, Poland, Russia, Sweden

Website: <https://www.cbss.org/>

Economic Community of West African States (ECOWAS)

ECOWAS was established in 1975 to promote trade and cooperation and contribute to development in West Africa. In 1981 it adopted the Protocol on Mutual

Assistance in Defence Matters. Its Commission, Court of Justice and Parliament are based in Abuja, Nigeria.

Members (15): Benin, Burkina Faso, Cabo Verde, Côte d'Ivoire, Gambia, Ghana, Guinea, Guinea-Bissau, Liberia, Mali, Niger, Nigeria, Senegal, Sierra Leone, Togo

Note: In June 2017 ECOWAS agreed in principle to admit Morocco as its 16th member.

Website: <https://www.ecowas.int/>

European Union (EU)

The EU is an organization of European states that cooperate in a wide field, including a single market with free movement of people, goods, services and capital, a common currency (the euro) for some members, and a Common Foreign and Security Policy (CFSP), including a Common Security and Defence Policy (CSDP). The EU's main bodies are the European Council, the Council of the European Union (also known as the Council of Ministers or the Council), the European Commission (the secretariat), the European Parliament and the European Court of Justice.

The CFSP and CSDP are coordinated by the High Representative of the Union for Foreign Affairs and Security Policy, assisted by the European External Action Service (EEAS).

The principle seat of the EU is in Brussels, Belgium.

Members (28): Austria, Belgium, Bulgaria, Croatia, Cyprus, Czechia, Denmark, Estonia, Finland, France, Germany, Greece, Hungary, Ireland, Italy, Latvia, Lithuania, Luxembourg, Malta, Netherlands, Poland, Portugal, Romania, Slovakia, Slovenia, Spain, Sweden, UK*

* The UK withdrew from the EU on 31 Jan. 2020, leaving 27 members. During a transition period until 31 Dec. 2020 (with the possibility of extension until 31 Dec. 2021 or 2022), the UK remains part of the EU's single market but no longer participates in its political institutions. The nature of the UK's future cooperation with the EU, including in foreign and security policies, and its possible participation in some EU agencies has yet to be agreed.

Website: <https://europa.eu/>

European Atomic Energy Community (Euratom, or EAEC)

Euratom was created by the 1957 Treaty Establishing the European Atomic Energy Community (Euratom Treaty) to promote the development of nuclear energy for peaceful purposes and to administer (in cooperation with the IAEA) the multinational regional safeguards system covering the EU member states. The Euratom Supply Agency, located in Luxembourg, has the task of ensuring a regular and equitable supply of ores, source materials and special fissile materials to EU member states.

Members (28): The EU member states*

* While Euratom is formally independent of the EU, all full members of Euratom must also be members of the EU. The UK thus withdrew from Euratom on 31 Jan. 2020, leaving 27 members, although its rules and arrangements will continue to apply to the UK during the transition period.

Website: <https://ec.europa.eu/euratom/>

European Defence Agency (EDA)

The EDA is an agency of the EU, under the direction of the Council. It was established in 2004 to help develop European defence capabilities, to promote European armaments cooperation and to work for a strong European defence technological and industrial base. The EDA's decision-making body is the Steering Board, composed of the defence ministers of the participating member states and the EU's High Representative for Foreign Affairs and Security Policy (as head of the agency). The EDA is located in Brussels, Belgium.

Participating member states (27): The EU member states other than Denmark*

* The UK withdrew from the EDA on 31 Jan. 2020, leaving 26 members.

Note: The EDA has signed administrative arrangements with Norway (2006), Switzerland (2012), Serbia (2013) and Ukraine (2015) that enable these states to participate in its projects and programmes.

Website: <https://eda.europa.eu/>

Gulf Cooperation Council (GCC)

Formally called the Cooperation Council for the Arab States of the Gulf, the GCC was created in 1981 to promote regional integration in such areas as economy, finance, trade, administration and legislation and to foster scientific and technical progress. The members also cooperate in areas of foreign policy and military and security matters. The Supreme Council (consisting of the head of each member state) is the highest GCC authority. Its headquarters are in Riyadh, Saudi Arabia.

Members (6): Bahrain, Kuwait, Oman, Qatar, Saudi Arabia, United Arab Emirates

Website: <https://www.gcc-sg.org/>

Intergovernmental Authority on Development (IGAD)

IGAD was established in 1996 to expand regional cooperation and promote peace and stability in the Horn of Africa. It superseded the Intergovernmental Authority on Drought and Development (IGADD), which was established in 1986. Its secretariat is in Djibouti.

Members (8): Djibouti, Eritrea, Ethiopia, Kenya, Somalia, South Sudan, Sudan, Uganda

Website: <https://www.igad.int/>

International Conference on the Great Lakes Region (ICGLR)

The ICGLR, which was initiated in 2004, works to promote peace and security, political and social stability, and growth and development in the Great Lakes region. In 2006 the member states adopted the Pact on Security, Stability and Development in the Great Lakes Region, which entered into force in 2008. Its executive secretariat is in Bujumbura, Burundi.

The ICGLR Joint Intelligence Fusion Centre (JIFC) was launched in 2012 in Goma, Democratic Republic of the Congo, to collect, analyse and disseminate information on armed groups in the region and recommend action to member states.

Members (12): Angola, Burundi, Central African Republic, Congo (Republic of the), Congo (Democratic Republic of the), Kenya, Rwanda, South Sudan, Sudan, Tanzania, Uganda, Zambia

Website: <http://www.icglr.org/>

League of Arab States

The Arab League was established in 1945 to form closer union among Arab states and foster political and economic cooperation. An agreement for collective defence and economic cooperation among the members was signed in 1950. In 2015 the Arab League agreed to create a joint Arab military force for regional peacekeeping, but no progress in its establishment has been subsequently made. The general secretariat of the Arab League is in Cairo, Egypt.

Members (22): Algeria, Bahrain, Comoros, Djibouti, Egypt, Iraq, Jordan, Kuwait, Lebanon, Libya, Mauritania, Morocco, Oman, Palestine, Qatar, Saudi Arabia, Somalia, Sudan, Syria*, Tunisia, United Arab Emirates, Yemen

   * Syria was suspended from the organization on 16 Nov. 2011.

Website: <http://www.leagueofarabstates.net/>

North Atlantic Treaty Organization (NATO)

NATO was established in 1949 by the North Atlantic Treaty (Washington Treaty) as a Western military alliance. Article 5 of the treaty defines the members' commitment to respond to an armed attack against any party to the treaty. Its headquarters are in Brussels, Belgium.

Members (29): Albania, Belgium, Bulgaria, Canada, Croatia, Czechia, Denmark, Estonia, France, Germany, Greece, Hungary, Iceland, Italy, Latvia, Lithuania, Luxembourg, Montenegro, Netherlands, Norway, Poland, Portugal, Romania, Slovakia, Slovenia, Spain, Turkey, UK, USA

   Note: In addition to the 29 members as of 1 Jan. 2020, North Macedonia became a member of NATO and the following subsidiary bodies on 27 Mar. 2020.

Website: <https://www.nato.int/>

Euro-Atlantic Partnership Council (EAPC)

The EAPC brings together NATO and its Partnership for Peace (PFP) partners for dialogue and consultation. It is the overall political framework for the bilateral PFP programme.

Members (50): The NATO member states and Armenia, Austria, Azerbaijan, Belarus, Bosnia and Herzegovina, Finland, Georgia, Ireland, Kazakhstan, Kyrgyzstan, Malta, Moldova, North Macedonia, Russia, Serbia, Sweden, Switzerland, Tajikistan, Turkmenistan, Ukraine, Uzbekistan

Website: <https://www.nato.int/cps/en/natohq/topics_67979.htm>

Istanbul Cooperation Initiative (ICI)

The ICI was established in 2004 to contribute to long-term global and regional security by offering practical bilateral security cooperation with NATO to countries of the broader Middle East region.

Participants (33): The NATO member states and Bahrain, Qatar, Kuwait, United Arab Emirates

Website: <https://www.nato.int/cps/en/natohq/topics_58787.htm>

Mediterranean Dialogue

NATO's Mediterranean Dialogue was established in 1994 as a forum for political dialogue and practical cooperation between NATO and countries of the Mediterranean. It reflects NATO's view that security in Europe is closely linked to security and stability in the Mediterranean.

Participants (36): The NATO member states and Algeria, Egypt, Israel, Jordan, Mauritania, Morocco, Tunisia

Website: <https://www.nato.int/cps/en/natohq/topics_60021.htm>

NATO–Georgia Commission (NGC)

The NGC was established in September 2008 to serve as a forum for political consultations and practical cooperation to help Georgia achieve its goal of joining NATO.

Participants (30): The NATO member states and Georgia

Website: <https://www.nato.int/cps/en/natohq/topics_52131.htm>

NATO–Russia Council (NRC)

The NRC was established in 2002 as a mechanism for consultation, consensus building, cooperation, and joint decisions and action on security issues. It focuses on areas of mutual interest identified in the 1997 NATO–Russia Founding Act on Mutual Relations, Cooperation and Security and new areas, such as terrorism, crisis management and non-proliferation.

Participants (30): The NATO member states and Russia

Note: In Apr. 2014, following Russian military intervention in Ukraine, NATO suspended all practical cooperation with Russia, although meetings of the NRC continue at the ambassadorial level or above.

Website: <https://www.nato.int/nrc-website/>

NATO–Ukraine Commission (NUC)

The NUC was established in 1997 for consultations on political and security issues, conflict prevention and resolution, non-proliferation, transfers of arms and technology, and other subjects of common concern.

Participants (30): The NATO member states and Ukraine

Website: <https://www.nato.int/cps/en/natohq/topics_50319.htm>

Organisation Conjointe de Coopération en matière d'Armement (OCCAR, Organisation for Joint Armament Cooperation)

OCCAR was established in 1996, with legal status since 2001, to provide more effective and efficient arrangements for the management of specific collaborative armament programmes. Its headquarters are in Bonn, Germany.

Members (6): Belgium, France, Germany, Italy, Spain, UK

Participants (7): Finland, Lithuania, Luxembourg, Netherlands, Poland, Sweden, Turkey

Website: <https://www.occar.int/>

Organismo para la Proscripción de las Armas Nucleares en la América Latina y el Caribe (OPANAL, Agency for the Prohibition of Nuclear Weapons in Latin America and the Caribbean)

OPANAL was established by the 1967 Treaty of Tlatelolco to resolve, together with the IAEA, questions of compliance with the treaty. Its seat is in Mexico City, Mexico.

Parties to the Treaty of Tlatelolco (33): See annex A

Website: <https://www.opanal.org/>

Organization for Democracy and Economic Development–GUAM

GUAM is a group of four states, established to promote stability and strengthen security, whose history goes back to 1997. The organization was established in 2006. The members cooperate to promote social and economic development and trade in eight working groups. Its secretariat is in Kyiv, Ukraine.

Members (4): Azerbaijan, Georgia, Moldova, Ukraine

Website: <https://guam-organization.org/>

Organization for Security and Co-operation in Europe (OSCE)

The Conference on Security and Co-operation in Europe (CSCE), which had been initiated in 1973, was renamed the OSCE in 1995. It is intended to be the primary instrument of comprehensive and cooperative security for early warning, conflict prevention, crisis management and post-conflict rehabilitation in its area. Its headquarters are in Vienna, Austria, and its other institutions are based elsewhere in Europe.

The OSCE Troika consists of representatives of the states holding the chair in the current year, the previous year and the succeeding year. The Forum for Security Cooperation (FSC) deals with arms control and confidence- and security-building measures.

Participants (57): Albania†, Andorra, Armenia, Austria, Azerbaijan, Belarus, Belgium, Bosnia and Herzegovina, Bulgaria, Canada, Croatia, Cyprus, Czechia, Denmark, Estonia, Finland, France, Georgia, Germany, Greece, Holy See, Hungary, Iceland, Ireland, Italy, Kazakhstan, Kyrgyzstan, Latvia, Liechtenstein, Lithuania, Luxembourg, Malta, Moldova, Monaco, Mongolia, Montenegro, Netherlands, North Macedonia, Norway, Poland, Portugal, Romania, Russia, San Marino, Serbia, Slovakia*, Slovenia, Spain, Sweden‡, Switzerland, Tajikistan, Turkey, Turkmenistan, UK, Ukraine, USA, Uzbekistan

* Chair in 2019.
† Chair in 2020.
‡ Chair in 2021.

Website: <https://www.osce.org/>

Joint Consultative Group (JCG)

The JCG is an OSCE-related body established by the 1990 Treaty on Conventional Armed Forces in Europe (CFE Treaty) to promote the objectives and implementation of the treaty by reconciling ambiguities of interpretation and implementation. Its seat is in Vienna, Austria.

Parties to the CFE Treaty (30): See annex A

Note: In 2007 Russia suspended its participation in the CFE Treaty, and in Mar. 2015 it announced that it had decided to completely halt its participation in the treaty, including the JCG.

Website: <https://www.osce.org/jcg/>

Minsk Group

The Minsk Group supports the Minsk Process, an ongoing forum for negotiations on a peaceful settlement of the conflict in Nagorno-Karabakh.

Members (13): Armenia, Azerbaijan, Belarus, Finland, France*, Germany, Italy, Russia*, Sweden, Turkey, USA*, OSCE Troika (Albania, Slovakia and Sweden)

* The representatives of these 3 states co-chair the group.

Website: <https://www.osce.org/mg/>

Open Skies Consultative Commission (OSCC)

The OSCC was established by the 1992 Treaty on Open Skies to resolve questions of compliance with the treaty.

Parties to the Open Skies Treaty (34): See annex A

Website: <https://www.osce.org/oscc/>

Organization of American States (OAS)

The OAS, which adopted its charter in 1948, has the objective of strengthening peace and security in the western hemisphere. Its activities are based on the four pillars of democracy, human rights, security and development. Its general secretariat is in Washington, DC, USA.

Members (35): Antigua and Barbuda, Argentina, Bahamas, Barbados, Belize, Bolivia, Brazil, Canada, Chile, Colombia, Costa Rica, Cuba*, Dominica, Dominican Republic, Ecuador, El Salvador, Grenada, Guatemala, Guyana, Haiti, Honduras, Jamaica, Mexico, Nicaragua, Panama, Paraguay, Peru, Saint Kitts and Nevis, Saint Lucia, Saint Vincent and the Grenadines, Suriname, Trinidad and Tobago, Uruguay, USA, Venezuela

 * By a resolution of 3 June 2009, the 1962 resolution that excluded Cuba from the OAS ceased to have effect; according to the 2009 resolution, Cuba's participation in the organization 'will be the result of a process of dialogue'. Cuba has declined to participate in OAS activities.

Website: <https://www.oas.org/>

Organization of the Black Sea Economic Cooperation (BSEC)

The BSEC initiative was established in 1992 and became a full regional economic organization when its charter entered into force in 1999. Its aims are to ensure peace, stability and prosperity and to promote and develop economic cooperation and progress in the Black Sea region. Its permanent secretariat is in Istanbul, Turkey.

Members (12): Albania, Armenia, Azerbaijan, Bulgaria, Georgia, Greece, Moldova, Romania, Russia, Serbia, Turkey, Ukraine

Website: <http://www.bsec-organization.org/>

Pacific Islands Forum

The forum, which was founded in 1971 as the South Pacific Forum, aims to enhance cooperation in sustainable development, economic growth, governance and security. It also monitors implementation of the 1985 Treaty of Rarotonga, which established the South Pacific Nuclear-Free Zone. Its secretariat is in Suva, Fiji.

Members (18): Australia, Cook Islands, Fiji, French Polynesia, Kiribati, Marshall Islands, Micronesia, Nauru, New Caledonia, New Zealand, Niue, Palau, Papua New Guinea, Samoa, Solomon Islands, Tonga, Tuvalu, Vanuatu

Website: <https://www.forumsec.org/>

Regional Centre on Small Arms in the Great Lakes Region, the Horn of Africa and Bordering States (RECSA)

The Nairobi Secretariat on Small Arms and Light Weapons was established to coordinate implementation of the 2000 Nairobi Declaration on the Problem of Illicit Small Arms and Light Weapons in the Great Lakes Region and the Horn of Africa. It was transformed into RECSA in 2005 to oversee the implementation of the 2004 Nairobi Protocol for the Prevention, Control and Reduction of Small Arms and Light Weapons. It is based in Nairobi, Kenya.

Members (15): Burundi, Djibouti, Central African Republic, Congo (Democratic Republic of the), Congo (Republic of the), Eritrea, Ethiopia, Kenya, Rwanda, Seychelles, Somalia, South Sudan, Sudan, Tanzania, Uganda

Website: <https://www.recsasec.org/>

Regional Cooperation Council

The RCC was launched in 2008 as the successor of the Stability Pact for South Eastern Europe that was initiated by the EU at the 1999 Conference on South Eastern Europe. It promotes mutual cooperation and European and Euro-Atlantic integration of states in South Eastern Europe in order to inspire development in the region for the benefit of its people. It focuses on six areas: economic and social development, energy and infrastructure, justice and home affairs, security cooperation, building human capital, and parliamentary cooperation. Its secretariat is in Sarajevo, Bosnia and Herzegovina, and it has a liaison office in Brussels, Belgium.

Participants (46): Albania, Austria, Bosnia and Herzegovina, Bulgaria, Canada, Council of Europe, Council of Europe Development Bank, Croatia, Czechia, Denmark, European Bank for Reconstruction and Development, European Investment Bank, European Union, Germany, Finland, France, Greece, Hungary, International Organization for Migration, Ireland, Italy, Kosovo, Latvia, Moldova, Montenegro, North Atlantic Treaty Organization, North Macedonia, Norway, Organisation for Economic Co-operation and Development, Organization for Security and Cooperation in Europe, Poland, Romania, Serbia, Slovakia, Slovenia, South East European Cooperative Initiative, Spain, Sweden, Switzerland, Turkey, UK, United Nations, UN Economic Commission for Europe, UN Development Programme, USA, World Bank

Website: <https://www.rcc.int/>

Shanghai Cooperation Organisation (SCO)

The SCO's predecessor group, the Shanghai Five, was founded in 1996; it was renamed the SCO in 2001 and opened for membership of all states that support its aims. The member states cooperate on confidence-building measures and regional security and in the economic sphere. Its secretariat is in Beijing, China. The SCO Regional Anti-Terrorist Structure (RATS) is based in Tashkent, Uzbekistan.

Members (8): China, India, Kazakhstan, Kyrgyzstan, Pakistan, Russia, Tajikistan, Uzbekistan

Website: <http://www.sectsco.org/>

Sistema de la Integración Centroamericana (SICA, Central American Integration System)

SICA was launched in 1993 on the basis of the 1991 Tegucigalpa Protocol. Its objective is the integration of Central America to constitute a region of peace, freedom, democracy and development, based on respect for and protection and promotion of human rights. The SICA headquarters are in San Salvador, El Salvador.

The **Comisión de Seguridad de Centroamérica (CSC, Central American Security Commission)** was established by the 1995 Framework Treaty on Democratic Security in Central America. Its objectives include following up on proposals on regional security, based on a reasonable balance of forces, strengthening civilian power, and eradicating violence, corruption, terrorism, drug trafficking and arms trafficking.

Members (8): Belize, Costa Rica, Dominican Republic, El Salvador, Guatemala, Honduras, Nicaragua, Panama

Website: <https://www.sica.int/>

Southern African Development Community (SADC)

SADC was established in 1992 to promote regional economic development and the fundamental principles of sovereignty, peace and security, human rights and democracy. It superseded the Southern African Development Coordination Conference (SADCC), established in 1980. Its secretariat is in Gaborone, Botswana.

The **SADC Organ on Politics, Defence and Security Cooperation (OPDS)** is mandated to promote peace and security in the region.

Members (16): Angola, Botswana, Comoros, Congo (Democratic Republic of the), Eswatini, Lesotho, Madagascar, Malawi, Mauritius, Mozambique, Namibia, Seychelles, South Africa, Tanzania, Zambia, Zimbabwe

Website: <https://www.sadc.int/>

Unión de Naciones Suramericanas (UNASUR, Union of South American Nations)

UNASUR is an intergovernmental organization with the aim of strengthening regional integration, political dialogue, economic development and coordination in defence matters among its member states. Its 2008 Constitutive Treaty entered into force on 11 March 2011 and it is intended to gradually replace the Andean Community and the Mercado Común del Sur (MERCOSUR, Southern Common Market). Its headquarters are in Quito, Ecuador.

The **Consejo de Defensa Suramericano (CDS, South American Defence Council)** met for the first time in March 2009. Its objectives are to consolidate South America as a zone of peace and to create a regional identity and strengthen regional cooperation in defence issues.

Members (7): Bolivia, Ecuador, Guyana, Peru, Suriname, Uruguay, Venezuela

Note: Argentina, Brazil, Chile, Colombia and Paraguay withdrew from UNASUR during 2019 and Ecuador Peru started the withdrawal process. At a summit in Santiago, Chile, on 22 Mar. 2019, Argentina, Brazil, Chile, Colombia, Ecuador, Guyana, Paraguay and Peru discussed forming a new regional group, known as the Forum for the Progress of South America (Foro para el Progreso de América del Sur, PROSUR)

Website: <http://www.unasursg.org/>

III. Strategic trade control regimes

Australia Group (AG)

The AG is an informal group of states and the European Commission formed in 1985. The AG meets annually to exchange views and best practices on strategic trade controls in order to ensure that dual-purpose material, technology and equipment are not used to support chemical and biological warfare activity or programmes.

Participants (43): Argentina, Australia*, Austria, Belgium, Bulgaria, Canada, Croatia, Cyprus, Czechia, Denmark, Estonia, European Commission, Finland, France, Germany, Greece, Hungary, Iceland, India, Ireland, Italy, Japan, Korea (South), Latvia, Lithuania, Luxembourg, Malta, Mexico, Netherlands, New Zealand, Norway, Poland, Portugal, Romania, Slovakia, Slovenia, Spain, Sweden, Switzerland, Turkey, UK, Ukraine, USA

> * Permanent chair.

Website: <https://www.australiagroup.net/>

Hague Code of Conduct against Ballistic Missile Proliferation (HCOC)

The principle of the 2002 HCOC is the need to curb the proliferation of ballistic missile systems capable of delivering WMD. Subscribing states must exercise restraint in the development, testing and deployment of such missiles. The Ministry for Foreign Affairs of Austria acts as the HCOC Secretariat.

Subscribing states (140): Afghanistan, Albania, Andorra, Antigua and Barbuda, Argentina, Armenia, Australia, Austria, Azerbaijan, Belarus, Belgium, Benin, Bosnia and Herzegovina, Bulgaria, Burkina Faso, Burundi, Cabo Verde, Cambodia, Cameroon, Canada, Central African Republic, Chad, Chile, Colombia, Comoros, Congo (Republic of the), Cook Islands, Costa Rica, Croatia, Cyprus, Czechia, Denmark, Dominica, Dominican Republic, Ecuador, El Salvador, Eritrea, Estonia, Ethiopia, Fiji, Finland, France, Gabon, Gambia, Georgia, Germany, Ghana, Greece, Guatemala, Guinea, Guinea-Bissau, Guyana, Haiti, Holy See, Honduras, Hungary, Iceland, India, Iraq, Ireland, Italy, Japan, Jordan, Kazakhstan, Kenya, Kiribati, Korea (South), Latvia, Lesotho, Liberia, Libya, Liechtenstein, Lithuania, Luxembourg, Madagascar, Malawi, Maldives, Mali, Malta, Marshall Islands, Mauritania, Micronesia, Moldova, Monaco, Mongolia, Montenegro, Morocco, Mozambique, Netherlands, New Zealand, Nicaragua, Niger, Nigeria, North Macedonia, Norway, Palau, Panama, Papua New Guinea, Paraguay, Peru, Philippines, Poland, Portugal, Romania, Russia, Rwanda, Saint Kitts and Nevis, Samoa, San Marino, Senegal, Serbia, Seychelles, Sierra Leone, Singapore, Slovakia, Slovenia, South Africa, Spain, Sudan, Suriname, Sweden, Switzerland, Tajikistan, Tanzania, Timor-Leste, *Togo*, Tonga, Tunisia, Turkey, Turkmenistan, Tuvalu, Uganda, UK, Ukraine, Uruguay, USA, Uzbekistan, Vanuatu, Venezuela, Zambia

> *Note*: In addition to the 140 subscribing states as of 1 Jan. 2020, Saint Vincent and the Grenadines subscribed to the HCOC on 27 Jan., Equatorial Guinea on 28 Jan. and Somalia on 19 Feb. 2020.

Website: <https://www.hcoc.at/>

Missile Technology Control Regime (MTCR)

The MTCR is an informal group of countries that since 1987 has sought to coordinate national export licensing efforts aimed at preventing the pro-liferation of missile systems capable of delivering WMD. The countries apply the Guidelines for Sensitive Missile-Relevant Transfers. The MTCR has no secretariat. A point of contact based in the Ministry for Foreign Affairs of France distributes the regime's working papers and hosts regular policy and information-exchange meetings.

Partners (35): Argentina, Australia, Austria[†], Belgium, Brazil, Bulgaria, Canada, Czechia, Denmark, Finland, France, Germany, Greece, Hungary, Iceland, India, Ireland, Italy, Japan, Korea (South), Luxembourg, Netherlands, New Zealand*, Norway, Poland, Portugal, Russia, South Africa, Spain, Sweden, Switzerland, Turkey, UK, Ukraine, USA

  * Plenary host in 2019 and MTCR chair in 2019/20.
  [†] Plenary host in 2020 and MTCR chair in 2020/21.

Website: <https://www.mtcr.info/>

Nuclear Suppliers Group (NSG)

The NSG, formerly also known as the London Club, was established in 1975. It coordinates national transfer controls on nuclear materials according to its Guidelines for Nuclear Transfers (London Guidelines, first agreed in 1978), which contain a 'trigger list' of materials that should trigger IAEA safeguards when they are to be exported for peaceful purposes to any non-nuclear weapon state, and the Guidelines for Transfers of Nuclear-Related Dual-Use Equipment, Materials, Software and Related Technology (Warsaw Guidelines). The NSG Guidelines are implemented by each participating state in accordance with its national laws and practices. The NSG has no secretariat. The Permanent Mission of Japan to the IAEA in Vienna acts as a point of contact and carries out practical support functions.

Participants (48): Argentina, Australia, Austria, Belarus, Belgium, Brazil, Bulgaria, Canada, China, Croatia, Cyprus, Czechia, Denmark, Estonia, Finland, France, Germany, Greece, Hungary, Iceland, Ireland, Italy, Japan, Kazakhstan*, Korea (South), Latvia, Lithuania, Luxembourg, Malta, Mexico, Netherlands, New Zealand, Norway, Poland, Portugal, Romania, Russia, Serbia, Slovakia, Slovenia, South Africa, Spain, Sweden, Switzerland, Turkey, UK, Ukraine, USA

  * Plenary host in 2019 and NSG chair in 2019/20.

  Note: In addition, the European Union and the chair of the Zangger Committee are permanent observers.

Website: <https://www.nuclearsuppliersgroup.org/>

Proliferation Security Initiative (PSI)

Based on a US initiative announced in 2003, the PSI is a multilateral forum focusing on law enforcement cooperation for the interdiction and seizure of illegal WMD, missile technologies and related materials when in transit on land, in the air or at sea. The PSI Statement of Interdiction Principles was issued in 2003. The PSI has no secretariat, but its activities are coordinated by a 21-member Operational Experts Group.

Participants (107): Afghanistan, Albania, Andorra, Angola, Antigua and Barbuda, Argentina*, Armenia, Australia*[†], Austria, Azerbaijan, Bahamas, Bahrain, Belarus, Belgium, Belize, Bosnia and Herzegovina, Brunei Darussalam, Bulgaria, Cambodia, Canada*, Chile,

Colombia, Croatia†, Cyprus, Czechia†, Denmark*, Djibouti†, Dominica, Dominican Republic, El Salvador, Estonia, Fiji, Finland, France*†, Georgia, Germany*†, Greece*, Holy See, Honduras, Hungary, Iceland, Iraq, Ireland, Israel, Italy*†, Japan*†, Jordan, Kazakhstan, Korea (South)*†, Kyrgyzstan, Kuwait, Latvia, Liberia, Libya, Liechtenstein, Lithuania†, Luxembourg, Malaysia, Malta, Marshall Islands, *Micronesia*, Moldova, Mongolia, Montenegro, Morocco, Netherlands*†, New Zealand*†, North Macedonia, Norway*†, Oman, Palau, Panama, Papua New Guinea, Paraguay, Philippines, Poland*†, Portugal*†, Qatar†, Romania, Russia*, Saint Lucia, Saint Vincent and the Grenadines, Samoa, San Marino, Saudi Arabia, Serbia, Singapore*†, Slovakia, Slovenia†, Spain*†, Sri Lanka, Sweden, Switzerland, Tajikistan, Thailand, Trinidad and Tobago, Tunisia, Turkey*†, Turkmenistan, UK*†, Ukraine†, United Arab Emirates†, USA*†, Uzbekistan, Vanuatu, Viet Nam, Yemen

* Member of the Operational Experts Group.
† PSI exercise host, 2003–19.

Website: <https://www.psi-online.info>

Wassenaar Arrangement on Export Controls for Conventional Arms and Dual-Use Goods and Technologies (Wassenaar Arrangement, WA)

The Wassenaar Arrangement was formally established in 1996. It aims to prevent the acquisition of armaments and sensitive dual-use goods and technologies for military uses by states whose behaviour is cause for concern to the member states. The WA Secretariat is in Vienna, Austria.

Participants (42): Argentina, Australia, Austria, Belgium, Bulgaria, Canada, Croatia†, Czechia, Denmark, Estonia, Finland, France, Germany, Greece*, Hungary, India, Ireland, Italy, Japan, Korea (South), Latvia, Lithuania, Luxembourg, Malta, Mexico, Netherlands, New Zealand, Norway, Poland, Portugal, Romania, Russia, Slovakia, Slovenia, South Africa, Spain, Sweden, Switzerland, Turkey, UK, Ukraine, USA

* Chair in 2019.
† Chair in 2020.

Website: <https://www.wassenaar.org/>

Zangger Committee

Established in 1971–74, the Nuclear Exporters Committee, called the Zangger Committee, is a group of nuclear supplier countries that meets informally twice a year to coordinate transfer controls on nuclear materials according to its regularly updated trigger list of items which, when exported, must be subject to IAEA safeguards. It complements the work of the Nuclear Suppliers Group.

Members (39): Argentina, Australia, Austria, Belarus, Belgium, Bulgaria, Canada, China, Croatia, Czechia, Denmark, Finland, France, Germany, Greece, Hungary, Ireland, Italy, Japan, Kazakhstan, Korea (South), Luxembourg, Netherlands, New Zealand, Norway, Poland, Portugal, Romania, Russia, Slovakia, Slovenia, South Africa, Spain, Sweden, Switzerland, Turkey, UK, Ukraine, USA

Website: <http://www.zanggercommittee.org/>

Annex C. Chronology 2019

IAN DAVIS

This chronology lists the significant events in 2019 related to armaments, disarmament and international security. Keywords are indicated in the right-hand column.

January

1–2 Jan.	Ethnic clashes in response to a suspected jihadist attack kill nearly 50 people in the Centre-Nord region of Burkina Faso.	Burkina Faso
3 Jan.	The Philippines ratifies the Convention on Cluster Munitions (CCM).	CCM; Philippines
10 Jan.	Venezuela enters a presidential crisis as opposition leader Juan Guaidó and the National Assembly declare incumbent President Nicolás Maduro 'illegitimate'.	Venezuela
15–16 Jan.	Al-Shabab militants kill at least 21 civilians in an attack on a Nairobi hotel and office complex.	al-Shabab; Kenya
16 Jan.	Adopting Resolution 2452 (2019), the United Nations Security Council establishes a UN Mission to support the Hodeidah Agreement (UNMHA).	UNMHA; UN Security Council; Yemen
16 Jan.	A four-month-old UN ceasefire in Tripoli breaks down after clashes between rival armed groups.	Libya
17 Jan.	A car bomb attack claimed by the National Liberation Army (ELN) at a police academy in Bogotá, Colombia, kills at least 21 people.	Colombia; ELN
21 Jan.	A referendum endorses the new Bangsamoro Autonomous Region in Muslim Mindanao in the Philippines—an essential part of the peace process.	Philippines
21 Jan.	A Taliban attack on an Afghan military base outside of Kabul kills more than 40 people.	Afghanistan; Taliban
23 Jan.	After Venezuelan opposition leader Guaidó declares himself president, he is supported by some countries including the United States. Venezuelan President Maduro severs diplomatic ties with the USA.	USA; Venezuela
23 Jan.	Russian President Vladimir Putin holds talks with Turkish President Recep Tayyip Erdogan on a joint Russian–Turkish plan to stabilize Idlib province in Syria.	Russia; Syria; Turkey
24 Jan.	The Central African Republic (CAR) Government and 14 armed groups begin peace negotiations in Khartoum, Sudan.	CAR; peace process

27 Jan.	The Islamic State claims responsibility for a cathedral bombing in Sulu province, the Philippines, that kills at least 20 people. The attack is blamed on the IS-aligned armed group Abu Sayyaf.	Islamic State; Philippines
28 Jan.	US and Taliban negotiators agree on a bilateral framework that includes a ceasefire and a promise from the Taliban not to harbour terrorists in exchange for US withdrawal from Afghanistan.	Afghanistan; Taliban; USA
28 Jan.	Turkish President Erdogan announces his intention to establish safe zones in northern Syria to allow the return of millions of Syrian refugees who currently reside in Turkey.	refugees; Syria; Turkey
28 Jan.	The US Justice Department charges Chinese tech firm Huawei with multiple counts of fraud, raising US–China tensions.	China; USA
28 Jan.	Israel announces that the mandate of the Temporary International Presence in Hebron (TIPH), a civilian observer mission established to protect residents in the Palestinian city of Hebron in the West Bank, will not be renewed.	Israel; Palestine; TIPH
31 Jan.	The European Union (EU) begins the formal process of registering the Special Purpose Vehicle (SPV), a financial mechanism aiming to preserve European trade with Iran in the face of unilateral US sanctions.	EU; Iran; JCPOA; SPV
February		
1 Feb.	The USA formally suspends the 1987 Treaty on the Elimination of Intermediate-Range and Shorter-Range Missiles (INF Treaty) with Russia. The next day Russia follows suit.	INF Treaty; Russia; USA
3 Feb.	The USA deploys an additional 3750 troops to the US–Mexican border, raising the total number of soldiers at the border to about 6000.	Mexico; USA
5 Feb.	Russia hosts Afghanistan peace talks between Taliban representatives and senior Afghan politicians, but excludes the Afghan Government.	Afghanistan; Russia; Taliban
6 Feb.	The CAR Government and 14 armed groups sign a peace agreement following talks in Sudan.	CAR; peace agreement
13 Feb.	Zimbabwe becomes the 168th state to ratify the Comprehensive Nuclear-Test-Ban Treaty (CTBT).	CTBT; Zimbabwe
14 Feb.	At least 45 Indian paramilitary police are killed in an attack on Indian security forces in Indian-administered Kashmir. The Pakistan-based militant group Jaish-e-Mohammad claims to have carried out the attack.	India; Kashmir; Pakistan
23 Feb.	Facing the longest wave of protests since independence, Sudanese President Omar al-Bashir declares a national state of emergency, dismisses the federal government and sacks all state governors.	Sudan
25 Feb.	The UN Secretary-General and the head of International Committee of the Red Cross (ICRC) pledge to strengthen efforts to combat sexual violence in conflict settings.	ICRC; sexual violence; UN

26–27 Feb.	India carries out an air strike against an alleged Jaish-e-Mohammad training camp in Balakot, Pakistan. During a counter-air strike on India the next day, Pakistan shoots down an Indian combat aircraft and detains one of the pilots. The pilot is freed on 1 March.	India; Kashmir; Pakistan
27–28 Feb.	US President Donald J. Trump and North Korean leader Kim Jong Un arrive in Hanoi, Vietnam, for a second bilateral summit on North Korea's nuclear programme. The talks break down after both sides fail to agree on conditions for relieving US sanctions.	North Korea; nuclear weapons; USA
March		
1 Mar.	The Organisation for the Prohibition of Chemical Weapons (OPCW) Fact-finding Mission in Syria reports 'reasonable grounds' for believing a chemical weapon attack took place in Douma in April 2018.	chemical weapons; OPCW; Syria
14 Mar.	Two rockets fired at Tel Aviv from the Gaza Strip lead to over 100 retaliatory air strikes by Israel.	Israel; Palestine
17 Mar.	The Philippines officially withdraws from the International Criminal Court (ICC), one year after announcing its intention to do so over the ICC's preliminary examination of President Rodrigo Duterte's drug war.	ICC; Philippines
21 Mar.	President Trump calls for US recognition of Israel's sovereignty over the Golan Heights, a region captured from Syria in 1967 and annexed in 1981.	Israel; USA
22 Mar.	Twenty-three soldiers are killed in a Boko Haram attack in south-western Chad.	Boko Haram; Chad
23 Mar.	The Kurdish-led Syrian Democratic Forces (SDF) alliance captures the Islamic State's last territory in Syria.	Islamic State; SDF; Syria
23 Mar.	Gunmen massacre about 160 Fulani herders in the village of Ogossagou in central Mali, following a cycle of increasing intercommunal tensions.	Mali
25–26 Mar.	Following military clashes between Hamas and Israel in Gaza, a ceasefire is brokered by Egypt.	ceasefire; Hamas; Israel
27 Mar.	India announces that it has successfully tested an anti-satellite weapon for the first time.	India; space security
29 Mar.	The Security Council extends the mandate of the UN Organization Stabilization Mission in the Democratic Republic of the Congo (MONUSCO) for nine months and calls for an independent strategic review of the mission, including consideration of an exit strategy.	DRC; MONUSCO; UN
29 Mar.	Azerbaijan and Armenia hold their first official summit on Nagorno-Karabakh and commit to strengthening the ceasefire, improving communications and implementing humanitarian projects.	Armenia; Azerbaijan; Nagorno-Karabakh
April		
4 Apr.	The Libyan National Army seizes the town of Gharian, 100 km south of Tripoli, in an escalation of the armed conflict in Libya.	Libya

8 Apr.	President Trump designates Iran's Islamic Revolutionary Guard Corps (IRGC) as a foreign 'terrorist' organization. Iran declares the USA a 'state sponsor of terrorism'.	Iran; USA
11 Apr.	Following four months of large-scale protests, Omar al-Bashir, President of Sudan since 1989, is deposed in a coup.	Sudan
18 Apr.	North Korea says it conducted a test of a new type of 'tactical guided weapon', its first such missile test in nearly six months.	North Korea; missile proliferation
21 Apr.	Suicide bombings kill 259 people and injure at least 500 in Colombo, Sri Lanka. The government blames a local Islamist militant group with foreign support; Islamic State also claims responsibility for the attack.	Islamic extremism; Sri Lanka
25 Apr.	North Korean leader Kim Jong Un and Russian President Vladimir Putin meet for their first-ever summit in the Russian city of Vladivostok.	North Korea; Russia
26 Apr.	President Trump announces that he will withdraw the USA from the international Arms Trade Treaty (ATT).	ATT; USA
29 Apr.–10 May	The Non-Proliferation Treaty (NPT) Preparatory Committee meets in New York, but divisions on several issues prevent any agreement on joint recommendations for the 2020 Review Conference.	NPT PrepCom
30 Apr.	Venezuelan opposition leader and disputed interim president Guaidó leads an attempted uprising against President Maduro.	Venezuela
May		
1 May	US and Taliban negotiators begin a new round (the sixth) of peace talks in Doha, Qatar.	Afghanistan; Taliban; USA
3 May	Parties to the armed conflict in South Sudan meeting in Addis Ababa, Ethiopia, agree a six-month extension of the deadline to form a transitional power-sharing government.	South Sudan
4–5 May	The Gaza–Israel conflict escalates after the Israeli military launches air strikes into Gaza killing at least 22 Palestinians.	Israel; Palestine
6 May	In its first report since 2005, the Intergovernmental Science-Policy Platform on Biodiversity and Ecosystem Services (IPBES) warns that biodiversity loss is 'accelerating', with over a million species now threatened with extinction.	climate change; IPBES
6 May	The Syrian Army launches a major ground offensive against one of the last rebel strongholds in Idlib province.	Syria
8 May	Iran announces that it will reduce its commitments under the Joint Comprehensive Plan of Action (JCPOA) every 60 days, unless the other parties manage to compensate for the US sanctions.	Iran; JCPOA
12 May	The United Arab Emirates (UAE) says four commercial ships off the coast of Fujairah 'were subjected to sabotage operations'.	UAE; Persian Gulf

14 May	Yemen's Houthi rebels launch drone attacks on Saudi Arabia, striking an oil pipeline and taking it out of service.	Houthis; Saudi Arabia; Yemen
19 May	A further allegation of chemical weapon use in Kabanah, north-western Syria is investigated by the OPCW.	chemical weapons; OPCW; Syria
30 May	A second round of talks in Norway between representatives of Venezuelan President Maduro and opposition leader Guaidó aimed at resolving the nation's political crisis end without agreement.	Venezuela
June		
3 June	Sudan's security forces kill at least 100 unarmed protesters outside the military's headquarters in Khartoum.	Sudan
6 June	The African Union (AU) suspends Sudan's membership with immediate effect after the Khartoum massacre.	AU; Sudan
9 June	Large-scale protests take place in Hong Kong against proposed legislation regarding extradition to China.	China; Hong Kong
9–10 June	A Boko Haram attack in the Far North region of Cameroon kills at least 16 soldiers and 8 civilians.	Boko Haram; Cameroon
10 June	An armed attack on a Dogon village in the region of Mopti in central Mali kills at least 95 people.	Mali
12 June	Russia and Turkey broker a ceasefire in Syria's Idlib province between Syrian Government forces and rebels, but it fails to halt the fighting.	Russia; Syria; Turkey
13 June	A Japanese and a Norwegian oil tanker are attacked in the Gulf of Oman. The USA accuses Iran of carrying out the attacks.	Gulf of Oman; oil tanker attacks; Iran; USA
16–17 June	At least 30 people are killed in multiple, unclaimed suicide attacks in the north-eastern state of Borno in Nigeria. A day later, 15 soldiers are killed in an attack on an army base by the Boko Haram group, Islamic State in West African Province (ISWAP).	Nigeria; ISWAP
19 June	Five years after Malaysia Airlines flight MH17 was shot down over Ukraine killing 298 people, a Dutch-led investigation announces charges against 4 suspects in the case (3 Russians and 1 Ukrainian).	Netherlands; Russia; Ukraine
19 June	A UN investigation finds the Saudi Arabian Government responsible for killing journalist Jamal Khashoggi.	Saudi Arabia
20 June	British arms sales to Saudi Arabia are ruled unlawful by the Court of Appeal in the United Kingdom, in a judgment that also accuses ministers of ignoring whether air strikes that killed civilians in Yemen broke humanitarian law.	arms transfers, Saudi Arabia; UK; Yemen
20–21 June	Iran shoots down a US military drone; the USA and Iran disagree about whether it was in international or Iranian airspace. The USA calls off a retaliatory air strike, instead responding with cyberattacks against Iranian intelligence and military assets.	Iran; USA

22 June	The USA unveils the economic part of its new Israeli–Palestinian peace initiative, including a pledge of $50 billion in investment in Palestine and neighbouring countries after a peace deal.	Israel; Palestine; USA
28–29 June	At the Group of 20 (G20) Summit in Japan, China and the USA agree to temporarily halt their trade war, with the USA pausing additional tariffs and China agreeing to purchase more US agricultural products.	China; G20; USA
30 June	Mass protests take place in Sudan following a military crackdown in June in which over 120 people were killed across the country.	Sudan
30 June	President Trump meets with North Korean leader Kim Jong Un in the Korean Demilitarized Zone and they agree to restart negotiations over the North Korean nuclear programme.	North Korea; nuclear weapons; USA
July		
1 July	The International Atomic Energy Agency (IAEA) confirms that Iran has exceeded a stockpile limit for low-enriched uranium established by the 2015 nuclear agreement (JCPOA).	IAEA; Iran; JCPOA
2 July	An air strike on a migrant detention centre outside Tripoli, Libya, kills at least 53 people. The UN condemns the attack as a possible war crime.	Libya
4 July	The British Navy seizes a tanker off the coast of Gibraltar suspected of carrying Iranian oil to a refinery in Syria in violation of EU sanctions.	Iran; UK; EU sanctions
5 July	The Sudanese Military Transition Council and a coalition of opposition and protest groups reach a power-sharing agreement following months of protests.	Sudan
7–8 July	A two-day peace conference in Qatar between the Taliban and influential Afghans, including government officials, agrees a 'roadmap for peace' designed to end the 18-year war.	Afghanistan; peace process
8 July	Bosco Ntaganda, a former militia leader in the Democratic Republic of the Congo (DRC), is convicted of war crimes by the ICC for offences committed in 2002–2003. He is subsequently sentenced to 30 years in prison.	DRC; ICC
8 July	Iran announces that it has passed the uranium enrichment cap set in its international nuclear deal (JCPOA). The IAEA verifies that the cap has been breached.	IAEA; Iran; JCPOA
8 July	The UAE announces a withdrawal from the Yemeni port city of Hodeidah in compliance with a UN-brokered ceasefire.	UAE; Yemen
9 July	A report by the OPCW suggests that Syria continues to possess chemical nerve agents and poison gas, in light of 'growing evidence of deliberately false declarations' by the Syrian Government.	chemical weapons; OPCW; Syria
12 July	An attack by the Islamist group al-Shabab on a hotel in Kismayo, Somalia, kills at least 26 people.	al-Shabab; Somalia

17 July	The World Health Organization (WHO) declares the Ebola outbreak in the DRC a 'public health emergency of international concern'.	DRC; Ebola; WHO
17 July	At a meeting of the Trilateral Contact Group (Ukraine, Russia and the Organization for Security and Co-operation in Europe), the parties commit to another ceasefire in eastern Ukraine.	Ukraine
17 July	The USA removes Turkey from the F-35 programme after Turkey accepts delivery of S-400 air defence systems from Russia.	Russia; Turkey; USA
17 July	Leaders of the Sudanese military and civilian opposition sign the power-sharing agreement (reached on 5 July), which provides for a transitional military-civilian council followed by a transitional civilian government and finally national elections.	Sudan; peace agreement
18 July	The Trump administration communicates to the UN Secretary-General that the USA does not intend to become a party to the ATT and thus has no future legal obligations stemming from signature.	ATT; USA
19 July	Iran seizes a British oil tanker in the Strait of Hormuz amid rising tensions in the Gulf.	Iran; UK
22 July	Multiple air strikes by Syrian Government forces target a market in a rebel-held region of north-western Syria, killing at least 43 people.	Syria
27 July	A Boko Haram attack on a funeral and villages near Maiduguri in north-eastern Nigeria kills over 70 people.	Boko Haram; Nigeria
August		
1 Aug.	The Mozambican Government and the Mozambican National Resistance (RENAMO) sign a peace agreement bringing an end to the recent six-year period of armed clashes.	Mozambique; RENAMO
2 Aug.	The USA announces its formal withdrawal from the INF Treaty.	INF Treaty; USA
5 Aug.	India revokes the special status of Kashmir under Article 370 of the Indian constitution and also moves to split the state into two federal territories.	India; Kashmir
7 Aug.	Turkey and the USA announce plans for a jointly managed buffer zone in north-eastern Syria.	Syria; Turkey; USA
10 Aug.	Southern separatists in Yemen aligned with the UAE seize the Yemeni city of Aden from the Saudi Arabian-backed government of President Abdrabbuh Mansur Hadi.	Saudi Arabia; UAE; Yemen
17 Aug.	At least 92 people are killed and 142 wounded in a suicide bombing in Kabul, Afghanistan. The Islamic State claims responsibility for the attack.	Afghanistan; Islamic State
17 Aug.	Sudan's pro-democracy movement and the country's ruling military council finalize a power-sharing agreement, paving the way for a transition to civilian-led government after months of unrest.	Sudan
18 Aug.	The USA tests a ground-launched cruise missile that would have been prohibited under the INF Treaty.	missile proliferation; USA

18 Aug.	Chad declares a state of emergency in two eastern provinces, after about 100 people died in violent intercommunal clashes earlier in the month.	Chad
24–26 Aug.	The Group of Seven (G7) Summit hosted by France ends without a formal joint declaration for the first time in its 44-year history.	G7 Summit
26–30 Aug.	The Fifth Conference of States Parties to the ATT is held in Geneva, Switzerland, and makes progress in establishing language on how key aspects of the treaty should be implemented.	ATT
29 Aug.	Three former senior rebel commanders from the Revolutionary Armed Forces of Colombia (FARC) announce their return to armed struggle in Colombia, becoming the highest-ranking rebels to withdraw from the 2016 peace deal.	Colombia; FARC
September		
3 Sep.	The USA imposes sanctions on Iran's civilian space agency and two research organizations, claiming that they are carrying out ballistic missile research.	Iran; USA
4 Sep.	Hong Kong announces the withdrawal of a controversial anti-extradition bill and sets up an independent study to review social and economic inequality within the territory.	China; Hong Kong
5 Sep.	As US–Taliban peace talks close in on an agreement, the Taliban claims responsibility for an attack near the US embassy in Kabul that kills at least 16 people, including a US soldier.	Afghanistan; Taliban; USA
7 Sep.	A major Russia–Ukraine prisoner exchange takes place with each side releasing 35 individuals, including the 24 Ukrainian sailors taken captive by Russia in November 2018.	Russia; Ukraine
8 Sep.	President Trump announces the cancellation of previously secret arrangements to meet with the Taliban and Afghan Government, declaring the peace talks 'dead'.	Afghanistan; Taliban; USA
8 Sep.	Two attacks by armed groups in the north of Burkina Faso kill at least 29 people.	Burkina Faso
14–15 Sep.	Two major oil installations are attacked in Saudi Arabia. Houthi rebels in Yemen claim responsibility for the attack, but the USA accuses Iran of direct involvement. President Trump tweets the day after the attack that the USA is 'locked and loaded'.	Iran; Saudi Arabia; USA; Yemen
15 Sep.	Talks to end Venezuela's protracted crisis collapse as the main opposition group pulls out of Norwegian-sponsored negotiations in Barbados.	Venezuela
16 Sep.	Russia and Turkey agree to create a buffer zone in Syria's Idlib province.	Russia; Syria; Turkey
16 Sep.	After almost two years, a review of the EU Common Position on Arms Exports is completed with the adoption of a new Council Decision.	EU Common Position
18–19 Sep.	As part of a wave of violence following the collapse of Afghan peace talks, an attack by the Taliban kills at least 22 people in Zabul province and a US air strike kills at least 30 people in Nangarhar province.	Afghanistan; Taliban; USA

20 Sep.	The USA imposes new sanctions on Iran that specifically target the country's central bank and national development fund.	Iran; USA
20–30 Sep.	Egyptian security forces crack down on anti-government protests, reportedly arresting around 2000 people.	Egypt
22 Sep.	At least 40 people are killed as a result of an attack by Afghan Government forces in Helmand province that was meant to target a Taliban cell.	Afghanistan; Taliban
23 Sep.	At least 30 people are killed in Indonesia's Papua province, as security forces clash with protesters in Wamena and Jayapura, the provincial capital.	Indonesia
23 Sep.	The UN Climate Action Summit ends with few significant new commitments. Russia announces that it will ratify the 2015 Paris Agreement on climate agreement.	climate change; Paris Agreement; Russia
25 Sep.	The 11th Conference on Facilitating the Entry into Force of the CTBT is held in New York, USA. The USA declines to participate for the first time.	CTBT; USA
26 Sep.	For the first time since the outbreak of the 2008 war between Georgia and Russia, their foreign ministers hold talks about the conflicts in Abkhazia and South Ossetia.	Georgia; Russia
27 Sep.	The Maldives accedes to the CCM.	CCM; Maldives
27 Sep.	China announces at the 74th Session of the UN General Assembly that it has initiated the domestic legal procedures to join the ATT.	ATT; China
28 Sep.	Afghanistan holds presidential elections that were originally scheduled to take place in April.	Afghanistan
October		
1–6 Oct.	The number of deaths from nearly a week of anti-government rallies in Iraq exceeds 100, with thousands more injured.	Iraq
2 Oct.	North Korea announces that it has test-launched 'a new type' of submarine-launched ballistic missile called the Bukkeukseong-3.	North Korea; missile proliferation
2 Oct.	Attacks on two army camps in Boulkessy and Mondoro in Mali kill 25 soldiers and leave 60 missing.	Mali
4–5 Oct.	Denuclearization negotiations between North Korea and the USA in Stockholm, Sweden, fail to break the deadlock.	North Korea; nuclear weapons; USA
6–7 Oct.	President Trump announces the withdrawal of US troops from north-eastern Syria, but the next day warns that he would 'destroy and obliterate' the Turkish economy if any offensive went too far.	Syria; Turkey; USA
7–11 Oct.	The Missile Technology Control Regime (MTCR) resumes holding an annual plenary (it was not held in 2018), this year in Auckland, New Zealand	MTCR
9 Oct.	Turkey announces the start of military operations in north-eastern Syria to create a 'safe zone' to allow for the return of Syrian refugees.	Syria; Turkey

11 Oct.	The Nobel Peace Prize is awarded to the Ethiopian Prime Minister, Abiy Ahmed Ali, for his contributions to ending Ethiopia's decades-long war with Eritrea and for his mediation assistance in Sudan.	Ethiopia; Nobel Peace Prize
14 Oct.	The Jalisco New Generation Cartel ambush and kill 14 police officers in the state of Michoacán, Mexico.	Mexico
14 Oct.	The USA imposes sanctions on Turkish Government agencies in response to Turkey's incursion into Syria. The sanctions are lifted 10 days later, although the incursion continued.	Syria; Turkey; USA
15 Oct.	The UN Mission for Justice Support in Haiti (MINUJUSTH) completes its mandate, ending 15 years of peacekeeping operations in the country. It is replaced by a political mission, the UN Integrated Office in Haiti (BINUH).	Haiti; BINUH; MINUJUSTH
17 Oct.	Turkey and the USA negotiate a five-day ceasefire in northern Syria to allow Kurdish fighters to withdraw from the safe zone, but fighting continues.	Syria; Turkey; USA
18 Oct.	An explosion at a mosque in eastern Afghanistan kills at least 60 people. No group claims responsibility for the attack.	Afghanistan
22 Oct.	Russia and Turkey agree deploy their forces across north-eastern Syria in order to force the withdrawal of Kurdish fighters from the region.	Russia; Syria; Turkey
26 Oct.	President Trump announces that Abu Bakr al-Baghdadi, the leader of the Islamic State, has been killed in a US military operation in Syria.	Islamic State; Syria; USA
30 Oct.–8 Nov.	150 delegates representing Syria's government, opposition and civil society groups meet in Geneva, Switzerland, in the first round of talks to draft a new Syrian constitution.	Syria
31 Oct.	The Islamic State announces that Abu Ibrahim al-Hashimi al-Qorashi is the group's new leader.	Islamic State
31 Oct.	The Iraqi Prime Minister, Adil Abdul Mahdi, resigns after weeks of anti-government protests.	Iraq
November		
1 Nov.	The Islamic State in the Greater Sahel (ISGS) kills 53 Malian soldiers and 1 civilian in an attack on an army base in Indelimane, near the Malian–Nigerian border.	ISGS; Mali
4 Nov.	The USA formally notifies the UN of its intention to withdraw from the Paris Agreement on climate change in Autumn 2020.	USA; climate change; Paris Agreement;
5 Nov.	The Yemeni Government and separatists represented by the Southern Transitional Council sign the Riyadh Agreement to end a power struggle in southern Yemen.	Riyadh Agreement; Yemen
6 Nov.	An attack on a Canadian mining company's convoy in Burkina Faso kills at least 37 people.	Burkina Faso
11 Nov.	On behalf of Rohingya Muslims, Gambia files a lawsuit against Myanmar at the International Court of Justice (ICJ), accusing Myanmar's leadership of genocide.	Gambia; ICJ; Myanmar

12–13 Nov.	An Israeli air strike in Gaza kills Baha Abu al-Ata, a senior commander of the militant group Palestinian Islamic Jihad (PIJ). PIJ responds with hundreds of rocket launches and further Israeli air strikes kill at least 34 Palestinians.	Israel; Palestine
15–19 Nov.	At least 100 protesters, in 21 cities across Iran, are killed in five days of protests that started in response to an increase in oil prices.	Iran
16 Nov.	Leaked files and internal documents reveal how the Chinese Government carried out an extensive programme to crack down on Uighurs in Xinjiang, while publicly presenting the efforts as benevolent.	China
18 Nov.	Ireland convenes the first of a series of open consultations about a political declaration on explosive weapons in populated areas (EWIPA), with a view to finalizing and adopting a declaration in 2020.	EWIPA; Ireland
18 Nov.	The USA announces that it will no longer consider Israeli settlements in the West Bank to be a violation of international law. Two days later, the 14 other members of the UN Security Council strongly oppose the announcement.	Israel; Palestine; UN Security Council; USA
18–22 Nov.	The Conference on the Establishment of a Middle East Zone Free of Nuclear Weapons and Other Weapons of Mass Destruction holds its first session at the UN in New York. It is boycotted by Israel and the USA, but adopts a political declaration.	WMD-free zone; Middle East
25 Nov.	Thirteen French troops are killed in a helicopter collision in Mali. It is the biggest single loss of life for the French military since the 1980s.	France; Mali
25 Nov.	The World Meteorological Organization reports that levels of greenhouse gases in the atmosphere have reached another new record high of 407.8 parts per million, with 'no sign of a slowdown, let alone a decline'.	climate change
25–29 Nov.	The Fourth Review Conference of the Anti-Personnel Mines Convention (APM Convention) is held in Oslo, Norway. Seven states parties are granted extensions to their mine clearance deadlines.	APM Convention
25–29 Nov.	The 24th Conference of the States Parties to the Chemical Weapons Convention (CWC) adopts two decisions to amend the Annex on Chemicals for the first time.	CWC
December		
2–13 Dec.	The annual UN Climate Change Conference (COP25) held in Madrid, Spain, ends with few new commitments. Australia, Brazil and the USA block action on several issues.	Australia; Brazil; climate change; UN; USA
3–4 Dec.	North Atlantic Treaty Organization (NATO) leaders meet in the UK for a 70th anniversary summit and agree to initiate a 'forward-looking reflection process' on how to strengthen its political dimension.	NATO

4–5 Dec.	The Wassenaar Arrangement (WA) holds its annual plenary in Vienna, Austria, and adopts a set of new control list items, including new controls on certain types of cyber-surveillance technologies.	WA
7 Dec.	Iran and the USA undertake a prisoner swap.	Iran; USA
9 Dec.	The leaders of Russia and Ukraine hold their first face-to-face talks at a summit in Paris, hosted by France and Germany. They agree to implement a ceasefire in eastern Ukraine by the end of the year.	Russia; Ukraine
10 Dec.	A revised version of the US–Mexico–Canada Agreement, a new trade deal, is signed in Mexico City	Canada; Mexico; USA
10–12 Dec.	Three days of public hearings of charges of genocide against Myanmar take place at the ICJ.	ICJ; Myanmar
11 Dec.	Islamist militants kill 71 soldiers in an attack on a military camp in Inatès, Niger, near the border with Mali.	Niger
12 Dec.	The USA tests a ground-launched ballistic missile that would have been prohibited under the INF Treaty.	USA; missile proliferation
18 Dec.	The US House of Representatives approves two articles of impeachment against President Trump on charges of abuse of power and obstruction of Congress.	USA
19 Dec.	Libya's Government of National Accord activates a cooperation accord with Turkey, allowing for a potential Turkish military intervention in Libya.	Libya; Turkey
20 Dec.	The USA founds the US Space Force, a branch of the US Armed Forces dedicated to space warfare.	space; USA
20 Dec.	Members of the British Parliament vote 358 to 234 in favour of a bill to leave the EU on 31 January 2020.	Brexit; EU; UK
22 Dec.	Afghanistan's election commission announces that President Ashraf Ghani is set to win a second five-year term as president, based on delayed preliminary results of the September presidential election.	Afghanistan
28 Dec.	A framework agreement for future direct talks is reached between the Sudanese Government and some armed groups in Darfur.	Sudan
28 Dec.	A truck bomb attributed to al-Shabab kills at least 81 people and wounds 125 in Mogadishu, Somalia.	al-Shabab; Somalia
29 Dec.	The Taliban's ruling council agrees to a temporary ceasefire in Afghanistan, opening for a potential peace agreement with the USA.	Afghanistan; Taliban; USA
31 Dec.	A pneumonia of unknown cause in Wuhan, China, is reported to the WHO Country Office in China.	China; COVID-19; WHO

About the authors

José Alvarado Cóbar (Guatemala) is a Research Assistant in SIPRI's Governance and Society Programme, conducting research on gender, peace processes and conflict. Prior to joining SIPRI, he completed his graduate thesis on the fragmentation of women's organizations during peace processes and the potential outcomes during post-conflict peacebuilding at Uppsala University. He has also conducted research on human trafficking, gang violence and mining conflicts in the United States and Guatemala, as well as on the monitoring and evaluation of health and education projects in Jordan. His most recent publications have focused on gender, peace processes, and arms transfers and arms transfer controls.

Dr Vincent Boulanin (France/Sweden) is a Senior Researcher at SIPRI, where his work focuses on the challenges posed by the advances of autonomy in weapon systems and the military applications of artificial intelligence (AI) more broadly. Before joining SIPRI in 2014, he completed a doctorate in political science at the École des Hautes Études en Sciences Sociales [School for Advanced Studies in the Social Sciences] in Paris. His recent publications include *Artificial Intelligence, Strategic Stability and Nuclear Risk* (SIPRI, June 2020, lead author); *Limits on Autonomy in Weapon Systems: Identifying Practical Elements of Human Control* (SIPRI–ICRC, June 2020, co-author); 'Cyber-incident management: Dealing with risk of escalation' (SIPRI, forthcoming 2020, co-author); and *Bio Plus X: Arms Control and the Convergence of Biology and Emerging Technology* (SIPRI, Mar. 2019, co-author).

Kolja Brockmann (Germany) is a Researcher in SIPRI's Dual-use and Arms Trade Control Programme. He joined SIPRI in 2017 and conducts research in the fields of export control, non-proliferation and technology governance. He focuses on the multilateral export control regimes, controls on emerging technologies, particularly additive manufacturing, intangible transfers of technology and the Arms Trade Treaty. He received his MA with distinction in Non-Proliferation and International Security from King's College London. His recent publications include *Bio Plus X: Arms Control and the Convergence of Biology and Emerging Technologies* (SIPRI, Mar. 2019, co-author) and *Challenges to Multilateral Export Controls: The Case for Inter-regime Dialogue and Coordination* (SIPRI, Dec. 2019).

Mark Bromley (United Kingdom) is the Director of SIPRI's Dual-use and Arms Trade Control Programme, where his work focuses on national, regional and international efforts to regulate the international trade in conventional arms and dual-use items. His recent publications include *Detecting, Investigating and Prosecuting Export Control Violations: European Perspectives on Key Challenges and Good Practices* (SIPRI, Dec. 2019, co-author); 'Measuring illicit arms and financial flows: Improving the assessment of Sustainable Development Goal 16', SIPRI Background Paper (July 2019, co-author).

Dr Marina Caparini (Canada) is a Senior Researcher and Director of SIPRI's Governance and Society Programme. Her research focuses on peacebuilding and the nexus between security and development. She is currently working on gender-sensitive and inclusive health services as a building block of peace. Prior to joining SIPRI in December 2016, she held senior positions at the Norwegian Institute for International Affairs, the International Center for Transitional Justice and the Geneva Centre for the Democratic Control of Armed Forces. Her recent publications include 'Gender training for police peacekeepers: Where are we now?', SIPRI Backgrounder (Oct. 2019); 'Police reform in Northern Ireland: Achievement and future challenges', SIPRI Backgrounder (Oct. 2019, co-author); and 'Connecting the dots on the triple nexus', SIPRI Backgrounder (Nov. 2019, co-author), on the interlinkages between humanitarian, development and peace efforts.

Dr Ian Davis (United Kingdom) is the Executive Editor of the SIPRI Yearbook and an Associate Senior Fellow within Conflict and Peace at SIPRI. From 2014–16 he was the Director of SIPRI's Editorial, Publications and Library Department. Prior to joining SIPRI, he held several senior positions and worked as an independent human security and arms control consultant. He has a long record of research and publication on international and regional security, and blogs on NATOrelated issues. His recent publications include 'Towards an open and accountable NATO' in eds I. Shapiro and A. Tooze, *Charter of NATO* (Yale University Press, 2018) and 'How much does the UK spend on nuclear weapons?', BASIC Research Report (Nov. 2018).

Dr Tytti Erästö (Finland) is a Senior Researcher in SIPRI's Nuclear Disarmament, Arms Control and Non-proliferation Programme. Her research interests include the Iran nuclear deal, the Treaty on the Prohibition of Nuclear Weapons (TPNW), efforts to establish a weapons of mass destruction-free zone in the Middle East, and the global disarmament and non-proliferation regime more generally. Previously, she worked at the Ploughshares Fund in Washington, DC; the Belfer Center for Science and International Affairs, Harvard Kennedy School; and the Vienna Center for Disarmament and Non-Proliferation. Her recent publications include 'The arms control–regional security nexus in the Middle East,' EU Non-proliferation and Disarmament Paper no. 68 (Apr. 2020); 'Will Europe's latest move lead to the demise of the Iran nuclear deal?,' SIPRI WritePeace blog (Jan. 2020); and 'Fifty years of the NPT: Cause for celebration or commemoration?', SIPRI WritePeace blog (May 2019).

Dr Aude Fleurant (Canada/France) is the Director of SIPRI's Arms and Military Expenditure Programme. Her research interests focus on the transformation of the military market and analysis of the interaction of supply and demand dynamics. Her recent publications include 'The SIPRI Top 100 arms-producing and military services companies, 2018', SIPRI Fact Sheet (Dec. 2019, co-author); and 'The European defence industry' in ed. A. T. H. Tan, *The Global Arms Trade: A Handbook* (Routledge, forthcoming in 2020).

Shannon N. Kile (United States) is the Director of SIPRI's Disarmament, Arms Control and Non-proliferation Programme. His principal areas of research are nuclear arms control and non-proliferation, with a special interest in the nuclear programmes of Iran and North Korea. His work also looks at regional security issues related to Iran and the Middle East. He has contributed to numerous SIPRI publications, including chapters on nuclear arms control and nuclear forces and weapon technology for the SIPRI Yearbook since 1994.

Hans M. Kristensen (Denmark) is the Director of the Nuclear Information Project at the Federation of American Scientists (FAS) and a SIPRI Associate Senior Fellow. He is a frequent consultant to the news media and institutes on nuclear weapon matters, and is co-author of the 'Nuclear notebook' column in the *Bulletin of the Atomic Scientists*.

Alexandra Kuimova (Russia) is a Research Assistant in SIPRI's Arms and Military Expenditure Programme. Working with SIPRI's databases on military expenditure, the arms industry and arms transfers, she focuses on developments in the Middle East and North Africa region and post-Soviet states. Her recent publications include 'Trends in international arms transfers, 2019', SIPRI Fact Sheet (Mar. 2020, co-author); 'The SIPRI Top 100 arms-producing and military services companies, 2018', SIPRI Fact Sheet (Dec. 2019, co-author); and 'Military spending and arms imports by Iran, Saudi Arabia, Qatar and the UAE', SIPRI Fact Sheet (May 2019, co-author).

Dr Moritz Kütt (Germany) is a Senior Researcher at the Institute for Peace Research and Security Policy at the University of Hamburg, working within Arms Control and Emerging Technologies. In his research, he develops new approaches and innovative tools for verification of nuclear arms control, non-proliferation and disarmament agreements. These approaches and tools seek in particular to enable non-nuclear weapon states to participate effectively in such verification activities. Prior to his time in Hamburg, Kütt was a Postdoctoral Research Associate with the Program on Science and Global Security at Princeton University.

Dr Filippa Lentzos (Norway) is a Senior Research Fellow at King's College London and an Associate Senior Researcher within Armament and Disarmament at SIPRI. She is also a Biosecurity Columnist at the *Bulletin of the Atomic Scientists*, an Editor of the social science journal *BioSocieties*, and the NGO Coordinator for the Biological and Toxin Weapons Convention. A biologist and social scientist by training, she has researched and been actively involved in biological disarmament and non-proliferation for over 15 years. Her 450-page edited volume, *Biological Threats in the 21st Century: The Politics, People, Science and Historical Roots*, was published by Imperial College Press in 2016.

Dr Jaïr van der Lijn (Netherlands) is the Director of SIPRI's Peace Operations and Conflict Management Programme. He is also an Associate Fellow at the Radboud University Nijmegen. His research interests include the future of peace operations, their evaluation and factors for success and failure, comprehensive approaches in missions and their relationship with local populations. His recent publications include Assessing the Effectiveness of the United Nations Mission in Mali (MINUSMA) (Norwegian Institute of International Affairs, 2019, lead editor); Towards Legitimate Stability in CAR and the DRC: External Assumptions and Local Perspectives, SIPRI Policy Report (Sep. 2019, co-author); and 'Multilateral peace operations and the challenges of irregular migration and human trafficking', SIPRI Background Paper (June 2019).

Dr Diego Lopes da Silva (Brazil) is a Researcher with SIPRI's Arms and Military Expenditure Programme. He holds a PhD in Peace, Defence and International Security Studies from São Paulo State University. His publications have mainly addressed issues of the arms trade, arms production and transparency in military expenditure. Prior to SIPRI, he held research positions at the Institute for Public Policy and International Relations (IPPRI) of the São Paulo State University and at the Latin American Network On Defense And Security (RESDAL). His recent publications include 'Reassessing Brazil's arms industry' in eds K. Hartley and J. Belin, *The Economics of the Global Defence Industry* (Routledge, 2019); and 'Filling arms production data gaps: South America as a case in point', *Economics of Peace and Security Journal* (2018).

Giovanna Maletta (Italy) is a Researcher in SIPRI's Dual-Use and Arms Trade Control Programme. Her research interests include export controls and trade compliance, with a particular focus on the dual-use and arms export control policies of the European Union (EU) and its member states. Her work also involves mapping cooperation and assistance activities in the field of arms transfer and SALW controls and of relevance to the implementation of the Arms Trade Treaty. Further, Maletta coordinates activities related to SIPRI's role in the EU Non-Proliferation and Disarmament Consortium. Her most recent publications include 'The inclusion of gender-based violence concerns in arms transfers decisions: The case of the Arms Trade Treaty', SIPRI WritePeace Blog (Aug. 2019, co-author), and 'Legal challenges to EU member states' arms exports to Saudi Arabia: Current status and potential implications', SIPRI Topical Backgrounder (June 2019).

Dr Caitríona McLeish (United Kingdom) is a Senior Fellow at the Science Policy Research Unit (SPRU), University of Sussex, and Co-Director of the Harvard Sussex Program on Chemical and Biological Weapons. The main focus of her research is on the governance of dual-use technologies in regard to the effective implementation of the prohibitions under both the Chemical Weapons Convention and the Biological Weapons Convention, and how to create effective mechanisms to prevent misuse of legitimate science and technology. Her recent work includes analysis of past chemical and biological warfare programmes; consideration of chemical weapons use and allegations of use; and various examinations of the roles that have and might be played in chemical and biological disarmament efforts by actors outside of government.

Dr Zia Mian (Pakistan/United Kingdom) is the Co-Director of the Programme on Science and Global Security at Princeton University, where he also directs the Project on Peace and Security in South Asia. A physicist, his work focuses on nuclear weapons, arms control and disarmament, and nuclear energy issues. He is co-editor of the journal *Science & Global Security* and co-chair of the International Panel on Fissile Materials. Mian is co-author of *Unmaking the Bomb: A Fissile Material Approach to Nuclear Disarmament and Nonproliferation* (MIT Press, 2014). He has contributed to the SIPRI Yearbook on fissile materials since 2007.

Dr Dylan O'Driscoll (Ireland) is a Senior Researcher and Director of SIPRI's Middle East and North Africa (MENA) Programme. His work focuses on the drivers of conflict and pathways to peace in the MENA Region and beyond. He is also an Associate Research Fellow at the LSE Middle East Centre. He previously held the Conflict Research Fellowship at the Social Science Research Council, New York, and worked as a Researcher and Lecturer at the Humanitarian and Conflict Response Institute (HCRI) at the University of Manchester. O'Driscoll has spent over two years working and conducting research in Iraq and has published widely in both policy and academia.

Moa Peldán Carlsson (Sweden) is a Research Assistant at SIPRI within emerging military and security technologies. Her focus spans autonomous weapon systems, artificial intelligence, cybersecurity, arms control and emerging technology. During her studies in Political Science, she developed a profile on gender and terrorism, and wrote her thesis on alternative paths for female empowerment in militarized societies. She has also studied South Asian perspectives on peace and conflict in India and Nepal, as well as contemporary global security topics, terrorism and gender in Australia.

Dr Pavel Podvig (Russia) is a Researcher in the Program on Science and Global Security at Princeton University and a Senior Researcher at the United Nations Institute for Disarmament Research (UNIDIR). Podvig directs his own research project, Russian Nuclear Forces (RussianForces.org). He is also a co-editor of *Science & Global Security* and a member of the International Panel on Fissile Materials.

Daniel Porras (United States) is a Space Security Fellow at the United Nations Institute for Disarmament Research (UNIDIR). He focuses on political and legal issues surrounding space security, in particular the progressive development of sustainable norms of behaviour for space. He conducts research on the emergence of new technologies and approaches to strategic stability in outer space. Porras has participated as the technical expert for multiple UN bodies working on space security issues, including the Group of Governmental Experts on the Prevention of an Arms Race in Outer Space and Subsidiary Group 3 (on PAROS) of the Conference on Disarmament.

Sofía Sacks Ferrari (Chile) is a Regional Data Curator at the office of the United Nations High Commissioner for Refugees (UNHCR). From 2019 to 2020, she was a Research Assistant in SIPRI's Peace Operations and Conflict Management Programme, where she collaborated with the programme's research on peace operation trends and women's participation in multilateral peace operations.

Timo Smit (Netherlands/Sweden) is a Researcher in SIPRI's Peace Operations and Conflict Management Programme. He is in charge of SIPRI's database on multilateral peace operations and conducts research on trends in peace operations and various related thematic issues. His recent research has focused on, among other things, women's participation in peace operations and the civilian Common Security and Defence Policy (CSDP) of the European Union.

Dan Smith (United Kingdom) is the Director of SIPRI. He has a long record of research and publication on a wide range of conflict and peace issues. His current work focuses on the relationship between climate change and insecurity, on peace and security issues in the Middle East and on global conflict trends. He is the author of successive editions of atlases of politics, war and peace, and the Middle East, and of a blog on international politics.

Dr Nan Tian (South Africa) is a Researcher in SIPRI's Arms and Military Expenditure Programme, where he leads the Military Expenditure Project. His regions of expertise are Africa and China, with research interests focused on the causes and impact of military expenditure and civil conflict, and the issues relating to transparency and accountability in military budgeting, spending and procurement. Previously, he was a Macroeconomics Lecturer at the University of Cape Town. He has published in *Defence and Peace Economics*; *The Economics of Peace and Security Journal*; and *Peace Economics, Peace Science and Public Policy*. His recent publications include 'Estimating the arms sales of Chinese companies', SIPRI Insights Paper (Jan. 2020, co-author).

Dr Petr Topychkanov (Russia) is a Senior Researcher in SIPRI's Nuclear Disarmament, Arms Control and Non-proliferation Programme, working on issues related to nuclear non-proliferation, disarmament, arms control and the impact of new technologies on strategic stability. Prior to joining SIPRI in 2018, he held the position of Senior Researcher at the Centre for International Security at the Primakov National Research Institute of World Economy and International Relations, Russian Academy of Sciences. His recent publications include *The Impact of Artificial Intelligence on Strategic Stability and Nuclear Risk, Volume III, South Asian Perspectives* (SIPRI, Apr. 2020, editor and co-author).

Pieter D. Wezeman (Netherlands/Sweden) is a Senior Researcher in SIPRI's Arms and Military Expenditure Programme. He has contributed to many SIPRI publications since 1994, including SIPRI's annual reviews of global trends in arms transfers, arms industry and military expenditure. Among other things, he has published on military expenditure and capabilities in the Middle East, multilateral arms embargoes, arms flows to Africa, and the

European arms industry. In 2003–2006 he also worked as a Senior Analyst on arms proliferation for the Dutch Ministry of Defence, and in 2017 as a Technical Expert for the United Nations Group of Governmental Experts during a review of the UN Report on Military Expenditure.

Siemon T. Wezeman (Netherlands) is a Senior Researcher in SIPRI's Arms and Military Expenditure Programme. His areas of research include the monitoring of arms transfers, military spending and arms-producing companies, with a particular focus on the Asia–Pacific and former Soviet regions, the use of weapons in conflicts, transparency in arms transfers, and the development of conventional military technologies. His recent publications include 'Reporting to the United Nations Register of Conventional Arms', SIPRI Background Paper (June 2019); *Arms Flows to South East Asia* (SIPRI, Dec. 2019); 'Trends in world military expenditure, 2019', SIPRI Fact Sheet (Apr. 2020, co-author); and 'Trends in international arms transfers, 2019', SIPRI Fact Sheet (Mar. 2020, co-author).

Index